Shooter's Bible®

D1119583

No. 73
1982 Edition

Shooter's Bible

EDITOR:
Robert F. Scott

MANAGING EDITOR:
Charlene S. Cruson

ASSOCIATE EDITOR:
Tucker Spirito

RESEARCHERS:
Hadassa J. Goldsmith
Lottie L. Nielsen
Robert D. Scott

ARTISTS:
Cheryl J.G. Handelman
Kathi Romeo
Caryn Seifer

CONSULTANTS:
Frank Ercolino
Frank Gologorsky
Hermann Koelling

COMPOSITOR:
Skilset Typographers, Inc.

COVER PHOTOGRAPHER:
Deaton, Wells & Koumjian

Stoeger Publishing Company

Published by Stoeger Publishing Company
55 Ruta Court
South Hackensack, New Jersey 07606

Library of Congress Catalog Card No.: 63-6200

International Standard Book No.: 0-88317-105-8

Manufactured in the United States of America

Distributed to the book trade and to the sporting goods trade by Stoeger Industries, 55 Ruta Court, South Hackensack, New Jersey 07606

In Canada, distributed to the book trade and to the sporting goods trade by Stoeger Trading Company, 165 Idema Road, Markham, Ontario, L3R 1A9.

Contents

Foreword

Last year, in a considerable departure from tradition, I used this space to discuss the subject of gun control, underscoring that it is an issue that generates much heated discussion but few solutions.

That piece must have struck a responsive chord among readers and reviewers, for it resulted in a great many letters of approbation plus numerous reviews and editorials quoting liberally from that foreword. One organization thought so highly of it that they reprinted it in their newsletter, which reaches an audience of more than a quarter of a million readers.

During the year just passed, New York legislators passed what they have trumpeted as "the toughest gun law in the United States." Unfortunately, they forgot to pass simultaneous appropriations bills to enlarge the prison system, with the result that the law is more honored in the breach than in the observance.

As a result of several killings and assassination attempts on public figures, the subject of gun control still pervades as a social issue of concern to people everywhere. It is fortunate, indeed, that President Reagan has not let the attempt on his life color an even-handed approach to a basic constitutional question.

What can one say about a book that has been published continuously since 1925? That it is a classic cannot be doubted. That in these times of runaway inflation, its 576 information-packed pages represent a good value. What many people may not appreciate is that each year we make subtle changes. This year, however, we have made significant changes that make your 1982 SHOOTER'S BIBLE not only a better buy, but a better reference book:

● Right up until press time, we have kept abreast of rapidly changing prices for sporting arms, equipment, accessories and ammunition. The prices shown for each item are manufacturers' suggested retail prices at the time of publication. We cannot, of course, guarantee the currency of these prices, but, for our part, we have detected a leveling off in the inexorable inflationary spiral.

● We have added a new and exclusive feature: the Gunfinder®. This easy-to-use and exclusive index to all guns in the SHOOTER'S BIBLE will enable readers to make comparisons between products of several manufacturers. Thus, no matter what type of guns you are looking for—automatic pistols or single-action revolvers, for example—the Gunfinder® at the back of the book will lead you to them.

● Also placed at the back of the book for quick reference is the new Directory of Manufacturers and Suppliers of all products featured in this year's BIBLE, which includes U.S. suppliers of foreign firearms and air guns as well as phone numbers and—for handy cross-reference—the type of product manufactured or supplied.

● As an adjunct to our continuing series on great weapons museums of the world, we have added to the reference section a comprehensive list of every major weapons and military museum in North America. This listing will enhance the value of the 1982 SHOOTER'S BIBLE to readers whose work or pleasure trips take them to other parts of the country.

● We have also completely revised and greatly expanded The Shooter's Bookshelf. Every entry—and there's about 2,000—includes the author, title, publisher and date of publication for every book in print of interest to the hunter and shooter. In addition, we have kept in titles that have recently gone out of print but that might still be available through a bookseller, sporting goods dealer or library.

● For the convenience of collectors, we have added a new feature. Certain guns are classified as curios and relics by the Bureau of Alcohol, Tobacco and Firearms of the U.S. Treasury Department. We have reproduced the ATF listing of all guns so classified.

As always, the articles section of the new 1982 SHOOTER'S BIBLE contains the work of some of the best-known gun writers in the world:

● Our lead article by John C. Rhodes concisely tells why the inexpensive handgun has been and probably always will be with us.

● The long-recoil autoloading shotgun has been popular throughout the 20th century, but not many shooters know of its long and distinguished history. In his informative article, James F. Brady makes us aware of the debt we all owe to John M. Browning for his ingenious invention.

● Black powder is one of the fastest growing areas of interest in the shooting sports. Robert Fisch, Curator of Firearms at the West Point Museum, opens up the exciting possibilities of the sport in his article on the renaissance of light slug rifles.

● Don B. Kates Jr., a California attorney, takes a long hard look at the issue of gun control in a sober examination entitled, "Gun Control: Can it Work?"

● Our continuing feature on the great museums of the world takes readers this time to Springfield, Massachusetts, and a veritable treasure house of history and arms technology: the long-neglected Springfield Armory Museum.

• Of all the military rifles in use in recent wars, none has been as much maligned as Canada's ill-starred Ross rifle. The brass swore by it, but the foot soldiers swore at it—and abandoned it whenever they could replace it with an Enfield. W. John Farquharson examines the checkered career of this gun in his definitive article.

• "They may be small but they are challenging." That's the opinion of everyone who has ever attempted to hunt squirrel. Don Lewis, perhaps America's top varmint hunter, describes the tricks of the squirrel hunter's trade.

• Continuing his highly praised feature of last year's SHOOTER'S BIBLE, John Traister adds more do's and don'ts to his gunsmithing tables.

• Collectors are turning to the many overlooked areas of gun collecting in their search for new collectibles. One such area has been the curios and oddities that have intrigued inventors over the years. In his "Knives That Shoot . . . and Other Firearms Oddities," Robert Dana explores this fascinating subject.

As always, we invite readers to correspond with us, to send us their comments and suggestions regarding the SHOOTER'S BIBLE. Only with your help can we continue to keep the book as useful and informative as it has always been.

—ROBERT F. SCOTT

Articles

A 41-caliber SWAMP ANGEL (top), a Suicide Special of unusually good quality, manufactured by Forehand & Wadsworth, of Worcester, Massachusetts. A nickel-plated RED JACKET NO. 1 (bottom), marked THE LEE ARMS CO., WILKES-BARRE, PA., manufactured in 22-caliber rimfire.

The Indestructible Saturday Night Special

John C. Rhodes

On a rainy March afternoon President Ronald Reagan, in office less than three months, left the Washington Hilton Hotel after addressing about 3,500 union delegates. As the President headed for his bulletproof limousine, flanked by aides and surrounded by watchful Secret Service agents, a small knot of newsmen and unauthorized spectators hovered at the hotel exit.

The sight of a president is still comparatively rare in Washington, and members of the Metropolitan Police detail openly gawked at the waving figure. Their backs were turned toward the crowd in an attitude of inattention that was nearly fatal.

Suddenly, it happened, recorded by the TV cameras in sickening full-color for all the world to see. One of the new breed of demented and discontented drifters that a free society tolerates opened fire on the President and his party, using a 22-caliber handgun purchased shortly before in Dallas, Texas, for $47.

This assassination attempt and the subsequent attack on the pope, coupled with the shooting of former Beatle John Lennon, unleashed a flood of editorial comment directed at firearms in general by a society seeking simple solutions to complex problems. The particular target of most editorial writers was so-called "Saturday Night Specials."

What went unnoticed by the quick-fix editorialists and the general public was the fact that inexpensive handguns are far from a recent phenomenon. During the latter part of the 19th century, a myriad of cheap, low-quality pocket revolvers was turned out by American gun manufacturers for mass distribution. Sociologists and cultural archaeologists, searching for an explanation to this handgun explosion and the violence that accompanies it, point to the makeup of American society. Answering the question, "What kind of society are we?" Robert Sherrill, author of *The Saturday Night Special* (Charter House, 1973) says, ". . . we have a trashy society. Emma Lazarus's most famous lines from the poem at the base of the Statue of Liberty are words supposedly uttered by our patroness:

'Give me your tired, your poor,
Your huddled masses yearning to breathe free,
The wretched refuse of your teeming shore.
Send these, the homeless, tempest-tost
   to me. . . .'

"And the rest of the world did just that. We became the world's greatest experiment in landfill. America is built on an awesome amount of wretched refuse."

One hundred years ago, the omnipresent handgun was not a luxury—it was a necessity in a violent time. Violence was everywhere, but it had its greatest expression in the Civil War—the bloodiest conflict in American history. In the span of four years, 714,245 people were killed or wounded in a nation of 32 million compared to 880,000 dead and wounded during World War II among a population of 133 million. To cite one example, the Second Battle of Bull Run in 1862 was a three-day slaughter that cost almost as many American casualties as the bitter battle for the island of Iwo Jima, which lasted 36 days and set a record for World War II with nearly 6,000 killed and more than 17,000 wounded.

With the end of the Civil War the standing army diminished in size, but the regulars continued to fight, this time against assorted Indian tribes doggedly resisting the successive waves of ranchers, farmers and miners that swept over their lands. Here the gun was not only a weapon; it was a tool.

If the frontier was a place of violence, the cities afforded no haven of safety. The backwash of the Civil War and the hardships of intermittent depressions converged on the expanding urban centers as well. Violent industrial strikers, roaming gangs of toughs and murderers and a small army of organized vice—gamblers, pickpockets and prostitutes—all engaged in violent combat with the outnumbered and baffled police of the day, who were untrained and poorly paid.

Here is Herbert Asbury's account of conditions in the old Fourth Ward of New York City from his *The Gangs of New York* (Alfred A. Knopf, 1927):

> Streets over whose cobblestones had rolled the carriages of the aristocrats were filled with dives which sheltered the members of such celebrated river gangs as the Daybreak Boys, Buckoos, Hookers, Swamp Angels, Slaughter Housers, Short Tails, Patsy Conroys, and the Border Gang.
>
> No human life was safe, and a well-dressed man venturing into the district was commonly set upon and murdered or robbed, or both, before he had gone a block. If the gangsters could not lure a prospective victim into a dive, they followed him until he passed beneath an appointed window, from which a woman dumped a bucket of ashes on his head. As he gasped and choked, the thugs rushed him into a cellar, where they killed him and stripped the clothing from his back, afterward casting his naked body upon the sidewalk.
>
> The police would not march against the denizens of the Fourth Ward except in parties of a half-dozen or more, and when their quarry sought refuge in a dive, they frequently besieged the place for a week or longer until the thug was driven forth by restlessness or hunger. The principal resorts were always well garrisoned and fully supplied with muskets, knives and pistols.

It is little wonder that the law-abiding citizen, venturing abroad in the land—whether on city streets or country roads, where tramps and highwaymen were common—found it advisable or even necessary to go armed. Understandably, the law of demand and supply went to work with a vengeance. Given such a tremendous demand for concealable weapons, American arms manufacturers quickly furnished a supply of small, low-cost handguns.

In addition to exposing a large percentage of the population to the carnage of battle, the Civil War demonstrated the immense potential of machine production, as the South was to learn after being humbled by the industrial colossus of the North. During the four years of this conflict, northern industry alone provided four million muskets and one and a quarter billion cartridges for the Union forces. The percussion cap gave dependability to small arms while the rear-loading cylinders of the revolver (once Rollin White's restrictive patent expired in 1869) introduced flexibility and speed of loading. Metallic cartridges and improved powders added even greater utility to the handgun. These factors made it attractive and easy for many manufacturers to make simple revolvers in quantity. And they did—by the millions. Enter the Suicide Special.

Everyman's Gun

Dubbed "Suicide Specials" by latter-day collectors, these interesting guns have been largely neglected until recently. Today they are widely sought, now that they are recognized as a distinct and separate genre of American firearms. Donald B. Webster Jr., one of the first to write on Suicide Specials, maintained that these guns were unique, if only because they had almost no historical significance. This is perhaps a severe judgment. While they may not have the romantic associations of, say, the Colt Single Action, their role in history has been large, albeit unsung.

Interestingly, the term "Suicide Special" and its modern counterpart, "Saturday Night Special," are both of recent origin. "Suicide Special" was apparently coined by Duncan McConnell in an article on these guns in the February 1948 issue of *The American Rifleman*. According to pioneer gun-value author Charles Edward Chapel, however, the late Dr. S. Traner Buck of Philadelphia referred to them as "suicide guns" even earlier. They were also known as "kill-and-run-guns." The point to remember is that they were intended to provide a cheap and not necessarily reliable weapon for emergency use. Their very cheapness apparently led to their popularity among those who wanted to commit suicide—thus the name. A few less charitable writers have suggested that underscoring the appelation was the fact that the guns were often so cheaply and poorly made that it was virtual suicide to ever fire one of them even in self-defense.

According to author Robert Sherrill, the origin of the term "Saturday Night Special" came about in this fashion:

Though it it has something of a Gay Nineties ring to it, the term "Saturday Night Special" has actually been around for only a few years. Fittingly, its place of birth was Detroit. Something is always happening there in the way of firearms. When Sidney Hillman, the labor leader, visited Detroit in the mid-1930s to help settle a strike, a group of union men met with him at his hotel room. He noted the bulges under their coats. "Guns! Always Guns!" he cried despairingly. "Why is it there are always guns in Detroit?"

Not that Detroit is the easiest place to buy a gun; it's just that a determined Detroiter won't be stopped when he wants one. So it was that in the late 1950s and early 1960s, when mischievous residents of Detroit could not get their hands on guns in their hometown, they would simply hop in their cars and tool down to Toledo, Ohio, less than an hour away, where guns were sold in candy stores, flower shops, filling stations, shoeshine stands, anywhere at all. Since a great many of these purchases were made to satisfy the passions of Saturday night, Detroit lawmen began to refer to the weapons as "Saturday Night Specials." And thus the language of America was enriched.

As employed by most collectors today, the term "Suicide Specials" refers to single-action cartridge revolvers with solid frames, spur triggers and rigid cylinders (i.e., they do not swing out), which are freed by the removal of a center pin. They were usually made under a sales or trade name which can be found stamped somewhere on the gun, although the manufacturer's name may not appear.

Some less-exacting collectors are inclined to include in the Suicide Special classification any gun that even comes close to being a purist's Suicide Special, including the Remington Iroquois revolvers made by Otis A. Smith, as well as other guns. To the dismay of some collectors, for example, French and Belgian pinfire revolvers, Colt New Line revolvers, double-action solid or hinged-frame revolvers dubbed "Bulldogs," and various lesser-known single-shot weapons, without regard for whether they are cartridge or percussion firearms, wind up in some collections of Suicide Specials.

Several qualities characterized the Suicide Specials: external flashiness (many were nickel-plated and exhibited pin-punch or floral or scroll engraving), internal crudeness and low price. As an example of the latter, Merwin, Hulburt & Company in 1888

offered in their catalog a ROBIN HOOD revolver absolutely free with the purchase of one of their 44-caliber Army revolvers. In 1890 this same firm advertised its "celebrated LIBERTY model" for $1.10 postpaid. Prices ranged as high as $10.00 for an engraved model with special grips—ivory or pearl grips could cost more than the guns themselves—but such "expensive" guns were the exception rather than the rule. The 60-cent BLUE JACKET, advertised by Merwin, Hulbert & Company in 1887, and Sears, Roebuck's 68-cent DEFENDER held the record for lowest price, at the same time helping to create a market that numbered in the millions.

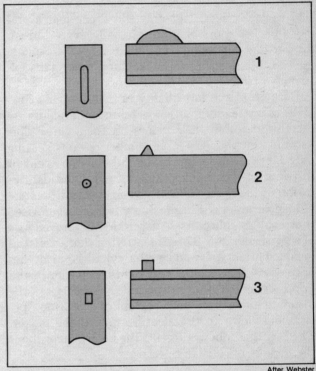

After Webster

Front sights: (1) half-disc blade in brass or steel, the most common sight on Suicide Specials; (2) cone-shaped brass bead; (3) rectangular or cylindrical brass bead.

Sales of Suicide Specials were usually handled through agents who acted as distributors to sporting goods stores and hardware stores, and sold directly to consumers through mail-order catalogs. Others reached the public via cigar and cigarette coupons. Suicide Specials were the favorite prizes for the armies of small boys who earned pin money as door-to-door salesmen of patent medicines, salves, soaps and perfumes. And these inexpensive guns were important accompaniments to Fourth of July

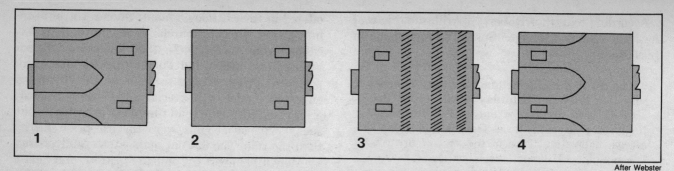

Cylinders: (1) fluted cylinder with locking notches at the rear, the most common form on Suicide Specials, especially on larger caliber models; (2) plain cylinder with locking notches at the rear, frequently found on 22 caliber guns; (3) plain cylinder (banded) with locking notches at the front; (4) a rare and unusual type of fluted cylinder with locking notches at the front.

celebrations. Suicide Specials became as widely carried as jackknives. Not only did every man's and boy's pocket sport one, but virtually every bureau drawer and nightstand in America held a Suicide Special. Many still do, thus making these guns extremely attractive to gun collectors.

Because of the low quality of most Suicide Specials, many manufacturers were understandably reluctant to stamp their names on their guns. This accounts for the very large number of guns bearing only fanciful trade names—or those of the agent or distributor. The absence of marks makes the identification of the maker difficult, so an elaborate system of identification of Suicide Specials has been devised that enables collectors to ascertain the provenance of a particular gun. These identifying characteristics include barrel types and lengths, cylinder-pin latches or releases, front sights, rear sights, grip frames and grips, cylinders and sideplates. Nevertheless, the ultimate aim of the identification of a Suicide Special boils down to the identification of the maker. The text that follows presents the known facts about the makers of Suicide Specials.

The Gun Makers

Albert J. Aubrey. This manufacturer, of Meriden, Connecticut, and Hopkinton, Massachusetts, held several patents issued between 1906 and 1908. Aubrey guns were sold by Sears, Roebuck & Company of Chicago through its mail-order catalogs. Because of their dates of manufacture, Aubrey guns are not classified by some purists as true Suicide Specials.

Bacon Manufacturing Company. This company, of Norwich, Connecticut, was well established in the gun business before it began the manufacture of Suicide Specials under the patent of Alonzo Louis Sweet (No. 210,725 issued December 10, 1878) covering a cylinder stop at the bottom of the cylinder at the rear in a cheap, single-action, rimfire, solid-frame, solid-top revolver with a round butt. (Sweet, a gunsmith in Norwich from 1873 to 1875, assigned one-half of his patent rights to the Bacon Manufacturing Company.)

Thomas K. Bacon had established Bacon & Company in Norwich in 1852 with a capital of $20,000; the firm name was changed to the Bacon Arms Company in 1853 and to the Bacon Manufacturing Company in 1855.

In addition to Suicide Specials, Bacon's company produced Bacon single-action underhammer pepperbox pistols, single-shot pistols, Briggs & Hopkins revolvers and the Bacon Navy revolver, made under the Charles W. Hopkins patent (No. 35,419 issued May 27, 1862).

Bacon Suicide Specials occasionally have false rifling notches at the muzzle, a feature of Hood Fire Arms Company guns. Some also utilize the blade-type cylinder-pin release patented by Freeman W. Hood (No. 160,192 issued February 23, 1875), leading to the suspicion that the Bacon and Hood companies worked closely together.

Among the trade names used on Bacon guns are BONANZA, CONQUEROR, DAISY, EXPRESS, GUARDIAN, LITTLE GIANT and U.S. ARMS CO.

Thomas K. Bacon sold his interest in the company to Charles A. Converse, as reported in the *Norwich Weekly Courier* of October 22, 1863. Since Bacon's headstone in Yantic Cemetery in Norwich bears a G.A.R. (Grand Army of the Republic) marker, the sale of his interest in the company may have been prompted by his joining the Union Army. Bacon died in 1873, but the company continued in existence until about 1890. The Crescent Fire Arms Company, also of Norwich, purchased the remaining stock about 1892, when it was founded.

Bliss & Goodyear. Frank D. Bliss began to make pocket-sized percussion and cartridge revolvers around 1856 at 16 Whitney Avenue in New Haven, Connecticut. Alfred D. Goodyear joined Bliss in this venture in 1859. The firm made Suicide Specials under the William H. Bliss patent (No. 202,627 issued April 23, 1878) covering a single-action, rimfire, solid-frame gun with circular left-side plate.

Among the trade names of Bliss & Goodyear products made under this patent are AMERICA, CHALLENGE, CRESCENT, DEFIANCE, DREADNOUGHT (?) EXCELSIOR, NONPAREIL, NORWICH ARMS CO., PATRIOT, PENETRATOR, PINAFORE, PRAIRIE KING, PROTECTOR, SCOTT ARMS CO. (?), SPY, TRUE BLUE and WINFIELD ARMS CO. (Note: The question mark after the DREADNOUGHT and the SCOTT ARMS CO. guns indicates that these were *probably* made by Bliss & Goodyear, but their origin is not unequivocally certain. This question mark designates probability also in the listings that follow.)

Bliss & Goodyear continued in operation until 1887, making only single-action revolvers.

Chicago Firearms Company. Best known for its patented 10-shot PROTECTOR palm pistol, a squeeze-type weapon with radial chambers (No. 273,644 issued March 6, 1883, to Jacques E. Turbiaux, of Paris, France), this company is believed to have made several Suicide Specials marked with the firm's name.

Continental Arms Company. One of the earliest makers of Suicide Specials, the firm was organized in 1866 in Norwich, Connecticut, to manufacture a five-shot pepperbox pistol known as the LADIES COMPANION under the patent of Charles A. Converse and Samuel S. Hopkins (No. 57,622 issued August 28, 1866). Their Suicide Specials were marked CONTINENTAL 1 and CONTINENTAL 2. The company became defunct after a short existence.

Edwin L. and J. Dickinson. The Dickinson brothers, of Springfield, Massachusetts, manufactured a single-shot rimfire pocket pistol in 22 and 32 calibers employing an unusual rack and pinion operated by means of a folding lever on the underside of the barrel. The brothers supposedly were in business between 1863 and 1888. Edwin L. Dickinson is listed in Springfield city directories as a manufacturer of pistols at 964 Main Street (Mill River) in 1876-77 and at Hanover Street from 1877 to 1888. D. L. Dickinson is listed as a pistol manufacturer from 1885 to 1887, with no business address. Charles C. Dickinson is listed as an employee of E. L. Dickinson from 1881 to 1886, after which he worked for the Smith & Wesson Company. Markings on their guns include EARL-

HOOD and RANGER NO. 2, with the name E. L. DICKINSON, SPRINGFIELD, MASS., MFG'R. also appearing.

Eagle Arms Company. Incorporated November 20, 1865, with offices at 262 Broadway, New York City, this company made the Plant Manufacturing Company front-loading pocket revolver as well as a small number of Suicide Specials. The Plant factory in New Haven, Connecticut, was destroyed by fire in December 1866; the Eagle Firearms Company continued in existence until 1870.

Enterprise Gun Works. Established in 1848 by Bown and Tetley at 136-138 Wood Street in Pittsburgh, Pennsylvania, to manufacture rifles. In 1862 James Bown became the sole proprietor. Despite the

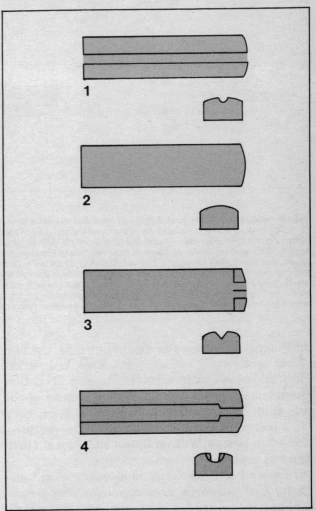

After Webster

Rear sights: (1) full-length groove in topstrap, the most common rear sight on Suicide Specials; (2) plain topstrap (i.e., no rear sight) found on many 22 caliber and cheap models; (3) notched raised lip, found on many models; (4) full-length groove in topstrap, narrow at rear; least often encountered and usually on better quality guns.

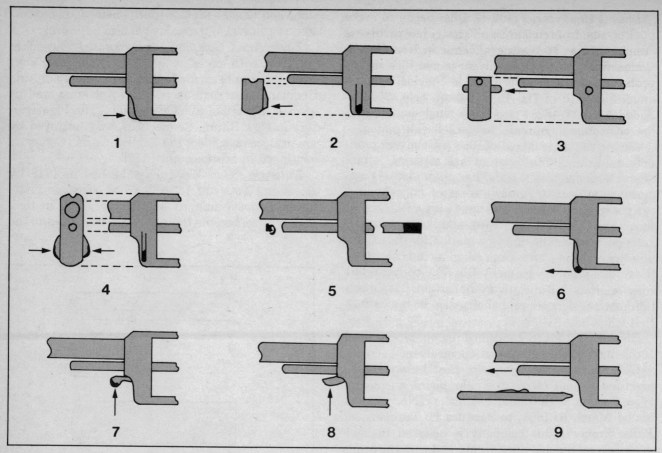

After Webster

Cylinder-pin releases: (1) push-in type at front end of frame described in Freeman Hood's patent issued February 23, 1875; (2) push-in type on left side of frame covered by Samuel S. Hopkins' patent issued March 28, 1871; (3) push-button on left side of frame — many Suicide Specials with this type of cylinder-pin release bear the patent date April 6, 1875, leading to the conclusion that they are of Hood manufacture; (4) double-blade pincer, evidence of Bacon Manufacturing Company manufacture; (5) threaded cylinder pin, the kind found on many cheap guns; (6) pull-out blade at front of frame, a rare type; (7) push-up spur at front of frame, covered by Ethan Allen's patent issued September 24, 1861, and evidence of Forehand & Wadsworth manufacture; (8) push-up type blade at front end of frame covered by Ethan Allen's patent issued September 24, 1861, also positive evidence of Forehand & Wadsworth manufacture; (9) internal spring release found on cheaper Rupertus guns and others.

fact that its rifles were of superior quality, the firm subsequently made Suicide Specials marked ENTERPRISE and JAMES BOWN & SON. Because we know that Bown's son William was not made a member of the firm until 1871, these guns must have been made after that date. Sometime after 1879, the company was taken over by William Brown and August Hirth and was operated by them until 1890.

Forehand & Wadsworth. Sullivan Forehand and Henry C. Wadsworth were sons-in-law and successors to Ethan Allen & Company upon Allen's death in 1871. The Forehand & Wadsworth name was adopted in 1872 and used until 1890, when the name was changed to the Forehand Arms Company. Wadsworth retired in 1890 and died in Brazil in 1892 while serving in the diplomatic corps. Forehand died in

1898, and the company was subsequently bought by Hopkins & Allen in 1902.

Trade names of Forehand & Wadsworth Suicide Specials include BULLDOG, ELECTRIC (?), FOREHAND & WADSWORTH, HALF BREED (?), SWAMP ANGEL and TERROR.

Great Western Gun Works. Established in 1866, by John H. Johnston at the corner of Penn and Wayne Streets in Pittsburgh, Pennsylvania, the plant was destroyed by fire in 1868 and reopened at 179 Smithfield Street; in 1874 it moved to larger quarters at 285 Liberty Street. Until 1870 this firm concentrated on the manufacture of small percussion revolvers, after which date they began making Suicide Specials, all of which can be identified by the name GREAT WESTERN. The company continued in business until about 1895.

Harrington & Richardson. This is one of the two firms still in existence whose name is currently associated with the manufacture of Suicide Specials (the other is Iver Johnson).

The history of Harrington & Richardson begins with Frank Wesson (1828-1899) who, in association with Nathan Harrington, began a gunsmithing business in 1859 at 18 Manchester Street in Worcester, Massachusetts. Twelve years later, Wesson and Gilbert H. Harrington, Nathan's nephew, formed a partnership, Wesson & Harrington, for the manufacture of pocket revolvers under Gilbert Harrington's patent (No. 11,534 issued February 7, 1871) which incorporated a sliding side-ejector working through a loading gate.

In 1874, Wesson sold his interest in the business to Harrington, who, with William A. Richardson, formed the Harrington & Richardson Arms Company and began making revolvers incorporating features covered by Richardson's patent (No. 177,887 issued May 23, 1876) for a method of attaching springs to revolver frames. In the fall of 1876 the factory was moved to larger quarters at 31 Hermon Street.

In addition to revolvers marked with the name HARRINGTON & RICHARDSON, their guns bear the trade names AETNA and VICTOR. With the introduction of double-action revolvers in the 1880s (including an unusual gun with a hinged bayonet under the barrel), the company stopped production of single-action revolvers and Suicide Specials. In 1894 the factory was moved to Park Avenue, corner of Chandler Street. The plant is now in Gardner, Massachusetts, on Industrial Rowe.

Hood Fire Arms Company. Located in Norwich, Connecticut, this company probably made more Suicide Specials than all other makers combined, thus giving the industrial city on the Thames River the dubious honor of being the Suicide Special Capital.

The company was headed by Freeman W. Hood, a prolific patentee of firearms devices. According to suicide special author Donald Webster, Hood's basic patent (No. 160,192 issued February 23, 1875) covered a feature that had been in general use for several years; therefore, it was not really patentable.

Curiously, only one revolver bears the Hood name, a fact that tends to play down Hood's role in the manufacture of Suicide Specials. In addition to the Hood Fire Arms Company, Freeman Hood controlled the Norwich Arms Company and the Norwich Lock Manufacturing Company. Moreover, he apparently held interests in the Continental Arms

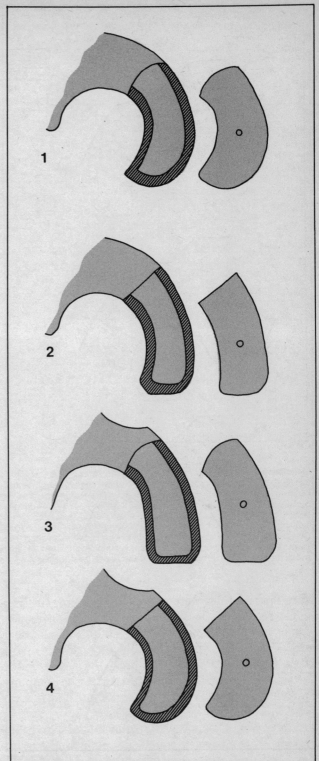

After Webster

Frames and grips: (1) birdhead, found on most Suicide Specials, especially on 22 caliber models; (2) square butt, the next most common type; (3) saw-handle square butt, often found on models of 32 caliber or larger; (4) saw-handle birdhead, an unusual configuration on Suicide Specials.

17

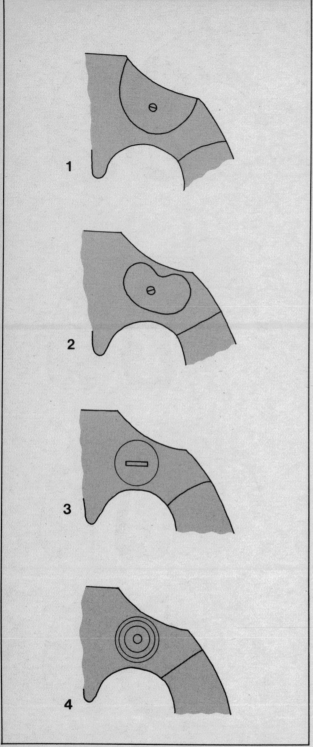

After Webster

Side plates: (1) removable side plate, giving access to the mechanism of the gun; **(2)** a variant of the removable side plate — note that types 1 and 2 are usually found on better quality guns; **(3)** round plate at the left side of frame, also serving as the hammer screw; **(4)** round plate at the left side of the frame, also serving as the nut holding the threaded end of the hammer screw.

Company and Bacon Manufacturing, also Norwich-based, as well as interests in a number of other firms. Hood was active until about 1885, when his last firearms patent was issued.

Among the trade names ascribed to Hood's companies are ALASKA, BOYS CHOICE, BRUTUS, CENTENNIAL, CZAR, EAGLE ARMS CO., HARD PAN, HARTFORD ARMS CO., INTERNATIONAL, JEWEL, LITTLE JOHN, SCOTT ARMS CO., SCOUT, TRAMPS TERROR, UNION JACK, and VICTORIA.

Hopkins & Allen. One of the major New England firearms manufacturers in the period during which it was in operation (1867-1915), the company was established by three brothers—Charles W., Henry H. and Samuel S. Hopkins—who held patents on many of the guns they manufactured.

In addition to Suicide Specials, the firm produced the Merwin, Hulbert & Company revolvers under contract to that firm. (Joseph Merwin and William Hulbert were not manufacturers themselves, but were dealers and sales agents.)

Some of Hopkins & Allen's Suicide Specials were of comparatively good quality, bearing names such as BLUE JACKET and XL. Other Hopkins & Allen trade names included ALLEN, CAPT. JACK, CZAR, DICTATOR, DREAMNOUGHT, ENCORE, GOVERNOR (?), HOPKINS & ALLEN, METROPOLITAN POLICE, MONARCH (?), NON-XL, RANGER, SCOTT, SECRET SERVICE (?), TOWER'S POLICE SAFETY, and XLCR.

Iver Johnson Arms Works. Iver Johnson and Martin Bye, former employees of Ethan Allen, established their gunmaking business in 1871 at 244 Main Street in Worcester, Massachusetts; 20 years later the company moved from their plant at 44 Central Street in Worcester to Fitchburg, Massachusetts, where it is still located. This is the second of the two surviving manufacturers whose names are associated with Suicide Specials.

The first guns that the Iver Johnson firm made were Suicide Specials, and it is to Suicide Specials that the firm owes its success. Their Suicide Specials have two unusual characteristics: All are virtually identical, with only the trade names varying, for neither the Iver Johnson name nor any patent date appears on any of their models. In the 1880s the company added double-action revolvers to their line, identifiable by the owl-head logo on the grips.

Among the Iver Johnson trade names are DEFENDER, ECLIPSE, FAVORITE, FAVORITE NAVY, LION (?), SMOKER, and TYCOON.

Lee Arms Company. This firm made nickel-plated metallic cartridge pocket revolvers marked RED JACKET and often with the maker's name as well. The

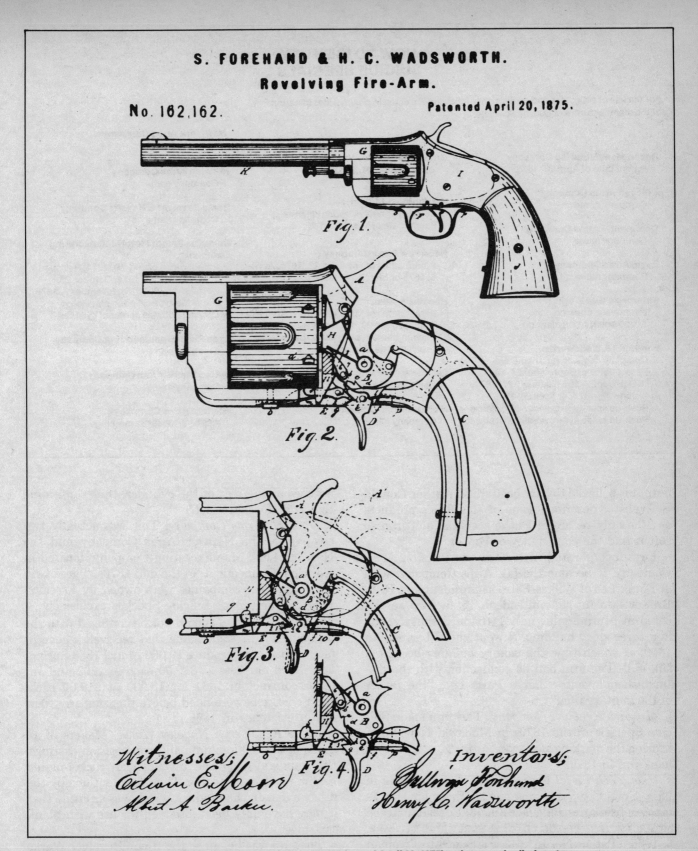

S. FOREHAND & H. C. WADSWORTH.
Revolving Fire-Arm.

No. 162,162.   Patented April 20, 1875.

Fig. 1.

Fig. 2.

Fig. 3.

Witnesses;   Fig. 4.   Inventors;
Edwin E. Moore   Sullivan Forehand
Albert A. Barker   Henry C. Wadsworth

Sullivan Forehand and Henry C. Wadsworth patented (No. 162, 162 issued April 20, 1875) an improved cylinder-stop device. The patent date on a Suicide Special is positive proof of Forehand & Wadsworth manufacture.

HOW TO IDENTIFY
SUICIDE SPECIALS

For the use of collectors and dealers, the following are clues to *positive* identification of the manufacturers of Suicide Specials:

Bacon Manufacturing Company
Patent date of April 23, 1878

Chicago Arms Company
Company name

Continental Arms Company
Company name

Eagle Arms Company
Company name

Enterprise Gun Works
ENTERPRISE marking
JAMES BOWN & SON marking

Forehand & Wadsworth
Company name or variant thereof
Patent dates of September 24, 1861,
October 22, 1861, January 27, 1871,
June 27, 1871, or April 20, 1875
Push-up spur-type cylinder-pin release
Push-up blade-type cylinder-pin release

Great Western Gun Works
GREAT WESTERN marking

Harrington & Richardson
Company name or variant thereof
Patent date of May 23, 1876

Hood Fire Arms Company
Patent dates of February 23, 1875, April
6, 1875 or March 14, 1876

Hopkins & Allen
Patent dates of March 28, 1871, April 27,
1875, June 20, 1875 or May 27, 1879
Push-in blade-type cylinder-pin release
on left side of frame

Lee Arms Company
Company name

Mohawk Arms Company
Company name

New York Arms Company
Company name

Norwich Arms Company
Company name

Rome Revolver & Novelty Company
Company name

Rupertus Patent Pistol Manufacturing Company
Patent dates of July 19, 1864, Reissued;
November 21, 1871; October 28,
1873; July 6, 1875; November 9, 1875
Rupertus-type cylinder-pin release
Locking notches at rear of cylinder

Ryan Pistol Manufacturing Company
Company name

United States Arms Company
Company name

Western Arms Company
WESTERN ARMS CO. marking

output is believed to have been small. Author Donald B. Webster described some of this firm's products as "the only revolvers I have seen made of iron so soft it had the consistency of copper."

First incorporated in 1877 as the Pittston Arms Company, it became the Lee Arms Company, with J. Frank Lee of Wilkes-Barre as president and R. L. Brewer as plant superintendent. Its factory was located in Sturmerville, near Pittston, Pennsylvania, in a three-story building. It went out of business in 1889, at which time the factory building became a silk mill. The firm had no connection with the distinguished inventor James Paris Lee, "the father of the military rifle."

Mohawk Revolver Company. This firm made Suicide Specials in the 1870s in Mohawk, New York, bearing the marking MOHAWK, MOHAWK, N. Y. It went bankrupt in 1879.

New York Pistol Company. With sales offices in New York City, this was one of Freeman Hood's many subsidiaries and made Suicide Specials marked MOHEGAN, N.Y. PISTOL CO. NEW YORK, and PAT. APR. 6, 1875. (Patent No. 161,613 was issued to Freeman W. Hood and covered a cylinder stop operating in

notches at the rear of the cylinder, thus confirming this as a Hood product.)

Norwich Arms Company. This was actually two companies, the Norwich Arms Company and the Norwich Lock Manufacturing Company, located in Norwich, Connecticut, in the mid 1870s. These twin post-Civil-War companies were owned by Freeman W. Hood and made Suicide Specials exclusively.

(Note: This firm should not be confused with the company of the same name that received a government contract to produce 10,000 Model 1863 Springfield rifled muskets at $18.00 each in 1863 and another contract in 1864 for 15,000 at $19.00 each. Both contracts were filled before the company went out of existence in 1866.)

Rome Revolver & Novelty Works. Makers of all kinds of brass, aluminum and composition castings, this company also had a 32-caliber, nickel-plated rimfire revolver in its line. They are identified by the firm's name on the product, which was so crude that it may have only been intended for use with blank cartridges.

The firm was begun as the Rome Revolver Works in 1879 by William J. Doyle, a machinist, and Solo-

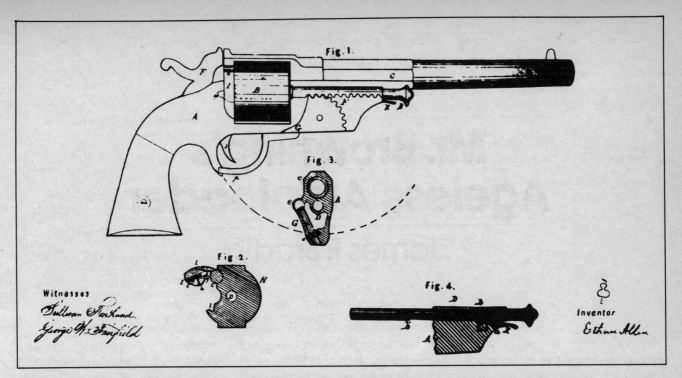

Ethan Allen's patent (No. 33,328 issued September 24, 1861) covered his cylinder pin and rammer release. It was used on Allen and on Forehand & Wadsworth guns. Note the signature of Sullivan Forehand, Allen's son-in-law, as a witness.

mon Butler, a pattern-maker, who bought out the bankrupt Mohawk Revolver Company, of Mohawk, N. Y. The revolver works in Rome did not last long; in 1880 Doyle bought out Butler, who retired. The original building in Rome is still standing.

Rupertus Patent Pistol Manufacturing Company. Founded in 1858 by Jacob Rupertus, this company remained in existence until 1900 and made a remarkable variety of firearms, including single-shot percussion and cartridge pistols, four-shot cartridge pistols (like the Sharps), eight-shot pepperboxes, rimfire double-barreled pistols (in which the firing pin is adjustable so as to strike either barrel), rifles and revolvers.

In 1888, Jacob Rupertus was living at 4505 Royal Street in Germantown and listed himself as a gunsmith; the following year the city directory shows him at the same address, listed as a machinist.

Rupertus Suicide Specials include trade names such as EMPIRE, HERO or NERO, PROTECTOR ARMS CO., and J. RUPERTUS PHILA. PA. and various Rupertus patent dates. Jacob Rupertus held at least 10 handgun patents, issued between 1859 and 1899, although the firm apparently ceased operations in 1888.

Ryan Pistol Manufacturing Company. Estab-lished in the 1870s with a factory in Norwich, Connecticut, this firm had an office and sales rooms on Franklin Street in New York City in 1874. The business was headed by Thomas J. Ryan. Trade names noted on the products of this company are NAPOLEON, PREMIERE, RYAN, and RYAN'S NEW MODEL.

United States Arms Company. This was the trade name for many of the revolvers made at Rockfall, Connecticut, by the Otis A. Smith Company. Offices were at 244 Plymouth Street in Brooklyn, New York, from 1870 to 1878. The firm also made double-action revolvers under the same name.

In the beginning, Suicide Specials competed for public favor with the more dependable large-bore single-shot pistols. Just as the single-shot pistol was doomed as a weapon for personal protection by the emergence of the multi-shot Suicide Special, so the Suicide Special was in turn made obsolete by the newer double-action revolver.

But untold numbers of Suicide Specials still repose in trunks, night tables and bureau drawers across the land. The irony is that these lowly guns that once sold for modest prices, now command hundreds of dollars and are finally coming into their own as a distinct and eminently collectible category of American firearms.

Mr. Browning's Ageless Autoloader

James F. Brady

The autoloader is gradually replacing the pump gun as America's most popular shotgun. Although the trend seems to be toward the gas-operated autoloader, the old tried-and-true, long-recoil system is still in high favor among knowledgeable shotgunners—duck and goose shooters, in particular. Long-recoil Brownings and Remingtons with worn bluing and scratched stocks appear to be the first choice of veteran turkey hunters as well. Why are long-recoil guns favored by so many of these and other shotgunners? Simply because they are second to none in reliability and ruggedness.

Birth of the Long-Recoil Shotgun

Invented by the greatest and most prolific firearms designer of all time, John Moses Browning, the long-recoil autoloader was the first autoloading shotgun and the first repeating shotgun with a solid breech and no exposed hammer. The system was patented on October 9, 1900, and first commercially manufactured by Fabrique Nationale (F.N.) in 1903. Interestingly, Browning filed a patent on the principle of gas-operated firearms in January 1890, more than 13 years before the very first autoloading shotgun—his long-recoil gun—appeared on the market.

Browning expended more time and effort on his long-recoil shotgun than on any of his other designs. His biggest problem was getting the gun to function with loads developing wide variances in recoil. Finally, Browning developed a simple friction device that could be adapted for light or heavy loads and manufactured for only a few cents. This device gave the gun designer a virtual monopoly on autoloading shotguns until the expiration of the gun's patent.

Browning, well aware of his advantage, was not inclined to sell the rights to the gun's manufacture. For this reason, and because he believed he had a revolutionary product in his autoloading shotgun, Browning demanded a royalty-basis arrangement with Winchester, similar to his arrangements with other companies such as Colt and F.N. Up until this time, Browning had sold Winchester the rights to manufacture and sell guns of his design while retaining the patents in his own name. Such famous and successful guns as the Winchester Single Shot Rifle, the Model 1886, 1892 and 1894 rifles, the Model 1897 Pump Action Shotgun and many others, were the result of this highly profitable arrangement. Winchester's president, T. G. Bennett, adamantly rejected the new proposal and Browning picked up his prototype guns and walked out. "It was not a very dignified parting," Browning later admitted. It was, however, historic. The incident marked the end of the close Browning-Winchester relationship that spanned 20 years.

Browning next turned his attention to the Remington Arms Company; however, just before preliminary discussions were to get under way, the company's president died, quickly dashing Browning's hopes that he'd found a manufacturer for his new autoloader. Finally, in February 1902, Browning took his revolutionary shotgun to Fabrique Nationale d'Armes de Guerre in Herstal, Belgium. F.N., which was already manufacturing Browning automatic pistols, was granted the exclusive rights to the

John Browning holds his most famous design, the long-recoil autoloading shotgun. Browning devoted more time and effort to the design and testing of this gun than to any of his other inventions.

The author's favorite grouse and woodcock gun, a Browning Light Twenty with a barrel-bored straight cylinder. It weighs slightly over six pounds. Brady can get on and hit a flying target faster with this gun than any other he owns (above).

The latest version of the Browning long-recoil autoloading shotgun, the Auto-5. The gun retains the most distinctive and functional feature of these Browning guns, the squared-off breech-back. Thousands of shooters find this breech configuration to be very helpful in obtaining consistent results in wingshooting (below).

manufacture and sale of the autoloading shotgun in March 1902. Because of restrictive American tariffs on foreign products, Browning arranged with F.N. to give Remington the rights to manufacture and sell the gun in the United States. Remington brought it out as the Remington Model 11 in 1905.

Browning showed his own faith in the gun by placing an order for 10,000, with a large deposit, at the time he signed his contract with F.N. The order had some risk attached to it: The guns were to be delivered to Shoverling, Daly, and Gales in New York for distribution in the U.S., but hunters in America had never heard of an automatic shotgun and never dreamed that such a thing existed.

Nevertheless, with the guns stamped "Browning Automatic Arms Company" the entire shipment was sold in one year. Browning's faith in his creation was justified.

A Sporting Arm for the 20th Century

For more than 75 years the long-recoil autoloader has remained one of the classic firearms and is still banging away in the fields, marshes, mountains and jungles of the world. In addition to Browning, the gun has been produced by Breda, Franchi, Remington, Savage and others. Total production of this sterling shooting machine is well into the millions—Browning alone has produced and sold more than a million.

Despite the number of firearms manufacturers who have produced the autoloading shotgun, its basic design has remained the same. The gun as designed by John Browning —and still made that way today by the Browning company—features an unusual innovation in that the rear of the receiver drops away sharply at almost 90 degrees from the top. Many shooters, accustomed to the old-fashioned rounded breech-back that has been around since muzzleloading days, are disconcerted by this functional design. In fact, when the gun first entered the marketplace, many shooters had custom gunsmithing firms restock their guns so the wood of the grip extended up to the rear of the receiver, thus giving them a more rounded look.

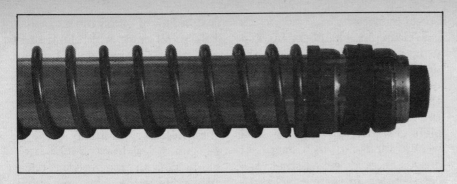

Browning's biggest problem in designing his autoloading shotgun was in getting the gun to function with loads giving wide variations in recoil. The answer lay in the simple friction brake shown here at the end of the recoil spring. This invention gave Browning a virtual monopoly on autoloading shotguns until the expiration of its patent.

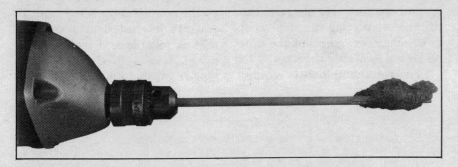

A clean chamber is an absolute necessity when using any autoloading shotgun. Extraction troubles due to dirty chambers are the main cause of malfunctions with these guns. After use, clean your guns with a wire brush and powder solvent. Several times each season, clean the chambers with the device shown here. It consists of a wad of steel wool wrapped around a slotted length of wooden doweling chucked in an electric drill. This rig will clean the dirtiest chambers.

To my mind, and the minds of thousands of other modern shooters, these folks were doing away with one of the best features of the gun. As designed by Browning, the innovation is a perfectly fine example of "design follows function." That squared-off receiver seems to be of great assistance in obtaining consistent results in wingshooting and mysteriously helps obtain consistent elevations from shot to shot. Although elevation consistency is usually a function of the stock drop at the comb—providing the shooter keeps his cheek solidly on that comb—the "square-stern" Browning seems to make it easier.

I have never used any gun with which I can get on a flying target—and hit it—as rapidly as I can with the Browning-type receiver.

My favorite woodcock and grouse gun is a Browning Light Twenty with a barrel-bored straight cylinder, though some of my fine doubles and over/unders would be well-suited to this hunting. I have an acquaintance who has killed hundreds of grouse with a 20-gauge Browning autoloader that he has carried at least a mile for every bird he took. (He is a jump-shooter and does not use a dog for grouse hunting, so you know he has to be quick.) I once asked him the secret of his success

on these birds and he replied, "My legs and my Browning."

Long-recoil shotguns are eminently reliable tools, more so than the gas-operated guns. I own several gas-operated guns and like them for some purposes—shooting trap doubles and skeet shooting, for instance. For goose, duck and turkey hunting, though, the long-recoil autoloader is best. The felt recoil from the gas guns is slightly softer than from the long-recoil guns, but both autoloading types are much easier on the shooter's shoulder and cheek than any fixed-breech gun. This is especially true when heavy loads are used.

At the moment of firing, the long-recoil system's barrel and breech bolt are locked together and recoil for several inches until the motion is arrested by a stop. Two separate return springs, one for the barrel and another for the breech block, are fully compressed when the breech block reaches the limit of its rearward motion. The breech block is caught and held in this position by a latch. The barrel return spring pushes the barrel forward and unlocks it from the breech bolt. The fired shell, held to the breech bolt by the extractor, is ejected as the barrel moves forward. When the barrel has reached its original forward position, it trips a lever that drops a latch allowing the beech bolt to come forward. As it does so, it picks up another shell from the carrier and chambers it. The gun is now ready to fire again. All of this happens so fast that it seems instantaneous. The recoil is spread out over a longer period than it would be with a fixed-breech gun, and the recoil felt by the shooter is much less.

Keeping a Reliable Gun Reliable

The reliability of long-recoil autoloaders is directly proportional to the care given them by their owners. Shooters should make every effort to keep the gas mechanisms, especially the chambers, as clean as possible. This avoids and, in fact, virtually eliminates extraction troubles, the bane of users of these guns. Merely running a patch moistened with powder solvent through barrel and chamber will not do the job.

Plastic residue from fired shells and other crud are not removed by ordinary cleaning methods and can lead to a rough chamber wall that can be felt with a finger. This roughness can cause a fired shell to be only partially extracted from the chamber, which jams the action. A really dirty chamber can be the cause of broken extractors that will put the gun completely out of business.

I clean my chambers by first using a wire brush to loosen the dirt and grime. Then I wrap the brush with fine steel wool to finish the job. Several times a year, give the chambers in your gun a complete cleaning by wrapping steel wool around a 10-inch length of quarter-inch doweling that has been slotted for a few inches to hold the steel wool. The other end is chucked in an electric drill and the steel wool is inserted into the chamber. A two-minute run with this rig will clean and polish the dirtiest chamber. Do not start the drill before placing the steel wool in the chamber, and shut the drill off before removing the wool.

Long-recoil autoloaders require a thin film of oil on the magazine tube at all times, which lubricates the recoil spring and friction brake. The operative word here is "thin." Too much oil will allow the barrel and breech block to recoil much faster and with greater force than necessary and may damage the gun. A few drops on the barrel guide slots in the receiver once in a while is the only other oiling recommended for these guns.

The long-recoil shotgun has been around longer than most of us and is still going strong. By no means has it been made obsolete by the newer gas-operated guns. If you are interested in a shotgun that is reliable and highly functional, take a hard look at the long-recoil shotgun.

Black Powder Renaissance: A New Look at Light Slug Rifles

Robert Fisch

For the firearm enthusiast, the 19th century would have been *the* period in which to have lived. During that time, firearms technology progressed from the flintlock muzzleloader to the machine gun, from black powder to smokeless powder, and to the point where the 30 caliber, previously suitable only for hunting squirrels and other "big" game, became the average caliber for military rifles.

As soon as practical metallic self-primed cartridges were developed, progress came in leaps and bounds. By the end of the Civil War, those countries which had commissions or boards searching for the perfect breechloading rifle had new rifles in the hands of their troops within a few years. Some countries, like Switzerland, took giant steps. Within four years, the Swiss advanced from muzzleloaders via single-shot metallic cartridge breechloaders to 12-shot, bolt-action repeaters.

Yet, with all of this development taking place, muzzleloading rifles were still the predominant arms used in competition by serious shooters through the 1860s and until the 1880s when their use finally tapered off, at least with regard to world competition. Certainly, very few mechanical devices enjoyed as long a period of popularity as did the muzzleloader, so there must have been good reason. Perhaps more than any other factor, the elongated rifle bullet, perfectly sized to the bore and held absolutely concentric to it at the moment of firing, can be credited for this Indian summer of muzzleloading. And, in a word, "accuracy" was the key.

Riflemen of the 19th century recognized the limitations of the patched round ball, but made little progress in improving it before the 1840s. The patch was a nuisance—it added to the labor and time in loading the rifle; and the shape and weight of the ball certainly did little to increase its range and trajectory. Rarely is anything all bad, and the round ball is no exception. One of its most noteworthy attributes is that when it connects with tissue or some other firm object, it tends to impart more of its energy to the object than pointed bullets. Some years ago this writer conducted a series of tests in a laboratory to illustrate the effectiveness of various projectile shapes. Bullets were shot into gelatin blocks, then the blocks were cut in half and the bullet channels photographed. Almost every type of ammo—minie balls, 5.56mm, 30-06—was tested, and all left very interesting channels with myriads of radiating fractures over which to muse and ponder—until a flintlock musket was fired. The 72-caliber round ball blew the gelatin block into every corner of the lab; pieces stuck to the ceiling, the floor, the walls. Later when we tried to duplicate the results of the musket with a modern rifle, it could only be done with soft-nosed bullets at very high velocity.

Still, when considering what is effective overall, the round ball admittedly needed improvement. In England, a belt was added around the ball which would engage the rifling and eliminate the cloth patch. A few years later in the 1850s, a British officer, General John Jacob, improved on the idea by elongating the mechanically fitted bullet. In France, Captain Claude Minie experimented with a hollow-based bullet, and, in Switzerland, a pointed bullet wrapped in a cloth patch was used in the 1840s. Stan-

Scottish sporting and target rifle made by Alexander Henry of Edinburgh in 1877. It is a 45 caliber and has Henry's patented elevating cheekpiece, which could be raised to the proper height to provide support no matter how high the tang sight was elevated.

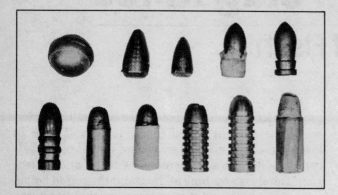

Rifle projectiles: (left to right, top row) (1) belted round ball, the first type of projectile which eliminated the need for a cloth patch; (2) 48 cal. Picket bullet; (3) 38 cal. Picket bullet for a Swiss hunting rifle; (4) 41 cal. Swiss bullet for the M1851 Federal Rifle as issued with a cloth patch tied in place; (5) M1851 Swiss bullet without the cloth patch; (bottom row) (6) modified M1851 Swiss bullet with a hollow base; (7) 42 cal. swaged bullet for paper patching; (8) same with paper patch in place; (9) pre-rifled 45 cal. compression-type bullet; (10) 45 cal. bullet which depends upon "compression expansion" alone; (11) 45 cal. pre-rifled swaged Whitworth bullet.

type rifling and the French-style Minie bullet.

In target shooting, however, where accuracy is the prime requisite, the use of a cloth-patched, elongated projectile did not go unnoticed. In fact, American riflemen of the 1840s were also experimenting with this system. Generally, the bullets were of a shorter, more pointed configuration, much like that of a loaf of sugar of the period, or picket from a fence. These "sugar loaf" or "picket" bullets produced some exceptionally fine groups in target shooting, and were occasionally used in hunting rifles. But in addition to the hindrance of loading any bullet with a cloth patch, the picket bullet had a very short bearing surface at the base end, and great care had to be exercised in keeping the point of the bullet exactly in the center of the bore. One device that assisted this operation and also had a number of side benefits was the false muzzle, patented in 1840 by Alvan Clark of Cambridge, Massachusetts. Even after picket bullet moulds began gathering dust in shooters' closets, the false muzzle remained in use because it afforded maximum protection to one of the most sensitive portions of an accurate muzzleloading rifle —the muzzle from which it must be both loaded and cleaned.

Although the picket bullet gave the decided advantage of long-range accuracy over the round ball, it still did not possess all the qualities necessary to extend the use of muzzleloading rifles for so long. Development and improvement rarely stand still. So it was that the experiments of an Englishman, Sir Joseph Whitworth, popularized a type of rifle toward which a number of other people had been striving: the "smallbore" rifle. In 1854, Whitworth, who was a mechanical engineer, conducted a series of tests for the British Government to determine whether its new Pattern 1853 Rifle/Musket was really the ultimate infantry arm. Was there perhaps something better, as others were suggesting? Whitworth was

dardized at 41 caliber in 1851, this small caliber was considered a novelty by some military minds of the time, but it would seem that the Swiss were very much on the right track. In 1855 the U.S. Army tested most of the latest, improved military rifles from Europe and fired the Swiss "Federal" rifle at 818 yards. One hundred shots were fired at a target 10 x 13 feet and *all* hit the target. The other rifles were fired from a distance of only 645 yards and the next best, the English Pattern 1853 Rifle/Musket, put only 40 bullets out of 100 in a target 9 x 13 feet. Some voices may have favored the adoption of the Swiss system for the U.S. Army, but loading the Swiss rifle was slower and more laborious than the others. Consequently, the U.S. adopted the English-

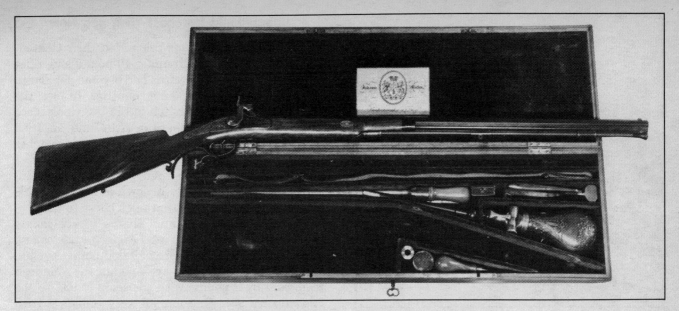

Cased Swiss 38-caliber Picket bullet sporting rifle made by Johann Müller of Bern circa 1850-55.

not bound by caliber, but his bullet would have to equal the 530-grain weight of the 577 service Minie bullet.

Sir Joseph's experiments spanned almost 10 years, and during the 1860s dominated the shooting matches held in England. No great benefits from his experiments were gained by the British Army because, as with everything, you give a little to get a little. His 45-caliber hexagonally rifled barrels definitely outclassed the range and accuracy of the Pattern 53, but were much more sensitive to careless cleaning, improper loading and changes in climate. Also, military minds were beginning to be assailed by thoughts of breechloaders and metallic cartridges. And tolerances had to be more precise in the bore or much of the accuracy advantage was lost. Cost, of course, was another factor. Even so, the Whitworth Rifle became well known in the U.S. because of its use by Confederate sharpshooters. In England, thousands of Whitworth and other smallbore rifles were privately purchased by militia volunteers; in fact, they were so popular among them that when a rifle of this type was built with military mountings, it became known as a "Volunteer" rifle.

Since Whitworth held a patent on his hexagonal bore, other British makers had to develop their own system of rifling. However, they did have some common denominators which would qualify the rifles for military use and the British National Rifle Association matches. They were all 10 pounds or under,

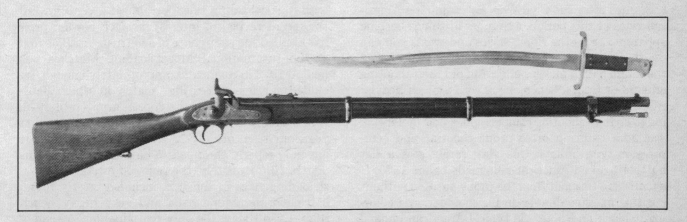

English Whitworth 45-caliber military rifles saw limited service in the United States during the Civil War and helped popularize compression bullet rifles for sporting purposes after the war.

Whitworth rear sight typical of the type found on the various British "Volunteer" rifles.

stocking and furniture in the military style, 45 caliber and shooting a bullet of about 530 grains. The bullets had parallel sides and could be paperpatched or merely greased lead. The fit could be a mechanical one to the shape of the bore or round in cross section. The bases of the bullets were flat or slightly concave; and the overall length was usually a bit over two-and-one-half times the diameter. This great length facilitated the expansion of the flat bases through compression. Upon firing, the rear of the bullet started to move before the front, with the resulting compression expanding the bullet's diameter.

The lightweight slug rifle using a compression bullet was firmly established in England in the early 1860s, but did not gather much of a following in the U.S. until after the Civil War. By examining American rifles of this period, a number of things become apparent. From the rifling styles and twists you can see that before the Civil War, Americans preferred the round ball or picket bullet, and did their shooting offhand or from a bench or log with a much heavier rifle. After the Civil War with many veterans returning to civilian shooting competition, a new dimension was added—unsupported prone shooting and compression-type bullets. One very rarely sees a flat buttplate on an American rifle made before 1870. If a man were to shoot from the prone position without creating massive dimples in his shoulder, and coloring it black and blue, the typical American hooked buttplate had to go.

International Matches: Then and Now

By the time Americans celebrated their Centennial, prone shooting with under-10-pound slug rifles at ranges of up to 1,000 yards had become popular in most of the English-speaking countries. In fact, the first international rifle match in the U.S. took place in 1874 between an American team and an Irish team, who were veterans of many long-range matches and winners of the "Elcho Shield" match, the most prestigious team match fired at Wimbledon, England. It is interesting to review the results of this match because the American team chose to use specially built Remington and Sharps *breechloading* rifles, while the Irish team used Rigby *muzzleloading* rifles. With a possible score of 1,000 points overall, and the value of one bull's-eye 4 points, the American team won by 3 points, with the score of 934 to the Irish team's 931. One undoubtedly unhappy Irish team member shot a bull's-eye on the wrong target, for which he received no credit, points or cheers from his fellow team members. That one shot would have made the difference between winning or losing for his team. Another thing which seemed to disturb John Rigby, maker of the Irish rifles and a shooting member on the team, was that the Americans cleaned their rifles between each shot, and at Wimbledon it was not customary to do so. This led Rigby to challenge the American team to an impromptu match the day following the international competition—an abbreviated 1,000-yard match with a possible of only 400, 25 shots per man, no cleaning between shots. The Irish won with a score of 321 to the American score of 201, quite a drubbing. No doubt the voyage back to Ireland was not so gloomy as it might have been.

The development of smokeless powder completely sealed the doom of international shooting matches with muzzleloading rifles for almost a century, but the recent revival of interest in black powder arms has kindled the resurgence of such matches. The first of the International Muzzleloading Matches was held in 1972 in Spain and, appropriately enough, included a prone "free rifle" match in which lightweight slug rifles were the chosen arm. Until 1976, American involvement was just a token; even in that year, our team of only 18 shooters did not include anyone properly equipped to be competitive in this match. Unfortunately, the renewed interest in muzzleloading rifles in the U.S. included mostly round ball shooting, Minie balls and very heavy bench rifles. Even today, the only reproduction "assembly line" lightweight slug rifles suited for prone shooting

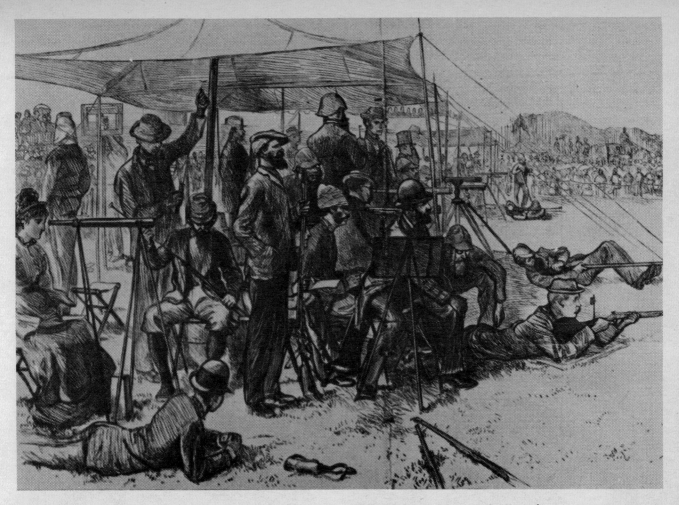

A scene from the 1,000-yard shooting during the 1877 International Rifle Match, reprinted from *Harper's Weekly* October 6, 1877.

are made by Parker-Hale in England.

By 1977, the U.S. had done its homework and went to Switzerland ready for Match No. 4, the "Free Rifle" match, the majority of its team members equipped with British smallbore rifles. The team borrowed knowledge from others—as well as rifles. In this competition, all of the rifles had to be originals, and finding suitable ones not only was time consuming, but often expensive and agonizing.

Although I was a member of the U.S. team in 1976, my first attempt in Match 4 was in 1977, with a borrowed English sporting and target rifle made by Thomas Turner. Having fired some reasonably good practice targets, I approached the shooting mat oozing confidence only to put my first .451 bullet into the 8 ring, followed by two more. By the fourth shot, I was in the 10 ring and stayed in the 9-10 ring area until the last shot. By that time, not only had confidence returned to me, but a pleasant euphoria

seemed to be guiding my actions. I remember how crowded the shooters were, and in trying not to crown my fellow competitors with my ramrod, I began performing a modified baton twirler's routine with it over my head, which the spectators seemed to enjoy immensely. I suppose I might have confused showmanship with marksmanship, because when I viewed my last shot through the spotting scope, the hole was definitely not in the 10 ring, more like the 6. Of course, at the time I was only too happy to take refuge in the observation, "The gun didn't sound right."

During the following three years, we all learned a great deal about the characteristics of various compression bullet rifles and their projectiles. Early models usually had more radically shaped bores and deeper rifling, such as the Whitworth and Alexander Henry systems, and generally were more difficult to master. When the rifle is fired, the bullet must totally upset to fill the grooves or gas will escape past it; a "gascut" bullet will not provide the maximum accuracy your rifle may be capable of. To obviate this, powder charges of 80 to 100 grains were common in the last century; they were also necessary to flatten the trajectory in 1,000-yard shooting, but were by no means comfortable loads to shoot from the prone position. By the 1870s, shallow grooves, seldom more than .004″ deep were favored in a conventional land-and-groove configuration, or the Rigby Rachet groove. In shooting these rifles today at only 100 meters, the smallest powder charge necessary to expand the bullet fully and give it a true course should be sought when "working in" a new rifle.

There are ways other than using larger powder charges to achieve the goal of full expansion in these rifles, but sometimes they are not as accurate, or are, at the least, more bothersome. A hollow base was one method employed to cure the ills of one 40-caliber rifle. It had too slow a twist—about 1 turn in 24 inches—and would not group well with a bullet which was long enough to expand fully with the compression system. It also had rifling of about .008 inches in depth, again a problem when using a compression bullet. Another method found to be effective is pre-grooving a bullet which is about .001 inches under groove diameter. The bullet can be pushed through the false muzzle a couple of times before loading, but a much better solution is to pre-rifle the bullet. If one has the ability to "fresh out" a barrel, use the same system with the barrel as a guide for rifling a short tube, which can then be formed into a die specifically for this purpose. The die can be made slightly undersize on the lands, and loading will be a breeze. The pre-grooved bullet is a real lifesaver in a rifle which has developed a slight powder bed and possibly dulled edges on the lands as well. This condition will often allow some stripping of the bullet as it starts up the bore, resulting in a loss of accuracy. The pre-grooved bullet is locked into the rifling at

Producing a good group with a slug rifle is sometimes dependent on very minor changes in the ammunition. The target on the left was fired at 100 meters from the prone position with the Warner underhammer rifle. The group covered by the white pasters was fired with alloy bullets of 1 part tin to 60 parts lead. Immediately after pasting the target, pure lead bullets were tried. The first shot went into the 9 ring and, after a sight correction, the next five stayed well in the 10 ring.

The target on the right was fired with Picket bullets from the Swiss Liegler rifle at 50 meters off-hand. The pasted holes are a group using "fresh" Hoppes 9 plus which was still thin and watery; then old Hoppes 9 plus which had become thick and milky was tried resulting in the unpasted group. It seems every rifle wants to be an individual.

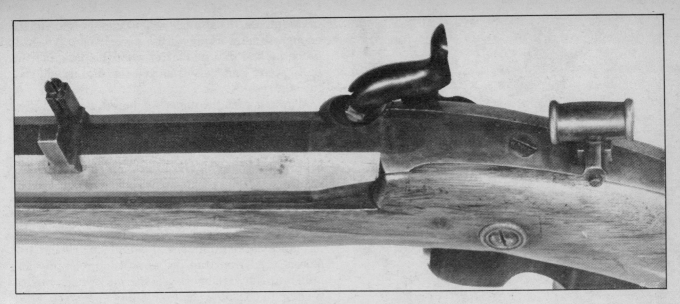

Swiss "lollypop" tang sight with windage adjustment and sunshade on the Liegler rifle.

the moment of discharge and given a chance to expand fully before commencing its journey to the 10 ring.

Whether the bullet is flatbased or hollowbased, it should have straight sides for at least three quarters of its length, with a slight shoulder where it begins to taper into the nose. Such a bullet will cut a clean hole in the target and be easier to spot when every second counts during a match. Also, it is easier to keep parallel to the bore when loading. If it has many grease grooves, this will aid in holding the fouling at a manageable level—not only by supplying lubrication, but because the front shoulder will act as a scraper.

If a rifle is stubborn about bullet expansion, and a flat base is preferred to a hollow base, the front rotating band or bands on the type of bullet just mentioned can be enlarged to engrave themselves with the rifling during loading. A simple method of enlarging a mould which has uniform rotating bands is to turn a piece of stock on a lathe to fit the diameter of what amounts to the bottom of the grease grooves in the mould. Grind a small toolbit to the shape of the rotating bands and insert it crossways into the shaft with a small set screw behind it for adjustment. If the entire mould is to be enlarged, start with the base ring and grind off the front of the shaft as you move deeper into the mould so you will maintain consistent support for the shaft. Of course, this system will only work with a mould in which the lead enters from the base end, or at least has the base exposed, such as the moulds made by The Gun Shop

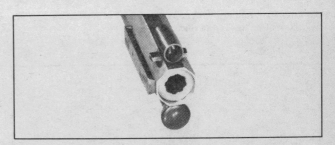

The most common form of target sight has no screw adjustment for windage but can be moved to the right or left in the dovetail which attaches it to the barrel. It is nothing more than a sunshade inside which is mounted a pinhead, post or aperture sight. The muzzle of this rifle by Liegler is recessed to center a false muzzle for starting the Picket bullet. Most Swiss ramrods have a large head for a better grip in ramming, which is evident in this photo, and could not be used in the field for cleaning.

British-style long-range front sight has windage adjustment and a set screw to lock the slide in place to protect the windage screw. The apertures are mounted in removable "barrels" which are locked into the sunshade.

An American folding "lollypop" tang sight with windage adjustment on the Tonks rifle.

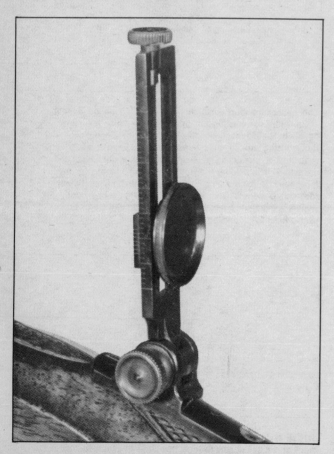

British-style tang sight which has the elevation screw mounted between the side rails for added protection.

in Montrose, Colorado. When you are fortunate enough to be working with a perfect bore, you will probably find that no matter what the design of the bullet, pure lead, as soft as you can find it, will give the best results.

Working with an imperfect bore, or when heavy powder charges are used in long-range shooting, a small amount of tin can be added, somewhere between 1:30 to 1:60 to ease loading problems or excessive deforming of the base. Composition bullets with a hard lead nose and soft base were also used in the long-range matches of the last century and even today are used in large-caliber heavyweight bench guns. If your concern is in squeezing every bit of performance out of an under-10-pound slug rifle at 100 meters fired from the prone position, composition bullets are not cost effective, especially when practice is going to consume about 50 bullets per week.

Likewise, paperpatched bullets and loading methods which include leisurely cleaning the bore between shots should be avoided; in an international match only 30 minutes are allowed to fire 14 shots, including one "warming" or "fouling" shot. Of the 13 shots fired at the target, the best 10 are added together and become your score. Sighting in is done on a Friday, and one or two days later when you return to the firing line, "It's for real." That 30 minutes gets eaten up when you're trying to scope your shots through everyone's smoke, or are forced to make a number of sight corrections. A rifle and load that requires no more than brushing the bore every second or third shot is a blessing. But if powder fouling is still building up to the point of difficult loading or reducing accuracy, then try more lubrication first. A wafer about ⅛- to ³⁄₁₆-inch thick of beeswax and tallow between the bullet and powder will often eliminate the problem. If not, a felt "sweeper" wad of about the same thickness, soaked in your favorite lubricant and used with or without the wafer wad, (but always placed at the base of the bullet) is another method. For more thorough scrubbing action, the sweeper wad can have stiff paper glued on both sides of the felt before lubricating the wads, creating a "stiff sandwich," so to speak.

For many years, the controversy of "gain twist" versus "uniform twist" rifling has occupied the minds of gunmakers and riflemen alike, and will probably continue to do so. If you were to look for comparisons you might begin with the first international matches in 1874, where the Irish Rigbys had gain twist, and the American Sharps and Remingtons had a uniform twist. The Americans won the matches overall, but as individuals, only one American shot a higher score

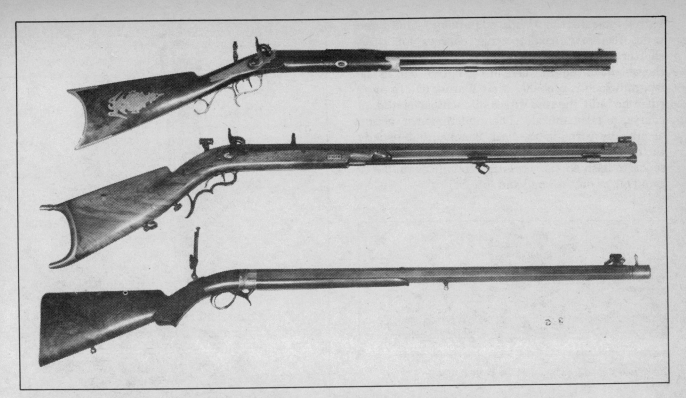

The American sporting rifle (top) by J. Tonks of Boston circa 1860-70 is rifled with a gain twist and was intended for round balls or Picket bullets. The Swiss privately purchased Military/Target rifle (center), made by Liegler in Olten, although appearing very "civilian," qualified for military matches and even had a bayonet bar at the muzzle. Below is the 45-caliber underhammer slug rifle attributed to Horace Warner circa 1880-85.

than the top Irish shooter. As always, there are too many other factors and variables to be able to draw valid conclusions. If you had to choose between either system, the uniform twist would seem to be better, as it allows the option of a mechanically fitted bullet or lapping the bore while the gain twist does not. The shape of the lands and grooves does not seem to be critical but, in general, because of the shallow depth of the grooves, it is beneficial to have at least seven or eight to reduce the tendency of stripping, and about twice the width of the lands. A bore without taper and no loose or tight spots will shoot very well, but most of the old slug rifles and especially the British ones, have a taper of .001 inch to .003 inch in the bore. It does make loading easier and guarantees that resistance will be maintained on the bullet as it heads toward the muzzle.

Bore and bullet are the heart of a good rifle, but other features add their own dimension to the overall effectiveness of the piece. A rifle intended primarily for target shooting will not have a rib under the barrel, or ramrod fitted to it. This ensures that as the gun heats during firing, there will be less tendency for distortion, or walking the bullets across the target. In Switzerland, where the owner of a target rifle might be required to have it qualify as a military arm also, to maintain the advantage of the target rifle, a ramrod is occasionally fitted and held by thimbles mounted on individual platforms instead of a solid rib—not very attractive, but a solution if one must have a ramrod.

The Warner Rifle: Unmatched in Performance

Sidelocks and underhammer action both have their advocates, but the looks and workmanship most often seen on the underhammer rifles were inferior, I thought, until I acquired one credited to Horace Warner of Syracuse, New York. This rifle has so many good features that perhaps a description of it would serve as a model for many of the finer American-made light slug rifles. It should be noted that during the 1880s and 1890s Warner was one of the most esteemed makers of super-accurate muzzle-loading target rifles.

The rifle was intended for 20- to 40-rod distances, not international shooting of 800, 900 and 1,000 yards. The height of the rear sight and length of the barrel indicate this. With a 10-pound limit, and using relatively small powder charges for these shorter distances, there is more benefit in putting the weight in the thickness of the barrel than in the length, which is probably what Warner had in mind when he built the rifle with a 30-inch barrel and, of course, a false muzzle. The underhammer action avoids any turns in the flash channel, but usually the nipple is mounted directly into the barrel, and a separate flash cup is necessary around the nipple to avoid burns on the hand and forearm.

Sharp's-designed front sight on the Warner under-hammer rifle (side view).

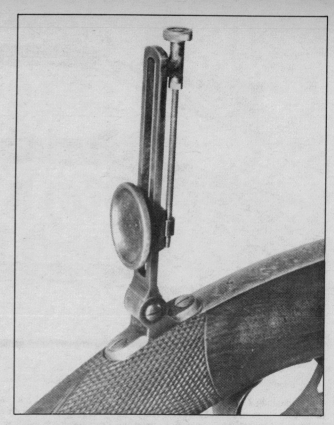

Typical American-style long-range tang sight on the Warner underhammer rifle.

In the construction of this rifle, the barrel is not attached directly to the frame, but instead has a separate "patent breech" with a built-in flash cup—a sturdier and far more attractive system. There is no halfcock notch on the hammer, as even with a fly guiding the sear over the notch, there can be a slight hesitation in hammer fall. With a screw mounted in the hammer, the weight of the trigger pull can be varied, and the screw which anchors the rear end of the mainspring/triggerguard also serves to eliminate trigger backlash. The folding rear tang sight has a vernier scale and is screw adjustable for elevation. The front sight is "stock" Sharps, windage adjustable, with removable apertures and a spirit level to provide amusement, if nothing else. Just concentrate and watch the bubble. It is equipped with a flat "shotgun" buttplate and a rather straight stock with a pistol grip suitable for offhand, bench or prone shooting. The butt is hollow to allow making the barrel heavier, but it also presents the option of adding about three pounds of lead in the butt to change the balance of the rifle and qualify it for the 10- to 13-pound class. It is difficult for me to believe how I could have walked away from a Warner Rifle at a gun show, actually get as far as a local restaurant and order my lunch before realizing that I was about to write another "stupid" chapter in my life. Fortun-

ately, my wife was more than understanding and fended off the management while I dashed back for the rifle. I have no doubt that without it I would have won one less gold medal in the 1980 International Matches.

Shooting light slug rifles can fill many challenging and enjoyable hours. If the subject interests you and your "quest" begins, give a generous amount of attention to the bore of a prospective rifle. Don't be prejudiced toward a particular type of action—they all have their merits—and don't be dissuaded if the gun's condition is less than perfect, especially when considering a "shooting" rifle. Some years ago when observing a rather "ratty" looking rifle in the hands of a competitor at the start of a match, a shooter made the remark, "Looks a bit rough, doesn't it?" The competitor replied, "You're looking at the good part," after which point he "cleaned house." Perhaps he was only partially right: the rifle was being held by "the good part." As in all types of shooting, success is a product of a weapon system, a good bullet and a good rifle—held in the confident, practiced hands of a good shooter.

Gun Control: Can It Work?

Don B. Kates Jr.

The assassination of John Lennon and the attempt on President Reagan occasioned much editorialization for "gun control." This is ironic, since the argument for such legislation has generally been that banning handguns would reduce domestic homicide—it being everywhere recognized that it would have little effect upon assassins or hardened criminals. After all, even in England authorities find that there are always sufficient illicit guns for any criminal who is really determined to have one. And it is difficult to imagine anyone more determined than an assassin who is willing to risk death or long imprisonment for the attempt.

For related reasons I am even skeptical that a handgun ban would reduce domestic and acquaintance homicide. But before discussing this, I would make some disclaimers. First, far from representing the "gun lobby," I am a liberal criminologist with a background in civil-rights law and a teacher of constitutional and criminal law and criminal procedure. Unlike those who typically oppose gun bans, I did not grow up with guns. I am happy to say that neither I nor the rest of my family has ever hunted. Nor am I going to espouse the Second Amendment right to keep and bear arms, or argue that people should own handguns for protection. Assuming that gun owners are completely wrong on those issues, two more basic questions remain: 1) Can we disarm the millions who believe that they have both constitutional right and urgent necessity for a handgun to protect their families? 2) Do the likely benefits of trying to disarm them outweigh the likely costs?

Unfortunately these questions find no answers in the vast literature for handgun prohibition. It consists mostly of polemics against the handgun, unalloyed by specifics as to how a ban could actually be implemented. Upon critical examination, this literature, which is supposed to have made the definitive case for handgun prohibition, turns out to show only that many progressive and humane scholars detest firearms and believe the world would be better off if they somehow disappeared.

Since the case for handgun prohibition is often treated as already established, it may be useful to quote at length some neutral evaluations of this literature. Social-policy analyst Barry Bruce-Briggs: "It is startling to note that no policy research worthy of the name has been done on the issue of gun control. The few attempts at serious work are of marginal competence at best, and tainted by obvious bias." Professor Philip Cook, director of Duke University's Center for the Study of Criminal Justice Policy: "While the consistent failure of gun-control proposals to pass Congress has often been blamed on lobbying efforts of the NRA, part of the problem may be that the case for more stringent gun-control regulation has not yet been made in a scientific fashion."

Indeed, the six states which forbid owning or buying a handgun without a permit (Hawaii, Michigan, Missouri, New Jersey, New York, North Carolina) consistently have higher homicide rates than demographically comparable states that allow any sane adult without criminal record to buy them. Contrary to the argument

IF GUNS ARE OUTLAWED
ONLY OUTLAWS WILL HAVE GUNS

by pro-gun groups, this does not show that widespread handgun ownership deters homicide. Rather it suggests that some states with peculiarly high homicide rates have tried to reduce them by banning handguns. But since that approach consistently fails, a high homicide rate comes to coincide with handgun bans. By the same token, the states which traditionally have had the lowest homicide rates have also had the most lax gun laws.

Banning handguns cannot reduce homicide because, no matter how strict the enforcement, murderers represent so tiny a proportion of the population that there will always be far more handguns (or other legal or illegal firearms) available than they need. Only one out of every 5,400 handguns is used to murder, and a ban can reduce homicide only if it affects possession of that particular weapon.

Prohibitionists have attempted to avoid this obvious truth by arguing that most murders are committed not by "criminals," but by the ordinary citizen in a moment of rage and with a handgun he keeps loaded to protect his home. Accepting (for the moment) this characterization of murderers, it is nevertheless impossible to square the unexamined assumption that a ban will disarm such citizens with our experience under Prohibition and under marijuana laws. People who think they need a handgun to protect their families would have a far stronger incentive to disobey than did marijuana smokers or most drinkers. And keeping (or acquiring in a single black-market transaction) a handgun obviously involves far less risk and effort than the long succession of black-market transactions engaged in by millions of marijuana-law and Prohibition violators. Realistically, compliance with a handgun ban would come only from sportsmen—whom no one really cares about disarming because they don't keep their guns loaded around the house.

Moreover, when the average murderer is accurately characterized, it becomes evident that he is even less likely to comply with the ban than the ordinary citizen. Unlike the ordinary protection owner, the average murderer is an impoverished, hopeless, often alcoholic or drug-dependent aberrant with a long history of taking out his frustrations in sudden violent outbursts against those around him. National data show that 68 percent of murderers have previously been arrested for at least one major felony. But arrest data substantially under-represent their true history since it typically involves violence against friends and acquaintances, who rarely press charges—or whose complaints are likely to be dismissed by the police as mere "family disputes." Thus in 90 percent of domestic homicides police had been to the home at least once before to stop a beating; in 50 percent of these murders the police had been there five or more times before.

It should surprise no one if people with such histories of actual violence have little more compunction about violating a handgun ban than the professional robber or burglar whom the prohibitionists themselves concede will never be disarmed. What is surprising is that handgun prohibitionists should be so oblivious to our experience with national Prohibition and marijuana laws as to argue that a national handgun ban would be more enforceable than the few state bans which now exist, e.g., New York's.

A national ban would require enforcement in areas far less well policed than New York and along our 12,000-mile borders. If handguns were illegally imported at the same volume as marijuana, 22 million weapons of the approximate size of the one which killed John Lennon could be smuggled in each year. Of course, since the country has already about 55 million handguns of all kinds, there would not be a market for 22 million new ones. Even now, when handgun sales are legal in 44 states, only about 2.5 million are sold each year—40 percent to sportsmen, who would presumably not violate a ban. But if we cannot prevent a million illegal immigrants or ten thousand metric tons of marijuana from entering the country each year, a ban will not prevent anyone who wants a handgun for self-defense or crime from getting one.

But what about all the evidence that handgun prohibition works in England and other countries? The most charitable characterization which a social scientist could make of this "evidence" is that it has been carefully selected to buttress a preconceived position. When the full range of foreign comparisons is made, what appears is this: The gun bans of the European countries commonly compared to the U.S. were not enacted to reduce general violence (with which those countries have been little affected). They were enacted to prevent the assassinations and political terrorism from which England, Germany, etc., still suffer far more than we.

In fact, prohibitionists abruptly stopped referring to England in 1971 with the appearance from Cambridge University of the first in-depth study of that country's handgun-permit law. This Cambridge study attributes England's comparatively low violence wholly to cultural factors, pointing out that until 1920 England had far fewer gun controls than most American states. Yet England had far less violence then than did those states or than England now has. Those who blame greater handgun availability for our greater rates of handgun homicide ignore the fact that rates of murder with knives or without any weapon (i.e., with hands and feet) are also far lower in England. The study's author has asked rhetorically whether it is claimed that knives are less available in England than in the U.S. or that the English have fewer hands and feet than Americans. As a subsequent British government publication puts it, although "one reason often given for American homicide is the easy availability of firearms . . . the strong correlation with racial and linked socio-economic variables suggests that the underlying determinants of the homicide rate relate to particular cultural factors."

European comparisons would be incomplete without mention of Switzerland, where violence rates are very low though every man of military age is required to own a handgun or fully automatic rifle. Israeli violence is similarly low, though the populace is even more intensively armed. The comparison to handgun-banning Japan's low homicide rate is plainly inappropriate because of our totally different culture and heritage and our substantial ethnic heterogeneity. (The only valid comparison reinforces the irrelevancy of gun bans: it is that Japanese-Americans, with full access to handguns, have a slightly lower homicide rate than their gunless counterparts in Japan.) An appropriate comparison to Japan might be Taiwan. Despite even more stringent anti-handgun laws, it has a homicide rate greater than

ours and four times greater than Japan's. Similarly, the U.S. might well be compared with South Africa, a highly industrialized and ethnically heterogeneous country which has very little political violence. Despite one of the world's most stringent "gun control" programs, South Africa's non-political homicide rate is twice ours.

Before concluding this part of the discussion I should emphasize that comparisons between differing societies are very difficult to make and dangerous to generalize from. Had the choice been mine I would have refrained from any such comparisons. But so much of the argument for handgun prohibition has been based upon specious reasoning from specially chosen foreign examples that clarification becomes almost obligatory.

States with Lowest Homicide Rates Have Laxest Gun Laws

While the benefits flowing from handgun prohibition have been greatly exaggerated, the costs have gone virtually unnoticed. From a civil-liberties point of view, the proposals of those few prohibitionists who have seriously considered enforcement techniques are truly scary. One is to "reinterpret" the Fourth Amendment to allow police to swoop down on strategically located streets, round up pedestrians en masse, and herd them through portable airport-type metal detectors. A formerly free populace will now be unable to work or run ordinary errands without the risk of being dragnetted into long lines such as they now encounter only when voluntarily traveling by air. Of course— for whatever consolation it may be to the rest of us—we may expect that the flying squad's attentions

will be focused on certain neighborhoods and on people of certain racial and economic characteristics.

But the metal-detector approach would only operate against transportation of handguns, not remove them from the home. So a respected liberal federal judge has recently urged the Supreme Court to abandon the constitutional requirement of probable cause in gun-search cases. In other words, the police would be empowered to break into any home, search any person or vehicle, simply at random or by whim. Yet another proposal is to offer bounties for people to turn in their friends, neighbors, and relatives. One is reminded of Pavel Morozov, the 14-year-old boy posthumously lionized by Stalin after he was murdered for having turned in his father as a violator of Soviet farm-collectivization policies.

Another proposal involves penalties so ferocious that people will be more frightened of the law than of giving up what they see as their families' only protection in a violent society. For the perhaps thirty million protection owners who could be expected to defy a ban, the law will require a mandatory year in prison. Beyond the moral implications of thus making war on so large a part of our society is the sheer impracticability. A year sentence for only 0.2 percent of these probable violators would mean more than a doubling of the federal prison system. Moreover, imprisonment could only follow trial and conviction. Even if the federal courts dismissed all other civil and criminal cases, trying 0.2 percent (or even 0.02 percent) of the probable violators would take so long that many would end up winning motions to dismiss for failure to provide a speedy trial.

NEVER MIND THE DOG • BEWARE OF OWNER!

United Press International Photo

My doubts about handgun prohibition do not betoken opposition to "gun controls" in general. Prohibiting firearms to minors, the insane, and violent felons is sensible, and so are most of our other twenty thousand present federal, state, and local gun-control laws. For their own purposes, both sides in the handgun-prohibition debate make it a practice to emphasize that present controls have not stemmed American violence. Progun groups proclaim this as proof that no gun controls can ever work. Conversely, anti-gun groups claim it only shows the need for total prohibition.

Of course, no gun law (nor all criminal laws together) can offset the fundamental cultural, socioeconomic, and institutional factors which create a violent society. Nevertheless, gun laws can be helpful. Instead of blindly enacting national prohibition we should systematically study our present controls (which, between federal and diverse state laws, include every conceivable gun law) to determine what approaches are helpful, what aren't, and why. The seminal work of this type is Bendis and Balkin's study which finds Illinois' moderate and sensible gun laws failing not because they are inherently insufficient but because they are virtually unenforced: "Based on the Chicago data it is difficult to argue that gun laws do not work or that stronger laws are needed . . . It is very possible that if gun laws do potentially reduce gun-related crime, the present laws are all that is needed if they are enforced. What good would stronger laws do when the courts have demonstrated they will not enforce them?"

In this connection, it may be remembered that last year John Hinckley was caught red-handed violating the federal ban on firearms in commercial aircraft. Had the charges not been dropped he would have been in federal prison instead of shooting the President. When we are not making even minimal efforts to enforce our present sensible controls, why should we move to a complete prohibition which all our experience shows could not be enforced however hard we tried?

Don Kates is an attorney who practices in California. His first book was Restricting Handguns: The Liberal Skeptics Speak Out. *He is currently editing a collection of scholarly papers on firearms regulation to be published by Ballinger under the auspices of the Pacific Institute for Public Policy Research.*

Great Weapons Museums of the World: The Springfield Armory Museum

George M. Horn

Americans are not much given to establishing shrines or known for an overweening fondness for the past. But if gun enthusiasts and history buffs wanted to create their own Mecca, they would make pilgrimages en masse to Springfield, the bustling little metropolis of western Massachusetts, lying along the east bank of the Connecticut River.

Situated high on a plateau overlooking this attractive city, the Springfield Armory is a group of buildings that literally were witnesses to history and should be enshrined. If their mute bricks and stones could speak, what stories they could tell.

Here it was that during the Revolutionary War in 1777, a "laboratory" and arms depot were established. The official birth date of the Springfield Armory, however, is April 2, 1794, when the Third Congress of the fledgling federal government established it as a "National Armory." By the 1790s, the supply of muskets available to the government from arms imported during the Revolutionary War had reached a dangerously low level. Because France, beset with her own domestic difficulties, could supply no more guns, and England—the former mother country—was then at war with France, Congress directed the establishment of two federal armories. The second armory was set up at Harper's Ferry, Virginia (now West Virginia). A succession of reliable small arms was developed at Springfield whose contributions to the history of the United States cannot be measured. It can be said without exaggeration that the Springfield Armory literally saved the nation from disaster on numerous occasions.

The first pattern adopted and copied at Springfield was the French Charleville Model 1763 flintlock musket, which had seen extensive service with Continental troops during the Revolution. This gun, named the 1795 Model, with minor improvements, served until 1844, when it was superseded by percussion-ignition models.

The first year's output of flintlocks at Springfield was only 245 muskets, all laboriously fashioned by hand. With the introduction of newly invented machinery, such as giant triphammers for welding barrels, barrel-turning lathes and an ingenious wood-turning lathe devised by self-taught inventor Thomas Blanchard (on view at the Springfield Armory Museum), production methods and facilities rapidly improved.

By 1830 annual production reached 16,500 muskets. In addition to the smooth-bore long arms, the Springfield Armory produced flintlock pistols and shorter, lighter muskets for the cadets at the U.S. Military Academy at West Point. In all, 471,346 flintlock muskets were built at the Springfield Armory from 1795 to 1844, when production was changed to smooth-bore percussion muskets of 69 caliber. Of the latter, 171,940 were made by 1855, when the 58-caliber rifled musket was adopted. Between 1855 and 1865, the astonishing total of 840,549 of these muzzleloaders was made at the Springfield Armory.

At the end of the Civil War, the government found

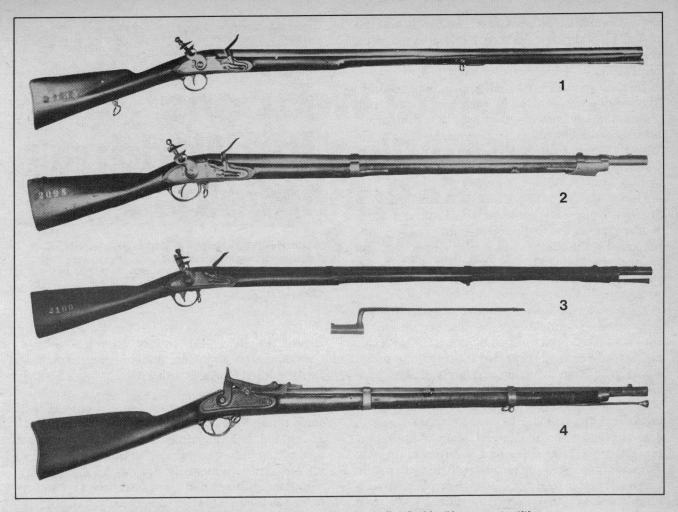

From top to bottom: (1) Model 1807 U.S. Flintlock Carbine, also called the "Indian Carbine" because quantities were ordered by the Indian Department to be issued to friendly Indians; (2) The Model 1816 U.S. Flintlock Musket enjoyed the largest production run of U.S. flintlock muskets (this is the shorter artillery model) (3) Cadets at the U.S. Military Academy at West Point were supplied with short muskets like this 1831 muzzleloader, probably to make the manual of arms easier and smarter-looking; (4) Erskine Allin's first (1865) conversion of the Civil War percussion rifle, which came to be known as the Trapdoor Springfield.

itself with hundreds of thousands of now-obsolete muzzleloading guns. Many of these were converted to breechloaders by Erskine S. Allin, master armorer at the Springfield Armory.

Allin's contributions to firearms development were many, but the greatest was his clever design for converting muzzleloaders to breechloaders. It consisted of a hinged "trapdoor" breech block with a loading latch, an extractor and a firing pin. A section was milled from the top of the breech of a muzzleloader, the new block was attached, the percussion hammer replaced by one designed to strike the new firing pin, and the conversion was complete. (It should be noted that Allin's system, preferred by the government, was only one of many approaches to the problem. Other systems included the Joslyn, Miller, Mont

Storm, Morse, Needham, Peabody, Phoenix, Remington, Roberts, Sharps and Whitney. This list does not include the many other inventors' systems submitted for government tests, but comprises only those contracted for by the government, produced in quantity or used by the militia of the individual states.)

In 1865, the Springfield Armory converted 5,000 percussion rifle muskets using the Allin system. Allin improved the extractor in 1866, and the Model 1866 rifles that resulted later underwent a second alteration, which reduced their caliber from 58 to 50 by brazing a liner in the bore. With further improvements, the Allin system was adopted for new arms, both rifles and carbines, and it remained the standard system for military long arms until 1892, when—with the introduction of smokeless powder—it was replaced by a slightly modified Norwegian magazine rifle, the Krag-Jorgensen, which remained in use only until 1903.

In that year an improved, clip-loading modified Mauser rifle was adopted by the army. Utterly reliable and widely known as the accurate "Springfield," it served with distinction throughout the First World War. By October 1918 a production rate of more than a thousand Springfields a day was achieved at the armory.

During the 1920s and 1930s the Springfield Armory developed and produced the Garand rifle of World War II, the first semiautomatic *military* rifle produced in the millions and used as a basic shoulder weapon. In the 1950s the Springfield Armory designed and manufactured the fully automatic M14 to take the NATO cartridge.

Despite the nature of its products, the Springfield Armory has led a relatively placid existence. Only a few times has it been touched by violence. One tragic incident had consequences that ultimately produced a stronger nation living under a newly ratified Constitution.

In Massachusetts, as in the other states, the Revolution and the period after it were times of social, economic and political upheaval. Many of the important leaders in commerce and government became Tories and followed the retreating British armies to Canada or even to England. In their place arose a new aristocracy that drew its wealth largely from maritime trade. More and more, the financial resources of the states were concentrated along the seaboard, leaving the dissatisfied farmers of the interior to struggle against the burden of mortgages, not to mention their stubborn soil.

Open rebellion resulted, fanned by the economic depression that swept over the infant nation after the war. In the hills of western Massachusetts, the impoverished farmers and small businessmen demanded legislative relief in the form of more paper money and laws to stay foreclosure by the hated sheriffs. These discontented elements united under the leadership of Daniel Shays, a Revolutionary War veteran. In 1786, he and his disheveled followers closed the courts in Worcester and marched up and down the countryside in an attempt to prevent the convening of the courts and the entering of judgments against debtors.

Although "Shays' Rebellion" won many sympathizers, it failed at Springfield, which became Shays' Waterloo, when his attempt to capture the stores of munitions there failed. The site of this engagement

Shooter's Bible photo

In addition to its designation as a national historic site, on February 19, 1980, the Springfield Armory became the 39th engineering landmark to be included in the history and heritage program of the American Society of Mechanical Engineers.

is near the Springfield Armory. Here U.S. soldiers, commanded by Maj.-Gen. William Shepard of Westfield, repulsed Shays' attack with a volley of artillery fire that killed four of Shays' followers.

Shays appealed to Shepard for a truce so that he could retrieve the bodies of the five men killed. Shepard replied that he could only count four bodies, but if Shays would attack again, he would be happy to furnish him with as many dead as he wanted. The ragtag army Shays had assembled broke up and returned to their homes, disappointed.

Shays' Rebellion had one positive effect: It was instrumental in galvanizing the propertied classes of the new nation to support and ratify the federal Constitution of 1787 as a bulwark against such outbreaks of violence in the states.

That Springfield would be selected as the location for a National Armory was almost inevitable, because it provided a natural site. It was far enough from the coast and from the Canadian border to be secure from attack by any potential enemy. The powerful Connecticut River was a capital asset, providing power for sawmills, gristmills and attracting entrepreneurs to establish machine shops. The arrival of the railroad about 1835 further stimulated trade and industry. Artisans, attracted by the opportunities in the city's numerous factories, poured in and created a reservoir of skilled workers that has remained one of Springfield's resources to this day.

The armory grew slowly after its establishment in 1794. In 1815, Maj. Roswell Lee took command of the installation, eventually becoming its civilian superintendent, a post he was to hold for more than

Construction on this imposing building, the New Arsenal, now called the Main Arsenal, was begun during the Mexican War. It still dominates the Springfield Armory complex and the skyline of the city of Springfield, on whose official seal it appears. Today it houses the extensive collections of the Springfield Armory Museum.

18 years. It was Lee who conceived the design for the facility as a "Grand National Armory," and who gave impetus to the plan for the quadrangular arrangement of the armory buildings that still dominate Springfield's skyline.

Maj. James Wolfe Ripley—a stormy petrel if there ever was one—took over as commanding officer in 1841. He was to direct the army's affairs for 13 years, and he was to leave his mark on it in no uncertain terms. Ripley embarked on an ambitious building construction program, perhaps taking advantage of the increased demands of the Mexican War, during which the armory was busy producing muskets and spare parts. During Ripley's tenure, he built the charming commanding officers' quarters, still standing today, which became the subject of a bitter and acrimonious investigation after which Ripley was eventually cleared.

Maj. Ripley's relationship with the community, never placid, is epitomized in the massive iron fence surrounding the Springfield Armory grounds. Taste-fully designed, it is both utilitarian and symbolic. The fence palings, appropriately, are nine-foot-high halberds and pikes; the gates are intricately patterned examples of the ironworker's art. It is a fence that invites no one to attempt to scale it or breach it.

In 1847 construction began on the Main Arsenal building, which today houses the collections of the Springfield Armory Museum. The original purpose of this building was to store the newly manufactured muskets until they could be sent to other arsenals or issued to troops. Three stories high, with a taller square tower, the building was capable of storing hundreds of thousands of guns in special racks constructed for this purpose. These are the same racks that impressed poet Henry Wadsworth Longfellow, who visited the Springfield Armory on his honeymoon. His wife remarked on the resemblance of the tiers of stored arms to the pipes of an organ. Longfellow later wrote his poem, "The Arsenal at Springfield," forever immortalizing this visual image.

Another who left his mark on the Springfield Ar-

The German MG42 machine gun (right) was developed by Dr. Grunow from a Polish design captured by the Germans in 1939. But copying is not always successful; the United States copied the MG42 as the T24 during World War II. The American copy (left) was unsuccessful because of a failure to make allowance for the difference in length between the U.S. caliber 30 and the German 7.92 mm Mauser cartridges. As a result, the bolt face of the T24 could not recoil far enough behind the ejection slot of the receiver.

Looking down the lined-up machine gun exhibit at the Springfield Armory Museum, which traces the history of automatic weapons. Here are arrayed 45- and 58-caliber Gatlings, a Gardner in 50-70 caliber, a Billinghurst Requa battery gun and an Ager "coffee mill" gun, both in 58 caliber.

mory was Maj. James G. Benton, who served as commanding officer between 1868 and 1881. This was a critical transition period in the development of American arms that saw the creation of the trapdoor Springfield. Although the Winchester Model 73 has earned the reputation of "The gun that won the West," the truth is that the title actually belongs to the trapdoor Springfield, which was the weapon that armed the U.S. cavalry and infantry units that opened the West to peaceful settlement. Col. Benton's stewardship is notable, too, because it marked the establishment of the first Springfield Armory Museum.

The Museum's Treasures

Thanks to the meticulous care taken in the site development of the armory and the harmonious design and placement of the buildings, unlike most New England mill towns, Springfield's "factory"—the armory—became esthetically beautiful, more like an attractive college campus than an ugly industrial establishment. As a consequence, Springfield's wealthy residents flocked to this neighborhood to build magnificent mansions, causing it to be called the "Gold Coast."

The city of Springfield is a delightful place to visit. Its situation on a succession of terraces and in gently rolling country produces an effect of spacious leisure.

Shooter's Bible photo

This formidable yet attractive iron fence, whose palings are pikes and halberds, completely surrounds the Springfield Armory grounds. Maj. James Wolfe Ripley had it forged by the Ames Sword Company in exchange for surplus and cast-off cannons.

Its imposing architecture and tree-shaded lawns, parks and wide boulevards give it an atmosphere of dignity, substance and comfort. Its diversified industries, superior transportation facilities, fine shops and comfortable homes give an all-around impression of prosperity. And its central location makes it easy to reach: 80 miles from Albany, 85 miles from Boston, 75 miles from Providence and 130 miles from New York City. The Massachusetts Turnpike (I-90) passes slightly to the north and I-91 carries traffic through the city (take Springfield Center exit for the museum and drive east on State Street). Museum hours are 8 a.m. to 4:30 p.m. every day except New Year's Day and Christmas.

The visitor to the Springfield Armory Museum will literally take a trip through time, for every period of American arms development is represented here. Amazingly, the extensive exhibits comprise only about 15 percent of the total holdings of the museum, much of which still remains to be processed and cataloged. Make no mistake about it—there is much to see here, and a full day will not be too much time to devote to absorbing the contents of this priceless collection.

The museum staff is small but specialized. It includes W. Douglas Lindsay Jr., superintendent of the site; William E. Meuse, curator; Larry Lowenthal, historian; Joseph A. Polcetti, museum technician; and John R. McCabe, park technician. Amy Lewontin is the librarian.

The exhibits cover a multitude of subjects: machine guns, rockets and bazookas, experimental weapons, Springfield muskets, Civil War muskets and rifled muskets, Erskine Allin's trapdoor Springfields, and swords and bayonets of all descriptions. Weapons with historical associations abound: the machine gun that guarded Woodrow Wilson's White House; the bayonet about which Theodore Roosevelt made some caustic comments; John F. Kennedy's birthday present—a Spencer Civil War carbine; Gen. Dwight D. Eisenhower's presentation M14 rifle; and the gun that was found in the effects of Confederate President Jefferson Davis when he was captured. There are examples of guns that have exploded, guns that have been struck by lightning, even a gun whose sweat-soaked stock had been gnawed by a porcupine seeking salt. And this enumeration hardly scratches the surface. The Springfield Armory Museum also boasts of having one of the largest collections of toy soldier miniatures in any museum.

One of the strengths of the Springfield Armory Museum is in its "firsts" and "lasts." Many guns bearing serial number 1 and also the last example of

An exhibit of rockets and bazookas. The first bazooka was a 2.36-inch rocket-launcher developed at the Aberdeen Proving Ground in 1942 and named after the homemade trombone-like musical instrument of hillbilly comedian Bob Burns, the "Arkansas Traveler" of radio and motion pictures. The Germans captured American bazookas in North Africa and developed their own shielded, larger caliber Raketenpanzerbuchse 54 (rocket tank gun), which their troops nicknamed "Panzerschreck"(tank wrecker) and "Ofenrohr" (stovepipe).

many weapons are housed here, including John Garand's last design, the T-31 made in 1948 and affectionately called the "bull pup," which was never accepted by the military. One of the Museum's "firsts" is Serial Number 1 of the famous 1903 Springfield which was issued in 1917 at an army camp near Syracuse, New York, to Frank C. Lynbaugh. When Pvt. Lynbaugh got to France, his lieutenant noticed the serial number during inspection. The rifle was taken from Lynbaugh, to be sent back to the Springfield Armory as a historical item. In 1974, Lynbaugh, then 80 years old, appeared at the museum and asked to see the rifle. To his surprise—and his pleasure—the rifle was produced. He exclaimed, "Yes, sir, that's my old gun. *I* got old, but it looks the same."

An interesting display demonstrates the hazards of the careless handling of muzzleloading weapons. During the Civil War, the standard weapon of both sides was a 58-caliber muzzleloading rifled musket. It had a number of drawbacks, not the least of which was that loading it was almost impossible in anything but a standing position. Despite the consequent exposure to enemy fire, an experienced soldier could load and fire three times a minute; under com-

bat conditions, he could be expected to keep up a steady fire of at least two shots a minute.

Even so, it sometimes happened that men were sent into battle who did not know how to load or fire their weapons (as occurred at Shiloh) or who were given such rudimentary instruction that in the shock of battle they simply did not know what to do. After the battle of Gettysburg, 27,574 rifles were found on the battlefield. Only about 6,000 of these were properly loaded; some 12,000 had from 3 to 10 loads. One piece found contained an astonishing 23 loads. From these statistics, it has been estimated that one-third of the fighting men on each side were incapable of firing their weapons. The soldiers who died with such guns in their hands *thought* they were firing their guns, but the sound of battle was so deafening, they often couldn't tell if their guns had fired when they pulled the trigger. Sometimes they failed to prime the rifle or they inserted the bullet and powder in the reverse order. If so, this error could only be undone by using a ballpuller to withdraw the charge. An extensive exhibit in the Springfield Armory Museum demonstrates graphically what happened to some of these guns.

Another display shows the results of penetration

In 1845 Maj. James Wolfe Ripley razed the former superintendent's quarters at the Springfield Armory and erected this charming residence. Outside pressure caused a court of inquiry to be convened to investigate charges of extravagance in building such a "palace." The court later exonerated Ripley, saying that "had equal care and judgment been observed in the erection of the old superintendent's house, the expense of erecting this would have been saved." Today it serves as headquarters for the Springfield Armory Museum.

"This is the Arsenal, from floor to ceiling, like a huge organ, rise the burnish'd arms." So wrote poet Henry Wadsworth Longfellow, who visited the Springfield Armory in 1843 while on his honeymoon and saw hundreds of thousands of muskets stored in racks like these. Two visitors read Longfellow's poem at one of the remaining "organ" gun racks, whose purpose was to provide security for the stored weapons but also to give ventilation and air circulation to them.

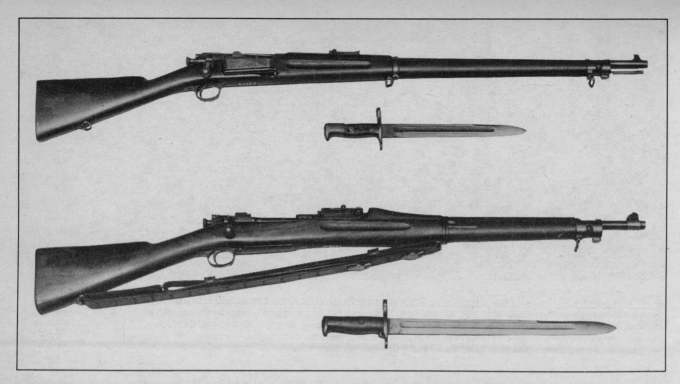

The Model 1892 Krag-Jorgensen bolt-action rifle (top), the first small-caliber smokeless powder repeating rifle adopted by the U.S. government. It was almost identical with the military rifle of Denmark. All Krags, as they came to be called, were of 30-40 caliber and were manufactured at the Springfield Armory. U.S. Model 1903 Springfield rifle, with 1905 knife bayonet (bottom). Earlier models had a rod bayonet, which were found to be flimsy and unsuitable for combat.

tests conducted at the Springfield Armory. These tests were an early method used by weapons designers to compare the relative power and effectiveness of weapons fired from a uniform distance. In the 17th and 18th centuries, blocks of white pine boards were employed, but later testers preferred seasoned oak, a denser and harder material.

Thus, from a distance of 25 feet, the caliber 45-70 Model 1873 Springfield rifle, whose 70-grain charge fired a bullet that developed a velocity of 1,315 feet per second (fps), penetrated only 3.5 inches into seasoned oak. By contrast, the 1893 Krag-Jorgensen, also developed at the Springfield Armory, firing a bullet of 30-40 caliber from the same distance, developed a velocity of 2,470 fps and penetrated 19.5 inches. And the 30-06 Model 1903 Springfield demonstrates the influence of bullet weight: A 150-grain bullet developing 2,700 fps penetrated 27.5 inches, while a 220-grain bullet traveled more slowly at 2,300 fps but achieved a startling 30.75 inches of penetration. No wonder the 1903 Springfield is still a respected and much-sought-after gun.

Despite the tremendous contributions of the Springfield Armory to the security of the United States, during the 1960s rumblings were heard of a shutdown of the installation. In the eyes of efficiency-minded bureaucrats, the lovely old buildings had outlived their usefulness; by modern standards, there is no doubt that they were inefficient. Weapons had changed and it was felt that the need for a small-arms manufacturing capability no longer existed, that private industry could mass-produce needed weapons as it had in the past. Overlooked, perhaps, was the reservoir of talent and know-how that the employees at the Springfield Armory represented. The final blow fell in 1968 when almost the entire armory was closed down and the complex was transferred to Springfield Technical Community College. A few buildings, including the museum, came under the jurisdiction of the National Park Service.

Today, the Springfield Armory stands partly deserted, its future cloudy at best. A few of its buildings have been demolished. Others echo the sounds of youthful voices as college students attend classes in their hallowed halls. Some of its structures have been sacrificed to make way for new college buildings, whose severely modern designs are in sharp contrast to the stately Greek Revival style of the gra-

On February 2, 1944, the two-millionth Garand M1 rifle was completed by the Springfield Armory. Choice pieces of wood were always saved for special guns, so this rifle was equipped with an unusual stock of beautiful tiger-striped walnut. Here machinist Norbert Bonneville shows the prized rifle to then commanding officer Col. George A. Woody at the presentation ceremony.

John C. Garand was a self-taught machinist whose greatest pleasure came when he could build his own prototype models of the gun designs he had conceived. Here he is seen at a drill press in his own workshop at the Springfield Armory.

cious old buildings they replaced and whose only relationship to the older buildings is that they are all of red brick.

Current plans call for the remodeling and modernizing of the museum, now under the aegis of the National Park Service, as a Historic Site. It is perhaps not out of place to hope that the Park Service will resist any temptation to reduce the Springfield Armory's extensive collections to a film show in an auditorium together with a few representative exhibits.

Although the museum proper has been concentrated in Col. Ripley's Main Arsenal building, it is not difficult for an imaginative visitor to people the lovely grounds of the armory with the ghosts of the past. These flagstone walks knew the tread of such distinguished ordnance experts as Capt. Alexander B. Dyer, who invented the Civil War Dyer artillery shell and later became Chief of Ordnance; Maj. Theodore T. S. Laidley, known for the Laidley carbine and the Laidley traveling forge, a veritable rolling black-

John Garand, developer of the Garand rifle, had a number of hobbies, one of which was figure skating. During the cold Springfield winters he would cover his parlor floor with canvas and flood it with water. When the windows were opened it would freeze, thus providing him with a small skating rink at home. After Garand's marriage, his wife convinced him to move the rink to the backyard.

smith shop; Lt. Col. A. R. Buffington, who commanded the Springfield Armory for almost 11 years and invented various improvements in firearms manufacturing methods; Col. Alfred Mordecai, a West Point graduate in the class of June 1861, whose father, also a West Point graduate (class of 1823) and a Southerner, decided that he could fight against neither side and so resigned his commission, while his son fought throughout the Civil War on the Union side and died a brigadier general; and Col. Jay E. Hoffer, associated with the development of the Thompson machine gun and whose name is memorialized in the Hoffer drum magazine.

No one's contributions can be felt more clearly at Springfield than those of John C. Garand. Born in St. Remi, Quebec, in 1888, Garand's family moved to Connecticut 10 years later. His working life began at the age of 12, when he went to work in a cotton mill. At the age of 13 he demonstrated his mechanical genius by obtaining the first of his many patents.

The outbreak of the First World War found him employed as a toolmaker in New York City, serving as a part-time soldier in the National Guard. He submitted a design for a light machine gun to the National Inventions Bureau, and he was commissioned by the National Bureau of Standards to build a model of his gun, which operated on a rather novel principle. The most novel thing about Garand's gun was that it worked.

A year after the Armistice, Garand found employment at the Springfield Armory at an annual salary of $3,500. Garand was to remain there for 34 years, until his retirement in 1953.

During that time, he created the T1920 rifle, a primer-actuated weapon, as were his Model 1921 and Model 1924 guns. In 1929, his gas-operated T-3 semi-automatic rifle was submitted for testing. (This was similar to the subsequent M1, but was chambered for the 276 Pedersen cartridge.) In 1931 Garand developed a 30-caliber version of this gun, which eventually evolved into the M1, adopted by the U.S. Army in 1936.

Endless tomes have been written to propound the philosophy of museum science and to expound the objectives of museum administration. But every museum curator knows why the objects of the past must be carefully preserved. They must be preserved that the dead may live, that what has gone before shall not be lost forever, that something may be salvaged from the dust and mold of time, that the past may color the present and give hope to the future. Careful preservation of hallowed objects from the past is the only payment we can make to reduce the debt we owe to those who, through the years, have fashioned and made secure the world in which we live.

Yesterday was yesterday. Today forgets. Tomorrow there may be nothing, no one left to remember, as the world picks up increased speed toward a dubious fate.

Ballistics Made Easy

Chuck Adams

The term "ballistics" is defined by Webster as: (1) "the science of the motion of projectiles in flight," or what is generally called *exterior ballistics* by firearms enthusiasts; and (2) "the study of the processes within a firearm as it is fired." This more limited definition covers *interior ballistics*. Everything that occurs inside a firearm from the instant the firing pin strikes the primer until the bullet exits the muzzle falls within the realm of interior ballistics. Once the bullet clears the muzzle and is on its own, so to speak, all physical and mathematical factors associated with it fall into the category of exterior ballistics.

It should be noted that there is a third type of ballistics, *terminal ballistics*, that considers the effect of the projectile on the target. Two additional related fields include shot ballistics and forensic ballistics (the study of receivered projectiles).

The study of projectile performance is important to all hunters and serious target shooters. To achieve maximum bullet performance, a shooter must carefully consider caliber, cartridge design, powder charge, bullet configuration and dozens of other factors that combine to produce superior shooting results. Actually, all these factors combine *every time* a trigger is pulled on a live round, but this combination generally produces less than satisfactory results unless it is carefully planned.

Ballistics From the Beginning

The history of ballistics as a science is more than 2,000 years old. The word "ballistics" stems from the Greek word used to describe the science of producing efficient throwing machines. Rough-hewn ballistics, however, undoubtedly entered into the daily life of Stone Age man, for archaeological evidence indicates that crude throwing instruments and deliberately manufactured projectiles were used many thousands of years before the Greeks. Still, the advent of warfare with firearms in Western Europe during the early 1400s is generally considered the official birth of ballistics as we know it today. Battles have been won through ballistic superiority from that time until the present, and governments have spared neither time nor expense to advance their knowledge of ballistics and to employ it to the best military advantage.

As a result of national military interests during the past five centuries, some of the world's most brilliant scientific minds have formulated modern ballistic science. A common notion during the early 14th century was that a bullet left a gun barrel, traveled in a completely straight line until it ran out of energy, then fell straight to the ground. An Italian scientist named Tartaglia refuted this belief in the mid-1500s, stating that a bullet travels along a continuous curve. A hundred years later, Galileo described theoretical bullet velocities based on the forces of gravity and air resistance. During the early 1700s, Sir Isaac Newton aided the study of ballistics by making important advances in both mathematics and physics. Among his most famous contributions in these areas were his "universal law of gravitation" and his formulation of the calculus necessary to compute bullet trajectory. In 1740, Benjamin Robins, using Newton's theories, invented a ballistic pendulum, the world's first means of actually measuring bullet velocity.

The rudimentary work of these and other early ballisticians has been advanced during the past 200 years. For example, the effects of internal chamber pressure, rifling pitch, bullet weight and shape, cartridge configuration, gunpowder ignition, bullet inertia and air drag on ballistic performance were well understood by the end of the 19th century. Through experimentation, military-conscious governments and manufacturers of sporting firearms have refined this understanding into a precise, effective science benefitting both target competitors and serious hunting riflemen. With the help of accurate ballistics tables a modern sportsman can achieve maximum performance from any given cartridge.

The Great Rifle/Cartridge Compromise

If a serious rifleman were offered one ballistic-oriented wish from a benevolent genie, it would probably be to own the ultimate rifle/cartridge combination. Such a combination would cause a bullet to travel on a perfectly straight line from muzzle to target without recoil or muzzle noise. It would also place all bullets in the same hole with a steady hold, and would impart exactly enough energy to kill hunted animals at any distance. Unfortunately, such a shooting combination cannot exist in physical reality, because certain factors limit the performance of any rifle/cartridge combination, regardless of basic design or components used. The intelligent shooter must make the best of the resources at his command.

Of the many factors that impede ballistic performance, internally, the variables include basic cartridge designs, composition of modern gunpowders, steels used in firearms, sectional densities of bullets and rifling pitches in gunbarrels. Externally, the limiting factors include amounts of recoil produced during a shot, levels of muzzle blasts, dramatic effects of gravity and air resistance on bullets in flight, levels of accuracy achievable at various muzzle velocities and the killing power of bullet designs on animals. Knowing how to emphasize certain ballistics factors and de-emphasize others, a gunner will be able to choose his ultimate rifle/cartridge combination and tailor various loads to perform specialized functions.

It is important to remember, however, that no single rifle/cartridge combination will perform every ballistic task to perfection. There are always trade-offs. Factors which limit *every* shooter include recoil level, muzzle-blast level, barrel-steel tolerances and the effects of gravity and air resistance on any bullet.

Generally, the heavier the bullet of a particular

The varmint shooter after prairie dogs or similar open-country rodents is primarily concerned with flat trajectory that eases aiming problems.

diameter, the better it resists air friction as it flies. However, propelling a heavy bullet requires ample cartridge-case capacity, a large amount of slow-burning propellant and a fairly long rifle barrel to take advantage of the propellant's ability to counteract bullet inertia and accelerate to a practical muzzle velocity. This results in heavier recoil and louder muzzle blast than that produced by a firearm shooting a lighter bullet. Very few shooters can comfortably handle combinations with bullets weighing over 200 grains when these combinations shoot flat enough to hit game or targets at long, unknown distances. A bullet leaving the muzzle at 2800 to 3200 feet per second (fps) produces a long-range trajectory ample for most hunting needs, with a heavier bullet always producing a flatter overall trajectory than a lighter one of identical diameter. Compare a 100-grain bullet starting at 3000 fps from a seven-

Open-country critters require ballistically excellent cartridges because flat trajectory and wind-bucking ability are key ingredients to success.

pound rifle versus a 300-grain bullet starting at the same velocity from a nine-pound rifle. The 100-grain bullet produces over 50 foot-pounds of tooth-jarring punishment on the rear end. The 180-grain bullet, however, shot at the same muzzle velocity from an eight-pound rifle produces recoil of slightly over 25 foot-pounds. The biggest, burliest shooter might be able to absorb recoil of 30 or 35 ft.-lbs. but this level is decidedly unpleasant for most gunners. As a result, a deer hunter should shoot a 180-grain bullet instead of a 300-grain bullet, even though the latter will retain its energy and flat-shooting qualities better than the lower grain bullet, all else being equal.

The quality of barrel steel, the effects of gravity and friction caused by air resistance may necessitate similar rifle cartridge trade-offs. Most factory gun-barrel chambers can handle pressures of up to 50,000 or 55,000 pounds per square inch without danger, and most can handle bullet velocities of up to 3500 fps without causing rapid barrel wear and sacrificing accuracy. Increasing chamber pressures past established limits or pushing bullets faster than 3500 fps

can be hazardous to a shooter, damaging to a rifle, and limits what the rifleman can do when handloading or designing a unique "wildcat" cartridge. The tug of gravity on a bullet is a constant that cannot be altered by any shooter. It may force him to turn to aerodynamic bullet design plus relatively high bullet velocity to help minimize gravity's effect on trajectory and the aiming adjustments he must make at various distances.

Accuracy levels and terminal ballistics qualities of bullets may present other problems for individual shooters. To the big-game hunter, pinpoint accuracy is usually not as important as flat trajectory, cancelling the need to tailor loads and closely match rifling pitch to velocities achieved. In contrast, such accuracy is extremely important to anyone intent on winning official silhouette or paper-target matches. A big-game hunter is concerned with the terminal ballistics qualities of his bullets, that is, how they mushroom and perform at various velocities; the target shooter couldn't care less about this because it does not affect his performance in the least.

Open-country animals, like Rocky Mountain goats, require the most ballistically sound cartridge/rifle combinations because accuracy, flat trajectory and knockdown power are all vital to success.

The geometric design of a particular cartridge also influences how it performs ballistically. Within certain general guidelines, most accepted modern hunting or shooting cartridges are well designed, but some are definitely superior to others in their ability to perform certain tasks. For example, the 280 Remington is generally viewed as the ideal theoretical choice for shooting deer at moderate to long range, because it combines efficient powder-burning, practical bullet velocities, tolerable recoil and muzzle blast and a bullet sectional density, that is, the relationship of a bullet's mass to the surface area of its cross-section. Bullet sectional density retains energy best over long range when deer-hunting bullets between 140 and 160 grains are used. Such a well-balanced cartridge is also less critical to load and produces excellent accuracy with a minimum of experimentation.

The 7mm Remington Magnum cartridge, however, shoots the same superior .284-diameter bullets at higher muzzle velocity, but its effects are more recoil, more muzzle blast, less efficient powder-burning and more fickle loading requirements for decent ac-

curacy. The fanatic elk hunter who feels he needs more power and a slightly flatter bullet trajectory may opt to use the 7mm Magnum, but increased bullet velocity is achieved at the expense of other important ballistics considerations.

Another velocity-designed cartridge that gives up a lot in other areas is the old 220 Swift, a once-popular varmint-sniping round shooting a 45-grain, 22-caliber bullet at nearly 4000 fps. This cartridge is grossly over bore capacity; its case size is huge when compared to its bullet diameter. The result is extremely inefficient powder-burning, quickly worn-out bores because of friction and powder erosion, and less-than-top-notch accuracy from most loads.

The fact that certain cartridges provide a practical compromise among limiting factors is the chief reason some designs have been popular for many years, despite attempts to improve upon them by enlarging chambers, altering case shapes and using exotic gunpowders. Improvements in gunpowder during the past 75 years have indeed made a few once-popular cartridges ballistically obsolete. A

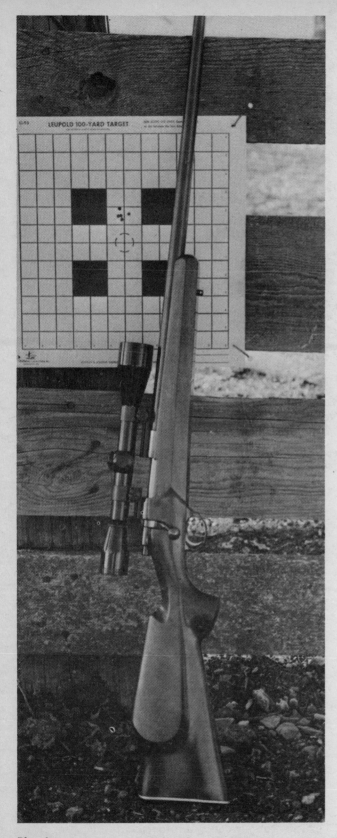

Pinpoint accuracy on targets is only one ballistic requirement of serious all-around shooters.

prime example is the 300 H&H Magnum, designed in the 1920s by the British firm of Holland & Holland to be used with now-antiquated long-stick cordite powder. Nevertheless, many others are still going strong after many years because they provide an efficient bore-diameter/case-capacity ratio and shoot bullets of acceptable weight at practical velocities. Good examples are the 30-06 Springfield introduced in 1906, the 250 Savage (1915), the 270 Winchester (1925) and the 280 Remington (1957; now called the 7mm Remington Express). So-called improvements on all of these cartridges have been made during the past several decades, but only by dipping into that area of diminishing returns where considerably more gunpowder must be used to achieve slightly flatter trajectories and slightly higher bullet energies.

Shooters often wonder why modern technology hasn't made more substantial improvements in cartridges since the introduction of the 30-06, for example. But factors such as recoil level and chamber-pressure limits on top-quality steel, plus unalterable physical laws involving efficient chamber-to-bore size ratios (given present gunpowders), most efficient case shapes (including body taper and shoulder angle), and similar cartridge properties have prevented earth-shaking cartridge improvement. Cartridge companies make phenomenal claims about new offerings, because cartridges are marketed and promoted the way automobiles, electric carving knives and shaving creams are. Nonetheless, barring some revolutionary breakthrough in propellant chemistry or the manufacture of firearm steel, conventional cartridge design has probably reached as high a level of perfection as it is ever likely to reach. Arms manufacturers have made the most of existing technology—chambering rifles for cartridges of known ballistics qualities and matching these chamberings with rifling twists and barrel lengths that enhance accuracy and trajectory.

As a result, the avid shooter would be wise to settle on a popular rifle/cartridge combination and concentrate his efforts on achieving ideal exterior ballistics. As a general rule, the slower the bullet moves or the longer it is in relation to its diameter, the steeper the rifling pitch needed to stabilize that bullet for peak accuracy. Similarly, the more over bore capacity a cartridge is, the longer the barrel and the slower-burning the powder needed to produce reasonable muzzle velocity.

A shooter's first responsibility is to choose a cartridge that exhibits the high-performance qualities required for his particular brand of sport. The most intelligent way to make this choice is to consult experts in the field, either by talking with experienced shooters or by reading.

What these desired qualities may be will vary dramatically from shooter to shooter. The long-range varmint gunner will emphasize pinpoint accuracy and ultra-flat trajectory with minimal recoil; the canyon-country deer hunter will seek relatively flat trajectory and decent accuracy from a big-game bullet with moderate recoil; the hunter after dangerous game will want raw stopping power in a big bullet at close range with little or no worry about recoil level; and the avid target buff will look for a combination of accuracy, flat trajectory and low recoil levels. In any case, a solid handle on how to use a ballistic table will help any shooter sensibly load for his chosen cartridge or at least choose adequate factory ammunition to perform a specific task. In addition, it will help him sight-in his rifle and compensate with the sights for distances other than his sighting zero.

How to Read a Ballistic Table

A ballistic table displays important information about particular bullets originating at specific muzzle velocities. In recent years, Hornady, Sierra, Speer and other major bullet manufacturers have made such tables readily available to the general public. Learning to use a ballistic table is relatively easy, provided common terms and concepts are fully understood.

Trajectory. The trajectory of a bullet is the actual path that bullet follows after leaving the muzzle of a rifle at a particular velocity. Many factors shape a bullet's trajectory, but the three primary ones are muzzle velocity, air resistance on the bullet and the constant downward tug of gravity.

An accurate, ballistically sound shooting combination is pure joy to use on targets and game.

Velocity. Velocity may be defined as the speed at which a bullet is moving at any given point along its trajectory. Velocity is measured in feet per second (fps) and constantly slows after a bullet leaves the muzzle because of air friction on the bullet. This slow-down rate will vary with the shape, weight and diameter of the bullet.

Bullet Energy. Bullet energy is measured in foot-pounds (ft.-lbs.) and is based on the mass of the bullet in conjunction with its velocity. The energy of a bullet can be calculated in a number of ways. A common method used by arms and munitions manufacturers is to multiply the weight of the bullet in pounds by the velocity squared and divide the result by twice the acceleration of gravity (64.32). This may be simplified by converting bullet pounds into grains in the following formula:

$$\text{Energy} = \frac{\text{Bullet Weight (grains) x Velocity}^2}{450240}$$

Bullet energy affects killing power on animals and knockdown power on kinetic targets like steel silhouettes and is usually listed for various shooting distances in a standard ballistic table.

Base Line. The base line on a trajectory diagram is a straight line drawn from the muzzle to the target. No matter what the range of a shot, the muzzle of the rifle must be elevated to raise the trajectory above this base line so the bullet crosses this line again directly on target.

Line of Sight. Because iron or telescopic sights are affixed *above* the bore, the line of sight is not exactly the same as the base line on a trajectory diagram. At practical shooting ranges, the base line and line of sight can be considered identical, but an accurate ballistic diagram always differentiates between the two.

Drop. Bullet-drop figures are usually included in a typical ballistic table to facilitate a straight-across trajectory comparison with another bullet originating at a different speed. Drop figures are computed when the bullet leaves the muzzle traveling parallel to the ground (along the base line). Such figures show how drastically gravity and air resistance affect bullet path.

Mid-range. Mid-range is the height above the base line to which a particular bullet traveling at a particular velocity rises when a rifle is zeroed for a particular range. For example, the mid-range of a setup zeroed at 200 yards might be 2.5 inches; the mid-range of a setup zeroed at 400 might be 6 inches, etc. In other words, if a rifle is zeroed for 200 yards, the bullet will rise 2.5 inches above point of aim

A RIFLEMAN'S TYPICAL BALLISTIC TABLE

.284 dia., 140 grain Spitzer Sectional Density: .248 Ballistic Coefficient: .490

RANGE YARDS	MUZZLE	100	200	300	400	500	600
Velocity FPS	3500.	3282.	3075.	2878.	2689.	2508.	2334.
Energy FT-LB	3807.	3348.	2939.	2574.	2247.	1954.	1693.
Drop In	0.0	-1.39	-5.99	-14.27	-26.74	-44.01	-66.79
Mid-Range In	0.0	0.38	1.61	3.87	7.38	12.36	19.13
Bullet Path In	-1.50	0.86	0.00	-4.53	-13.25	-26.78	-45.82
Velocity FPS	3400.	3187.	2985.	2791.	2606.	2428.	2257.
Energy FT-LB	3593.	3157.	2769.	2421.	2111.	1832.	1584.
Drop In	0.0	-1.47	-6.36	-15.14	-28.38	-46.73	-70.96
Mid-Range In	0.0	0.40	1.71	4.11	7.83	13.14	20.34
Bullet Path In	-1.50	0.96	0.00	-4.85	-14.16	-28.59	-48.89
Velocity FPS	3300.	3092.	2894.	2704.	2523.	2348.	2180.
Energy FT-LB	3385.	2972.	2603.	2273.	1978.	1714.	1478.
Drop In	0.0	-1.56	-6.75	-16.09	-30.17	-49.71	-75.55
Mid-Range In	0.0	0.42	1.81	4.37	8.33	13.99	21.68
Bullet Path In	-1.50	1.06	0.00	-5.21	-15.17	-30.58	-52.28
Velocity FPS	3200.	2997.	2803.	2617.	2439.	2268.	2103.
Energy FT-LB	3183.	2791.	2442.	2129.	1849.	1598.	1375.
Drop In	0.0	-1.66	-7.19	-17.14	-32.15	-53.01	-80.61
Mid-Range In	0.0	0.45	1.93	4.66	8.89	14.93	23.17
Bullet Path In	-1.50	1.18	0.00	-5.60	-16.27	-32.78	-56.03
Velocity FPS	3100.	2901.	2712.	2530.	2355.	2187.	2026.
Energy FT-LB	2987.	2616.	2285.	1989.	1723.	1486.	1275.
Drop In	0.0	-1.78	-7.67	-18.29	-34.34	-56.65	-86.21
Mid-Range In	0.0	0.48	2.06	4.97	9.50	15.97	24.81
Bullet Path In	-1.50	1.31	0.00	-6.03	-17.49	-35.21	-60.19
Velocity FPS	3000.	2806.	2620.	2442.	2270.	2106.	1948.
Energy FT-LB	2797.	2447.	2134.	1853.	1602.	1378.	1180.
Drop In	0.0	-1.90	-8.21	-19.57	-36.76	-60.69	-92.44
Mid-Range In	0.0	0.51	2.20	5.32	10.17	17.13	26.65
Bullet Path In	-1.50	1.45	-0.00	-6.51	-18.85	-37.92	-64.82
Velocity FPS	2900.	2710.	2528.	2353.	2186.	2025.	1871.
Energy FT-LB	2614.	2283.	1987.	1721.	1485.	1274.	1088.
Drop In	0.0	-2.04	-8.80	-20.99	-39.45	-65.18	-99.38
Mid-Range In	0.0	0.55	2.36	5.71	10.93	18.42	28.70
Bullet Path In	-1.50	1.61	0.00	-7.04	-20.36	-40.94	-69.99
Velocity FPS	2800.	2614.	2436.	2265.	2101.	1943.	1794.
Energy FT-LB	2437.	2124.	1845.	1595.	1372.	1174.	1000.
Drop In	0.0	-2.19	-9.45	-22.57	-42.45	-70.20	-107.14
Mid-Range In	0.0	0.59	2.54	6.14	11.77	19.87	31.00
Bullet Path In	-1.50	1.79	0.00	-7.64	-22.04	-44.32	-75.77
Velocity FPS	2700.	2519.	2344.	2176.	2016.	1863.	1717.
Energy FT-LB	2266.	1971.	1708.	1472.	1263.	1078.	917.
Drop In	0.0	-2.36	-10.19	-24.34	-45.81	-75.83	-115.85
Mid-Range In	0.0	0.64	2.74	6.63	12.72	21.50	33.59
Bullet Path In	-1.50	1.99	-0.00	-8.31	-23.94	-48.11	-82.29
Velocity FPS	2600.	2422.	2252.	2088.	1931.	1782.	1642.
Energy FT-LB	2101.	1824.	1576.	1355.	1159.	987.	838.
Drop In	0.0	-2.55	-11.01	-26.32	-49.59	-82.17	-125.68
Mid-Range In	0.0	0.69	2.96	7.18	13.79	23.34	36.52
Bullet Path In	-1.50	2.21	0.00	-9.05	-26.07	-52.39	-89.65
Velocity FPS	2500.	2326.	2159.	2000.	1847.	1703.	1567.
Energy FT-LB	1943.	1682.	1449.	1243.	1060.	901.	764.
Drop In	0.0	-2.76	-11.93	-28.55	-53.85	-89.33	-136.78
Mid-Range In	0.0	0.74	3.21	7.79	14.99	25.42	39.84
Bullet Path In	-1.50	2.46	0.00	-9.90	-28.48	-57.24	-97.98

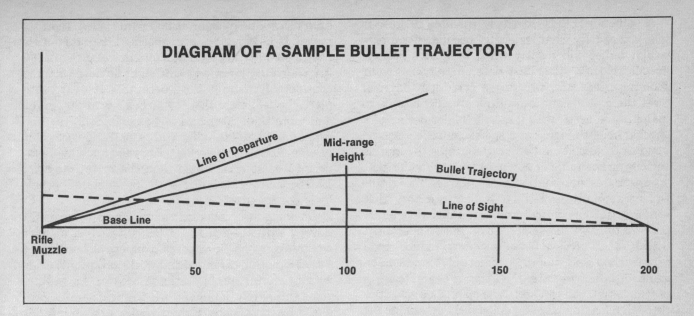

DIAGRAM OF A SAMPLE BULLET TRAJECTORY

Line of Departure

Mid-range Height

Bullet Trajectory

Line of Sight

Base Line

Rifle Muzzle

50   100   150   200

about halfway between the shooter and a 200-yard target. Mid-range figures tell a shooter precisely how much he must hold *under* a target at distances closer than the distance he is sighted in for. For example, if a rifle's 200-yard mid-range is 2.5, the shooter must hold 2.5 inches *under* the target at 100 yards and somewhat less than this at closer or longer ranges between zero and 200 yards.

Bullet Path. The bullet path figures on a standard ballistic table tell exactly where a bullet will hit at ranges other than a standard, practical sight-in zero (for instance, 200 yards for a deer hunter). Because a rifle's sights are normally above the bore line between .75 of an inch (the average height of iron sights) and 1.5 inches (the average height of a scope), the muzzle reading on a bullet-path table is normally −1.5 for calibers most often used with telescopic sights and −.75 for calibers most often used with iron sights. (See the trajectory diagram and sample ballistic table for clarification). From this minus muzzle reading, the bullet rises to a plus reading at 100 yards, falls back to the rifle's zero (say, 200 yards), and begins to drop steadily past this distance in minus readings for 300 yards, 400 yards, etc. These figures accurately predict where a bullet will strike in relation to the line of sight, i.e., where the sights are, at 0 yards, 100 yards, 200 yards, 300 yards, and so on.

Sectional Density and Ballistic Coefficient. These two terms usually accompany ballistics tables describing the characteristics of particular bullet designs—designs like the Sierra 140-grain, 284-caliber Spitzer; the Remington 130-grain, 277-caliber Pointed Soft-Point Core-Lokt, etc.

The sectional density of a bullet is calculated from its mass and diameter. A common formula for sectional density (SD) is: $SD = W/7000\ D^2$, where W is the bullet weight in grains, 7000 the number of grains in a pound and D^2 the bullet diameter in inches. Sectional density, coupled with a mathematical determination of a bullet's aerodynamic shape, is the chief factor in how well that bullet resists air friction in flight and retains its energy and velocity over the long haul. All else being equal, the higher the computed sectional density of a bullet, the better it will retain its energy and velocity as it flies.

The ballistic coefficient of a bullet is more meaningful to a shooter than its sectional density. The ballistic coefficient is a precise, mathematical coupling of section density with a "form factor" that takes into account an individual bullet's aerodynamic shape. The general formula for ballistic coefficient (C) is $C = SD/I$, where SD is sectional density and I is a predetermined form factor. The published ballistic coefficients of various commercial bullets allow a shooter to determine which one will retain its velocity and energy best during a long shot. The higher a bullet's ballistic coefficient, the better that bullet resists air friction during flight.

Here's a helpful comparison to clarify ballistic coefficient: Two 160-grain, .284-diameter bullets have precisely the same sectional density, but if one is a slender-nosed boattail and the other a blunt-nosed flat base, the boattail will have a much higher ballistic coefficient because a slender nose penetrates air better than a blunt nose and because a boattail penetrates air better than a flat base. If flat trajectory is a shooter's overriding priority, the slender-nosed boattail is the only logical choice.

A ballistic table is extremely valuable because it tells you exactly what trajectory peculiarities a particular bullet will display when fired at a specific muzzle velocity. After first determining what your shooting needs are, selecting a cartridge that will meet these needs and consulting a ballistic table to match these needs with a specific bullet design of a specific weight moving at a specific muzzle velocity, you can handload ammo that duplicates the muzzle velocity in the table or purchase factory fodder that approximates information in the table. The result will be a totally predictable bullet trajectory that conforms to the energy, drop, mid-range and bullet path sections of the table. If you must experiment with loads to achieve better accuracy, reduce recoil or muzzle blast, improve bullet performance on game, or otherwise alter the exterior characteristics of your setup, you can keep tabs on muzzle velocities through reloading tables and instantly determine the trajectory of your altered shooting combination by going back to ballistics tables.

Once you have settled on a particular cartridge/powder/bullet combination that produces a known muzzle velocity, the rest is incredibly easy. Simply sight in for a standard zero recommended by ballistics tables and reloading manuals, memorize some pertinent mid-range and bullet path figures and head for the field to enjoy your shooting sport. At this point you know where your bullet will strike in relation to line of sight at any distance, and as long as you estimate the distance to the target and adjust accordingly, you'll score a hit every time with a careful hold and trigger squeeze.

If you are hunting big game, like deer, with a flat shooter like the 280 Remington and 140-grain boat-tail bullets leaving the muzzle at 2900 fps, a ballistic table lets you know you can hold dead on any animal out to 300 yards without fear of shooting over or under with a 200-yard zero, because the 200-yard mid-range for this combo is less than 2.5 inches and the drop below line of sight at 300 yards is less than six inches. If, however, you are shooting 170-grain bullets from a 30-30 Winchester at a muzzle velocity of 2200 fps, trajectory knowledge and sight holdover become considerably more critical, because a 100-yard zero places bullets more than 10 inches low at 200 yards and more than 20 inches low at 300. Still, the big, round-nosed 30-30 bullet with a ballistic coefficient of only .182 is a much better bet for bucking dense deer cover at close range than the more frangible, faster-moving 280 bullet with its outstanding ballistic coefficient of .449.

A shooter who makes it his business to acquaint himself with the science of ballistics has a distinct advantage when he chooses a practical hunting or target-shooting cartridge and works up specific loads which perform specific tasks. Moreover, he will become intimately familiar with the trajectories produced by these loads. Extensive research on interior ballistics over the past decades has made modern cartridge selection a snap, and published data on the exterior ballistic traits of various factory-produced bullets moving at specific muzzle velocities provides a major shortcut for the shooter who doesn't want to spend many years experimenting before competing on the target range or hunting for game. The ballistic ins and outs of shooting for sport are really cut and dried for those who understand the limitations imposed by interior ballistics, stick with tried-and-true rifle/cartridge combinations, use ballistics tables to help them settle on practical bullet/load combinations, and thoroughly familiarize themselves with the mid-range and bullet path peculiarities of these combinations to facilitate aiming in the field. The results are superior accuracy, consistent shooting and the greatly heightened enjoyment that always comes from being completely in control.

Editor's Note: A separate section with complete ballistics tables can be found on pages 473-499.

Canada's Ill-Fated Ross Rifle

W. John Farquharson

The Ross rifle, "made by the mile and chopped off at both ends," was one of the most controversial weapons of World War I, and is memorable today for its colorful but unillustrious history.

For about 14 years the Canadian-made Ross rifle usurped the long Lee-Enfield rifle as Canada's chosen military arm because it was heralded to be lighter, stronger and more accurate. Unfortunately, although the gun was slightly lighter, withstood greater breech pressures than the Lee-Enfield and was an accurate sporting rifle, it was totally unreliable as a military arm. Compounding the Ross' shortcomings, probably no other service rifle invented and manufactured in large quantity was riddled with the "teething problems" the Ross rifle experienced. Despite several design overhauls, the problems inherent in the Ross rifle were never fully resolved and, in the end, the gun that was to be Canada's ace military weapon was abandoned as an unsalvageable failure.

To appreciate the history of the Ross rifle fully, knowledge of the rifle's inventor and Canada's social and political climate in the 1900s is helpful. Until the turn of this century, the Dominion of Canada, like other nations and colonies comprising the great British Empire, was completely dependent upon the mother country for rifles, ammunition and all uniforms and military supplies for its militia. The Boer War (1899-1902) proved this to be a most unsatisfactory arrangement. During that war, in which 7,000 Canadians served alongside the British, Canada placed an order for 15,000 British Lee-Enfield rifles but failed to receive a single one. The War Office in Whitehall was exercising its own priorities

to re-equip the British Army and cover the losses and wastage incurred in South Africa.

Result? The liberal government of Sir Wilfred Laurier made a policy stating that Canada must manufacture its own rifles, a solution embraced by the entire nation. Nationalism was an adhesive force in Canada and the pervasive belief among its people was that no nation should have to depend upon foreign countries for its basic armaments. Soon after the establishment of this new policy, an attempt was made to persuade the Birmingham Small Arms Company to manufacture Lee-Enfield rifles in Canada. The attempt was unsuccessful, but it readied the way for the Ross.

The Conception of the Ross Rifle

The year was 1901. Enter Sir Charles Ross, a wealthy Scots nobleman, the ninth Baronet of Balnagown, Ross-shire, Scotland, and Major of the Lovat Scouts. Sir Charles was not a typical British aristocrat; he was a man of action who looked upon the young dominion as a land of unlimited promise. Lord and master of 350,000 acres and 3,000 rent-paying tenants in Ross-shire, his estate included a distillery from whence came the finest scotch and gin for Sir Charles' tables. He arrived in Canada in 1897, invested in a street railway in Vancouver, and later that year built the West Kootenay Power and Light Company, a hydroelectric complex in Rossland, British Columbia. Simultaneously, he acquired mining interests in China.

A shrewd entrepreneur, his undertakings and investments never failed to make a profit. He was an

McCord Museum of McGill University

Sir Charles Ross, circa 1897.

engineer by profession and an inventor by choice. Because of a deep interest in guns that stemmed from boyhood, Sir Charles' inventive mind turned periodically to the design and operation of firearms. In fact, while a student at Cambridge, he bought and studied a Mannlicher rifle—the gun whose action was to be refitted into his own rifle.

When Sir Charles Ross appeared in Ottawa, Canada, in early 1901, he brought with him several rifles of his own design, which were manufactured by his American agent, gunsmith Joseph A. Bennett of Hartford, Connecticut. Parts for these Ross rifles were being supplied by Billings & Spencer of Hartford and by the Frank Mossberg Company of Attleboro, Massachusetts.

However, as is often the case with inventors, Ross had some blind spots when it came to his own patents and inventions and failed to see or recognize their faults. His rifle was in many ways a product of his own lack of patience for detail. Critics pointed out that the early Model 1897 and 1900 Rosses were nothing but modifications of the straight-pull rifle action of the Model 1890 Mannlicher, whose faults had been discovered by the Americans during the American rifle trials of 1892: Mannlicher rifles depend upon near-perfect ammunition for efficient firing, especially in the poor weather conditions of the battlefield.

Thus, Sir Charles' rifle differed considerably from standard Mauser-type bolt-action rifles because, like the M-1890 Austrian Mannlicher, the Ross was of the straight-pull type. That is, before pulling the bolt handle to the rear, it was unnecessary to lift the bolt handle to rotate the bolt lugs so the locking lugs could be released from their receiver recesses. In the Ross, the handle was pulled straight to the rear, an action that automatically rotated the locking lugs on the forward end of the bolt-sleeve assembly.

Public Archives of Canada

Interior of the Ross Rifle Company factory in Quebec City, circa 1905, with racks of finished and unfinished 303 Mark II Ross rifles. Note the racks of finished Ross rifle actions. American authority E.C. Crossman tested one of them, the interrupted thread Mark III in 280 Ross caliber, literally to destruction: 107,000 pounds per square inch — breech pressures that wrecked both the Mausers and Springfields.

National Photographs Collection, Public Archives of Canada

The first Canadian army returning from drill practice with their 303 Mark III Ross rifles at Valcartier Camp, 16 miles northwest of Quebec City. Swiftly erected through the energetic efforts of Col. Sir Sam Hughes, KCMG, the camp was equipped with more than 1500 targets by August 1914 and the men readied for active duty.

Despite the disadvantages of the Ross rifle's similarity to the early Austrian Mannlicher, Sir Frederick Borden, Minister of Militia and Defence, seized upon the hope that a factory could be built in Canada to manufacture these rifles. He promptly drafted an initial order for 12,000 Ross rifles and 10,000 more for each consecutive year for the following five years, at $30.00 per delivered rifle. Thanks to mass production, the price of a 303 Lee-Enfield rifle, which at the time was Canada's service weapon, was only $12.50 —a fact Sir Charles well knew. The price of each Ross Mark II rifle, originally set at $25.00 was later raised to $28.00.

At the same time he drafted the order, Sir Frederick Borden also appointed a commission of military and civilian rifle experts to evaluate the new rifle and report their findings to him. (The commission included Col. Sir Sam Hughes, who was later to bet his political career on the Ross rifle.) After carefully examining the merits of this new Ross, the commission proposed a total of six improvements in the bolt, extractor, magazine and rear sight. Once the changes were made the committee proposed that a series of trials be fired simultaneously with the 303 Lee-Enfield.

These trials took place in Quebec in August of 1901. The Ross rifle, designed for a breech pressure of 44,000 pounds per square inch (psi), was proofed with a 303 British cartridge loaded to give that pressure. The Ross jammed every time it was fired, and the only way the bolt could be opened was by hammering back its handle. The rear-locking 303 Lee-Enfield, designed for 40,000 psi breech pressure, flawlessly fired proof cartridges loaded to that pressure. In an endurance test of 1,000 rounds, the Ross rifle worked very stiffly, jammed and misfired on an average of one in every 50 rounds. After the 300th round was fired, the solder holding the front sight assembly to the barrel melted, and the front sight fell off. The Boer War-tested Lee-Enfield easily passed the entire rifle trials.

Sir Charles Ross blamed the ammunition for his rifle's miserable showing. He claimed that the Canadian and British 303 ammo did not have the precision or quality of the American and Austrian ammunition that he had used in his original testing. He also claimed that the problems were minor ones and could be solved without difficulty.

The committee took his word. After all, Sir Charles was a major, a field-grade officer of brilliant achieve-

At Barriefield, Ontario, June 1915, Canadian Mounted Infantry troopers grinned happily as they turned in their Mark II Ross rifles. They were issued the more-reliable British-made Short Lee Enfields. In retrospect, it seemed unnecessary, because by 1916-17 Canadian armorers had solved the basic problems connected with the Ross rifles.

ments—and a gentleman. In its report, the committee concluded that the Ross had some advantages over the Lee-Enfield. For instance, the rifle could be shot more rapidly because of its straight back-and-forth action. A good shooter could get off five accurate shots in 20 seconds because the Ross could be worked back and forth rapidly without interfering with on-target shoulder hold. Other pluses included its lightness, the strength of its front-locking breech mechanism and its capability to be dismantled without tools. Only a penknife was needed to reassemble the first trial Mark I Ross rifle.

On March 27, 1902, the Canadian liberal government signed a contract with Sir Charles Ross similar to the one initially drawn up, calling for the manufacture of his rifles. The Canadian government, for better or for worse—and mostly for worse—got their new Canadian army rifle.

The Problem-Plagued Rosses

Sir Charles Ross, a millionaire, an Eatonian and a Light Blue, said he had found $1 million and would finance construction of the rifle factory himself. In effect, this meant that no one but Sir Charles served on any board of directors of the Ross Rifle Company

—only the inventor knew what went on inside the walls of the factory. Construction began in 1902, and by mid-1903 the Ross Rifle Company was manufacturing the sealed-pattern Ross Mark I, sometimes known as the Model 1903.*

The Ross Mark I weighed 7½ lbs.; the rifling was four-grooved, one turn in 10 inches; the barrel was 28 inches and, like all Ross military rifles, was chambered for the Mark VI and VII rimmed British 303 cartridges. The breech action cocked on the closing stroke, and the fired case was extracted from the hot chamber by a blow to the extractor by the bolt sleeve as it was quickly withdrawn. The back sight, originally an open-leaf calibrated to a maximum of 2,500 yards, as for open plains *veldt* shooting, was later shortened to 2,200 yards maximum. There was no provision for a bayonet attachment on this first Ross Militia military rifle.

Soon after the 1903 Mark I was issued, criticism began. The militia complained that the Ross rear

*A sealed-pattern rifle is a specimen of the type officially adopted by the Canadian government for its armed forces—with Canadian-specified dimensions followed exactly in manufacture. The specimen bears the government insignia in red sealing wax: hence the term "sealed pattern."

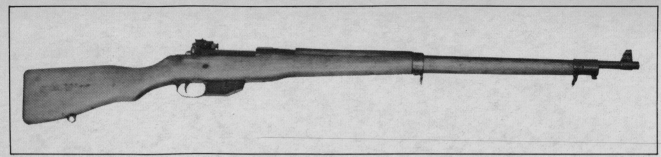

A humped-back buttstock and comb, a squat, low-sided receiver with flat, wide-bolt tracks and a square-cut end combined to make the Mark III "Long Ross" rifle the most homely looking version of the Ross rifles. The receiver bridge carried the Ross-patented open-aperture battle sight and was slotted at the forward edge for charger loading with five-round clips.

backsight was easily knocked out of alignment, the rifle stock was weak at the grip and the sharp edges of the unfinished wood and metal surfaces cut the hands and tore the uniforms of the soldiers during rifle drill. The most serious complaint, however, was that the rifle jammed badly during rapid fire.

To this list of complaints, the Royal North-West Mounted Police, who had been issued the Ross rifles in 1904, added one more: The springs of the bolt stop were defective, causing the rifle bolts to fall out of the rear of the action and become lost.

In 1904, a permanent Standing Small Arms Committee was appointed to recommend improvements for the Ross Mark I. As soon as these rifle improvements were made, the 303 Ross Mark II was born.

The new Mark II Ross weighed approximately 8½ lbs. and its 28-inch barrel was slightly heavier than the Mark I. The barrel was screwed into the receiver ring with a very coarse thread; the receiver itself was high sided. The rifle's four-groove rifling had a bore diameter of .303 inches and a groove diameter of .312 inches. Depth of groove was .0056 inches; rifling twist to the left was between 9.75 inches to one turn in 10 inches. Its rear portions resembled that of the American Mauser-type Model 1903 Springfield.

The bolt sleeve of the Mark II was neat and compact: The bolt head lugs were solid and locked horizontally and unlocked to a vertical position on opening. The action was cocked on the opening stroke; the flat-sheet steel extractor had a claw on its front and extraction of the fired case from the rifle chamber was done by the camming action of the bolt on opening.

The bolt release on the newest Ross rifle was a vertical sliding plunger located on the left side of the receiver near the rear end and firing pin. To remove the bolt the shoooter had to depress the release. Operation of the rifle required that the bolt handle

be pushed to the left to engage the safety and to the right to release and fire. The safety—which was actually a button—was located on top of the right-hand bolt handle. Although it was a bit inconvenient to operate, the safety was a very reliable mechanism in the engaged position.

The five-round magazine was a vertical, staggered-round Harris box entirely enclosed by the wooden stock. The magazine depressor, or lifter, was on the right side and protruded from the forearm about two inches in front of the breech ring. For quick dump loading of rounds, the operator simply depressed the magazine follower. The magazine cut-off, which curved to form a hook for the thumb, was a steel stem passing behind the magazine and through a hole in the top of the trigger guard. Rounding out the features of the Mark II Ross was a provision for a short, knife-type handle bayonet attached below the barrel muzzle.

Shortly after the first 3,000 Mark II rifles were delivered in February 1907, it was apparent that the sights were still flimsy and would not hold their zero, and that the guns still suffered from rapid-fire jamming. The Standing Small Arms Committee recommended that the defects be corrected, and, once again, the Ross rifle was sent back to the factory for repair.

All incorporated changes were designated by adding a small star (*) behind the Mark II until five stars had been added. In fact, it is correct to regard the variations on the basic Mark II arm as transitional models to the next Ross refinement. Thus the Mark II*, which was equipped with a magazine lever and a tangent-curve rear sight, was a transition toward the next further-improved version, the Mark II**.

The Mark II** incorporated the most radical changes—in the barrel, safety catch and sights. An-

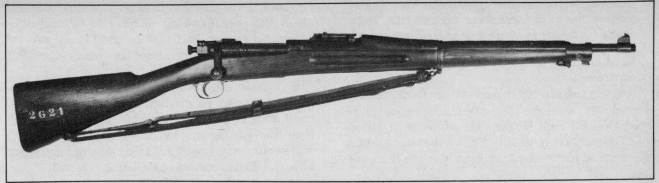

The Model 1903 Springfield Mauser-type bolt-action rifle served the U.S. Armed Forces reliably and admirably in both world wars. With an accurate sight range on 36-inch Bull's-eye targets of 1,000 to 1,200 yards, the M1903 easily outperformed the 303 Mark II Ross rifle, which failed miserably in the mire and mud of Flanders.

other version of the basic Ross Mark II★★, called the Sniper Model, was equipped with a sight that attached to the stock by a stock bolt. (This rifle also had the BSA Martin vernier aperture target sight that brought the Ross rifle its early fame as a target rifle, winning the Queen's and King's Prize at Bisley.) The Mark II★★ was probably the best-working Ross military rifle. It was made in three grades—$35.00 Military Standard, $40.00 Military Target and the deluxe $48.00 Military Presentation Grade.

In November 1911, the manufacture of the Ross Rifle Mark III began. All the faults and defects found in the earlier Rosses were to be completely eliminated in this new model.

The "Long Ross" Mark III, or Model 1912, was very different from the two earlier Rosses. The Mark III action was an unattractive, squat-sided affair with flat and comparatively wider bolt tracks than its predecessors. In fact, its ungainly, hump-backed buttstock, its single-row, five-round, sheet-metal box magazine projecting below the action and stock and its extra-long 30.5-inch barrel added nothing to the looks of the gun.

Still, this was the first Ross rifle with a rear receiver bridge located directly in front of the right-hand bolt handle. The forward edge of this bridge was milled out to accept a charger clip to permit fast loading. This receiver bridge also had a Ross-patented open-aperture rear sight. Lying flat, it was an open battle sight; flipped up, it provided an aperture and open sight combination. The Mark III sight screw adjustment provided both windage and elevation.

The all-new locking lugs on the bolt head were of the interrupted screw, or thread, type, which had withstood over 100,000 psi maximum pressure tests in Hercules Powder Company experiments. The bolt

lugs were not positioned horizontally and became vertical upon locking. Also, the solid bolt-head lugs of the Mark II could fit into the bolt sleeve of the screw-interrupted Mark III lugs, and vice versa. But, of course, neither of these Ross bolts would fit into the receiver-locking recesses of the other rifle's breech.

On this new Mark III, the magazine cut-off and bolt release were incorporated into one small rotatable lever located on the left side of the rear receiver bridge. When rotated downward, this lever prevented the entire bolt from coming all the way back and acted as a magazine cut-off. Turning the lever upward allowed the bolt to travel backward to the full length of the magazine. In this system the rim of the top 303 British round could rise in front of the bolt and be driven forward into the waiting chamber as the bolt was thrust forward into the locked position. When the rotatable lever was clicked to project at right angles to the receiver, the bolt assembly could be completely drawn out to the rear.

It was this rifle, the "Long Ross" Mark III, that failed so miserably on European battlefields. Author Larry Worthington in his book on the Canadian Expeditionary Corps, 1914-1919, *Amid the Guns Below*, succinctly states the facts:

The Ross rifle could not have been worse for active service. It was a fine precision-made sporting rifle, and as such Colonel Hughes knew it to be extremely accurate at long range. But its length made it unsuitable for the cavalry; the artillery found that it slipped in the limber brackets (made for the slimmer Lee-Enfields) and fouled the wheels; and as a weapon it failed the infantry when it was most needed. The gun required special care and special ammunition that was unavailable overseas. A few rounds of rapid fire caused it to heat and jam, and the heel of a heavy boot, or an entrenching tool was needed to release the bolt, when seconds meant the difference between life and death. Canadians in battle soon learned to salvage British Lee-Enfields from the dead, but since they had to account for the Ross at inspection, many carried two rifles.

Reports from the front and articles in the Ottawa newspapers about the Ross rifle inadequacies infuriated Col. Sir Sam Hughes, the Minister of Militia and Defence. He refused to believe that in rapid fire the moving parts seized, making it worse than useless.

At home by mid-1916, Sir Charles had only delivered 66,590 of the 100,000 Mark III Ross rifles ordered by the British War Office in September of 1914. Sick and tired of waiting, the War Office canceled the order.

If the uproar over deliveries and troubles overseas with the Mark III rifle bothered Sir Charles, he never showed it. Always aloof, his address at 590 Laurier Avenue in Quebec City was only a mailing address. The always-on-the-go Sir Charles was busy supervising his Quebec factory, his overseas Scottish estates, touring French battlefields, fishing at his Labrador retreat or—early in 1915—badgering the Tsar of Russia into buying some of his Mark III Rosses. On one visit to a Canadian military camp in England, it was said that Ross reacted to a complaint about the poor handling of his rifle by muttering something to the effect that he was bloody well not going to play nursemaid to the whole Canadian Army.

Sir Charles could afford to be brash; he had the unflagging support of Hughes. Many times in Parliament, Hughes said that he would stand or fall on the Ross rifle. Challenging his colleagues, he taunted, "I will swallow any Lee-Enfield that does not jam when I fire it." The Members of Parliament jeered.

In the summer of 1916, Gen. Sir John French ordered all Rosses withdrawn from service and reinstated the British Lee-Enfields. The fall of the rifle was soon followed by the fall of Hughes. On November 11, 1916, Prime Minister Sir Robert Borden fired him. Five months later the Ross Rifle Company ceased to exist.

A View of the Ross from the Present

The Mark III Ross rifle failed in trench warfare because the battle grime worked itself into the receiver locking wells, causing it to freeze. The straight-pull bolt action, which unlocked by the camming effect of the spiral bolt ribs riding inside the sleeve, could not provide the sufficient camming power of a turning-bolt Lee-Enfield operating against a screw

S & K Manufacturing Co.

The British Lee-Enfield, or S.M.L.E., with a 4X Bushnell Banner hunting scope. The rear-locking, S.M.L.E. turning bolt action proved vastly superior to the straight-pull action of the Ross. In the battlefield mud of Flanders, the Mark III failed to extract its fired shells and jammed shut.

thread to draw out fired cases from heat-swollen chambers. Of course, constant swabbing out with a chamber cleaning stick would have prevented this from happening; however, such care was a near impossibility in the trenches.

A test of the Ross Mark III by general headquarters in June 1915, revealed that the Canadian 303 ammunition was .010 inches *smaller* in caliber than the standard British equivalent, because the Ross chamber was smaller than the .303-inch Lee-Enfield's.

The Lee-Enfield chamber measured .339 inches at the neck and .462 inches at the base. Comparable measurements for the Ross chamber were .338 inches and .460 inches. After modifications, the rechambered Ross Mark III measured an enlarged .341 inches at the neck and .464 inches at the cartridge-case base just in front of the rim.

The hardness of the Canadian-made Dominion Arsenal brass had been increased to lessen the amount of expansion in firing, but even the "hard" Canadian brass couldn't stop the extraction troubles of the Mark III rifles.

Then there was the disastrous Mark III bolt stop. The real reason for the gun jamming in rapid fire lay in the thin outer edge of the rearmost "saw-tooth" locking lug, which came into sharp, hammer-blow contact with the unyielding steel bolt stop. This pounding caused the locking cam to bend or crack,

until it finally deformed enough to cause the bolt head to jam when it was closed against the resisting shoulders in the receiver. In violent ejection during rapid fire—especially when cases were sticky in extraction—impact between cam and stop was increased, deformation was accelerated and jamming resulted. This discovery was made in June 1915 by Major R. M. Blair, Assistant Inspector of Small Arms for Canadian Ordnance.

Major Blair and his staff worked out a design for foolproofing all Mark IIIs in France. First, the diameter of the bolt stop at the area of impact was increased from .01007 square inches to .021607 square inches. This adjustment cut in half the stress per square inch at each blow. Second, although the Ross bolt could be assembled in such a way that it would lock, the rifle could still be fired. To correct this fault of improperly assembled bolt sleeves, Major Blair and his ordnance experts put a rivet through the sleeve, which followed a recess cut, by filing down three threads of one of the bolt spirals. Also, the extractor groove slope was eliminated in all later Mark IIIs.

None of the Ross rifle models, Marks I, II or III, was a good service weapon, but they all might have been. Had their inventor taken a deeper interest in detail, it is probable that all the faults of the Ross rifle could have been corrected. The jamming was corrected but the repair came too late—every soldier in

The Foote Collection, Manitoba Archives

Boys' Rifle Team in 1914 just before the outbreak of "The Guns of August." The Ross Cadet rifles shown above were used for smallbore indoor target rifle training, and prepared the youngsters for competition with older team members shooting full-bore Ross Marks I and II.

On a 1916 visit to the front, Hon. Lt.-Gen. and first War Minister of Militia and Defence Sir Sam Hughes and the commanding officer watch as the Canadian troops parade with their Mark III 303 Ross rifles in hand. Later the same year, after the soldiers had thrown away their Ross rifles in disgust, three Canadian divisions had been rearmed with British Lee-Enfields.

the entire Canadian Corps' four divisions had already utterly lost confidence in the Ross rifle and reverted to using the British 303 S.M.L.E. Further, had all of the problems been solved, Canadian soldiers might have carried their Canadian-made Ross rifles into World War II—and proudly. According to Ross-rifle expert Jerome Knap, in his article: "The Saga of the Ross Rifle":

> . . . some Canadian snipers preferred the Ross Mark III Sniper Rifle over the P-14 Enfield, or S.M.L.E. One battalion intelligence report of the Canadian Corp in 1917 had this to say: "GOOD SHOOTING—During the Second Battle of Ypres, over 200 deliberate shots were fired at close range at advancing Germans by a King's Prize winner. He must have accounted for nearly 150 casualties."

Ironically, as a sporting rifle, the Ross had few rivals in its day and many of the very early gun experts sang its praises. Capt. Edward C. Crossman wrote a long article on the Ross for *Arms and the Man* magazine, calling it "The Rifle of My Dreams."

On the open-target range or on a big game hunt, the Ross rifle performed well. Along with the 303 British cartridge, the Ross was chambered for three others: 35 Winchester, 375 Eley and 280 Ross.

In 1908, Eley cartridge designer F. W. Jones dazzled the shooting world by winning all five 1,000-yard matches with the new 280 Ross Match Rifle and ammunition made by Sir Charles Ross.

In the big game arena the Ross also won acclaim. The 280 Ross was the original high-velocity Magnum, projecting a 140-grain bullet at 3,100 feet per second. Today, it can be loaded to velocities equal to that of the new 7mm Remington belted Magnum.

In 1912 Cluny C. Luke of Alberni, British Columbia, wrote a letter to the manager of the Ross Rifle Company, telling how pleased he was with his recent purchase of a 280 Model 10 Ross rifle on a hunting trip to Cassiar, B.C.:

> I went after 13 head and bagged the lot, at ranges varying from 60 to 500 yards, in 27 shots . . . (taking) 3 black bears, 4 grizzlies, 2 goats, 2 caribou, and 2 moose. In my estimation there is no rifle to compare with it, the balance being perfect, the action fast and smooth, while the flatness of trajectory quite does away with all judging of distances. I shot a goat at over 500 yards with exactly the same sight that I take at 100 yards . . . Three grizzlies were killed in under a minute.

In 1920, the Canadian government settled all debts and contracts with Sir Charles Ross. Claiming that his contract called for 100,000 rifles at $28.50 each, Ross demanded expropriation of just under $9 million; the government paid him $2 million. During the 1920s the Ross plant, which had manufactured a total of 342,000 Ross military rifles was razed and a park was built on its site. The Ross rifle story was over.

Editor's Note: Mr. Farquharson is seeking to borrow or buy two mint-condition 303 British-caliber Ross military rifles with perfect bores and chambers for testing .303 British commercial hunting ammunition. Any reader willing to lend or sell such a rifle is invited to write to the author, c/o Editor, Stoeger Publishing Company, 55 Ruta Court, South Hackensack, NJ 07606.

Varmint Hunting in Miniature

Don Lewis

The veteran hunter stood behind a scarred hemlock. Silently, he watched a towering beechnut tree 50 yards in the distance. A flash of gray had assured him his quarry was hidden in the maze of limbs. Sweeping the canopy of twigs and branches with compact binoculars, he stopped at his barely visible target: a squirrel's head and neck. It was a tough shot—the kind the rifleman squirrel hunter dreams about.

Resting the 22 rimfire against the hemlock, the hunter centered the dot reticle of the 6X scope on the neck of his target and squeezed the trigger. The thud of the striking bullet echoed as the squirrel hung for several seconds before plummeting to the ground. It was precision shooting at its best. The hunter felt a sense of accomplishment only the rimfire rifle squirrel hunter experiences.

There are no hard statistics on how many hunters here and in Canada specialize in this fascinating sport, but the figure has to be low. It is unfortunate that so many hunters fail to take squirrel hunting seriously and, consequently, do not consider it a sport. Many times, squirrel shooting falls into the residual class—when other game is in short supply, hunters head for the squirrel woods. But squirrel hunting, especially with the 22-rimfire cartridge, has all the ingredients to qualify it as a major hunting sport. While it lacks the camaraderie of a deer camp, the chilling sight of a Cape buffalo or the majestic beauty of a Dall ram high on a mountain crag, squirrel hunting has its own built-in frustrations and disappointments. The squirrel hunter with the rimfire rifle faces greater shooting challenges than does the deer or bear hunter. The big game hunter seeks the prize—a wide set of antlers, a full curl of horns or the pelt of a massive Kodiak bear. The squirrel hunter, on the other hand, derives complete satisfaction from knowing how to hunt the high-top aerialists, finds tranquility in the silence of a timber stand and warms with inner delight when patience and shooting skill bring success.

In Search of the Squirrel

Hunting the wary tree climber requires a great deal of knowledge about its feeding habits and habitat. For instance, *Sciurus carolinensis*, or the common gray squirrel, the most frequently hunted of all rodents, often visits large timber stands and is especially fond of beechnuts, white oak acorns and shellbark hickory nuts plus other types of mast food. The diet of his larger cousin, *Sciurus niger*, or the fox squirrel, is similar, except its favorite habitat is small woodlots or one or two large trees along a fence row. It will even nest and raise a family within sight of farm buildings. It has an insatiable desire for corn, while big timber grays show little interest in it.

Although no cut-and-dried method exists for finding squirrels, the veteran hunter can find signs that indicate squirrel country. Heavy concentrations of large beechnut or white oak trees point to ample mast food. Scars and scratches on a dead chestnut tree may indicate a den. Overturned leaves where cached nuts have been dug up are also sure signs of squirrel activity. Of course, remains of nuts and acorns that have been chiseled open are the most obvious giveaways.

As important as habitat may be, game biologists

All photos by Helen Lewis

The author used a discontinued Model 64 Savage/ Anschutz scoped with a 1-inch Unertl target scope to collect these two gray squirrels—one a black-phased gray. Note the "Dial-A-Shell" container on Lewis' coat, which drops one round at a time by turning the dial—very convenient for a single-shot rifle like his.

shot many squirrels silhouetted against the dimly lit sky in the pre-dawn hours. Grays are most active up to mid-morning and again in late afternoon, especially on very bright days. Overcast, cloudy days will keep the gray from sunning itself during early afternoon.

Weather conditions aren't all that critical to hunting squirrel. The old belief that squirrels will not venture out in a high wind is false. True, windy conditions may make it difficult for squirrels to navigate across tree tops, but a hungry gray or fox will tackle considerably heavy winds to get the succulent buds at the very tips of high limbs. Under strong, gusty conditions, the experienced hunter watches the ground. That's where the action will be.

Although the wily tree climber may spend a day or two in a den or nest if a severe storm is in progress, weather conditions will not affect a squirrel's desire for food. Sub-zero temperatures and heavy snow will not keep the nut eater from finding buried food. In fact, the keen nose of a gray or fox can pinpoint a nut under eight inches of snow with unerring accuracy. Inveterate nut hoarders, the gray and the fox

are at a loss to explain why one patch of timber will have squirrels and a similar one several miles away is void of bushytails. The wise hunter will spend plenty of time prior to the season looking for good squirrel territory. It's time consuming and requires a lot of patience but, in the end, it will enhance the success ratio.

What time of day is best to hunt squirrels? Old-time hunters used to hit the woods long before daylight and would have left no later than 10 in the morning. Squirrel activity, they believed, ceased until late afternoon when they came back on watch. The patient, watchful hunter today, however, will see squirrels at all hours of the day. Squirrels tend to feed all day long and will even do so very late in the evening. Many experienced squirrel hunters, in fact, will not hunt the morning after a full moon because they believe squirrels feed in bright moonlight. But full moon or not, gray squirrels are generally early risers. Before the days of shooting schedules, hunters

You can use a tree for a rest on a long shot. Rifle is Model 82 Kimber with a Weaver T-6 silhouette scope.

will bury practically every nut they can find. Usually the one who succumbs to the weather is the hunter.

Dispelling Squirrel Myths

The large family of rodents has added intrigue, color, mirth and myths to American folklore. For example, in the 1800s western packrats supposedly cached prospectors' gold nuggets that, when found, brought fortune to the finder. Porcupines, it was believed, could throw their quills. And every February, a Pennsylvania groundhog, Punxsutawney Phil, forecasts winter weather for the entire nation. The squirrel has had its share of myths, too.

Some hunters refuse to look for the larger squirrels in a wood infested with pine squirrels. There is still a deep-rooted belief that pine squirrels castrate gray squirrels, although no real evidence supports this belief. The myth started when old-time hunters killed male squirrels that had no visible testes. In many cases, the scrotum was shrunken and gave the appearance that it had been removed. Biologists now know that the testes of a male squirrel do not enter the scrotum until the young squirrel is sexually mature. Also, certain larvae may destroy the testes. This evidence, plus the fact that a very young squirrel's underdeveloped scrotum with no fur looks somewhat like scar tissue, deals a severe blow to the emasculation theory.

The migration myth is another fable from yesteryear that needs to be put to rest. Practically every veteran squirrel hunter claims to have seen a real live squirrel migration with dozens of big grays deserting an area in search of better living conditions.

What was actually seen, however, was nothing more than a fall mating ritual. Perhaps it began an hour before with one male chasing a female. The commotion attracted more males that joined in the mad chase down logs, over brushland and through the dizzy heights of massive hardwoods. It all ended with one large male being the victor, leaving the rest to wander back to their dens. For those who hunted many years ago, the chase, with all its noise and excitement, could have included 40 to 50 males, if it covered enough territory. If the story were told to-

Practically any 22-rimfire rifle can be used for squirrel hunting. Shown are 13 of the author's squirrel outfits, any of which serve him well in the squirrel woods.

A top squirrel rifle can keep all of its shots in one inch or less at 50 yards. Here Lewis tests the Model 82 Kimber scoped with a Weaver T-6 silhouette. Ammo is CCI Green Tag Competition 22 long rifle. The following photo attests to this rifle's accuracy.

day, the figure would be more like 10 to 15 because of drastically reduced squirrel populations. Still, even that number lends some credence to hunters' tales of migration. The only real migrations encompassing literally tens of thousands of squirrels ended in the Civil War days when squirrels began losing their hardwood habitats.

The Weapon Debate: Shotgun vs. Rifle

The table-pounding argument within the squirrel hunting fraternity nowadays is the choice between the shotgun and the rifle. The shotgunner is positive the rifleman makes the countryside unsafe with flying ricochets, and the rifleman swears the scatter-gun hunter is a despicable sight in squirrel territory. Curiously, there seems to be no middle ground; but there is room in the squirrel woods for both groups and, in fact, both are needed.

The shotgunner, it's fair to say, will have an easier time collecting his game. Unlike the rifleman who is forced to wait for his quarry to become motionless, the shotgun hunter can take practically any shot that is safe and within range. This doesn't make squirrel hunting with a shotgun a matter-of-fact affair; a squirrel gliding through a maze of grapevines or across interlocking limbs of high hemlock trees is not an easy target. The shotgun has a distinct advantage in heavy vegetation, dense entanglements of vines and with on-moving targets. Since this type of habitat fits nicely into a squirrel's life, there are plenty of areas where the shotgunner will find ample challenge, but it's safe to say his ratio of success will not be impressive.

Through the decades, the shotgun squirrel hunter has pretty much stuck with the 12-gauge boring in a full-choke barrel topped off with a high brass load of No. 4 shot. Other modern hunters put their faith in smaller gauges and lighter shot right down to the No. 7½ pellet.

A look at ballistics may throw some light on this matter and lessen the controversy. It's the pattern that kills—not so much the size of the pellet. A shotgun pellet cannot be guided, and the hunter must depend on the density of the pattern to make the kill. Every pellet that strikes the target contributes in some manner to the kill; consequently, dense patterns put more pellets into the target. It is also true that heavier shot retains its velocity longer and offers more kinetic energy, which, in layman's terms, is killing power. But then, an ounce of No. 4 shot contains roughly 135 pellets, while one ounce of No. 6 shot jumps the count to 225. Going to 7½ brings it

Three 5-shot groups fired at 50 yards into 1-inch squares with top squirrel outfits: The top one-holer was cut by a Remington 541S with a Weaver T-6 scope and Remington target long-rifle (lot 6600) ammo. The middle group was printed by a Kimber Model 82 topped with a Weaver T-6 scope; ammo was CCI Green Tag target long rifle. The bottom group was shot with the Savage/Anschutz Model 54 Sporter scoped with a 6X Redfield Widefield; ammo was Federal Champion long rifle (lot 711).

up to 350. The hunter must decide his own needs. For extreme ranges up to 40 yards, Nos. 4 and 5 would offer the necessary killing power, even though the pattern would have gaps in it. In country that offers shorter shots, No. 6 or 7½ shot would be more than adequate.

Regarding gauge, the debate is just as heated. The false belief that the larger the gauge, the harder the shotgun shoots, leads a lot of hunters down the wrong path. In the velocity column, there is little difference between the tiny .410 bore and the mighty 10-gauge Magnum. Velocities run from 1,100 feet per second (fps) to 1,375. The differences rest in the size of the shot charge. The standard .410 shell is capable of throwing a half-ounce of shot from the muzzle at more than 1,200 fps. The 12-gauge can equal that velocity with 1¼ ounces of shot. The 3½ inch, 10-gauge Magnum will match that speed with a full two ounces of shot. The more pellets, the denser the pattern and, again, it's the pattern that spells success or failure.

A Case for the 22 Rimfire

For the hunter who seeks the ultimate in squirrel shooting, a switch to the common 22-rimfire cartridge in a super-accurate rifle will bring to fruition a new style of hunting: varmint hunting in miniature. Now it's a single projectile that must be guided accurately to a small, distant target. The shooting is very selective and disappointment comes more often than success.

For many years, the long-rifle cartridge reigned as the cartridge of choice. With the advent of the more powerful 224 cartridge in the 22 Hornet in 1930, the little rimfire began a slow journey to oblivion as a hunting cartridge. During the last 20 years, the common 22-rimfire cartridge has been relegated by hunters to the ranks of the unwanted. A fair segment of the modern hunting fraternity looks upon the 22 rimfire as a toy; it's far from that in the squirrel woods.

First and foremost, no other cartridge is better equipped for squirrel shooting—and that includes the 22-rimfire Magnum series. Both the Remington 5mm Magnum and the Winchester 22 Magnum, which have muzzle velocities of close to 2,000 fps, are too powerful and destructive for squirrel hunting. Further, their 40-grain slugs have a bad tendency to ricochet. Reduced loads in centerfire cartridges add flavor to squirrel shooting, but they have the same inherent drawbacks as the 22-rimfire Magnums. This leaves the old 22-rimfire, long-rifle cartridge in a class by itself.

The little rimfire outfit is very temperamental. For

Lewis watches as his wife touches off a shot in the squirrel woods. Don is using a discontinued Model 64 Savage/Anschutz 22 single-shot scoped with a 6X Unertl 1-inch target scope. Helen is using a KKJ Walther 22 rimfire scoped with a Redfield 6X.

some strange reason, it will not handle all brands of long-rifle ammunition with the same degree of accuracy. While super-high speed brands of 22 ammo may appear to have more to offer, they seldom have the tight group potential needed for long-distance squirrel shooting. A step in the right direction is target ammunition. The fear that it is too low in velocity at roughly 1,050 fps is groundless. Velocity charts show that high-speed fodder adds only a couple of hundred feet more speed at the muzzle, inconsequential at distances of up to 50 yards.

While target ammunition is more expensive, it is also manufactured under tighter controls. It's more dependable and consistent, right from the priming charge to the 40-grain bullet, which is more uniform and free from defects. The low noise level of target ammo is a plus for the squirrel shooter, too, but its accuracy potential is by far its greatest virtue.

Admittedly, any 22 rifle can be used with fair suc-

cess in the squirrel woods, especially if the shots are under 30 yards. Beyond that distance, a rifle is required that can put all of its bullets from a benchrest at 50 yards into a one-inch group or less. As simple as this may sound, relatively few mass-produced rifles will attain that goal even with target ammo. For the most part, semi-target rifles or ones falling into higher price brackets will consistently meet the one-inch requirement. Accuracy doesn't just happen; it's the product of a good rifle, fine ammunition and the shooter's ability to get the best from his equipment. But a rifle should not be discarded until it has been tested from a solid rest at 50 yards.

No hunter can shoot beyond his visual range, and that goes double for the squirrel buff. No rifle is any better than its sighting arrangement. Iron sights may be steeped in history, but faced with dull morning haze and late evening shadows, the rifleman squirrel hunter needs high-quality optics. For decades, the

22 rifle has been the victim of poor optics. The varmint and big game rifles carried the best, but the rimfire wore whatever could be cranked out for a few dollars. Low magnification, poor optics and a crosswire that covered an inch at 50 yards was standard for years.

A good squirrel rifle warrants a fine scope—and that means money. Normally, a 6 power gathers enough light for early-morning and late-evening shooting and also provides adequate magnification for shots up to 60 yards. A regular 6X big game or

The shotgun is preferable for the young hunter. Here is Darrel Lewis, the author's son, at age 15. He wouldn't have bagged this many squirrels with a rifle.

varmint-type scope will do, and if it is to be used strictly as a squirrel hunting scope, it should be returned to the manufacturer to be parallax corrected at 75 yards. Most big game hunting scopes are adjusted for parallax at 125 yards or more, which makes close appear hazy. Setting it at a closer range will put the target in sharp focus.

Squirrel hunting with the rimfire can be done several ways. The sit-and-wait method is probably the best. A good idea is to stake out a position from which 50-yard shots are available on all sides. This permits the hunter to cover a full 100 yards of woods. Shooting half the length of a football field is no problem for the hunter who knows his rifle will put all of its bullets in less than one inch at the same distance. In fact, it's the long shot that the rifle-bearing squirrel shooter looks for.

A second method is similar to shotgun hunting. The hunter slips quietly along, watching for moving squirrels, dangling tails or quick flashes of gray. (Always stop by a tree, since it will offer a natural rest for the long shot.) The hunter walks a few yards and then surveys the surroundings for 10 minutes or longer, if he has the slightest suspicion squirrels are in the area. The wily tree dwellers can be extremely cautious and will remain motionless for an agonizing amount of time. Squirrels, too, have extremely keen eyesight and are almost always gone before the hunter can act, even with a shotgun. The rifleman faces even more frustration, since it's unlikely he will get a shot at more than two of every five squirrels seen in range. His success ratio might run to only 60 percent.

The Tasty Rewards

The pleasures of squirrel hunting include more than just shooting success. Squirrels are fine table fare; and when properly prepared, they are sweet and tender. But there's work to be done before they can be fried or stewed; the squirrel must be skinned and this is not always an easy task.

There are a variety of skinning methods, but a simple one is to cut the hide around the squirrel's midsection. After making a shallow cut around the body, work the fingers of both hands under the hide on each side of the cut and pull in opposite directions. The hide will peel off. Young squirrels present few skinning problems, but a gray or fox that has reached the old age of five years will test the hunter's strength. For best results, skinning should be done before the entrails are removed. Some hunters do not field dress a squirrel immediately after bagging it, but will wait and dress out their kill after the hunt.

Squirrels with their captor, who used the Ithaca Model 72 scoped with a Bushnell 4X (left), the Marlin 39A with 6X Weaver (center) and the discontinued Savage/Auschutz Model 64 scoped with 6X Uertl target scope.

However, in very warm weather it is wise to field dress immediately after the kill.

Squirrel recipes vary depending on what part of the country the cook comes from. My wife, Helen, sticks with this simple and delicious recipe:

Deep Fried Squirrel
(Serves 3-4)

Cut up two or three squirrels into frying-size pieces and cook with one onion and one stalk of chopped celery in boiling water until tender, about 20-30 minutes. Dry between paper towels and cool.

For batter, combine:

½ cup flour	½ teaspoon salt
½ cup corn meal	1 egg
1 teaspoon baking powder	¾ cup milk

Mix well. Dip pieces of squirrel into batter and fry in hot oil until golden brown.

Despite the pleasures and challenges inherent in the sport, squirrel hunting may be in trouble. Squirrels are basically a product of large stands of hardwoods, and with the steady decline of these forests, squirrels face an uncertain future. The hunter is also to blame for a lack of interest—not only in hunting but also in maintaining a healthy habitat for *Sciurus carolinensis*. But if it's true that squirrel hunting is moribund and will eventually take its place in Americana with the kerosene lamp, the butter churn and the one-room school, we will have lost another rural tradition.

To the person who sees hunting in terms of credit-card junkets for exotic game in faraway places or who specializes in trophy hunting only, the passing of the simple gray squirrel will go unnoticed. Sadder, yet, when the last squirrel rifle cracks in this land and the country kid has no patches of oak and beech in which to hunt squirrel, urbanization will have claimed another victory.

More Do's and Don'ts of Home Gunsmithing

John Traister

Nothing is more frustrating than to begin a repair or alteration on your favorite firearm and find—about half-way through—you don't have the proper tools or materials to complete it, or the knowledge to make the most of the tools you do have. The 1981 SHOOTER'S BIBLE discussed the basic gunsmithing tools and their use, safety precautions for the home gunsmith to follow, recommended reference books and some of the most frequent problems encountered by the amateur gunsmith. (See "Do's and Don'ts of Home Gunsmithing," 1981 SHOOTER'S BIBLE, pp. 52-62.)

When you begin home gunsmithing, you'll need some sound fundamentals before you loosen even one screw. Jumping into the task of taking your pride-and-joy apart without first considering some of the rudimentary techniques can be discouraging, if not

downright disastrous. For example, if you use the wrong kind of screwdriver on a tightly seated screw, you will certainly damage the screw slot. Once the firearm has been disassembled, what plans did you make to get it back together again? Some owners apply heat to a firearm, say, to anneal the receiver of a bolt-action rifle to enable drilling and tapping for a telescope sight. If the job is done precisely, okay; if not, the practice can lead to such inconveniences as a forehead full of brass particles or a couple of missing fingers and, in some cases, the results could mean "curtains."

The following charts are designed to show you at a glance what certain jobs involve and whether you should attempt them or not. But don't take them as gospel since everyone's knowledge, capabilities and tools will vary considerably. If a particular proj-

ect seems to be beyond your capabilities, by all means get some help. On the other hand, if you are certain that you can tackle a project described as needing a professional, don't let the charts talk you out of attempting it. The projects listed as "do's" are those that have been found over a number of years to be best suited for the hobbyist or home gunsmith and, consequently, the ones which are less likely to end up as failures. Those projects under the heading of "don'ts" are just the opposite. Granted, many amateurs have sucessfully completed some of these projects, such as shaping, inletting and finishing a gun stock from a walnut blank. But although I've seen several reasonably good jobs come out of hobbyists' basements, more times than not I've seen these half-finished blanks end up as expensive kindling. Don't let this happen to you.

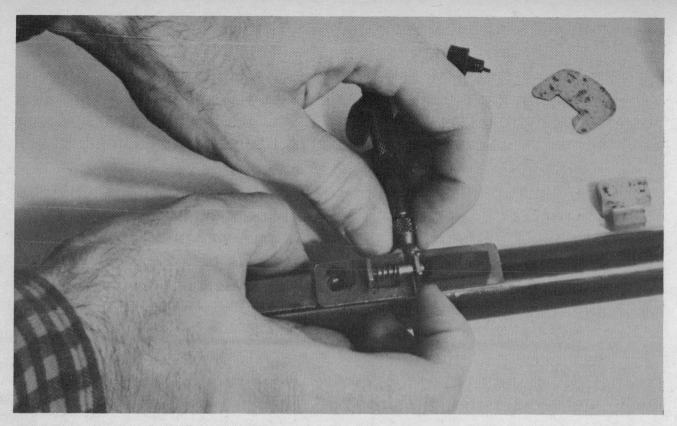

Once you disassemble this Winchester Model 37 shotgun, are you sure you can get it back together?
A good bit of the professional's work consists of correcting amateur's work.

Drilling and tapping a receiver for scope mounts is best left to the professional gunsmith.

GENERAL GUN REPAIRS

Type of Project	Do	Don't	Comments	Tools Needed
Trigger adjustments Screw adjustments	X		Adjust by trial-and-error method.	Screwdriver and, preferably, trigger-pull gauge
By honing		X	Amateur can take off too much metal or obtain wrong angle, either ruining trigger mechanism or making firearm unsafe.	
Remodeling military firearms Altered model	X		If altered, collector's value is lost or at least diminished.	A variety of gunsmithing tools, depending on extent of remodeling
Unaltered		X	Most military weapons have collector's value if in original condition.	
Accurizing Competitive arms		X	Very specialized work, suited only for specialist.	
Hunting arms	X		Methods include stock bedding with Brownell's Acraglas®, trigger adjustments, smoother metal-to-metal contact, etc.	
Mounting rifle sights On factory pre-drilled models	X		Mount sight or scope using pre-drilled holes; bore sight first before zeroing in.	Screwdriver, Loc-Tite or other substances to "freeze" screws to threads
Rifles not drilled and tapped at factory		X	Aligning holes is often a problem without proper jigs and fixtures. Also, certain hardened receivers must be annealed to accept drill bit. Too risky for amateur.	
Rechoking shotguns		X	Job strictly for pros; tools too expensive and skill normally above capabilities of home gunsmith.	
Tightening dovetail slots By peening shoulders		X	Finish will sometimes be damaged.	
By raising craters in slot	X		Use center punch to raise enough craters to tighten dovetail sight.	Center punch, hammer and vise to hold gun

Type of Project	Do	Don't	Comments	Tools Needed
Polishing shotgun chambers	X		Use special barrel-polishing tool available from Frank Mittermeier, Inc. Use ¼-in. drill motor for power and fine emery.	Polishing head, cloth drill and vise to hold gun
Polishing shotgun bores		X	Choke may be removed from bore if care is not taken.	
Lapping rifle barrel		X	Initial setup is rather complicated and rifling can be damaged if not done precisely.	
Recrowning burred muzzle Inexpensive rifle	X		Cut barrel back about ⅛ in. Use rotary file in hand brace to start; finish with brass ball and lapping compound.	Hand brace, rotary file, brass ball, lapping compound, vise, hacksaw and mill file (for truing muzzle after cut)
Expensive rifle		X	Amateur may make mistake and lower value of gun.	

Installing sling swivels presents few problems if a little care is taken.

GENERAL GUN REPAIRS (CONT.)

Type of Project	Do	Don't	Comments	Tools Needed
Correcting burred chambers in expensive 22 rimfire rifles	X		Use small bastard file only on ridge; don't touch any other portion of chamber.	22 caliber ironing tool is safest way if tool is available
Removing metal fouling from rifles	X		Apply small amount of bore cleaner on patch and swab bore; run clean patches through bore and oil.	J-B Bore Cleaner, patches and cleaning rod
Relining 22 rimfire barrels		X	Equipment too expensive for hobbyist. Requires skill and knowledge.	
Tightening loose single-barreled shotgun Around forward semicircular cutout	X		Use center punch and hammer to peen lightly around cutout.	Center punch, hammer and vise
Around rear lug		X	Unless barrel is plugged exactly right, barrel can be flattened by applying too much pressure.	
Removing dents from shotgun barrels Inexpensive gun	X		Use expanding barrel plug; insert and tighten; peen lightly around dent until it raises flush with surface.	Expanding barrel plug, ball-peen hammer, long-shanked screwdriver
Expensive gun		X	Leave for professional gunsmith.	
Mounting sling swivels One-piece stock		X	If front stud is not fitted precisely, accuracy of the rifle may be impaired.	
Two-piece stocks like Win. 94	X		Front swivel normally clamps around magazine tube.	Hand drill, tape for marking depth on bit, bits, screwdriver
Jeweling bolts	X		If the pattern is messed up on the first go-around, it can easily be polished out and started over.	Drill press, jeweling fixture to hold part and abrasive rods
Removing pits and scratches in metal parts Shotgun barrels		X	Barrels are very thin and can be weakened by draw filing.	

GENERAL GUN REPAIRS (CONT.)

Type of Project	Do	Don't	Comments	Tools Needed
Removing pits and scratches in metal parts Rifle barrels	X		The amount of pressure you use on the file is very important: too little will scratch the metal, too much will clog the file and cause scratches. When pits are removed, polish in normal way and then reblue.	10-in. mill file

HANDGUNS

Type of Project	Do	Don't	Comments	Tools Needed
SAUER MODEL 1913 Replacing rear sight and extractor		X	Both of these parts are tempered to be their own springs and will probably have to be made by a gunsmith.	
Replacing trigger bar and magazine catch spring	X		If this spring breaks, it is not difficult to make.	
SAUER MODEL 38H Replacement of cocking lever spring		X	Can be cold-formed from round-wire stock, but not a job for the amateur.	
MAUSER HSC Replacement of firing pin	X		The WW II Models frequently have firing-pin breakage, but replacements are available.	Conventional disassembly tools
MAUSER MODEL 1896 Replacing extractor	X		The extractor is tempered to be its own spring, and when a replacement part can be found, it's a relatively simple operation.	
Replacing rear sight spring	X		This is a blade-type spring that is easy to reproduce.	
Replacing safety extension		X	The tempered safety extension snaps into two notches in the sub-frame, but if this should break, it's a job for the pro.	

Type of Project	Do	Don't	Comments	Tools Needed
WEBLEY REVOLVER Replacing main spring	X		Remove grips for the repair.	Screwdriver and pliers

WEBLEY AUTO PISTOL
    Disassembly for cleaning
    Partial
	X		The Model 1909 strips down to four basic groups for cleaning.	Basic disassembly tools

Complete		X	Not recommended for amateur.	
Replacement of V-spring	X		Remove grips to reveal V-spring and lever, which act as the recoil system.	Screwdriver and pliers
COLT LIGHTNING REVOLVER Replacement of trigger spring arm		X	Replacement parts are available, but these require careful fitting by a gunsmith.	

IVER JOHNSON REVOLVER
    Tightening barrel latch
    Welding
		X	Requires detailed stripping of the frame, adding a spot of steel weld to the back of each latching lug, and recutting them to fit.	

By peening	X		Place small steel block tightly between lugs to prevent bending and peen an impression on the side of each lug. A slight bump on the back of each lug will tighten latch.	Hammer, blunt punch and anvil
REMINGTON MODEL 51 Field-stripping	X		The pistol easily disassembles into about 10 pieces for cleaning and minor repairs.	Drift punches
Complete disassembly		X	It is not advisable to remove all parts from this pistol due to possible breakage of unavailable parts.	

CENTERFIRE RIFLES

Type of Project	Do	Don't	Comments	Tools Needed
GERMAN GEWHER 88 Replacing ejector	X		The separate bolt head is easily removable so the tiny ejector can be easily removed.	
Replacing extractor	X		The extractor, which is tempered to be its own spring, is also in the bolt head and is easily replaced.	
Replacing firing pin		X	Replacing the firing pin and complete disassembly of the bolt is best left to a professional.	
MARLIN MODEL 1894 Correcting spring lever		X	A very slight deformation of the lever can cause a failure to depress the trigger block—preventing the trigger from being pulled. The lever can be straightened, but is a job for a pro.	
Replacing firing pin spring	X		Remove breech block and replace spring.	Drift punch and screwdriver
Replacement of ejector spring		X	This leaf-type spring must be properly aligned with the ejector track in the breech block and can be tricky.	
MAUSER MODEL 98 Installing low scope safety	X		Low scope safeties, which are easy to install, are available from Numrich Arms Corp.	No tools needed
WINCHESTER MODEL 70 **(Pre-64)** Replacing extractor	X		If replacement part is not available, use extractor from 1917 Enfield after thinning it down.	

SHOTGUNS

Type of Project	Do	Don't	Comments	Tools Needed
MOSSBERG MODEL 500 Repairing broken action slides By brazing		X	Heat required to braze will weaken and ruin hardness of metal.	
Silver solder	X		Use silver solder of lowest melting point and take care to get a good flow.	Torch, silver solder, flux and clamps
H&R TOPPER Replacing broken barrel lug		X	These lugs have been known to break and, while they may be repaired by silver soldering, the job is strictly for the pro.	
WINCHESTER MODEL 37 Replacement of firing pin retainer screw	X		Make sure striker is in forward position, move top lever to right and remove screw immediately under top-lever thumb notch.	Screwdriver
WINCHESTER MODEL 42 Replacing extractor	X		Left extractor will break more frequently than main extractor, but installation is not difficult.	
Replacing ejector	X		Narrow ejector mounted in a recess in left inside wall of receiver is not difficult to replace.	
Tightening screws	X		Many screws on this shotgun come loose and should be checked and tightened periodically.	
WINCHESTER MODEL 24 Replacement of internal action parts	X		If you can obtain replacement parts, the operation is not difficult. Merely remove buttstock, which allows access to the inside of the receiver.	

22 RIMFIRE RIFLES

Type of Project	Do	Don't	Comments	Tools Needed
H&R MODEL 760 Replacing fiber buffer	X		If replacement parts cannot be found, use 16-gauge shotshell wad.	Screwdriver and drift punches
22 MAUSER TRAINER Removing extractor from bolt		X	Unless absolutely necessary, the extractor of this rifle should not be removed.	
Repairing broken extractor		X	Weld must be of steel, recut to shape and then retempered—a job for the gunsmith.	
NOBLE MODEL 235 Repairs of any kind	X		Repairs on this rifle by a professional gunsmith will often cost more than the gun is worth, and is therefore a good gun for the amateur to practice on.	
REMINGTON MODEL 552 Replacing seer and trigger springs		X	The degree of tension of both springs is critical to proper functioning—but it is a job for the pro.	
Tightening magazine-tube retaining screw	X		This screw should be checked often to prevent losing magazine tube.	Screwdriver
Replacing ejector	X		First remove bolt and then pull ejector out by its forward end.	

STOCK WORK

Type of Project	Do	Don't	Comments	Tools Needed
Shaping and inletting semi-finished stock	X		Semi-finished stocks from Fajen and Bishop are within the capabilities of most amateurs. Take off only the amount of wood necessary for a close fit.	Stock-making set from Frank Mittermeier, Inc., inletting black; glass bedding kit optional
Finishing semi-finished stock (as described above)	X		Many stock-finishing kits are available that produce very fine, professional-quality jobs.	Abrasive cloth from 80 to 400 grit, wood filler and oil finish, steel wool

Type of Project	Do	Don't	Comments	Tools Needed
Refinishing existing stock On modern abused firearm	X		Remove old finish with varnish remover; raise dents with steam; sand out remaining dents; then sand smooth and finish with stock finish.	Varnish remover, abrasive paper, steel wool, flat iron or soldering iron, damp cloth, wood filler and finish
On classic guns		X	Altering original finish, regardless of its condition, may lower value. Any restoration should be done by a professional.	
Filling dents and gouges Inexpensive stock	X		Heat pallet knife, rub against shellac stick to melt it on pallet; quickly "swipe" it across the area to be repaired.	Shellac stick of proper color, pallet knife and source of heat
Expensive stock		X		
Building finished stock from walnut blank		X	Amateurs usually do not have the skill, tools or patience to shape a stock from scratch. This often discourages beginners from attempting other jobs within their capabilities.	Stockmaker's action screw spokeshave, rasps, many sizes of chisels, bottoming tools and others not normally found in the home gun shop

Knives That Shoot... and Other Firearms Oddities

Robert Dana

You are rummaging through some old walking sticks at a neighborhood garage sale, and a heavy cane catches your eye. While you are inspecting it, the handle comes apart and you find yourself with a pistol in one hand and a stick in the other. You have just come upon a gun popular in the 19th century for self-defense and widely used by poachers—a cane gun.

Whether you report your "find" to the owner is a matter between yourself and your conscience. But you are foolish if you do not buy the cane at any reasonable price. Cane guns are only one of the many firearms curiosa that are coming to the attention of collectors. If you are intrigued by these oddities or already have some in your collection, here are some of the things you should look for in unlikely places or in unusual guises.

Cane Guns. By itself, a cane or walking stick can be a formidable weapon. When a gun has been added, the combination is potentially lethal, even in the hands of an unaggressive person.

Some cane guns are genuine firearms; others are air guns. We sometimes forget that air guns have a long and honorable history, dating back in their present form at least until the early 16th century. A few cane guns were actually made of cane or wood, but most were of metal. In all cases, the presence of a gun was usually well concealed.

One early cane gun fired a gunpowder-propelled bullet, but its striker was mouth-blown by the shooter, much like a primitive blowgun. A cartridge was loaded in the chamber; a hollow tube with a floating dart ran back to the handle, which was fitted with a silver screw cap. To fire this gun, you removed the cap on the handle and the ferrule at the other end raised the muzzle to let the dart slide back, and blew. The pointed dart detonated the primer of the special 7mm centerfire cartridge. (To serve as a safety, a small hole was bored about an inch above the cartridge head and a nail or rod was inserted here.)

Many of the cane guns of the late 1800s were not straight walking sticks like the one just described, but had traditional curved handles. Remington made a popular model for 22 and 32 rimfire cartridges, which was advertised as being "Protection against Dogs and Highwaymen." To load such a gun, you inserted a cartridge in the chamber after the handle had been pulled back "until a flat spring jumped up and prevented forward motion." The action was entirely enclosed in the curved handle, and the gun was cocked by drawing back on the handle. The spring catch also served as the rear sight, and this and the concealed button trigger were the only clues that a firearm was hidden in the cane. Remington's advertising stressed the usefulness of the cane for taxidermists and ornithologists, a message that would certainly raise the eyebrows of today's Audubon Society members.

Some cane guns were made in attachable sections; often one section was a concealable shoulder stock which could be screwed to the gun at the appropriate moment. Other cane guns had no barrel to speak of, being hollow for only a short distance at the handle end. When the curved handle was

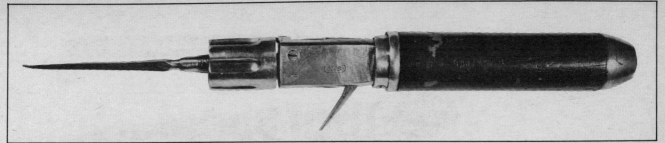

The business end of a walking stick six-shot revolver with attached stiletto. Note the spur trigger.

separated from the stick portion, a pistol or even a pepperbox was at hand.

Cane guns are often marked with the name of the maker. One maker whose signed cane guns were world-famous was John Day, a prolific inventor from Barnstable, Devon, whose 1823 British patent covered a percussion-cap gun built into a cane.

Of all the patented cane guns, perhaps the most unusual was that of British inventor Henry William Vander Kleft, who, in 1814, proposed a nine-part "walking staff to contain a pistol, powder, ball, and screw telescope, pen, ink, paper, pencil, knife and drawing utensils." Imagine finding one of these versatile walking sticks at a tag sale!

Cane guns utilizing gas (usually carbon dioxide) as a propellant came into use early in the 19th century. The gas was supplied in cylinders much like it is today; but cane air guns had to be hand-pumped to fill the gun's air reservoir, which often took up as much as half the cane's length. A few experimental air cane guns incorporated a pump into the cane, but the commercially successful versions all employed a separate pump. The spring-driven air gun mechanism was unsuitable for use in cane guns.

Air cane guns operated like other pneumatic guns. Pressure on the trigger (which was cocked by turning a lever or key) opened a valve, releasing a burst of air from the reservoir and propelling the bullet down the barrel. One charge of the reservoir could be good for 25 to 30 shots.

A word of caution to the person lucky enough to find an air cane gun: The basic rules of gun safety should always apply, especially when handling such a disguised weapon. A pneumatic air cane gun is an especially powerful device, and its bullets have great penetrating power and shock effect. The first discharge of air may easily deliver a muzzle velocity and penetration similar to

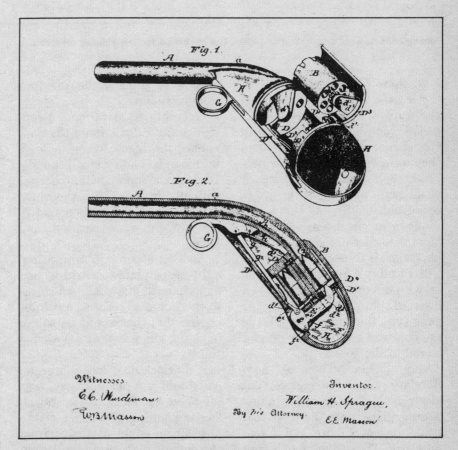

William H. Sprague, of Jamestown, New York, in 1888 patented this ingenious revolver, whose curved barrel extended into the butt, presaging guns used in World War II for firing around corners.

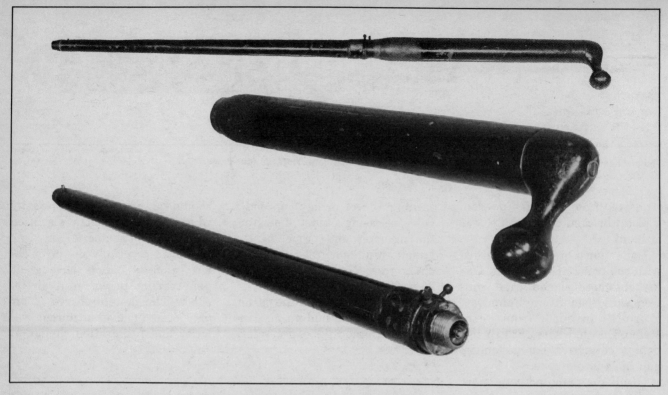

Rare air cane gun, shown together and apart. The thickened section is the air reservoir.

a 22 short rifle cartridge.

Air cane guns can be found in the same shapes as powder-propelled cane guns—that is, with straight or curved handles—and they were made for the same purposes: self-defense, poaching or small-game hunting of targets of opportunity.

When not in use as a weapon, like its powder-propelled counterpart, the air cane gun was carried with its muzzle capped by a ferrule or with a cork or wood tampon inserted. In muzzle-loaded air guns (yes, these existed, too), the tampon was a full-length ramrod stored in the bore.

Alarm Guns. Then, as now, burglary was commonplace, but electronic devices were not in use. Alarm guns were devices that could be set to fire and sound an alarm. The explosion of a gunpowder charge may have been accompanied by other warning sounds to protect the premises from intruders.

One unusual alarm gun, a sundial gun, did little more than announce the hours by means of a burning glass and a small cannon. Because the sun's position changes with the seasons, both the burning glass and the cannon had to be adjustable in position and angle.

Another alarm gun, which fired a 16-gauge pinfire cartridge, had a mechanism like a modern clockwork kitchen timer with a pointer on the dial that could be set to have the gun go off at a specified time.

A flintlock door-lock alarm, an early and complicated gun, was intended to ward off intruders. Those knowing the secret of the mechanism could disarm it from the outside by turning the key in an unusual way. Conventional key turning procedures would explode the charge.

As one goes further back in time, alarm guns become more elaborate. With the introduction of percussion caps and metallic cartridges, however, we find increased simplicity. Intended to be fastened to a door joint or window frame, 19th century alarms fired blank cartridges when a spring-driven hammer was triggered by the opening of a door or window.

Some early devices were designed not only to sound an alarm but to light a match which "exposes the burglar and at once shows the location of the attempted entry," as its inventor, Hudson Ferris, of Chicago, described it in his 1883 patent specifications for an "improved match-lighting alarm."

Twenty years earlier, A. F. Hammond of Houston, Ohio, had patented a burglar alarm in which a match was ignited by the burning powder of the alarm, which also featured a clamp for attaching the device to a mantel, window sill or door frame.

One sturdy and commanding alarm gun was of solid bronze and came in a fitted leather case. You filled the barrel with black powder, capped the nipple, drew back the hammer and placed it on the floor at the edge of a closed door, much like a wedge-shaped doorstop. Pressure on the door by an intruder forced down a long sloping trigger that released the hammer. A later doorstop-style alarm utilized a 22 blank cartridge to sound the alarm.

Another alarm gun, the drop alarm, was intended to be dislodged and fall when a door was opened. Shaped like a fish-line sinker, it was suspended by a cord from the door and held a 32 S&W blank cartridge which detonated upon striking the floor. This alarm operated equally well on windows.

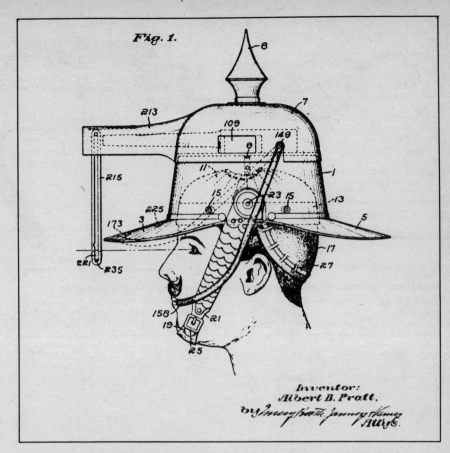

A multipurpose 1916 invention of Albert B. Pratt of Lyndon, Vermont. The blowback automatic in this hat was aimed by looking at the target. The crown also served as a cooking pot.

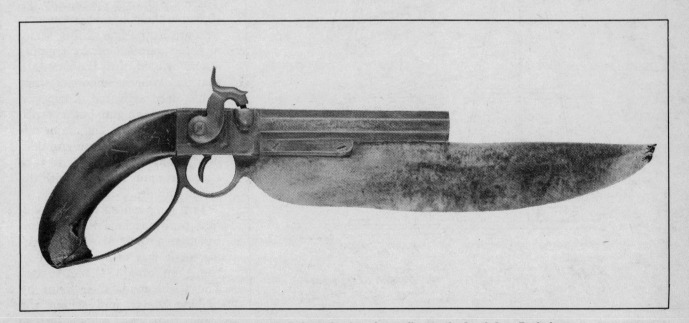

George Elgin's cutlass pistol, patented in 1837 and actually issued to American sailors on the South Seas Exploring Expedition.

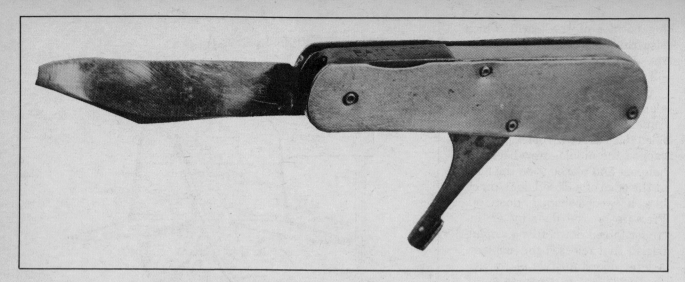

Pocketknife/pistol combination showing knife blade extended and spur trigger.

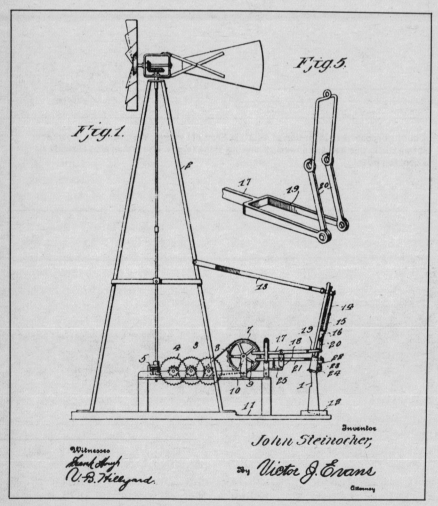

This 1913 windmill automatically fired an autoloading shotgun to scare off birds and animals. Invented by John Steinocher of West Texas.

Types of alarm guns to look for include those made or patented by Simeon Coon and David Coon, B. F. Cheesebrough, Noah Chaffee, The American Portable Alarm, Ruff & McDowell, Reichard's Patented Burglar Alarm and Conklin & Hauser.

Trip Guns and Trap Guns. These are devices specifically designed to shoot animals or humans who are in the line of fire. Many of these were set off by tripping a wire or cord, thus the name. In that its discharge announces that it has been activated, a trip gun is also an alarm gun, but one with a deadly purpose. The major difference is that an alarm gun does not "follow" the intruder to take aim; a trip gun will move with the victim and fire.

Trip guns whose intended victims were poachers were not uncommon in England, where poaching was a way of life for some in the 17th and 18th centuries. Those who made their living by robbing graves and selling the bodies to medical schools for use in anatomical studies (they were

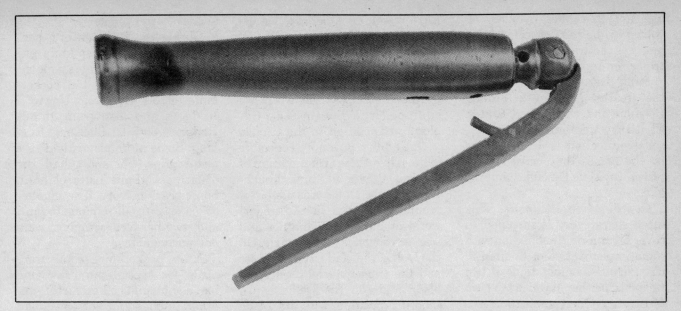

Unusual muzzleloading squeeze gun employing pill-type fulminate primer, squeezed by compressing the lever with the hand.

sometimes called "resurrectionists") had to face the hazard of trip guns set up in graveyards. Guns of this type were outlawed in England in 1827.

In 1857, an American named Reuthe patented a "Trap for Capturing and Destroying Wild Animals," which was manufactured in large quantities in Hartford, Connecticut. The Reuthe trap gun had two barrels that fired simultaneously when two baited springs were pulled out by an animal that seized the bait attached to them.

Two years later, John O. Couch and Henry S. North obtained a patent for their invention, a six-barreled "Game Shooter," which later became popular in Australia for taking kangaroos. Like the Reuthe gun, this was held in place by a wire running to a tree or post and was discharged when an animal took the bait fastened near the muzzle. Unlike the Reuthe, it had a traditional pistol grip and a spur trigger, and could do double duty as a self-defense weapon.

In the early 20th century, under a patent issued in 1914 to C. D. Lovelace, F. C. Taylor of St. Louis manufactured his "Fur Getter," a breechloader that fired modern cartridges in 22 caliber or 10 gauge.

Collectors of trip guns seek out the French-made all-metal "Chicken Thief," in both flintlock and pinfire. These trip guns, which probably saw more use in homes and stores than in chicken houses, are characterized by clamps at the butt to permit fastening to a firm support. A pull on a string or wire that ran to a bar under the barrel fired these guns.

Because of their failure to discriminate in the selection of targets, trip guns are a highly controversial subject. Today's courts have tended to take a dim view of such protective devices and to make substantial awards to victims who have been injured or maimed by trip guns, whether they were trespassing or not.

Palm Pistols. Guns in this category are those which are held in the palm of the hand and fired by squeezing or compressing the fist. For this reason they are also known as "squeezer pistols." Most palm pistols were fired by squeezing the main spring until the hammer or firing pin became disengaged and struck the cartridge.

Palm pistols may be found in various shapes, ranging from the Webber single-shot tube with a hard-rubber knob at one end, to the round shape of the Chicago palm pistol, a seven-shot double-action model whose cylinder was a flat disc and whose chambers radiated like the spokes of a wheel.

Other palm pistols included the Shatuck Unique (often misspelled "Shattuck") with four short barrels and chambers bored in one solid steel block, which drops down for loading. Of the European squeezer pistols, perhaps the best known is the Gaulois, which is sometimes found concealed in a fine leather cigar case.

One of the most unusual palm pistols is the "Little All Right," patented by Edward Boardman and Andrew Peavey of Lawrence, Massachusetts, in 1876. Resembling a tiny revolver, it was held in the palm of the hand. The small five-shot 22-caliber cylinder revolved, while the concealed firing pin was activated by a folding trigger on top of the barrel.

Palm pistols were produced in the greatest numbers in France, Belgium and the United States. That they were intended for personal protection is demonstrated by the names they carried: Protector, Invisible Defender, and the like.

Combination Weapons. This catch-all category is intended to cover firearms in combination with some implement, tool or utensil, but excludes combinations of two weapons, neither of which is a gun. Most often, the combination is a gun with a cutting or piercing weapon. Moreover, the firearm may not be the primary weapon, but a back-up weapon. Combination weapons came into use in the earliest days of firearms, when they were often combined with battle axes, maces, or pole arms such as pikes and halberds.

Some combination weapons made good sense: a gun combined with a shield for defense or with a sword for offense. But others had an element of the ridiculous, as, for example, a gun with a table fork or a gun with a plow.

A very rare and highly desirable collector's item is a wheel lock combined with an edged weapon having a calendar blade (a blade etched with a perpetual ecclesiastical calendar). Another gun/cutting weapon combination much sought after by collectors is the

Elgin pistol, an American percussion pistol with a heavy Bowie-type or cutlass blade fastened under the barrel. Patented by George Elgin in 1837 and ordered by the U.S. Navy, Elgin's pistol equipped the South Seas Exploring Expedition to the Pacific.

One oddity prized by collectors is the triple-threat combination of revolver, dagger and brass knuckles called the Dolne Apache pistol reputedly favored in the underworld of Paris. Still another and scarcer version is the Delhaxie. On the Dolne, the blade, the knuckles and the trigger all fold; only the blade folds on the Delhaxie. In shooting position with its blade extended for thrusting, the Dolne's handle cannot be used for striking; with the Delhaxie in shooting position, its handle is clutched for striking and the opened blade points downward for use as a dagger.

The American "My Friend" pistol is a knuckleduster and a cartridge pepperbox with an unconventional grip, patented in 1865 by James Reid of Catskill, New York. This all-metal (brass or steel) weapon came in seven-shot 22 caliber and five-shot 32 and 41 calibers. (The odd number of rounds was dictated by the type of safety employed.)

Another much-earlier, all-metal pistol designed for use as a striking weapon was made by the famous Irish gunmaking firm of Rigby in Dublin. It had percussion-cap ignition and came in three-, four-

and six-barrel versions.

During the 20th century, penknife pistols and clasp-knife pistols and revolvers became popular. The best known of the pocketknife pistols were from Unwin & Rodgers and also from James Rodgers, both of Sheffield, England. Some knife pistols had true pistol grips, but most had the usual pocketknife hafts of horn, bone, pearl or ivory. The number of blades ranged from one to four, and two-barreled weapons were not uncommon.

A few pocketknife pistols were made for special purposes. One had a shotgun-shell extractor; another, intended for horsemen, had a hook for cleaning horses' hooves; sailors could select one with a marlin spike.

There is almost no limit to the varieties of weapons, implements, tools and utensils with which firearms have been combined. Guns were married to whips, smokers' briar pipes, belt buckles, bicycle handlebars, door keys, umbrellas, purses, torches, plows, watches, helmets, fishhooks, cameras, wrenches, even table knives, forks and spoons. Some patented inventions never got off the drafting table, but many cane guns, pen pistols and knife revolvers were widely sold.

So the next time you are at a garage sale or in a second-hand store, don't pass up that innocent-looking umbrella or walking stick. There may be more to it than meets the eye.

Reference

Weapons and Military Museums of North America

ALABAMA
Daviston. Horseshoe Bend National Military Park, Rte. 1, Box 3, 36256.
Ft. McClellan. Military Police Corps Museum, Bldg. 3182, 36205.
Ft. Rucker. U.S. Army Aviation Museum, Bldg. 6007, 36362.
Gulf Shores. Ft. Morgan Museum, Star Rte., Box 2780, 36542.
Huntsville. Alabama Space and Rocket Center, Tranquility Base, 35807.
Mobile. USS Alabama Battleship Commission, P.O. Box 65, 36601.
Montgomery. Alabama Dept. of Archives and History, 624 Washington Ave., 36130.

ARIZONA
Camp Verde. Ft. Verde State Historic Park, P.O. Box 397, 86322.
Ft. Huachuca. Ft. Huachuca Historical Museum, P.O. Box 766, 85613.
Ganado. Hubbell Trading Post National Historic Site, Box 150, 86505.
Tombstone. Tombstone Courthouse State Historic Park, 219 Toughnut St., 85638.
Tucson. Arizona Historical Society, 949 E. 2nd St., 85719.
Ft. Lowell Museum, 2900 N. Craycroft Rd., 85710

ARKANSAS
Berryville. Saunders Memorial Museum, 113-15 Madison St., 72616.
Ft. Smith. Ft. Smith National Historic Site, P.O. Box 1406, 72902.
Gillett. Arkansas Post County Museum, Hwy. #1-The Great River Rd., 72055.
Arkansas Post National Memorial, 72055.
Helena. Phillips County Museum, 623 Pecan St., 72342.
Jonesboro. Arkansas State Univ. Museum, Learning Resources Center, 72401.
Little Rock. Arkansas History Commission, 1 Capitol Mall, 72202.
Museum of Science and History, MacArthur Park, 72202.
Pea Ridge. Pea Ridge National Military Park, 72751.
Prairie Grove. Prairie Grove Battlefield State Park, P.O. Box 306, 72753.
Rogers. Daisy International Air Gun Museum, U.S. Hwy. 71, 72756.
Washington. Old Washington Historic State Park, 71862.

CALIFORNIA
Auburn. Placer County Museum, 1273 High St., Gold Country Fair Ground, 95603.
Bakersfield. Cunningham Memorial Art Gallery, 1930 R. St., 93301.
Kern County Museum, 3801 Chester Ave., 93309.
Beverly Hills. The Francis E. Fowler, Jr. Foundation Museum, 9215 Wilshire Blvd., 90210.
Dorris. Herman's House of Guns, 204 S. Oregon St., 96023.
El Monte. El Monte Historical Museum, 3150 N. Tyler Ave., 91731.
Ft. Jones. Ft. Jones Museum, Main St., 96032.
Lakeport. Lake County Museum, 255 N. Forbes St., 95453.
Lebec. Ft. Tejon State Historic Park, 93243.
Los Angeles. Amer. Society of Military History, Patriotic Hall, 1816 S. Figueroa St., 90015.
Monterey. Monterey State Historic Park, 210 Olivier, 93940.
Presidio of Monterey Museum, 93940.
Port Hueneme. Civil Engineer Corps/Seabee Museum, Naval Construction Battalion Center, Code 2232, 93043.
San Diego. San Diego Historical Society, 2727 Presidio Dr., 92103.
San Francisco. Ft. Point and Army Museum Assn., Funston Ave. at Lincoln Blvd., 94129.
Ft. Point National Historic Site, Presidio of San Francisco, 94129.
Presidio Army Museum, Bldg. 2, Presidio of San Francisco, 94129.
Wells Fargo Bank History Room, 420 Montgomery St., 94104.
Shasta. Shasta State Historic Park, P.O. Box 507, 96087.
Woodside. Woodside Store, 471 Kings Mountain Rd., 94062.

COLORADO
Colorado Springs. Pioneers' Museum, 215 S. Tejon, 80903.
Estes Park. Estes Park Area Historical Museum, Hwy 36, 80517.
Ft. Carson. Ft. Carson Museum of the Army in the West, 849 Oconnel Blvd., 80913.
Ft. Garland. Old Fort Garland, P.O. Box 208, 81133.
Ft. Morgan. Ft. Morgan Heritage Foundation, P.O. Box 184, 80701.
Golden. Buffalo Bill Memorial Museum, Rte. 5, 80401.
Grand Junction. Museum of Western Colorado, 4th and Ute Sts., 81501.
Hugo. Lincoln County Museum, P.O. Box 626, 80821.
Julesburg. Ft. Sedgwick Depot Museum, 202 W. 1st St., 80737.
La Junta. Bent's Old Fort National Historic Site, Box 581, 81050.
LaVeta. Ft. Francisco Museum, 81055.
Leadville. House with the Eye Museum, 127 W. Fourth St., 80461.

Meeker. The White River Museum, 565 Park St., 81641.
Sterling. Overland Trail Museum, Junction I-76 and Hwy 6 East, 80751.
Walsenburg. Ft. Francisco Museum, 119 E. Cedar St., 81089.

CONNECTICUT
Guilford. Henry Whitfield Museum, Whitfield St., 06437.
Hartford. Museum of Connecticut History, Connecticut State Library, 231 Capitol Ave., 06115.
Wadsworth Atheneum, 600 Main St., 06103.
Meriden. Meriden Historical Society, Inc., 424 W. Main St., 06450.
Norwich. The Slater Memorial Museum, 108 Crescent St., 06360.
Washington. Historical Museum of the Gunn Memorial Library, Wykeham Rd., 06793.
West Redding. Colonial Musuem, Putnam Memorial State Park, Connecticut Rte. 58, 06896.

DELAWARE
Delaware City. Ft. Delaware, Pea Patch Island in Delaware River, 19706.

DISTRICT OF COLUMBIA
Washington, D.C. Anderson House, Headquarters and Museum of the Society of the Cincinnati, 2118 Massachusetts Ave., N.W., 20008.
Bureau of Alcohol, Tobacco and Firearms Museum, 1200 Pennsylvania Ave., N.W., 20226.
Daughters of the American Revolution Museum, 1776 D St. N.W. 20006.
Ford's Theatre (Lincoln Museum), 511 10th St., N.W., 20004.
National Museum of History and Technology, 14th St. and Constitution Ave., N.W. 20560.
National Rifle Association Firearms Museum, 1600 Rhode Island Ave., N.W., 20036.
U.S. Marine Corps Museum, Marine Corps Historical Center, Navy Yard, 20374.
U.S. Navy Memorial Museum, Bldg. 76, Washington Navy Yard, 20374.

FLORIDA
Boca Raton. Boca Raton Center for the Arts, Inc., 801 W. Palmetto Park Rd., 33432.
Eglin Air Force Base. Air Force Armaments Museum, 3201/AFAM, 32542.
Ft. Pierce. St. Lucie County Historical Museum, 414 Seaway Dr., 33450.
Jacksonville. Ft. Caroline National Memorial, 12713 Ft. Caroline Rd., 32225.
Key West. East Martello Gallery and Museum, S. Roosevelt Blvd., 33040.
Lighthouse Military Museum, 938 Whitehead at Truman, 33040.
Olustee. Olustee Battlefield State Historic Site, P.O. Box 2, U.S. 90, 2 miles east, 32072.
Orlando. Orange County Historical Commission, 812 E. Rollins, St., 32803.
Pensacola. Naval Aviation Musuem, U.S. Naval Air Station, 32508.
St. Petersburg. St. Petersburg Historical Museum, 335 2nd Ave., N.E. 33701.

GEORGIA
Atlanta. Atlanta Historical Society, 3101 Andrews Drive, N.W., 30355.
Atlanta Museum, 537-39 Peachtree St., N.E., 30308.
Cyclorama, Boulevard at Atlanta, 30303.
Columbus. Columbus Museum of Arts and Sciences, Inc., 1251 Wynnton Rd., 31906.
Cordele. Georgia Veterans Memorial Museum, 31015.
Crawfordville. Confederate Museum, Alexander H. Stephens State Park, 30631.
Darien. Ft. King George, P.O. Box 711, 31305.
Ft. Benning. National Infantry Museum, U.S. Army Infantry Center, 31905.
Ft. Oglethorpe. Chickamauga-Chattanooga National Military Park, 30741.
Marietta. Cobb County Youth Museum, 649 Cheatham Hill Dr., 30064.
Kennesaw Mountain National Battlefield Park, Jct. Stilesboro Rd. and Old Hwy. 41, 30060.
Midway. Sunbury Historic Site, Rte. 1, 31320.
Richmond Hill. Ft. McAllister, P.O. Box 198, 31324.
St. Simons Island. Ft. Frederica National Monument, Rte. 4, 31522.
Savannah. Old Ft. Jackson, Box 782, 31402.
Tybee Island. Ft. Pulaski National Monument, Box 98, 31328.
Tybee Museum, 31328.

HAWAII
Ft. DeRussy. U.S. Army Museum, Hawaii, Battery Randolph, Kalia Rd., 96815.
Pearl Harbor. Pacific Submarine Museum, Naval Submarine Base, 96860.

IDAHO
Rexburg. Upper Snake River Valley Historical Society, Rte. 2, 83440.

ILLINOIS
Aurora. Aurora Historical Museum, 304 Oak Ave., 60506.
G.A.R. Memorial & Veterans Museum, 23 E. Downer Pl., 60505.
Chicago. American Police Center & Museum, 1130 S. Wabash Ave., 60605.
Chicago Historical Society, Clark St. at North Ave., 60614.
Chicago Public Library Cultural Center, 78 E. Washington St., 60602.
George F. Harding Museum, 86 E. Randolph St., 60601.
Polish Museum of America, 984 N. Milwaukee Ave., 60622.
Clinton. The Homestead Museum, 219 E. Woodlawn St., 61727.
Edwardsville. Madison County Historical Museum, 715 N. Main St., 62025.
Kankakee. Kankakee County Historical Society Museum, 8th Ave. & Water St., 60901.
Marion. Williamson County Historical Society, 105 S. Van Buren, 62959.
Mendota. Time Was Village Museum, US 51-52, 4 Miles S., 61342.
Moline. Rock Island County Historical Society, 822 11 Ave., 61265.
Paxton. Ford County Historical Society, 145 W. Center St., 60957.
Prairie du Rocher. Ft. de Chartres Historic Site Museum, Ft. de Chartres Historic Site, 62277.
Rock Island. John M. Browning Memorial Museum, Rock Island Arsenal, 61299.
Sandwich. Stone Mill Museum, 315 East Railroad St., 60548.
Sterling. Sterling-Rock Falls Historical Society, 212 Third Ave., 61081.
Watseka. Iroquois County Historical Society Museum, Old Courthouse, 2nd & Cherry, 60970.
Wauconda. Andrew Cook Museum, North Main St., 60084.
Lake County Museum, Lakewood Forest Preserve, 60084.
Waukegan. Waukegan Historical Society, 1917 N. Sheridan Rd., 60085.
Wheaton. Cantigny, 1 S. 151 Winfield Rd., 60187.
Dupage County Historical Museum, 102 E. Wesley St., 60187.

INDIANA
Battle Ground. Battle Ground Historical Corp., Box 225, 47920.
Columbus. Bartholomew County Historical Society, 524 Third St., 47201.
Crawfordsville. General Lew Wallace Study (or Studio), East Pike St., 47933.
Evansville. Evansville Museum of Arts and Science, 411 S.E. Riverside Dr., 47713.
Ft. Wayne. Historic Fort Wayne, Inc., 46302.
Franklin. Johnson County Historical Museum, 150 W. Madison St., 46131.
Kokomo. Howard County Historical Museum, 1200 W. Sycamore St., 46901.
La Porte. La Porte County Historical Museum, La Porte County Complex, Court House Square, 46350.
Lafayette. Tippecanoe County Historical Museum, 909 South St., 47901.
Mishawaka. Hannah Lindahl Children's Museum, 410 Lincoln Way East, 46544.
Peru. Puterbaugh Museum, 11 N. Huntington St., 46970.
Rensselaer. Jasper County Historical Society, 624 Clark St., 47978.
Richmond. Wayne County Historical Museum 1150 North "A" St., 47374.
Salem. Washington County Historical Society, Inc., 307 E. Market St., 47167.
South Bend. The Northern Indiana Historical Society, 112 S. Lafayette Blvd., 46601.
Terre Haute. Historical Museum of the Wabash Valley, 1411 S. 6th St., 47802.
Versailles. Ripley County Historical Society Museum, P.O. Box 224, 47042.
Vincennes. George Rogers Clark National Historical Park, 401 S. Second St., 47591.

IOWA
Cedar Falls. Cedar Falls Historical Society Museum, 303 Clay St., 50613.
University of Northern Iowa Museum, 31st and Hudson Rd., 50614.
Decorah. Vesterheim, Norwegian-American Museum, 502 W. Water St., 52101.
Des Moines. Iowa State Historical Department Division of Historical Museum & Archives, E. 12th and Grand Ave., 50319.
Dubuque. Mathias Ham Museum, 2241 Lincoln Ave., 52001.
Glenwood. Mills County Historical Society and Museum, Glenwood Lake Park, 51534.
Osage. Mitchell County Historical Museum, North 6th, 50461.
Sibley. McCallum Museum, City Park, 51249.

KANSAS
Abilene. Dickinson County Historical Society, 412 S. Campbell St., 67410.
Ashland. Pioneer Museum, 430 W. 4th, 67831.
Baldwin. Baker University, William A. Quayle Bible Collection, Spencer-Quayle Wing, Library, 8th St., 66006.
Old Castle Museum, 5th and Dearborn Sts. 66006.
Chanute. Martin and Osa Johnson Safari Museum, Inc., 16 S. Grant St., 66720.
Dodge City. Boot Hill Museum, Inc., 500 W. Wyatt Earp, 67801.
Ft. Leavenworth. Fort Leavenworth Museum, Reynolds & Gibbon Aves., 66027.
Ft. Riley. U.S. Cavalry Museum, United States Cavalry Museum, 66442.
Ft. Scott. Ft. Scott National Historic Site, Old Fort Blvd., 66701.
Fredonia. Wilson County Historical Society Museum, 416 N. 7th, 66736.
Garnett. Anderson County Historical Museum, Court House, 66032.
Kanopolis. Ft. Harker Museum, 67454.
Larned. Ft. Larned National Historic Site, Rte. 3, 67550.
Logan. Dane G. Hansen Memorial Museum, 67646.
Manhattan. Riley County Historical Museum, 2309 Claflin Rd., 66502.
Mankato. Jewell County Historical Museum, 66956.
Marysville. Original Pony Express Home Station, Inc., 809 North St., 66508.
North Newton. Kauffman Museum, E. 27th St., 67117.
Osawatomie. John Brown Memorial Museum, 10th and Main Sts., 66064.
Ottawa. Franklin County Historical Society, Inc., Box 145, 66067.
Phillipsburg. Old Ft. Bissell, 67661.
Republic. Pawnee Indian Village Museum, Rte. 1, 66964.
Salina. Smoky Hill Historical Museum, Oakdale Park, 67401.
Wichita. Wichita-Sedgwick County Historical Museum Assoc., 204 S. Main, 67202.

KENTUCKY
Bowling Green. Kentucky Museum, Western Kentucky University, 42101.
Columbus. Columbus-Belmont Civil War Museum, Columbus-Belmont State Park, 42032.
Ft. Campbell. Don F. Pratt Memorial Museum, Wickham Hall, 42223.
Ft. Knox. Patton Museum of Cavalry and Armor, Keyes Park, 40121.
Frankfort. . Kentucky Historical Society, Broadway at the St. Clair Mall, 40602.
Kentucky Military History Museum, East Main St., 40602.
Lexington. Waveland State Shrine, Higbee Mill Rd., 40503.
London. Mountain Life Museum, Levi Jackson Wilderness Road State Park, 40741.
Louisville. The Filson Club, 118 W. Breckinridge St., 40203.
Museum of Natural History and Science, 727 W. Main St., 40202.
Perryville. Perryville Battlefield Museum, 40468.
Richmond. Ft. Boonesborough Museum, Ft. Boonesborough State Park, Route 5, 40475.
Jonathan Truman Dorris Museum, Eastern Kentucky University, Perkins Bldg., 40475.

LOUISIANA
Chalmette. Chalmette National Historical Park, St. Bernard Hwy., 70043.
Mansfield. Mansfield State Commemorative Area, Hwy. 175, 3 miles SE of Mansfield, 71052.
New Orleans. Confederate Museum, 929 Camp St., 70130.
Ft. Pike State Monument, Rte. 6, Box 194, 70119
Louisiana State Museum, 751 Chartres St., 70116.

MAINE
Augusta. Ft. Western Museum, Bowman St., 04330.
Bangor. Bangor Historical-Penobscot Heritage Museum, 159 Union St., 04401.
Brunswick. Pejepscot Historical Society, 11 Lincoln St., 04011.
Bucksport. Bucksport Historical Society, Inc. Main St., 04416.
Eastport. Border Historical Society, Inc., Washington St., 04631.
Newfield. Willowbrook at Newfield, Main St., 04056.
Portland. Maine Historical Society, 485 Congress St., 04101.
Prospect. Ft. Knox State Memorial, State Hwy. 174, 04981.
Rockland. Shore Village Museum, 104 Limerock St., 04841.
Waterville. Redington Museum, 64 Silver St., 04901.

MARYLAND
Aberdeen Proving Ground. U.S. Army Ordnance Museum, % U.S. Army Ordnance Center and School, 21040.
Annapolis. United States Naval Academy Museum, 21402.
Baltimore. Baltimore Seaport & the Baltimore Maritime Museum, Pier 4, Pratt St., 21202.
Ft. McHenry National Monument and Historic Shrine, 21230.
Star-Spangled Banner Flag House, 844 E. Pratt St., 21202.
Walters Art Gallery, Charles and Centre Sts., 21201.
Big Pool. Ft. Frederick State Park, 21711.
Cumberland. George Washington's Headquarters, Dept of Parks and Recreation, City Hall, 21502.
Ft. Meade. Ft. George G. Meade Army Museum, 4674 Griffin Ave., 20755.
Oxon Hill. Ft. Washington Park, off Ft. Washington Rd., 20021.

St. Michaels. Chesapeake Bay Maritime Museum, P.O. Box 636, 21663.
Sharpsburg. Antietam National Battlefield Site-Visitor Center, P.O. Box 158, 21782.

MASSACHUSETTS
Abington. Dyer Memorial Library, Centre Ave., 02351.
Berlin. Art and Historical Collections, 01503.
Beverly. Beverly Historical Society and Museum, 117 Cabot St., 01915.
Boston. Ancient and Honorable Artillery Company of Massachusetts, Faneuil Hall, 02109.
USS Constitution Museum Foundation, Inc., Boston National Historical Park, 02129.
Canton. Canton Historical Society, 1400 Washington St., 02021.
Chelmsford. Chelmsford Historical Society, 40 Byam Rd., 01824.
Concord. Concord Antiquarian Society, 200 Lexington Rd., 01742.
Danvers. Danvers Historical Society, 13 Page St., 01923.
Deerfield. Memorial Hall Museum, Pocumtuck Valley Memorial Assn., Memorial St., 01342.
Duxbury. Duxbury Rural and Historical Society, Box 176, Snug Harbor Station, 02332.
Fall River. Fall River Historical Society, 451 Rock St., 02720.
Fitchburg. Fitchburg Historical Society, 50 Grove St., 01420.
Groton. Groton Historical Society, Main St., 01450.
Longmeadow. Longmeadow Historical Society, 697 Longmeadow St., 01106.
Mattapoisett. Mattapoisett Museum and Carriage House, 5 Church St., 02739.
Middleborough. Middleborough Historical Association, Inc., Jackson St., 02346.
North Oxford. Clara Barton Birthplace, Clara Barton Rd., 01537.
Northborough. Northborough Historical Society, Inc. 52 Main St., 01532.
Oxford. Oxford Library Museum, 339 Main St., 01540.
Plymouth. Plimoth Plantation Inc., Warren Ave., 02360.
Sandwich. Heritage Plantation of Sandwich, Grove St., 02563.
Scituate. Scituate Historical Society, 121 Maple St., 02066.
South Carver. Edaville Railroad Museum, Rochester Rd., 02366.
Springfield. Springfield Armory National Historic Site, 1 Armory Center, 01105.
Sturbridge. Old Sturbridge Village, 01566..
Taunton. Old Colony Historical Society, 66 Church Green, 02780..
Worcester. John Woodman Higgins Armory, Inc., 100 Barber Ave., 01606.
Worcester Historical Museum, 39 Salisbury St., 01608.

MICHIGAN
Adrian. Lenawee County Historical Museum, 104 E. Church, 49221.
Copper Harbor. Ft. Wilkins State Park, 49918.
Dearborn. Dearborn Historical Museum, 915 Brady St., 48124.
Detroit. Ft. Wayne Military Museum, 6325 W. Jefferson Ave., 48209.
Wayne State University Museum of Anthropology, Merrick and Anthony Wayne Dr., 48202.
Escanaba. Delta County Historical Society, Ludington Park, 49829.
Hastings. Charlton Park Village and Museum, 2545 S. Charlton Park Rd., 49058.
Leland. Leelanau Historical Museum, P.O. Box 246, 49654.
Ludington. Rose Hawley Museum, 305 E. Filer St., 49431.
Mackinac Island. Mackinac Island State Park Commission, Box 370, 49757.
Madison. Lac Qui Parle County Historical Society, West side of Fairgrounds, 56256.
Manistee. Manistee County Historical Museum, 425 River St., 49660.
Marshall. Honolulu House Museum, P.O. Box 15, 49068.
Menominee. Menominee County Historical Museum, 904 11th Ave., 49858.
Niles. Ft. St. Joseph Museum, 508 E. Main St., 49120.
Plymouth. Plymouth Historical Museum, 155 S. Main St., 48170.
Port Sanilac. Sanilac Historical Museum, 228 S. Ridge St., 48469.
St. Ignace. Ft. de Buade Museum, Inc. 334 N. State St., 49781.

MINNESOTA
Bagley. Clearwater County Historical Society, 56621.
Brown Valley. Sam Brown Log House, 56219.
Carlton. Carlton County Historical Society, Dental Bldg. 55718.
Crookston. Polk County Historical Society, Hwy. 2, 56716.
Grand Marais. Cook County Museum, 55604.
Henderson. Sibley County Historical Society, 56044.
Litchfield. G.A.R. Hall and Museum, Meeker County Historical Society, 318 N. Marshall, 55355.
Mantorville. Dodge County Old Settlers and Historical Society, 55955.
Morris. Stevens County Historical Museum, 6th & Nevada, 56265.
Preston. Fillmore County Historical Museum, 55965.
Red Wing. Goodhue County Historical Society, 1166 Oak St., 55066.

South St. Paul. Dakota County Historical Museum, 130 3rd Ave., N., 55075.
Stillwater. Washington County Historical Museum, 602 N. Main St., 55082.
Windom. Cottonwood County Historical Society, 812 Fourth Ave., 56101.

MISSISSIPPI
Biloxi. Beauvoir, the Jefferson Davis Shrine, Box 200 W. Beach Blvd., 39531.
Carrollton. Old Jail Museum, Carrollton Green & Magnolia Streets, 38917.
Columbus. The Columbus and Lowndes County Historical Society Museum, 316 7th St. No, 39701.
Holly Springs. Marshall County Historical Museum, P.O. Box 806, 38635.
Jackson. Mississippi Military Museum, 120 N. State St., 39201.
Lyman. JP Museum of Indian Artifacts, Hwy. 49, 39574.
Port Gibson. Grand Gulf Military State Park, Rte. 2, 39150.
Vicksburg. Old Court House Museum-Eva Whitaker Davis Memorial, 1008 Cherry St., 39180.
Washington. Historic Jefferson College, College St., 39190.

MISSOURI
Charleston. Mississippi County Historical Society, 403 N. Main, 63834.
Clayton. General Daniel Bissell Home, Jefferson Barracks Historical Park, 7900 Forsythe, 63105.
Hazelwood. Little Red School House, 450 Brookes Lane, 63042.
Kansas City. The Liberty Memorial Museum, 100 West 26th St., 64108.
Kennett. Dunklin County Museum, Inc. 122 College, 63857.
Kirksville. E. M. Violette Museum, Northeast Missouri State University, 63501.
Laclede. General John J. Pershing Boyhood Home State Historic Site, 64651.
Lexington. Battle of Lexington, State Historic Site, 64060.
Liberty. Clay County Historical Museum, 14 N. Main, 64068.
Lone Jack. Jackson County Civil War Museum and Battlefield, Jackson County Park Dept., 64070.
Mexico. Audrain County Historical Society, 501 S. Muldrow, 65265.
Point Lookout. The Ralph Foster Museum, School of the Ozarks, 65726.
Republic. Wilson's Creek National Battlefield, 521 No. Hwy. 60, 65738.
St. Charles. St. Joseph Museum, 11th and Charles, 64501.
St. Louis. Soldiers' Memorial, 1315 Chestnut St., 63103.
Sedalia. Pettis County Historical Society, % Sedalia Public Library, Third & Kentucky, 65301.
Sibley. Ft. Osage, 64088.

MONTANA
Billings. Yellowstone County Museum, Logan Field, 59103.
Missoula. Ft. Missoula Historical Museum, Bldg. 322, 59801.
Sidney. J. K. Ralston Museum & Art Center, 221 Fifth S.W., 59270.
Wisdom. Big Hole National Battlefield, P.O. Box 237, 59761.

NEBRASKA
Bellevue. Strategic Aerospace Museum, 2510 Clay St., 68005.
Burwell. Ft. Hartsuff State Historical Park, 68823.
Chadron. Museum of the Fur Trade, Rte. 2, 69337.
Crawford. Ft. Robinson Museum, Box 304, 69339.
Ft. Calhoun. Ft. Atkinson State Historical Park, Box 237, 68023.
Washington County Historical Museum, 14th and Monroe Sts., 68023.
Gering. North Platte Valley Historical Association, Inc., 11th & J Sts., near Hwy. 92 & 71, 69341.
Gothenburg. Pony Express Station, Ehmen Park, 69138.
Hastings. Hastings Museum, 1330 N. Burlington, 68901.
North Platte. Buffalo Bill's Ranch, R.R. 1, 69101.
Sioux Lookout D.A.R. Log Cabin Museum, Memorial Park, 69101.
Omaha. General George Crook House, Ft. Omaha, 68111.
Union Pacific Historical Museum, 1416 Dodge St., 68179.
Osceola. Polk County Historical Museum, South end of Hawkey St., 68651.
Plattsmouth. Cass County Historical Society Museum, 644 Main St., 68048.
Red Cloud. Webster County Historical Museum, 721 W. 4th Ave., 68970.
Tecumseh. Johnson County Historical Society, Inc. Third and Lincoln Sts., 68450.
Weeping Water. Heritage House Museum, 68463.
Wilber. Wilber Czech Museum, Box 253, 68465.
York. Anna Palmer Museum, 211 E. 7th St., 68467.

NEVADA
Reno. Nevada Historical Society, 1650 N. Virginia St., 89504.

NEW HAMPSHIRE
Charlestown. Old Ft. Number 4 Associates, Rte. 11, 03603.
Dover. Annie E. Woodman Institute, 182-192 Central Ave., 03820.
Manchester. Manchester Historic Association, 129 Amherst St., 03103.
New London. New London Historical Society, Little Sunapee Rd., 03257.
Portsmouth. Portsmouth Historical Society, 43 Middle St., 03801.

NEW JERSEY

Camden. Camden County Historical Society, Park Blvd & Euclid Ave., 08103.
Cape May Court House. Cape May County Historical Museum, Rte. 9-R.D. #1, 08210.
Freehold. Monmouth County Historical Association, 70 Court St., 07728.
Greenwich. Cumberland County Historical Society, YeGreate St., 08323.
Highlands. Sandy Hook Museum, P.O. Box 437, Gateway National Recreation Area, 07732.
Hopewell. Hopewell Museum, 28 E. Broad St., 08525.
Morristown. Morristown National Historical Park, Morris Ave. W. and Washington Pl., 07960.
Mount Holly. Historic Burlington County Prison Museum, 128 High St., 08060.
Neptune. Neptune Historical Museum, 25 Neptune Blvd, 07753.
Paterson. Passaic County Historical Society, Lambert Castle, Valley Rd., 07503.
Ridgewood. Paramus Historical and Preservation Society, Inc., 650 E. Glen Ave., 07450.
Ringwood. Ringwood Manor House Museum, Sloatsburg Rd., 07456.
Salem. Salem County Historical Society, 79-83 Market St., 08079.
Sussex. Space Farms Zoological Park and Museum, Beemerville Rd., 07461.
Titusville. Johnson Ferry Museum and Vistors Center, Washington Crossing State Park, 08560.
Trenton. Old Barracks Association, S. Willow St., 08608.
Woodbury. Gloucester County Historical Society, 58 N. Broad St., 08096.

NEW MEXICO

Albuquerque. National Atomic Museum, Kirtland Air Force Base East, 87115.
Lincoln. Old Lincoln County Courthouse Museum, Lincoln State Monument, 88338.
Radium Springs. Fort Selden State Monument, Box 58, 58054.
Ramah. El Morro National Monument, 87321.
Taos. Governor Bent Museum, Bent St., 87571.
Watrous. Ft. Union National Monument, 87753.

NEW YORK

Albany. New York State Office of Parks and Recreation, Division for Historic Preservation, Executive Dept., Agency Bldg. No. 1, Nelson A. Rockefeller Empire State Plaza, 12238.
Auburn. Seward House, 33 South St., 13021.
Batavia. The Holland Land Office Museum, 131 W. Main St., 14020.
Bellport. Bellport-Brookhaven Historical Society-Museum, Bellport Lane, 11713.
Bronx. The Bronx County Historical Society, 3266 Bainbridge Ave., 10467.
Brooklyn. Harbor Defense Museum of New York City, Fort Hamilton, 11252.
Caledonia. Big Springs Museum, Main St., 14423.
Canaan. Canaan Historical Society, Inc., Warner's Crossing Rd., 12029.
Castile. Castile Historical House, 17 E. Park Rd., 14427.
Cattaraugus. Cattaraugus Area Historical Center, 23 Main St., 14719.
Chazy. The Alice T. Miner Colonial Collection, Box 157, 12921.
Clayton. 1000 Islands Museum, 401 Riverside Dr., Old Town Hall, 13624.
Corning. The Rockwell-Corning Museum, Baron Steuben Pl., Market at Centerway, 14830.
Cortland. Cortland County Historical Society, Inc., 25 Homer Ave., 13045.
Crown Point. Crown Point State Historic Site, 12928.
East Durham. Durham Center Museum, Inc., 12423.
Elizabethtown. Adirondack Center Museum, Court St., 12932.
Elmira. Chemung County Historical Society, Inc., 304 Williams St., 14901.
Fabius. Pioneer's Museum, Highland Forest, 13063.
Fishers. Valentown Museum, Valentown Sq., 14453.
Fishkill. Van Wyck Homestead Museum, Rte. 9, 12524.
Ft. Edward. Ft. Edward Historical Association, P.O. Box 106, 12828.
Ft. Johnson. Montgomery County Historical Society, N.Y. Rte. 5, 12070.
Geneva. Geneva Historical Society and Museum, 543 S. Main St., 14456.
Gouverneur. Gouverneur Museum, Rte. 2, Leadmine Rd., 13642.
Hoosick Falls. Bennington Battlefield State Historic Site, State Rt. 67, 12090.
Hurleyville. Sullivan County Historical Society, Inc. P.O. Box 247, 12747.
Ilion. Remington Gun Museum, Catherine St., 13357.
Lake George. Ft. William Henry Museum, Canada St., 12845.
Little Falls. Herkimer House State Historic Site, Rte. 169, 13365.
Narrowsburg. Ft. Delaware, 12764.
New City. Historical Society of Rockland County, 20 Zukor Rd., 10956.
New York. Dyckman House and Museum, 204th St. & Broadway, 10021.
Fraunces Tavern Museum, 54 Pearl St., 10004.
General Grant National Memorial, Riverside Dr. and W. 122nd St., 10031.
The Metropolitan Museum of Art, 5th Ave. at 82nd St., 10028.
Museum of the City of New York, Fifth Ave. at 103rd St., 10029.

New York City Police Academy Museum, 235 E. 20th St., 10003.
The New York Historical Society, 170 Central Park West, 10024.
Newburgh. Washington's Headquarters State Historic Site, 84 Liberty St., 12550.
Oriskany. Oriskany Battlefield State Historic Site, State Rte. 69, 13424.
Ossining. Ossining Historical Society Museum, 196 Croton Ave., 10562.
Oswego. Ft. Ontario State Historic Site, East 7th St., 13126.
Owego. Tioga County Historical Society Museum,110 Front St., 13827.
Oyster Bay. Sagamore Hill National Historic Site, Cove Neck Road, 11771.
Riverhead. Suffolk County Historical Society, 300 W. Main St., 11901.
Rochester. Rochester Museum and Science Center, 657 East Ave., Box 1480, 14603.
Rome. Ft. Stanwix National Monument, 112 E. Park St., 13440.
Sackets Harbor. Pickering-Beach Historical Museum, 503 W. Main, 13685.
Sackets Harbor Battlefield State Historic Site, 13685.
Sag Harbor. Suffolk County Whaling Museum of Sag Harbor, Long Island, Main St., 11963.
Schoharie. Old Stone Fort Museum & William W. Badgley Historical Museum, N. Main St., 12157.
Staten Island. Staten Island Historical Society, 441 Clarke Ave., 10306.
Stillwater. Saratoga National Historical Park, Box 113-C, 12170.
Stony Point. Stony Point Battlefield State Historic Site, U.S. 9W, 10980.
Tarrytown. The Historical Society of the Tarrytowns, Inc., 1 Grove St., 10591.
Ticonderoga. Ft. Mt. Hope, Burgoyne Rd., 12883.
Ft. Ticonderoga, Box 390, 12883.
Tonawanda. Historical Society of the Tonawandas, Inc., 113 Main St., 14150.
Tuckahoe. Westchester County Historical Society, 43 Read Ave., 10707.
Vails Gate. Knox Headquarters State Historic Site, Box 207, 12584.
New Windsor Cantonment State Historic Site, Temple Hill Rd., 12584.
Warsaw. Warsaw Historical Museum, 15 Perry Ave., 14569.
Warwick. Warwick Historical Society, P.O. Box 353, 10990.
Waterloo. Waterloo Library and Historical Society, 31 E. Williams St., 13165.
Waterloo Memorial Day Museum, 35 E. Main St., 13165.
West Point. West Point Museum, United States Military Academy, 10996.
Westfield. History Center and Museum, Main and Portage Sts., Center of Village Park, 14787.
Windsor. Old Stone House Museum, 10 Chestnut St. 13865.
Wyoming. Middlebury Historical Society Museum, 32 S. Academy St., 14591.
Youngstown. Old Ft. Niagara Association, Ind., Old Ft. Niagara, Box 169, 14174.

NORTH CAROLINA

Burlington. Alamance Battleground State Historic Site, Rte. 1, 27215.
Durham. Bennett Place State Historic Site, 4409 Bennett Memorial Rd, 27705.
Fort Bragg. 82nd Airborne Division War Memorial Museum, Ardennes St., 28307.
Greensboro. Guilford Courthouse National Military Park, New Garden Rd. & Old Battleground Rd., 27408.
Hickory. The Hickory Museum of Art, 3rd St. & First Ave., N.W., 28601.
Hillsborough. Orange County Historical Museum, King St., 27278.
Kure Beach. Ft. Fisher State Historic Site, Box 68, 28449.
Murfreesboro. Murfreesboro, North Carolina Museum, P.O. Box 3, 27855.
Murphy. Cherokee County Historical Museum, Inc., Peachtree St., 28906.
Newton. Catawba County Historical Museum, 1716 S. College Dr., Hwy. 321, 28658.
Newton Grove. Bentonville Battleground State Historic Site, Box 27, 28366.
Raleigh. North Carolina Museum of History, 109 E. Jones St., 27611.
Shelby. Cleveland County Historical Museum, Courtsquare, 28150.
Southport. Brunswick Town State Historic Site, Box 356, 28461.
Wilmington. New Hanover County Museum, 814 Market St., 28401.
USS North Carolina Battleship Memorial, Cape Fear River on Eagles Island, P.O. Box 417, 28402.

NORTH DAKOTA

Abercrombie. Ft. Abercrombie Historic Site, 58001.
Bismarck. State Historical Society of North Dakota, North Dakota Heritage Center, 58505.
Ft. Ransom. Ransom County Historical Society, 58033.
Jamestown. Ft. Seward Historical Society, Inc., 321 3rd Ave., 58401.
Mandan. Ft. Abraham Lincoln State Historical Park, Rte. 2 Box 139, 58554.
Great Plains Museum, Hwy. 1806, 58554.
Valley City. Barnes County Historical Museum, County Courthouse, 58072.

OHIO

Bellefontaine. Logan County Historical Museum, W. Chillicothe Ave. at Seymour, 43311.
Burton. Geauga County Historical Society Century Village, 14653, E. Park St., 44021.

Cambridge. Guernsey County Museum, P.O. Box 741, 43725.
Carrollton. Caroll County Historical Society, P.O. Box 174, 44615.
Celina. Mercer County Historical Museum, The Riley Home, 130 E. Market, 45883.
Chillicothe. Mound City Group National Monument, 16062 State Rte. 104, 45601.
Fremont. The Rutherford B. Hayes Library and Museum, 1337 Hayes Ave., 43420.
Granville. Granville Historical Museum, Broadway, 43023.
Greenville. Garst Museum, 205 N. Broadway, 45331.
Marion. Stengel-True Museum, 504 S. State St. 43302.
Massillon. The Massillon Museum, 212 Lincoln Way, 44646.
Medina. Munson House, Medina County Historical Society, 231 E. Washington, 44256.
Niles. National McKinley Birthplace Memorial Association Museum, 40 N. Main St., 44446.
Norwalk. Firelands Historical Society Museum, 4 Case Ave., 44857.
Piqua. Piqua Historical Area, 9845 N. Hardin Rd., 45356.
Sheffield Lake. 103rd Ohio Volunteer Infantry Memorial Foundation, 5501 E. Lake Rd., 44054.
Tiffin. Seneca County Museum, 28 Clay St., 44883.
Urbana. Champaign County Historical Society Museum, 809 E. Lawn Ave., 43078.
Wooster. Wayne County Historical Society, 546 E. Bowman St., 44691.
Wright-Patterson AFB. United States Air Force Museum, 45433.
Xenia. Greene County Historical Society, 74 W. Church St., 45385.
Zanesville. Dr. Increase Mathews House, 304 Woodlawn Ave., 43701.

OKLAHOMA
Bartlesville. Woolaroc Museum, State Hwy. 123, 74003.
Cheyenne. Black Kettle Museum, 73628.
Claremore. J. M. Davis Gun Museum, Fifth and Hwy. 66, 74017.
Cookson. Ft. Chickamauga, 74427.
Ft. Sill. U.S. Army Field Artillery and Ft. Sill Museum, 73503.
Okemah. Territory Town, Rte. 2, Box 297-A, 74859.
Oklahoma City. National Cowboy Hall of Fame and Western Heritage Center, 1700 N.E. 63rd St., 73111.
Oklahoma Historical Society, Historical Bldg., 73105.
Sapulpa. Sapulpa Historical Museum, 100 E. Lee, 74066.
Tishomingo. Chickasaw Council House Museum, Rte. 1, Box 14, 73460.

OREGON
Haines. Eastern Oregon Museum, Rte. 1, Box 109, 97833.
Kerby. Josephine County Kerbyville Museum, 24195 Redwood Hwy., Box 34, 97531.
Klamath Falls. Favell Museum of Western Art and Indian Artifacts, 125 W. Main St., 97601.
Lakeview. Schminck Memorial Museum, 128 "E" St., 97630.
Portland. Portland Children's Museum, 3037 S.W. 2nd Ave., 97201.
Roseburg. Douglas County Museum, Box 1550, County Fairgrounds, 97470.
The Dalles. Fort Dalles Museum, 16th St. & Garrison St., 97058.

PENNSYLVANIA
Athens. Tioga Point Museum, 724 S. Main St., 18810.
Boalsburg. Christopher Columbus Family Chapel, Boal Mansion and Museum, 16827.
Pennsylvania Military Museum, 28th Division Shrine, Box 148, 16827.
Carlisle Barracks. United States Army Military History Institute, 17013.
Easton. Northampton County Historical Society, 101 S. 4th St., 18042.
Gettysburg. Gettysburg National Military Park, 17325.
Harrisburg. Pennsylvania Historical and Museum Commission, 3rd & North Sts., 17120.
Haverford. Haverford Township Historical Society, Karakung Dr., Powder Mill Park, 19083.
Hellertown. Gilman Museum, at the Cave, 18055.
Jeannette. Bushy Run Battlefield, Bushy Run Rd., 15644.
Ligonier. Ft. Ligonier Memorial Foundation, Inc., S. Market St., 15658.
Meadville. Baldwin-Reynolds House Museum, 639 Terrace St., 16335.
Middleburg. The Snyder County Historical Society, Inc., Dr. Geo. F. Dunkleberger Memorial Library, 30 E. Market St., 17842.
Pennsburg. Schwenkfelder Museum, Seminary St., 18072.
Philadelphia. Independence National Historical Park, 313 Walnut St., 19106.
Philadelphia Maritime Museum, 321 Chestnut St., 19106.
War Library and Museum of the Military Order of the Loyal Legion of the United States, 1805 Pine St., 19103.
Pittsburgh. The Ft. Pitt Blockhouse, Point State Park, 15222.
Ft. Pitt Museum, Point State Park, 15222.
Strasburg. Eagle Americana Shop and Gun Museum, R.D. 1, 17579.
Sunbury. Ft. Augusta, 1150 N. Front St., 17801.

Valley Forge. The Valley Forge Historical Society, 19481.
Valley Forge National Historical Park, 19481.
Wilkes-Barre. Wyoming Historical and Geological Society, 69 S. Franklin St., 18701.
York. The Historical Society of York County, 250 E. Market St., 17403.

RHODE ISLAND
Bristol. Bristol Historical and Preservation Society, 48 Court St., 02809.
Newport. Naval War College Museum, Naval War College, Coasters Harbor Island, 02840.
Newport Artillery Company Museum, 23 Clarke St., 02840.
Providence. Rhode Island Historical Society, 52 Power St., 02906.
Rhode Island State Archives, Rm. 43, State House, Smith St., 02903.
Westerly. Westerly Public Library, Broad St., 02891.

SOUTH CAROLINA
Aiken. Aiken County Historical Museum, 226 Chesterfield, 29801.
Beaufort. Beaufort Museum, Craven St., 29902.
Blacksburg. Kings Mountain National Military Park, 29702.
Camden. Camden District Heritage Foundation, Historic Camden, P.O. Box 710, 29020.
Charleston. Citadel Archives-Museum, The Citadel, 29409.
Patriots Point Naval and Maritime Museum, 29464.
Powder Magazine, 79 Cumberland St., 29401.
Columbia. South Carolina Confederate Relic Room and Museum, World War Memorial Bldg, 920 Sumter St., 29201.
South Carolina Criminal Justice Hall of Fame, 5400 Broad River Rd., 29210.
Florence. Florence Air and Missile Museum, U.S. Hwy. 301, North Airport Entrance, 29503.
Fort Jackson. Fort Jackson Museum, Bldg. 4442, 29207.
Greenwood. The Museum, Phoenix St., 29646.
Hampton. Hampton County Historical Society Museum, 1st West, 29924.
Pendleton. Pendleton District Historical and Recreational Commission, 125 E. Queen St., 29670.
Spartanburg. Spartanburg County Regional Museum, 501 Otis Blvd., 29302.
Sullivan's Island. Ft. Sumter National Monument, Middle St. 29482.
Union. Union County Historical Museum, Drawer 220, 29379.
Winnsboro. Fairfield County Museum, South Congress St., 29180.

SOUTH DAKOTA
Chamberlain. Old West Museum, West Hwy. 16, 57325.
Deadwood. Adams Memorial Hall Museum, 54 Sherman, 57732.
Lake City. Ft. Sisseton State Park Visitors Center, 57247.
Pierre. Robinson Museum, Memorial Bldg, 57501.
Rapid City. Horseless Carriage Museum, Box 2933, 57708.
Sturgis. Old Ft. Meade Museum and Historic Research Association, 1113 Poisley Terrace, 57785.
Watertown. Kampeska Heritage Museum, 27 First Ave. S.E., 57201.

TENNESSEE
Dover. Ft. Donelson National Military Park, Hwy. 79, 37058.
Franklin. Carter House, APTA, 1140 Columbia AVe., 37064.
Knoxville. Confederate Memorial Hall "Bleak House," 3148 Kingston Pike, 37919.
Murfreesboro. Stones River National Battlefield, Rte. 10, Box 401, Old Nashville Hwy., 37130.
Nashville. Association for the Preservation of Tennessee Antiquities, 110 Leake Ave., 37205.
Tennessee State Museum, War Memorial Bldg., 37219.
Shiloh. Shiloh National Military Park and Cemetery, 38376.

TEXAS
Austin. Texas State Library, 1201 Brazos St., 78711.
Cameron. Milan County Historical Museum, P.O. Box 966, 76520.
Canyon. Panhandle-Plains Historical Museum, 2401 Fourth Ave., 79015.
Cleburne. Layland Museum, 201 N. Caddo, 76031.
Del Rio. Whitehead Memorial Museum, 1308 S. Main St., 78840.
Denton. North Texas State University Historical Collection, West Mulberry and Ave. A, 76203.
Egypt. Northington-Heard Memorial Museum, Box 277, 77436.
El Paso. El Paso Museum of History, 12901 Gateway West, 79927.
Falfurrias. The Heritage Museum at Falfurrias, Inc., Box 86, 78355.
Ft. Bliss. Ft. Bliss Replica Museum, Pleasonton & Sheridan Rds., 79916.
Ft. Davis. Ft. Davis National Historic Site, Box 1456, 79734.
Ft. Worth. Ft. Worth Museum of Science and History, 1501 Montgomery St., 76107.
Museum of Aviation Group, 300 North Spur 341, 76108.

Ft. Hood. Second Armored Division Museum, 76546.
Harlingen. Confederate Air Force, Rebel Field, 78550.
Hillsboro. Confederate Research Center and Gun Museum, P.O. Box 619, 76645.
Kingsville. John E. Conner Museum, Texas A&I University, 78363.
La Porte. Battleship Texas, 3527 Battleground Rd., 77571.
Livingston. Polk County Memorial Museum, 601 W. Church, P.O. Drawer 511, 77351.
Marshall. Harrison County Historical Museum, Old Courthouse, Peter Whetstone Square, 75670.
Nacogdoches. Stone Fort Museum, Stephen F. Austin University, 75962.
New Braunfels. Sophienburg Museum, 401 W. Coll St., 78130.
Newcastle. Ft. Belknap Museum and Archives, Box 68, 76372.
Ozona. Crockett County Museum, P.O. Drawer B, Courthouse Annex, 76943.
Panhandle. Carson County Square House Museum, 5th and Elsie Sts., 79068.
San Angelo. Ft. Concho National Historic Landmark, 213 East Ave. D., 76903.
San Antonio. Ft. Sam Houston Military Museum, Bldg. 123, 78234.
  History and Traditions Museum, Military Training Center/LGH, Lackland Air Force Base, 78236.
  Lone Star Brewing Company, Buckhorn Hall of Horns, Fins, Feathers and Boar's Nest, 600 Lone Star Blvd., 78297.
  Memorial Bldg., 3805 Broadway, 78209.
  San Jose Mission, 6539 San Jose Dr., 78214.
Sunset. Sunset Trading Post-Old West Museum, Rte. 1, 76270.
Teague. Burlington-Rock Island Railroad Museum, 218 Elm St., 75860.
Tyler. Goodman Museum, 624 N. Broadway, 75702.
Uvalde. Garner Memorial Museum, 333 N. Park St., 78801.
Van Horn. Culberson County Historical Museum, Main St., 79855.

UTAH
Farmington. Pioneer Village, Box N, 84025.
Ft. Douglas. Ft. Douglas Museum, Bldg. 32, 84113.
Ft. Duchesne. Ute Tribal Museum, Hwy. 40, Bottle Hollow Resort, 84026.
Ogden. Ogden Union Station Museums, Rm 212, Union Station, 25th & Wall Ave., 84401.

VERMONT
Brownington. The Old Stone House, 05860.
Hubbardton. Hubbardton Battlefield Museum, 05749.
Montpelier. Vermont Museum, Pavilion Bldg, 05602.
Northfield. Norwich University Museum, on Rte. 12 (Main St.) ¼ mile north of Jct. 12&12A, 05663.
Reading. Reading Historical Society, 05062.
Shelburne Museum, Inc., U.S. Rte. 7, 05482.
Windsor. Old Constitution House, North Main St., 05089.

VIRGINIA
Alexandria. Ft. Ward Museum and Park, 4301 W. Braddock Rd., 22304.
Bridgewater. Reuel B. Pritchett Museum, Bridgewater College, East College St., 22812.
Charles City. Berkeley Plantation, Rte. 5, 23030.
Fredericksburg National Military Park, 1301 Lafayette Blvd., 22401.
Front Royal. Warren Rifles Confederate Museum, 95 Chester St., 22630.
Glen Allen. Meadow Farm Museum, Mountain & Courtney Rds., 23060.
Lexington. Stonewall Jackson House, 8 E. Washington St., 24450.
  VMI Museum, Virginia Military Institute, Jackson Memorial Hall, 24450.
Manassas. Manassas National Battlefield Park, P.O. Box 1830, 22110.
New Market. New Market Battlefield Park, P.O. Box 1864, 22844.
Newport News. The Mariners Museum, Museum Dr., 23606.
  The War Memorial Museum of Virginia, 9285 Warwick Blvd., Huntington Park, 23607.
Norfolk. General Douglas MacArthur Memorial, MacArthur Square, 23510.
  Naval Amphibious Museum, NAB Little Creek, 23521.
Petersburg. Centre Hill Mansion Museum, Franklin St., 23803.
  Petersburg National Battlefield, P.O. Box 549, 23803.
  Siege Museum, c/o Dept. of Tourism, 15 W. Bank St., 23803.
Portsmouth. Portsmouth Naval Museum, 2 High St., 23705.
Quantico. United States Marine Corps Aviation Museum, Brown Field, Marine Corps Base, 22134.
Richmond. Museum of the Confederacy, 1201 E. Clay St., 23219.
  Richmond National Battlefield Park, 3215 E. Broad St., 23223.
  Virginia Historical Society, 428 North Blvd., 23221.
Spotsylvania County. Spotsylvania Historical Association, Inc., P.O. Box 64, 22553.
Williamsburg. Colonial Williamsburg, Goodwin Bldg., 23185.
Winchester. Winchester-Frederick County Historical Society, Inc., Box 58, 22601.
Yorktown. Colonial National Historical Park, P.O. Box 210, 23690.

WASHINGTON
Anacortes. Anacortes Museum, 1305 8th, 98221.
Bremerton. Naval Shipyard Museum, Washington State Ferry Terminal Bldg., 98310.
Brewster. Ft. Okanogan Interpretive Center, Bridgeport State Park, 98812.
Chinook. Fort Columbia State Park, P.O. Box 172, 98614.
Coulee Dam. Ft. Spokane Museum, Box 37, 99116.
Coupeville. Ft. Casey Interpretive Center, Ft. Casey State Park, 12805 St. Casey Rd., 98239.
Davenport. Lincoln County Historical Museum, P.O. Box 585, 99122.
Ft. Lewis. Ft. Lewis Military Museum, Bldg. T4320, 98433.
Goldendale. Maryhill Museum of Fine Arts, 98620.
Grandview. Ray E. Powell Museum, 313 Division, 98930.
Kelso. Cowlitz County Historical Museum, 5th & Allen St., 98626.
North Bend. Snoqualmie Valley Historical Museum, 222 North Bend Blvd, 98045.
Port Townsend. The Coast Artillery Museum at Ft. Worden, 98368.
  Jefferson County Historical Society, City Hall, 98368.
Prosser. Benton County Museum & Historical Society, Inc., P.O. box 591, 99350.
Seattle. Museum of History and Industry, 2161 E. Hamlin St., 98112.
Spokane. Ft. Wright College Historical Museum, W. 4000 Randolph Rd., 99204.
Vancouver. Ft. Vancouver National Historic Site, 98661.
Walla Walla. Ft. Walla Walla Museum Complex, P.O. Box 1616, 99362.
White Swan. Ft. Simcoe Interpretive Center, Rte. 1, Box 39, 98952.
Yakima. Yakima Valley Museum and Historical Association, 2105 Tieton Dr., 98902.

WEST VIRGINIA
Ansted. Hawks Nest State Park, P.O. Box 417, 25812.
Charleston. West Virginia Dept. of Culture & History, Capitol Complex, 25305.
Harpers Ferry. Harpers Ferry National Historical Park, Shenandoah St., 25425.
Huntington. The Huntington Galleries, Inc., 2033 McCoy Rd., 25701.
Lewisburg. Ft. Savannah Inn, 204 N. Jefferson, 24901.
Weston. Jackson's Mill Museum, 26452.
Wheeling. Oglebay Institute-Mansion Museum, Oglebay Park, 26003.

WISCONSIN
Ashland. Ashland Museum, 500 W. 2nd St., 54806.
Beloit. Bartlett Memorial Historical Museum, 2149 St. Lawrence Ave., 53511.
Green Bay. Neville Public Museum, 129 S. Jefferson, 54301.
Hatfield. VI Teeples' Thunderbird Museum, P.O. Merrillan, 54754.
Janesville. Rock County Historical Society, 10 S. High St., 53545.
  The Tallman Restorations, 440 N. Jackson St., 53545.
Kenosha. Kenosha County Historical Museum, 6300 3rd Ave., 53140.
King. Wisconsin Veterans Museum, Veterans Home, 54946.
Madison. Grand Army of the Republic Memorial Hall Museum, State Capitol, 419 N. 53702.
  State Historical Society of Wisconsin, 816 State St., 53706.
Milton. Milton House Museum, Hwy. 26 & 59, 53563.
Milwaukee. Milwaukee County Historical Society, 910 N. Third St., 53203.
  Milwaukee Public Museum, 800 W. Wells St., 53233.
New Glarus. Chalet of the Golden Fleece, 618 2nd St., 53574.
New Holstein. New Holstein Historical Society, 2025 Randolph Ave., 53061.
Oshkosh. Oshkosh Public Museum, 1331 Algoma Blvd, 54901.
Prairie du Chien. Villa Louis and Museum, Villa Rd. and Boilvin, 53821.
Racine. Racine County Historical Museum, Inc. 701 St. Main St., 53403.
River Falls. Area Research Center, Chalmer Davee Library, University of Wisconsin, 54022.
Stoughton. Stoughton Historical Society, 324 S. Page St., 53589.
Superior. Douglas County Historical Museum, 906 E. 2nd St., 54880.
Waupaca. Hutchinson House, P.O. Box 173, 54981.

WYOMING
Buffalo. Johnson County, Jim Gatchell Memorial Museum, 10 Fort St., 82834.
Casper. Ft. Caspar Museum and Historic Site, 14 Fort Caspar Rd., 82601.
Cheyenne. Warren Military Museum, Bldg. 210, Francis E. Warren Air Force Base, 82001.
  Wyoming State Museum, Barrett Bldg, 22nd & Central Ave., 82002.
Cody. Buffalo Bill Historical Center, Box 1020, 82414.
Douglas. Ft. Fetterman State Museum, 82366.
Ft. Laramie. Ft. Laramie National Historic Site, 82212.
Ft. Bridger. Ft. Bridger State Museum, 82933.
Gillette. Rockpile Museum, Hwy. 14-16 West Gillette, 82716.
Green River. Sweetwater County Museum, 50 W. Falming Gorge Way,

Guernsey. Guernsey State Museum, Guernsey State Park, 82214.
Jackson. Jackson Hole Historical Museum, 101 N. Glenwood, 83001.
Lander. Pioneer Museum, 630 Lincoln St., 82520.
Riverton. Riverton Museum, 700 E. Park, 82501.

CANADA

ALBERTA
Calgary. Princess Patricia's Canadian Light Infantry Regimental Museum, Currie Barracks, T3E IT8.
Drumheller. Homestead Antique Museum, P.O. Box 700, T0J 0Y0.
Ft. Macleod. Ft. Macleod Historical Association, Box 776, TOL OZO.
Wetaskiwin. Reynolds Museum, Hwy. 2A, Box 6780, T9A 2G4.

BRITISH COLUMBIA.
Ft. Langley. Langley Centennial Museum & National Exhibition Centre, Mavis & King Sts., VOX 1JO.
Kamloops. Kamloops Museum, 207 Seymour, V2C 2E7.
New Westminster. The Regimental Museum/The Armory, 530 Queens Ave., V3L 1K3.
Powell River. Powell River Historical Museum Association, Museum Bldg, Box 42, V8A 425.
Prince Rupert. Museum of Northern British Columbia, Corner McBride St. and First Ave., V8J 3S1.
Vancouver. Pacific National Exhibition, British Columbia Pavilion, Exhibition Park, V5K 4A9.
Regimental Museum, Seaforth Highlanders of Canada, 1650 Burrard St., V6J 3G4.
Vedder Crossing. Canadian Military Engineers Museum, Canadian Forces School of Military Engineering, Local 263, MPO 612, C.F.B. Chilliwack, VOX 2E0.
Victoria. Ft. Rodd Hill National Historic Park, 604 Ft. Rodd Hill Rd., V9C-1B5
Maritime Museum of British Columbia, 28-30 Bastion Sq., V8W 1H9.

MANITOBA
Shilo. Royal Canadian Artillery Museum, Canadian Forces Base, R0K 2A0.
Winnipeg. Royal Winnipeg Rifles Museum, 969 St. Mathews Ave., R2C 1X8.

NEW BRUNSWICK.
Aulac. Ft. Beausejour National Historic Park, E0A 3C0.
Oromocto. Canadian Forces Base Gagetown Museum, CFB Gagetown, EOG 1PO.
St. Andrews. Block House Historic Site and Centennial Park, 40 Town Hall, E0G 2X0.
St. John. Ft. Howe Blockhouse, P.O. Box 1971, E2L 4L1.
The New Brunswick Museum, 277 Douglas Ave., E2K 1E5.

NEWFOUNDLAND
Placentia. Castle Hill National Historic Park, P.O. Box 10, Jerseyside, A0B 2G0.
St. John's. Cape Spear National Historic Park, P.O. Box 5879.

NOVA SCOTIA
Annapolis Royal. Ft. Anne National Historic Park, St. George St., B0S 1A0.
Halifax. Halifax Citadel National Historic Park, P.O. Box 1480, North Postal Station, B3K 5H7.
Halifax South. The Army Museum-Halifax Citadel, P.O. Box 3666, B3J 3K6.
Louisbourg. Fortress of Louisbourg National Historic Park, P.O. Box 160, B0A 1M0.

ONTARIO
Alliston. South Simcoe Pioneer Museum, Municipal Office, L0M 1A0.
Amherstburg. Ft. Malden National Historic Park, Laird Ave., Box 38, N9V 2Z2.
Borden. Base Borden Military Museum and Worthington Park, Canadian Forces Base, L0M 1C0.
Dundas. Dundas Historical Society Museum, 139 Park St., L9H 5G1.
Dunvegan. Glengarry Pioneer Museum, P.O. Box 5, KOC 1JC.
Gananoque. Gananoque Historical Museum, 10 King St., E., K7G 2T7.
Golden Lake. Algonquin Museum, Via Algonquin Park, K0J 1X0.
Guelph. Colonel John McCrae Birthplace Society, 102 Water St., N1H 6L3.
Kingston. Murney Tower Museum, P.O. Box 54, K7L 4V6.
Old Ft. Henry, Box 213, K7L 4V8.
Royal Military College of Canada Museum, K7L 2W3.
London. London Historical Museums, 325 Queens Ave., N6B 3L7.
The Royal Canadian Regiment Museum, Wolseley Hall, Wolseley Barracks, N5Y 4T7.
Merrickville. Blockhouse Museum, R.R. 4, P.O. Box 294, K0G 1N0.
Milton. Halton Museum, R.R. 3, L9T 2X7.
Niagara-on-the-Lake. Ft. George National Historic Park, P.O. Box 787, L0S 1J0.
Ottawa. Canadian War Museum, 330 Sussex Dr., K1A 0M8.
Regimental Museum, Governor General's Foot Guards, Drill Hall, Cartier Sq., K1P 5R3.
Penetanguishene. Historic Naval and Military Establishments, P.O. Box 160, Midland L4R 4K8.
Prescott. Ft. Wellington National Historic Park, 400 Dibble St., E., KOE 1TO.
St. Catharines. St. Catharines Historical Museum, 343 Merritt St., L2T 1K7.
Sutton. Eildon Hall, Sibbald Memorial Museum, Sibbald Point Park, R.R. 2 L0E 1R0.
Toronto. Black Creek Pioneer Village, 1000 Murray Ross Pkwy. M3N 1S4
Fort York, Garrison Rd. at Fleet and Strachan Ave. M6K 3C3
Marine Museum of Upper Canada, Exhibiton Place, M6K 3C3.
Toronto Historical Board, Exhibition Park, M6K 3C3.
Windsor. Hiram Walker Historical Museum, 254 Pitt St. W., N9A 5L5.

PRINCE EDWARD ISLAND
Rocky Point. Ft. Amherst National Historic Park, C0A 1H0.

QUEBEC
Beebe. Stanstead County Historical Society, 110 Main St.
Chambly. Ft. Chambly National and Historic Parks, 2 Richelieu St., J3L 2B9.
Cookshire. Compton County Historical and Museum Society, J0B 1M0.
Coteau-du-lac. Ft. Coteau-du-Lac.
Ile-aux-Noix. Ft. Lennox National Historic Park, St. Paul.
Knowlton. Brome County Historical Museum, P.O. Box 690, JOE 1VO.
Montreal. The Saint Helen's Island Museum, The Fort. H3C 2W9.
Royal Canadian Ordnance Corps Museum, 6560 Hochelaga St., H3C 3H7.
Rigaud. Musee du College Bourget, 65 rue St. Pierre, J0P 1P0.

SASKATCHEWAN
Batoche. Batoche National Historic Site S0M 0E0.
Battleford. Battleford National Historic Park, Box 70, S0M 0E0.
Regina. Royal Canadian Mounted Police Museum, Box 6500, S4P 3J7.
Riverhurst. F.T. Hill Museum, S0H 3P0.
Weyburn. Soo Line Historical Museum, 411 Industrial Lane, S.E.

PUERTO RICO
San Juan. Museum of Military and Naval History, Ft. San Jeronimo beside Caribe Hilton Hotel, 00905.

Where to Hunt What in the U.S. and Canada
A Guide for All Who Hunt with Gun or Camera

(The name of an animal in italics indicates that it is one of the most popular species sought in that state or province.)

United States
Alabama
Deer, rabbit, squirrel, *bobwhite quail, mourning dove* and waterfowl.

Alaska
Moose, caribou, Dall sheep, mountain goat, grizzly bear, brown bear, black bear, polar bear, deer, elk, bison, musk ox, wolf, snowshoe hare, arctic hare, seal, walrus, ptarmigan, grouse and waterfowl.

Arizona
Mule deer, white-tailed deer, elk, pronghorn antelope, *javelina,* black bear, cougar, quail, *white-winged dove,* wild turkey, band-tailed pigeon and waterfowl.

Arkansas
Deer, rabbit, *squirrel,* duck, wild turkey, *mourning dove* and *bobwhite quail.*

California
Mule deer, elk, pronghorn antelope, black bear, wild boar, rabbit, squirrel, *dove, waterfowl, quail, pheasant,* chukar, Hungarian partridge, grouse, wild turkey and pigeon.

Colorado
Elk, mule deer, bighorn sheep, pronghorn antelope, black bear, cougar, waterfowl, pheasant, chukar, grouse, quail and mourning dove.

Connecticut
Rabbit, squirrel, raccoon, *ruffed grouse* and woodcock.

Delaware
Deer, rabbit, squirrel, *waterfowl,* bobwhite quail, mourning dove and woodcock.

Florida
Deer, wild hog, cottontail rabbit, marsh rabbit, *gray squirrel,* fox squirrel, *bobwhite quail,* wild turkey, *waterfowl* and *mourning dove.*

Georgia
Deer, rabbit, squirrel, *bobwhite quail,* mourning dove, ruffed grouse, woodcock, wild turkey and waterfowl.

Hawaii
Feral sheep, wild goat, wild pig, deer, barred dove, lace-necked dove, mourning dove, ring-necked pheasant, chukar, francolin and quail.

Idaho
Mule deer, white-tailed deer, elk, mountain sheep, mountain goat, moose, pronghorn antelope, black bear, cottontail rabbit, snowshoe hare, jack rabbit, *pheasant,* Hungarian partridge, chukar, quail, grouse, dove, wild turkey and waterfowl.

Illinois
Rabbit, squirrel, deer, *mourning dove, quail,* pheasant, *duck* and *goose.*

Indiana
Rabbit, squirrel, deer, pheasant and quail.

Iowa
Squirrel, cottontail rabbit, deer, *pheasant, quail,* Hungarian partridge, ruffed grouse and waterfowl.

Kansas
Cottontail rabbit, jack rabbit, fox squirrel, gray squirrel, *waterfowl, pheasant, prairie chicken* and *quail.*

Kentucky
Deer, *gray squirrel,* rabbit, red fox, *mourning dove,* quail, wild turkey, ruffed grouse and goose.

Louisiana
White-tailed deer, fox squirrel, gray squirrel, swamp rabbit, cottontail rabbit, *mourning dove, bobwhite quail, waterfowl* and wild turkey.

Maine
White-tailed deer, black bear, snowshoe hare, squirrel, ruffed grouse, pheasant, *woodcock,* snipe, rail and *black duck.*

Maryland
Deer, *squirrel, rabbit, waterfowl, mourning dove,* quail and ruffed grouse.

Massachusetts
Deer, squirrel, rabbit, *pheasant,* ruffed grouse, quail, waterfowl, snipe, rail and woodcock.

Michigan
Deer, bear, squirrel, rabbit, *ruffed grouse,* woodcock, waterfowl, *pheasant* and quail.

Minnesota
Deer, moose, black bear, squirrel, snowshoe hare, rabbit, *pheasant, ruffed grouse, waterfowl,* sharp-tailed grouse and woodcock.

Mississippi
White-tailed deer, gray squirrel, fox squirrel, cottontail rabbit, swamp rabbit, *bobwhite quail, mourning dove, wild turkey* and waterfowl.

Missouri
Deer, *squirrel, cottontail rabbit,* swamp rabbit, *bobwhite quail,* dove, wild turkey and waterfowl.

Montana
Elk, mule deer, white-tailed deer, pronghorn antelope, mountain goat, mountain sheep, moose, black bear, pheasant, grouse, Hungarian partridge, chukar, wild turkey and waterfowl.

Nebraska
White-tailed deer, mule deer, pronghorn antelope, cottontail rabbit, squirrel, *ring-necked pheasant,* bobwhite quail, sharp-tailed grouse, prairie chicken, *waterfowl* and *wild turkey.*

Nevada
Mule deer, elk, pronghorn antelope, desert bighorn sheep, cougar, cottontail rabbit, jack rabbit, mourning dove, chukar, quail, grouse and waterfowl.

New Hampshire
Deer, black bear, rabbit, snowshoe hare, gray squirrel, raccoon, *ruffed grouse* and *woodcock.*

New Jersey
Deer, squirrel, *cottontail rabbit,* quail, pheasant, ruffed grouse, woodcock, *waterfowl* and rail.

New Mexico
Mule deer, white-tailed deer, elk, pronghorn antelope, javelina, black bear, cougar, squirrel, cottontail rabbit, wild turkey, quail, mourning dove, sandhill crane and waterfowl.

New York
Deer, black bear, rabbit, snowshoe hare, squirrel, *ruffed grouse, pheasant,* wild turkey, woodcock and waterfowl.

North Carolina
Deer, black bear, wild boar, rabbit, *squirrel, mourning dove,* quail, ruffed grouse, wild turkey and *waterfowl.*

North Dakota
White-tailed deer, mule deer, pronghorn antelope, fox squirrel, gray squirrel, cottontail rabbit, jack rabbit, *sharp-tailed grouse*, duck, Hungarian partridge, sage grouse, ruffed grouse, pheasant and wild turkey.

Ohio
Deer, *rabbit*, *squirrel*, raccoon, ruffed grouse, *pheasant*, Hungarian partridge, quail, waterfowl and wild turkey.

Oklahoma
White-tailed deer, mule deer, fox squirrel, gray squirrel, cottontail rabbit, jack rabbit, *bobwhite quail*, mourning dove, prairie chicken, *wild turkey* and waterfowl.

Oregon
Black-tailed deer, *mule deer*, *elk*, black bear, rabbit, squirrel, *waterfowl*, *pheasant*, *chukar*, Hungarian partridge, quail, grouse, wild turkey, *band-tailed pigeon* and mourning dove.

Pennsylvania
Deer, *black bear*, squirrel, rabbit, woodcock, mourning dove, *wild turkey*, waterfowl, ruffed grouse, quail and pheasant.

Rhode Island
Deer, *cottontail rabbit*, snowshoe hare, *squirrel*, pheasant, quail, ruffed grouse and waterfowl.

South Carolina
Deer, rabbit, squirrel, *quail*, *mourning dove*, wild turkey and waterfowl.

South Dakota
White-tailed deer, mule deer, pronghorn antelope, mountain goat, cottontail rabbit, fox squirrel, gray squirrel, *ring-necked pheasant*, sharp-tailed grouse, bobwhite quail, Hungarian partridge, mourning dove, jacksnipe, prairie chicken, sage grouse, Hungarian partridge, wild turkey and waterfowl.

Tennessee
Deer, wild boar, *squirrel*, *rabbit*, *mourning dove*, ruffed grouse, *quail* and waterfowl.

Texas
White-tailed deer, *mule deer*, javelina, cottontail rabbit, jack rabbit, squirrel, *mourning dove*, *bobwhite quail*, *scaled quail*, ring-necked pheasant, wild turkey, prairie chicken, prairie grouse and waterfowl.

Utah
Mule deer, elk, moose, pronghorn antelope, desert bighorn sheep, cougar, squirrel, snowshoe hare, jack rabbit, cottontail rabbit, *pheasant*, mourning dove, chukar, grouse, quail and *waterfowl*.

Vermont
White-tailed deer, black bear, cottontail rabbit, snowshoe hare, raccoon, gray squirrel, *ruffed grouse*, woodcock and waterfowl.

Virginia
Deer, black bear, *squirrel*, *rabbit*, *bobwhite quail*, *mourning dove*, ruffed grouse, wild turkey and waterfowl.

Washington
Deer, elk, mountain goat, black bear, cougar, rabbit, *pheasant*, quail, chukar, Hungarian partridge, grouse, dove, band-tailed pigeon, wild turkey and *waterfowl*.

West Virginia
Deer, rabbit, squirrel, *ruffed grouse*, woodcock, mourning dove and quail.

Wisconsin
Deer, black bear, rabbit, squirrel, fox, *ruffed grouse*, sharp-tailed grouse, Hungarian partridge, pheasant and woodcock.

Wyoming
Mule deer, *white-tailed deer*, *elk*, antelope, moose, mountain sheep, mountain goat, bear, *pheasant*, *chukar*, Hungarian partridge, *sage grouse*, wild turkey and waterfowl.

Canada
Alberta
Mule deer, white-tailed deer, *moose*, elk, mountain sheep, caribou, mountain goat, antelope, grizzly bear, black bear, cottontail rabbit, snowshoe hare, jack rabbit, *waterfowl*, pheasant. *Hungarian partridge*, *sharp-tailed grouse*, *ruffed grouse*, blue grouse, spruce grouse and ptarmigan.

British Columbia
Mule deer, *black-tailed deer*, white-tailed deer, *moose*, mountain goat, Dall sheep, Stone sheep, bighorn sheep, elk, caribou, grizzly bear, black bear, cougar, wolf, coyote, wolverine, fox, snowshoe hare, grouse, ptarmigan, *waterfowl*, mourning dove, pheasant, California quail, Hungarian partridge and chukar.

Manitoba
White-tailed deer, *moose*, elk, woodland caribou, black bear, snowshoe hare, fox, wolf, lynx, wolverine, *sharp-tailed grouse*, spruce grouse, ruffed grouse, ptarmigan grouse, Hungarian partridge, pheasant, wild turkey and *waterfowl*.

New Brunswick
White-tailed deer, moose, black bear, snowshoe hare, ruffed grouse, spruce grouse, *woodcock* and waterfowl.

Newfoundland and Labrador
Moose, *caribou*, black bear, snowshoe hare, arctic hare, *ptarmigan*, spruce grouse, ruffed grouse and waterfowl.

Northwest Territories
Black bear, grizzly bear, *moose*, *caribou*, Dall sheep, mountain goat, wolf, wolverine, *waterfowl*, *ptarmigan* and *grouse*.

Nova Scotia
White-tailed deer, black bear, moose, *snowshoe hare*, *ruffed grouse*, pheasant, Hungarian partridge, woodcock and *waterfowl*.

Ontario
White-tailed deer, *moose*, black bear, cottontail rabbit, snowshoe hare, *ruffed grouse*, spruce grouse, sharp-tailed grouse, ptarmigan, Hungarian partridge, pheasant, bobwhite quail, *waterfowl* and woodcock.

Prince Edward Island
Snowshoe hare, red fox, woodcock, Wilson's snipe, ruffed grouse, Hungarian partridge, ring-necked pheasant and *waterfowl*.

Quebec
White-tailed deer, *moose*, caribou, black bear, snowshoe hare, *ruffed grouse*, spruce grouse, sharp-tailed grouse, ptarmigan, Hungarian partridge and *waterfowl*.

Saskatchewan
Mule deer, white-tailed deer, *moose*, elk, caribou, antelope, black bear, cottontail rabbit, snowshoe hare, jack rabbit, fox, coyote, *waterfowl*, *sharp-tailed grouse*, ruffed grouse, spruce grouse, *Hungarian partridge*, pheasant and ptarmigan.

Yukon Territory
Black bear, grizzly bear, polar bear, *moose*, *caribou*, Dall sheep, Stone sheep, snowshoe hare, arctic hare, *grouse*, ptarmigan and *waterfowl*.

Federal, State and Provincial Agencies Concerned with Wildlife Protection and Exploitation

FEDERAL GOVERNMENT

Bureau of Sport Fisheries and Wildlife
Fish and Wildlife Service
Department of the Interior
18th and C Streets, N.W.
Washington, D.C. 20240

Environmental Protection Agency
401 M Street, S.W.
Washington, D.C. 20460

Forest Service
Department of Agriculture
Building E
Rosslyn Plaza
Rosslyn, Virginia 22209

Migratory Bird Conservation
    Commission
Department of the Interior Building
Washington, D.C. 20240

National Zoological Park
Smithsonian Institution
Adams Mill Rd.
Washington, D.C. 20009

STATE GOVERNMENTS

ALABAMA
Game and Fish Division
Department of Conservation and
    Natural Resources
64 North Union Street
Montgomery, Alabama 36104

ALASKA
Department of Fish and Game
Subport Building
Juneau, Alaska 99801

ARIZONA
Game and Fish Department
2222 West Greenway Road
Phoenix, Arizona 85023

ARKANSAS
Game and Fish Commission
Game and Fish Commission Building
Little Rock, Arkansas 72201

CALIFORNIA
Department of Fish and Game
Resources Agency
1416 Ninth Street
Sacramento, California 95814

Wildlife Conservation Board
Resources Agency
1416 Ninth Street
Sacramento, California 95814

COLORADO
Division of Wildlife
Department of Natural Resources
6060 Broadway
Denver, Colorado 80216

CONNECTICUT
Fish and Wildlife Unit
Department of Environmental
    Protection
State Office Building
165 Capitol Avenue
Hartford, Connecticut 06115

DELAWARE
Division of Fish and Wildlife
Department of Natural Resources and
    Environmental Control
Tatnall Building
Legislative Avenue and D Street
Dover, Delaware 19901

DISTRICT OF COLUMBIA
Department of Environmental Services
1875 Connecticut Avenue, N.W.
Washington, D.C. 20009

FLORIDA
Game and Fresh Water Fish
    Commission
Farris Bryant Building
620 South Meridian Street
Tallahassee, Florida 32304

GEORGIA
Game and Fish Division
Department of Natural Resources
270 Washington Street, S.W.
Atlanta, Georgia 30334

HAWAII
Fish and Game Division
Department of Land and Natural
    Resources
1179 Punchbowl Street
Honolulu, Hawaii 96813

IDAHO
Fish and Game Department
600 South Walnut
P.O. Box 25
Boise, Idaho 83707

ILLINOIS
Wildlife Resources Division
Department of Conservation
605 State Office Building
400 South Spring Street
Springfield, Illinois 62706

INDIANA
Fish and Wildlife Division
Department of Natural Resources
State Office Building
Indianapolis, Indiana 46204

Land, Forests, and Wildlife
Resources Advisory Council
Department of Natural Resources
State Office Building
Indianapolis, Indiana 46204

IOWA
Fish and Wildlife Division
Conservation Commission
300 Fourth Street
Des Moines, Iowa 50319

KANSAS
Forestry, Fish and Game Commission
P.O. Box 1028
Pratt, Kansas 67124

KENTUCKY
Department of Fish and Wildlife
    Resources
State Office Building Annex
Frankfort, Kentucky 40601

LOUISIANA
Game Division
Wildlife and Fisheries Commission
Box 44095
Capitol Station
Baton Rouge, Louisiana 70804

MAINE
Department of Inland Fisheries
    and Game
284 State Street
Augusta, Maine 04330

MARYLAND
Wildlife Administration
Department of Natural Resources
Tawes State Office Building
580 Taylor Avenue
Annapolis, Maryland 21401

MASSACHUSETTS
Department of Natural Resources
Leverett Saltonstall Building
100 Cambridge Street
Boston, Massachusetts 02202

MICHIGAN
Wildlife Division
Department of Natural Resources
Mason Building
Lansing, Michigan 48926

MINNESOTA
Game and Fish Division
Department of Natural Resources
Centennial Office Building
St. Paul, Minnesota 55155

MISSISSIPPI
Game and Fish Commission
Game and Fish Building
402 High Street
P.O. Box 451
Jackson, Mississippi 39205

MISSOURI
Game Division
Department of Conservation
2901 North Ten Mile Drive
P.O. Box 180
Jefferson City, Missouri 65101

MONTANA
Game Management Division
Department of Fish and Game
Helena, Montana 59601

NEBRASKA
Game and Parks Commission
2200 North 33rd Street
P.O. Box 30370
Lincoln, Nebraska 68503

NEVADA
Department of Fish and Game
P.O. Box 10678
Reno, Nevada 89510

NEW HAMPSHIRE
Game Management and Research
  Division
Department of Fish and Game
34 Bridge Street
Concord, New Hampshire 03301

NEW JERSEY
Wildlife Management Bureau
Fish, Game and Shellfisheries Division
Department of Environmental
  Protection
Labor and Industry Building
P.O. Box 1809
Trenton, New Jersey 08625

NEW MEXICO
Game Management Division
Department of Game and Fish
State Capitol
Sante Fe, New Mexico 87503

NEW YORK
Division of Fish and Wildlife
Department of Environmental
  Conservation
50 Wolf Road
Albany, New York 12233

NORTH CAROLINA
Wildlife Resources Commission
Albermarle Building
325 North Salisbury Street
P.O. Box 27687
Raleigh, North Carolina 27611

NORTH DAKOTA
Department of Game and Fish
2121 Lovett Avenue
Bismarck, North Dakota 58505

OHIO
Wildlife Division
Department of Natural Resources
1500 Dublin Road
Columbus, Ohio 43224

OKLAHOMA
Department of Wildlife Conservation
1801 North Lincoln Boulevard
P.O. Box 53465
Oklahoma City, Oklahoma 73105

OREGON
Wildlife Commission
1634 Southwest Alder Street
P.O. Box 3503
Portland, Oregon 97208

PENNSYLVANIA
Game Commission
P.O. Box 1567
Harrisburg, Pennsylvania 17120

RHODE ISLAND
Division of Fish and Wildlife
Department of Natural Resources
83 Park Street
Providence, Rhode Island 02903

SOUTH CAROLINA
Department of Wildlife Resources
1015 Main Street
P.O. Box 167
Columbia, South Carolina 29202

SOUTH DAKOTA
Department of Game, Fish and Parks
State Office Building No. 1
Pierre, South Dakota 57501

TENNESSEE
Game and Fish Commission
Ellington Agricultural Center
P.O. Box 40747
Nashville, Tennessee 37220

TEXAS
Fish and Wildlife Division
Parks and Wildlife Department
John H. Reagan State Office Building
Austin, Texas 78701

UTAH
Division of Wildlife Resources
Department of Natural Resources
1596 West North Temple
Salt Lake City, Utah 84116

VERMONT
Department of Fish and Game
Agency of Environmental Conservation
Montpelier, Vermont 05602

VIRGINIA
Commission of Game and Inland
  Fisheries
4010 West Broad Street
P.O. Box 11104
Richmond, Virginia 23230

WASHINGTON
Department of Game
600 North Capitol Way
Olympia, Washington 98501

WEST VIRGINIA
Division of Wildlife Resources
Department of Natural Resources
1800 Washington Street, East
Charleston, West Virginia 25305

WISCONSIN
Game Management Bureau
Forestry, Wildlife and Recreation
  Division
Department of Natural Resources
P.O. Box 450
Madison, Wisconsin 53701

WYOMING
Game and Fish Division
P.O. Box 1589
Cheyenne, Wyoming 82001

CANADA

ALBERTA
Alberta Fish and Wildlife Division
Natural Resources Building
9833 - 109th Street
Edmonton, Alberta T5K 2E1

BRITISH COLUMBIA
Environment and Land Use
  Commission
Parliament Building
Victoria, British Columbia V8V 1X4

Department of Land, Forest and
  Water Resources
Parliament Building
Victoria, British Columbia V8V 1X4

MANITOBA
Department of Lands, Forests and
Wildlife Resources
9-989 Century Street
Winnipeg, Manitoba R3H 0W4

NEWFOUNDLAND
Canadian Wildlife Service
Sir Humphrey Gilbert Building
Duckworth St.
St. John's, Newfoundland A1C 1G4

Department of Tourism
Wildlife Division
Confederation Building, 5th Floor
St. John's, Newfoundland

NORTHWEST TERRITORIES
Game Management Branch
Government of the Northwest
Territories
Yellowknife, Northwest Territories

NOVA SCOTIA
Department of Environment
Box 2107
Halifax, Nova Scotia

Department of Land and Forests
Dennis Building
Granville Street
Halifax, Nova Scotia

ONTARIO
Wildlife Branch
Ministry of Natural Resources
Whitney Block
Toronto, Ontario M7A 1W3

PRINCE EDWARD ISLAND
Department of Fish and Wildlife
Environmental Control Commission
Box 2000
Charlottetown, Prince Edward Island
C1A 7N8

Department of Environment and
Tourism
Box 2000
Charlottetown, Prince Edward Island
C1A 7N8

QUEBEC
Department of Tourism, Fish and
Game
150 St. Cyrille East - 15th Floor
Quebec, Quebec G1R 4Y3

SASKATCHEWAN
Department of Natural Resources
Fisheries and Wildlife Branch
Administrative Building
Regina, Saskatchewan S4S 0B1

YUKON TERRITORY
Game Branch
Government of the Yukon Territory
Whitehorse, Yukon Territory

Organizations and Associations of Interest to the Hunter and Shooter

AMATEUR TRAPSHOOTING ASSOCIATION
P.O. Box 246, West National Road   Phone: (513) 898-4638
Vandalia, Ohio 45377
David D. Bopp, General Manager
Founded 1923
Members: 100,000
Persons interested in the sport of trapshooting. Sanctions and determines rules governing shoots held by local, state, and provincial trapshooting associations: maintains permanent records for each shooter participating in 16 yard, handicap and doubles classifications in registered class competitions in state and provincial meets. Sponsor of Grand American Trapshooting Tournament held annually at Vandalia, Ohio, where historical exhibit and Hall of Fame are maintained. Publications: (1) *Trap and Field Magazine,* monthly; (2) *Official Trapshooting Rules,* annual; (3) *Trap and Field Official ATA Averages,* annual.

AMERICAN ASSOCIATION FOR CONSERVATION INFORMATION
Manitoba Dept. of Renewable   Phone: (204) 786-9495
Resources & Transportation Services
Box 22, 1495 St. James Street
Winnepeg, MB, Canada R3H OW9
Don Keith, President
Members: 68
Professional society of officials of state and provincial conservation agencies. Sponsors annual awards program whereby winners in various categories of conservation education work are selected by a panel of judges. Publications: (1) *Balance Wheel,* bimonthly; (2) *Yearbook.* Convention/Meeting: Annual — always June.

AMERICAN COMMITTEE FOR INTERNATIONAL CONSERVATION
c/o Natural Resources Defense   Phone: (202) 737-5000
Council, Inc.   Founded 1930
917 15th Street, NW   Affiliates: 20
Washington, D.C. 20005
Thomas B. Stoel, Secretary-Treasurer
A council of organizations concerned with international conservation of species and habitats. Serves as a national committee of the International Union for Conservation of Nature and Natural Resources (IUCN).

AMERICAN CONSERVATION ASSOCIATION
30 Rockefeller Plaza   **INACTIVE**
New York, N.Y. 10020
George R. Lamb, Executive Vice-President
Founded: 1958
Trustees: 11
Not a membership group. A private foundation established "to advance knowledge and understanding of conservation and to preserve and develop natural and living resources for public use, either directly or in cooperation with federal, state, local and private conservation agencies."

AMERICAN COON HUNTERS ASSOCIATION
Ingraham, Illinois 62434   Phone: (618) 752-6691
Floyd E. Butler, Secretary
Founded 1948
Members: 500

Persons interested in coon hunting. To promote and encourage the great sport of coon hunting; to seek to encourage proper practices of conservation of our raccoons and their natural habitats; to encourage the propagation of raccoons; to encourage liberation of live raccoons so that their numbers will increase rather than decrease; to promote and maintain friendly relations between land-owners and coon hunters, everywhere; to seek to restore decency and fairness in the sale of coonhounds, placing the ability to hunt, strike, trail and tree raccoons and stay treed, above all other qualities; to discourage the breeding of worthless ones; and so far as possible, place the coon-hunting fraternity upon the highest standard of sportsmanship so that it can pass on to posterity a sport unsurpassed in wholesome recreation, enjoyment, pleasure and delight. Convention/Meetings: World Championship for coon hounds held each year in October. Meeting held first day of World Championship.

AMERICAN DEFENSE PREPAREDNESS ASSOCIATION
1700 North Moore Street, Suite 900   Phone: (703) 522-1820
Arlington, Virginia 22209
Henry A. Miley Jr., President
Founded 1919
Members: 33,000
Staff: 25
Local groups: 48

Manufacturers, military personnel and engineers interested in industrial preparedness for the national defense of the United States. Divisions: Air Armament; Artillery; Chemical-Biological; Combat and Surface Mobility; Electronics; Fire Control; Management; Materials; Missiles and Astronautics; Packaging, Handling, and Transportability; Research; Small Arms Systems; Standards and Metrology; Technical Documentation; Underwater Ordnance; Cost and Value Management. Publications: (1) *Common Defense,* monthly newsletter; (2) *National Defense,* bimonthly magazine. Formerly: American Ordnance Association. Absorbed: (1965) Armed Forces Chemical Association; (1974) Armed Forces Management Association. Convention/Meeting: Annual—during May in Washington, D.C.

AMERICAN INSTITUTE OF BIOLOGICAL SCIENCES
1401 Wilson Boulevard   Phone: (703) 527-6776
Arlington, Virginia 22209
Arthur Gentile, Ph.D., Executive Director
Founded: 1947
Members: 9,000
Federation of professional biological associations and individuals with an interest in the life sciences. To promote unity and effectiveness of effort among persons engaged in biological research, teaching or application of biological data; to further the relationships of biological sciences to other sciences, the arts, and industries. Conducts symposium series; arranges for prominent biologists to lecture at small liberal arts colleges and radiation biologists to visit certain medical schools; provides advisory committees and other services to the Atomic Energy Commission, Office of Naval Research, and National Aeronautics and Space Administration. Created in 1966 on Office of Biological Education which serves as a clearing-house for information and conducts programs relative to several facets of biological education. Maintains placement service. Committees: Education; Environmental Biology; Exobiology; Hydrobiology; Microbiology; Oceanic Biology; Physiology; Public Responsibilities. Publications: Scientific Manpower Commission. Publications: (1) *BioScience,* monthly; (2) *Directory of Bioscience Departments and Facilities in the U.S. and Canada.*

AMERICAN PHEASANT AND WATERFOWL SOCIETY
Route 1   Phone: (715) 238-7291
Granton, Wisconsin 54436
Lloyd Ure, Secretary-Treasurer
Founded 1936
Members: 1,750
Hobbyists, aviculturists, zoos. To perpetuate all varieties of up-

land game, ornamental birds and waterfowl. Publications: (1) *Bulletin,* bimonthly; (2) *Membership Roster,* annual. Formerly: (1962) American Pheasant Society. Convention/Meeting: Annual.

AMERICAN PISTOL AND
REVOLVER ASSOCIATION, INC.   INACTIVE
512 East Wilson Avenue, Suite 301   Phone: (213) 247-1100
Glendale, California 91206
Elliott Stone Graham, President
Founded 1975
Members: 4500
Staff: 3
Officers and directors: 50
Regional groups: 3
Collectors of firearms, target shooters and individuals concerned about preserving the constitutional right to keep and bear arms. To inform and alert citizens on current anti-gun legislation, particularly owners of pistols and revolvers. To oppose legislation that would in any way infringe upon the ownership of handguns (pistols) and to oppose any candidate favoring such restrictions. Urges repeal of Federal Firearms Act of 1968. Publications: *Hot Pistol News* and *The Pistol Owners Legislative Handbook.* Convention/meeting: Biennial.

AMERICAN SECURITY COUNCIL
Washington Communications Center   Phone: (703) 825-8336
Boston, Virginia 22713
John M. Fisher, President
Founded 1955
Members: 300,000
Staff: 45
Corporations and individuals from all walks of life. Research and education in the field of national security. Publications: Monthly newsletter, *The Washington Report; American Security Council and Council Foundation,* quarterly journal.

ASSOCIATION OF AMERICAN ROD AND
GUN CLUBS, EUROPE OCPA
First Perscom APO MSD
New York, New York 09081
Lee E. Miethke, Executive Officer
Founded 1952
Members: 65,000
Local groups: 70
Federation of rod and gun clubs connected with American military forces in Europe, North Africa and the Near East. To encourage hunting, fishing, archery and allied sports; to promote the principles of sportsmanship and game conservation. Maintains library on conservation and European wildlife, with majority of books in German language. Publication: *Rod and Gun,* monthly. Convention/Meeting: Annual.

ASSOCIATIONS OF MIDWEST
FISH AND GAME COMMISSIONERS
Forestry, Fish and Game Commission   Phone: (316) 672-6473
Box 1028
Pratt, Kansas 67124
Fred Warders, Treasurer
Founded 1934
Members: 17
Fish and game commissioners and directors of 15 midwestern states and 3 Canadian provinces. Promotes conservation of wildlife and outdoor recreation. Sponsors Midwest Pheasant Council; Dove Committee. Committees: Federal-State Relations; Federal Aid; Legislation; Federal Farm Program; Wetlands. Publication: *Proceedings,* annual. Convention/Meeting: Annual.

BIG THICKET ASSOCIATION
Box 198   Phone: (713) 274-2971
Saratoga, Texas 77585
Gene Fiegelson, President
Founded 1964
Members: 1,350
Conservationists and others interested in preserving the wilderness area of southeast Texas known as the "Big Thicket." The Thicket is one of the major resting places along the Gulf Coast for migratory birds; in addition, at least 300 species live there permanently, many of them endangered species. Members of the Association have succeeded in having parts of the area declared a national biological preserve. Other activities include assisting scientists with research projects, operating a tourguide service, helping to maintain a Big Thicket Museum at Saratoga, Texas, a Big Thicket collection at the Lamar University Library in Beaumont, Tex., and coordinating programs aimed at preserving the area with other conservation organizations. Publication: *Big Thicket Bulletin,* quarterly; also publishes informational pamphlets, a bibliography and other materials. Convention/Meeting: Annual—always May or June, Saratoga, Tex.

BOUNTY INFORMATION SERVICE
c/o Stephens College Post Office   Phone: (314) 474-6967
Columbia, Missouri 65201
H. Charles Laun, Director
Founded 1965
Members: 2,000
Individuals interested in the removal of wildlife bounties in the U.S. and Canada. Organizes bounty removal programs, publishes literature on the bounty system and methods for removal, compiles yearly summary of bounties in North America and executes individual studies of areas (i.e. cougar bounty in Texas). Maintains library. Publications: *Bounty News,* 1-3/year; has also published *"Guide for the Removal of Bounties"* and *"A Decade of Bounties."* Convention/Meeting: Annual or Biennial.

BRIGADE OF THE AMERICAN REVOLUTION
The New Windsor Cantonment   INACTIVE
P.O. Box 207   Phone: (914) 561-1765
Vails Gate, New York 12584
Robert Showalter, Commander
Founded 1962
Members: 1000
Staff: 9
Units: 80
The men and women of the Brigade are dedicated to the authentic re-creation of soldier life during the period of the American Revolution. The Brigade fosters and encourages the exhibition and display of crafts and skills of the 18th century in general and specifically those closely relating to the life of the armies of the time. Each member regiment assumes the identity and organization of an original unit known to have participated in the Revolutionary War. All clothing, arms and equipment are researched for historical accuracy and no substitutions or modern materials are permitted. Various performances of a pageant-like nature are staged, usually at some historic site, involving military drills and exercises and demonstrations of camp life and craft skills designed to educate and entertain. Publications: Quarterly journal, *The Brigade Dispatch;* Monthly newsletter. Convention/Meeting: Brigade events commence in March and generally take place every other weekend through November.

CITIZENS COMMITTEE FOR THE RIGHT TO
KEEP AND BEAR ARMS
1601 114th SE, Suite 151   Phone: (206) 454-4911
Bellevue, Washington 98004
Alan M. Gottlieb, Chairman
Founded 1971
Members: 205,000
Staff: 24

A national independent non-profit mass membership organization concerned solely with preserving the right to keep and bear arms. The committee also maintains a public affairs office in the nation's capital (600 Pennsylvania Avenue, S.E., Suite 205). The Committee's National Advisory Council, made up of businessmen, educators, legislators, religious leaders, and includes 90 members of the U.S. Congress. Issues action bulletins, pro-gun rights brochures, bumper strips, decals, buttons and patches, and legislative action materials. Supported by membership fees and voluntary contributions. Publication: *Point Blank,* monthly.

CITIZENS COMMITTEE ON NATURAL RESOURCES
1000 Vermont Ave., N W   **INACTIVE**
Washington, D.C. 20005   Phone: (202) 638-3396
Spencer M. Smith, Jr., Executive Director
Founded 1954
Staff: 2
Individuals interested in lobbying in behalf of conservation program dealing with government departments.

COMPANY OF MILITARY HISTORIANS
North Main Street   Phone: (203) 399-9460
Westbrook, Connecticut 06498
Major William Reid, Administrator
Founded 1951
Members: 2,500
Staff: 4
Professional society of military historians, museologists, artists, writers, and private collectors interested in the history of American military units, organization, tactics, uniforms, arms, and equipment. Publications: (1) *Military Collector and Historian,* quarterly; (2) *Military Uniforms in America,* quarterly; (3) *Military Music in America* (records), irregular. Formerly: (1962) Company of Military Collectors and Historians. Convention/Meeting: Annual. Open to the public Mon.-Fri., 9-4.

CONSERVATION EDUCATION ASSOCIATION
c/o Robert A. Darula   Phone: (414) 465-2480
School University Programs   Members: 950
University of Wisconsin, Green Bay
Green Bay, Wisconsin 54302
Dr. Richard W. Presnell, Secretary-Treasurer
Founded 1947
Conservationists, educators and others interested in improving conservation education in public schools, teacher training institutions, and organization programs. Outstanding state, local and organizational conservation publications, especially those of normally limited distribution, are circulated bimonthly to members. Publications: (1) *Newsletter,* bimonthly; (2) *Proceedings,* annual. Formerly: (1953) National Committee on Policies in Conservation Education. Convention/Meeting: Annual – always August.

CONSERVATION FOUNDATION
1717 Massachusetts Avenue, NW   Phone: (202) 797-4300
Washington, D.C. 20036
William K. Reilly, President
Founded 1948
Staff: 50
Not a membership organization. Conducts research, education and information programs to develop knowledge, improve techniques, and stimulate public and private decision-making and action to improve the quality of the environment. Carries out environmental studies, demonstration planning programs, and offers a variety of conservation services at home and abroad. Publication: *CF Letter,* monthly; also publishes books, pamphlets, studies, guides, reports, and reprints.

CONSERVATION AND RESEARCH FOUNDATION
Box 1445   Phone: (203) 873-8514
Connecticut College
New London, Connecticut 06320
Richard H. Goodwin, President
Founded 1953
Not a membership organization. To encourage biological research and promote conservation of renewable natural resources. Makes research grants; offers Jeanette Siron Pelton Award for outstanding published contributions in experimental plant morphology. Publishes A *Five Year Report* (last one in 1978). Convention/Meeting: Annual.

CONSERVATION SERVICES
Massachusetts Audubon   Staff: 5
South Great Road
Lincoln, Massachusetts 01773
Wayne Hanley, Editor
Founded 1965
Members: 5
Small Audubon and conservation groups, comprising 34,000 individual members. Purpose is to publish magazines, newsletters and environmental brochures for New England conservation organizations, and to develop television, radio and audiovisual materials that can be used in New England. Maintains extensive source files. Publications: (1) *Massachusetts Audubon Society Newsletter,* 10/year; (2) *Man and Nature Yearbook,* quarterly. Formerly: Conservation Services Center.

DEFENDERS OF WILDLIFE
1244 19th Street, NW   Phone: (202) 659-9510
Washington, D.C. 20036
John W. Grandy, Executive Vice-President
Founded 1925
Members: 50,000
Persons interested in wildlife and conservation. To promote, through education and research, the protection and humane treatment of all mammals, birds, fish and other wildlife, and the elimination of painful methods of trapping, capturing and killing wildlife. Publication: *Defenders of Wildlife News,* bi-monthly. Formerly: Anti-Steel-Trap League; Defenders of Furbearers. Convention/Meeting: Semi-annual.

DESERT PROTECTIVE COUNCIL
P.O. Box 4294   Phone (714) 397-4264
Palm Springs, California 92263
Glenn Vargas, Executive Director
Founded 1954
Members: 700
Persons interested in safeguarding desert areas that are of unique scenic, scientific, historical, spiritual, and recreational value. Seeks to educate children and adults to a better understanding of the desert. Works to bring about establishment of wildlife sanctuaries for protection of indigenous plants and animals. The Desert Protective Council Education Foundation, a subdivision of the Council formed in 1960, handles educational activities and distributes reprints of desert and wildlife conservation articles. Publication: *El Paisano* (by Foundation), quarterly, and a yearly publication on a special topic. Convention/Meeting: Annual—Oct.

DUCKS UNLIMITED
P.O. Box 66300   Phone: (312) 299-3334
Chicago, Illinois 60666   Regional groups: 1,450
Dale E. Whitesell, Executive Vice President
Founded 1937
Members: 350,000
Staff: 65
State groups: 50
Conservationists in the United States and Canada interested in migratory waterfowl conservation. To restore or build natural

breeding habitats for migratory waterfowl primarily in the prairie provinces of Canada, which provides 80% of North America's wild geese and ducks. The American group raises funds for this construction and rehabilitation work, carried on by the field operating unit in Canada. Publications: (1) *Ducks Unlimited Magazine,* bi-monthly; (2) *Annual Report;* also publishes *The Ducks Unlimited Story.* Affiliated with: Ducks Unlimited (Canada). Absorbed: (1936) More Game Birds in America. Convention/Meeting: Annual.

FEDERATION OF WESTERN OUTDOOR CLUBS

208 Willard North   Phone: (415) 386-6544
San Francisco, California 94118
Winchell T. Hayward, President
Founded 1932
Members: 46
Outdoor clubs (41) in western United States with combined membership of 48,000, associate members 1300. Promotes conservation of forests, wildlife, and natural features. Publication: *Western Outdoor,* semi-annually. Convention/Meeting: Annual — always late August.

FIREARMS LOBBY OF AMERICA   INACTIVE

325 Pennsylvania Avenue S.E   Phone: (202) 547-1670
Washington, D.C. 20003
Morgan Norval, National Director
Founded 1968
Members: 18,000
A national, independent, voluntary, non-profit association of American citizens concerned with preserving their right to keep and bear arms. Publication: Quarterly newsletter, *Aim & Fire.*

FRIENDS OF THE EARTH

124 Speer Street   Phone: (415) 495-4770
San Francisco, California 94105
David Brower, Founder & Board Chairman
Founded 1969
Members: 25,000
Regional groups: 50
Not Man Apart, monthly newspaper.

FRIENDS OF NATURE, INC.

Brooksville, Maine 04617
Martin R. Haase, Executive Secretary
Founded 1953
Conservationists "dedicated to maintaining the balance of nature for the mutual benefit of man and his plant and animal friends." Carries on educational work and maintains several nature sanctuaries. Holds annual meeting.

FRIENDS OF THE WILDERNESS   INACTIVE

3515 East Fourth St.   Phone: (218) 724-7227
Duluth, Minn. 55804
William H. Magie, Exec. Sec.
Founded 1949
Members: 17,364
Persons interested in preservation of the Boundary Water Canoe Area of Minnesota, the wilderness canoe country of the Superior National Forest. Maintains library of 400 volumes pertaining to the area. Holds annual meeting.

GAME CONSERVATION INTERNATIONAL

900 NE Loop 410, Suite D-211   Phone: (512) 824-7509
San Antonio, Texas 78209
Bob Holleron, Executive Director
Founded 1967
Members: 1,000
Staff: 2
Individuals interested in wildlife conservation. Administers Hunters' Legal Defense Fund. Publications: *Hook n' Bullet,*

quarterly. Convention/Meeting: Biennial Hunters and Fishermen's Conservation Conference.

INTERNATIONAL ASSOCIATION OF WILDLIFE AGENCIES

1412 16th Street, NW   Phone: (202) 232-1652
Washington, D.C. 20036
Jack H. Berryman, Executive Vice President
Founded 1902
Members: 310
State and provincial game, fish and conservation departments (61) and officials (316). To educate the public to the economic importance of conserving natural resources and managing wildlife properly as a source of recreation and a food supply; to seek better conservation legislation, administration and enforcement. Publications: (1) *Proceedings,* annual; (2) *Newsletter,* bimonthly. Formerly: (1917) National Association of Game Commissioners and Wardens. Convention/Meeting: Annual — always second Monday in September.

INTERNATIONAL BENCHREST SHOOTERS

c/o Evelyn Richards   Staff: 1
411 North Wilbur Avenue
Sayre, Pennsylvania 18840
Robert A. White, President
Founded 1970
Members: 1,600
Gunsmiths, research engineers, gun writers, other interested persons. "To develop the ultimate in gun accuracy." Sponsors tournaments with demonstrations of new inventions or idea developments in the field. Also sponsors seminars. Publication: *Precision Shooting Magazine,* monthly. Convention/Meeting: Annual.

INTERNATIONAL UNION FOR CONSERVATION OF NATURE AND NATURAL RESOURCES

Founded 1948
Members: 449
International federation of national governments (39) and national and international organizations (393) in 97 countries. For the preservation of the natural environment of man and the conservation of the world's natural resources. Serves as a forum for discussion of conservation problems and studies; sponsors international youth camps; intercedes with governments on conservation matters; maintains Van Tienhoven Library. Conducts research on measures to promote and protect national parks, nature reserves, wildlife and its habitat. Provides advisory field missions. International headquarters located in Morges, Switzerland. Technical Commissions: Conservation Education; Ecology; Environmental Policy, Law and Administration; Landscape Planning; Law and Administration; National Parks and protected areas; Survival Service. Publications (must be ordered from Switzerland: (1) *IUCN Bulletin,* monthly; (2) *Proceedings* (of conferences); also publishes *Red Data Book* (endangered species), technical reports and a UN List of National Parks and Equivalent Reserves. Formerly: (1956) International Union for the Protection of Nature. General Assembly/Technical Meeting: Triennial.

INTERNATIONAL WILD WATERFOWL ASSOCIATION (IWWA)

Box 1075   Phone: (701) 252-1239
Jamestown, North Dakota 58401
Carl E. Strutz, Secretary
Founded 1958
Members: 500

Persons concerned with conservation and the preservation of wild waterfowl. Works toward protection, conservation and reproduction of any species considered in danger of eventual extinction; encourages the breeding of well known and rare species in captivity so that more people may learn about them by observation and enjoy them in the natural habitats created for this purpose. Has established Avicultural Hall of Fame. Publications: (1) *Bulletin,* bimonthly; (2) *Membership list,* annual; has published books on keeping cranes, wild geese, and wild ducks in captivity. Convention/Meeting: Annual

IZAAK WALTON LEAGUE OF AMERICA
1800 North Kent Street, Suite 806   Phone: (703) 528-1818
Arlington, Virginia 22209
Jack Lorenz, Executive Director
Founded 1922
Members: 53,000
Staff: 18
State divisions: 22
Local chapters: 450
Promotes means and opportunities for educating the public to conserve, maintain, protect and restore the soil, forest, water and other natural resources of the U.S. and promotes the enjoyment and wholesome utilization of those resources. Committees: Energy Resources, Environmental Education, Fish and Wildlife, Public Lands, Urban Environment, Water and Wetlands, Water Quality, and Youth. Publication: *Outdoor America.* Absorbed: (1962) Friends of the Land. Convention/Meeting: Annual — always July.

J.N. "DING" DARLING FOUNDATION
3663 Grand, Suite 608   Phone: (515) 255-9860
Des Moines, Iowa 50312
Sherry R. Fisher, Chairman
Founded 1962
Trustees: 36
"To initiate plans and to coordinate, guide and expedite programs, research and education which will bring about conservation and sound management of water, woods and soil; to restore and preserve historical sites; to create and assist in wildlife management plans; to improve and assure outdoor recreational opportunities for present and future generations." Established 1700-acre wildlife and waterfowl sanctuary on Sanibel Island, off the west coast of Florida. Awards scholarships at Iowa State University for wildlife management students. Named for the late J. N. "Ding" Darling, a professional cartoonist long active in conservation activities. Holds annual meeting.

LEAGUE TO SAVE LAKE TAHOE
Box 10110   Phone: (916) 541-5388
South Lake Tahoe, California 95731
Cameron W. Wolfe Jr., President
Staff: 2
Membership comprised of individuals and organizations who give financial support to the League. Purpose is to "do all things and to perform all acts necessary to keep Lake Tahoe blue and to protect and preserve the natural beauty and grandeur of the Lake Tahoe area of California and Nevada; to promote and encourage the concept that all developments, improvements and man-made changes of any kind, which may be required to accommodate the proper and desirable growth of the area and provide the maximum recreational values, should place primary emphasis on preserving the natural beauty of the lake." Publication: *Newsletter,* quarterly. Convention/Meeting: Annual.

NATIONAL AUDUBON SOCIETY
950 Third Avenue   Phone: (212) 832-3200
New York, New York 10022
Russell W. Peterson, President
Founded 1905

Members: 400,000
Local groups: 440
Affiliated groups: 146
Persons interested in conservation and restoration of natural resources, with emphasis on wildlife, wildlife habitats, soil, water, and forests. Sponsors four Audubon camps for teachers and youth leaders; nature lectures; and wildlife tours. Supports a force of 18 wardens to patrol wildlife refuge areas and sanctuaries; produces teaching materials for schools. Divisions: Educational Services; Lecture; Nature Centers; Research; Sanctuary; Service. Publications: (1) *Audubon Leader,* semimonthly; (2) *Audubon Magazine,* bimonthly; (3) *American Birds,* bimonthly; (4) *Nature Bulletins,* quarterly. Formerly: (1935) National Association of Audubon Societies for the Protection of Wild Birds and Animals, Inc. Convention/Meeting: Biennial.

NATIONAL BENCHREST SHOOTERS ASSOCIATION
5735 Sherwood Forest Drive   Phone: (216) 882-6877
Akron, Ohio 44319
Stella Buchtel, Secretary-Treasurer
Founded 1951
Rifle enthusiasts interested in precision shooting. Conducts registered shoots and certifies records. Sections: Bench Rest Rifle; Heavy Varmint; Light Varmint; Sporter Classes. Publication: *Rifle,* bimonthly. Holds annual directors' meeting.

NATIONAL BOARD FOR THE PROMOTION OF RIFLE PRACTICE
Forrestal Building West, Room 1E053   Phone: (202) 693-6460
Washington, D.C. 20314
Col. Jack R. Rollinger, Executive Officer
Founded 1903
Members: 25
Staff: 14
Local clubs: 2,100
Civilian shooting clubs and marksmanship clubs in high schools and colleges. An agency of the U.S. Department of the Army, "to promote marksmanship training with rifled arms among able bodied citizens of the U.S. and to provide citizens outside the active services of the Armed Forces with means whereby they may become proficient with such arms." Provides arms and ammunition to member clubs; exhibits national marksmanship trophies; maintains records and distributes awards for national and international marksmanship competitions. Publication: *National Board Directory.* Convention/Meeting: Annual—always Washington, D.C.

NATIONAL MUZZLELOADING RIFLE ASSOCIATION
Friendship, Indiana 47021   Phone: (812) 667-5131
Maxine Moss, Office Manager-Editor
Founded 1933
Members: 25,000
Regional groups: 350
Persons interested in black powder shooting. To preserve the heritage left to us by our forefathers, and to promote safety in the use of arms. Maintains National Range located at Friendship, Ind. Sponsors Beef Shoot in Jan., Spring Shoot, National Shoot in the fall, and Turkey Shoot in Oct. Committees: Long Range Planning; Property; Fund Raising; Range Officers; Grounds; Commercial Row; Traffic; Safety; Camping; Memorial; Public Relations; Scoring; Award. *Muzzle Blasts,* monthly. Convention/Meeting: Annual.

NATIONAL PRAIRIE GROUSE TECHNICAL COUNCIL
College of Natural Resources   Phone: (715) 346-3665
University of Wisconsin   Members: 120
Stevens Point, Wisconsin 55481   State groups: 17
Raymond K. Anderson, Chairman
Founded 1952

Sponsors biennial meeting for technical personnel and administrators of state, provincial and federal agencies, and individuals from private groups involved in preservation, research, and management of the prairie chicken and sharp-tailed grouse. Conference makes possible exchange of information on current research and management of these species and reviews local and national legislation affecting the prairie grouse resource. Publications: (1) *P.G. News,* semiannual; (2) *Proceedings,* biennial. Formerly: (1956) National Committee on the Prairie Chicken; (1961) Prairie Chicken Technical Committee. Conference: Biennial.

NATIONAL RIFLE ASSOCIATION OF AMERICA

1600 Rhode Island Avenue, NW   Phone: (202) 828-6000
Washington, D.C. 20036
Harlan B. Carter, Executive Vice President
Founded 1871
Members: 1,500,000
Staff: 275
State groups: 54
Local groups: 9,000
Target shooters, hunters, gun collectors, gunsmiths, police officers, and others interested in firearms. Promotes rifle, pistol, and shotgun shooting, hunting, gun collecting, hunter and home firearms safety, conservation, etc. Encourages civilian marksmanship in interests of national defense. Maintains national records of shooting competitions; sponors teams to compete in the Olympic Games and other world championships. Committees: Twenty-nine standing committees and four standing committees all with a charter of responsibilities to cover every phase of the shooting sport. Publications: (1) *The American Rifleman,* monthly; (2) *The American Hunter,* monthly; (3) *The American Marksman,* monthly. Other publications include a large variety of training, educational, and informational pamphlets, brochures, and pamphlets. Meeting. Annual—always April.

NATIONAL SHOOTING SPORTS FOUNDATION

1075 Post Road   Phone: (203) 637-3618
Riverside, Connecticut 06878
Arnold H. Rohlfing, Executive Director
Founded 1961
Members: 120
Staff: 10
Chartered to promote in the American public a better understanding and more active participation in the recreational shooting sports. Organizes the annual observance of National Hunting and Fishing Day. Prints and distributes over 3 million copies of various shooting and hunting/conservation publications. Write for catalog of publications.

NATIONAL SKEET SHOOTING ASSOCIATION

P.O. Box 28188   Phone: (512) 688-3371
San Antonio, Texas 78228
Ann Myers, Executive Director
Founded 1935
Members: 18,000
Staff: 11
State groups: 54
Local groups: 650
Amateur skeet shooters. Registers competitive shoots and supervises them through formulation and enforcement of rules. Publication: *Skeet Shooting Review,* monthly. Convention/Meeting (World Championship Shoot): Annual.

NATIONAL SPORTING GOODS ASSOCIATION

717 North Michigan Avenue   Phone: (312) 944-0205
Chicago, Illinois 60611
James L. Faltinek, Executive Director
Founded 1929

Members: 8,000
Staff: 50
Manufacturers, wholesalers, retailers, and importers of athletic equipment, sporting goods, and supplies. Provides data on cost-of-doing-business, store modernization, etc. Sponsors annual Gold Medal Award Program of the Sports Foundation for excellence in park and recreation management and in pollution control. Divisions: Athletic Goods Team Distributors; Awards Specialists; Outdoor Sports Stores; Ski Retailers International. Publications: (1) *Selling Sporting Goods,* monthly; (2) *Memo to Management,* monthly; (3) *NSGA Buying Guide,* annual; also publishes research and statistical studies. Convention/Meeting: Annual.

NATIONAL TRAPPERS ASSOCIATION

15412 Tau Road   Phone: (616) 781-3472
Marshall, Michigan 49068
Don Hoyt Sr., President
Founded 1959
Members: 10,000
State groups: 38
Trappers of animals for the purpose of selling skins and furs; fur dealers, outdoorsmen. Researches animal control techniques; compiles statistics. Committees: Conservation. Publications: *Voice of the Trapper,* quarterly. Convention/Meeting: Annual.

NATIONAL WATERFOWL COUNCIL

c/o Arizona Game and Fish Dept.   Phone: (602) 942-3000
222 West Greenway Road   States: 49
Phoenix, Arizona 85023
Harold F. Olson, Chairman
Founded 1952
Members: 50
State and provincial fish and game departments. To coordinate waterfowl planning, research, and management. Convention/Meeting: Semiannual—Mar. and Aug., held in conjunction with conventions of North American Wildlife Conference and Bureau of Sport Fish and Wildlife Service Waterfowl Regulations.

NATIONAL WILDLIFE FEDERATION

1412 16th Street, NW   Phone: (202) 797-6800
Washington, D.C. 20036
Thomas L. Kimball, Executive Vice President
Founded 1936
Members: 4,100,000
Staff: 400
Local groups: 6,500
Federation of 53 state conservation organizations and 1.1 million associate members, plus individual conservationist-contributors. Represents in its structure 3.6 million supporters. To encourage the intelligent management of the life-sustaining resources of the earth, and to promote a greater appreciation of these resources, their community relationship and wise use. Gives organizational and financial help to local conservation projects; annually awards fellowships for graduate study of conservation; publishes conservation-education teaching materials. Compiles and distributes annual survey of compensation in the fields of fish and wildlife management. Maintains library of conservation publications. Sponsors National Wildlife Week; many public service television and radio announcements. Activities are financed by sales of Wildlife Conservation Stamps and nature-related materials. Publications: (1) *Conservation Report,* weekly; (2) *Conservation News,* semimonthly; (3) *Ranger Rick's Nature Magazine,* 10/year; (4) *National Wildlife Magazine,* bimonthly; (5) *International Wildlife Magazine,* bimonthly; (6) *Conservation Directory,* annual; also publishes numerous free and lowcost conservation materials. Convention/Meeting: Annual.

NATURAL RESOURCES COUNCIL OF AMERICA

1025 Connecticut Ave., N.W. **INACTIVE**
Suite 914
Washington, D.C. 20036 Phone: (202) 293-3200
Hamilton K. Pyles, Exec. Sec.
Founded: 1946
Members: 47

Federation of national and regional conservation organizations and scientific societies interested in conservation of natural resources. Sponsors special natural resource studies and surveys. Committee: Scientific Advisory. Publications: (1) *Legislative News Service* (actions taken by Congress on natural resources), weekly; (2) *Executive News Service* (actions taken by Executive Branch on natural resources), weekly; also publishes books on selected natural resource topics. Convention/Meeting: Semi-annual—always held with North American Wildlife and Natural Resources Conference.

NEW ENGLAND ADVISORY BOARD
FOR FISH AND GAME PROBLEMS

115 Summit Avenue Phone: (401) 821-9096
West Warwick, Rhode Island 02839
Theodore Boyer, Secretary
Founded 1951
Members: 64,200

Sportsmen. To promote and improve conservation, hunting, fishing and recreation in New England. All New England states affiliated. Convention/Meeting: 3/year.

NORTH AMERICAN WILDLIFE FOUNDATION

709 Wire Building Phone: (202) 347-1774
Washington, D.C. 20005
L.R. Jahn, Secretary
Founded 1911
Trustees: 50
Contributing members: 400
Trustees: 30

"To insure, through financial support, the continuity of practical and systematic investigation into management practices and techniques throughout North America, to the end that the latest, most effective local, national, and international programs for wildlife and other natural resources will be adopted in the public interest." Foundation is not an action organization and does not attempt the actual mechanics of wildlife restoration; works through cooperating agencies, organizations, institutions. Owns Delta Waterfowl Research Station in Manitoba, Canada. Maintains library of 450 volumes on natural science subjects and wildlife restoration and management. Formerly: (1935) American Game Protective Association; (1946) American Wildlife Institute; (1951) American Wildlife Foundation.

NORTH-SOUTH SKIRMISH ASSOCIATION, INC.

Route 1, Box 226A Phone: (703) 635-5715
Bentonville, Virginia 22610
John L. Rawls, Executive Secretary
Founded 1950
Members: 3,400
Regional groups: 12
Local groups: 178

to promote marksmanship with the small arms and artillery of the Civil War era, fired in the original manner." Sponsors semi-annual national skirmishes at Ft. Shenandoah, Virginia and some 40 regional skirmishes throughout the eastern United States, in which competitors, dressed as were Union and Confederate soldiers, compete. Skirmishes feature: individual matches with muskets, carbines, and revolvers; 6-man artillery matches; 5-man team carbine matches; and 8-man musket matches. Publication: *The Skirmish Line,* bimonthly. Affiliated with: National Rifle Association of America. Convention/Meeting: Semi-annual.

OUTDOOR WRITERS ASSOCIATION OF AMERICA

4141 West Bradley Road Phone: (414) 354-9690
Milwaukee, Wisconsin 53209
Edwin W. Hanson, Executive Director
Founded 1927
Members: 1,450
Staff: 3

Professional organization of newspaper, magazine, radio, television, and motion picture writers and photographers (both staff and free-lance) on outdoor recreation and conservation. Gives awards for outstanding writing and films in the field; conducts surveys for educational and industrial organizations; compiles market data for writer members, and offers liaison aid in writer assignments. Committees: Awards; Educational and Scholarship; Ethics; Youth Program. Publications: (1) *Outdoors Unlimited,* monthly; (2) *Spotlight,* quarterly; (3) *Outdoor Writers' Association of America Directory;* also publishes *Communicating the Outdoor Experience.*

PACIFIC INTERNATIONAL TRAPSHOOTING
ASSOCIATION

3847 Glenwood Loop, SE Phone: (503) 364-1042
Salem, Oregon 97301
Gordon P. Hull, Secretary-Manager
Founded 1928
Members: 6,000

Sponsors state, provincial, international and individual registered trapshoots. "Grand Pacific Trapshoot"/Meeting: Annual, Reno, Nevada, mid July.

PHEASANT TRUST

Great Witchingham
Norwich, Norfolk, England
Philip Wayre, Honorary Director
Founded 1959
Members: 550
Staff: 3

Purposes are: to breed rare and threatened species of game birds for release in suitable reserves in their native lands; to maintain the world's largest collection of rare pheasants for education and scientific research; to promote the conservation of rare game birds throughout the world. Has received several first breeding awards from Agricultural Society of Great Britain. Publication: Annual report. Formerly: Ornamental Pheasant Trust.

PRAIRIE CHICKEN FOUNDATION

4122 Mineral Point Road Phone: (608) 233-5474
Madison, Wisconsin 53705
Paul J. Olson, President
Founded 1958

Persons dedicated to preservation of the prairie chicken in Wisconsin. Raises funds and acquires land to develop prairie chicken habitat in the state. Owns some 5000 acres, at a cost of $200,000; makes some purchases cooperatively with the Society Tympanuchus Cupido Pinnatus. Publication: *Prairie Chicken,* irregular.

RUFFED GROUSE SOCIETY

994 Broadhead Road, Suite 304 Phone: (412) 262-4044
Corapolis, Pennsylvania 15108 State chapters: 12
Samuel R. Pursglove Jr., Executive Director Local groups: 16
Founded 1961
Members: 4,300
Staff: 5

Ruffed grouse hunters; game biologists; conservationists. Actively supports ruffed grouse and woodcock research and habitat improvement. Cooperates with state conservation departments, paper and pulp industries, and strip mining companies in habitat improvement and encourages conservation measures. Endows research into ecological aspects of the ruffed grouse and woodcock. Publications: *The Drummer,* semi-monthly. Convention/Meeting: Annual.

SAFARI CLUB INTERNATIONAL
5151 East Broadway, Suite 1680   Phone: (602) 747-0260
Tuscon, Arizona 85711
Holt Bodinson, Administrative Director
Founded 1970
Staff: 12
Regional groups: 59
Members: Regular, 2200; associate, 4700; affiliate, 500,000
Staff: 9
Regional groups: 39
To promote good fellowship among those who love the outdoors and the sport of hunting. To promote the conservation of the wildlife of the world through selective trophy hunting of aged and infirm animals, leaving prime animals to procreate. To educate youth in the safe and proper use of firearms and to interest them in the conservation and preservation of forests and animals, our natural heritage. Publication: *Safari* magazine. Convention/Meetings: Annual convention in Las Vegas; quarterly director's meetings; monthly chapter meetings.

SAINT HUBERT SOCIETY OF AMERICA
Dean Witter Reynolds, Inc.   Phone: (212) 986-3180
5 World Trade Center
New York, New York 10006
Thomas C. Keister Jr., President
Founded 1958
Members: 100
Individuals interested in wildlife, conservation, hunting, and the lore of the outdoors. "Dedicated to the promulgation of conservation, hunting, fishing, and the preservation of the great American heritage of the outdoors and those traditions of sportsmanship and fair play which have become associated with the American way of life." Sponsors outings for members including shoots, hunts, and fishing expeditions. Named in honor of the patron saint of hunters who was born in Belgium in the middle of the seventh century. Similar organizations have been in existence in Europe since the eighth century. Meet bimonthly.

SHOOTERS CLUB OF AMERICA   INACTIVE
591 Camino de la Reina, Suite 200
San Diego, California 92108
Founded 1963
Hunters, shooters, gun dealers, collectors, industry personnel, and others interested in "protecting the fundamental right of citizens to keep and bear arms and in combatting restrictive anti-gun legislation on local, state, and national levels." Conducts educational and public relations program on behalf of gun sportsmen and in support of "pro-gun" legislation.

SIERRA CLUB
530 Bush Street   Phone: (415) 981-8634
San Francisco, California 94108
Michael McCloskey, Executive Director
Members: 183,000
Staff: 130
Regional chapters: 325
All who feel the need to know more of nature, and know that this need is basic to man. "To protect and conserve the natural resources of the Sierra Nevada, the United States and the World; to undertake and publish scientific and educational studies concerning all aspects of man's environment and the natural ecosystems of the World; and to educate the people of the United States and the World to the need to preserve and restore the quality of that environment and the integrity of those ecosystems." Works on urgent campaigns to save threatened areas, wildlife, and resources; conducts annual environmental workshops for educators; schedules wilderness outings; presents awards; maintains library. Chapters and committees schedule talks, films, exhibits, and conferences. Committees: Economics; Energy; Environmental Education; Environmental Research; Forest Practices; International Environment; Mountaineering; National Land Use; National Water Resources; Native American Issues; Outings; Population; Wilderness; Wildlife and Endangered Species. Departments: Conservation; Outings. Publications: (1) *National News Report,* weekly; (2) *Sierra Club Bulletin,* monthly; (3) *Ascent,* Sierra Club mountaineering journal, annual; also publishes books and produces films, posters, and exhibits. Member of: United Nations (with non-government organization status). Convention/Meeting (Wilderness Conference): Biennial.

SOCIETY FOR THE PRESERVATION OF BIRDS OF PREY
c/o Encyclopedia of Associations   Members: 250
Gale Research Co.   Staff: 1
Book Tower
Detroit, Michigan 48226
Founded 1966
Professional ornithologists, bird watchers, and raptor enthusiasts. Seeks to stress the value of birds of prey (raptors) and to encourage their protection; disseminates information and promotes communication among members; discourages harvesting of raptorial birds for purposes of falconry and research; denounces caging, selling and trading, display, or exhibition of the birds; urges reasonable and biologically sound pest control measures and supports abolition of accumulative, wide-target insecticides. Publications: *The Raptor Report,* 3/year; also publishes numerous bulletins and pamphlets. Formerly: (1966) Palisades Hawking Club.

SOCIETY OF TYMPANUCHUS CUPIDO PINNATUS
433 East Michigan   Phone: (414) 271-6755
Milwaukee, Wisconsin 53202
Robert T. Foote, President
Founded 1960
Sportsmen dedicated to preserving the prairie chicken and to "doing so with humor, excellent taste, and efficiency—at the same time having a bit of fun along the way." (The prairie chicken or prairie hen, also called a pineated grouse, is a game bird of the northern hemisphere, related to the pheasant and having mottled plumage. The Society calls itself by the scientific name for the prairie chicken.) Members' contributions are used to buy land for prairie chicken habitat, specifically to add acres to the Buena Vista Reservation in Portage County, Wisconsin. As of June, 1971, the Society had bought over 6300 acres of land, which is leased to the Wisconsin Conservation Department for clearing, restoration, and maintenance on chicken range. Only other organized activity is an annual cocktail party and business meeting held in December in Milwaukee where many of the members live. Publications: (1) *Boom,* quarterly; (2) *Membership Roll.*

SOUTHEASTERN ASSOCIATION OF FISH AND WILDLIFE AGENCIES
P.O. Box 40747   Phone: (615) 741-1431
Nashville, Tennessee 37204
Gary T. Myers, Secretary-Treasurer
Directors of state game and fish commissions in 16 southern states. To protect the right of jurisdiction of southeastern states over their wildlife resources on public and private lands; study state and federal wildlife legislation and regulations as they affect the area; consult with and make recommendations to federal wildlife and public land agencies on federal management programs and programs involving federal aid to southeastern states; serve as a clearing house for exchange of ideas on wildlife management and resarch techniques. Sponsors statistical studies at North Carolina.

SPORTING ARMS AND AMMUNITION MANUFACTURERS' INSTITUTE, INC.
420 Lexington Avenue   Phone: (212) 986-6920
New York, New York 10017
Harry L. Hampton Jr., Executive Director
Founded 1926
Members: 13
Staff: 4

Manufacturers of sporting firearms, ammunition and powder. Promotes shooting sports, safe handling of firearms, technical research, etc. Committees: Legislative and Legal Affairs; Promotional Guidance; Internat'l Trade; Traffic; Technical. Meeting: Semi-annual.

UNITED STATES REVOLVER ASSOCIATION
59 Alvin Street   Phone: (413) 734-5725
Springfield, Massachusetts 01104
Stanley A. Sprague, Executive Secretary
Founded 1900
Members: 1,350
Staff: 2

To foster and develop revolver and pistol shooting; to establish and preserve records; and to encourage and conduct pistol matches between members and clubs of this country as well as marksmen of other countries. Publication: *U.S. Handgunner,* bimonthly. Convention/Meeting: Annual—always Springfield, Mass.

WATERFOWL ADVISORY COMMITTEE   INACTIVE
Group of thirteen national organizations interested in waterfowl management. Meets each Aug. in Washington, D.C. to hear reports on the status of waterfowl, and to recommend annual hunting regulations to the director of Bureau of Sports Fisheries and Wildlife of U.S. Department of the Interior.

WESTERN ASSOCIATION OF STATE GAME AND FISH COMMISSIONERS
Box 25   Phone: (208) 384-3771
Boise, Idaho 83707
Robert L. Salter, Secretary-Treasurer
Founded 1922
Members: 16

Officials of state and provincial game and fish agencies of western states and provinces. Promotes fish and game conservation in West. Publication: *Proceedings of WASGFC,* annual. Convention/Meeting: Annual.

WILDERNESS SOCIETY
1901 Pennsylvania Avenue, NW   Phone: (202) 293-2732
Washington, D.C. 20006
William A. Turnage, Executive Director
Founded 1935
Members: 55,000
Staff: 35

Persons interested in preserving wilderness through educational programs, scientific studies, and cooperation with local and state citizen organizations in resisting the destruction of wildland resources and wildlife. Conducts leadership training programs for citizen conservationists. Sponsors book award program for young people. Sponsors "A Way to the Wilderness" trip program. Publication: *Living Wilderness,* quarterly; also publishes *Wilderness Reports,* notices, and conservation alerts on critical conservation issues. Convention/Meeting: Semi-annual.

WILDLIFE MANAGEMENT INSTITUTE
709 Wire Building   Phone: (202) 347-1774
Washington, D.C. 20005
Daniel A. Poole, President
Founded 1946
Staff: 18

To promote better management and wise utilization of all renewable natural resources in the public interest. Publications: (1) *Outdoor News Bulletin,* biweekly; (2) *Transactions of Annual North American Wildlife and Natural Resources Conference* (and cumulative index); also publishes various books and monographs. Holds annual conference.

WILDLIFE SOCIETY
7101 Wisconsin Avenue, NW, Suite 611   Phone: (301) 986-8700
Washington, D.C. 20014
Richard N. Denney, Executive Director
Founded 1937
Members: 7,500
Regional groups: 7

Professional society of wildlife biologists and others interested in resource conservation and wildlife management on a sound biological basis. Publications: (1) *Journal of Wildlife Management,* quarterly; (2) *Wildlife Society Bulletin,* quarterly; (3) *Wildlife Monographs,* irregular. Formerly: (1937) Society of Wildlife Specialists. Convention/Meeting: Annual—held with North American Wildlife and Natural Resources Conference.

WORLD WILDLIFE FUND
1601 Connecticut Avenue, NW   Phone: (202) 387-0800
Washington, D.C. 20009
Russel E. Train, President
Founded 1961
Staff: 28

Supported by contributions from individuals, funds, corporations, and foundations with a concern for conservation of wildlife and its habitat. Emphasizes preservation of endangered and vanishing species of wildlife, plants, and natural areas anywhere in the world. Makes grants for land acquisition, habitat protection and maintenance and scientific ecological research around the globe. Support is given existing conservation societies, agencies, and governments to carry out projects and services. Maintains small library. Committee: Scientific Advisory. Affiliated with: World Wildlife Fund International, and International Union for Conservation of Nature and Natural Resources, both headquartered at Morges, Switzerland. Holds quarterly board meetings. WWF includes 26 national affiliates.

(NOTE: Organizations and associations which are national in scope and who desire to be listed in this directory should send detailed information about themselves in the format shown here. Address: The Editor, SHOOTER'S BIBLE, 55 Ruta Court, South Hackensack, NJ 07606.)

The Shooter's Bookshelf

EXPLANATION OF A TYPICAL ENTRY

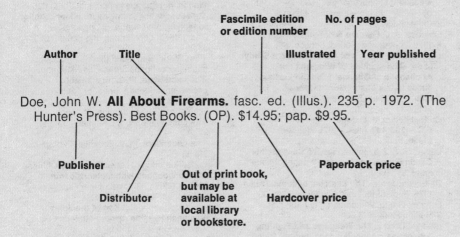

Doe, John W. **All About Firearms.** fasc. ed. (Illus.). 235 p. 1972. (The Hunter's Press). Best Books. (OP). $14.95; pap. $9.95.

- Author
- Title
- Fascimile edition or edition number
- No. of pages
- Illustrated
- Year published
- Publisher
- Distributor
- Out of print book, but may be available at local library or bookstore.
- Hardcover price
- Paperback price

AIR GUNS

Bowyer, Chaz. **Guns in the Sky: The Air Gunners of World War Two.** (Illus.). Date not set. Scribner's. $14.95.

Fanta, Ladd & Lewis, Jack. **Airgun Digest.** 1977. pap. DBI Books. $6.95.

Wesley, L. **Air Guns and Air Pistols.** new and enl. ed. (Illus.). 1977. A. S. Barnes. $9.95.

Carden, G. V., rev. by. **Air-Guns and Air-Pistols.** (Illus.). 208 p. 1980. A. S. Barnes. $14.50.

AMMUNITION

Central Intelligence Agency. **CIA Ammunition and Explosives Supply Catalog.** (Illus.). 1975. pap. Paladin Press. $7.95.

—**CIA Explosives for Sabotage Manual.** (Illus.). 1975. pap. Paladin Press. $5.95.

Guns and Ammo Magazine Editors, ed. **Guns and Ammo Annual, 1981.** (Illus.). 320 p. 1980. pap. Petersen Publishing. $6.95.

Labbett, Peter. **Military Small Arms Ammunition of the World, 1945-1980.** (Illus.). 160 p. 1980. Presidio Press. $18.95.

Matunas, Edward. **American Ammunition and Ballistics.** (Illus.). 1979. Winchester Press. $12.50.

Parkerson, Codman. **A Brief History of Bullet Moulds.** Pioneer Press. $1.75.

Sears & Roebuck Ammunition Catalog. (Illus.). pap. Sand Pond. $1.50.

Steindler, R. A. **Reloader's Guide.** 3rd ed. (Illus.). 1975. softbound. Stoeger. $7.95.

Suydam, Charles R. **U.S. Cartridges and Their Handguns: 1795-1975.** (Illus.). 1978. Beinfeld. (OP). $14.95; pap. $9.95.

Warner, Ken. **Handloader's Digest Bullet and Powder Update.** 96 p. 1980. Follett. pap. $4.95.

Williams, Mason. **The Law Enforcement Book of Weapons, Ammunition and Training Procedures: Handguns, Rifles and Shotguns.** (Illus.). 1977. C. C. Thomas. $32.50.

Wootters, John. **The Complete Book of Practical Handloading.** (Illus.). 1977. softbound. Stoeger. $6.95.

—**The Complete Book of Practical Handloading.** (Illus.). 1976. Winchester Press. $12.50.

ANTELOPES

Bere, Rennie. **Antelopes.** (Illus.). 1971. Arco. (OP). $3.95.

Bronson, Wilfrid S. **Horns and Antlers.** (Illus.). 1942. Harcourt Brace Jovanovich. $4.95.

Caton, John D. **The Antelope and Deer of America: A Scientific Treatise Upon the Natural History, Habits, Affinities and Capacity for Domestication of the Antilocapra and Cervidae of North America.** (Illus.). 1974. Repr. Arno Press. $22.00.

Chace, G. Earl. **Wonders of the Pronghorn.** (Illus.). (gr 3-7). 1977. Dodd, Mead & Co. $5.95.

ANTI-TANK GUNS

Chamberlain, Peter & Gander, Terry. **Anti-Tank Weapons.** (Illus.). 1975. Arco. (OP). $5.95; pap. $3.95.

—**Self Propelled Anti-Tank and Anti-Aircraft Guns.** (Illus.). 1975. pap. Arco. $3.95.

Foss, Christopher. **Jane's Pocket Book of Towed Artillery.** 1979. pap. Macmillan. $7.95.

Hoffschmidt, Edward J. & Tantum, William H. **German Tank and Antitank of World War Two.** 1968. Paladin Enterprises. $12.50.

ARCHERY

American Alliance for Health, Physical Education & Recreation. **Archery: A Planning Guide for Group and Individual Instruction.** 1972. pap. AAHPER. (OP). $4.25.

—**Archery Selected Articles, 1971.** pap. AAHPER. $.60.

Annarino, A. **Archery: Individualized Instructional Program.** 1973. pap. P-H. $2.75.

Archery. 1976. pap. British Book Center. $2.50.

Archery-Fencing Guide 1978-80. 1978. pap. AAHPER. $2.50.

Ascham, Roger. **Toxophilus, the Schole of Shootinge,** 2 bks. 1969. Repr. of 1545 ed. Walter J. Johnson, Inc. $25.00.

—**Toxophilus, 1545.** Arber, Edward, ed. 1971. Repr. of 1895 ed. Scholarly Press. $17.00.

Barrett, Jean **Archery.** 3rd ed. 1980. Goodyear. $5.95.

Barrett, Jean A. **Archery.** 2nd ed. 1973. pap. Goodyear. $5.50.

Barrington, Daines. **Archery in England.** pap. British American Books. $3.95.

Bear, Fred. **Archer's Bible.** (Illus.). 1980. pap. Doubleday. $3.95.

—**Fred Bear's World of Archery.** (Illus.). 1979. Doubleday. $14.95.

Burke, Edmund. **Archery.** (Illus.). 1963. pap. Arc Books. $1.75.

Burke, Edmund H. **Archery Handbook.** (Illus.). 1954. Arco. $4.95.

—**Archery Handbook.** 1976. pap. Arco. $2.95.

—**Field and Target Archery.** (Illus.). 1961. Arco. $4.00.

—**History of Archery.** 1971. Repr. of 1957 ed. Greenwood Press. $15.75.

Butler, David F. **The New Archery.** rev. ed. (Illus.). 1973. A. S. Barnes. $6.95.

Campbell, Donald W. **Archery.** 1970. pap. Prentice-Hall. $3.95.

Ford, Horace A. **Archery, Its Theory and Practice.** 1971. Repr. of 1856 ed. George Shumway Publisher. $10.00.

Foy, Tom. **Archery.** 1976. pap. Charles River Books. $2.50.

—**Beginner's Guide to Archery.** Transatlantic Arts, Inc. (OP). $8.75.

Gillelan, G. Howard. **Complete Book of the Bow and Arrow.** rev. ed. 1977. Stackpole Books. $9.95.

—**Archery at Home: How to Practice Daily and Stay Sharp for Target Shooting, Field Archery, and Bowhunting.** (Illus.). 1980. McKay, David, Co. $10.95.

Health, E. G. **Archery. The Modern Approach.** rev. 2nd ed. (Illus.). 1978. Faber & Faber. $12.95; pap. $6.50.

—**A History of Target Archery.** (Illus.). 1974. A. S. Barnes. $9.95.

Helgeland, G. **Archery World's Complete Guide to Bowhunting.** (Illus.). 1975. Prentice-Hall. $8.95; pap. $3.95.

Helgeland, Glenn. **Archery World's Complete Guide to Bowhunting.** 1977. Prentice-Hall. $8.95; pap. $3.95.

Herrigel, Eugen. **Zen in the Art of Archery.** 1971. pap. Random House. $1.95.

Hochman, Louis. **Complete Archery Book.** (Illus.). 1957. Arco. $4.95.

Hodgkin, Adrian E. **The Archer's Craft.** 2nd ed. (Illus.). 1974. (Pub. by Faber & Faber). Merrimack Book Service. $22.00.

Hougham, Paul. **Encyclopedia of Archery.** (Illus.). 1957. A. S. Barnes. $6.95.

Johnson, Dewayne J. & Oliver, Robert A. **Archery.** 51 p. 1980. pap. text ed. American Press. $2.95.

—**Archery.** (Illus.). 51 p. (Orig.). 1980. pap. text ed. American Press. $2.95.

Klann, Margaret L. **Target Archery.** 1970. pap. Addison-Wesley. $7.50.

Latham, J. D., ed. **Saracen Archery.** (Illus.). Saifer, Albert, Pub. $30.00.

Laubin, Reginald & Laubin, Gladys. **American Indian Archery.** (Illus.). 1980. University of Oklahoma Press. $12.50.

Laycock, George & Bauer, Erwin. **Hunting with Bow and Arrow.** 1965. Arco. $3.95.

Learn, C. R. **Bowhunter's Digest.** 1974. Follett. pap. $6.95.

Lewis, Jack, ed. **Archer's Digest.** 2nd ed. (Illus.). 1977. pap. Follett. $7.95.

McKinney, Wayne C. **Archery.** 4th ed. 1980. pap. Brown, William C., Co. $3.25.

Markham, Gervase. **The Art of Archerie.** facs. ed. 1968. Repr. of 1634 ed. George Shumway Publisher. $15.00.

Mosely, Walter M. **An Essay on Archery.** 1976. Charles River Books. $17.50.

Neade, William. **The Double Armed Man.** facs. ed. (Illus). 1971. George Shumway Publisher. $10.00.

Niemeyer, Roy K. & Zabik, Roger. **Beginning Archery.** 3rd ed. 1978. pap. Wadsworth Publisher. $3.95.

Pszczola, Lorraine. **Archery.** 2nd ed. (Illus). 1976. pap. Holt, Rinehart & Winston. $3.95.

Reichart, N. & Keasey, G. **Archery.** 3rd ed. (Illus). 1961. Ronald Press. (OP) $5.95.

Richardson, M.E. **Archery.** 1975. pap. McKay, David, Co. (OP) $2.95.

Roberts, Daniel. **Archery for All.** 1976. David & Charles. (OP) $4.95.

Smith, Mike. **Archery.** 1978. Arco. $6.95.

Stamp, Don. **Archery—an Expert's Guide.** pap. Wilshire Book Co. $2.00.

——**Archery: An Expert's Guide.** pap. Borden. $2.00.

——**Challenge of Archery.** (Illus). 1971. International Pubns. Service. $16.50.

——**The Challenge of Archery.** 2nd ed. (Illus). 1980. Transatlantic Arts, Inc. $16.95.

——**Field Archery.** (Illus). 1980. Transatlantic Arts, Inc. $12.95.

Richardson, Margherita E. **Teach Yourself Archery.** rev. ed. (Illus). 1979. pap. McKay, David, Co. $3.50.

Tinsley, Russell. **Bow Hunter's Guide.** (Illus). 1975. softbound. Stoeger. $5.95.

Williams, John. **Archery for Beginners.** (Illus). 1976. pap. Contemporary Books. $5.95.

With Stick & String: Adventures with Bow and Arrow. (Illus). Avery Color Studios. $4.95.

Wood, Sir William. **The Bowman's Glory or Archery Revived.** 1976. Charles River Books. $7.50.

Wood, Sir William. **The Bowman's Glory or Archery Revived.** Repr. of 1969 ed. Ridgeway Books. $10.00.

ARMS AND ARMOR

Albion, Robert G. **Introduction to Military History.** (Illus). 1971. Repr. of 1929 ed. AMS Press. $29.00.

American Machines & Foundry Co. **Acoustic Study Program.** (Illus). 1972. pap. Paladin Press. $7.95.

Archer, Denis, ed. **Jane's Infantry Weapons 1977.** 1977. Watts, Franklin, Inc. $72.50.

——**Jane's Infantry Weapons 1978.** 1978. Watts, Franklin, Inc. $72.50.

Ashdown, Charles H. **Armour and Weapons in the Middle Ages.** (Illus). Saifer, Albert, Publisher. $18.00.

——**British and Continental Arms and Armour.** (Illus). Peter Smith. $9.00.

——**British and Continental Arms and Armour.** (Illus). 1970. pap. Dover. $4.00.

Barker, A. J. **Russian Infantry Weapons of World War Two.** 1971. Arco. $3.50.

Barnes, Duncan. **History of Winchester Firearms, Eighteen Sixty-Six to Nineteen Eighty.** rev. ed. (Illus). 1980. Winchester Press. $21.95.

Bearse, Ray. **Sporting Arms of the World.** 1977. Harper & Row. $15.95.

Berenstein, Michael. **The Armor Book.** (Illus). 1979. McKay, David, Co. $6.95.

Birla Institute of Scientific Research, Economic Research Division & Agarwal, R. J. **Defense Production and Development.** 1978. Verry, Lawrence, Co. $7.50.

Brassey's Infantry Weapons of the World. 2nd ed. 1978. Crane-Russak Co. $47.50.

Brodie, Bernard & Brodie, Fawn M. **From Crossbow to H-Bomb.** rev. ed. (Illus). 1973.

Indiana University Press. $10.00; pap. $2.95.

Central Intelligence Agency. **CIA Special Weapons Supply Catalog.** (Illus). 1975. pap. Paladin Enterprises. $5.95.

Chappelear, Louis E. **Japanese Armor Makers.** 1978. Hawley, W. M. (OP) $25.00.

Collier, Basil. **Arms and the Men: The Arms Trade and Governments.** (Illus). 1980. (Pub. by Hamish Hamilton England). David & Charles. $35.00.

Cormack, A. J. **German Small Arms.** (Illus). 1979. International Pubns. Service. $20.00.

Cowper, H. S. **The Art of Attack: Being a Study in the Development of Weapons and Appliances of Offense, from the Earliest Times to the Age of Gunpowder.** (Illus). 1977. Repr. of 1906 ed. Rowman & Littlefield, Inc. $21.50.

Curtis, Howard M. **European Helmets, 800 B.C.–1700 A.D.** (Illus). 1978. Beinfeld. (OP) $19.95.

Daniel, Larry J. & Gunter, Riley W. **Confederate Canon Foundries.** Pioneer Press, ed. Pioneer Press. $17.95.

De Gheyn, Jacob. **The Exercise of Arms.** (Illus). 1976. Repr. of 1607 ed. Arma Press. $65.00.

Diagram Group. **Weapons.** (Illus). 1980. St. Martin's Press. $25.00.

Draeger, Donn F. **The Weapons and Fighting Arts of the Indonesian Archipelago.** (Illus). 1972. C. E. Tuttle. (OP) $12.50.

Elgood, Robert, ed. **Islamic Arms and Armour.** (Illus). 1979. Biblio Distribution Center. $175.00.

Featherstone, Donald. **Weapons and Equipment of the Victorian Soldier.** (Illus). 1978. (Pub. by Blandford Press England). Sterling. $14.95.

Feist, Uwe. **Aero-Armor Series, Vol. 12.** 52 p. (gr. 7-12). 1980. pap. Aero Press. $3.95.

Ffoulkes, Charles & Hopkinson, E. C. **Sword, Lance & Bayonet.** (Illus). 1967. Arco. (OP) $7.50.

Ffoulkes, Charles J. **Armourer and His Craft.** (Illus). 1967. Repr. of 1912 ed. Arno Press. $18.50.

Finlay, Ian H. & Bann, Stephen. **Heroic Emblems.** (Illus). 1978. pap. Z Press. $3.50.

Fitzsimons, Bernard, ed. **The Illustrated Encyclopedia of Twentieth Century Weapons and Warfare.** (Illus). 1978. Purnell Reference Books. $249.50.

Foss. **Armour and Artillery 1979-1980.** 1980. Franklin Watts, Inc. $99.50.

——**Combat Support Equipment 1980-1981.** 1980. Franklin Watts, Inc. $125.00.

Foss, Christopher. **Infantry Weapons of the World.** 1977. Scribner's. $7.95.

Frost, H. Gordon. **Blades and Barrels: Six Centuries of Combination Weapons.** Walloon Press. $16.95; deluxe ed. $25.00; presentation ed. $50.00.

Funcken, Liliane & Funcken, Fred. **Arms and Uniforms: Lace Wars, Pt. 1.** 1978. Hippocrene Books. $17.95.

——**Arms and Uniforms: Lace Wars, Pt. 2.** 1978. Hippocrene Books. $17.95.

——**Arms and Uniforms —Ancient Egypt to the Eighteenth Century.** Hippocrene Books. $11.95.

——**Arms and Uniforms—Late Eighteenth Century to the Present Day.** Hippocrene Books. (OP) $11.95.

——**Arms and Uniforms—the First World War, Pt. 1.** Hippocrene Books. (OP) $11.95.

——**Arms and Uniforms—the First World War, Pt. 2.** Hippocrene Books. (OP) $11.95.

——**Arms and Uniforms—The Napoleonic Wars, Pt. 1.** Hippocrene Books. (OP) $11.95.

——**Arms and Uniforms—The Napoleonic Wars, Pt. 2.** Hippocrene Books. (OP) $11.95.

——**Arms and Uniforms—the Second World War, Pt. 1.** Hippocrene Books. (OP) $11.95.

——**Arms and Uniforms—the Second World War, Pt. 2.** Hippocrene Books. (OP) $11.95.

——**Arms and Uniforms—the Second World War, Pt. 3.** Hippocrene Books. (OP) $11.95.

——**Arms and Uniforms—the Second World War, Pt. 4.** Hippocrene Books. (OP) $11.95.

——**British Infantry Uniforms from Marlborough to Wellington.** (Arms and Uniforms Ser.) (Illus). 1977. pap. Hippocrene Books. (OP) $4.95.

——**First World War, 2 pts.** (Illus). 1974. International Pubns Service. $12.50/ea.

——**The Lace Wars, Pt. 1.** (Illus). 1977. International Pubns Service. $17.50.

——**The Lace Wars, Pt. 2.** (Illus). 1977. International Pubns Service. $17.50.

——**The Lace Wars, Pt. 1.** Beekman Publishers. $13.95.

——**The Lace Wars, Pt. 2.** Beekman Publishers. $13.95.

Gettens, Rutherford J., et al. **Two Early Chinese Bronze Weapons with Meteoritic Iron Blades.** (Illus). 1971. pap. Freer Gallery of Art, Smithsonian Institution. $5.00.

Grancsay, Steven V. **Catalog of the John Woodman Higgins Armory Museum.** (Illus). Mowbray Co. (OP) $10.00.

Gruzanski, C. V. **Spike and Chain.** Wehman Brothers, Inc. $5.25.

Guthman, William, ed. **Guns and Other Arms.** (Illus). 1980. pap. Mayflower Books. $7.95.

Halbritter, Kurt. **Halbritter's Arms Through the Ages: An Introduction to the Secret Weapons of History.** (Illus). 1979. Viking Press. $9.95.

——**Halbritter's Arms Through the Ages: An Introduction to the Secret Weapons of History.** Muir, Jamie, tr. (Illus). 1980. pap. Penguin Books. $5.95.

Hamilton, T. M. **Firearms on the Frontier: Guns at Fort Michilimackinac 1715-1781.** Armour, David A., ed. (Illus). 1976. pap. Mackinac Island State Park Commission. $3.00.

Hart, Harold H., ed. **Weapons and Armor.** 1977. Hart. (OP) $23.95; pap. $7.95.

Hawley, W. M. **Introduction to Japanese Swords.** 1973. pap. Hawley, W. M. $3.00.

Held, Robert, ed. **Arms and Armor Annual.** 1973. pap. DBI Books. $9.95.

Hoff, Arne. **Feuerwaffen.** 2 vols. (Illus). 1976. Arma Press. Set $95.00.

Hogg, I. V. **Military Pistols and Revolvers.** (Illus). 1970. pap. Arco. $1.95.

Hogg, Ian. **Military Small Arms of the Twentieth Century.** 1973. pap. Follett. (OP) $7.95.

Hughes, B. P. **Firepower: Weapon Effectiveness on the Battlefield, 1630-1815.** (Illus). 1974. Scribner's. (OP) $12.50.

Hulton, A. **Sword and the Centuries.** Wehman Brothers, Inc. $8.50.

International Institute for Strategic Studies. **Military Balance 1980-1981.** 1980. Facts on File. $17.95.

Jane's Infantry Weapons: 1980. Date not set. Franklin Watts, Inc. $95.00.

Jane's Weapon Systems: 1980-81. 11th ed. Date not set. Franklin Watts, Inc. $99.50.

Johnson, Thomas M. **Collecting the Edged Weapons of the Third Reich,** 2 vols. Bradach, Wilfrid, tr. (Illus). T. M. Johnson. Vol. 1: $18.50; pap. $10.00. Vol. 2: $18.50.

——**Collecting the Edged Weapons of the Third Reich.** Vol. 3. Bradach, Wilfrid, tr. (Illus). 1979. T. M. Johnson. $20.00.

——**Wearing the Edged Weapons of the Third Reich.** Brodach, Wilfrid, tr. (Illus). 1977. pap. T. M. Johnson. $10.00.

Johnson, Thomas M. & Bradach, Wilfrid. **Third Reich Edged Weapons Accounterments.** (Illus). 1978. pap. T. M. Johnson. $10.00.

Joly, H. L. **Naunton Collection of Japanese Sword Fitting.** 1973. Repr. of 1912 ed. Hawley, W. M. $50.00.

Journal of the Arms and Armour Society. Vol. 1. (Illus). 1970. George Shumway Publisher. $12.00.

Keller, May L. **The Anglo-Saxon Weapon Names, Treated Archaeologically and Etymologically.** 1967. Repr. of 1906 ed. International Pubns Service. $30.00.

Kelly, Francis M. & Schwabe, Randolph. **Short History of Costume and Armour, Chiefly in England 1066-1800.** 2 vols. in 1. (Illus). 1968. Repr. of 1931 ed. Arno Press. $16.00.

—**A Short History of Costume and Armour 1066-1800,** 2 vols in 1. (Illus). 1972. Arco. $12.50.

Laking, Guy F. **A Record of European Armour and Arms Through Seven Centuries,** 5 vols. (Illus). Repr. AMS Press. set. $295.00.

Lindsay, Merrill. **The Lure of Antique Arms.** (Illus). 1978. softbound. Stoeger. $5.95.

—**Miniature Arms.** (Illus). 1976. Arma Press. (OP). $7.95.

—**Twenty Great American Guns.** (Illus). 1976. pap. Arma Press. $1.75.

Long, Franklin A. & Reppy, Judith, eds. **The Genesis of New Weapons: Decision Making for Military R&D.** 1980. Pergamon Press. $22.50.

Mango, Karin. **Armor: Yesterday and Today.** (Illus). (gr. 4 up). 1980. Messner, Julian. $8.29.

Mason, Richard O. **Use of the Long Bow with the Pike.** 1970. limited ed. George Shumway Publisher. $10.00.

Matunas, Edward. **Handbook of Metallic Cartridge Reloading.** (Illus). 1980. Winchester Press. $14.95.

Mavrodin, Valentin, compiled by. **Fine Arms from Tula.** (Illus). 1978. Harry N. Abrams, Inc. $28.50.

Milton, Roger. **Heralds and History.** (Illus). 1978. Hippocrene Books. $14.95.

Mowbray, E. Andrew, ed. **Arms-Armor: From the Atelier of Ernst Schmidt, Munich.** (Illus). 1967. Mowbray Co. $15.00.

Moyer, Frank A. **Special Forces Foreign Weapons Handbook.** (Illus). 1970. Paladin Press. $15.95.

Neal, W. Keith & Back, D. H. **Great British Gunmakers 1740-1790: The History of John Twigg and the Packington Guns.** (Illus). 1975. Biblio Distribution Center. $80.00.

Norman, A. V. & Pottinger, Don. **History of War and Weapons 449-1660: English Warfare from the Anglo-Saxons to Cromwell.** Orig. Title: **Warrior to Soldier: 449-1660.** 1967. T. Y. Crowell. $7.95.

Owen, J. I. ed. **Brassey's Infantry Weapons of the World 1975.** (Illus). 1975. Westview Press. (OP). $39.50.

—**Brassey's NATO Infantry and Its Weapons.** 1976. Westview Press. (OP). $14.50.

—**Brassey's Warsaw Pact Infantry and Its Weapons: Defence Publications.** 1976. Westview Press. $17.00.

Peterson, Harold L. **The American Sword. 1775-1945.** (Illus). 1977. Riling, Ray, Arms Books. $18.50.

Pretty, Ronald T., ed. **Jane's Weapon Systems.** 1976. Watts, Franklin, Inc. $72.50.

—**Jane's Weapon Systems 1977-78.** (Illus). 1977. Watts, Franklin, Inc. $72.50.

Reid, William. **Arms Through the Ages.** (Illus). 1976. Harper & Row. $39.95.

Robinson, H. Russell. **The Armour of Imperial Rome.** (Illus). 1974. Scribner's. $17.50.

Royal United Services Institute for Defense Studies, ed. **International Weapon Developments: A Survey of Current Developments in Weapon Systems,** 4th ed. (Illus). 1980. pap. Pergamon Press. $13.25.

Rusi & Brassey's Defense Yearbook. 1978/79. 89th ed. 1979. Crane-Russak Co. $27.50.

Sampson, Anthony. **The Arms Bazaar: From Lebanon to Lockheed.** 1978. pap. Bantam Books. $2.95.

Schreir, Konrad F., Jr. **Marble Knives and Axes.** (Illus). 1978. pap. Beinfeld. $4.95.

Schroeder, Joseph J., Jr. ed. **Arms of the World: 1911.** pap. DBI Books. $5.95.

Schuyler-Hartley-Graham Military Furnishers. **Illustrated Catalog Arms and Military Goods.** facs. ed. (Illus). 1864. Flayderman, N. & Co. $9.50.

Seitz, Heribert. **Blankwaffen,** 2 vols. (Illus). 1976. Arma Press. set. $90.00.

Shepperd, G. A. **A History of War and Weapons, 1660-1918.** (Illus). 1972. T. Y. Crowell. $7.95.

Snodgrass, A. M. **Arms and Armour of the Greeks.** (Illus). 1967. Cornell University Press. $22.50.

Stephens, Frederick J. **Edged Weapons, a Collector's Guide.** (Illus). 1977. (OP). Hippocrene Books. $14.95.

Tantum, W. V. & Hoffschmidt, E. J., eds. **German Combat Weapons of World War II.** 1968. Sycamore Island Books. $12.95.

Thomas, B., et al. **Armi e Armature Europee.** (Illus., Lt.). 1964. Arma Press. $64.50.

Thomas, Donald S. **U.S. Silencer Patents,** 2 vols. new ed. Brown, Robert K. & Lund, Peder C., eds. (Illus). 1973. Paladin Press. Incl. Vol. 1. 1888-1935. $15.95; Vol. 2. 1936-1972. $15.95. Set. $29.95.

Traister, John. **Learn Gunsmithing: The Troubleshooting Method.** (Illus). 1980. Winchester Press. $12.95.

Truby, J. David. **Silencers, Snipers and Assassins.** Brown, Robert K. & Lund, Peder C., ed. (Illus). 1972. Paladin Press. $17.95.

—**Quiet Killers.** (Illus). 1972. Paladin Press. $6.95; pap. $6.00.

U.S. Army Foreign Science & Technology Center, Washington, D.C. **Typical Foreign Unconventional Warfare Weapons.** 1976. Paladin Press. pap. $4.00.

U.S. Army Munitions Command. **Silencers: 1896.** (Illus). 1971. Paladin Press. $10.95; pap. $6.95.

U.S. Army Sniper Training Manual. (Illus.) 1975. Paladin Press. $12.95.; pap. $8.95.

Vangen, Roland D. **Indian Weapons.** (Illus). 1972. Filter Press. $4.50; pap. $1.50.

Von Mellenthin, F. W. **Panzer Battles: A Study of the Employment of Armor in the Second World War.** Turner, L. C., ed. Betzler, H., tr. (Illus). 1971. University of Oklahoma Press. $14.50.

Werner, E. T. **Chinese Weapons.** Wehman Brothers, Inc. $3.50.

—**Chinese Weapons.** Alston, Pat, ed. (Illus). 1972. pap. Ohara Pubns. $3.50.

West, Bill. **Junior Arms Library 1849-1970.** 5 vols. West, Bill. Set. $98.00.

—**U.S.A. Arms Manufacturers Catalogues, 1877-1900.** 3 vols. West, Bill. Set. $30.00.

Wilkinson-Latham, Robert. **Swords and Other Edged Weapons.** (Illus). 1978. Arco. $8.95; pap. $5.95.

Williams, John. **Atlas of Weapons and War.** 1976. John Day. $12.95.

Wintringham, Thomas H. **Story of Weapons and Tactics.** facs. ed. 1943. Arno Press. $16.00.

Woikinson, Frederick. **World War I Weapons and Uniforms.** (Illus). Beekman Publishers. $10.95.

Yumoto, J. M. **Samurai Sword.** Wehman Brothers, Inc. $9.50.

ARTILLERY

Archer, Denis, ed. **Jane's Pocket Book of Naval Armament.** (Illus). 1976. pap. Macmillan. $5.95.

Batchelor, John. **Artillery.** 1973. pap. Ballantine Books. $4.95.

Batchelor, John H. & Hogg, Ian. **Artillery.** (Illus). 1972. Scribner's. $9.95.

Behrend, Arthur. **As from Kemmel Hill.** (Illus). 1975. Repr. of 1963 ed. Greenwood Press. $13.00.

Bidwell, R. G., ed. **Brassey's Artillery of the World: Defence Publications.** 1977. Westview Press. (OP). $39.50.

Bourne, William. **The Arte of Shooting in Great Ordnaunce.** 1969. Repr. of 1587 ed. W. J. Johnson. $13.00.

Chamberlain, Peter & Gander, Terry. **Heavy Artillery.** (Illus). 1975. pap. Arco. $3.95.

Foss, Christopher. **Artillery of the World.** 2nd ed. (Illus). 1976. Scribner's. $8.95.

— **Jane's Pocket Book of Towed Artillery.** 1979. pap. Macmillan. $7.95

Gibbon, John, ed. **Artillerist's Manual.** Repr. of 1860 ed. Greenwood Press. $29.50.

Hogg, Ian. **Artillery in Color: 1920-1963.** (Illus). 1980. Arco. $11.95; pap. $7.95.

— **Guns, 1939-45.** 1976. pap. Ballantine Books. $2.50.

Hogg, Ian V. **British & American Artillery of World War Two.** (Illus). 1979. Hippocrene Books. $24.95.

Hogg, O. F. **Artillery: Its Origin, Heyday and Decline.** (Illus). 1970. Shoe String Press. $17.50.

Hughes, B. P. **Firepower: Weapon Effectiveness on the Battlefield, 1630-1815.** (Illus). 1974. Scribner's. (OP). $12.50.

Macchiavelli, Niccolo. **The Arte of Warre (Certain Waies of the Orderyng of Souldiours).** Whitehorne, P., tr. 1969. Repr. of 1562 ed. W. J. Johnson. $42.00.

Marsden, E. W. **Greek & Roman Artillery: Technical Treatises.** 1971. Oxford University Press. $18.95.

Norton, Robert. **The Gunner, Showing the Whole Practise of Artillerie.** 1973. Repr. of 1628 ed. W. J. Johnson. $40.00.

Patrick, John M. **Artillery & Warfare During the Thirteenth & Fourteenth Centuries.** 1961. pap. Utah State University Press. $3.00.

Rogers, H. B. **A History of Artillery.** (Illus). 1974. Citadel Press. $7.95.

Rogers, H. C. **A History of Artillery.** 1977. pap. Citadel Press. $4.95.

Simienowicz, Casimir. **The Great Art of Artillery.** 1976. Charles River Books. $20.00.

—**The Great Art of Artillery.** Chevlet, George, tr. from Fr. 1973. Repr. of 1729 ed. British Book Center. (OP). $17.95.

Tousard, Louis De. **American Artillerists Companion.** 3 vols. 1809-1813. Repr. Set. Greenwood Press. $106.00.

BALLISTICS

Matunas, Edward. **American Ammunition and Ballistics.** (Illus). 1979. Winchester Press. $12.50.

Wilber, Charles G. **Ballistic Science for the Law Enforcement Officer.** (Illus). 1977. C. C. Thomas. $30.00.

—**Forensic Biology for the Law Enforcement Officer.** (Illus). 1974. C. C. Thomas. $24.25.

Williams, M. **Practical Handgun Ballistics.** 1980. C. C. Thomas. $17.50.

BAYONETS

Carter, Anthony. **The History and Development of the Sword, Sabre and Knife Bayonet.** 1974. Scribner's. $3.95.

Carter, J. Anthony. **Allied Bayonets of World War Two.** (Illus.). 1969. Arco. $3.50.

Hardin, Albert N. **The American Bayonet: 1776-1964.** (Illus.). 1977. Hardin. $24.50.

Stephens, Frederick J.A. **A Collector's Pictorial Book of Bayonets.** (Illus.). 1976. pap. Hippocrene Books. $3.95.

BIRD DOGS

Brown, William F. **National Field Trial Champions, 1956-1966.** (Illus.). 1966. A. S. Barnes. $12.00.

Davis, Henry P. **Training Your Own Bird Dog.** rev. ed. (Illus.). 1970. Putnam. $8.95.

Evans, George Bird. **Troubles with Bird Dogs and What to Do About Them: Training Experiences with Actual Dogs Under the Gun.** (Illus.). 1975. Winchester Press. $10.00.

Falk, John R. **The Complete Guide to Bird Dog Training.** 1976. Winchester Press. $10.95.

---**The Practical Hunter's Dog Book.** (Illus.). 1975. softbound. Stoeger. $5.95.

Long, Paul. **All the Answers to All Your Questions About Training Pointing Dogs.** (Illus.). 1974. pap. Capital Bird Dog Enterprises. $4.95.

Mueller, Larry. **Bird Dog Guide.** rev. ed. (Illus.). 1976. softbound. Stoeger. $6.95.

Seminatore, Mike & Rosenburg, John M. **Your Bird Dog and You.** (Illus.). 1977. A. S. Barnes. $9.95.

Webb, Sherman. **Practical Pointer Training.** (Illus.). 1974. Winchester Press. $6.95.

BLACK POWDER GUNS

Buchele, William & Shumway, George. **Recreating The American Longrifle.** Orig. Title: Recreating The Kentucky Rifle. (Illus.). 1973. pap. George Shumway Publisher. $10.00.

Lauber, George. **How to Build Your Own Flintlock Rifle or Pistol.** Seaton, Lionel, tr. from Ger. (Illus.). 1976. pap. Jolex. $6.95.

---**How to Build Your Own Percussion Rifle or Pistol.** Seaton, Lionel, tr. from Ger. (Illus.). 1976. pap. Jolex. $6.95.

---**How to Build Your Own Wheellock Rifle or Pistol.** Seaton, Lionel, tr. from Ger. (Illus.). 1976. Jolex. $6.95.

Lewis, Jack & Springer, Robert, eds. **Black Powder Gun Digest,** 2nd ed. (Illus.). 1977. pap. DBI Books. $7.95.

National Muzzle Loading Rifle Association. **Muzzle Blasts: Early Years Plus Vol. I & II. 1939-41.** 1974. pap. George Shumway Publisher. (OP). $15.00.

Nonte, George C., Jr. **Black Powder Guide.** 2nd ed. (Illus.). 1976. softbound. Stoeger. $7.95.

---**Home Guide to Muzzle Loaders.** (Illus.). 1974. pap. Stackpole Books. $6.95.

Steindler, R. A., ed. & illus. **Shooting the Muzzle Loaders.** (Illus.). 1975. Jolex. $11.95; pap. $6.95.

BOW AND ARROW

Barwick, Humphrey. **Concerning the Force and Effect of Manuall Weapons of Fire.** 1974. Repr. of 1594 ed. W. J. Johnson. $8.00.

Hamilton, T. M. **Native American Bows: Their Types and Relationships.** (Illus.). 1972. George Shumway Publisher. (OP). $10.00.

Hardy, Robert. Longbow: **A Social and Military History.** (Illus.). 1977. Arco. (OP). $19.95.

Mason, Richard O. **Use of the Long Bow with the Pike.** 1970. limited ed. George Shumway Publishers. $10.00.

Murdoch, John. **Study of the Eskimo Bows in the U.S. National Museum.** facs. ed. (Illus.). Repr. of 1884 ed. pap. Shorey. $2.00.

A New Invention of Shooting Fireshafts in Long-Bowes. 1974. Repr. of 1628 ed. W. J. Johnson. $3.50.

Pope, Saxton T. **Bows and Arrows.** 1974. University of California Press. $12.50.

Smythe, John. **Bow Versus Gun.** 1974. Repr. of 1590 ed. text ed. British Book Center. (OP). $17.50.

Tinsley, Russell. **Bow Hunter's Guide.** (Illus.). 1975. softbound. Stoeger. (OP). $5.95.

CARIBOU

Georgeson, C. C. **Reindeer & Caribou.** facs. ed. (Illus.). Repr. of 1904 ed. pap. Shorey. $1.50.

Murie, Olaus J. **Alaska Yukon Caribou.** facs. ed. (Illus.). 1935. pap. Shorey. (OP). $10.00.

Rearden, Jim. **Wonders of Caribou** (gr. 5 up). 1976. Dodd, Mead & Co. $5.95.

CARTRIDGES

Barnes, Frank. **Cartridges of the World.** 4th ed. 1980. pap. Follett. $9.95.

Bartlett, W. A. & Gallatin, D. B. **B and G Cartridge Manual.** Pioneer Press. $2.00.

Datig, Fred A. **Cartridges for Collectors,** 3 vols. Borden. $7.50 ea.

Nonte, George. **The Home Guide to Cartridge Conversions.** rev. ed. Gun Room Press. $12.95.

Steindler, R. A. **Reloader's Guide.** 3rd ed. (Illus.). 1975. softbound. Stoeger. $7.95.

Suydam, **American Cartridge.** Borden. $8.50.

Suydam, Charles R. **U.S. Cartridges and Their Handguns: 1795-1975.** (Illus.). 1978. DBI Books. (OP). $14.95; pap. $9.95.

Thomas, Gough. **Shotguns and Cartridges for Game and Clays.** 3rd ed. (Illus.). 1976. Transatlantic Arts, Inc. $15.00.

Treadwell. **Cartridges, Regulation and Experimental.** Pioneer Press. $2.00.

Whelen, Townsend. **Why Not Load Your Own?** (Illus.). A. S. Barnes. $7.95.

COLLECTING

Chapel, Charles E. **The Gun Collector's Handbook of Values: 1980-81.** 13th rev. ed. (Illus.). 1979. Coward, McCann and Geoghegan. $16.95; pap. $8.95.

Liu, Allan J., ed. **The American Sporting Collector's Handbook.** (Illus.). 1977. softbound. Stoeger. $5.95.

COLT REVOLVERS

Bady, Donald B. **Colt Automatic Pistols,** rev. ed. 1973. Borden. $15.00.

Barnard, Henry. **Armsmear: The Samuel Colt Biography.** (Illus.). 1978. Beinfeld. (OP). $24.95.

Keating, Bern. **The Flamboyant Mr. Colt and His Deadly Six-Shooter.** 1978. Doubleday. $9.95.

Larson, E. Dixon. **Colt Tips.** Pioneer Press. $3.95.

McClernan, John B. **Slade's Wells Fargo Colt.** (Illus.). 1977. Exposition Press. (OP). $5.00.

Serven, James E. **Firearms from Eighteen Thirty-Six.** 1979. Stackpole Books. $22.95.

Shumaker, P. L. **Colt's Variations of the Old Model Pocket Pistol.** 1957. Borden. $8.95.

Smith, Loren W. **Home Gunsmithing: The Colt Single Action Revolvers.** (Illus.). 1971. Ray Riling, Arms Books. $7.95.

Swayze, Nathan L. **Fifty One Colt Navies.** (Illus.). 1967. Gun Hill. $15.00.

Virgines, George. **Saga of the Colt Six Shooter: And the Famous Men Who Used It.** 1969. Fell, Frederick, Publishers. $7.95.

Wilson, R. L., **The Book of Colt Engraving.** 1978. Follett. (OP). $39.95.

CROSSBOWS

Bilsom, Frank. **Crossbows.** (Illus.). 1975. Hippocrene Books. (OP). $8.95.

Payne-Gallwey, R. **Crossbow.** Newbury Books Inc. (OP). $27.50.

Payne-Gallwey, Ralph. **Cross-Bow, Medieval and Modern.** Saifer, Albert, Pub. $30.00.

Wilbur, C. Martin. **History of the Crossbow.** (Illus.). Repr. of 1936 ed. pap. Shorey. $1.50.

DECOYS

Barber, Joel. **Wild Fowl Decoys.** (Illus.). pap. Dover. $6.00.

---**Wild Fowl Decoys.** (Illus.). Peter Smith. $12.50.

Becker, A. C., Jr. **Decoying Waterfowl.** (Illus.). 1973. A. S. Barnes. (OP). $12.00.

Berkey, Barry R., et al. **Pioneer Decoy Carvers: A Biography of Lemuel and Stephen Ward.** (Illus.). 1977. Cornell Maritime, Press. $17.50.

Brown, Ercil. **Thrills of the Duck Hunt for the Officebound.** (Illus.). 1973. Dorrance. (OP). $2.50.

Casson, Paul W. **Decoy-Collecting Primer.** (Illus.). pap. Eriksson, Paul S., Pubs. $5.95.

Connett, Eugene. **Duck Decoys.** 1980. Durrell. $12.50.

Coykendall, Ralf. **Duck Decoys and How to Rig Them.** (Illus.). 1965. Holt, Rinehart & Winston. $7.95.

Decoys. (Illus.). 1974. Applied Arts. (OP). $1.50.

Delph, John & Delph, Shirley. **Factory Decoys of Mason Stevens.** (Illus.). Schiffer. $35.00.

Earnest, Adele. **The Art of the Decoy.** (Illus.). 1965. Crown. $10.00.

Fleckenstein, Henry A. **Decoys of the Mid-Atlantic Region.** (Illus.). 1979. Schiffer. $19.95.

Frank, Charles W., Jr. **Louisiana Duck Decoys.** 1979. Pelican. $24.95.

Humphreys, John. **Hides, Calls and Decoys.** (Illus.). 1979. pap. International Pubns. Service. $7.50.

Johnsgard, Paul A. ed. **The Bird Decoy: An American Art Form.** (Illus.). 1976. University of Nebraska Press. $17.95.

Le Master, Richard. **Wildlife in Wood.** 1978. Model Technology, Inc. $19.95.

MacKay, William F., Jr. & Colio, Quinton. **American Bird Decoy.** (Illus.). 1979. Repr. of 1965 ed. Schiffer. $19.95.

MacKay, William, Jr. **American Bird.** (Illus.). 1979. Repr. of 1965 ed. Schiffer. $19.95.

McKinney, J. Evans. **Decoys of the Susquehanna Flats and Their Makers.** 1979. pap. Holly Press. $12.95.

Murphy, Charles F. **Working Plans for Working Decoys.** (Illus.). 1979. Winchester Press. $12.50.

Parmalee, Paul W. & Loomis, Forrest D. **Decoys and Decoy Carvers of Illinois.** 1969. pap. Northern Illinois University Press. $25.00.

Starr, George. **Decoys of the Atlantic Flyway.** 1974. Winchester Press. $19.95.

Starr, George R., Jr. **How to Make Working Decoys.** 1978. Winchester Press. $15.00.

Webster, David S. & Kehoe, William. **Decoys at Shelburne Museum.** 1961. pap. Shelburne Museum, Inc. $7.50.

DEER HUNTING

Anderson, Luther A. **Hunting The Uplands with Rifle and Shotgun.** (Illus.). 1977. Winchester Press. $10.00.

Bauer, Erwin A. **The Digest Book of Deer Hunting.** (Illus.). 1979. pap. Follett. $2.95.

Cartier, John O. **The Modern Deer Hunter.** (Illus.). 1977. T. Y. Crowell. $10.95.

Conway, Bryant W. **Successful Hints on Hunting White Tail Deer.** 2nd ed. 1967. pap. Claitors. $1.98.

Dalrymple, Byron W. **Complete Book of Deer Hunting.** (Illus.). 1975. softbound. Stoeger. $6.95.

——**Complete Book of Deer Hunting.** 1973. Winchester Press. $8.95.

Dickey, Charley. **Charley Dickey's Deer Hunting.** (Illus.). 1977. pap. Oxmoor House. $3.95.

Donovan, Robert E. **Hunting Whitetail Deer.** (Illus.). 1978. Winchester Press. $12.50.

Elman, Robert, Ed. **All About Deer Hunting in America.** 1976. Winchester Press. $12.95.

Hayes, Tom. **How to Hunt the White Tail Deer.** A.S. Barnes. rev. ed. $8.95; pap. $6.95

Hewett, H. P. **Fairest Hunting: Hunting and Watching Exmoor Deer.** 1974. British Book Center. $4.95.

——**The Fairest Hunting.** (Illus.). J. A. Allen. $3.25.

James, M. R. **Bowhunting: For Whitetail and Mule Deer.** 1976. Jolex. $10.95; pap. $6.96.

Kittredge, Doug & Wambold, H. R. **Bowhunting for Deer.** rev. ed. 1978. Stackpole Books. $8.95.

Koller, Lawrence, R. **Shots at Whitetails.** rev. ed. (Illus.). 1970. Knopf. $12.50.

Laycock, George. **Deer Hunter's Bible.** rev. ed. (Illus.). 1971. pap. Doubleday. $2.50.

——**The Deer Hunter's Bible.** 2nd rev. ed. (Illus.). 1977. pap. Doubleday. $3.50.

McNair, Jack. **Shooting for the Skipper: Memories of a Veteran Deerstalker.** (Illus.). 1971. Reed, A.H. & A.W. Books. (OP) $6.75.

Nelson, Norm. **Hunting the Whitetail Deer: How to Bring Home North America's Number-One Big Game Animal.** (Illus.). 1980. McKay, David, Co. $12.50.

Outdoor Life Editors. **Outdoor Life's Deer Hunting Book.** (Illus.). 1975. Harper & Row. $10.95.

Sisley, Nick. **Deer Hunting Across North America.** (Illus.). 1975. Freshet Press. $12.95.

Smith, Richard P. **Deer Hunting.** 1978. Stackpole Books. $9.95.

Strung, Norman. **Deer Hunting.** (Illus.). 1973. Lippincott. (OP) $7.95.

Tillett, Paul. **Doe Day: The Antlerless Deer Controversy in New Jersey.** 1963. pap. Rutgers University Press. $3.25.

Tinsley, Russell. **Hunting the Whitetail Deer.** (Illus.). 1974. pap. Barnes & Noble. $1.95.

——**Hunting the Whitetail Deer.** rev. ed. (Illus.). 1977. Funk & Wagnalls. $7.95; pap. $4.95.

——**Hunting the Whitetail Deer.** rev. ed. (Illus.). 1977. T. Y. Crowell. $7.95; pap. $4.50.

Wallack, L. R. **The Deer Rifle.** (Illus.). 1978. Winchester Press. $10.95.

Weiss, John. **The Whitetail Deer Hunter's Handbook.** (Illus.). 1979. Winchester Press. $10.95.

Whitehead, Kenneth. **Hunting and Stalking Deer Throughout the Ages.** (Illus.). 1980. David & Charles. $50.00.

Wootters, John. **Hunting Trophy Deer.** 1977. Winchester Press. $14.95.

DUCK SHOOTING

Adams, Chuck. **The Digest Book of Duck and Goose Hunting.** (Illus.). 1979. pap. Follett. $2.95.

Barber, Joel. **Wild Fowl Decoys.** (Illus.). Peter Smith. $12.50.

——**Wild Fowl Decoys.** (Illus.). pap. Dover. $6.00.

Coykendall, Ralf. **Duck Decoys and How to Rig Them.** (Illus.). 1965. Holt, Rinehart & Winston. $7.95.

Gresham, Grits. **The Complete Wildfowler.** (Illus.). 1975. softbound. Stoeger. $5.95.

Hinman, Bob. **The Duck Hunter's Handbook.** (Illus.). 1976. softbound. Stoeger. $6.95.

——**The Duck Hunter's Handbook.** 1974. Winchester Press. $10.95.

DUCKS

Dethier, Vincent G. **Fairweather Duck.** 1970. Walker & Co. $4.95.

Ellis, Melvin R. **Peg Leg Pete.** 1973. (OP). Holt, Rinehart & Winston. $5.95.

Holderread, Dave. **The Home Duck Flock.** rev. ed. (Illus.). 1980. pap. Garden Way Publishing. $5.95.

Hyde, Dayton. **Raising Wild Ducks in Captivity.** 1974. Dutton. (OP). $15.00.

Jaques, Florence P. **Geese Fly High.** (Illus.). 1964. Repr. of 1939 ed. University of Minnesota Press. $8.95.

Kortright, E. H. **Ducks, Geese and Swans of North America.** rev. ed. Bellrose, Frank C. rev. by (Illus.). 1975. Stackpole Books. $17.95.

McKane, John G. **Ducks of the Mississippi Flyway.** (Illus.). 1969. pap. North Star Press. $2.98.

Ogilvie, M. A. **Ducks of Britain and Europe.** 1975. R. Curtis Books. $14.50.

——**Ducks of Britain and Europe.** (Illus.). 1975. Bueto. $18.00.

Ripley, Dillon. **Paddling of Ducks.** (Illus.). 1969. Smithsonian Institution Press. (OP) $6.95.

Romashko, Sandra D. **Wild Ducks and Geese of North America.** (Illus.). 1978. pap. Windward Publishing. $2.95.

Sowls, Lyle K. **Prairie Ducks: A Study of Their Behavior, Ecology and Management.** (Illus.). 1978. University of Nebraska Press. $11.50; pap. $3.50.

Walters, John & Parker, Michael. **Keeping Ducks, Geese and Turkeys.** 1976. Merrimack Book Service. $8.95.

DUELING

Bacon, Francis. **The Charge of Sir F. Bacon Touching Duells.** Repr of 1614 ed. Johnson, Walter J., Inc. $8.00.

Baldick, Robert. **The Duel: The History of Dueling.** (Illus.). 1966. Crown. $8.50.

Bennetton, Norman A. **Social Significance of the Duel in Seventeenth Century Drama.** Repr. of 1938 ed. Greenwood Press. $15.50.

Coleman, J. Winston. **Famous Kentucky Duels.** (Illus.). 1969. Henry Clay. $3.95.

Douglas, William. **Duelling Days in the Army.** 1977. Scholarly Press. $30.00.

Gamble, Thomas. **Savannah Duels & Duellists: 1733-1877.** (Illus.). 1974. Repr. of 1923 ed. $18.50.

Hutton, Alfred. **The Sword and the Centuries; or, Old Sword Days and Old Sword Ways.** (Illus.). 1973. Repr. of 1901 ed. C. E. Tuttle. $8.50.

McCarty, Clara S. **Duels in Virginia and Nearby Bladenburg.** 1976. Dietz Press. $8.50.

Melville, Lewis & Hargreaves, Reginald. **Famous Duels and Assassinations.** (Illus.). 1974 Repr. of 1929 ed. Gale Research Co. $14.00.

Risher, James F. **Interview with Honor.** 1975. Dorrance. $6.95.

Sietz, Don C. **Famous American Duels.** facs. ed. 1929. Arno Press. $18.00.

Thimm, Carl A. **Complete Bibliography of Fencing and Dueling.** (Illus.). 1968. Repr. of 1846 ed. Arno Press. $23.00.

Trachtman, Paul. **The Gunfighters.** 1974. Silver Burdett Co. $9.95.

Williams, Jack K. **Dueling in the Old South: Vignettes of Social History.** Texas A & M University Press. $9.95.

FALCONRY

Ap Evans, Humphrey. **Falconry.** (Illus.). 1974. Arco. $15.00.

——**Falconry for You.** Branford. $6.50.

Beebe, F. L. **Hawks, Falcons and Falconry.** (Illus.). 1976. Hancock House. $25.00.

Beebe, Frank L. & Webster, Harold M., eds. **North American Falconry and Hunting Hawks.** 4th ed. (Illus.). 1976. North American Falconry and Hunting Hawks. $30.00.

Berners, Juliana. **The Boke of Saint Albans Containing Treatises on Hawking, Hunting and Cote Armour.** 1976. Repr. of 1881 ed. Scholarly Press. $25.00.

——**The Book of Hawking, Hunting and Blasing of Arms.** 1969. Repr. of 1486 ed. W. J. Johnson. $42.00.

Bert, Edmund. **An Approved Treatise of Hawkes and Hawking Divided into Three Bookes.** 1968. Repr. of 1619 ed. W. J. Johnson. $16.00.

Brander, Michael. **Dictionary of Sporting Terms.** (Illus.). 1968. Humanities Press. $7.00.

Burton, Richard F. **Falconry in the Valley of the Indus.** 1971. Falcon Head Press. $13.50.

Danielsson, Bror, ed. **Middle English Falconry Treatises, Pt. 1.** 1978. pap. Humanities Press. Write for info.

Falconer's Club of America Journals: 1941-1961. 1974. Falcon Head Press. $32.50.

Fisher, Charles H. **Falconry Reminiscences.** 1972. Falcon Head Press. $15.00; deluxe ed. $25.00.

Fleming, Arnold. **Falconry and Falcons: Sport of Flight.** (Illus.). 1976. Repr. of 1934 ed. Charles River Books. $20.00.

——**Falconry and Falcons: Sport of Flight.** (Illus.). Repr. text ed. Charles River Books. $20.00.

Frederick Second of Hohenstaufen. **The Art of Falconry.** Wood, Casey A. & Fyfe, F. Marjorie, eds. (Illus.). 1943. Stanford University Press. $28.50.

Freeman, Gage E. & Salvin, Francis H. **Falconry: Its Claims, History and Practice.** 1972. Falcon Head Press. $12.50; deluxe ed. $25.00.

Glasier, Philip. **Falconry and Hawking.** (Illus.). 1979. Branford. $15.50.

Gryndall, William. **Hawking, Hunting, Fouling and Fishing;** Newly Corrected by W. Gryndall Faulkener. 1972. Repr. of 1596 ed. Walter J. Johnson, Inc. $13.00.

Hands, Rachel, ed. **English Hawking and Hunting in the Boke of St. Albans.** facs. ed. (Illus.). 1975. Oxford University Press. $48.00.

Illingworth, Frank. **Falcons and Falconry.** 3rd rev. ed. 1964. British Book Center. (OP) $8.95.

Jameson, E. W. Jr. & Peeters, Hans J. **Introduction to Hawking.** 2nd ed. (Illus.). 1977. pap. Jameson & Peeters. $6.95.

Jameson, Everett W., Jr. **The Hawking of Japan, the History and Development of Japanese Falconry.** (Illus.). Repr. of 1962 ed. Jameson & Peeters. $24.50.

Lascelles, Gerald. **Art of Falconry.** (Illus.). 1971. Repr. of 1895 ed. Charles T. Branford, Co. (OP) $7.25.

Latham, Simon. **Lathams Falconry, 2 pts.** 1977. Repr. of 1615 ed. Walter J. Johnson, Inc. $32.50.

McElroy, Harry. **Desert Hawking.** (Illus.). 1977. H. C. McElroy. $17.00.

Madden, D. H. **Chapter of Mediaeval History.** 1969. Repr. of 1924 ed. Kennikat. $12.50.

Mellor, J. E. **Falconry Notes by Mellor.** 1972. Falcon Head Press. $8.50.

Michell, E. B. **Art and Practice of Hawking.** Bradford. $8.50.

Phillott, D. C. & Harcourt, E. S., trs. from Persian Urdu. **Falconry—Two Treatises.** 1968. text ed. Falcon Head Press. $30.00.

Salvin, Francis H. & Broderick, William. **Falconry in the British Isles.** 1970. Repr. of 1855 ed. North American Falconry and Hunting Hawks. $22.50.

Samson, Jack. **Falconry Today.** (Illus.). 1975. Walck, Henry Z., Inc. (OP) $8.95.

Schlegel, H. & Verster De Wulverhorst, J. A. **The World of Falconry.** 1980. Vendome Press. $60.00.

Schlegel, H. & Wulverhorst, A. H. **Traite De Fauconnerie: Treatise of Falconry.** Hanlon, Thomas, tr. (Illus.). 1973. Chasse Pubns. $32.50.

Summers, Gerald. **The Lure of the Falcon.** 1973. Simon & Schuster. $7.95.

Turberville, George. **The Books of Faulconrie or Hawking.** 1969. Repr. of 1575 ed. Walter J. Johnson, Inc. (OP) $44.00.

Woodford, Michael H. **Manual of Falconry.** Branford, Charles T., Co. (OP) $12.00.

FIREARMS

Ackley, Parker O. **Home Gun Care and Repair.** (Illus.). 1974. pap. Stackpole Books. $4.95.

Amber, John T. **Gun Digest Treasury.** 5th ed. 1977. pap. DBI Books. $7.95.

Amber, John T., ed. **Handloader's Digest.** 1978. pap. DBI Books. $7.95.

——**Handloader's Digest.** 7th ed. 1975. pap. DBI Books. $7.95.

Askins, Charles. **Askins on Pistols and Revolvers.** Bryant, Ted & Askins, Bill, eds. 1980. National Rifle Association. $25.00; pap. $8.95.

Baer, L. R. **The Parker Gun: An Immortal American Classic.** (Illus.). 1978. Beinfeld. (OP) $24.95.

Barker, A. J. **Principles of Small Arms.** (Illus.). 1977. pap. Paladin Press. $4.00.

Barnes, Leslie W. **Canada's Guns: An Illustrated History of Artillery.** (Illus.). 1979. pap. University of Chicago Press. $9.95.

Barwick, Humphrey. **Concerning the Force and Effect of Manuall Weapons of Fire.** 1974. Repr. of 1594 ed. W. J. Johnson. $8.00.

Bearse, Ray. **Sporting Arms of the World.** (Illus.). 1977. Harper & Row. $15.95.

Bianchi, John. **Blue Steel and Gunleather.** 1978. Follett. (OP) $9.95.

Bowman, Hank W. **Famous Guns from the Winchester Collection.** (Illus.). 1958. Arco. (OP) $3.50.

Bristow, Allen P. **The Search for an Effective Police Handgun.** (Illus.). 1973. C. C. Thomas. $20.00.

Brophy, William S. **Krag Rifles.** (Illus.). Beinfeld. (OP).

Browne, Bellmore H. **Guns and Gunning.** (Illus.). Repr. of 1908 ed. Shorey. $6.00.

Burch, Monte. **Gun Care and Repair.** 1978. Winchester Press. $10.95.

Cadiou, Yves & Richard, Alphonse. **Modern Firearms.** (Illus.). 1977. William Morrow & Co. $19.95.

Carmichel, Jim. **The Modern Rifle.** (Illus.). 1976. softbound. Stoeger. (OP) $5.95.

Chant, Chris. **Armed Forces of the United Kingdom.** (Illus.). 1980. David & Charles. $14.50.

Chapel, Charles E. **Complete Guide to Gunsmithing: Gun Care and Repair.** rev. ed. (Illus.). 1962. A. S. Barnes. $9.95.

Consumer Guide. **The Consumer Guide: Guns.** 1972. pap. Pocket Books. $1.95.

Corbin, David R. **Discover Swaging.** 1979. Stackpole Books. $14.95.

Cromwell, Giles. **The Virginia Manufactory of Arms.** 1975. University Press of Virginia. $20.00.

Cullin, William H. **How to Conduct Foreign Military Sales: The 80-81 United States Guide.** 1980. Bureau of National Affairs. $95.00.

Daenhardt, Rainer, ed. **Espingarda Perfeyta; or The Perfect Gun: Rules for Its Use Together with Necessary Instructions for Its Construction and Precepts for Good Aiming.** Daenhardt, Rainer & Neal, W. Keith, trs. from Port. (Illus., Eng. & Port.). 1975. Biblio Distribution Centre. $46.00.

Davis, John E. **Introduction to Tool Marks, Firearms and the Striagraph.** (Illus.). 1958. C. C. Thomas. $11.00.

Dewar, Michael. **Internal Security Weapons and Equipment of the World.** (Illus.). 1979. Scribner's. $12.50.

Dunlap, Roy. **The Gunowner's Book of Care, Repair & Maintenance.** (Illus.). 1974. Harper & Row. $12.95.

Durham, Douglass. **Taking Aim.** 1977. Seventy-Six Press. $7.95.

Editors of Gun Digest. **Gun Digest's Book of Gun Accessories.** Schroeder, Joseph J., ed. (Illus.). 1979. pap. DBI Bks. $8.95.

Edsall, James. **The Story of Firearm Ignition.** Pioneer Press. $3.50.

——**Volcanic Firearms and Their Successors.** Pioneer Press. $2.50.

Educational Research Council of America. **Firearms Examiner.** Ferris, Theodore N. & Marchak, John P., eds. (Illus.). 1977. Changing Times Education Service. $2.25.

Ezelle, Edward C. & Smith, W. H. **Small Arms of the World.** 11th ed. (Illus.). 1979. Repr. of 1943 ed. Stackpole Books. $25.00.

Fairbairn, W. E. & Sykes, E. A. **Shooting to Live.** 1974. Repr. of 1942 ed. Paladin Press. $5.95.

Flayderman, Norm. **Flayderman's Guide to Antique Firearms and Their Values.** 1977. pap. DBI Books. $12.95.

Foss, Christopher. **Infantry Weapons of the World.** rev. ed. (Illus.). 1979. Scribner's. $12.50.

George, John N. **English Pistols and Revolvers.** Albert Saifer, Pub. $15.00.

Grennell, Dean A. **ABC's of Reloading.** 1974. pap. DBI Books. $6.95.

Grennell, Dean A., ed. **Law Enforcement Handgun Digest.** 2nd rev. ed. 1976. pap. Follett. $6.95.

Guns and Ammo Magazine Editors, ed. **Guns and Ammo Annual.** 1981. (Illus.). 1980. pap. Petersen Publishing. $6.95.

Hamilton, T. M. **Early Indian Trade Guns: 1625-1775.** (Contributions of the Museum of the Great Plains Ser.: No. 3). (Illus.). 1968. pap. Museum of the Great Plains Pubns. Dept. $2.50.

Hanauer, Elsie. **Guns of the Wild West.** (Illus.). A. S. Barnes. $12.00.

Hatcher. **The Book of the Garand.** Gun Room Press. $11.95.

Hatcher, et al. **Firearms Investigation, Identification and Evidence.** 1977. Repr. Stackpole Books. $22.50.

Hatcher, Julian S. **Hatcher's Notebook.** rev. ed. (Illus.). 1962. Stackpole Books. $13.95.

Held, Robert. **Age of Firearms.** (Illus.). 2nd rev. ed. pap. DBI Books. (OP) $4.95.

Helmer, William J. **The Gun That Made the Twenties Roar.** (Illus.). rev. and enl. ed. 1977. Gun Room Press. $16.95.

Hertzberg, Robert. **The Modern Handgun.** 1977. Arco. $4.95; pap. $2.50.

Hoff, Arne. **Dutch Firearms.** Stryker, Walter A., ed. (Illus.). 1978. S. B. Barnes. $85.00.

Hoffschmidt, Edward J. **Know Your Gun. Incl. Know Your .45 Auto Pistols; Know Your Walther P. .38 Pistols; Know Your Walther P.P. and P.P.K. Pistols; Know Your M1 Garand Rifles; Know Your Mauser Broomhandle Pistol; Know Your Anti-Tank Rifle.** 1976. Borden. pap. $4.50.

Hogg, Brig., fwrd. by. **The Compleat Gunner.** (Illus.). 1976. Repr. Charles River Books. $10.50.

Hogg, Ian V. **The Complete Illustrated Encyclopedia of the World's Firearms.** (Illus.). 1978. A & W Pubs. $24.95.

——**Guns and How They Work.** (Illus.). 1979. Everest House. $16.95.

Hogg, Ian V. & Weeks, John. **Military Small Arms of the Twentieth Century.** 3rd ed. (Illus.). 1977. Hippocrene Books. $19.95.

Howe, James V. **Amateur Guncraftsman.** (Illus.). 1967. pap. Funk & Wagnalls. $1.95.

Howe, Walter J. **Professional Gunsmithing.** (Illus.). 1946. Stackpole Books. $14.95.

Huebner, Siegfried. **Silencers for Hand Firearms.** Schreier, Konrad & Lund, Peder C., eds. 1976. pap. Paladin Press. $9.95.

Huntington, R. T. **Hall's Breechloaders: John H. Hall's Invention and Development of a Breechloading Rifle with Precision-Made Interchangeable Parts, and Its Introduction into the United States Service.** (Illus.). 1972. pap. George Shumway Publisher. $15.00.

Ingram, M. V. **The Bellwitch.** Pioneer Press. (OP) $3.00.

Jackson & Whitelaw. **European Hand Firearms.** 1978. Albert Saifer, Pub. $22.50.

James, Garry, ed. **Guns for Home Defense.** (Illus.). 1975. pap. Petersen Publishing. $3.95.

——**Guns of the Gunfighters.** (Illus.). 1975. pap. Petersen Publishing. $4.95.

Journal of the Historical Firearms Society of South Africa. Vol. I. (Illus.). 1964. Repr. of 1958 ed. Lawrence Verry Co. (OP) $7.50.

Kennedy, Monty. **Checkering and Carving of Gunstocks.** rev. ed. (Illus.). 1952. Stackpole Books. $15.95.

Koller, Larry. **How to Shoot: A Complete Guide to the Use of Sporting Firearms—Rifles, Shotguns and Handguns—on the Range and in the Field.** rev. ed. Elman, Robert, ed. (Illus.). 1976. Doubleday. (OP) $9.95.

Larson, E. Dixon. **Remington Tips.** Pioneer Press. $4.95.

Lauber, George. **How to Build Your Own Flintlock Rifle or Pistol.** Seaton, Lionel, tr. from Ger. (Illus.). 1976. pap. Jolex. $6.95.

——**How to Build Your Own Percussion Rifle or Pistol.** Seaton, Lionel, tr. from Ger. (Illus.). 1976. pap. Jolex. $6.95.

——**How to Build Your Own Wheellock Rifle or Pistol.** Seaton, Lionel, tr. from Ger. (Illus.). 1976. pap. Jolex. $6.95.

Lenk, Torsten. **Flintlock: Its Origin and Development.** Albert Saifer, Pub. $35.00.

The Lewis Gun. 1976. Paladin Press. $17.95.

Lewis, Jack. **Gun Digest Book of Modern Gun Values.** 1976. pap. DBI Books. $7.95.

——**Law Enforcement Handgun Digest.** 3rd ed. 1980. pap. DBI Books. $8.95.

Lewis, Jack & Springer, Robert, eds. **Black Powder Gun Digest.** 2nd ed. 1977. pap. DBI Books. $7.95.

Lindsay, Merrill. **Twenty Great American Guns.** (Illus.). 1976. Repr. pap. Arma Press. $1.75.

——**The Lure of Antique Arms.** (Illus.). 1978. softbound. Stoeger. $5.95.

Liu, Allan, J. **The American Sporting Collector's Handbook.** 1977. softbound. Stoeger. $5.95.

Miller, Martin. **Collector's Illustrated Guide to Firearms.** (Illus.). 1978. Mayflower Books. $24.95.

Murtz, Harold A. **Guns Illustrated 1979.** 10th ed. (Illus.). 1977. pap. Follett. $7.95.

Murtz, Harold A., ed. **Gun Digest Book of Exploded Firearms Drawings.** 2nd ed. 1977. pap. DBI Books. $7.95.

National Muzzle Loading Rifle Association. **Muzzle Blasts: Early Years Plus Vol. I and II 1939-41.** 1974. pap. George Shumway Publisher. $18.00.

Nonte, George C., Jr. **Black Powder Guide.** 2nd ed. (Illus.). 1976. pap. Stoeger. $7.95.

—**Firearms Encyclopedia.** (Illus.). 1973. Harper & Row. $19.95.

—**Handgun Competition.** (Illus.). 1978. Winchester Press. $12.95.

—**Handloading for Handgunners.** 1978. pap. $7.95.

—**Home Guide to Muzzle Loaders.** (Illus.). 1975. pap. Stackpole Books. $6.95.

—**Pistol Guide.** 1980. Stoeger. $8.95.

—**Revolver Guide.** 1980. Stoeger. $8.95.

Nonte, George C., Jr., & Jurras, Lee. **Handgun Hunting.** (Illus.). 1976. softbound. Stoeger. $5.95.

Nonte, George C., Jr. **Combat Handguns.** Jurras, Lee F., ed. (Illus.). 1980. Stackpole Books. $17.95.

Norton (R. W.) Art Gallery. **E. C. Prudhomme: Master Gun Engraver.** (Illus.). 1973. pap. Norton Art Gallery. $3.00.

Owen, J. I., ed. **Brassey's Infantry Weapons of the World, 1975.** (Illus.). 1975. Westview Press. $39.50.

Page, Warren. **The Accurate Rifle.** 1975. softbound. Stoeger. $6.95.

Peterson & Elman. **The Great Guns.** 1977. Grosset & Dunlap. $10.95.

Peterson, Harold L. **Encyclopedia of Firearms.** (Illus.). 1964. E. P. Dutton. $16.95.

Pollard, Hugh B. **The History of Firearms.** 1974. Burt Franklin, Pub. $25.50; pap. $8.95.

Reese, Michael, II. **Nineteen Hundred Luger—U.S. Test Trials.** 2nd rev. ed. Pioneer Press, ed. (Illus.). Pioneer Press. $4.95.

Rice, F. Philip. **Outdoor Life Gun Data Book.** (Illus.). 1975. Harper & Row. $12.95.

Richardson, H. L. & Wood, Wallis W. **Firearms and Freedom.** Seventy Six Press.

Riviere, Bill. **The Gunner's Bible.** rev. ed. 1973. pap. Doubleday. $3.50.

Roberts, Willis J. & Bristow, Allen P. **Introduction to Modern Police Firearms.** Gourley, Douglas, ed. (Illus.). 1969. text ed. Glencoe. $10.95.

Rosa, Joseph G. **Gunfighters: Man or Myth.** (Illus.). 1980. pap. University of Oklahoma Press. $5.95.

Russell, Carl. **Firearms, Traps and Tools of the Mountain Men.** (Illus.). 1977. pap. University of New Mexico Press. $6.50.

Schroeder, Joseph J., Jr., ed. **Gun Collector's Digest.** 2nd ed. 1976. pap. DBI Books. $7.95.

Scott, Robert F., ed. **Shooter's Bible, 1982, No. 73.** (Illus.). 1981. softbound. Stoeger. $10.95.

Sell. **Handguns Americana.** 1973. Borden. $8.50.

Sherrill, Robert. **The Saturday Night Special.** 1975. pap. Penguin Books. $2.75.

Shotgun Shooting. 4th ed. (Illus.). 1974. pap. Charles River Books. $2.50.

Smythe, John & Barwick, Humphrey. **Bow vs. Gun.** 1976. Repr. Charles River Books. $15.00.

Smith, W. H. B. **Small Arms of the World.** (Illus.). 1975. pap. A & W Visual Library. $9.95.

Stack, Robert. **Shotgun Digest.** 1974. pap. DBI Books. $6.95.

Stanford, J. K. **Complex Gun.** Soccer. $15.00.

Steindler, R. A. **Firearms Dictionary.** (Illus.). 1975. pap. Paladin Press. $6.95.

—**Reloader's Guide.** (Illus.). 3rd ed. 1975. softbound. Stoeger. $7.95.

—**Rifle Guide.** (Illus.). 1978. softbound. Stoeger. $7.95.

Steindler, R. A., ed. & illus. **Shooting the Muzzle Loaders.** (Illus.). 1975. Jolex. $11.95; pap. $6.95.

Stockbridge, V. D. **Digest of U.S. Patents Relating to Breech-Loading & Magazine Small Arms, 1836-1873.** (Illus.). 1963. N. Flayderman & Co. $12.50.

Suydam, Charles R. **U.S. Cartridges & Their Handguns: 1795-1975.** (Illus.). 1978. DBI Books. $14.95; pap. $9.95.

Sybertz, Gustav. **Technical Dictionary for Weaponry.** (Ger.-Eng.). 1969. pap. French & European Pubns., Inc. $120.00.

Tappon, Mel. **Survival Guns.** 1978. Janus Press. $12.95.

—**Survival Guns.** 1977. pap. Janus Press. $9.95.

Thomas, Donald G. **Silencer Patents, Vol. III: European Patents 1901-1978.** (Illus.). 1978. Paladin Press. $15.00.

Truby, J. David. **The Lewis Gun.** (Illus.). 1977. Sycamore Island Books. $17.95.

Truby, J. David & Minnery, John. **Improvised Modified Firearms.** 2 vols. Lund, Peder C., ed. (Illus.). 1975. Paladin Press. $9.95 each.

Truby, J. David, et al. **Improvised Modified Firearms.** 2 vols.1975. Paladin Press. $19.95 set.

U.S. Army. **Forty-MM Grenade Launcher: M79.** (Illus.). pap. Paladin Press. $4.00.

U.S. Cartridge Company. **U.S. Cartridge Company Collection of Firearms.** (Illus.). Sycamore Island Books. $6.00.

Van Rensselaer, S. **American Firearms.** (Illus.). 1978. Century House. $16.00.

Virgines, George E. **Famous Guns & Gunners.** (Illus.). 1980. Pine Mountain Press. $10.95; pap. $6.95.

Wahl, Paul. **Gun Trader's Guide.** (Illus.). 9th ed. 1981. softbound. Stoeger. $9.95.

Waite, M. D. & Ernst, Bernard. **The Trapdoor Springfield.** 1979. Beinfeld. $19.95.

Warner, Ken. **The Practical Book of Guns.** (Illus.). 1978. Winchester Press. $10.95.

Warner, Ken, ed. **Gun Digest Nineteen Eighty.** 34th ed. (Illus.). 1979. pap. Follett. $9.95.

West, Bill. **Know Your Winchesters: General Use, All Models and Types, 1849-1969.** (Illus.). B West. $12.00.

—**Winchester, Cartridges, and History.** (Illus.). B West. $29.00.

—**Winchester-Complete: All Wins & Forerunners, 1849-1970.** (Illus.). 1975. B West. $28.00.

—**Winchester Encyclopedia.** (Illus.). B West. $12.00.

—**Winchester Lever-Action Handbook.** (Illus.). B West. $29.00.

—**The Winchester Single Shot.** (Illus.). B West. $12.00.

Weston, Paul B. **The New Handbook of Handgunning.** (Illus.). 1980. C. C. Thomas.

Willett, Roderick. **Gun Safety.** (Illus.). 1967. International Pubns. Service. $5.25.

Williams, John J. **Survival Guns and Ammo: Raw Meat.** (Illus.). 1979. pap. Consumertronics. $15.00.

Williams, Mason. **The Law Enforcement Book of Weapons, Ammunition & Training Procedures: Handguns, Rifles and Shotguns.** (Illus.). 1977. C. C. Thomas. $35.75.

Winant, Lewis. **Firearms Curiosa.** (Illus.). 1961. Ray Riling, Arms Books. $9.95.

Wirnsberger, Gerhard. **Standard Directory of Proof Marks.** Steindler, R. A. tr. from Ger. (Illus.). 1976. pap. Jolex. $5.95.

Wood, J. B. **The Gun Digest Book of Firearms Assembly: Centerfire Rifles, Pt. IV.** 1980. pap. Follett. $8.95.

—**Gun Digest Book of Firearms Assembly-Disassembly: Rimfire Rifles, Pt. I.** (Illus.). 1979. pap. Follett. $8.95.

—**Gun Digest Book of Firearms Assembly-Disassembly: Revolvers, Pt. II.** (Illus.). 1979. pap. Follett. $8.95.

—**Gun Digest Book of Firearms Assembly-Disassembly: Rimfire Rifles, Pt. III.** (Illus.). 1980. pap. Follett. $8.95.

—**Troubleshooting Your Handgun.** 1978. pap. Follett. $5.95.

Wootters, John. **The Complete Book of Practical Handloading.** (Illus.). 1977. softbound. Stoeger. $6.95.

Wycoff, James. **Famous Guns That Won the West.** (Illus.). 1975. pap. Arco. $2.00.

FIREARMS—CATALOGS

Byron, D. **The Firearms Price Guide.** (Illus.). 1977. pap. Crown. $9.95.

Byron, David. **The Firearm's Price Guide.** rev. ed. (Illus.). 1980. pap. (Michelman Books.) Crown. $9.95.

Eighteen-Sixty Two Ordnance Manual. Pioneer Press. $1.50.

Guns, Value & Identification Guide. (Illus.). Wallace-Homestead Book Co. $2.95.

House of Collectibles, Inc. **Official Price Guide to Antique and Modern Firearms.** (Illus.). 1980. pap. House of Collectibles. $9.95.

Hoxie Bullet Catalog. Pioneer Press. $0.75.

Lewis, Jack. **Gun Digest Book of Modern Gun Values.** (Illus.). 1978. pap. DBI Books. $7.95.

Murtz, Harold A., ed.**Guns Illustrated, 1979.** 11th ed. 1978. pap. DBI Books. $6.95.

Murtz, Harold A., ed. **Guns Illustrated 1981** 13th ed. 1980. pap. DBI Books. $8.95.

Owen, J. I., ed. **Brassey's Infantry Weapons of the World, 1974-75: Infantry Weapons and Combat Aids in Current Use by the Regular and Reserve Forces of All Nations.** (Illus.). 1974. text ed. British Book Center. $49.00.

Quertermous, Russel C. & Quertermous, Stephen C. **Modern Guns: Identifications & Values.** 1979. Crown. $11.95.

Remington Gun Catalog 1877. Pioneer Press. $1.50.

Schroeder, Joseph J., ed. **Gun Collector's Digest.** 2nd ed. 1976. pap. DBI Books. $7.95.

Scott, Robert F., ed. **Shooter's Bible. 1982, No. 73.** (Illus.). 1981. softbound. Stoeger. $10.95.

Sears & Roebuck Ammunition Catalog. (Illus.). pap. Sand Pond. $1.50.

Sellers, Frank. **Sharps Firearms.** (Illus.). 1978. Follett. $34.95.

Smith Brothers-Boston Mass. Sand Pond. $3.00.

Tarassuk, L. **Antique European and American Firearms at the Hermitage Museum.** Drapkin, R., tr. (Illus., Eng. & Rus.). 1973. Arco. $20.00.

—**Antique European and American Firearms at the Hermitage Museum.** 1973. State Mutual Book and Periodical Service, Ltd. $15.00.

Tarassuk, Leonid, ed. **Antique European and American Firearms at the Hermitage Museum.** (Illus., Eng. & Rus.). 1976. Arma Press. $30.00.

Tinkham, Sandra S., ed. **Catalog of Tools, Hardware, Firearms, and Vehicles.** 1979. incl. color microfiche. Somerset House. $260.00. pap. $30.00.

United States Cartridge Co.-Lowell, Mass. Sand Pond. $2.50.

U.S. Cartridge Company's Collection of Firearms. 1971. We Inc. $6.00.

Wahl, Paul. **Gun Trader's Guide.** (Illus.). 9th ed. 1978. softbound. Stoeger. $9.95.

Warner, Ken, ed. **Gun Digest 1982** 36th ed. 1981. pap. DBI Books. $10.95.

—**Gun Digest Review of Custom Guns.** 1980. pap. DBI Books. $8.95.

West, Bill. **Remington Arms Catalogues, 1877-1899.** 1st ed. (Illus.). 1971. B West. $10.00.

—**Stevens Arms Catalogues, 1877-1899.** 1st ed. (Illus.). 1971. B West. $12.00.

Wilson, Loring D. **The Handy Sportsman.** 1977. softbound. Stoeger. $5.95.

Winchester Shotshell Catalog 1897. (Illus.). pap. Sand Pond. $1.25.

FIREARMS—COLLECTORS AND COLLECTING

Akehurst, Richard. **Antique Weapons.** (Illus.). 1969. Arco. (OP). $5.95.

Amber, John T. **Gun Digest Treasury.** 5th ed. 1977. pap. DBI Books. $7.95.

—**Gun Digest 1978.** 32nd ed. pap. DBI Books. $8.95.

Bowman, Hank W. **Antique Guns from the Stagecoach Collection.** (Illus.). 1964. lib. bdg. Arco. $3.50.

Chapel, Charles E. **Gun Collector's Handbook of Values: 1980-1981.** 13th rev. ed. 1979. Coward, McCann & Geoghegan. $16.95; pap. $8.95.

DiCarpengna, N. **Firearms in the Princes Odescalchi Collection in Rome.** (Illus.). 1976. Repr. of 1969 ed. Arma Press. $20.00.

Dixie Gun Works Antique Arms Catalog. Pioneer Press. $10.00.

Early Firearms of Great Britain and Ireland from the Collection of Clay P. Bedford. (Illus.). 1971. Metropolitan Museum of Art. $17.50; pap. $4.95.

Flayderman, Norm. **Norm Flayderman's Book of Antique Gun Values.** 1977. pap. DBI Books. $12.95.

Flayderman, Norm. **Norm Flayderman's Guide to Antique American Firearms and Their Values.** 1977. pap. DBI Books. $12.95.

Guns, Value and Identification Guide. (Illus.). Wallace-Homestead Book Co. $2.95.

Gusler, Wallace B. & Lavin, James D. **Decorated Firearms, 1540-1870, from the Collection of Clay P. Bedford.** 1977. University Press of Virginia. $25.00.

Hake, Ted. **Six Gun Hero Collectibles.** 1976. Wallace-Homestead Book Co. $7.95.

Kennard, A. M. **French Pistols and Sporting Guns.** 1972. Transatlantic Arts Inc. $2.95.

Lindsay, Merrill. **The Lure of Antique Arms.** (Illus.). 1978. softbound. Stoeger. $5.95.

Liu, Allan J. **The American Sporting Collector's Handbook.** (Illus.). 1977. softbound. Stoeger. $5.95.

Murtz, Harold A., ed. **Guns Illustrated 1978.** 10th ed. (Illus.). 1977. pap. DBI Books. $6.95.

Neal, Robert J. & Jinks, Roy G. **Smith and Wesson, 1857-1945.** rev. ed. 1975. A. S. Barnes. $25.00.

Quertermous, Russel & Quertermous, Steve. **Modern Guns, Identification and Values.** 2nd rev. ed.(Illus.).1980. pap. Collector Books.$11.95.

Quertermous, Russell & Quertermous, Steve. **Modern Guns, Identification and Values.** 3rd ed. 1980. pap. Collector Books. $11.95.

Quertermous, Russell & Quertermous, Steve. **Modern Guns, Identification and Values.** (Illus.). pap. Wallace-Homestead Book Co. $11.95.

Schroeder, Joseph J., Jr. ed. **Gun Collector's Digest.** 2nd ed. 1976. pap. DBI Books. $7.95.

Schroeder, Joseph J. **Gun Collector's Digest.** 1974. pap. DBI Books. $6.95.

Serven, James. **Rare and Valuable Antique Arms.** 1976. Pioneer Press. $4.95.

Shumaker, P. L. **Colt's Variations of the Old Model Pocket Pistol.** 1957. Borden. $8.95.

Steinwedel, Louis W. **Gun Collector's Fact Book.** 1975. Arco. $10.00; pap. $5.95.

Tarassuk, L. **Antique European and American Firearms at the Hermitage Museum.** Drapkin, R., tr. (Illus., Eng. & Rus.). 1973. Arco. $20.00.

U.S. Cartridge Company's Collection of Firearms. 1971. We Inc. $6.00.

Wahl, Paul. **Gun Trader's Guide.** 9th ed. (Illus.). 1981. softbound. Stoeger. $9.95.

Wilkinson, Frederick. **Antique Firearms.** (Illus.). 276 p. 1980. Sterling. $17.95.

Wilkinson-Latham, Robert. **Antique Guns in Color: 1750-1865.** (Illus.). 1978. Arco. $8.95; pap. 6.95.

Wilson, R. L. **The Book of Colt Engraving.** (Illus.). 1978. Beinfeld. $39.95.

FIREARMS—HISTORY

Ayalon, David, **Gunpowder and Firearms in the Mamluk Kingdom: A Challenge to Midaeval Society.** 2nd ed. 1978. Biblio Distribution Centre.

Baer, L.R. **The Parker Gun: An Immortal American Classic.** (Illus.). 1978. Beinfeld. (OP) $24.95.

Berger, Michael. **Firearms in American History.** (Illus.).(gr. 5 up). 1979. Franklin Watts, Inc. $5.45.

Blanch, H.J.A. **A Century of Guns: A Sketch of the Leading Types of Sporting and Military Small Arms.** (Illus.). 1977. Repr. of 1909 ed. Charles River Books. $25.00.

Bowman, Hank W. **Famous Guns from the Smithsonian Collection.** (Illus.). 1966. lib. bdg. Arco. $3.50.

Bowman, Hank W. & Cary, Lucian. **Antique Guns.** (Illus.). 1953. Arco. $3.50.

Brophy, William S. **Krag Rifles.** (Illus.). 1978. Beinfeld. (OP). $19.95.

—**L. C. Smith Shotguns.** (Illus.). 1978. Beinfeld, (OP). $24.95.

Brown, M. L. **Firearms in Colonial America: The Impact of History and Technology 1492-1792.** (Illus.). 1980. Smithsonian Institution Press. $40.00.

Buchele, W. & Shumway, G. **Recreating the American Longrifle.** Orig. Title: **Recreating the Kentucky Rifle.** (Illus.). 1973. pap. George Shumway Publisher. $10.00.

Burrell, Brian. **Combat Weapons: Handguns and Shoulder Arms of World War 2.** (Illus.). 1974. Transatlantic Arts, Inc. $9.50.

Campbell, Hugh B. **The History of Firearms.** (Illus.). 1977. pap. B. Franklin. (OP). $8.95.

DuMont, John S. **Custer Battle Guns.** (Illus.). 1974. Old Army Press. $10.00.

Editors of Outdoor Life, ed. **The Story of American Hunting and Firearms.** 1976. Dutton. $12.95.

Fuller, Claud E. **Breech-Loader in the Service 1816-1917.** (Illus.). 1965. Flayderman, N. & Co. $14.50.

Fuller, Claude E. & Steward, Richard D. **Firearms of the Confederacy.** 1977. Repr. of 1944 ed. Quarterman. $25.00.

Gaier, Claude. **Four Centuries of Liege Gunmaking.** (Illus.). 1977. Arma Press. $80.00.

Grancsay, Stephen V. & Lindsay, Merrill. **Master French Gunsmith's Designs from the XVII to the XIX Centuries.** (Illus.). 1976. Ltd. ed. (1000 copies). Arma Press. $89.00.

Greener, William W. **The Gun and Its Development: With Notes on Shooting.** 1975. Repr. of 1881 ed. Gale Research Co. $26.00.

Gusler, Wallace B. & Lavin, James D. **Decorated Firearms, 1540-1870 from the Collection of**

Clay P. Bedford. 1977. (Colonial Williamsburg Foundation.) University Press of Virginia. $25.00

Hackley, F. W., et al. **History of Modern U.S. Military Small Arms Ammunition: Vol. 2, 1940-1945.** Gun Room Press. $25.00.

Hartzler, Daniel D. **Arms Makers of Maryland.** (Illus.). 1976. George Shumway Publisher. $35.00.

Held, Robert. **Age of Firearms.** (Illus.). 2nd ed. rev. pap. DBI Books. (OP). $4.95.

Helmer, William J. **The Gun That Made the Twenties Roar.** Gun Room Press. $16.95.

Hetrick, Calvin. **The Bedford County Rifle and Its Makers.** (Illus.). 1975. pap. George Shumway Publisher. (OP). $5.00.

Hogg, Ian & Batchelor, John. **Naval Gun.** (Illus.). 1979. Sterling. $24.95.

Holme, N. & Kirby, E. L. **Medal Rolls: Twenty-Third Foot Royal Welch Fusiliers, Napoleonic Period.** 1979. S. J. Durst. $39.00.

Hutslar, Donald A. **Gunsmiths of Ohio: 18th and 19th Centuries.** Vol. I. (Illus.). casebound. George Shumway Publisher. $35.00.

Jackson, Melvin H. & De Beer, Charles. **Eighteenth Century Gunfounding.** (Illus.). 1974. Smithsonian Institution Press. $19.95.

Jinks, Roy G. **History of Smith and Wesson.** (Illus.). 1978. Beinfeld.

Kennet, Lee & Anderson, James L. **The Gun in America.** (Illus., Orig.). 1975. pap. text ed. Greenwood Press. $3.95.

Kindig, Joe Jr. **Thoughts on the Kentucky Rifle in Its Golden Age.** 1980. casebound. George Shumway Publisher. $59.50.

Lindsay, Merrill. **The New England Gun: The First 200 Years.** (Illus.). 1976. Arma Press. $20.00. pap. $12.50.

—**One Hundred Great Guns.** (Illus.). 1967. Walker & Co. $25.00.

Neal, Keith W. & Back, D. H. **Great British Gunmakers 1740-1790: The History of John Twigg and the Packington Guns.** (Illus.). 1975. S. P. Bernet. $80.00.

North & North. **Simeon North: First Official Pistol Maker of the United States.** Repr. Gun Room Press. $7.95.

Peterson, Harold. **Historical Treasury of American Guns.** Benjamin Co. $4.95; pap. $2.95.

Pollard, Hugh B. **History of Firearms.** (Illus.). 1974. B. Franklin. $25.50.

Reese, Michaell II. **Nineteen-Hundred Luger-U.S. Test Trials.** 2nd rev. ed. (Illus.). pap. Pioneer Press. $4.95.

Ritchie, Carson I. **The Decorated Gun.** (Illus.). Date not set. A. S.Barnes. $15.00.

Rosebush, Waldo E. **American Firearms and the Changing Frontier.** 1962. pap. Eastern Washington State Historical Society. $3.00.

Rywell, Martin. **American Antique Pistols.** Pioneer Press. $2.00.

—**Confederate Guns.** Pioneer Press. $2.00.

Schreier, Konrad F., Jr. **Remington Rolling Block Firearms.** (Illus.). pap. Pioneer Press. $3.95.

Schroeder, Joseph J., Jr. **Arms of the World—1911.** 1972. pap. DBI Books. $5.95.

Serven, James. **Two Hundred Years of American Firearms.** (Illus., Orig.). 1975. pap. Follett. $7.95.

—**Colt Firearms from 1836.** 1974. Fountain Press. $19.95.

—**Conquering the Frontiers.** 1974. Fountain Press. $19.95.

Shelton, Lawrence P. **California Gunsmiths.** (Illus.). 302p. 1977. casebound. George Shumway Publisher. $29.65.

SIPRI. **Anti-Personnel Weapons.** 1978. Crane-Russak Co. $29.95.

Smythe, John & Barwick, Humphrey. **Bow Versus Gun: Certain Discourses, and a Breefe Discourse.** 1974. George Shumway Publisher. $10.00.

Suydam, Charles R. **U.S. Cartridges and Their Handguns: 1795-1975.** (Illus.). 1978. Beinfeld. (OP) $14.95; pap. $9.95.

Tarassuk, Leonid. **Antique European and American Firearms at the Hermitage Museum.** limited ed. (Illus., Eng. & Rus.). 1973. Arma Press. (OP). $30.00.

---**Antique European and American Firearms at the Hermitage Museum.** 1973. State Mutual Book and Periodical Service, Ltd. $15.00.

Tout, Thomas F. **Firearms in England in the Fourteenth Century.** (Illus.). 1969. pap. (OP). George Shumway Publisher. $5.00.

West, Bill. **Browning Arms and History, 1847-1973.** (Illus.). 1972. B. West. $20.00.

---**Marlin and Ballard, Arms and History, 1861-1971.** (Illus.). 1972. B. West. $29.00.

---**Remington Arms and History, 1816-1971.** (Illus.). 1972. B. West. $22.00.

---**Savage Stevens, Arms and History, 1849-1971.** (Illus.). 1971. B. West. $29.00.

---**Winchester-Complete: All Wins and Forerunners, 1849-1970.** (Illus.). 1975. B. West. $28.00

Wilkinson,Frederick. **Antique Firearms.** 1978. Repr. Presidio Press. $14.95.

Wilkinson-Latham, Robert. **Antique Guns In Color: 1250-1865.** 1978. Arco. $8.95; pap. $6.95.

Williamson, Harry F. **Winchester: The Gun That Won the West.** (Illus.). A. S. Barnes. (OP). $7.98.

Wycoff, James. **Famous Guns That Won the West.** (Illus.). 1975. pap. Arco. $2.00.

FIREARMS—IDENTIFICATION

Ahern, Jerry & Hart, Dave. **Peace Officer's Guide to Concealed Handguns.** 1978. pap. Follett. (OP). $7.95.

Byron, David. **Gunmarks.** (Illus.). 1980. Crown. $10.00.

Grancsay, Stephen V. & Lindsay, Merrill. **Illustrated British Firearms Patents, 1718-1853.** (Illus.). 1976. ltd. ed. Arma Press. $75.00.

Mathews J. Howard. **Firearms Identification: Original Photographs and Other Illustrations of Hand Guns, Vol. 2.** 1973. Repr. of 1962 ed. C. G. Thomas. $56.75.

---**Firearms Identification: Original Photographs and Other Illustrations of Hand Guns, Data on Rifling Characteristics of Hand Guns & Rifles, Vol. 3.** Wilimovsky, Allan E., ed. (Illus.). 1973. C. C. Thomas. $88.00.

---**Firearms Identification: The Laboratory Examination of Small Arms, Rifling Characteristics in Hand Guns, and Notes on Automatic Pistols, Vol. 1.** 1973. Repr. of 1962 ed. C. C. Thomas. $56.75.

Quertermous, Russel & Quertermous, Steve. **Modern Guns, Identification and Values.** 2nd, rev. ed. (Illus.). 1980. pap. Collector Books. $11.95.

Quertermous, Russell & Quertermous, Steven. **Modern Guns.** 2nd ed. (Illus.). 1980. pap. Crown. $11.95.

---**Modern Guns Identification and Values.** (Illus.). pap. Wallace-Homestead Book Co. $11.95.

Wilber, Charles G. **Ballistic Science for the Law Enforcement Officer.** (Illus.). 1977. C. C. Thomas. $30.00.

The World's Submachine Guns. TBN Enterprises. $19.95.

FIREARMS—INDUSTRY AND TRADE

Farley, Philip J., et al. **Arms Across the Sea.** 1978. Brookings Institution. $8.95.

Gervasi, Tom. **Arsenal of Democracy: American Weapons Available for Export.** (Illus.). 1978. Grove Press. $19.50.

Grancsay, Stephen V. & Lindsay, Merrill. **Illustrated British Firearms Patents 1718-1853.** limited ed. (Illus.). Arma Press.$75.00.

Hanifhen, Frank C. & Engelbrecht, Helmuth C. **Merchants of Death: A Study of the International Armaments Industry.** Garland Pub. $33.00.

Hartzler, Daniel D. **Arms Makers of Maryland.** 1975. George Shumway Publisher. $35.00.

Russell, Carl P. **Guns on the Early Frontiers: A History of Firearms from Colonial Times through the Years of the Western Fur Trade.** 1980. University of Nebraska Press. $19.50. pap. $6.95.

Kennett, Lee & Anderson, James L. **The Gun in America.** (Illus.). pap. Greenwood Press. $3.95.

Kirkland, Turner. **Southern Derringers of the Mississippi Valley.** Pioneer Press. $2.00.

Lindsay, Merrill. **One Hundred Great Guns.** (Illus.). 1967. Walker & Co. $25.00.

Noel-Baker, Philip. **Private Manufacture of Armaments.** 1971. pap. Dover. $6.00.

Smith, Merritt R. **Harper's Ferry Armory and the New Technology: The Challenge of Change.** (Illus.).1977. Cornell University Press. $22.50; pap. $7.95.

Stockholm International Peace Research Institute (SIPRI). **The Arms Trade Registers.** 1975. MIT Press. $16.00.

---**Arms Trade with the 3rd World.** rev. ed. (Illus.). 1975. Holmes & Meier. $27.00.

West, Bill. **Browning Arms and History, 1842-1973.** (Illus.).1972. B. West. $29.00.

FIREARMS—LAWS AND REGULATIONS

Davidson, Bill R. **To Keep and Bear Arms.** 2nd ed. 1979. Sycamore Island Books. $12.95.

Dolan, Edward F. Jr. **Gun Control: A Decision for Americans.** (Illus.). 1978. Watts, Franklin, Inc. $4.90.

Gottlieb, Alan B. **The Gun Owner's Political Manual.** 1976. pap. Green Hill. $1.95.

Gun Control. 1976. pap. American Enterprise Institute for Public Policy Research. $2.00.

Gun Control Means People Control. 1974. Independent American. $1.75.

Kates, Don B., Jr. **Gun Control: The Liberal Skeptic Speaks Out.** 1979. North River Press. price not set.

Kennet, Lee & Anderson, James L. **The Gun in America.** (Illus.). text ed. pap. Greenwood Press. $3.95.

Krema, Vaclav. **Identification and Registration of Firearms.** (Illus.). 1971. C. C. Thomas. $14.50.

Kukla, Robert J. **Gun Control: A Written Record of Efforts to Eliminate the Private Possesssion of Firearms in America.** Orig. Title: Other Side of Gun Control. 1973. pap. Stackpole Books. $4.95.

Scanlon, Robert A. ed. **Law Enforcement Bible.** (Illus.). 1978. softbound. Stoeger. $7.95.

---**Law Enforcement Bible No. 2** (Illus.). 1981. softbound. Stoeger. $11.95.

Sherrill, Robert. **The Saturday Night Special.** 1975. pap. Penguin Books. $2.75.

FOWLING

Bauer, Erwin A. **Duck Hunter's Bible.** pap. Doubleday. $2.95.

Becker, A. C. Jr. **Waterfowl in the Marshes.** (Illus.) 1969. A. S. Barnes. $9.95.

Bell, Bob. **Hunting the Long Tailed Bird.** (Illus.). 1975. Freshet Press. $14.95.

Bourjaily, Vance. **Unnatural Enemy.** (Illus.). 1963. Dial Press. $6.95.

Carroll, Hanson, et al. **The Wildfowler's World.** 1973. Winchester Press. (OP) $12.95.

Day, J. Wentworth. **The Modern Fowler.** 1973. Repr. of 1934 ed. British Book Center. (OP) $18.50.

Dickey, Charley. **Quail Hunting.** (Illus.). 1975. softbound. Stoeger. $3.95.

Gresham, Grits. **The Complete Wildfowler.** (Illus.). 1975. softbound. Stoeger. $5.95.

Gryndall, William. **Hawking, Hunting, Fouling and Fishing; Newly Corrected by W. Gryndall Faulkner.** 1972. Repr. of 1596 ed. W. J. Johnson. $13.00.

Hastings, Macdonald. **Shooting—Why We Miss: Questions and Answers on the Successful Use of the Shotgun.** 1977.David McKay Co. $6.95; pap. $3.95.

Hinman, Bob. **The Duck Hunter's Handbook.** (Illus.). 1976. softbound. Stoeger. $6.95.

Knap, Jerome, ed. **All About Wildfowling in America.** 1976. Winchester Press. (OP) $10.00.

Petzal, David E., ed. **The Expert's Book of Upland Bird and Water-Fowl Hunting.** 1975. Simon & Schuster. $9.95.

Rice, F. Philip & Dahl, John. **Game Bird Hunting.** rev. ed. (Illus.). 1977. Funk & Wagnalls. $7.95; pap. $4.95.

Russell, Dan M. **Dove Shooter's Handbook.** 1974. Winchester Press. $6.95.

Waterman, Charles F. **Hunting Upland Birds.** (Illus.). 1975. softbound. Stoeger. $5.95.

Wood, Shirley E. Jr. **Gunning for Upland Birds and Wildfowl.** 1976. Winchester Press. $10.00.

Youel, Milo A. **Cook the Wild Bird.** (Illus.). 1976. A. S. Barnes. $17.50.

GAME AND GAME BIRDS

Anderson, Luther A. **Hunting the Uplands with Rifle and Shotgun.** (Illus.). 1977. Winchester Press. $10.00.

Becker, A. C., Jr. **Game and Bird Calling.** (Illus.). 1972. A. S. Barnes. (OP) $7.95.

Bell, Bob. **The Digest Book of Upland Game Shooting.** 1979. pap. Follett. $2.95.

Brakefield, Tom. **The Sportsman's Complete Book of Trophy and Meat Care.** (Illus.). 1975. Stackpole Books. $8.95.

Bucher, Ruth & Gelb, Norman. **The Book of Hunting.** (Illus.). 1977. Paddington Press. $60.00.

Burk, Bruce. **Game Bird Carving.** (Illus.). 1972. Winchester Press. $17.50.

Colby, C. B. **Big Game: Animals of the Americas, Africa and Asia.** (Illus.). 1967. Coward, McCann & Geoghegan. $5.29.

Cone, Arthur L. Jr. **The Complete Guide to Hunting.** (Illus.). 1978. softbound. Stoeger. $5.95.

Dalrymple, Byron. **How to Call Wildlife.** (Illus.). 1975. Funk & Wagnalls. $7.50; T. Y. Crowell. pap. $4.50.

---**North American Big Game Hunting.** (Illus.). 1978. softbound. Stoeger. $5.95.

Dasmann, Raymond F. **Wildlife Biology.** (Illus.). 1964. John Wiley & Sons, Inc. $13.50.

Dickey, Charley. **Dove Hunting.** (Illus.). 1976. Oxmoor House. $2.95.

---**Quail Hunting.** (Illus.). 1974. softbound. Stoeger. $3.95.

Elliott, Charles. **Care of Game Meat and Trophies.** (Illus.). 1975. Funk & Wagnalls. $7.50; pap. $4.50.

Gage, Rex. **Game Shooting with Rex Gage.** (Illus.). 1977. pap. International Pubns. Service. $5.00.

Gooch, Bob. **Conveys and Singles.** (Illus.). 1980. A. S. Barnes. $10.95.

——**Squirrels and Squirrel Hunting.** Cornell Maritime Press. $6.00.

Gresham, Grits. **The Complete Wildfowler.** (Illus.). 1975. softbound. Stoeger. $5.95.

Hagerbaumer, David. **Selected American Game Birds.** 1972. Caxton. $30.00.

Hinman, Bob. **The Duck Hunter's Handbook.** (Illus.). 1976. softbound. Stoeger. $5.95.

McCristal, Vic. **Top End Safari.** Soccer. $14.95.

Ormond, Clyde. **Small Game Hunting.** (Illus.). 1974. pap. Barnes & Noble. $1.95.

——**How to Track and Find Game.** (Illus.). 1975. Funk & Wagnalls. $7.50; pap. $4.50.

Rue, Leonard L. **Sportsman's Guide to Game Animals.** (Illus.). 1968. Harper & Row. $13.95.

Rue, Leonard L., III. **Game Birds of North America.** (Illus.). 1973. Times Mirror Mag. $12.50.

Scheid, D. **Raising Game Birds.** 1974. Scribner's. $2.50.

Scott, P. **Coloured Key to the Wildfowl of the World.** rev. ed. (Illus.). 1972. Heinman. $12.50.

Scott, Peter. **A Coloured Key to the Wildfowl of the World.** rev. ed. (Illus.). 1972. International Pubns. Service. $8.50.

Waterman, Charles F. **Hunting Upland Birds.** (Illus.). 1975. softbound. Stoeger. $5.95.

Youel, Milo A. **Cook the Wild Bird.** (Illus.). 1976. A. S. Barnes. $17.50.

GAME AND GAME BIRDS—FRANCE

Villenave, G. M. **Chasse.** (Illus., Fr.). Larousse & Co. $19.75.

GAME AND GAME BIRDS—MEXICO

Tinker, Ben. **Mexican Wilderness and Wildlife.** (Illus.). 1978. University of Texas Press. $9.95.

GAME AND GAME BIRDS—NEW ZEALAND

Poole, A. L. **Wild Animals in New Zealand.** (Illus.). 1969. Reed, A. H. & A. W., Books. $14.25.

GAME AND GAME BIRDS—NORTH AMERICA

Alaska Magazine Editors. **Alaska Hunting Guide.** (Illus.). 1976. pap. Alaska Northwest Publishing Co. $3.95.

Bromhall & Grundle. **British Columbia Game Fish.** pap. International School Book Service. $9.95.

Dalrymple, Byron. **North American Big Game Hunting.** (Illus.). 1974. softbound. Stoeger. $5.95.

——**North American Game Animals.** (Illus.). 1978. Crown. $14.95.

Dickey, Charley. **Quail Hunting.** (Illus.). 1974. softbound. Stoeger. $3.95.

Elman, Robert. **The Hunter's Field Guide.** 1974. Knopf. $12.50.

Gresham, Grits. **The Complete Wildfowler.** (Illus.). 1975. softbound. Stoeger. $5.95.

Hinman, Bob. **The Duck Hunter's Handbook.** (Illus.). 1976. softbound. Stoeger. $6.95.

Holland, Dan. **Upland Game Hunter's Bible.** (Illus.). pap. Doubleday. $3.50.

Jacques, Florence P. **Geese Fly High.** (Illus.). 1964. Repr. of 1939 ed. University of Minnesota Press. $6.95.

Johnsgard, Paul A. **North American Game Birds of Upland and Shoreland.** (Illus.). University of Nebraska Press. $11.95; pap. $6.95.

Knap, Jerome. **All About Wildfowling in America.** 1976. Winchester Press. $10.00.

Leopold A. Starker & Darling, F. Fraser. **Wildlife in Alaska.** 1973. Repr. of 1953 ed. Greenwood Press. $11.25.

Mullin, John M., ed. **Game Bird Propagation.** 1978. North American Game Breeders & Shooting Preserves Association,Inc.(OP). $12.95.

Phillips, John C. **American Game Mammals and Birds: A Catalog of Books, Sports, Natural History and Conservation. 1582-1925.** 1978. Repr. of 1930 ed. Arno Press. $37.00.

Rice, F. Philip & Dahl, John I. **Game Bird Hunting.** (Illus.). 1974. pap. Barnes & Noble. $1.95.

Rue, Leonard L. **Game Birds of North America.** 1973. Harper & Row. $13.50.

Tinsley, Russell, ed. **Small-Game Hunting.** 1977. softbound. Stoeger. $5.95.

——ed. **All About Small-Game Hunting in America.** 1976. Winchester Press. $10.00.

Walsh, H. M. **Outlaw Gunner.** 1971. Cornell Maritime Press. $8.50.

Walsh, Roy. **Gunning the Chesapeake.** 1960. Cornell Maritime. $7.00.

Waterman, Charles F. **Hunting Upland Birds.** (Illus.). 1975. softbound. Stoeger. $5.95.

Zim, Herbert S. & Sprunt, Alexander, 4th. **Game Birds.** 1961. Western Publishing. $5.50; pap. $1.95.

GAME COOKERY

Backus, David. **European Recipes for American Fish and Game.** 1978. pap. Willow Creek. $4.50.

Billmeyer, Pat. **The Encyclopedia of Wild Game Cleaning and Cooking.** (Orig.). 1979. pap. write for info. ABC Publishing.

Candy, Robert. **Getting the Most from Game and Fish.** Hard, Walter, ed. (Illus.). 1978. pap. Garden Way Publishing. $9.95.

Cone, Joan. **Easy Game Cooking: One Hundred and Twenty-Four Savory, Home-Tested Money-Saving Recipes and Menus for Game Birds and Animals.** 1974. EPM Publications. spiral bdg. $4.95.

Fink, Edith & Day, Avenelle. **Hot Birds and Cold Bottles.** 320p. 1972. Delacorte. $10.00.

Goolsby, Sam. **Great Southern Wild Game Cookbook.** 193p. 1980. Pelican. $13.95.

Gorton, Audrey A. **Venison Book: How to Dress, Cut up and Cook Your Deer.** 1957. pap. Greene. $3.95.

Green, Karen & Black, Betty. **How to Cook His Goose: And Other Wild Games.** 1973. Winchester Press. $6.95.

Hanle, Zack. **Cooking Wild Game.** 1974. Liveright. $12.95.

Hull, Raymond & Sleight, Jack. **Home Book of Smoke-Cooking Meat, Fish and Game.** 1971. Stackpole Books. $9.95.

Jenkins, Susan. **Wildgame: Florida's Panhandle Cookbook.** (Florida's Panhandle Cookbook Ser.: No. 3). (Illus.). 48p. (Orig.). 1977. pap. Owen & Jenkins. $2.25.

Johnson, L. W., ed. **Wild Game Cookbook: A Remington Sportsmen's Library Bk.** pap. Benjamin Co. $3.95.

Knight, Jacqueline E. **The Hunter's Game Cookbook.** (Illus.). 1978. Winchester Press. $10.95.

Michigan United Conservation Clubs. **The Wildlife Chef.** new ed. 1977. pap. Mich United Conserv. $3.95.

Rojas-Lombardi, Felipe. **Game Cookery.** (Illus.). 1973. dura. Livingston. $2.95.

——**Game Cookery.** (Illus.). 1973. plastic bdg. Harrowood Books. $2.95.

Rywell, Martin. **Wild Game Cook Book.** 74p. 1952. pap. Buck Hill. $3.75.

Sleight, Jack & Hull, Raymond. **The Home Book of Smoke Cooking, Meat, Fish and Game.** 1975. pap. BJ Pub Group. $1.50.

Steindler, Geraldine. **Game Cookbook.** 209p. 1965. softbound. Stoeger. $6.95.

Wongrey, Jan. **Southern Wildfowl and Wildgame Cookbook.** 1976. Sandlapper Store. $4.95.

Youel, Milo A. **Cook the Wild Bird.** (Illus.). 1976. A. S. Barnes. $17.50.

GATLING GUNS

Johnson, F. Roy & Stephenson, Frank, Jr. **The Gatling Gun and Flying Machine of Richard and Henry Gatling.** (Illus.). 1979. Johnson NC. $9.50.

Wahl, Paul & Toppel, Donald R. **The Gatling Gun.** (Illus.). 1978. pap. Arco. $5.95.

GUNS

Carmichel, Jim. **The Modern Rifle.** (Illus.). 1976. softbound. Stoeger. $5.95.

Daenhardt, Rainer. **Espingarda Perfeyta: or the Perfect Gun: Rules of Its Use Together with Necessary Instructions for Its Construction and Precepts for Good Aiming.** Daenhardt, Rainer, tr. from Port. (Illus., Eng. & Port.). 1975. S. P. Bernet. $46.00.

George, John N. **English Pistols and Revolvers.** Saifer, Albert, Pub. $15.00.

Lindsay, Merrill. **The Lure of Antique Arms.** (Illus.). 1978. softbound. Stoeger. $5.95.

Liu, Allan J., ed. **The American Sporting Collector's Handbook.** (Illus.). 1977. softbound. Stoeger. $5.95.

Luger Manual. (Reprint of original English-language edition.). 1967. softbound. Stoeger. $1.95.

Mauser Manual. (Facs. ed. of early English language Mauser Catalog and Manual.). 1974. softbound. Stoeger. $1.95.

Nonte, George C., Jr. **Black Powder Guide.** 2nd ed. (Illus.). 1976. softbound. Stoeger. $7.95.

——**Pistol Guide.** (Illus.). softbound. Stoeger. $8.95.

——**Revolver Guide.** (Illus.). softbound. Stoeger. $8.95.

O'Connor, Jack. **The Hunting Rifle.** (Illus.). 1975. softbound. Stoeger. $5.95.

Page, Warren. **The Accurate Rifle.** (Illus.). 1975. softbound. Stoeger. $6.95.

Peterson, Harold. **Historical Treasury of American Guns.** Benjamin Co. $4.95; pap. $2.95.

Scott, Robert F., ed. **1982 Shooter's Bible , No. 73.** (Illus.). 1981. softbound. Stoeger. $10.95.

Steindler, R. A. **Rifle Guide.** (Illus.). 1978. softbound. Stoeger. $7.95.

Wahl, Paul. **Gun Trader's Guide.** 9th ed. (Illus.). softbound. Stoeger. $9.95.

GUNSMITHING

Ackley, Parker O. **Home Gun Care and Repair.** (Illus.). 1974. Stackpole Books. $3.95.

Angier, R. H. **Firearms Blueing and Browning.** 1936. Stackpole Books. $9.95.

Bailey, De Witt and Nic, Douglas A. **English Gunmakers: The Birmingham and Provincial Guntrade in the 18th and 19th Century.** (Illus.). 1978. Arco. $18.95.

Bish, Tommy. **Home Gunsmithing Digest.** 2nd ed. 1971. pap. Follett. $7.95.

Bowers, William S. **Gunsmiths of Pen-Mar-Va, Seventeen Ninety to Eighteen Forty.** (Illus.). 1979. Irwinton. $25.00.

Carmichel, Jim. **Do-It-Yourself-Gunsmithing.** (Illus.). 1978. Harper & Row. $13.95.

Demeritt, Dwight B., Jr. **Maine Made Guns and Their Makers.** (Illus.). Maine State Museum Pubns $22.00.

Dunlap, Roy F. **Gunsmithing.** 1963. Stackpole Books. $14.95.

Gaier, Claude. **Four Centuries of Liège Gunmaking.** (Illus.). 1977. Biblio. Distribution Center. $90.00.

Gill, Harold B., Jr. **Gunsmithing in Colonial Virginia.** (Illus.). 1974. University Press of Virginia. $7.50; pap. $4.50.

Gill, Harold, Jr. **The Gunsmith in Colonial Virginia.** 1974. pap. Colonial Williamsburg Foundation. $4.50.

Grancsay, Stephen A. & Lindsay, Merrill. **Master French Gunsmith's Designs: From the Twelfth to Fourteenth Century.** limited ed. (Illus.). Arma Press. $89.00.

Hartzler, Daniel D. **Arms Makers of Maryland.** (Illus.). 1977. George Shumway Publisher. $35.00.

Howe, James V. **Amateur Guncraftsman.** (Illus.). 1967. pap. Funk & Wagnalls. $1.95.

Howe, Walter J. **Professional Gunsmithing.** (Illus.). 1946. Stackpole Books. $14.95.

Hutslar, Donald A. **Gunsmiths of Ohio: 18th and 19th Centuries.** (Illus.). 1973. George Shumway Publisher. $29.50.

Lindsay, Merrill. **The New England Gun: The First 200 Years.** (Illus.). 1976. David McKay Co. $20.00; pap. $12.50.

MacFarland, Harold E. **Gunsmithing Simplified.** (Illus.). A. S. Barnes. $12.00.

——**Introduction to Modern Gunsmithing.** (Illus.). 1975. pap. Barnes & Noble. $2.95.

Newell, A. Donald. **Gunstock Finishing and Care.** (Illus.). 1949. Stackpole Books. $12.95.

Norton Art Gallery. **Artistry in Arms: The Art of Gunsmithing and Gun Engraving.** (Illus.). 1971. pap. Norton Art Gallery. $2.50.

Shelton, Lawrence P. **California Gunsmiths.** (Illus.). 1977. George Shumway Publisher. $26.95.

Smith, Loren W. **Home Gunsmithing: The Colt Single Action Revolvers.** (Illus.). 1971. Ray Riling, Arms Books. $7.95.

Steindler, R. A. **Home Gunsmithing Digest.** 2nd ed. 1978. pap. Follett. $7.95.

Stelle & Harrison. **The Gunsmith's Manual: A Complete Handbook for the American Gunsmith.** (Illus.). Repr. of 1883 ed. Gun Room Press. $9.95.

Traister, John E. **Basic Gunsmithing.** (Illus.). pap. TAB Books. $8.95.

——**Gun Digest of Gunsmithing Tools and Their Uses.** 1980. pap. DBI Books. $7.95.

Walker, Ralph. **Hobby Gunsmithing.** (Illus.). 1972. pap. Follett. $6.95.

——**Black Powder Gunsmithing.** 1978. pap. Follett. $6.95.

GUNSTOCKS

Arthur, Robert. **Shotgun Stock: Design, Construction and Embellishment.** (Illus.). 1970. A. S. Barnes. (OP) $17.50.

HAWKEN RIFLES

Baird, John D. **Fifteen Years in the Hawken Lode.** (Illus.). Gun Room Press. $12.95.

——**Hawken Rifles. The Mountain Man's Choice.** Gun Room Press. $12.95.

HUNTING

Acerrano, Anthony J. **The Practical Hunter's Handbook.** (Illus.). 1978. Winchester Press. $10.00.

Amory, Cleveland. **Man Kind? Our Incredible War on Wildlife.** 1974. Harper & Row. $12.50.

Anderson, Luther A. **Hunting the Woodlands for Small and Big Game.** (Illus.). 1980. A S Barnes. $12.00.

Ardrey, Robert. **The Hunting Hypothesis.** 1977. pap. Bantam Books. $2.25.

Babcock, Havilah. **Jaybirds Go to Hell on Friday.** 1964. Holt, Rinehart & Winston. (OP) $4.95.

Bashline, L. James. ed. **The Eastern Trail.** (Illus.). 1972. Freshet Press. $8.95.

——**Hunter's Digest.** 1973. DBI Books. $6.95.

Bauer, Erwin. **Hunter's Digest.** DBI Bks. 1973. pap. $7.95.

Bauer, Erwin A., ed. **Hunter's Digest.** 2nd ed. (Illus.). 1979. pap. Follett. $7.95.

Beckford, Peter. **Thoughts on Hunting.** (Illus.). Repr. British Book Center. price not set.

Berners, Juliana. **The Boke of St. Albans Containing Treatises on Hawking, Hunting and Cote Armour.** 1976. Repr. of 1881 ed. Scholarly Press. $25.00.

——**The Book of Hawking, Hunting and Blasing of Arms.** 1969. Repr. of 1486 ed. W. J. Johnson. $42.00.

Bourjaily, Vance. **Country Matters: Collected Reports from the Fields and Streams of Iowa and Other Places.** 1973. Dial Press. $8.95.

——**Unnatural Enemy.** (Illus.). 1963. Dial Press. $6.95.

Bowring, Dave. **How to Hunt.** (Illus.). 1978. Winchester Press. $10.95.

Brakefield, Tom. **Small Game Hunting.** (Illus.). 1978. Lippincott. $10.00.

Brister, Bob. **Shotgunning: The Art and The Science.** 1976. Winchester Press. $12.95.

Bucher, Ruth & Gelb. Norman. **The Book of Hunting.** (Illus.). 1977. Paddington Press. $60.00.

Buckle, Esme, compiled by. **Dams of National Hunt Winners, 1963-64.** pap. (Dist. by Sporting Book Center). J. A. Allen. $3.75.

——**Dams of National Hunt Winners, 1966-73.** (Illus.). pap. (Dist. by Sporting Book Center). J. A. Allen. $15.75.

——**Dams of National Hunt Winners: 1973-75.** J. A. Allen. $15.00.

Cadman, Arthur. **A Guide to Rough Shooting.** (Illus.). 1975. David & Charles. $11.50.

Cartier, John O. ed. **Twenty Great Trophy Hunts.** 1980. David McKay Co. $17.50.

Clarke, I. A. **An Introduction to Beagling.** (Illus.). 1974. British Book Center. $4.95.

Clayton, Michael. **A-Hunting We Will Go.** 1972. British Book Center. $8.50.

Cone, Arthur L., Jr. **The Complete Guide to Hunting.** (Illus.). 1978. softbound. Stoeger. $5.95.

——**Complete Guide to Hunting.** 1970. Macmillan. $6.95.

Coon, Carleton S. **The Hunting Peoples.** 1972. Rowman. $10.00.

Dalrymple, Byron W. **the Complete Book of Deer Hunting.** (Illus.). 1976. softbound. Stoeger. $5.95.

——**North American Big Game Hunting.** (Illus.). 1975. softbound. Stoeger. $5.95.

DeRuttie, Andrew. **Hunting on a Budget—for Food and Profit.** 1975. pap. Major Books. $1.25.

Dickey, Charley. **Quail Hunting.** (Illus.). 1974. softbound. Stoeger. $3.95.

——**Charley Dickey's Bobwhite Quail Hunting.** (Illus.). 1975. Oxmoor House. $9.95.

——**Charley Dickey's Bobwhite Quail Hunting.** (Illus.). 1974. pap. (Family Guide Book Set). Oxmoor House. $3.95.

Dodd, Ed. **Mark Trail's Hunting Tips.** (Illus.). 1969. pap. Essandess. $1.00.

——**Mark Trail's Hunting Tips.** pap. Pocket Books. $1.00.

Dougherty, Jim. **Varmint Hunter's Digest.** 1977. pap. Follett. $6.95.

East, Ben. **The Ben East Hunting Book.** (Illus.). 1974. Harper & Row. $13.95.

Eggert, Richard. **Fish and Hunt the Back Country.** 1978. Stackpole Books. $9.95.

Elliott, William. **Carolina Sports by Land and Water: Incidents of Devil-Fishing. Wild-Cat, Deer and Bear Hunting.** (Illus.). 1978. Repr. of 1859 ed. Attic Press. $10.00.

Elman, Robert. **The Hunter's Field Guide.** 1974. Knopf. $12.50.

——**One Thousand One Hunting Tips.** (Illus.). 1978. Winchester Press. $15.95.

Fadala, Sam. **Blackpowder Hunting.** 1978. Stackpole Books. $10.95.

Ferber, Steve. Ed. **All About Rifle Hunting and Shooting in America.** 1977. Winchester Press. $10.00.

Field & Stream. **Field & Stream Reader.** facs. ed. 1946. Arno. $19.50.

Frankenstein, Alfred. **After the Hunt.** (Illus.). 1974. University of California Press. $35.00.

Gilsvik, Bob. **All-Season Hunting.** (Illus.). 1977. softbound. Stoeger. $5.95.

——**The Guide to Good Cheap Hunting.** (Illus.). 1979. Stein & Day. $10.95; pap. $5.95.

——**All Season Hunting.** 1976. Winchester Press. $9.95.

Gooch, Bob, Conveys and Singles. (Illus.). 1980. A. S. Barnes. $10.95.

——**Land You Can Hunt.** (Illus.). 1980. A S Barnes. $12.00.

Gresham, Grits. **The Complete Wildfowler.** (Illus.). 1975. softbound. Stoeger. $5.95.

Grey, Hugh, ed. **Field & Stream Treasury.** 1971. Holt, Rinehart & Winston. (OP) $12.95.

Grey, Zane. **Zane Grey, Outdoorsman: Zane Grey's Best Hunting and Fishing Tales.** Reiger, George, ed. (Illus.). 1972. Prentice-Hall. $9.95.

Grinnel, George B. & Sheldon, Charles, eds. **Hunting and Conservation.** 1970. Repr. of 1925 ed. Arno. $25.00.

Gryndall, William, **Hawking, Hunting, Fouling and Fishing: Newly Corrected by W. Gryndall Faulkener.** 1972. Repr. of 1596 ed. W. J. Johnson. $13.00.

Hagel, Bob. **Game Loads and Practical Ballistics for the American Hunter.** (Illus.). 1978. Knopf. $12.95.

Hammond, Samuel H. Wild. **Northern Scene in Sporting Adventures with Rifle and the Rod.** (Illus.). 1979. Repr. of 1857 ed. Harbor Hill Books. $12.50.

Hanenkrat, William F. **The Education of a Turkey Hunter.** 1974. Winchester Press. $8.95.

Harbour, Dave. **Hunting the American Wild Turkey.** (Illus.). 1975. Stackpole Books. (OP) $8.95.

Harker, Peter & Eunson, Keith. **Hunting with Harker.** (Illus.). 1976. Reed, A. H. & A. W., Books. (OP) $9.75.

Hastings, Macdonald. **Churchill's Gameshooting.** 1974. (Pub. by Michael Joseph.) Merrimack Book Service. $19.95.

Heacox, Cecil E. & Heacox, Dorothy. **The Gallant Grouse: All About the Hunting and Natural History of Old Ruff.** (Illus.). 1980. David McKay Co. $14.95.

Hill, Gene. **A Hunter's Fireside Book: Tales of Dogs, Ducks, Birds and Guns.** (Illus.). 1972. Winchester Press. $9.95.

——**Mostly Tailfeathers.** 1975. Winchester Press. $8.95; limited ed. $20.00.

Hinman, Bob. **The Duck Hunter's Handbook.** (Illus.). 1976. softbound. Stoeger. $6.95.

Holden, Philip. **Hunter by Profession.** (Illus.). 1974. International Pubns. Service. $9.90.

Hunting Magazine Eds., ed. **Hunting Annual 1981.** (Illus.). 1980. pap. Petersen Publishing. $6.95.

James, Davis & Stephens, Wilson, eds. **In Praise of Hunting.** (Illus.). 1961. Devin-Adair Co. $10.00.

Janes, Edward C. **Boy and His Gun.** (Illus.). 1951. A S Barnes. $6.95.

——**Ringneck! Pheasants and Pheasant Hunting.** (Illus.). 1975. Crown. $8.95.

Johnson, et al. **Outdoor Tips.** pap. Benjamin Co. $2.95.

Klineburger, Bert & Hurst, Vernon W. **Big Game Hunting Around the World.** (Illus.). 1969. Exposition Press. $15.00.

Knap, Jerome. **The Digest Book of Hunting Tips.** 1979. pap. Follett. $2.95.

——**Hunter's Handbook.** 1973. Scribner's. $3.50.

Knap, Jerome J. **Complete Hunter's Almanac: A Guide to Everything the Hunter Needs to Know About Guns, Game, Tracking and Gear with a Special Section on Hunting Locations in North America.** (Illus.). 1978. Pagurian Press.

Laycock, George. **Shotgunner's Bible.** (Illus.). 1969. pap. Doubleday. $2.95.

Lindner, Kurt. **The Second Hunting Book of Wolfgang Birkner.** (Illus.). 1976. with case Arma Press. $175.00.

McCristal, Vic. **Top End Safari.** Sportshelf & Soccer Associates. $14.95.

McNair, Paul C. **The Sportsman's Crafts Book.** 1978. Winchester Press. $10.95.

Madden, D. H. **Chapter of Mediaeval History.** 1969. Repr. of 1924 ed. Kennikat Press. $15.00.

Madden, Dodgson H. **Diary of Master William Silence: A Study of Shakespeare and Elizabethan Sport.** 1970. Repr. of 1897 ed. Haskell Booksellers. $51.95.

Marchington, John. **Game Shooting: Management and Economics.** (Illus.). 1976. Merrimack Book Service. $10.95.

Merrill, William K. **Hunter's Bible.** (Illus.). 1968. Doubleday. $2.95.

Mosher, John A. **The Shooter's Workbench.** 1977. Winchester Press. $10.95.

Mueller, Larry. **Bird Dog Guide.** (Illus.). 1976. softbound. Stoeger. $6.95.

Needwood. **The Hunting Quiz Book.** pap. British Book Center. $2.95.

Nonte, George C., Jr. & Jurras, Lee E. **Handgun Hunting.** (Illus.).1976. softbound.Stoeger. $5.95.

O'Connor, Jack. **The Hunting Rifle.** (Illus.). 1975. softbound. Stoeger. $5.95.

——**Shotgun Book.** (Illus.). 1978. Knopf. $15.00; pap. $8.95.

Ormond, Clyde. **Complete Book of Hunting.** rev. ed. (Illus.). 1972. Harper & Row. $10.95.

——**Small Game Hunting.** 1970. Dutton. $4.95.

——**Outdoorsman's Handbook.** 1975. pap. Berkeley Publishing. $1.95.

Page, Warren. **One Man's Wilderness.** 1973. Holt, Rinehart & Winston. (OP). $8.95.

Petzal, David E. ed. **Experts' Book of the Shooting Sports.** Simon & Schuster. $9.95.

Pollard, Hugh B. **The Mystery of Scent.** 1972. British Book Center. $4.95.

Pollard, Jack. **Straight Shooting.** Sportshelf & Soccer Associates. $14.50.

Pryce, Dick. **Hunting for Beginners.** (Illus.). 1978. softbound. Stoeger. $5.95.

Pulling, Pierre. **Game and the Gunner: Common-Sense Observations on the Practice of Game Conservation and Sport Hunting.** 1973. Winchester Press. $8.95.

Randolph, J. W. **World of Wood, Field and Stream.** 1962. Holt, Rinehart & Winston. $3.95.

Rees, Clair & Wixom, Hartt. **The Penny-Pinching Guide to Bigger Fish and Better Hunting.** (Illus.). 1980. Winchester Press. $9.95.

Robinson, Jerome B. **Hunt Close!** (Illus.). 1978. Winchester Press. $10.00.

Scharff, Robert. **Hunter's Game, Gun and Dog Guide.** 1963. pap. Macmillan. $1.95.

Schwenk, Sigrid, et al. eds. **Multum et Multa: Beitraege zur Literatur, Geschichte und Kultur der Jagd.** (Illus.). 1971. De Gruyter. $75.00.

Scott, Robert F. **Shooter's Bible 1982, No. 73.** (Illus.). 1981. softbound. Stoeger. $10.95.

Sell, Francis. **Art of Small Game Hunting.** 1973. pap. Stackpole Books. (OP). $3.95.

Sparano, Vin T. **The Complete Outdoors Encyclopedia.** (Illus.). 1973. Harper & Row. $18.95.

Spiller, Burton. **Grouse Feathers.** (Sportsmen's Classics Ser.). (Illus.). 1972. Crown. (OP). $8.95.

Spiller, Burton L. **More Grouse Feathers.** (Illus.). 1972. Crown. (OP). $7.50.

Stehsel, Donald L. **Hunting the California Black Bear.** (Illus.). pap. Donald Stehsel. $4.95.

Strung, N. **Complete Hunter's Catalog.** (Illus.). 1978. pap. Lippincott. $8.95.

Tapply, Horace G. **Sportsman's Notebook.** 1964. Holt, Rinehart & Winston. (OP). $7.95.

Taylor, Zack. **Successful Waterfowling.** (Illus.). 1974. Crown. (OP). $8.95.

Tinsley, Russell. **Bow Hunter's Guide.** (Illus.). 1975. softbound. Stoeger. $5.95.

——**Small-Game Hunting.** (Illus.). 1977. softbound. Stoeger. $5.95.

Trueblood, Ted. **The Ted Trueblood Hunting Treasury.** (Illus.). 1978. David McKay Co. $14.95.

Washburn, O. A. **General Red.** (Illus.). Jenkins. $5.50.

Waterman, Charles F. **Hunter's World.** (Illus.). 1970. Random House. $15.00.

——**Hunting Upland Birds.** (Illus.). 1975. softbound. Stoeger. $5.95.

——**The Part I Remember.** (Illus.). 1974. Winchester Press. $8.95.

Wehle, Robert G. **Wing and Shot.** (Illus.). 1971. Country Press. $8.50; deluxe ed. $20.00.

Whisker, James. B. **The Right to Hunt.** 1980. Caroline House. $7.95.

——**The Right to Hunt.** 1981. North River Press. $7.95.

Willett, Roderick. **Gun Safety.** (Illus.). 1967. International Pubns. Service. $5.25.

Wilson, James. **The Rod and the Gun.** (Illus.). 1973. Repr. of 1844 ed. British Book Center. $16.95.

Wilson, Loring. **The Handy Sportsman.** (Illus.). 1977. softbound. Stoeger. $5.95.

Woodcock, E. N. **Fifty Years a Hunter and Trapper.** pap. Fur-Fish-Game A. R. Harding. $2.50.

Woolner, Frank. **Timberdoodle: A Thorough Guide to Woodcock Hunting.** (Illus.). 1974. Crown. $7.95.

Woolner, Lionel. **Hunting of the Hare.** 1972. British Book Center. $7.50.

Zutz, Don. **Handloading for Hunters.** 1977. Winchester Press. $12.50.

HUNTING—DICTIONARIES

Brander, Michael. **Dictionary of Sporting Terms.** (Illus.) 1968. Humanities Press. $7.00.

Burnand, Tony. **Dictionnaire chasse. (Dictionnaires de l'homme du vingtieme siecle).** (Fr.) 1970. Larousse & Co. $7.75.

——**Dictionnaire De la Chasse.** 250p. (Fr.) 1970. pap. French & European Pubns. Inc. $7.50.

Frevert, W. **Woerterbuch der Jaegerei.** 4th ed. (Ger.) 1975. French & European Pubns. Inc. $12.00.

Kehrein, Franz. **Woerterbuch der Weidmannssprache.** (Ger.) 1969. French & European Pubns. Inc. $36.00.

Kirchoff, Anne. **Woerterbuch der Jagel. (Ger., Eng. & Fr. Dictionary of Hunting).** 1976. French & European Pubns. Inc. $27.50.

Sparano, Vin T. **The Sportsman's Dictionary of Fishing and Hunting Lingo.** (Illus.). 1980. David McKay Co. $12.95.

Wisconsin Hunting Encyclopedia. 1976. pap. Wisconsin Sportsman. $2.95.

HUNTING—HISTORY

Butler, Alfred J. **Sport in Classic Times.** (Illus.). 1975. W. Kaufman. $11.95.

Cheney, Roberta & Erskine, Clyde. **Music, Saddles and Flapjacks: Dudes at the Oto Ranch.** 1978. Mountain Press. $12.95.

Danielsson, Bror, ed. **William Twiti's the Art of Hunting, Vol. 1.** (Illus.). 1977. pap. Humanities Press. $31.50.

Greene, Robert. **The Third and Last Part of Conny-Catching.** 1923. Arden Library. $12.50.

Harding, Robert S. ed. **Omnivorous Primates: Gathering and Hunting in Human Evolution.** Teleki, Geza P. (Illus.). 1981. Columbia University Press. $35.00.

Petersen, Eugene T. **Hunters' Heritage: A History of Hunting in Michigan.** Lowe, Kenneth S., ed. (Illus.). 1979. Michigan United Conservation Clubs. $4.65.

Rick, John W. **Prehistoric Hunters of the High Andes.** (Studies in Archaeology Ser.) 1980. Academic Press. $27.50.

Spiess, Arthur E. **Reindeer and Caribou Hunters: An Archaeological Study.** (Studies in Archaeology Ser.). 1979. Academic Press. $27.00.

HUNTING—PRIMITIVE

Clarke, Grahame. **Stone Age Hunters.** 1967. McGraw-Hill. $5.50; pap. $2.95.

Coon, Carleton. **The Hunting Peoples.** 1971. Little, Brown & Co. (OP) $10.00; pap. $3.95.

——**The Hunting Peoples.** (Illus.). 1979. Merrimack Book Service. $9.50.

Frison, George C. **Prehistoric Hunter's of the High Plains.** 1978. Academic Press. $29.50.

Gerstacker, Friedrich. **Wild Sports in the Far West.** Steeves, Edna L. & Steeves, Harrison R., eds. 1968. Duke University Press. $14.75.

Lee, Richard B. & De Vore, Irven. eds. **Man the Hunter.** 1968. pap. Aldine. $10.95.

Marks, Stuart A. **Large Mammals and a Brave People: Subsistence Hunters in Zambia.** (Illus.). 1976. University of Washington Press. $16.00.

Sergeant, R. B. **South Arabian Hunt.** 1976. text ed. Verry, Lawrence Co. $20.00.

Service, Elman R. **Hunters.** (Illus.). 1966. pap. Prentice-Hall. $3.95.

HUNTING—AFRICA

Capstick, Peter H. **Death in the Long Grass.** (Illus.). 1978. St. Martin's Press. $10.00.

Cloudsley-Thompson, J. L. **Animal Twilight, Man and Game in Eastern Africa.** (Illus.). 1967. Dufour Editions, Inc. $10.50.

Findlay, Frederick R. N. & Croonwright-Schreiner, S. C. **Big Game Shooting and Travel in Southeast Africa: Account of Shooting Trips in the Cheringoma and Gorongoza Divisions of Portuguese South-East Africa and in Zululand.** Repr. of 1903 ed. Books for Libraries. $40.25.

Gilmore, Parker. **Days and Nights by the Desert.** Repr. of 1888 ed. Books for Libraries. $20.50.

Haardt, Georges M. & Audouin-Dubreuil, Louis. **Black Journey: Across Central Africa with Citroen Expedition.** (Illus.). Repr. of 1927 ed. Negro University Press. $18.25.

Hemingway, Ernest. **Green Hills of Africa.** 1935. Scribner's. $7.95; pap. $4.95.

Herne, Brian. **Ugandi Safaris.** 1980. Winchester Press. $12.95.

Holub, Emil. **Seven Years in South Africa.** 2 vols. 1881. Set. Scholarly Press. $45.00.

—**Seven Years in South Africa: Travels, Researches and Hunting Adventures Between the Diamond Field and the Zambesi, 1827-79.** 2 vols. 1971. Repr. of 1881 ed. Johnson Reprint Corp. $57.00.

MacQueen, Peter. **In Wildest Africa.** 1909. Scholarly Press. $29.00.

Mazet, Horace S. **Wild Ivory.** 1971. Galloway. $6.95.

Mohr, Jack. **Hyenas in My Bedroom.** (Illus.). 1969. A S Barnes. (OP) $5.95.

Nassau, Robert H. **In an Elephant Corral: And Other Tales of West African Experiences.** Repr. of 1912 ed. Negro University Press. $8.00.

Pohl, Victor. **Farewell the Little People.** (Illus.). 1968. pap. Oxford University Press. $3.75.

HUNTING—ALASKA

Alaska Hunting Guide: (Illus.). 1976. pap. Alaska Northwest. $3.95.

Alaska Hunting Guide 1978-79. rev. ed. (Illus.). pap. Alaska Northwest. $5.95.

Alaska Magazine Editors. **Selected Alaska Hunting and Fishing Tales. Vol. 4.** 1976. pap. Alaska Northwest. $3.95.

Hubback, T. R. **Ten Thousand Miles to Alaska for Moose and Sheep.** facs. ed. 1921. Shorey. $4.00.

Joll, Gary. **To Alaska to Hunt.** (Illus.). 1978. pap. International Publications Service. $8.50.

Keim, Charles J. **Alaska Game Trails with a Master Guide.** pap. Alaska Northwest. $6.95.

Waugh, Hal & Keim, Charles J. **Fair Chase with Alaskan Guides.** (Illus.). 1972. pap. Alaska Northwest. $3.95.

HUNTING—ARCTIC REGIONS

Nelson, Richard K. **Hunters of the Northern Ice.** 1969. University of Chicago Press. $17.50.

Stefansson, Vilhjalmur. **Hunters of the Great North.** 1922. AMS Press. $22.00.

HUNTING—AUSTRALIA

Byrne, Jack. **Duck Hunting in Australia and New Zealand.** (Illus.). 1974. Reed, A. H. & A. W., Books. (OP) $9.25.

Stewart, Allan. **The Green Eyes Are Buffaloes.** Sportshelf & Soccer Associates. $17.50.

HUNTING—FRANCE

Villenave, G. M. **Chasse.** (Illus., Fr.). Larousse & Co. $19.75.

HUNTING—GREAT BRITAIN

Danielsson, Bror, ed. **William Twiti's the Art of Hunting.** Vol. 1. (Illus.). 1977. pap. text ed. Humanities Press. $31.50.

Edward of Norwich. **Master of Game: Oldest English Book on Hunting.** Baillie-Grohman, William A. & Baillie-Grohman, F. eds. (Illus.). Repr. of 1904 ed. AMS Press. $45.00.

Hands, Rachel, ed. **English Hawking & Hunting in the Boke of St. Albans.** facs ed. (Illus.). 1975. Oxford University Press. $48.00.

Hewitt, H. P. **Fairest Hunting: Hunting and Watching Exmoor Deer.** 1974. British Book Center. $4.95.

Jeffries, Richard. **The Gamekeeper at Home and the Amateur Poacher.** 1978. pap. Oxford University Press. $5.95.

Thomas, William B. **Hunting England: A Survey of the Sport and of Its Chief Grounds.** 1978. Repr. of 1936 ed. R West. $30.00.

HUNTING—GREECE

Butler, Alfred J. **Sport in Classic Times.** (Illus.). 1975. W. Kaufmann. $11.95.

Hull, Denison B. **Hounds and Hunting in Ancient Greece.** (Illus.). 1964. University of Chicago Press. $15.00.

HUNTING—INDIA

Jaipal. **Great Hunt.** 1980. Carlton Press. $9.50.

Taylor, John. **Wild Life in India's Tiger Kingdom.** 1980. Carlton Press. $11.00.

HUNTING—NEW ZEALAND

Byrne, Jack. **Duck Hunting in Australia and New Zealand.** (Illus.). 1974. Reed, A. H. & A. W., Books. (OP) $9.25.

Forrester, Rex & Illingworth, Neil. **Hunting in New Zealand.** (Illus.). 1967. Reed, A. H. & A. W., Books. (OP) $8.25.

Joll, Gary. **Big Game Hunting in New Zealand.** (Illus.). 1968. International Pubns. Service. $9.00.

Roberts, Gordon. **Game Animals in New Zealand.** (Illus.). 1968. Reed, A. H. & A. W., Books. (OP) $7.50.

HUNTING—NORTH AMERICA

Anderson, Luther A. **How to Hunt American Small Game.** (Illus.). 1969. Funk & Wagnalls. (OP) $5.95.

Dalrymple, Byron W. **North American Big Game Hunting.** (Illus.). 1975. softbound. Stoeger. $5.95.

Elman, Robert. **The Hunter's Field Guide.** 1974. Knopf. $12.50.

Elman, Robert & Peper, George, eds. **Hunting America's Game Animals and Birds.** (Illus.). 1975. Winchester Press. $12.95.

Holland, Dan. **Upland Game Hunter's Bible.** (Illus.). pap. Doubleday. $3.50.

Knap, Jerome. **Where to Fish and Hunt in North America: A Complete Sportsman's Guide.** (Illus.). Pagurian Press. $8.95.

Leopold, Luna B., ed. **Round River: From The Journals of Aldo Leopold.** (Illus.). 1972. pap. Oxford University Press. $2.50.

O'Connor, Jack. **The Art of Big Game Hunting in North America.** 2nd ed. 1977. Knopf. $13.95.

Ormond, Clyde. **Small Game Hunting.** rev. ed. (Illus.). 1977. Funk & Wagnalls. $7.95; pap. $4.95.

Petzal, David E. **The Expert's Book of Big Game Hunting in North America.** (Illus.). 1976. Simon & Schuster. $10.95.

Smith. **The One-Eyed Poacher.** 1980. Repr. Downeast. $4.50.

HUNTING—U.S.

Abbott, Henry. **Birch Bark Books of Henry Abbott: Sporting Adventures and Nature Observations in the Adirondacks in the Early 1900s.** (Illus., Repr. of 1914 & 1932 eds.). 1980. Harbor Hill Books. $19.95.

Babcock, H. **My Health Is Better In November.** (Illus.). 1960. Holt, Rinehart & Winston. $5.95.

Bailey's Hunting Directory. 1978-79. (Illus.). 1978. J A Allen. $23.25.

Cadbury, Warder, intro. by. **Journal of a Hunting Excursion to Louis Lake. 1851.** (Illus.).1961. Syracuse University Press. $7.95.

Cone, Arthur L. **The Complete Guide to Hunting.** (Illus.). 1978. softbound. Stoeger. $5.95.

Cory, Charles B. **Hunting and Fishing in Florida, Including a Key to the Water Birds.** 1970. Repr. of 1896 ed. Arno. $14.00.

Dalrymple, Bryon W. **The Complete Book of Deer Hunting.** (Illus.). 1975. softbound. Stoeger. $6.95.

—**North American Big Game Hunting.** (Illus.). 1975. softbound. Stoeger. $5.95.

Duffy, M. **Hunting and Fishing in Louisiana.** 1969. Pelican. (OP). $4.95.

Elman, Robert, ed. **All About Deer Hunting in America.** 1976. Winchester Press. $12.95.

Gilsvik, Bob. **All-Season Hunting.** (Illus.). 1976, softbound. Stoeger. $5.95.

Gohdes, Clarence, ed. **Hunting in the Old South: Original Narratives of the Hunters.** (Illus.). 1967. Louisiana State University Press. $7.50.

Kaplan, Meyer A. **Varmint Hunting.** 1977. pap. Monarch Press. $2.95.

Lang, Varley. **Follow the Water.** (Illus.). 1961. Blair, John F. $4.50.

McTeer, Ed. **Adventures in the Woods & Waters of the Low Country.** Beaufort Book Co. $5.95.

Mitchell, John G. **The Hunt.** 1980. Knopf. $10.95.

Murray, William H. **Adventures in the Wilderness.** Verner, William K., ed. (Illus.). 1970. Repr. Syracuse University Press. $10.50.

O'Connor, Jack. **The Hunting Rifle.** (Illus.). 1975. softbound. Stoeger. $5.95.

Palliser, John. **Solitary Rambles and Adventures of a Hunter in the Prairies.** (Illus.). 1969. Repr. of 1853 ed. C E Tuttle. $5.00.

Pryce, Dick. **Hunting for Beginners.** (Illus.). 1978. softbound. Stoeger. $5.95.

Rearden, Jim, ed. **Alaska Magazine's Alaska Hunting Guide** (Illus.). 1979. pap. Alaska Northwest. $5.95.

Richardson, Larry. **A Guide to Hunting in Tennessee.** (Illus.). 1980. pap. Thomas Press. $7.95.

Roosevelt. Theodore. **Hunting Trips of a Ranchman.** 1970. Repr. of 1885 ed. Gregg Press. $12.50.

—**Hunting Trips of a Ranchman.** Repr. of 1885 ed. Irvington. $17.50.

—**Outdoor Pastimes of an American Hunter.** 1970. Repr. of 1905 ed. Arno Press. $24.00.

—**Ranch Life and the Hunting-Trail.** 1970. Repr. of 1901 ed. Arno Press. $12.00.

—**Ranch Life and the Hunting-Trail.** 1966. Repr. of 1899 ed. University Microfilms International. $8.95.

—**Ranch Life in the Far West.** (Illus.). 1968. Northland Press. $6.00.

—**Theodore Roosevelt's America.** Wiley, Farida, ed. (Illus.). 1955. Devin-Adair Co. $7.50.

—**Wilderness Hunter.** 1970. Repr. of 1900 ed. Irvington. $16.00.

Sandoz, Mari. **The Buffalo-Hunters: The Story of the Hide Men.** 1978. pap. University of Nebraska Press. $4.50.

Tillett, Paul. **Doe Day: the Antlerless Deer Controversy in New Jersey.** 1963. Rutgers University Press. $6.00; pap. $3.25.

Tome, Philip. **Pioneer Life or Thirty Years a Hunter: Being Scenes and Adventures in the Life of Philip Tome.** (Illus.). 1971. Repr. of 1854 ed. Arno Press. $10.00.

Wootters, John. **A Guide to Hunting in Texas.** 1979. pap. Pacesetter Press. $5.95.

HUNTING DOGS

Baily's Hunting Directory 1974-1975. 1975. British Book Center. $22.50.

Bernard, Art. **Dog Days.** 1969. Caxton. $5.95.

Brown, William F. **Field Trials.** (Illus.). 1977. A S Barnes. $12.00.

Drabble, Phil. **Of Pedigree Unknown: Sporting and Working Dogs.** (Illus.). 1977. Transatlantic Arts, Inc. $8.75.

Duffey, Dave. **Hunting Dog Know-How.** (Illus.). 1972. Winchester Press. $6.95.

——**Hunting Hounds: How to Choose, Train and Handle America's Trail and Tree Hounds.** (Illus.). 1972. Winchester Press. $6.95.

Duffey, David M. **Dave Duffey Trains Gun Dogs.** (Illus.). 1974. Dreenan Press. $7.95.

——**Expert Advice on Gun Dog Training.** 1977. Winchester Press. $11.95.

Erlandson, Keith. **Gundog Training.** 1978. Barrie & Jenkins. $11.95.

Falk, John R. **The Practical Hunter's Dog Book.** (Illus.). 1975. softbound. Stoeger. $5.95.

Goodall, Charles. **How to Train Your Own Gun Dog.** (Illus.). 1978. Howell Book House, Inc. $8.95.

Hartley, Oliver. **Hunting Dogs.** pap. Fur-Fish-Game (A. R. Harding Pub.) $2.50.

——**Hunting Dogs.** pap. A. R. Harding Pub. $3.00.

Henschel, Stan. **How to Raise and Train a Chesapeake Bay Retriever.** 1965. pap. TFH Pubns. $1.50.

——**How to Raise and Train a Coonhound.** pap TFH Pubns. $1.79.

——**How to Raise and Train a Labrador Retriever.** (Illus.). pap. TFH Pubns. $1.29.

Irving, Joe. **Training Spaniels.** (Illus.). 1980. David & Charles. $18.50.

Knap, Jerome. **The Digest Book of Hunting Dogs.** (Illus.). 1979. pap. DBI Books. $2.95.

Lent, Patricia A. **Sport with Terriers.** (Illus.). 1973. Arner Pubns. $8.95.

Mueller, Larry. **Bird Dog Guide.** (Illus.). 1976. softbound. Stoeger. $6.95.

Rice, F. Philip & Dahl, John. **Hunting Dogs.** 1967. Harper & Row. $10.95.

——**Hunting Dogs.** rev. ed. (Illus.). 1978. T Y Crowell. $7.95; pap. $4.50.

Russell, Joanna. **All About Gazehounds.** (Illus.). 1976. Merrimack Book Service. $9.95.

Salmon, H. M. **Gazehounds and Coursing.** (Illus.). 1977. North Star Press. $18.50.

Stetson, Joe. **Hunting with Scenthounds.** 1965. pap. TFH Pubns. $1.79.

——**Handbook of Gundogs.** 1965. pap. TFH Pubns. $1.79.

——**Hunting with Flushing Dogs.** 1965. pap. TFH Pubns. $1.79.

Tarrant, Bill. **Best Way to Train Your Gun Dog: The Delmar Smith Method.** 1977. McKay, David, Co. $10.95.

Wehle, Robert G. **Wing and Shot.** 1964. Country Press NY. $12.00.

Whitney, Leon F. & Underwood, Acil B. **Coon Hunter's Handbook.** Hart, Ernest, ed. (Illus.). 1952. Holt, Rinehart & Winston. $5.95.

Wolters, Richard A. **Gun Dog. Revolutionary Rapid Training Method.** (Illus.). 1961. Dutton. $9.95.

HUNTING DOGS—POINTERS

Hart, Ernest H. **How to Raise and Train a Pointer.** (Illus.). 1966. TFH Pubns. $1.79.

Pet Library Ltd. **Know Your Setters and Pointers.** (Illus.). pap. Doubleday. $1.50.

Spirer, L. Z. & Spirer, H. F. **German Short-Haired Pointer.** 1970. TFH Pubns. $5.95.

Steinfeldt, Cecilia. **The Onderdonks: A Family of Texas Pointers.** 1975. Trinity University Press. $25.00.

Stetson, Joe. **Hunting with Pointing Dogs.** 1965. pap. TFH Pubns. $1.50.

HUNTING DOGS—RETRIEVERS

Coykendall, Ralph W., Jr. **You and Your Retriever.** (Illus.). 1963. Doubleday. $5.95.

Fowler, Ann & Walters, D. K., eds. **Charles Morgan on Retrievers.** (Illus.). 1968. October House. $17.50.

Free, James L. **Training Your Retriever.** 5th rev. ed. (Illus.). 1974. Coward, McCann & Geoghegan. $8.95.

Kersley, J. A. **Training the Retriever: A Manual.** (Illus.). 1971. Howell Book House. $11.95.

Leclerc, Maurice J. **Retriever Trainer's Manual.** (Illus.). 1962. Ronald Press. (OP.) $8.50.

Pet Library Ltd. **Know Your Retriever.** (Illus.). pap. Doubleday. $1.50.

Stetson, Joe. **Hunting with Retrievers.** pap. TFH Pubns. $1.79.

Wolters, Richard A. **Water Dog.** (Illus.). Dutton. $9.95.

HUNTING DOGS—SETTERS

Pet Library Ltd. **Know Your Setters and Pointers.** (Illus.). pap. Doubleday. $1.50.

HUNTING STORIES

Alaska Magazine Editors. **Selected Alaska Hunting and Fishing Tales.** Vol. 3. 1974. pap. Alaska Northwest. $3.95.

Bear, Fred. **Fred Bear's Field Notes.** Doubleday. $10.00.

Brister, Bob. **Moss, Mallards and Mules: And Other Hunting and Fishing Stories.** 1973. Winchester Press. (OP.) $8.95.

Hill, Gene. **Hill Country: Stories About Hunting and Fishing and Dogs and Such.** (Illus.). 1978. Dutton. $9.95.

Holden, Philip. **Backblocks.** (Illus.). 1974. International Pubns. Service. $9.25.

MacQuarrie, Gordon. **Stories of the Old Duck Hunters.** 1979. pap. Willow Creek Press. $5.95.

Neasham, V. Aubrey. **Wild Legacy: California Hunting and Fishing Tales.** (Illus.). 1973. Howell-North. $6.50.

HUNTING WITH BOW AND ARROW

Adams, Chuck. **The Complete Book of Bowhunting.** (Illus.). 1978. Winchester Press. $14.95.

Bear, Fred. **Archer's Bible.** (Illus.). 1980. pap. Doubleday. $3.95.

Conaster, Dean. **Bowhunting the White-Tailed Deer.** (Illus.). 1977. Winchester Press. $10.00.

Elliott, Cheri. **The Digest Book of Bowhunting.** (Illus.). 1979. pap. Follett. $2.95.

Gillelan, G. Howard. **Complete Book of the Bow and Arrow.** rev. ed. 1977. Stackpole Books. $9.95.

Helgeland, Glenn. **Archery World's Complete Guide to Bowhunting.** 1977. Prentice-Hall. $8.95; pap. $3.95.

James, M. R. **Bowhunting for Whitetail and Mule Deer.** (Illus.). 1976. Jolex. $10.95; pap. $6.96.

Kittredge, Doug & Wambold, H. R. **Bowhunting for Deer.** rev. ed. 1978. Stackpole Books. $8.95.

Laycock, George & Bauer, Erwin. **Hunting with Bow and Arrow.** 1965. Arco. $3.95.

Learn, C. R. **Bow Hunter's Digest.** 1974. pap. DBI Books. $6.95.

Schuyler, Keith C. **Bow Hunting for Big Game.** (Illus.). 1974. Stackpole Books. $5.95.

Smythe, John & Barwick, Humphrey. **Bow Vs. Gun.** 1976. Repr. Charles River Bks. $15.00.

Tinsley, Russell. **Bow Hunter's Guide.** (Illus.). 1975. softbound. Stoeger. $5.95.

KNIFE-THROWING

Echanis, Michael D. **Knife Fighting, Knife Throwing for Combat.** (Illus.). 1978. pap. Ohara Publications. $7.95.

McEvoy, H. K. **Knife-Throwing.** Wehman Brothers, Inc. $3.95.

McEvoy, Harry K. **Knife Throwing: A Practical Guide.** (Illus.). 1973. pap. C. E. Tuttle. $3.95.

KNIVES

Barney, Richard W., and Loveless, Robert W. **How to Make Knives.** 1977. pap. Beinfeld Publ. (OP.) $9.95.

Blandford, Percy. **How to Make Your Own Knives.** (Illus.). 1979. TAB Books. $10.95; pap. $6.95.

Boye, David. **Step-by-Step Knifemaking.** 1977. softbound. Stoeger. $7.95.

Cassidy, William. **Knife Digest.** Peterson, Harold L., et al. eds. (Illus.). 1974. Knife Digest. $15.00; pap. $5.95.

Cassidy, William L. **The Complete Book of Knife Fighting.** Lund, Peder C., ed. 1975. Paladin Press. $10.95.

——**Knife Digest: Second Annual Edition.** (Illus.). 1976. pap. Paladin Enterprises. $7.95.

Ehrhardt, Larry. **Encyclopedia of Pocket Knives: Book Three Price Guide.** (Illus.). Heart of America Press. $6.95.

Erhardt, Roy & Ferrell, J. **Encyclopedia of Pocket Knives: Book One and Book Two Combined.** (Illus.). Heart of America Press. $6.95.

Hardin, Albert N., Jr. & Hedden, Robert W. **Light but Efficient: A Study of the M1880 Hunting and M1890 Intrenching Knives and Scabbards.** (Illus.). 1973. Albert N. Hardin. $7.95.

Hughes, B. R. **American Hand-Made Knives of Today.** Pioneer Press. $2.95.

Hughes, B. R. & Lewis, Jack. **Gun Digest Book of Knives.** pap. DBI Books. $7.95.

Latham, Sid. **Knifecraft.** Stackpole Books. $16.95.

——**Knives and Knifemakers.** (Illus.). 1974. pap. Macmillan. $5.95.

——**Knives and Knifemakers.** 1973. Winchester Press. $15.00.

Levine, Bernard R. **Knifemakers of Old San Francisco.** (Illus.). 1978. Badger Books. $12.95.

Lewis, Jack & Hughes, B. R. **Gun Digest Book of Folding Knives.** 1977. pap. Follett. $7.95.

Mayes, Jim. **How to Make Your Own Knives.** (Illus.). 1979. Everest House. $7.95.

Parker & Voyles. **Official 1981 Price Guide to Collector Knives.** 2nd rev. ed. (Illus.). pap. Stoeger. $9.95.

——**Official Guide to Pocket Knives.** 2nd rev. ed. 1979. pap. House of Collectibles. $9.95.

Parker, James & Voyles, Bruce. **Official Price Guide to Collector Pocket Knives.** 4th ed. (Illus.). pap. Wallace-Homestead. $9.95.

Parker, James F. & Voyles, Bruce. **Official Price Guide to Collector Knives.** 3rd ed. (Illus.). 1980. pap. House of Collectibles. $9.95.

Peterson, Harold L. **American Knives.** (Illus.). 1958. Scribner's. $5.95.

——**American Knives.** 1975. pap. Scribner's. $4.95.

——**American Knives.** Gun Room Press. $12.95.

——**History of Knives.** (Illus.). 1966. Scribner's. $5.95.

Schreir, Konrad F., Jr. **Marble Knives and Axes.** (Illus.). 1978. pap. Beinfeld. $4.50.

Schroeder, William. **A Collector's Illustrated Price Guide to Pocket Knives.** 1977. pap. Collector Books. $2.95.

Strung, Norman. **The Encyclopedia of Knives.** (Illus.). 1976. Lippincott. $12.50.

Tappan, Mel, ed. **Guide to Handmade Knives and the Official Directory of the Knifemaker's Guild.** limited ed. Janus Press. $19.50.

—**A Guide to Handmade Knives and the Official Directory of the Knifemaker's Guild.** (Illus.). 1977. pap. Janus Press. $9.50.

Wallace, George B. **Knife Handling for Self Defense.** 1973. pap. Walmac Books. (OP). $5.00.

Warner, Ken. **Practical Book of Knives.** (Illus.). 1976. softbound. Stoeger. $5.95.

— ed. **Knives 81.** 1980. pap. DBI Books. $5.95.

LEE-ENFIELD RIFLES
Chamberlain, Peter & Gander, Terry. **Machine Guns.** (Illus.). 1975. Arco. $5.95; pap. $3.95.

MAUSER PISTOLS
Belford & Dunlap, **Mauser Self-Loading Pistol.** Borden. $13.50.

Holland, Claude V. **The Military Four.** pap. Hol-Land Bks. $2.98.

Mauser Manual. (Facs. ed. of early English language Mauser Catalog and Manual). 1974. softbound. Stoeger. $1.95.

Pender. **Mauser Pocket Pistols: 1910-1946.** Borden. $14.50.

MOOSE
Berry, William D. **Deneki: An Alaskan Moose.** 1965. Macmillan. $4.50.

Jenkins, Marie M. **Deer, Moose, Elk and Their Family.** (Illus.). 1979. Holiday House. $7.95.

Mason, George F. **Moose Group.** (Illus.). 1968. pap. Hastings House Pubs. $3.84.

Peterson, Randolph L. **North American Moose.** 1955. University of Toronto Press. $15.00.

Van Wormer, Joe. **The World of the Moose.** (Illus.). 1972. Lippincott. (OP). $6.95.

NATURAL HISTORY—OUTDOOR BOOKS
Barrus, Clara, ed. **The Heart of Burrough's Journals.** 1979. Repr. of 1928 ed. Arden Lib. $30.00.

Bedichek, Roy. **Adventures with a Texas Naturalist.** (Illus.). 1961. University of Texas Press. $11.95; pap. $4.95.

Beston, Henry. **Outermost House.** 1976. pap. Penguin Books. $2.95.

Borland, Hal. **Beyond Your Doorstep.** (Illus.). 1962. Knopf. (OP). $6.95.

—**Hal Borland's Book of Days.** 1976. Knopf. $10.00.

Borland, Hal G. **This Hill, This Valley.** 1963. Lippincott. (OP). $10.00.

Brown, Vinson. **How to Explore the Secret Worlds of Nature.** (Illus.). 1962. Little, Brown & Co. (OP). $4.95.

—**Knowing the Outdoors in the Dark.** (Illus.). 1973. pap. Macmillan. $2.95.

Burroughs, John. **Under the Apple-Trees.** 1916. Folcroft. $7.50.

—**Wake-Robin.** 1896. Folcroft. $7.50.

—**Winter Sunshine.** 1879. Folcroft. $15.00.

—**A Year in the Fields.** 1901. Folcroft. $15.00.

Cooper, Susan F. **Rural Hours.** (Illus.). 1968. Repr. of 1887 ed. Syracuse University Press. $7.95.

Davids, Richard C. **How to Talk to Birds and Other Uncommon Ways of Enjoying Nature the Year Round.** (Illus.). 1972. Knopf. (OP). $7.95.

Errington, Paul L. **The Red Gods Call.** (Illus.). 1973. Iowa State University Press. $6.95.

Fuller, Raymond T. **Now That We Have to Walk: Exploring the Out-of-Doors.** facsimile ed. Repr. of 1943 ed. Arno Press. $17.00.

Gibbons, Euell. **Euell Gibbons' Beachcombers Handbook: Field Guide Edition.** 1967. pap. David McKay Co. (OP). $2.95.

Halle, Louis J. **Spring in Washington.** Peter Smith. (OP). $5.00.

—**Spring in Washington.** (Illus.). 1963. pap. Atheneum. $1.25.

Hanenkrat, Frank T. **Wildlife Watcher's Handbook.** (Illus.). 1979. Winchester Press. $10.00; pap. $7.95.

Harrison, Hal H. **Outdoor Adventures.** (Illus.). Vanguard. (OP). $5.95.

Jefferies, Richard. **Old House at Coate.** 1948. Arno Press. $16.00.

Kieran, John F. **Nature Notes.** facs. ed. 1941. Arno Press. $14.50.

Leopold, Aldo. **Sand County Almanac: With Other Essays on Conservation from Round River.** (Illus.). 1966. Oxford University Press. $11.95.

—**Sand County Almanac Illustrated.** new ed. 1977. Tamarack Press. $25.00.

O'Kane, Walter C. **Beyond the Cabin Door.** 1957. William L. Bauhan, Inc. (OP). $4.50.

Olson, Sigurd F. **Listening Point.** (Illus.). 1958. Knopf. $8.95.

—**Open Horizons.** (Illus.). 1969. Knopf. $8.95.

—**Singing Wilderness.** (Illus.). 1956. Knopf. (OP). $6.95.

—**Sigurd F. Olson's Wilderness Days.** (Illus.). 1972. Knopf. $15.00.

Ormond, Clyde. **Complete Book of Outdoor Lore.** (Illus.). 1965. Harper & Row. $9.95.

Pearson, Haydn S. **Sea Flavor.** facs. ed. 1948. Arno Press. $15.00.

Quinn, John R. **The Winter Woods.** (Illus.). 1976. Chatham Press. $8.95.

Rood, Ronald, et. al. **Vermont Life Book of Nature.** Hard, Walter, Jr., ed. (Illus.). 1967. Stephen Greene Press. (OP). $7.95.

Rowlands, John J. **Cache Lake County.** (Illus.). 1959. W. W. Norton & Co. $12.95.

Sharp, Dallas L. **Face of the Fields.** facs. ed. 1911. Arno Press. $15.00.

—**Sanctuary! Sanctuary!** facs. ed. 1926. Arno Press. $10.00.

Sharp, William. **Where the Forest Murmurs.** 1906. Arno Press. $19.50.

Shepard, Odell. **Harvest of a Quiet Eye: A Book of Digressions.** facs. ed. Repr. of 1927 ed. Arno Press. $19.50.

Teale, Edwin W. **American Seasons.** 4 vols. (Illus.). 1966. Dodd, Mead & Co. $10.00 ea; Set. $40.00.

—**Autumn Across America.** (Illus.). 1956. Dodd, Mead & Co. $10.00.

—**Journey into Summer.** (Illus.). 1960. Dodd, Mead & Co. (OP) $10.00; pap. $2.25.

—**North with the Spring.** (Illus.). 1951. Dodd, Mead & Co. $10.00.

—**Wandering Through Winter.** (Illus.). 1965. Dodd, Mead & Co. $10.00.

Wiley, Farida, ed. **John Burroughs' America.** (Illus.). Devin-Adair Co. $7.50; pap. $5.25.

Wood, Robert S. **Mountain Cabin.** 1977. pap. Chronicle Books. $4.95.

Working from Nature. (Color Crafts Ser.). 1975. Franklin Watts, Inc. $6.95.

ORDNANCE
Bruce, Robert V. **Lincoln and the Tools of War.** (Illus.). 1974. Repr. of 1956 ed. Greenwood Press. $17.25.

Carman, W. Y. **History of Firearms from Earliest Times to 1914.** 1955. St. Martin's Press. (OP). $6.50.

Chamberlain, Peter & Gander, Terry. **Infantry, Mountain and Airborne Guns.** 1975. Arco. $5.95; pap. $3.95.

—**Light and Medium Artillery.** (Illus.). 1975. Arco. pap. $3.95.

—**Mortars and Rockets.** 1975. Arco. $5.95; pap. $3.95.

Cipolla, Carlo M. **Guns, Sails and Empires: Technological Innovation and the Early Phases of European Expansion 1400-1700.** Funk & Wagnalls. pap. $1.95.

Colby, C. B. **Civil War Weapons: Small Arms and Artillery of the Blue and Gray.** (Illus.). 1962. Coward, McCann & Geoghegan. $5.29.

Ffoulkes, Charles. **The Gun Foundaries of England.** (Illus.). 1969. George Shumway Publisher. (OP). $20.00.

Foss, Christopher. **Infantry Weapons of the World.** rev. ed. (Illus.). 1979. Scribner's. $12.50.

Hoffschmidt, Edward J. & Tantum, William H. **Second World War Combat Weapons: Japanese Combat Weapons, Vol. 2.** (Illus.). We Inc. (OP). $10.00.

Norton, Robert. **The Gunner, Shewing the Whole Practise of Artillerie.** 1973. Repr. of 1628 ed. W. J. Johnson. $40.00.

Office of Strategic Services. **OSS Sabotage and Demolition Manual.** (Illus.). 1973. pap. Paladin Enterprises. $12.95.

Simon, Leslie E. **Secret Weapons of the Third Reich: German Research in World War II.** (Illus.). 1970. We Inc. (OP). $10.00.

—**Secret Weapons of the Third Reich: German Research in World War II.** (Illus.). 1970. Paladin Enterprises. pap. $8.95.

ORIENTATION
Atkinson, George & Bengtsson, Hans. **Orienteering for Sport and Pleasure.** (Illus.). 1977.Stephen Greene Press.$10.95; pap. $6.95.

Disley, John. **Orienteering.** (Illus.). 1973. Stackpole Books. pap. $4.95.

Henley, B. M. **Orienteering.** (Illus.). 1976. Charles River Books. $6.95.

Kjellstrom, Bjorn. **Be Expert with Map and Compass: The Orienteering Handbook.** 1976. pap. Scribner's. $6.95.

Kreitler, Hans & Kreitler, Shulamith. **Cognitive Orientation and Behavior.** 1976. Springer Publishing. $27.50.

Mooers, Robert L., Jr. **Finding Your Way in the Outdoors.** 1972. Dutton. $6.95.

—**Orienteering.** 1976. British Book Center. pap. $2.50.

Rand, Jim & Walker, Tony. **This is Orienteering.** (Illus.).1977.Transatlantic Arts Inc. (OP). $12.50.

Ratliff, Donald E. **Map, Compass and Campfire.** (Illus.). 1970. Binford & Mort Pubs. pap. $2.00.

Rutstrom, Calvin. **Wilderness Route Finder.** 1973. Macmillan. pap. $1.95.

Watson, J. D. **Orienteering.** (Illus.). 1975. Charles River Books. pap. $2.50.

OUTDOOR COOKERY
Allen, Gale & Allen, Robert F. **The Complete Recreational Vehicle Cookbook: For Campers, Motor Homes, RV's and Vans.** Moulton, Jocelyn, ed. 1977. Celestial Arts. pap. $4.95.

Ames, Mark & Ames, Roberta. **Barbecues.** 1973. pap. Warner Books. (OP). $0.95.

Anderson, Beverly M. & Hamilton, Donna M. **The New High Altitude Cookbook.** (Illus). 1980. Random House. $14.95.

Anderson, Ken. **The Sterno Outdoor Living Book.** 1977. Dorison House. $5.95.

Angier, Bradford. **Food-from-the-Woods-Cooking.** (Illus.). 1973. Macmillan. pap. $1.50.

—**Wilderness Cookery.** (Illus.). 1970. pap. Stackpole Books. (OP) $3.95.

Banks, James E. **Alferd Packer's Wilderness Cookbook.** (Illus.). 1969. Filter Press. $7.00. pap. $1.50;

Barker, Harriett. **One Burner Gourmet.** 1975. pap. Contemporary Books. $4.95.

Bartmess, Marilyn A., ed. **Woodall's Campsite Cookbook.** 1971. pap. Simon & Schuster. (OP) $2.95.

Bates, Joseph D., Jr. **Outdoor Cook's Bible.** (Illus.). 1964. Doubleday. $3.50.

Beard, James A. **Fireside Cookbook.** (Illus.). 1969. Simon & Schuster. $15.95.

Berglund, Berndt & Bolsby, Clare. **Wilderness Cooking.** 1973. Scribner's. $4.95; pap. $3.95.

Better Homes & Gardens Editors. **The Better Homes & Gardens All-Time Favorite Barbecue Recipes.** 1980. pap. Bantam. $2.25.

Blanchard, Marjorie. P. **The Outdoor Cookbook.** (Illus.). 1977. Franklin Watts, Inc. $5.90.

Bock, Richard. **Camper Cookery.** 1977. pap. Lorenz Press. $5.95.

Bond, Jules. **The Outdoor Cookbook.** 1976. pap. Pocket Books. $1.95.

Brent, Carol D., ed. **Barbecue: The Fine Art of Charcoal, Gas and Hibachi Outdoor Cooking.** (Illus.). 1971. Doubleday. (OP). $4.95.

Bultmann, Phyllis. **Two Burners and an Ice Chest: The Art of Relaxed Cooking in Boats, in Campers and Under the Stars.** (Illus.). 1977. Prentice-Hall. $11.95; pap. $5.95.

Bunnelle, Hasse. **Food for Knapsackers: And Other Trail Travelers.** 1971. pap. Sierra Club Books. $4.95.

Bunnelle, Hasse & Sarvis, Shirley. **Cooking for Camp and Trail.** 1972. pap. Sierra Club. $4.95.

Burros, Marian & Levine, Lois. **The Summertime Cookbook.** 1980. pap. Macmillan. $4.50.

Carhart, Arthur H. **Outdoorsman's Cookbook.** rev. ed. 1962. pap. Macmillan. $0.95.

Crocker, Betty. **Betty Crocker's New Outdoor Cookbook.** (Illus.). 1967. Western Publishing. (OP). $3.95.

Cross, Margaret & Fiske, Jean. **Backpacker's Cookbook.** 1973. Ten Speed Press. $3.00.

Culinary Arts Institute Editorial Staff. **The Master Chef's Outdoor Grill Cookbook.** 1975. pap. Grosset & Dunlap. $2.95.

Dawson, Charlotte. **Recreational Vehicle Cookbook.** (Illus., Orig.). 1970. Trail-R Club of America. $3.95.

—**Trailerists Cookbook.** Trail-R Club of America. $3.50.

Dodd, Ed. **Mark Trail's Cooking Tips.** 1971. pap. Essandess. (OP) $1.00.

Douglas, Luther A. & Douglas, Conda E. **The Explorers Cookbook.** (Illus.). 1971. Caxton Printers. (OP). $14.95.

Drew, Edwin P. **The Complete Light-Pack Camping and Trail-Food Cookbook.** 1977. pap. McGraw-Hill. $3.95.

Farmer, Charles. **The Digest Book of Outdoor Cooking.** (Illus.). 1979. pap. DBI Books. $2.95.

Farmer, Charles J. & Farmer, Kathy, eds. **Campground Cooking.** 1974. pap. DBI Books. (OP). $6.95.

Fears, J. Wayne. **Backcountry Cooking.** (Illus.). 1980. East Woods Press. $11.95; pap. $6.95.

Ferguson, Larry & Lister, Priscilla, eds. **The Outdoor Epicure.** (Illus.). 1979. pap. Signpost Book Publishing. $2.95.

Fitzgerald. **Easy to Bar-B-Q Cook Book: A Guide to Better Barbecuing.** pap. Pacifica House. $3.50.

Fleming, June. **The Well-Fed Backpacker.** 1979. pap. Victoria House. $4.95.

Groene, Janet. **Cooking on the Go.** rev. ed. (Illus.). 1980. W. W. Norton & Co. $12.50.

Hemingway, Joan & Maricich, Connie. **The Picnic Gourmet.** (Illus.). 1977. Random House. $12.95; pap. $5.95.

Holm, Don. **Old-Fashioned Dutch Oven Cookbook.** 1969. pap. Caxton Printers. $14.95.

Holsman, Gale T. & Holsman, Beverly. **The Great Outdoors Cookbook.** 1980. pap. Bantam. $2.50

Hughes, Stella. **Chuck Wagon Cookin'.** 1974. pap. University of Arizona Press. $8.50.

Hunter, Rob. **Camping and Backpacking Cookbook.** (Illus.). 1978. pap. Hippocrene Books. $2.95.

Jones, Phil. **Cooking over Wood.** 1976. pap. Drake Pubs. $4.95.

Kaatz, Van. **The Thrifty Gourmet's Chopped Meat Book.** (Illus.). 1976. pap. Major Books. $1.50.

Kamins, James. **The Cookout Conspiracy.** Young, Billie, ed. 1974. Ashley Books. $9.95.

Kinmont, Vikki, & Axcell, Claudia. **Simple Foods for the Pack.** (Illus.). 1976. pap. Sierra Club Books. $5.95.

Kirschbaum, Gabrielle. **Picnics for Lovers.** 1980. Van Nostrand Reinhold. $12.95.

Kitchin, Frances. **Cook-Out.** (Illus.). 1978. David & Charles. $11.50.

Knap, Alyson. **The Outdoorsman's Guide to Edible Wild Plants of North America: an Illustrated Manual** (Illus.). 1975. Pagurian Press. $8.95.

Logan, Barbara. **Barbecue and Outdoor Cookery.** (Illus.). 1978. pap. Beekman Publishers. $6.95.

Lund, Duane R. **Camp Cooking ... Made Easy and Kind of Fun.** Adventure Publications. 1978. $3.95.

MacDonald, Barbara and Culinary Arts Institute Staff. **Outdoor Cookbook.** (Illus.). 1975. pap. Delair Consolidated. $3.95.

McElfresh, Beth. **Chuck Wagon Cookbook.** pap. Swallow Press. $2.50.

Macklin, Harvey. **Backpacker's Cookbook: A Complete Manual and Handbook for Cooking Freeze-Dried and Wild Foods on the Trail and in the Wilderness.** (Illus.). 1978. Pagurian Press.

Macmillan, Diane D. **The Portable Feast.** (Illus.). 1973. 101 Productions. $7.95; pap. $4.95.

McMorris, Bill & McMorris, Jo. **The All Outdoors Cookbook.** (Illus.). 1974. David McKay Co. (OP). $9.95.

McNair, James K. **The Complete Book of Picnics.** 1980. pap. Ortho Books. $4.95.

Mandeville, Terry M. **Backpacking Menus.** 1980. pap. Price Guide. $3.95.

Marshall, Mel. **Cooking Over Coals.** 1975. softbound. Stoeger. $5.95.

—**Cooking Over Coals.** 1971. Winchester Press. $8.95.

—**The Family Cookout Cookbook.** 1973. pap. Ace Books. $0.95.

Martin, George W. **The Complete Book of Outdoor Cooking.** (Illus.). 1975. A. S. Barnes. (OP). $7.95.

Mendenhall, Ruth D. **Backpack Cookery.** (Illus.). 1974. pap. La Siesta. $1.50.

Messner, Yvonne. **Campfire Cooking.** (Illus. Orig.). 1973. pap. David C. McKay Publishing Co. $1.95.

Miller, Dorcas S. **The Healthy Trail Food Book.** (Illus.). 1980. East Woods Press. $7.25; pap. $3.95.

Mohney, Russ. **Trailside Cooking.** (Illus). 1976. pap. Stackpole Books. $2.95.

Morris, Dan & Morris, Inez. **The Complete Fish Cookbook.** (Illus.). 1978. softbound. Stoeger. $5.95.

—**Complete Outdoor Cookbook.** 1979. Dutton. $6.95.

Nagy, Jean. **Brown Bagging It: A Guide to Fresh Food Cooking in the Wilderness.** 1976. pap. Marty-Nagy Bookworks. $2.50.

The Outdoor Cookbook. (Illus.). 1976. Oxmoor House. $5.95.

Popper, Kathryn. **Honorable Hibachi.** (Illus.). 1965. Simon & Schuster. $4.95.

Powledge, Fred. **The Budget Backpacker's Food Book: How to Select and Prepare Your Provision from Supermarket Shelves with Over 50 Trail-Tested Recipes.** 1977. pap. David McKay Co. (OP). $3.95.

Raup, Lucy G. **Camper's Cookbook.** 1967. pap. Tuttle. $3.75.

Reimers, Emil. **Cooking for Camp and Caravan.** 1976. British Book Center. (OP). $5.95.

Riviere, William A. **Family Campers' Cookbook.** (Illus.).1965. Holt, Rinehart & Winston. (OP). $4.95.

Schubert, Ruth L. **The Camper's Cookbook.** 1974. pap. Little, Brown & Co. $3.50.

Steindler, Geraldine. **Game Cookbook.** (Illus.). 1965. softbound. Stoeger. $7.95.

Strom, Arlene. **Cooking on Wheels.** (Illus.). 1970. pap. Bond Wheelwright Co. $3.95.

Tarr, Yvonne Y. **The Complete Outdoor Cookbook.** (Illus.). 1973. Quadrangle. $8.95.

Taylor, Joan C. **Picnics.** (Illus.). 1979. Random House. $4.95.

Thomas, Dian. **Roughing It Easy: A Unique Ideabook on Camping and Cooking.** (Illus.). 1974. pap. Brigham Young University Press. $8.95. pap. $4.95.

Tonn, Maryjane H., ed. **Ideals Outdoor Cookbook.** 1975. pap. Ideals. (OP). $2.25.

Wallace, Aubrey. **Natural Foods for the Trail.** 1977. Vogelsang Press. $3.95.

Western Publishing Editors, ed. **Betty Crocker's New Outdoor Cookbook No. 10.** 1976. pap. Bantam Books. (OP). $1.50.

Wood, Jane. **Elegant Fare from the Weber Kettle.** (Illus.). 1977. Western Publishing. $6.95.

Woodall's Campside Cookbook. pap. Woodall. $3.95.

OUTDOOR LIFE

Acerrano, Anthony J. **The Outdoorsman's Emergency Manual.** 1976. softbound. Stoeger. $5.95.

—**The Outdoorsman's Emergency Manual.** 1976. Winchester Press. $11.95.

Allison, Linda. **The Sierra Club Summer Book.** (Illus.). 1977. Sierra Book Club. $4.95.

Andreson, Steve. **The Orienteering Book.** (Illus.). 1977. pap. World Pubns. (OP). $3.50.

—**The Orienteering Book.** (Illus.). 1980. pap. Anderson World. $3.50.

Angier, Bradford. **Food-from-the-Woods-Cooking.** (Illus.). 1973. pap. Macmillan. $1.50.

—**How to Stay Alive in the Woods.** Orig. Title. **Living off the Country.** 1962. pap. Macmillan. $1.95.

—**One Acre and Security: How to Live off the Earth Without Ruining It.** 1973. pap. Random House. $3.95.

—**Skills for Taming the Wilds: A Handbook of Woodcraft Wisdom.** 1972. pap. Pocket Books. (OP). $1.50.

—**Survival with Style.** (Illus.). 1974. pap. Random House. $4.95.

—**Wilderness Gear You Can Make Yourself.** (Illus.). 1973. pap. Macmillan. $2.95.

—**The Master Backwoodsman.** 1979. pap. Fawcett Book Group. $4.95.

—**The Master Backwoodsman.** 1978. Stackpole Books. $10.95.

Angier, Bradford & Angier, Vena. **Wilderness Wife.** (Illus). 1976. Chilton Book Co. (OP). $7.95.

Bourjaily, Vance. **Country Matters: Collected Reports from the Fields and Streams of Iowa and Other Places.** 1973. Dial Press. $8.95.

Boy Scouts of America. **Boy Scout Fieldbook.** new ed. (Illus). 1978. pap. Workman Publishing. $4.95.

Bradford, William.**Survival Outdoors.** 1977. pap. Macmillan. (OP). $2.95.

Bridge, Raymond. **High Peaks and Clear Roads: A Safe and Easy Guide to Outdoor Skills.** (Illus). 1978. Prentice-Hall. $10.95; pap. $4.95.

Brittain, William. **Survival Outdoors.** (Illus). 1977. pap. Monarch Press. $2.95.

Brown, Terry & Hunter, Rob. **Map and Compass.** rev. ed. (Illus). Hippocrene Books. $2.95.

Brown, Vinson. **Knowing the Outdoors in the Dark.** (Illus). 1973. pap. Macmillan. $2.95.

—**Knowing the Outdoors in the Dark.** 1972. Stackpole Books. (OP). $7.95.

Carrighar, Sally. **Home to the Wilderness.** (Illus). 1973. Houghton Mifflin. $7.95.

Cartier, John O. **The Modern Deer Hunter.** 1977. Crowell. $10.95.

Colby, C. B. **Camper's and Backpacker's Bible.** (Illus). 1977 softbound. Stoeger. $7.95.

Crawford, John S. **Wolves, Bears and Bighorns: Wilderness Observations and Experiences of a Professional Outdoorsman.** (Illus). 1981. Alaska Northwest. $19.95; pap. $12.95.

Eastman, P.F. **Advanced First Aid for All Outdoors.** 1976. pap. Cornell Maritime Press. $6.00.

Explorers Limited, compiled by. **Explorers Ltd. Source Book.** (Illus). 1977. Harper & Row. $15.00; pap. $7.95.

Fear, Daniel E., ed. **Surviving the Unexpected: A Curriculum Guide for Wilderness Survival and Survival from Natural and Man Made Disasters.** (Illus). 1974. Survival Education Association. $5.00.

Fleming, June, ed. **The Outdoor Idea Book.** (Illus). 1978. pap. Victoria House. $6.50.

Fodor's Outdoors America. (Illus). 1980. David McKay Co. $12.95.

Frederickson, Olive A. & East, Ben. **The Silence of the North.** 1973. pap. Warner Books. (OP). $1.50.

Gearing, Catherine.**Field Guide to Wilderness Living.** 1973. pap. Southern Publishing Association. $3.95.

Gode, Merlin. **Winter Outdoor Living.** 1978. pap. text ed. Brighton Publishing. $2.75.

Gregory, Mark, **The Good Earth Almanac.** 1973. pap. Grosset & Dunlap. (OP). $4.95.

Hall, Bill. **A Year in the Forest.** (Illus). 1975. McGraw-Hill. (OP). $6.95.

Hamper, Stanley R. **Wilderness Survival.** 3rd ed. 1975. Repr. of 1963 ed. Peddlers Wagon. $1.79.

Hanley, Wayne. **A Life Outdoors: A Curmudgeon Looks at the Natural World.** (Illus). 1980. Stephen Greene Press. $10.95; pap. 5.95.

Heacox, Cecil E. **The Education of an Outdoorsman.** 1976. Winchester Press. $8.95.

Henderson, Luis M. **Campers' Guide to Woodcraft and Outdoor Life.** Orig. Title: **Outdoor Guide.** 1972. pap. Dover. $3.50.

Hickin, Norman. **Beachcombing for Beginners.** 1976. pap. Wilshire Book Co. $2.00.

Hollatz, Tom. **The White Earth Snowshoe Handbook.** (Illus). 1973. pap. North Star Press. $3.50.

Humphreys, J. **Living off the Land.** (Illus). 1979. pap. International Pubns. Service. $8.50.

Hunter, Rodello. **Wyoming Wife.** 1969. Knopf. $7.95.

Jeneid, Michael. **The Outdoors Adventure Book.** (Illus). 1975. Henry Z. Walck. (OP). $8.95.

Johnson, et al. **Outdoor Tips: A Remington Sportsmen's Library Book.** pap. Benjamin Co. $2.95.

Jones, James C., ed. **The National Outdoor Living Directory, No. 2.** (Illus). 1975. Live Free. (OP). Price not set.

Kephart, Horace. **Camping and Woodcraft.** (Illus). 1948. Macmillan. $8.95.

Kodet, E. Russel & Angier, Bradford. **Being Your Own Wilderness Doctor.** (Illus). 1975. Stackpole Books. $4.95.

Labostille, Anne. **Woodswoman.** (Illus). 1978. pap. E. P. Dutton. (OP) $3.95.

Lamoreaux, Bob & Lamoreaux, Marcia. **Outdoor Gear You Can Make Yourself.** (Illus). 1976. pap. Stackpole Books. (OP). $3.95.

Lueders, Edward. **The Clam Lake Papers: A Winter in the North Woods.** 1977. Harper & Row. $7.95.

McGuire, Thomas. **Ninety-Nine Days on the Yukon: An Account of What Was Seen and Heard in the Company of Charles A. Wolf, Gentleman Canoeist.** 1977. pap. Alaska-Northwest. $7.95.

McManus, Patrick. **A Fine and Pleasant Misery.** 1978. Holt, Rinehart & Winston. $7.95.

McPhee Gribble Publishers. **Out in the Wilds.** (Illus). 1977. pap. Penguin Books. $1.50.

Merrill, W. K. **The Survival Handbook.** (Illus). 1972. Winchester Press. $6.95.

Mitchell, Jim & Fear, Gene. **Fundamentals of Outdoor Enjoyment: Text or Teaching Guide for Coping with Outdoor Environments, All Seasons.** (Illus). 1976. pap. Survival Education Association. $5.00.

Mohney, Russ. **Wintering: The Outdoor Book for Cold-Weather Ventures.** 1976. pap. Stackpole Books. $2.95.

Nichols, Maggie. **Wild, Wild Woman.** 1978. pap. Berkeley Publishing. $4.95.

Olsen, Larry D. **Outdoor Survival Skills.** rev. ed. 1973. Brigham Young University Press. $8.95; pap. $4.95.

—**Outdoor Survival Skills.** 1976. pap. Pocket Books. $1.95.

Olson, Sigurd F. **Sigurd F. Olson's Wilderness Days.** (Illus). 1972. Knopf. $15.00.

Ormond, Clyde. **Complete Book of Outdoor Lore.** (Illus). 1965. Harper & Row. $9.95.

—**Outdoorsman's Handbook.** 1971. E. P. Dutton. (OP) $6.95.

—**Outdoorsman's Handbook.** 1975. pap. Berkley Publishing. $1.95.

Outdoor Living Skills Instructor's Manual. 1979. pap. American Camping Association. $5.00.

The Outdoors Survival Manual. (Illus). 1978. pap. Sterling. $6.95.

Owings, Loren C., ed. **Environmental Values, 1860-1972: A Guide to Information Sources.** 1976. Gale Research Co. $28.00.

Patmore, J. Allan. **Land and Leisure in England and Wales.** 1971. Fairleigh Dickinson. $22.50.

Petzoldt, Paul. **The Wilderness Handbook.** (Illus). 1977. pap. W.W. Norton & Co. $5.95.

Platten, David. **The Outdoor Survival Handbook.** David & Charles. $12.95.

Rae, William E. **Treasury of Outdoor Life.** (Illus). 1975. Harper & Row. $12.95.

Rand, William M. **Just Fishin' and Huntin'.**1978. Vantage Press. $7.50.

Rawick, George P. **From Sundown to Sunup.** 1972. pap.Greenwood Press. $15.00; pap. $3.95.

Robinson, David. **The Complete Homesteading Book: Proven Methods for Self-Sufficient Living.** 1974. Garden Way Publishing. $12.95. pap. $5.95.

Rood, Ronald. **It's Going to Sting Me: A Coward's Guide to the Great Outdoors.** 1977. pap. McGraw-Hill. $3.95.

Rutstrum, Calvin. **New Way of the Wilderness.** (Illus). 1966. Macmillan. $4.95; pap. $2.95.

—**Once Upon a Wilderness** (Illus). 1973. Macmillan. $6.95.

Ruxton, George F. **Adventures in Mexico and the Rocky Mountains.** Rio Grande Press. $12.00.

Thomas, Gordon. **Mostly in Fun: Rhymes and Reflections on Outdoor Experiences.** (Illus). 1977. pap. Signpost Book Publishing. $3.95.

Van Der Smissen, Betty, et al. **Leader's Guide to Nature-Oriented Activities.** 2nd ed. (Illus). 1968. pap. Iowa State University Press. $4.95.

Vogt, Bill. **How to Build a Better Outdoors: The Action Manual for Fishermen, Hunters, Backpackers, Hikers, Canoeists, Riders, and All Other Outdoor Lovers.** (Illus). 1978. David McKay Co. $9.95. pap. $4.95;

Waterman, Charles F. **The Part I Remember.** (Illus). 1974. Winchester Press. (OP). $8.95.

Woolner, Frank. **My New England.** (Illus). 1972. Stone Wall Press. $10.00.

Wurman, Richard S. et al. **The Nature of Recreation: A Handbook in Honor of Frederick Law Olmstead.** 1972. pap. MIT Press. $5.95.

PISTOLS

Archer, Denis, ed. **Jane's Pocketbook of Pistols and Submachine Guns.** 1977. pap. Macmillan. $6.95.

Askins, Charles. **Askins on Pistols and Revolvers.** Bryant, Ted & Askins, Bill, eds. 1980. National Rifle Association. $25.00; pap. $8.95.

Best, Charles W. **Cast Iron Toy Pistols, 1870-1940: A Collector's Guide.** (Illus). 1973. Best Antiques. $15.00.

Bianchi, John. **Blue Steel and Gun Leather.** 1978. Beinfeld. (OP). $9.95.

Blair, Claude. **Pistols of the World.** (Illus). 1969. Viking Press. (OP). $30.00.

Chamberlain, Peter & Gander, Terry. **Allied Pistols, Rifles, and Grenades.** 1976. pap. Arco. $3.95.

—**Axis Pistols, Rifles and Grenades.** 1977. pap. Arco. $4.95.

Datig, Fred A. **Luger Pistol.** rev. ed. Borden. $9.50.

Dixon, Norman. **Georgian Pistols: The Art and Craft of the Flintlock Pistol, 1715-1840.** 1972. George Shumway Publisher. $18.00.

Dunlap, H. J. **American, British and Continental Pepperbox Firearms.** (Illus). 1967. Repr. of 1964 ed. Pacific Books. $17.95.

Dyke, S. E. **Thoughts on the American Flintlock Pistol.** (Illus). 1974. George Shumway Publisher. $5.00.

Grennell, Dean A. **A Pistol and Revolver Digest.** 1976. pap. Follett. $7.95.

—**Pistol and Revolver Digest.** 2nd ed. (Illus). 1979. pap. Follett. $7.95.

Hertzberg, Robert. **Modern Handguns.** (Illus). 1977. Arco. $4.95; pap. $2.50.

Hogg, I. V. **Military Pistols and Revolvers.** (Illus). 1970. Arco. $3.50; pap. $1.95.

Holland, Claude V. **The Military Four.** C. V. Holland. $4.95; pap. $2.98.

Horlacher, R., Ed. **The Famous Automatic Pistols of Europe.** Seaton, L. & Steindler, R. A., trs. from Ger. (Illus). 1976. pap. Jolex. $6.95.

Kirkland, Turner. **Southern Derringers of the Mississippi Valley.** Pioneer Press. $2.00.

Klay, Frank. **The Samuel E. Dyke Collection of Kentucky Pistols.** Gun Room Press. $1.75.

Koch, R. W. **The FP-45 Liberato-Pistol 1942-45.** (Illus.). 1977. Research. $10.00.

Leithe. **Japanese Hand Pistols.** Borden. $9.95.

Luger Manual. (Reprint of original English-language edition). 1967. softbound. Stoeger. $1.95.

Mauser Manual (Facs. ed. of early English language **Mauser Catalog and Manual**).). 1974. softbound. Stoeger. $1.95.

Millard J. T. **A Handbook on the Primary Identification of Revolvers and Semi-Automatic Pistols.** (Illus.). 1974. C. C. Thomas. $13.50; pap. $10.25.

Mitchell, Jack. **The Gun Digest Book of Pistolsmithing.** 1980. pap. Follett. $8.95.

Neal, Robert J. & Jinks, Roy G. **Smith & Wesson 1857-1945.** 1972. A. S. Barnes. $25.00.

—**Pistol Guide.** 1980. Stoeger. $8.95.

—**Pistol and Revolver Guide.** 3rd ed. (Illus.). 1975. softbound. Stoeger. (OP.) $6.95.

—**Pistolsmithing.** (Illus.). 1974. Stackpole Books. $15.95.

Nonte, George C., Jr. **Combat Handguns.** Jurras, Lee F. ed. (Illus.). 1980. Stackpole. $17.95.

—**Pistolsmithing.** (Illus.).1974. Stackpole $15.95.

Nonte, George C., Jr. & Jurras, Lee E. **Handgun Hunting.** (Illus.). 1976. softbound. Stoeger. $5.95.

Nonte, George C., Jr. & Jurras, Lee E. **Handgun Hunting.** (Illus.). 1975. Winchester Press. $8.95.

North & North. **Simeon North: First Official Pistol Maker of the United States.** Repr. Gun Room Press. $7.95.

Olson, John, compiled by. **The Famous Automatic Pistols of Europe.** (Illus.). 1975. Jolex. (OP.) $9.95; pap. $6.95.

Reese, Michael. **Collector's Guide to Luger Values.** 1972. pap. Pelican. $1.95.

—**Luger Tips.** 1976. Pioneer Press. $6.95.

Sawyer, Charles W. **United States Single Shot Martial Pistols.** 1971. We Inc. $5.00.

Van Der Mark, Kist & Van Der Sloot, Puype. **Dutch Muskets and Pistols.** (Illus.). 1974. George Shumway Publisher. $25.00.

Wallack, L. R. **American Pistol and Revolver Design and Performance.** 1978. Winchester Press. $13.95.

Whittington, Robert D. **German Pistols and Holsters, 1943-45: Military—Police—NSDAP.** (Illus.). Gun Room Press. $15.00.

Wilkerson, Frederick. **British and American Flintlocks.** 1972. Transatlantic Arts, Inc. $2.95.

Wilkinson, F. J. **Flintlock Pistols.** (Illus.). 1976. pap. Hippocrene Books. $2.95.

Williams, Mason. **The Sporting Use of the Handgun.** (Illus.). 1979. C. C. Thomas. $14.75.

RELOADING

Anderson, Robert S. L., ed. **Reloading for Shotgunners.** 1981. pap. DBI Books. $7.95.

Scott, Robert F., ed. **Shooter's Bible 1982, No. 73.** (Illus.). 1981. softbound. Stoeger. $10.95

Steindler, R. A. **Reloader's Guide.** 3rd ed. (Illus.). 1975. softbound. Stoeger. $7.95.

Wootters, John. **The Complete Book of Practical Handloading.** (Illus.). 1977. softbound. Stoeger. $6.95.

REVOLVERS

Askins, Charles. **Askins on Pistols and Revolvers.** Bryant, Ted & Askins, Bill, eds. 1980. National Rifle Association. $25.00; pap. $8.95.

Chamberlain, W. H. & Taylorson, A. W. **Adam's Revolvers.** 1978. Barrie & Jenkins. $29.95.

Grennell, Dean A. **Pistol and Revolver Digest.** (Illus.). 1976. pap. DBI Books. $7.95.

—**Pistol and Revolver Digest.** 2nd ed. (Illus.). 1979 pap. Follett. $7.95.

Hertzberg, Robert. **Modern Handgun.** (Illus.). 1977. Arco. $4.95; pap. $2.50.

Hogg, I. V. **Military Pistols and Revolvers.** (Illus.). 1970. Arco. $3.50; pap. $1.95.

James, Garry, Ed. **Guns of the Gunfighters.** (Illus.). 1975. pap. Petersen Publishing (OP) $4.95.

Jinks, Roy G. **History of Smith & Wesson.** (Illus.). 1978. Beinfeld. (OP.) $15.95.

Millard, J.T. **A Handbook on the Primary Identification of Revolvers and Semi-Automatic Pistols.** (Illus.). 1974. C. C. Thomas. $13.50; pap. $10.25.

Neal, Robert J. & Jinks, Roy G. **Smith and Wesson, 1857-1945.** 1975. A. S. Barnes. $25.00.

Nonte, George C. Jr. **Revolver Guide,** 1980. Stoeger. $8.95.

—**Pistol and Revolver Guide.** 3rd ed. (Illus.). 1975. softbound. Stoeger. (OP.) $6.95.

Nonte, George C., Jr. & Jurras, Lee E. **Handgun Hunting.** (Illus.). 1976. softbound. Stoeger. $5.95.

Report of Board on Tests of Revolvers and Automatic Pistols 1970. (Illus.). Sand Pond. $3.00.

Williams, Mason. **The Sporting Use of the Handgun.** (Illus.). 1979. C. C. Thomas. $14.75.

RIFLES

Archer, Denis. **Jane's Pocket Book of Rifles and Light Machine Guns.** 1977. pap. Macmillan. $6.95.

Beard, Ross E., Jr. **Carbine: The Story of David Marshall Williams.** 1977. Sandlapper Store. $12.50; ltd. ed., signed. $25.00.

Behn, Jack. **Fourty-Five—Seventy-Five Rifles.** Repr. of 1956 ed. Gun Room Press. $7.95.

Brophy, William S. **Krag Rifles.** (Illus.). 1978. Beinfeld. $19.95.

Buchele, William and Shumway, George. **Recreating the American Longrifle.** Orig. Title: **Recreating the Kentucky Rifle.** (Illus.). 1973. pap. George Shumway Publisher. $10.00.

Carmichel, Jim. **The Modern Rifle.** (Illus.). 1976. softbound. Stoeger. $5.95.

Chamberlain, Peter & Gander, Terry. **Allied Pistols, Rifles and Grenades.** 1976. pap. Arco. $3.95.

—**Axis Pistols, Rifles, and Grenades.** 1977. pap. Arco. $4.95.

—**Submachine Guns and Automatic Rifles: World War II Facts.** 1976. pap. Arco. $3.95.

Chapman, John R. **Improved American Rifle.** (Illus.). 1978. Beinfeld. (OP.) $5.95.

Colby, C. B. **First Rifle: How to Shoot It Straight and Use It Safely.** (Illus.). 1954. Coward, McCann & Geoghegan. $5.29.

Davis, Henry. **A Forgotten Heritage: The Story of the Early American Rifle.** 1976. Repr. of 1941 ed. Gun Room Press. $9.95.

De Haas, Frank. **Bolt Action Rifles.** Amber, John T., ed. 1971. pap. DBI Books. (OP.) $7.95.

—**Bolt Action Rifles.** Amber, John T., ed. pap. DBI Books. (OP.) $6.95.

—**Single Shot Rifles and Actions.** (Illus.). 1976. pap. DBI Books. (OP.) $8.95.

Dillin, John G. **The Kentucky Rifle.** 5th ed. (Illus.). 1967. George Shumway Publisher. (OP.) $35.00.

Editors of Gun Digest. **NRA Collector's Series: 1885-1888-1906-1923.** pap. DBI Books. (OP.) $2.95.

Edsall, James. **The Golden Age of Single Shot Rifles.** Pioneer Press. $2.75.

—**The Revolver Rifles.** Pioneer Press. $2.50.

Grant, James J. **More Single Shot Rifles.** (Illus.). Gun Room Press. $12.50.

Hanson. **The Plains Rifle.** Gun Room Press. $11.95.

Hatcher, Julian S. **The Book of the Garand.** Edwards, Douglas & Wick, Patricia, eds. (Illus.). 1977. Repr. of 1948 ed. Pine Mountain Press. $22.50.

Huddleston, Joe D. & Shumway, George. **Rifles in the American Revolution.** 1978. George Shumway Publisher. (OP).

Huddleston, Joe D. **Colonial Riflemen in the American Revolution.** (Illus.). 1978. George Shumway Publisher. $15.00.

Kindig, Joe, Jr. **Thoughts on the Kentucky Rifle in Its Golden Age.** (Illus.). 1971. George Shumway Publisher. $39.50.

Lachuk, John. **The Gun Digest Book of the .22 Rimfire.** 1978. pap. DBI Books. $6.95.

Lindsay, Merrill. **The Kentucky Rifle.** (Illus.). 1976. Arma Press. $15.00.

Mauser Manual (Facs. ed. of early English language **Mauser Catalog and Manual**). 1974. softbound. Stoeger. $1.95.

O'Connor, Jack, et al. **Complete Book of Shooting: Rifles, Shotguns and Handguns.** 1966. Harper & Row. (OP.) $10.95.

—**Complete Book of Rifles and Shotguns.** rev. ed. (Illus.). 1966. Harper & Row. $12.50.

—**The Hunting Rifle.** (Illus.). 1975. softbound. Stoeger. $5.95.

—**Rifle Book.** 3rd ed. (Illus.). 1978. Knopf. $13.95; pap. $7.95.

Olson, John. **John Olson's Book of the Rifle.** (Illus.). 1974. Jolex. $9.95; pap. $5.95.

Otteson, Stuart. **The Bolt Action: A Design Analysis.** 1976. Winchester Press. $12.95.

Page, Warren. **The Accurate Rifle.** (Illus.). 1975. softbound. Stoeger. $6.95.

—**The Accurate Rifle.** Winchester Press. $8.95.

Perkins, Jim. **American Boys Rifles.** (Illus.). 1980. pap. Collector Books. $9.95.

Petzal, David. **.22 Caliber Rifle.** (Illus.). 1973. Winchester Press. $6.95.

Pullum, Bill & Hanenkrat, Frank T. **Position Rifle Shooting.** (Illus.). 1975. softbound. Stoeger. $5.95.

Roberts, Ned H. **The Muzzle-Loading Cap Lock Rifle.** (Illus.). 1978. Repr. George Shumway Publisher. $24.50.

Rywell, Martin. **American Antique Rifles.** Pioneer Press. $2.50.

—**U.S. Muskets, Rifles and Carbines.** Pioneer Press. $2.00.

Schedelman, Hans. **Vienna Kunsthistorisches Die Grossen Buchsenmacher.** (Illus.). 1976. Arma Press. $235.00.

Shumway, George. **Pennsylvania Longrifles of Note.** (Illus.). 1977 pap. George Shumway Publisher. $6.50.

—**Rifles of Colonial America.** 2 vols. incl. Vol. 1; Vol. 2. (Illus.). 1980. casebound. George Shumway Publisher. ea. $49.50.

Steindler, R. A. **Rifle Guide.** (Illus.). 1978. softbound. Stoeger. $7.95.

Taylor. **African Rifles and Cartridges.** Gun Room Press. $16.95.

U.S. Rifle Caliber .30 Model 1903. Pioneer Press. $2.00.

U.S. Rifle Model 1866 Springfield. Pioneer Press. $2.00.

U.S. Rifle Model 1870 Remington. Pioneer Press. $2.00.

Wahl, Paul. **Carbine Handbook.** (Illus.). 1964. Arco. (OP.) $6.00; pap. $4.95.

Waite, M. D. & Ernst, Bernard. **The Trapdoor Springfield.** 1979. Beinfeld. (OP.) $19.95.

Wallack, L. R. **American Rifle Design and Performance.** 1977. Winchester Press. $14.95.

Waterman, Charles. **The Treasury of Sporting Guns.** (Illus.). 1979. Random House. $24.95.

Wood, J. B. **Troubleshooting Your Rifle and Shotgun.** (Illus.). 1978. pap. DBI Books. $5.95.

The World's Assault Rifles. TBN Enterprises. $19.95.

SHARPS RIFLES

Manual of Arms for the Sharps Rifle. Pioneer Press. $1.50.

Rywell, Martin. **Sharps Rifle: The Gun That Shaped American Destiny.** Pioneer Press. $2.95.

Sellers, Frank. **Sharps Firearms.** (Illus.). 1978. Beinfeld. $34.95.

SHIELDS

Chase, G. H. **The Shield Devices of the Greeks in Art and Literature.** (Illus.). 1978. Repr. of 1902 ed. Arno Press. $10.00.

Davison, Betsy. **Shields of Ancient Rome.** (Illus.). 1969. pap. Westerfield. Malter-Westerfield. (OP). $2.00.

Wright, Barton. **Pueblo Shields.** (Illus.). 1976. Northland Press. $9.50.

SHOOTING

Anderson, Gary. **Marksmanship.** 1972. pap. Simon & Schuster. $2.95.

Arnold, Richard. **Clay Pigeon Shooting.** (Illus.). International Pubns Service. $9.00.

——**Clay Pigeon Shooting.** (Illus.). 1974. text. ed. Sportshelf & Soccer Associates. $14.50.

Bell, Bob. **The Digest Book of Upland Game Shooting.** 1979. pap. DBI Books. $2.95.

Brister, Bob. **Shotgunning: The Art and the Science.** (Illus.). 1976. Winchester Press. $12.95.

Carmichel, Jim. **The Modern Rifle.** (Illus.). 1976. softbound. Stoeger. $5.95.

Chapman, John R. **Improved American Rifle Instructions to Young Marksmen.** (Illus.). 1978. pap. DBI Books. (OP). $5.95.

Cogwell & Harrison. **Shooting.** 1973. pap. McKay, David, Co. (OP). $2.95.

Davidson, Bill R. **To Keep and Bear Arms.** 2nd ed. Sycamore Island Books. $12.95.

Day, J. Wentworth. **The Modern Shooter.** 1976. Repr. of 1952 ed. Charles River Books. $15.00.

——**The Modern Shooter.** 1976. Repr. Dynamic Learn Corp. (OP). $15.00.

Evans, G. P. **Small Game Shooting.** Sportshelf & Soccer Associates. $14.50.

Ferber, Steve, ed. **All About Rifle Hunting and Shooting in America.** 1977. Winchester Press. $10.00.

Fuller, W. H. **Small-Bore Target Shooting.** rev. ed. Palmer, A. J., ed. 1978. Barrie & Jenkins. $11.95.

Grennell, Dean A. **ABC's of Reloading.** 1974. pap. DBI Books. $6.95.

Hastings, MacDonald. **Shooting—Why We Miss: Questions and Answers on the Successful Use of the Shotgun.** 1977. pap. McKay, David, Co. $3.95.

Janes, Edward C. **Boy and His Gun.** (Illus.). 1951. A. S. Barnes. $6.95.

Koller, Larry. **How to Shoot: A Complete Guide to the Use of Sporting Firearms—Rifles, Shotguns, and Handguns—on the Range and in the Field.** (Illus.). 1976. Doubleday. (OP). $9.95.

Lind, Ernie. **Complete Book of Trick and Fancy Shooting.** (Illus.). 1972. Citadel Press. $6.95.

——**Complete Book of Trick and Fancy Shooting.** (Illus.). 1972. Winchester Press. $6.95.

McCawley, E. S. **Shotguns and Shooting.** 1965. pap. Van Nos Reinhold. $5.95.

McGivern, Ed. **Ed McGivern's Book of Fast and Fancy Revolver Shooting, Centennial Edition.** (Illus.). 1975. Follett. $10.00.

Marchington, John. **Shooting: A Complete Guide for Beginners.** (Illus.). 1972. Merrimack Book Service. $11.95.

Mason, James D. **Combat Handgun Shooting.** (Illus.). 1976. C. C. Thomas. $24.75.

Missildine, Fred & Karas, Nick. **Score Better at Trap and Skeet.** (Illus.). 1977. softbound. Stoeger. $6.95.

Montague, Andrew A. **Successful Shotgun Shooting.** (Illus.).1971. Winchester Press.$6.95.

Mosher, John A. **The Shooter's Workbench.** (Illus.). 1977. Winchester Press. $10.95.

O'Connor, Jack. **Complete Book of Shooting: Rifles, Shotguns, Handguns.** (Illus.). 1966. Harper & Row. (OP). $9.95.

——**Rifle Book.** 2nd rev. ed. (Illus.). 1978. Random House. $13.95; pap. $7.95.

——**Shotgun Book.** (Illus.). 1978. Knopf. $15.00; pap. $8.95.

O'Connor, Jack, et al. **Complete Book of Shooting: Rifles, Shotguns, Handguns.** (Illus.). 1975. Times Mirror Mag. (OP). $8.95.

Page, Warren. **The Accurate Rifle.** (Illus.). 1975. softbound. Stoeger. $6.95.

Petzal, David E., ed. **Experts' Book of the Shooting Sports.** Simon & Schuster. $9.95.

Pryce, Dick. **Hunting for Beginners.** 1978. softbound. Stoeger. $5.95.

Pullum, Bill & Hanenkrat, Frank T. **Position Rifle Shooting.** (Illus.). 1975. softbound. Stoeger. $5.95.

Riviere, Bill. **Gunner's Bible.** 1973. pap. Doubleday. $3.50.

Rees, Clair F. **Beginner's Guide to Guns & Shooting.** 1978. Follett. $6.95.

Reynolds, E. G. & Fulton, Robin. **Target Rifle Shooting.** 1978. Barrie & Jenkins. $11.95.

Roberts, Willis J. & Bristow, Allen P. **Introduction to Modern Police Firearms.** Gourley, Douglas, ed. (Illus.). 1969. Glencoe. $9.95.

Ruffer, J. E. **The Art of Good Shooting.** (Illus.). 1976. David & Charles. $4.95.

——**Good Shooting.** (Illus.). 1980. David & Charles. $21.50.

Scott, Robert F., ed. **Shooter's Bible, 1982, No. 73.** (Illus.). 1981. softbound. Stoeger. $10.95.

Sherrod, Blackie. **Blackie Sherrod ... Scattershooting.** 1975. Strode. $6.95.

Shotgun Shooting. 1976. pap. British Book Center. $2.50.

Stanbury, Percy & Carlisle, G. L. **Shotgun Marksmanship.** rev. ed. (Illus.). 1978. Barrie & Jenkins. $11.95.

Steindler, R. A. ed. **Shooting the Muzzleloaders.** (Illus.). 1975. Jolex. $11.95; pap. $6.95.

Weston, Paul B. **Combat Shooting for Police.** 2nd ed. (Illus.). 1978. C. C. Thomas. $11.75.

Wilkinson, Frederick, ed. **The Book of Shooting for Sport and Skill.** (Illus.). Crown. $19.95.

Willett, Roderick & Grattan, Gurney A. **Rough Shooting.** (Illus.). 1975. Merrimack Book Service. $15.95.

SHOTGUNS

Anderson, Robert S. L., ed. **Reloading for Shotgunners.** 1981. DBI Books. $7.95.

Arthur, Robert. **Shotgun Stock: Design, Construction and Embellishment.** (Illus.). 1970. A. S. Barnes. (OP). $17.50.

Baer, L. R. **The Parker Gun: An Immortal American Classic.** 1978. Beinfeld. (OP). $24.95.

Barker, A. J. **Shotguns and Shooting.** Brown, Robert K. & Lund, Peder C., eds. (Illus.). 1973. Paladin Press. $6.50; pap. $4.00.

Boy Scouts of America. **Rifle and Shotgun Shooting.** (Illus.). 1967. pap. Boy Scouts of America. $0.55.

Brister, Bob. **Shotgunning: The Art and the Science.** (Illus.). 1976. Winchester Press.$12.95.

Brophy, William S. **L. C. Smith Shotguns.** (Illus.). 1978. Beinfeld. (OP). $24.95.

Burch, Monte. **Shotgunner's Guide.** 1980. Winchester Press. $12.95.

Crudgington, I. M. & Baker, D. J. **The British Shotgun: 1850-1870.** Vol. 1. (Illus.). 1978. Barrie & Jenkins. $21.95.

Garwood, G. T. **Gough Thomas's Gun Book.** (Illus.). 1970. Winchester Press. (OP). $8.95.

——**Gough Thomas's Second Gun Book.** (Illus.). 1972. Winchester Press. (OP). $8.95.

Hastings, Macdonald. **Shooting—Why We Miss: Questions and Answers on the Successful Use of the Shotgun.** 1977. pap. McKay, David, Co. $3.95.

Hinman, Bob. **Golden Age of Shotgunning.** (Illus.). 1972. Winchester Press. (OP). $8.95.

Jinks, Roy G. **History of Smith and Wesson.** (Illus.). 1978. Beinfeld. (OP). $15.95.

Knight, Richard A. **Mastering the Shotgun.** (Illus.). 1975. Dutton, E. P. (OP). $7.95.

Laycock, George. **Shotgunner's Bible.** (Illus.). 1969. pap. Doubleday. $2.95.

Lewis, Jack & Mitchell, Jack. **Shotgun Digest.** 2nd ed. 1980. pap. DBI Books. $8.95.

McCawley, E. S. **Shotguns and Shooting.** 1976. pap. Van Nos Reinhold. $5.95.

McIntosh, Michael. **The Best Shotguns Ever Made in America.** 1980. McKay, David, Co. $14.95.

O'Connor, Jack. **Shotgun Book.** (Illus.). 1965. Knopf. $15.00; pap. $8.95.

Olson, John. **John Olson's Book of the Shotgun.** (Illus.). 1975. Jolex. (OP). $9.95; pap. $6.95.

Robinson, Roger H. **The Police Shotgun Manual.** (Illus.). 1973. C. C. Thomas. $13.50.

Stanbury, Percy & Carlisle, G. L. **Shotgun Marksmanship.** (Illus.). Barrie & Jenkins. $11.95.

——**Shotgun and the Shooter.** 1978. Barrie & Jenkins. $11.95.

Thomas, Gough. **Shotgun Shooting Facts.** 1979. Winchester Press. $10.00.

——**Shotguns and Cartridges for Game and Clays.** 3rd ed. (Illus.). 1976. Transatlantic Arts Inc. $15.00.

Wallack, L. R. **American Shotgun Design and Performance.** 1977. Winchester Press. $13.95.

Waterman, Charles. **The Treasury of Sporting Guns.** (Illus.). 1979. Random House. $24.95.

Whillett, Roderick F. **The Good Shot.** 1980. A. S. Barnes. $12.95.

Williams, Mason. **The Defensive Use of the Handgun: For the Novice.** rev. ed. (Illus.). C. C. Thomas. $12.75; pap. $7.75.

Wood, J. B. **Gun Digest Book of Firearms Assembly-Disassembly: Shotguns.** 1980. pap. DBI Books. $8.95.

——**Troubleshooting Your Rifle and Shotgun.** (Illus.). 1978. pap. DBI Books. $5.95.

Zutz, Don. **The Double Shotgun.** (Illus.). 1978. Winchester Press. $14.95.

SURVIVAL

Acerrano, Anthony J. **The Outdoorsman's Emergency Manual.** (Illus.). 1977. softbound. Stoeger. $5.95.

Allaby, Michael. **The Survival Handbook.** Tension, Marika H., ed. (Illus.). 1977. State Mutual Book & Periodical Service. $14.95.

Angier, Bradford. **How to Stay Alive in the Woods.** Orig. Title: **Living off the Country.** 1966. pap. Macmillan. $1.25.

—**Survival with Style.** (Illus.). 1972. Stackpole Books. (OP). $6.95.

Belisle, David A. **The American Family Robinson: The Adventures of a Family Lost in the Great Desert of the West.** 1976. Repr. of 1854 ed. Scholarly Press. (OP). $25.00.

Biggs, Don. **Survival Afloat.** (Illus.). 1976. McKay, David & Co. $9.95; pap. $5.95.

Boswell, John. **The Complete Survival Manual.** 1980. Times Books.

Brown, Terry & Hunter, Rob. **The Concise Book of Survival and Rescue.** 1978. pap. Vanguard Press. $2.95.

Colby, C. B. **Survival: Training in Our Armed Services.** (Illus.). 1965. Coward, McCann & Geoghegan. $5.29.

Dalrymple, Byron. **Survival in the Outdoors.** 1972. Dutton, E. P. $6.95.

Dennis, Lawrence. **Operational Thinking for Survival.** 1969. R. Myles. $5.95.

Dept. of the Air Force. **Survival: Air Force Manual 64-5.** (Illus.). 1976. pap. Paladin Enterprises. $8.00.

Fear, Daniel E., ed. **Surviving the Unexpected: A Curriculum Guide for Wilderness Survival and Survival from Natural and Man Made Disasters.** (Illus.). rev. ed. 1974. Survival Education Association. $5.00.

Fear, Eugene H. **Surviving the Unexpected Wilderness Emergency.** 6th ed. (Illus.). 1979. pap. Survival Education Association. $5.00.

Fear, Gene. **Where Am I: A Text and Workbook for Personal Navigation Anywhere.** 1974. pap. Survival Education Association. (OP). $4.50.

Gibbons, Euell. **Stalking the Good Life.** 1971. David McKay Co. (OP) $8.95.

Graves, Richard. **Bushcraft: A Serious Guide to Survival and Camping.** (Illus.). 1972. pap. Schocken Books. $7.95.

Greenbank, Anthony. **A Handbook for Emergencies: Coming Out Alive.** (Illus.). 1976. Doubleday. $6.95; pap. $3.95.

Hal, Betty L. **Survival Education.** 1976. pap. Binford. $4.50.

Hersey, John R. **Here to Stay.** 1963. Knopf. $6.95.

Jones, Tristan. **Ice!** 1978. Sheed, Andrews & McMeel. $8.95.

Koller, James, ed. **The Best of Live Free.** (Illus.). 1977. pap. Live Free. (OP). $3.95.

LaValla, Rick. **Survival Teaching Aids.** 1974. pap. Survival Education Association. (OP). $2.00.

Lee, E. C. & Lee, Kenneth. **Safety and Survival at Sea.** (Illus.). 1972. W. W. Norton & Co. $10.00.

Merrill, Bill. **The Survival Handbook.** 1974. pap. Arc Books. $1.95.

Nelson, Dick & Nelson, Sharon. **Desert Survival.** (Illus.). 1977. pap. Tecolote Press. $3.95.

Nesbitt, Paul, et al. **Survival Book.** (Illus.). 1969. pap. Funk & Wagnalls. pap. $1.95.

Olsen, Larry D. **Outdoor Survival Skills.** rev. ed. 1973. Brigham Young University Press. $8.95; pap. $4.95.

Platt, Charles. **Outdoor Survival.** (Illus.). 1976. Watts, Franklin, Inc. $4.33.

Read, Piers Paul. **Alive: The Story of the Andes Survivors.** (Illus.). 1974. Lippincott. $12.50; Avon. pap. $2.50.

Shea, John G. **Perils of the Ocean and Wilderness: Or, Narratives of Shipwreck and Indian Captivity, Gleaned from Early Missionary Annals.** 1976. Repr. of 1857 ed. lib. bdg. Garland Publishing. $40.00.

Stoeffel, Skip. **Disaster-Survival Education Lesson Plans.** 1974. pap. Survival Education Association. (OP). $2.50.

Szczelkun, Stefan A. **Survival Scrapbook 1: Shelter.** (Illus.). pap. Shocken Books. $3.95.

Thygerson, Alton L. **Disaster Survival Handbook.** (Illus.). 1979. pap. Brigham Young University Press. $7.95.

Troebst, Cord-Christian. **Art of Survival.** Coburn, Oliver, (tr. from Ger.) (Illus.). 1975. pap. Doubleday. $3.50.

Vignes, Jacques. **The Rage to Survive.** Voukitchevitch, Mihailo, tr. (Illus.). 1976. Morrow, William & Co. $6.95.

Western Electric. **Survival in the North.** Wehman Brothers, Inc. $7.95.

SWORDS

Akehurst, Richard. **Antique Weapons.** (Illus.). 1969. Arco. $5.95.

Campbell, Archibald. **Scottish Swords from the Battlefield at Culloden.** Mowbray, E. Andrew, ed. (Illus.). Mowbray Co. $5.00.

Castle, Egerton. **Schools and Masters of Fence from the Middle Ages to the Eighteenth Century.** (Illus.). 1969. casebound. George Shumway Publisher. $20.00.

Dobree, Alfred. **Japanese Sword Blades.** 3rd ed. (Illus.). 1971. pap. George Shumway Publisher. $6.00.

Draeger, Donn F. & Warner, Gordon. **Japanese Swordsmanship: Technique and Practice.** (Illus.). 1981. C. E. Tuttle. $19.95.

Ffoulkes, Charles & Hopkinson, E. C. **Sword, Lance and Bayonet.** (Illus.). 1967. Arco. $7.50.

Gunsaulus, H. C. **Japanese Sword-Mounts.** (Illus.). 1923. pap. Kraus Reprint. $16.00.

Hamilton, John. **Collection of Japanese Sword Guards with Selected Pieces of Sword Furniture.** 1975. pap. Peabody Museum of Salem. $9.75.

Hawley, Willis M. **Japanese Swordsmiths.** 2 vols. 1966-67. W. M. Hawley. Vol. 1. $15.00; Vol 2. $10.00.

Hutton, Alfred. **The Sword and the Centuries; or, Old Sword Days and Old Sword Ways.** (Illus.). 1973. Repr. of 1901 ed. C. E. Tuttle. $14.50.

Japanese Swordsmiths. 1980. W. M. Hawley. $60.00.

Johnson, Thomas M. **Collecting the Edged Weapons of the Third Reich.** Vol 3. Bradach, Wilfred, tr. (Illus.). 1978. T. M. Johnson $20.00.

—**Wearing the Edged Weapons of the Third Reich.** Bradach, Wilfrid, tr. 1977. pap. T. M. Johnson. $10.00.

Joly, Henri. **Shosankenshu: Japanese Sword Mounts.** Albert Saifer Pub. $35.00.

Joly, Henry. **Japanese Sword Fittings.** (Illus.). 1978. Saifer, Albert, Pub. $48.00.

Kammer, Reinhard, ed. **Zen and Confucius in the Art of Swordsmanship.** Fitzgerald, Betty, tr. (Illus.). 1978. Routledge & Kegan. $9.75.

Ogasawara, Nobuo. **Japanese Swords.** Kenny, Don, tr. from Jap. (Illus.). 1976. pap. $3.95. Japan Publications $3.95.

Peterson, Harold L. **The American Sword, 1775-1945.** (Illus.). 1977. Ray Riling, Arms Books. $18.50.

Rankin, Robert H. **Small Arms of the Sea Services: A History of the Firearms and Edged Weapons of the U.S. Navy, Marine Corps and Coast Guard from the Revolution to the Present.** (Illus.). 1972. Flayderman, N. & Co. $14.50.

Rawson, Philip S. **Indian Sword.** (Illus.). 1967. Arco $8.50.

Sasano, Mesayki. **Early Japanese Sword Guards: Sukashi Tsuba. (Pierced Work).** (Illus.). 1972. Japan Publications $15.00.

Schnorr, Emil. **Japanese Sword Guards.** (Illus.). 1976. pap. C. E. Tuttle. $5.00.

Silver, George. **Paradoxes of Defence, Wherein Is Proved the True Grounds of Fight to Be in the Short Ancient Weapons.** 1968. Repr. of 1599 ed. Johnson, Walter J. $8.00.

Tsuba, Sukashi. **Early Japanese Sword Guards.** $19.50. Wehman Brothers, Inc.

Wilkinson-Latham, Robert. **Swords and Other Edged Weapons.** 1978. Arco. $8.95. pap. $5.95.

Yumoto, John M. **Samuri Sword: A Handbook.** (Illus.). 1958. Tuttle, C.E., $9.50.

TAXIDERMY

Brakefield, Tom. **The Sportsman's Complete Book of Trophy & Meat Care.** (Illus.).1975. Stackpole Books. $8.95.

Cappel, Leo J. **A Guide to Model Making and Taxidermy.** (Illus.). 1973 Reed, A.H. & A. W., Books. pap. $5.95.

Farnham, Albert B. **Home Taxidermy for Pleasure and Profit.** (Illus.). pap. A. R. Harding Publishing. $3.00.

Grantz, Gerald J. **Home Book of Taxidermy and Tanning.** (Illus.). 1970. Stackpole Books. $9.95.

Harrison, James M. **Bird Taxidermy.** (Illus.). 1977. David & Charles. $11.50.

Labrie, Jean. **The Amateur Taxidermist.** (Illus.). 1972. Hart. (OP) $7.50; pap. $4.95.

McFall, Waddy F. **Taxidermy Step by Step.** (Illus.). 1975. Winchester Press. $8.95.

Maurice, Michael. **Complete Taxidermist's Guide to Books, Instructions and Supplies.** 1975. pap. Reel Trophy. $1.00.

Migdalski, Edward C. **How to Make Fish Mounts and Other Fish Trophies.** 1960. Ronald Press. $14.95.

Moyer, John W. **Practical Taxidermy: A Working Guide.** (Illus.). 1953. Ronald Press. (OP) $9.50.

Pray, Leon L. **Taxidermy.** (Illus.). 1943. Macmillan. $4.95.

Roberts, Nadine H. **The Complete Handbook of Taxidermy.** (Illus.). 1979. TAB Books. $12.95; pap. $9.95.

Tinsley, Russell. **Taxidermy Guide.** (Illus.). 1977. softbound. Stoeger. $7.95.

TRAP AND SKEET SHOOTING

Campbell, Robert, ed. **Skeet Shooting with D. Lee Braun.** pap. Benjamin Co. $4.95; pap. $1.95.

—**Trapshooting with D. Lee Braun and the Remington Pros.** Benjamin Co. $5.95; pap. $3.95.

Chapel, C. E. **Field, Skeet and Trapshooting.** pap. Funk & Wagnalls. (OP). $2.95.

Hartman, Barney. **Hartman on Skeet.** (Illus.). 1973. Stackpole Books. (OP). $8.95.

Migdalski, Edward C. **Clay Target Games.** (Illus.). 1978. Winchester Press. $12.95; pap. $6.95.

Missildine, Fred with Nick Karas. **Score Better at Trap and Skeet.** (Illus.). 1977. softbound. Stoeger. $6.95.

—**Score Better at Trap and Skeet.** (Illus.). 1978. Winchester Press. $10.95.

Rees, Clair F. **The Digest Book of Trap and Skeet Shooting.** 1979. pap. DBI Books. $2.95.

Sports Illustrated Staff. **Sports Illustrated Book of Shotgun.** (Illus.). Lippincott. $4.95.

TRAPPING

Argus Archives. **Traps and Trapping: Furs and Fashion.** 1977. pap. Argus Archives. (OP). $2.50.

Bateman, James. A. **Animal Traps and Trapping.** (Illus.). 1971. Stackpole Books. $9.95.

Chansler, Walter S. **Successful Trapping Methods: A Guide to Good Trapping.** 2nd ed. (Illus.). 1968. pap. Van Nos Reinhold. $4.95.

Clawson, George. **Trapping and Tracking.** (Illus.). 1977. Winchester Press. $8.95.

Dearborn, Ned. **Trapping on the Farm.** Repr. of 1910 ed. pap. Shorey. $2.00.

Errington, Paul L. **Muskrats and Marsh Management.** (Illus.). 1978. University of Nebraska Press. $10.95; pap. $3.25.

Finnerty, Edward W. **Trappers, Traps and Trapping.** (Illus.). 1976. A. S. Barnes. $9.95.

Gilsvik, Bob. **The Complete Book of Trapping.** 1976. Chilton Book Co. $12.50.

——**The Modern Trapline: Methods and Materials.** 1980. Chilton Book Co. $12.50.

Glendinning, Richard. **When Mountain Men Trapped Beaver.** (Illus.). 1967. Garrard. (OP). $3.68.

Harbottle, Jeanne & Credeur, Fern. **Woman in the Bush.** Pelican. $6.00.

Harding, A. R. **Deadfalls and Snares.** (Illus.). pap. A. R. Harding Publishing. $3.00.

——**Fox Trapping.** (Illus.). pap. A. R. Harding Publishing. $3.00.

——**Mink Trapping.** (Illus.). pap. A. R. Harding Publishing. $3.00.

——**Steel Traps** (Illus.). pap. A. R. Harding Publishing. $3.00.

——**Trappers' Handbook.** 1975. pap. A. R. Harding Publishing. $1.50.

——**Trapping as a Profession.** 1975. pap. A. R. Harding Publishing. $1.50.

——**Wolf and Coyote Trapping.** (Illus.). pap. A. R. Harding Publishing. $3.00.

Karras, A. L. **North to Cree Lake.** (Illus.). 1971. Trident Press. $7.95.

Kreps, E. **Science of Trapping.** (Illus.). pap. A. R. Harding Publishing. $3.00.

Lindsay, Neil M. **Tales of a Wilderness Trapper.** 1973. pap. A. R. Harding Publishing. $1.00.

Lynch. V. E. **Trails to Successful Trapping.** pap. A. R. Harding Publishing. $3.00.

McCracken, Harold & Van Cleve, Harry. **Trapping.** (Illus.). 1974. A. S. Barnes. $8.95.

Mascall, Leonard. **A Booke of Fishing with Hooke and Line.** 1973. Repr. of 1590 ed. Walter J. Johnson. $9.50.

Mason, Otis T. **Traps of the American Indians.** facs. ed. (Illus.). 1901. pap. Shorey. $2.00.

Russell, Andy. **Trails of a Wilderness Wanderer.** 1975. Knopf. $7.95.

Russell, Carl. **Firearms, Traps and Tools of the Mountain Men.** (Illus.). 1967. Knopf. (OP). $15.00.

——**Firearms, Traps and Tools of the Mountain Men.** 1977. pap. University of New Mexico Press. $8.95.

Russell, Osborne. **Journal of a Trapper.** Haines, Aubrey L., ed (Illus.). 1965. University of Nebraska Press. $13.50; pap. $3.50.

Ruxton, George F. **Mountain Men.** Rounds, Glen, ed. & illus. (Illus.). 1966. Holiday House. (OP). $3.95.

Sandoz, Mari. **The Beaver Men: Spearheads of Empire.** (Illus.). 1978. pap. University of Nebraska Press. $4.50.

Speck, F. G. et al. **Rappahannock Taking Devices: Traps, Hunting and Fishing.** (Illus.). 1946. University Museum of the University of Pennsylvania. $1.00.

The Trapper's Companion. (Illus.). pap. A. R. Harding Publishing. $2.00.

Woodcock, E. N. **Fifty Hears a Hunter and Trapper.** pap. A. R. Harding Publishing. $3.00.

WHITE-TAILED DEER

Conaster, Dean. **Bowhunting the White-Tailed Deer.** (Illus.). 1977. Winchester Press. $10.00.

Conway, Bryant W. **Successful Hints on Hunting White Tail Deer.** 2nd ed. 1967. pap. Claitors. $1.98.

Hayes, Tom. **How to Hunt the Whitetail Deer.** new & rev. ed. A. S. Barnes. $8.95; pap. $6.95.

Koller, Lawrence R. **Shots at Whitetails.** rev. ed. (Illus.). 1970. Knopf. $12.50.

La Bastille, Anne. **White-Tailed Deer.** Bourne, Russell & Lawrence, Bonnie S., eds. (Illus.). 1973. National Wildlife Federation. $2.50.

Rue, Leonard L. **World of the White-Tailed Deer.** 1962. Lippincott. $8.95.

Stadtfeld, Curtis K. **The Whitetail Deer: A Year's Cycle.** (Illus.). 1975. Dial Press. $7.95.

Tinsley, Russell. **Hunting the Whitetail Deer.** (Illus.). 1974. pap. Barnes & Noble (OP). $1.95.

——**Hunting the Whitetailed Deer.** 1977. T. Y. Crowell. $7.95; pap. $4.50.

WINCHESTER RIFLES

Barnes, Duncan. **History of Winchester Firearms, 1866-1980.** rev. ed. (Illus.). 1980. Winchester Press. $21.95.

Butler, David F. **Winchester 1873 and 76: The First Repeating Centerfire Rifles.** (Illus.). 1970. Winchester Press. (OP). $11.95.

Colby, C. B. **Firearms by Winchester: A Part of U.S. History** (Illus.). 1957. Coward, McCann & Geoghegan. $5.29.

Madis, George. **Winchester Book.** 3rd ed. (Illus.). 1979. Art & Reference House. $39.50.

Watrous, George R. **History of Winchester Firearms 1866-1966.** 1975. Winchester Press. (OP). $15.00.

West, Bill. **Know Your Winchester: General Use, All Models and Types, 1849-1969.** (Illus.). B. West. $12.00.

——**Winchester-Complete: All Wins and Forerunners, 1849-1976.** (Illus.). 1975. B. West. $33.00.

——**Winchester Encyclopedia.** (Illus.). B. West. $12.00.

——**Winchester Lever-Action Handbook.** (Illus.). B. West. $29.00.

——**The Winchester Single Shot.** (Illus.). B. West. $12.00.

——**Winchesters, Cartridges and History.** (Illus.). B. West. $29.00.

Williamson, Harry F. **Winchester: The Gun That Won the West.** (Illus.). 1978. pap. A. S. Barnes. $10.95.

The Shooter's Magazine Rack

Alaska (M)
Established 1935
Circulation: 182,000
Robert A. Henning, Editor and Publisher
Alaska Northwest Publishing Company
Box 4-EEE
Anchorage, Alaska 99509
(907) 274-0521

Alaska Geographic (Q)
Established 1972
Circulation: 8000
Robert A. Henning, Editor
The Alaska Geographic Society
Box 4-EEE
Anchorage, Alaska 99509
(907) 274-0521

The American Blade (BM)
Established 1973
Circulation: 20,000
Wallace Beinfeld, Editor and Publisher
Beinfeld Publishing, Inc.
12767 Saticoy Street
North Hollywood, California 91605
(213) 982-3700

American Field (W)
Established 1874
Circulation: 15,000
W. F. Brown, Editor
American Field Publishing Company
222 West Adams Street
Chicago, Illinois 60606
(312) 372-1383

American Firearms Industry (11 x yr.)
Established 1972
Circulation: 23,000
Andrew Molchan, Editor and Publisher
National Association of Federally
   Licensed Firearms Dealers
7001 North Clark Street
Chicago, Illinois 60626
(312) 338-7600

American Handgunner (BM)
Established 1976
Circulation: 107,000
Jerome Rakusan, Editor
Publishers' Development Corporation
591 Camino de la Reina, Suite 200
San Diego, California 92108
(714) 297-5350

The American Hunter (M)
Established 1973
Circulation: 107,000
Earl Shelsby, Managing Editor
National Rifle Association of America
1600 Rhode Island Avenue, N.W.
Washington, D.C. 20036
(202) 783-6505

The American Rifleman (M)
Established 1871
Circulation: 1,100,000
William F. Parkerson, III, Editor
National Rifle Association of America
1600 Rhode Island Avenue, N.W.
Washington, D.C. 20036
(202) 783-6505

The American Shotgunner (M)
Established 1973
Circulation: 180,000
Bob Thruston, Editor
Celebrity Sports
P.O. Box 3351
Reno, Nevada 89505
(702) 329-2521

The American West (BM)
Established 1964
Circulation: 22,000
Thomas W. Pew Jr., Editor
American West Publishing Company
3033 N. Campbell Avenue
Tucson, Arizona 85717
(602) 881-5850

Archery World (BM)
Established 1952
Circulation: 96,000
Glenn Helgeland, Editor
Market Communications, Inc.
225 E. Michigan Ave.
Milwaukee, Wisconsin 53202
(414) 276-6600

The Arizona Shooter (M)
Established 1979
Circulation: 6,000
Norma Jankofsky, Editor and Publisher
5931 E. Sharon Drive
Scottsdale, Arizona 85254
(602) 996-2606

Arms Gazette (M)
Established 1973

MERGED WITH MAN AT
ARMS MAGAZINE

Army (M)
Established 1904
Circulation: 12,000
L. James Binder, Editor
Association of the U.S. Army
2421 Wilson Boulevard
Arlington, Virginia 22201
(703) 841-4300

Bow & Arrow (BM)
Established 1963
Circulation: 87,000
Cheri Elliott, Editor
Gallant Publishing Company, Inc.
34249 Camino Capistrano
Capistrano Beach, California 92624
(714) 493-2101

Bowhunter (BM)
Established 1971
Circulation: 105,000
M. R. James, Editor
Bowhunter
9715 Saratoga Road
Fort Wayne, Indiana 46804
(219) 744-1373

Chase Magazine (M)
Established 1920
Circulation: 3,000
Jo Brandenburg, Editor
The Chase Publishing Co., Inc.
1150 Industry Road
Lexington, Kentucky 40555
(606) 254-4262

Ducks Unlimited Magazine (BM)
Established 1937
Circulation: 325,000
Lee D. Salber
Ducks Unlimited, Inc.
P.O. Box 66300
Chicago, Illinois 60666
(312) 299-3334

Enforcement Journal (Q)
Established 1963
Circulation: 43,000
Frank J. Schira, Editor
National Police Officers Association of
   America
609 West Main Street
Louisville, Kentucky 40202
(502) 845-4141

Field & Stream (M)
Established 1895
Circulation: 2,000,000
Jack Samson, Editor
CBS Consumer Publishing
1515 Broadway
New York, N.Y. 10036
(212) 975-7435

Fins & Feathers (M)
Established 1972
Circulation: 110,000
Steve Grooms, Editor
Fins & Feathers
318 West Franklin Avenue
Minneapolis, Minnesota 55404
(612) 874-8404

Fishing and Hunting News (W)
Established 1944
Circulation: 140,000
Vence Malernee, Editor
Outdoor Empire Publishing, Inc.
511 Eastlake Avenue E.
Seattle, Washington 98109
(206) 624-3845

Florida Sportsman (M)
Established 1969
Circulation: 75,500
Vic Dunaway, Editor
Wickstrom Publishers, Inc.
2701 S. Bayshore Dr.
Miami, Florida 33133
(305) 858-3546

Fur-Fish-Game (Harding's Magazine) (M)
Established 1905
Circulation: 190,000
A. R. Harding, Editor
A. R. Harding Publishing Co.
2878 East Main Street
Columbus, Ohio 43209
(614) 231-9585

Gray's Sporting Journal (7 x yr.)
Established 1975
Circulation: 60,000
Edward E. Gray, Editor and Publisher
Gray's Sporting Journal Company
1330 Beacon Street
Brookline, Massachusetts 02146
(617) 731-8691

Grit and Steel (M)
Established 1899
Circulation: 6,000
Mary M. Hodge, Editor
DeCamp Publishing Company
Drawer 208
Gaffney, South Carolina 29340
(803) 489-2324

The Gun Report (M)
Established 1955
Circulation: 8000
Kenneth W. Liggett, Editor
World-Wide Gun Report, Inc.
113-115 South College Avenue
Aledo, Illinois 61231
(309) 582-5311

Gun Week (W)
Established 1966
Circulation: 35,000
James C. Schneider, Editor
Amos Press, Inc.
911 Vandemark Road
Sidney, Ohio 43537
(513) 492-4141

Gun World (M)
Established 1960
Circulation: 126,000
Jack Lewis, Editor
Gallant Publishing Company, Inc.
34249 Camino Capistrano
Capistrano Beach, California 92624
(714) 493-2101

Guns (M)
Established 1954
Circulation: 128,000
Jerome Rakusan, Editor
Publishers' Development Corporation
591 Camino de la Reina, Suite 200
San Diego, California 92108
(714) 297-5350

Guns and Ammo (M)
Established 1958
Circulation: 475,000
Howard French, Editor
Petersen Publishing Company
8490 Sunset Boulevard
Los Angeles, California 90069
(213) 657-5100

**Handloader: The Journal of Ammunition
  Reloading (BM)**
Established 1966
Circulation: 36,000
David R. Wolfe, Editor
Wolfe Publishing Company, Inc.
138 North Montezuma Street
Prescott, Arizona 86301
(602) 445-7810

Hobbies, The Magazine for Collectors (M)
Established 1931
Circulation: 46,000
Pearl Ann Reeder, Editor
Lightner Publishing Company
1006 South Michigan Avenue
Chicago, Illinois 60605
(312) 939-4767

Hounds & Hunting (M)
Established 1903
Circulation: 14,000
R. F. Slike, Editor
Hounds & Hunting
Box 372
Bradford, Pennsylvania 16701
(814) 368-6154

Hunter Safety News (BM)
Established 1972
Circulation: 20,000
Leslie Hunter, Editor
Outdoor Empire Publishing, Inc.
511 Eastlake Avenue East
Seattle, Washington 98109
(206) 624-3845

Hunter's Horn (M)
Established 1921
Circulation: 10,000
George Slankard, Editor
The Hunter's Horn Publishing
  Company, Inc.
P.O. Box 426
Sand Springs, Oklahoma 74063
(918) 245-9571

Law and Order (M)
Established 1953
Circulation: 25,000
Frank G. MacAloon, Editor
Copp Organization, Inc.
5526 N. Elston Avenue
Chicago, Illinois 60630
(312) 792-1838

Man at Arms (BM)
Established 1978
Circulation: 13,000
E. Andrew Mowbray, Editor
  and Publisher
222 W. Exchange Street
Providence, Rhode Island 02903
(401) 861-1000

Michigan Out-of-Doors (M)
Established 1947
Circulation: 110,000
Kenneth Lowe, Editor
Michigan United Conservation Clubs, Inc.
P.O. Box 30235
Lansing, Michigan 48909
(517) 371-1041

Michigan Sportsman (BM)
Established 1976
Circulation: 20,000
Thomas Petrie, Editor
Michigan Sportsman, Inc.
P.O. Box 2483
Oshkosh, Wisconsin 54903
(414) 231-9338

Minnesota Sportsman (BM)
Established 1977
Circulation: 12,000
Bob Gilsvik, Editor
Minnesota Sportsman, Inc.
P.O. Box 3003
Oshkosh, Wisconsin 54903
(414) 231-8160

Muzzle Blasts (M)
Established 1932
Circulation: 23,000
Maxine Moss, Editor
National Muzzle Loading Rifle Association
P.O. Box 67
Friendship, Indiana 47021
(812) 667-5131

The Muzzleloader (BM)
Established 1974
Oran Scurlocks Jr., Editor and Publisher
Route 5, Box 347-M, Dept. TW-6
Texarkana, Texas 75503
(214) 832-4726

Mzuri Drumbeat (Q)
Established 1972
Circulation: 30,000
Bob Dill, Editor and Publisher
Dill & Associates
41 East Taylor
Reno, Nevada 89501
(702) 323-0779

National Defense (BM)
Established 1920
Circulation: 31,000
R. E. Lewis, Editor
American Defense Preparedness
  Association
819 Union Trust Building
740 15th Street, N.W.
Washington, D.C. 20005
(202) 347-7250

Outdoor Life (M)
Established 1897
Circulation: 1,700,000
John Culler, Editor
Times Mirror Magazines, Inc.
380 Madison Avenue
New York, N.Y. 10017
(212) 687-3000

Outdoor Press (W)
Established 1966
Circulation: 6,000
Fred L. Peterson, Editor and Publisher
The Outdoor Press, Inc.
N. 2012 Ruby Street
Spokane, Washington 99207
(509) 328-9392

Outdoors Today (50 x yr.)
Established 1970
Circulation: n.s.
Gary Dotson, Editor
Outdoors Today, Inc.
P.O. Box 6852
St. Louis, Missouri 63144
(314) 727-2722

Pennsylvania's Outdoor People (M)
Established 1959
Circulation: 70,000
Tom Price, Editor
Dardanell Publications, Inc.
610 Beatty Road
Monroeville, Pennsylvania 15146
(412) 373-7900

Petersen's Hunting (M)
Established 1973
Circulation: 200,000
Basil C. Bradbury, Editor
Petersen Publishing Company
8490 Sunset Boulevard
Los Angeles, California 90069
(213) 657-5100

Point Blank (M)
Established 1971
Circulation; 209,000
John M. Snyder, Editor
Citizens Committee for the Right
to Keep and Bear Arms
1601 114th S.E.,
Bellevue, Washington 98004
(206) 454-4911

The Police Marksman (Q)
Established 1975
Circulation: 19,000
James Collins, Editor
Police Marksman Association
217 South Court Street
Montgomery, Alabama 36140
(205) 262-5761

Police Times (M)
Established 1964
Circulation: 97,000
Donald Anderson, Editor
American Law Enforcement Officers'
Association
1100 N.E. 125th Street
North Miami, Florida 33161
(305) 891-1700

Popular Guns (BM)
Established 1969
Circulation: 150,000
Herbert Bradford, Editor
Country Wide Publications, Inc.
257 Park Avenue South
New York, New York 10010
(212) 777-4200

Popular Mechanics (M)
Established 1902
Circulation: 1,670,000
John A. Linkletter, Editor
The Hearst Corporation
224 West 57th Street
New York, N.Y. 10019
(212) 262-4282

Popular Science (M)
Established 1872
Circulation: 1,833,000
Hubert P. Luckett, Editor
Times Mirror Magazines, Inc.
380 Madison Avenue
New York, N.Y. 10017
(212) 687-3000

Precision Shooting (M)
Established 1956
Circulation: 2500
Ritchie Moorhead, Editor
Precision Shooting, Inc.
P.O. Box 6
Athens, Pennsylvania 18810
(717) 888-7801

Rifle: The Magazine for Shooters (BM)
Established 1969
Circulation: 27,000
David R. Wolfe, Editor
Wolfe Publishing Company, Inc.
138 North Montezuma Street
Prescott, Arizona 86301
(602) 445-7810

Saga (M)
Established 1950
Circulation: 209,000
David J. Elrich, Editor
Gambi Publishing Corporation
333 Johnson Avenue
Brooklyn, N.Y. 11206
(212) 456-8600

The Shooting Industry (M)
Established 1956
Circulation: 24,000
Jerome Rakusan, Editor
Publishers' Development Corporation
591 Camino de la Reina, Suite 200
San Diego, California 92108
(714) 297-5350

Shooting Times (M)
Established 1960
Circulation: 179,000
Alex Bartimo, Editor
P J S Publications, Inc.
P.O. Box 1790
Peoria, Illinois 61656
(309) 682-6626

Shootin' Trap (M)
Established 1979
Circulation: 15,000
Frank Kodl, Editor and Publisher
2500A Valley Road
Reno, Nevada 89512
(702) 329-4519

Shotgun News (SM)
Established 1946
Circulation: 120,000
Jim Weaver, Editor
Snell Publishing Company
P.O. Box 669
Hastings, Nebraska 68901
(402) 463-4589

Skeet Shooting Review (M)
Established 1946
Circulation: 18,000
Milo Mims, Editor
National Skeet Shooting Association
P.O. Box 28188
San Antonio, Texas 78228
(512) 688-3560

Soldier of Fortune (BM)
Established 1975
Circulation: 80,000
Robert K. Brown, Editor and Publisher
Omega Group, Ltd.
P.O. Box 693
Boulder, Colorado 80302
(303) 449-3750

Southern Outdoors (8 x yr.)
Established 1953
Circulation: 200,000
Dave Ellison, Editor
Bass Anglers Sportsman Society
P.O. Box 17915
Montgomery, Alabama 36117
(205) 272-9530

Sporting Goods Business (M)
Established 1968
Circulation: 23,000
Robert Carr, Editor
Gralla Publications
1515 Broadway
New York, N.Y. 10036
(212) 869-1300

Sporting Goods Dealer (M)
Established 1899
Circulation: 16,000
C. C. Johnson Spink, Editor
Sporting Goods Publishing Co.
1212 North Lindbergh Boulevard
St. Louis, Missouri 63166
(314) 997-7111

Sports Afield (M)
Established 1887
Circulation: 500,000
Tom Paugh, Editor
The Hearst Corporation
250 W. 55th Street
New York, N.Y. 10019
(212) 262-8852

Sports and Recreation (BM)
Established 1946
Circulation: 35,000
Robert Bushnell, Editor
Nystrom Publishing Co.
9100 Cottonwood Lane
Maple Grove, Minnesota 55369
(612) 425-7900

Sports Merchandizer (M)
Established 1968
Circulation: 24,000
Eugene R. Marnell, Editor
1760 Peachtree Road, Northwest
Atlanta, Georgia 30357
(404) 874-4462

Sports Illustrated (W)
Established 1954
Circulation: 2,250,000
Roy Terrell, Editor
Time, Inc.
Time-Life Bldg.
New York, N.Y. 10020
(212) 586-1212

Texas Sportsman Magazine (BM)
Established 1971
Circulation: 25,000
R. Allan Charles, Editor and Publisher
Neptune Publications
P.O. Box 10411
San Antonio, Texas 78210
(512) 533-8991

Trap and Field (M)
Established 1890
Circulation: 24,000
Betty Ann Foxworthy, Editor
Curtis Publishing Company
1100 Waterway Boulevard
Indianapolis, Indiana 46202
(317) 634-1100

Turkey Call (BM)
Established 1973
Circulation: 31,000
Gene Smith, Editor
The National Wild Turkey Federation
P.O. Box 467
Edgefield, South Carolina 29824
(803) 637-3106

West Virginia Hills and Streams (M)
Established 1970
Circulation: 1400
Julia P. Young, Editor
West Virginia Hills and Streams, Inc.
Box 38
Durbin, West Virginia 26264
(304) 456-4789

Western Outdoor News (W)
Established 1953
Circulation: 80,000
Bill Rice, Editor
Western Outdoors Publications
3197 East Airport Loop Drive
Costa Mesa, California 92626
(714) 546-4370

Western Outdoors (M)
Established 1960
Circulation: 128,000
Burt Twiligar, Editor
Western Outdoors Publications
3197 East Airport Loop Drive
Costa Mesa, California 92626
(714) 546-4370

Wildlife Harvest (M)
Established 1973
Circulation: 1,000
John M. Mullin, Editor
North American Game Breeders &
    Shooting Preserves Association, Inc.
Goose Lake, Iowa 52750
(319) 577-2267

Wildlife Review (Q)
Established 1935
Circulation: 5,000
Kenneth J. Chiavetta, Editor
Aylesworth Hall, Room 263
Colorado State University
Fort Collins, Colorado 80523
(303) 491-7002

Wisconsin Sportsman (BM)
Established 1972
Circulation: 48,000
Thomas C. Petrie, Editor and Publisher
Wisconsin Sportsman, Inc.
P.O. Box 2266
Oshkosh, Wisconsin 54903
(414) 233-1327

Canadian Periodicals
B.C. Outdoors (M)
Established 1945
Circulation: 30,000
Donald Stainsby, Editor
S.I.P. Division of MacLean-Hunter, Ltd.
#202-1132 Hamilton Street
Vancouver, British Columbia V6B 2S2
(604) 687-1581

Canada Gunsport (M)
Established 1975
Circulation: 20,000
Canada Gun Sports
G. N. Dentay, Editor
14th Avenue, RR2
Gormley, Ontario L0H 1G0
(416) 881-8446

*The Canadian Journal of
    Arms Collecting (Q)*
Established: 1962
Circulation: 1300
S. J. Gooding, Editor
Museum Restoration Service
P.O. Box 390
Bloomfield, Ontario K0K 1G0
(613) 393-2980

Ontario Fisherman & Hunter (M)
Established 1967
Circulation: 32,000
Burton J. Myers, Editor
Ontario Fisherman and Hunter
5 Guardsman Road
Thornhill, Ontario L3T 2A1
(416) 881-1033

Québec Chasse & Pêche (M, French)
Established 1971
Circulation: 64,000
Jeannot Ruel, Editor
5786 Av. Christophe-Colomb
Montréal, Québec H2S 2G1

Sporting Goods Canada (8 x yr.)
Established 1973
Circulation: 9300
Dan Wilton, Editor and Publisher
Maclean-Hunter, Ltd.
481 University Avenue
Toronto, Ontario M5W 1V5
(416) 595-1811

Sporting Goods Trade (7 x yr.)
Established 1973
Circulation: 9,000
Gordon Bagley, Editor
Page Publications
380 Wellington Street West
Toronto, Ontario M5V 1E3
(416) 366-4608

Western Angling (BM)
Established 1965
Circulation: 14,000
J. L. Grundle, Editor and Publisher
Western Fish & Game Magazine, Ltd.
205-1591 Bowser Street
Vancouver, British Columbia V7P 2Y2
(604) 980-5821

Wildlife Crusader (M)
Established 1944
Circulation: 36,000
Paul F. Murphy, Editor
Stovel Advocate Press
365 Bannatyne Avenue
Winnipeg, Manitoba R3A 0E5
(204) 774-2926

Explanation of Symbols: (M) Monthly; (BM) Bimonthly; (SM) Semimonthly; (W) Weekly; (Q) Quarterly

Firearms Curios and Relics

The curios and relics listed below have currently been determined by the Bureau of Alcohol, Tobacco and Firearms (ATF) to have special value as collectors' items as of 1981. To be recognized as curios or relics, firearms must satisfy at least one of the following requirements:

1. The weapon (not including replicas) must have been manufactured at least 50 years ago;

2. The weapon must be certified by the curator of a municipal, state or federal museum exhibiting firearms to be of museum interest;

3. A substantial part of the weapon's monetary value must be derived from the fact that it is novel, rare or bizarre, or was associated with some historical figure, period or event.

Collectors who wish to obtain a curio or relic determination from the ATF on a specific firearm not appearing in this listing may submit a letter to the Chief of the Firearms Technology Branch, Bureau of Alcohol, Tobacco and Firearms, Washington, DC 20226. The letter should include a complete physical description of the firearm, reasons why the collector believes that the weapon in question merits classification as a relic or curio, as well as any supporting data concerning the history of the firearm.

Armand Gevage .32ACP caliber semiautomatic pistols, as manufactured in Belgium prior to World War II.

Astra M 300 pistol, calibers 7.65mm and 9mm Kurz, marked with German Waffenamt acceptance stamp, 1939-1945.

Astra M 400 pistol, German Army Contract, caliber 9mm Bergmann-Bayard, Serial Number range 97351-98850.

Astra Model 400 semiautomatic pistol, second German Army Contract, caliber 9mm Bergmann-Bayard, in the serial number range 92851 through 97350.

Astra M 600 pistol, caliber 9mm Parabellum, marked with German Waffenamt acceptance stamp, 1939-1945.

Astra M 800 Condor Model, pistol, caliber 9mm Parabellum.

Baker Gun and Forging Company, all firearms manufactured from 1899 to to 1919.

Bannerman Model 1937, Springfield rifle, caliber 30-06.

Bayard Model 1923 semiautomatic pistol, caliber 7.65mm or .380, Belgian manufacture.

Beretta Model 1915 pistols, caliber 6.35mm, 7.65mm, and 9mm Glisenti.

Beretta Model 1915/1919 (1922) pistol (concealed hammer), caliber 7.65mm.

Beretta Model 1919 pistol (without grip safety), caliber 6.35 mm.

Beretta Model 1923 pistol, Caliber 9mm Glisenti.

Beretta Model 1931 pistol, bearing Italian Navy Crest consisting of the letters "RM" and an anchor on the grip medalion, caliber 7.65 mm.

Beretta Model 1932 pistol, having smooth wooden grips with "PB" medallion, caliber 9mm.

Beretta Model 1934 pistols, caliber 9mm post war variations bearing Italian Air Force eagle markings.

Beretta Model 1934 pistols, caliber 9mm, produced during 1945 or earlier and having serial numbers within the following ranges—500000 to 999999, F00001 to F120000, G0001 to G80000, 00001AA to 10000AA, or 00001BB to 10000BB. This classification does not include any post war variations dated subsequent to 1945 or bearing post war Italian proof marks.

Beretta Model 1934 pistol, light weight model marked "Tipo Alleggerita" or "All" having transverse ribbed barrel, caliber 9mm.

Beretta Model 1935 pistol, Rumanian Contract, marked "P. Beretta—Cal. 9 Scurt—Mo. 1934—Brevet." on the slide, caliber 9mm.

Beretta Model 1935 pistol, Finnish Home Guard Contract, marked "SKY" on the slide, caliber 7.65mm.

Beretta Model 1935 pistols, caliber 7.65mm, produced during 1945 and earlier and having serial numbers below 620799.

Beretta M1951 pistol, Egyptian Contract, caliber 9mm Parabellum.

Beretta M1951 pistol, Israeli Contract, caliber 9mm Parabellum.

Bergmann-Bayard M1908 pistol, caliber 9mm Bergmann-Bayard.

Bernardelli Model 1956, experimental pistol, caliber 9mm Parabellum.

Bern Arsenal Experimental Gas Locked pistol, caliber 9mm Parabellum.

Bern Arsenal Experimental 16-shot pistol, caliber 9mm Parabellum.

FN Browning, Model 1902 (usually known as the Model 1903) semiautomatic pistol, caliber 9mm Browning long.

Browning Centennial Model High-Power Pistol, caliber 9mm Parabellum.

Browning Centennial Model 92 lever action rifle, caliber .44 Magnum.

Browning Superposed Centennial, consisting of a 20 gauge superposed shotgun, supplied with an extra set of .30-06 caliber superposed barrels.

Browning Hi-Power pistols, caliber 9mm having German Waffenamt inspector's marks.

Browning M1935 Hi-Power pistol, Canadian, Congolese, Indian and Nationalist Chinese Contracts, caliber 9mm Parabellum.

Browning "Baby" Model pistol, Russian Contract, caliber 6.35mm.

Browning M1910 and M1922 pistol, Contract pieces; M1910 Dutch Navy, M1922 Dutch or French Navy, and M1922 Yugoslavian Army calibers 7.65mm and 9mm Kurz.

Browning M1922 pistol, caliber 7.65 mm bearing German Navy acceptance stamps.

Browning M1922 pistol, caliber 9mm, bearing German Waffenamt acceptance stamp, 1939-1945.

Browning Model 1922 pistol, caliber 7.65mm, bearing German NSDAP or RFV markings.

Browning Model 1922 pistol, caliber 7.65mm or 9mm Kurz, marked with the Greek letters Epsilon Sigma denoting issue to the Greek Army.

Browning Model 1922 pistol, caliber 7.65mm or 9mm Kurz, marked "T.C. Subay" denoting issue to the Army of the Turkish Republic.

Browning Model 1922 pistol, caliber 7.65mm or 9mm Kurz, marked "C.P.I.M." denoting issue to the Belgian Political Police.

Browning Model 1922 pistol, caliber 7.65mm or 9mm Kurz, marked "S.P." and/or bearing the crest of the Kingdom Thailand.

Budischowsky, Model TP70, semiautomatic pistol, caliber .25 ACP, with custom serial number DB1.

Campo-Giro Model 1913 and 1913/16 pistol, caliber 9mm Largo.

Chinese Communist types 51 and 54 Tokarev pistols, caliber 7.62mm.

Chinese, Peoples Republic of China, copy of Japanese Type Sigiura Shiki semiautomatic pistol, caliber 7.65 mm.

Chylewski semiautomatic pistol manufactured by S.I.G. Switzerland, caliber 6.35mm (.25 ACP).

Clement pistol, Belgian manufacture, caliber 5mm Clement.

Colt Ace Service Model semiautomatic pistol, caliber .22, manufactured by Colt from 1935 to 1945, serial number range from SM1 to SM13803 including those marked "UNITED STATES PROPERTY" on the right side of the frame.

Colt Ace semiautomatic pistol, caliber .22, manufactured by Colt from 1931 to 1947, serial number range from 1 to 10935 including those marked "UNITED STATES PROPERTY" on the right side of the frame.

Colt Aircrewman revolver produced between 1951 and 1959, caliber .38 Special, marked "Property of U.S. Air Force" on back strap, having

Air Force issue numbers of 1 thru 1189 and in the serial number range 1902LW thru 90470I W.

Colt Army Model double action revolver, any caliber, manufactured between 1899 and 1907.

Colt, First Model, Match Target Woodsman, caliber .22, semiautomatic pistol, manufactured from 1938 to 1944, serial numbers MT1 to MT15,000.

Colt, J frame, Officer's Model Match, .38 Special revolver manufactured from 1970 to 1972, identified by a J serial number prefix.

Colt Lightning Model double action revolver, any caliber manufactured between 1899 and 1909

Colt Model 1900 semiautomatic pistol, caliber .38, in original configuration.

Colt Model 1902 semiautomatic pistol, sporting model, caliber .38, in original configuration.

Colt Model 1902 semiautomatic pistol, military model, caliber .38, in original configuration.

Colt Model 1903 Pocket (exposed hammer), semiautomatic pistol caliber .38 ACP.

Colt Model 1903 Pocket (hammerless), semiautomatic pistol, caliber .32.

Colt Model 1908, .25 ACP caliber, hammerless semiautomatic pistol having a grip safety, originally manufactured in Connecticut by Colt prior to 1956.

Colt Model 1908 Pocket (hammerless) semiautomatic pistol caliber .380.

Colt Model 1911 Commercial semiautomatic pistols, caliber .45 ACP, serial numbers C1 thru C130,000.

Colt Model 1911 pistol, English Contract, caliber .455.

Colt Model 1911-A1, commercial model, in caliber .45 and bearing Egyptian inscription meaning police, on the upper forward right-hand side of the trigger guard and having serial numbers within the range of C186000 to C188000.

Colt Model 1911-A1, .45 caliber pistol, manufactured by Union Switch and Signal Company, prototype model, bearing serial number US & S Exp. 1 to US & S Exp. 100.

Colt Fourth Model Derringer, caliber .22 short rimfire, cased as a set of two pistols in a leather book titled "Colt Derringer, Limited Edition, by Colt," on the spine of the book and "A Limited Edition by Colt," on the cover.

Colt Government Model pistols in caliber .45 ACP, BB Series.

Colt Mk IV Series 70 semiautomatic pistols in all calibers, which were incorrectly marked at the factory with both Colt Government Model markings and Colt Commander markings.

Colt, Ned Buntline Commemorative, caliber .45. revolver.

Colt New Service revolvers as manufactured between 1898 and 1944, all variations, all calibers.

Colt Officers Model (1904-1930), .38 caliber revolver.

Colt Officers Model (1930-1949), .22 caliber revolver.

Colt Officers Model Match (1953-1969), .22 and .38 caliber revolvers.

Colt Officers Model Special (1949-1952), .22 and .38 caliber revolvers.

Colt Officers Model Target (1930-1949), .32 and .38 caliber revolvers.

Colt, single action Army (Bisley, Standard, and target variations), all original, manufactured from 1899 to 1946, serial number range from 182000 to 357869.

Colt, Abercrombie and Fitch, "Trailblazer," .45 New Frontier.

Colt, Alabama Sesquicentennial, .22.

Colt, Alamo, .22 and .45.

Colt, Abilene, .22 (Kansas City-Cow Town).

Colt, Appomattox Court House Centennial, .22 and .45.

Colt, Arizona Ranger Model Commemorative, .22 revolver.

Colt, Arizona Territorial Centennial, .22 and .45.

Colt, Arkansas Territory Sesquicentennial, .22.

Colt, Battle of Gettysburg Centennial, .22.

Colt, Belleau Wood, .45 Pistol, (World War I Series).

Colt, California Bicentennial, .22.

Colt, California Gold Rush, .22 and .45.

Colt, Camp Perry Single Shot, Target Pistols, .22 long rifle or .38 Special caliber.

Colt, Carolina Charter Tercentenary, .22 and .22/.45.

Colt, Chamizal Treaty, .22 and .45.

Colt, Chateau Thierry, .45 Pistol, (World War I Series).

Colt, Cherry's Sporting Goods 35th Anniversary, .22/.45.

Colt, Chisholm Trail, .22 (Kansas Series-Trails).

Colt, Civil War Centennial Single Shot, .22.

Colt, Coffeyville, .22 (Kansas Series-Cow Town).

Colt, Colorado Gold Rush, .22.

Colt, Colonel Samuel Colt, Sesquicentennial, .45.

Colt, Colt's 125th Anniversary, .45.

Colt, Columbus (Ohio) Sesquicentennial, .22.

Colt, H. Cook, "1 of 100," .22/.45.

Colt, Dakota Territory, .22.

Colt, Des Moines, Reconstruction of Old Fort, .22 and .45.

Colt, Dodge City, .22 (Kansas Series-Cow Town).

Colt, Wyatt Earp, Buntline Special, .45 (Lawman Series).

Colt, Wyatt Earp, .22 and .45 (Lawman Series).

Colt, European Theater, .45 Pistol (World War II Series).

Colt, Florida Territory Sesquicentennial, .22.

Colt, General Nathan Bedford Forrest, .22.

Colt, Fort Findlay (Ohio) Sesquicentennial, .22.

Colt, Fort Hays, .22 (Kansas Series-Forts).

Colt, Fort Larned, .22 (Kansas Series-Forts).

Colt, Fort McPherson (Nebraska) Centennial Derringer, .22.

Colt, Fort Scott, .22 (Kansas Series-Forts).

Colt, Fort Stephenson (Ohio) Sesquicentennial, .22.

Colt, Fort-Niner Miner, .22.

Colt, Pat Garrett, .22 and .45 (Lawman Series).

Colt, Genesco (Illinois) 125th Anniversary, Derringer, .22.

Colt, Golden Spike Centennial, .22.

Colt, Wild Bill Hickok, .22 and .45 (Lawman Series).

Colt, General Hood, Tennessee Campaign Centennial, .22.

Colt, Idaho Territorial Centennial, .22.

Colt, Indiana Sesquicentennial, .22.

Colt, Kansas Centennial, .22.

Colt, Maine Sesquicentennial, .22 and .45.

Colt, Bat Masterson, .22 and .45 (Lawman Series).

Colt, General George Meade, Pennsylvania Campaign, .22 and .45.

Colt, Meuse Argonne, .45 Pistol (World War I Series).

Colt, Montana Territory Centennial, .22 and .45.

Colt, Missouri Sesquicentennial, .22.

Colt, General John Hunt Morgan, Indiana Raid, .22.

Colt, Joaquin Murrieta, "1 of 100," .22/.45.

Colt, Nebraska Centennial, .22.

Colt, Nevada Centennial, .22 and .45.

Colt, Nevada Centennial "Battle Born," .22 and .45.

Colt, New Jersey Tercentenary, .22 and .45.

Colt, New Mexico Golden Anniversary, .22.

Colt, NRA Centennial, single action revolver, in calibers .357 Magnum and .45.

Colt, NRA Centennial, Gold Cup National Match pistol, in caliber .45.

Colt, Oklahoma Territory Diamond Jubilee, .22.

Colt, Oregon Trail, .22 (Kansas Series-Trails).

Colt, Pacific Theater, .45 Pistol (World War II Series).

Colt, Pawnee Trail, .22 (Kansas Series-Trails).

Colt, Peacemaker Commemorative, .22 and .45 revolver.

Colt, Pony Express, Russell, Majors and Waddell, Presentation Model .45.

Colt, Pony Express Centennial, .22.

Colt, Rock Island Arsenal Centennial Single Shot, .22.

Colt, St. Augustine Quadricentennial, .22.

Colt, St. Louis Bicentennial, .22 and .45.

Colt, Santa Fe Trail, .22 (Kansas Series-Trails).

Colt, Second (2nd) Marne, .45 Pistol (World War I Series).

Colt, Shawnee Trail, .22 (Kansas Series-Trails).

Colt, Sheriff's Model, .45.

Colt Single Action Army revolver, caliber .45, serial #85163A, Engraved and inlaid with a bust of President Abraham Lincoln.

Colt, Texas Ranger, .45.

Colt, "The Right to Keep and Bear Arms" commemorative, .22 caliber Peacemaker Buntline, single action revolver having a 7½-inch barrel with the inscription "The Right to Keep and Bear Arms" inscribed on the barrel and a serial number range of G0001RB thru G3000RB.

Colt, United States Bicentennial Commemorative, Python revolver, caliber .357.

Colt, United States Bicentennial Commemorative, single action army revolver, caliber .45.

Colt, West Virginia Centennial, .22 and .45.

Colt, Wichita, .22 (Kansas Series-Cow Town).

Colt, Woodsman, caliber .22, semiautomatic target pistol, manufactured from 1915 to 1943, serial number 1 to 157,000.

Colt, Wyoming Diamond Jubilee, .22.

Colt, 1873 Peacemaker Centennial 1973, single action revolver, 44/.40 or .45.

Czechoslovakian CZ50 pistol, caliber 7.65mm.

Czechoslovakian CZ52 pistol, caliber 7.62mm.

Czechoslovakian CZ27 pistol, caliber 7.65mm, with flanged barrel for silencer and bearing German Waffenamt acceptance stamp, 1939-1945.

Czechoslovakian CZ38 pistol, caliber 9mm Kurz, with or without German Waffenamt acceptance stamp.

Czechoslovakian Model 24 pistol, caliber 9mm Kurz, marked with German Navy acceptance stamps, Navy proof marks or issuance marks.

Czechoslovakian Model 27 pistol, caliber 7.65mm, marked with German Navy acceptance stamps, Navy proof marks or issuance marks.

Czechoslovakian Model 1927 pistol, caliber 7.65mm, bearing German Waffenamt acceptance markings.

Czechoslovakian Model 1952 and 1952/57, 7.62 x 45mm and 7.62 x 39mm caliber, semiautomatic rifles (Puska Vzor 52, 7.62 x 45mm, and Puska Vzor 52/57, 7.62 x 39mm).

Danish M1910/1921 Bayard, pistol, caliber 9mm Bergmann-Bayard.

Davis Warner Infallible, semiautomatic pistol, caliber .32.

Dreyse Military Model 1910 pistol, caliber 9mm.

Egyptian Hakim (Ljungman) 7.92mm semiautomatic rifle as manufactured in Egypt.

Esser-Barratt, English manufacture, slide action rifle, caliber .303.

French S.A.C.M. Model 1935A pistol, caliber 7.65 Long, marked with German Navy acceptance stamps, Navy proof marks or issuance marks.

French M1935 pistol, caliber 7.65 French Long, bearing German Waffenamt acceptance stamp for period of 1939-1945.

French Model 1949, caliber 7.5mm, semiautomatic rifle (Fusil Mle. 1949 (MAS) 7.5mm).

German P38 pistols, caliber 9mm Parabellum manufactured prior to 1947.

Gustloff semiautomatic pistol, in caliber 7.65mm, manufactured by Gustloff Werke, Suhl, Germany.

Hammond or Grant Hammond pistols, all models, variations or prototypes, made by Grant Hammond Corporation, New Haven, Connecticut.

Hammond/Hi-Standard semiautomatic pistols, in caliber .45.

Harrington and Richardson, Abilene Anniversary, .22 revolver.

Harrington and Richardson, Centennial Officer's Model Springfield rifle, .45-70 Govt.

Harrington and Richardson, Centennial Standard Model Springfield rifle, .45-70 Govt.

Harrington and Richardson, Self-loading semiautomatic pistol, caliber .32.

Hartford Arms and Equipment Company single shot target pistol, caliber .22LR.

Hartford Arms and Equipment Company repeating pistol, caliber .22LR.

Hartford Arms and Equipment Company Model 1928 pistol, caliber .22LR.

Hi-Standard experimental electric free pistol, caliber .22 long rifle.

Hi-Standard Model P38, semiautomatic pistol, caliber .38 special.

Hi-Standard experimental Model T-3 semiautomatic pistol, caliber 9mm Luger.

High-Standard Model C/S smoothbore .22 caliber shot semiautomatic pistols, bearing serial numbers 59279, 59473, 59478, or 59460.

Hi-Standard experimental ISU rapid fire semiautomatic pistol, caliber .22 short.

High Standard Model A pistol, caliber .22LR.

High Standard Model B pistol, caliber .22LR.

High Standard Model C pistol, caliber .22Short.

High Standard Model D pistol, caliber .22LR.

High Standard Model E pistol, caliber .22LR.

High Standard Model H-A pistol, caliber .22LR.

High Standard Model H-B pistol, first model, caliber .22LR.

High Standard Model H-B pistol, second model, caliber .22LR.

High Standard Model H-D pistol, caliber .22LR.

High Standard Model H-E pistol, caliber .22LR.

High Standard Model USA-HD pistol, caliber .22LR.

High Standard Model HD-Military pistol, caliber .22LR.

High Standard Model G-380 pistol, caliber .380.

High Standard Model G-B pistol, caliber .22LR.

High Standard Model G-D pistol, caliber .22LR.

High Standard Model G-E pistol, caliber .22LR.

High Standard Model G-O (First Model Olympic) pistol, caliber .22 Short.

High Standard Supermatic Trophy, Model 107, .22 pistol Olympic Commemorative Model.

Hungarian Frommer Model 1937 pistol, caliber 7.65mm, marked with German Navy acceptance stamps, Navy proof marks or issuance marks.

Hungarian Model 1937 pistol, caliber 7.65mm, bearing German Waffenamt acceptance markings.

Italian Brixia M1906, pistol, caliber 9mm Glisenti.

Italian Glisenti M1910. pistol, caliber 9mm Glisenti.

Ithaca double barrel shotguns actually manufactured in New York by the Ithaca Gun Company, Ithaca, New York. All gauges and all models, having barrels at least 18 inches in length and an overall length of at least 26 inches, manufactured before 1950.

Ithaca Gun Company single barrel trap guns, break open all gauges, all models actually manufactured at Ithaca, New York, before 1950.

Ithaca, St. Louis Bicentennial, Model 49, .22 rifle.

Japanese Type I Hamada (1941) pistol, caliber 7.65mm.

Japanese Type II Hamada, pistol, caliber 7.65mm.

Japanese Type 14 (1925) pistol, caliber 8mm Nambu.

Japanese Type 94 (Model 1934), pistol, caliber 8mm Nambu (8 x 21mm cartridge), manufactured in Japan 1934-1945.

Japanese "Grandpa" Nambu, Model 1904, pistol, caliber 8mm Nambu.

Japanese "Baby" Nambu pistol, caliber 7mm Nambu.

Japanese Type Sigiura Shiki semiautomatic pistol, caliber 7.65mm and 6.35mm.

Jieffeco pistol, Belgian manufacture, caliber 7.65mm.

Jieffeco, semiautomatic pistol, in caliber .25 ACP, marked "Davis Warner Arms Corp., N.Y."

Kimball pistols, all models, all calibers.

Kolibri pistols, calibers 2.7mm and 3mm Kolibri.

L. C. Smith Shotguns manufactured by Hunter Arms Company and Marlin Firearms Company from 1899 to 1971.

Lahti L-35 pistol, Finnish manufacture, caliber 9mm Parabellum.

Luger, pistol, all models and variations manufactured prior to 1946.

Luger, Mauser commercal manufacture, semiautomatic pistol, 70 Jahre, Parabellum-Pistole, Keiserreich Russland, commemorative, caliber 9mm.

Luger, Mauser commercial manufacture, semiautomatic pistol, 75 Jahre, Parabellum-Pistole, 1900-1975, commemorative, caliber 7.65mm.

Luger, Mauser commercial manufacture, semiautomatic pistol, 75 Jahre, Parabellum-Pistole, Konigreich Bulgarien, commemorative, caliber 7.65mm.

MAB Model D pistol, caliber 7.65mm bearing German Navy acceptance stamp.

MAB Model D pistol, caliber 7.65mm bearing German Waffenamt acceptance stamp for the period 1939-1945.

MAB Model R pistol, caliber 9mm Parabellum.

Makarov pistol, Russian and East German, caliber 9mm Makarov.

Mannlicher pistol, M1900, M1901, M1903 and M1905, caliber 7.63mm Mannlicher.

Marlin 90th Anniversary, Model 39-A, .22 Rifle.

Marlin 90th Anniversary, Model 39-A, .22 Carbine.

Original military bolt action and semiautomatic rifles manufactured between 1899 and 1946.

Mauser, semiautomatic pistols manufactured prior to 1946, any caliber.

Menz Liliput, German manufacture, caliber 4.25mm.

Menz PBIII, in caliber 7.65mm, manufactured by August Menz, Suhl, Germany.

Menz PBIIIA, in caliber 7.65mm, manufactured by August Menz, Suhl, Germany.

Menz PBIV, in caliber 7.65mm, manufactured by August Menz, Suhl, Germany.

Menz PBIVa, in caliber 7.65mm, manufactured by August Menz, Suhl, Germany.

Menz Special, in caliber 7.65mm, manufactured by August Menz, Suhl, Germany.

Mexican Obregon, pistol, caliber .45 ACP.

Mugica Model 120, pistol, caliber 9mm Parabellum.

North Korean Type 1964, pistol, caliber 7.62mm Tokarev.

Norwegian M1914, pistol, caliber .45 ACP.

PAF "Junior" semiautomatic pistol, caliber .25, manufactured by the Pretoria Arms Factory Ltd. of South Africa.

PAF pistol, marked "BRF," caliber .25, manufactured by the Pretoria Arms Factory Ltd. of South Africa.

Phoenix (U.S.A.) pistol, caliber .25 ACP.

Polish FB "VIS," M1935 (Radom), pistol, caliber 9mm Parabellum, Original Republic of Poland model with an eagle crest and Polish inscription on left side of slide. Dated 1936, 1937, 1938, or 1939 and having small sized serial numbers in the range 1 through 50,000 without letter or number prefix or suffix.

Polish VB "VIS" Model 1935 (Radom) pistol, caliber 9mm Parabellum, bearing German military acceptance markings.

Reising .22 caliber, semiautomatic pistol.

Remington Canadian Territorial Centennial, Model 742, Rifle.

Remington, Model 51, semiautomatic pistol, calibers .32 ACP or .380 ACP.

Remington 150th Anniversary Model 1100SA semiautomatic shotgun, caliber 12 gauge.

Remington 150th Anniversary Model 870SA slide action shotgun, caliber 12 gauge.

Remington 150th Anniversary Model 742ADL semiautomatic rifle, caliber .30/06.

Remington 150th Anniversary Model 760ADL slide action rifle, caliber .30/06.

Remington 150th Anniversary Model 552A semiautomatic rifle, caliber .221r.

Remington 150th Anniversary Model 572A slide action rifle, caliber .221r.

Remington 150th Anniversary Model Nylon 66 semiautomatic rifle, caliber .221r.

Remington Montana Territorial Centennial, Model 600, Rifle.

Roth Steyr 1907, semiautomatic pistol, caliber 8mm.

Ruger Canadian Centennial, Matched No. 1 Rifle Sets, Special Deluxe.

Ruger Canadian Centennial, Matched No. 2 Rifle Sets.

Ruger Canadian Centennial, Matched No. 3 Rifle Sets.

Ruger Canadian Centennial, Model 10/22, Carbine.

Ruger, flattop, "Blackhawk" revolvers, calibers .44 Magnum and .357 Magnum, all barrel lengths, made from 1955 through 1962.

Ruger, flattop, single-six, .22 caliber revolvers with flat side loading gate, all barrel lengths, made from 1953 through 1956.

Sauer 38(h), pistol, caliber 7.65mm marked with Third Reich police acceptance stamps of Eagle C, F, K or L.

Sauer 38H pistol, caliber 7.65mm bearing German Waffenamt acceptance markings.

Savage Arms, semiautomatic pistols, caliber .45 ACP, all models.

Savage, Prototype pistols, caliber .25, .32 and .38 made between 1907 and 1927.

Savage, Model 1907 Pistols, caliber .32 and .380.

Savage, Model 1907 Pistols, caliber .45 military contract.

Savage, Model 1911 Pistol, caliber .45, Prototype.

Savage, Model 1915 Pistol, caliber .32 and .380.

Savage, Model 1917 Pistol, caliber .32 and .380.

Smith and Wesson, U.S. Border Patrol 50th Anniversary Commemorative, Model 66, stainless steel, caliber .357 Magnum, revolvers.

Smith & Wesson, Model .22/32 Hand Ejector (Bekeart Model), caliber .22 LR, serial numbers 138220 to 534636 (no letter).

Smith & Wesson, K-22 Hand Ejector, caliber .22 LR, serial numbers 632132 to 696952 (no letter).

Smith & Wesson, K-32 Hand Ejector (K-32 Masterpiece), caliber .32 S&W Long, serial numbers 653388 to 682207 (no letter).

Smith & Wesson, .38 Hand Ejector Military and Police, caliber .38, serial numbers 1 to 241703 (no letter).

Smith & Wesson, .357 Magnum Hand Ejector, caliber .357 Magnum, serial numbers 45768 to 60000 (no letter).

Smith & Wesson, .44 Hand Ejector, all calibers, serial numbers 1 to 62488 (no letter).

Smith & Wesson, .455 Mark II Hand Ejector, caliber .455.

Smith & Wesson Mercox Dart Gun, caliber .22 rimfire, blank.

Smith & Wesson, .22/32 Kit Gun, caliber .22 LR, serial numbers 525670 to 534636 (no letter).

Smith & Wesson, .32 Double Action Top Break, caliber .32 S&W, serial numbers 209302 and higher.

Smith & Wesson, .32 Safety Hammerless Top Break (New Departure), caliber .32 S&W, serial numbers 91401 and higher.

Smith & Wesson, .38 Double Action Top Break, caliber .38 S&W, serial numbers 382023 and higher.

Smith & Wesson, .38 Double Action Top Break Perfected Model, caliber .38 S&W.

Smith & Wesson, .38 Safety Hammerless Top Break (New Departure), caliber .38 S&W, serial number 119901 and higher.

Smith & Wesson, pistol, caliber .35, all variations.

Smith & Wesson, 2nd Model, single shot pistol, calibers .22 rimfire, .32 S & W and .38 S & W.

Smith & Wesson, 3rd Model, single shot pistol, caliber .22 rimfire, .32 S & W and .38 S & W.

Smith & Wesson, 1st Model, Ladysmith revolver, caliber .22 rimfire long.

Smith & Wesson, 2nd Model, Ladysmith revolver, caliber .22 rimfire long.

Smith & Wesson, 3rd Model, Ladysmith revolver, caliber .22 rimfire long.

Smith & Wesson Model 39-1 (52-A), pistol, caliber 9mm Parabellum.

Smith & Wesson Model 39, steel frame pistol, caliber 9mm Parabellum.

Smith & Wesson, pistol, caliber .32 ACP.

Smith & Wesson Model Straight Line, single shot pistol, caliber .22 rimfire long rifle.

Smith & Wesson, Model 16 (K-32 Masterpiece), caliber .32 S&W Long, "K" serial number series.

Smith & Wesson, .38/44 Outdoorsman & Heavy Duty, caliber .38, serial numbers 36500 to 62023 (no letter).

Smith & Wesson 150th Anniversary Texas Ranger Commemorative Model 19 revolver.

Smith and Wesson, Model 10 Victory Models, identified by the letter "V" prefix to the serial number, in the original .38 Special chambering, with U.S. Navy acceptance marks.

Smith & Wesson, U.S. Army Model of 1917, caliber .45, serial numbers 1 to 163476.

Standard Arms Co., rifle/shotgun combination, U.S., Model "Camp," slide action caliber .50.

Standard Arms Co., rifle Model G, slide action or gas operated, caliber unknown.

Standard Arms Co., rifle Model M, slide action caliber .25-.35, .30 Rem. and .35 Rem.

Star Model B semiautomatic pistol, caliber 9mm Parabellum, having German military acceptance marks and in the serial number range 21597 through 249687.

Steyr-Hahn M1912, pistol, caliber 9mm Steyr.

Steyr-Hahn M1912, pistol, caliber 9mm Parabellum marked with Third Reich police acceptance stamps of Eagle C, F, K or L.

Sosso pistols manufactured by Guilio Sosso, Turin, Italy, or Fabrica Nationale D'Armi, Brescea Italy, caliber 9mm.

Tauler Model military and police pistol.

Tokagypt 58, pistol, caliber 9mm Parabellum.

Unique Model 17 pistol, French manufacture, caliber 7.65mm bearing German Waffenamt acceptance stamp for period of 1939-1945.

Unique Kriegsmodell pistol, French manufacture, caliber 7.65mm, bearing German Waffenamt acceptance stamp for period 1939-1945.

U.S. Model 1911 semiautomatic pistol, military series, caliber .45, serial-number range from 1 to 629500, all original variations regardless of manufacture including: The North American Arms Company, Model 1911; the Springfield Armory, Model 1911 with NRA markings; the Remington Arms-UMC, Model 1911; and any Model 1911 cutaways.

U.S. pistols, Model 1911-A1, caliber .45, manufactured by the Singer Manufacturing Company in 1942, serial-number range from S800001 to S800500.

U.S. Model 1911-A1 semiautomatic pistol, caliber .45, manufactured by Remington Rand, bearing serial number prefix of ERRS.

U.S. Model 1911-A1 semiautomatic pistol, caliber .45, produced as original factory cutaways.

U.S. Rifle, caliber .30 MC-1952, equipped with telescopic sight mount MC, telescopic sight MC1, marked U.S.M.C. or kollmorgan.

Walther pistols, Manufactured at Zella-Mehlis prior to 1946, all models any caliber.

Webley Model 1909, pistol, caliber 9mm Browning Long.

Webley and Scott, Model 1910 and 1913 high velocity pistols, caliber .38 ACP.

Webley and Scott, M1913, Navy or Commercial, self-loading pistol, caliber .455.

Webley-Fosbury, semiautomatic revolvers, all calibers, all models.

Winchester 1980 Alberta Diamond Jubilee Commemorative carbines, Model 94, in caliber .38/55.

Winchester Alaskan Purchase Centennial, Model 1894, carbine.

Winchester Antlered Game Commemorative, Model 94, carbine, caliber .30-30.

Winchester Apache Commemorative carbine, commemorative edition of Model 1894 Winchester with serial number prefix of AC.

Winchester Bicentennial 76, Model 94 carbine.

Winchester Buffalo Bill, Model 1894, carbine.

Winchester Buffalo Bill, Model 1894, Rifle.

Winchester Canadian 1967, Centennial Model 1894, carbine.

Winchester Canadian 1967, Centennial Model 1894, Rifle.

Winchester Centennial, Model 1866, carbine.

Winchester Centennial, Model 1866, Rifle.

Winchester Comanche Commemorative carbine, commemorative edition of Model 1894 Winchester with serial number prefix of CC.

Winchester Cowboy Commemorative, Model 94, carbine.

Winchester Golden Spike, Model 1894, carbine.

Winchester Illinois Sesquicentennial, Model 1894, carbine.

Winchester Klondike Gold Rush Commemorative Model 94, carbine.

Winchester Legendary Lawman Commemorative, Model 94, carbine, caliber .30-30.

Winchester Legendary Frontiersman Model 94 rifle, caliber .38-55.

Winchester "Limited Edition II" Model 94 rifle, caliber .30-30.

Winchester Little Big Horn Centennial, Model 94, carbine.

Winchester Lone Star Commemorative, Model 94, carbine.

Winchester Lone Star Commemorative, rifle, Model 94, .30-30.

Winchester "Ducks Unlimited" shotgun, Model 12, bearing serial numbers DU-001 through DU-800 (Commemorative).

Winchester "Matched Set of 1000," a cased pair consisting of a Winchester Model 94 rifle, caliber .30-30 and a Winchester Model 9422 rifle, caliber .22.

Winchester Model 52, rifle, bearing serial numbers 1 to 6,500.

Winchester Model 53, all original, manufactured from 1924 to 1947 with 16 inch or longer barrel, and 26 inch or longer overall length.

Winchester Model 54, rifle, speed lock variation, caliber .270.

Winchester Model 65, all original, manufactured from 1933 to 1947 with 16 inch or longer barrel and 26 inch or longer overall length.

Winchester Model 70 Ultra Match Target Special Grade rifle, caliber .308.

Winchester rifles, Model 70, .308, .270 Winchester, and 30-06 caliber, 19 inch barrel and Mannlicher type stock, made from 1968 to 1971.

Winchester Model 71, all original, manufactured from 1936 to 1958, with 16 inch or longer barrel and 26 inch or longer overall length.

Winchester Limited Edition, Model 94 carbine, caliber .30-30, serial numbers 77L1 through 77L1500.

Winchester Model 1873, all original, manufactured from 1899 to 1925, with 16 inch or longer barrel and 26 inch or longer overall length.

Winchester Model 1885 (single shot rifle), all original, manufactured from 1899 to 1920, with 16 inch or longer barrel, and 26 inch or longer overall length.

Winchester Model 1886, all original, manufactured from 1899 to 1935, with 16 inch or longer barrel and 26 inch or longer overall length.

Winchester Model 1892, all original, manufactured from 1899 to 1947, with 16 inch or longer barrel and 26 inch or longer overall length.

Winchester Model 1894 rifles and carbines manufactured prior to January 2, 1964, and having a serial number of less than 2,700,000, provided their barrel length is at least 16 inches and their overall length at least 26 inches.

Winchester Model 1895, all original manufactured from 1899 to 1938, with 16 inch or longer barrel and 26 inch or longer overall length.

Winchester Nebraska Centennial, Model 1894, carbine.

Winchester NRA Centennial rifle, Model 94, .30-30.

Winchester Model NRA Centennial, Model 94 carbine.

Winchester Mounted Police, Model 94, carbine.

Winchester Northwest Territories Centennial rifle.

Winchester rifle, Model 70, caliber .308 rifle, 19 inch barrel and Mannlicher type stock, made from 1968 to 1971.

Winchester Royal Canadian Mounted Police Centennial, Model 94 carbine.

Winchester 150th Anniversary Texas Ranger Commemorative, Model 1894, carbine.

Winchester Theodore Roosevelt, Model 1894, carbine.

Winchester Theodore Roosevelt, Model 1894, Rifle.

Winchester Wells Fargo and Company Commemorative, Model 94 carbines.

Winchester Wyoming Diamond Jubilee, Model 94 carbine.

Winchester Yellow Boy Indian, Model 94 carbine.

Handguns

ASTRA PISTOLS & REVOLVERS

ASTRA MODEL 44

4″ barrel

6″ barrel

ASTRA 357, 357 MAG. & 38 SPECIAL

Potent, powerful and smooth as silk: the Astra 357. Chambered for the hot 357 Magnum cartridge, this large-frame revolver also handles the popular 38 Special, making it equally suitable for the serious target shooter and for the sportsman.

All forged steel and highly polished to a rich blue, the Astra 357 has a heavyweight barrel with integral rib and ejector shroud. The rear sight is click-adjustable for windage and elevation. The hammer is of the wide-spur target type, and the trigger is grooved. The grips are of checkered hardwood. The cylinder is recessed, and the gun utilizes a spring-loaded, floating firing pin for additional safety.

The internal lockwork of the Astra 357 is as finely fitted and finished as the exterior, giving it a smoothness second to none. There's even a four-stage adjustment to control spring tension on the hammer.

The Astra 357 is available with 4″, 6″ and 8½″ barrel. The 4″ and longer-barreled models have square butts and are supplied with comfortable, hand-filling oversized grips. Length overall with 6″ barrel is 11¼″.

Barrel Length	Finish	Caliber	Weight	
4″	Blue	357 Mag.	38 oz.	**$300.00**
3″	Blue	357 Mag.	38 oz.	**300.00**
6″	Blue	357 Mag.	39 oz.	**300.00**
8½″	Blue	357 Mag.	41 oz.	**315.00**

ASTRA CONSTABLE 22 L.R. & 380 ACP

The Astra Constable is a double-action, all steel small-frame auto, so you can safely carry it fully loaded with a round in the chamber and the safety off. A single pull of the trigger then cocks and fires the pistol without the necessity of cocking the hammer manually, as is necessary with most autos. The thumb safety completely blocks the hammer and actually locks the firing pin in place until released. The barrel is rigidly mounted in the frame for greater accuracy and the gun features quick, no-tool takedown, integral non-glare rib on the slide, push-button magazine release and a round, non-snagging hammer spur.

22 L.R. & 380 ACP Blue		**$320.00**
22 L.R. & 380 ACP Chrome		**350.00**
22 L.R. & 380 ACP Blue Engraved		**440.00**
22 L.R. & 380 ACP Chrome Engraved		**475.00**

Meet the Astra Model 44 Magnum. Designed around the popular lines of its forerunner, the Astra 357, this revolver features wide-spur target hammers and a four-position main spring adjustment device which allows for custom tuning of trigger pull. The Astra M44 has features all its own, too. For instance, oversized, beefed-up frame and target-style grips to provide balanced weight distribution and minimize the apparent recoil of the 44 Magnum round.

The revolver, finished in a deep astral blue, is available with a 6-inch barrel which features an integral sight rib and shroud for the ejector rod. Grooved triggers, ramp front sights and fully adjustable rear sights are standard on all 44 Magnum models.

6″	Blue	44 Mag.	**$395.00**
6″	Blue	41 Mag.	**395.00**
6″	Blue	45 Colt	**395.00**

BERETTA PISTOLS

MODEL 70S PISTOL

This pistol is available in 22 Auto and 380 Auto and has a frame of steel alloy. Longer barrel guide; safety lever blocking the hammer; push button magazine release; sloping grip; sight and rear sight blade fixed on the breech block.

SPECIFICATIONS:
Total Length: 6.5". Barrel Length: 3.5". Height: 4.8". Weight (mag. empty): 1 lb. 7 ozs. Magazine Capacity, 380 Auto: 7 rounds. Magazine Capacity, 22 Auto: 8 rounds.

Model 70S **$274.00**

MODEL 81/84 PISTOLS

These pistols are pocket size with a large magazine capacity. The lockwork is of double-action type. The first shot (with hammer down, chamber loaded) can be fired by a double-action pull on the trigger without cocking the hammer manually.

The pistols also feature a favorable grip angle for natural pointing, positive thumb safety (uniquely designed for both right- and left-handed operation), quick take-down (by means of special take-down button) and a conveniently located magazine release. The magazine capacity is 13 rounds in 380 caliber (Model 84) and 12 rounds in the 32 auto caliber (Model 81). Black plastic grips. Wood grips available at extra cost.

SPECIFICATIONS — Model M-81
Caliber: 32 Auto (7.65mm). Weight: 1 lb. 8 oz. Barrel Length: 3¾" (Approx.). Overall Length: 6½" (Approx.). Sights: Fixed - Front and Rear. Magazine Capacity: 12 Rounds. Height, overall: 4¼" (Approx.).

SPECIFICATIONS — Model M-84
Caliber: 380 Auto (9mm Short). Weight: 1 lb. 7 oz. (Approx.). Barrel Length: 3¾" (Approx.). Overall Length: 6½" (Approx.). Sights: Fixed - Front and Rear. Magazine Capacity: 13 Rounds. Height, overall: 4¼" (Approx.).

Model 81 (with plastic grips) **$408.00**
Model 81 (with wood grips) 425.00
Model 84 (with plastic grips) 408.00
Model 84 (with wood grips) 425.00

MODEL 76 PISTOL

Designed for target shooting the M-76 features built-in, fixed counterweight for correct balance and control of recoil; raised, matted rib on which both front and rear sights are solidly mounted; rear sight fully adjustable for windage and elevation; front sight supplied in three interchangeable widths. Trigger pull is factory adjusted to a weight between 3 lbs. 5 oz. and 3 lbs. 12 oz.

Grips are plastic, shaped and checkered to give a firm hold. Pistols are equipped with a positive thumb safety. All metal parts are finished in blue-black. Checkered wood grips available at extra cost.

SPECIFICATIONS:
Caliber: 22 LR. Magazine Capacity: 10 Rounds. Overall Length: 8.8" (223mm). Barrel Length: 6" (150mm). Sight Radius: 6.9" (176mm). Weight (mag. empty): 2 lbs. 1 oz. (930 grams). Height: 5.6" (143mm). Rifling: 6 lands & grooves, R.H. pitch.

Model 76 (with plastic grips) **$370.00**
Model 76 (with wood grips) 415.15

MODEL 92S PISTOL

A heavy-duty handgun, chambered for the high-velocity 9mm Parabellum (Luger) cartridge. The pistol's unique "Hammer Drop" safety feature blocks the firing pin from the hammer, releases the hammer and breaks the connection between the trigger and sear. Double-action lockwork —pistol may be fired by a double-action trigger pull (with hammer down), as well as in the regular single-action mode. Magazine has extra-large capacity of 15 rounds, although of standard length (another cartridge may be carried in the chamber). Pistol is fully locked at time of firing. Extractor acts as loaded chamber indicator visually and by feel. Both front and rear sights are mounted on the slide. All metal parts are finished in blue-black. Grips are black plastic, checkered and grooved. Wood grips extra.

SPECIFICATIONS:
Caliber: 9mm Parabellum (Luger). Magazine Capacity: 15 Rounds. Overall Length: 8.54" (217mm). Barrel Length: 4.92" (125mm). Sight Radius: 6.1" (155mm). Weight (mag. empty): 2 lbs. 1½ oz. (950 grams). Height: 5.39" (137mm). Width: 1.45" (37mm). Rifling: 6 lands & grooves, R.H. pitch.

Model 92S (with plastic grips) **$515.00**
Model 92S (with wood grips) 543.00

BERNARDELLI PISTOLS

MODEL 80

Caliber: .22 L.R.-10 Shot; 380 ACP-7 Shot. **Barrel:** 3.54". **O.A. Length:** 6.45". **Weight:** 26.8 oz. **Stock:** Checkered plastic w/thumb rest (Wrap Around). **Sights:** Adjustable. **Features:** Hammer-blocking slide safety which locks firing pin to permit loading or clearing of chamber w/safety engaged. Loaded round indicator, adjustable rear sight. White outline rear sight and white dot front sight. Dual recoil buffer springs. Serrated trigger. Inertia type firing pin. Magazine follower interlock holds slide open after last round is fired.

Model 80 .... **$220.00**

MODEL 100

Caliber: .22 L.R. only—10 shot. **Barrel:** 5.9". **O.A. Length:** 9.00". **Weight:** 37.75 oz. **Features:** Target barrel weight included. Heavy sighting rib with interchangeable front sight. Rear sight adjustable for elevation and windage. Serrated trigger, inertia type firing pin. Comfortable checkered walnut grips with thumb rest. Accessories include cleaning equipment and assembly tools. Case included.

Model 100 .... **$395.00**

BERSA PISTOLS

MODEL 644

Caliber: 22 L.R.
Barrel Length: 3½"
Overall Length: 6½".
Height: 4¼".
Magazine Capacity: 7 rounds.
Empty Weight: 26½ oz.

Model 644 with extra magazine .. **$175.00**
      extra 22 L.R. magazine 16.00

BROWNING AUTOMATIC PISTOLS

22 CHALLENGER II

The 22 Challenger II has a unique wedge locking system (patent pending) that prevents the slightest instability or loosening. The screw adjustable rear sight is recoil-proof. It does not move with the operating slide, so the Challenger remains sighted in, shot after shot. The 6¾″ barrel is cleanly rifled, and the muzzle is recessed. This barrel length also offers a long sighting plane, which contributes to accuracy.

The Challenger II's frame is all steel, deeply blued. All the parts are machined and hand fitted for long wear. The wide, gold-plated trigger has a positive, crisp action.

The grips are made of tough impregnated hardwood that resist scarring and scraping. After you fire the last cartridge, the slide stays open, a convenience in determining the pistol's safety status and in facilitating safe reloading.

The Challenger II's spring-loaded magazine stores 10 Long Rifle 22 cartridges. A magazine follower button allows you to depress the magazine spring to make the loading fast and easy.

Challenger II **$224.95**
Extra magazine **14.95**

9mm HI-POWER

The Browning 9mm Parabellum, also known as the 9mm Browning Hi-Power has a 14-cartridge capacity and weighs two pounds. The push-button magazine release permits swift, convenient withdrawal of the magazine.

The 9mm is available with either a fixed blade front sight and a windage adjustable rear sight or a non-glare rear sight, screw adjustable for both windage and elevation. The front sight is a ⅛-inch wide blade mounted on a ramp. The rear surface of the blade is serrated to prevent glare.

In addition to the manual safety, the firing mechanism includes an external hammer so it is easy to ascertain whether the pistol is cocked.

Standard **$474.95**
Standard with adjustable sights **519.95**
Silver Chrome with adjustable sights **539.95**
Extra magazine **36.25**

SPECIFICATIONS:

Magazine Capacity: 10. **Overall length:** 10⅞″. **Barrel length:** 6¾″. **Height:** 5¼″. **Weight:** 38 oz. **Sight radius:** 9⅛″. **Ammunition:** 22 L.R. **Grips:** Impregnated hardwood. **Front sights:** ⅛″ wide. **Rear sights:** Screw adjustable for vertical correction. Drift adjustable for windage. **Grades available:** Standard.

BDA-380. A high-powered, double-action pistol with fixed sights in 380 caliber.

BDA-380 nickel ... **$424.95**   BDA-380 standard . **$369.50**
Extra magazine ...   **25.00**   Extra magazine ...   **20.75**

AUTOMATIC PISTOL SPECIFICATIONS

	22 Challenger II	9 mm Hi-Power		BDA-380
		Fixed Sights	Adjustable Sights	(Double Action)
Capacity of Magazine	10	13	13	12
Overall Length	10⅞″	7¾″	7¾″	6¾″
Barrel Length	6¾″	4²¹⁄₃₂″	4²¹⁄₃₂″	3¹³⁄₁₆″
Height	5¼″	5″	5″	4¾″
Weight (Empty)	39 oz.	32 oz.	32-1/5 oz.	23 oz.
Sight Radius	9⅛″	6⁵⁄₁₆″	6⅜″	4¹⁵⁄₁₆″
Ammunition	22LR	9 mm Luger	9 mm Luger	380 Auto
Grips	Impregnated hardwood	Checkered walnut [1]	Checkered walnut [1]	Walnut
Front Sights	⅛″ wide	Fixed blade	⅛″ wide blade on ramp	Fixed blade with white dot
Rear Sights	Screw adjustable for vertical correction. Drift adjustable for windage.	Drift adjustable for windage.	Screw adjustable horizontal and vertical.	White outlined square notch. Drift adjustable for windage.
Grades Available	Standard	Standard [2] and Renaissance [3]	Standard [2] and Renaissance [3]	Standard

[1] Renaissance models come with Nacrolac pearl grips.   [2] The Standard 9 mm caliber pistol comes in lined, padded vinyl, flexible, zipper case.   [3] The Renaissance 9 mm caliber is encased in a deluxe black vinyl pistol case.

BAUER PISTOLS

25 CALIBER AUTOMATIC
$122.85

SPECIFICATIONS:
Caliber: 25 automatic
Capacity: 6 shot
Barrel length(s): 2¼″
Weight: 10 oz.
Overall length: 4″
Safety: Positive manual
Grips: Pearl or genuine walnut
Finish: Neutral Satin Stainless

CHARTER ARMS REVOLVERS

POLICE BULLDOG
38 SPECIAL 6-SHOT REVOLVER

SPECIFICATIONS:
Caliber: 38 Special. **Type of Action:** 6-shot single and double action. **Barrel length:** 4 inches. **Overall length:** 9 inches. **Height:** 5⅛ inches. **Weight:** 20½ ounces. **Grips:** Square butt, American walnut hand-checkered. **Sights:** Full-length ramp front; fully adjustable combat rear. **Finish:** High-luster Service Blue $184.00

TARGET BULLDOG 357 MAG.
44 SPECIAL

SPECIFICATIONS:
Caliber: 357 Mag., 44 spl. **Type of action:** 5 shot, single and double action. **Barrel length:** 4 inches. **Overall length:** 9 inches. **Height:** 5⅛ inches. **Weight:** 20½ ounces. **Grips:** American walnut square butt. **Sights:** Full length ramp front sight; fully adjustable, milled channel, square notch rear sight. **Finish:** High-luster Service Blue.
357 Mag. $215.50
44 Special 216.50
Finish: High-luster Service Blue.

PATHFINDER
22 MAGNUM

SPECIFICATIONS:
Caliber: 22 Magnum. **Type of action:** 6 shot, single and double action. **Barrel length:** 3 or 6 inches. **Overall length:** 7¾″ (3″ bbl.), 10⅝″ (6″ bbl.). **Height:** 4¾″ (3″ bbl.), 5″ (6″ bbl.). **Weight:** 20 oz. (3″ bbl.), 22½ oz. (6″ bbl.). **Grips:** Hand-checkered square butt grips. **Sights:** Patridge-type ramp front sight, fully adjustable notch rear sight. **Finish:** High luster Service Blue.

With 3″ barrel $196.00
With 6″ barrel 202.00

CHARTER ARMS REVOLVERS

UNDERCOVER   32 S & W Long
Blue finish with regular grips $173.00

SPECIFICATIONS:
Caliber: 32 S & W Long. **Type of Action:** 6 Shot, single and double action. **Barrel Length:** 2". **Overall Length:** 6¼". **Height:** 4⅛". **Weight:** 16 ounces. **Grips:** Smooth American walnut, uncheckered. **Sights:** Wide Patridge type front; notch rear 9/64". **Rifling:** One turn in 17", right hand twist. **Finish:** High luster Service Blue.

PATHFINDER   22 L.R.

Blue finish with regular grips
   3" barrel $187.00
Blue finish with square butt grips
   6" barrel 201.50

SPECIFICATIONS:
Caliber: 22 Long Rifle. **Type of Action:** 6 shot, single and double action. **Barrel Length:** 3 or 6 inches. **Overall Length:** 7⅛" (3" bbl.), 10⅝" (6" bbl.). **Height:** 4¼" (3" bbl.), 5" (6" bbl.) **Weight:** 19 oz. (3" bbl.), 22½ oz. (6" bbl.). **Grips:** Smooth American walnut, uncheckered. Optional: Bulldog grips American walnut hand-checkered. **Sights:** Fully adjustable rear; Patridge-type ramp front. **Rifling:** One turn in 16 inches, right hand twist. **Finish:** High luster Service Blue.

UNDERCOVER   38 Special

2" barrel blue finish with
   regular grips $173.00
2" barrel stainless steel finish
   with checkered panel grips ... 229.50
3" barrel blue finish with
   regular grips 173.00

BULLDOG 44 SPECIAL

Blue finish with Bulldog grips $168.00
Stainless Steel finish with Bulldog grips 244.00

SPECIFICATIONS:
Caliber: 38 Special (Mid-Range & Standard). **Type of Action:** 5 shots, single and double action. **Barrel Length:** 2" or 3". **Overall Length:** 6¼" (2" bbl.), 8" (3" bbl.). **Height:** 4¼" (2" bbl.), 4¾" (3" bbl.). **Weight:** 16 oz. (2" bbl.), 17½ oz. (3" bbl.). **Grips:** Smooth American walnut. **Sights:** Patridge type ramp front, square-notched rear. **Finish:** High-luster Service Blue or Stainless Steel.

SPECIFICATIONS:
Caliber: 44 Special. **Type of Action:** 5 shot, single and double action. **Barrel length:** 3 inches. **Overall Length:** 7¾". **Height:** 4¾". **Weight:** 19 oz. **Grips:** American walnut hand-checkered bulldog grips. **Sights:** Patridge-type, 9/64-inch wide front; square-notched rear. **Finish:** High-luster Service Blue or Stainless Steel.

CHARTER ARMS REVOLVERS

**22 LR SEMI-AUTO PISTOL
EXPLORER II**

Black finish with regular grips
6", 8", 10" barrels $99.00

SPECIFICATIONS:
Caliber: .22 Long Rifle. **Type of Action:** 8-shot magazine. **Barrel Length:** 6, 8, or 10 inches. **Overall Length:** 13½" (6" bbl.), 15½" (8" bbl.), 17½" (10" bbl.). **Height:** 6½ inches. **Weight:** 28 ounces. **Grips:** Shur-hold, simulated walnut. **Sights:** Snag-free blade front; adjustable square-notched rear; elevation reference lines; definite click indicator. **Finish:** Black, heat cured, semi-gloss textured enamel.

**357 MAGNUM REVOLVER
BULLDOG "TRACKER"**

Blue finish with Square Butt grips
4", 6" barrels $205.00

SPECIFICATIONS:
Caliber: .357 Magnum. **Type of Action:** 5 shot. **Barrel Length:** 4 or 6 inches. **Overall Length:** 9" (4" bbl.), 11" (6" bbl.). **Height:** 5⅛ inches. **Weight:** 27.5 ounces. **Grips:** Hand-checkered walnut, square butt design. **Sights:** Ramp front sight; adjustable square-notched rear; elevation reference lines; definite click indicator. **Finish:** Service Blue.

COLT REVOLVERS

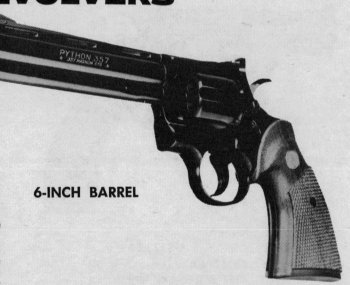

6-INCH BARREL

PYTHON 357 MAGNUM
PYTHON 357 MAGNUM & 38 SPECIAL

**357 Magnum Barrels: 2½", 4", 6"
38 Special Barrel: 8"**

The Colt Python revolver, suitable for hunting, target shooting and police use, is chambered for the powerful 357 Magnum cartridge as well as the 38 Special. Python features include ventilated rib, fast cocking, wide-spur hammer, trigger and grips, adjustable rear and ramp-type front sights, ⅛" wide.

The sighting radius of the revolver with a 6" barrel is 7⅝"; overall length, 11¼"; weight, 43½ ounces. Both the 357 Magnum and the 38 Special come fitted with handsome fully checkered walnut stocks and a finish of either Colt royal blue or polished nickel.

Caliber	Barrel	Finish	Price
357 Mag.	2½"	blue	$475.95
357 Mag.	4"	blue	486.50
357 Mag.	4"	nickel	506.95
357 Mag.	6"	blue	493.95
357 Mag.	6"	nickel	508.95
357 Mag.	8"	blue	504.50
357 Mag.	8"	nickel	519.50
38 Spec.	8"	blue	504.50
38 Spec.	8"	nickel	519.50

COLT REVOLVERS

COLT DIAMONDBACK

22 L.R., 6″ bbl., blue	$361.95
22 L.R., 4″ bbl., blue	353.95
38 Spec., 4″ bbl., blue	353.95
38 Spec., 6″ bbl., blue	361.95

The Colt Diamondback all-steel revolver was designed along the lines of the Python and includes the features of the bigger Python on a medium-size frame. These features include the ventilated rib, which dissipates barrel heat, reduces mirage effect and provides the preferred flat sighting plane . . . the wide spur target hammer which has a new cross-cut design which assures non-slip cocking . . . a grooved trigger and shrouded ejector rod, which protects the ejector rod and minimizes "barrel bounce."

The Diamondback is equipped with a fully adjustable rear sight for windage and elevation. The front sight is an integral ramp type.

SPECIFICATIONS:
Calibers: 22 L.R. and 38 Special.
Barrel lengths: 2½″ and 4″.
Sights: Adjustable rear sight, ramp-type front.
Trigger: Smooth.
Hammer: Wide-spur, checkered.
Stocks: Checkered walnut target stock.
Weights: 2½″ bbl. 38 Spec. (24 ozs.);
 4″ bbl. 38 Spec. (27 oz.); 4″ bbl. 22 L.R. (31¾ oz.).
Finish: Colt Blue. Polished nickel. (38 only).

COLT DETECTIVE SPECIAL IN 38 SPECIAL WITH 2″ BARREL (All Steel)

Blue Finish	$299.95
Nickel Finish	329.95

SPECIFICATIONS:
Caliber: 38 Special. **Barrel Length:** 2″ barrel.
Overall Length: 6⅞″. **Weight:** 21½ ounces. **Sights:** Fixed-type ramp-style, glare proofed. **Trigger:** Smooth. **Stocks:** Full checkered walnut, round butt. **Finish:** Colt Blue. Polished Nickel.

COLT LAWMAN MK III
357 MAGNUM REVOLVER

SPECIFICATIONS:
Caliber: 357 Magnum
Barrel length(s): 2″ & 4″
Weight: 2″ barrel 32 oz.; 4″ barrel 35 oz.
Overall length: 2″ barrel 7¼″; 4″ barrel 9⅜″
Sights: Fixed blade front; fixed square notch rear
Hammer: Target
Stock: 2″ barrel round-butt checkered walnut only; 4″ barrel square butt checkered walnut
Finish: Colt blue or polished nickel

Blue finish	$274.95
Polished Nickel	292.50

COLT SINGLE-ACTION REVOLVERS

SINGLE ACTION ARMY

The Colt Single Action Army, also known as the original "Peacemaker," offers superb balance, rugged design and is equipped with fixed rear square notch and fixed front blades. In addition, all three models of this classic Colt feature authentic grips and three hammer positions: one for carrying, one for loading and one for firing.

S.A. Army .357 Mag. w/5½" bbl., nickel **$555.95**
S.A. Army 44 Spec., 45 Colt w/4¾" or 5½" bbl.,
  blue **479.95**
S.A. Army 45 Colt w/7½" bbl., blue **491.95**

Calibers: 357 Magnum, 44-Special, 44/40 and 45 Colt.
Barrel length(s): 4¾", 5½", 7½", 12".
Weight: 45 caliber w/5½" barrel, 37 oz.; .357 caliber w/ 5½" barrel, 41½ oz.
Overall length: 4¾" barrel, 10⅛"; 5½" barrel, 10⅞"; 7½" barrel, 12⅞".

Sights: Fixed front blade; fixed rear square notch.
Stock: Black composite rubber or walnut.
Finish: Colt blue or polished nickel.

NEW FRONTIER SINGLE ACTION ARMY

The Colt New Frontier Single Action Army Revolver iş made in three calibers: 44-Special, 44/40 and 45 Colt. It features an adjustable rear sight with flat-top frame and ramp-front sight; also smooth trigger, knurled hammer spur and walnut stocks. Available in blue finish.

New Frontier S.A. Army, 45 Colt w/4¾" bbl. . . . **$555.95**
All calibers w/7½" bbl. **571.50**

Calibers: 357 Magnum, 44-Special 44/40 and 45 Colt .
Length of Barrel: 7½"; 4¾" w/45 Colt.
Length Overall: 12⅞" with 7½" bbl.
Weight: 39½ oz.
Sights: Ramp front; adjustable rear.
Sight Radius: With 7½" barrel—8⅝".

Finish: Case-hardened frame; blued barrel, cylinder, trigger guard & backstrap.
Stock: Walnut.

COLT SINGLE ACTION REVOLVERS

Deluxe Colt Single Action revolvers are also available in highly decorated form. Degree of decoration is dependent only on the individual customer's taste. Colt Single Action Army illustrated at left provides coverage for approximately two thirds of the barrel, portions of the cylinder and partial coverage of the frame and sideplate.

More highly decorated models provide larger coverage of engraving, including the side of the top strap, the backstrap down to the stock, the butt, trigger guard and the crane.

COLT REVOLVERS & PISTOLS

TROOPER MK III
357 Mag., 22 Win. Mag. RF, 22 LR, Barrels: 4", 6"

Tremendous penetrating power in the Magnum caliber makes this handgun suitable for hunters of big game or for police officers. Its quick draw type, ramp-style front sight and adjustable rear sight makes this a target-sighted general purpose revolver. Features include: wide target trigger; wide serrated hammer; full checkered walnut stocks. Trooper MKIII, 357 Magnum, 22 Win. Mag. Rimfire, 22 Long Rifle. 4" or 6" barrel.

4" barrel, blue finish	$323.95
4" barrel, nickel finish	343.50
6" barrel, blue finish	324.95
6" barrel, nickel finish	350.00
6" barrel, blue finish, 22 Win. Mag. RF or 22 LR only	324.95

Trooper Specifications: Caliber: 357 Magnum, 22 Win. Mag. RF, 22 LR. **Barrel Length:** 4", 6". With target stocks: 1/8" longer. **Weight (Oz.):** 39 oz. with 4" bbl. 42 oz. with 6" bbl. **Sights:** Fixed ramp-type front sight with 1/8" blade. Rear sight adjustable for windage and elevation. **Trigger:** Wide target trigger. **Hammer:** Wide checkered spur on target hammer. Target—case hardened finish. **Stocks:** Target stocks, checkered walnut. **Finish:** Colt blue and polished nickel finishes. **Cylinder Capacity:** 6 shot counterbored. **Overall Length:** 9 1/2" with 4" barrel.

GOLD CUP NATIONAL MATCH MK IV SERIES '70
45 ACP $470.95

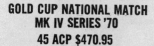

SPECIFICATIONS:
Caliber: 45 ACP
Capacity: 7 rounds
Barrel length(s): 5"
Weight: 38 1/2 oz.
Overall length: 8 3/8"
Sights: Undercut front; Colt-Elliason adjustable rear
Hammer: Serrated target hammer
Stock: Checkered walnut
Finish: Colt blue

GOVERNMENT MODEL MKIV/SERIES '70

These full-size automatic pistols, available exclusively with 5-inch barrels, may be had in 45 ACP, 9mm Luger, 38 Super and 22 LR. The Government Model's special features include fixed military sights, grip and thumb safeties, grooved trigger, sand-blasted walnut stocks and Accurizor barrel and bushing.

Caliber	Weight	Overall Length	Magazine Rounds	Finish	Price
45 ACP	38 oz.	8 3/8"	7	Blue	$352.95
				Nickel	376.50
38 Super	39 oz.	8 3/8"	9	Blue	375.50
9mm Luger	39 oz.	8 3/8"	9	Blue	358.95
22 LR/"Ace"	42 oz.	8 3/8"	10	Blue	382.50

Note: A 22 LR Conversion Unit containing 8 separate components converts 45 ACP and 38 Super Government Models to 22 LR. .... $206.50.

MK IV/Series '70 GOVERNMENT MODEL 5" barrel only

COLT AUTOMATIC PISTOLS

LIGHTWEIGHT COMMANDER

This lightweight, shorter version of the Government Model offers increased ease of carrying with the firepower of the 45 ACP. The Lightweight Commander features alloy frame, fixed-style sights, grooved trigger, lanyard-style hammer and walnut stocks.

Weight	Overall Length	Magazine Rounds	Finish	Price
27 oz.	7⅞″	7	Blue	$348.95

LIGHTWEIGHT COMMANDER
4¼″ barrel only

COMBAT COMMANDER

The semi-automatic Combat Commander, available in 45 ACP, 38 Super or 9mm Luger, boasts an all-steel frame that supplies the pistol with an extra measure of heft and stability. This outstanding Colt also offers fixed square-notch rear and fixed blade front, lanyard-style hammer and thumb and grip safety.

Caliber	Weight	Overall Length	Magazine Rounds	Finish	Price
45 ACP	36 oz.	7⅞″	7	Blue	$352.95
				Nickel	369.95
38 Super	36½ oz.	7⅞″	9	Blue	352.95
9mm Luger	36½ oz.	7⅞″	9	Blue	358.95

COMBAT COMMANDER
4¼″ barrel only

EMF DAKOTA REVOLVERS

**MODEL SA511E
1873 ARMY REVOLVER**

$485.00

Custom engraved single-action revolver. Custom blue finish, one-piece walnut grips. Available with 4⅝″, 5½″ and 7½″ barrels, in 357 Mag., 44/40, and 45 L.C.

MODEL SA511

$229.00

Genuine Dakota fast-draw single-action revolver with 4⅝″ barrel. Exact shooting copy of the original Colt Single Action Revolver. Colt-type hammer with firing pin, beautiful blue finish, case-hardened frame, one-piece walnut grips and solid brass back strap and trigger guard. Available in 22 L.R., 357 Mag., 30 MI, 44/40, 45 L.C. Optional barrels available in 4⅝″, 5½″, 7½″ and 12″ barrels.

EMF DAKOTA REVOLVERS

MODEL SA511T
$249.00

Modern version of the Old Single Action Revolver. It is available with a ramp front blade target sight and adjustable rear sight. Polished blue finish with case-hardened frame, brass back and trigger guard, one-piece walnut grips. Available in 357 Mag., 44/40, and 45 L.C. with 5½" or 7½" barrels.

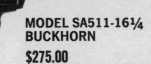

MODEL SA511-16¼ BUCKHORN
$275.00

Dakota Buckhorn shown with shoulder stock. Equipped with 16¼" barrel for precision shooting. Can be obtained without the shoulder stock, or with, which transforms it to a revolving carbine. Available in either 357 Mag. or 45 L.C. a revolving carbine. Available in 357 Mag., 44/40 and 45 L.C.

FREEDOM ARMS

FA-S 22 LR $124.75

Caliber	22 Short, Long and Long Rifle—High Speed or Standard Velocity
Action	Single
Cylinder	5 Shot—Fluted Design
Construction	All Stainless Steel
Finish	Semi-Matte
Barrel length	1¾ inches
Overall length	4¾ inches
Weight	4¼ oz.
Sights	Blade Front, Notched Rear
Safety	Notch on Hammer

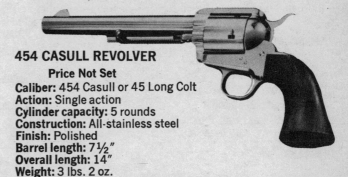

454 CASULL REVOLVER
Price Not Set
Caliber: 454 Casull or 45 Long Colt
Action: Single action
Cylinder capacity: 5 rounds
Construction: All-stainless steel
Finish: Polished
Barrel length: 7½"
Overall length: 14"
Weight: 3 lbs. 2 oz.
Sights: Blade front, notched rear
Grips: Genuine hardwood
Safety: Hammer down

FA-L 22 LR
$129.50

Caliber	22 Short, Long or Long Rifle—High Speed or Standard Velocity
Action	Single
Cylinder	5 Shot—Fluted Design
Construction	All Stainless Steel
Finish	Semi-Matte
Barrel length	1 inch

These mini-revolvers feature a serrated hammer spur, new patented cylinder locking system, a "birds head" grip frame with black ebonite grips, blade front sight, sheathed trigger, luxurious semi-matte finish, and more. Included is also a fully lined presentation case.

Overall length	4 inches
Weight	4 oz.
Sights	Blade Front, Notched Rear
Safety	Notch on Hammer

RENATO GAMBA

Gamba RGP81
Double Action Auto Pistol
$435.00

SPECIFICATIONS

- **Calibers:** 32 ACP, 380 ACP and 9 x 18 Ultra.
- **Capacities:** 14 rounds in 32 ACP; 13 rounds in 380 ACP and 9 x 18 Ultra, plus one in chamber.
- **Grips:** Stippled walnut
- **Barrel Length:** 3.34".
- **Overall Length:** 6.29.
- **Weight:** 1.65 lbs. empty.
- **Sights:** Open, fixed.
- **Safety:** Double safety.
- **Features:** Exposed hammer; combat trigger guard; matted sight channel; magazine extension.

H&R REVOLVERS

H&R Model 732
6-Shot Revolver

The H&R Model 732 features an easy-loading swing-out cylinder and comes with either 2½ or 4-inch barrel in blue finish.

2½" $99.50
4" 99.50

SPECIFICATIONS

- **Caliber:** 32 S&W long.
- **Capacity:** 6 shots.
- **Grips:** Black Cycolac.
- **Barrel Length:** 2½" and 4".
- **Weight:** 23½ oz., and 26 oz.

- **Action:** Single and double. Swing-out cylinder.
- **Sights:** 4" barrels have windage adjustment on rear sight.
- **Finish:** H&R Crown-Lustre Blue.

H&R Model 733
6-Shot Revolver

Model 733: Offering the same features as the Model 732, this revolver is finished in a high-lustre, protective nickel. With

2½" $110.00
4" 110.00

SPECIFICATIONS

- **Caliber:** 32 S&W long.
- **Capacity:** 6 shots.
- **Grips:** Black Cycolac.
- **Barrel Length:** 2½", 4".
- **Weight:** 23½ oz.; 26 oz.

- **Action:** Single and double. Swing-out cylinder.
- **Sights:** Blade front sight.
- **Finish:** Nickel.

H&R REVOLVERS

H&R Model 999

9-Shot 22 Short, Long & Long Rifle
Also available in 6-Shot 32 S&W Long

H&R's Model 999 is a break-open type 9-shot revolver featuring a wide hammer spur for fast and easy cocking. Made with unbreakable coil springs throughout.

With 6″ ventilated rib barrel. **$165.00**
With 4″ barrel **165.00**
Engraved Model 999 .... **395.00**

Caliber: 22 short, long, and long rifle.
Capacity: 9 shots.
Grips: Checkered walnut.
Barrel Length: 6″ ventilated.
Weight: 30 oz.

Action: Single and double. Top break-open.
Sights: Adjustable front and rear.
Finish: H&R Crown-Lustre Blue.

H&R Model 949

9-Shot 22 Short, Long & Long Rifle—Barrel: 5½″

H&R's Model 949 is a modern 9-shot 22 caliber revolver with frontier features. With automatic rebound hammer, wide cocking spur and unbreakable coil spring construction. **$99.50**

FEATURES AND SPECIFICATIONS

Caliber: 22 short, long, and long rifle.
Capacity: 9 shots.
Grips: One-piece walnut grip.
Barrel Length: 5½″.
Weight: 31 oz.

Action: Single and double. Side loading and ejection.
Sights: Adjustable rear sight; Western type front blade sight.
Finish: H&R Crown-Lustre Blue; (or nickel—Model 950 $94.50.

Available with color-cased frame, 7½″ barrel as Model 976 .... **$139.50**

H&R Model 929

9-Shot Revolver

9-Shot 22 Short, Long & Long Rifle—Barrel: 2½″, 4″, & 6″

H&R's Model 929 revolver features a 9-shot swing-out cylinder. Made in 22 caliber, it is available with 2½″, 4″ and 6″ barrel lengths. The 4″ and 6″ barrels have windage adjustment on rear sight. Blue finish. 2½″ **$99.50** 4″ and 6″ **$99.50**. **Model 930** has identical features, but is finished in durable, protective nickel, and comes with 2½″ or 4″ barrels. Matte finish on top frame. 2½″ **$110.00**; 4″ **$110.00**.

FEATURES AND SPECIFICATIONS

Caliber: .22 short, long, and long rifle;
Capacity: 9 shots.
Grips: Black Cycolac.
Barrel Length: 2½″, 4″, and 6″.
Weight: 22 oz., 26 oz., and 28 oz.

Action: Single and double. Swing-out cylinder.
Sights: 4″ and 6″ barrels have windage adjustment on rear sight.
Finish: H&R Crown-Lustre Blue.

H&R REVOLVERS

H&R Model 649

SPECIFICATIONS:
Caliber: 22 Long rifle; 22 Win. Magnum
Capacity: 6 shot
Barrel length(s): 5½", 7½"
Weight: 32 oz.
Sights: Western-type front blade sight; adjustable rear
Action: Single action and double action side loading and ejecting
Grips: One piece wrap around genuine walnut
Finish: H&R Crown Lustre Blue barrel, blue satin-finish frame
Price: $120.00
Model 650: Same as Model 649 except with nickel finish
$130.00

H&R Model STR 022

FEATURES AND SPECIFICATIONS
Caliber: .22 blank. **Capacity:** 9 shots. **Grips:** Black Cycolac. **Barrel Length:** 2½". **Weight:** 19 oz. **Action:** Single and double. Pull pin cylinder. **Finish:** Blue satin finished frame.
Available with nickel finish as Model STR 122 .... **$74.50**

NOTE: *If a louder report is required, the 6-shot Model STR 032 is available at the same price, and with features identical to those of the Model STR 022. It is chambered for 32 caliber S&W center-fire, blank cartridges* **$69.50**
Available with nickel finish as Model STR 132. .... **$74.50**

H&R Model 622

The **H&R Model 622** is a 6-shot single and double action 22 caliber revolver which handles 22 long rifle and features a safety rim cylinder. Available in 2½" and 4" barrel lengths. Blue finish. **$79.50**

FEATURES AND SPECIFICATIONS
Caliber: 22 long rifle.
Capacity: 6 shots.
Grips: Black Cycolac. Round Butt.
Barrel Length: 2½" and 4".
Weight: 20 oz. and 26 oz.
Action: Single and double. Pull pin cylinder.
Sights: Blade front sight.
Finish: Satin finished frame. H&R Crown-Lustre Blue barrel.

Also in 32 S&W Long as Model 632 2½" & 4". Blue Finish **$79.50**

HECKLER & KOCH PISTOLS

**P9S DOUBLE ACTION 45 ACP
& 9MM LUGER**

**VP70Z DOUBLE-ACTION
AUTOMATIC PISTOL**

HK4 AUTOMATIC PISTOL

The HK4 provides the choice of 380, 32, 25 ACP or 22 LR. A dust-proof self-sealed auto with multiple safety features and double-action trigger.

SPECIFICATIONS:
Calibers: 380 - 22 LR - 32 - 25
Length: 6³⁄₁₆″ (157 mm)
Height: 4²¹⁄₆₄″ (110 mm)
Width at Butt: 1¹⁷⁄₆₄″ (32 mm)
Barrel Length: 3¹¹⁄₃₂″ (85 mm)
Sight Radius: 4⁴⁹⁄₆₄″ (121 mm)
Weight of Pistol: 16,9 oz (480 g)
Weight of Magazine: 1,4 oz (40 g)
Magazine Capacity: 7 8 8 8

Model HK4 (380 cal.) **$430.00**
Model HK4 380 caliber with 22 caliber conversion kit **480.00**
Model HK4 380 caliber with set of 3 conversion kits in
22LR, 25, and 32 .... **590.00**

MODEL P9S Cal. 45 ACP PISTOL

The P9S double action 45 ACP embodies the same features of the P9S 9mm—Polygonal rifling and the delayed roller-locked bolt system in the slide.

SPECIFICATIONS:
Caliber: 45 ACP
Magazine: 7 rounds (plus 1 in chamber)
Barrel Length: 4″
Length of Pistol: 7.6 in.
Height of Pistol: 5.4 in.
Sight radius: 5.8 in.
Weight without Magazine: approx. 30 oz.
Weight of Magazines Empty: 2.6 oz.

Model P9S Caliber 45 (w/Combat Sight) **$645.00**
Also available in 45 Target Model **728.00**

HECKLER & KOCH PISTOLS
MODEL P9S AUTOMATIC PISTOL

The P9S is an automatic pistol with a stationary barrel and sliding delayed roller-locked system which reduces recoil. The polygonal twist barrel affords 5% to 6% increase in muzzle velocity.

SPECIFICATIONS:
Caliber: 9 mm parabellum (9 mm Luger)
Weight: 32 oz.
Barrel Length: 4″
Overall Length: 7⅝″
Magazine Capacity: 9 rounds
Sights: Fixed, square-blade quick-draw front; square-notch rear
Sights Radius: 5¾″
Rifling: Polygonal, right twist

Model P9S (w/combat sights) **$645.00**
Also available in Target pistol as Model P9S Target **728.00**
30 Luger cal. Conversion Kit
(w/barrel and 2 magazines), must be ordered with P9S 9mm **95.00**

VP70Z DOUBLE-ACTION
AUTOMATIC PISTOL

The VP70 Automatic Pistol is recoil operated, with an inertia bolt and stationary barrel. The receiver is of solid plastic material. The parallel-type revolver trigger (double-action trigger only) and the direct **firing pin ignition** ensure constant **readiness to fire** and permit the weapon to be safely carried while **loaded and** uncocked until the trigger is pulled. The cartridges are fed from an 18-round magazine.

The sights on the VP70 are based on the light-and-shadow principle. Targets can be aimed at even under unfavorable lighting and vision conditions.

SPECIFICATIONS:
Magazine: 18 rounds
Caliber: 9 mm x 19 (Parabellum)
Sight, Front: Ramp type, channelled
Length of Pistol: 8.03 in.
Height of Pistol: 5.67 in.
Length of Barrel: 4.57 in.
Sight Radius: 6.89 in.
Pistol, without Magazine: 29 oz.
Weight of Magazine Empty: 3.5 oz.

Model VP70Z (w/Combat Sights & Two 18-Round Magazines)..**$489.00**

HIGH STANDARD AUTO PISTOLS

VICTOR MILITARY MODEL
TARGET PISTOL

High Standard's Victor is available with a restyled rib, and an interchangeable front sight. The rib, which reduces the overall weight of the 5½″ Victor by three ounces is vented. The 5½″ Victor, less barrel weight, is now ISU qualified. All models feature push button barrel takedown. The wide target trigger can be adjusted for travel and weight of pull. The rear sight is stationary (mounted on rib), and is micro adjustable for elevation and windage—adjustment screws are positive click spring loaded. The Victor comes fitted with checkered American walnut military grips with thumb rest. Front and backstrap are stippled for a positive grip. Equipped with positive double-action safety, and automatic slide lock, holding the action open after the last round has been fired. Additional features include 24 carat gold-plated trigger, safety and magazine release, with identifying roll marks gold-filled. Available with 5½″ barrel, in blue finish **$348.00.**

FEATURES AND SPECIFICATIONS: Caliber: 22 L.R. **Capacity:** 10 rounds. **Barrel:** 4½ inch and 5½ inch, specially molded and contoured barrels. **Sights:** Adjustable micrometer rear sight mounted on rib. **Trigger:** Wide target trigger—2-2¼ lb. pull. **Grips:** Checkered walnut military. **Weight:** 47 oz. for 5½-inch model. **Overall Length:** 9¾″ for 5½-inch model. **Finish:** Blue.

TROPHY GRADE—MILITARY MODEL AUTOMATICS

MILITARY TROPHY
10 Shot 22 L.R.
5½″ Bull Barrel
$304.00

MILITARY TROPHY
10 Shot 22 L.R.
7¼″ Fluted Barrel
$323.50

The High-Standard "Trophy" grade automatics come in military models only with a choice of a 5½″ bull barrel, or a 7¼″ fluted barrel. They differ only in length and style of barrel. The trigger pull is 2 to 2¼ lbs. and has a trigger travel adjustment, enabling the shooter to limit the amount of backward travel of trigger to a minute distance beyond the firing point. Also, there is a trigger-pull adjustment (a positive, click-stop adjusting screw) which adjusts the degree of tension on Trophy and Citation model triggers. A uniform trigger pull is achieved because the sear engages the hammer on the outside periphery, making the engaging surfaces further away from the hammer pivot point. The Trophy models are ground, polished, buffed and blued and come with a gold, target-size trigger and gold identification. The back and front strap are stippled and the mechanical parts are machined and hand-honed. The rear sight is new in that the bracket is rigidly fixed to the frame—the slide moves through the yoke, making it completely vibration and shock free. The fixed ramp type front sight, dovetail slots in the barrel. The military grip is a faithful duplicate of the Military 45 and comes with thumbrest in checkered American walnut. Automatic slide lock holds action open after last shot is fired. When the safety is in position, the sear is blocked and the sear bar is disconnected, thereby completely disconnecting the firing mechanism. It cannot discharge.

SPECIFICATIONS FOR MILITARY TROPHY MODELS (5½″ & 7¼″ BARRELS)

CALIBER: 22 Long Rifle.
CAPACITY: 10 shot.
BARREL: 5½″ bull barrel; 7¼″ fluted barrel.
SIGHTS: Stationary bracket type, deep notched rear; fixed ramp type dovetail front sight.
SIGHT RADIUS: With 5½″ barrel—8¾″; with 7¼″ barrel—10″.

TRIGGER: Wide target trigger, with trigger travel adjustment and trigger-pull adjustment (2-2¼ lbs.).
SAFETY: Double acting safety. Automatic side lock.
LENGTH OVERALL: With 5½″ bbl.—9¾″; with 7¼″ bbl.—11½″.
WEIGHT: 44.5 ounces for both models.
FINISH: Ground, polished, buffed and blued.

HIGH STANDARD AUTO PISTOLS

CITATION MILITARY MODEL AUTOMATICS

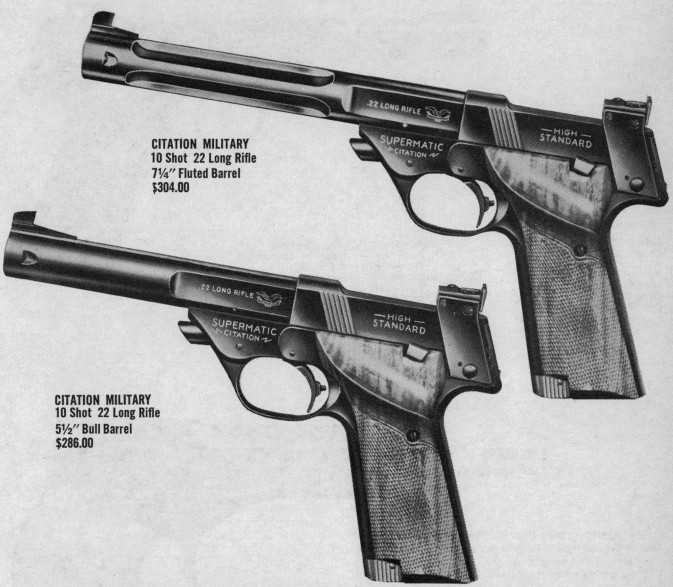

CITATION MILITARY
10 Shot 22 Long Rifle
7¼" Fluted Barrel
$304.00

CITATION MILITARY
10 Shot 22 Long Rifle
5½" Bull Barrel
$286.00

The Supermatic "Citation" grade military models are available in two barrel lengths—5½" bull barrel, and 7¼" fluted barrel. The trigger pull and trigger travel adjustment are standard on all Citation models. The military models have a stationary type near sight with a dovetail, fixed ramp type front sight. Back and front straps are stippled. The grips are checkered American walnut and come with thumb rest, in right or left hand design. All Citation models come with positive double-action safety and side lock features. Barrel interchangeability is also standard with all Citation models. Mechanical parts are machined and hand-honed.

SPECIFICATIONS

CALIBER: 22 Long Rifle.
CAPACITY: 10 shot.
BARREL: 5½" bull barrel; 7¼" fluted barrel.
SIGHTS: Stationary bracket type, deep notched rear; fixed ramp type dovetail front sight.
SIGHT RADIUS: With 5½" barrel—8¾"; with 7¼" barrel—10".
TRIGGER: Wide target trigger, with trigger travel adjustment and trigger-pull adjustment (2-2¼ lbs.).
SAFETY: Positive, double action. Side lock.
GRIPS: Military type checkered American walnut with thumb rest.
LENGTH OVERALL: With 5½" barrel—9¾"; with 7¼" barrel—11½".
WEIGHT: 44.5 ounces for both models.
FINISH: Ground, polished, blued.

HIGH STANDARD PISTOLS

SHARPSHOOTER
10-Shot 22 Long Rifle
5½″ Bull Barrel
$253.00

Model: 9210
Caliber: 22 LR
Rounds: 10
Barrel: 5½″ Bull
Weight: 42 oz.
Overall Length: 10¼″
Overall Height: 5¼″

Sights: Front—⅛″ Blade Serrated
Ramp; **Rear**—Adjustable—Micrometer
Click—Windage & Elevation
Grips: Walnut—Checkered with
Thumbrest
Finish: Blue
Features: Wide Serrated Target Trigger;
Military Grip; Pushbutton Barrel
Takedown.

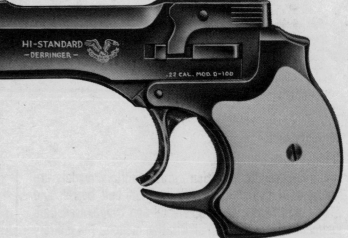

DERRINGERS
3½″ 2-Shot Dual Barrels

The Derringers from High Standard offer the traditional look of the old, with the safety design features of the new. They feature hammerless design.

Their double action is safety-engineered—the High Standard Derringer cannot ever fire accidentally—even if dropped.

They're available in either onyx black with black grips or polished nickel with black grips. These derringers have an overall width of less than 1″ and weigh 11 oz. Chambered to fire 22 Magnum.

NO. 9306 MAGNUM DERRINGER							
9194	22 Mag.	2	Blue	Black	3½″	5″	11	$130.00
9306	22 Mag.	2	Nickel	Black	3½″	5″	11	151.00

HIGH STANDARD REVOLVERS

HIGH SIERRA DELUXE
9-Shot 22 Long Rifle

The High Sierra Western-style revolver features a steel frame and comes with a 7" octagonal barrel with a custom blue finish, complemented by hand-rubbed walnut grips. Trigger guard and backstraps are gold-plated. Available with dual cylinders (22L.R./22 Magnum). High Sierra deluxe comes equipped with an adjustable rear sight. Price: High Sierra with adjustable rear sight and two cylinders (22LR/mag), **$214.50.**

DOUBLE NINE
9-Shot 22 Long Rifle

The Double Nine with steel frame and 5½" barrel comes with interchangeable cylinders for standard 22 L.R. and 22 Magnum ammunition. Features include nine-shot capacity, double action and swing-out cylinders. Available with adjustable rear sight in blue finish, priced at **$210.50.**

The Longhorn Deluxe: Same as Double Nine except with 9½" "Buntline" barrel. Available in trophy blue with dual cylinders with adjustable rear sights **$214.50.**

Western Revolvers (9-shot) Double Action

MODEL NO.	NAME	FEATURES	FINISH	CAL.	BBL. LGTH.
9324	Double Nine Deluxe	Adj. Rear Sight	Trophy Blue	2 Cyl 22 LR/mag	5½"
9328	Longhorn Deluxe	Adj. Rear Sight	Trophy Blue	2 Cyl 22 LR/mag	9½"
9375	High Sierra Deluxe	Adj. Rear Sight	Trophy Blue	2 Cyl 22 LR/mag	7" Oct

HIGH STANDARD PISTOLS

SPORT KING

Model: 9258 & 9259
Caliber: 22 L.R.
Barrel: 9258—4½"
     9259—6¾"
Weight: 4½"—39 oz.
     6¾"—42 oz.
Overall Length: 4½"—9¼"
     6¾"—11½"
Overall Height: 5"
Sights: Front—⅛" blade; Rear—⅛" square notch,
  adjustable for windage.
Grips: Checkered walnut.
Finish: Blue
Price: $225.00

MODEL 10-X
Custom-Made Target Pistol

Model: 9372
Caliber: 22 L.R.
Barrel: 5½" bull barrel.
Sights: Adjustable rear sight mounted on the frame
  and free of the slide.
Grips: Walnut
Finish: Non-reflective blue
Features: Military grip; target trigger with
  overtravel adjustment; trigger pull adjust-
  ment; stippled frontstrap and backstrap;
  automatic slide lock and two extra maga-
  zines. The pistol has a five-year warranty.
Price: $599.50

IVER JOHNSON PISTOLS

X300 PONY

X300 PONY

All-steel, the X300 Pony is chambered for 380 ACP. The magazine holds six rounds. For maximum security, the pistol features an inertia firing pin, and the large thumb safety cams the hammer out of contact with the sear. The windage-adjustable rear sight is rounded on its outer dimensions so it won't snag on clothing. Grips are of solid walnut, and the backstop is extra long to protect a hand from being bitten by the hammer.
Length: 6"; **Height:** 4".

Model	Grips	Finish	Cal.	Barrel	Sights	Price
		X300 PONY .380 AUTO PISTOL				
A3380-B	Walnut	Blue	.380	3"	Adjustable	$240.70
A3380-N	Walnut	Nickel	.380	3"	Adjustable	254.50
A3380-M	Walnut	Military	.380	3"	Adjustable	240.70
Pocket Pistol	Walnut (Avail.)	Blue	.250	3"	Non-Adjustable	183.24

INTERARMS
VIRGINIAN REVOLVERS

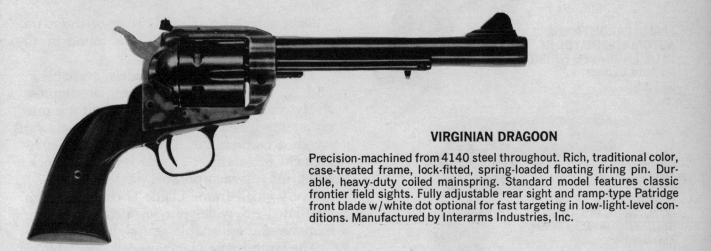

VIRGINIAN DRAGOON

Precision-machined from 4140 steel throughout. Rich, traditional color, case-treated frame, lock-fitted, spring-loaded floating firing pin. Durable, heavy-duty coiled mainspring. Standard model features classic frontier field sights. Fully adjustable rear sight and ramp-type Patridge front blade w/white dot optional for fast targeting in low-light-level conditions. Manufactured by Interarms Industries, Inc.

VIRGINIAN DRAGOON SINGLE ACTION REVOLVERS		
VIRGINIAN BUNTLINE	.44 Magnum, 12″ VAV25190	$289.00
	.357 Magnum, 12″ VAV25790	249.00
	.45 Colt, 12″ VAV25090	269.00
	.41 Magnum, 12″ VAV21490	269.00
VIRGINIAN DRAGOON	.45 Colt, 5″ VAV15010	$219.00
	.357 Magnum, 5″ VAV15710	199.00
	.44 Magnum, 6″ VAV15130	239.00
	.45 Colt, 6″ VAV15030	219.00
	.357 Magnum, 6″ VAV15730	199.00
	.44 Magnum, 7½″ VAV15160	239.00
	.45 Colt, 7½″ VAV15060	219.00
	.357 Magnum, 7½″ VAV15760	199.00
	.41 Magnum 7½″ VAV11460	219.00
	.44 Magnum 8⅜″ VAV15170	239.00
VIRGINIAN DRAGOON STAINLESS STEEL	.44 Magnum 6″ VAV15131	$279.00
	.45 Colt, 6″ VAV15031	279.00
	.44 Magnum, 7½″ VAV15161	279.00
	.45 Colt, 7½″ VAV15061	279.00
	.44 Magnum, 8⅜″ VAV15171	279.00
	.44 Magnum, 10½″ VAV15181	299.00
VIRGINIAN DRAGOON HOLSTER (Without Belt)	6″ or 7½″ BHL00001	$36.00
VIRGINIAN DRAGOON DELUXE PRESENTATION CASE Walnut with Velvet Lining	6″ or 7½″ VAE00001	77.00

LLAMA AUTOMATIC PISTOLS

LLAMA LARGE FRAME AUTOMATIC PISTOL IN BLUE ENGRAVED FINISH
45 Auto Caliber
$433.95

LLAMA SMALL FRAME AUTOMATIC PISTOL IN BLUE ENGRAVED FINISH
380 Caliber
$358.95

Llama's time-proven design, enhanced by individual hand-fitting and hand-honing of all moving parts, has resulted in handguns that provide smooth operation, pin-point accuracy, and rugged reliability under the toughest conditions.

Deluxe features, all indicative of the extra care lavished on each gun, are found in all Llama handguns.

The small-frame Llama models, available in 22 L.R., 32 Auto. and 380 Auto., are impressively compact handguns. All frames are precision machined of high strength steel, yet weigh a featherlight 23 ounces. A full complement of safeties . . . side lever, half-cock, and grip . . . is incorporated.

Every small-frame Llama is complete with ventilated rib, wide-spur serrated target-type hammer and adjustable rear sight.

The large-frame Llama models, available in potent 45 ACP, 38 Super and 9mm Parabellum, are completely crafted of high strength

LLAMA LARGE FRAME AUTOMATIC WITH DEEP BLUE FINISH
9mm, 38 Super & 45 Auto
$366.95

LLAMA SMALL FRAME AUTOMATIC WITH DEEP BLUE FINISH
22, 32 & 380 Caliber
$283.95

LLAMA AUTOMATIC PISTOLS

steel, machined and polished to perfection. Complete with ventilated rib for maximum heat dissipation, wide-spur checkered target-type hammer, adjustable rear sight and genuine walnut grips, make these truly magnificent firearms.

In addition to High Polished Deep Blue, these superb handguns are available in deluxe fancy finishes:

- High Polished Deep Blue Engraved (380 Auto., 45 ACP).
- Handsome Satin Chrome (22 L.R., 380 Auto., 45 ACP).
- Satin Chrome Engraved (380 Auto., 45 ACP).
- Gold Damascened. (380 Auto.). Richly engraved Spanish Gold for those who will be satisfied with nothing but the best.

Extra Magazines $24.95

LLAMA LARGE FRAME AUTOMATIC IN SATIN CHROME ENGRAVED FINISH
45 Auto Caliber
$466.95

LLAMA SMALL FRAME AUTOMATIC WITH SATIN CHROME ENGRAVED FINISH
380 Caliber
$366.95

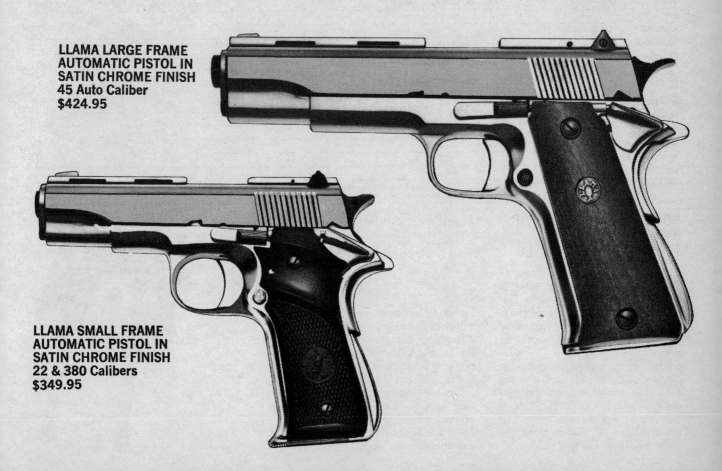

LLAMA LARGE FRAME AUTOMATIC PISTOL IN SATIN CHROME FINISH
45 Auto Caliber
$424.95

LLAMA SMALL FRAME AUTOMATIC PISTOL IN SATIN CHROME FINISH
22 & 380 Calibers
$349.95

LLAMA AUTOMATIC PISTOLS

LLAMA 45 DOUBLE ACTION AUTOMATIC
Also available in 9mm

LLAMA Automatic Pistol Specifications

TYPE:	Small Frame Auto Pistols			Large Frame Auto Pistols		
CALIBERS:	.22 L.R.	.32 Auto.	.380 Auto.	.38 Super	9mm	.45 Auto.
FRAME:	Precision machined from high strength steel. Serrated front strap, checkered (curved) backstrap.			Precision machined from high strength steel. Plain front strap, checkered (curved) backstrap.		
TRIGGER:	Serrated.			Serrated.		
HAMMER:	External. Wide spur, serrated.			External. Wide spur, serrated.		
OPERATION:	Straight blow-back.			Locked breech.		
LOADED CHAMBER INDICATOR:	No	Yes	Yes	Yes	Yes	Yes
SAFETIES:	Side lever thumb safety, half-cock safety			Side lever thumb safety, half-cock safety.		
GRIPS:	Modified thumb-rest black plastic grips.			Genuine walnut on blue models. Genuine teakwood on satin chrome, satin chrome engraved and blue engraved models.		
SIGHTS:	Square notch rear, and Patridge-type front, screw adjustable rear sight for windage.			Square notch rear, and Patridge-type front, screw adjustable rear sight for windage.		
SIGHT RADIUS:	4¼"			6¼"		
MAGAZINE CAPACITY:	8-shot	7-shot	7-shot	9-shot	9-shot	7-shot
WEIGHT:	23 ounces			2 lbs., 8 ozs.		
BARREL LENGTH:	3¹¹/₁₆"			5"		
OVER-ALL LENGTH:	6½"			8½"		
HEIGHT:	4⅜"			5¼"		
FINISH:	Std. models; High-polished, deep blue. Deluxe models; satin chrome (.22, .380, .45); satin chrome engraved (.380, .45); blue engraved (.380, .45); Gold Damascened with simulated pearl grips (.380, .45).					

GOLD DAMASCENED FINISH
380 Caliber
$1670.00

In the centuries-old tradition of Toledo steel, this superb example of a nearly lost art . . . Gold Damascened. Rich Spanish gold, magnificently engraved by old world craftsmen to create true works of art.

Crafted in the mountainous Basque Region of Spain, Llama handguns have enjoyed a reputation of rugged dependability since 1910. This is the same ageless tradition that made blades of Toledo steel the most prized in Europe.

Today, Gabilondo y Cia, S.A., maker of Llama handguns, occupies a huge, modern factory . . . one of the largest in Europe devoted entirely to handguns. Built in 1960, the factory, equipped with the best and most modern machinery available from the United States, Switzerland and West Germany, produces handguns that are unequaled anywhere in the world.

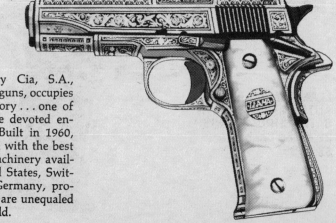

LLAMA REVOLVERS

**LLAMA SUPER COMANCHE IV
IN HIGH POLISHED DEEP BLUE FINISH
44 Magnum 6″ barrel
Also available in 8½″ barrel
$481.95**

SUPER COMANCHE, LLAMA'S ALL-NEW 44 MAGNUM DOUBLE ACTION . . . THE MOST RUGGED, ACCURATE REVOLVER BUILT.

Three years of intensive product development and generations of prototypes evolved before final specifications were set for this all-new Super Comanche. If ever a handgun was conceived, designed and built to fit the exacting requirements of big-bore handgunners, this one is it.

Take the frame for example: it's massive. The most solid, most rugged of any other double-action revolver. Its weight and balance are such that the heavy recoil generated by the powerful 44 Magnum cartridge is easily and comfortably controlled, even when rapid firing in the double-action mode. In the single-action mode, the broad, serrated hammer-spur makes cocking easy and fast.

Instead of a single cylinder latch, the new Llama has two. In addition to the conventional center pin at the rear of the ratchet, there's a second latch up front which locks the crane to the frame at the underside of the barrel ring. Using this two-lock system, the cylinder and crane are locked in a more positive manner than can be achieved using the common detent/ball arrangement found on other revolvers.

Only coil springs are used throughout. Not only does this provide added strength in a critical area, but the added rigidity raises the gun's accuracy potential as well. Also aiding accuracy is the heavyweight barrel measuring .815″ in diameter. A matte-finish rib reduces glare and helps get on target faster.

But building the strongest and most accurate revolver were only two of the three basic goals Llama engineers set for themselves; they also wanted to build the safest. To that end, the hammer is mounted on an eccentric cam, the position of which is controlled by the trigger. Only when the latter is fully depressed can the firing pin contact the primer. Accidental discharge is virtually impossible.

LLAMA REVOLVERS

IN REVOLVERS TODAY, THERE'S A NEW NAME IN EXCELLENCE. IT'S THE LLAMA COMANCHE® SERIES. Designed for you and incorporating every feature worth having to make these Llamas the finest revolvers made today . . . at any price.

All the Comanche models — 22 L.R., 38 Special, and the sledgehammer 357 Magnum caliber utilize massively forged solid–steel frames for tremendous strength and enduring reliability.

Up front, Llama added a precision-bored heavyweight barrel of target quality, complete with a solid shroud to protect the ejector rod, and a raised ventilated-rib that dissipates heat from the barrel to give you a clear, sharp sight image even when the action gets hot.

The sights are fully adjustable, with a square notch, rear sight and a quick-draw ramp front.

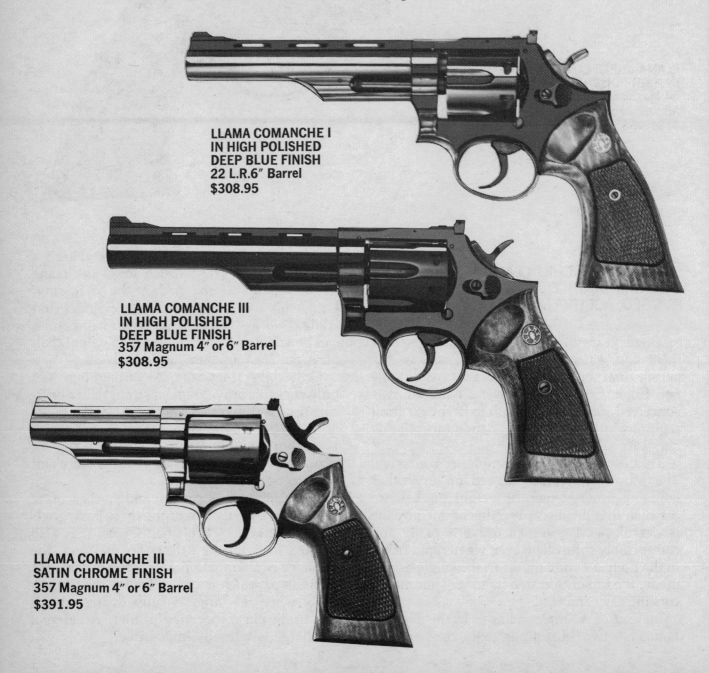

**LLAMA COMANCHE I
IN HIGH POLISHED
DEEP BLUE FINISH
22 L.R.6" Barrel
$308.95**

**LLAMA COMANCHE III
IN HIGH POLISHED
DEEP BLUE FINISH
357 Magnum 4" or 6" Barrel
$308.95**

**LLAMA COMANCHE III
SATIN CHROME FINISH
357 Magnum 4" or 6" Barrel
$391.95**

LLAMA REVOLVERS

The frame topstrap and the integral ventilated-rib are matte finished to eliminate glare along the sight plane.

The deeply-colored, case-hardened hammer and trigger are target quality. Both the wide spur on the hammer and the wide trigger itself are cleanly serrated for greater ease in cocking and firing.

On the inside, everything is finely fitted and polished, for a double action that's slick and smooth, and a single-action trigger-pull that's light, crisp and clean. Llama gave all Comanches a floating firing pin, for greater safety and dependability . . . a feature you'll find only on the finest handguns.

Every Llama revolver is hand fitted with generously over-sized target grips of deeply-checkered genuine walnut. As you would expect on a revolver of this quality, the finish is superb . . . flawlessly polished and richly blued.

LLAMA COMANCHE II IN HIGH POLISHED DEEP BLUE FINISH
38 Special 6" Barrel
$308.95

LLAMA COMANCHE II IN HIGH POLISHED DEEP BLUE FINISH
38 Special 4" Barrel
$308.95

LLAMA "Comanche"® Specifications

CALIBERS:	.357 Magnum	.38 Special (Hi-speed or Mid-range)	.22 L.R.
BARREL LENGTH:	4 and 6-inch	4 and 6-inch	6-inch
NUMBER OF SHOTS:	6 shots	6 shots	6 shots
FRAME:	Forged high tensile strength steel. Serrated front and back strap.		
ACTION:	Conventional double-action. Floating firing pin.		
TRIGGER:	Wide grooved target trigger. Case-hardened.		
HAMMER:	Wide spur target hammer with serrated gripping surface. Case-hardened.		
SIGHTS:	Square notch rear sight with windage and elevation adjustments; serrated quick-draw front sight on ramp.		
SIGHT RADIUS:	With 4-inch barrel — 5¾"; with 6-inch barrel — 7¾".		
GRIPS:	Oversized target, walnut. Checkered.		
WEIGHT:	w/4" bbl. — 2 lbs., 4 ozs. / w/6" bbl. — 2 lbs., 7 ozs.	w/4" bbl. — 2 lbs., 1 oz. / w/6" bbl. — 2 lbs., 4 ozs.	2 lbs., 8 ozs.
OVER-ALL LENGTH:	With 4-inch barrel — 9¼"; with 6-inch barrel — 11".		
FINISH:	High-polished, deep blue. Deluxe models; satin chrome (.357 w/4" & 6" bbl.); Gold Damascened with simulated pearl grips (.357 w/4" bbl.).		

LLAMA REVOLVERS

LLAMA "Super Comanche"® Revolver Specifications

CALIBER:	.44 Magnum
BARREL LENGTH:	6"
NUMBER OF SHOTS:	6 shots
FRAME:	Forged high tensile strength steel
ACTION:	Conventional double action
TRIGGER:	Smooth extra wide
HAMMER:	Wide spur, deep positive serrations
SIGHTS:	Rear-click adjustable for windage and elevation, leaf serrated to cut down on glare. Front-ramped blade.
SIGHT RADIUS:	8"
GRIPS:	Oversized target, walnut. Checkered
WEIGHT:	3 lbs., 2 ozs.
OVER-ALL LENGTH:	11¾"
FINISH:	High polished, deep blue
SAFETY FEATURE:	The hammer is mounted on an eccentric cam, the position of which is controlled by the trigger. Only when the latter is fully depressed can the firing pin contact the primer.

LUGER 22 AUTOMATIC PISTOLS

New Steel Frame

LUGER AUTOMATIC PISTOL
22 LR 4½" Barrel
$182.95

Chambered for the economical 22 LR, the newest Luger handles both standard and high velocity cartridges interchangeably. The Luger features a one-piece solidly forged and machined steel frame for total strength and accuracy, and all moving parts are engineered for steel-to-steel contact.

Luger Accessories:

Extra Luger Magazines	$21.95
Luger Magazine Charger	4.95
Standard Luger Holster	21.95
Basket Weave Luger Holster	24.95
Carrying Case	21.95

LUGER 22 AUTOMATIC PISTOL

MODELS:	Standard Luger
CALIBER:	.22 Long Rifle, standard or high-velocity.
MAGAZINE:	Ten-shot capacity clip type magazine.
BARREL LENGTHS:	4½".
SIGHTS:	Square bladed front sight with square notch, stationary rear sight.
SIGHT RADIUS:	8"
FRAME:	High tensile strength steel
GRIPS:	Genuine American black walnut, fully checkered.
APPROX. WEIGHT:	1 lb., 13½ ozs.
OVER-ALL LENGTH:	8⅞"
SAFETY:	All models; Positive side lever safety, (Green Dot-Safe) (Red Dot-Fire)
FINISH:	Non-reflecting black.

NO. 4 LUGER KIT
$224.95

NO. 4 LUGER COMBO
$234.95

No. 4 Luger Kit contains Luger, complete with leather holster, easy loading magazine charger and extra magazine.

No. 4 Luger Combo (not illustrated) contains everything but the ammo. Includes Luger, leather holster, easy loading magazine charger, extra magazine and carrying case.

MERRILL

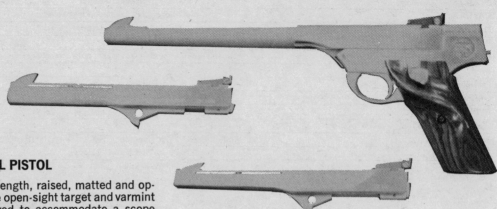

MERRILL PISTOL

This pistol features a full-length, raised, matted and optional vented rib barrel for the open-sight target and varmint shooter. The barrel is grooved to accommodate a scope without additional drilling or tapping. Cocking indicator visible from rear of gun. Features a precision spring-loaded barrel lock.

Caliber: 22 LR Sil.; 22 MRE, 22 Hornet; 256 Win. Mag.; 357 Mag., 357/44 B&D, 30 Herrett; 357 Herrett; 44 Rem. Mag.; 41 Rem. Mag.; 7mm Merrill; 30 Merrill.

Barrel: 9" or 10¾" semi-octagonal, matted to prevent glare; 14" tapered barrel available in all calibers except 22.

Sights: Front .125" blade standard; .080" blade optional. Rear adjustable for windage and elevation.

Trigger: Roller trigger adjustable for weight of pull.
Finish: Polished blue; hard chrome finish optional.
Stock: Smooth walnut or pauferro with thumb and heel rest.
Features: Barrel is grooved for scope mounting; cocking indicator visible from rear of gun; spring-loaded barrel lock and positive thumb safety.

9" complete $410.00
10¾" complete 445.00
14" complete 530.00

NAVY ARMS PISTOL

TWISTER $79.95

SPECIFICATIONS:
Caliber: 22 long rifle, 9mm rimfire.
Capacity: 2 separate barrels, 1 round each.
Barrel Length: 3⅜".
Weight: 1½ lbs.
Finish: Blue barrel with pearlite grips.
Features: Book-style presentation box.
Rimfire ammunition: 9mm, box of 50 **$8.00.**

ROSSI REVOLVERS

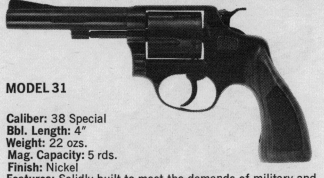

MODEL 31

Caliber: 38 Special
Bbl. Length: 4"
Weight: 22 ozs.
Mag. Capacity: 5 rds.
Finish: Nickel
Features: Solidly built to meet the demands of military and police service. Swing out 5-shot cylinder. Target trigger and wide-spur target hammer. Medium weight 4" barrel w/ramp front sight. Checkered wood grips. Crisp double-action and exceptional balance.
Model 31, blue **$139.00**
Model 31, nickel **144.00**

MODEL 51 SPORTSMAN

Caliber: 22 LR
Bbl. Length: 6"
Finish: Deep blue
Features: Checkered wood grips. Rear sight fully adjustable.
Model 51 Sportsman **$159.00**

MODELS 68, 69 & 70

Caliber: 22 short—mod. 70
32 S&W—mod. 69
38 Special—mod. 68
Bbl. Length: 3"
Weight: 22 ozs.
Mag. Capacity: 6 rds.—22 L.R. & 32 S&W; 5 rds.—38 Spec.
Features: Rugged, all-steel small frame. Smooth double-action pull and combat styling. Ramp front sight and low profile adjustable rear sight. Thumb-latch operated swingout cylinder. Checkered wood grips.
Models 68 & 69, blue **$139.00**
nickel **144.00**
Model 70, blue **144.00**
nickel **150.00**

RUGER REVOLVERS

POLICE SERVICE-SIX
357 Mag., 38 Special & 9mm

The Ruger Police Service-Six has all of the basic features built into the Ruger Security-Six revolvers. The grip of both the Police Service-Six and the Security-Six has been subtly redesigned to permit rapid, accurate double-action firing without any tendency for the revolver to shift during operation. The new Police Service-Six differs from the Security-Six in that it has fixed (non-adjustable) sights to eliminate any potential for accidental sight misalignment with resulting error in aim, and comes in 2¾" and 4" barrel lengths but not in 6" length. 357 Mag. w/2¾" & 4" barrel, blue only.
357 Mag., blue, 2¾" bbl., 4" bbl. & 4" heavy bbl... **$178.00**
357 Mag., stainless steel, 4" bbl. & 4" heavy bbl. .. **198.00**
38 Special, blue, 2¾" bbl., 4" bbl. **178.00**
38 Special, stainless steel, 4" bbl. & 4" heavy bbl... **198.00**
9mm, blue, 4" bbl. **194.00**

SECURITY-SIX 357 Mag.

SPECIFICATIONS: Six Shots. Calibers: 357 Magnum caliber (handles 38 Spec.), 38 Special. **Barrel:** 2¾", 4", 6", five-groove-rifling 18¾" right twist. **Weight:** 33½ ounces (4" barrel). **Overall Length:** 9¼" (4" barrel). **Sights:** Ruger adjustable rear (elevation and windage adjustments). Front sight is ⅛" wide, serrated. **Grips:** Checkered walnut, semi-target style. **Finish:** Polished all over and blued. Stainless steel models have brushed satin finish.
357 Mag., blue, 2¾" bbl., 4" bbl.,
4" heavy bbl. & 6" bbl. **$211.00**
357 Mag., stainless steel, 2¾" bbl., 4" bbl.,
4" heavy bbl., & 6" bbl. **233.00**
357 Mag., blue, big grip, 4" heavy bbl. & 6" bbl. **228.00**
357 Mag., stainless steel, big grip,
4" heavy bbl. & 6" bbl. **250.00**

RUGER REVOLVERS

SPEED-SIX

Double Action, Round Butt
(Checkered Walnut Grip Panels)

The Speed-Six is a round butt lightened version of the Security-Six, designed for the use by off-duty and plainclothes officers where weight and concealability are essential. The Speed-Six is available on special order with a spurless hammer. The mechanism and construction are identical to the Security-Six. (Models 207 and 208 can be had with a spurless hammer.)

Model 208— 38 Spec. Caliber-Fixed Sights
2¾" barrel $178.00

Model 207— 357 Mag. Caliber-Fixed Sights
2¾" barrel $178.00
4" barrel 178.00

Stainless Steel
Model 737—357 Mag. Caliber-Fixed Sights
2¾" barrel $198.00
4" barrel 198.00

Model 738—38 Spec. Caliber-Fixed Sights
2¾" barrel $198.00

SUPER SINGLE-SIX CONVERTIBLE
(With two cylinders— 22 L.R. & 22 WMR)

Features: Ruger single action mechanism. Transfer bar ignition. Interlocked gate, transfer-bar, cylinder latch functions. Gate controlled loading. All stressed components hardened chrome-molybdenum steel. Music wire springs throughout. Improved patridge front sight. **Calibers:** 22 Short, Long, Long Rifle and 22 WMR. **Barrel:** 6 groove, 14" twist. **Cylinders:** 2-interchangeable. **Ignition mechanism:** transfer-bar. Independent-alloy steel firing pin mounted in frame.

Sights: Adjustable rear and ramp front blade sight. **Grips:** Genuine walnut. **Finish:** Polished and blued or stainless steel.

NR4-4⅝" Barrel (with interchangeable 22WMR cyl.) .. **$157.50** stainless steel .... not available
NR5-5½" Barrel (with interchangeable 22WMR cyl.) ... 157.50 stainless steel **$224.00**
NR6-6½" Barrel (with interchangeable 22WMR cyl.).... 157.50 stainless steel 224.00
NR9-9½" Barrel (with interchangeable 22WMR cyl.).... 157.50 stainless steel .... not available

RUGER REVOLVERS

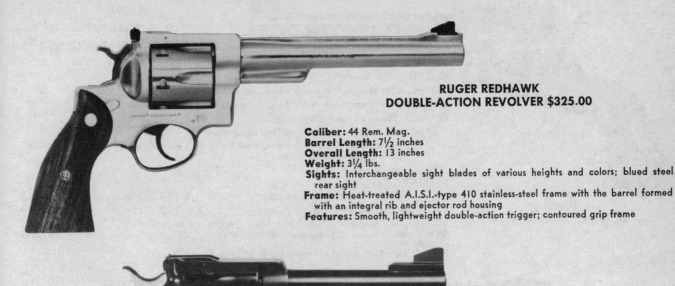

RUGER REDHAWK
DOUBLE-ACTION REVOLVER $325.00

Caliber: 44 Rem. Mag.
Barrel Length: 7½ inches
Overall Length: 13 inches
Weight: 3¼ lbs.
Sights: Interchangeable sight blades of various heights and colors; blued steel rear sight
Frame: Heat-treated A.I.S.I.-type 410 stainless-steel frame with the barrel formed with an integral rib and ejector rod housing
Features: Smooth, lightweight double-action trigger; contoured grip frame

RUGER NEW MODEL BLACKHAWK/CONVERTIBLE BLACKHAWK
SINGLE-ACTION REVOLVER
45 Caliber $197.50
45 Caliber Convertible $217.00

Calibers: 45 and 45/45 ACP
Barrels: Nos. BN-44 and BN-44X (conv.) 4⅝-in. barrels; Nos. BN-45 and BN-45X (conv.) 7½-in. barrels; with 6 groove rifling and 16″ twist
Weight: 38 oz. (4⅝″); 40 oz. (7½″)
Overall Length: 10⅛″ w/4⅝″ bbl.; 13⅛″ w/7½″ bbl.
Sights, grips, ignition mechanism, springs screws, cylinder frame: Same as 44 Magnum Blackhawk specifications.
Features: Convertible model includes extra cylinder for 45 ACP cartridge.

BLACKHAWK SINGLE-ACTION REVOLVER
(IN 30 CARBINE CALIBER) $197.50

Caliber: 30 Carbine
Barrel Length: 7½″, 6 groove rifling 20″ twist
Overall Length: 13⅛ inches
Weight: 44 ounces
Springs: Unbreakable music wire springs used throughout; no leaf springs.
Screws: For security, Nylok® screws are used at all five locations that might be affected by recoil.
Sights: Patridge style, ramp front sight with ⅛″ wide blade, matted to eliminate glare. Rear sight adjustable for windage and elevation.
Ignition System: Independent alloy steel firing pin, mounted in frame, transfer-bar
Frame: Same cylinder frame as 44 Mag. Super Blackhawk
Grips: Genuine walnut
Finish: Polished, blued and anodized

RUGER REVOLVERS

RUGER BLACKHAWK SINGLE ACTION REVOLVER

CALIBER: 357 Magnum; 38 Special interchangeably.

BARREL: 4⅝" and 6½", 8 groove rifling, 16" twist.

FRAME: Chrome molybdenum steel with bridge reinforcement and rear-sight guard.

SPRINGS: Music wire springs throughout.

WEIGHT: 40 ounces with 4⅝" barrel and 42 ounces with 6½" barrel.

SIGHTS: Patridge style, ramp front matted blade ⅛" wide. Rear sight click adjustable for windage and elevation.

GRIPS: Genuine walnut.

FINISH: Polished and blued; or stainless steel.

BN34—4⅝" Barrel, 357 Magnum caliber .... $197.50 Stainless Steel $237.50
BN36—6½" Barrel, 357 Magnum caliber .... 197.50 Stainless Steel 237.50
BN34-X—4⅝" Barrel ⎱ fitted with 9mm Parabellum extra
BN36-X—6½" Barrel ⎰ cylinder. Walnut panels 217.00

Note: (Convertible model not available in Stainless Steel)

Handles 38 Special Interchangeably

RUGER BLACKHAWK SINGLE ACTION REVOLVER

CALIBER: 41 Magnum.

BARREL: 4⅝ and 6½", Buttoned rifling 1 turn in 20" twist.

FRAME: Chrome molybdenum steel with bridge reinforcement and rear-sight guard.

SPRINGS: Music wire springs throughout.

WEIGHT: 38 ounces with 4⅝" barrel and 40 ounces with 6½" barrel.

SIGHTS: Patridge style, ramp front matted blade ⅛ wide. Rear sight click adjustment for windage and elevation.

GRIPS: Genuine walnut.

OVERALL LENGTH: 12⅛" (6½" bbl.); 10¼" (4⅝" bbl.).

FINISH: Polished and blued.

BN-41—4⅝" Barrel $197.50
BN-42—6½" Barrel 197.50

RUGER SUPER BLACKHAWK SINGLE ACTION REVOLVER

CALIBER: 44 Magnum; 44 Special interchangeably.

BARREL: 6 groove rifling, 20" twist.

FRAME: Chrome molybdenum steel with bridge reinforcement and rear sight guard.

SPRINGS: Music wire springs throughout.

WEIGHT: 48 ounces.

SIGHTS: Patridge style, ramp front matted blade ⅛" wide. Rear sight click adjustable for windage and elevation.

GRIP FRAME: Chrome molybdenum steel enlarged and contoured to minimize recoil effect.

TRIGGER: Wide spur, low contour, sharply serrated for convenient cocking with minimum disturbance of grip.

OVERALL LENGTH: 13⅜".

FINISH: Polished and blued.

S47N—7½" Barrel, with steel grip frame $228.00
S410N—10½" Barrel, with steel grip frame 228.00

Handles 44 Special Interchangeably

RUGER 22 AUTOMATIC PISTOLS

STANDARD MODEL AUTO PISTOL
$120.00

CALIBER: 22 Long Rifle only
BARREL: Length, 4¾" or 6" medium weight, 6 groove rifling, 14" twist.
SPRINGS: Music wire springs.
WEIGHTS: 36 ozs. for 4¾" barrel; 38 ozs. for 6" barrel.
OVERALL LENGTH: 8¾" or 10" depending on barrel length.
SIGHTS: Front fixed; rear adjustable.
MAGAZINE: Detachable, 9-shot capacity.
TRIGGER: Grooved, curved finger surface, ⅜" wide. Two stage pull.
SAFETY: Locks sear and bolt. Cannot be put in safe position unless gun is cocked.
GRIPS: Hard rubber.

MARK 1
TARGET PISTOL
$157.00

CALIBER: 22 Long Rifle only.
BARREL: Length, 6⅞" heavy weight, burnish reamed.
SPRINGS: Music wire springs.
WEIGHT: 42 ounces.
OVERALL LENGTH: 10⅞".
SIGHTS: Patridge style, front blade, .125" wide, undercut to prevent glare. Micro rear sight, click adjustment for windage and elevation. Sight radius, 9⅜".
MAGAZINE: Detachable, 9-shot capacity.
TRIGGER: Light crisp pull, no backlash.
SAFETY: Locks sear and bolt. Cannot be put in safe position unless gun is cocked.
GRIPS: Hard rubber.

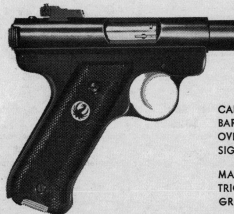

MARK 1
BULL BARREL TARGET PISTOL
$157.00

CALIBER: 22 Long Rifle only
BARREL: 5½" heavyweight bull barrel.
OVERALL LENGTH: 9½".
SIGHTS: Patridge style, front blade, .125" wide, undercut Micro rear sight, click adjustments for windage and elevation.
MAGAZINE: Detachable, 9-shot capacity.
TRIGGER: Light crisp pull, no backlash.
GRIPS: Hard rubber.

SMITH & WESSON AUTO PISTOLS

9MM AUTOMATIC PISTOL
DOUBLE ACTION
(MODEL NO. 39)

BLUE
$284.50

NICKEL
$313.50

CALIBER:	9mm Luger (Parabellum)
MAGAZINE CAPACITY:	8 (2-eight round magazines furnished)
BARREL:	4 inches
LENGTH OVER ALL:	7 7/16 inches
WEIGHT:	26 1/2 ounces without magazine
SIGHTS:	Fixed, 1/8-inch serrated ramp front; Patridge type rear adjustable for windage only
STOCKS:	Checked walnut with S & W monograms
FINISH:	S & W Blue or Nickel

22 CAL. AUTOMATIC PISTOL
(MODEL NO. 41)

BLUE ONLY
(7 3/8" BARREL)
$325.25

CALIBER:	22 Long Rifle
MAGAZINE CAPACITY:	10 rounds
BARREL:	7 3/8 inches
LENGTH OVERALL:	With 7 3/8" barrel, 12 inches
SIGHT RADIUS:	With 7 3/8" barrel, 9 5/16 inches
WEIGHT:	With 7 3/8" barrel, 43 1/2 ounces
SIGHTS:	Front: 1/8-inch Patridge undercut. Rear: S & W Micrometer Click Sight, adjustable for windage and elevation
STOCKS:	Checked walnut with modified thumb rest, equally adaptable to right- or left-handed shooters
FINISH:	S & W Bright Blue
TRIGGER:	3/8-inch width, with S & W grooving and an adjustable trigger stop
MUZZLE BRAKE:	Detachable (7 3/8" barrel only)

NOTE: Model 41 is also available in 22 Short caliber for international shooting

22 AUTOMATIC PISTOL (HEAVY BARREL)
(MODEL NO. 41)

BRIGHT BLUE ONLY
$325.25

CALIBER:	22 Long Rifle
MAGAZINE CAPACITY:	10 rounds
BARREL:	5 1/2, 7 3/8 inches
LENGTH OVERALL:	9 inches
SIGHT RADIUS:	8 inches
WEIGHT:	44 1/2 oz
SIGHTS:	Front: 1/8" Patridge on ramp base. Rear: New S & W Micrometer Click Sight with wide 7/8" sight slide
STOCKS:	Checked walnut with modified thumb rest, equally adaptable to right- or left-handed shooters
FINISH:	S & W Bright Blue
TRIGGER:	3/8-inch width, with S & W grooving and an adjustable trigger stop

SMITH & WESSON AUTO PISTOLS

38 MASTER (MODEL NO. 52)

BRIGHT BLUE ONLY
$536.00

CALIBER:	38 S & W Special for Mid Range Wad Cutter only
MAGAZINE CAPACITY:	5 rounds (2-five round magazines furnished)
BARREL:	5 inches
LENGTH OVERALL:	8⅝ inches
SIGHT RADIUS:	6¹⁵⁄₁₆ inches
WEIGHT:	41 oz. with empty magazine
SIGHTS:	Front: ⅛" Patridge on ramp base. Rear: New S & W Micrometer Click Sight with wide ⅞" sight slide.
STOCKS:	Checked walnut with S & W monograms
FINISH:	S & W Bright Blue with sandblast stippling around sighting area to break up light reflection
TRIGGER:	⅜-inch width with S & W grooving and an adjustable trigger stop

9MM AUTOMATIC PISTOL DOUBLE ACTION (MODEL NO. 59)

BLUE
$340.75

NICKEL
$372.00

CALIBER:	9mm Luger (Parabellum)
MAGAZINE CAPACITY:	2-14 round magazines furnished
BARREL:	4 inches
LENGTH OVERALL:	7⁷⁄₁₆ inches
WEIGHT:	27 oz. without magazine
SIGHTS:	Front: ⅛-inch serrated ramp. Rear: Square notch with Micrometer Click adjustment for windage only.
STOCKS:	Checked high impact molded nylon
FINISH:	S & W Blue or Nickel

9MM AUTOMATIC PISTOL DOUBLE ACTION (MODEL 459)

BLUE $382.75
NICKEL 411.00

CALIBER:	9mm Luger	**WEIGHT:**	28 oz.
MAGAZINE CAPACITY:	Two 14-round magazines, furnished	**SIGHTS:**	Front—square ⅛-in. serrated ramp; Rear—square notch rear sight blade fully Micrometer Click adjustable
BARREL:	4 inches	**STOCKS:**	Checkered high-impact molded nylon grips
OVERALL LENGTH:	7⁷⁄₁₆ inches	**FINISH:**	Blue or nickel

9MM AUTOMATIC PISTOL DOUBLE ACTION (MODEL 439)

BLUE $326.25
NICKEL 352.75

CALIBER:	9mm Luger	**WEIGHT:**	27 oz.
MAGAZINE CAPACITY:	Two 8-round magazines, furnished	**SIGHTS:**	Front—square ⅛-in. serrated ramp; Rear—square notch rear sight blade fully Micrometer Click adjustable
BARREL:	4 inches	**STOCKS:**	Checkered walnut grips with S & W monograms
OVERALL LENGTH:	7⁷⁄₁₆ inches	**FINISH:**	Blue or nickel

SMITH & WESSON REVOLVERS

38 MILITARY & POLICE
(MODEL NO. 10)

CALIBER:	38 S & W Special
NUMBER OF SHOTS:	6
BARREL: LENGTH	2, 4, 5 and 6 inches; also 4-inch heavy barrel
OVERALL:	With 4-inch barrel, 9¼ inches
WEIGHT:	With 4-inch barrel, 30½ oz
SIGHTS:	Front: Fixed, ⅛-inch serrated ramp. Rear: Square notch
STOCKS:	Checked walnut Service with S & W monograms, round or square butt
FINISH:	S & W Blue or Nickel

**BLUE
$171.75**

**NICKEL
$185.50**

38 MILITARY & POLICE (AIRWEIGHT)
(MODEL NO. 12)

CALIBER:	38 S & W Special.
NUMBER OF SHOTS:	6.
BARREL:	2 or 4 inches.
LENGTH OVERALL:	With 2-inch barrel and round butt, 6⅞ inches.
WEIGHT:	With 2-inch barrel and round butt, 18 oz.
SIGHTS:	Front: Fixed, ⅛-inch serrated ramp. Rear: Square notch.
STOCKS:	Checked walnut Service with S & W monograms, round or square butt.
FINISH:	S & W Blue or Nickel.

**BLUE
$218.00**

**NICKEL
$247.50**

(Illus. with round butt)

357 MILITARY & POLICE (HEAVY BARREL)
(MODEL NO. 13)

CALIBER:	357 Magnum and 38 S&W Special.
ROUNDS:	6-shot cylinder capacity.
BARREL:	4 inches.
LENGTH OVERALL	9¼ inches.
WEIGHT:	34 oz.
SIGHTS:	Front: ⅛-inch serrated ramp. Rear: Square notch.
STOCKS:	Checked walnut Service with S&W monograms, square butt.
FINISH:	S&W Blue or Nickel.

**BLUE
$176.50**

**NICKEL
$192.75**

9mm MILITARY & POLICE
(MODEL NO. 547)

CALIBER:	9mm
NUMBER OF SHOTS:	6
BARREL:	3 or 4 inches
OVERALL LENGTH:	8⅛" with 3-in. barrel; 9⅛" with 4-in. barrel
WEIGHT:	32 oz. with 3-in. barrel; 34 oz. with 4-in. barrel
SIGHTS:	Front is ⅛" serrated ramp; rear is ⅛" square notch
STOCKS:	Checkered walnut target round butt with speedloader cutaway (3"); checkered square butt Magna Service (4")
FINISH:	S&W Blue

BLUE ONLY $246.00

SMITH & WESSON REVOLVERS

K-38 MASTERPIECE
(MODEL NO. 14)

CALIBER:	38 S & W Special.
NUMBER OF SHOTS:	6.
BARREL:	6, 8⅜ inches.
LENGTH OVERALL:	With 6-inch barrel, 11⅛ inches.
WEIGHT LOADED:	With 6-inch barrel, 38½ oz.; 8⅜-inch, 42½ oz.
SIGHTS:	Front: ⅛-inch plain Patridge. Rear: S & W Micrometer Click Sight, adjustable for windage and elevation.
STOCKS:	Checked walnut Service with S & W monograms.
FINISH:	S & W Blue.
FEATURES:	Available in single action, blue only, by special order.

6" $242.50
8⅜" 254.75
**With target hammer,
trigger and stocks**
6" $278.77
8⅜" $291.00

38 COMBAT MASTERPIECE
WITH 4-INCH BARREL
(MODEL NO. 15)

CALIBER:	38 S & W Special
NUMBER OF SHOTS:	6
BARREL:	2 & 4 inches.
LENGTH OVERALL:	9⅛ inches
WEIGHT LOADED:	with 4-inch barrel, 34 oz.
SIGHTS:	Front: ⅛-inch Baughman Quick Draw on plain ramp. Rear: S & W Micrometer Click Sight, adjustable for windage and elevation
STOCKS:	Checked walnut Service with S & W monograms
FINISH:	S & W Blue or Nickel

BLUE $196.50
NICKEL $211.50
**Blue with target hammer
and trigger, 4" barrel $216.25**

K-22 MASTERPIECE
(MODEL NO. 17)

CALIBER:	22 Long Rifle
NUMBER OF SHOTS:	6.
BARREL:	6, 8⅜ inches.
LENGTH OVERALL:	With 6-inch barrel, 11⅛ inches.
WEIGHT LOADED:	With 6-inch barrel, 38½ oz.; 8⅜-inch, 42½ oz.
SIGHTS:	Front: ⅛-inch plain Patridge. Rear: S & W Micrometer Click Sight, adjustable for windage and elevation.
STOCKS:	Checked walnut Service with S & W monograms.
FINISH:	S & W Blue.

BLUE ONLY
6" $257.75
8⅜" 269.50
**with target hammer,
trigger and stocks**
6" barrel $294.00
8⅜" barrel 305.75

SMITH & WESSON REVOLVERS

22 COMBAT MASTERPIECE
WITH 4-INCH BARREL
(MODEL NO. 18)

CALIBER:	22 Long Rifle
NUMBER OF SHOTS:	6
BARREL:	4 inches
LENGTH OVERALL:	9 1/8 inches
WEIGHT LOADED:	36 1/2 oz.
SIGHTS:	Front: 1/8-inch Baughman Quick Draw on plain ramp. Rear: S & W Micrometer Click Sight, adjustable for windage and elevation
STOCKS:	Checked walnut Service with S & W monograms
FINISH:	S & W Blue

BLUE ONLY
$241.75
With target hammer and trigger $261.50

"357" COMBAT MAGNUM
(MODEL NO. 19)

CALIBER:	357 Magnum (Actual bullet dia. 38 S & W Spec.)
NUMBER OF SHOTS:	6
BARREL:	2 1/2, 4, 6 inches
LENGTH OVERALL:	9 1/2 inches with 4" barrel; 7 1/2 inches with 2 1/2" barrel; 11 1/2 inches with 6" barrel
WEIGHT:	35 oz. (2 1/2" model weighs 31 oz.)
SIGHTS:	Front: 1/8" Baughman Quick Draw on 2 1/2" or 4" barrel, 1/8" Patridge on 6" barrel. Rear: S & W Micrometer Click Sight, adjustable for windage and elevation
STOCKS:	Checked Goncalo Alves Target with S & W monograms.
FINISH:	S & W Bright Blue or Nickel

BRIGHT BLUE OR NICKEL
$228.00—$262.00

Price based on accessories such as round or square butt, adjustable sights, target trigger, target hammer, target stocks, white outline rear or red ramp front.

1955 45 TARGET
(MODEL No. 25)

CALIBER:	45 A. C. P.
NUMBER OF SHOTS:	6
BARREL:	6 1/2 inches
LENGTH OVERALL:	11 7/8 inches
WEIGHT:	45 oz.
SIGHTS:	Front: 1/8-inch plain Patridge. Rear: S & W Micrometer Click Sight, adjustable for windage and elevation
STOCKS:	Checked walnut Target with S & W monograms
HAMMER:	Checked target type
TRIGGER:	Grooved target type
FINISH:	S & W Blue

BLUE ONLY
$399.33

SMITH & WESSON REVOLVERS

357 MAGNUM
(MODEL NO. 27)

CALIBER:	357 Magnum (Actual bullet dia. 38 S & W Spec.)
NUMBER OF SHOTS:	6
BARREL:	3½, 5, 6, 8⅜ inches
LENGTH OVERALL:	With 6-inch barrel, 11¼ inches.
WEIGHT:	With 3½-inch barrel, 41 oz.; 5-inch, 42½ oz.; 6-inch, 44 oz.; 8⅜-inch, 47 oz.
SIGHTS:	Front: Choice of any S & W target sight. Rear: S & W Micrometer Click Sight, adjustable for windage and elevation.
STOCKS:	Checked walnut Service with S & W monograms.
FRAME:	Finely checked top strap and barrel rib.
FINISH:	S & W Bright Blue or Nickel.

BRIGHT BLUE OR NICKEL
With presentation box
4" $419.83
6" 405.75
8⅜" 433.07
Without presentation box
4" $383.00
6" 369.00
8¾" 398.00

HIGHWAY PATROLMAN
(MODEL NO. 28)

CALIBER:	357 Magnum (Actual bullet dia. 38 S & W Spec.)
NUMBER OF SHOTS:	6
BARREL:	4, 6 inches
LENGTH OVERALL:	With 6-inch barrel, 11¼ inches.
WEIGHT:	With 4-inch barrel, 41¾ oz.; 6-inch, 44 oz.
SIGHTS:	Front: ⅛-inch Baughman Quick Draw on plain ramp. Rear: S & W Micrometer Click Sight, adjustable for windage and elevation.
STOCKS:	Checked walnut Service with S & W monograms (Walnut Target stocks at additional cost).
FINISH:	S & W Satin Blue with sandblast stippling or barrel rib and frame edging.

BLUE ONLY
$261.75
With target stocks (Illus.)
$282.00

44 MAGNUM
(MODEL NO. 29)

CALIBER:	44 Magnum
NUMBER OF SHOTS:	6
BARREL:	4, 6, 8⅜ inches
LENGTH OVERALL:	With 6½-inch barrel, 11⅞ inches.
WEIGHT:	With 4-inch barrel, 43 oz.; 6½-inch, 47 oz.; 8⅜-inch, 51½ oz.
SIGHTS:	Front: ⅛-inch S & W Red Ramp. Rear: S & W Micrometer Click Sight adjustable for windage and elevation. White Outline notch.
STOCKS:	Special oversize Target type of checked Goncalo Alves, with S & W monograms.
HAMMER:	Checked target type.
TRIGGER:	Grooved target type.
FINISH:	S & W Bright Blue or Nickel.

BRIGHT BLUE OR NICKEL
with presentation box
4", 6" $419.83
8⅜" 433.07

SMITH & WESSON REVOLVERS

41 MAGNUM
(MODEL NO. 57)

CALIBER:	.41 Magnum.
NUMBER OF SHOTS:	6.
BARREL:	4, 6, 8⅜ inches.
LENGTH OVERALL:	With 6-inch barrel, 11⅜ inches.
WEIGHT:	With 6-inch barrel, 48 oz.
SIGHTS:	Front: ⅛-inch S & W Red Ramp. Rear: S & W Micrometer Click Sight adjustable for windage and elevation. White Outline notch.
STOCKS:	Special oversize Target type of checked Goncalo Alves, with S & W monograms.
HAMMER:	Checked target type.
TRIGGER:	Grooved target type.
FINISH:	S & W Bright Blue or Nickel.

**BRIGHT BLUE
OR NICKEL**
with presentation box
4", 6" $419.83
8⅜" 433.07

1953 22/32 KIT GUN
(MODEL NO. 34)

CALIBER:	22 Long Rifle
NUMBER OF SHOTS:	6
BARREL:	2, 4 inches
LENGTH OVERALL:	With 4-inch barrel and round butt, 8 inches
WEIGHT:	With 4-inch barrel and round butt, 22¼ oz.
SIGHTS:	Front: ⅒-inch serrated ramp. Rear: S & W Micrometer Click Sight, adjustable for windage and elevation.
STOCKS:	Checked walnut Service with S & W monograms, round or square butt
FINISH:	S & W Blue or Nickel

**BLUE
$211.00**

**NICKEL
$229.25**

STAINLESS STEEL MODELS

1977 22/32 KIT GUN
(MODEL NO. 63)

SPECIFICATIONS: Caliber: 22 Long Rifle. **Number of shots:** 6. **Barrel Length:** 4 inches. **Weight:** 24½ oz. (empty). **Sights:** ⅛-inch red ramp front sight. Rear sight is the black stainless steel S&W Micrometer Click square-notch, adjustable for windage and elevation. **Stocks:** Square butt. **Finish:** Satin.

**STAINLESS STEEL
$243.50**

38 CHIEFS SPECIAL STAINLESS
MODEL NO. 60

SPECIFICATIONS: Caliber: 38 S&W Special. **Number of shots:** 5. **Barrel:** 2 Inch. **Length Overall:** 6½ inches. **Weight:** 19 oz. **Sights:** Front Fixed, 1/10-inch serrated ramp. Rear: Square notch. **Stocks:** Checked walnut Service with S&W monograms. **Finish:** Satin

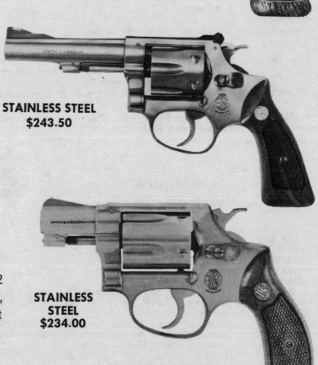

**STAINLESS
STEEL
$234.00**

SMITH & WESSON REVOLVERS

38 MILITARY & POLICE STAINLESS
MODEL NO. 64

SPECIFICATIONS: Caliber: 38 S&W Special. **Number of Shots:** 6. **Barrel:** 4 Inch heavy barrel, square butt. 2-inch regular barrel, round butt. **Length Overall:** With 4-inch barrel, 9¼ inches 2-inch barrel, 6⅞ inches. **Weight:** With 4-inch barrel, 34 ounces. **Sights:** Fixed, ⅛-inch serrated ramp front; square notch rear. **Stocks:** Checked walnut Service with S&W monograms. **Finish:** Satin. **Ammunition—** 38 S&W Special, 38 S&W Special Mid Range.

Stainless
Steel
$185.00

357 Military & Police Stainless
Heavy Barrel
MODEL NO. 65

SPECIFICATIONS: Caliber: 357 Magnum and 38 S&W Special. **Rounds:** 6-shot cylinder capacity. **Barrel:** 4-inch heavy barrel. **Length Overall:** With 4-inch barrel, 9¼ inches. **Weight:** With 4-inch barrel, 34 oz. **Sights:** Fixed, ⅛-inch serrated ramp front; square notch rear. **Stocks:** Checked walnut Service with S&W monograms, square butt. **Finish:** Satin.

Stainless
Steel
$196.75

357 COMBAT MAGNUM REVOLVER
MODEL NO. 66

SPECIFICATIONS: Caliber: 357 Magnum (Actual bullet diam. 38 S&W Spec.). **Number of shots:** 6. **Barrel:** 6 or 4 Inch with square butt; 2½ inches with round butt. **Length Overall:** 9½″ with 4″ barrel; 7½ inches with 2½-inch barrel. **Weight:** 35 ounces with 4″ barrel. **Sights:** Front: ⅛″ Rear: S&W Red Ramp on ramp base, S&W Micrometer Click Sight, adjustable for windage and elevation. **Stocks:** Checked Goncalo Alves target with square butt with S&W monograms. **Finish:** Satin. **Trigger:** S&W grooving with an adjustable trigger stop. **Ammunition:** 357 S&W Magnum, 38 S&W Special Hi-Speed, 38 S&W Special, 38 S&W Special Mid Range.

Stainless
Steel
$244.00

K-38 COMBAT MASTERPIECE REVOLVER
MODEL NO. 67

SPECIFICATIONS: Caliber: 38 S&W Special. **Number of shots:** 6. **Barrel:** 4 Inch. **Length Overall:** 9⅛″ with 4″ barrell. **Weight Loaded:** 34 oz. with 4″ barrel. **Sights:** Front: ⅛″ Rear: S&W Red Ramp on ramp base, S&W Micrometer Click Sights, adjustable for windage and elevation. **Stocks:** Checked walnut Service with S&W Monograms square butt. **Finish:** Satin. **Trigger:** S&W grooving with an adjustable trigger stop. **Ammunition:** 38 S&W Special, .38 S&W Special Mid Range.

Stainless
Steel
$228.75

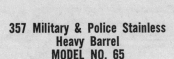
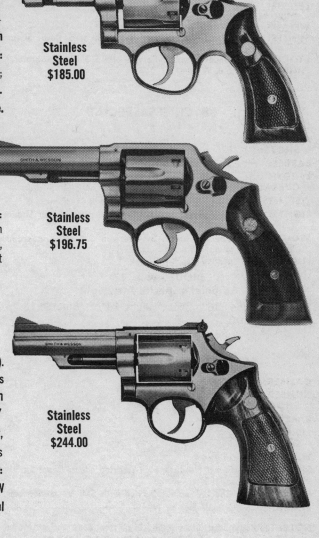

SMITH & WESSON REVOLVERS

32 REGULATION POLICE

CALIBER:	32 S & W Long.
NUMBER OF SHOTS:	6.
BARREL:	2, 3 inches.
LENGTH OVERALL:	With 4-inch barrel, 8½ inches.
WEIGHT:	With 4-inch barrel, 18¾ oz.
SIGHTS:	Front: Fixed, 1/10-inch serrated ramp. Rear: Square notch.
STOCKS:	Checked walnut Service with S & W monograms.
FINISH:	S & W Blue.

(MODEL NO. 31)
BLUE ONLY $211.25

38 CHIEFS SPECIAL

CALIBER:	38 S & W Special
NUMBER OF SHOTS:	5.
BARREL:	2 or 3 inches. (3"—blue only)
LENGTH OVERALL:	With 2-inch barrel and round butt, 6½ inches.
WEIGHT:	With 2-inch barrel and round butt, 19 oz.
SIGHTS:	Front: Fixed, 1/10-inch serrated ramp. Rear: Square notch.
STOCKS:	Checked walnut Service with S & W monograms, round or square butt.
FINISH:	S & W Blue or Nickel.

MODEL NO. 37
38 Chief's Special Airweight

Same as Model 36 except: weight 14 oz. **Blue $215.75; Nickel $244.00.**

BLUE $194.00
NICKEL $210.00   **(MODEL No. 36)**

38 BODYGUARD "AIRWEIGHT"

CALIBER:	38 S & W Special.
NUMBER OF SHOTS:	5.
BARREL:	2 inches.
LENGTH OVERALL:	6⅜ inches.
WEIGHT:	14½ oz.
SIGHTS:	Front: Fixed, 1/10-inch serrated ramp. Rear: Square notch.
STOCKS:	Checked walnut Service with S & W monograms.
FINISH:	S & W Blue or Nickel.

NOTE: The Bodyguard also supplied in all-steel construction, Model 49, weighing 20½ oz. Price: Blue, **$208.75**; Nickel, **$227.00**.

BLUE $224.75
NICKEL $253.75   **(MODEL No. 38)**

K-22 MASTERPIECE M. R. F.

CALIBER:	22 Magnum Rim Fire.
NUMBER OF SHOTS:	6.
BARREL:	4, 6, 8⅜ inches.
LENGTH OVERALL:	With 6-inch barrel, 11⅛ inches.
WEIGHT:	With 6-inch barrel, 39 oz.
SIGHTS:	Front: ⅛-inch plain Patridge. Rear: S & W Micrometer Click Sight, adjustable for windage and elevation.
STOCKS:	Checked walnut Service with S & W monograms.
FINISH:	S & W Blue.
	Auxiliary cylinder available in 22 LR.

BLUE ONLY
4", 6" $272.00
8⅜" 284.75

(MODEL NO. 48)

SMITH & WESSON REVOLVERS

DISTINGUISHED COMBAT MAGNUM

CALIBER:	357 Magnum
NUMBER OF SHOTS:	6
BARREL LENGTH:	4 or 6 inches
OVERALL LENGTH:	9¾" with 4-in. barrel; 11½" with 6-in. barrel
WEIGHT:	42 oz. with 4-in. barrel; 46 oz. with 6-in. barrel
SIGHTS:	Front is S&W Red Ramp; rear is S&W Micrometer Click adjustable for windage and elevation; White outline notch. Option with 6-in. barrel only—plain Patridge front with black outline notch.
STOCKS:	Checkered Goncalo Alves with speedloader cutaway
FINISH:	S&W Blue or Nickel

MODEL 686, same as Model 586 except finish is stainless steel, **$268.00**

**BLUE OR NICKEL $246.00
(MODEL NO. 586)**

STAR AUTOMATIC PISTOLS

STAR PD
45 ACP BLUE

Chambered for the sledgehammer 45 ACP, the PD has the same capacity— 7 rounds —as the U.S. Government Model, yet it weighs nearly a pound less, as well as being smaller in every dimension. Just a fraction over 7" long, it weighs only 25 ounces.
45 ACP Blue $360.00

STAR BKM & BM
9mm LUGER BLUE
9mm LUGER CHROME

Overall Length: 7.17". Barrel Length: 3.9".
Magazine Capacity: 8 rounds.
Model BM Blue   34.06 oz..........**$300.00**
Model BM Chrome 34.06 oz.......... **330.00**
Model BKM Blue 25.59 oz.......... **300.00**

The Model BM offers all steel construction and the BKM offers a high strength, weight-saving duraluminum frame. An improved thumb safety locks both the slide and hammer with hammer cocked or uncocked; further, an automatic magazine safety locks the sear when the magazine is removed.

STERLING AUTOMATIC PISTOLS

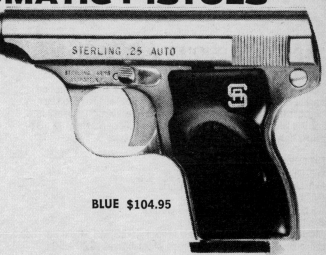

25 AUTO MODEL 300

Sterling Arms introduces the dependable MODEL 300, a personal sized automatic, constructed of ordnance steel, featuring indestructable Cycolac grips.

SIZE: 4½" x 3½"	**CONSTRUCTION:** All steel
WEIGHT: 13 oz.	**GRIPS:** Cycolac—Black
CAPACITY: 6 shots	**FINISH:** Blue or Stainless Steel
CALIBER: 25 ACP	

Model 300S: Same as Model 300 except has stainless steel construction and finish. **$124.95**

BLUE $104.95

STERLING AUTOMATIC PISTOLS

22 AUTO MODEL 302

Performance and standards of the potent little MODEL 302, chambered for the 22 LR cartridge, provides companionship above the ordinary.

SIZE: 4½" x 3½"
WEIGHT: 13 oz.
CAPACITY: 6 shots
CALIBER: 22 Long Rifle

CONSTRUCTION: All steel
GRIPS: Cycolac—Black
FINISH: Blue

Model 302S: Same as Model 302 except has stainless steel construction and finish. **$124.95**

BLUE $104.95

380 DOUBLE ACTION
AUTO MODEL 400 MK II

Your *security* is assured with the MODEL 400 featuring both double and single action, combined with the powerful 380 cartridge.

SIZE: 6½" x 4¾"'
WEIGHT: 26 oz.
CAPACITY: 7 shots
CALIBER: 380

CONSTRUCTION: All ordnance steel
GRIPS: Walnut hand checkered
FINISH: Blue

Model 400S: Same as Model 400 except has stainless steel construction and finish. **$259.95**

BLUE $209.50

32 DOUBLE ACTION
MODEL 402S MK II

This slim and compact automatic pistol is ideal for police and security use. Features a low-profile, target-type rear sight fully adjustable for windage and elevation; safety is a rolling block design; slide lock remains open after the last shot; hammer is a low-profile serrated type.

SIZE: 6½" x 4¾"
WEIGHT: 26 oz.
MAGAZINE CAPACITY: 8 rounds
CALIBER: 32 ACP
GRIPS: Checkered American walnut
FINISH: Stainless Steel
Model 402 MK II: Same as Model 402S MK II except has deep blue finish with stainless steel barrel. **$209.50**

STEYR PISTOLS

**STEYR GB80
Semi-Auto Pistol
$585.00**

Caliber: 9mm Parabellum
Magazine Capacity: 18 rounds
Action: Double. Gas-operated, blowback delayed action
Barrel Length: 5.4"
Overall Length: 8.9"
Weight: 2.09 lbs. (empty)
Height: 5.7"
Sights: Fixed, open. Notch rear, post front
Trigger Pull: Approx. 4 lbs. (with hammer cocked);
    approx. 14 lbs. (with hammer uncocked)
Muzzle Velocity: 1,184 fps

TAURUS REVOLVERS

SPECIFICATIONS:
Caliber: 38 Special
Capacity: 6 shot
Barrel length(s): 4"
Weight: 34 oz.
Sights: 2/8" on ramp front; micrometer click adjustable
    rear for windage and elevation.
Action: Double
Stock: Checkered walnut
Finish: Blue or satin

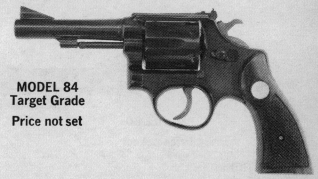

**MODEL 84
Target Grade**

Price not set

SPECIFICATIONS:
Caliber: 38 Special
Capacity: 6 shot
Barrel length(s): 6"
Weight: 34 oz.
Sights: Patridge-type front; micrometer click adjustable
    rear for windage and elevation
Action: Double
Stock: Checkered-walnut target
Finish: Bright royal blue

Model 96 Target Scout: Same as Model 86 Target Master
    except 22 L.R. caliber. Blue.

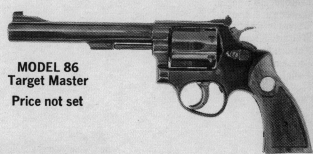

**MODEL 86
Target Master**

Price not set

SPECIFICATIONS:
Caliber: 38 Special
Action: Double
Number of Shots: 6
Barrel Length: 4" only
Weight: 34½ oz.
Sights: 2/8" on Ramp, Front.
    Rear Micrometer Click
    Adjustable for Windage
    and Elevation
Finish: Blue or satin
Stocks: Checkered Walnut Target

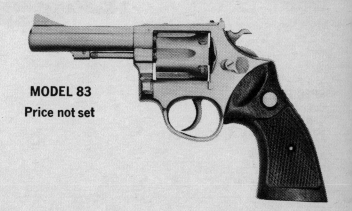

MODEL 83

Price not set

TAURUS REVOLVERS

MODEL 73
Price not set

SPECIFICATIONS:
Caliber: 32 Special
Capacity: 6 shot
Barrel length(s): 3" Heavy barrel
Weight: 20 oz.
Sights: Rear, square notch
Action: Double
Stock: Standard checkered
Finish: Blue or satin

MODEL 80
Price not set

SPECIFICATIONS:
Caliber: 38 Special
Capacity: 6 shot
Barrel length(s): 3", 4"
Weight: 33 oz.
Action: Double
Stock: Checkered walnut
Finish: Blue or satin

MODEL 82
Heavy Barrel
Price not set

SPECIFICATIONS:
Caliber: 38 Special
Capacity: 6 shot
Barrel length(s): 3", 4"
Weight: 34 oz.
Action: Double
Stock: Checkered walnut
Finish: Blue or satin

TAURUS REVOLVERS

MODEL 65
Price not set

SPECIFICATIONS:
Caliber: 357 Magnum
Capacity: 6 shot
Barrel Length: 3", 4"
Weight: 34 oz.
Sights: Rear—square notch, front ramp
Action: Double
Stock: Checkered walnut target
Finish: Royal blue or satin

MODEL 66
Price not set

SPECIFICATIONS:
Caliber: 357 Magnum
Capacity: 6 shot
Barrel Length: 3", 4", 6"
Weight: 35 oz.
Sights: Serrated ramp, front. Rear Micrometer Click
   adjustable for windage and elevation
Action: Double
Stock: Checkered walnut magna grips (3"); checkered
   walnut target grips (4" & 6")
Finish: Royal blue or satin

MODEL 85 "Protector"
Price not set

SPECIFICATIONS:
Caliber: 38 Special
Capacity: 5 shot
Barrel Length: 3"
Weight: 21 oz.
Sights: Notch rear sight, fixed sight
Action: Double
Stock: Brazilian hardwood
Finish: Blue or satin

WALTHER PISTOLS

DOUBLE ACTION AUTOMATIC PISTOLS

The Walther double action system combines the principles of the double action revolver with the advantages of the modern pistol . . . without the disadvantages inherent in either design. Published reports from independent testing laboratories have cited Walther superiority in rugged durability, positive performance and reliability. Special built-in safety design and a simple disassembly procedure combine to make these one of the safest and most easily maintained handguns.

Models PP and PPK/S differ only in the overall length of the barrel and slide. Both models offer the same features, including compact form, light weight, easy handling and absolute safety—both models can be carried with a loaded chamber and closed hammer, but ready to fire either single or double action. Both models in calibers 32 ACP and 380 ACP are provided with a live round indicator pin to signal a loaded chamber. An automatic internal safety blocks the hammer to prevent accidental striking of the firing pin, except with a deliberate pull of the trigger. Sights are provided with white markings for high visibility in poor light.

Rich Walther blue/black finish is standard and each pistol is complete with extra magazine with finger rest extension. Available in calibers 22 L.R., 32 ACP and 380 ACP.

The Walther P-38 is a double action, locked breech, semi-automatic pistol with an external hammer. Its compact form, light weight and easy handling is combined with the superb performance of the 9mm Luger Parabellum cartridge.

The P-38 is equipped with both a manual and automatic safety, which allows it to be safely carried while the chamber is loaded.

Available in calibers 9mm Luger Parabellum, 30 Luger and 22 L.R. with either a rugged non-reflective black finish or in a polished blued finish.

Overall length: model PP (6.7″); PPK/S (6.1″); P-38 (8½″) P-38IV (8″); P-38K (6⅜″). Height: models PP, PPK/S (4.28″); P-38 (5.39″) P-38IV (5.39″); P-38K (5.39″). Weight: model PP (23.5 oz.); PPK/S (23 oz.); P-38 (28 oz.) P-38IV (29 oz.); P-38K (26 oz.).

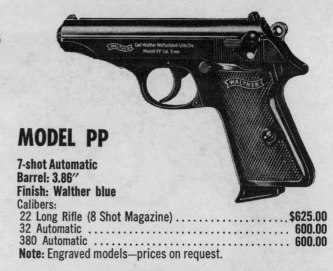

MODEL PP

7-shot Automatic
Barrel: 3.86″
Finish: Walther blue
Calibers:
22 Long Rifle (8 Shot Magazine) $625.00
32 Automatic 600.00
380 Automatic 600.00
Note: Engraved models—prices on request.

MODEL PPK/S

7-shot Automatic
Barrel: 3.27″
Finish: Walther blue
Calibers:

Model PPK/S American, 380ACP $290.00
Note: Engraved models—prices on request.

MODEL P-38K

8-shot Automatic
Barrel: 2¾″
Finish: matte

Calibers:
9mm Luger $750.00
Same as Model P-38 except for slide mounted front sight and rear sight adjustable for windage.

MODEL P-38

8-shot Automatic
Barrel: 4¹⁵/₁₆″ (9mm & 30 Luger)
 5¹/₁₆″ (.22 L.R.)
Finish: matte
Calibers:
22 Long Rifle $830.00
30 Luger 750.00
9mm Luger 750.00
Note: Engraved models—prices on request.

P-38IV AUTO-PISTOL

8-shot Automatic
Barrel: 4½″
Finish: Matte
Caliber:
9mm Luger $750.00
Same as the P-38K except for longer barrel, O.A. length and weight. Sights are non-adjustable. Imported by Interarms.

WALTHER PISTOLS

WALTHER GSP MATCH PISTOL

Calibers: 22 L.R. & 32 S&W wadcutter

WALTHER OSP

22 Short only
$1150.00

with carrying case

Models:

GSP—22 Long Rifle w/carrying case	$1150.00
GSP-C—32 S&W wadcutter w/carrying case	1300.00
22 caliber L.R. conversion unit for GSP-C	740.00
22 Short Cal. Conversion Unit for GSP-C	790.00

Walther match pistols are built to conform to ISU and NRA match target pistol regulations. The model GSP, caliber 22 L. R. is available with either 2.2 lb. (1000 gm) or 3.0 lb. (1360 gm) trigger, and comes with 4½" barrel and special hand-fitting design walnut stock. Sights consist of fixed front, and adjustable rear sight. The

GSP-C 32 S&W wadcutter center fire pistol is factory tested with a 3.0 lb. trigger. The 22 L. R. conversion unit for the model GSP-C consists of an interchangeable barrel, a slide assembly and two magazines. The 22 caliber model weighs 44.8 oz; 32 S&W weighs 49.4 oz. Overall length is 11.8". Magazine capacity is 5-shot.

DAN WESSON REVOLVERS

FEATURE INTERCHANGEABLE BARREL CAPABILITY WITHIN CALIBER

The Dan Wesson 38 special and 357 Magnum revolver features interchangeable barrel capability. It may be had with a choice of 2½", 4", 6" & 8" barrel lengths, and comes equipped with Sacramento-, Combat- or Target-type walnut grips. Extra interchangeable barrel assemblies (includes barrel shroud) are available. To change barrel one simply removes the barrel nut with wrench (supplied), slip off barrel shroud and unscrew barrel from frame. Screw new barrel to clearance gauge (supplied), slip corresponding

shroud over barrel, screw on barrel nut and tighten with wrench. Sight adjustment remains constant when changing barrel lengths.

Shown are two handguns designed and developed by Wesson Arms. Each gun can accommodate three different sizes of interchangeable barrels in both 357 Magnum and 38 caliber size. Engraved designs can also be provided and alternate grips in three styles are available—each handcarved in genuine walnut.

Model 8— 38 Special   Model 14— 357 Magnum   (with fixed sights)

SPECIFICATIONS:

Caliber: 357 Magnum (Standard)
38 Special (Optional)

Ammunition: 357 Magnum, 38 Special, Hi-Speed, 38 Special Mid-Range.

Number of Shots: 6 (Double Action & Single Action)

Barrel Lengths: 2½", 4" & 6" (Optional & Interchangeable)

Weight: 2½", 30 oz.; 4", 34 oz.; 6", 38 oz.; 8", 42 oz.
Dimensions: 4"—9¼" x 5⅜"

Sights: Front — ⅛" Serrated Blade
Rear — Integral with frame
Trigger: Wide Tang (⅜") with adjustable overtravel stop.

Hammer: Wide Spur (⅜") with short double action travel.

Plate Screws: Socket head high torque.

Grips: Walnut, interchangeable and optional.

Finish: Satin Blue

2½" barrel	**$187.00**
4" barrel	193.00
6" barrel	199.00

DAN WESSON REVOLVERS

MODEL SERIES 15– 2VH

Model 9– 38 Special
Model 15– 357 Magnum
Model 22– 22 LR
(with adjustable rear sights)

SPECIFICATIONS:

Caliber: 357 Magnum (Standard)
38 Special (Optional)
22 LR (Optional)

Ammunition: 357 Magnum, 38 Special, Hi-Speed, 38 Special Mid-Range.

Number of Shots: 6 (Double Action & Single Action)

Barrel Lengths: 2½", 4", 6", 8", 10", 12", 15" (Optional & Interchangeable)

Weight: 2½", 32 oz.; 4", 36 oz.; 6", 40 oz.; 8", 44 oz.; 10", 50 oz.; 12", 54¼ oz.; 15", 59¼ oz.

Dimensions: 4" — 9¼" x 5½"

Sights: Front — ⅛" Serrated Interchangeable Blade
Rear — Adjustable for Windage & Elevation Click graduated — 1 click — ⅜" at 25 Yds.

Trigger: Wide Tang (⅜") with adjustable overtravel stop.

Hammer: Wide Spur (⅜") with short double action travel.

Plate Screws: Socket head high torque

Grips: Walnut, interchangeable and optional.

Finish: Brite Blue

Model 9, Model 15-2VH & Model 22-VH:
2½" bbl. $282.00
4" bbl. 291.00
6" bbl. 301.00
8" bbl. 310.00
Model 15-2VH only:
10" bbl. $334.00
12" bbl. 356.00
15" bbl. 390.00

Also available: The Dan Wesson Pistol Pac. This special offering consists of one 8" Model Series revolver plus three more interchangeable barrel assemblies (2½", 4", 6"), an extra grip, four additional colored front sight blades and a Dan Wesson belt buckle and emblem all in a special carrying case. **$634.00**

Rifles

BEEMAN RIFLES

BEEMAN/WEIHRAUCH HW60 SMALLBORE RIFLE
FROM $495.00

22-caliber LR, single shot. Improved bolt action. Adjustable match trigger with push button safety. Precision rifled barrel. Stippled forearm and pistol grip. Precision aperture sights, hooded front sight ramp. Barrel length: 26.8". Length: 45.7". Weight: 10.8 lbs.

BEEMAN/FWB 2000
FROM $795.00

22-caliber long rifle. Micrometer match aperture sights. Foresight with interchangeable inserts. Meets ISU standard rifle specifications. Short lock time. Precision match trigger adjustable for weight, release point, finger length, lateral position, etc. Barrel length: 22" and 26¼". Length: 39" and 43¾". Weight: 9⅛ lbs. and 9¾ lbs.

BROWNING RIFLES

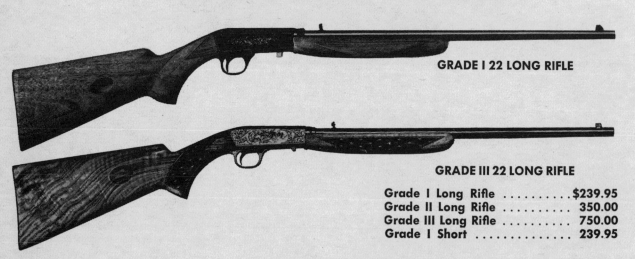

GRADE I 22 LONG RIFLE

GRADE III 22 LONG RIFLE

Grade I Long Rifle	$239.95
Grade II Long Rifle	350.00
Grade III Long Rifle	750.00
Grade I Short	239.95

SPECIFICATIONS

Caliber: 22 Long Rifle in Grades I, II, III; 22 Short in Grade I only. **Action:** Semi-automatic, double extractors with bottom ejection. **Barrel length:** 22 LR, 19¼"; 22 Short, 22". **Magazine:** Tubular with loading port in stock. **Capacity:** 22 LR, 11 rounds; 22 Short, 16 rounds. **Sights:** Gold bead front. Adjustable, folding leaf rear. **Length of pull:** 13¾". **Overall length:** Long Rifle, 37". Short, 40". **Weight:** Long Rifle, 4 lbs. 12 oz.; Short, 4 lbs. 15 oz. **Grade II**—(not illus.) Chrome plated receiver in satin finish with small game scenes engraved on all surfaces. Select walnut and forearm, hand checkered in diamond design.

BROWNING RIFLES

**MODEL BL-22 LEVER ACTION RIFLE
GRADE I $219.95**

**MODEL BL-22 LEVER ACTION RIFLE
GRADE II $249.95**

BL-22 SPECIFICATIONS

ACTION — Short throw lever action. Lever travels through an arc of only 33 degrees and carries the trigger with it, preventing finger pinch between lever and trigger on the upward swing. The lever cycle ejects the fired shell, cocks the hammer, and feeds a fresh round into the chamber.

MAGAZINE — Rifle is designed to handle 22 caliber ammunition *in any combination* from tubular magazine. Magazine capacity is 15 Long Rifles, 17 Longs, and 22 Shorts. The positive magazine latch opens and closes easily from any position.

SAFETY — A unique disconnect system prevents firing until the lever and breech are fully closed and pressure is released from and reapplied to the trigger. An inertia firing pin and an exposed hammer with a half-cock position are other safety features.

RECEIVER — Forged and milled steel. Grooved. All parts are machine finished and hand fitted.

TRIGGER — Clean and crisp without creep. Average pull 5 pounds. Trigger gold-plated on Grade II model.

STOCK AND FOREARM — Forearm and straight grip butt stock are shaped from select, polished walnut. Hand checkered on Grade II model. Stock dimensions:

Length of Pull......................13½"
Drop at Comb.....................1⅝"
Drop at Heel.........................2¼"

SIGHTS — Precision, adjustable folding leaf rear sight. Raised bead front sight.

SCOPES — Grooved receiver will accept the Browning 22 riflescope (Model 1217) and two-piece ring mount (Model 9417) as well as most other groove or tip-off type mounts or receiver sights.

ENGRAVING — Grade II receiver and trigger guard are hand-engraved with tasteful scroll designs.

BARREL — Recessed muzzle. Barrel length: 20 inches.

OVERALL LENGTH — 36¾ inches.

WEIGHT — 5 pounds.

**BLR RIFLE
243 Winchester, 308 Winchester & 358 Winchester
$364.95**

BLR SPECIFICATIONS

CALIBERS: 243 Win., 308 Win. and 358 Win.

APPROXIMATE WEIGHT: 6 pounds, 15 ounces.

OVERALL LENGTH: 39¾ inches.

ACTION: Lever action with rotating head, multiple lug breech bolt with recessed bolt face. Side ejection.

BARREL: Individually machined from forged, heat treated chrome-moly steel. Length: 20 inches. Crowned muzzle. Rifling: 243 Win.—one turn in 10 inches. 308 and 358 Win.—one turn in 12 inches.

MAGAZINE: Detachable, 4-round capacity.

TRIGGER: Wide, grooved finger piece. Short crisp pull of 4½ pounds. Travels with lever.

RECEIVER: Non-glare top. Drilled and tapped to accept most top scope mounts. Forged and milled steel. All parts are machine-finished, and hand-fitted. Surface deeply polished.

SIGHTS: Low profile, square notch, screw adjustable rear sight. Gold bead on a hooded raised ramp front sight. Sight radius: 17¾ inches.

SAFETY: Exposed, 3-position hammer. Trigger disconnect system. Inertia firing pin.

STOCK AND FOREARM: Select walnut with tough oil finish and sure-grip checkering, contoured for use with either open sights or scope. Straight grip stock. Deluxe recoil pad installed.

Length of pull ....13¾ inches
Drop at comb ....1¾ inches
Drop at heel ....2⅜ inches

ACCESSORIES: Extra magazines are available as well as sling swivel attachment for forearm bolt and butt-stock eyelet for sling mounting..**$19.75**

BROWNING AUTOMATIC RIFLES

Browning Arms Company has added a center fire (semi) Rifle to their line of sporting arms. Called simply the Browning Automatic Rifle, it is gas operated, and has the strong, precision locking principle of a bolt action rifle. It weighs less than 7⅜ pounds and is offered in 30-06 Sprg., 308 Win., 270 Win., 243 Win., 7mm Rem. Mag. and 300 Win. Mag. calibers.

The Browning Automatic is a magazine-fed rifle with a new "trap door" design, box type magazine that is attached to the hinged floor plate. The magazine may be loaded while attached to the gun or is easily detached for conventional loading.

The receiver is machined from a solid bar of steel and is completely free of exposed screws, pins or holes, except provisions for scope mountings. A multiple head breech bolt locks directly into the barrel, engaging 7 sturdy lugs.

The stock and forearm are of select French walnut, sharply checkered and hand finished. Sights consist of: a gold bead on a hooded ramp front sight, and a folding leaf-type rear sight adjustable for windage and elevation.

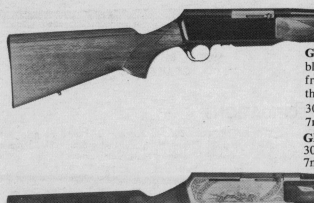

GRADE I—Quiet Browning quality. The receiver is deeply blued and left smooth as silk. Stock and forearm are carved from dense-grained French walnut, sharply checkered on the pistol grip and forearm for a good steady hold.

30/06 Sprg., .270 Win., .308 Win. & 243 Win.	**$539.95**
7mm Rem. Mag. & 300 Win. Mag.	**594.95**

GRADE III—Features beautiful scrollwork.

30/06 Sprg., 270 Win., 308 Win. & 243 Win.	**$1000.00**
7mm Rem. Mag. & 300 Win. Mag.	**1060.00**

GRADE IV—The ultimate big-game rifle. The Grade IV's receiver is grayed steel with intricate hand-engraved game scenes. Standard calibers have running deer on one side, running antelope on the other. Magnum calibers have moose on one side, elk on the other. The floor plate and trigger guard are covered with intricate hand engraving too.

The stock on this rifle is the very finest, highly figured French walnut. Flawless hand-checkering covers the pistol grip and forearm, bordered by ornate hand carving. As a final touch, the trigger is gold-plated.

30/06 Sprg., .270 Win., 308 Win. & 243 Win.	**$1900.00**
7mm Rem. Mag. & 300 Win. Mag.	**1960.00**

Extra Magazines

Grade I	**$19.75**
Grade III	**27.75**
Grade IV	**27.75**

BAR-22 22 Caliber Automatic Rifle

grade I	**$229.95**

BPR-22 22 Caliber Pump Rimfire Rifle

grade I	22 Long Rifle	**$229.95**
grade I	22 Magnum	**249.95**
grade II	22 Magnum	**349.95**

BAR-22 SPECIFICATIONS

MODELS: 22 Long Rifle, Grade I.

ACTION: Self-loading and ejecting. Shoots as rapidly as trigger is pulled. Side ejection.

BARREL: Recessed muzzle — 20¼".

OVERALL LENGTH: 38¼".

MAGAZINE: Tubular. Latch closes from any position.

MAGAZINE CAPACITY: 22 Long Rifle — 15.

STOCK: French walnut. Pistol grip and forearm cut checkering.

STOCK DIMENSIONS: Length of pull 13¾". Drop at comb 1½". Drop at heel 2¼".

SAFETY: Cross-bolt safety on rear of trigger guard.

SIGHTS: Front: Gold bead. Rear: Folding leaf with calibrated adjustments.

SIGHT RADIUS: 16".

APPROXIMATE WEIGHT: 6 lbs. 4 oz.

TRIGGER: Black anodized. Average pull 5 lbs.

RECOMMENDED SCOPE & MOUNTS: 4x 22 rifle scope. Receiver grooved to accept scope mount base.

BPR-22 SPECIFICATIONS

MODELS: BPR-22, Grade I only. BPR-22 Magnum, Grade I only.

ACTION: Short, positive pump stroke. Finger must be released and re-applied to trigger at end of stroke. Side ejection.

BARREL: Recessed muzzle, both models: 20¼".

OVERALL LENGTH: Both Models: 38¼".

MAGAZINE: Tubular. Latch closes from any position.

MAGAZINE CAPACITY: BPR-22—22 Long Rifle: 15. BPR-22 Magnum—22 Magnum: 11.

STOCK: French walnut. Pistol grip and forearm—cut checkering.

STOCK DIMENSIONS: Length of pull 13¾". Drop at comb 1½". Drop at heel 2¼".

SAFETY: Cross bolt safety on rear of trigger guard.

SIGHTS: Front: Gold bead. Rear: Folding leaf with calibrated adjustments.

SIGHT RADIUS: 16".

APPROXIMATE WEIGHT: 6 lbs. 4 oz.

TRIGGER: Black anodized. Average pull 5 lbs.

RECOMMENDED SCOPE AND MOUNTS: 4x 22 Riflescope. Receiver grooved to accept scope mount base.

BROWNING RIFLES

BBR BOLT ACTION RIFLE
Calibers — 25-06 Rem., 270 Win., 30-06
Sprg., 7mm Rem. Mag., 300 Win. Mag.
$429.95

SPECIFICATIONS:

ACTION: Short throw bolt of 60-degrees. The large diameter bolt and fluted surface reduce wobble and friction. The rotary bolt head has 9 engaging locking lugs and a recessed bolt face. Plunger-type ejector.

MAGAZINE: Detachable. Depress the magazine latch and the hinged floorplate swings down. The magazine can be removed from the floorplate for reloading or safety reasons.

TRIGGER: Adjustable within the average range of 3 to 6 pounds. Also grooved to provide sure finger control.

STOCK AND FOREARM: Anti-warp inlays of structural aluminum ⅛″ thick and 8″ long in the barrel channel.

Stock is select grade American walnut cut to the lines of a Monte Carlo sporter with a full pistol grip and high cheek piece. Stock dimensions:

Length of Pull ....13⅜″
Drop at Comb .... 1⅝″
Drop at Heel .... 2⅛″

SCOPES: Closed. Clean tapered barrel. Receiver is drilled and tapped for a scope mount..

BARREL: Hammer forged rifling where a precision machined mandrel is inserted into the bore. The mandrel is a reproduction of the rifling in reverse. As hammer forces are applied to the exterior of the barrel, the barrel is actually molded around the mandrel to produce flawless rifling and to guarantee a straight bore. 24″ long.

OVERALL LENGTH: 44½″ **WEIGHT:** 8 pounds.

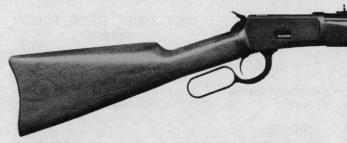

BROWNING 92
44 Rem. Magnum Grade I **$299.95**

TRIGGER: Gold plated. Trigger pull approximately 5½ lbs.

MAGAZINE: Tubular. Loading port in right side of receiver. Magazine capacity 11 rounds.

STOCK AND FOREARM: Seasoned French walnut with high gloss finish. Straight grip stock and classic forearm style. Steel modified crescent butt plate.

Length of pull—12¾″
Drop at comb—2″
Drop at heel—2⅞″

OVERALL LENGTH: 37½″
APPROXIMATE WEIGHT: 5½ lbs.
HAND ENGRAVED RECEIVER: Hand engraved scrollwork on both receiver sides.

SPECIFICATIONS:

ACTION: Lever operated with double verticle locks. Exposed 3 position hammer with half cock position. Top ejection.

RECEIVER: Forged and milled from high strength steel.

BARRELS: Machined from forged, heat-treated billets of steel. Chambered and rifled for 44 Rem. Magnum caliber. Rifling twist 1 turn in 38″. Barrel length 20″.

SIGHTS: Classic cloverleaf rear with notched elevation ramp. Steel post front. Sight radius 16⅝″.

CHARTER AR-7 EXPLORER RIFLE

**MODEL 9220
EXPLORER RIFLE**
(22 Long Rifle Caliber)
$98.00

The Explorer rifle is a semiautomatic 22 Long Rifle caliber with a 16″ barrel and is fitted with a plastic stock which floats if accidentally dropped in water. For transport, the Explorer compacts into its own stock, measuring 16½″ overall. The rear sight is a hooded peep with the aperture adjustable for elevation changes. Windage may be accomplished by moving the front sight back and forth.

CALIBER: 22 Long Rifle. **ACTION:** Semiautomatic. **LOAD:** Detachable box, magazine fed. **SIGHTS:** Square blade front, adjusting rear peep. **CAPACITY:** 8 rounds. **BARREL:** High test alloy with rifled steel liner. **STOCK:** Full pistol grip, recessed to carry barrel and action. **WEIGHT:** 2¾ pounds. **OVERALL LENGTH:** 34½″. **LENGTH STOWED:** 16½″.

COLT HIGH POWER RIFLES

COLT SAUER SPORTING RIFLE
standard calibers $ 996.95
magnum calibers $1030.50

Caliber: 25-06, 270, 30-06, 7mm Rem. Mag., 300 Win. Mag., 300 Weatherby Mag.
Capacity: 3 round with detachable magazines
Barrel length(s): 24"
Weight: Standard 8 lb.; mag. 8 lbs. 10 oz.
Overall length: 43 ¾"
Sights: Drilled and tapped for scope mounts

Action: Bolt action
Safety: Tang-type safety that mechanically locks the sear
Stock: American walnut, cast-off Monte Carlo design with cheek piece; fore-end tip and pistol-grip cap are rosewood with white line spacers, hand checkering and black recoil pad
Features: Unique barrel/receiver union, non-rotating bolt with 3 internal articulating locking lugs.

COLT SAUER SHORT ACTION
$996.95

Caliber:	22-250, 243 and 308 (7.62mm NATO)
Barrel Length:	24"
Overall Length:	43 ¾"
Barrel Type:	Krupp Special Steel, hammer forged
Stock:	American walnut, Monte Carlo cheek piece with rosewood fore-end tip and pistol grip cap
Weight (empty):	7 lbs. 8 oz.
Safety:	Tang
Sights:	Drilled and tapped for scope mounts

Magazine Capacity: 3 rounds in detachable magazine
Finish: Colt Blue with polyurethane

FEATURES:
Now the Colt Sauer Rifle is available in 22-250, 243 and 308. Features the same revolutionary non-rotating bolt with three large locking lugs. American walnut stock with high-gloss finish, 18-line-per-inch checkering, rosewood forend tip and grip cap, black recoil pad. Cocking indicator, loaded chamber indicator, and Safety-on bolt opening capability.

COLT SAUER GRAND AFRICAN
$1108.95

Caliber: 458 Win. Mag. **Capacity:** 3 rounds with detachable magazines. **Barrel length(s):** 24" round tapered. **Weight:** 10 lbs. without sights. **Overall length:** 44½". **Sights:** Hooded ramp style front; fully adjustable rear. **Action:** Bolt action. **Safety:** Tang type that mechanically locks the sear.

COLT SAUER GRAND ALASKAN
$1058.50

Caliber: 375 H&H. **Capacity:** 3 rounds with detachable magazine. **Barrel length:** 24". **Weight:** 8 lbs. 10 oz. **Overall length:** 43 ¾". **Sights:** Drilled and tapped for scope mounts.

Stock: Solid African bubinga wood, cast-off Monte Carlo design with cheek piece, contrasting rosewood, forend tip and pistol-grip cap with white line spacers, and checkering on the forend and pistol grip. **Features:** Unique barrel/receiver union, non-rotating bolt with 3 internal articulating locking lugs.

Safety: Tang. **Stock:** American walnut, Monte Carlo cheek piece with rosewood fore-end tip and pistol grip cap and black recoil pad.

COLT RIFLES

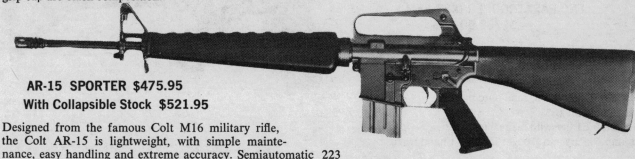

COLT SAUER DRILLING
THREE-BARREL SHOTGUN-RIFLE
$3355.00

The Colt Sauer Drilling is a three-barrel combination side-by-side 12-gauge shotgun available in 30-06 Springfield or 243 calibers. This addition to the Colt Sauer line is 41¾-inches overall. Its 25-inch barrels are mounted on a selected, oil-finish, American walnut stock. The barrels are made from fine steel, finished in traditional Colt Blue, as are other metal parts, with an engraved rib that reduces glare and a brass-bead front sight. The left shotgun barrel is bored with modified choke and the right barrel with full choke. The barrel has four-groove rifling with a right hand twist. A thumb activated device on the tang raises or lowers the rear sight for firing of the rifle barrel. A system of double triggers fires the two shotgun and one rifle barrels. The safety is located on the left side of the stock for convenient thumb operation. When the safety button is moved, a red dot indicates "fire" position. Checkering on the stock at forend and pistol grip is 16-lines per inch. Each Colt Sauer Drilling is individually engraved at the receiver with game scenes. The recoil pad and pistol grip cap are black composition.

AR-15 SPORTER $475.95
With Collapsible Stock $521.95

Designed from the famous Colt M16 military rifle, the Colt AR-15 is lightweight, with simple maintenance, easy handling and extreme accuracy. Semiautomatic 223 (5.56 mm) with 5-round magazine capacity. Front sight post adjustable for elevation. Quick flip rear sight assembly with short-range and long-range tangs, adjustable for windage. Weight: 7½ lbs. Overall Length: 39" Barrel Length: 20"; with collapsible stock 16"

FABRIQUE NATIONALE SEMI-AUTOMATIC RIFLES

F.N.-LAR COMPETITION (308 MATCH)
$1975.00

The F.N.-LAR Competition 308 Win. Match gas-operated semi-automatic has a rifled bore with 4-lands and grooves, plus right-hand twist, one turn in 12 inches. The rear sight is adjustable from 200 to 600 yards in 100 yard increments. Sight radius is 21¾". Synthetic stock with ventilated forend. **Weight** (without magazine): 9 lbs. 7 oz. **Overall Length:** 44½". **Barrel Length:** 21" (24½" with flash hider).

F.N.-LAR PARATROOPER (308 MATCH)
$2088.00

FABRIQUE NATIONALE
SEMI-AUTOMATIC RIFLES

F.N.-LAR H.B. (Heavy Barrel) (308 MATCH)
With wood stock & metal bipod $2617.00
With synthetic stock $2418.00

FNC PARATROOPER (223 REM.)
$1798.00

SPECIFICATIONS:
Caliber: 223 Rem. (5.56mm)
Capacity: 30-round magazine
Action: Gas-operated, semi-automatic
Barrel Length: 18"
Weight: 9.61 lbs. with magazine
Rifling: 6 lands and grooves with right-hand twist

RENATO GAMBA RIFLES

THE MUSTANG
$10,519.20

A break-open, single barrel rifle with side locks of the Holland & Holland type and fitted with set trigger. The barrel is of monoblock design from Boehler Blitz steel, with right-handed rifling. The frame is made of heat-treated high-alloy steel, and the locking is of Triple Greener design, equipped with a double safety. Stock and forend are of walnut with hand-checkering. Stock has a pistol grip and cheekpiece. Forend is of the Schnabel style. The Mustang is hand engraved and available in a choice of 222 Rem., 243 Win., 270 Win. and 30-06 calibers. Standard Model supplied with Zeiss scope, claw mounts and fitted leather case.

THE SAFARI 77
$9134.60

The Safari, an over-and-under big-game rifle, has a monoblock barrel of steel, pearl front-sight on checkered anti-reflecting ramp, and sight notch. It is made with clockwise rifling. The frame is of high-resistance heat-treated steel. Locking is by a three-lug Greener system side locks. Engraving depicts hunting scenes in relief, signed by the artist. Available in 7 x 65R, 375 H&H Mag. and 458 Win. Mag. calibers.

H&R COMMEMORATIVE CARBINES

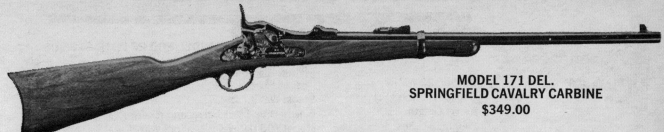

MODEL 171 DEL.
SPRINGFIELD CAVALRY CARBINE
$349.00

Caliber: 45-70 GOVT.
Stock: American walnut with saddle ring and bridle
Action: Trap door, single shot
Weight: 7 lbs.
Barrel Length: 22"
Overall Length: 41"
Sights: Blade front sight; original military-style rear
Metal Finish: Blue-black and color cased. Engraved action.

MODEL 174
LITTLE BIG HORN COMMEMORATIVE
SPRINGFIELD CARBINE
$349.00

Caliber: 45-70 GOVT.
Stock: American Walnut with metal grip adapter
Action: Trap door, single shot
Barrel Length: 22"

Sights: Tang mounted aperture sight adjustable for windage and elevation. Blade front sight.
Weight: 7 lbs. 8 oz.
Overall Length: 41"
Metal Finish: Barrel—Blue-Black
Action—Color case hardened

H&R CENTERFIRE RIFLES

BOLT-ACTION MODEL 300
$450.00

Caliber: 22-250 Rem., 243 Win., 25-06 Rem., 270 Win., 30-06, 308 Win., 7mm Rem. Mag., 300 Win. Mag.
Capacity: 7mm Rem., Mag. and 300 Win. Mag. calibers have 3 round magazine. All others have 5 round magazine.
Stock: One piece genuine American walnut stock with roll-over cheek piece, and pistol grip. Hand checkered, contrasting wood on forearm tip and pistol grip cap. Rifle recoil pad.
Action: Mauser type bolt action with hinged floor plate and adjustable trigger.

Barrel Length: 22" tapered.
Weight: 7¾ lbs.
Sights: Fully adjustable rear sight drilled and tapped for scope mounts and receiver sight. Gold bead front sight grooved for hood.
Overall Length: 42½"
Safety: Sliding safety.
Also Available: Model 301 carbine with full length Mannlicher style stock and 18 inch barrel. Available in most of the above calibers. **$495.00**

H & R RIMFIRE RIFLES

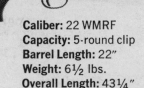

MODEL 700 22 WMR $185.00

Caliber: 22 WMRF
Capacity: 5-round clip
Barrel Length: 22"
Weight: 6½ lbs.
Overall Length: 43¼"

Sights: Blade front; folding leaf rear; drilled and tapped for scope bases
Stock: Walnut stock
Finish: Blue-black barrel and receiver
Model 700 Deluxe, 22 caliber WMRF with 22" barrel $295.00

MODEL 750 $74.50

Caliber: 22 long rifle; standard and high velocity cartridge
Capacity: Single shot
Weight: 5 lbs.
Barrel Length: 22" tapered. **Overall Length:** 39"

Stock: Walnut-finished American hardwood. Hard rubber buttplate, white liner
Action: Self-cocking bolt action
Safety: Side thumb lever
Sights: Blade front; open rear sight with elevator; grooved for tip-off scope mounts

MODEL 865 $84.50

Caliber: 22 long rifle; standard and high velocity cartridge
Capacity: 5-round magazine
Weight: 5 lbs.
Barrel Length: 22" tapered. **Overall Length:** 39"
Stock: Walnut-finished American hardwood. Hard rubber

buttplate, white liner
Action: Self-cocking bolt action
Safety: Side thumb level
Sights: Blade front; open rear sight with elevator; grooved for tip-off scope mounts

MODEL 5200 MATCH $325.00

Caliber: 22 long rifle match
Action: Turn bolt, single shot
Weight: 11 lbs.
Barrel Length: 28". **Overall Length:** 46"

Stock: American walnut, semi-gloss finish
Sights: None supplied with rifle. Receiver drilled and tapped for receiver sight. Barrel drilled and tapped for front sight. Scope bases supplied.
Metal Finish: Polished blue-black

H & R SINGLE-SHOT RIFLES

MODEL 155
44 Rem. Mag., 45-70 Govt.
$110.00

SPECIFICATIONS:

Caliber: 44 Rem. Mag., 45-70 Govt.
Barrel length(s): 44 Rem. Mag., 24"; 45-70 Govt., 24", 28"
Weight: 44 Rem. Mag., 7 lbs.; 45-70 Govt., 7 lbs., 7½ lbs.

Overall length: 44 Rem. Mag., 39"; 45-70 Govt., 39", 43"
Sights: Blade front with ramp; folding leaf rear
Action: Single shot
Stock: Walnut–finished hardwood with hard-rubber butt plate
Finish: Blue-black barrel with color-cased frame
Accessories: Brass cleaning rod

H&R SINGLE-SHOT RIFLES

MODEL 157
30-30 Win., 22 Hornet
22 WMRF $110.00

Caliber: 30-30 Win., 22 Hornet, 22 WMRF
Barrel length(s): 22"
Weight: 6¼ lbs.
Overall length: 37"

Sights: Blade front; folding leaf rear; drilled and tapped for scope bases
Action: Single shot
Stock: Walnut-finished hardwood with hard-rubber butt plate
Finish: Blue-black barrel with color-cased frame
Accessories: Swivels front and rear

MODEL 158
30-30 Win. & 22 Hornet
$89.50

Caliber: 30-30 Win., 22 Hornet
Barrel length(s): 22"
Weight: 6 lbs.
Overall length: 37"

Sights: Blade front with ramp; folding leaf rear; drilled and tapped for scope bases
Action: Single shot
Stock: Walnut finished hardwood with a hard-rubber butt plate
Finish: Blue-black barrel with color case-hardened frame

MODEL 173
SPRINGFIELD OFFICER'S MODEL
$375.00

Caliber: 45-70 Govt.
Barrel length(s): 26"
Weight: 8 lbs.
Overall length: 45"

Sights: Blade front; tang mounted aperature rear
Action: Trap door, single shot
Stock: American walnut with hand checkering
Finish: Blue-black; color cased receiver

MODEL 058 COMBO GUN
30-30 Win. and 22 Hornet
$110.00

Gauge: 20 gauge modified choke shotgun
Barrel length(s): 26" mod. Rifle 22"
Weight: 5¼ lbs., 6 lbs. with rifle barrel
Overall length: Shotgun barrel, 41½"; rifle barrel, 37½"
Sights: Front bead on shotgun barrel; blade front, folding leaf rear on rifle barrel
Action: Single shot
Stock: Walnut–finished hardwood with hard-rubber butt plate
Finish: Blue-black; color cased frame
Accessories: 30-30 Win. or 22 Hornet 22" barrels

HECKLER & KOCH
SEMI-AUTOMATIC RIFLES

HK93 SEMI-AUTOMATIC RIFLES
223 Caliber

HK93 SPECIFICATIONS:	A-2	A-3
Length of rifle:	37.0 in.	29.92 in.
Length of barrel:	16.14 in.	16.14 in.
Sight radius:	19.09 in.	19.09 in.
Weight of rifle without magazine:	7.94 lbs.	8.60 lbs.
Weight of 40 round magazine, empty	11 oz.	

Weight of 25 round magazine, empty	8.84 oz.
Weight of 5 round magazine, empty	2.11 oz.
Sight adjustments	200, 300, 400 m and V-notch rear
Telescopic sight mount	HK clamp mount

Model HK93 (w/25-round magazine & sling) **$638.00**
With retractable metal stock **812.00**

HK91 SEMI-AUTOMATIC RIFLES
308 Caliber

HK91 SPECIFICATIONS:	A-2	A-3
Length of rifle:	40.35 in.	33.07 in.
Length of barrel:	17.71 in.	17.71 in.
Sight radius:	22.44 in.	22.44 in.
Weight of rifle without magazine:	9.70 lbs.	10.56 lbs.
Weight of 20 round magazine, empty	9.88 oz.	

Weight of 5 round magazine, empty	3.17 oz.
Sight adjustments	200, 300, 400 m and V-notch rear
Telescopic sight mount	HK clamp mount

Model HK91 (w/20-round magazine & sling) **$656.00**
With retractable metal stock **830.00**

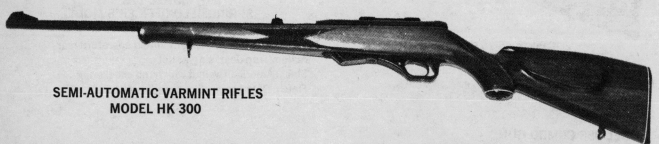

SEMI-AUTOMATIC VARMINT RIFLES
MODEL HK 300

The Model HK 300 features a European walnut checkered stock. All metal parts are finished in a high luster custom blue. The receiver is fitted with special bases for a HK 05 quick snap-on clamp mount with 1″ rings that will fit all standard scopes. The positive locking action of the HK 05 provides for instant scope mounting with no change in zero, even after hundreds of repetitions. The rifle has a V-notch rear sight, adjustable for windage, and a front sight adjustable for elevation. Scope mounts are available as an additional accessory.
Caliber: 22 Winchester Magnum.
Weight: 5.7 lbs.

Barrel: Hammer forged, polygonal profile.
Overall length: 39.4″.
Magazine: Box type, 5 and 15 rounds capacity.
Sights: V-notch rear, adjustable for windage; post front, adjustable for elevation.
Trigger: Single stage, 3½ lb. pull.
Action: Straight blow-back inertia bolt.
Stock: Top-grade European walnut, Monte Carlo style with cheek rest, checkered pistol grip and forearm.
Accessories: HK 05 clamp mount with 1″ rings to fit most U.S. made telescopic sights **$420.00**

HECKLER & KOCH RIFLES

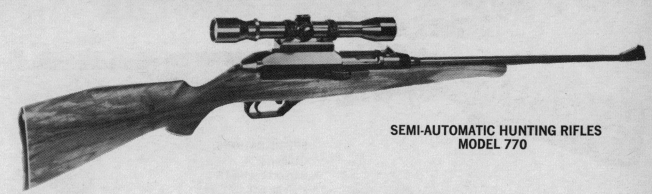

**SEMI-AUTOMATIC HUNTING RIFLES
MODEL 770**

SPECIFICATIONS:
Caliber: 308 Win., 243 Win.
Weight: (308 cal.) 8 lbs.
Barrel: Hammer forged, standard or polygonal profile.
Overall Length: 44.5″
Magazine: 3 and 10 rounds
Sights: V-notch rear, adjustable for windage; post front, adjustable for elevation

Trigger: Single stage
Action: Delayed Roller locked
Stock: European walnut with Monte Carlo cheek rest

Model 770 (308 cal. w/scope and 3-round
  magazine) **$640.00**
Model 940 same as **Model 770**,
  except is 30-06 caliber **$770.00**

IVER JOHNSON RIFLES

**PLAINFIELD MODEL M-1 CARBINES
PM 30P $257.60**

SPECIFICATIONS:
Caliber: 30
Weight: 5½ lbs.
Magazine: 15 and 30 rounds
Barrel Lengths: 12″ and 18″
Sights: Adjustable
Finish: Blue
Stock: Telescoping American walnut permits packing in
  backpack or saddlebag for campers and hunters
PM 30G & PM 30S, new military and military sporter
  versions of PM 30P **$221.76**

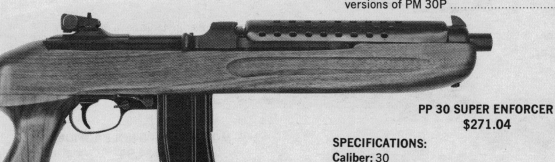

**PP 30 SUPER ENFORCER
$271.04**

SPECIFICATIONS:
Caliber: 30
Weight: 4 lbs.
Magazine: 15 and 30 rounds
Action: Based on carbine action
Barrel Length: 9½″
Sights: Adjustable
Stock: American walnut

IVER JOHNSON RIFLES

SPITFIRE $257.60

SPECIFICATIONS:
Caliber: 224
Barrel Length: 18"
Weight: 5 lbs.
Safety: Rotary blocks trigger
Stock: American hardwood

KASSNAR RIFLES

MODEL M-1500 BOLT ACTION
$129.95

SPECIFICATIONS:
Caliber: 22 mag., 22 MRF
Barrel: Tapered sporter-weight barrel
Weight: 6½ lbs.
Sights: Open sight sporter-type

Action: Bolt
Safety: Positive sliding thumb safety
Stock: Nato wood, with Monte Carlo comb. Receiver grooved for tip-off scope mount.

MODEL M-16 SEMI-AUTOMATIC
$129.95

SPECIFICATIONS:
Caliber: 22 L.R.
Barrel Length: 19"
Weight: 6 lbs. 12 oz.

Sights: Ramp front; adjustable peep rear sight
Stock: Black painted mahogany
Features: Sling and sling swivels included

MODEL M-1400 BOLT ACTION
$124.95

SPECIFICATIONS:
Caliber: 22 L.R.
Barrel: Tapered sporter weight barrel
Weight: 6 lbs.
Sights: Hooded ramp front sight; open rear sporter-type
Action: Bolt

Safety: Positive sliding thumb safety
Stock: Hand-checkered nato wood, with Monte Carlo comb. Receiver grooved for tip-off scope mount.

KASSNAR RIFLES

MODEL M-20S SEMI-AUTOMATIC
$99.95

Weight: 5 lbs., 14 oz.
Sights: Open sights sporter-type
Safety: Positive sliding thumb safety
Stock: Nato wood, receiver grooved for tip-off scope mount. Hand checkered.

SPECIFICATIONS:
Caliber: 22 L.R.
Capacity: 15-round clip
Barrel Length(s): 19½"

KASSNAR/PARKER-HALE RIFLES

PARKER-HALE SUPER

SPECIFICATIONS:
Caliber: 22/250, 243, 6mm, 25/06, 270, 30/06, 308, 7mm Mag., 300 Mag.
Capacity: 5 shot, magnum 4 shot
Barrel Length(s): 24"
Overall Length: 45"
Sights: Hooded bead front sight; folding adjustable rear sight
Action: Bolt action. Receiver drilled and tapped for standard scope mounts
Safety: Slide thumb safety, locks trigger, bolt and sear
Stock: Two-tone walnut stock with a rollover Monte Carlo cheek piece, skip-line checkering and rosewood at forend and grip cap
Standard calibers **$369.95**
Magnum calibers **374.95**

PARKER-HALE VARMINT

SPECIFICATIONS:
Caliber: 22/250, 243, 6mm, 25/06
Capacity: 5 shot
Barrel Length(s): 24"
Overall Length: 45"
Action: Glass-bedded, bolt action. Receiver drilled and tapped for standard scope mounts
Safety: Slide thumb safety, locks trigger, bolt and sear
Stock: Two-tone European walnut stock has high comb with rollover cheek piece, skip checkering, Wundhammer grip and ventilated recoil pad **$374.95**

KASSNAR/PARKER-HALE MIDLAND RIFLE

SPECIFICATIONS:
Caliber: 243, 270, 30/06, 308
Capacity: 4 shot

Barrel Length: 24"
Overall Length: 45"
Sights: Bead front sight, folding adjustable rear sight
Action: Long Mauser-type non-rotating claw extractor and one-piece forged construction with an extra safety lug
Safety: Tang safety catch which locks sear and trigger
Stock: Hand-checkered seasoned walnut
Price: (including 1-inch scope mounts, base blocks and fixing screws) **$249.95**

KIMBER RIFLES

KIMBER MODEL 82 CLASSIC

KIMBER MODEL 82

The Model 82 bolt-action, 22-caliber rifle is available in two styles, the Classic version with a satin sheen finish and plain buttstock or the Cascade model with Monte Carlo comb and cheekpiece. Both styles feature hand-checkered walnut stock, checkered steel buttplate, polished steel pistol grip and a one-piece trigger guard and floorplate. The trigger is adjustable for weight of pull, overtravel and depth of sear engagement. Accidental readjustment after setting is avoided because of two adjustment lock screws within the action housing.

The LR Sporter is available with a 4- or 10-shot magazine; the Magnum Sporter, available with a 4-shot magazine only. The barrel is 22″ and has 6-groove, right-hand twist rifling with a pitch of one turn in 16″. Special Kimber one-inch scope mount rings, machined from steel to fit the dove-tailed receiver, are available in two heights. Also offered are open iron sights, hooded ramp front sight with bead and adjustable folding leaf rear sight.

Model 82 Classic, 22 LR Sporter, plain barrel, without sights **$430.00**
Model 82 Cascade, 22 LR Sporter, plain barrel, without sights **450.00**
Model 82 Classic, 22 Magnum Sporter, plain barrel, without sights **$465.00**
Model 82 Cascade, 22 Magnum Sporter, plain barrel, without sights **480.00**

KLEINGUENTHER RIFLES

K-15 INSTA-FIRE IMPROVED $975.00

Available in Calibers:
243; 25-06; 270, 7X57; 30-06; 308 Win.; 308 Norma; 300 Win. Mag.; 7mm Reg. Mag.; 375 H and H Mag.; 270 Weatherby Mag.; 300 Weatherby Mag.; 257 Weatherby Mag.

SHORTEST IGNITION TIME: Striker travels 158 thousandths of one inch only . . . The extremely light striker is accelerated by a powerful striker spring . . . A patented two cocking cam design enables a very light and smooth cocking of the striker assembly . . . Two-piece firing pin.
CLIP FEATURE: Also will feed from top.
3 LOCKING LUGS: With large contact area as found on designs with multiple locking lugs involved . . . Providing perfect fit . . . A feature which can not be duplicated by designs with multiple lugs . . . also Stellite locking insert.
60 DEGREE BOLT LIFT ONLY: For fast reloading.
SAFETY: Located on right hand side . . . locking trigger and sear . . . Most convenient location . . . Also locks bolt . . . Combined with cocking indicator.
FINE ADJUSTABLE CRISP TRIGGER: 2 lbs. — 7 lbs. . . . Two major moving parts only.
STOCKS: American & European Walnut Monte-Carlo stock with 1″ recoil pad . . . Rosewood fore-end with white spacer . . . Rosewood pistol grip cap . . . 20 line hand checkering . . . Quick detachable swivels . . . Bedded with three major contact points to metal . . . Barrel has one contact area, other than that it is free floating . . . High luster finish or full oil finish . . . Choice of wood color, blond thru dark. Available in right or left hand stocks . . . AAA grade stocks available as an option.
SPECIFICATIONS: Barrel length — Standard-24″, Magnum-26″ . . . Trigger pull weight — Micro-adjustable between 2-7 lbs. . . . Magazine capacity — Standard-5 cartridges, Magnum-3 cartridges . . . Trigger pull lengths — 14⅜″. Overall length — Standard 44⅞″, Magnum 46⅞″ . . . Overall weight 7 lbs. 8 to 10 oz.
RECEIVER DRILLED AND TAPPED FOR FOLLOWING SCOPE MOUNTS: Buehler two-piece and one-piece base mounts, Redfield one-piece base mount, Conetrol mount . . . Three different Kleinguenther two-piece base mounts and Quick Detachable.
QUALITY CONTROL — WARRANTY WORK: Quality control is performed on each gun prior to shipment to our nationwide customers. An ample supply of spare parts is always in inventory. Warranty service is performed by Kleinguenther of Seguin in their modern facilities by well trained gunsmiths.
PROOF TEST: Performed in accordance to International Standards.
OPTIONS: Iron sights . . . Set trigger . . . Engravings, wood carvings, wood inlays, etc.

MARLIN LEVER-ACTION CARBINES

MARLIN 444S $250.95

Caliber: .444 Marlin

Capacity: 4-shot tubular magazine

Action: Lever-action; solid top receiver; side ejection; gold plated steel trigger; deeply blued metal surfaces; receiver top sand-blasted to prevent glare.

Stock: Two-piece genuine American black walnut with fluted comb; rubber rifle butt pad; full pistol grip; white butt plate and pistol grip spacers; tough Mar-Shield® finish; quick detachable sling swivels and leather carrying strap.

Weight: 7½ lbs.

Barrel: 22″ with Micro-Groove® rifling (12 grooves)

Sights: Adjustable folding semi-buckhorn rear, hooded-ramp front sight with brass bead and Wide-Scan™ front sight hood; solid top receiver tapped for scope mount or receiver sight; offset hammer spur for scope use—works right or left.

Overall Length: 40½″

MARLIN GOLDEN 39A

MARLIN GOLDEN 39

The Marlin lever action 22 is the oldest (since 1891) shoulder gun still being manufactured. In fact, the only older gun design still being manufactured is Colt's 1873 Single Action Army revolver.

Solid Receiver Top. You can easily mount a scope on your Marlin 39 by screwing on the machined scope adapter base provided. The screw-on base is a neater, more versatile method of mounting a scope on a .22 sporting rifle. The solid top receiver and scope adapter base provide a maximum in eye relief adjustment. If you prefer iron sights, you'll find the 39 receiver clean, flat and sand-blasted to prevent glare.

Exclusive Brass Magazine Tube. A small point perhaps, but not if you've ever had a steel tube rust.

Micro-Groove® Barrel. Marlin's famous rifling system of multi-grooving has consistently produced fine accuracy because the system grips the bullet more securely, minimizes distortion, and provides a better gas seal. And the Model 39 maximizes accuracy with the heaviest barrels available on any lever action .22.

MARLIN GOLDEN 39A $214.95 (less scope)

Caliber .22 Short, Long and Long Rifle

Capacity: Tubular magazine holds 26 Short, 21 Long and 19 Long Rifle Cartridges

Action: Lever action; solid top receiver; side ejection; gold plated steel trigger; one-step take-down; deeply blued metal surfaces; receiver top sand-blasted to prevent glare.

Stock: Two-piece genuine American black walnut with fluted comb; full pistol grip and forend. Blued-steel forend cap; sling swivels; grip cap; white butt plate and pistol-grip spacers; tough Mar-Shield® finish.

Barrel: 24″ with Micro-Groove® rifling (16 grooves)

Sights: Adjustable folding semi-buckhorn rear, ramp front sight with new Wide-Scan™ hood. Solid top receiver tapped for scope mount or receiver sight; scope adapter base; offset hammer spur for scope use—works right or left.

Overall Length: 40″

Weight: About 6½ lbs.

MARLIN GOLDEN 39M $214.95 (less scope)

Caliber: .22 Short, Long and Long Rifle.

Capacity: Tubular magazine holds 21 Short, 16 Long or 15 Long Rifle Cartridges.

Action: Lever action with square finger lever; solid top receiver; side ejection; gold-plated steel trigger; one-step take-down; deeply blued-metal surfaces; receiver top sandblasted to prevent glare.

Stock: Two-piece straight-grip genuine American black walnut with full forend. Blued steel forend cap; sling swivels; white butt plate spacer; tough Mar-Shield® finish.

Barrel: 20″ with Micro-Groove® rifling (16 grooves).

Sights: Adjustable folding semi-buckhorn rear, ramp front sight and new Wide-Scan™ hood. Solid top receiver tapped for scope mount or receiver sight; scope adapter base; offset hammer spur for scope use—works right or left.

Overall Length: 36″

Weight: About 6 lbs.

MARLIN LEVER-ACTION CARBINES

MARLIN 1895S $309.95

Caliber: .45/70 Government
Capacity: 4-shot tubular magazine.
Action: Lever action; solid top receiver; side ejection; gold-plated steel trigger; deeply blued metal surfaces; receiver top sandblasted to prevent glare.
Stock: Two-piece genuine American black walnut with fluted comb; rubber rifle butt pad; full pistol grip; white butt and pistol grip spacers; tough Mar-Shield® finish; quick-detachable sling swivels and leather carrying strap.
Barrel: 22″ with Micro-Groove® rifling (12 grooves); honed chamber.
Sights: Adjustable semi-buckhorn folding rear, ramp front sight with brass bead and Wide-Scan™ hood. Solid top receiver tapped for scope mount or receiver sight; offset hammer spur for scope use; adaptable for right or left hand use.
Overall Length: 40½″
Weight: About 7½ lbs.

MARLIN 1894 $232.95

Caliber: .44 Rem. Magnum
Capacity: 10-shot tubular magazine
Action: Lever action with traditional squared finger lever; solid top receiver; side ejection; gold-plated steel trigger; deeply blued metal surfaces; receiver top sandblasted to prevent glare.
Stock: Two-piece straight-grip genuine American black-walnut butt plate white spacer; blue-steel forend cap; tough Mar-Shield® finish.
Barrel: 20″ with Micro-Groove® rifling (12 grooves). Honed chamber.
Sights: Adjustable semi-buckhorn folding rear, hooded-ramp front sights; solid top receiver tapped for scope mount or receiver sight; offset hammer spur for scope use—works right or left.
Overall Length: 37½″
Weight: About 6 lbs.

MARLIN 1894C 357 MAGNUM $232.95

Caliber: 357 Magnum
Capacity: 9-shot tubular magazine
Action: Lever action; side ejection; solid top receiver; gold-plated steel trigger; deeply blued metal surfaces; receiver top sandblasted to prevent glare.
Stock: Straight-grip two-piece genuine American black walnut with white butt plate spacer.
Barrel: 18½″ with modified Micro-Groove® rifling (12 grooves)
Sights: Adjustable semi-buckhorn folding rear, bead front. Solid top receiver tapped for scope mount or receiver sight; offset hammer spur for scope use—adjustable for right or left hand use.
Overall Length: 36″
Weight: 6 lbs.

MARLIN LEVER-ACTION CARBINES

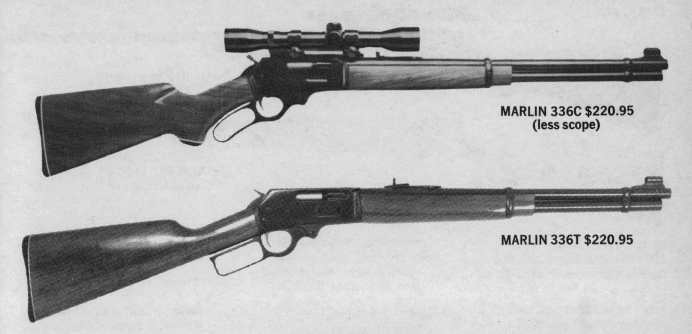

MARLIN 336C $220.95
(less scope)

MARLIN 336T $220.95

The 336C with full pistol grip and the 336T saddle gun both feature side-ejecting, solid top receivers, heat-treated machined steel forgings, American black-walnut stock with Mar-shield® finish, Micro-Groove® rifling, and folding semi-buckhorn rear sights.

Marlin 336C Specifications
Caliber: .30/30 Win., or .35 Rem.
Capacity: 6-shot tubular magazine
Action: Lever action; solid top receiver tapped for scope mount or receiver sight; offset

metal surfaces; receiver top sand-blasted to prevent glare
Stock: Two-piece genuine American black walnut with fluted comb and full pistol grip. Grip cap; white butt plate and pistol-grip spacers; tough Mar-Shield® finish
Barrel: 20" with Micro-Groove® rifling (12 grooves)
Sights: Adjustable semi-buckhorn folding rear, ramp front sight with brass bead and Wide-Scan™ front sight hood. Solid top receiver; side ejection; gold-plated steel trigger; deeply blued

hammer spur for scope use—works right or left.
Overall Length: 38½"
Weight: About 7 lbs.

Marlin 336T Specifications
Same action as 336C, available in .30/30 Win. only, with straight-grip stock, squared finger lever, and 18½" barrel.
Approx. 6¾ lbs.

Forgings. Marlin uses six forged parts in the manufacture of all high rifles: receiver, lever, trigger plate, carrier, hammer, and locking bolt.

MARLIN 375 $250.95

Barrel: 20" with Micro-Groove® rifling (12 grooves).
Sights: Adjustable, folding semi-buckhorn rear, ramp front sight with brass bead and Wide-Scan™ hood. Solid top receiver tapped for scope mount or receiver sight; offset hammer spur for scope use; adaptable for right or left handers.
Overall Length: 38½"
Weight: About 6¾ lbs.

Caliber: 375 Winchester
Capacity: 5-shot tubular magazine
Action: Lever action; side ejection; solid top receiver; gold plated steel trigger;

deeply blued metal surfaces; receiver top sand-blasted to prevent glare.
Stock: Two-piece genuine American black walnut, with fluted comb, full pistol grip and rubber rifle butt pad. Pistol grip cap, white pistol grip and butt spacers. Tough Mar-shield® finish, quick-detachable sling swivels and leather carrying strap.

MARLIN BOLT-ACTION RIFLES

700 SERIES IN 22 CALIBER

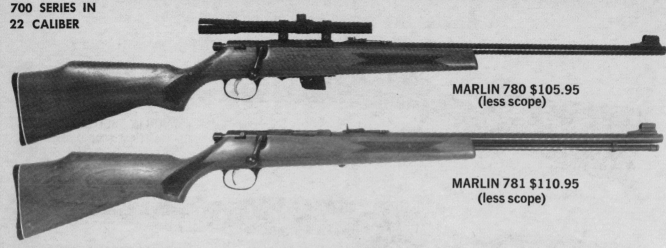

MARLIN 780 $105.95
(less scope)

MARLIN 781 $110.95
(less scope)

Marlin 780 Specifications
Caliber: .22 Short, Long or Long Rifle
Capacity: Clip magazine holds 7 Short, Long or Long Rifle Cartridges.

Action: Bolt action; serrated, anti-glare receiver top; gold-plated steel trigger; positive thumb safety; red cocking indicator.
Stock: Monte Carlo genuine American black walnut with full pistol grip; checkering on pistol grip and underside of fore-end; white butt plate spacer; tough Mar-Shield® finish.
Barrel: 22″ with Micro-Groove® rifling (16 grooves)
Sights: Adjustable folding semi-buckhorn rear, ramp front, Wide-Scan™ front sight hood; receiver grooved for tip-off scope mount.

Overall Length: 41″
Weight: About 5½ lbs.
 Marlin 781. Specifications same as Marlin 780, except with tubular magazine that holds 25 Short, 19 Long or 17 Long Rifle Cartridges. Weight: About 6 lbs.

700 SERIES IN 22 MAGNUM

MARLIN 783 MAGNUM $122.95
(less scope)

Marlin 783 Magnum Specifications
Caliber: .22 Win. Magnum Rimfire (Not interchangeable with any other .22 cartridge)

Capacity: 12-shot tubular magazine with patented closure system

Action: Bolt action; serrated, anti-glare receiver top; gold-plated steel trigger; positive thumb safety; red cocking indicator.
Stock: Monte Carlo genuine American black walnut with full pistol grip; checkering on pistol grip and underside of fore-end; white butt plate spacer; sling swivels and handsome leather carrying strap; tough Mar-Shield® finish.

Barrel: 22″ with Micro-Groove rifling (20 grooves)
Sights: Adjustable folding semi-buckhorn rear, ramp front with new Wide-Scan™ hood; receiver grooved for tip-off scope mount.
Overall Length: 41″
Weight: About 6 lbs.

MARLIN 782 MAGNUM $117.95
(less scope)

Marlin 782 Magnum Specifications
Same as 783 Magnum, except with 7-shot clip magazine.

MARLIN RIFLES

MARLIN 990 $110.95

SPECIFICATIONS:
Caliber: 22 Long Rifle
Capacity: 18-shot tubular magazine
Barrel: 22" with Micro-Groove® rifling
(16 grooves)
Stock: Monte Carlo genuine American black
walnut with fluted comb and full
pistol grip; checkering on pistol
grip and forend; tough Mar-shield® finish.
Sights: Adjustable folding semi-buckhorn
rear, ramp front sight with brass bead;
Wide-Scan™ hood.
Overall Length: 40¾"
Weight: About 5½ lbs.
Features: Receiver grooved tip-off scope;
bolt hold-open device; cross-bolt safety.

MARLIN 995 $103.95

SPECIFICATIONS:
Caliber: 22 Long Rifle
Capacity: 7-shot clip magazine
Barrel: 18" with Micro-Groove® rifling
(16 grooves)
Stock: Monte Carlo genuine American black
walnut with full pistol grip;
checkering on pistol grip and fore-end.
Sights: Adjustable folding semi-buckhorn
rear; ramp front sight with brass bead;
Wide-Scan™ front sight hood.
Overall Length: 36¾"
Weight: About 5½ lbs.
Features: Receiver grooved for tip-off scope
mount; bolt hold-open device; cross-bolt
safety.

GLENFIELD SERIES

GLENFIELD 15 $82.95

SPECIFICATIONS:
Caliber: 22 Short, Long or Long Rifle
Capacity: Single shot
Barrel Length: 22" (16 grooves)
Weight: 5½ lbs.
Overall Length: 41"
Sights: Adjustable open rear, ramp front
sight
Features: Receiver grooved for tip-off scope
mount; checkering on pistol grip;
thumb safety; red cocking indicator.
Stock: One-piece walnut finished hardwood
Monte Carlo stock with full pistol grip;
checkering on pistol grip.

GLENFIELD 20 $90.95
(less scope)

SPECIFICATIONS:
Caliber: 22 Short, Long or Long Rifle
Capacity: Clip magazine holds 7 Short,
Long or Long Rifle cartridges
Barrel Length(s): 22"
Weight: 5½ lbs.
Overall Length: 41"
Sights: Ramp front sight; adjustable open
rear; receiver grooved for tip-off scope
mount
Action: Bolt action; serrated anti-glare
receiver top; chrome-plated steel
trigger; positive thumb safety; red
cocking indicator
Stock: One-piece walnut-finished
hardwood stock with full pistol grip;
checkering on pistol grip
Shown here with Glenfield 200C, 4X scope

MARLIN RIFLES
GLENFIELD SERIES

SPECIFICATIONS:
Caliber: 22 Long Rifle
Capacity: 18-shot tubular magazine with patented closure system
Barrel Length: 22"
Weight: 5½ lbs.
Overall Length: 40½"
Sights: Ramp front sight; adjustable open rear. Receiver grooved for tip-off scope mount
Action: Semi-automatic; side ejection; bolt hold-open device; receiver top has serrated, non-glare finish; cross-bolt safety
Stock: One-piece walnut-finished

GLENFIELD 60 $85.95
(less scope)

hardwood Monte Carlo stock with full pistol grip; checkering on pistol grip and forend
Shown here with Glenfield 200C, 4X scope

SPECIFICATIONS:
Caliber: 30/30 Win.
Capacity: 6-shot tubular magazine
Barrel Length: 20"
Weight: 7 lbs.
Overall Length: 38¼"
Sights: Ramp front sight; adjustable open rear. Solid top receiver tapped for scope mount or receiver sight; offset hammer spur for scope use—adaptable for right- or left-handed use
Action: Lever action; solid top receiver; side ejection; deeply blued metal

GLENFIELD 30A $205.95
(less scope)

surfaces; blued steel trigger; receiver top sandblasted to prevent glare
Stock: Two-piece walnut-finished hardwood stock with full pistol grip; checkering on pistol grip and forend
Shown here with Glenfield 400 A, 4X scope

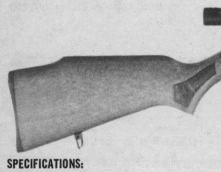

SPECIFICATIONS:
Caliber: 22 Long Rifle
Capacity: Chrome-plated 7-shot clip magazine
Barrel Length: 18"
Weight: 4½ lbs.
Overall Length: 36½"
Sights: Adjustable open rear, ramp front sight. Receiver grooved for tip-off scope mount

GLENFIELD 70 $85.95

Action: Semiautomatic; side ejection; bolt hold-open device; receiver top has serrated, non-glare finish; chrome-plated trigger; cross-bolt safety
Stock: One-piece walnut finished hardwood Monte Carlo stock with full pistol grip; checkering on pistol grip; sling swivels

MOSSBERG RIFLES

Caliber: 22 Super Target Rifle
Capacity: 7-shot clip magazine; also loads as single shot
Barrel Length: 27"
Weight: About 8 lbs. with sights
Overall Length: 44½"
Sights: Lyman 17A hooded front sight with 7 interchangeable inserts. Receiver grooved for scope mounting;

MODEL 144 $169.95

furnished with Mossberg S331 receiver peep sight
Action: Hammerless bolt action; grooved trigger with adjustable trigger pull
Stock: American walnut; beavertail forend, cheekpiece, adjustable hand stop pistol grip and special 1¼" target sling swivels

MOSSBERG RIFLES

22 CALIBER RIMFIRE

MODEL 377 PLINKSTER $109.95

Action—Semi-automatic. **Caliber**—22 Long Rifle. **Capacity**—15 Long Rifle Cartridges. Brass tubular magazine through buttstock; bright orange follower. **Barrel**—20" tapered with AC-KRO-GRUV rifling; ordnance steel. **Stock**—Straight-line, molded one-piece thumb hole of modified polystyrene foam, Monte Carlo comb and roll-over cheek piece. Sling swivel studs and fore-end checkering. Serrated, non-slip butt plate. **Color**—Walnut finish with blued barrel and receiver. Black butt plate and trigger guard. **Sight**—4 power scope with cross hair reticle. **Safety**—Positive, thumb operated; bolt locks in open position. **Receiver**—Milled ordnance steel, complete with scope mount base. Shell deflector included. **Length**—40". **Weight**—About 6.25 lbs. with scope.

MODEL 353 $114.95

With exclusive two-position, extension forend of black Tenite for steady firing from the prone position, up to 7 shots in less than 2 seconds. **Action**—Shoots 22 cal. Long Rifle, regular or High Speed cartridges. Automatic self loading action from 7-shot clip. Receiver grooved for scope mounting.

Stock—Genuine American walnut with Monte Carlo. Checkered at forend and pistol grip. Sling swivels and web strap on left of stock. Butt plate with white liner. **Barrel**—18" AC-KRO-GRUV® 8-groove rifled barrel. **Sights**—Open rear with "U" notch, adjustable for windage and elevation; ramp front with bead. **Weight**—About 5½ lbs. Length overall 38½".

MODEL 341 $104.95

Action—Hammerless bolt rifle action with Mossberg's "Magic 3-Way" 7-shot clip magazine which adjusts instantly to load, Short, Long or Long Rifle cartridges. Positive safety at side of receiver. Receiver grooved for scope mounting, tapped and drilled for peep sights. (Mossberg No. S330 receiver peep sight.) **Stock**—Genuine American walnut with Monte Carlo and cheek piece. Custom checkering on pistol grip and forend. Sling swivels. Butt plate with white line spacer. **Barrel**—24" AC-KRO-GRUV® 8-groove rifled barrel. **Sights**—Open rear with "U" notch, adjustable for windage and elevation; ramp front with bead. **Weight**—About 6¼ lbs. Length overall 43½".

MODEL 377 PLINKSTER **MODEL 353** **MODEL 341**

MOSSBERG RIFLES

MODEL 380 Price Not Set

Caliber—22 L.R. **Action**—Autoloader. **Barrel**—20″ tapered with AC-KRO-GRUV®. **Receiver**—Milled ordnance steel, grooved for scope mounting. **Capacity**—15, tube fed through buttstock. **Safety**—Positive, thumb operated, bolt locks in open position. **Stock**—Rifleman style, walnut finished, black non-slip butt plate. **Sights**—Adjustable rear bead front sight. Optional 4 power scope with cross hair reticle. **Overall Length**—40″. **Weight**—About 5½ lbs. with scope.

NEW HAVEN BRAND MODEL 453 T Price Not Set

Action—Semi-automatic. **Caliber**—22 Long Rifle. **Capacity**—7-shot, clip feed. **Stock**—One-piece birch in walnut finish. **Model 453 TS** available with 4x scope and mounts.

NEW HAVEN BRAND MODEL 740 T Price Not Set

Action—Bolt-action. **Caliber**—22 Magnum. **Capacity**—5-shot, clip feed. **Barrel**—24″ heavy barrel, chambered for 22 WMR cartridge. **Stock**—Walnut-finished birch. **Model 740 TS** available with 4x scope and mounts.

22 CALIBER MAGNUM

MODEL 640K 22 Win. Magnum $119.95

Especially designed for the powerful and accurate 22 WMRF Magnum cartridge. Our exclusive Mossberg AC-KRO-GRUV® rifling assures your long-range shots. **Action**—Hammerless, bolt action, with extra-heavy receiver and bolt. (Caution: Do not use any other 22 RF cartridge.) Double shell extractors, grooved trigger and 5-shot detachable clip. Thumb operated safety on right-hand side of receiver. Receiver grooved for scope mounting, tapped and drilled for Mossberg S330 peep sight. **Stock**—Genuine American walnut with Monte Carlo and cheekpiece. Sling swivels. Custom checkered at pistol grip and forend. Butt plate and pistol grip cap with white spacers. **Barrel**—24″ special gun quality steel. **Sights**—Fully adjustable, folding leaf rear sight. Ramp front with bead. **Weight**—About 6¼ lbs. **Overall Length** –44¾″.

REMINGTON AUTOLOADING 22 RIFLES

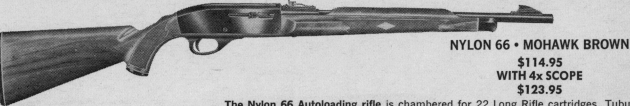

NYLON 66 • MOHAWK BROWN
$114.95
WITH 4x SCOPE
$123.95

The Nylon 66 Autoloading rifle is chambered for 22 Long Rifle cartridges. Tubular magazine thru butt stock holds 15 long rifle cartridges. Remington's Nylon 66 receiver parts, stock and barrel are interlocked with steel and structural nylon. There's no need for lubrication because friction-free parts glide on greaseless bearings of nylon. Barrel made of Remington proof steel. Stock is made of DuPont "Zytel" nylon, a new gunstock material. Resembles wood, weighs less than wood, outwears, outlasts wood. Stock features fine-line non-slip checkering, white diamond inlays and white line spacers at grip cap, butt plate and forend tip and has a lifetime warranty. Receiver is grooved for "tip-off" scope mounts.

Nylon 66 Black Diamond	**$114.95**
Nylon 66 Black Diamond w/4x Scope	**123.95**
Sling Strap and Swivels Installed	**11.50**

The Nylon 66 is also made in an Apache Black deluxe model. The stock is jet black nylon and both the barrel and the receiver cover are chrome plated. $121.95

	NYLON 66 "MOHAWK BROWN"	NYLON 66 "APACHE BLACK"
ACTION	Autoloading.	Autoloading.
CALIBER	22 Long Rifle Rim Fire.	22 Long Rifle Rim Fire.
CAPACITY	Tubular magazine thru butt stock. Holds 15 long rifle cartridges.	Tubular magazine thru butt stock. Holds 15 long rifle cartridges.
STOCK	DuPont "ZYTEL" nylon, checkered grip & fore-end with white diamond inlays, white line spacers on butt plate, grip cap & fore-end. Black fore-end tip.	DuPont "ZYTEL" nylon, checkered grip & fore-end with white diamond inlays, white line spacers on butt plate, grip cap & fore-end.
SIGHTS	Rear sight adjustable for windage and range, blade front, common sight line for iron sights and scope.	Rear sight adjustable for windage and range, blade front, common sight line for iron sights and scope.
SAFETY	Top-of-grip, Positive.	Top-of-grip, Positive.
RECEIVER	Grooved for "tip-off" scope mounts. Double extractors.	Grooved for "tip-off" scope mounts. Double extractors. Chrome Plated Receiver and Barrel.
OVER-ALL LENGTH	38½".	38½".
WEIGHT	4 lbs.	4 lbs.

MODEL 541-S "CUSTOM" SPORTER • Clip Repeater

Remington Model 541-S "Custom" Sporter	**$329.95**
Extra 5-Shot Clip Magazine	**5.00**
Extra 10-Shot Clip Magazine	**6.00**
Sling Strap and Quick Release Swivels Installed	**18.50**

A customized 22 rimfire rifle. An excellent choice for rimfire metallic silhouette shooting. American walnut stock with fine-line cut checkering in an attractive, raised diamond pattern, and protected by Du Pont's rugged RK-W finish. Receiver and bowed trigger guard handsomely scroll engraved. Matching rosewood-colored forend tip, pistol grip cap and checkered butt plate fitted with white line spacers.

Hand polished exterior metal surfaces richly blued to a tasteful, medium high lustre. Receiver is drilled and tapped for regular scope mounts or receiver sights as well as grooved for "tip-off" type mounts. Barrel also drilled and tapped for open sights. Supplied with a 5-shot clip magazine. 5- and 10-shot extra magazines are available.

REMINGTON AUTOLOADING 22 RIFLES

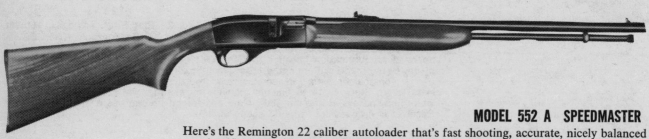

MODEL 552 A SPEEDMASTER

Here's the Remington 22 caliber autoloader that's fast shooting, accurate, nicely balanced ... the rifle you'll want for small game hunting, controlling crop-destroying and marauding pests, or for just plain fun-shooting. The Model 552 has every feature the shooter wants, such as: twenty shots as fast as you can squeeze the trigger, rich walnut stock, cross bolt safety, receiver grooved for "tip-off" scope mounts. **$148.95**

MODEL 552 BDL DeLuxe

A deluxe model with all the tried and proven dependable mechanical features on the inside, plus special design and appearance extras on the outside. The 552 BDL includes new tasteful Remington custom impressed checkering on both stock and for new DuPont RK-W tough lifetime finish that brings out the lustrous beauty of the walnut while protecting it, and rugged big-game type fully adjustable rear sight with ramp front sight. **$166.95**
Sling Strap and Swivels **17.50**

SPECIFICATIONS FOR MODELS 552A, 552BDL

ACTION:	Autoloading. Tubular Magazine.
CALIBER:	22 Short, Long and Long Rifle rim fire.
CAPACITY:	Holds 20 Short, 17 Long, 15 Long Rifle cartridges.
STOCK:	American Walnut. DuPont RK-W tough lustrous finish and fine-line custom checkering.
SIGHTS:	552 A —Adjustable rear, bead front. 552 BDL—Fully adjustable rear, ramp front. Screw removable.

SAFETY:	Positive cross bolt.
RECEIVER:	Grooved for "tip-off" scope mounts.
OVER-ALL LENGTH:	40″
BARREL LENGTH:	21″
AVERAGE WEIGHT:	5¾ lbs.

REMINGTON AUTOLOADING RIFLES

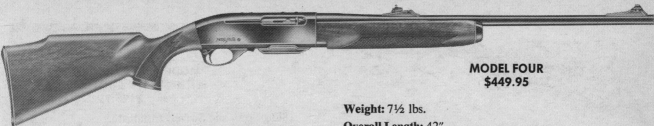

MODEL FOUR
$449.95

Calibers: 6mm, 243 Win., 270 Win., 7mm Express Rem., 30-06 and 30-06 "Accelerator," 308 Win. and 308 "Accelerator"

Capacity: 5-shot in all calibers (4 in the magazine, 1 in the chamber); extra 4-shot magazine available

Action: Gas operated; receiver drilled and tapped for scope mounts; positive safety switch

Barrel Length: 22"

Weight: 7½ lbs.

Overall Length: 42"

Sights: Blade ramp front; adjustable sliding ramp rear

Stock: Checkered American walnut; Monte Carlo stock with full cheekpiece; pistol grip; flared and checkered forend

Model Four special order: D Peerless and F Premier Grades (both engraved) and F Premier Grade (engraved with gold inlay)

Length of Pull: 13⁵⁄₁₆" **Drop at Heel:** 2½" **Drop at Comb:** 1¹¹⁄₁₆" (with Monte Carlo: 1¹³⁄₁₆")

MODEL 7400
$399.95

Calibers: 6mm Rem., 243 Win., 270 Win., 7mm Express Rem., 30-06 and 30-06 "Accelerator," 308 Win. and 308 "Accelerator"

Capacity: 5 centerfire cartridges (4 in the magazine, 1 in the chamber); extra 4-shot magazine available

Action: Gas operated; receiver drilled and tapped for scope mounts

Barrel Length: 22"

Weight: 7½ lbs.

Overall Length: 42"

Sights: Standard blade ramp front, sliding ramp rear

Stock: Checkered American walnut stock and forend; curved pistol grip

Length of Pull: 13⅜" **Drop at Heel:** 2¼" **Drop at Comb** 1¹³⁄₁₆"

REMINGTON BOLT-ACTION RIFLES

MODELS 581 & 582 IN 22 L. R. CALIBER

The 581 series 22 Long Rifle rimfire bolt-action rifles feature the look, feel and balance of big-game center-fire rifles. They are available in styles—a clip repeater with single-shot adapter, and a tubular-magazine repeater. The bolt is an artillery type with rear lock-up and has six extra-heavy, rotary locking lugs at the back that engage grooves in the solid-steel receiver. A bolt cover at rear keeps dirt and bad weather outside. Two extractors are standard on this 581 series of 22 rifles. Hunting-type trigger is wide and the trigger guard is roomy enough to accommodate a gloved finger. The stock is Monte Carlo style with pistol grip suitable for use with or without a scope. Sights consist of a bead front sight and U-notch lock-screw adjustable rear. Precise bedding into the stock is achieved by a new round receiver. The receiver is also grooved for tip-off scope mounts. There are no slots or notches cut into the receiver and the bolt handle isn't used as lock-up lugs. The barrel is of ordnance steel, crowned at the muzzle, polished and blued. The non-slip thumb safety is located at the right rear of the receiver. With positive safety.

MODEL 581 BOYS' RIFLE $125.95

REMINGTON BOLT-ACTION RIFLES

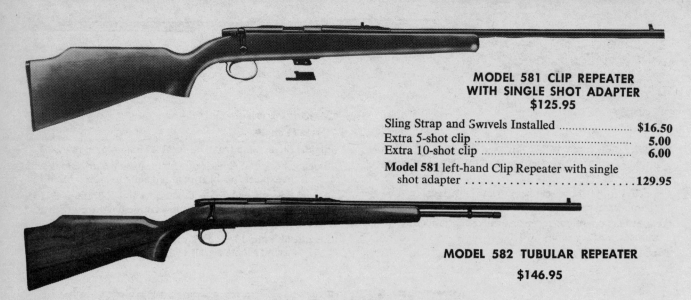

MODEL 581 CLIP REPEATER WITH SINGLE SHOT ADAPTER
$125.95

Sling Strap and Swivels Installed **$16.50**
Extra 5-shot clip **5.00**
Extra 10-shot clip **6.00**
Model 581 left-hand Clip Repeater with single
    shot adapter **129.95**

MODEL 582 TUBULAR REPEATER
$146.95

MODEL 581 & MODEL 582

SPECIFICATIONS:

Stock & Forend: Walnut-finished hardwood with Monte Carlo, full size, black butt plate. Single-screw takedown.
Receiver: Round, ordnance steel, grooved for scope mounts.
Capacity: M/581 6-shot clip repeater with single-shot adapter. M/582 20 Short, 15 Long, 14 Long Rifle cartridges.

Sights: Front: bead, dovetail adjustable. Rear: U-notch type, lock-screw adjustable.
Safety: Positive, serrated thumb-type. Left-hand safety on left-hand model.
Weight: M/581 4¾ lbs.; M/582 5 lbs.
Overall Length: 42⅜"
Sling Strap and Swivels Installed **$12.50**

MODEL 700ADL

MODEL 700 ADL "Deluxe": Calibers— 222 Remington, 22-250 Remington, 6mm Remington, 243 Winchester, 25-06 Remington, 270 Winchester, 30-06, 308 Winchester, 7mm Express Remington **$334.95**
MODEL 700 ADL "Deluxe" MAGNUM: Caliber—7mm Rem. Mag.... **349.95**

MODEL 700BDL

MODEL 700 BDL "Custom Deluxe": Calibers—222 Remington, 22-250 Remington, 6mm Remington, 243 Winchester, 25-06 Remington, 7mm-08 Remington, 270 Winchester, 30-06, 308 Winchester, 7mm Express Remington **$399.95**
17 Remington caliber **414.95**
Left-Hand Model in 270 Win. & 30-06 .... **414.95**
MODEL 700 BDL "Custom Deluxe" MAGNUM: Calibers—7mm Remington Mag., 8mm Rem. Mag., 300 Winchester Mag. **$414.95**
Left-Hand Model in 7mm Rem. Magnum **429.95**
MODEL 700 SAFARI in 375 H&H Mag., 458 Win. Mag. **649.95**

REMINGTON BOLT-ACTION RIFLES

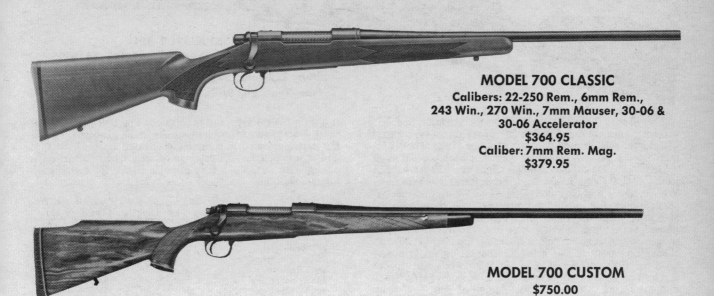

MODEL 700 CLASSIC
**Calibers: 22-250 Rem., 6mm Rem.,
243 Win., 270 Win., 7mm Mauser, 30-06 &
30-06 Accelerator
$364.95
Caliber: 7mm Rem. Mag.
$379.95**

MODEL 700 CUSTOM
$750.00

SPECIFICATIONS:

Calibers: Same as Model 700 BDL except 17 Remington, 375 H&H Mag. and 458 Win. Mag.

Capacity: Same as Model 700 BDL.

Barrel: Choice of 22″ or 24″ length in Remington high-proof ordance steel. With or without sights. Not available with stainless steel barrel.

Bolt: Jeweled with shrouded firing pin.

Receiver: Drilled and tapped for scope mounts. Fixed magazine with or without hinged floor plate.

Stock: Cut-checkered selected American walnut with quick detachable sling swivels installed. Recoil pad standard equipment on Magnum rifles. Installed at extra charge on others.

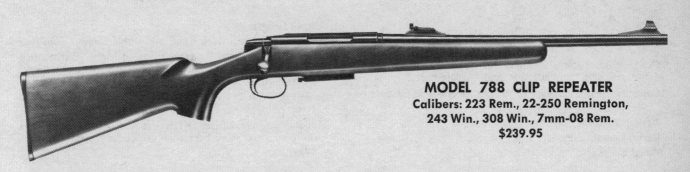

MODEL 788 CLIP REPEATER
**Calibers: 223 Rem., 22-250 Remington,
243 Win., 308 Win., 7mm-08 Rem.
$239.95**

Now the shooter can get bolt-action accuracy in three favorite big game calibers—the 243 Win., 308 Win. and the new 7mm-08 Rem. with the moderately priced Remington Model 788. And for the varmint shooter, it's available in two of the hottest calibers, the 22-250 Rem. and the 223 Rem. Features are: Artillery type bolt with nine extra-heavy locking lugs, removable clip magazine, precision-rifled ordnance steel barrel, detachable blade front sight and lock screw, adjustable rear sight, well-positioned safety at rear of receiver, bolt cover, hunting-type trigger, all-purpose stock designed for scope or open sights, receiver drilled and tapped for scope mounts and receiver sights. Stock dimensions are as follows: 13⅝″ length of pull; 2⅝″ drop at heel; 1⅞″ drop at comb (from open sight line).

Model 788 Sling Strap and Swivels	$	16.50
Extra clip		7.75
Model 788 with 4x Scope		284.95

Calibers	Clip Mag. Cap.	Barrel Length	Overall Length	Av. Wt. Lbs.
Model 788				
223 Remington	4	24″	43⅝″	7½
22-250 Remington	3	24″	43⅝″	7½
243 Winchester	3	18½″	38½″	7¼
308 Winchester	3	18½″	38½″	7¼
7mm-08 Remington	3	18½″	38½″	7¼

REMINGTON BOLT-ACTION RIFLES

MODEL 700 BDL
HEAVY BARREL VARMINT SPECIAL $419.95
Calibers: 222 Rem., 223 Rem., 22-250 Rem., 25-06 Rem., 6mm Rem., 243 Win., 308 Win. and 7mm-08 Rem.

The Model 700 BDL heavy barrel "Varmint Special" version comes equipped with a 24″ heavy target-type barrel with target-rifle (Remington 40XB) scope bases. The "Varmint Special" is available in a wide range of popular high velocity, varmint calibers which include the 222 Rem., 223 Rem., 22-250 Rem., 25-06 Rem., 6mm Rem., 308 Win., 243 Win. calibers and 7mm-08 Rem. The "Varmint Special" was designed for maximum-range precision shooting—suitable for chucks, foxes and other varmints. Features include hinged floor plate; quick release swivels and strap; crisp trigger pull; American walnut stock, Monte Carlo style with cheekpiece, positive cut skip-line checkering on grip and all three sides of forend, grip cap with white line spacer and butt plate; Du Pont developed RK-W wood finish. Stock dimensions are as follows: 13⅜″ length of pull; 1⅜″ drop at heel; ½″ drop at comb (from open sight line). The safety is a thumb-lever type and is serrated. The bolt knob is oval shaped, serrated top and bottom. As in the Model 700 BDL, the cartridge head is completely encased by the bolt face and is supported by three rings of steel when the action is closed. This model is a very popular choice for metallic silhouette shooting.

Calibers	Clip Mag. Cap.	Barrel Length	Overall Length	Av. Wt. Lbs.
22-250 Remington	5	24″	43½″	9
222 Remington	6	24″	43½″	9
223 Remington	6	24″	43½″	9
25-06 Remington	5	24″	44½″	9
6mm Remington	5	24″	43½″	9
243 Winchester	5	24″	43½″	9
308 Winchester	5	24″	43½″	8¾
7mm-08 Remington	5	24″	43½″	8¾

MODEL SIX $399.95

Calibers: 6mm Rem., 243 Win., 270 Win., 30-06 and 30-06 "Accelerator," and 308 Win. and "Accelerator"

Capacity: 5-shot capacity in all six calibers (4 in the removable clip, 1 in the chamber)

Action: Pump action

Barrel Length: 22″

Weight: 7½ lbs.

Overall Length: 42″

Sights: Blade ramp front sight; adjustable sliding ramp rear

Stock: Cut-checkered American walnut Monte Carlo stock with full cheekpiece; flared forend has full wraparound positive-cut checkering

Length of Pull: 13⁵⁄₁₆″ **Drop at Heel:** 2½″ **Drop at Comb:** 1¹¹⁄₁₆″ (with Monte Carlo: 1¹³⁄₁₆″)

Model Six special order: D Peerless and F Premier Grades (both engraved) and F Premier Grade (engraved with gold inlay)

MODEL 7600 $349.95

Barrel Length: 22″

Weight: 7½ lbs.

Overall Length: 42″

Sights: Standard blade ramp front sight; sliding ramp rear, both removable

Stock: Checkered American walnut

Length of Pull: 13⅜″. **Drop at Heel:** 2⅛″. **Drop at Comb:** 1¹¹⁄₁₆″

Calibers: 6mm Rem., 243 Win., 270 Win., 30-06 and 30-06 "Accelerator," 308 Win. and 308 "Accelerator"

Capacity: 5-shot capacity in all six calibers (4 in the removable magazine, 1 in the chamber)

Action: Pump action

REMINGTON PUMP-ACTION RIFLES

MODEL 572 A FIELDMASTER • 22 Short, Long, Long Rifle

For the shooter who likes a pump action 22 caliber rifle. the "Fieldmaster" Model 572 A is best ...
Exclusive cartridge-feeding design prevents jamming, permits easy single loading. By simply removing the inner magazine tube, parent or instructor can convert the Model 572 into a single-shot rifle for the beginning shooter; when shooter is experienced, magazine tube can be put back again to make the Model 572 a repeater. $154.95

MODEL 572 BDL Deluxe • 22 Short, Long, Long Rifle

Features of this rifle with big-game feel and appearance are: DuPont beautiful but tough RK-W finish, center-fire-rifle-type rear sight fully adjustable for both vertical and horizontal sight alignment, big-game style ramp front sight, beautiful Remington impressed checkering on both stock and forend.

Model 572 BDL DELUXE $171.95
Sling Strap & Swivels installed 15.50

MODELS 572A & 572 BDL DELUXE SPECIFICATIONS:

ACTION:	Pump repeater	**SIGHTS:**	A—Adjustable rear, bead front. BDL—Fully adjustable rear, ramp front. Screw removable
CALIBER:	22 Short, Long and Long Rifle rimfire	**SAFETY:**	Positive cross bolt
CAPACITY:	Tubular magazine holds 20 Short, 17 Long, 15 Long Rifle cartridges	**RECEIVER:**	Grooved for "tip-off" scope mounts
		OVERALL LENGTH:	40"
STOCK AND FOREND:	A—Walnut finished hardwood BDL—American Walnut with DuPont RK-W tough lustrous finish and fine line custom checkering	**BARREL LENGTH:**	21"
		AVERAGE WEIGHT:	5½ lbs

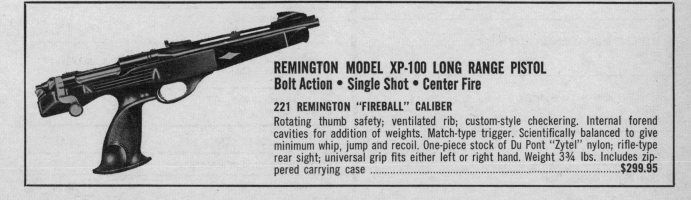

REMINGTON MODEL XP-100 LONG RANGE PISTOL
Bold Action • Single Shot • Center Fire

221 REMINGTON "FIREBALL" CALIBER

Rotating thumb safety; ventilated rib; custom-style checkering. Internal forend cavities for addition of weights. Match-type trigger. Scientifically balanced to give minimum whip, jump and recoil. One-piece stock of Du Pont "Zytel" nylon; rifle-type rear sight; universal grip fits either left or right hand. Weight 3¾ lbs. Includes zippered carrying case $299.95

REMINGTON TARGET RIFLES

MODEL 40-XB "RANGEMASTER"
Center Fire Rifle

Barrels are unblued stainless steel. Choice of either standard weight or heavy barrel. Comb grooved for easy bolt removal. Mershon White Line non-slip rubber butt plate supplied. See below for complete specifications and prices.

MODEL 40XB-BR • Bench Rest Center Fire Rifle

Built with all the features of the extremely accurate Model 40-XB-CF but modified to give the competitive bench rest shooter a standardized rifle that provides the inherent accuracy advantages of a short, heavy, extremely stiff barrel. Wider, squared off fore-end gives a more stable rest on sandbags or other supports and meets weight limitations for the sporter and light-varmint classes of National Bench Rest Shooters Association competition.

	MODEL 40-XB CENTER FIRE	MODEL 40XB-BR CENTER FIRE
ACTION	Bolt—Single shot in either standard or heavy barrel versions. Repeater in heavy barrel only. Receiver bedded to stock. Barrel is free floating	Bolt, single shot only
CALIBERS	See listing below	222 Rem., 22 Bench Rest Rem., 7.62 NATO (308 Win.), 6mm Bench Rest Rem., 223 Rem., 6x47
SIGHTS	No sights supplied. Target scope blocks installed	Supplied with target scope blocks
SAFETY	Positive thumb operated	Positive thumb operated
RECEIVER	Drilled and tapped for scope block and receiver sights	Drilled and tapped for target scope blocks
BARREL	Drilled and tapped for scope block and front target iron sight. Muzzle diameter S2—approx. ¾", H2—approx. ⅞". Length: 27¼". Unblued stainless steel only	Unblued stainless steel only. 20" barrel for Light Varmint Class. 24" barrel for Heavy Varmint Class.
TRIGGER	Adjustable from 2 to 4 lbs. pull. Special 2 oz. trigger available at extra cost. Single shot models only	Adjustable from 1½ to 3½ lbs. Special 2 oz. trigger available at extra cost
STOCK	American Walnut. Adjustable front swivel block on rail. Rubber non-slip butt plate	Selected American Walnut. Length of pull—12"
OVERALL LENGTH	Approx. 47"	38" with 20" barrel. 42" with 24" barrel
AVERAGE WEIGHT	S2—9¼ lbs. H2—11¼ lbs.	Light Varmint Class (20" barrel) 9¼ lbs. Heavy Varmint Class (24" barrel) 12 lbs.

MODEL 40-XB CENTER FIRE	PRICE
40XB-CF-S2 Stainless steel, standard weight barrel	
40XB-CF-H2 Stainless steel, heavy barrel	$719.95

CALIBERS: Single-shot: 222 Rem., 22-250 Rem., 6mm Rem., 243 Win., 7.62mm NATO (308 Win.), 30-06, 30-338 (30-7mm Mag.), 300 Win. Mag., 25-06 Rem., 7mm Rem. Mag.

MODEL 40-XB CENTER FIRE	PRICE
Heavy barrel version only Extra for repeating models	$47.95
CALIBERS: Repeating 222 Rem., 22-250 Rem., 6mm Rem., 243 Win., 7.62mm NATO (308 Win.).	
Single shot version only Extra for two ounce trigger	$79.95

MODEL 40XB-BR CENTER FIRE	PRICE
40XB-BR Heavy barrel without sights	$759.95
Extra for two-ounce trigger	$79.95

REMINGTON TARGET RIFLES

MODEL 40-XR
Rim Fire Position Rifle

Stock designed with deep fore-end for more comfortable shooting in all positions. Butt plate vertically adjustable. Exclusive loading platform provides straight line feeding with no shaved bullets. Crisp, wide, adjustable match trigger. Meets all International Shooting Union standard rifle specifications. **$569.95**

MODEL 40-XC National Match Course Rifle

Chambered for the 7.62mm NATO cartridge solely, this match rifle was designed to meet the needs of competitive shooters firing the national match courses. Position style stock, five shot repeater with top loading magazine, anti-bind bolt and receiver and in the bright stainless steel barrel. Meets all International Shooting Union Army Rifle specifications. **$779.95**

MODEL 540-XR, 540-XRJR RIM FIRE POSITION RIFLE / MODEL 40-XR RIM FIRE POSITION RIFLE

	MODEL 540-XR, 540-XRJR RIM FIRE POSITION RIFLE	MODEL 40-XR RIM FIRE POSITION RIFLE
ACTION	Bolt action single shot	Bolt action single shot
CALIBER	22 Long Rifle rim fire	22 Long Rifle rim fire
CAPACITY	Single loading	Single loading
SIGHTS	Optional at extra cost. Williams Receiver No. FPTK and Redfield Globe front match sight	Optional at extra cost. Williams Receiver No. FPTK and Redfield Globe front match sight
SAFETY	Positive serrated thumb safety	Positive thumb safety
LENGTH OF PULL	540-XR—Adjustable from 12¾" to 16" 540-XRJR—Adjustable from 11" to 14¼"	13½"
RECEIVER	Drilled and tapped for receiver sight	Drilled and tapped for receiver sight or target scope blocks
BARREL	26" medium weight target barrel countersunk at muzzle. Drilled and tapped for target scope blocks. Fitted with front sight base	24" heavy barrel
BOLT	Artillery style with lock-up at rear. 6 locking lugs, double extractors	Heavy, oversized locking lugs and double extractors
TRIGGER	Adjustable from 1 to 5 lbs.	Adjustable from 2 to 4 lbs.
STOCK	Position style with Monte Carlo, cheekpiece and thumb groove. 5-way adjustable butt plate and full length guide rail	Position style with front swivel block on fore-end guide rail
OVER-ALL LENGTH	540-XR—Adjustable from 42½" to 46¾" 540-XRJR—Adjustable from 41¾" to 45"	42½"
AVERAGE WEIGHT	8 lbs. 13 oz. without sights. Add 9 oz. for sights	10 lbs. 2 oz.

MODEL 540-XR
Rim Fire Position Rifle

An extremely accurate 22 caliber single shot match rifle. Extra fast lock time contributes to this fine accuracy. Specially designed stock has deep fore-end and 5 way adjustable butt plate for added comfort and better scores in all positions.

Pistol grip designed to eliminate wrist-twisting and assures straight-back trigger pull. Adjustable match trigger. Match style sling strap with adjustable front swivel block and set sight available as accessories at extra charge. **$299.95**

MODEL 540-XR, 540-XRJR
Front Swivel Block and Sling Strap Assembly (Optional Accessory at Extra Charge). **$15.50**

MODEL 540-XRJR • Junior Rim Fire Position Rifle

A match rifle with all the features of the Model 540-XR but fitted with 1¾" shorter stock to fit the junior shooter. **$299.95**

ROSSI RIFLES

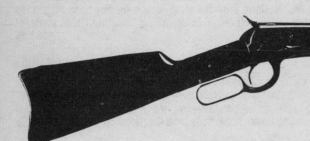

The tubular magazine holds 20 short, 16 long, and 13 long rifle 22 rimfire cartridges interchangeably. Available in blue finish.

ROSSI SLIDE-ACTION GALLERY MODEL
Standard or Carbine

Model	Finish	Weight	Barrel Length	Price
Standard	Blue	5¾ lbs.	23"	$152.00
Standard	Nickel	5¾ lbs.	23"	166.00
Carbine	Blue	5½ lbs.	16½"	152.00
Carbine	Nickel	5½ lbs.	16½"	166.00

ROSSI SADDLE-RING LEVER ACTION CARBINE
357 Mag. or 38 Special

Model	Finish	Weight	Barrel Length	Price
Carbine	Blue	5¾ lbs.	20"	$283.00
Carbine	Blue Engraved	5¾ lbs.	20"	325.00

RUGER CARBINES

No. 3 CARBINE SINGLE-SHOT $284.00

Caliber—45/70, 223, 22 Hornet, 375 Win., Single-shot.
Barrel—22 inches.
Weight—6 pounds.
Overall Length—38½ inches.
Rear Sight—Folding leaf adjustable.
Front Sight—Gold bead.
Safety—Sliding tang.
Stock and Forearm—Solid American Walnut.

RUGER MINI-14
Blued $269.50
Stainless Steel $310.00

General:

MATERIALS—Heat-treated Chrome molybdenum and other alloy steels, as well as music wire coil springs, are used throughout the mechanism to ensure reliability under field operating conditions.

SAFETY—The safety blocks both the hammer and sear. The slide can be cycled when the safety is on. The safety is mounted in the front of the trigger guard so that it may be set to Fire position without removing finger from trigger guard.

FIRING PIN—The firing pin is retracted mechanically during the first part of the unlocking of the bolt. The rifle can only be fired when the bolt is safely locked.

STOCK—One-piece American hardwood reinforced with steel liner at stressed areas. Handguard and forearm separated by air space from barrel to promote cooling under rapid-fire conditions.

FIELD STRIPPING—The Carbine can be field stripped to its eight (8) basic subassemblies in a matter of seconds and without the use of tools. All of these subassemblies are significant in size and not subject to loss. Further disassembly can be accomplished, if desired, without the use of special tools. This should, however, not be necessary for cleaning or field maintenance.

SPECIFICATIONS—CALIBER: 223 (5.56mm). **LENGTH:** 37¼". **WEIGHT:** 6 lbs. 4 oz. **MAGAZINE:** 5 round, detachable box magazine. 10-shot and 20-shot magazines available from Ruger dealers. **BARREL LENGTH:** 18½".

RUGER AUTOLOADING CARBINES
IN 22 LONG RIFLE AND 44 MAGNUM CALIBERS

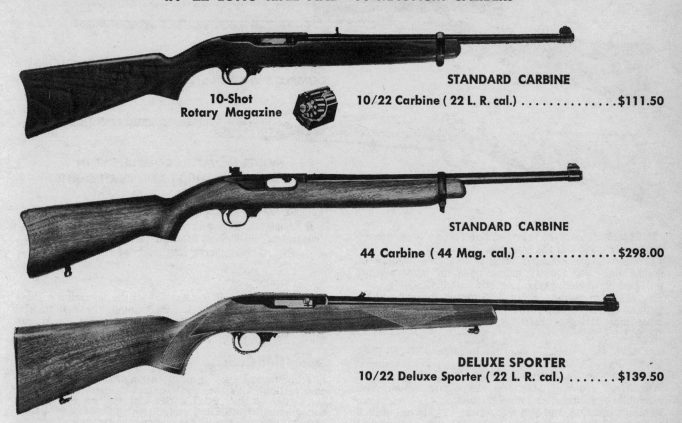

10-Shot Rotary Magazine

STANDARD CARBINE

10/22 Carbine (22 L. R. cal.) $111.50

STANDARD CARBINE

44 Carbine (44 Mag. cal.) $298.00

DELUXE SPORTER

10/22 Deluxe Sporter (22 L. R. cal.) $139.50

Model 10/22 Carbine
22 LONG RIFLE CALIBER

Identical in size, balance and style to the Ruger 44 Magnum Carbine and nearly the same in weight, the 10/22 is a companion to its high-power counterpart. Construction of the 10/22 Carbine is rugged and follows the Ruger design practice of building a firearm from integrated sub-assemblies. For example, the trigger housing assembly contains the entire ignition system, which employs a high-speed, swinging hammer to insure the shortest possible lock time. The barrel is assembled to the receiver by a unique dual-screw dove-tail system that provides unusual rigidity and strength—and accounts, in part, for the exceptional accuracy of the 10/22.

Specifications: Caliber: 22 long rifle, high-speed or standard velocity loads. **Barrel:** 18½" length. Barrel is assembled to the receiver by unique dual-screw dove-tail mounting for added strength and rigidity. **Weight:** 5 pounds. **Overall Length:** 37". **Sights:** 1/16" gold bead front sight. Single folding leaf rear sight, adjustable for elevation. Receiver drilled and tapped for scope blocks or tip-off mount adapter. **Magazine:** 10-shot capacity, exclusive Ruger rotary design. Fits flush into stock. **Trigger:** Curved finger surface, ⅜" wide. **Safety:** Sliding cross-button type. Safety locks both sear and hammer and cannot be put in safe position unless gun is cocked. **Stocks:** Solid American walnut, oil finished. Available in 2 styles. The Standard Carbine and The Sporter. **Finish:** Polished all over and blued or anodized.

Model 44 Carbine
44 MAGNUM CALIBER

The carbine is gas-operated, with the slide energized by a short-stroke piston driven by a very small quantity of gas tapped from the barrel during firing. The mechanism is exceptionally smooth in operation, strong, reliable and safe; the breech remains locked until it is opened automatically *after* the bullet has left the barrel. The receiver is machined from a solid block of hot-rolled chrome molybdenum steel. The tubular magazine is located in the fore-end, capacity is 4 shots, with an additional shot in the chamber. When the last shot has been fired, the breech remains open until it is released by operating the latch located just ahead of the trigger guard.

Specifications: Caliber: 44 Magnum only, using all factory loads. The use of jacketed bullets is recommended to insure optimum accuracy and maximum stopping power. **Barrel:** 18½" long, 12 groove rifling, 38" twist. Barrel is permanently assembled to the receiver by 20 pitch screw threads. **Weight:** 5 pounds, 12 ounces. **Overall Length:** 36¾". **Sights:** 1/16" gold bead front sight. Single folding leaf rear sight, adjustable for elevation. Receiver drilled and tapped. **Magazine:** Fixed, tubular type located in fore-end. **Capacity:** 4 rounds plus 1 round in chamber. **Trigger:** Two stage pull. Curved finger surface ⅜" wide. **Safety:** Sliding cross-button type. Safety locks both sear and hammer and cannot be put in safe position unless gun is cocked. **Stock:** Genuine American walnut.

RUGER M-77 BOLT ACTION RIFLE

**MODEL No. M77R (TELESCOPE NOT INCLUDED)
COMPLETE WITH 1" STEEL RUGER RINGS (NO SIGHTS)**

**MODEL No. M77RS COMPLETE WITH 1"
STEEL RUGER RINGS AND OPEN SIGHTS**

Calibers: 22-250 Remington, 243 Winchester, 6mm Remington, 25-06 Remington, 220 Swift, 257 Roberts 250-3000, 7x57mm, 270 Winchester, 30-06, 7mm Remington Magnum, 300 Winchester Mag., 338 Winchester Mag., and 458 Win. Magnum.

Action. The M-77 is available in two action lengths—the Short Stroke and the Magnum.

The Short Stroke action is designed to take advantage of the accuracy and ballistic efficiency of the modern short series of cartridges. (Magazine box length: 2.920")

The Magnum action—about ½" longer than the Short Stroke—assures smooth and faultless feeding of the versatile long series of cartridges. (Magazine box length: 3.340")

The M-77 short stroke is available in calibers 22-250, 243, 6mm, 220 Swift, and 308. The M-77 Magnum is chambered for 270, 25-06, 7x57mm 30-06, 7mm Rem. Magnum, 300. Win. Mag., 338 Win. Mag. and 458 Win. Magnum. Also available in calibers 22-250, 220 Swift, 243 Win., 6mm Remington, 25-06, and 308 with a heavy 24" barrel, drilled and tapped for target-scope blocks, and supplied with 1" Ruger steel rings. 26" barrel in 220 Swift.

The M-77 Round top (Magnum Action only) is equipped with open sights. The receiver is shaped and tapped to accommodate standard commercial scope mount bases. The Round top is not milled for Ruger scope rings. Available only in 25/06, 270, 30-06, 7mm Rem. Mag., and 300 Win. Mag.

In the rare event of a cartridge case failure, the mechanism of the Model 77 has been provided with numerous vents to minimize the effect of escaping gas. A vent of the usual type is provided on the right side of the receiver. Gas which flows along the locking lug channel is largely diverted by the rugged bolt stop and vented through a special opening. In addition, the substantial flange on the bolt sleeve is designed to deflect gas away from the shooter. The one-piece bolt of the Model 77 avoids the brazed joints which are now commonly used as an economy measure. Two massive front locking lugs and a positive long extractor, combined with one-piece construction, result in extraordinary strength and reliability.

The external bolt stop, held in position by a strong hidden spring, is conveniently located on the left rear of the receiver. No tools are needed to open the bolt stop and remove the bolt.

The serrated steel-trigger is adjustable to a minimum pull of 3½ pounds. Trigger action is smooth, crisp and free from creep at all adjustments.

The safety, which is securely mounted in the heavy metal of the tang, is of the desired shotgun type; positive and readily accessible.

For added safety and convenience, the magazine floor plate is hinged to allow emptying of the magazine without having to work the cartridges through the action. The floor plate can be easily opened by pressing the release lever located at the inside front of the trigger guard.

Specifications:

ACTION: Short-stroke or magnum lengths. **BOLT:** One-piece construction, with two massive locking lugs. **EXTRACTOR:** Long external type. **BOLT STOP:** Left side of receiver, coil spring action. **TRIGGER:** Serrated steel, adjustable for weight of pull. **SPRINGS:** Music wire coil springs throughout (except for special magazine follower spring). **MAGAZINE:** Staggered box type with stainless steel follower and quick release hinged floor plate. Capacity: five rounds (plus one in chamber), three rounds in Magnum calibers. **BARREL:** 22", Chrome-molybdenum alloy steel. Except calibers 25/06, 300 Win. Mag., 338 Win. Mag., 458 Win. Magnum and 7mm Remington Magnum and all M77V which are 24". **SAFETY:** Sliding shotgun-type, mounted on receiver tang. **STOCK:** Genuine American Walnut, thoroughly seasoned, hand-checkered, and hand rubbed. Pistol grip cap with Ruger medallion. Swivel studs. Live rubber recoil pad. **STOCK DIMENSIONS:** Drop at heel: 2⅛". Drop at comb: 1⅝". **LENGTH OF PULL:** 13¾". **STOCK BEDDING:** Ruger diagonal-front-mounting-screw system (Patented) insures consistent bedding of receiver barrel assembly in stock. **LENGTH OVERALL:** 42 inches. **WEIGHT:** Approximately 6½ pounds without scope. (M77V 9 lbs.) and 458 mag. model, approx. 8¾ lbs.

MODELS AND PRICES

M77R—with scope rings only	$325.00
M77ST—(Round Top) with open sights	325.00
M77R — 338 Mag.	325.00
M77RS—with rings and sights	341.25
M77RS—338 Win. Mag.	341.25
M77RS— 458 Win. Mag.,	429.50
M77V—with 24" heavy barrel	325.00
M77B/A—Barreled actions	$262.50 to 357.50
D-71—Ruger 1" Steel Extra Rings (pr.)	23.00

RUGER NO. 1 SINGLE-SHOT RIFLES

RUGER NUMBER ONE STANDARD RIFLE

General Description

The RUGER No. 1 SINGLE-SHOT action belongs in the under-lever, falling-block category and follows in many characteristics the Farquharson design. In all mechanical details, however, the RUGER No. 1 action is completely new and is in no sense a replica of any older action. The action has been engineered to use the most powerful of the modern magnum cartridges with safety and reliability.

Receiver Design.

The heart of the design is the massive receiver which forms a rigid connection between the barrel and butt stock. The butt stock is mortised into the receiver in such a way as to reinforce the grip section against splitting or cracking. A longitudinal bolt which passes through the butt stock binds the butt stock and receiver together into a solid, rigid structure. Projecting forward from the main part of the receiver and lying directly below the barrel is a heavy steel extension formed integrally with the receiver to facilitate forearm attachment. Because of this forearm hanger, it is possible to arrange the forearm to be completely clear of the barrel or to have any desired pressure on the barrel. The side walls of the receiver are .218″ thick; these side walls are joined behind the breech block by a massive solid section. It is in this area that the RUGER No. 1 receiver represents the major improvement over the Farquharson type. In these older actions, there is only a thin web of steel effectively joining the side walls behind the breech block.

Firing Pin Hammer Design.

The advantages of the No. 1 hammer-firing pin design are:
1. The mainspring located in the forearm, is in an area where ample space is available for a large, lightly stressed spring.
2. Mounting of the hammer on the lever pivot simplifies the mechanism.
3. Hammer notch located on the periphery of the hammer greatly reduces the pressure on the sear.
4. The swinging transfer block, located in the upper interior of the breech block, functions to virtually lock the firing pin in its forward position against gas pressure during firing.
5. The ignition mechanism requires no openings in the rear of the breech block and, accordingly, no gas can issue in the direction of the shooter's face as it might in some older designs where some leakage can pass along the sides of the firing pin and exit at the rear surface of the breech block.
6. The hammer is retracted upon the first opening motion of the lever and can never actuate the firing pin unless the breech block is fully elevated into firing position.

Ejector Design.

The provisions for removal of fired cartridge cases from the chamber are particularly complete. The action readily handles any type of cartridge case i.e., rimmed, semi-rimmed, belted, rimless, etc. The extractor-ejector mechanism is designed to provide great leverage between the hand-lever and the point where the ejector actually engages the rim or groove of the cartridge case. It is so powerful, in fact, that if the case does not come out, the extractor will usually pull through the rim by use of a moderate force on the lever. With this mechanism, the shells will be thrown clear of the gun when the action is opened and the mechanism is in effect, a powerful spring-actuated automatic ejector. However, if the auto ejector feature is not desired, the ejector spring may be removed.

Trigger and Safety.

The trigger mechanism is adjustable for sear engagement, over travel, and weight of pull. The minimum pull at the present time is slightly under three pounds. The mechanism is free of take-up motion and trigger release is notably crisp. The crispness of this pull is attained by simply establishing leverages which greatly multiply, at the point of sear engagement, the movement of the trigger finger. The safety engages both the sear and the hammer directly to provide an absolute maximum of real security. The safety cannot be put on if the hammer is not cocked, but the action may be opened and closed whether the safety is on or off. The safety is of the sliding shotgun type.

Sights.

The mounting of telescopic sights has been carefully studied in connection with the RUGER No. 1 Single Shot. The rifle is sold complete with scope mounts of RUGER design, made particularly for this rifle. These mounts are split horizontally and fit 1″ diameter scope tubes. They are the tip-off type, made entirely of steel. RUGER No. 1 rifles are equipped with ¼ rib scope mount only, unless open sights are also ordered. This ¼ rib functions primarily as a base for the RUGER scope mounts and may also be used for mounting open sights which are optional.

Two forearms are available: a semi beaver-tail modern type of forearm and a short slender design patterned after the typical designs of Alexander Henry.

When the short Henry type forearm is used, the front sling swivel is mounted on a barrel band and a sling in this event would be regarded as primarily a carrying sling. The front swivel is mounted in the forearm.

Both pistol grip and forearm are hand-checkered in an ample area to a borderless design. The finish completely reveals the character and grain of the carefully selected American walnut from which the stocks and forearms are made.

RUGER NO. 1 SINGLE-SHOT RIFLES

These five illustrations show the variations which are currently offered in the Ruger No. 1 Single-Shot Rifle. Orders for variations or calibers other than those listed are not available from Ruger. The Ruger No. 1 rifles come fitted with selected American walnut stocks. Pistol grip and forearm are hand-checkered to a borderless design. Price for any listed model is **$405.00**. Barreled action is **$286.50**.

RUGER Number One Light Sporter
Calibers: 243 Win., 30/06, 270 Win. 7x57mm
Barrel: 22 inches.
Sights: Open.
Weight: 7¼ pounds.

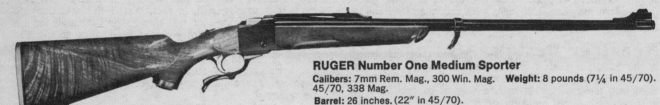

RUGER Number One Medium Sporter
Calibers: 7mm Rem. Mag., 300 Win. Mag. 45/70, 338 Mag.
Barrel: 26 inches. (22″ in 45/70).
Sights: Open.
Weight: 8 pounds (7¼ in 45/70).

RUGER Number One Standard Rifle
Calibers: 22/250, 243 Win., 6mm Rem., 25/06, 270 Win., 30/06, 7mm Rem. Mag., 300 Win. Mag., 220 Swift, 333 Mag.
Barrel: 26 inches.
Sights: Ruger steel tip-off scope rings, 1″.
Weight: 8 pounds.

RUGER Number One Special Varminter
Caliber: 22/250, 25/06, 220 Swift
Barrel: 24 inches.
Sights: Ruger Steel blocks and Tip-off scope rings, 1″.
Weight: 9 pounds.

RUGER Number One Tropical Rifle
Calibers: 375 H & H Mag., 458 Win., Mag.
Barrel: 24 inches.
Sights: Open.
Weight: 8¼ pounds for 375, 9 pounds for 458.

AC-556® Selective Fire Automatic Rifle

Cal. 223 (5.56mm)

The Ruger AC-556 automatic rifle is a selective fire weapon equipped with a reinforced one-piece American hardwood stock and heat-resistant, ventilated fiberglass handguard. The fire control mechanism consists of a positive three-position selector lever which provides semi-automatic, three-shot burst, or fully automatic modes of fire. The selector lever is readily accessible and both the safety and the selector lever can be reached without removing the hand from the normal firing position. The AC-556 automatic rifle is equipped with a muzzle flash hider, military bayonet stud type protected front sight, and fiberglass handguard, and can be provided with the blued steel folding stock, available at additional cost. Choice of a high cyclic rate of fire, 3-shot burst, or semi-automatic operation, coupled with low recoil, folding stock option, compact size and light weight, in either blued or stainless steel models, make the Ruger AC-556 automatic rifle the ideal choice

AC-556 F® Selective Fire Automatic Rifle

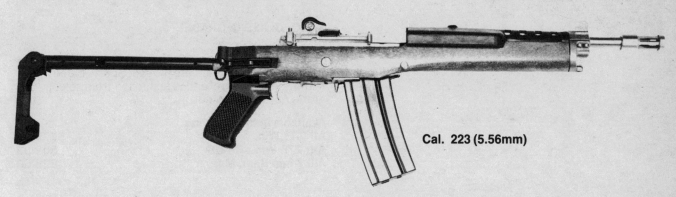

Cal. 223 (5.56mm)

The Ruger AC-556 F automatic rifle is a short barrel, selective fire weapon based on the mechanism of the AC-556 automatic and is ideal for applications where accurate fire combined with compactness and short overall length are required. Both the AC-556 and AC-556 F automatic rifles have been specifically designed to complement the ballistic and dimensional advantages of the highly efficient .223 (5.56mm) caliber cartridge which has a very flat trajectory and excellent energy retention at long ranges.

	AC-556	AC-556 F
Weight of Basic Rifle (Loaded)	6 Lbs. 6 Oz.	7 Lbs. 15 Oz.
Overall Length (Folding Stock Opened)	37.25"	33.5"
Overall Length (Stock Folded)	—	23.75"
Barrel Length	18.5"	13"
Cyclic Rate of Fire (Full Auto., Approx.)	750 R.P.M	750 R.P.M

Model	Description	Price
AC-556	Selective Fire Automatic Rifle	$309.00
AC-556 F	Selective Fire Folding Stock Model with 20-shot Magazine	343.00
K AC-556	Stainless Steel Selective Fire Automatic Rifle	373.00
K AC-556 F	Stainless Steel Selective Fire Automatic Rifle with Stainless folding Stock	407.50

SAKO RIFLES

LIMITED EDITION SAKO SAFARI GRADE

Features extended magazine for storing four back-up rounds plus one in the chamber; barrel band swivel; express-type rear sight rib for extra strength; a satin or matte bluing for extra durability.

**Available in 300 Win. Mag.,
338 Win. Mag., 375 H&H Mag.**   **$1660.00**

SAKO CLASSIC GRADE

This incredibly accurate Sako Classic Grade is the rifle by which all others are judged. Sports blued, satin-finished barrel and is fashioned from select grade American walnut.

Available in the following:
AII 243 Win. **$775.00**
AIII 270 Win., 30-06 .... **809.00**
AIII 7 mm Rem. Mag. **825.00**

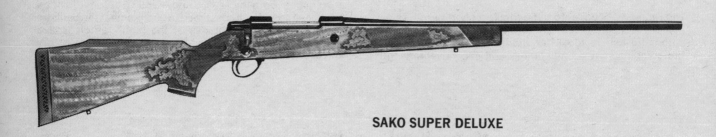

SAKO SUPER DELUXE

Sako offers the Super Deluxe to the most discriminating gun buyer. This one-of-a-kind beauty is available on special order.

**Special order. Available in AI,
AII, AIII Calibers** **$1660.00**

SAKO RIFLES

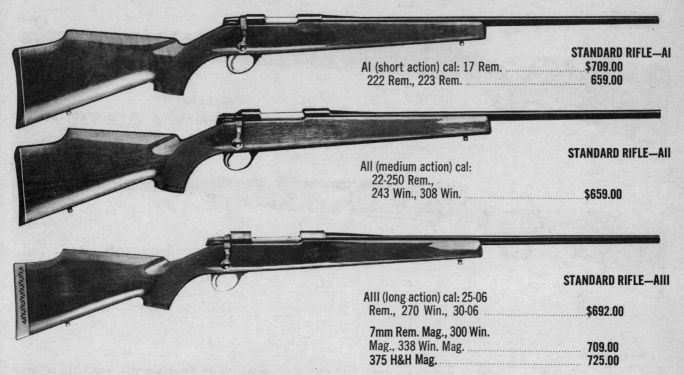

STANDARD RIFLE—AI

AI (short action) cal: 17 Rem. $709.00
222 Rem., 223 Rem. 659.00

STANDARD RIFLE—AII

AII (medium action) cal:
22-250 Rem.,
243 Win., 308 Win. $659.00

STANDARD RIFLE—AIII

AIII (long action) cal: 25-06
Rem., 270 Win., 30-06 .... $692.00

7mm Rem. Mag., 300 Win.
Mag., 338 Win. Mag. 709.00
375 H&H Mag. 725.00

THE SAKO TRIGGER IS A RIFLEMAN'S DELIGHT... SMOOTH, CRISP AND FULLY ADJUSTABLE.

If these were the only Sako features, it would still be the best rifle available. But the real quality that sets Sako apart from all others is its truly outstanding accuracy.

While many factors can affect a rifle's accuracy, 90% of any rifle's accuracy potential lies in its barrel. And the creation of superbly accurate barrels is where Sako is unique.

The care that Sako takes in the cold-hammering processing of each barrel is unparalleled in the industry. As an example, after each barrel blank is drilled, it is diamond-lapped and then optically checked for microscopic flaws. This extra care affords the Sako owner lasting accuracy and a finish that will stay "new" season after season.

You can't buy an unfired Sako. Every gun is test fired using special overloaded proof cartridges. This ensures the Sako owner total safety and uncompromising accuracy. Every barrel must group within Sako specifications or it's scrapped. Not recycled. Not adjusted. Scrapped. Either a Sako barrel delivers Sako accuracy, or it never leaves the factory.

And hand-in-hand with Sako accuracy is Sako beauty. Genuine European walnut stocks, flawlessly finished and checkered by hand.

Sako rifles are available in the following:
- Standard, with AI, AII and AIII actions.
- Deluxe, with AI, AII and AIII actions.
- Varmint, with heavy-barrel and Varminter forend in AI and AII.
- Carbine—with full-length stock. AII action in 243. AIII action in 270 and 30-06.
- Super Deluxe, with AI, AII and AIII actions.
- Classic Grade, with AII, (243), and AIII action in (270, 30-06, and 7mm Rem. Mag.)
- Safari Grade, with AIII Mag. calibers: 300 Win. Mag., 338 Win. Mag. and 375 H&H Mag.

SAKO RIFLES

Sako Carbine
Caliber: 243 Win., 270 Win., 30-06 ....**$825.00**

Sako Varmint (Heavy Barrel)
AI (short action) cal: 222 Rem.,
223 Rem. **$709.00**
AII (medium action) cal:
22-250 Rem., 243 Win., 308 Win. **709.00**

1) COMPLETE RIFLES:

Calibers	*Available Models	Action Type	Magazine Capacity	Barrel Length	Approx. Wt.: S, D, SD, CL,	Approx Wt. (Varmint)	Approx. Wt. (Carbine)	Approx. Wt. (Safari)	Twist R.H. 1 Turn-in	Length of Pull
.17 Rem*	S/SD	AI-1	5	23½"	6½ lbs.				9"	13½"
.222**	S/D/V/SD	AI-1	5	23½"	6½ lbs.	8¼ lbs.			14"	13½"
.223**	S/D/V/SD	AI-1	5	23½"	6½ lbs.	8¼ lbs.			13"	13½"
.22-250**	S/D/V/SD	AII-3	5	23½"	7¼ lbs.	8½ lbs.			14"	13½"
.243**	S/D/V/C/CL/SD	AII-1	5	23" (20"C)	7¼ lbs.	8½ lbs.	7½ lbs.		10"	13½"
.308**	S/D/V/SD	AII-1	5	23"	7¼ lbs.	8½ lbs.			12"	13½"
.25-06**	S/D/SD	AIII-1	5	24"	8 lbs.				10"	13½"
.270**	S/D/C/CL/SD	AIII-1	5	24" (20"C)	8 lbs.		7½ lbs.		10"	13½"
.30-06**	S/D/C/CL/SD	AIII-1	5	24"(20"C)	8 lbs.		7½ lbs.		10"	13½"
7mm Rem. Mag.**	S/D/CL/SD	AIII-2	4	24"	8 lbs.				9½"	13½"
.300 Win. Mag.**	S/D/SD/SF	AIII-3	4	24"	8 lbs.			8 lbs.	10"	13½"
.338 Win. Mag.**	S/D/SD/SF	AIII-3	4	24"	8 lbs.			8 lbs.	10"	13½"
.375 H&H Mag.**	S/D/SD/SF	AIII-4	4	24"	8 lbs.			8 lbs.	12"	13½"

*CODE: S=Standard D=Deluxe SD=Super Deluxe V=Varmint C=Carbine CL=Classic Grade SF=Safari Grade
**Sako Super Deluxe Rifles are available for these calibers on special order only.

Stock: Standard — European walnut, high gloss finish, hand checkered, 20 lines to the inch. Deluxe — European walnut, high gloss finish, French-type hand checkered, 22 lines to the inch, rosewood grip cap and forend tip, semi beavertail forend. Super Deluxe — Select European walnut, high gloss finish, deep oak leaf hand engraved design. Classic Grade — Select American walnut, oil finish, hand checkered, 20 lines to the inch. Safari Grade — European walnut, oil finish, hand checkered, 20 lines to the inch. Carbine — Full length stock, European walnut, oil finish, hand checkered, 20 lines to the inch. Varmint — European walnut, oil finish, hand checkered, 20 lines to the inch, bull beavertail forend.

Metal finish: Carbine, Varmint, Standard, Classic Grade, Safari Grade: Blued satin finish. Deluxe, Super Deluxe: super high polished deep blue finish.

2) SAKO BARRELED ACTIONS: Standard barreled actions are available for calibers listed above.

3) SAKO ACTIONS:

Action Type	Calibers	Barrel Thread	Over-All Length	Approx. Weight	Magazine Length
AI₁	.17, .222, .222 Rem. Mag., .223	.866 x 16w	6½"	2½ lbs.	2.32"
AII₁	.243, .308	1 x 16 unified	7⅜"	2½ lbs.	2.85"
AII₃	.22-250	1 x 16 unified	7⅜"	2½ lbs.	2.72"
AIII₁	.25-06, .270, .30-06	1³/₆₄ x 16 unified	8⅜"	2¾ lbs.	3.64"
AIII₂	7mm Rem. Mag.	1³/₆₄ x 16 unified	8⅜"	2¾ lbs.	3.64"
AIII₃	.300 Win. Mag., .338 Win. Mag.	1³/₆₄ x 16 unified	8⅜"	2¾ lbs.	3.64"
AIII₄	.375 H&H Mag.	1³/₆₄ x 16 unified	8⅜"	2¾ lbs.	3.64"

SAKO RIFLES

SAKO HIGH-POWERED RIFLES ARE
UNIQUE IN THAT THEY ARE MADE
IN THREE DIFFERENT ACTIONS.

- AI (Short action) • AII (Medium action) • AIII (Long action)

Each action is customized to fit a specific set of individual hunting needs, each designed, engineered and scaled for a specific range of cartridges:

- AI (Short action) 17 Rem., 222 Rem., 223 Rem.

- AII (Medium action) 22-250 Rem., 243 Win., 308 Win.

- AIII (Long action) 25-06 Rem., 270 Win., 30-06, 7mm Rem. Mag., 300 Win. Mag., 338 Win. Mag., 375 H&H Mag.

Every Sako rifle, regardless of caliber, is built on an action with no unnecessary bulk or excess weight and with a bolt action as short as it is smooth.

Not only is the action scaled to the cartridge, the entire rifle is beautifully proportioned and perfectly scaled.

SAKO DELUXE RIFLES
AI (short action)
cal: 222 Rem.,
223 Rem. $875.00

AII (medium action)
22-250 Rem., 243
Win., 308 Win. $875.00

AIII (long action)
cal: 25-06 Rem.,
270 Win., 30-06 ...$917.00
7mm Rem. Mag. 934.00
300 Win Mag. 934.00
338 Win Mag. 934.00
375 H&H Mag. 950.00

- The Sako AI, (Short action) chambered for 222 Rem., will weigh an easy-to-carry 6½ lbs.

- The Sako AII (Medium action), chambered for 243 Win., comes in at 7¼ lbs.

- The Sako AIII (Long action), chambered for the big 375 H&H Mag., will tip the scales at a recoil-absorbing 8 lbs.

As a result, every Sako delivers better handling, faster swing and less fatigue.

The scope mounting system on these Sakos is among the strongest in the world. Instead of using separate bases, a tapered dovetail is milled right into the receiver, to which the scope rings are mounted. A beautifully simple system that's been proven by over twenty years of use. Sako scope rings are available in: low (2½ to 3-power scopes); medium (4-power scopes) and high (6-power scopes). Available in 1" only.

SAKO RIFLES

SAKO BARRELLED ACTIONS:

FOR THE PRIVATE OR PROFESSIONAL GUNSMITH WHO WISHES TO BUILD HIS OWN CUSTOM RIFLE, SAKO OFFERS BARRELLED ACTIONS IN STANDARD DEEP BLUE. AVAILABLE IN AI (SHORT ACTION), AII (MEDIUM ACTION) AND AIII (LONG ACTION).

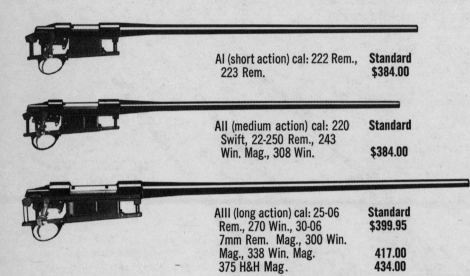

AI (short action) cal: 222 Rem., 223 Rem. — **Standard $384.00**

AII (medium action) cal: 220 Swift, 22-250 Rem., 243 Win. Mag., 308 Win. — **Standard $384.00**

AIII (long action) cal: 25-06 Rem., 270 Win., 30-06 7mm Rem. Mag., 300 Win. Mag., 338 Win. Mag. — **Standard $399.95**
417.00
375 H&H Mag. 434.00

SAKO ACTIONS: ONLY WHEN YOU BUY A SAKO RIFLE DO YOU HAVE THE CHOICE OF THREE DISTINCT ACTIONS. EACH CUSTOMIZED TO FIT A SPECIFIC SET OF INDIVIDUAL HUNTING NEEDS. EACH DESIGNED, ENGINEERED AND SCALED FOR A SPECIFIC RANGE OF CARTRIDGES. AS A RESULT, SAKO DELIVERS BETTER HANDLING, FASTER SWING AND LESS FATIGUE. SAKO ALSO OFFERS THESE ACTIONS ALONE IN AI (SHORT ACTION), AII (MEDIUM ACTION) AND AIII (LONG ACTION). AVAILABLE IN THE WHITE ONLY.

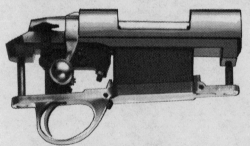

AI (SHORT ACTION) CALIBERS:
17 Rem.
222 Rem.
222 Rem. Mag.
223 Rem.
In white only $266.95

AII (MEDIUM ACTION) CALIBERS:
22-250 Rem.
243 Win.
308 Win.
In white only $266.95

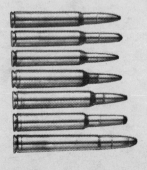

AIII (LONG ACTION) CALIBERS:
25-06 Rem.
270 Win.
30-06
7mm Rem. Mag.
300 Win. Mag.
338 Win. Mag.
375 H&H Mag.
In white only $284.95

SAVAGE CENTERFIRE RIFLES

MODEL 99-A
Calibers: 250 Savage 243, 308 and 375 Winchester

The 99-A features a straight (saddle) stock with schnabel forend **$326.10**

MODEL 99-C
Calibers: 308 & 243 Winchester, 7mm/08 Remington

The 99-C North American Classic features select walnut stock designed with a high Monte Carlo and deeply fluted comb. Stock and grooved forend skip-line checkered. Stock is fitted with whiteline recoil pad and pistol-grip cap. Detachable hooded ramp front sight, rear sight adjustable for elevation and windage. **$333.50**

MODEL 99-E
Calibers: 300 Savage, 243 and 308 Winchester

The 99-E lever-action carbine comes with a 22″ barrel. The fully enclosed box-type magazine with rotary carrier has a 5-shot capacity; plus one in chamber. With blued steel lever, grooved trigger and corrugated buttplate. Walnut finished Monte Carlo stock has grooved forend. Finger tip safety on right side of trigger locks trigger and lever. **$296.60**

SPECIFICATIONS—FEATURES

MODEL	Barrel Length	Barrel Steel	Steel Receiver	Tapped For Top Mount Scope	Sights Front	Sights Rear	Cocking Indicator	Magazine Type	Cartridge Counter	Capacity	Safety	Stock and Fore-end	Checkered	Flut. Comb.	Capped Grip	Butt Plate	Avg. Wgt. (Lbs.)
99-A	22″	Chrome Moly	Blued	X	Removable Ramp	Removable Adjustable	X	Rotary	X	6	Top Tang	Select Walnut		X		Steel	7
99-C	22″	Chrome Moly	Blued	X	Removable Hooded Ramp	Removable Adjustable	X	Clip		5	Top Tang	Select Walnut	X	X	X	Hard Rubber	8
99-E	22″	Chrome Moly	Blued	X	Removable Ramp	Removable Adjustable	X	Rotary		6	Slide Bottom Tang	Wal. Fin. Hardwood	X	X		Hard Rubber	7

MODELS 99 A, C and E Stock: Length 13½″; Drop at Comb 1⅝″ (1½″ for 99-A); Drop at Monte Carlo 1½″; Drop at Heel 2½″. Length Overall 41¾″.

RATE OF TWIST (R.H.) 1 turn in 9½″ for 7mm/08; 1 turn in 10″ for 243 and 250 Savage; 1 turn in 12″ for 300 Savage, 375 and 308.

SAVAGE CENTERFIRE RIFLES

MODEL 170 PUMP–ACTION RIFLE
30-30 Winchester & 35 Rem.
$204.45

The Model 170 pump-action rifle was designed to handle the 30-30 Winchester and 35 Rem. cartridge; pump stroke is 3-¾". Savage claims to have reduced friction in the action by an automatic vibrating process. It's Savage's answer to what hand-honing is meant to do. It includes the slide, bolt and sear. All locking surfaces between receiver and bolt are heat hardened. The receiver is machined from 8.9 pounds of solid tempered steel. The receiver is drilled and tapped for scope mounts.

Features include a top tang safety (under the shooter's thumb). The 170 comes with a selected walnut Monte Carlo style stock with checkered pistol grip and slide handle. Savage designed the slide handle of the 170 to slightly overlap the receiver while in the forward position. The action is hammerless, and the trigger must be released and squeezed for each shot. With 22" barrel, the 170 weighs 6¾ lbs.

SPECIFICATIONS — FEATURES

MODEL	Barrel Length	Tapped For Top Mount Scope	Sights Front	Sights Rear	Safety Fire Control	Maga-zine Type	Ca-pacity	Top Tang Safety	Stock and Slide Handle	Silent-Lok	Check-ered	Monte Carlo	Sling Studs	Stock Finish	Butt Plate	Avg. Wgt. (Lbs.)
170	22"	X	Hooded Removable Ramp	Folding Leaf	X	Tubular	4	X	Select Walnut	X	X	X	X	Electro-Cote	Hard Rubber	6¾

MODEL 170 Stock: Length 14"; drop 1½" at comb, 1½" at Monte Carlo, 2½" at heel. Length over-all 41½".   RATE OF TWIST (R.H.) 1 turn in 12" for 30-30 & 35.

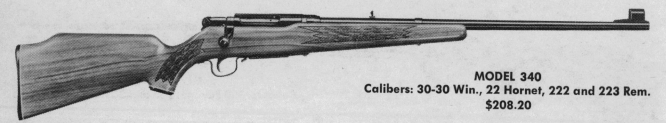

MODEL 340
Calibers: 30-30 Win., 22 Hornet, 222 and 223 Rem.
$208.20

The Savage 340 bolt-action center-fire rifle comes in calibers 30-30 Win., 22 Hornet, 222 and 223 Remington. The bolt locks up in front, assuring strength and accuracy. The barrel is precision-rifled and the muzzle is crowned.

The bolt handle is curved. Features include a Monte Carlo style stock of American walnut; checkering; pistol-grip cap and white-line spacers. Other features include detachable clip magazine (the clip pops out when the release lever is pushed) and metal open sights.

SPECIFICATIONS—FEATURES

MODEL	Barrel Length	Tapped for Scope Mount	Sights Front	Sights Rear	Thumb Safety	Clip Maga-zine	Ca-pacity	Checkered Stock Select Walnut	Checkered Stock Fluted Comb.	White Line Butt Plate	White Line Grip Cap	Monte Carlo Stock	Roll-Over Cheek Piece	Butt Plate	Avg. Wgt. (Lbs.)
340	22 Hornet, 223, 222:24"	Side Mount	Hooded Removable Ramp	Folding Leaf	X	X	5	X	X	X	X	X		Hard Rubber	7½
	30-30 22"	Side Mount	Hooded Removable Ramp	Folding Leaf	X	X	4	X	X	X	X	X		Hard Rubber	7¼

MODEL 340 Stock: Length 13½"; drop 1¾" at comb, 1¾" at Monte Carlo, 2½" at heel.
RATE OF TWIST (R.H.) 1 turn in 12" for 30-30 and 14" for 222, 223; 16" for 22 Hornet.

SAVAGE & STEVENS CENTERFIRE RIFLES

MODEL 110 BOLT ACTION CENTERFIRE RIFLES

MODEL 110-C (right hand)
MODEL 110-CL (left hand)

Features ejector clip magazine for convenient loading and unloading. To unload, press the recessed button and out pops the clip with the shells neatly held and tips protected. An extra loaded clip provides additional fire power. Exclusive twin gas ports in receiver, gas baffle lugs on bolt and bolt end cap give most complete protection. Extra clip, **$9.55** (specify caliber).

Calibers for right and left hand: 30-06 Sprg., 270 Win. & 243 Mag. Caliber: 7mm Rem. Mag.
Right hand only: 25-06, 22-250 Rem. 24″ barrels only

Standard calibers:	.... right-hand	$296.60
"	.... left-hand	298.45
Magnum caliber :	.... right-hand	305.90
	.... left-hand	307.75

SPECIFICATIONS — FEATURES

| MODEL | Free Floating Barrel | | Steel Receiver | Gas Ports | Tapped For Top Mount Scope | Sights | | Satin Slide Bolt | Recessed Bolt Face | Safety Gas Baffles | Cocking Indicator | Magazine | Capacity | Top Tang Safety | Checkered Stock | Cheek Piece | Butt Plate | Avg. Wgt. (Lbs.) |
	Barrel Length	Barrel Steel				Front	Rear											
110-C,CL	22″*	Chrome Moly	Blued	2	X	Hooded Removable Ramp	Removable Adjustable	X	X	3	X	Clip	5	X	Select Walnut	X	Hard Rubber	7
110-C,CL (Mag)	24″	Chrome Moly	Blued	2	X	Removable Ramp	Removable Adjustable	X	X	3	X	Clip	4	X	Select Walnut	X	Recoil Pad	7¾

LEFT-HAND rifles built to same specifications, except with left-hand stock and action.
ALL MODELS Stock: Length 13½″; drop 1⅝″ at comb, 1½″ at Monte Carlo. 2¼″ at heel. Length over-all: 42½″-45″.

*RIGHT HAND 25-06, 22-250 Rem. 24″ barrel only.
RATE OF TWIST (R.H.) 1 turn in 9½″ for 7mm Rem. Mag.; 1 turn in 10″ for 25-06, 243, 30-06 and 270; 1 turn in 14″ for 22-250; 1 turn in 12″ for 308.

MODEL 110-S Silhouette Rifle
Caliber: 308 Win., 7mm/08 Rem.
$298.45

LENGTH	OVERALL	43″
	BARREL	22″
	STOCK	13½″
DROP AT	COMB	1⅜″
	MONTE CARLO	1¼″
	HEEL	2¼″
AVERAGE WEIGHT (LBS.)		(MAX. 8 lbs. 10 oz.)
CARTRIDGE CAPACITY		5

Features: A heavy 22″ tapered barrel, ⅞″ diameter at muzzle, allows for greater accuracy. Receiver is drilled and tapped for scope mounting, satin blue finish on receiver to reduce light reflection. The barrel is free floating in special "Silhouette" stock of select walnut, has high fluted comb, hard filling, Wundhammer swell pistol grip for both right and left-hand use. Anschutz style stippled checkering on pistol grip and under fore-end. Stock is fitted with rifle recoil pad.

STEVENS MODEL 110-ES
Calibers: 30-06 Sprg., 243 and 308 Win.
with 4X Scope and Mount

Features walnut-finished, hardwood stock with high Monte Carlo cheekpiece and 5-shot internal box magazine. Removable, adjustable rear sight and removable front ramp sight. **$257.80**
Model 110-E: Same as Model 110-ES but without 4X Scope and Mount. **$217.40**

SAVAGE 22 RIFLES

SAVAGE MODEL 980-DL
22 Long Rifle
$136.40

The Model 980-DL features Monte Carlo stock with fluted comb; decorative white-lined butt is checkered on grip and forend. Deep blue, solid steel, square-look receiver is grooved for scope mounting. Equipped with hooded ramp front sight and folding leaf adjustable rear sight. Easy loading magazine holds 15 long-rifle cartridges.

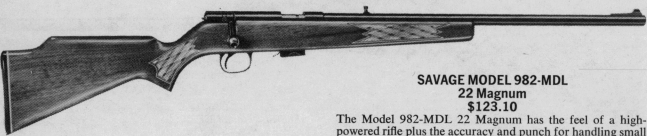

SAVAGE MODEL 982-DL
22 Long Rifle
$128.65

The 982-DL is equipped with flush-fit, push-button release 5-shot magazine similar to centerfire rifles. Monte Carlo stock is American walnut with cut checkering on pistol grip and forend. Deep blued, solid steel receiver is matted to reduce glare and grooved for scope mounting. Tapered, free-floating barrel has ramp front sight and folding leaf rear sight.

SAVAGE MODEL 982-MDL
22 Magnum
$123.10

The Model 982-MDL 22 Magnum has the feel of a high-powered rifle plus the accuracy and punch for handling small game and pests. Monte Carlo stock is American walnut with deep blued, solid steel receiver and barrel. Matted receiver is grooved for scope mounting and has ramp front sight and folding leaf rear sight. Also features a 5-shot detachable clip magazine and double extractors for positive ejection.

STEVENS MODEL 987-T AUTOLOADER
22 Long Rifle with 1541 4X Scope and Mount
$102.80

The Model 987-T has top tang safety and 15-shot capacity tubular magazine. Autoloading is with 22 long rifle only. Trigger must be pulled and released for each shot. Monte Carlo stock is walnut-finished hardwood.
Model 987 22 Long Rifle: Same as Model 987-T except without 4X Scope and Mount. **$92.70**

SAVAGE/STEVENS/FOX 22 RIFLES

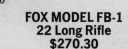

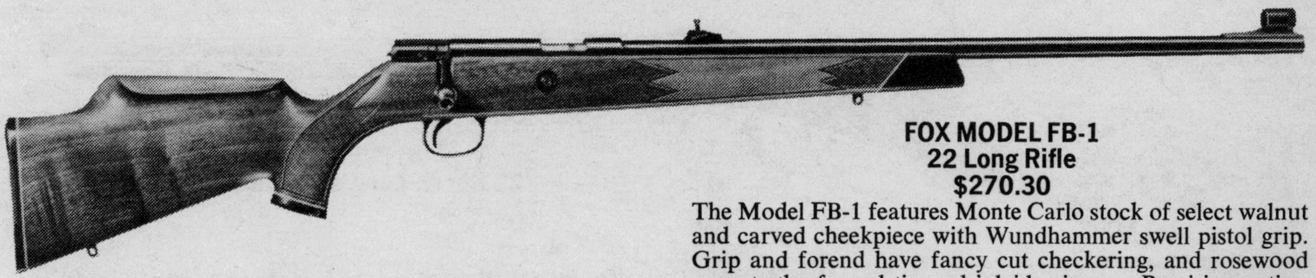

FOX MODEL FB-1
22 Long Rifle
$270.30

The Model FB-1 features Monte Carlo stock of select walnut and carved cheekpiece with Wundhammer swell pistol grip. Grip and forend have fancy cut checkering, and rosewood accents the forend tip and inlaid grip cap. Precision action has removable bolt with double extractors. Receiver is grooved for tip-off scope mounting and drilled and tapped for scope mounting bases. Also features 5-shot detachable magazine and hooded ramp front and rear sights, adjustable for windage and elevation.

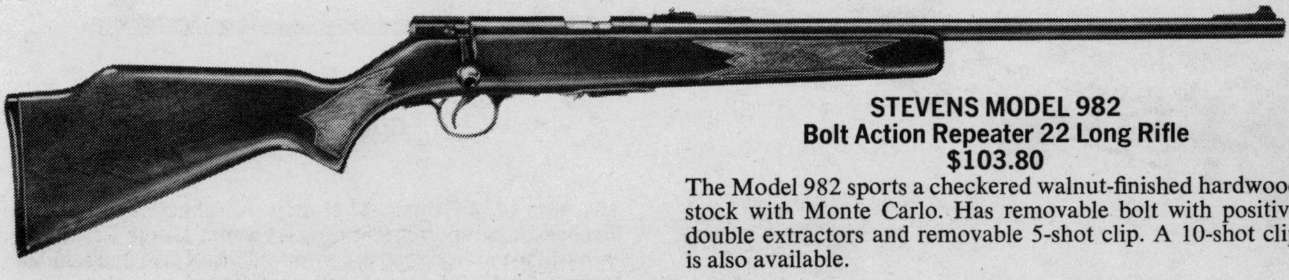

STEVENS MODEL 982
Bolt Action Repeater 22 Long Rifle
$103.80

The Model 982 sports a checkered walnut-finished hardwood stock with Monte Carlo. Has removable bolt with positive double extractors and removable 5-shot clip. A 10-shot clip is also available.

SPECIFICATIONS—FEATURES

	FB-1	982	980-DL	982-DL	982-MDL	987
Overall Length	43″	41″	40½″	41″	41″	40½″
Barrel Length	24″	22″	20″	22″	22″	20″
Length of Pull	14″	14″	14″	14″	14″	14″
Drop at Comb	1¾″	1½″	1½″	1¾″	1¾″	1½″
Drop at Monte Carlo	1¾″	1⅝″	1⅝″	1¾″	1¾″	1⅝″
Drop at Heel	2⅝″	2½″	2½″	2⅝″	2⅝″	2½″
Average Weight	6½ lbs.	5¾ lbs.	6 lbs.	6 lbs.	6 lbs.	6 lbs.

RATE OF TWIST (R.H.) 1 turn in 16″ for 22 L.R. and 22 Magnum.

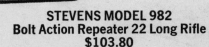

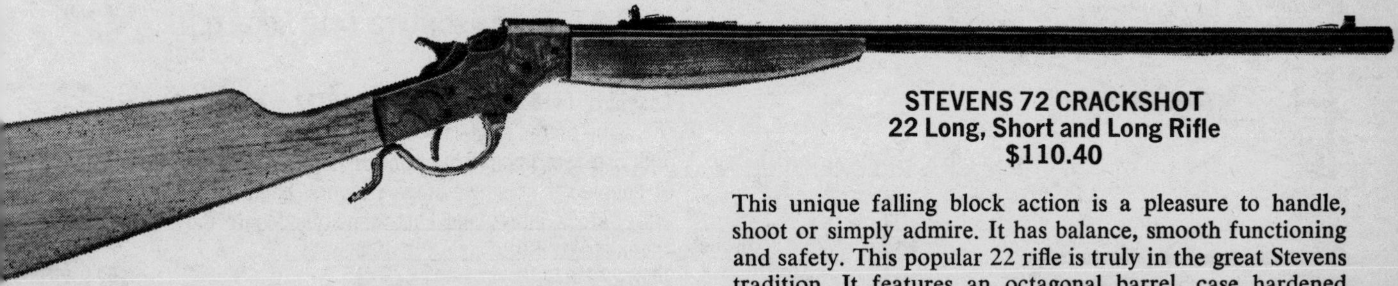

STEVENS 72 CRACKSHOT
22 Long, Short and Long Rifle
$110.40

This unique falling block action is a pleasure to handle, shoot or simply admire. It has balance, smooth functioning and safety. This popular 22 rifle is truly in the great Stevens tradition. It features an octagonal barrel, case hardened frame, walnut stock and forend with oil finish.

STEVENS & SAVAGE/ANSCHUTZ RIFLES

STEVENS 89
22 Short, Long and Long Rifle

This little single shot has the balance and feel of a traditional western carbine. Featuring western-style lever action with a rugged Martini-type breech block, automatic ejection. Hammer must be cocked by hand independent of the lever prior to firing. Ideal for that young beginner. **$71.25**

ANSCHUTZ 1432
CUSTOM SPORTER

Anschutz 1432 Caliber: 22 Hornet. Anschutz has introduced this handsome sporter featuring a custom Monte Carlo stock with roll over cheek piece, contoured pistol grip and schnabel forend. Grip and forend are lavishly hand-checkered in a skip-line pattern. The stock is of fine French walnut. Receiver is grooved for scope mount and drilled and tapped for scope bases. **$669.70**

SPECIFICATIONS — FEATURES

MODEL	Barrel Length	Grooved for Scope	Tapped for Scope Mount	Sights Front	Sights Rear	Thumb Safety	Clip Magazine	Capacity	Checkered Stock Select Walnut	Checkered Stock Fluted Comb.	White Line Butt Plate	White Line Grip Cap	Monte Carlo Stock	Roll-Over Cheek Piece	Butt Plate	Avg. Wgt. (Lbs.)
1432	22 Hornet, 24″	X	Top Mount	Hooded Ramp	Folding Leaf	Wing	X	5	X	X	X	X	X	X	Hard Rubber	6¾

1432 Stock: Length 14″; drop 1¼″ at comb, 1¼″ at Monte Carlo, 1¼″ at heel.
RATE OF TWIST (R.H.) 1 turn in 14″ for 222; 16″ for 22 Hornet.

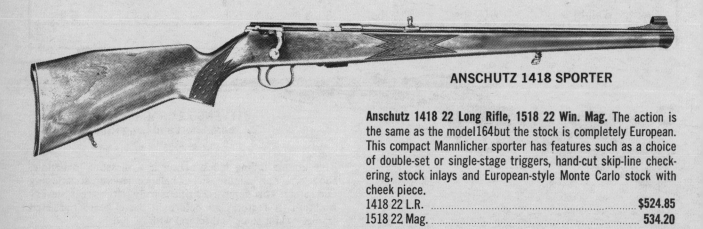

ANSCHUTZ 1418 SPORTER

Anschutz 1418 22 Long Rifle, 1518 22 Win. Mag. The action is the same as the model 164 but the stock is completely European. This compact Mannlicher sporter has features such as a choice of double-set or single-stage triggers, hand-cut skip-line checkering, stock inlays and European-style Monte Carlo stock with cheek piece.

1418 22 L.R. **$524.85**
1518 22 Mag. **534.20**

SAVAGE/ANSCHUTZ RIFLES

54 SPORTER (22 L.R. or 22 Mag.)

54 Sporter 22 long rifle, 54-M 22 Magnum. The model 54 Sporter combines the smallbore action with a handsome sporting Monte Carlo stock of fine French walnut. Strictly custom grade from the hand-carved roll-over cheek-piece and contoured pistol grip to the graceful schnabel fore-end. Both fore-end and pistol grip are hand checkered in a skip-line pattern.

The action is the Anschutz Match 54 that has dominated smallbore rifle shooting in recent years. Receiver is grooved for scope mount and drilled and tapped for scope bases. 54 Sporter, 22 L. R. **$621.30**

The 54-M magnum offers Anschutz - accurate shooting up to 100-125 yards for the varmint and small game hunter. 54-M, 22 Magnum. **$628.60**

164 CUSTOM GRADE 22 SPORTERS

164 22 long rifle, 164-M 22 magnum. The action of the 164— is the same one used on the Savage/Anschutz model 64 target rifle. The barrel is precision bored for pinpoint accuracy. Receiver is grooved for instant scope mounting. The select European walnut stock has all the custom grade features,—Monte Carlo with cheek-piece, Wundhammer swell pistol grip, schnabel fore-end and checkering. **$352.80**

The 164-M is chambered for the 22 magnum cartridge for those longer range shots. **$360.45**

SPECIFICATIONS — FEATURES

| MODEL | Barrel Length | Grooved for Scope | Tapped For Scope Mount | Sights | | Trigger Factory set for crisp trigger pull. | Clip Magazine | Capacity | Safety | Checkered Stock | | | Fluted Comb. | White Liner | Butt Plate | Length Overall | Average Weight (Lbs.) |
				Front	Rear					Cheek-piece	Monte Carlo	Wal-nut					
54, 54-M	24″	X	X	Hooded Ramp	Folding Leaf	X	X	6*,5†	Wing	X	X	X	X	X	Hard Rubber	43″	6¼
164, 164-M	23″	X		Hooded Ramp	Folding Leaf	X	X	6*,5†	Slide	X	X	X	X	X	Hard Rubber	40¾″	6
1418 1518	19¾″	X		Hooded Ramp	Folding Leaf	X	X	6*,5†	Slide	X	X	X	X	X	Hard Rubber	37⅝″	5½

Models 54, 164 and 1418 are chambered for 22 long rifle ONLY.   †Models: 1518, 164-M and 54-M chambered for 22 W.M.R. ONLY. Clip capacity 4.
   MODELS 164   Stock: Length 14″; drop 1½″ at comb, 1½″ at Monte Carlo, 2¼″ at heel.
        54   Stock: Length 14″; drop 1¼″ at comb, 1¼″ at Monte Carlo, 1¼″ at heel. RATE OF TWIST (R.H.) 1 turn in 16″ for 22 L.R., 22 Mag.
        1418, 1518   Stock: Length 13½″; drop 1⅛″ at comb, 2⅛″ at Monte Carlo, 2⅜″ at heel.

ANSCHUTZ & SAVAGE/ANSCHUTZ TARGET RIFLES

With Adjustable Cheek Piece, Combination Hand Stop / Sling Swivel and Variable Angle Hook Butt Plate

1413 Super Match 54.

You can have the Super Match 54 in three models (1413, 1407, 1411).

Model 1413 Super Match 54. The free-style international target rifle that dominates international competition for these reasons: a new superb Match 54 bolt design that is satin smooth; very short firing pin travel for extremely fast lock time; new conveniently located side safety. The new model 5071 Match Two-Stage Triggers are faster, more precise and more reliable. The mechanism reaction time is reduced. Other features include combination hand-stop/sling swivel, hook butt plate for right- and left-hand use, adjustable palm-rest, butt plate and cheek piece. **1413 Super Match 54 $1070.25. 1813-L**, left-hand stock **$1225.75.**

Model 1407 Match 54. Meets all International Shooting Union requirements and is suitable for all N.R.A. matches. Has new satin smooth Match 54 bolt design, new Match Two-Stage for precise and reliable adjustments and new convenient side safety. The whole stock and pistol grip are sculptured to fit the shooter in either a prone or standing position match. Hand-stop/sling swivel is included. **1407 ISU Match 54 $663.75 1807-L**, left-hand stock **$764.60.**

Model 1411 Match 54. The famous Anschutz prone rifle with the new Match 54 bolt design. Very short firing pin travel for extremely fast lock time. New conveniently located side safety, new single stage triggers are even faster, even more precise and reliable. The mechanism reaction time is reduced. Other features include adjustable cheek piece, combination hand-stop/sling swivel and adjutable butt plate. **1411 Match 54,** prone stock **$746.15. 1811-L**, left-hand stock **$913.30.**

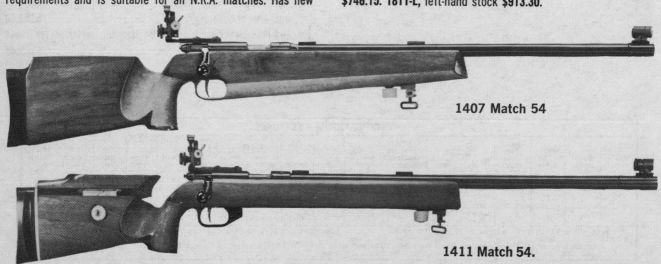

1407 Match 54

1411 Match 54.

ANSCHUTZ & SAVAGE/ANSCHUTZ TARGET RIFLES

1408ED "Super" Running Boar Rifle.
Available on special order only. $770.10; 1808ED, left hand, $860.10.

SAVAGE/ANSCHUTZ 64. The 64 offers shooters a superior but moderately priced, medium weight entry into the world of international champions. Target stock has checkered pistol grip, contoured thumb groove, Wundhammer swell, beavertail fore-end and adjustable butt plate with new blackline spacer—allows you to adjust length of trigger pull to your own specifications. Three-pound single stage trigger is adjustable for weight of pull, take-up and over-travel. 64-S models are equipped with the Anschutz 6723 Match Sight Set. 64 right hand **$343.25**, 64-L Left hand **$362.75**, 64-S right hand (with sights) **$431.70**, 64-SL left hand (with sights **$502.20.**

SAVAGE/ANSCHUTZ MARK 12. A target rifle with true target rifle features designed in the Anschutz tradition. Action is similar to Model 64. The heavy ⅞"-diameter, 26"-long barrel is precision rifled. Other features include an authentic target rifle stock with cheekpiece, thumb groove and Wundhammer swell pistol grip, adjustable hand stop and sling swivel. Comes fully equipped with front and rear target sights. The rear micrometer sight has click adjustments for windage and elevation. The globe front sight has seven aperture and post inserts for various shooting conditions and individual preferences. **$159.30.** Target sling, for right or left hand **$17.65.**

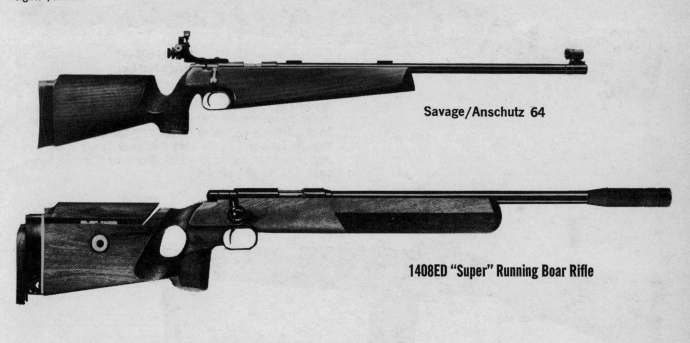

Savage/Anschutz 64

1408ED "Super" Running Boar Rifle

SPECIFICATIONS—FEATURES

	64	Mark 12
BARREL	Precision rifled. 22 long rifle only.	
LENGTH	26" Medium heavy 1¹⁄₁₆" diameter.	26" ⅞" diameter.
ACTION	Single shot. Large loading platform.	
TRIGGER	3 lbs. Single stage, adjustable for weight of pull, take-up, over-travel.	Factory set for crisp trigger pull.
SAFETY	Slide safety locks sear and bolt.	Slide safety locks trigger.
STOCK	Walnut finished hardwood Cheek-piece. Swivel rail.	Walnut finished hardwood.
SIGHTS	Receiver grooved for Anschutz sights. Scope blocks. Front sight base. 64-S models are equipped with Anschutz 6723 match sight set.	Front—Insert type globesight. Rear—(Micrometer click adjustments)
LENGTH	44"	43"
WEIGHT (avg.)	7¾ lbs.	8 lbs.

Left hand rifles built to same specifications, except with left-hand stock, cast-off.

RATE OF TWIST (RH) 1 turn in 16" for 22 LR.

SPRINGFIELD ARMORY

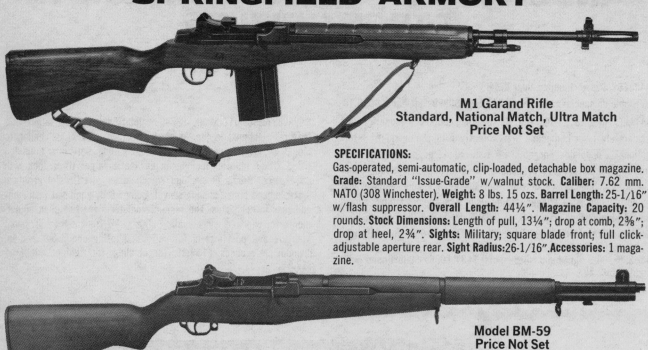

M1 Garand Rifle
Standard, National Match, Ultra Match
Price Not Set

SPECIFICATIONS:
Gas-operated, semi-automatic, clip-loaded, detachable box magazine. **Grade:** Standard "Issue-Grade" w/walnut stock. **Caliber:** 7.62 mm. NATO (308 Winchester). **Weight:** 8 lbs. 15 ozs. **Barrel Length:** 25-1/16" w/flash suppressor. **Overall Length:** 44¼". **Magazine Capacity:** 20 rounds. **Stock Dimensions:** Length of pull, 13¼"; drop at comb, 2⅜"; drop at heel, 2¾". **Sights:** Military; square blade front; full click-adjustable aperture rear. **Sight Radius:** 26-1/16". **Accessories:** 1 magazine.

Model BM-59
Price Not Set

SPECIFICATIONS:
Gas-operated, semi-automatic, clip-fed. **Grade:** Standard "Issue-Grade" w/walnut stock. **Caliber:** 30M2 (30-06) and 308 (7.62mm). **Weight:** 9 lbs. 8 ozs. **Barrel Length:** 24". **Overall Length:** 43½". **Magazine Capacity:** 8 rounds. **Stock Dimensions:** Length of pull, 13"; drop at comb, 2"; drop at heel, 2½". **Sights:** Front, military square blade; rear, full click-adjustable aperture.

Standard Rifle M1A, Match
Grade M1A, Super Match M1A
Rifle with heavy premium bbl.
Price Not Set

SPECIFICATIONS:
Gas-operated, semi-automatic (standard model); semi-auto/full auto selective fire (auto model); detachable box magazine. **Caliber:** 7.62 mm NATO (308 Winchester). **Magazine Capacity:** 20 rounds. **Accessories:** folding alpine paratrooper stock; muzzle brake; flash suppressor; grenade launcher combo; bipod; grenade launcher/winter trigger; grenade launcher sights; bayonet; field oiler cleaning equipment. Limited availability.

STEYR
MANNLICHER RIFLES

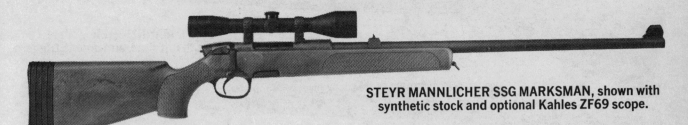

STEYR MANNLICHER SSG MARKSMAN, shown with synthetic stock and optional Kahles ZF69 scope.

SPECIFICATIONS:
Calibers: 243 Win., 308 Win. (7.62x51)
Barrel: 26"
Weight: 8.6 lbs. (9.9 lbs. with Kahles scope)
Overall Length: 44.5"
Stock: Choice of synthetic half stock of ABS "CYCOLAC" or walnut. Removable spacers in butt section adjusts length of pull from 12¾" to 14".
Sights: Hooded blade front; folding rear leaf sight.

Features: Parkerized finish. Choice of interchangeable single or double set triggers. Detachable 5-shot rotary straight-line feed magazine of "Makrolon." 10-shot magazine optional. Heavy duty receiver drilled and tapped for scope mounting. 6 rear locking lugs.

Cycolac half stock	$ 729.00
Walnut half stock	845.00
Cycolac half stock, with mounted Kahles ZF69 scope	1482.00
Optional 10-shot magazine	66.00
Spare 5-shot magazine	25.00

STEYR MANNLICHER SSG MATCH

Same as the Model SSG MARKSMAN, except with 26" heavy barrel, match bolt, Walther target peep sights, and adjustable rail in forend to adjust sling travel. Weight: 11 lbs.

Cycolac half stock	$ 996.00
Walnut half stock	1106.00
Spare 5-shot magazine	25.00

**STEYR MANNLICHER ML 79   LUXUS
(MODELS L & M)**

SPECIFICATIONS:
Calibers:
   Model L (standard calibers) 22-250 Rem., 243 Win., 308 Win.
   Model L (optional metric calibers) 5.6x57
   Model M (standard calibers) 25-06 Rem., 270 Win., 7x57, 7x64, 30-06
   Model M (optional metric calibers) 6.5x55, 6.5x57, 7.5x55, 9.3x62
Barrel: 20" (full stock); 23.6" (half stock)
Weight: 6.8 lbs. (full stock); 6.9 lbs. (half stock)
Overall Length: 39" (full stock); 43" (half stock)
Stock: Hand-checkered walnut with Monte Carlo cheekpiece. Either full Mannlicher or half stock. European hand-rubbed oil finish or high gloss lacquer finish.

Sights: Ramp front—adjustable for elevation; open U-notch rear—adjustable for windage.
Features: Single combination trigger (becomes hair trigger when moved forward before firing). Detachable 3-shot steel straight-line feed magazine (6-shot optional). 6 rear locking lugs. Drilled and tapped for scope mounts.

Full stock	$1172.00
Half stock	1097.00
Optional metric calibers	add 50.00
Spare 3-shot magazine	41.50
Spare 6-shot magazine	78.65

STEYR MANNLICHER RIFLES

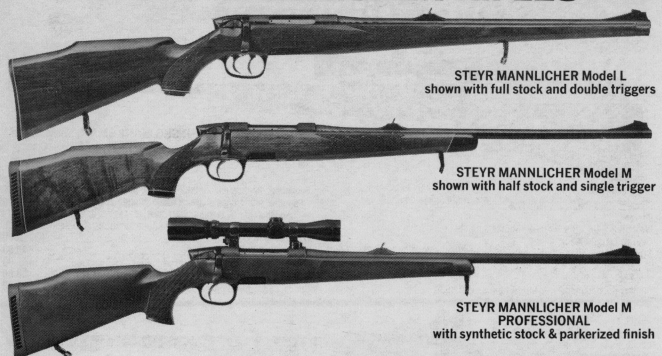

STEYR MANNLICHER Model L
shown with full stock and double triggers

STEYR MANNLICHER Model M
shown with half stock and single trigger

STEYR MANNLICHER Model M PROFESSIONAL
with synthetic stock & parkerized finish

SPECIFICATIONS:
Calibers:
Model SL (standard calibers only) 222 Rem. 222 Rem. Mag., 223 Rem.
Model L (standard calibers) 22-250 Rem., 6mm Rem., 243 Win, 308 Win.
Model L (optional metric caliber) 5.6x57
Model M (standard calibers) 25-06 Rem., 270 Win, 7x57, 7x64, 30.06 Spr.
Model M (optional metric calibers) 6.5x55, 6.5x57, 7.5x55, 8x57JS, 9.3x62

Barrel: 20" (full stock); 23.6" (half stock)
Weight: 6.8 lbs. (full stock); 6.9 lbs. (half stock); 7.5 lbs. (Professional)
Overall Length: 39" (full stock); 43" (half stock)
Stock: Full Mannlicher or standard half stock with Monte Carlo cheekpiece and rubber recoil pad. Hand-checkered walnut in skip-line pattern. The Model M with half stock is also available in a "Professional" version with a parkerized finish and synthetic stock made of ABS "CYCOLAC" (made with right-handed action only). Note: Model M is available with left-handed action in full stock and half stock.

Features: Choice of fine-crafted single or double set triggers. Detachable 5-shot rotary magazine of "Makrolon." 6 rear locking lugs. Drilled and tapped for scope mounting.

Full stock	$ 958.00
Full stock, with left-handed action	1082.00
Half stock	893.00
Half stock, with left-handed action	1020.00
Professional, with iron sights	715.00
Professional, without sights	690.00
Optional metric calibers add	50.00
Spare magazine	25.00

STEYR MANNLICHER Model S/T Magnum
with heavy barrel shown with
optional butt magazine inletted in stock

SPECIFICATIONS:
Caliber: Model S—257 Weatherby Mag., 264 Win. Mag., 300 Win. Mag., 338 Win. Mag., 7mm Rem. Mag., 300 H&H Mag., 375 H&H Mag.
Model S (Optional calibers)—6.5x68, 8x68S, 9.3x64
Model S/T (Heavy barrel)—375 H&H Mag., 458 Win. Mag.
Model S/T (Optional caliber)—9.3x64
Barrel: 26", Model S/T (with 26" heavy barrel)
Weight: 8.4 lbs. (Model S); 9.02 lbs. (Model S/T); add .66 lbs. for butt mag. opt.
Overall Length: 45"

Stock: Half stock with Monte Carlo cheekpiece and rubber recoil pad. Hand-checkered walnut in skip-line pattern. Available with optional spare magazine inletted in butt stock.
Features: Choice of fine-crafted single or double set triggers. Detachable 4-shot rotary magazine of "Makrolon." 6 rear locking lugs. Drilled and tapped for scope mounting.

Model S or S/T	$ 962.00
Model S or S/T, with opt. butt magazine	1032.00
Optional calibers add	50.00
Spare magazine	25.00

STEYR MANNLICHER RIFLES

STEYR MANNLICHER VARMINT
Models SL & L $965.00

SPECIFICATIONS:
Calibers:
  Model SL Varmint—222 Rem.
  Model L Varmint—22-250 Rem., 243 Win., 308 Win.
  Model L (Optional caliber)—5.6x57
Barrel: 26″ heavy barrel
Weight: 7.92 lbs.

Overall Length: 44″ / L (Varmint)
Sights: without sights.
Features: Choice of interchangeable single or double set triggers, 5-shot detachable "Makrolm" rotary magazine; 6 rear locking lugs; drilled and tapped for scope mounts.
Optional caliber $50.00
Spare magazine 25.00

TIKKA RIFLES

TIKKA M65 STANDARD $685.00

Calibers: 25-06, 6, 5 x 55, 7 x 64, 270 Win., 308 Win., 30-06, 7mm Rem. Mag., 300 Win. Mag.; **Weight:** 3,3 kg. **Barrel Length:** 560mm; **Overall Length:** 1080mm; **Magazine:** Clip magazine, 5 cartridges; **Stock:** Walnut with palm-swell in pistol grip.

TIKKA M55 DELUXE $749.00

Specifications: Calibers: 17 Rem., 222 Rem., 22-250 Rem., 6mm Rem., 243 Win., 308 Win. **Weight:** 3,3 kg. **Barrel Length:** 580mm. **Overall Length:** 1070mm. **Magazine:** Clip magazine, 3 cartridges. **Stock:** Walnut with rosewood forend tip and grip cap. Roll-over cheekpiece. Palm-swell in pistol grip. **Accessories:** Magazine, 5 cartridges.

TIKKA M65 WILDBOAR $820.00
Calibers: 7x64, 300 Win. Mag., 308 Win., 30-06

WEATHERBY RIFLES

VARMINTMASTER $679.95
Calibers: 22-250 Rem. & 224 W.M.
(without sights)

Mark V VARMINTMASTER—Calibers: 22-250 Rem. and 224 Weatherby Magnum. **Action:** Mark V bolt action scaled down, six locking lugs, enclosed cartridge case head, three gas ports. **Sights:** shown with 3X to 9X Weatherby Variable Scope on Buehler Mount. **Stock:** Monte Carlo with cheek piece and hand checkering. Fore-end tip, pistol grip and rubber butt pad.

MARK V DELUXE RIFLE $989.95
Calibers: 240 W.M., 257 W.M., 270 W.M.
7 mm W.M., 300 W.M., 340 W.M.,
378 W.M., 460 W.M. & 30-06

MARK V DELUXE RIFLE—Calibers: 257, 270, 7m/m, 300, 340, 378 and 460 Weatherby Magnum and 30-06 calibers. **Action:** Weatherby Mark V with recessed bolt face, nine locking lugs, three gas escape ports. 54° bolt lift. **Sights:** shown with hooded ramp front sight and receiver peep sight. **Stock:** Monte Carlo with cheek piece and checkering, fore-end tip, pistol grip cap, fitted rubber recoil pad.

Mark V Deluxe Rifle, less sights, in 240, 257, 270, 7mm, 300 W.M. and 30-06 calibers **$699.95.** In 340 W.M., less sights **$714.95;** 378 W.M. less sights **$859.95;** and in 460 W.M. caliber less sights **$989.95.** Rifles with factory-mounted scopes at extra cost. (Left-hand deluxe model, **$15.00**)

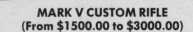

MARK V CUSTOM RIFLE
(From $1500.00 to $3000.00)

MARK V CUSTOM RIFLE—Specifications same as Deluxe rifle except with fancy grade walnut stock and full metal engraving. Prices range from $1000.00 to $3000.00 depending upon degree of decoration and sights desired by the shooter. Mark V Custom rifle shown is equipped with 3X to 9X Weatherby Variable scope on Buehler mount. Customs require approximately 18 months to produce.

RIFLE SPECIFICATIONS

CALIBER	224	22/250	240	257	270	7mm	30-06	300	340	378	460
Model	Right hand 24" or 26" bbl. Left hand model not available.		Right or left hand 24" bbl. Right hand 26" bbl. Left hand 26" bbl. available in 300 cal. only						Right or left hand 26" bbl. only.	Right or left hand 26" bbl. only.	Right or left hand 26" bbl. only.
Weight w/o sights	6½ lbs.		7¼ lbs.						8½ lbs.		10½ lbs.
Overall length	43¼" or 45¼" dependent on barrel length		44½" or 46½" dependent on barrel length						46½"		
Capacity	5 shots: 4 in magazine; 1 in chamber	4 shots: 3 in mag.; 1 in chamber	6 shots: 5 in mag.; 1 in chamber	4 shots: 3 in magazine; 1 in chamber			5 shots: 4 in mag.; 1 in chamber	4 shots: 3 in magazine; 1 in chamber		3 shots: 2 in magazine; 1 in chamber	
Barrel	24" standard or 26" semi-target		24" standard or 26" #2 contour						26" #2 contour	26" #3 contour	26" #4* contour
Rifling	1-14" twist		1-10" twist		1-10" twist	1-10" twist		1-10" twist	1-10" twist	1-12" twist	1-16" twist
Sights	Scope or iron sights extra										
Stock	American walnut, individually hand-bedded to assure precision accuracy. High-lustre, durable stock finish. Quick detachable sling swivels. Basket weave checkering. Monte Carlo style with cheek piece, especially designed for both scope and iron sighted rifles. Length of pull 13½". Length of pull of 460-13⅞".										French walnut only.
Action	A scaled-down version of the popular Mark V action with 6 precision locking lugs in place of 9.		Featuring the Mark V action. The nine locking lugs have almost double the shear area of the lugs found on conventional bolt rifles. The cartridge case head is completely enclosed in the bolt and barrel. 460 action includes hand honing, bolt knob fully checkered, bolt and follower damascened, custom engraved floor plate.								
Safety	Forward moving release accessible and positive										

BARRELED ACTION SPECIFICATIONS

CALIBER	224	22/250	240	257	270	7mm	30-06	300	340	378	460
Model	Right hand 24" or 26" bbl. Left hand model not available.		Right or left hand 24" bbl. Right hand 26" bbl. Left hand 26" bbl. available in 300 cal. only						Right or left hand 26" bbl. only.	Right or left hand 26" bbl. only.	Right or left hand 26" bbl. only.

*Pendleton Dekicker is an integral part of the barrel.
Prices for barreled action models
22-250 and 224 Varmintmaster calibers $400.00 240 W.M. 257 W.M., 270 W.M., 7mm W.M., 300 W.M., and 30-06 calibers $415.00, 340 W.M. $425.00 378 W.M. $495.00, 460 W.M. $555.00

WEATHERBY RIFLES

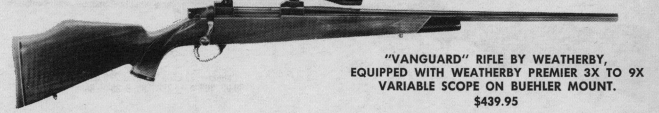

"VANGUARD" RIFLE BY WEATHERBY, EQUIPPED WITH WEATHERBY PREMIER 3X TO 9X VARIABLE SCOPE ON BUEHLER MOUNT.
$439.95

The Vanguard by Weatherby is now available in the following calibers: 243 Win., 25-06, 270 WCF 7mm Rem. Mag., 30-06, and 300 Win. Mag.

The "hammer-forging" method of barrel manufacture, guarantees a glass-smooth bore with optimum dimensional stability from breech to muzzle. It is this "hammer-forging" technique which gives the Vanguard rifle its accuracy and long life.

The Vanguard action is based on one of the most highly acclaimed designs in the gun industry, yet sports many of the modern safety advancements. The bolt face is recessed and it in turn is recessed into the barrel forming 3 concentric bands of steel around the cartridge case head. In addition to this case support, the Vanguard also features a completely enclosed bolt sleeve to prevent escaping gases from flowing back through the bolt into the shooter's face. Other safety features include a gas ejection port, two massive bolt lugs, and side operated safety lever. The action

has a knurled bolt knob for a better grip, a hinged floor plate for easy removal of loaded cartridges from the magazine, and a drilled and tapped receiver for simplified scope installation. The action is forged out of high strength chrome moly steel, polished and blued to a rich deep hue. The trigger guard and floor plate are black chromed for maximum durability.

The Vanguard has a fully adjustable trigger mechanism providing a crisp and clean pull down to 3 pounds.

The Vanguard stock is made of select American walnut and bedded for accuracy, it sports a Weatherby butt pad, 45° rosewood fore-end tip and pistol grip cap, white line spacers, and the traditional Weatherby diamond inlay. The finish of the Vanguard stock is the same high luster type found on the Mark V . . . scratch resistant and impervious to water, perspiration, or solvents. The Vanguard stock has a 13½" pull and just the right amount of cast-off and drop for the average shooter.

SPECIFICATIONS
Vanguard Rifles available in right-hand models only

Calibers	243 Win.	25-06 Rem.	270 WCF	7mm Rem. Mag.	30-06	300 Win. Mag.
Weight (approximate)	7 lb. 14 oz.	7 lb. 14 oz.	7 lb. 14 oz.	7 lb. 14 oz.	7 lb. 14 oz.	7 lb. 14 oz.
Overall Length	44 "	44½"	44½"	44½"	44½"	44½"
Magazine Capacity	5 rds.	5 rds.	5 rds.	3 rds.	5 rds.	3 rds.
Barrel Length	24"	24"	24"	24"	24"	24"
Rifling	1-10"	1-10"	1-10"	1-10"	1-10"	1-10"
Sights	Scope or iron sights at extra cost.					
Stocks	American Walnut, 13½" pull, fore-end tip & pistol grip cap					
Action	Vanguard action of the improved Mauser type					
Safety	Side operated, forward moving release, accessible & positive					
Scope Mounts	The Vanguard accepts any Mark V scope mount					

MARK XXII
22 LR SEMI-AUTOMATIC CLIP-FED
$279.95 (with open sights)

Also available with 15-shot tubular magazine (not illus.), with open sights. . . **$289.95**

MARK XXII RIMFIRE RIFLE—Caliber: 22 Long Rifle Rimfire. **Action:** semi-automatic, clip magazine (5 and 10 shot). Single shot selector. Bolt stays open after last shot. Shotgun-type tang safety. Receiver grooves for scope mounting. **Sights:** folding rear leaf and ramp front sight. **Stock:** Monte Carlo with cheek piece and hand checkering. Rosewood pistol grip cap and fore-end tip, and a "non-skid" rubber butt plate. Sling swivels. **Overall length:** 42¼". **Weight:** approximately 6 lbs.

WINCHESTER RIFLES

MODEL 70 XTR Standard
$412.00

Calibers: 22-250, 243 Win., 270 Win.,
30-06, 308 Win., 222 Rem. & 25-06 Rem.

MODEL 70 XTR Magnum $428.00
375 H&H Magnum $652.00

Calibers: 264 Win. Mag., 7mm Rem. Mag.,
300 Win. Mag., 338 Win. Mag. & 375 H&H Mag.

Model 70 XTR

Model 70 XTR advantages: Versatility and broad selection of calibers. Inherent accuracy due to barrel construction and precise chambering. High strength and durability from machined steel components. Dependable, smooth operation because of anti-bind bolt; fully machined and polished internal surfaces. Three-position safety; easy removal of firing pin assembly from bolt.

Features include Monte Carlo stock of American walnut with cheek-piece. Fine cut checkering. Tough, high-luster finish on wood. Black fore-end tip and pistol grip cap with white spacers. Black serrated butt plate. Hooded ramp front sight; new adjustable rear sight. Receiver drilled and tapped for scope. High polish and blueing. Engine-turned bolt. Detachable sling swivels. Hinged floor plate for fast unloading. Crisp trigger pull. Swaged rifling for accuracy.

Sets the standard for accuracy, ruggedness and dependability for hunters

22 in. barrel, right hand twist, 1 turn in 10 in., except 308 caliber which is 1 turn in 12 in., and 222 Rem., and 22-250 calibers which is 1 turn in 14 in.

Hooded front bead and adjustable rear sights. Stock dimensions: length of pull 13½ in., drop at comb 1¾ in., drop at heel 2⅛ in., drop at Monte Carlo 1½ in.; with cheek piece. Magazine holds 5 cartridges plus 1 in chamber.

Model 70 XTR Magnum

In a range of calibers for knocking over hyenas and other predators to large game animals such as elk, moose, caribou or Kodiak bear.

24 in. barrel except the 375 H & H Magnum which has a heavyweight barrel. Hooded bead front and adjustable rear sights except for 375 H & H Magnum which is furnished with a shallow V-notch adjustable rear sight. Stock dimensions: length of pull 13½ in., drop at comb 1¾ in.; with cheek piece. Winchester rubber recoil pad. Magazine holds 3 cartridges plus 1 in chamber.

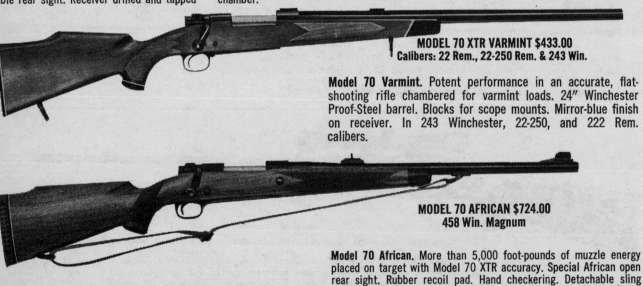

MODEL 70 XTR VARMINT $433.00
Calibers: 22 Rem., 22-250 Rem. & 243 Win.

Model 70 Varmint. Potent performance in an accurate, flat-shooting rifle chambered for varmint loads. 24″ Winchester Proof-Steel barrel. Blocks for scope mounts. Mirror-blue finish on receiver. In 243 Winchester, 22-250, and 222 Rem. calibers.

MODEL 70 AFRICAN $724.00
458 Win. Magnum

Model 70 African. More than 5,000 foot-pounds of muzzle energy placed on target with Model 70 XTR accuracy. Special African open rear sight. Rubber recoil pad. Hand checkering. Detachable sling swivels. Carrying strap. Twin steel stock reinforcing bolts. Ebony forend tip.

WINCHESTER RIFLES

MODEL 70 XTR BOLT ACTION FEATHERWEIGHT $433.00
Calibers: 243, 270 and 308 Win., 30-06 Spr., 257 Roberts & 7mm Mauser

The Model 70 XTR Featherweight features special tapered 22" cold-formed barrel of Winchester-proof steel. Receiver drilled and tapped for scope mounting. Barrel and all external metal surfaces polished to a richly blued XTR finish. Stainless steel magazine follower. Three-position safety and detachable sling swivels. Stock is schnabel-style, satin-finished American walnut with straight comb and new red buttpad with black spacer. Approx. wt.: 6¾ lbs.

Made entirely in U.S.A.

Caliber	Magazine Capacity (a)	Barrel Length	Overall Length	Length of Pull	Drop at Comb	Drop at Heel	Drop at Monte Carlo	Nominal Weight (lbs.)	Rate of Twist (R.H.) 1 turn in
M/70 XTR Standard									
222 Rem.	5	22"	42½"	13½"	1¾"	2⅛"	1½"	7½	14"
22-250 Rem.	5	22"	42½"	13½"	1¾"	2⅛"	1½"	7½	14"
243 Winchester	5	22"	42½"	13½"	1¾"	2⅛"	1½"	7½	10"
25-06 Rem.	5	24"	44½"	13½"	1¾"	2⅛"	1½"	7½	10"
270 Winchester	5	22"	42½"	13½"	1¾"	2⅛"	1½"	7½	10"
30-06 Springfield	5	22"	42½"	13½"	1¾"	2⅛"	1½"	7½	10"
308 Winchester	5	22"	42½"	13½"	1¾"	2⅛"	1½"	7½	12"
M/70 XTR Varmint (with heavy barrel)									
222 Rem.	5	24"	44½"	13½"	*9/16"	*15/16"	*3/8"	9¾	14"
22-250 Rem.	5	24"	44½"	13½"	*9/16"	*15/16"	*3/8"	9¾	14"
243 Winchester	5	24"	44½"	13½"	*9/16"	*15/16"	*3/8"	9¾	10"
M/70 XTR Magnum (with Recoil Pad)									
264 Win. Mag.	3	24"	44½"	13½"	1¾"	2⅛"	1½"	7¾	9"
7mm Rem. Mag.	3	24"	44½"	13½"	1¾"	2⅛"	1½"	7¾	9½"
300 Win. Mag.	3	24"	44½"	13½"	1¾"	2⅛"	1½"	7¾	10"
338 Win. Mag.	3	24"	44½"	13½"	1¾"	2⅛"	1½"	7¾	10"
375 H & H Mag.**	3	24"	44½"	13½"	1¾"	2⅛"	1½"	8½	12"
M/70 African (with Recoil Pad)									
458 Win. Mag.**	3	22"	42½"	13½"	1⅜"	2⅜"	1¾"	8½	14"
M/70 XTR Featherweight									
243 Winchester	5	22"	42½"	13½"	1⅜"	1¾"	—	6¾	10"
257 Roberts	5	22"	42½"	13½"	1⅜"	1¾"	—	6¾	10"
270 Winchester	5	22"	42½"	13½"	1⅜"	1¾"	—	6¾	10"
7mm Mauser (7x57)	5	22"	42½"	13½"	1⅜"	1¾"	—	6¾	8¾"
30-06 Springfield	5	22"	42½"	13½"	1⅜"	1¾"	—	6¾	10"
308 Winchester	5	22"	42½"	13½"	1⅜"	1¾"	—	6¾	12"

(a) Add one round for cartridge in chamber.
*From Center Line of bore. All others from line of sight.
**Not XTR

LEVER-ACTION XTR RIMFIRE
Model 9422 XTR Standard $276.00
Model 9422M XTR Magnum $283.00

The Model 9422 XTRs have been designed with a lever action that operates quickly and smoothly, with superior control during cartridge feeding. Both the Standard and Magnum rifles are grooved for scope mounting and include these features: coldformed Winchester-proof steel barrel; forged steel receiver, frame, and finger lever; side ejection; front ramp sight with dovetail bead and hood; adjustable semi-buckhorn rear sight; simplified takedown; scalloped tangs; solid American walnut stock and forearm. **SPECIFICATIONS: Calibers:** 22 rimfire; 22 Win. Mag. (XTR Mag.). **Magazine Capacity:** 21 Shorts, 17 Longs or 15 Long Rifles; 11 W.M.R. (XTR Mag.). **Weight:** 6¼ lbs. **Overall Length:** 37⅛". **Barrel Length:** 20½". **Length of Pull:** 13½". **Drop at Comb:** 1¾". **Drop at Heel:** 2½". **Rate of Twist:** (R.H.) 1 turn in 16.

WINCHESTER RIFLES

MODEL 94 REGULAR 30-30 Winchester $223.00

Model 94 Lever Action Carbine. Straight tang-to-toe lines of the American West. Hooded front sight. Sporting rear sight. Barrel band. Half-cock safety. In 30-30 Winchester, 32 Winchester Special.

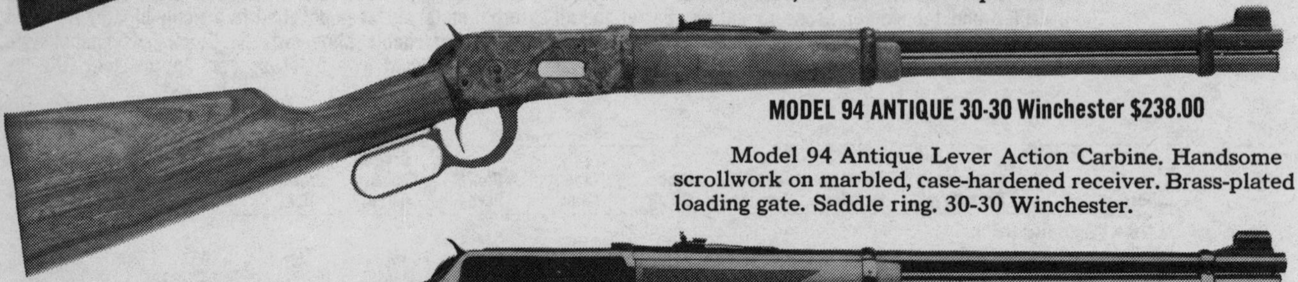

MODEL 94 ANTIQUE 30-30 Winchester $238.00

Model 94 Antique Lever Action Carbine. Handsome scrollwork on marbled, case-hardened receiver. Brass-plated loading gate. Saddle ring. 30-30 Winchester.

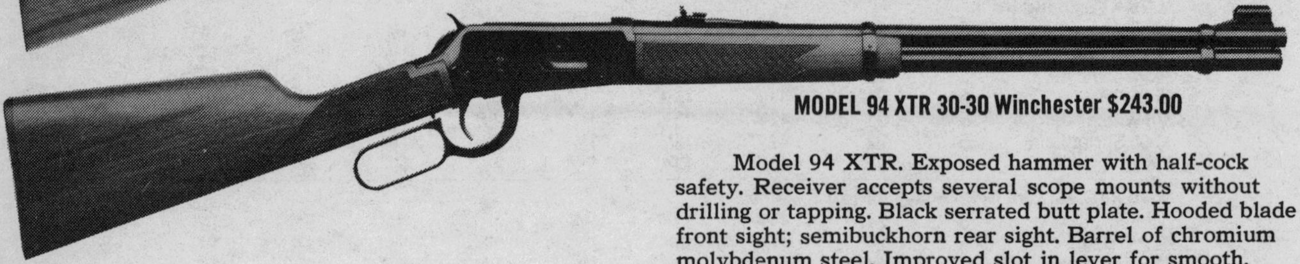

MODEL 94 XTR 30-30 Winchester $243.00

Model 94 XTR. Exposed hammer with half-cock safety. Receiver accepts several scope mounts without drilling or tapping. Black serrated butt plate. Hooded blade front sight; semibuckhorn rear sight. Barrel of chromium molybdenum steel. Improved slot in lever for smooth, fast action and feeding. 30-30 Winchester.

Model 94 XTR Big Bore. Non-glare finish on walnut; fine cut checkering on forearm and butt stock; high polish and deep blueing on the metal; beefed-up side panels; rubber butt pad reduces recoil. 375 Winchester. **$283.00**

MODEL 94 TRAPPER $176.00
30-30 Winchester

Model 94 Trapper Lever Action Carbine. Exposed hammer with half-cock safety. Full-length magazine tube holds five cartridges. Dovetailed blade front and semi-buckhorn rear sights. Straight-grip buttstock and forearm made of American walnut.

Model 94 Specifications

	Model 94 Carbine 30-30 Win.	Model 94 Antique Carbine 30-30 Win.	Model 94 XTR 30-30 Win.	94 XTR Big Bore 375 Win.	Model 94 Trapper Carbine 30-30 Win.
Mag. Capacity (a)	6	6	6	6	5
Overall Length	37¾″	37¾″	37¾″	37¾″	33¾″
Barrel Length	20″	20″	20″	20″	16″
Length of Pull	13″	13″	13″	13¼″	13″
Drop at Comb	1¾″	1¾″	1¾″	1¾″	1¾″
Drop at Heel	2½″	2½″	2½″	2½″	2½″
Weight (lbs.)	6½	6¼	6½	6⅛	6⅛″
Rate of Twist (R.H.) 1 turn in	12″	12″	12″	12″	12″

(a) Add one round for cartridge in chamber

WINSLOW RIFLES

STANDARD SPECIFICATIONS FOR ALL WINSLOW RIFLES

Stock: Hand rubbed black walnut. Length of pull—13½ inches. Plainsmaster ⅜ inch castoff. Bushmaster 3/16 inch castoff. All rifles are drilled and tapped to incorporate the use of telescopic sights. Rifles with receiver or open sights are available on special order. All rifles are equipped with quick detachable sling swivel studs and white line recoil pad. Choice of two standard stock models; Plainsmaster stock, and Bushmaster stock. **Magazine:** Staggered box type, four shot. (Blind in the stock has no floor plate.) **Action:** Mauser Mark x Action. **Overall Length:** 43 inches (Standard Model); 45 inches (Magnum). All Winslow rifles have company name and serial number and grade engraved on the action and caliber engraved on barrel. **Barrel:** Douglas barrel premium grade, chrome moly-type steel. All barrels 20 caliber through 35 caliber have six lands and grooves. All barrels larger than 35 caliber have eight lands and grooves.

All barrels are finished to (.2 to .4) micro inches inside the lands and grooves. **Total Weight (without scope):** 24 inch barrel—Standard calibers 243, 308, 270, etc. 7 to 7½ lbs.

26 inch barrel—Magnum calibers 264 Win., 300 Wby., 458 Win., etc. 8 to 9 lbs.

Winslow rifles are made in the following calibers:

Standard cartridges—22-250, 243 Win., 244 Rem., 257 Roberts, 308 Win., 30-06, 280 Rem., 270 Win., 25-06, 284 Win., 358 Win. and 7mm (7x57).

Magnum Cartridges—300 Weatherby, 300 Win., 338 Win., 358 Norma, 375 H.H., 458 Win., 257 Weatherby, 264 Win., 270 Weatherby, 7mm Weatherby, 7mm Rem., 300 H.H., 308 Norma.

Left-handed models available in most calibers.

The Winslow rifle can be fitted to suit your needs through choice of two models of stock. The Plainsmaster—Pinpoint accuracy in open country with full curl pistol grip and flat forearm. The Bushmaster—Lighter weight for bush country. Slender pistol with palm swell. Beavertail forend for light hand comfort.

All Winslow stocks incorporate a slight castoff to deflect recoil, minimizing flinch and muzzle jump.

WINSLOW BASIC RIFLE

The Basic Rifle, available in the Bushmaster stock, features one ivory diamond inlay in a rosewood grip cap and ivory trademark in bottom of forearm. Grade 'A' walnut jewelled bolt and follower **$1150.00.** Plainsmaster stock **$100.00** extra. **Left-hand** model **$1250.00**

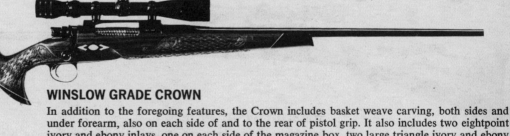

WINSLOW GRADE CROWN

In addition to the foregoing features, the Crown includes basket weave carving, both sides and under forearm, also on each side of and to the rear of pistol grip. It also includes two eightpoint ivory and ebony inlays, one on each side of the magazine box, two large triangle ivory and ebony inlays, one on each side of the buttstock. **Price upon request**

WINSLOW VARMINT

This 17 caliber is available in the Bushmaster stock and the Plainsmaster stock, which is a miniature of the original high roll-over cheek piece and a round leading edge on the forearm, modified spoon billed pistol grip. Available in 17/222, 17/222 mag. 17/233, 222 Rem. and 223. Regent grade shown. **Price upon request**

WINSLOW RIFLES

WINSLOW GRADE ROYAL

In addition to foregoing features, the Winslow Royal includes carving under forearm tip, carving on each side of magazine box, carving grip cap, carving belly behind pistol grip, carving in front of and in back of cheek piece, carving on each side of buttstock. **Price upon request.**

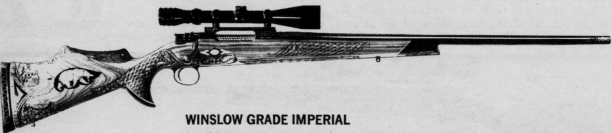

WINSLOW GRADE IMPERIAL

In addition to foregoing features, the Winslow Imperial includes barrel engraved from receiver to point eleven inches forward of receiver, engraving on the forward receiver ring, engraving on rear receiver ring, engraving on bolt handle and trigger guard, engraving on scope mounts and rings. **Price upon request.**

WINSLOW GRADE EMPEROR

In addition to the foregoing features, the Winslow Emperor is engraved in gold raised relief from receiver to point six inches forward of receiver and on tip of barrel, 1 animal on each side of front receiver, 1 animal on rear receiver, 1 animal head top each scope ring, 1 animal head on bolt handle and 1 animal head on trigger guard. **Price upon request.**

Shotguns

ASTRA SHOTGUNS

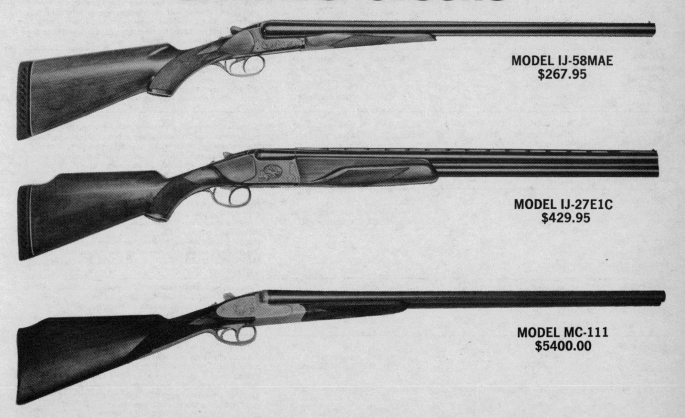

MODEL 750E
$639.00

Model No.	650	650E	750	750E	750 Skeet Skeet	750 Trap
Gauge	12	12	12	12	12	12
Barrel length	28″	28″	28″	28″	28″	30″
Chokes	MF	MF	MF	MF	SS	MF
Stock	walnut: plastic butt	walnut: plastic butt	walnut: plastic butt	walnut: plastic butt	walnut: Monte Carlo*	walnut: Monte Carlo*
Extractors	yes	no	yes	no	no	no
Selective ejectors	no	yes	no	yes	yes	yes
Triggers	2	2	1	1	1	1
Price	$452.04	$566.84	$562.65	$639.00	$735.72	$735.72

*With rubber recoil pad

BAIKAL SHOTGUNS

MODEL IJ-58MAE
$267.95

MODEL IJ-27E1C
$429.95

MODEL MC-111
$5400.00

BAIKAL SHOTGUNS

Model No.	Grade Style	Gauge	Chamber Lgth.	Barrel Lgth.	Choke	Weight*	Additional Features/Price
IJ-18 IJ-18E	Std. Plain Barrel	12, 20, or .410	2¾" or 3"	26", 28", or 30"	Mod or Full	5¾ lb.	IJ-18: extractor. IJ-18E: selective ejector. Walnut-stained hardwood. Hand-checkered pistol grip. Fore-end center latch. Cross bolt safety in trigger guard. Cocking indicator. Engraved receiver. IJ-18 **$73.50**; IJ-18E **$79.95**.
IJ-58MA IJ-58MAE	Side-by-Side	12 or 20	2¾" or 3"	26" or 28"	Imp. Cyl./Mod or Mod/Full	6¾ lb.	IJ-58MA: extractors. IJ-58MAE: selective ejectors/extractors. Select walnut. Hand-checkered pistol grip and fore-end. Hinged front trigger. Fore-end center latch. Engraved receiver. IJ-58MA **$239.95**; IJ-58MAE **$267.95**.
IJ-27IC IJ-27EIC	Over-Under/ Vent Rib (Field or Competition)	12	2¾" or 3"	26", 28", or 30"	Imp. Cyl./Mod or Mod/Full	6¾ lb.- 7½ lb.	IJ-271C: extractors. IJ-27EIC: selective ejectors/extractors. Select walnut. Hand-checkered pistol grip and fore-end. White spacers at pistol grip and recoil pad. Fore-end center latch. Single selective trigger. Engraved receiver. Skeet and trap models available. IJ-271C **$390.00**; IJ-27E1C **$429.95**; IJ-27E1C Silver **$585.95**; IJ-27E1C Super **$895.95**.
TOZ-34E	Over-Under/ Vent Rib (except 28 ga: solid rib)	12, 20, or 28	2¾"	26" or 28"	Imp. Cyl./Mod or Mod/Full	7 lb.	TOZ-34E: selective ejectors. Select walnut. Hand-checkered pistol grip and fore-end. Recoil pad. White spacers at pistol grip and butt. Cocking indicators. Engraved receiver. Available in Souvenir and Special models with engraved hunting scenes on polished nickel receiver and chiseled stock. Also available in two barrel sets. **$675.00**
IJ-25	Competition Over-Under/ Vent Rib (Hand-Fitted)	12	2¾"	26", 28", or 30"	Skeet/ Skeet, Mod/Full, or Imp. Mod/Full	7¾ lb.	Select walnut. Hand-checkered pistol grip. Ventilated fore-end. Monte Carlo stock. Internal action parts chromed. Target-grade single selective trigger. Hand-engraved; silver-inlayed receiver, trigger guard, and fore-end latch. Extractors or ejectors. White spacers at pistol grip and recoil pad. **Price Not Set.**
MC-5 MC-6	Hand-Made Over-Under/ Hand-Fitted Solid Raised Rib (Field or Competition)	12 or 20	2¾"	26" or 28"	Skeet/ Skeet, Imp. Cyl./ Mod, or Mod/Full	7 lb.	Select fancy walnut. Hand-checkered pistol grip or straight stock, with or without cheek piece and Monte Carlo. Hand-checkered fore-end permanently attached. Internal action parts chromed. Double triggers on separate base plate. Fully engraved receiver, trigger guard, and tang. Extractors or ejectors. Available in two barrel sets. MC-5 **$1295.00**; MC-6 **$1900.00**.
MC-7	Hand-Made/ Over-Under/ Hand-Fitted Solid Raised Rib	12 or 20	2¾"	26", 28", or 30"	Imp. Cyl./Mod, Mod/Full, or Full/Full	7½ lb.	Select fancy walnut. Hand-checkered straight stock or pistol grip, with or without cheek piece. Hand-checkered beavertail fore-end with pushbutton release. Internal action parts chromed. Double or single selective triggers. Hand-chiseled and engraved receiver, trigger guard, and tang. Extractors or ejectors. **$2730.00.**
MC-8-0 (skeet) MC-8-01 (trap)	Hand-Made Competition Over-Under/ Hand-Fitted Raised Vent Target Rib	12	2¾"	26" or 28"	Special Parabolic Skeet or Trap Chokes	7¾ lb.	Select fancy walnut. Hand-checkered pistol grip, fore-end, and butt. Monte Carlo stock. Fore-end permanently attached. Hand-engraved receiver, trigger guard, and tang. All internal action parts chromed. Single trigger with extractors or ejectors. Available in two barrel sets. **$2450.00.**
MC-21	Automatic (five-shot)/ Hand-Fitted Vent Rib/ Gas Operated with Recoiling Barrel	12	2¾"	26", 28", or 30"	Imp. Cyl., Mod, or Full	7¼ lb.	Select walnut. Hand-checkered pistol grip and fore-end with cheek piece. White spacers at pistol grip and butt. Hand-engraved receiver. All internal action parts chromed. Left or right safety. Instant takedown, including trigger housing. Target grade trigger. Magazine cut-off. Interchangeable barrel. **Price Not Set.**
MC-109	Hand-Made Sidelock/ Over-Under	12	2¾"	To customer specification	To customer specification	7¼ lb.	Extra fancy walnut. Hand-checkered straight stock or pistol grip, with or without cheek piece and Monte Carlo. Gold inlays in stock available. Removable sideplates. All internal action parts chromed. Cocking indicators. Single selective trigger. Hand-chiseled hunting scenes on receiver and trigger guard, with gold and silver inlays available. MANUFACTURED TO CUSTOMER SPECIFICATIONS. **$5035.00.**
MC-110	Hand-Made Side-by-Side/ Hand-Fitted Solid Raised Rib	12 or 20	2¾"	26" or 28"	Imp. Cyl./Mod or Mod/Full	6½ lb.	Fancy walnut. Straight or pistol grip stock. Hand-checkered grip and fore-end. Pushbutton fore-end release. Fully engraved receiver with hunting scenes. All internal action parts chromed. Double trigger. Extractors or selective ejectors. **$3200.00.**
MC-111	Hand-Made Sidelock/ Side-by-Side	12	2¾"	To customer specification	To customer specification	7 lb.	Extra fancy walnut. Straight or pistol grip stock, with or without cheek piece and Monte Carlo. Hand-checkered and carved. Gold and silver inlays in stock available. Removable sideplates. All internal parts chromed. Cocking indicators. Selective ejectors. Single selective or double triggers. Hand-chiseled scenes on receiver, trigger guard, and tang, with gold and silver inlays available. MANUFACTURED TO CUSTOMER SPECIFICATIONS. **$5400.00.**

*Approximate: weight varies according to barrel length, wood density, and other factors.

BERETTA SHOTGUNS

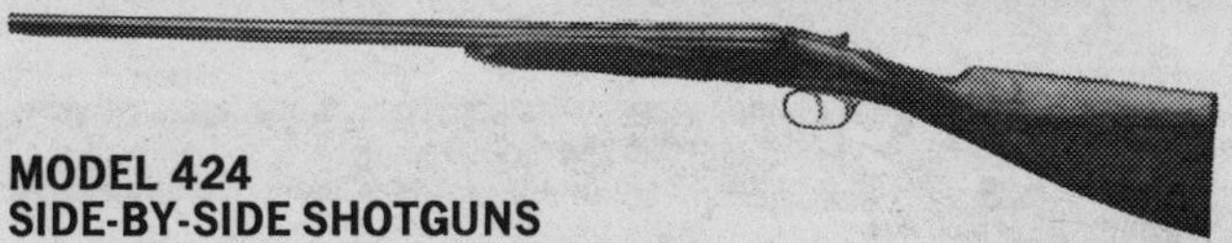

MODEL 424
SIDE-BY-SIDE SHOTGUNS

The action body, made of solid forged alloy steel, is of Boxlock design (Beretta patent) with coil springs throughout, and is nicely finished with light border engraving on rust-resistant, satin-chrome frame. Lockup is by means of double underlugs and bolts.

Barrels of steel "S" (chrome-moly) are joined on the "Mono Bloc" system giving alignment and rigidity. They are finished in a rich blue-black and are chrome lined. A hollow, matted rib is fitted to the barrels.

Model 424 shotguns are equipped with double triggers (front trigger hinged), automatic safety and plain, positive extractors.

Stocks are of the "English" straight grip type, fore-ends and stocks are made of fine, seasoned European walnut and hand-checkered.

STANDARD DIMENSIONS

Length of Pull: 14⅛″ (358mm)
Drop at Comb: 1 9/16″ (40mm)
Drop at Heel: 2 9/16″ (65mm)

Note: Gun weights may vary due to different stock wood densities, etc.

Model 424 (12 & 20 ga.) **$900.00**

Ga.	Length	Chamber	Description	Approx. Weight
12	26″	2¾″	Imp Cyl./Mod.	6 lbs. 10 oz.
12	28″	2¾″	Mod./Full	6 lbs. 10 oz.
20	26″	3″	Imp. Cyl./Mod.	5 lbs. 14 oz.
20	28″	3″	Mod./Full	5 lbs. 14 oz.

MODEL A-301
GAS-OPERATED, SEMIAUTOMATIC SHOTGUNS

The gas system absorbs a considerable part of the recoil. All parts in contact with the powder gases are made of stainless steel. The gas piston allows the use of all 2¾″ (70mm) shotshells, loaded to all standard pressure levels, without any adjustment to the gun. Those models chambered for 3″ (76mm) magnum shells need no adjustment for the various 3″ loads and will fit most standard 2¾″ field loads as well. The breech bolt is locked into the steel barrel extension at time of firing. Barrels are made of steel "S" (chrome-moly) and have chrome-lined bores. The lightweight receivers are decorated with scroll patterns and finished in blue-black, as are the barrels. Stocks and forearms are of choice European walnut, hand-checkered and richly finished.

Standard Dimensions

Length of Pull, Field Guns: 14⅛″ (358mm)
Drop at Comb: 1⅜″ (35mm)
Drop at Heel: 2⅜″ (60mm)
Magazine Capacity: 3 Rounds

All barrels fitted with ventilated ribs, except for "Slug" barrels which have adjustable rifle sights.

All stocks are of pistol grip (capped) style, fore-ends are shaped for a firm grip. Trap gun and 3″ Magnum gun stocks are fitted with recoil pads.

Safety is push button type, in trigger guard.

Model A301 Automatic w/VR (12 & 20 ga.) **$485.00**
Model A301 Mag. Automatic w/VR (12 & 20 ga.) **530.00**
Model A301 Automatic Slug Gun (12 ga.) **485.00**

Ga.	Length	Chamber	Description	Approx. Weight
12	22″	2¾″	Slug choke w/rifle sights	6 lbs. 14 oz.
12	26″	2¾″	Imp. Cyl.	6 lbs. 14 oz.
12	28″	2¾″	Mod.	6 lbs. 14 oz.
12	28″	2¾″	Full	6 lbs. 14 oz.
12	30″	2¾″	Full	7 lbs.
20	28″	3″	Full, Magnum	6 lbs. 8 oz.
20	28″	2¾″	Mod.	6 lbs. 5 oz.
20	28″	2¾″	Full	6 lbs. 5 oz.

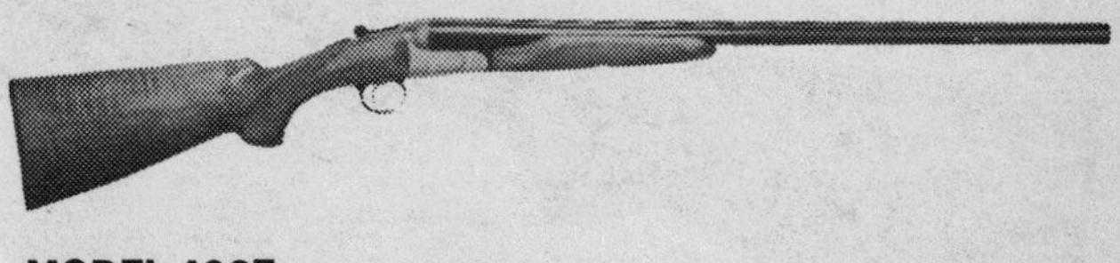

MODEL 426E
SIDE-BY-SIDE SHOTGUNS

The 426E is basically the same as the 424, with the following added features:

The action body is decorated with fine engraving. A silver pigeon is inlaid into the top lever. The action is fitted with a selective single trigger (selector button on safety slide) and the gun has selective automatic ejectors. A hollow matted rib is joined to the barrels. The pistol-grip style stock and fore-end are of select European walnut, hand-checkered and richly finished.

Standard Dimensions

Length of Pull: 14⅛″ (358mm)
Drop at Comb: 1 9/16″ (40mm)
Drop at Heel: 2 9/16″ (65mm)

Note: Gun weights may vary due to different stock wood densities, etc.

Model 426E (12 & 20 ga.) **$1115.00**

Ga.	Length	Chamber	Description	Approx. Weight
12	26″	2¾″	Imp. Cyl./Mod.	6 lbs. 10 oz.
12	28″	2¾″	Mod./Full	6 lbs. 10 oz.
20	26″	3″	Imp. Cyl./Mod.	5 lbs. 14 oz.
20	28″	3″	Mod./Full	5 lbs. 14 oz.

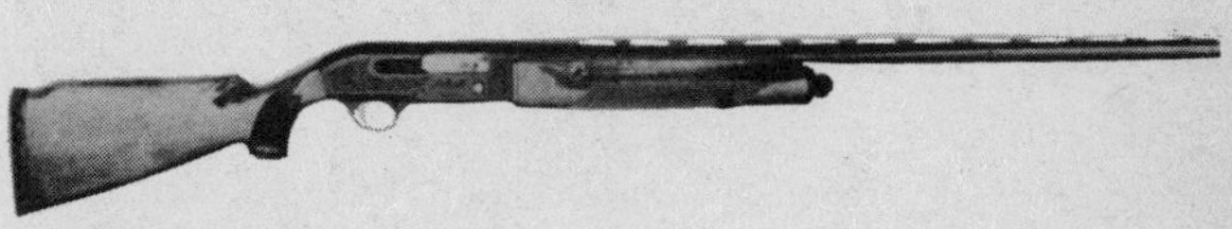

MODEL A-301
SKEET AND TRAP SHOTGUNS

These guns incorporate the same design features and materials as the A-301 field guns but are crafted for target shooting. The Trap gun has a Monte Carlo stock, fitted with recoil pad, and is choked for trap shooting The trigger is gold plated. The Skeet gun has choke and stock dimensions suitable for skeet shooting. The trigger is gold plated.

SPECIFICATIONS—TRAP GUN MODEL A-301

Ga.	Length	Chamber	Description	Approx. Weight
12	30″	2¾″	Full Choke	7 lbs. 10 oz.

Standard Dimensions

Length of Pull: 14⅜″ (362mm)
Drop at M.C.: 1⅜″ (35mm) to 1 9/16″ (40mm)
Drop at Heel: 1⅝″ (40mm)

SPECIFICATIONS—SKEET GUN MODEL A-301

12	26″	2¾″	Skeet Choke	7 lbs., 8 oz.

Standard Dimensions

Length of Pull: 14¼″ (362mm)
Drop at Comb: 1⅜″ (35mm)
Drop at Heel: 2⅜″ (60mm) to 2 9/16″ (65mm)

Model A-301 Skeet (12 & 20 ga.) **$485.00**
Model A-301 Trap (12 ga.) **500.00**

BERETTA SHOTGUNS

MODEL 685 FIELD GRADE

GAUGE: 12 ga. with 26" imp. cylinder & modified barrel; 28" and 29½" modified & full barrel; 29½" full barrel.
ACTION: Matte, silver-gray finished sides with reinforced receiver.
TRIGGER: Selective single trigger.
STOCK: Fine European walnut, hand checkered and finished.
WEIGHT: 7 lbs. 2 oz.
PRICE: $820.00

MODEL 686 FIELD GRADE

GAUGE: 12 ga. with 26" imp. cylinder & modified barrel; 28" and 29½" modified & full barrel; 29½" full barrel.
ACTION: Thick side walls, with Beretta's famous low profile and high security lockup.
TRIGGER: Selective single trigger.
STOCK: Choice European walnut, hand checkered and hand finished with a tough gloss finish.
WEIGHT: 7 lbs. 2 oz.
PRICE: $980.00

MARK II SINGLE-BARREL TRAP GUN

12GA. 32" or 34" BBL. Full Choke (2¾" chambers). Wt. approx. 8 lbs. Auto ejector. Recoil pad. Monte Carlo-type stock made of fine European walnut, hand-finished and hand-checkered. Forend is special hand filling design. Length of pull 14⅜". Drop at Monte Carlo comb 1⅜". Drop at heel 1⅝".
PRICE **$580.00**

MODEL A302 MAG-ACTION SYSTEM

The A302 with improved gas system can handle either 2¾" or 3" magnum shells with only a change of barrels. It has a lever operated cut-off switch, enabling the shooter to substitute or remove the shotshell while keeping the barrel empty without emptying the magazine first.
PRICE **$565.00**

BERETTA SHOTGUNS

SERIES 680 TRAP

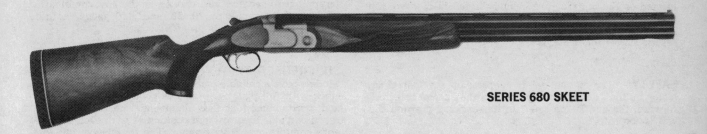

SERIES 680 SKEET

Beretta makes the 680 Series Trap and Skeet guns with competition features such as true box-locks and a patented firing mechanism to give the shortest possible firing time. A specially designed trigger presents slipping. The finely sculpted receiver is reinforced with thick walls and a high security lockup. The low-profile design of the 680 makes recoil much more controllable. The technology and quality of the Beretta 680 Series makes for an ideal competition shotgun.

GAUGE:
 TRAP: 12 ga. with 29½″ barrel, 2¾″ chamber. Choked imp mod/full.
 SKEET: 12 ga. with 26″ and 28″ barrel, 2¾″ chamber. Choked skeet/ skeet.
ACTION: Thick walled and heat treated for durability and strength, with Beretta's low profile.
TRIGGER: Selective gold-plated trigger.
STOCK: Hand-finished select figured European walnut. Dimensions are: 1¼″-1½″ drop at comb. 2⅛″ drop at heel and 14⅜″ length of pull.
WEIGHT:
 TRAP: 8⅛ lbs.
 SKEET: 8 lbs.
PRICE: $1580.00.

SERIES 680 COMBO

GAUGE: 12 ga. with 30″ over/under barrel. Choked imp. mod/full with extra fitted single barrel 32″ or 34″ with full choke.
ACTION: Thick walled and heat treated for durability and strength, with Beretta's low profile.
TRIGGER: Single selector, gold plated.
STOCK: Hand-finished, select figured European walnut stock and forend. Dimensions are: 1¼″-1½″ drop at comb, 2⅛″ drop at heel and 14⅜″ length of pull.
WEIGHT: 8½ lbs.
PRICE: $2100.00.

BROWNING PRESENTATION
SUPERPOSED SHOTGUNS

TWO GUNS IN ONE — The Superposed is a two-barreled shotgun with one barrel positioned directly over the other, rather than side by side. The first shot causes little disturbance to aim, since the veritcal barrel positioning reduces muzzle jump to the minimum and since the under barrel, containing the more open choke, is usually fired first, delivering recoil to the lower, steadier portion of the shoulder.

SINGLE SELECTIVE TRIGGER — You may fire either the tighter choked over barrel or the more open choked under barrel first by the quick movement of the "barrel selector button" to the right or to the left. This selector button is located on the top tang just behind the receiver, where the thumb naturally rests in the shooting position. After the first shot, the gun's mechanism automatically readies the second barrel for firing.

SAFETY — The manual safety operates off the "barrel selector button" described above. With the "barrel selector" forward, the gun is "off-safe." In its rearward position the gun is "on safe."

AUTOMATIC EJECTORS — Fired shells are automatically ejected by an ejection system upon each opening of the breech. Unfired shells remain in the chamber or chambers upon opening but are lifted above the level of the chamber so that they can be lifted out by hand.

TAKEDOWN SYSTEM — The barrels and forearm portion of the gun may be separated from the receiver and stock portion. A latch in the forearm unlocks the two sections after which they need only be unhinged. The forearm does not separate from the barrels in this maneuver.

FINISH — The stock and forearm are made from seasoned walnut individually hand-adjusted to each gun. The checkering of the stock and forearm not only adds to the gun's beauty but affords a sure grip. The receiver is hand engraved.

SUPERPOSED MODELS — Twelve and 20 gauge models are available in two weights: Lightning and the Super-Light. The 28 and .410 gauge models are provided in one weight.

The 12 gauge 3-inch Magnum Superposed will handle the lightest available 2¾-inch loads or the big 3-inch, carrying 1⅞ ounces of shot. For extra shooting comfort, the Magnum is fitted with a deluxe recoil pad. The Super-Light Model is an ultra light field gun with the classic straight grip stock favored by many upland bird hunters. It weighs only 6 lbs. 8 ounces in 12 gauge and 6 lbs. in 20 gauge.

A special feature of all Browning 20 gauge Superposed hunting models, except in the fast-handling Super-Light model, is 3-inch chamber boring.

SUPERPOSED SKEET — The Superposed Skeet models come in 12, 20, 28 and .410 gauge with a short over-all length. Each model features a special skeet stock complete with a full pistol grip and comfortable recoil pad, hand-filling beavertail forearm, plus front and center ivory sight beads. Available with 26½- or 28-inch barrels, all have special Skeet chokes. Browning's Skeet Set has 4 sets of barrels all perfectly matched in 12, 20, 28 and .410 gauge. Each barrel is hand fitted to a single 12-gauge frame and a single removable beavertail forearm. All Browning Superposed target guns may be ordered with one or more extra sets of barrels fitted to the same receiver, each with its own forearm. They may be of the same gauge with different barrel lengths and chokes, or in any combination of 12 and 20 gauge, or 20, 28, and .410 gauge. A fitted luggage type gun case is provided.

SUPERPOSED TRAP — Both Broadway and Ligntning Models have a reliable mechanical trigger. The special trap stock with full pistol grip affords good control of the gun and assists consistent face alignment. The contoured trap recoil pad aids identical gun positioning with each shot and adds comfort over a long shoot. The long beavertail forearm places the hands in the same horizontal plane for natural pointing. Front and center ivory sights quickly show any error in pointing. *Broadway Trap:* Its unusually wide ⅝-inch sighting plane quickly aligns eye to target and, without effort, facilitates holding a true bearing on the target during flight. *Lightning Trap:* The Lightning model carries carefully proportioned 30-inch barrels and a 5/16-inch-wide full ventilated rib.

PRESENTATION GRADE — The Presentation Series in Superposed Shotguns offers a choice of four basic receiver engraving styles and engraved animal or bird scenes. *Presentation One (P-1):* A combination of oak leaf engraving with scrollwork covering the outer edges of the silver grey receiver. The bottom of the receiver sports an oak leaf cluster. The scrollwork extends along the trigger guard, with an oak leaf cluster in the center. One of six animal scenes may be chosen for the receiver. Also available is the P-1 Superposed with gold inlaid birds or dogs and choice of blued or grey finish receiver.

Presentation Two (P-2): The P-2 offers a fleur-de-lis engraving with a choice from three sets of game scenes on both sides and the bottom of the receiver, plus a higher grade of walnut and more elaborate checkering than the P-1 series. Any of these animal scenes are available in gold inlay on either the regular silver grey receiver or a satin blued finish.

Presentation Three (P-3): The P-3 Superposed is offered in three bird and dog scene combinations. All birds and dogs are inlaid with gold on a grey or blue receiver.

Presentation Four (P-4): The basic motif of the P-4's grey receiver is the fleur-de-lis engraving. The deep floral carving covers the sides, top, bottom, forearm, latch and trigger guard. One engraving motif is available. Also available are gold inlaid game birds and dog's head.

BROWNING PRESENTATION SUPERPOSED SHOTGUNS

OVER/UNDER SUPERPOSED SPECIFICATIONS

STOCK—

	12 Gauge Hunting	20, 28 and .410 Gauge Hunting
Length of Pull	14¼″	14¼″
Drop at Comb	1⅝″	1½″
Drop at Heel	2½″	2⅜″

EXTRA SET OF BARRELS — Presentation Series Superposed in any of the specifications listed below are available in gauge combinations of 12 & 12, 12 & 20, 20 & 20, 20 & 28, and/or .410, 28 & .410. A choice of either Hunting, Skeet or Trap stock.

SIGHTS — Medium raised steel bead. Trap and Skeet models: Ivory Front and Center sights.

CHOKE — On all models any combination of Full — Improved-Modified — Modified — Improved-Cylinder — Skeet — Cylinder.

TRIGGER — Gold plated on all models except the Super Light. Fast, crisp, positive.

Model and Gauge HUNTING	Barrel Length	Average Weight (1)	Rib
Lightning 12	28″	7 lbs. 8 oz.	5⁄16″ Vent
Lightning 12	26½″	7 lbs. 6 oz.	5⁄16″ Vent
Super Light 12	26½″	6 lbs. 8 oz.	5⁄16″ Vent
Magnum 12 (2)	30″	8 lbs. 1 oz.	5⁄16″ Vent
Magnum 12 (2)	28″	7 lbs. 15 oz.	5⁄16″ Vent
Lightning 20	28″	6 lbs. 6 oz.	¼″ Vent
Lightning 20	26½″	6 lbs. 4 oz.	¼″ Vent
Super Light 20	26½″	6 lbs.	¼″ Vent
Lightning 28	28″	6 lbs. 10 oz.	¼″ Vent
Lightning 28	26½″	6 lbs. 7 oz.	¼″ Vent
Lightning .410	28″	6 lbs. 14 oz.	¼″ Vent
Lightning .410	26½″	6 lbs. 10 oz.	¼″ Vent

TARGET GUN SPECIFICATIONS
SKEET MODELS

SUPERPOSED	Barrel Length (in.)	Approx. Weight (lbs.-oz.)	Vent. Rib. (width, in.)	Length of Pull (in.)	Drop at Comb (in.)	Drop at Heel (in.)	Chokes	Grades Available
Lightning 12	26½	7 lbs. 9 oz.	5⁄16	14⅜	1½	2	S-S	All
Lightning 12	28	7 lbs. 11 oz.	5⁄16	14⅜	1½	2	S-S	All
Lightning 20	26½	6 lbs. 8 oz.	¼	14⅜	1½	2	S-S	All
Lightning 20	28	6 lbs. 12 oz.	¼	14⅜	1½	2	S-S	All
Lightning 28	26½	6 lbs. 11 oz.	¼	14⅜	1½	2	S-S	All
Lightning 28	28	6 lbs. 14 oz.	¼	14⅜	1½	2	S-S	All
Lightning .410	26½	6 lbs. 13 oz.	¼	14⅜	1½	2	S-S	All
Lightning .410	28	7 lbs.	¼	14⅜	1½	2	S-S	All
Skeet Set 12, 20, 28, .410	26½	7 lbs. 10 oz.	¼	14⅜	1½	2	S-S	All
Skeet Set 12, 20, 28, .410	28	7 lbs. 12 oz.	¼	14⅜	1½	2	S-S	All

TRAP MODELS

SUPERPOSED	Barrel Length (in.)	Approx. Weight (lbs.-oz.)	Vent. Rib. (width, in.)	Length of Pull (in.)	Drop at Comb (in.)	Drop at Monte Carlo (in.)	Drop at Heel (in.)	Chokes	Grades Available
Lightning 12*	30	7 lbs. 13 oz.	5⁄16	14⅜	1⁷⁄16		1⅝	F-F, IM-F, M-F	All
Broadway 12*	30	7 lbs. 15 oz.	⅝	14⅜	1⁷⁄16		1⅝	F-F, IM-F, M-F	All
Broadway 12*	32	8 lbs.	⅝	14⅜	1⁷⁄16		1⅝	F-F, IM-F, M-F	All
*These models also available with Monte Carlo comb				14⅜	1⅜	1⅜	2		

BROWNING PRESENTATION SUPERPOSED SHOTGUNS

HUNTING MODELS

Lightning 12 and 20, 3" Magnum 12 gauges

Presentation 1 Engraved	$4140.00
Presentation 1 Gold Inlay	4700.00
Presentation 2 Engraved	5040.00
Presentation 2 Gold Inlay	6050.00
Presentation 3 Gold Inlay	7390.00
Presentation 4 Engraved	8500.00
Presentation 4 Gold Inlay	9630.00

Super-Light 12 and 20 gauges

Presentation 1 Engraved	$4190.00
Presentation 1 Gold Inlay	4750.00
Presentation 2 Engraved	5090.00
Presentation 2 Gold Inlay	6100.00
Presentation 3 Gold Inlay	7440.00
Presentation 4 Engraved	8550.00
Presentation 4 Gold Inlay	9680.00

Lightning 28 gauge and .410 bore

Presentation 1 Engraved	$4250.00
Presentation 1 Gold Inlay	4810.00
Presentation 2 Engraved	5150.00
Presentation 2 Gold Inlay	6150.00
Presentation 3 Gold Inlay	7500.00
Presentation 4 Engraved	8600.00
Presentation 4 Gold Inlay	9750.00

TRAP MODELS

Lightning 12 gauge

Presentation 1 Engraved	$4200.00
Presentation 1 Gold Inlay	4760.00

Presentation 2 Engraved	$5100.00
Presentation 2 Gold Inlay	6110.00
Presentation 3 Gold Inlay	7450.00
Presentation 4 Engraved	8560.00
Presentation 4 Gold Inlay	9700.00

BROADway 12 gauge

Presentation 1 Engraved	$4300.00
Presentation 1 Gold Inlay	4860.00
Presentation 2 Engraved	5200.00
Presentation 2 Gold Inlay	6210.00
Presentation 3 Gold Inlay	7550.00
Presentation 4 Engraved	8660.00
Presentation 4 Gold Inlay	9800.00

SKEET MODELS

Lightning 12 and 20 gauges

Presentation 1 Engraved	$4200.00
Presentation 1 Gold Inlay	4760.00
Presentation 2 Engraved	5100.00
Presentation 2 Gold Inlay	6110.00
Presentation 3 Gold Inlay	7450.00
Presentation 4 Engraved	8560.00
Presentation 4 Gold Inlay	9700.00

Lightning 28 gauge and .410 bore

Presentation 1 Engraved	$4310.00
Presentation 1 Gold Inlay	4870.00
Presentation 2 Engraved	5210.00
Presentation 2 Gold Inlay	6220.00
Presentation 3 Gold Inlay	7560.00
Presentation 4 Engraved	8670.00
Presentation 4 Gold Inlay	9800.00

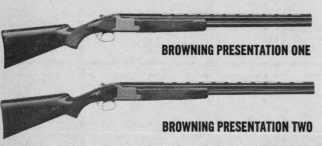

BROWNING PRESENTATION ONE

BROWNING PRESENTATION TWO

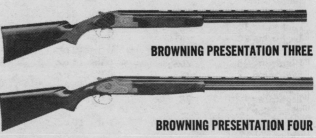

BROWNING PRESENTATION THREE

BROWNING PRESENTATION FOUR

LIMITED EDITION WATERFOWL SUPERPOSED
$7000.00

Limited to 500 Belgian-made guns. Each gun comes with a form-fitted, velvet-lined, handcrafted black walnut case.

GAUGE: 12 gauge

BARREL: 28". Choke is modified/full.

RECEIVER: Gold inlaid and engraved gray steel.

STOCK AND FOREARM: High-grade, dark French walnut with hand-oiled finished stock. Hand-checkered forearm; rounded pistol grip and checkered butt.

BROWNING SHOTGUNS

SUPERPOSED CONTINENTAL
20 GAUGE $5200.00

ACTION: Superposed 20 gauge action, engineered to function with extra set of 30-06 Sprg. over and under rifle barrels.

SHOTGUN BARRELS: 20 gauge, 26½". Choked, modified and full with 3-inch chambers. Engine turned ventilated rib with medium raised German nickel silver sight bead.

RIFLE BARRELS: 30-06 Springfield caliber, 24". Right hand rifling twist, 1 turn in 10 inches. Crowned muzzles. Folding leaf rear sight finely calibrated for elevation. Flat face gold bead front sight mounted on matted ramp. Sight radius — 16¹⁵⁄₁₆". Maximum distance between centers of impact of a 2 shot group from each barrel, using commercially available 150 grain 30-06 ammunition, is 1½ inches at 100 yards.

TRIGGER: Single, selective, inertia. Gold plated, fast and crisp. Let off approximately 4½ lbs.

AUTOMATIC SELECTIVE EJECTORS: Fired shells ejected from chambers upon opening of action. Unfired shells elevated for easy removal.

SAFETY: Manual thumb safety on top tang incorporated with barrel selector mechanism. Either over or under barrel can be selected to fire first.

STOCK AND FOREARM: Select high grade American walnut with deluxe oil finish. Straight grip stock and Schnabel forearm with 25 line hand checkering.

	With Shotgun Barrels Installed	With Rifle Barrels Installed
Length of pull	14¼"	14¼"
Drop at comb	1½"	1¹¹⁄₁₆"
Drop at heel	2⁷⁄₃₂"	2½"

OVERALL LENGTH: With 20 gauge shotgun barrels 43½". With 30-06 rifle barrels 41".

APPROXIMATE WEIGHT: With 20 gauge shotgun barrels 5 lbs. 14 oz. With 30-06 rifle barrels 6 lbs. 14 oz.

SUPERPOSED CONTINENTAL MODEL: 20 Gauge Over/Under Shotgun with extra set of 30-06 Over/Under Rifle barrels, including fitted luggage.

BPS PUMP SHOTGUN
12 GAUGE

GAUGE: 12 gauge only.

BARRELS: Choice of 26", 28", or 30" with high post ventilated rib. Trap model has front and center ivory sight beads. Hunting model has German nickel sight bead.

ACTION: Pump action with double-action bars. Bottom loading and ejection. Magazine cut-off to switch loads in chamber without disturbing shells in magazine and to convert gun from repeating to single shot operation.

CHOKE: Your choice of full, modified, or improved cylinder.

TRIGGER: Crisp and positive.

CHAMBER: Hunting model: All 2¾", 2¾" magnum and 3" magnum shells, Target models: 2¾" shells only.

SAFETY: Convenient top receiver safety. Slide forward to shoot.

APPROXIMATE WEIGHT: 28" barrel model weighs 7 lbs. 12 oz.

OVERALL LENGTH: 26" barrel 46¾". 28" barrel 48¾". 30" barrel 50¾".

STOCK AND FOREARM: Select walnut, weather resistant finish, sharp 20-line checkering. Full pistol grip. Semi-beavertail forearm with finger grooves, Length of pull — 14¼". Drop at comb — 1½". Drop at heel — 2½".

Grade I, Hunting, 12 ga., Ventilated Rib	$334.95
Grade I, Trap, 12 ga., Ventilated Rib	349.95
Grade I, Buck Special, 12 ga., no accessories	354.95
Grade I, Buck Special, 12 ga., with accessories	374.95

ST-100 SUPERPOSED TRAP SPECIAL $3575.00

RECEIVER: Grade I blued steel hand engraved with ST-100 insignia in laurel background.

BARRELS: 30 inch. Five position impact adjustment device allows points of impact adjustment. Fluting under barrel expands and contracts naturally during heated shooting.

CHOKES: Choice of Full-Full, Improved Modified-Full, or Modified-Full.

CHAMBERS: 12 gauge. 2¾" shells only.

TRIGGER: Single selective. Mechanical with deep contour for sure control. Fast, crisp, positive.

SIGHTS: Front and center ivory sight beads.

RIB: ½" rib with full length and transverse serrations to break up reflection. Full floating, high post design.

RECOIL PAD: Deluxe contoured trap style.

AUTOMATIC EJECTION: Fired shells ejected automatically on opening action. Unfired shells elevated from chamber for convenient removal.

STOCK AND FOREARM: Select walnut, high gloss finish with hand checkering for sure grip. Full pistol-grip stock; semi-beavertail forearm.

Length of pull: 14⅜"
Drop at comb: 1⁷⁄₁₆"
Drop at heel: 1⅝"

APPROXIMATE WEIGHT: 8 pounds.

BROWNING AUTOMATIC SHOTGUNS

**LIGHT 12 AND LIGHT 20 GAUGE
WITH VENT. RIB $474.95
3" MAGNUM 12 AND MAGNUM 20 GAUGE
WITH VENT. RIB $484.95**

AUTOMATIC-5 MODELS—The Browning Automatic-5 Shotgun is offered in an unusually wide variety of models and specifications. The Browning 12-gauge 3-inch Magnum accepts up to and including the 3-inch, 1⅞ ounce, 12-gauge Magnum load, which contains only ⅛ ounces of shot less than the maximum 3½-inch 10-gauge load. The 2¾-inch Magnums and 2¾-inch high-velocity shells may be used with equal pattern efficiency. Standard features include a special shock absorber and a hunting-style recoil pad. The kick is not unpleasant with even the heaviest 3-inch loads.

Browning also offers the 20 gauge in a 3-inch Magnum model. This powerful, light heavyweight offers maximum versatility to 20-gauge advocates. It handles the 20-gauge, 2¾-inch high velocity and Magnums, but it literally thrives on the 3-inch, 1¼ ounce load which delivers real 12-gauge performance in a 20-gauge package.

The 12-gauge Automatic-5, chambered for regular 2¾-inch shells handles all 12-gauge, 2¾-inch shells, from the very lightest 1 ounce field load to the heavy 1½ ounce Magnums. The Browning 20-gauge Automatic is lightweight and a top performer for the upland hunter. Yet, with 2¾-inch high velocity or 2¾-inch Magnums, it does a fine job in the duck blind.

All models and gauges of the Automatic-5 are available in the Buck Special version, which is designed to accurately fire the rifled slug or buckshot loads. In addition, its specially bored 24-inch barrel will deliver nice open patterns with standard field loads.

SKEET MODELS—Special 26-inch skeet barrels fit all Browning Automatic-5's of like gauge and model so an owner may easily convert his favorite hunting gun to a skeet gun by a quick change of barrels. **$534.95**

HUNTING MODELS—

Light 12, and Light 20 gauge	**$534.95**
3" magnum 12 gauge and magnum 20 gauge	544.95
Buck Special without accessories	
Light 12, and Light 20 gauge	544.95
3" magnum 12 gauge and magnum 20 gauge	559.95
Buck Special with accessories	
Light 12, and Light 20 gauge	**$564.95**
3". magnum 12 gauge and magnum 20 gauge	579.95

2000 GAS AUTOMATIC SHOTGUNS

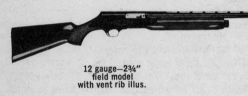

12 gauge—2¾"
field model
with vent rib illus.

TRAP AND SKEET MODELS

12 Ga. 2¾" Trap and Skeet (with receiver rib and high post vent rib)	**$514.95**
20 Ga. 2¾" Skeet (with standard receiver and standard target rib)	**$474.95**

HUNTING MODELS

12 and 20 Ga. 2¾" Field Model	
Ventilated Rib	**$474.95**
12 and 20 Ga. 3" Mag. Model	
Ventilated Rib	**$474.95**

2000 12 Gauge Specifications

Gauge—12 gauge.

Barrel—Choice of 26", 28" or 30" barrel in 2¾" Field models. 28", 30" or 32" in 3" Magnum models. Plain or ventilated rib. Plain barrels have matted sighting surface. All barrels are completely interchangeable within the same gauge.

Chamber—All 2¾" standard and 2¾" Magnum loads with 2¾" chambered barrel. 3" Magnum loads with Magnum barrel.

Choke—Choice of Full, Modified, Improved Cylinder or Cylinder in 2¾" models. Full of Modified in 3" Magnum models.

Capacity—Five 2¾" loads; Four 3" Magnum loads. Reduced to three 2¾" or 3" Magnum loads with magazine plug.

Trigger—Crisp. Positive.

Safety—Cross bolt. Red warning band visible when in "fire" position. Easily reversible by gunsmith for left hand shooter.

Receiver—Engraved with handsome scroll designs. Machined and forged from high grade steel.

Sight—Medium raised bead. German nickel silver.

Stock and Forearm—French walnut, skillfully checkered. Full pistol grip. No recoil pad.

Length of pull—14¼"
Drop at comb—1⅝"
Drop at heel—2½"

Overall Length
26" Barrel—45⅜"
28" Barrel—47⅜"
30" Barrel—49⅜"
32" Barrel—51⅜"

Approximate Weight—Ventilated Rib Models. (Plain barrel models weigh 3 oz. less.)

26" Barrel—7 lbs. 10 oz.
28" Barrel—7 lbs. 11 oz.
30" Barrel—7 lbs. 12 oz.
32" Barrel—7 lbs. 13 oz.

Also available in Buck Special: 12 & 20 gauge 2¾", 12 gauge 3" Magnum with 24" barrel.

With accessories $494.95, without accessories **$474.95.**

2000 20 Gauge Specifications

Barrel—Ventilated Rib only. Front and center ivory sight beads on skeet barrel. Available in 26" & 28" lengths.

Chamber—All 2¾" standard and 2¾" Magnum loads with 2¾" chambered barrel. 3" Magnum loads only with Magnum barrel.

Capacity—Five 2¾" loads; four 3" loads. Reduced to three 2¾" or 3" Magnum loads with magazine plug provided.

Trigger—Crisp, positive.

Safety—Cross bolt. Red warning band. Easily reversible.

Receiver—Engraved with scroll designs. Cold forged and machined from high-grade steel.

BROWNING SHOTGUNS

CITORI STANDARD

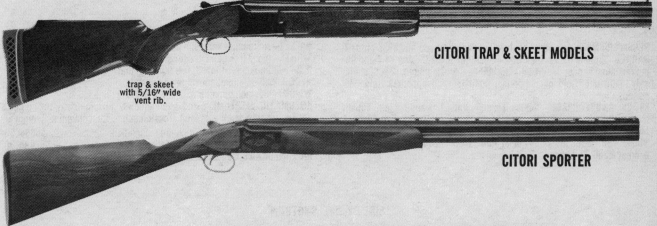

CITORI TRAP & SKEET MODELS

trap & skeet with 5/16" wide vent rib.

CITORI SPORTER

FIELD GRADE

Gauge—12, 20, 28 and 410 gauge.

Barrels—Choice of 30", 28" or 26" in 12 gauge. 28" or 26" in 20 gauge. Ventilated rib with matted sighting plane. Medium raised German nickel silver sight bead. 26" or 28" in 28 gauge. 26" or 28" in 410 gauge.

Overall Length—12, 20, 28 and 410 gauge.
- With 26" barrels—43"
- With 28" barrels—45"
- With 30" barrels—47"

Chokes—Choice of Full-Full or Mod-Full in 30" barrels; choice of Mod-Full or Imp Cyl-Mod in 28" and 26" barrels.

Trigger—Single selective. Gold plated. Fast and crisp.

Chamber—All 20 gauge Field models and all 12 gauge Field models accept all 3" magnum loads, as well as 2¾" loads. 28 gauge accepts 2¾" loads. 410 gauge accepts 2½", 3" or 3" mag. loads.

Safety—Manual thumb safety. Combined with barrel selector mechanism.

Automatic Ejectors—Fired shells thrown out of gun; unfired shells are elevated for easy removal.

APPROXIMATE WEIGHT—

	12 gauge	20 gauge
26" barrels	7 lbs. 9 oz.	6 lbs. 11 oz.
28" barrels	7 lbs. 11 oz.	6 lbs. 13 oz.
30" barrels	7 lbs. 13 oz.	

Stock and Forearm—Dense walnut. Skillfully checkered. Full pistol grip. Hunting Beavertail forearm. Field type recoil pad installed on 12 gauge models.

	12 gauge	20 gauge
Length of pull	14¼"	14¼"
Drop at comb	1⅝"	1½"
Drop at heel	2½"	2⅜"

HUNTING MODELS

Standard 12 and 20 Ga. & Sporter 12 and 20 Ga.

Grades I	$ 689.95
Grades II	1195.00
Grades V	1800.00

Standard 28 Ga. and .410 Bore & Sporter 28 Ga. and .410 Bore

Grades I	$ 719.95
Grades II	1235.00
Grades V	1850.00

TRAP MODELS

Standard 12 Ga.

Grade I (High Post Target Rib)	$ 769.95
Grade II (High Post Target Rib)	1295.00
Grade V (High Post Target Rib)	1925.00

COMBO TRAP SET

(Furnished with fitted luggage case for gun and extra barrel.)

Standard 12 Guage with 32" Over/Under barrels and 34" single barrel. One removable forearm supplied.

Grade I (High Post Target Rib)	$1295.00

SKEET MODELS

Standard 12 and 20 Ga.

Grade I (High Post Target Rib)	$ 769.95
Grade II (High Post Target Rib)	1295.00
Grade V (High Post Target Rib)	1925.00

Standard 28 Ga. and 410 Bore

Grade I (High Post Target Rib)	$ 799.95
Grade II (High Post Target Rib)	1295.00
Grade V (High Post Target Rib)	1925.00

(Furnished with fitted luggage case for gun and extra barrel.)

BROWNING SHOTGUNS

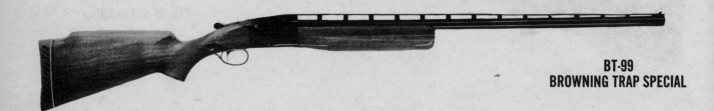

**BT-99
BROWNING TRAP SPECIAL**

RECEIVER—Machined steel, tastefully hand-engraved and richly blued.
BARREL—Choice of 32 inch or 34 inch. **CHOKE**—Choice of Full, Improved Modified or Modified. **CHAMBER**—for 12 gauge, 2¾" shells only. **TRIGGER**—Gold plated, crisp, positive, pull approximately 3½ pounds.
STOCK AND FOREARM—Select French walnut, hand-rubbed finish, sharp 20-line hand-checkering. Monte Carlo or Conventional stock available.
Stock: Full pistol grip; **Length of Pull:** 14⅜"; **Drop at Comb:** 1⅜"; **Drop at Heel:** 2"; **Forearm:** Full beavertail.

SAFETY—No manual safety, a feature preferred by trap shooters.
SIGHTS—Ivory front and center sight beads.
RIB—High post, ventilated, full floating, matted, 11/32 inch wide.
RECOIL PAD—Deluxe, contoured trap style.
WEIGHT—32 inch barrel 8 lbs., 34 inch barrel 8 lbs. 3 oz.
AUTOMATIC EJECTION—Fired shell ejected automatically on opening action, unfired shell elevated from chamber for convenient removal.
GRADE I COMPETITION: 32" & 34" barrel .... $ 659.95
  With extra barrel (includes case) 935.00
PIGEON GRADE COMPETITION 1500.00

SIDE-BY-SIDE SHOTGUN

**BROWNING "B-SS"
SIDE-BY-SIDE SHOTGUN
12 & 20 GAUGE**

**12 GAUGE
B-SS SPECIFICATIONS:**

BARRELS: Choice of 26", 28" or 30" barrels. Solid rib with matted top. Sight bead is German nickel silver.
CHOKE: 30" barrels choked full or modified and full. 28" barrel model choked modified and full. 26" barrels choked, modified and full, or improved cylinder and modified.
TRIGGER: Single mechanical trigger fires right barrel first (the more open choke). Gold plated on all models.
CHAMBER: 2¾", 2¾" Mag. and 3" mag. shells.
AUTOMATIC SAFETY: Goes on safe when breech is opened and remains there until manually moved to off safe.
AUTOMATIC EJECTORS: Fired shells are thrown out of gun. Unfired shells are elevated for easy removal.
WEIGHT: With 30" barrels approx. 7 lbs. 7 oz., with 26" barrels approx. 7 lbs. 3 oz., with 28" barrels approx. 7 lbs. 5 oz.
OVERALL LENGTH: 26" barrels 43". 28" barrels 45". 30" barrels 47".

STOCK AND FOREARM: Select walnut, hand-rubbed finish, sharp 20-line hand checkering. Full pistol grip. Full grip beavertail forearm.
Length of pull: 14¼"
Drop at comb: 1⅝"
Drop at heel: 2½"
The Browning Side by Side has a "mechanical" trigger which differs from the "inertia" trigger found on many two barreled guns in that the recoil of the first shot is not used to set up the mechanism for the second shot. The first pull of the trigger fires the right barrel. The next pull fires the left barrel. The positive linkage of the B-SS mechanical trigger prevents doubling (both barrels firing at the same instant) or balking. The chromed trigger lets off crisply at about 4½ pounds.

Grade I Standard 12 & 20 ga. with Barrel Selector $549.95
Grade II Standard 12 & 20 ga. with Barrel Selector 975.00
Grade I Sporter 12 & 20 ga. with Barrel Selector 549.95
Grade II Sporter 12 & 20 ga. with Barrel Selector 975.00

FIE SHOTGUNS

THE S.O.B.

Gauge	BBL	Overall Length	Price
12	18"	27½"	$99.95
20	18"	27½"	99.95
.410	18"	27½"	99.95

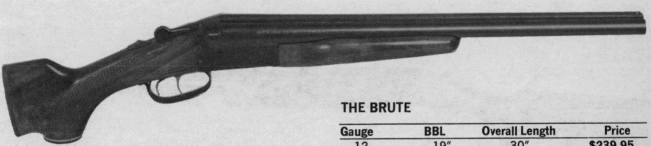

THE BRUTE

Gauge	BBL	Overall Length	Price
12	19"	30"	$239.95
20	19"	30"	239.95
.410	19"	30"	239.95

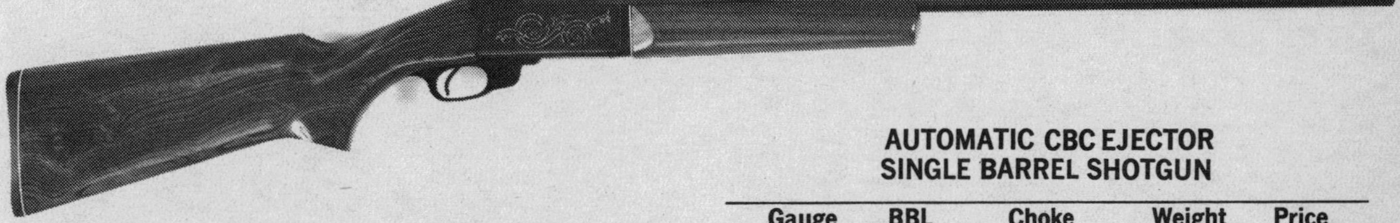

**HAMMERLESS RIFLE/SHOTGUN COMBO
20 GAUGE/30-30 CALIBER
$129.95**

AUTOMATIC CBC EJECTOR SINGLE BARREL SHOTGUN

Gauge	BBL	Choke	Weight	Price
12—2¾"	28"	Full	6¼ lb.	$74.95
20—2¾"	28"	Full	6 lbs.	74.95
.410—3"	26"	Full	5½ lb.	74.95
12—2¾"	28"	Hammerless Full	6½ lb.	99.95
20—2¾"	28"	Hammerless Full	6½ lb.	99.95

FIE SHOTGUNS

ERA DELUXE
SINGLE BARREL SHOTGUN

Gauge	BBL	Choke	Weight	Price
12—2¾"	28"	Full	6½ lb.	$74.95
12—2¾"	30"	Full	6½ lb.	74.95
20—2¾"	28"	Full	6½ lb.	74.95
410—3"	26"	Full	6½ lb.	74.95
16—2¾"	28"	Full	6½ lb.	74.95

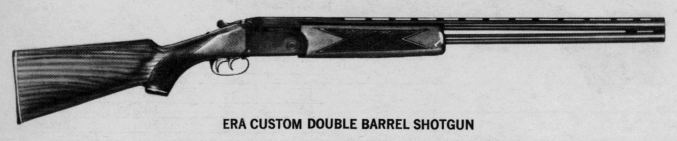

ERA CUSTOM DOUBLE BARREL SHOTGUN

Gauge	BBL	Choke	Weight	Price
12—2¾"	28"	Modified & Full	6 lb. 14 oz.	$199.95
16—2¾"	28"	Modified & Full	6 lb. 11 oz.	199.95
20—2¾"	28"	Modified & Full	6 lb. 11 oz.	199.95
410—3"	26"	Modified & Full	6 lb. 4 oz.	199.95
Coach 12—2¾"	18" or 20"	Cylinder Bore	6 lb. 6 oz.	229.95
Coach 20—2¾"	18" or 20"	Cylinder Bore	6 lb. 3 oz.	229.95

ERA DELUXE OVER AND UNDER SHOTGUN

Gauge	BBL	Choke	Weight	Price
12—2¾"	28"	Modified & Full	9.8 lb.	$279.95
20—2¾"	28"	Modified & Full	9.8 lb.	279.95

FRANCHI SHOTGUNS

2003 O/U TRAP

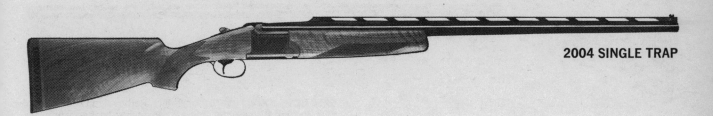

2004 SINGLE TRAP

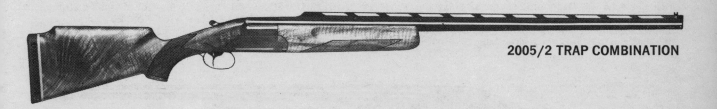

2005/2 TRAP COMBINATION

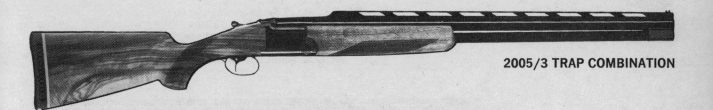

2005/3 TRAP COMBINATION

SERIES 2000 SPECIFICATIONS
GAUGE: 12 gauge (chambered for all 2¾" shells).
BARRELS: Model 2003: 30" or 32"; Model 2004: 32" or 34";
Models 2005/2 and 2005/3: 30", 32" or 34".
CHOKES: Model 2003—improved modified-full and full-full;
Model 2004—full; Model 2005/2—improved modified-full and
full; Model 2005/3—any combination.
TRIGGER: Trap trigger anatomically designed. O/U barrel
selector located on the trigger.
SAFETY: Manual thumb safety.
SIGHTS: Raised steel middle bead with ⁷⁄₁₆" translucent red
front sight.

STOCKS: Oil-finished, European walnut. All stocks are hand
checkered and interchangeable; buttstocks are drilled for a
recoil reducer.
WEIGHT: All models between 8 lbs. 4 oz. and 8 lbs. 6 oz.

3000/2 TRAP UNDERGUN COMBINATION

GAUGE: 12 gauge only.
BARRELS: 32" O/U; 34" underbarrel.
CHOKE: Full, improved-modified and modified.
WEIGHT: 8 lbs. 6 oz.

FRANCHI SHOTGUNS

STANDARD AUTOMATIC SHOTGUN WITH VENT RIB
ALSO AVAILABLE WITH 22" SLUG BBL.

MAGNUM AUTOMATIC WITH VENT RIB

SPECIFICATIONS
GAUGES: 12 and 20 (Standard models chambered for all 2¾" shells; Magnum models chambered for all 3" shells).
BARRELS: Standard models: 24", 26" and 28". Standard 12 gauge only: 30". Magnum 12 gauge: 32"; Magnum 20 gauge: 28".
CHOKES: Standard models: cylinder, improved cylinder, modified and full. Magnum models: full.

SAFETIES: Lateral push button safety. Removal of two lateral pins, located through the receiver permits the trigger-safety lifter mechanism to be removed as a single unit.
STOCKS: Stock and forend with fully machine cut checkered pistol grip and foregrip. Magnum models equipped with factory-fitted recoil pad (optional on other 12-gauge models).
WEIGHTS: Standard 12 gauge: 6 lbs. 4 oz.; Standard 20 gauge: 5 lbs. 2 oz.; Magnum 12 gauge: 8 lbs. 4 oz.; 20 gauge Magnum: 6 lbs.
OVERALL LENGTH: 47½" with 28" barrel.

GAS-OPERATED MODEL 500 WITH VENT RIB

GAUGE: 12 gauge (chambered for 2¾" shells).
BARRELS: 26", 28" and 30".
CHOKES: 26" improved cylinder; 28" modified or full: 30" full.
WEIGHT: Approx. 7 lbs.
STOCK: Semi-gloss finish.

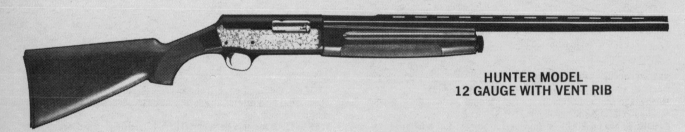

HUNTER MODEL 12 GAUGE WITH VENT RIB

Franchi Hunter features include: specially selected European stock, forend; fully engraved million-dollar lightweight receiver covered by a lifetime guarantee; the automatic safety, which securely locks the hammer, is silent and positive; hand safety can be reversed for left–handed shooters; chrome-lined barrel for light weight and maximum strength; checkered pistol grip; reliable recoil action requiring no maintenance and no cleaning. Chambered for 2¾ shells.

GALEF SHOTGUNS

Monte Carlo — Single Barrel Trap Shotgun

**MONTE CARLO
SINGLE BARREL TRAP GUN
$349.95**

Barrel Assembly:	Monobloc. Barrel tubes of superior quality hi-tensil chromoly steel with extra heavy walls. Chambered for 2¾" shells.
Rib:	5/16" tapered wide track Ventilated Rib with front and rear bead sights.
Action:	Monte Carlo design with release forward of trigger guard. Handsomely engraved and finished in a non-glare blue. Automatic type extractor. Gold plated trigger and forend screw.
Safety:	Slide type mounted on upper tang.
Stock Dimensions:	Drop at Comb: 1⅛", Drop at Heel: 1⅝", Length of Pull: 14½", Pitch: ½". Straight without cast-off or cast-on. Monte Carlo comb. Full pistol grip with cap. Trap style recoil pad.
Forearm Dimensions:	Length: 12½", Width: 2⅝". Beavertail semi-pear shaped.
Stock And Forearm:	Selected European Walnut. Custom finished and fitted. Generously hand checkered in two point panel design.
Weight:	Approximately 8¼ pounds.

Specifications of the "Monte Carlo" single barrel trap shotgun

Gauge:	12 gauge only
Barrel Length:	32 inches
Choke:	Trap

COMPANION FOLDING SINGLE BARREL SHOTGUNS
(12, 16, 20, 28 & 410 Gauges)

COMPANION, w/plain barrel $138.00

COMPANION w/vent rib barrel $167.20

Specifications:

Gauge:	12, 16, 20, 28, and 410 gauge, 12 and 20 gauge chambered for 3" magnum shells. 16 and 28 gauge are chambered for 2¾" shells. 410 with 3 inch chamber.
Style:	Single barrel, folding shotgun.
Breech Assemby: (Barrel)	Monobloc. Special alloy steel drawn from a single block including the rib extension and locking lug. Greatest elasticity and strength are thus obtained, especially as the barrel tubes are completely inserted to coincide with the breech face. Also available in Ventilated Rib Barrel with specifications same throughout.
Receiver:	Machined from solid stock and handsomely engraved in satin chrome.
Safety:	Non-automatic shotgun type, positioned at upper tang.

Sights:	Gold bead front. Receiver notched for alignment in pointing.
Stock and Forearm:	Selected European Walnut, hand checkered two point panel design. Full pistol grip with cap and hard plastic butt plate.
Approximate Weights:	12 gauge 30" barrel ....5 lbs. 9 ounces 410 gauge 28" barrel ....4 lbs. 8 ounces

Standard Stock Dimensions:		
Drop at Comb ..... 1½"		Approximate for all gauges and lengths
Drop at Heel ...... 2⅝"		
Length of Pull ......14"		
Pitch .... 3"		

Barrel Length & Choke Combinations:	Gauge:		Barrel-Chokes:
	12	30"	Full—Magnum
	12	28"	Full—Magnum
	16	28"	Full
	20	28"	Full—Magnum
	28	28"	Full
	410	26"	Full

RENATO GAMBA SHOTGUNS

Grade: Field model with hand-engraved scroll work on case-hardened receiver
Gauge: 28 gauge chambered for 2¾" shells
Barrels: Chrome-lined demi-block barrels of Boehler steel
Barrel Length & Choke Combinations: 26" Imp. Cyl. & Modified. 28" Modified & Full
Trigger: Single or double
Action: Box-lock

PRINCIPESSA SIDE-BY-SIDE SHOTGUN 28 GAUGE

Ejectors: Non-automatic ejector
Stock: Select European walnut with hand-checkered straight English grip and slim English-style forend. Beavertail forend available. Hand-rubbed oil finish. Fitted with rubber recoil pad
Stock Dimensions: Length of pull—14½"; drop at comb—1¼"; drop at heel—2"
Weight- 5 lbs. 8 ozs.
PRINCIPESSA with double trigger $1566.00
PRINCIPESSA with single trigger 1695.00

AMBASSADOR SIDE-BY-SIDE MODELS

Made to customer's specifications on special order
Executive Grade $23,698.00
Gold/Black Grade 15,798,00
English Grade 12,020.00

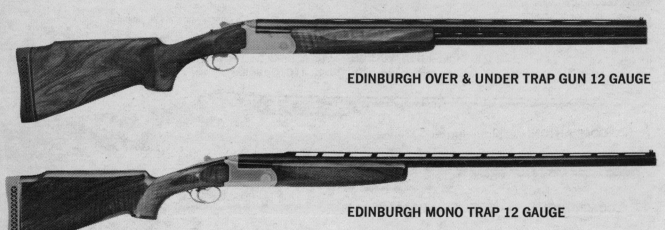

EDINBURGH OVER & UNDER TRAP GUN 12 GAUGE

EDINBURGH MONO TRAP 12 GAUGE

SPECIFICATIONS:
Gauge: 12 chambered for 2¾" shells
Barrels: Chrome-lined demi-block barrels of special Boehler steel with file cut top rib.
Barrel Length & Choke Combinations: O/U Trap—30" or 32" (F/F, IM/F, M/F); O/U Skeet—26" or 28" (Skeet chokes); Mono Trap—32", 34" (F, IM, M)
Trigger: Shaped single trigger (selective available)
Action: Patented Anson system
Ejectors: Automatic ejectors
Receiver: Chrome-nickel molybdenum heat-treated steel
Stock & Forend: Selected walnut with Monte Carlo design trap stock with shaped pistol grip and ventilated rubber recoil pad. Hand checkering and European oil finish on

trap models. Skeet model comes with high gloss lacquer finish stock and skeet pad.

Stock Dimensions:	TRAP	SKEET
Length of pull:	14½"	14"
Drop at comb:	1½"	1¼"
Drop at heel:	2¼"	2"
Drop at Monte Carlo:	2"	N/A
Weights (Approx.): Trap—7¾ lbs.; Skeet—7¼ lbs.		

Trap Combo Set (with O/U bbl.—30" or 32" and single bbl.—32" or 34") $2856.30
O/U TRAP 1995.00
O/U SKEET 1995.00
MONO TRAP 1995.00

RENATO GAMBA SHOTGUNS

OXFORD SIDE-BY-SIDE SHOTGUN
12, 20 & 20 GAUGE MAGNUM

Grade: Field model with receiver hand engraved in English scroll

Gauges: 12 and 20 gauge chambered for 2¾" shells; 20 gauge with 3" chambers

Barrels: Chrome-lined demi-block barrels of Boehler steel

Barrel Length & Choke Combinations: 26" Imp. Cyl. & Modified; 28" Modified & Full (other combinations available on request)

Trigger: Single or double trigger (double trigger with articulated front trigger)

Action: Box-lock based on the Anson and Deeley system

Ejectors: Automatic ejectors

Receiver: Chrome-nickel molybdenum, heat-treated steel frame

Stock: European walnut with hand-checkered straight grip. Checkered butt for non-slip surface. European oil finish

Forend: European walnut, hand-checkered. English style with Anson type pushbutton release

Stock Dimensions: Length of pull—14½"; drop at comb—1½"; drop at heel—2½"

Weights (Approx.): Depending on density of wood, gauge and barrel length. 12 gauge—6 lbs. 8 ozs.; 20 gauge—5 lbs. 10 ozs.

OXFORD 12, 20 or 20 gauge mag., with double trigger $1768.80

OXFORD 12, 20 or 20 gauge mag., with single trigger 1919.40

LONDON SIDE-BY-SIDE SHOTGUNS 12 & 20 GAUGE

Grade: Field model with bright or case-hardened receiver. Hand engraved in rose bouquet and scroll work

Gauges: 12 & 20 chambered for 2¾" shells only

Barrels: Chrome-lined demi-block barrels of Boehler steel

Barrel Length & Choke Combinations: 26" Imp. Cyl. & Modified; 28" Modified & Full (other combinations available on request)

Trigger: Single or double trigger

Action: Side-locks based on the Holland & Holland system with double safety, and three-lug Purdey locking system

Ejectors: Automatic ejectors

Receiver: Chrome-nickle molybdenum heat-treated steel frame

Stock: European walnut with hand-checkered straight grip, and butt inlaid gold oval. Checkered butt for non-slip surface. Hand-rubbed European oil finish

Forend: European walnut, hand checkered. Slim English style with Anson-type pushbutton release

Stock Dimensions: Length of pull — 14½"; drop at comb — 1½"; drop at heel — 2½"

Weights (Approx.): Depending on density of wood, gauge and barrel length. 12 gauge, 6 lbs. 8 ozs.; 20 gauge, 5 lbs. 10 ozs.

LONDON 12 or 20 gauge, with double trigger $3806.50

LONDON 12 or 20 gauge, single trigger 3978.20

GARBI SHOTGUNS

MODEL 60-A WITH EXTRACTORS $790.00 (shown)
MODEL 60-B WITH EJECTORS $1085.00
Gauges: 12, 16 and 20
Action: Sidelock with Purdey locking system.
Stock: Select walnut with hand checkering.
Barrel Lengths: 26", 28" or 30".
Features: Several choke options; extensive scroll engraving on receiver; double triggers and extractors; made to customer's dimensions.

MODEL 62-A WITH EXTRACTORS $790.00
MODEL 62-B WITH EJECTORS $1065.00
Gauges: 12, 16 and 20
Stock: Select walnut with hand-checkering.
Barrel Lengths: 26", 28" or 30". Barrels are special steel demi-bloc.
Features: Several choke options; jointed trigger (double trigger); plain receiver with engraved border; gas exhaust valves; made to customer's dimensions.

MODEL 51 $490.00
Gauges: 12, 16 and 20
Chokes: Modified and full.
Action: Box-lock.
Stock: Hand-checkered stock and forend.
Features: Double trigger and extractors; hand-engraved receiver.

H&R SINGLE BARREL SHOTGUNS

Model 162, 12-and 20-gauge, single shot shotgun with cylinder bore barrel, fires rifled slugs for deer hunting. Also can be used for birds and small game.

MODEL 162
12/24" Cyl. Bore and
20/24" Cyl. Bore
$94.50

Gauge: 12 and 20 chambered for 3" shells.
Capacity: Single shot
Stock: Walnut finished American hardwood.

Overall Length: 40"
Weight: 5½ lbs.
Barrel Length: 24" with fully adjustable rear sight and dovetail front sight.

H&R MODEL 088 and 088JR

$72.50

Gauge: Model 088 available in 12, 16, 20, and .410; Model 088JR available in 20 and .410.
Capacity: Single shot
Stock: Semi-pistol grip walnut finished Semi-beavertail forend.

Overall Length: 40" to 47"
Weight: 5 to 6½ lbs.
Barrel Lengths: 12 ga.—28", 30", 32"; 16 ga.—28"; 20 ga.—26"; 410 ga.—25"; 20 ga. JR—25"; 410 ga. JR—25".

H&R SINGLE BARREL SHOTGUNS

Model 058 has self-adjusting barrel lock, positive shell ejection, rebounding hammer.
Model 490, with identical features, is designed for young shooters and overall length is 3″ shorter.
Model 098, available in .410 and 20 gauge, features a rich ebony-finished stock and distinctive chrome frame.

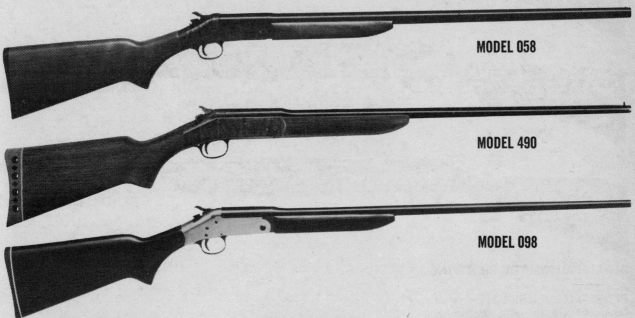

MODEL 058

MODEL 490

MODEL 098

MODEL 058 $79.50

Gauge: 12, 20 & 410 chambered for 3″; 16 & 28 chambered for 2¾″.

Capacity: Single shot.

Stock: Walnut-finished hardwood.

Overall length: 12/36″-51″; 12/32″-47″; 12/30″-45″; 12/28″-43″; 16/28″-43″; 20/28″-43″; 28/26″-41″; 410/26″-41″.

Weight: 5½ -6 lbs.

Choke combinations: 12/30″ full; 12/28″ full; 12/28″ mod.; 16/28″ mod.; 20/28″ full; 20/28″ mod.; 28/26″ mod.; 410/26″ full.

MODEL 490 $79.50

Gauge: 20 gauge, modified, 3″ chamber; .410 gauge, full, 3″ chamber; 28 gauge, modified, 2¾″ chamber.

Capacity: Single shot.

Stock: Walnut finished American hardwood with recoil pad.

Overall Length: 40″.

Weight: 5 lbs.

Barrel Length: 26″ barrel.

Greenwing: $89.50

MODEL 098 $79.50

Gauge: 12, 20 gauge, modified & .410 gauge, full chambered for 6-3″.

Capacity: Single shot.

Stock: Ebony finished American hardwood with recoil pad.

Overall Length: 41″.

Weight: 5½ lbs.

Barrel Length: 26″ with brass bead front sight.

MODEL 176 10 Gauge

Gauge: 10 full, 12 full, 16 full, 20 full.

Chamber: 10 Ga., 3½-inch Magnum; 12 Ga., 3-inch Magnum; 16 Ga., 12¾-Magnum; 20 Ga., 3-inch Magnum.

Stock: Walnut-finished hardwood with recoil pad.

Metal Finish: Blue-black barrel. Color cased frame.

Stock Dimensions: Length 13¼″; Drop at comb 1½″; Drop at heel 2½″.

Sights: Brass bead front.

Overall Length: 47-51 in.

Weight & Price: 10 ga. 36″ bbl. 10 lbs. **$99.50;** 10 ga. 32″ bbl. 9½ lbs. **$99.50;** 12 ga. 36″ bbl. 9 lbs. **$89.50;** 12 ga. 32″ bbl. 8½ lbs. **$89.50;** 16 ga. 32″ bbl. 8¼ lbs. **$89.50;** 20 ga. 32″ bbl. 8½ lbs. **$89.50.**

HECKLER & KOCH BENELLI SHOTGUNS

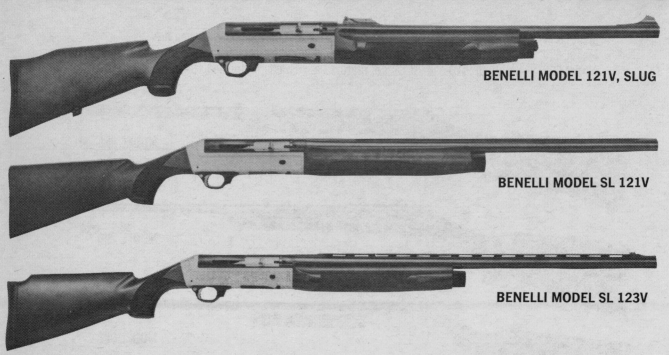

BENELLI MODEL 121V, SLUG

BENELLI MODEL SL 121V

BENELLI MODEL SL 123V

BENELLI AUTOMATIC SHOTGUNS

BENELLI MODEL SL 121V
Gauge: 12 (5 shot); 3-shot plug furnished
Action: Tubular steel receiver, bolt group and alloy trigger group
Barrel length: 26" or 28"
Stock: Walnut; hand-checkered pistol grip and forearm
Weight: 6¾ lbs.
121V, SLUG $458.00
SL 121V, ventilated rib, modified choke, standard model 418.00

SL 123V, 12 gauge, ventilated rib, modified choke, deluxe model, engraved receiver $489.00
Also available:
SL 123V with full choke 489.00
SL 201, 20 gauge, ventilated rib, 26-inch barrel, improved modified choke 421.00
Benelli spare barrels 220.00

ITHACA SHOTGUNS

MODEL 37 ULTRA FEATHERLIGHT™ PUMP SHOTGUN $378.00

The Ultra Featherlight™ features bottom ejection, which puts empties conveniently at your feet for easy recovery. The gun may be fired right- or left-handed with no worry about shells ejecting across your line of sight.

Orange iridescent Raybar™ sight points out game even against dense foliage and in poor light conditions. The Ultra Featherlight™ also features high-gloss American walnut stock, streamlined forend, gold trigger, Sid Bell grip cap and ventiated rib.

SPECIFICATIONS:
Gauge: 20
Chamber length: 2¾"
Barrel length: 25"
Choke: Full, Modified, Imp. Cyl.
Length of pull: 14"
Drop at comb: 1½"
Drop at heel: 2¼"
Weight: 5 lbs.

ITHACA SHOTGUNS

MODEL 37 STANDARD WITH VENTLIATED RIB
$345.00

A versatile gun that shoots squirrel, rabbit, duck, geese, even waterfowl. The Model 37 is suitable for both right- and left-handed shooters, with left-handed safety available. Pumping the action requires only a slight movement of your arm. With the ejection port on the bottom of the gun instead of on the side, rain, dirt and debris stay outside of the Model 37's Featherlight™ action.

Model	Grade	Gauge	Chamber Length	Barrel Length	Choke	Length of Pull	Drop at Comb	Drop at Heel	Weight (lbs)	Price
37	Standard, Standard Vent, or Deluxe Vent	12	2¾"	30"	Full	14"	1½"	2¼"	6¾	Standard $299.00
		12	2¾"	28"	Mod.	14"	1½"	2¼"	6¾	Standard Vent $345.00
		12	2¾"	26"	Imp. Cyl.	14"	1½"	2¼"	6¾	
		20	2¾"	28"	Full or Mod.	14"	1½"	2¼"	6¼	Deluxe Vent
		20	2¾"	26"	Imp. Cyl.	14"	1½"	2¼"	6¼	$357.00

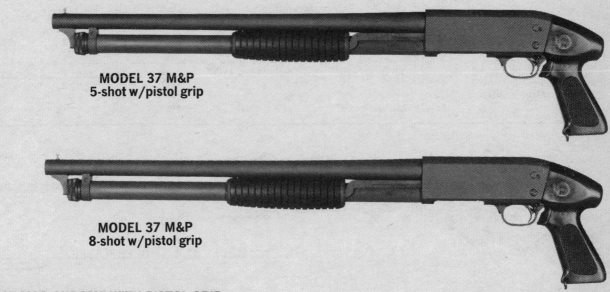

MODEL 37 M&P
5-shot w/pistol grip

MODEL 37 M&P
8-shot w/pistol grip

MODEL 37 M&P CHROME WITH PISTOL GRIP
$350.00

These shotguns are the original military and police versions of the Model 37. Their bottom ejection makes it possible to fire from either the left or right shoulder without the possible distraction of shells ejected across the shooter's field of vision. Metal parts are either Parkerized or matte-chrome finished. Wood has a non-glare, maintenance-free tung oil finish.

Model	Grade	Gauge	Chamber Length	Barrel Length	Choke	Length of Pull	Drop at Comb	Drop at Heel	Weight (lbs.)	Price Without Pistol Grip
37 M&P	5-shot	12	2¾"	18," 20"	Cyl.	14"	1½"	2¼"	6½	$283.00
37 M&P	8-shot	12	2¾"	20"	Cyl.	14"	1½"	2¼"	6¾	296.00
37 M&P Chrome	8-shot	12	2¾"	20"	Cyl.	14"	1½"	2¼"	6¾	330.00

ITHACA SHOTGUNS

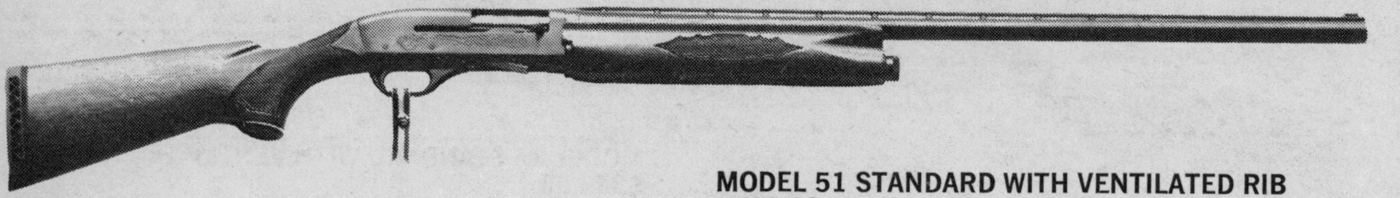

MODEL 51 STANDARD WITH VENTILATED RIB
$433.00

The Model 51 is a gas-operated, semi-automatic shotgun featuring a machined, solid-steel receiver and a triple-lug lock-up that makes the bolt and barrel act as one integral piece. The gun's barrel is Roto-Forged® from a 15-inch billet of steel; its stock is solid American walnut.

Model 51 Deluxe target gun has full-fancy hand-checkered wood and target-grade barrel. Model 51 Standard comes with a plain or vent-rib barrel, or 3″ Magnum version.

Model	Grade	Gauge	Chamber Length	Barrel Length	Choke	Length of Pull	Drop at Comb	Drop at Heel	Weight (lbs)	Price
51	Standard Vent	12	2¾″	30″	Full	14″	1½″	2¼″	7½	Standard Vent
		12	2¾″	28″	Full or Mod.	14″	1½″	2¼″	7½	$433.00
		12	2¾″	26″	Imp. Cyl.	14″	1½″	2¼″	7½	
		20	2¾″	28″	Full or Mod.	14″	1½″	2¼″	7¼	
		20	2¾″	26″	Imp. Cyl.	14″	1½″	2¼″	7¼	
51	Vent Magnum	12	3″	30″	Full	14″	1½″	2¼″	8	$466.00
		20	3″	28″	Full	14″	1½″	2¼″	7¾	
51	Deluxe Trap	12	2¾″	30″	Full	14½″	1⁵⁄₁₆″	1⁷⁄₁₆″	8	$558.00
51	Deluxe Trap M.C.	12	2¾″	30″	Full	14½″	1½″	1½″-2″	8	590.00
51	Deluxe Skeet	12	2¾″	26″	SKT	14″	1½″	2¼″	7½	550.00
		20	2¾″	26″	SKT	14″	1½″	2¼″	7½	

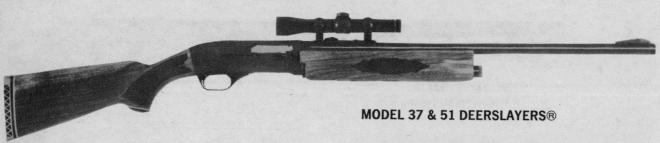

MODEL 37 & 51 DEERSLAYERS®

Ithaca now has four Deerslayer® models for firing rifled slugs with famous Deerslayer® accuracy. You'll bring home Whitetails with this gun that you'd be lucky to get with regular shotguns. With shotshells, these barrels also provide effective 35-yard patterns on upland game.

Model	Grade	Gauge	Chamber Length	Barrel Length	Choke	Length of Pull	Drop at Comb	Drop at Heel	Weight (lbs)	Price
37	Standard and	12	2¾″	26″	RS	14″	1½″	2¼″	6¾	Standard
	Super Deluxe	12	2¾″	20″	RS	14″	1½″	2¼″	6½	$335.00
		20	2¾″	26″	RS	14″	1½″	2¼″	6¼	Super Deluxe
		20	2¾″	20″	RS	14″	1½″	2¼″	6	$378.00
37	Ultra-Deerslayer	20	2¾″	20″	RS	14″	1½″	2¼″	5	$355.00
51	Deerslayer	12	2¾″	24″	RS	14″	1½″	2¼″	7½	$423.00

KASSNAR–FIAS SHOTGUNS

FIAS SK-3

Brescia, the firearms capital of Italy and maybe of all Europe, is the home of the Fias line of over-and-unders. Featured in three grades, 12 and 20 gauge and all popular barrel lengths and chokes. Weight 6-6½ lbs.

SK-1: Featuring double triggers, European walnut stock and forend, chrome-lined Breda steel barrels, hand checkered, hand fitted, with Anson and Deely lock mechanism. **$449.95**

SK-3: Features all of the above with a single selective trigger and standard extractors. **$469.95**

SK-4D: Deluxe engraved, beavertail fore-end, automatic ejectors, ventilated rib and single selective trigger. . **$529.95**

SK-4DT: Features all the same features as the SK-4D but includes double ventilated rib and right-hand palm swell for trap shooting. **$559.95**

KASSNAR–ZABALA SHOTGUNS

KASSNAR SIDE BY SIDE SHOTGUNS

The Kassnar-Zabala side by side shotguns offer the sportsman as complete a line of doubles as is available. Zabalas are available in 10, 12, 20 and .410 gauge in all popular chokes and barrel lengths. Of added interest is the 20 gauge,

24″ M-F which affords the young beginner a light weight and shorter stock piece which is easy to handle and carry. 12, 20 and .410 gauge **$399.95**
10 gauge **469.95**

KRIEGHOFF SHOTGUNS

MODEL TRUMPF $3995.00
Boxlock Drilling

Gauges: 12 or 16.
Chamber: 2¾″.
Calibers: 243 Win., 6.5x55, 6.5x57 R, 7x57 R, 7x65 R, 7x64, 308 Win., 30-06, 8x57 JRS, 9.3x74 R.
Barrel Length: 25″ soldered. Optional free-floating rifle barrel.
Chokes: Imp. Cyl.; Imp. Mod.
Action: Boxlock; Greener crossbolt and double barrel lug locking. Steel receiver or optional special aluminum alloy (Dural). Receivers are hard nickel-plated (satin finish).
Triggers: Double; optional single trigger available. Front trigger activates upper right barrel. If manual rifle selecting feature is activated this trigger becomes the rifle trigger with a standard pull. May also be set for a finer trigger pull. Rear trigger fires upper left barrel.
Stock: Oil-finished German-styled stock with pistol grip and cheekpiece. Optional custom stock available.
Forearm: Semi-beavertail.
Engraving: Light scrollwork. Various engravings avail.

Weight: Approx. 7.5 lbs. with steel receiver; approx. 6.8 lbs. with special aluminum alloy receiver (Dural).
Features: Custom leather case; special-caliber drillings avail.

MODEL NEPTUN $6980.00
Sidelock Drilling

The Model Neptun is the same as the Model Trumpf except for the following specifications:
Action: Sidelocks for shot barrels and rifle barrel lock mounted on the trigger plate. Separate manual rifle cocking feature. Greener crossbolt and double-barrel locking.
Engraving: Standard engraving features hunting scenes with leaf arabesques. Custom engravings avail. at add'l. cost.
Weight: Approx. 7.5 lbs. with steel receiver; approx. 7 lbs. with special aluminum alloy receiver (Dural).

MODEL NEPTUN-PRIMUS $8370.00
Sidelock Drilling

The Neptun-Primus is a deluxe version of the Model Neptun.

KRIEGHOFF SHOTGUNS

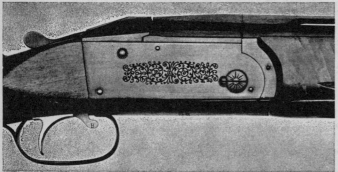

Standard

Features unique Krieghoff split barrel design, simplified construction. Internal parts are specially hardened, heat-treated steel. Single trigger is mechanical, dependable. Selected European stocks and forends.

Standard Grade Trap	$3995.00
Standard Grade Hunting	4495.00
Standard Grade Skeet ..	4495.00
Standard Vandalia Rib Trap	4495.00
Standard Low Rib 2 Barrel Trap Combo Set ...	on request
Standard Vandalia Rib 2 Barrel Trap Combo Set	on request
Standard Grade 4 Barrel Skeet Set	9995.00

San Remo (Vandalia Grade only)

Fine American walnut wood. Relief engraving meticulously insculpted. Polished mechanism. Krieghoff weight is between the hands for perfect balance, fast pointing. All Krieghoffs have special short hammer fall for instant response.

San Remo Grade 4 Barrel Skeet Set	$16,995.00
San Remo Vandalia Trap	on request
San Remo Vandalia Combo Trap Set	on request
San Remo Low Rib Combo Trap Set	on request
San Remo Low Rib Trap	on request

Monte Carlo

Superb relief engraving, silver inlaid figurines. Fancy grade walnut. All Krieghoffs have light recoil, straight back, no barrel whip, better position for second shot. In Monte Carlo grade.

Monte Carlo Grade 4 Barrel Skeet Set	$25,995.00
Monte Carlo Trap	13,995.00
Monte Carlo or Crown Combo Trap	16,995.00

Crown

The finest Krieghoff. Gold inlaid figurines. Superbly grained, polished, epoxy-finished woods. Polished mechanism. Double and triple checking of every Krieghoff assures matchless quality.

Crown Grade 4 Barrel Skeet Set	$27,995.00
Crown Trap	14,995.00

Super Crown

The ultimate version of the Crown Krieghoff. Relief engraving with gold and silver inlaid figurines. Polished mechanism. Epoxy-finished woods, superbly grained and polished. Peerless performance.

Super Crown Grade 4 Barrel Skeet Set	$35,000.00

München

The München is hand-forged from Böhler ordnance steel. The stock is handrubbed American Claro walnut. And, like all Krieghoffs, the München has an interchangeable barrel system that comes boxed in a leather case.

München Grade 4 Barrel Skeet Set	$11,995.00

EXTRA BARRELS:

Skeet, Hunting, Vandalia (High Rib Trap)	$1595.00
Low Rib Trap	1395.00

KRIEGHOFF SHOTGUNS

MODEL KS2 $17,500.00
Side/Side Sidelock Field

Gauge: 20.
Chamber: 3".
Barrel Length: 28".
Choke: Right: mod. Left: full.
Rib: Low, narrows, tapered.
Trigger: Single trigger, non-selective right-left. Sidelocks with V-springs.
Stock: Oil-finished, exhibition-grade English walnut. **Length:** 14¼"; **Drop at Comb:** 1½" **Drop at Heel:** 2½".
Forearm: Semi-beavertail.
Engraving: Hunting scenes with gold inlays in banknote-style engraving; outlined with English scrolls.
Weight: Approx. 6 lbs.

MODEL U.L.M.-P. $9950.00
Over/Under Sidelock Live Pigeon

Gauge: 12.
Chamber: 2¾".
Barrel Length: 30".
Chokes: Bottom: imp. mod. Top: full.
Rib: Tapered, ventilated.
Trigger: Single trigger, non-selective bottom-top. Hand detachable sidelocks with coil springs and safety catching sears.
Stock: Oil-finished, selected fancy English walnut. **Length:** 14⅜"; **Drop at Comb:** 1⅜"; **Drop at Heel:** 1⅜". Optional custom-made stock available.
Forearm: Semi-beavertail.
Engraving: Optional.
Weight: Approx. 8 lbs.

MARLIN SHOTGUNS

**MARLIN
SUPERGOOSE 10
$238.95**

SPECIFICATIONS:
Gauge: 10, 3½" Magnum or 2⅞" reg shells
Capacity: 2-shot clip magazine
Barrel length: 34"
Weight: 10½ lbs.

Overall length: 55½"
Sights: Bead front sight & new U-groove rear sight
Action: Bolt action
Trigger: Gold-plated steel
Safety: Positive thumb
Stock: Extra long genuine American black

walnut with pistol grip and Pachmayr® ventilated recoil pad; white butt spacer, quick-detachable steel swivels and deluxe leather carrying strap; Mar-Shield® finish.

**ORIGINAL GOOSE GUN
12 GAUGE 3" MAGNUM—36" BARREL
(FULL CHOKE ONLY)
$144.95**

High-flying ducks and geese are the Goose Gun's specialty. The Marlin Goose Gun has an extra-long 36" full-choked barrel and Magnum capability, making it the perfect choice for tough shots at wary waterfowl. It also features a quick-loading 2-shot clip magazine, a convenient leather carrying strap and a quality ventilated recoil pad.

Marlin Goose Gun Specifications
Gauge: 12 gauge; 2¾" Magnum 3" Magnum or 2¾" Regular shells
Choke: Full
Capacity: 2-shot clip magazine
Action: Bolt action; gold-plated steel trigger; positive thumb safety; red cocking indicator.

Stock: Genuine American walnut with pistol grip and ventilated recoil pad; white butt spacer; swivels and leather carrying strap; tough Mar-Shield® finish.
Barrel: 36" with bead front sight & new U-groove rear sight
Overall length: 56¾"
Weight: About 8 lbs.

MARLIN SHOTGUNS
MARLIN MODEL 120 12-GAUGE MAGNUM PUMP-ACTION SHOTGUN

MARLIN 120 MAGNUM PUMP SHOTGUN WITH VENTILATED RIB
$297.95
(extra barrels $91.95)

After years of design study, Marlin has introduced a pump action shotgun that is designed to fill the demand for a solid, reliable, pump action gun. An all-steel receiver is made from a solid block of high tensile steel. New-design, exclusive slide lock release lets you open the action to remove unfired sheel even with gloved hands. All-steel floating concave ventilated rib, serrated on top, provides clean sighting, reduces mirage when trap and skeet shooting. Front and middle sights help the eye align barrel and target. Handsomely engine turned bolt, shell carrier and bolt slide add elegance and double action bars provide smoothest possible operation with no binding or twisting. Matte finish, grooved receiver top eliminates glare, aids natural gun pointing and sighting. Big reversible safety button—serrated and located where it belongs, in front of the trigger—operates the cross-bolt safety that positively blocks the trigger. Choice of barrels—26″ improved cylinder choke, 28″ modified choke, 30″ full choke, 20″ slug barrel (with rifle sights), and 38″ full choke barrel. Select the length and boring of your choice. Extra barrels are completely interchangeable. 5-shot magazine capacity (4 with 3″ shells) 3-shot plug furnished. Stainless steel, non-jamming shell follower. Like all Marlins, the 120 Magnum has a genuine American walnut stock and fore-end. The buttstock design is made to fit American shooters with its full dimensions. Semi-beavertail fore-end is full and fits a full range of hands. Both stock and fore-end are checkered with a handsome pattern and feature Mar-Shield® finish. Deluxe recoil pad is standard.

MARLIN 120 MAGNUM SPECIFICATIONS: 12 gauge, 2¾″ or 3″ Magnum or regular shells interchangeably; 5 shots in magazine (4 with 3″ shells), 3-shot plug furnished; approx. 7¾ #; 20″, 26″, 28″ or 30″ barrels with steel ventilated ribs, front and middle sights; recoil pad; grip cap; white butt and grip spacers; stock dimensions: 14″ long including recoil pad, 1½″ drop at comb, 2⅜″ drop at heel; genuine American walnut stock and fore-end are finely checkered and Mar-Shield™ finished; all-steel receiver; cross bolt safety.

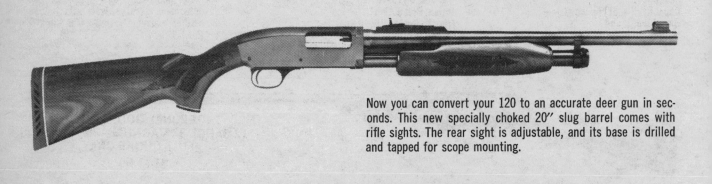

Now you can convert your 120 to an accurate deer gun in seconds. This new specially choked 20″ slug barrel comes with rifle sights. The rear sight is adjustable, and its base is drilled and tapped for scope mounting.

MARLIN GLENFIELD 778
12 GAUGE PUMP
Plain $216.95   Vent. Rib $245.95

778 SPECIFICATIONS:

Gauge: 12 gauge; handles 2¾″ Magnum, 3″ Magnum, or 2¾″ Regular shells interchangeably.

Choke: Modified

Capacity: 5-shot tubular magazine (4-shot with 3″ shells); 3-shot plug furnished.

Stock: Two-piece walnut finish hardwood with full pistol grip; semi-beavertail fore-end. Ventilated recoil pad; checkering on pistol grip.

Action: Pump; engine-turned bolt, shell carrier and bolt slide; double action bars; slide lock release; stainless steel shell follower; reversible crossbolt safety; blued steel trigger; deeply blued metal surfaces.

Barrel: 26″ Improved Cylinder, with or without vent rib. 28″ Modified Choke, with or without vent rib. 30″ Full Choke, with or without vent rib. 38″ MXR, Full Choke, without rib. 20″ Slug Barrel (Improved Cylinder), with semi-buckhorn rear, ramp front sight with brass bead and Wide-Scan™ hood. Drilled and tapped for scope mount.

Approx. Weight: 7¾ lbs.

MOSSBERG SHOTGUNS

**BOLT-ACTION SHOTGUNS
VENTILATED RIB**

MODEL 183K

MODEL 395K

MODEL 385K

The most popular bolt action shotguns are those made by Mossberg, in 12 and 20 gauge and 410 bore. Proof tested in our factory and chambered for all standard and Magnum factory loads. A modern streamline designed self-cocking action with **positive safety on top—right under your thumb.** The design and dimensions of these guns make them ideal for fast shooting. All Mossberg shotguns shoot rifled slugs accurately for deer or other big game.

Model 183K 410 bore bolt-action with C-LECT-CHOKE **$111.95**

The only 410 bore shotgun that gives you the advantage of finger-operated adjustable choke. **Action**—Fixed-type top loading magazine holds two shells, plus one in chamber. Chambered for all 2½" and 3" factory loaded shells. Convenient thumb-operated safety.
Stock—Walnut finish Monte Carlo design. Rubber recoil pad with white liner. Molded trigger guard. **Barrel**—25" tapered blued steel barrel, including C-LECT-CHOKE. Mossberg's exclusive factory installed adjustable choke lets you instantly choose Full Choke, Modified Choke, Improved Cylinder Bore or points in between. Gold bead front sight. **Weight**—About 5¾ lbs. Length overall 45¼".

Model 395K 12 ga. bolt-action with C-LECT CHOKE **$129.95**

With 3" Magnum shells and number 2 shot this becomes a great goose gun.
Action—Strong bolt action chambered for 3" Magnum as well as 2¾" factory loaded shells.

Double locking lugs for added strength. Quick removable bolt with double extractors. Detachable clip magazine. Magazine holds two shells plus one in chamber. Positive Safety on Top—"Right Under Your Thumb". **Stock**—Walnut finish, modern Monte Carlo design, pistol grip and cushion rubber recoil pad. **Barrel**—28" including C-LECT-CHOKE. **Sights**—Grooved rear sight for accurate alignment. Shotgun bead front. **Weight**—About 7½ lbs. Length overall 45¾".

Model 385K 20 ga. bolt action with C-LECT-CHOKE **$121.95**

Identical to Model 395K except that it is a 20 gauge shotgun with 28" barrel, including C-LECT-CHOKE. Chambered for 3" Magnum as well as 2¾" factory loaded shells. **Weight**—About 6⅜ lbs. Length overall 45¾".

NEW HAVEN BRAND BOLT-ACTION SHOTGUNS

Model 283 T .410 bore bolt-action repeater, Standard Grade. Full choke. Chambered for all 2½" and 3" factory loaded shells. **Barrel**—24". **Stock**—Walnut finish Monte Carlo design. **Weight**—About 6¾ lbs. Length overall 43½". **Price not set.**

Model 495 T 12 ga. bolt action repeater, Standard Grade. Full choke. Chambered for all 2½" and 3" factory loaded shells. **Barrel**—28". **Price not set.**

Model 485 T 20 ga. bolt action repeater, Standard Grade. Full choke. Chambered for all 2½" and 3" factory loaded shells. **Barrel**—26". **Price not set.**

MOSSBERG SHOTGUNS

NEW HAVEN BRAND
BOLT-ACTION SHOTGUNS PLAIN BARRELS AND VENTILATED RIB

MODEL 600 AKT

MODEL 600 SLUGSTER

Slide Action 600"T" offers a lightweight action, high tensile strength alloy. It also features the famous Mossberg "Safety on Top" and a full range of interchangeable barrels. The stock is walnut-finished birch with serrated buttplate and has a fluted comb and grooved beavertail forend.

Model 600 AT: 12 ga. Std. grade, 30" full or 28" mod., plain barrel. 26" Imp. Cyl. .... **Price not set**
Model 600 CT: 20 ga. Std. grade, 28" full or 28" mod., plain barrel. 26" Imp. Cyl. .... **Price not set**
Model 600 ET: .410 Std. grade, 26" full, plain barrel.
Model 600 ATV: 12 ga. Std. grade, 30" full or 28" mod., vent. rib barrel. 26" Imp. Cyl. .... **Price not set**
Model 600 CTV: 20 ga. Std. grade, 28" full or 28" mod., vent. rib barrel. 26" Imp. Cyl. .... **Price not set**

Model 600 ETV: .410 Bore, Std. grade, 26" Full, vent. rib barrel. .... **Price not set**
Model 600 AKT: 12 ga. Std. grade, 28" C-LECT-CHOKE, plain barrel. .... **Price not set**
Model 600 CKT: 20 ga. Std. grade, 28" C-LECT-CHOKE, plain barrel. .... **Price not set**
Model 600 AKTV: 12 ga. Std. grade, 28" C-LECT-CHOKE, vent. rib barrel. .... **Price not set**
Model 600 CKTV: 20 ga. Std. grade, 28" C-LECT-CHOKE, vent. rib barrel. .... **Price not set**
Model 600 SLUGSTER: 12 ga. Std. grade, 28" Slugster barrel with rifle sights .... **Price not set**

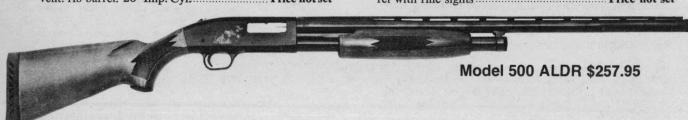

Model 500 ALDR $257.95

MODEL 500 SPECIFICATIONS:
Action—Positive slide-action. **Barrel**—12 or 20 gauge with free-floating vent. rib. ACCU-CHOKE interchangeable choke tubes. Chambered for 2¾" standard and Magnum and 3" Magnum shells. **Receiver**—Aluminum alloy, deep blue/black finish. Ordnance steel bolt locks in barrel extension for solid "steel-to-steel" lockup. **Capacity**—6-shot (one less when using 3" Magnum shells). Plug for 3-shot capacity included. **Safety**—Top tank, thumb-operated. Disconnecting trigger. **Stock & Forend**—Walnut-finished American hardwood with checkering. Both models with rubber recoil pad. **Standard Stock Dimensions**—14" length of pull; 2½" drop at heel; 1½" drop at comb. **Sights**—Metal bead front. **Overall Length** —48" with 28" barrel. **Weight**—12 ga. 7¼ lbs.; 20 ga. 6¾ lbs. (Varies slightly due to wood density.).

500 HI-RIB TRAP
Model 500-AHTD 12 ga. 28" ACCU-CHOKE w/ Imp., Mod., Mod. & Full choke tubes **$449.50**

Model 500-AHT 12 ga. 30" Full choke **$436.95**
500-COMBO PACK w/EXTRA SLUGSTER BAR
Model 500 ALDRX 12 ga. 28" ACCU-CHOKE, Vent. rib & 24" Slugster **$302.95**

Model 500 CLDRX 20 ga. 28" ACCU-CHOKE, Vent rib & 24" Slugster **$302.95**

500—VENT. RIB
Model 500ALDR 12 ga. w/ Vent. Rib. 3 interchangeable choke tubes: full; modified; improved cylinder. Chambered for 2¾" and 3" factory loaded shells. Barrel length—28". Overall length—48". Weight—7¼ lbs. **$257.95**

Model 500CLDR 20 ga. Same as model 500ALDR. Weight—6¾ lbs. **$257.95**

MOSSBERG SHOTGUNS

LAW ENFORCEMENT SHOTGUNS:

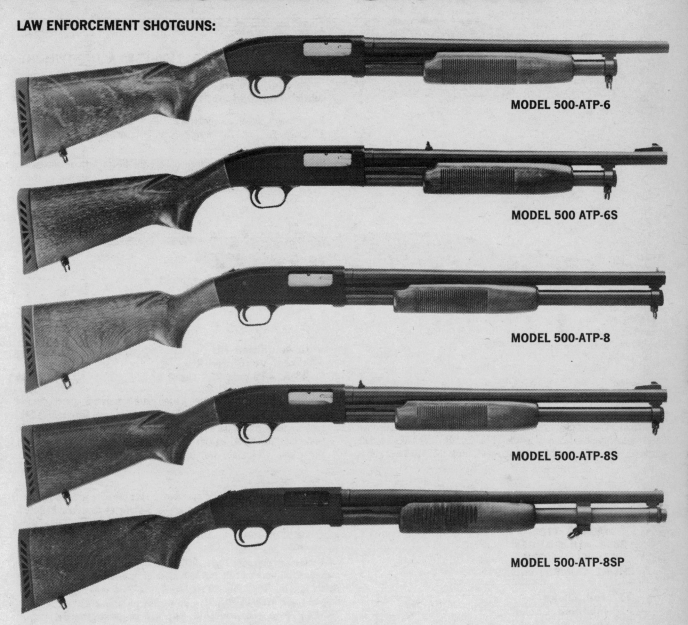

MODEL 500-ATP-6

MODEL 500 ATP-6S

MODEL 500-ATP-8

MODEL 500-ATP-8S

MODEL 500-ATP-8SP

Model 500 ATP-8 8-shot 20″ barrel **$221.50**
Model 500 ATP-8S 8-shot 20″ barrel w/sights **230.50**
Special firepower, 12 gauge, 8-shot, pump action shotgun in Cylinder Bore. 20″ Barrel. Magazine tubes hold seven standard 2¾″ shells, plus one in the chamber for 8-shot capacity (capacity is one less with 3″ mag.). Lustre-deep bluing. Walnut stained stock and forearm. Deluxe recoil pad. Drilled and tapped for scope and factory installed sling swivels.

Model 500 ATP-6 6-shot 18½″ barrel **$209.50**
Model 500 ATP-6S 6-shot 18½″ barrel **218.50**
Special 12 gauge, 6-shot pump action shotgun in Cylinder Bore. 18½″ Barrel. Magazine tube holds five standard 2¾″ shells, plus one in the chamber for 6-shot capacity. (Capacity is one less with 3″ mag.). Lustre-deep bluing. Walnut-stained stock and forearm. Deluxe recoil pad.

Model 500 ATP-8SP 8-shot 20″ barrel Special Defense/Enforcement Shotgun **$248.95**
Special 12 gauge, 8-shot pump action shotgun in Cylinder Bore Choke. 20″ Barrel. Magazine tube holds seven standard 2¾″ shells, plus one in the chamber (capacity is one less with 3″ mag.) non-glare, military-style metal finish. Stock and forearm oil finished. Equipped with bayonet lug for U.S. M-7 Bayonet.

REMINGTON AUTOLOADING SHOTGUNS

MODEL 1100 LT-20 • LIGHTWEIGHT
20 Gauge only

with plain barrel $391.95
with ventilated rib 431.95

Barrel length and choke combinations for the Model 1100 lightweight in 20 gauge: 28" full; 28" modified; and 26" improved Cylinder. Weight, 6½ pounds.

Model 1100 SA Skeet 20 gauge lightweight LT-20, with ventilated rib barrel. $446.95

MODEL 1100 • SMALL GAUGES
28 & 410 Gauges

with ventilated rib $438.95
SA Skeet Ventilated Rib,
28 & .410 ga., 25" skeet bbl. 453.95

The Remington Model 1100 Autoloading shotguns in 28 and .410 gauges are scaled-down models of the 12 gauge version. Built on its own receiver and frame, these small gauge shotguns are available in a wide selection of chokes with either plain or ventilated rib barrels. The .410 bore field grade will handle 2½" and 3" shotgun shells, while the .410 Skeet gun is supplied with a 2½" chambered barrel. Extra barrels are interchangeable within gauge regardless of chamber length of original barrel. Bore .410 guns are designed for the exclusive use of plastic shells. The Model 1100 field grade 28 and .410 gauge guns are equipped with American walnut stocks and forends and feature a scratch resistant RK-W wood finish.

MODEL 1100
28 & 410 GAUGES
BARREL LENGTH
& CHOKE COMBINATIONS

25" Full Choke
25" Modified Choke
25" Imp. Cyl. Choke

SPECIFICATIONS: STYLE — Gas operated. 5 shot capacity with 28 ga. shells — 4 shot capacity with 3" - 410 ga. shells. 3 shot plug furnished. **BARREL** — Special Remington ordnance steel. Extra barrels interchangeable within gauge **CHAMBER** — 2½" in .410 ga. skeet; 3" in field grades; 2¾" in 28 ga. field and skeet models. **OVER-ALL LENGTH** — 45½". **SAFETY** — Convenient cross-bolt type. **RECEIVER** — Made from solid steel, top matted, scroll work on bolt and both sides of receiver. **STOCK DIMENSIONS,** walnut in .410, 28 ga., and 20 ga. — 14" long, 2½" drop at heel, 1½" drop at comb. **AVERAGE WEIGHT** — 28 ga. skeet-6¾ lbs.; .410 ga. skeet-7¼ lbs.; 28 ga. plain barrel-6¼ lbs.; .410 ga. plain barrel-6¾ lbs.; 28 ga. vent. rib-6½ lbs.; .410 ga. vent. rib-7 lbs.

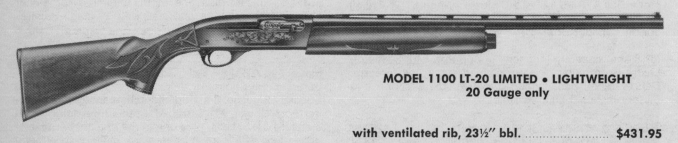

MODEL 1100 LT-20 LIMITED • LIGHTWEIGHT
20 Gauge only

with ventilated rib, 23½" bbl. $431.95

The Model 1100 LT-20 autoloading shotgun is the same as the Model 1100 except it is 4½" shorter overall.

REMINGTON AUTOLOADING SHOTGUNS

The Remington Model 1100 is a 5-shot gas operated autoloading shotgun with a gas metering system designed to reduce recoil-effect. This design enables the shooter to use all 2¾" standard velocity, "Express," and 2¾" magnum loads without any gun adjustments. Barrels, within gauge and versions, are interchangeable. The 1100 is made in gauges of 12, 20, 28 and .410, with a choice of different chokes, barrel lengths, and gauge combinations. The solid-steel receiver features decorative scroll work. Stocks come with fine-line checkering in a fleur-de-lis design combined with American walnut and a scratch-resistant finish developed by DuPont called RK-W. Features include decorative receiver scrolls, white-diamond inlay in pistol-grip cap, white-line spacers, full beavertail forend, fluted-comb cuts and chrome-plated bolt.

Model 1100 D Tournament with vent. rib barrel	**$1650.00**
Model 1100 F Premier vent. rib barrel	**3300.00**
Model 1100 F Premier with gold inlay	**4950.00**

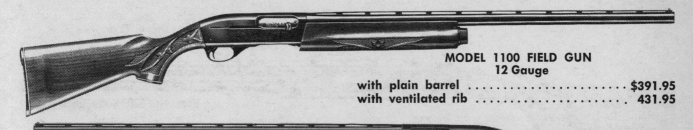

MODEL 1100 FIELD GUN
12 Gauge

with plain barrel **$391.95**
with ventilated rib **431.95**

**REMINGTON MODEL 1100
LEFT HAND ACTION — 12 GAUGE**

MODEL 1100 LEFT HAND

A complete mirror image of the regular Model 1100, these left hand shotguns put an end to the bothersome flying hulls that left-handed shooters had to face. Ejection is on the left side—all other specifications are the same as the regular Model 1100, 12 gauge. Left hand Monte Carlo stock available on trap model.

Model	Barrel length, in.	Choke	Price
1100LH with Vent. Rib Barrel	30	Full	$457.95
	28	Mod.	457.95
	26	I.C.	457.95
1100LH Mag. with Vent. Rib Barrel	30	Full	497.95
1100LH SA Skeet with Vent. Rib Barrel	26	Skeet	471.95

Model	Barrel length, in.	Choke	Price
1100 LH TA Trap	30	Full	$481.95
1100 LH TA Trap Monte Carlo	30	Full	491.95

12 & Lightweight-20 Gauges
For 3" & 2¾" Magnum Shells Only

MODEL 1100 MAGNUM

with plain barrel **$432.95**
with ventilated rib **472.95**

Designed for 3" and 2¾" Magnum shells but accepts and functions with any 1100 standard 2¾" chambered barrel. Available in 12 gauge 30" full or 28" modified choke, plain or ventilated rib and 28" full or modified choke in 20 gauge, plain or ventilated rib barrels. Stock dimensions: 14" long including pad, 1½" drop at comb. Furnished with recoil pad. Weight: about 8 lbs.

MODEL 1100 DEER GUN
12 & Lightweight-20 Gauges

22" barrel, improved cylinder choke. Rifle sights adjustable for windage and elevation. Recoil pad. Weight: about 7¼ lbs. Choked for both rifled slugs and buck shot. **$430.95**

REMINGTON O&U SHOTGUNS

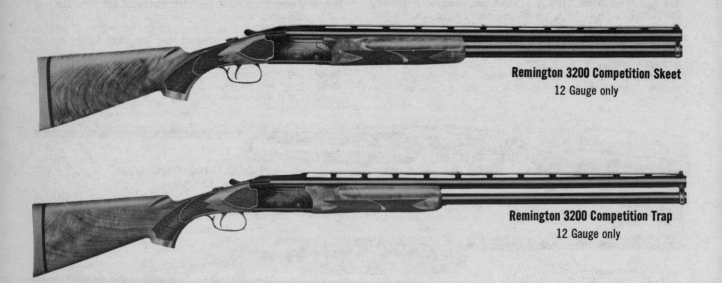

Remington 3200 Competition Skeet
12 Gauge only

Remington 3200 Competition Trap
12 Gauge only

3200 OVER/UNDER SHOTGUNS

SPECIFICATIONS:

Stock and Fore-end: Specially selected fancy walnut stock and fore-end. (Special Trap select but not fancy grade.) Cut checkering, 20 lines to the inch. Full beavertail fore-end. Satin finish standard on Competition grade guns. Optional 1⅜" or 1½" drop on Monte Carlo stocks in Competition grade guns. All with recoil pad.

Frame: Machined steel with sliding top lock. Shield-covered breech. Hammers cock on opening. Sides richly embellished.

Ejection: Automatic. Fired shells eject on opening. Unfired shells remain in chamber but are raised above chamber level for easy manual extraction.

Safety and Barrel Selector: Combination manual safety and barrel selector mounted on top tang. Left for bottom barrel; right for top barrel; middle position for safety on.

Trigger: Single selective. ⁵⁄₁₆" wide. Crisp with extra-fast lock time.

Sights: Ivory bead front, white-metal middle.

3200 Trap

Nominal Stock Dimensions: 14⅜" long. 2" drop at heel. 1½" drop at comb. 1⅜" drop at comb.

Over-all Length: 48" with 30" barrels and recoil pad.

Average Weight: 8¼ lbs. for guns with 30" barrels.

3200 Skeet

Nominal Stock Dimensions: 14" long, 2⅛" drop at heel. 1½" drop at comb.

Over-all Length: Skeet—44¼" with 26" barrels. Competition Skeet—43" with 26" barrels.

Average Weight: 7¾ lbs. with 26" barrels.

3200 Skeet Gun Set Limited-Edition "Competition"
Contains the Model 3237, 12 ga., 28 in. barrel skeet gun with new small-gauge barrel set—20 ga., 28 ga. and .410—complete in case.

3200 Models	Barrel Length	Type of Choke	Price
Competition Skeet	28"	Skeet & Skeet	$1525.00
	26"	Skeet & Skeet	1525.00
Competition Trap	32"	Imp. Modified & Full	1525.00
	30"	Full & Full	1525.00
	30"	Imp. Modified & Full	1525.00
Competition Trap with Monte Carlo Stock	32"	Imp. Modified & Full	1525.00
	32"	Imp. Modified & Full	1525.00
	30"	Full & Full	1525.00
	30"	Imp. Modified & Full	1525.00
	30"	Imp. Modified & Full	1525.00
Live Bird	28"	Imp. Modified & Full	1525.00
Skeet Set	28"	Skeet & Skeet	5750.00

REMINGTON PUMP SHOTGUNS

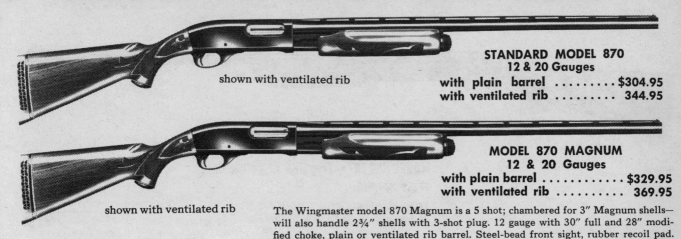

shown with ventilated rib

STANDARD MODEL 870
12 & 20 Gauges
with plain barrel $304.95
with ventilated rib 344.95

shown with ventilated rib

MODEL 870 MAGNUM
12 & 20 Gauges
with plain barrel $329.95
with ventilated rib 369.95

The Wingmaster model 870 Magnum is a 5 shot; chambered for 3" Magnum shells—will also handle 2¾" shells with 3-shot plug. 12 gauge with 30" full and 28" modified choke, plain or ventilated rib barrel. Steel-bead front sight, rubber recoil pad. Stock: 14" long including pad, 2½" drop at heel, 1⅝" drop at comb. 20 gauge furnished in 28" full or modified choke ventilated rib and plain barrels. Weight 12 gauge about 8 lbs., 20 gauge about 7 lbs.

MODEL 870 DEER GUN
12 & 20 Gauges
Brushmaster Deluxe (illus.) $324.95
Standard Deer Gun 306.95
Brushmaster 20 ga. Lightweight   324.95

shown with rifle sight barrel

The Model 870 Brushmaster is made to handle rifled slugs and buck shot. With 20" barrel and fully adjustable rifle-type sights. Stock fitted with rubber recoil pad and white line spacer. Other specifications same as standard 870. Also available in standard model. Same as Deluxe Brushmaster above, but with lacquer finish; no checkering, recoil pad, grip cap; special handy short fore-end. The Lightweight 20 ga. Brushmaster includes rifle sights and has a 20" barrel.

MODEL 870 SA SKEET GUN
WITH VENTILATED RIB BARREL
12, 20, 28 Gauges and .410 bore

The Wingmaster Model 870SA skeet gun comes with 26" barrel, special skeet boring, ventilated rib with ivory-bead front and white-metal middle sight. Also available in 28 & 410 gauge .

12 ga. about 7 lbs., 20 ga. about 6½ lbs. Also available in SC grade with selected wood and hand checkering.

870SA Skeet, vent rib, Rem. Skeet choke (12 & 20 gauges) $352.95
870SA Skeet, vent rib, Rem. Skeet choke (28 & .410 gauges) 360.95

MODEL 870
12 & 20 GAUGE
BARREL LENGTH
& CHOKE COMBINATIONS

30"	Full Choke
28"	Full Choke
28"	Modified Choke
26"	Imp. Cyl. Choke
Deer Gun 20" Imp. Cyl.	

SPECIFICATIONS: STYLE—5 shot pump action shotgun. Take down. 3 shot plug furnished. GAUGES—12 and 20. BARREL—Special Remington ordnance steel. Extra barrel is interchangeable within gauge: OVERALL LENGTH—48½" with 28" barrel. SAFETY—Convenient cross-bolt type, positive. RECEIVER—Made from solid steel, top matted. STANDARD STOCK DIMENSIONS—Stock and fore-end rich American walnut; beautiful checkering. 14" long, 2½" drop at heel, 1⅝" drop at comb. Trap reg.—14⅜" long, 1⅞" drop at heel, 1½" drop at comb. Monte Carlo—14⅜" long, 1⅞" drop at heel, 1⅜" drop at comb, 1⅜" drop at M.C. AVERAGE WEIGHT—12 ga. - 7 lbs.; 20 ga. - 6½ lbs.

REMINGTON PUMP SHOTGUNS

MODEL 870 TA • Trap Gun 12 GAUGE ONLY

SPECIFICATIONS:

TA Trap Ventilated Rib 30″ barrel Full $352.95
TA Trap with Monte Carlo 30″ barrel Full 362.95

Model	Barrel length, in.	Choke	
870TB with Vent. Rib Barrel	30	Full	$392.95
870TB with Vent. Rib Barrel & Monte Carlo Stock	30	Full	$402.95
870TBLH with Vent. Rib Barrel	30	Full	$414.95
870LH with Monte Carlo Stock	30	Full	$424.95

MODEL 870 TB • Trap Gun 12 GAUGE ONLY

SPECIFICATIONS: Available with 30″ full or modified trap, ventilated rib barrel. Ivory bead front and white metal rear sight. Recoil pad. Special target grade hammer, sear and trigger assembly. Beautiful "B" grade walnut stock with lustrous DuPont RK-W finish, fleur-de-lis checkering, special small pistol grip with cap. Regular stock dimensions: drop at comb 1½″, drop at heel 1⅞″, length of pull 14⅜″. Monte Carlo stock dimensions: drop at comb 1⅜″, drop at Monte Carlo 1⅜″, drop at heel 1⅞″, length of pull 14⅜″ . . . Extra 34″ full choke trap gun barrels available.

MODEL 870 TB • Left Hand Trap Gun

The only pump action trap gun built specifically for the left handed shooter. True "mirror image" design offers left hand feeding and ejection. Produced in 30″ full choke ventilated rib barrels with either regular or Monte Carlo stocks. Other specifications same as above.

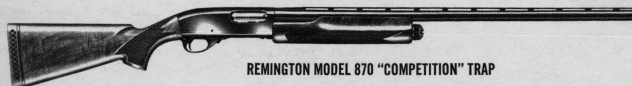

REMINGTON MODEL 870 "COMPETITION" TRAP

The 870 "Competition" is a single-shot trap gun which features a unique gas-assisted recoil-reducing system, a completely new choke design, a high step-up ventilated rib and a redesigned stock and fore-end with cut checkering and a satin finish. Length of pull 14⅜ in., drop at heel 1⅞ in., drop at comb 1⅜ in. Weight 8½ lbs. Barrel 30 in. $518.95

MODEL 870 HIGH GRADE

D Tournament Ventilated Rib, all gauges and versions $1650.00
F Premier Ventilated Rib, all gauges and versions 3300.00
F Premier Ventilated Rib with Gold Inlay, all gauges and versions 4950.00

REMINGTON PUMP SHOTGUNS

MODEL 870 LEFT HAND • Field Gun "WINGMASTER"
12 and 20 Gauges

A complete mirror image of the regular Model 870, these left hand shotguns put an end to the bothersome flying hulls that left-handed shooters had to face. Ejection is on the left side—all other specifications are the same as the regular Model 870, 12 and 20 gauge. Left hand Monte Carlo stock available on trap model.

Model	Barrel length, in.	Choke	Price
870LH	30	Full	$366.95
With Vent.	28	Full	366.95
Rib Barrel	28	Mod.	366.95
	26	I.C.	366.95
870LH Mag. with Vent. Rib Barrel	30	Full	$391.95

SPECIFICATIONS

STYLE	5 shot pump action shotgun.
GAUGES	12 and 20.
BARREL	Special Remington proof steel. Extra barrels are interchangeable within version (reg. or left hand) and gauge without fitting.
OVER-ALL LENGTH	48½" with 28" barrel.
SAFETY	Convenient positive cross-bolt type. Reversed on left hand models.
RECEIVER	Made from solid steel, top matted.
STANDARD STOCK DIMENSIONS	Stock and fore-end: Rich American walnut. Beautiful checkering. 14" long including recoil pad, 2½" drop at heel, 1⅝" drop at comb.
AVERAGE WEIGHT	20 ga.-6½ lbs.; 12 ga.-7 lbs.

MODEL 870 • 20 Gauge Lightweight (shown)
MODEL 870 • 20 Gauge Lightweight Magnum

20 Gauge Lightweight
20 Gauge Lightweight 3 Inch Magnum

This is the pump action designed for the upland game hunter who wants enough power to stop fast flying game birds but light enough to be comfortable on all day hunting. The 20 gauge Lightweight handles all 20 gauge 2¾ in. shells. The magnum version handles all 20 gauge shells including the powerful 3 in. shells. American walnut stock and forend.

Model	Barrel length, in.	Choke	Price
870L.W.	28	Full	$304.95
With Plain	28	Mod.	304.95
Barrel	26	I.C.	304.95
870L.W.	28	Full	$344.95
With Vent.	28	Mod.	344.95
Rib Barrel	26	I.C.	344.95
870L.W. Mag. With Plain Barrel	28	Full	$329.95
870L.W. Mag. With Vent. Rib Barrel	28	Full	$369.95

MODEL 870 • 28 & .410 Gauges

These small gauges are scale models of the famous Model 870 "Wingmaster" in the larger gauges. Built on their own receiver and frame, they give the shooter unique handling and pointing characteristics. Beautiful fleur-de-lis fine line checkering, white line spacers at butt plate and grip cap, chrome plated bolt, and steel bead front sight are bonus features. American walnut stock and fore-end.

Model 870	Barrel length, in.	Choke	
with Vent. Rib Barrel	25	Full	$354.95
	25	Mod.	354.95
	25	I.C.	354.95

REMINGTON TRAP & SKEET GUNS

BARREL LENGTH & CHOKE COMBINATIONS

26″	Rem. Skeet 12/20
25″	Rem. Skeet 28/410

Model 1100SA Skeet Gun: is made in 12, 20, LT-20, 28 gauge and .410 bore. It comes with 26″ barrel, skeet boring, ventilated rib, ivory bead front sight and white metal rear sight. Stock dimensions are 14″ long, 2½″ drop at heel, 1½″ drop at comb. Weight, about 7½ lbs.

Model 1100 SA Skeet, with ventilated rib barrel	**$446.95**
Model 1100 Tournament Skeet 12 and LT-20 gauge	526.95
Model 1100 Tournament Skeet small bore version .410 and 28 gauge	533.95

BARREL LENGTH & CHOKE COMBINATIONS

30″	Full Choke

Model 1100TA Trap Gun: is made in 12 gauge only and is equipped with rubber recoil pad and ventilated rib barrel. Stock is of selected grade wood and features fineline fleur-de-lis design checkering and white spacers on butt plate and grip cap. Fore-end has swept back design and fluting to give secure gripping area. Trap stock dimensions: 14⅜″ long including recoil pad, 1¾″ drop at heel, 1⅜″ drop at comb. Weight: about 8 lbs. Available in 30″ full choke only. Ivory bead front sight, white metal rear sight. Also available with Monte Carlo stock $10.00 extra.

Model 1100 TA Trap, w/vent rib barrel	**$456.95**
Model 1100 TA Trap, w/ vent rib & Monte Carlo stock	466.95
Model 1100 Tournament Trap 30″ barrel Full	536.95
Model 1100 Tournament Trap 30″ barrel Monte Carlo stock Full	546.95

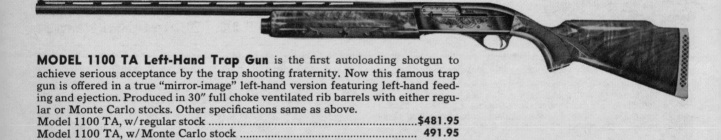

MODEL 1100 TA Left-Hand Trap Gun is the first autoloading shotgun to achieve serious acceptance by the trap shooting fraternity. Now this famous trap gun is offered in a true "mirror-image" left-hand version featuring left-hand feeding and ejection. Produced in 30″ full choke ventilated rib barrels with either regular or Monte Carlo stocks. Other specifications same as above.

Model 1100 TA, w/regular stock	**$481.95**
Model 1100 TA, w/Monte Carlo stock	491.95

SPECIFICATIONS: STYLE—5 shot gas operated shotgun. 3 shot plug furnished. GAUGE—Made in 12 and 20 gauge. BARREL—Special Remington ordnance steel. Extra barrel is interchangeable within gauge. OVERALL LENGTH—48″ (with 28″ barrel). SAFETY—Convenient cross-bolt type. RECEIVER—Made from solid steel, top matted, scroll work on bolt and both sides of receiver. STANDARD STOCK DIMENSIONS—Stock and forend; rich American walnut. 14″ long 2½″ drop at heel, 1½″ drop at comb. Trap reg., 14⅜″ long, 1¾″ drop at heel, 1⅜″ drop at comb. Monte Carlo, 14⅜″ long, 1¾″ drop at heel, 1¼″ drop at comb, 1¼″ drop at M.C. AVERAGE WEIGHT—12 ga. - 7½ lbs., 20 ga. - 6½ lbs.

MODEL 1100
12 & LT-20 Gauges
BARREL LENGTH & CHOKE COMBINATIONS

30″	Full Choke
28″	Full Choke
28″	Modified Choke
26″	Imp. Cyl. Choke

Note: 20 gauge model is not available in 30″ barrel length.

ROSSI SHOTGUNS

OVERLAND MODEL II

SQUIRE MODEL 14

OVERLAND MODEL II: Available in a 410 bore and 12 or 20 gauge for both standard 2¾-inch shells or 3-inch magnum. The 12 and 20 gauges are offered in the Coach Gun version with abbreviated 20 inch-barrels with improved and modified chokes. Overlands feature a raised rib with matted sight surface, hardwood stocks, rounded semi-pistol grips, color case-hardened hammers, triggers and locking lever.

Gauge	Barrel Length	Choke	Price
12	20" 28"	IC&M M&F	$273.00
20	20" 26"	IC&M	273.00
410	26"	F&F	289.00

SQUIRE MODEL 14: Available in 410 bore or 12 or 20 gauge, the Squire has 3-inch chambers to handle the full range of shotgun loads. Features double triggers, raised matted rib, beavertail forend and pistol grip. Twin underlugs mesh with synchronized sliding bolts for double-safe solid lockup.

Gauge	Barrel Length	Choke	Price
12	26" 28"	IC&M M&F	$287.00
20	26"	IC&M	287.00
410	26"	F&F	303.00

SQUIRE CHROME ENGRAVED:

410	26"	F&F	$340.00

ROTTWEIL SHOTGUNS

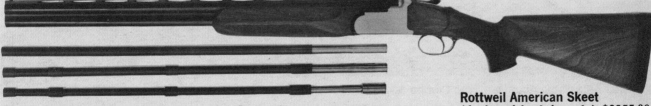

Rottweil Supreme Field Over/Under Shotgun

SPECIFICATIONS:
Gauge: 12 ga. only
Action: Boxlock
Barrel: 28" (Mod. & Full, Imp. Cyl. & Imp. Mod. & Full), vent. rib.
Weight: 7¼ lbs.
Length: 47" overall
Stock: European walnut, hand-checkered and rubbed

Sight: Metal bead front
Features: Removable single trigger assembly with button selector; retracting spring mounted firing pins; engraved action. Extra barrels available.
Price: 28" Mod. & Full $2255.00
28" Imp. Cyl. & Imp. Mod. 2255.00
28" Live Pigeon, Mod. & Full, overall length 45½" 2255.00

Rottweil American Skeet (designed for tube sets) $2255.00

SPECIFICATIONS:
Gauge: 12 ga.
Action: Boxlock, Skeet and Skeet choke
Barrel: 27" Skeet and Skeet, vent rib
Weight: 7½ lbs.
Length: 44½" overall
Stock: Selected European walnut, hand-checkered, modified forend

Sights: Plastic front housed in metallic sleeve with additional center bead
Features: Interchangeable inertia-type trigger group. Receiver milled from solid block of special gun steel. Retracting firing pins are spring mounted. All coil springs. This was the first shotgun specially designed for tube sets.

ROTTWEIL SHOTGUNS

Rottweil Montreal Trap $2255.00

SPECIFICATIONS:
Gauge: 12 ga. only
Action: Boxlock
Barrel: 30″ Imp. Mod. & Full
Weight: 8 lbs.
Length: 48½″ overall

Stock: European walnut, hand-checkered
Sights: Metal bead front
Features: Inertia-type trigger, interchangeable for any system. Frame and lock milled from solid-steel block. Retracting firing pins are spring mounted. All coil springs. Selective single trigger. Action engraved. Extra barrels available.

Rottweil American Trap Combo $2255.00

SPECIFICATIONS:
Gauge: 12 ga. only
Action: Boxlock ¾ & 1/1 choke
Barrels: O/U 32″ separated, ¾ & 1/1 choke. Single 34″, high vent rib, 1/1 choke.
Weight: O/U 8½ lbs. Single 8½ lbs.
Stock: European walnut, hand-checkered and rubbed. (Unfinished stocks available.)

Sights: Plastic front housed in metallic sleeve with additional center bead.
Features: Interchangeable inertia-type trigger groups, 2 standard. Lower tang surface milled to accommodate fast change. Receiver milled from solid block of special gun steel. Barrel locking lugs are recessed into breech face. Chokes are hand-honed, test-fired and then reworked until each shoots flawless patterns. Retracting firing pins spring mounted. All coil springs. Action engraved.

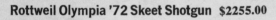

Rottweil Olympia '72 Skeet Shotgun $2255.00

SPECIFICATIONS:
Gauge: 12 ga. only
Action: Boxlock
Barrel: 27″ (special skeet choke), vent. rib.
Weight: 7¼ lbs.
Length: 44½″ overall
Stock: European walnut, hand-checkered,

modified beavertail fore-end.
Sights: Metal bead front
Features: Inertia-type trigger, interchangeable for any system. Frame and lock milled from solid-steel block. Retracting firing pins are spring mounted. All coil springs. Selective single trigger. Action engraved. Extra barrels available.

Rottweil Adjustable American Trap Combo $3455.00

Available single barrel only: 2525.00
Available double barrel only: 2255.00

SPECIFICATIONS:
Gauge: 12 ga.
Action: Rebounding lock, ejector
Barrels: Double barrel, 12 ga., length 32″, improved modified and full choke, exposed lower barrel, muzzle-collar-fitted
Weight: 8½ lbs.
Stock: European Walnut, hand checkered and rubbed

Sights: Plastic front housed in metallic sleeve with additional center bead
Features: The trap shooter adjusts the point of impact of the barrel with an L-wrench. Solid-block, special gun steel receiver. Recessed barrel-locking lugs. Interchangeable stocks, firing pins and bolts. Double-vented recoil pad. Sandblasted receiver.

RUGER SHOTGUNS

RUGER OVER AND UNDER SHOTGUN
$760.00

Hardened 4140 chrome molybdenom and other alloy steels and music wire coil springs are used throughout the frame. Single selective trigger. Automatic top safety serves as the selector that determines which ot the two barrels will be fired first. Standard gold bead front sight. Stock and semi-beavertail forearm are shaped from American walnut with hand cut checkering. Pistol grip cap and rubber recoil pad are standard and all wood surtaces are polished and weatherproof-sealed.

SPECIFICATIONS:

Gauge	20
Chambers	3"
Barrel Lengths	26", 28"
Overall Length (26" Barrels)	43"
Chokes	Skeet & Skeet, Improved Cylinder & Modified, Full & Modified
Length of Pull	14"
Drop at Comb	1½"
Drop at Heel	2½"
Weight	Approximately 7 lbs.

SAVAGE & STEVENS SHOTGUNS

MODEL 94-C $81.85-$83.60

Stevens 94-C: Single barrel shotgun with hammer style action. Opening lever on top tang swings either way, automatic ejectors, checkered walnut finished hardwood stock and forend. Available with 36" "Long Tom" barrel in 12 gauge .... **$81.85-$83.60**

94-Y Youth Model: 20 & 410 gauges, top lever opening. Has shooter stock with rubber recoil pad, 26" barrel. **$91.80**

Model 9478: A single barrel shotgun in 10, 12, 20, or 410 gauges. Features manual cocking, visible hammer, unbreakable coil springs. Automatic ejection and bottom-opening lever. Color, case-hardened finish. **$75.60**

Model 9478 10 gauge Waterfowl: With 36-in. barrel, stock is fitted with rubber recoil pad, and grooved forend. **$95.30**

Model 9478-Y Youth Model. With 20 and 410 gauges. Bottom opening lever, shorter stock with hard rubber butt plate, 26-in. barrel. 20 ga. modified or 410 full choke. .. **$81.85**

Price: 9478, 9478 Waterfowl and 9478-Y .... **Price Not Set**

SPECIFICATIONS: BARREL—CHOKE—CHAMBER

MODEL			9478*—94-C				9476-Y—94-Y	
GAUGE		10	12	16	20	410	20	410
BARREL LENGTHS & CHOKES	26" F					•		•
	26" M						•	
	28" F		•	•	•			
	30" F		•					
	32" F		•					
	36" F	•	•					
CHAMBERED FOR OVERALL LENGTHS		2⅞" &3½"	2¾" &3"	2¾"	2¾" &3"	2½" &3"	2¾" &3"	2½" &3"
LENGTH	OVERALL		42"—52"				40½"	
	TAKEN DOWN		26"—36"				26"	
	STOCK		14"				12½"	
DROP AT	COMB		1½"				1½"	
	HEEL		2½"				2½"	
AVERAGE WEIGHT (LBS.)		9½	6—6¼				5½	

*MODEL 9478 NOT AVAILABLE IN 16 GAUGE OR 12 GAUGE 32" F

FEATURES

MODEL	94-C—94-Y	9478—9478-Y
REBOUNDING HAMMER	•	
2-WAY TOP LEVER OPENING	•	
BOTTOM OPENING LEVER		•
AUTO EJECTOR	•	
POSITIVE EXTRACTION		•
STOCK WAL. FIN. HARDWOOD	•	•
FORE-END WAL. FIN. HARDWOOD	•	•

MODEL 24-V $203.90

24-V Combinations: 30-30 Win./20 ga.; 222 Rem./20 ga.; 223 Rem./20 ga.; 357 Mag./20 ga.; 22 Hornet/20 ga. Takes regular 3" Magnum shells for small game, use a 20-gauge slug for larger game.

SAVAGE & FOX SHOTGUNS

STEVENS MODEL 311
12, 20 & .410 Gauges
$214.20

This double barrel shotgun has many refinements usually found only in higher priced guns. It offers sturdy construction, solid lockup, excellent balance and superior shooting qualities. Three-inch Magnum available in 12 and 20 gauges.

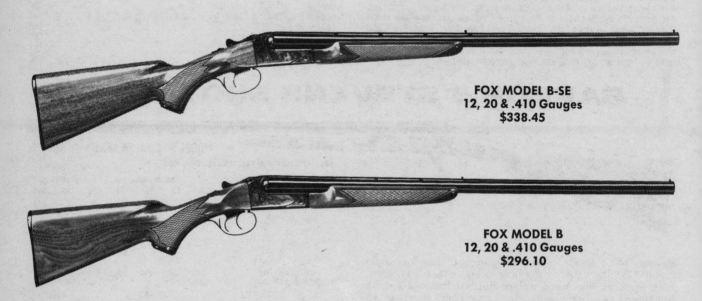

FOX MODEL B-SE
12, 20 & .410 Gauges
$338.45

FOX MODEL B
12, 20 & .410 Gauges
$296.10

Fox B-SE Gauges 12, 20 and 410. Automatic ejectors are standard equipment on the Fox B-SE. Other fine gun features are the single trigger and ventilated rib. The B-SE has the lines found only in a double gun, enriched with materials and finishes typical of expensive custom guns. Its selected walnut stock has a deeply fluted comb and checkering on pistol grip. The gracefully tapered beavertail fore-end is also attractively checkered. The frame has color case hardened finish with decoration on bottom. Convenient top tang safety.

Fox B 12 and 20 Gauge. This American-made shotgun features ventilated rib, double triggers for instant choke selection, walnut stock, plus fast handling and precise balance. The Fox B sports fluted comb with cut-checkering on the pistol grip and beaver tail forend.

| | | | | | | | Trigger | | Frame | | | | |
MODEL	Vent Rib	Solid Rib	Bead Sights	Automatic Top Tang Safety	Extractors	Selective Ejectors	Single	Double	Case Hardened	Coil Springs	White Line Butt Plate	Average Weight (Lbs.)
B-SE	X		2	X		X	X		X	X		7—8
B	X		2	X	X			X	X	X		6½—8
311		X	1	X	X			X	X	X	X	7¼—8

SPECIFICATIONS — FEATURES

ALL MODELS Stock: Length 14"; drop 1½" at comb, 2½" at heel.
Length overall 41¾"-45", take down 26"-30". All Models proof tested.

SAVAGE RIFLE/SHOTGUNS

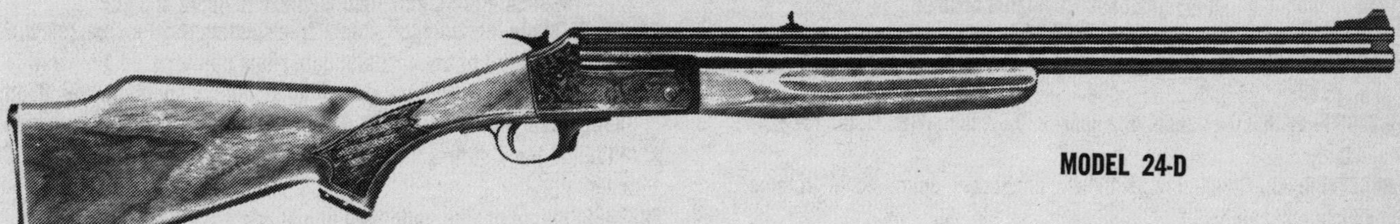

MODEL 24-D

MODEL 24 FIELD GRADE

24-C Campers Companion Combination: 22 long rifle/20 gauge. At 5¾ pounds, it's a pound lighter and five inches shorter than other 24's. When stored in special case, it measures just 5″ x 22″. The case has handles for carrying, thongs for tieing to pack or saddle. Recess in stock holds extra shells. **$149.60**

24-D Deluxe Combinations: 22 long rifle/20 or .410 gauge; 22 magnum/20 gauge. A breech and separated barrels on this handsome deluxe model means lighter weight and better balance. Two-way top opening lever swings either way for right- or left-hand use. The checkered walnut stock and fore-end are protected for lasting beauty with our new electro-cote finish. The decorated receiver adds a final deluxe touch. This combination gun is ideal for small game, pests and varmints as well as plinking. A 20 gauge slug can be used for larger game; the 22 magnum adds extra power and range for bobcat, fox, turkey **$175.00**

24 Field Grade Combinations: 22 long rifle/20 or .410 gauge; 22 magnum/20. A combination gun at a field grade price makes this model an ideal first gun—combines the ever popular 22 cartridge with either of two popular shotgun gauges. New top lever opening. Walnut finished hardwood stock and forend are coated with sturdy electro-cote. **$135.40**

MODEL	Caliber Gauge	Barrel 24″ F	20″ C	Chambered For
24-V	223, 20	X		2¾″ & 3″
	351 Mag., 20	X		2¾″ & 3″
	30-30, 20	X		2¾″ & 3″
	22 Hornet, 20	X		2¾″ & 3″
	222, 20	X		2¾″ & 3″
24-D	22 L.R., 20	X		2¾″ & 3″
	22 L.R., 410	X		2½″ & 3″
	22 Mag., 20	X		2¾″ & 3″
24-F.G.	22 L.R., 20	X		2¾″ & 3″
	22 L.R., 410	X		2½″ & 3″
	22 Mag., 20	X		2¾″ & 3″
24-C	22 L.R., 20		X	2¾″

F—Full C—Cylinder

SPECIFICATIONS—FEATURES

MODELS	Barrels Length	Scope Mounting	Grooved For Scope	Sights Front	Sights Rear	Color Case Hardened Frame	Rebounding Hammer	Hammer Selector	Top Lever Opening	Takedown	Stock Select Walnut	Stock Walnut Finished Hardwood	Checkered Stock	Monte Carlo	White Line Butt Plate	White Line Grip Cap	Length Over-all	Avg. Wgt. (Lbs.)
24-V	24″	Tapped		Ramp	Folding Leaf	X	X	X	X	X	X		X	X	X	X	40″	6¾–7½
24-D	24″		X	Ramp	Sporting	X	X	X	X	X	X		X	X	X	X	40″	7½
24-F.G.	24″		X	Ramp	Sporting	X	X	X	X	X		X					40″	6½
24-C	20″		X	Ramp	Sporting	X	X	X	X	X		X					36½″	5¾

MODELS 24-V, 24-D Stock: Length 14″; drop 2″ at comb, 1¾″ at Monte Carlo, 2⅝″ at heel; taken down 24″.
24-C Stock: Length 14″; drop 1¾″ at comb, 2¾″ at heel; taken down 20″.
24-F.G. Stock: Length 14″; drop 1¾″ at comb, 2¾″ at heel; taken down 24″.

RATE OF TWIST (R.H.) 1 turn in 12″ for 30-30, 357 Mag.; 14″ for 222, 223; 16″ for 22 Mag., 22 L.R., 22 Hornet.

SHOTGUNS OF ULM

K-80 SPECIAL HUNTING MODEL
$3700.00

BARREL: Soldered 28" with ¼ and ¾ chokes; 8mm tapered ventilated rib.

WEIGHT: With steel receiver: approx. 7¾ lbs. With Dural receiver: 7 lbs.

RECEIVER: Oil-finished and lightly arabesque-engraved with small hunting scene.

STOCK: Length: 14⅜" with drops of 1.6" and 2.4".

Note: Extra barrel sets with separate barrels cannot be fitted to the Hunting Model.

MODEL K-80 OVER AND UNDER TRAP AND SKEET

BARRELS: Made of Boehler steel; free-floating bottom barrel with adjustable point of impact; standard rib is non-tapered 12mm wide. Tapered 12mm rib or straight rib available on special order. Trap, Skeet, Live Pigeon and International barrels all interchangeable.

RECEIVERS: Hard satin-nickel finish; blue finish available as special order.

TRIGGERS: Wide profile, quick-set adjustable .

EJECTORS: Selective automatic.

SIGHTS: Strong metal front sight with insert and metal center bead.

STOCKS: Hand-checkered and oil-finished select walnut stock and forearm; silver soldered metal-to-metal assemblies. Removable palm swell stocks available in five different engraving patterns.

STANDARD GRADE I

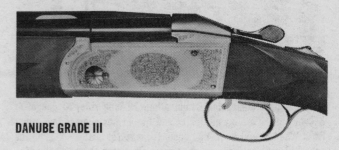

DANUBE GRADE III

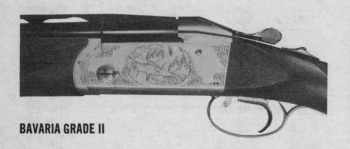

BAVARIA GRADE II

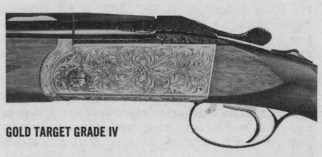

GOLD TARGET GRADE IV

GRADE	K 80 TRAP			K 80 SKEET		
	O/U	Unsingle	O/U-Unsingle Combo	O/U 12 ga. Regular Skeet Chokes	O/U International Skeet Tula Chokes	4-barrel set 12, 20, 28, .410 Tula Chokes and gas vents bottom barrel
I STANDARD	$3,380.00	$3,990.00	$5,150.00	$3,380.00	$3,495.00	$7,150.00
II BAVARIA	5,500.00	6,175.00	7,215.00	5,500.00	5,580.00	9,230.00
III DANUBE	6,860.00	7,555.00	8,580.00	6,860.00	7,000.00	10,595.00
IV GOLD TARGET	8,870.00	9,595.00	11,000.00	8,870.00	9,000.00	13,975.00
V CUSTOM	Made to customer specifications			Made to customer specifications		

SMITH & WESSON SHOTGUNS

MODEL 1000 AUTO SHOTGUN

MODEL 3000 PUMP SHOTGUN

MODEL 1000 SPECIFICATIONS

STYLE: 4-Shot (Plugged for 2 Shots) Autoloading gas-operated shotgun with pressure compensator and floating piston for light recoil.

GAUGE: 12 & 20 (2¾" Chamber) ; 12 3" Magnum Chamber

BARREL: Smith & Wesson Proof-Tested Chrome Molybdenum Steel.

RECEIVER: Light Weight High Tensile Strength Alloy, Scroll Engraved both sides ; 12 gauge 3" magnum has steel receiver.

LENGTH: 48" Over-all (with 28" Barrel).

SAFETY: Positive Cross-Bolt Type, Interchangeable left or right hand.

STOCK: Selected American Walnut: Length of Pull 14", Drop at Comb 1½", Drop at Heel 2⅜".

WEIGHT: 7½ lbs. with 28" barrel (12 gauge, 2¾" chamber); 6½ lbs. with 28" barrel (20 gauge, 2¾" chamber); 8 lbs. with 30" barrel (12 gauge, 3"chamber)

PRICE: 12 ga. w/vent. rib & 3" Magnum chamber, **$472.95**.
12 and 20 ga., w/vent. rib & 2¾" chamber, **$431.95**.

26"	Skeet	
26"	Improved Cylinder	with
28"	Modified	Vent.
28"	Full	Rib and 2¾"
30"	Full	Chamber

30"	Modified	with Vent. Rib and 3"
30"	Full	Chamber

MODEL 3000 PUMP SHOTGUN SPECIFICATIONS

STYLE: 5 Shot Pump Action Shotgun.

GAUGE: 12 (3" Chamber).

BARREL: Cold hammer forged Molybdenum Steel. Optional extra barrel: 22" Cylinder Bore Slug barrel with fully adjustable rifle sights.

RECEIVER: Machined steel.

LENGTH: 48½" (with 28" barrel).

SAFETY: Cross Bolt safety. Interchangeable left or right hand.

STOCK: American walnut stock and fore-end; hand-cut checkering; hand-rubbed and lacquered finish. Length of Pull 14", Drop at Comb 1⅜", Drop at Heel 2¼".

WEIGHT: 7 lbs., 7 oz. with 28" barrel.

PRICE: For vent. rib, **$354.95**; for slug gun, **$324.95**. Extra barrel for vent. rib, **$119.95**. Slug barrel, **$97.95**.

26"	Improved Cylinder	with Plain or
28"	Modified	Vent. Rib and 3"
30"	Full	Chamber

MODEL 916
with vent rib & recoil pad
in 12 and 20 GAUGE

MODEL 916 SPECIFICATIONS

STYLE: 6 shot pump-action shotgun, plugged for 3 shots.

GAUGE: 12 and 20 gauge chambered to accept both 2¾" and 3" magnum shells.

BARREL: Model 916-T offers interchangeable barrel capacity.

RECEIVER: From solid chrome molybdenum steel with hardened lock areas, satin, non-glare top.

LENGTH: 48" overall with 28" barrel.

SAFETY: Convenient top tang type.

STOCK: Genuine American walnut with fluted comb and finger grooved walnut fore-end; 14" length of pull; 2½" drop at heel; 1⅝" drop at comb.

WEIGHT: 7¼ lbs. with a 28" plain barrel.

MODEL	GAUGE	BARREL LENGTH	CHOKE	
MODEL 916-T PLAIN BARREL	12	30"	Full	
	12	28"	Modified	$197.95
	12	26"	Imp. Cylinder	
	20	26"	Imp. Cylinder	
	20	28"	Full	
	20	28"	Modified	
MODEL 916-T RIFLE SIGHTS	12	20"	Cylinder (recoil pad)	233.50
MODEL 916 PLAIN BARREL	12	30"	Full	
	12	28"	Modified	
	12	26"	Imp. Cylinder	190.95
	20	28"	Full	
	20	28"	Modified	
	20	26"	Imp. Cylinder	
MODEL 916-T VENTILATED RIB AND VENTILATED RECOIL PAD	12	30"	Full	
	12	28"	Modified	
	12	26"	Imp. Cylinder	234.95
	20	28"	Full	
	20	28"	Modified	
	20	26"	Imp. Cylinder	
MODEL 916 VENTILATED RIB AND VENTILATED RECOIL PAD	12	30"	Full	
	12	28"	Modified	
	12	26"	Imp. Cylinder	
	20	28"	Full	227.95
	20	28"	Modified	
	20	26"	Imp. Cylinder	
MODEL 916 RIFLE SIGHTS	12	20"	Cylinder (8 shot)	218.95
	12	20"	Cylinder (8 shot, recoil pad)	226.50

VENTURA SHOTGUNS

CONTENTO O/U SHOTGUNS

GAUGE: 12 only (2¾" chamber).
ACTION: Boxlock, with Woodward side lugs and double internal bolts for extra-low profile.
BARRELS: Field, 26" and 28". Skeet, 28". Pigeon, 29½". Trap, 32". Trap models have high post sighting ribs with option of screw-in chokes in both O/U and single barrels. All models have ventilated side ribs.
WEIGHTS: Superlight Field, 6 lb. 7 oz.; Skeet, 7 lb. 7 oz; Pigeon, 7 lb. 10 oz; Trap O/U, 8 lb. 2 oz.
STOCK: Trap: Hand-checkered Monte Carlo-style in European walnut. 14½" x 1⁷⁄₁₆". Recoil pad for individual fitting.

STANDARD TRAP

FEATURES: Single selective triggers, auto ejectors. Extra Lusso Trap has fancy walnut and extensive Florentine engraving. All models available in three grades: Standard, Lusso and Extra Lusso.

Field	$1195.00 to 2395.00
*Skeet (not available in Standard)	1625.00 to 2550.00
Pigeon	1265.00 to 2550.00
Trap	1350.00 to 2725.00

MODEL 51 DOUBLE
MODEL 51 XXV-BL

GAUGE: 12 only (2¾" chamber).
ACTION: Anson & Deeley with double underlugs.
BARRELS: 25" (XXV), 26", 28", 30", with chokes according to use.
WEIGHTS: With 28" bbls. 6 lbs. 10 ozs.; XXV 6 lbs. 6 ozs.
STOCKS: Select European walnut, hand checkered. Straight English or pistol grip stock with slender beavertail forend.
FEATURES: Single selective triggers, automatic ejectors, hand engraved action. XXV deluxe model with 25" barrels and Churchill rib.

MODEL 51 DOUBLE

Model 51 Double	$645.00
Model XXV-BL	775.00

MODEL 53

GAUGE: 28 (2¾" chamber) 36(.410") (3" chamber).
ACTION: Anson & Deeley boxlock with double underlugs.
BARRELS: 25", 26" and 28" with chokes according to gauge and use.
WEIGHTS: 28 gauge, 5 lbs. 5 ozs.; 36 gauge, 5 lbs.
STOCKS: Select European walnut, hand checkered. Straight English or pistol grip stock with slender beavertail forend.

MODEL 53 36 (410) GAUGE

FEATURES: Single selective or double triggers, automatic ejectors, hand engraved scalloped frames. 36(.410") gauge illustrated.

Model 53	$995.00-1195.00

MODEL 64-XXV

MODELS 62, 64 and 66 DOUBLES

GAUGE: 12 (2¾" chamber) & 20 (3" chamber).
ACTION: H&H sidelock with double underbolts; Model 66 with treble bolting and side clips.
BARRELS: 25" (62 XXV-SL), 26", 28" and 30" with chokes according to gauge and use.
WEIGHTS: 20 gauge from 5 lbs. 8 ozs.; 12 gauge from 6 lbs. 7 ozs.
STOCKS: Select figured European walnut, hand checkered. Straight English or pistol grip stock with slender beavertail forend. Model 66 has fancy walnut.

FEATURES: Single selective or double triggers, automatic ejectors. Model 62 has Purdy style engraving, Model 64-XXV (illustrated) and Model 66 have Florentine engraving. All models have cocking indicators, gas escape valves, and intercepting safeties.

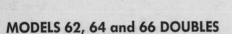

Model 62, from	$1120.00
Model 64, from	1200.00
Model 66, from	1895.00

WEATHERBY SHOTGUNS

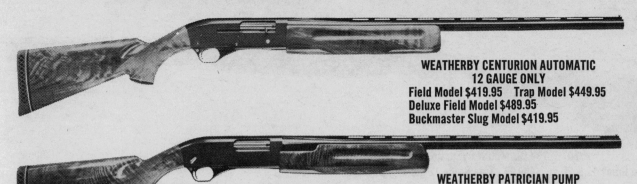

WEATHERBY CENTURION AUTOMATIC
12 GAUGE ONLY
Field Model $419.95   Trap Model $449.95
Deluxe Field Model $489.95
Buckmaster Slug Model $419.95

WEATHERBY PATRICIAN PUMP
12 GAUGE ONLY
Field Model $399.95   Trap Model $429.95
Deluxe Field Model $469.95
Buckmaster Slug Model $399.95

SPECIFICATIONS
for
PATRICIAN and CENTURION SHOTGUNS

WEATHERBY CENTURION AUTOMATIC

Gas operated means no friction rings and collars to adjust for different loads. The barrel holds stationary instead of plunging backward with every shot.

To these natural advantages of the gas-operated automatic, Weatherby has added revolutionary "Floating Piston" action. In the Weatherby Centurion, the piston "floats" freely on the magazine tube completely independent of every other part of the action. Nothing to get out of alignment. Nothing to cause drag or friction.

WEATHERBY PATRICIAN PUMP

The super-fast slide action operates on double rails for precision and reliability. No twists, no binds, no hang-ups.

To remove a loaded round, push the gold-plated forearm release lever to its forward position. Now the forearm is unlocked and the action can be opened.

Gauges:	12 ga. only		
Chamber length:	2¾" chamber and 3" Mag.		
Barrel lengths & chokes:	30" Full	28" Mod	26" Imp Cyl 30" Full 3" Mag
	28" Full	26" Mod	26" Skeet 30" Full Trap
Stock dimensions	**Field**	**Trap**	
Length of pull:	14¼"	14¾"	
Drop at comb:	1⅜"	1⅜"	
Drop at heel:	2¼"	1¾"	
Approx. weight:			
Patrician pump shotguns:	30" bbl — 7 lb.	9 oz.	
	28" bbl — 7 lb.	7 oz.	
	26" bbl — 7 lb.	5¼ oz.	
Centurion auto shotguns:	30" bbl — 7 lb.	11¾ oz.	
	28" bbl — 7 lb.	10½ oz.	
	26" bbl — 7 lb.	9¼ oz.	
Safety:	Cross bolt type, right or left hand		
Stock:	Figured American walnut, fine line hand checkering.		
Interchangeable barrels:	Available in above lengths and chokes.		
Price of extra barrels:	Patrician pump — $164.95		
	Centurion auto — 164.95		

WEATHERBY REGENCY SHOTGUN
12 & 20 GA. FIELD & SKEET $1269.95
12 GA. TRAP 1369.95

RECEIVER . . . The Regency receiver houses a strong, reliable box lock action, yet it features side lock type plates to carry through the fine floral engraving. The hinge pivots, are made of a special high strength steel alloy. The locking system employs the time-tested Greener cross bolt design.
SINGLE SELECTIVE TRIGGER . . . It is mechanically rather than recoil operated. This provides a fully automatic switch-over, allowing the second barrel to be fired on a subsequent trigger pull, even in the event of a misfire.

The Regency trigger is selective, as well. A flick of the trigger finger and the selector lever, located just in front of the trigger, is all the way to the left enabling you to fire the lower barrel first, or to the right for the upper barrel.
SELECTIVE AUTOMATIC EJECTORS . . . The Regency contains ejectors that are fully automatic both in selection and action. SLIDE SAFETY . . . The safety is the traditional slide type located conveniently on the upper tang on top of the pistol grip **BARRELS** . . . The breech block is hand fitted to the receiver, providing closest possible tolerances. Every Regency is equipped with a matted, ventilated rib and bead front sight.

REGENCY SHOTGUN SPECIFICATIONS

	Field and Skeet Models		Trap Models
Gauges	12 ga.	20 ga.	12 ga. (20 ga. not avail.)
Chamber Length	2¾" chamber	3" chamber	2¾" chamber
Barrel Lengths & Chokes	26" M/IC. S/S	26" F/M M/IC. S/S	30" F/F. F/IM.
	28" F/M. M/IC. S/S	28" F/M M/IC. S/S	32" F/F. F/IM. F/M
	30" F/M		
Stock Dimensions			
Length of pull	14¼"	14¼"	14⅜"
Drop at comb	1½"	1½"	1⅜"
Drop at heel	2½"	2½"	1⅞"
Approx. Weight	26" 7 lbs. 3 oz.	26" 6 lbs. 11 oz.	30" 7 lbs. 12 oz.
	28" 7 lbs. 6 oz.	28" 6 lbs. 14 oz.	32" 8 lbs.
	30" 7 lbs. 9 oz.		

Safety on all models—Slide operated rear tang
Stock on all models—Select American Walnut

WEATHERBY SHOTGUNS

WEATHERBY OLYMPIAN OVER/UNDER

Field Grade 12 & 20 ga. $999.95   Trap Grade 12 ga. only $1099.95

Specifications	Field and Skeet Models		Trap Models
Gauges	12 ga.	20 ga.	12 ga. (20 ga. not avail.)
Chamber Length	2¾" chamber 3" chamber (for 30" barrel only)	3" chamber	2¾" chamber
Barrel Lengths & Chokes	30" F/M 28" F/M, M/IC, S/S 26" M/IC, S/S	28" F/M, M/IC, S/S 26" F/M, M/IC, S/S	32" F/M, F/IM 30" F/M, F/IM

Stock Dimensions			
Length of pull	14³⁄₁₆"	14"	14⅜"
Drop at Comb	1½"	1½"	1⁷⁄₁₆"
Drop at heel	2½"	2½"	1¹⁵⁄₁₆"
(Monte Carlo)*			1¹¹⁄₁₆"
Approx. Weight	28" 7 lbs. 12 oz.	28" 7 lbs. 1 oz.	30" 8 lbs.
	26" 7 lbs. 8 oz.	26" 6 lbs. 14 oz.	

Safety on all models—Tang' thumb operated and combined with automatic barrel selector.
Stocks on all models—American Walnut.

*Trap models only.

WINCHESTER CUSTOM SHOTGUNS

DOUBLE BARREL SHOTGUNS
WINCHESTER MODEL No. 21

Custom Grade

Choice of gauge—12, 16 or 20 gauge; choice of barrel lengths—

    12 gauge—32, 30, 28 and 26 in.
    16 gauge—30, 28 and 26 in.
    20 gauge—30, 28 and 26 in.

Choice of choke combination; matted rib barrel, 2¾ in. chamber, rounded frame. Stock and beavertail forearm of Grade AA full-fancy American walnut. Stock built to individual specifications (within manufacturing limits). Straight or pistol grip—includes cheek piece, Monte Carlo and/or offset. Choice of forearm—field, skeet or trap; black insert in forearm tip. Fancy checkering on stock and forearm; steel pistol grip cap. Choice of composition butt plate, recoil pad or checkered butt. Panel in top rib inscribed "Custom built by Winchester for (Customer's Name)." Automatic or non-automatic safety (optional). Choice of front and middle bead sights.

Engine turned standing breech, frame, barrel flats, barrel lug, extractors, barrel breech, forearm retainer and inside upper surfaces of forearm shoe. Custom style ornamentation. Gold plated trigger. Gold oval name plate (optional). Choice of three initials engraved on name plate or trigger guard.

Custom Grade .... Special Order

Pigeon Grade

Carries all features of the Custom Grade plus the following added refinements: Matted rib or ventilated rib. 2¾ or 3 in. chamber (3 in. chamber not available in 16 gauge). Full leather covering on recoil pad (optional). Style "A" carving on stock and beavertail forearm. No. 6 engraving on frame and barrels. Gold inlaid pistol grip cap. Gold oval name plate or three initials gold inlaid on trigger guard.

Pigeon Grade .... Special Order

Grand American

Carries all features of the Custom and Pigeon Grades plus the following: Style "B" carving on stock and beavertail forearm. No. 6 engraving with all figures gold inlaid. Set of interchangeable barrels complete with extra beavertail forearm suitably engraved and carved to match balance of gun. Leather trunk gun case with canvas cover—both case and cover embossed with three initials in gold or black.

Grand American .... Special Order

WINCHESTER AUTOMATIC SHOTGUNS

SUPER-X MODEL 1 XTR GAS-OPERATED AUTOMATIC SHOTGUN

SUPER-X MODEL 1 XTR

Receiver and all other metal parts machined steel.

All Ventilated Rib models have a mid-rib sight.

1. Super-X Model 1 Field Gun. With ventilated rib barrel and bead front sight. 12 gauge chambering 2¾″ shells available in 26″ improved cylinder, 28″ with modified or full choke, and 30″ full choke.

2. Super-X Model 1 Trap Gun. 12 gauge. 30″ ventilated rib barrel Full choke. Selected walnut regular or Monte Carlo stock and wide forearm. Engraved receiver. Black-rubber recoil pad with white spacer. Red-bead front sight.

3. Super-X Model 1 Skeet Gun. 12 gauge with 26″ ventilated rib barrel. Skeet choke. Selected walnut stock with wide forearm. Engraved receiver.

Super-X Model 1 XTR

Trap Gun, w/reg. trap stock & vent rib	**$654.00**
Trap Gun, w/Monte Carlo trap stock & vent rib	**669.00**
Skeet Gun, w/vent rib	**659.00**

Extra Barrels:

Field, plain	**121.95**
Field, vent rib	**149.95**
Trap or Skeet	**163.50**

Super-X Model 1 XTR Specifications

Model	Gauge	Chamber	Mag. Cap*	Choke	Length Barrel	Length Overall	Length Pull	Drop at Comb	Drop at Heel/ Monte Carlo	Sights
Field V.R.	12	2¾″	4	IC, M, F	26″– 28″-30″	46¼″-50¼″	14¼″	1½″ 1⅜″	2½″ 2½″	MB, F & M
Trap	12	2¾″	4	IM, F	30″	50⅝″	14⅝″	1⅜″	1⅞″	WB, F; MB, M
Trap MC	12	2¾″	4	IM, F	30″	50⅝″	14⅝″	1⁵/₁₆″	2⅛″– 1⅜″	WB, F; MB, M
Skeet V.R.	12	2¾″	4	S	26″	46½″	14¼″	1½″	2″	WB, F; MB, M

*Add one round for shell in chamber. Super X Model 1 has a five-round capacity with factory-installed plug removed and one round in chamber.
MBF — Metal Bead Front; MB, F & M — Metal Bead, Front & Middle; RTFR — Rifle Type, Front & Rear; IC — Improved Cylinder; M — Modified;
F — Full; S — Skeet.
WB, F — White Bead Front; MB, M — Metal Bead Middle

WINCHESTER SEMI-AUTOMATIC SHOTGUNS

MODEL 1500 XTR
12 and 20 GAUGE

The Winchester Model 1500XTR gives you a gas-operated, semi-automatic field gun with the option of interchangeable barrels or with the Winchoke® system. This shotgun comes supplied with plain or ventilated rib barrel. Extra interchangeable field barrels in popular lengths and chokes are available at an additional charge. Metal bead front sight.

Model 1500 XTR Winchoke. This shotgun is available with a special barrel adapted for the Winchoke system. Improved Cylinder, Modified, and Full Winchoke tubes are supplied with the gun. One winchoke tube on the gun and two ready in your pocket.

The Model 1500 XTR features a streamlined forearm design, fluted and cut-checkered.

This semi-automatic shotgun delivers reliable performance with reduced recoil. Front-locking, rotating bolt of machined steel locks precisely into the barrel to form one unit.

WINCHESTER
SEMI-AUTOMATIC SHOTGUNS

Model 1500 XTR Specifications:

Model Symbol	Gauge	Mag.* Cap.	Choke	Chamber	Barrel Length	Overall Length	Length of Pull	Drop at Comb	Drop at Heel	Sights	Weight [lbs.]	
Field with V.R.												
G15051 *XTR*	12	3	Full	2¾"	30"	50⅝"	14"	1½"	2½"	MB, F	7¼	
G15053 *XTR*	12	3	Modified	2¾"	28"	48⅝"	14"	1½"	2½"	MB, F	7⅛	
G15055 *XTR*	12	3	Imp. Cyl.	2¾"	26"	46⅝"	14"	1½"	2½"	MB, F	7	$396.00
G15071 *XTR*	20	3	Full	2¾"	28"	48⅝"	14"	1½"	2½"	MB, F	6⅞	
G15073 *XTR*	20	3	Modified	2¾"	28"	48⅝"	14"	1½"	2½"	MB, F	6⅞	
G15075 *XTR*	20	3	Imp. Cyl.	2¾"	26"	46⅝"	14"	1½"	2½"	MB, F	6¾	
†Extra Barrels												
Field												98.95
Field w/V.R.												126.95

Model 1500 *XTR* Semi-Automatic with Winchoke

Model Symbol	Gauge	Mag.* Cap.	Choke	Chamber	Barrel Length	Overall Length	Length of Pull	Drop at Comb	Drop at Heel	Sights	Weight [lbs.]	
Field												
G15081 *XTR*	12	3	Mod., Full	2¾"	28"	48⅝"	14"	1⅜"	2⅜"	MB, F	7	$381.00
G15083 *XTR*	20	3	& Imp. Cyl.	2¾"	28"	48⅝"	14"	1⅜"	2⅜"	MB, F	6½	
Field with V.R.												
G15085 *XTR*	12	3	Mod., Full	2¾"	28"	48⅝"	14"	1½"	2½"	MB, F	7¼	415.00
G15087 *XTR*	20	3	& Imp. Cyl.	2¾"	28"	48⅝"	14"	1½"	2½"	MB, F	6¾	
†Extra Barrels												
Field with Winchoke (Full, Mod., & Imp. Cyl.)												113.95
Field V.R. with Winchoke (Full, Mod., & Imp. Cyl.)												141.95

*Includes one round in chamber. Model 1300s have factory installed plug which, when removed, increases magazine capacity to four shells.   V.R. — Ventilated Rib   MBF — Metal Bead Front
•Winchoke in 12 or 20 gauge Models; supplied with Full and Improved Cylinder Winchoke tubes, with Modified unit installed.

WINCHESTER SIDE-BY-SIDE SHOTGUNS

MODEL 23 XTR PIGEON GRADE $1150.00
MODEL 23 XTR PIGEON GRADE LIGHTWEIGHT $1175.00
Side-by-side; selective single trigger; tapered ventilated rib with serrated sighting plane; white bead front sight and black butt plate with white spacers; chrome-lined bores; automatic ejectors; comes with Deluxe Case.

MODEL 23 XTR PIGEON GRADE LIGHTWEIGHT

MODEL 23 XTR PIGEON GRADE & LIGHTWEIGHT PIGEON GRADE SPECIFICATIONS:

Model	Gauge	Chamber	Choke	Barrel Length	Overall Length	Length of Pull	Drop at Comb	Drop at Heel	Sights	Weight
Field	12-20	3"	M & F	28"	44¾"	14"	1½"	2½"	WB, F&M	6½-7 lbs.
Field	12-20	3"	IC & M	26"	42¾"	14"	1½"	2½"	WB, F&M	6½-7 lbs.
Ltwt Field	12	3"	IC & IM	25½"	42¼"	14⅜"	1½"	2½"	WB, F&M	6¾ lbs.
Ltwt Field	20	3"	IC & M	25½"	41¼"	14⅜"	1½"	2½"	WB, F&M	6¼ lbs.

WINCHESTER
SLIDE-ACTION SHOTGUNS

MODEL 1300 XTR / MODEL 1300 XTR DEER GUN

All Model 1300 XTR 12 and 20 gauge field guns are chambered for 3" shells. They will chamber 3" Magnum, 2¾" Magnum and Standard 2¾" shot shells interchangeably. This eliminates the need to buy a separate Magnum field gun.

The hunter can select an interchangeable barrel or the Winchoke system. Extra interchangeable field barrels in popular lengths and chokes are also available at additional charge.

Model 1300 XTR Winchoke is available with a plain or ventilated rib barrel specially adapted for the Winchoke systems. Improved Cylinder, Modified, and Full Winchoke tubes are supplied with the gun. Three interchangeable chokes on one shotgun to cover a broad range of game and shooting situations.

It has a shortened, tapered forearm, cut-checkered on the underside for sure gripping. Nickel-plated carrier. High-luster finish on wood. High polish and blueing. Front-locking, rotating bolt of machined steel locks precisely into the barrel to form one unit.

Model 1300 XTR Deer Gun available in 12 gauge only, is fitted with folding leaf rear sights, recoil pad and sling swivels.

Model 1300 XTR Specifications:

Model	Gauge	Mag.* Cap.	Choke	Chamber	Barrel Length	Overall Length	Length of Pull	Drop at Comb	Drop at Heel	Sights	Weight [lbs.]	
Field Gun												
Deer Gun	12	5	Cyl. Bore	3"	22"	42⅝"	14"	1½"	2⅜"	RTFR	6½	
G13001 *XTR*	12	5	Full	3"	30"	50⅝"	14"	1⅜"	2⅜"	MB, F	6¾	
G13003 *XTR*	12	5	Modified	3"	28"	48⅝"	14"	1⅜"	2⅜"	MB, F	6⅝	
G13005 *XTR*	12	5	Imp. Cyl.	3"	26"	46⅝"	14"	1⅜"	2⅜"	MB, F	6½	$289.00
G13021 *XTR*	20	5	Full	3"	28"	48⅝"	14"	1⅜"	2⅜"	MB, F	6⅜	
G13023 *XTR*	20	5	Modified	3"	28"	48⅝"	14"	1⅜"	2⅜"	MB, F	6⅜	
G13025 *XTR*	20	5	Imp. Cyl.	3"	26"	46⅝"	14"	1⅜	2⅜"	MB, F	6¼	
Field with V.R.												
G13051 *XTR*	12	5	Full	3"	30"	50⅝"	14"	1½"	2½"	MB, F	6⅞	
G13053 *XTR*	12	5	Modified	3"	28"	48⅝"	14"	1½"	2½"	MB, F	6⅞	
G13055 *XTR*	12	5	Imp. Cyl.	3"	26"	46⅝"	14"	1½"	2½"	MB, F	6¾	$323.00
G13071 *XTR*	20	5	Full	3"	28"	48⅝"	14"	1½"	2½"	MB, F	6⅝	
G13073 *XTR*	20	5	Modified	3"	28"	48⅝"	14"	1½"	2½"	MB, F	6⅝	
G13075 *XTR*	20	5	Imp. Cyl.	3"	26"	46⅝"	14"	1½"	2½"	MB, F	6½	
†Extra Barrels												
Field												$94.95
Field w/V.R.												122.95

Model 1300 *XTR* with Winchoke

Model	Gauge	Mag.* Cap.	Choke	Chamber	Barrel Length	Overall Length	Length of Pull	Drop at Comb	Drop at Heel	Sights	Weight [lbs.]	
Field												
G13081 *XTR*	12	5	Mod., Full	3"	28"	48⅝"	14"	1⅜"	2⅜"	MB, F	7	$307.00
G13083 *XTR*	20	5	& Imp. Cyl.	3"	28"	48⅝"	14"	1⅜"	2⅜"	MB, F	7	
Field with V.R.												
G13085 *XTR*	12	5	Mod., Full	3"	28"	48⅝"	14"	1½"	2½"	MB, F	7¼	$341.00
G13087 *XTR*	20	5	& Imp. Cyl.	3"	28"	48⅝"	14"	1½"	2½"	MB, F	7¼	
†Extra Barrels												
Field w/Winchoke (Full, Mod., & Imp. Cyl.)												$109.95
Field V.R. with Winchoke (Full, Mod., & Imp. Cyl.)												137.95
Deer Slug (Cyl. Bore)												107.95

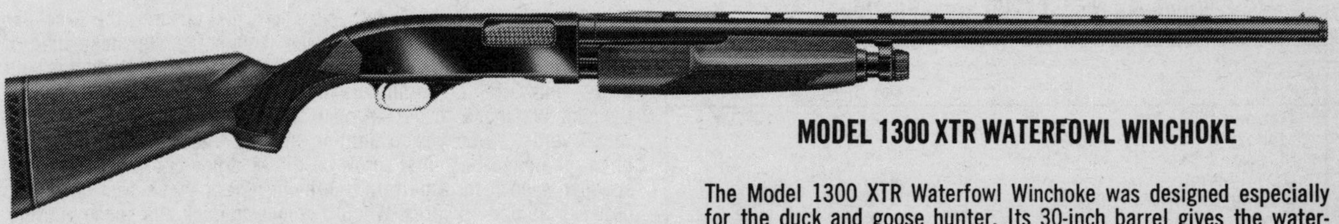

MODEL 1300 XTR WATERFOWL WINCHOKE

The Model 1300 XTR Waterfowl Winchoke was designed especially for the duck and goose hunter. Its 30-inch barrel gives the waterfowler the longer sighting plane preferred for pass-shooting. The gun also features three Winchoke tubes—improved modified, full and extra full—plus a spanner wrench for quick, convenient tube changing. The buttstock is fitted with a ventilated, black rubber recoil pad. In 12 gauge only with 3-inch chamber.
Model 1300 XTR Waterfowl Winchoke $341.50

WINCHESTER PUMP SHOTGUNS

MODEL 1200 IN 12 & 20 GAUGES

Hunters and shooters know that they've got to have a reliable shotgun that practically points by itself. They want a gun light enough to carry through a long day but just heavy enough to swing smoothly and surely when the chance comes. That's why more and more sportsmen are turning to a Model 1200—a shotgun that's lightweight, versatile, and trouble-free.

The Winchester Model 1200 slide-action shotguns blend fit, feel and performance with advanced engineering. Twin action slide bars give the Model 1200s a self-starting action designed to move back in a quick, effortless motion. Exclusive front-locking, rotating bolt-head locks the steel bolt securely into the steel breech for superb strength and safety. High-strength rustproof forged aluminum receiver. Crossbolt safety. Extended beavertail forend. Postive checkering. Weather-resistant stock finish. Engine turned steel bolt. American walnut stock and forearm. Fluted comb.

Model 1200 Extra barrels:

Riot	$90.95
1200—Field	90.95
1200—Field, w/winchoke (full, mod., & imp. cyl.)	105.95
1200—Field, w/vent rib	116.95
1200—Field, vent rib, w/winchoke (full, mod. & imp. cyl.)	131.95
Deer Barrel	105.95
Trap/Skeet	130.50
Winchoke:	
Extra tube	8.95
Tube wrench	2.10

Model 1200	12 Ga.	20 Ga.	Barrel Length	Type of Choke
Field Grade	x	—	30"	Full
Plain or Ventilated	—	x	28"	Full
Rib	x	x	28"	Modified
	x	x	26"	Imp. Cyl.
3" Magnum Plain or Ventilated	x	—	30"	Full
Rib	—	x	28"	Full

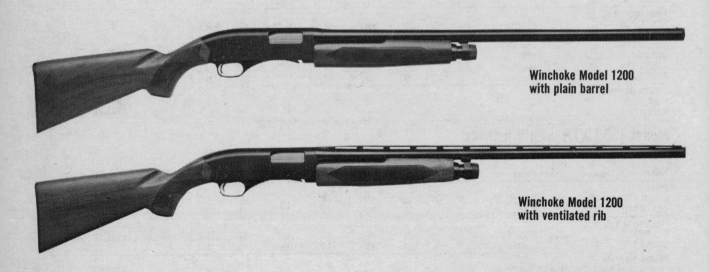

Winchoke Model 1200 with plain barrel

Winchoke Model 1200 with ventilated rib

MODEL 1200 WITH WINCHOKE

To change shot patterns to suit your sport, just unscrew the Winchoke in your slide-action shotgun. Replace it with the Winchoke tube of your choice, screw it in snugly and you're ready to go. If quail is your game—bobwhite, mountain or valley quail—pick up the Improved Cylinder Winchoke to get an open pattern that's most effective up to 30 yards. When you're hunting one of America's favorite game birds—the pheasant—just screw on the Modified choke tube with the spanner wrench for a pattern-tightening effect that's best on ranges between 25 and 45 yards. When it comes to duck and goose hunting, you can change to a Winchoke Full choke unit. For waterfowl long shots a Full choke can do the job.

Winchoke Model 1200 Field Gun with plain or ventilated rib barrels; 28" barrel; chambers 2¾" shells $254.00

Winchoke Model 1200 Specifications

Type	Field Plain Barrel	Field V.R.
Gauge	12-20●	12-20●
Magazine Capacity M/1200 *	5	5
Magazine Capacity M/1400 **	3	3
Barrel Length	28"	28"
Overall Length	48⅝"	48⅝"
Length of Pull	14"	14"
Drop at Comb	1⅜"	1½"
Drop at Heel	2⅜"	2½"
Weight (lbs.)	6½-7	6½-7¼
Sights	MBF	MBF

WINCHESTER O&U SHOTGUNS

Model 501 Grand European Skeet Gun

Features 27-inch side ventilated barrels and tapered ventilated rib; inertia-type single selective trigger; slide button combined barrel selector and safety; selective automatic ejectors. In 12 gauge only. Skeet or Trap version. $1800.00

Pigeon Grade XTR Skeet Gun

The Pigeon Grade XTR Field and Skeet version. Pigeon Grade Models feature receiver with silver gray satin finish and fine-line scroll engraving, hand-checkered stock and forearm of select walnut. Inertia trigger on 12 and 20 gauge models; mechanical trigger on 28 gauge and 410 bore.

Pigeon Grade XTR Field Gun. In 12 or 20 gauge	$1250.00
Pigeon Grade XTR Skeet Gun. In 12 or 20 gauge	1250.00
Pigeon Grade XTR Skeet Gun in 28 or .410 gauge	1300.00
Pigeon Grade XTR Skeet Gun 3-gauge set in 20, 28 or .410 gauge	3100.00

Pigeon Grade XTR Trap Gun

Trap Gun, w/std. trap stock and recoil pad	$1300.00
Trap Gun, w/Monte Carlo trap stock and recoil pad	1300.00

Pigeon Grade XTR Featherweight Field Gun

The Pigeon Grade XTR Featherweight Field Gun features 25½-inch, side-ventilated barrels; choked improved cylinder and improved modified in 12 gauge; and improved cylinder and modified in 20 gauge. Both gauges have 3-inch barrels. The 12 gauge gun weighs approximately 6¾ lbs.; the 20 gauge, about 6¼ lbs. $1400.00

Pigeon Grade XTR Lightweight Winchoke Field Gun

The new Winchester Pigeon Grade XTR Lightweight Winchoke Field Gun, in 12 and 20 gauge, features six Winchoke tubes—two each in improved cylinder, modified and full chokes—plus a newly designed wrench with wooden handle. The gun weighs approximately 7 lbs. in 12 gauge, 6½ lbs. in 20 gauge. $1450.00

WINCHESTER O&U SHOTGUNS

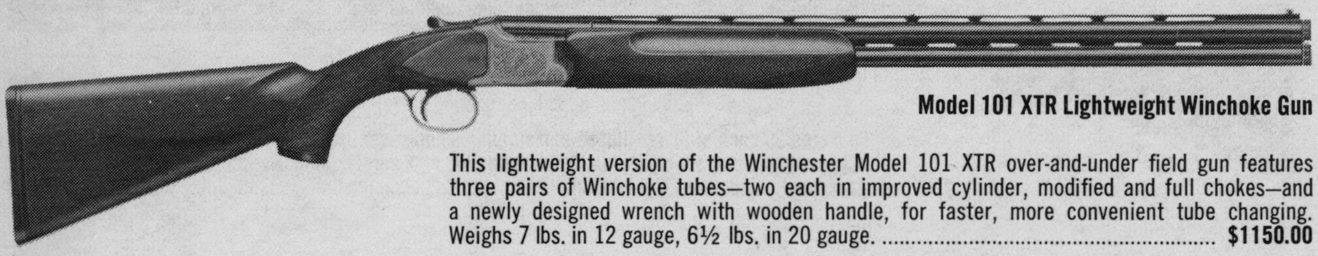

Model 101 XTR Lightweight Winchoke Gun

This lightweight version of the Winchester Model 101 XTR over-and-under field gun features three pairs of Winchoke tubes—two each in improved cylinder, modified and full chokes—and a newly designed wrench with wooden handle, for faster, more convenient tube changing. Weighs 7 lbs. in 12 gauge, 6½ lbs. in 20 gauge. **$1150.00**

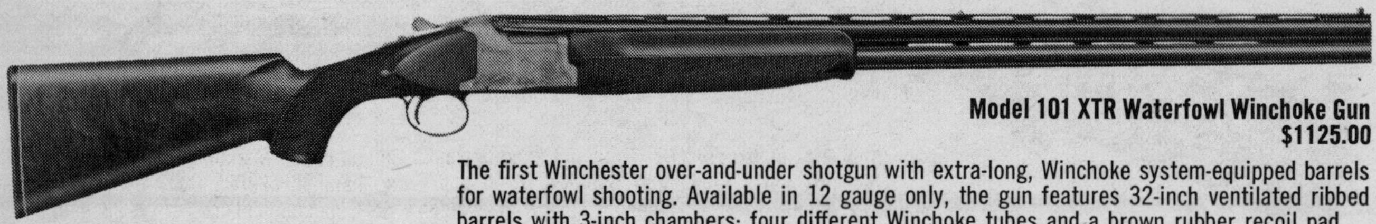

Model 101 XTR Waterfowl Winchoke Gun
$1125.00

The first Winchester over-and-under shotgun with extra-long, Winchoke system-equipped barrels for waterfowl shooting. Available in 12 gauge only, the gun features 32-inch ventilated ribbed barrels with 3-inch chambers; four different Winchoke tubes and a brown rubber recoil pad.

Model	Gauge	Chamber	Choke	Barrel Length	Overall Length	Length of Pull	Drop at Comb	Drop at Heel	Drop at MC	Sights	Nominal Weight
Model 501 Grand European Over-and-Under											
Skeet	12	2¾″	S & S	27″	43¾″	14⅛″	1½″	2½″		WB, F&M	7½ lbs.
Trap	12	2¾″	IM & F	30″	47⅛″	14½″	1¼″	1¾″		WB, F&M	8¼ lbs.
Trap	12	2¾″	IM & F	32″	49⅛″	14½″	1¼″	1¾″		WB, F&M	8½ lbs.
Trap, MC	12	2¾″	IM & F	30″	47⅛″	14½″	1⁵⁄₁₆″	2¼″	1⅜″	WB, F&M	8½ lbs.
Trap, MC	12	2¾″	IM & F	32″	49⅛″	14½″	1⁵⁄₁₆″	2¼″	1⅜″	WB, F&M	8½ lbs.
Model 101 XTR Over-and-Under											
Ltwt Field Winchoke	12-20	3″	W6	27″	43¾″	14⅛″	1½″	2¼″		WB, F&M	7 & 6½ lbs.
Waterfowl	12	3″	W4	32″	49⅛″	14⅛″	1½″	2¼″		WB, F&M	8¼ lbs.
Pigeon Grade XTR Over-and Under											
Fwt Field	12	3″	IC & IM	25½″	42¼″	14⅛″	1½″	2¼″		WB, F&M	6¾ lbs.
Fwt Field	20	3″	IC & M	25½″	42¼″	14⅛″	1½″	2¼″		WB, F&M	6¼ lbs.
Ltwt Field Winchoke	12-20	3″	W6	27″	43¾″	14⅛″	1½″	2¼″		WB, F&M	7 & 6½ lbs.
Skeet	12	2¾″	S & S	27″	43¾″	14″	1½″	2½″		WB, F&M	7½ lbs.
Skeet	20	2¾″	S & S	27″	43¾″	14″	1½″	2½″		WB, F&M	6¾ lbs.
Skeet	28	2¾″	S & S	28″	44¾″	14″	1½″	2½″		WB, F&M	6¾ lbs.
Skeet	410	2½″	S & S	28″	44¾″	14″	1½″	2½″		WB, F&M	6¾ lbs.
Skeet set	20/28/410	2¾″	S & S	28″	44¾″	14″	1½″	2½″		WB, F&M	6¾ lbs.
Trap, MC	12	2¾″	IM & F	30″	47⅛″	14⅜″	1⅜″	1⅞″	1⅜″	WB, F&M	8¼ lbs.
Trap, MC	12	2¾″	IM & F	32″	49⅛″	14⅜″	1⅜″	1⅞″	1⅜″	WB, F&M	8½ lbs.
Trap	12	2¾″	IM & F	30″	47⅛″	14⅜″	1⅜″	1⅞″		WB, F&M	8¼ lbs.
Trap	12	2¾″	IM & F	32″	49⅛″	14⅜″	1⅜″	1⅞″		WB, F&M	8½ lbs.
Trap Winchoke	12	2¾″	W4	30″	47⅛″	14⅜″	1⅜″	1⅞″		WB, F&M	8¼ lbs.
Trap Winchoke, MC	12	2¾″	W4	30″	47⅛″	14⅜″	1⅜″	2¼″	1⅜″	WB, F&M	8¼ lbs.
Trap Winchoke	12	2¾″	W4	32″	49⅛″	14⅜″	1⅜″	1⅞″		WB, F&M	8½ lbs.
Trap Winchoke, MC	12	2¾″	W4	32″	49⅛″	14⅜″	1⅜″	2¼″	1⅜″	WB, F&M	8½ lbs.

Black Powder Guns

BROWNING

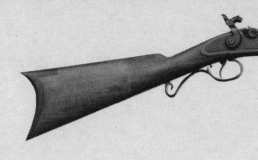

JONATHAN BROWNING MOUNTAIN RIFLE

Models: Browned steel model has tinned forend tip and natural-finished wedge plates. Barrel, lock, hammer, butt plate, trigger guard and other metal parts are traditional browned steel.

Brass model has brass forend tip, wedge plates, lock plate screw escutcheon, trigger guard, thimbles, toe plate and butt plate. All other parts including the barrel, lock, and hammer are browned steel.

SPECIFICATIONS:

Barrel: 30″ octagonal. 1 inch across the flats. Twist is 1 turn in 56″ on 45 caliber, 1 turn in 62″ on 50 caliber and 1 turn in 66″ on 54 caliber. Hooked breech.

Trigger: Single set design with roller bearing sear.

Sights: Traditional buck horn rear sight, screw adjustable for elevation, drift adjustable for windage. Blade front sight. Sight radius is 21⅞″.

Stock: Half stock with semi-cheek piece. Seasoned stock with oil finish. Traditional curved butt plate. Hickory ramrod with brass fittings threaded for cleaning jag and patch retriever.

Stock Dimensions: Length of pull—13½″, Drop at comb—2½″, Drop at heel—4″.

Overall Length: 47″

Approximate Weight: 9 lbs. 10 oz.

Price: $449.95

COLT

SPECIFICATIONS:

Caliber: 44

Barrel: 9″, 7 groove, right-hand twist

Weight: 73 oz.

Cylinder: 6 chambers, 1 safety lock pin, scene of soldiers fighting Indians.

Sight: German silver

Finish: Color case-hardened frame, hammer, loading lever and plunger. Blue barrel, cylinder, backstrap, trigger and wedge. Polished-brass trigger guard and oil finish grip.

Price: $500.95

1ST MODEL DRAGOON

SPECIFICATIONS:

Caliber: 44

Barrel: 7½″, part round, part octagonal, 7 grooves, left-hand twist

Weight: 66 oz.

Cylinder: 6 Chambers, ranger-Indian scene

Sights: German silver

Finish: Color case-hardened frame, loading lever, plunger; blue barrel, cylinder, trigger and wedge. Polished-brass backstrap and trigger guard; one-piece oil finish walnut stocks.

Price: 1st, 2nd and 3rd Model Dragoons **$399.95** each.

BABY DRAGOON

SPECIFICATIONS:

Caliber: 31

Barrel: 4″, 7 groove, right-hand twist

Cylinder: 5-shot unfluted, straight with ranger and Indian scene, oval bolt cuts

Sight: Brass pin

Finish: Color case-hardened frame and hammer, blue barrel, trigger, wedge, cylinder and screws; silver backstrap and trigger guard and varnished grips.

Price: $361.50

COLT

1851 NAVY REVOLVER

SPECIFICATIONS:
Caliber: 36
Barrel: 7½", 7 groove, left-hand twist
Weight: 42 oz.
Cylinder: 6 chambers with Naval scene
Sights: Brass front sight
Finish: Color case-hardened frame, loading lever, plunger, hammer and latch. Blue cylinder, trigger, barrel, screws and wedge. Silver-plated trigger guard and backstrap. Varnished one-piece walnut grips.
Price: $374.50

1861 NAVY REVOLVER

SPECIFICATIONS:
Same as 1851 Navy Revolver except:
Sights: German silver front
Price: $374.50

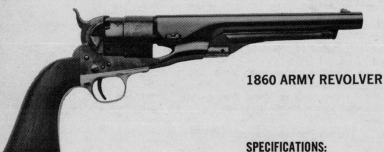

1860 ARMY REVOLVER

SPECIFICATIONS:
Caliber: 44
Barrel: 8", 7 groove, left-hand twist
Overall Length: 13¾"
Weight: 42 oz.
Sights: German silver; radius—10½"
Finish: Colt blue, color case-hardened frame, hammer loading lever, plunger; one-piece walnut grip.
Price: $383.95

COLT

1862 POCKET POLICE

SPECIFICATIONS:
Caliber: 36
Barrel: 5½" round, 7 groove, left-hand twist
Weight: 25 oz.
Cylinder: 5 chambers, rebated, fluted
Sights: Brass front
Finish: Color case-hardened frame, hammer, loading lever, plunger and latch. Blue barrel, wedge, cylinder, trigger and screws. Silver-plated trigger guard and backstrap, Varnished one-piece walnut grips.
Price: $351.50

1862 POCKET NAVY REVOLVER

SPECIFICATIONS:
Caliber: 36
Barrel: 5½", octagonal, 7 groove, left-hand twist
Weight: 27 oz.
Cylinder: 5 chambers, round-rebated with stage coach scene, 1³⁄₁₆" overall, rebated ⁹⁄₁₆"
Sights: Brass pin front
Finish: Color case-hardened frame, hammer loading lever, plunger and latch; blue barrel, wedge, cylinder, trigger guard and backstrap. Varnished one-piece walnut grips.
Price: $351.50

CVA

FRONTIER RIFLE $199.95

Lock: Color case-hardened, engraved percussion-style, bridle with fly and tumbler; screw-adjustable, sear engagement; authentic V-type mainspring.
Barrel: 28" octagon; ¹⁵⁄₁₆" across the flats; barrel tenon, hooked breech, round brass thimbles, deep-grooved.
Overall Length: 44".
Caliber: 45 and 50 percussion.
Weight: 6 lbs. 14 oz.

Stock: American hardwood.
Triggers: Double set will fire set and unset.
Sights: Brass blade front sight; screw-adjustable, dovetailed rear.
Finish: Blue steel; brass wedge plates; brass nose cap; trigger guard and butt plate.
Accessories: Stainless steel nipple, hardwood ramrod with brass tips, cleaning jag; kits available.

CVA

HAWKEN RIFLE　　**Percussion $249.95**
　　　　　　　　　　　Flintlock　　259.95

Caliber: 50 and 54 percussion or flintlock.
Ignition: Color case-hardened; bridle, fly, screw adjustable sear engagement and authentic V-type mainspring; two lock screws.
Barrel: 28″ octagon rifled one turn in 66″; 1″ across the flats, barrel tenon, hooked breech.
Overall Length: 44″
Weight: 7 lbs. 15 oz.

Finish: Solid brass patchbox, wedge plates, nose cap, ramrod thimbles, trigger guard and butt plate; blued steel finish.
Triggers: Double set, will fire set and unset; fully adjustable for trigger pull.
Sights: Dovetail, beaded blade front sight; fully adjustable, dovetail, open hunting rear sight.
Stock: Select walnut with fully formed beavertail cheek piece.
Accessories: Stainless steel nipple or flash hole liner; hardwood ramrod with brass tips and cleaning jag; chamois cloth rifle cover with finished rifle only; kits available.

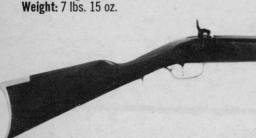

KENTUCKY RIFLE　　**Percussion $167.95**
　　　　　　　　　　　　Flintlock　　177.95

Ignition: Engraved color case hardened v-type mainspring.
Caliber: 45 percussion or flintlock.
Barrel: 33½″, rifled, octagon.
Overall Length: 48″.

Weight: 7 lbs. 4 oz.
Finish: Deep-luster blue, polished brass hardware.
Sights: Kentucky-style front and rear.
Stock: Dark, walnut tone.
Accessories: Brass-tipped, hardwood ramrod, stainless steel nipple; kits available.

MOUNTAIN RIFLE　　**Percussion $269.95**
　　　　　　　　　　　　Flintlock　　284.95

Ignition: Engraved percussion color case-hardened lock with adjustable sear engagement, fly and bridle, authentic V-type mainspring.
Caliber: 45 and 50 percussion or flintlock.
Barrel: 32″, custom rifled, octagon, 15/16″ across the flats, hooked breech with two barrel tenons.
Overall Length: 48″.

Weight: 7 lbs. 14 oz.
Finish: Brown steel, German silver patch box and wedge plates, pewter-type nose cap.
Triggers: Double set, will fire both set and unset.
Sights: German silver blade front, screw adjustable dovetail rear.
Stock: American maple with fully formed cheek piece.
Accessories: Stainless steel nipple, hardwood ramrod, cleaning jag; kits available.

"BIG BORE" MOUNTAIN RIFLE $279.95

Caliber: 54 and 58 percussion.
Lock: Color case-hardened, engraved percussion and flint lock style; adjustable sear engagement; bridle and fly in tumbler; authentic V-type mainspring.
Barrel: 32″ octagon; 1″ across the flats; hooked breech with two barrel tenons; rifled 1 turn 66″ for patch ball accuracy; authentic round thimbles; especially smooth rifling for fast break-in.

Overall Length: 48″
Weight: 8 lbs. 2 oz.
Triggers: Double set, will fire set and unset.
Stock: American maple with fully-formed cheekpiece.
Sights: German silver front sight; screw-adjustable dovetail rear.
Finish: Rich browned steel and wedge plates; authentic pewter-type nose cap.
Accessories: Stainless-steel nipple; hardwood ramrod with brass-tips; cleaning jag; kit available for 54 flintlock and both caliber percussions.

CVA

MOUNTAIN PISTOL

MOUNTAIN PISTOL $119.95

Ignition: Engraved percussion color case-hardened lock with adjustable sear engagement, fly and bridle.
Caliber: 45 or 50 percussion.
Barrel: 9″ octagon, $^{15}/_{16}$″ across the flats, hooked breech, custom rifling.
Overall Length: 15″.
Weight: 43 oz.
Finish: Brown steel, German silver wedge plates.
Trigger: Early style.
Sights: German silver blade front, fixed primitive rear.
Stock: American maple.
Accessories: Stainless steel nipple, hardwood ramrod, belt hook; kits available.

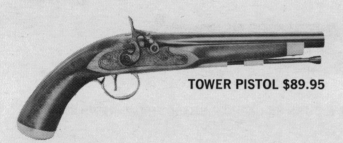

TOWER PISTOL $89.95

KENTUCKY PISTOL $89.95

Ignition: Engraved lock, screw adjustable sear engagement, V-type mainspring.
Caliber: 45 (451 bore) percussion.
Barrel: 9″, octagon at breech, tapers to round at muzzle.
Overall Length: 15¼″.
Weight: 36 oz.
Finish: Case-hardened lock, blued barrel, brass hardware.
Stock: Dark-grained walnut tone.
Accessories: Steel ramrod, stainless steel nipple; kits available for percussion and flintlock.

Ignition: Engraved percussion lock on finished pistol, adjustable sear.
Caliber: 45 (451 bore) percussion.
Barrel: 10¼″, rifled, octagon.
Overall Length: 15¼″.
Weight: 40 oz.
Finish: Case-hardened lock, blued barrel, brass hardware.
Sights: Dovetailed Kentucky front and rear.
Accessories: Brass-tipped, hardwood ramrod; kits available for percussion and flintlock.

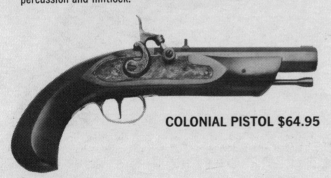

COLONIAL PISTOL $64.95

PHILADELPHIA DERRINGER $54.95

Ignition: Engraved lock.
Caliber: 45 (451 bore) percussion.
Barrel: 6½″, rifled, octagon.
Overall Length: 12¾″.
Weight: 31 oz.
Finish: Case-hardened lock, blued barrel, brass hardware.
Sights: Dovetail rear, brass blade front.
Stock: Dark, walnut tone.
Accessories: Steel ramrod, stainless steel nipple; kits available for percussion and flintlock.

Ignition: Percussion, coil-spring back-action lock.
Caliber: 45 percussion.
Barrel: 5¼″, rifled.
Overall Length: 7⅛″.
Weight: 16 oz.
Finish: Case hardened with brass hardware, blued barrel.
Stock: Walnut toned.
Accessories: Stainless steel nipple; kit available.

DIXIE

DIXIE NAVY REVOLVER
Plain Model $78.95
Engraved Model   92.50

This 36 caliber revolver was a favorite of the officers of the Civil War. Although called a navy type, it is somewhat misnamed since many more of the army personnel used it. Made in Italy. Use .376 mold or ball to fit. Use number 11 caps. Blued steel barrel and cylinder with brass frame.

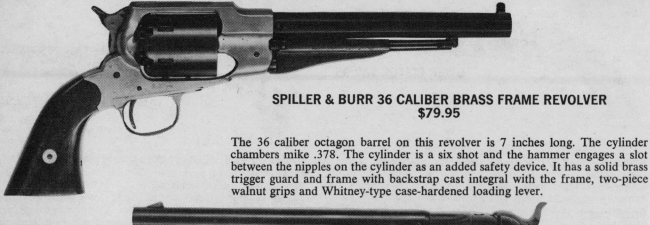

SPILLER & BURR 36 CALIBER BRASS FRAME REVOLVER
$79.95

The 36 caliber octagon barrel on this revolver is 7 inches long. The cylinder chambers mike .378. The cylinder is a six shot and the hammer engages a slot between the nipples on the cylinder as an added safety device. It has a solid brass trigger guard and frame with backstrap cast integral with the frame, two-piece walnut grips and Whitney-type case-hardened loading lever.

DIXIE KENTUCKY PISTOL
$89.95

This is the first reproduction black powder pistol and an authentic replica of a typical Kentucky pistol. Features Kentucky-type rifling and sights, brass furniture, dark cherry-stained maple stocks. Barrel length: 9″, 13⁄16″ across the flats. Caliber: 45. Recommended ball size: .445.

DIXIE 1860 ARMY REVOLVER
$125.00

The Dixie 1860 Army has a half-fluted cylinder and its chamber diameter is .447. Use .451 round ball mold to fit this 8-inch barrel revolver. Cut for shoulder stock.

THE TROPHY WINNER 44 SINGLE SHOT PISTOL
$125.00

The Trophy Winner 44 has a smooth bore shotgun pistol barrel that will interchange with the rifle barrel that is on the pistol. The gun is equipped with a 10-inch blued octagon barrel and has 7 grooves and 7 lands of equal width. Groove to groove diameter mikes .445, land to land diameter mikes .442. It has a fixed ramp front sight and adjustable rear sight. Overall length 12¾″. Weight 42 oz. **SHOTGUN PISTOL BARREL:** 28-gauge blued octagon smooth bore barrel, 10 in. long, brass front sight. . . . **$19.95**

"WYATT EARP" REVOLVER
$85.00

12″ octagon rifled barrel; cylinder is rebated and is 44 caliber. Highly polished brass frame, backstrap and trigger guard. The barrel and cylinder have a deep blue lustre finish. Hammer, trigger, and loading lever are case-hardened. Walnut grips. Recommended ball size is .451.

Shoulder stock for Dixie's "Wyatt Earp" Revolver... **$45.00**

DIXIE

DSB-58 SCREW BARREL DERRINGER
$69.95

Overall length 6½ inches; unique loading system; sheath trigger, color case-hardened frame, trigger and center-mounted hammer; European walnut, one-piece, "bag"-type grip. Uses #11 percussion caps.

DW-105 WALKER REVOLVER
$125.00

This 4½-pound, .44 caliber pistol is the largest ever made; back strap and guard are brass with Walker-type rounded-to-frame walnut grips; all other parts are blued; chambers measure .445 and take a .450 ball slightly smaller than the originals.

DPR-56 THIRD MODEL DRAGOON
$140.00

This engraved-cylinder, 4-and-a-half pounder is a reproduction of the last model of Colt's .44 caliber "horse" revolvers. Barrel measures 7⅜ inches, ⅛ inch shorter than the original; color case-hardened steel frame, one-piece walnut grips. Recommended ball size: .454.

DIXIE PENNSYLVANIA PISTOL
Percussion $ 95.00
Flintlock   110.00

Available in percussion or flint. Barrels have a bright lustre blue finish, ⅞" octagon, rifled, 44 caliber, brass front and rear sight, 10" length and takes a .430 ball. The barrel is held in place with a steel wedge and tang screw. The brass trigger guard, thimbles, nosecap, wedge plates and side plates are highly polished. Locks are fine quality with early styling. Plates measure 4¾" x ⅞". Percussion hammer is engraved and both plates are left in the white. Flint is an excellent style lock with the gooseneck hammer having an early wide thumb piece. Stock is walnut stained and has a wide bird head type grip.

MX 3 OVERCOAT PISTOL
$26.95

39 caliber with 4-inch smooth bore barrel. The breech plug and engraved lock have a burnished-steel finish and the octagon barrel and guard are blued.

MX 3S OVERCOAT PISTOL

Same as MX 3 but with engraved barrel, lock, trigger guard and breech plug. $34.50

SPANISH PERCUSSION PISTOL
$45.00

40 caliber smooth bore which takes a .395 ball. Checkered grip and steel fittings with ramrod.

DCW-712 FRENCH CHARLEVILLE FLINT PISTOL
$125.00

Reproduction of the Model 1777 Cavalry, Revolutionary War-era pistol. Has reversed frizzen spring; fore end and lock housing are all in one; case-hardened, round-faced, double-throated hammer; walnut stock; case-hardened frizzen and trigger; shoots .680 round ball loaded with about 40 grains ffg black powder.

DIXIE DUELING PISTOL
$79.95

This 9-inch smooth bore barreled pistol will vary from about a 44 to 50 caliber and generally is octagon shaped with front-action locks. The rubbed maple wood is stained assorted shades and the grips are checkered.

PHILADELPHIA DERRINGER
$39.95

41 caliber, 3½-inch blued barrel with walnut stocks.

LINCOLN DERRINGER
$144.95

41 caliber, 2-inch browned barrel with 8 lands and 8 grooves and will shoot a .400 patch ball.

DIXIE BRASS FRAMED "HIDEOUT" DERRINGER
Plain $43.95
Engraved   54.95

Made with brass frame and walnut grips and fires a .395 round ball.

ABILENE DERRINGER
$44.95

This gun is an all-steel version of Dixie's brass-framed derringers. The 2½-inch, 41-caliber barrel is finished in a deep blue black; frame and hammer are case hardened. Bore is rifled with six lands and grooves. Uses a tightly patched .395 round ball and 15 or 20 grains of FFFg powder. Walnut grips. Comes with wood presentation case.

DIXIE

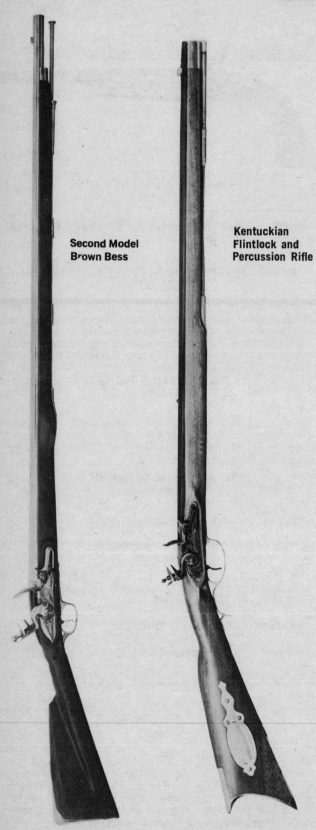

**Second Model
Brown Bess**

**Kentuckian
Flintlock and
Percussion Rifle**

SECOND MODEL BROWN BESS MUSKET
$265.00

74 caliber with a 41¾-inch smooth bore barrel which takes a .715 round ball. In keeping with the traditional musket it has brass furniture on a walnut-stained stock. The lock is marked "Tower" and has the crown with the "GR" underneath. Barrel, lock and ramrod are left bright.

THE KENTUCKIAN FLINTLOCK AND PERCUSSION RIFLE
$165.00

This rifle has a 33½-inch octagon blued barrel which is 13/16 inches across the flats. The rifle comes in 45 caliber only. The bore is rifled with 6 lands and grooves of equal width and about .006 inch deep. Land to land diameter is .453 and groove to groove diameter is .465. You will need a ball size .445 to .448. The rifle has a brass blade front sight and a steel open rear sight. Overall length of the rifle is 48 inches. The Kentuckian is furnished with brass butt plate, trigger guard, patch box, side plate, thimbles and nose cap. It has a case-hardened and engraved lock plate. Weight is about 6¼ pounds. Has a highly polished and finely finished stock in European walnut.

KENTUCKIAN FLINTLOCK & PERCUSSION CARBINE
Flintlock .$155.00
Percussion 155.00

This carbine is made exactly like the Kentuckian Rifle with the exception that it has a 27½" long barrel and the gun is 43" in length overall. Land-to-land diameter is .453 and groove-to-groove diameter is .465; will take a .445 to .488 ball. **Caliber:** 45 only. **Weight:** 5½ lbs.

DIXIE DOUBLE BARREL MUZZLE LOADING SHOTGUN
$260.00

A full 12-gauge, high-quality, double-barrelled percussion shotgun with browned barrels that are 30 inches long. Will take the plastic shot cups for better patterns. Bores are choked modified and full. Lock, barrel tang and trigger are case hardened in a light gray color and are nicely engraved. Also available: 10-gauge, double-barrel-choke cylinder bored, otherwise same specs as above. $315.00

SINGLE BARREL PERCUSSION SHOTGUNS
$59.95

Spanish–made percussion shotgun, 28 ga. with a 32-inch blued barrel. Most will have steel furniture with cap-box.

DIXIE

DIXIE STANDARD KENTUCKY RIFLE
Percussion $260.00

The Dixie Kentucky rifles have single set triggers; the stock is of hard plain straight-grain maple with a Tennessee-style cheek piece. Regular Kentucky rifle sights, and a "candy-stripe" ramrod. The barrel is made of Siemens-Martin steel, and is polished and blued. The gun has a bolster-type plug. Barrel is 40 inches long and comes in 45 caliber. Rifled with six lands and six grooves .007″ deep. Twist is one turn in 48 inches.

DIXIE HAWKEN PERCUSSION RIFLE
$189.95

DIXIE TENNESSEE MOUNTAIN RIFLE
Percussion or Flint $225.00

This 50-caliber rifle features double set triggers with adjustable set screw, bore rifled with six lands and grooves, barrel of $^{15}/_{16}″$ across the flats, brown finish and cherry stock. Length: 41½ in. Left-hand version in flint or percussion. **$245.00**

45 and 50 caliber with 28-inch blued barrel. Overall length 45½ inches. Recommended round ball size is .445 for 45 caliber, .495 for 50 caliber. Double set triggers, blade front sight, adjustable rear sight and case-hardened bar-style percussion lock.

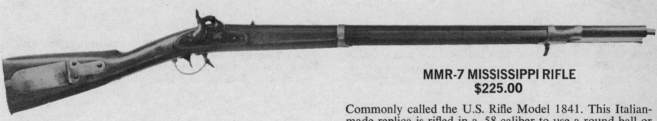

MMR-7 MISSISSIPPI RIFLE
$225.00

Commonly called the U.S. Rifle Model 1841. This Italian-made replica is rifled in a .58 caliber to use a round ball or a minie ball; 3 grooves and regulation sights; solid brass furniture; case-hardened lock.

YORK COUNTY, PENNSYLVANIA RIFLE
Percussion $152.95
Flintlock 162.95

A lightweight at just 7½ pounds, the 36-inch blued rifle barrel is fitted with a standard open-type brass Kentucky rifle rear sight and front blade. The maple one-piece stock is stained a medium darkness that contrasts with the polished brass butt plate, toe plate, patchbox, side plate, trigger guard, thimbles and nose cap. Featuring double-set triggers, the rifle can be fired by pulling only the front trigger, which has a normal trigger pull of four to five pounds; or the rear trigger can first be pulled to set a spring loaded mechanism that greatly reduces the amount of pull needed for the front trigger to kick off the sear in the lock. The land-to-land measurement of the bore is an exact .450 and the recommended ball size is .445 . Overall length is 51½ inches.

DIXIE

WINCHESTER '73 CARBINE
$359.95
ENGRAVED WINCHESTER '73 RIFLE
$395.00

44-40 caliber which may use modern or black powder cartridges. Overall length is 39 inches with the round barrel being 20 inches long. Its full tubular magazine will hold 11 shots. The walnut forearm and buttstock complement the high-lustre bluing of the all steel parts such as the frame, barrel, magazine, loading lever and butt plate. Comes with the trap door in the butt for the cleaning rod. It comes with the leaf rear sight and blade front sight. This carbine is marked "Model 1873" on the tang and caliber "44-40" on the brass carrier block.

ZOUAVE, MODEL 1863, 58 CAL. RIFLE
$250.00

The Zouave is a copy of an original Remington Zouave rifle which saw service in the Civil War and was acknowledged to be the most accurate military rifle of its day. In the hands of many a Civil War veteran, it helped open the West and furnished necessary food and protection. With its walnut stock, blued barrel, brass fittings and case-hardened lock, it is the most colorful rifle of its day. 58 caliber, rifled barrel. Use .570 ball or .575 Minie bullet.

ZOUAVE CARBINE
$215.00

Same as the regular Zouave rifle, but with a short 20-inch steel barrel. This carbine takes a .570 ball or .575 bullet.

BUFFALO HUNTER
$215.00

This sporterized version of Dixie's Italian-made Zouave uses a .570 ball or bullet and has the same 58 caliber rifled bore. Features walnut halfstock, checkering around the wrist, case-hardened lock, fine blued barrel and brass patchbox.

EUROARMS OF AMERICA

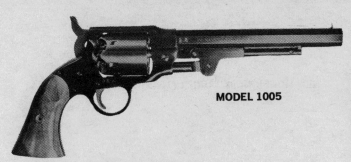

MODEL 1005

ROGERS & SPENCER REVOLVER
MODEL 1005 $160.00

Caliber: 44 Percussion; #11 percussion cap
Barrel Length: 7½ inches
Sights: Integral rear sight notch groove in frame, truncated cone front sight of brass
Overall Length: 13¾ inches
Weight: 47 ounces
Recommended Ball Diameter: 451 round or conical, pure lead

MODEL 1006

ROGERS & SPENCER ARMY REVOLVER
MODEL 1006, TARGET $200.00

Caliber: 44; takes .451 round or conical lead balls; #11 percussion cap
Weight: 47 ounces
Barrel Length: 7½ in.
Overall Length: 13¾ inches
Finish: High-gloss blue, walnut grip, solid-frame design, precision rifled barrel
Sights: Rear fully adjustable for windage and elevation; ramp front sight

ROGERS & SPENCER REVOLVER
MODEL 1007, LONDON GRAY
Revolver is the same as Model 1005, except for London Gray finish, which is heat treated and buffed for rust resistance; same recommended ball size and percussion caps.

ROGERS & SPENCER REVOLVER
MODEL 1008, ENGRAVED
Revolver is the same as Model 1007, except for engraving.

NEW MODEL ARMY (1020)

NEW MODEL ARMY REVOLVER
MODEL 1020 $155.00
This model is equipped with blued steel frame, brass trigger guard in 44 caliber.
Weight: 40 oz.
Barrel Length: 8 in.
Overall Length: 14¾ in.
Finish: Deep luster blue rifled barrel, polished walnut stock, brass trigger guard.

NEW MODEL NAVY REVOLVER
MODEL 1010 $155.00
Same as Model 1020 except with 6½″ barrel and 36 caliber.

NEW MODEL ARMY (TARGET)
MODEL 1030 $186.00
Caliber: 44
Weight: 41 oz.
Barrel: 8 inches; octagonal, blued, rifled
Overall Length: 14¾ in.
Sights: Rear sight adjustable for windage and elevation; ramp front sight.

NEW MODEL ARMY ENGRAVED
MODEL 1040 $228.00
Classical 19th-century style scroll engraving on this 1858 Remington New Model revolver.
Caliber: 44 Percussion; #11 cap
Barrel Length: 8 inches
Overall Length: 14¾ inches
Weight: 41 ounces
Sights: Integral rear sight notch groove in frame, blade front sight
Recommended Ball Diameter: .451 round or conical, pure lead

EUROARMS OF AMERICA

NEW MODEL ARMY TARGET
MODEL 1045 $233.00
Caliber: 44 Percussion; #11 cap
Barrel Length: 8 inches; precision rifled
Overall Length: 14¾ inches
Weight: 41 ounces
Sights: Integral rear sight notch groove in frame; dovetailed stainless steel front sight adjustable for windage
Finish: Stainless steel; polished yellow brass trigger guard; walnut grips
Recommended Ball Diameter: .451 round or conical, pure lead

NEW MODEL ARMY TARGET (1045)

REMINGTON 1858 NEW MODEL
ARMY REVOLVER MODEL 1046 $175.00
Caliber: 36
Weight: 41 oz.
Barrel Length: 6½ in.
Overall Length: 14¾ in.
Finish: Stainless steel with polished walnut stock
MODEL 1047: 44 Cal., 6½" barrel
MODEL 1048: 44 Cal., 8" barrel

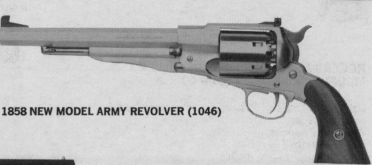

1858 NEW MODEL ARMY REVOLVER (1046)

1851 COLT NAVY SHERIFF (1080)

1851 COLT NAVY SHERIFF
MODEL 1080 $95.00
Caliber: 36 Percussion; #11 cap
Barrel Length: 5 inches
Overall Length: 11½ inches
Weight: 38 ounces
Sights: Rear sight is traditional 'V' notch groove in hammer, truncated cone front sight of brass
Finish: High-gloss blue on barrel and cylinder; backstrap frame and trigger guard polished yellow brass; walnut grips; hammer and loading lever color case-hardened
Recommended Ball Diameter: .375 round or conical, pure lead
1851 COLT NAVY SHERIFF
MODEL 1090 $99.00
Same as Model 1080 except in 44 caliber, with .451 round or conical ball diameter

1851 COLT NAVY CONFEDERATE (1100)

1851 COLT NAVY CONFEDERATE BRASS FRAME
MODEL 1100 $95.00
Caliber: 36 Percussion; #11 cap
Barrel: 7½ inches; octagonal to round, precision rifled
Overall Length: 13 inches
Weight: 41 ounces
Sights: Rear sight is traditional 'V' notch groove in hammer; truncated cone front sight of brass
Recommended Ball Diameter: .375 round or conical, pure lead
Finish: Blued barrel and cylinder; frame, backstrap and trigger guard are polished yellow brass; color case-hardened hammer and loading lever; walnut grips
1851 COLT NAVY CONFEDERATE BRASS FRAME
MODEL 1110 $99.00
Same as Model 1100 except in 44 caliber, with recommended ball diameter of .451 round or conical, pure lead

EUROARMS OF AMERICA

NAVY 1851 REVOLVER
44 CALIBER MODEL 1130 ......$123.00

Weight: 42 oz.
Barrel Length: 7½ in.
Overall Length: 13 in.
Finish: Brass frame, backstrap and trigger guard, blued octagon rifled barrel. Case-hardened hammer and loading lever, engraved cylinder with naval battle scene.

NAVY 1851 REVOLVER
36 CALIBER MODEL 1120 ......$119.00

A 44 caliber Navy Revolver with rebated cylinder.
Weight: 42 oz.
Barrel Length: 7½ in.
Overall Length: 13 in.
Finish: Steel frame, brass back strap and trigger guard, octagon rifled barrel, case-hardened hammer and loading lever, engraved cylinder with naval battle scene.

1851 SHERIFF REVOLVER
36 CALIBER MODEL 1170 ......$119.00
44 CALIBER MODEL 1180 ......$123.00

Shortened version of the Navy Revolver
Weight: 39 oz.
Barrel Length: 5 in.
Overall Length: 11½ in.
Finish: Steel frame, brass backstrap and trigger guard, blued octagon rifled barrel, case-hardened hammer and loading lever, engraved cylinder with naval battle scene.

1851 COLT NAVY REVOLVER (1190)

1851 COLT NAVY REVOLVER
MODEL 1190 $150.00

Police, 36 caliber, fluted cylinder, steel frame, 5-inch octagonal barrel, lanyard ring in butt of revolver.
Weight: 38 oz.
Barrel Length: 5 in.
Overall Length: 10½ in.
Finish: Deep luster blue rifled octagon barrel

NAVY 1851 REVOLVER SILVER PLATED
36 CALIBER MODEL 1150 ......$150.00

Weight: 42 oz.
Barrel Length: 7½ in.
Overall Length: 13 in.
Finish: Silver Plated back strap and trigger guard, octagon rifled barrel, case-hardened hammer and loading lever, engraved cylinder.

NAVY 1851 REVOLVER SILVER PLATED
44 CALIBER MODEL 1160 ......$154.00

Weight: 42 oz.
Barrel Length: 7½ in.
Overall Length: 13 in.
Finish: Silver Plated back strap and trigger guard, octagon rifled barrel, case-hardened hammer and loading lever, engraved cylinder.

1851 COLT NAVY MODEL 1140

1851 COLT NAVY SQUAREBACK TRIGGER GUARD
MODEL 1140 $131.00
Caliber: 36 Percussion; #11 cap
Barrel Length: 7½ inches
Overall Length: 13 inches
Weight: 43 ounces
Sights: Rear sight is traditional 'V' notch groove in hammer; truncated cone front sight of brass
Recommended Ball Diameter: .375 round or conical, pure lead
Finish: Steel frame; barrel and cylinder of high-gloss blue; cylinder has roll engraved classic Naval battle scene; hammer, frame and loading lever color case-hardened; backstrap and trigger guard in yellow brass; walnut grips

EUROARMS OF AMERICA

1851 COLT NAVY REVOLVER
MODEL 1200 $150.00
Same as Model 1190 except with 7½ in. octagonal barrel.
Weight: 41 oz.
Barrel Legth: 7½ in.
Overall Length: 13 in.

ARMY 1860 REVOLVER
44 CALIBER MODEL 1210 ......$145.00

The historic Army Model 1860 needs no introduction to shooter and collector. The cylinder is authentically roll engraved with a highly polished brass trigger guard and steel frame cut for shoulder stock. The frame, loading lever and hammer are beautifully finished in color case hardening.
Weight: 41 oz.
Barrel Length: 8 in., streamlined barrel.
Overall Length: 13⅝ in.
Caliber: 44
Finish: Brass trigger guard and backstrap, steel frame, round barrel, rebated cylinder engraved battle scene. Frame cut for shoulder stock.

44 CALIBER MODEL 1220
  (with 5" barrel) **$145.00**
44 CALIBER MODEL 1215
  (in stainless steel) **$194.00**

1862 POLICE REVOLVER
MODEL 1250 $160.00
Police revolver with a steel frame, fluted cylinder and 7½-inch barrel in 36 caliber, lanyard ring in butt of revolver
Weight: 40 oz.
Barrel: 7½ in.
Overall Length: 13 in.
Finish: Deep luster blue rifled round barrel

SCHNEIDER & GLASSICK CONFEDERATE REVOLVER
36 CALIBER MODEL 1050 ....$95.00
44 CALIBER MODEL 1060 ....$99.00

A modern replica of a Confederate Percussion Army Revolver. Polished brass frame, rifled high-luster blued octagonal barrel and polished walnut grips.
Weight: 40 oz.
Barrel Length: 7½ in.
Overall Length: 13 in.
Finish: Brass frame, backstrap and trigger guard, blued rifled barrel, case-hardened hammer and loading lever, engraved cylinder with naval battle scene.

1860 ENGRAVED COLT ARMY
MODEL 1230 $198.00
Caliber: 44 Percussion; #11 cap
Barrel Length: 8 inches, streamlined round barrel
Overall Length: 13⅝ inches
Weight: 41 ounces
Sights: Rear sight is traditional 'V' notch in hammer, blade front sight of brass
Recommended Ball Diameter: .451 round or conical, pure lead
Finish: Engraved with a beautiful 19th-century scroll pattern; engraved backstrap and trigger guard are of polished yellow brass; walnut grips

1861 COLT NAVY REVOLVER
MODEL 1240 $160.00
This is Sam Colt's modernized version of the popular Navy Model, with round barrel and the creeping loading lever "borrowed" from the 1860 Army model.
Caliber: 36
Weight: 41 oz.
Barrel Length: 7½ in.
Overall Length: 13 in.
Finish: Blue with polished brass backstrap and guard; color case-hardened hammer, frame and loading lever; one-piece walnut grip; engraved cylinder with naval battle scene.

1862 POLICE REVOLVER (1250)

SCHNEIDER & GLASSICK CONFEDERATE REVOLVER

EUROARMS OF AMERICA

PENNSYLVANIA RIFLE
MODEL 2130—45 Percussion $249.00
MODEL 2135—50 Percussion 249.00
MODEL 2140—45 Flint 288.00
MODEL 2145—50 Flint 288.00

SPECIFICATIONS:

Caliber: 45 (actual bore size .453) Deep rifling.
Barrel: Octagonal 13/16" across flats, length of barrel 36".
Lock Plate: Flint or Percussion. Case-hardened with flash shield on percussion guns.
Stock: Full-length one-piece walnut stock.
Ramrod: Made in a single piece, brass tipped at both ends and threaded at bottom end.
Mountings: Polished brass, including a large original-type patch box. Light engraving on lock plate.
Overall Length: 50".
Weight: 6½ to 7 lbs., depending on density of walnut stock.

HAWKEN RIFLE
MODEL 2210A $235.00

Traditional styling based on the original St. Louis rifle of Sam and Jake Hawken with hooked breech system.
Caliber: 50-caliber percussion
Barrel: 28 inches long; blued, precision rifled, octagonal
Weight: 9½-9¾ lbs., depending on density of wood
Stock: Solid one-piece walnut
Ramrod: Wooden, with brass tips threaded for cleaning jay, worm or ball puller.
Sights: Target rear sight adjustable for windage and elevation
Triggers: Double set triggers adjustable for hair trigger, if desired
Furniture: Polished brass mountings, barrel key

HAWKEN RIFLE ....
MODEL 2220A $256.00 ....
Same 50-caliber model as the 2210A, except with flintlock assemby.

REMINGTON 1862 RIFLE
MODEL 2255 $250.00

SPECIFICATIONS:

Caliber: 58
Ignition: Case-hardened percussion lock
Barrel: 32½" rifled
Overall length: 48½"
Weight: 9½ lbs.
Finish: High-polished round barrel, polished brass mountings and cap box, beech stock
Sights: Original 3-leaf rear sight, blade front sight
Ramrod: Heavy one-piece steel

EUROARMS OF AMERICA

2260 LONDON ARMORY COMPANY
3-BAND ENFIELD RIFLED MUSKET $311.00

Caliber: 58
Barrel Length: 39"
Overall Length: 54"
Weight: 11 lbs.
Stock: One-piece walnut. Polished "bright" brass butt plate, trigger guard and nose cap, blued barrel bands.
Ramrod: Steel.

2270 LONDON ARMORY COMPANY
2-BAND RIFLE MUSKET $295.00

Caliber: 58
Barrel Length: 33"
Overall Length: 49"
Weight: 10 lbs.
Stock: One-piece walnut.
Sights: Inverted 'V' front sight; Enfield folding ladder rear.
Ramrod: Steel.

LONDON ARMORY COMPANY
ENFIELD MUSKETOON
MODEL 2280 $264.00

Caliber: 58. Minie ball.
Barrel Length: 24".
Overall Length: 40¼".
Weight: 7 to 7½ lbs., depending on density of wood.
Barrel: Round high-luster blue barrel.
Stock: Seasoned walnut stock, with sling swivels.
Ramrod: Steel.
Ignition: Heavy-duty percussion lock.
Sights: Graduated military-leaf sight.
Furniture: Brass trigger guard, nose cap and butt plate. Blued barrel bands and lock plate, and swivels.

EUROARMS OF AMERICA

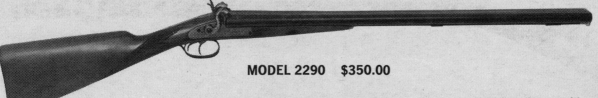

MODEL 2290 $350.00

A beautifully designed 12-gauge percussion muzzle-loading shotgun with modified and full choke. Tastefully engraved side locks and blue barrels. A wooden ramrod, brass tipped, capable of taking a brush or worm. The weight is approximately 6 lbs., making it an easy-to-handle lightweight field gun.

2295 SINGLE-BARRELED MAGNUM CAPE GUN $295.00

Euroarms of America offers a beautiful reproduction of a classic English-styled 12-gauge single barreled shotgun. It is a true 12 gauge with a 32-inch open choked barrel. Although the single barrel muzzleloader weighs only 7½ pounds, the English-styled stock is well proportioned and recoil with even relatively heavy powder charges is moderate. The stock is of European walnut with a satin oil finish. The barrel, underrib, thimbles, nose cap, trigger guard and butt plate are finished with EOA deep, rich blue. The lock is left in the white and displays a scroll engraving, as does the bow of the trigger guard. Overall length of the single barreled shotgun is 47½ inches. Uses #11 percussion caps and recommended wads are felt overpowder and cardboard overshot.

COOK & BROTHER CONFEDERATE CARBINE
MODEL 2300 $274.00

Classic re-creation of the rare 1861, New Orleans-made Artillery Carbine. Lockplate is marked "Cook & Brother N.O. 1861" and is stamped with a Confederate flag at rear of hammer.

Caliber: 58
Barrel Length: 24 in.
Overall Length: 40⅓ in.
Weight: 7½ lbs.
Sights: Adjustable dovetailed front and rear sights
Ramrod: Steel.
Finish: Barrel is antique brown; buttplate, trigger guard, barrel bands, sling swivels and nosecap are polished brass; stock is walnut.
Recommended Ball Sizes: .575 r.b., .577 minie and .580 maxi. Uses musket caps.

FIE

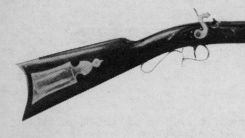

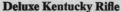

Kentucky Rifle

Cavalry Carbine
Remington Cavalry Carbine replica 58 cal. rifled barrel, case-hardened hammer and lock, polished brass fittings. Weight 7 lbs. **$159.95**

Berdan Rifle w/Brass Breech
Muzzle-loading 45 cal. percussion rifle. Adjustable sights, double-set adjustable trigger, solid brass patch box and fittings. Overall length: 42¾". Weight: 7 lbs. ... **$154.95**

Deluxe Kentucky Rifle
Muzzle-loading Kentucky rifle. 45 cal. rifled 35" octagonal barrel—polished solid-brass patch box, trigger guard, butt plate and stock fittings. Weight 7 lbs. **$149.95**
Flintlock model **$179.95**

Baby Dragoon Revolver
Baby Dragoon 31 cal. revolver replica engraved cylinder 4" or 6" octagonal barrel, polished-brass frame, square back trigger guard, one-piece walnut grip.
Weight 23 oz.—4"; 26 oz.—6" **$84.95**
Also available in engraved model **$94.95**

Colt Navy Revolver
1851 Model Colt Navy 36 cal. cap and ball revolver, 7½" octagonal barrel, polished-brass frame, one-piece walnut grip. Weight 40 oz. **$79.95**

Colt Navy Revolver
1851 Model Colt Navy 44 cal. cap and ball revolver, 7½" octagonal barrel, polished-brass frame, one-piece walnut grip. Weight 40 oz. **$79.95**
Full steel model **$109.95**

Tower Flintlock Pistol
Tower Flintlock pistol 69 cal. smooth bore, cherrywood stock with solid-brass trim, ramrod 9" barrel, 15½" long. Weight 48 oz. **$59.95**

Remington New Army Revolver
New Army Remington replica 44 cal. Revolver model 1858 with polished-brass frame, 7½" blued octagonal barrel, walnut grips. Weight 42 oz. **$89.95**
Full steel model 44 caliber **$119.95**
Also available in 36 caliber **$89.95**

Model HAW50 Hawken
50 caliber percussion or flintlock. Oil finished European walnut stock. Highly polished brass furniture, double triggers, sights fully adjustable for windage and elevation.
Percussion model **$219.95**
Flintlock model **$269.95**

INTERARMS

REPLICA

THE GEORGIA TREE GUN
$239.00

Ideal for both offhand and bench shooting. Of same design as original Allen & Thurber except for walnut forend. 1″ diameter, octagon barrel is blued to fine finish. Machined sights are open, adjustable for windage. Highly polished Inco brass furniture.
Caliber: 54, 58
Overall Length: 38″
Weight: 7½ lbs.

ALLEN & THURBER REPLICA
$229.00

Manufactured using only American materials and craftsmanship. Is individually and carefully hand-crafted with cut rifling, hand-formed lines and each part is individually fitted. Stock is made of rich walnut and has a hand-rubbed finish.
Caliber: 50, 54, 58
Barrel Length: 32″
Overall Length: 48″
Rifling: 8 grooves with a twist of 1 in 60″
Weight: 10 lbs.

KASSNAR

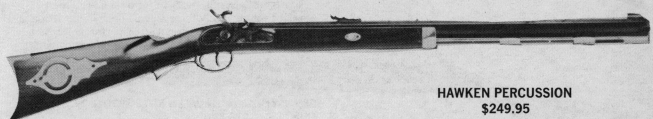

HAWKEN PERCUSSION
$249.95

"The Hawken", a favorite for nearly half of the nineteenth century, as well as playing an important part in the shaping of American history, has once again emerged as a favorite among muzzle-loading enthusiasts. Available in 45, 50, 54 and 58 caliber in flintlock or percussion.

HOPKINS & ALLEN ARMS

BOOT PISTOL
$75.25

The Boot Pistol is available in 45 caliber and comes with a sculptured walnut pistol grip and a full 6″ octagonal barrel. It measures 13″ overall in length. The 15/16″ octagon barrel is fitted with open sights—post type front sight and open rear sight with step elevator. The H&A Boot Pistol features a rich blueblack finish and is equipped with a match trigger.

HOPKINS & ALLEN ARMS

KENTUCKY PISTOL MODEL 10
Flint $97.62
Percussion $88.06

This 44-caliber pistol has a ¹⁵⁄₁₆″ x 10″ rifled barrel and features a convertible ignition system, heavy-duty ramrod and special Hopkins & Allen breech and tang. **Overall Length:** 15½ in. **Weight:** 3 lbs.

KENTUCKY RIFLE MODEL 34
Flint $150.90 (shown)
Percussion $148.40
Caliber: 45
Lock Mechanism: Flintlock or percussion
Barrel: 34″ octagonal; ¹⁵⁄₁₆″ across the flats
Overall Length: 50 in.
Weight: 8½ lbs.
Special Features: Convertible ignition system; heavy-duty ramrod

UNDERHAMMER RIFLE MODEL 25
$159.00
Calibers: 36 and 45
Stock: American walnut with cap box and walnut forend
Barrel: octagonal; avail. in lengths of 20″ 25″ or 32″; ¹⁵⁄₁₆″ across the flats; rifled with uniform round ball twist
Special Features: Only three moving parts in the action give the shooter years of trouble-free performance; uninterrupted sighting plane; target trigger; positive ignition

PENNSYLVANIA HAWKEN RIFLE MODEL 29
Flint $189.00
Percussion $179.00 (shown)
Caliber: 50
Lock Mechanism: Flintlock or percussion
Barrel: 29 in. long; octagonal; ¹⁵⁄₁₆″ across the flats; rifled with round ball twist
Overall Length: 44 in.
Weight: 7¼ lbs.
Stock: Walnut with cheekpiece and dual barrel wedges for added strength
Furniture: Brass fixtures, incl. patch box
Special Feature: Convertible ignition system

THE MINUTEMAN RIFLE
Flint $289.95
Percussion $274.95

(Available in Kit only)

Caliber: 45
Lock Mechanism: Exactly like that of the Minuteman era, in flintlock or percussion.
Stock: In the classic Kentucky style, figured maple stock is 55 inches long with rich oil finish.
Furniture: Brass patch box, butt plate and trigger guard.
Barrel: 39 in. octagonal barrel; 15/16 in. across the flats.
Sights: Precision "Silver Blade" front sight; notched "Kentucky" rear sight.
Weight: 9 lbs.

LYMAN REVOLVERS

NEW MODEL ARMY 44
$159.95

This rugged replica of Remington's 1858 New Model Army 44 has been the favorite of target shooters and other experienced muzzle loaders. The sturdy top strap, besides strengthening the basic frame design, provides an excellent platform for installation of an adjustable rear sight. Features include a deep-blue finish on the machined steel frame, barrel, cylinder and loading lever. The trigger and hammer are color case-hardened. The trigger guard is polished brass and the two-piece grips are well-finished European walnut. Available in 44 caliber; barrel length: 8″; overall length: 13½″; weight: 2 lbs. 9 oz.

1860 ARMY 44
$159.95

This revolver was the most widely used sidearm during the Civil War. Both sides prized the 1860 for its reliability and advanced features such as the "creeping" loading lever system. This, the last U.S. military percussion revolver, was the most advanced of the open-top revolvers. After the War, this gun went West and helped the pioneers survive and settle. Lyman's 1860 Army 44 is patterned exactly after the original and features one-piece walnut grips, color case-hardened frame, hammer and loading lever. The barrel and rebated engraved cylinder are polished blued steel while the backstrap and trigger guard are **nickel-plated** brass. The four-screw frame is cut for a shoulder stock. Available in 44 caliber; barrel length: 8″; overall length: 13⅝″; weight: 2 lbs. 9 oz.

1851 SQUAREBACK NAVY 36
$149.95

This 36 caliber replica is patterned after what may be the most famous percussion revolver ever made. Its classic lines and historic appeal make it as popular today as it was when Sam Colt was turning out the originals. Like the Remingtons, this replica of the second model 1851 (about 5,000 made) is made of quality material. The revolver features a color case-hardened steel frame, hammer and loading lever. The blued cylinder is engraved with the same naval battle scene as were the originals. The nickel-plated backstrap, square-back trigger guard and one-piece walnut grips combine to make Lyman's 1851 a real classic. Available in 36 caliber; barrel length: 7½″; overall length: 13″; weight: 2 lbs. 9 oz.

LYMAN

LYMAN PLAINS PISTOL
$159.95

This replica of the pistol carried by the Western pioneers of the 1880s features a pistol-sized Hawken lock with dependable coil spring and authentic rib and thimble styling. It has a richly stained walnut stock, blackened iron furniture and polished brass trigger guard and ramrod tips. Equipped with a spring-loaded target trigger and a fast twist barrel for target accuracy, the Plains Pistol is available in 50 or 54 caliber.

PLAINS RIFLE
Percussion $259.95

The Lyman Plains Rifle is patterned after the reliable and accurate guns used by the early plainsmen who opened the West and Northwest. Traditionally styled, this black-powder firearm features a double-set trigger and fully adjustable sight. In addition, its hooked breech makes takedown and cleaning a breeze. The handsome European walnut stock is highlighted by a gleaming brass trigger guard, buttplate, and a distinctive, easy-to-open patch box. Available in 50 caliber; barrel length: 28"; overall length: 45"; weight: 8¾ lbs.

GREAT PLAINS RIFLE
Percussion $339.95
Flintlock   354.95

The Great Plains Rifle has a 32" deep-grooved barrel and 1 in 66" twist to shoot patched round balls. Browned steel furniture including the thick steel wedge plates and steel toe plate; correct lock and hammer styling with coil spring dependability; and a walnut stock without a patch box. A Hawken-style trigger guard protects double set triggers. Steel front sight and authentic buckhorn styling in an adjustable rear sight. Available in 50 or 54 caliber.

LYMAN TRADE RIFLE
Percussion $259.95
Flintlock   274.95

The Lyman Trade Rifle features a 28-inch octagonal barrel, rifled one turn at 48 inches, designed to fire both patched roundball and the popular maxistyle conical bullets; overall length 45 inches; polished brass furniture with blued finish on steel parts; walnut stock; hook breech; single trigger, spring-loaded; coil-spring percussion lock; fixed steel sights; steel barrel rib and ramrod ferrules; available in 50 or 54 caliber percussion only.

NAVY ARMS

SPILLER & BURR REVOLVER

A brass-frame copy of the Whitney revolvers made in the Confederacy. Available in 36 caliber only with 7" full-octagon barrel. Weight 2½ lbs., overall length 12½".

SPILLER & BURR
$100.00

36 CALIBER 1861 NAVY

The Officer model 1861 Navy Replica comes in 36 caliber with a 7½" barrel and may be had with a 6-shot round or fluted cylinder and choice of brass or iron straps. The model with iron straps is also available with a square back guard. Features include: case hardened frame, lever, and hammer; balance of gun is blued. The 1861 Navy comes cut for a shoulder stock.

Shoulder Stock .... $ 50.00
Single Cased Set $191.00

1861 NAVY
$130.00

COLT WALKER 1847

The 1847 Walker replica comes in 44 caliber with a 9" barrel.   The full size Walker 44 weighs 4 lbs. 8 oz. and is well suited for the collector as well as the black powder shooter. Features include: rolled cylinder scene; blue and case hardened finish; and brass guard. Proof tested.

Engraved with gold bands at muzzle .... On Request

COLT WALKER 1847
$150.00

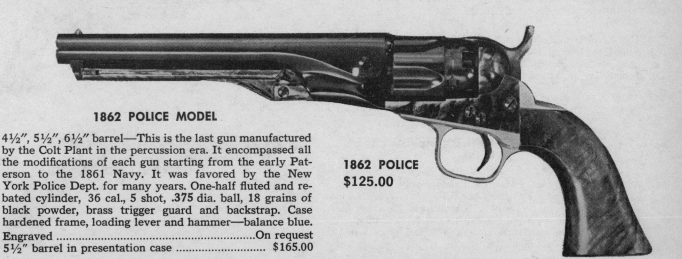

1862 POLICE MODEL

4½", 5½", 6½" barrel—This is the last gun manufactured by the Colt Plant in the percussion era. It encompassed all the modifications of each gun starting from the early Paterson to the 1861 Navy. It was favored by the New York Police Dept. for many years. One-half fluted and rebated cylinder, 36 cal., 5 shot, .375 dia. ball, 18 grains of black powder, brass trigger guard and backstrap. Case hardened frame, loading lever and hammer—balance blue.

Engraved ....On request
5½" barrel in presentation case $165.00

1862 POLICE
$125.00

NAVY ARMS

ARMY 1860
$130.00

These guns from the Colt line are 44 caliber and all six shot. The cylinder was authentically roll engraved with a polished brass trigger guard and steel strap cut for shoulder stock. The frame, loading lever and hammer are finished in high-luster color case-hardening. Walnut grips. **Weight:** 2 lbs. 9 oz. **Barrel Length:** 8". **Overall Length:** 13⅝". **Caliber:** 44. **Finish:** Brass trigger guard, steel back strap, round barrel creeping cylinder, rebated cylinder engraved. Navy scene. Frame cut for s/stock (4 screw).

Shoulder Stock	$50.00
Single Cased Set	194.00

ROGERS & SPENCER NAVY REVOLVER
$160.00

This revolver features a six-shot cylinder, octagonal barrel, hinged-type loading lever assembly, two-piece walnut grips, blued finish and case-hardened hammer and lever. **Caliber:** 44. **Barrel Length:** 7½ in. **Overall Length:** 13¾ in. **Weight:** 3 lbs.

TARGET MODEL REMINGTON REVOLVER
$135.00

With its top strap and frame, the Remington Percussion Revolver is considered the magnum of Civil War revolvers and is ideally suited for the heavy 44 caliber charges. Based on the Army Model, the target gun has target sights for controlled accuracy. Ruggedly built from modern steel and proof tested. Also available in 36 caliber.

REB MODEL 1860
$85.00

A modern replica of the confederate Griswold & Gunnison percussion Army revolver. Rendered with a polished brass frame and a rifled steel barrel finished in a high-luster blue with genuine walnut grips. **All Army Model 60's are completely proof-tested by the Italian government to the most exacting standards. Calibers:** 36 and 44. **Barrel Length:** 7¼" **Overall Length:** 13". **Weight:** 2 lbs. 10 oz.-11 oz. **Finish:** Brass frame, back strap and trigger guard, round barrel hinged rammer on the 44 cal. rebated cylinder.

Matching Shoulder Stock	**$45.00**
Single Cased Set	141.00

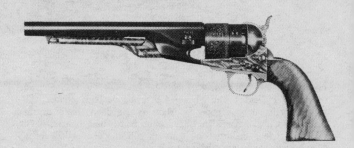

LEECH & RIGDON
$125.00

A modern version of the famous Leech & Rigdon Army Revolver. Manufactured during the Civil War in Augusta, Georgia, and furnished to many of the Georgia Cavalry units. It is basically a copy of the Colt Navy Revolver, but with a round Dragoon-type barrel. **Weight:** 2 lbs. 10 oz. **Barrel Length:** 7¼". **Overall Length:** 13". **Caliber:** 36. **Finish:** Steel case-hardened frame. Round barrel, hinged rammer.

NAVY ARMS

ARMY 60 SHERIFF'S MODEL $130.00

A shortened version of the Army Model 60 Revolver. The Sheriff's model version became popular because the shortened barrel was fast out of the leather. This is actually the original snub nose. The predecessor of the detective specials or belly guns designed for quick-draw use. A piece of traditional Americana, the Sheriff's model was adopted by many local police departments. Available in 36 and 44 calibers.

ENGRAVED ARMY

Engraving type "A"	.... On Request
type "B"	.... On Request
type "C"	.... On Request

REMINGTON NEW MODEL ARMY REVOLVER
Blue $125.00
Nickel 140.00

The most advanced design of the time, the Remington was considered the most accurate cap & ball revolver. A rugged, dependable, battle-proven Civil War veteran. With its top strap and rugged frame these guns are considered the magnum of C. W. revolvers and are ideally suited for the heavy 44 charges. Nickel finish in 44 cal. only. **Calibers:** 36, 44. **Barrel Length:** 8 in. **Overall Length:** 13½" in. **Weight:** 2 lbs. 9 oz.

| Single cased set, blue | $189.00 |
| Single cased set, nickel | 204.00 |

"YANK" REVOLVER $110.00

One of the most famous guns in all American history. During the Civil War it served both the North and South. Later, when the rush to open the west began, it became "standard equipment" for every man who ventured on a horse or rode a covered wagon to the virgin lands of wheat, cattle and gold. Due to its light recoil and lightning-fast action, it is still selected by many quick draw artists as the fastest single-action revolver in the world. Cylinder roll engraved with classic naval battle scene. Backstrap and trigger guard are polished brass. Case-hardened frame, hammer and loading lever. **Caliber:** 36. **Barrel Length:** 7½". **Overall Length:** 13 in. **Weight:** 2 lbs. 9 oz.

| Shoulder Stock | $ 45.00 |
| Single Cased Set | 171.00 |

CIVILIAN MODEL "YANK" NAVY. 36 cal., cylinder roll engraved with classic naval battle scene. Backstrap and trigger guard silver plated. $115.00

ENGRAVED "YANK"
Price on request

Just for that special spot in a collection. Hand-engraved to your specifications with gold inlay. Special grips of pearl, ivory and ebony plastic available.

LE PAGE DUELING PISTOL $300.00

This replica of a French percussion pistol has an octagonal barrel, single-set trigger and adjustable rear sight. The buttstock is made of European walnut. **Caliber:** 44. **Barrel Length:** 9 in. **Overall Length:** 15 in. **Weight:** 2 lbs. 2 oz.

NAVY ARMS

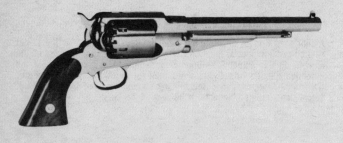

STAINLESS STEEL 1858 REMINGTON $180.00

Exactly like the standard 1858 Remington except that every part with the exception of the grips and trigger guard is manufactured from corrosion-resistant stainless steel. This gun has all the style and feel of its ancestor with all of the conveniences of stainless steel. 44 Caliber.

PATTERSON COLT

This famous arm saw service in the Mexican and Indian wars and is the most sought after of all the Colt weapons by collectors. Reproduced in a limited edition of 500 units. Deluxe limited edition (illustrated) of 50 units to be made with original styled engraving on special order only.
Specifications: Caliber: 36. Barrel Length: 9". Overall Length: 14". Weight: 2½" lbs. $195.00
Engraved Model 500.00

KENTUCKY PISTOLS

PERCUSSION

The Kentucky Pistol is truly a historical American gun . . . carried during the Revolution by the Minutemen . . . the sidearm of "Andy" Jackson in the Battle of New Orleans. Now Navy Arms Company has gone through great research to manufacture a pistol truly representative of its kind and with the balance and handle of the original for which it became famous.

FLINTLOCK

Flint	$125.00
Flint Brass-barrel model	140.00
Single Cased Set—Flint	191.00
Single Cased Set—Flint Brass Barrel	206.00
Percussion	$110.00
Percussion Brass-barrel model	125.00
Single Cased Set—Percussion	176.00
Single Cased Set—Percussion Brass Barrel	191.00

HARPER'S FERRY PISTOLS

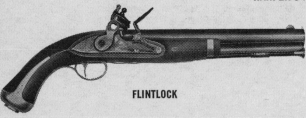

FLINTLOCK

HARPER'S FERRY

Of all the early American martial pistols, Harper's Ferry is one of the best known. They were carried by both the Army and the Navy. **NAVY ARMS COMPANY** has authentically reproduced the Harper's Ferry to the last minute detail. Well balanced and well made. $150.00

SPECIFICATIONS:
Weight: 2 lb. 9 oz. **Barrel length:** 10". **Over-all length:** 16". **Caliber:** 58 smoothbore.   **Finish:** Walnut stock, case hardened lock, brass mounted browned barrel.

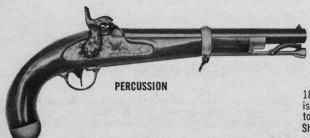

PERCUSSION

HARPER'S FERRY
MODEL 1855 DRAGOON PISTOL

Developed at Harpers Ferry Arsenal as a holster pistol for the U.S. mounted rifles, this pistol was later fitted with a shoulder stock and designated the Springfield Pistol Carbine Model 1855. In .58 cal., this pistol fires the standard 500 gr. minie ball and is the most powerful pistol ever made. Issued in pairs and designed to be carried in saddle holsters $200.00
Shoulder stock (not illus.) 45.00

NAVY ARMS

HENRY CARBINE
This arm first utilized by the Kentucky Cavalry. Available in either original 44 rimfire caliber or in 44/40 caliber. Oil stained American walnut stock, blued finish with brass frame. Also available in a limited deluxe edition of only 50 engraved models to be made complete with deluxe American walnut stock, original styled engraving and silver plated frames.
Specifications: Caliber: 44 rimfire & 44/40. Barrel Length: 23⅝"
Overall Length: 45". **$500.00**
Engraved Model 1500.00

J.P. MURRAY ARTILLERY CARBINE $265.00

Copy of the carbine used by the Southern artillery units during the Civil War. This carbine has been carefully reproduced with a browned, 23½" barrel in 58 cal.

MORSE/NAVY
SINGLE BARREL PERCUSSION 12 GAUGE SHOTGUN

The Morse/Navy single barrel 12-gauge Muzzle-Loading Shotgun is a well-balanced, American-made replica featuring a highly polished brass receiver with select American walnut stock. Navy Arms has improved upon the old Morse design to modernize this into a contemporary and exciting muzzle-loading configuration. **$149.95**

KENTUCKY RIFLE— 45 CALIBER PERCUSSION $225.00   FLINT $250.00

No weapon, before or since, has been so imbued with Americana as the Kentucky Rifle. The Kentucky was the wilderness weapon, Pennsylvania-born and universally used along the frontier. First called simply the long rifle, it was designated "the Kentucky" by gun lovers after the Civil War because Daniel Boone used it most effectively in opening up the Kentucky territory. In the hands of those who know how to use it, the Kentucky still can give many modern rifles a run for the money. The frontiersman could, with ease, pot a squirrel high in an oak tree or drop a deer at 100 yards. Barrel length is 35". Available in flint or percussion.

MORSE MUZZLE-LOADING RIFLE

Improved production techniques and modern engineering have produced this traditionally styled, muzzle-loading rifle. Quality plus custom craftsmanship is evident throughout this rifle with careful attention being paid to the most minute detail. It features Navy Arms "pre-straightened" precision rifled ordnance steel barrel, 45, 50 or 58 caliber. **$149.95**
Also available in 12-gauge. 149.95

NAVY ARMS

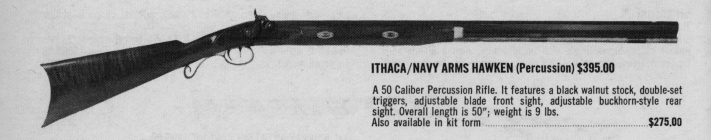

ITHACA/NAVY ARMS HAWKEN (Percussion) $395.00

A 50 Caliber Percussion Rifle. It features a black walnut stock, double-set triggers, adjustable blade front sight, adjustable buckhorn-style rear sight. Overall length is 50"; weight is 9 lbs.
Also available in kit form $275.00

ITHACA/NAVY ARMS HAWKEN (Flintlock) $425.00

A 50-caliber rifle, the Ithaca/Navy Arms Hawken flintlock features Hawken-style furniture, octagonal 32-inch barrel, double set triggers, buckhorn-style rear sight and Hawken-style toe and butt plates. Weight approx. 9 lbs.

HAWKEN HUNTER $225.00

A big 58-caliber riflle with select oil-finished, American walnut stock and highly polished brass furniture and Navy Arms prestraightened octagonal barrel. A design specifically for use with the hollow base Minie bullet.

HAWKEN HURRICANE $225.00

Designed specifically for the hollow base Minie bullet with a choice of 45 or 50 caliber featuring Navy's famous precision, pre-straightened octagonal barrel and polished brass furniture.

NAVY ARMS

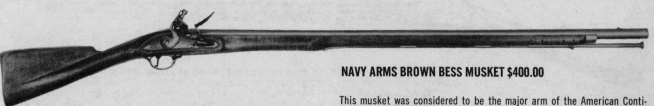

NAVY ARMS BROWN BESS MUSKET $400.00

This musket was considered to be the major arm of the American Continental Army during the American Revolution. The "Bess" was derived from Queen Elizabeth I and "Brown" came from the barrel's finish. This carefully reproduced replica carries the Colonial Williamsburg mark of authenticity and features a polished barrel and lock with brass trigger guard and buttplate. **Caliber:** 75. **Barrel Length:** 42 in. **Overall Length:** 59 in. **Weight:** 9½ lbs.

BUFFALO HUNTER $265.00

A percussion rifle designed to handle a 58-caliber 500-grain slug, it comes with a walnut-colored wood stock and features a color case-hardened lock and hammer. Barrel is precision rifled of ordnance steel

1863 SPRINGFIELD RIFLE $350.00

An authentically reproduced replica of one of America's most historical firearms, the 1863 Springfield rifle features a full-size, three-band musket and precision-rifled barrel. **Caliber:** 58. **Barrel Length:** 40 in. **Overall Length:** 56 in. **Weight:** 9½ lbs. **Finish:** Walnut stock with polished metal lock and stock fittings.

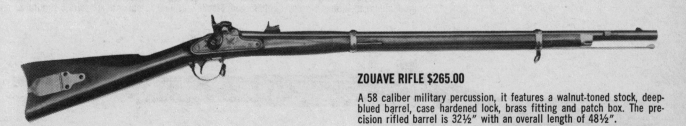

ZOUAVE RIFLE $265.00

A 58 caliber military percussion, it features a walnut-toned stock, deep-blued barrel, case hardened lock, brass fitting and patch box. The precision rifled barrel is 32½" with an overall length of 48½".

12-GA. CLASSIC SIDE-BY-SIDE SHOTGUN PERCUSSION $250.00

This 12-gauge shotgun features a color case-hardened lock, plates and hammers. All internal parts are steel. The walnut stock is hand checkered. The 28" barrels are blued. The shotgun will shoot all 12, 10 and light 8 gauge equivalent percussion loads. **Choke:** improved cylinder and modified. **Weight:** 7 lbs. 12 oz.

NAVY ARMS

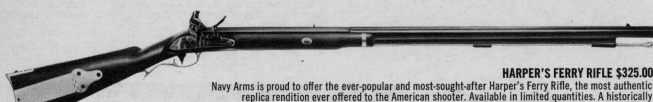

MISSISSIPPI RIFLE MODEL 1841 $275.00

The historic percussion lock weapon that gained its name as a result of its performance in the hands of Jefferson Davis' Mississippi Regiment during the heroic stand at the battle of Buena Vista. Also known as the "Yager" (a misspelling of the German Jaeger), this was the last rifle adopted by Army Ordnance to fire the traditional round ball. In 58 caliber, the Mississippi is handsomely furnished in brass, including patch box for tools and spare parts. **Weight:** 9½ lbs.; **Barrel length:** 32½"; **Overall length:** 48½"; **Caliber:** 58; **Finish:** Walnut finish stock, brass mounted.

HARPER'S FERRY RIFLE $325.00

Navy Arms is proud to offer the ever-popular and most-sought-after Harper's Ferry Rifle, the most authentic replica rendition ever offered to the American shooter. Available in limited quantities. A historically significant weapon complete with precision rifled 58 caliber browned barrel with attractive highly polished brass furniture.

1853 ENFIELD RIFLE MUSKET $300.00

The Enfield Rifle Musket marked the zenith in design and manufacture of the military percussion rifle and this perfection has been reproduced by Parker-Hale with reference to the original 120-year-old gauges. This and the other Enfield muzzle loaders reproduced by Parker-Hale were the most coveted rifles of the Civil War, treasured by Union and Confederate troops alike for their fine quality and deadly accuracy. **Caliber:** 577; **Barrel Length(s):** 39"; **Weight:** 9 lbs.; **Overall length:** 55"; **Sights:** Fixed front, graduated rear; **Rifling:** 3 groove, cold forged; **Stock:** Seasoned walnut with solid brass furniture.

1858 ENFIELD RIFLE $290.00

In the late 1850s the British Admiralty, after extensive experiments, settled on a pattern of rifle which had a 5-groove barrel of heavy construction, sighted to 1100 yards, and this was designated the Naval rifle, Pattern 1858. In the recreation of this famous rifle Parker-Hale has referred to the original 1858 Enfield Rifle in the Tower of London and has closely followed the specification even to the progressive depth rifling. **Caliber:** 577; **Barrel length(s):** 33"; **Weight:** 8 lbs. 8 oz.; **Overall length:** 48.5"; **Sights:** Fixed front, graduated rear; **Rifling:** 5 groove; cold forged; **Stock:** Seasoned walnut with solid brass furniture.

1861 ENFIELD MUSKETOON $275.00

The 1861 Enfield Musketoon is a Limited Collector's edition, individually serial numbered with certificate of authenticity. Supplied complete with many extras: Facsimile 1859 "Instructions of Musketry" Handbook. Replica 8-part Combination Tool. **Caliber:** 577; **Barrel length(s):** 24"; **Weight:** 7 lbs. 8 oz.; **Overall length:** 40.25"; **Sights:** Fixed front, graduated rear; **Rifling:** 5 groove; cold forged; **Stock:** Seasoned walnut with solid brass furniture.

NAVY ARMS

The firearms on this page are Navy Arms replicas, but are not black powder arms.

1875 REMINGTON
Blue $215.00
Nickel 275.00

Replica Arms first cartridge gun—copy of the 1875 Remington that was used by the James boys and Butch Cassidy. Available in 357 Magnum, 44/40 and 45 Long Colt. Two-piece walnut grips, all blue, case-hardened frame, 7½" barrel.

ROLLING BLOCK MAGNUM
SINGLE-SHOT PISTOL $175.00

This pistol is an exact copy of the famous Number Three Remington Rolling Block Pistol. It has a precision ordnance steel barrel in the traditional half-round, half-octagonal pattern, finished in a high-luster custom blue. The authentically reproduced action is finished in a rich color-case-hardening. The stocks are genuine walnut with a deep oil finish. Available in the popular 357 Magnum caliber. Also 22 L.R. and 22 Hornet.

REMINGTON-STYLE PERCUSSION REVOLVING CARBINE $225.00

An additional carbine model to be a companion piece to the Army Revolver. In matching 44 caliber with 20" barrel. Finished in a beautiful high-luster blue with buckhorn rear sight and adjustable blade front sight. A beautiful, light, handy six-shot repeating carbine which affected the design stimulus of the automatic weapon. **Caliber:** 44. **Barrel Length:** 20 in. **Overall Length:** 38 in. **Weight:** 5 lbs. **Finish:** Walnut stock; brass mounts; solid frame with top strap.

REMINGTON ROLLING BLOCK BUFFALO RIFLE & CARBINE

Navy Arms is proud to introduce the creation of the famous Remington Rolling—Block Action. Authentically reproduced in modern steels to the very finest detail. Each rifle is barreled with a famous octagonal Numrich Arms Corp. barrel featuring the famous hook rifling which is a process that every groove is singularly cut. The actions are case hardened complemented by a solid highly polished brass trigger guard and walnut colored stock. There are four models available. A Standard model with a full-length octagonal barrel for both rifle and carbine, a Creedmoor model which features half-round, half-octagonal barrel in both rifle and carbine model. All models are available in 45/70 or 50-70 caliber: 18" & 26" **$305.00**; 30" **$310.00**; 30" Creedmoor **$330.00**

ROLLING BLOCK BABY CARBINE $225.00

A beautiful Rolling Block Rifle. An ideal lightweight brush buster based on the small rolling block action. It features a beautiful precision rifle 22" round barrel in 22/L.R., 22 hornet or 357 magnum. The action is finished in beautiful rich color case hardening, while the barrel has a high luster blue. The trigger guard and buttplate are highly polished brass. The ensemble is completed by a beautiful, richly grained walnut stock.

NAVY ARMS

WHITWORTH MILITARY TARGET RIFLE

Recreation of Sir Joseph Whitworth's deadly and successful sniper and target weapon of the mid-1800s. Devised with a hexagonal bore with a pitch of 1 turn in 20 inches. Barrel is cold forged from ordnance steel, reducing the build-up of black powder fouling. Globe front sight; open military target rifle rear sight has interchangeable blades of different heights. Walnut stock is hand checkered. Caliber: 451; Barrel length: 36 inches; Weight: 9½ lbs. Price includes kit of accessories **$575.00**

PARKER-HALE 2 BAND RIFLE—MODEL 1858
Barrel: 33″, Overall length: 48½″, Weight: 8½ lbs. **$370.00**

PARKER-HALE MUSKETOON—MODEL 1861
Barrel: 24″, Overall length: 40¼″, Weight: 7½ lbs. **$300.00**

PARKER-HALE 3 BAND MUSKET—MODEL 1853
Barrel: 39″, Overall length: 55″, Weight: 9 lbs. **$400.00**

PARKER-HALE 451 VOLUNTEER RIFLE

Originally designed by Irish gunmaker, William John Rigby, this relatively small-caliber rifle was issued to volunteer regiments during the 1860s. Today it is rifled by the cold-forged method, making one turn in 20″. Sights are adjustable: globe front and ladder-type rear with interchangeable leaves; hand-checkered walnut stock; weight: 9½ lbs. Price includes comprehensive kit of accessories **$575.00**

RUGER BLACK POWDER REVOLVER

Ruger Old Army cap and ball revolver. 44 caliber, 7½ in. barrel, 46 ounces, American Walnut grips, adjustable rear sight, stainless steel nipples. Made to same best quality standard as the Ruger cartridge revolvers. Note: Use with lead ball or conical bullet of .457 diameter.

OLD ARMY . . . $196.00
OLD ARMY—STAINLESS STEEL . . . $257.50

SPECIFICATIONS of the OLD ARMY

Frame, Cylinder, and other **Working Components** are of heat-treated chrome-moly steel.

Caliber: 44. Bore .443 in., groove .451 in.

Weight: 2 pounds 14 ounces (46 ounces).

Barrel: 7½ in. Six grooves, right twist, 1 in 16 in.

Sights: Target rear (adjustable for elevation and windage) and ramp front.

Nipples: Stainless steel for standard caps.

Grips: American Walnut.

Finish: Polished all over;   blued and anodized.

The Lockwork is the same as that in the original Ruger Super Blackhawk. All Springs are coil, made from the highest quality steel music wire.

SHILOH
"Sharps Old Reliable" Metallic Cartridge Rifles

MODEL 1874 MILITARY RIFLE
$590.00

45-70 and 50-70 calibers. 30" round barrel. Blade front and Lawrence-style sights. Military style forend with 3 barrel bands and 1¼" swivels. Receiver group, butt plate and barrel bands case-colored, barrel—dark blue, wood—oil finish. 8 lbs. 12 oz.

MODEL 1874 CARBINE
$490.00

45-70 and 45-90 calibers. 24" round barrel, single trigger, blade front and sporting rear sight, butt stock straight grip, steel rifle butt plate, forend sporting Schnabble style. Case-colored receiver group and butt plate; barrel—dark blue; wood—oil finish; 8 lbs. 4 oz.

MODEL 1874 BUSINESS RIFLE
$535.00

45-70, 45-90, 45-120, 50-70, 50-90 and 50-140 calibers. 28" heavy-tapered round barrel, double set triggers adjustable set, sights, blade front and sporting rear with leaf. Butt stock is straight grip rifle butt plate, forend sporting Schnabble style. Receiver group and butt plate case-colored, barrel—dark blue, wood—American Walnut oil finished. 9 lbs. 8 oz.

MODEL 1874 SPORTING RIFLE NO. 3
$599.00

45-70, 45-90, 45-120, 50-70, 50-90 and 50-140 calibers. 30" tapered octagon barrel, double set triggers with adjustable set, blade front sight, sporting rear with elevation leaf and sporting tang sight adjustable for elevation and windage. Butt stock is straight grip with rifle butt plate, trigger plate is curved and checkered to match pistol grip. Forend is sporting Schnabble style. Receiver group and butt plate is case colored, barrel—high finish blu-black, wood—American Walnut oil finished. 9 lbs. 12 oz.

MODEL 1874 SPORTING RIFLE NO. 1
$695.00

45-70, 45-90, 45-120, 50-70, 50-90 and 50-140 calibers. 28" or 30" tapered octagon barrel. Double-set triggers with adjustable set, blade front sight, sporting rear with elevation leaf and sporting tang sight adjustable for elevation and windage. Butt stock is pistol grip, shotgun butt, sporting forend Schnabble style. Receiver group and butt plate case colored, barrel—high finish blu-black, wood—American Walnut oil finish. 9 lbs. 8 oz.

SHILOH

MODEL 1874 LONG-RANGE EXPRESS SPORTING RIFLE
$775.00

Calibers: 45-70-2 1/10", 45-90-2 4/10", 45-100-2 6/10", 45-110-2⅞", 45-120-3¼", 50-110-2½" and 50-140-3¼". 34" medium-weight tapered octagon barrel, globe front sight, sporting Tang sight, double set triggers with adjustable set; shotgun-style butt stock, pistol grip and traditional cheek rest with accent line; forend is tapered with Schnabble tip; stock is American black walnut oil finished; overall length—51 inches; 10 lbs. 8 oz.

Breech-loading Percussion Rifles

NEW MODEL 1863 CAVALRY CARBINE
$490.00

54 caliber (Calibers 45 and 50—Special Order). 22" round barrel with blade front and Lawrence rear sight with elevation leaf. Military forend with barrel band butt stock Military-style straight grip. Walnut finish. 8 lbs. 12 oz.

NEW MODEL 1863 MILITARY RIFLE
$590.00

54 caliber (Calibers 45 and 50—Special Order). 30" round barrel with blade front sight. Lawrence rear sight with elevation leaf. Forend 24" in length with steel nose cap, 3 barrel bands, 1¼" sling swivels. Butt stock straight grip Military-style, steel butt plate and patch box. 8 lbs. 12 oz.

MODEL 1863 SPORTING RIFLE
$590.00

54 caliber. 30" tapered octagon barrel, blade front sight, sporting rear with elevation leaf, double set triggers with adjustable set; curved trigger plate, pistol grip butt stock with steel butt plate, forend Schnabble style; optional Tang sight; 9 lbs.

THOMPSON/CENTER

CONTENDER

Standard Models:

This Contender may be purchased with a standard barrel of your choice, in any of the standard calibers listed. Barrel is available in 10″ length. 357 or 44 Magnum calibers are available either with or without patented choke. All standard barrels are supplied with iron sights; however, the rear sight may be removed for scope mounting. 357 and 44 Magnum calibers are available with the Thompson/Center patented detachable choke for use with the Hot Shot Cartridge. When the choke is removed, standard factory ammo may be fired from the same barrel without accuracy loss. **$235.00**

7mm T.C.U., 22 Long Rifle, 22 Win. Mag., 22 Hornet, 221 Fireball, 222 Rem., 223 Rem., 256 Win. Mag., 30/30 Win., 357 Mag. with and without choke, 41 Mag., 44 Mag. with and without choke, 45 ACP, 45 Colt with and without choke. (All calibers available with choke unless indicated).

Ventilated Rib/Internal Choke Models:

Featuring a raised ventilated (7/16″ wide) rib, this Contender model is available in either 357 or 44 Magnum caliber. Its rear leaf sight folds down to provide an unobstructed sighting plane when the pistol is used with Hot Shot Cartridges. A patented detachable choke (1⅞″ long) screws into muzzle internally. Overall barrel length 10″. . **$250.00**

Bull Barrel Models:

This pistol with 10-inch barrel features fully adjustable Patridge-style iron sights.

Standard and Custom calibers available:

22 Long Rifle, 22 Hornet, 221 Fireball, 222 Rem., 223 Rem., 256 Win. Mag., 7mm T.C.U., 30/30 Win., 30 Herrett, 357 Herrett, 357 Mag., 41 Mag., 44 Mag., 45 Colt and 45 Win. Mag.
Less internal choke **$235.00**
Standard calibers available with internal choke: 357 Mag., 44 Mag., 45 Colt **$240.00**

CONTENDER
SUPER "14" MODELS

Chambered in ten calibers (222 Remington and 223 Remington, 7mm T.C.U., 30 Herrett, 30/30 Winchester, 357 Herrett, 35 Remington, 41 Mag., 44 Mag. and 45 Win. Mag.), this gun is equipped with a 14″ bull barrel, fully adjustable target rear sight and ramped front sight (Patridge style). It offers a sight radius of 13½″, beavertail forend and grips designed by Steve Herrett. Overall length is 18¼″; weight is 3½ lbs. **$255.00**

THOMPSON/CENTER

THE PATRIOT
45 caliber

Featuring a hooked breech, double-set triggers, first-grade American walnut stock, adjustable (patridge-type) target sights, solid-brass trim, beautifully decorated and color case-hardened lock with a small dolphin-shaped hammer, the Patriot weighs approximately 36 ounces. Inspired by traditional gallery and dueling-type pistols, its carefully selected features retain the full flavor of antiquity, yet modern metals and manufacturing methods have been used to ensure its shooting qualities.

Patriot Pistol 45 caliber **$155.00**

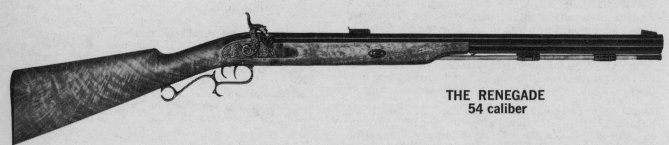

THE RENEGADE
54 caliber

Available in 50, 54 or 56 caliber percussion, the Renegade was designed to provide maximum accuracy and maximum shocking power. Constructed from superior modern steel with investment cast parts carefully fitted to an American walnut stock, the rifle features a precision-rifled (26″ carbine-type) octagon barrel, hooked-breech system, coil spring lock, double-set triggers, adjustable hunting sights and steel trim.

Renegade 50 and 54 caliber Caplock and 56 caliber smoothbore **$195.00**
Renegade 50 and 54 caliber Flintlock **200.00**

THE SENECA
36 & 45 caliber

Available in either 36 or 45 caliber percussion, the Seneca rifle is patterned on the style of an early New England hunting rifle. Six pounds light, this graceful little half-stock features a hooked breech, double-set triggers, first-grade American walnut, adjustable hunting sights, solid-brass trim, coil mainspring and finely patterned color case-hardened lock.

Seneca 36 or 45 caliber Caplock **$255.00**

THE HAWKEN
45, 50 and 54 caliber

Similar to the famous Rocky Mountain rifles made during the early eighteen hundreds, the Hawken is intended for serious shooting. Button-rifled for ultimate precision, the Hawken is available in 45 or 50 caliber, flint or percussion. Featuring a hooked breech, double-set triggers, first-grade American walnut, adjustable hunting sights, solid-brass trim, beautifully decorated and color case-hardened lock.

Hawken 45, 50 or 54 caliber Caplock **$255.00**
Hawken 45, 50 or 54 caliber Flintlock **265.00**

Air Guns

AIR RIFLE HEADQUARTERS

SPECIFICATIONS:
Caliber: 177
Barrel Length: 7½"
Weight: 2 lbs., 10 oz.
Overall Length: 14.9"
Sights: Slotted front sight; adjustable rear sight

**FEINWERKBAU
F-65 M-X
$498.50**

SPECIFICATIONS:
Caliber: 177
Barrel Length: 18¼"
Weight: 7 lbs. 6 oz.
Overall Length: 43½"
Sights: Hooded ramp front sight; open rear sight

**FEINWERKBAU
F-12 DELUXE
$287.50 ($308.50 Left Hand)**

**FEINWERKBAU F-12 CX
$528.50 ($548.50 LEFT HAND)**

SPECIFICATIONS:
Caliber: 177
Barrel: 18¼", rifled, hinged type.
Length: 43½ inches overall. **Weight:** 8 lbs. 14 oz.
Power: Spring air, single-stroke barrel cocking.
Stock: Walnut-finished hardwood with curved rubber butt-plate, pistol-grip cap with spacer, hand-cut checkering, Monte Carlo cheekpiece.

Sights: 2x-6x 1-inch tube, widefield scope included.
Features: Equipped with 1-inch sling, detachable swivels, filler screws, trigger shoe. Internally accurized for exceptional velocity.

**FEINWERKBAU F-124 SCX
$398.50**

SPECIFICATIONS:
Caliber: 177
Barrel: 18¼-inches, rifled, hinged type.
Length: 43½ inches overall. **Weight:** 8 lbs. 14 oz.
Power: Spring air, single-stroke barrel cocking.
Stock: Walnut-finished hardwood.
Sights: 3x-7x ⅞-inch tube widefield scope included.

Features: Equipped with 1-inch sling, detachable swivels, filler screws, and internal accurization for optimum velocity and accuracy.

AIR RIFLE HEADQUARTERS

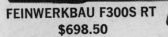

FEINWERKBAU F300S RT
$698.50

SPECIFICATIONS:
Caliber: 177
Barrel: 20", rifled, fixed solid with receiver.
Length: 43 inches overall. **Weight:** 10 lbs. 4 oz.
Power: Single-stroke sidelever, spring piston.
Stock: Adapted for fixed and moving target use. Walnut with adjustable buttplate, pistol-grip cap.
Sights: Shipped without sights; scope optional.

Features: Recoilless, vibration free. Permanent lubrication and seals. Barrel stabilizer weight included. Single-stage trigger.

SPECIFICATIONS:
Caliber: 177
Barrel Length: 18½"
Weight: 7¾ lbs. with 9½ oz. match sight installed
Overall Length: 43½"
Safety: Mainspring may be uncocked without firing
Stock: Walnut with checkering, soft curved rubber buttplate

WEIHRAUCH
HW 55
TYROLEAN
$448.50

SPECIFICATIONS:
Caliber: 177
Barrel Length: 6¼"
Weight: 2 lbs. 6 oz.
Overall Length: 12¾"
Sights: Front sight is a post enclosed within a tunnel system; rear sight is square notched
Safety: Auto-safety engages during loading; barrel may be tilted back to rearrange

WEIHRAUCH
HW 70
$114.50

BSA AIR GUNS

SPECIFICATIONS:
Caliber: 177
Barrel Length: 7⅞"
Weight: 3.6 lbs.
Overall Length: 15¾"
Safety: Safety catch is automatically applied on loading
Sights: Extra-long sight base; rear sight fully adjustable for windage and elevation.
Features: Precision-bored, all-steel barrel with mirror finish; hammer release system with independent sear for light consistent let-off; trigger weight is externally adjustable
MK8 Pistolscope, designed for use with
Scorpion Pistol **$39.50**

BSA SCORPION
$119.95

BSA AIR GUNS

SPECIFICATIONS:
Calibers: 177 and 22
Barrel Length: 19.5"
Weight: 8 lbs.
Overall Length: 44.7"
Sights: Open; ramp foresight with reversible bead/blade element adjustable for height
Stock: Oil-finished French walnut with high comb Monte Carlo cheekpiece; checkered pistol grip and forend; ventilated recoil pad
Features: Positive underlever action; precision-engineered breech plug; heavy barrel with cold-formed rifling

BSA AIRSPORTER SUPER
$350.00

SPECIFICATIONS:
Calibers: 177 and 22
Barrel Length: 18.5"
Weight: 7 lbs.
Overall Length: 43.5"
Sights: Adjustable bead/blade foresight and tangent rear sight with click adjustment for windage and elevation; reversible "V" and "U" elements
Stock: Polished hardwood with broad forend; Monte Carlo cheekpiece; ventilated rubber recoil pad
Features: High pressure "power seal" unit; match-type, single-stage trigger mechanism

BSA MERCURY
$199.50

BSA METEOR
$119.95

SPECIFICATIONS:
Calibers: 177 and 22
Barrel Length: 18.5"
Weight: 6 lbs.
Overall Length: 42"
Sights: Adjustable bead/blade foresight; tangent rear sight with click adjustment for windage and elevation; reversible "V" and "U" elements
Stock: Polished hardwood; **Meteor Super** features sculptured Monte Carlo cheekpiece and ventilated rubber recoil pad

BSA METEOR SUPER
$132.50

BEEMAN AIR RIFLES

ANSCULTZ MODEL 250
$725.00
($765.00 Left Hand)

SPECIFICATIONS:
Caliber: 177
Barrel Length: 18.5"
Weight: 10.8 lbs.
Overall Length: 45.2"
Sights: Moveable tunnel foresight with inserts; micrometer rear sight
Stock: French walnut with adjustable buttplate

BEEMAN AIR RIFLES

BEEMAN MODEL 100 $154.50
This 177-caliber rifle has a two-stage adjustable trigger, micro-click adjustable rear sight, hooded post front, and a walnut-finished hardwood stock. Barrel length; 18.7"; overall length: 42"; weight: 6½ lbs.

BEEMAN MODEL 250 $210.00
This new Model 250 comes in both 177 and 22 calibers and comes equipped with spring piston, micrometer rear sight, automatic safety and adjustable trigger with 40 lbs. cocking force. Velocity: 820 fps; barrel length: 20.4"; weight: 7.7 lbs.

BEEMAN MODEL 400 $555.00

The Model 400 features recoilless operation with double-piston construction, fixed barrel and side-cocking lever. The sights are micrometer peepsight. The stock is oil-polished walnut with adjustable curved butt pad. Weight: 10.8 lbs. Barrel: Cal. 177, 4.5mm rifled—length 480mm with barrel sleeve and detachable weight 100 g. Length: 1130mm. **$585.00** (left hand). Universal stock also available: **$650.00** (right hand), **$680.00** (left hand).

BEEMAN/FEINWERKBAU 124/127
MAGNUM SPORTER $230.00-$295.00
Available in two calibers—177 (124) and 22 (127)—this high-velocity, barrel-cocking sporter comes equipped with spring piston and adjustable target sights. In standard or deluxe model (shown). Velocity: 820+ fps (177), 680 fps (22); barrel length: 18.3"; weight: 6.9 lbs.; cocking force: 17 lbs.

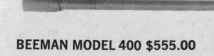

BEEMAN/FEINWERKBAU 300S MATCH
$675.00
This 177-caliber rifle is available in a 17.2-inch (barrel length) Junior Model; has five-way adjustable match trigger; match aperture rear sight with tunnel front sight; interchangeable inserts; in left- or right-hand configuration. Standard barrel length: 19.9"; weight: 8.8-10.8 lbs.; 640 fps. **$728.00** (left hand).

BEEMAN AIR RIFLES

BEEMAN/FEINWERKBAU 300S RUNNING BOAR TH $699.00

The 177-caliber "Running Boar" will aid every stalking hunter with its vibration-free action; grooved for scope only; sidelever cocking; single-stage tripper; spring piston; adjustable walnut comb, thumbhole grip; contoured adjustable buttplate. Barrel length: 19.9"; weight: 10.9 lbs.; 640 fps velocity. **$760.00** (left hand).

BEEMAN/FEINWERKBAU 300S UNIVERSAL $760.00

Extremely versatile, this 177-caliber, spring-piston powered rifle has two detachable front sights, two interchangeable cheekpieces and a special riser rail to raise the scope to higher cheekpiece levels. Barrel length: 19.9"; weight: 10.2 lbs. (**$820.00** for left-handed).

BEEMAN/WEBLEY OSPREY $259.95

The Osprey Air Rifle with a fixed barrel and side lever loading in 22 and 177 caliber has these features: Easy to load side lever; side lever ratchet for extra safety; trigger pull adjustment from 8 lbs. to 3 lbs.; micro-click adjustable rear sight; manual safety catch.

BEEMAN/WEBLEY VULCAN $160.00

This relatively inexpensive and light-weight rifle is designed with a new space-age piston head to insure a low friction fit; Monte Carlo comb stock, grooved for scopes. Calibers: 177 or 22; barrel length: 17"; weight: 6.8 lbs.; velocity: 790-815 fps.

BEEMAN/WEIHRAUCH HW 30S $140.00 (Standard)
30M $170.00 (Match)

On this 177-caliber rifle, the breech seal apparently never needs oiling. It has a double-jointed cocking lever; spring piston; match-grade trigger block, solid aluminum-grooved trigger and micro adjustable rear sight. Barrel length: 17"; weight: 5.8 lbs.

BEEMAN AIR RIFLES

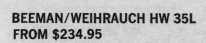

BEEMAN/WEIHRAUCH HW 35L
FROM $234.95

Available in 177 caliber. Adjustable heavy-duty match trigger. Walnut stock with cheekpiece and checkered grip. Weight: 8 lbs. Barrel: 19.6". Length: 44.7" overall.

BEEMAN/WEIHRAUCH HW 35EB
FROM $260.00 (177); $280.00 (22)

Available in two calibers, this 8-pound rifle sports thumb-release barrel latch; heavy-duty adjustable match trigger; spring piston; micro-click rear sight, tunnel front with inserts; automatic safety; rubber buttplate; and distinctly "American" cheekpiece. Barrel length: 19.6"; velocity: 755 fps (.177), 570-585 fps (.22).

BEEMAN/WEIHRAUCH HW 35 TH $240.00

This 177-caliber, spring-pistoned air rifle bears a tunnel foresight with five inserts and a click micrometer rear sight; also adjustable trigger and receiver grooved for scopes. Barrel length: 19.6"; weight: 8 lbs; velocity: 755 fps.

BEEMAN/WEIHRAUCH HW 50M $209.95 (MATCH)

Available in 177 Caliber. Barrel-cocking, spring piston mechanism. May be uncocked. Adjustable 2-stage, cast and grooved trigger. Monte Carlo comb and rubber buttplate. Barrel length: 18.3"; overall length: 43.1"; weight: 7.1 lbs. Standard model: $170.00

BEEMAN/WISCHO MODEL 55S $190.00 (177)
200.00 (22)

This spring-pistoned rifle, available in two calibers, features a beechwood stock, two-stage adjustable trigger and adjustable open rear sight. Barrel length: 16"; weight: 5 lbs.; velocity: 760 fps (.177), 580 fps (.22).

BEEMAN AIR RIFLES/PISTOLS

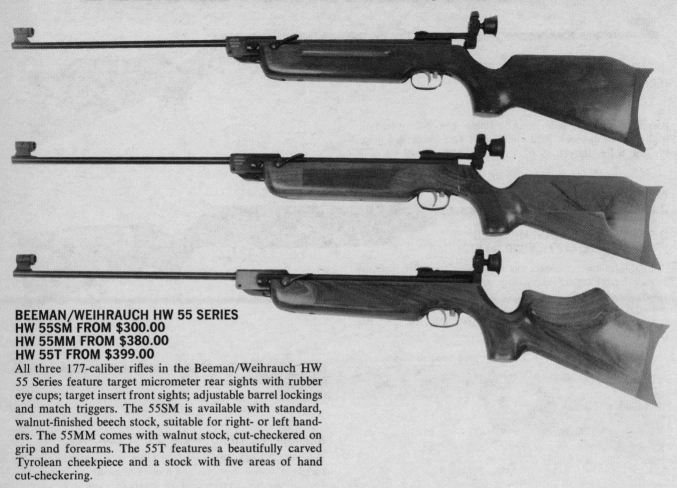

BEEMAN/WEIHRAUCH HW 55 SERIES
HW 55SM FROM $300.00
HW 55MM FROM $380.00
HW 55T FROM $399.00

All three 177-caliber rifles in the Beeman/Weihrauch HW 55 Series feature target micrometer rear sights with rubber eye cups; target insert front sights; adjustable barrel lockings and match triggers. The 55SM is available with standard, walnut-finished beech stock, suitable for right- or left handers. The 55MM comes with walnut stock, cut-checkered on grip and forearms. The 55T features a beautifully carved Tyrolean cheekpiece and a stock with five areas of hand cut-checkering.

BEEMAN MODEL 700 $115.00

This 177-caliber air pistol features adjustable double-pull trigger; auto safety; adjustable rear sight; hooded front; spring-piston; checkered synthetic stocks. Barrel length: 7″; weight: 3.1 lbs.; velocity: 460 fps. For left hand: **$117.00**

BEEMAN MODEL 800 $185.00

With recoilless action, this 177-caliber pistol has hooded front sight with interchangeable inserts; micro-click rear sight and synthetic grips. Barrel length: 7″; weight 3.2 lbs. **$187.00** (left hand).

BEEMAN AIR PISTOLS

BEEMAN MODEL 850 $215.00

Like the 800, the Model 850 also features recoilless action. This 177-caliber pistol has rotating barrel-housing; adjustable sights and optional muzzle weight. Barrel length: 7"; weight: 3.2 lbs. For left-handers: **$217.50.**

BEEMAN MODEL 900 $425.00

This 7-inch barrelled air arm has adjustable trigger, auto safety; micro-click rear sight with notch inserts and adjustable walnut stocks. Caliber: .177; weight: 3.2 lbs. **$460.00** for left-handers.

BEEMAN/FEINWERKBAU MODEL 65 MK I $485.00-$575.00
NON-ADJUSTABLE STOCK

The spring-pistoned, 177-caliber Model 65 MK I sports two mainsprings for more power; also recoilless action; sidelever cocking; lifetime internal lubrication; permanent seals. Adjustable grip, left-hand version and International Match model available. Barrel length: 7.5"; weight: 2.6 lbs. to 3.1 lbs.

BEEMAN/FEINWERKBAU MODEL 80
MATCH PISTOL $595.00 ($625.00 for left-handers)

Available in 177 caliber. Spring piston, single stroke sidelever cocking. Interchangeable blade front; adjustable rear sights. Features two-stage trigger adjustable for finger length, pull, and release. Weight: 2.8-3.2 lbs. Barrel: 7.5", twelve-grooved rifled steel. Length: 16.4" overall.

BEEMAN/WEBLEY HURRICANE $125.00

Available in 177 and 22 caliber. Features an adjustable rear sight and trigger pull, manual safety and scope mount. Weight: 2.4 lbs.; 11½" overall; 8" barrel

BEEMAN AIR PISTOLS

BEEMAN/WEBLEY TEMPEST $89.95

The **Tempest** is available in 177 caliber for target shooting
or 22 caliber for field work. Both feature an adjustable rear
sight and trigger pull; steel piston in steel liner for maximum
performance. Unique rearward spring expansion simulates
firearm recoil. Weight 2 lbs. Length 9″.

BEEMAN/WEIHRAUCH HW 70 $98.50

This pneumatic-powered air gun features a two-stage trigger;
adjustable rear sight with hooded front; and molded grip
with thumbrest. Barrel length: 6¼″; weight: 38 oz.; caliber:
.177; velocity: 410 fps.

BEEMAN/WISCHO CUSTOM MATCH $145.00

Featuring a spring piston, adjustable sights and 24-oz. trigger
pull, this 177-caliber pistol has a walnut stock with thumbrest. Barrel length: 7″; weight: 2 lbs. 2 oz. velocity: 450 fps.

BEEMAN/WISCHO S-20 STANDARD $115.00

The S-20 sports a front sight hood, an adjustable rear sight,
24-ounce trigger pull, spring piston and plain walnut stock
suitable for right- or left-handers. Barrel length: 7″; weight:
2 lbs. 2 oz. caliber: .177; velocity: 450 fps.

BENJAMIN AIR RIFLE

MODELS 3100, 3120: Benjamin Super Repeater Air Rifles with Monte Carlo stock. Cal. BB or 22 . **$89.05**

MODELS NO. 340, 342, 347: Benjamin Super Single Shot Air Rifle with Monte Carlo stock. Cal. BB or 177 or 22 has new rugged square top ramp-type front sight **$89.05**

No. 273 Detachable Rear Peep

Sight. Adjustable. For Models 340 - 342 - 347 - 310 - 312 - 317 - 720 - BENJAMIN AIR RIFLES. Advise Model. Each $6.00
Extra Discs; Small, Medium, Large. Each $3.05

BAR-O Detachable Rear Peep

Sight. Adjustable. For all Models Benjamin Rifles with BAR-V Sight. Advise Model. Each $2.70

Extra Discs; Small, Medium, Large. Each $1.35

Benjamin BAR-V Rear

Sight. It Rotates! Provides Quick, Sensitive Adjustment of Elevation and Windage. Each. $2.70

BENJAMIN H-C LEAD PELLETS
"Sized and Lubricated"

	Per Can
Benjamin H-C Lead Pellets Cal. 177 (250) . . .	**$1.85**
Benjamin H-C Lead Pellets Cal. 177 (500)	3.40
Benjamin H-C Lead Pellets Cal. 22 (250)	2.40
Benjamin H-C Lead Pellets Cal. 22 (500)	4.40

BENJAMIN ROUND BALL SHOT

Benjamin Steel Air Rifle Shot—BB 500	**$1.15**
Benjamin Steel Air Rifle Shot—BB 1 lb.	2.35
Benjamin Lead Air Rifle Shot—BB 500	3.60
Benjamin Lead Air Rifle Shot—BB—4.5 mm 1 lb.	**$5.60**
Benjamin Round Lead Shot—Cal. 22—5.5 mm. 1 lb.	**$5.60**

**MODELS 130, 132, 137
Single Shot Air Pistol
Cal. BB or 177 or 22
$72.30**

STANDARD SIZE JET KING CO$_2$ CARTRIDGE

For use in Benjamin Super Gas Rifles and Pistols. 10 in a box. **$4.55**
Size 2⅝" x 47/64". 8.5 Gram.

CROSMAN AIR & GAS PISTOLS

MODEL 454
SEMI-AUTO
BB MATIC
$28.50

Positive force feed magazine holds 16 Super BBs • Contoured grips with thumbrest for left- or right-handed shooters • Over 80 shots per CO_2 Power-let • Average muzzle velocity—375 f.p.s. • Positive slide-action safety • Rear sights adjustable for windage and elevation • Barrel length—7¾″ • Overall length—11⅜″ • Weight—29 Oz.

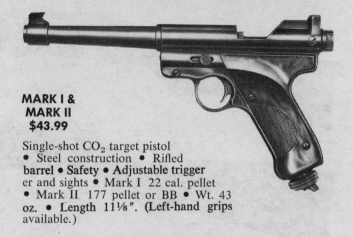

MARK I &
MARK II
$43.99

Single-shot CO_2 target pistol • Steel construction • Rifled barrel • Safety • Adjustable trigger er and sights • Mark I 22 cal. pellet • Mark II 177 pellet or BB • Wt. 43 oz. • Length 11⅛″. (Left-hand grips available.)

MODELS 1322 & 1377
$37.50

MODEL 1322: Single-shot 22 caliber pump pistol. Heavy duty pump link with sure grip checkered forearm. Selective pump power. Fully adjustable sights. Cross-bolt safety. Button rifled solid steel barrel. Gun blued steel parts.

MODEL 1377: Single-shot 177 caliber pump pistol. Heavy duty pump link with sure grip checkered forearm. Selective pump power. Fully adjustable sights. Cross-bolt safety. Button rifled, solid steel barrel. Gun blued steel parts.

MODEL 38-T
$38.50

MODEL 38-C: Combat. CO_2 177 Pellet Revolver. Holds six 177 caliber Pells. Single and Double action and revolving cylinder. Length 9½″. Weight 46 ozs. 10 lands R.H. twist. 3¼″ barrel. **$38.50**

MODEL 38-T: CO_2 177 Pellet Revolver. For Target shooting. Length 11¾″. Weight 46 ozs. Rifling: 10 lands R.H. twist, 1 turn in 16″, button rifled. 6″ barrel. **$38.50**

MODEL 1861 SHILOH $23.93

Six-shot CO_2-powered pistol • Shoots BBs and 177 caliber pellets • Features cross-bolt safety, wood styled grips and 6¾″ rifled steel barrel • Length 12¾″.

MODEL 1600 POWERMATIC
$23.95

MODEL 1600 POWERMATIC

Automatic firing 16-shot BB repeater • Leakproof CO_2 powered • Length 11⅜″ • Weight 29 oz.

CROSMAN AIR & GAS RIFLES

MODEL 1: 22 caliber pneumatic air rifle. Micrometer adjustable rear sights. Single-shot bolt action. Grooved metal receiver for scope mounting. Features an American hardwood stock and forearm. Rifled brass barrel for maximum accuracy. Length: 39"; weight: 5 lbs. 1 oz. **$67.43**

MODEL 73: 16-shot BB repeater. CO_2 powered. Solid steel barrel. Positive lever safety. Also shoots 177 caliber pellets. Length: 34¾"; weight: 3 lbs. 4 oz. Average muzzle velocity: BB—425 fps; Pellet—435 fps. **$24.99**

MODEL 760: 180-shot BB repeater, pump action. Shoots 177 or BB Caliber. BB's from storage chamber are metered into visual loading magazine. **$35.99**

MODEL 788 BB SCOUT: Starter gun with selective pump-up power and gravity-feed magazine, open rear sights adjustable for windage and elevation, positive bolt action, butt plate on stock and a solid-steel barrel and cross-bolt safety. Magazine holds 20 BBs and one BB in chamber. Overall length is 31". **$21.99**

CROSMAN RIFLES & ACCESSORIES

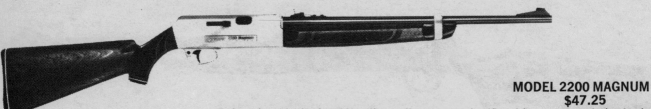

MODEL 2200 MAGNUM
$47.25

Bolt action, single shot 22 caliber pellet pneumatic rifle with a contoured pistol-grip stock, pumping mechanism with selective power; fixed blade front sight; butt plate with white line spacer and metal rear sights that are adjustable for windage and elevation. Weight is 4 lbs. 12 oz. Overall length is 39¾".

MODEL 766 $43.99

American Classic Model 766 features rifled barrel, bolt action receiver and a positive cross-bolt safety. 177 caliber, single-shot pneumatic rifle. Rear sight adjustable for windage and elevation with a fixed blade front sight. Weight 4 lbs. 14 oz. Length 39¾".

CROSMAN COPPERHEAD™ BBs

Perfectly round copper-plated steel shots assure greatest accuracy and in-flight stability; waisted diabolo design assures maximum weight distribution from head to skirt.

CROSMAN COPPERHEAD™ CO₂ POWERLETS®

These CO_2 Powerlets® are leakproof, corrosion-resistant and uniform in pressure.
5 Powerlets® to a pack $1.85

Model 617—72 packs of 200 BBs to a carton ....$ **.25** per pack
Model 627—48 packs of 400 BBs to a carton ....   **.49** per pack
Model 727—25 packs of 400 BBs to a carton ....   **.49** per pack
Model 737—12 packs of 1500 BBs to a carton ...... **1.49** per pack
Model 747—12 packs of 2500 BBs to a carton ...... **2.49** per pack
Model 757—6 packs of 5000 BBs to a carton .... **4.69** per pack

DAISY AIR GUNS

DAISY 179 SIX GUN
$19.50

The "Spittin' Image" of the famed Colt Peacemaker in style and action. Forced-feed, 12-shot repeating action. Single-action cocking hammer. Blued barrel, receiver; wood-grained molded grips. 11½" length.

MODEL 188 B·B/PELLET PISTOL
$19.50

• **SPRING ACTION AIR PISTOL. CALIBER:** 177 cal. **OVERALL LENGTH:** 12". **MUZZLE VELOCITY:** B•B's, 215 feet-per-second (65.5 mps); pellets, 180 feet-per-second (55 mps). **ACTION:** Under barrel cocking lever. **SIGHTS:** Blade and ramp front, notched rear. **GRIPS:** Checkered and contoured with thumb rest. **FEED:** Gravity, easy-loading port, 24 B•B shot capacity or single shot pellet.

MODEL 1188 B·B PISTOL
$19.50

A new concept in controlled velocity, spring-action air pistols. **GRIP & RECEIVER:** Black, die-cast metal, contoured grip with thumb rest, checkering. **BARREL:** Smooth bore steel. **ACTION:** Under-barrel cocking lever. **SIGHTS:** Blade and ramp front, notched rear. **FEED:** Gravity, easy-loading port, 24 B•B shot repeater. **SAFETY:** Manual. **MUZZLE VELOCITY:** 215 fps (65.5 mps). **LENGTH:** 12" (30.4 cm). Boxed.

MODELS 717 & 722
$61.50

• **MATCH QUALITY PNEUMATIC AIR PELLET PISTOLS. CALIBER:** Model 717, 177 cal.; Model 722, 22 cal. **OVERALL LENGTH:** 13½". **ACTION:** Single pump pneumatic, side-operating pump lever. **MUZZLE VELOCITY:** Model 717, 360 feet-per-second (109.7 mps); Model 722, 290 feet-per-second (88.3 mps). **SIGHTS:** Blade and front ramp, match grade fully adjustable notch rear with micrometer adjustments. **GRIPS:** Super-strength molded, woodgraining and checkering; contoured with thumb rest. Left-hand grips available.

DAISY AIR GUNS

POWER LINE 777
$183.75

RECEIVER: Black, die-cast metal. **BARREL:** Rifled steel. **ACTION:** Recoilless, single pump pneumatic. Side operating pump lever. **AMMO:** 177 cal. (4.5 mm) lead pellets. **FEED:** Single shot. **GRIPS:** Fully contoured anatomical. Hardwood, available right or left hand. **SIGHTS:** Blade and ramp front, match grade rear with adjustable width notch and micrometer click adjustments. **SAFETY:** Manual cross-bolt trigger block with red indicator. Muzzle velocity: 360 fps (109.7 mps). **LENGTH:** 13½″. **WEIGHT:** 3.1 lbs.

POWER LINE 780 & 790*
$61.25

RECEIVER: Black, die-cast metal. **BARREL:** Rifled steel. **ACTION:** CO_2 gas operated, manual cocking. **FEED:** Single shot. **AMMO:** Model 780, 22 cal. lead pellets; model 790, 177 cal. lead pellets. **GRIPS:** Super-strength molded, woodgrained and checkered, contoured to fit right or left hand. **SIGHTS:** Blade and ramp front, fully adjustable notch rear. **SAFETY:** Manual cross-bolt trigger block. Muzzle velocity: Model 780, 330-365 fps.; Model 790, 355-425 fps. **LENGTH:** 11.3″

*Models 780 and 790 formerly Smith & Wesson models 786 and 796.

MODEL 1200 CUSTOM CO_2 B•B PISTOL
$30.95

GRIP: Contoured, checkered, molded wood grained. **BARREL:** Smoothbore, heavy wall, seamless. **ACTION:** CO_2 gas operated. **SIGHTS:** Blade and ramp front, fully adjustable square notch rear. **CALIBER:** 177 B•B repeater, 60 B•B shot reservoir. **VELOCITY:** 420/450 fps. **LENGTH:** 12⅛″.

DAISY MODEL 840
$30.00

DAISY MODEL 840. Single pump pneumatic rifle with straight pull bolt action. Single shot .155 caliber pellet or 350-shot B•B repeater. Molded wood-grained stock and forearm; steel butt plate. Forearm forms pump lever. Adjustable open rear sight, ramp front. Cross bolt trigger safety. Muzzle velocity: B•Bs 310 fps; pellets 270 fps.

DAISY AIR GUNS

MODEL 845 TARGET GUN $36.00

SPECIAL TARGET VERSION OF MODEL 840. Designed for the young shooter with an interest in developing marksmanship skills; **Barrel:** Steel, smooth bore, steel shroud; **Sights:** Hooded front sights with aperture inserts, adjustable peep rear; **Action:** Pneumatic, single pump, straight pull bolt; **Magazine:** Single shot pellet or B•B repeater with 350 shot capacity, side loading port; **Receiver:** Structural molded, black finish; **Stock/forearm:** Sport styling, super-strength molded, woodgraining, checkered pistol grip, fluted comb, steel butt plate, grooved grip forearm; **Safety:** Manual; **Muzzle Velocity:** B•Bs 325 fps (99 mps); pellets 300 fps (91 mps); **Length:** 37⅛″ (94 cm). Recommended for ages 10 and older with adult supervision.

POWER LINE MODEL 850 $57.95

POWER LINE MODEL 850 SINGLE PUMP PNEUMATIC B•B/ PELLET RIFLE. Magazine: 100-shot B•B reservoir; **Ammo:** 177 cal. Daisy pellets, Daisy Bullseye® B•Bs; **Barrel:** Rifled steel. **Stock/Forearm:** Full length molded. Sporter styling with hand-wiped checkered woodgrain finish. Separate butt plate; **Receiver:** Black die cast metal. Dovetail scopt mount; **Safety:** Manual cross-bolt trigger block with red indicator; **Sights:** Ramp front, fully adjustable open rear; **Weight:** 4.3 lbs.; **Overall Length:** 38⅜″; Muzzle velocity: 177 cal. pellets, 480 fps.; B•Bs, 520 fps.

POWER LINE MODEL 880 $46.50

POWER LINE MODEL 880 PUMP-UP B•B REPEATER AND SINGLE SHOT PELLET GUN IN ONE. Great for shooters 14 and over. Pneumatic pump-up for variable power (velocity and range) increasing with pump strokes. Only 10 strokes required for maximum power. 100-shot capacity B•B magazine. Single-shot 177 caliber pellets. Ramp front and open rear sights. Scope mount. Monte Carlo design, molded stock with cheek piece and molded forearm. Cross bolt safety with red indicator and positive cocking valve safety prevents hang-fires. Length: 37¾″.

POWER LINE MODEL 881 $56.00

POWER LINE MODEL 881 PNEUMATIC PUMP-UP AIR GUN. Burnished receiver. Molded Monte Carlo stock with cheek piece and white spacer before the butt plate and grip cap. Checkered, molded forearm. It's a B•B repeater and a single-shot pellet gun in one. With pneumatic pump-up for variable power (velocity and range) increasing with pump strokes. Only 10 strokes for maximum power. Shoots 177 caliber pellets. 100 B•B shot capacity magazine. Ramp front sight and open rear sight. Cross bolt trigger safety with red indicator and positive cocking valve. Length: 37¾″.

DAISY AIR GUNS

DAISY MODEL 95
$30.65

DAISY 95 WOODSTOCK. Modern sporter style with real gun heft and feel. Full Seasoned wood stock, sporter forearm. Gravity-feed 700-shot repeating action. Controlled velocity. Ramp front, adjustable "V" slot rear sights. Length: 35".

MODEL 499
$44.95

WORLD'S MOST ACCURATE B·B GUN. Official model of the NRA-sanctioned Daisy/ U.S. Jaycees Shooting Education Program and the gun that has set every national record in 5-meter air gun competition. The 499 is used to train more than a million young shooters each year in proper gun handling and marksmanship. **Stock:** Monte Carlo, stained hardwood; **Forearm:** Semi-beavertail, stained hardwood with internal compartments for addition of weight for competitive shooting; **Sights:** Hooded front with aperture inserts, adjustable rear peep; **Barrel:** Steel, smooth bore; **Feed:** Single B·B shot, muzzle loading, magnetic B·B retainer; **Action:** Lever; **Safety:** Manual; **Muzzle Velocity:** 230 fps (70 mps); **Length:** 36¼" (92 cm); Recommended for ages 10 and older with adult supervision.

POWER LINE MODEL 922, 917
$61.95

Action: Pneumatic pump-up clip-fed pellet repeater. Straight pull bolt; **Feed System:** 5-shot positive index clip. Single shot adapter included; **Ammo:** Daisy Match pellets. **922:** .22 cal. (5.5 mm). **917:** .177 cal. (4.5 mm); **Barrel:** 20.8" (52.8 cm) Decagon rifled brass. Twist 1 turn in 16" (40.6 cm); **Barrel Shroud:** Tapered steel; **Stock/Forearm:** Monte Carlo stock, super-strength molded, hand-wiped finish, wood-graining, checkering, thumb grooves, separate butt plate and grip cap, white spacers, checkered forearm, diamond inlay; **Receiver:** Engraved gold tone filled; black finish. Dovetail scope mount; **Safety:** Manual cross bolt trigger block. Red indicator and open bolt; **Trigger Pull Weight:** 5 lbs. (2.3 kg); **Sights:** Ramp front, fully adjustable open rear, dovetail on receiver; **Weight:** 5 lbs. (2.2 kg); **Overall Length:** 37¾" (95.8 cm); **Pumping Effort:** 4 to 18.5 lbs., 1 to 10 pumps.

977 TARGET RIFLE
$75.95

MODEL 977 PNEUMATIC PUMP-UP TARGET RIFLE. The 977 features Power Line's 5-shot clip system and precision sights for fast, easy, accurate shooting. **Action:** Clip fed pneumatic pump-up pellet repeater. Straight pull bolt; **Feed System:** 5-shot positive index clip; **Ammo:** .177 cal. (4.5mm) Daisy pellets; **Barrel:** Rifled; **Stock/ Forearm:** Molded Monte Carlo stock, checkered forearm; **Receiver:** Engraved black finish; **Safety:** Manual cross bolt trigger block, red indicator and open bolt; **Sights:** Hooded front with aperture inserts, fully adjustable precision rear with micrometer calibrations; **Weight:** 5 lbs. (2.2 kg); **Overall Length:** 37¾" (98.5 cm); **Pumping Effort:** 4 to 18.5 lbs., 1 to 10 pumps.

DAISY AIR GUNS

DAISY MODEL 105
$20.50

DAISY 105 PAL. Lever action with automatic trigger block safety. Post front sight, open rear sight. Extra strength molded stock. Gravity feed, 350 shot. 260' controlled velocity. Length:30½".

DAISY MODEL 111
$25.50

DAISY 111 WESTERN CARBINE. Lever-cocking western carbine style with under-barrel rapid-loading port. Famed Daisy gravity-feed 700-shot repeating action with controlled velocity. Post front, adjustable "V" slot rear sights. Simulated gold receiver engraving. Length 35".

DAISY MODEL 1938
RED RYDER COMMEMORATIVE
$36.75

DAISY MODEL 1938 RED RYDER COMMEMORATIVE. The B•B gun Dads remember. Wood stock burned with Red Ryder lariat signature, wood forearm, saddle ring with leather thong. Lever cocking, 700-shot repeating action. Post front, adjustable V-slot, rear sights. Length: 35".

DAISY MODEL 1894
$39.00

DAISY 1894 SPITTIN' IMAGE B•B GUN. The "Spittin' Image" of the famed "carbine that won the West." 2-way lever cocking, side-loading port. 40-shot controlled-velocity repeated. 38".

GAMO AIR RIFLES

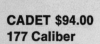

CADET $94.00
177 Caliber

The Gamo Cadet is specifically scaled to the young shooter but has the heft, feel and look of an adult air rifle. Features an automatic trigger block safety, which must be moved before firing; an all-steel, precision-rifled barrel; micro-adjustable 2-way click rear sight and grooved receiver for mounting scopes using 11mm bases. Stock is lacquered hard beechwood. One cocking stroke provides 570 fps muzzle velocity. The Cadet carries a one-year warranty.

EXPO $110.00
177 and 22 Calibers

The Gamo Expo target rifle has a 12-grooved, precision-rifled barrel with fully adjustable sights. Trigger tension is externally adjustable for a smooth, crisp pull; barrel is all steel and precision rifled for maximum rigidity and accuracy. The Expo also features a single cocking stroke to expose the breech for manual loading and provide a full 600 fps velocity. A year's warranty is provided.

EXPOMATIC $144.00
177 Caliber

The Gamo Expomatic, a high-performance target rifle, features a 25-pellet and spring-loaded tubular magazine. As the barrel is cocked, a pellet is automatically fed into the chamber, so reloading is fast and rapid-fire action is easy and accurate. This air gun also features an all-steel barrel in a heavy-weight contour; adjustable trigger; micro-adjustable rear sight and hooded front sight and lacquered beechwood stock. One-year warranty.

GAMO AIR RIFLES

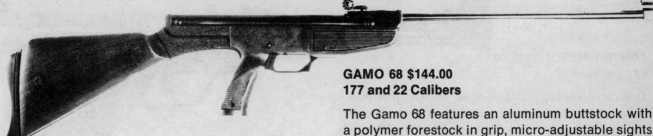

GAMO 68 $144.00
177 and 22 Calibers

The Gamo 68 features an aluminum buttstock with a polymer forestock in grip, micro-adjustable sights and a precision-rifled barrel that provides exceptional accuracy. Because the Gamo 68 pistol grip is usually held during the cocking operation, a special safety device blocks the trigger until the barrel is fully locked. The trigger is externally adjustable for weight of pull. A single cocking stroke provides 600 fps muzzle velocity. One-year warranty.

GAMATIC $178.00
177 Caliber

The Gamatic, available in 177 caliber only, offers the same quality features as the Gamo 68 but also boasts a 25-pellet, spring-loaded tubular magazine, allowing rapid fire action. When the barrel is cocked, a pellet is automatically fed into the chamber, making reloading fast and effortless. A year's warranty accompanies the gun.

MODEL 600 $144.00
177 and 22 Calibers

The Model 600 is an adult-size gun with all the performance needed for plinking and target shooting. A precision-rifled, target-quality barrel delivers quarter-inch groups at 25 feet; trigger is fully adjustable for crisp release; rear sight is micro-adjustable for windage and elevation; receiver is grooved to accept 11 millimeter scope mounts; stock is lacquered beechwood. One cocking stroke provides 660 fps muzzle velocity. The Model 600 carries a year's warranty.

GAMO AIR GUNS & ACCESSORIES

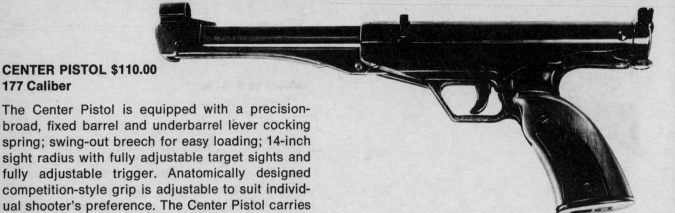

CENTER PISTOL $110.00
177 Caliber

The Center Pistol is equipped with a precision-broad, fixed barrel and underbarrel lever cocking spring; swing-out breech for easy loading; 14-inch sight radius with fully adjustable target sights and fully adjustable trigger. Anatomically designed competition-style grip is adjustable to suit individual shooter's preference. The Center Pistol carries a one-year warranty.

Model	Caliber	Type	Weight	Overall Length	Trigger	Sights	Approx. Velocity Feet Per Second	Stock
EXPO	177 & 22	Bbl. cocking spring type	5.5 lbs.	42"	Adjustable	front: hooded frt. sight rear: micro-sight	600 fps.	laquered beechwood
EXPOMATIC	177	Bbl. cocking spring type repeater version	5.5 lbs.	42"	Adjustable	front: hooded frt. sight rear: micro-sight	600 fps.	laquered beechwood
GAMATIC	177	Bbl. cocking spring type repeater version	6.5 lbs.	38"	Adjustable	front: hooded frt. sight rear: micro-sight	600 fps.	aluminum buttstock w/polymer forestock in grip
GAMO 68	177 & 22	Bbl. cocking spring type	6.5 lbs.	38"	Adjustable	front: hooded frt. sight rear: micro-sight	600 fps.	aluminum buttstock w/polymer forestock in grip
MODEL 600	177 & 22	Bbl. cocking spring type	7 lbs.	44"	Adjustable	front: hooded frt. sight rear: micro-sight	660 fps.	laquered beechwood
CENTER (PISTOL)	177	Underbarrel lever Cocking spring type	2.8 lbs.	14"	Adjustable	front: hooded frt. sight rear: micro-sight	400-435 fps.	anatomically designed competition style grip.
MODEL 300	22 only	Bbl. cocking spring type	7 lbs.	44"	Adjustable	front: hooded frt. sight rear: micro-sight	600 fps.	laquered beechwood
CADET	177 only	Bbl. cocking spring type	5 lbs.	37"		front: hooded frt. sight rear: micro-sight	570 fps.	laquered beechwood

PRECISION PELLETS

	Caliber	Price Per Can
Diabolo Pellets (500 in Can)	177	$2.70
Diabolo Pellets (250 in Can)	177	1.90
Diabolo Pellets (250 in Can)	22	2.70

ACCESSORIES

	Price
Catch Pellet	$15.00
Catch Pellet Rocker	50.00
Bullet Trap	30.00
Target Transport Device	100.00
Flat Catch Pellet	10.00

MARKSMAN AIR GUNS & ACCESSORIES

MODEL 1741
177 caliber
Price Not Set

SPECIFICATIONS:
Caliber: 177 BB's, pellets, darts
Capacity: 100 rds.
Barrel Length: 15½"
Weight: 5.08 lbs.
Action: Spring, break action
Safety: Automatic safety sets after each firing
Finish: One-piece walnut finished stock

PLAINSMAN MODEL 1049
CO$_2$ AIR PISTOL
Price Not Set

SPECIFICATIONS:
Caliber: 177 BB shot
Capacity: 100 rds.
Barrel Length: 5⅞"
Weight: 1¾ lbs.
Sights: Sport blade front; fixed notched rear
Action: Double-action trigger pull
Safety: Thumb
Finish: Durable black epoxy with walnut wood-grain plastic grips

SPECIFICATIONS:
Caliber: 177 BB's, pellets, darts
Capacity: 20 rounds
Barrel Length: 2½"
Weight: 1 lb. 8 oz.
Sights: Sport blade front; fixed notch rear
Action: Spring
Safety: Thumb
Finish: Durable black epoxy frame
MODEL 1020 AIR PISTOL: Same as Model 1010, except shoots BB's only.

MARKSMAN 1010 AIR PISTOL
Price Not Set

MARKSMAN AIR GUN PELLETS
Price Not Set

For all makes of air pistols and air rifles. These "waisted design" lead pellets ensure positive grip on rifling and expansion on targets. Produced to close size and weight tolerances.

177 caliber (4.5mm) lead pellets:
  No. 1212 (200 pellets)
  No. 1215 (500 pellets)

22 caliber (5.5mm) lead pellets:
  No. 1222 (200 pellets)
  No. 1225 (500 pellets)

MARKSMAN AIR GUNS
& ACCESSORIES

MARKSMAN WRIST LOCK SLINGSHOT #30-06
Price Not Set

Versatile and powerful wrist slingshot makes precise long-distance shooting easy. High velocity tubular latex thrust bands are formulated for excellent resistance to ozone and weathering. Rolled steel frame has a non-glare finish.

MARKSMAN BIG GAME SHOOTING GALLERY 2020
Price Not Set

For indoor or outdoor shooting. For use with 177 and 22 caliber air pistols and air rifles. Improve skills by safely shooting at moving animals, flying ducks, Ring-the-Bell Bull's-Eye and rotating skill targets. Features safety-angled backplate of 18-gauge steel that deflects BB's and pellets and traps them in gallery base. Additional targets available.

MARKSMAN FIRING RANGE 2040
Price Not Set

For use with most 177 and 22 caliber air pistols and air rifles. No batteries or electric power required. Center target with three figures rotates on pivot post when hit. Durable all-steel construction. Features safety-angled backplate of 18-gauge steel that deflects and traps BB's in gallery base. Additional targets available.

MARKSMAN INDOOR/OUTDOOR ROLL-UP
TARGET 2050 Price Not Set

New indoor/outdoor target features an exclusive roll-up target design with seven different scenes: Sea Battle, Shootin' Stars, Prehistoric Dinosaurs, Pub Darts, Space Wars, Save the Giant and Minefield Maneuvers. A urethane treated ballistic cloth serves as a backstop, and a nylon safety netting controls rebound and prevents ricochet. Designed for controlled velocity airguns with muzzle velocity up to 450 fps. Can also be used with standard NRA-type targets. Comes fully assembled and ready for use. Replacement target rolls available.

SHOOTIN DARTS 1300
Price Not Set

A new challenge to dart and air gun enthusiasts. This two-sided 12″ wound paper dartboard offers a choice of 12 popular dart games. Complete with one dozen authentic English mohair darts and the Marksman 1010 air pistol.

PRECISE AIR GUNS

RO-72 AIR PISTOL
$40.00

SPECIFICATIONS:
Caliber: 177
Capacity: Single shot
Barrel Length: 6"
Weight: 2 lbs. 3 oz.
Sights: Four interchangeable front sights; four rotating rear sights, micro-adjustable for windage and elevation
Action: Break action, barrel cocking
Muzzle Velocity: 310 fps

SPECIFICATIONS:
Caliber: 177
Capacity: Single shot
Barrel Length: 14"
Weight: 5½ lbs.
Sights: Hooded front sight; micrometer adjustable rear
Action: Spring, barrel cocking
Finish: Dark hardwood with cheekpiece; receiver grooved for scope mounting
Muzzle Velocity: 525 fps

PRECISE MINUTEMAN® MARSHALL
$64.95

SPECIFICATIONS:
Caliber: 177
Capacity: Single shot
Barrel Length: 19.4"
Weight: 7 lbs. 4 oz.
Sights: Hooded front sight; micrometer adjustable rear
Action: Spring; underlever cocking
Finish: Dark hardwood Monte Carlo stock with raised cheekpiece and buttplate; receiver grooved for mounting scope
Muzzle Velocity: 575 fps

PRECISE MINUTEMAN® MAGNUM
$99.00

SHERIDAN AIR GUNS

MODEL EB-CO₂ PISTOL
$55.90

SPECIFICATIONS:
Caliber: 20, 5mm
Barrel Length: 6½"
Weight: 27 oz.
Sights: Blade front sight; fully adjustable rear
Power: 12 gram CO_2 cylinders
Action: Turn bolt, single action
Finish: Durable blue with checkered simulated walnut grips

SHERIDAN AIR GUNS

PNEUMATIC RIFLES

Blue Streak Model CB   Single Shot: 5 MM.

Silver Streak Model C

A rifle for target or small game shooters. Full-length Mannlicher stock is made of genuine hand rubbed walnut. All working parts are precision engineered to assure accuracy and dependability.

- Controlled velocity. Pump action permits the shooter to determine the exact amount of velocity required for each shot. Improved valving mechanism assures long, trouble-free, high-quality performance.
- "Over and under" design with precision-rifled rigid mount barrel.
- Take-down walnut stock is readily removable.
- Single shot, bolt action design.
- Manual safety, mounted for easy thumb control.
- Choice of blue (BLUE STREAK) or satin-silver (SILVER STREAK) finish.
- Overall length: 37 in. Weight: 5¼ lbs.

MODELS AVAILABLE

MODEL	DESCRIPTION	PRICE
With Standard Open Sight		
CB	Blue Streak	$ 94.05
C	Silver Streak	97.60
With Receiver Sight		
CBW	Blue Streak	109.40
CW	Silver Streak	112.90
With Scope Sight		
CBS	Blue Streak	140.00
CS	Silver Streak	143.60

GAS-POWERED CO₂ RIFLES

Blue Streak Model FB   Single Shot: 5MM

Silver Streak Model F

35 Power Packed Shots

The Gas-Powered CO_2 Rifle is a companion line to the Pneumatics for those who enjoy or need faster shooting or who can't or just don't like to pump an air rifle.

- Blade type front sight.
- 5mm (20 cal.) precision-rifled rust proof barrel.
- Lightweight (6 lbs.).
- Compact length (37 in.).
- Over and under type construction with rigid mount barrel.
- Open sight easily adjustable for windage and elevation.
- Choice of blue or durable silver-satin plated finish.
- Bolt action (single shot).
- "Fireproof" safety.
- Sturdy valving mechanism with "locked in" charge.
- Easy takedown design.
- Full sporter length walnut stock.

Note—All rifles listed on this page are available in left hand versions at the same price. Add "LH" to above

MODELS AVAILABLE

MODEL	DESCRIPTION	PRICE
With Standard Open Sight		
FB	Blue Streak	$ 94.05
F	Silver Streak	97.60
With Receiver Sight		
FBW	Blue Streak	109.40
FW	Silver Streak	112.90
With Scope Sight		
FBS	Blue Streak	140.00
FS	Silver Streak	143.60

SHERIDAN ACCESSORIES

SHERIDAN INTERMOUNT

The Sheridan Intermount will accept any scope and mount made to fit the ⅜ in. standard dove tail. We can of course also furnish an excellent low-priced scope sight that we feel best suited to the needs of Sheridan owners. Prices are shown below.

No. 61—Wt. each 3 oz. **$11.70**

SHERIDAN INTERMOUNT AND SCOPE
Supplied with Weaver D4 scope.

No. 62—Wt. each 2 lbs. **$44.00**

LOW COST SHERIDAN AMMUNITION

The 5mm (.20 caliber) ammo is solid-nosed, bullet-shaped, super-penetrating, matched to the precision-rifled Sheridan barrels for proper sectional density and best ballistic coefficient. New plastic, reusable pellet box holds 500 rounds. Inset, hinged dispenser permits removal of pellets, one at a time.

No. 50—500 in a box **$5.35**

No. 51—500 in a box **$5.35**

PELLETRAP

Sheridan's Pelletrap is a compact, inexpensive, versatile target holder and backstop for air rifle practice. Wall hanger and flat base permit use most anywhere, indoors or out.

Weight each 6 lbs. **$17.60**

No. 24—Pelletrap Target Faces per 100 . . . .**$2.35**

SHERIDAN CO_2 CARTRIDGES

Standard 12.5 gram size and may be used in any CO_2 rifle or pistol calling for a 12.5 gram cartridge.

No. 63—5 in a box . . . .**$3.35** per box

Genuine leather holster for Sheridan CO_2 pistol. Features snap buttons on belt loop and safety snap.

No. 66 . . . .**$14.70**

Cleaning rod for Sheridan products.

No. 41 . . . .**$4.70**

SIG-HAMMERLI AIR GUNS

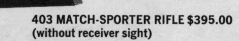

403 MATCH-SPORTER RIFLE $395.00
(without receiver sight)

Caliber: 177
Weight: 9 lbs. 4 ozs.
Overall Length: 45"
Sights: Front sight is globe tunnel with interchangeable sight inserts; rear sight is adjustable match-micrometer type.
Stock: Beechwood
Muzzle Velocity: 700-740 fps
Features: Raised cheekpiece; oversized rubber recoil pad; side-lever cocking; square forends.

MILITARY LOOK 420 $295.00
(without scope)

Calibers: 177 or 22
Barrel Length: 19"
Weight: 7½ lbs.
Overall Length: 43"
Sights: Front sight is globe tunnel with interchangeable sight inserts; rear sight is open and adjustable for windage.
Stock: Dark green, high-impact plastic
Muzzle Velocity: 700-740 fps

WALTHER AIR GUNS

WALTHER MODEL LP3
$450.00

SPECIFICATIONS:
Caliber: 177
Capacity: Single shot
Barrel Length(s): 9⅜"
Weight: 45.8 oz.
Overall Length: 13³⁄₁₆"
Sights: Micro-click rear sight, adjustable for windage and elevation
Action: Lever
Features: Power is compressed air. Recoilless operation, cocking in grip frame. 4-way adjustable trigger. Plastic thumbrest grips

WALTHER MODEL LP3 MATCH $540.00
SPECIFICATIONS:
Same as Model LP3 except with improved target grips with adjustable hand shelf

WALTHER MODEL LP53 $250.00
SPECIFICATIONS:
Caliber: 177
Capacity: Single shot
Barrel Length(s): 9⅜"
Weight: 40.5 oz.
Overall Length: 12⅜"
Sights: Micrometer rear sight; interchangeable rear sight blades
Features: Power is spring air. Target grips. Optional equipment includes barrel weight for improved balance

WALTHER LGR MATCH AIR RIFLE
$850.00

SPECIFICATIONS:
Caliber: 4.5mm (177)
Barrel Length: 19½
Overall Length: 44¼"
Weight: 10 lbs. 2 oz.

Stock: Same as LGR Air with exception of a high comb stock.
Sights: Same as LGR Air with the exception that sights are mounted on riser blocks.
Features: Same as LGR Air Rifle.

WALTHER MODEL LGR
$750.00

SPECIFICATIONS:
Caliber: 4.5mm (177)
Barrel Length(s): 19½"
Weight: 10 lbs. 2 oz.
Overall Length: 44¼"
Sights: Globe front sight; fully adjustable micrometer rear sight
Stock: Heavy walnut target stock with adjustable butt plate and adjustable muzzle weight
Features: Lever cocking, static pressure system provides constant velocity, shot after shot. Recoilless and vibration free. Adjustable trigger

WALTHER MODEL LGV SPECIAL
$600.00

SPECIFICATIONS:
Caliber: 4.5mm (177)
Capacity: Single shot
Barrel Length(s): 16"
Weight: 10 lbs. 4 oz.
Overall Length: 41⅜"
Sights: Globe front sight; micrometer adjustable rear sight
Trigger: Adjustable
Stock: Heavy walnut target stock matches styling and weight of the Walther small-bore target rifles, with fully adjustable butt plate

Sights, Scopes & Mounts

BUEHLER SAFETY & GUN SCREWS

BUEHLER LOW-SCOPE SAFETY

The Buehler Safety operates on the same mechanical principles as the manufacturer's original safety. In the "ON" position, pressure of the striker spring locks it securely. It will not cam over into firing position. Safety holds BOTH BOLT and STRIKER in locked position.

This safety operates on the right side of the action, rotating through an arc of 70 degrees with definite stops in the OFF and ON positions. It can be used equally well with or without a scope, and will be found to be faster and more convenient than the original safety. Complete with instructions for installation.

For following models:
MAUSER (M98, F.N.), KRAG, SPRINGFIELD WINCHESTER M54, 1891 ARGENTINE MAUSER

M93 (Fits most small ring Mauser actions which cock on closing such as M93, M95 and M96 Spanish, Mexican, Swedish) M94
Price each $14.75

FILLISTER HEAD & PLUG SCREWS

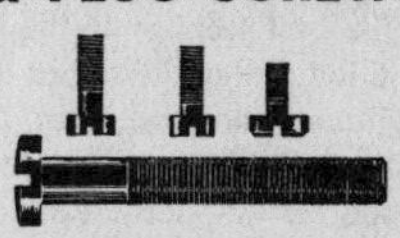

	Prices
6x48 SCREWS (1/8, 1/4, 5/16, 1/2" Mixed)	12-$2.00
6x48 PLUG SCREWS 3/32" .	12- 2.00
8x40 SCREWS (1/4 & 3/8" Mixed)	12- 2.00
8x40 PLUG SCREWS 3/32".	12- 2.00
10x32 PLUG SCREWS 3/32".	12- 2.00

GUARD SCREWS:

	Prices
UNIVERSAL	$1.75 Ea.
ENFIELD GUARD SCREW SCREWS UNIVERSAL	1.75 Ea.
SPRINGFIELD (KRAG) GD. MAUSER GUARD SCREWS	Set 4.00

RIFLE ACTION CHART—TOP MOUNT BASES

(Mount bases listed by our Code. Use this code in ordering.)

Catalog No. 35 1980	Micro Dial	Long 1-Piece Base	Short 1-Piece Base	2-Piece Base
BRNO Mauser Commercial				
Flat Top	BLU-WCC②	5/16BBWCC②		B2②
Round Rec. Ring	HV-U④		SR-S	H2①
BROWNING				
F.N. Action .264 thru .458	FI-U	FM	FI-S	F
Automatic Rifle (All Grades)				BA-2
Lever Action High Power				BL2
Bolt Action Rifle BBR New 1978 Model			BR	
B.S.A. Monarch Round Receiver				R
COLT SAUER				CS
ENFIELD Remington 30 Conversion			E-S	
Bridge flat up to .075 low	E-U③		E7-S	
Bridge shaped like M70	70-U			W③
Bridge shaped like R700	21-U③	21③	21-S③	R③
HARRINGTON & RICHARDSON, 22's				S2②
H&R 300 Ultra Bolt F.N. Action	FI-U	FM	FI-S	F
H&R 300, 301, Sako cal. .270 up				HS
GOLDEN EAGLE			GE	
HERTERS J9				F
HIGGINS–SEARS ROEBUCK				
50 & 51½" Bridge Hole Spacing	FI-U	FM	FI-S	F
51L, 51C, 52C	HV-U			H2
53C	70-U	70	70-S	W
237C, 238C			36	
29, 31, 33			60	
HUSQVARNA				
HVA crown grade rifles	HV-U		SR-S	H2
8000 & 9000 Series				8-9
HVA-Carl Gustaf				8-9
JAPANESE ARISKA			E-S④	
KLEINGUENTHER K-15				K5
MARLIN				
1894			M9	
336, 1895, 444			36	
455	FI-U	FM	FI-S	F
39A, 56, 57, 62			36⑥	
80, 81, 88, 89, 98				S2
MAUSER				
M98 Military Com. (1.4-1.42 dia.)	FI-U④	FM	FI-S	98
Small Ring (1.3 dia.) M91-M98 etc.	HV-U④		SR-S	95
1891 Argentine	HV-U④		91-S	
F.N. & Mark X Actions	FI-U	FM	FI-S	F
Mauser 3000 R.H., L.H. Models				M3
MOSSBERGS–Most Models .22 Cal.				S2②
M800				M8
RM-7				RM7
PARKER-HALE Super 1200 Series⑥	FI-U	FM	FI-S	F

(Circled numbers following certain Codes refer to Footnotes)

	Micro Dial	Long 1-Piece Base	Short 1-Piece Base	2-Piece Base
REMINGTON				
M600 & XP-100, M660			XP-1	
M700, 721, 725 long actions	21-U	21	21-S	R
M700, 722, 725 short actions			XP-1	R
M700 L.H. short or long action				R
760, 740, 742			60	
M788				78
510, 511, 512, 513, 514, 521, 550, 560				S2
12, 121, 552, 572, 24, 241			60②	
40X, 40XB				R
RUGER 44 CARBINE				RC2
M77 Round Receiver Long Act.	21-U	21	21-S	R
No.3 Carbine Single Shot				R3
10/22 Carbine				R1
Mini-14 Bridges 1/16" higher than Rec. Ring			14-H②	
Mini-14 Bridge and Rec. Ring same height			14-T②	
No. 1 Varminter			RN-1⑩	
SAVAGE 99–All Models		99		
110, 111, 112 R.H., L.H. short or long				V2
110, 111, 112 R.H. long action only	10-U			V2
SCHULTZ & LARSEN 54, 60, 64, 65, 68				L2
SHILEN DGA Single Shot				SH
SMITH & WESSON Model 1500				R
SPRINGFIELD				
1906-03, A1	S-U	S	S-S	
A3	A-U		A3-S	
STEYR—MANNLICHER Mod. L, SL (metric screws)				SL
Models M, S, ST, 79 (metric screws)				SM
Mannlicher-Schonauer M72 All models (metric screws)				72
THOMPSON HAWKEN			HK	
Renegade			RG	
Seneca			SC	
WEATHERBY F.N. Actions	FI-U	FM	FI-S	F
Mark V R.H., L.H. long action				R
Mark V R.H., long action only	21-U	21	21-S	R
Mark V Varmintmaster .224, .22/250				SV
Vanguard (all calibers)	21-U	21	21-S	R
WINCHESTER				
M70 Std.⑤ M670, 770	70-U	70	70-S	W
M70 Prewar (WWII) M54	54-U			W4
M70 Mag. H&H .300, .375 & N.M.	70-U			W
M70 Mag. .375 (Ser. No. 700,000 UP)	70-U			
M88, M100			88	
69, 72, 75, 74				S2
M52 (specify hole spacing)				T2
07, 61, 63, 77			60②	
BLANK BASES, flat on bottom for special installations	BL-U BL-UWCC	5/16, 3/8, 7/16, 1/2 Full Blanks		B-2⑨

SPECIALS: We can fit many rifles and actions that do not warrant a production run of bases. If you have something unusual, write us about it.

FOOTNOTES (indicated by circled numbers above)

① If clip lips and hump removed.
② Mounted with screws.
③ Rear screw hole matches hole in bridge.
④ File small flat at top of clip lips.
⑤ Serial numbers above 66,350, incl. Win. Magnums.
⑥ May be adapted with minor changes.
⑨ 2-piece available flat on the bottom 3/8" thick.
⑩ Drill and tap two additional holes.

BUEHLER SCOPE MOUNTS

BUEHLER TELESCOPIC SIGHT MOUNTS: By using one of the five basic styles of mount bases, you may position the scope of your choice in the best possible location. The best location is the one that positions the scope in such a way as to give a full field of view when the shooter's face is nestled in a comfortable, natural position against the stock. Scopes vary in eye relief from 3 to 5 inches. Sight adjustment turrets are in different locations. The amount of space available on the scope for the mount varies. Most important of all is the difference in shooters and in the way each one holds a rifle. One of the five styles of mounts will locate your scope in the best position for you. A good gunsmith or experienced sporting goods dealer is a great help in making this choice. All Buehler mount rings fit and are interchangeable with all Buehler bases.

4 AND 5-INCH BASES

SHORT ONE-PIECE BASES

The short one-piece base locates the front ring over the top of the receiver ring about 1 inch aft of the long one-piece base. The rear ring is in about the same location. Thus, ring spacing averages 4 inches. The short base is recommended for shorter scopes, scopes with large and long objective bells, and scopes with turrets near the center of the tube.

LONG ONE-PIECE BASES

This base is made to fit most of the rifles in common use. In most models it has the rings spaced about 5 inches apart with the front ring located *ahead* of the receiver on all bolt action rifles. The long base gives the greatest possible support to the scope and the longest amount of eye relief. It is recommended for long scopes and scopes with adjustment turrets located ahead of center.

One Piece Scope Mount base, 4" or 5" $21.50

TWO-PIECE BASES

Two-piece bases locate the front ring over the receiver ring in the same place as the short one-piece base. The rear ring, however, is over the bridge on bolt action rifles, not ahead of it as is the case with the one-piece bases. The ring spacing averages 4½ inches. Will accommodate scopes described under the *short* one-piece bases. The eye relief is shorter than either one-piece base but adequate for the average installation.

Two-Piece Scope Mount Base............$21.50

ENGRAVED SPLIT RINGS
Beautiful fully engraved
one-inch Split Rings.
Available in Codes 6,7,8.
Per Set $69.50

BUEHLER RINGS FOR BOTH ONE- AND TWO-PIECE MOUNTS

SOLID RINGS   **SPLIT RINGS**

A double split type ring with the added beauty of a smoothly rounded "ball turret top." The steel spacer at the top of each ring not only fills up an unsightly gap, but is made of 16 laminations .002 thick which may be peeled off one or more at a time, thus accurately fitting all scopes up to .010 smaller in size than the normal dimension of the ring.

BUEHLER RINGS AND HEIGHTS:

CODE	SOLID RINGS	Height
3	¾" Solid	.040
6	1" Split (Standard) (Low)	.075
7	1" High Split (Medium)	.136
8	1" Extra High Split (High)	.212
10	26 mm. (Standard)	.125
11	26 mm. High	.200

SOLID & DOUBLE RING

Solid rings, per set	$15.00
Double split rings, codes 6, 7 & 8	28.00
Double split rings, codes 5, 10 and 11	36.00

A SCOPE MOUNT WITH BUILT IN WINDAGE AND ELEVATION

MICRO DIAL MOUNT

Both windage and elevation features are built in. A twist of the fingers dials the elevation desired on a dial clearly marked in minutes (one inch at 100 yards). With ¼ minute clicks. Another twist on the lock wheel directly below the dial securely locks the setting. The windage screws also are calibrated in minutes on both sides. The Micro Dial is designed primarily for all scopes with internal adjustments, such as the Balvar 2½ to 8 (use Code 7 Rings for Balvar), but can be used to advantage with many other scopes—the reticule can always be perfectly centered. The Micro Dial also makes it possible to switch scopes between rifles. The ring spacing is 4 inches.

Micro-Dial Base, Ruger Mini 14	$33.25
Solid Rings Only, per set	$15.00
Split Rings Only, per set, codes 6, 7 & 8	28.00
Special Rings Only, per set, codes 10 and 11	36.00

BURRIS SCOPES

3X-9X FULLFIELD

A versatile scope for big game and varmint hunting. The most popular variable power scope because it fulfills a variety of purposes from long-range varmint shooting to shorter ranges of heavy brush shooting. A rugged, factory sealed hunting scope with a big 15 foot field of view at 9X and a 40 foot field at 3X.

3X-9X FULLFIELD

Plex	$206.95
Crosshair	206.95
Post Crosshair	211.95
1"-3" Dot	216.95

2X-7X FULLFIELD (not illus.)
Field of view: at 7X, 19 ft.; at 2X 50 ft.

Plex	$192.95
Crosshair	192.95
Post Crosshair	197.95

1¾ X-5X FULLFIELD (not illus.)
Field of view: at 5X, 27 ft.; at 1¾ X, 70 ft.

Plex	$173.95
Crosshair	173.95
Post Crosshair	178.95

3X-9X and 2X-7X available with Safari Finish, a Burris-developed low-lustre, high-performance finish, $10.00 extra. Storm Queen Lens Cover for all three scopes, $6.95.

4X-12X

6X-18X

4X-12X FULLFIELD

The ideal scope for long range varmint hunting and testing hand loads. Can also be used for big game hunting.

Crisp resolution, accurate parallax settings and a big field of view are some of the features of this scope. Friction type parallax settings from 50 yards to infinity with positive stop to prevent overturning. Fully sealed to withstand the worst field conditions and designed to deliver years of excellent service.

4X-12X FULLFIELD

Plex	$236.95
Fine Crosshair	236.95
.7"-2." Dot	246.95
Storm Queen Lens Cover	6.95

6X-18X FULLFIELD

This is a versatile scope that can be used for hunting, testing hand loads or shooting bench rest.

This high magnification variable scope features excellent optics, a precise parallax adjustment from 50 yards to infinity, accurate internal adjustments and a rugged, reliable mechanical design that will give years of dependable service.

Fully sealed against moisture and dust.

6X-18X FULLFIELD

Plex	$240.95
Fine Crosshair	240.95
.7"-2." Dot	250.95
Storm Queen Lens Cover	6.95

BURRIS SCOPES

Mini 4X
Mini 6X
Mini 8X
Mini 3X-9X
Mini 2X-7X
2X LER
3X LER

MINI SCOPES WITH POST CROSSHAIR RETICLE:

Mini 4X	$103.95
Mini 6X	111.95
Mini 8X	116.95
Mini 3X-9X	152.95
Mini 2X-7X	146.95

LONG EYE RELIEF SCOPE WITH CROSSHAIR RETICLE:

2X	$ 98.95
3X	106.95
4X	111.95
6X	121.95

BURRIS RINGS, BASES AND MOUNTS

SIGHT-THRU MOUNT
$16.95

**MEDIUM RINGS,
UNIVERSAL DOVETAIL**
$23.95

**SUPREME BASE,
UNIVERSAL DOVETAIL**
$15.95

**MEDIUM EXTENSION FRONT RING,
STANDARD REAR RING,
UNIVERSAL DOVETAIL**
$27.95

**LONG EYE RELIEF
UNIVERSAL BASE (LU)**
$13.95

**TRUMOUNT BASE,
UNIVERSAL DOVETAIL**
$13.95

BUSHNELL RIFLE SCOPES

1.3X BUSHNELL MAGNUM PHANTOM®

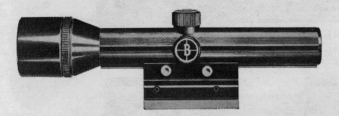

The Phantom increases clarity of sight picture and permits accurate holding on the target because the crosshair and target are on the same plane. The scope has micrometer reticle adjustments, and is made in crosshair reticle only.

This scope was designed specifically for handguns, and has an eye-relief of 7" thru 21" which takes the shooter easily from "two hand" varmint to "arms length," target position. All optics are hard coated.

1.3x all purpose game & target **$64.95**
2.5x varmint & long range **69.95**

BANNER RIFLESCOPES

Banner riflescopes feature the Multi-X® reticle and are available with the Bullet Drop Compensator. The neoprene eye guard combines with the long eye relief to give that extra margin of safety (except in wide angles).

Fixed Powers

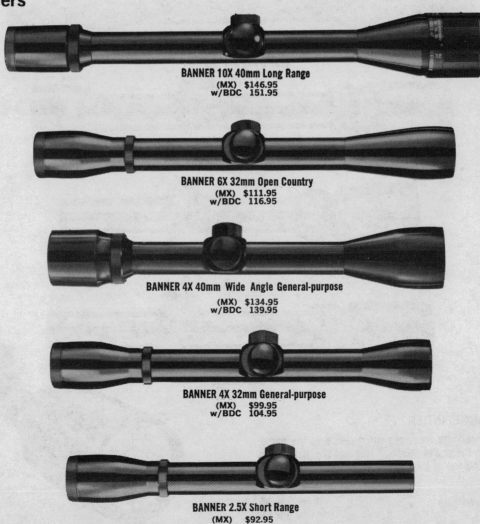

BANNER 10X 40mm Long Range
(MX) $146.95
w/BDC   151.95

BANNER 6X 32mm Open Country
(MX) $111.95
w/BDC   116.95

BANNER 4X 40mm Wide Angle General-purpose
(MX) $134.95
w/BDC   139.95

BANNER 4X 32mm General-purpose
(MX) $99.95
w/BDC   104.95

BANNER 2.5X Short Range
(MX) $92.95

BUSHNELL RIFLE SCOPES

Variable Power

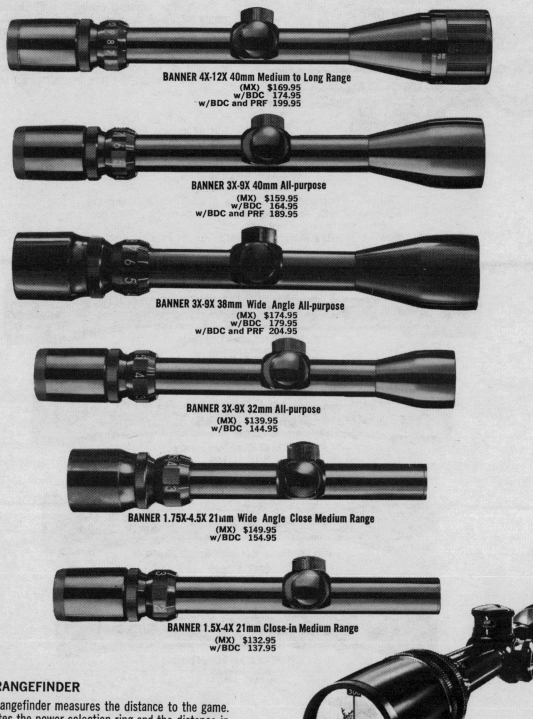

BANNER 4X-12X 40mm Medium to Long Range
(MX) $169.95
w/BDC 174.95
w/BDC and PRF 199.95

BANNER 3X-9X 40mm All-purpose
(MX) $159.95
w/BDC 164.95
w/BDC and PRF 189.95

BANNER 3X-9X 38mm Wide Angle All-purpose
(MX) $174.95
w/BDC 179.95
w/BDC and PRF 204.95

BANNER 3X-9X 32mm All-purpose
(MX) $139.95
w/BDC 144.95

BANNER 1.75X-4.5X 21mm Wide Angle Close Medium Range
(MX) $149.95
w/BDC 154.95

BANNER 1.5X-4X 21mm Close-in Medium Range
(MX) $132.95
w/BDC 137.95

PRISMATIC RANGEFINDER

The Prismatic Rangefinder measures the distance to the game. The hunter rotates the power selection ring and the distance in yards appears at the top of the field of view.

Scopechief $224.95
Banner, 3 models available .... from 189.95
to 204.95

BUSHNELL RIFLE SCOPES

CUSTOM 22

3X-7X All Purpose $42.95
w/BDC 44.95

4X All Purpose $34.95
w/BD 36.95

Custom 3x-7x 22 Variable

Magnifications:	3x	4x	5x	6x	7x
Field at 100 yards (ft.):	33	23	17	15	13.6
Exit pupil (mm):	6	4.5	3.6	3	2.6

Overall length: 10"; overall weight: 6½ oz.; clear aperture of objective lens: 18mm; outside diameter, eyepiece end: 1⅛"; outside diameter, objective end: ⅞"; eye relief: 2¼"-2½"; adjustment scale graduations equal: 1" at 100 yds.

Custom 4x 22
Field at 100 yards (ft.): 28.4; exit pupil: 4.5mm; overall length: 10⁵⁄₁₆"; overall weight: 5¼ oz.; clear aperture of objective lens: 18mm; outside diameter, eyepiece end: 1"; outside diameter, objective end: ⅞"; eye relief: 2½"; adjustment scale graduations equals: 1" at 100 yds.

SCOPECHIEF VI

(MX) **SCOPECHIEF® VI WITH MULTI-X® RETICLE**

With its MULTI-X RETICLE, Bushnell brings to the shooter in one reticle the advantage of the popular crosshairs, plus — post and crosshair, and rangefinding reticles.
The heavier portions of the new reticle lead the eye to the center aiming point providing improved accuracy under dawn and dusk shooting conditions. At the same time, the crosshairs at the center offer superior accuracy under normal shooting conditions for even the small target.

The ScopeChief VI Riflescope also comes with the Bullet Drop Compensator feature (BDC) and provides two scopes in one. BDC's whole purpose is to take the guesswork out of hold-over. Range still has to be estimated as it would with any scope. But BDC gives the hunter a choice: he can simply dial the estimated distance to the target and aim dead-on. Or he can preset it at the distance at which he zeroed in and allow for hold-over as he would with a regular scope. Scopes equipped with BDC come with three calibrated dials to cover normal factory loads. Additionally, there's a fourth dial for wildcat loads.

SCOPECHIEF VI 1.5x-4.5x $159.95
w/BDC 164.95

SCOPECHIEF VI 2.5x-8x $164.95
w/BDC 169.95

SCOPECHIEF VI SPECIFICATION CHART

	VARIABLE POWERS			FIXED POWER
Magnification	3x-9x	2.5x-8x	1.5x-4.5x	4x
Objective Lens Aperture (mm)	40	32	20	32
Field of View @ 100 yards (ft)	3x-35 9x-12.6	2.5x-45 8x-14	1.5x-73.7 4.5x-24.5	29
Weight (oz)	14.3	12.1	9.5	9.3
Length (in)	12.6	11.2	9.6	12
Eye Relief (in)	3x-3.5 9x-3.3	2.5x-3.7 8x-3.3	1.5x-3.5 4.5x-3.5	3.5
Exit Pupil (mm)	3x-13.3 9x-4.4	2.5x-12.8 8x-4	15x-13.3 4.5x-4.4	8
Relative Light Efficiency	3x-267 9x-30	2.5x-247 8x-96	1.5x-267 4.5x-30	96
MX Center CH Width @ 100 yards	3x-.67 9x-.22	2.5x-.8 8x-.25	1.5x-1.3 4.5x-.44	.5
MX Distance Post Tip to Post Tip (in) @ 100 yards	3x-24 9x-8	2.5x-28.8 8x-9	1.5x-48 4.5x-16	18
100 yards (in)	.5			

SCOPECHIEF VI 3x-9x ... $194.95
w/BDC 199.95
w/BDC and PRF 224.95

SCOPECHIEF VI 4x ... $119.95
w/BDC 124.95

BUSHNELL RIFLE SCOPES

BANNER RIFLESCOPE SPECIFICATION CHART

Magnification	BULLET DROP COMPEN-SATOR	Field of view at 100 yds. (ft.)	Weight (oz.)	Length (inches)	Eye distance (inches)	Entrance pupil (mm)	Exit pupil (mm)	Relative Light Efficiency	MX center CH width at 100 yds. (inches)	MX distance post tip to post tip (inches)	Graduation at 100 yds. (inches)
4x-12x 40mm	BDC	29 at 4x 10 at 12x	15.5	13.5	3.2	40	10 at 4x 3.3 at 12x	150 17	0.5 .17	18 6	.75
3x-9x 40mm	BDC	**35 at 3x** **12.6 at 9x**	13	13	3.5	40	13.3 at 3x 4.4 at 9x	267 30	.66 .22	24 8	.75
3x-9x 38mm	BDC	43 at 3x WIDE ANGLE 14.6 at 9x	14	12.1	3	38	12.7 at 3x 4.2 at 9x	241 26.5	.66 .22	24 8	1.0
3x-9x 32mm	BDC	39 at 3x 13 at 9x	11	11.5	3.5	32	10.7 at 3x 3.6 at 9x	171 19	.66 .22	24 8	1.0
1.75x-4.5x 21mm	BDC	71 at 1.75x WIDE ANGLE 27 at 4.5x	11.5	10.2	2.9	21	12 at 1.75x 4.7 at 4.5x	216 33	1.18 .44	45.7 17.8	1.5
1.5x-4x 21mm	BDC	63 at 1.5x 28 at 4x	10.3	10.5	3.5	21	14 at 1.5x 5 at 4x	294 41	1.3 0.5	48 18	1.5
10x 40mm	BDC	12	14.0	14.5	3	40	4	24	0.2	7.2	.66
6x 32mm	BDC	19.5	10.5	13.5	3	32	5.3	42	0.3	12	.66
4x 40mm	BDC	37.3 WIDE ANGLE	12	12.3	3	40	10	150	0.6	21	1.0
4x 32mm	BDC	29	10	12.0	3.5	32	8	96	0.5	18	1.0
2.5x 20mm		45	8	10.9	3.5	20	8	96	0.8	28.8	1.5

BUSHNELL 45° SPACEMASTER®
60mm Prismatic telescope, without eyepiece, 20-year limited warranty, Model 78-2300 .... **$283.00**

TRUSCOPE® POCKET BORE SIGHTER

This pocket-size bore sighter gives you the flexibility to carry it in your shirt or hunting jacket pocket. Rugged plastic case; comes complete with weatherproof cap and adjustable arbor. Fits any bore from 243 to 308 caliber.

TruScope will work on all scopes and most rifles, excluding rifles with tubular magazines, full stocks or extra wide barrels (bull barrels). **Color—gray; weight 3.6 oz.; size 3½" x 2¾" x 1⅛"** **$19.95**

BUSHNELL ARMORED SPORTVIEW® BINOCULARS
Model 13-8330, 8 x 30 wide-angle center focus, one-year limited warranty **$94.00**

GRIFFIN & HOWE

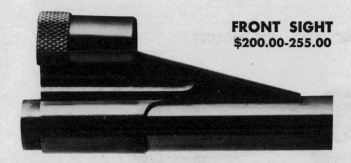

FRONT SIGHT
$200.00-255.00

BARREL BAND
$85.00

The Griffin & Howe type matted ramp front sight is hand-fitted to the barrel by means of a band. When fitted with a gold or ivory bead front sight and removable front sight cover, this sight gives a pleasing appearance and maximum efficiency. Available only on an installed basis.

The forward swing swivel may be attached by a barrel band in front of the forearm or a barrel band through the forearm. Available only on an installed basis.

QUARTER RIB EXPRESS SIGHT
$575.00 and up

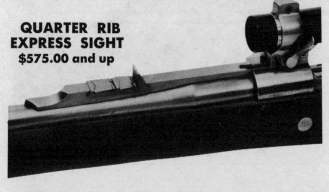

This sight may be made with fixed standing bar and folding leaves sighted in for any range desired. All leaves are marked for distance; the surface is matted with a gold directional line extending down from a wide V. Available only on an installed basis.

Top Ejection Mount   Standard Double-Lever Side Mount

TELESCOPE MOUNT

This mount has a locking cam action and is available for all models of rifles and is obtainable with 1″ or 26mm brackets, there are models to fit both domestic and imported telescopes. The mount holds the scope immovable in its split ring brackets. It can be mounted either low or high enough to enable using the iron sights when the telescope is mounted. It is readily detachable and, when replaced, it will always return to its original position with no scope mount adjustment necessary. It comes in the following models:

Side Mount $110.00
Side Mount, installed 200.00
Top Mount* .... $275.00 and up

*Available only on an installed basis.

Standard double-lever side mount with split rings, for telescopes with built in elevation and windage adjustment; Top ejection mount, for rifles similar to the Winchester 94, where the fired cases extract upwards. This mount, of necessity, has to be fitted in the off-set position; Garand mount, designed for use on the Garand and new M-14 military rifles, is mounted on the left side of the receiver to permit clip loading and top ejection.

JAEGER MOUNTS & ACCESSORIES

JAEGER QUICK DETACHABLE SIDE MOUNT

The Jaeger mount permits removing and attaching scope within a few seconds without the use of any coins or tools. The construction combines light weight with great rigidity. The unique clamping device locks the slide to the base securely, and insures return to zero. All mounts have windage adjustment at the rear ring.

Made for most bolt action rifles as well as Remington 740 & 760, Savage 99, Winchester 88 and other lever action rifles.

Especially well suited for Mannlicher Schoenauer rifles. $135.00

All mounts have split rings and are made in the following ring sizes and heights:

Mod. 20—1″ low
Mod. 21—1″ medium
Mod. 22—1″ high

Low rings for most scopes in low position, medium height rings for large objective scopes in low position, high rings for use of iron sights below scope.

JAEGER

M2 SAFETY

For low mounted scope. Available in two models: For Springfield and Mauser.
$15.00

KAHLES OF AMERICA

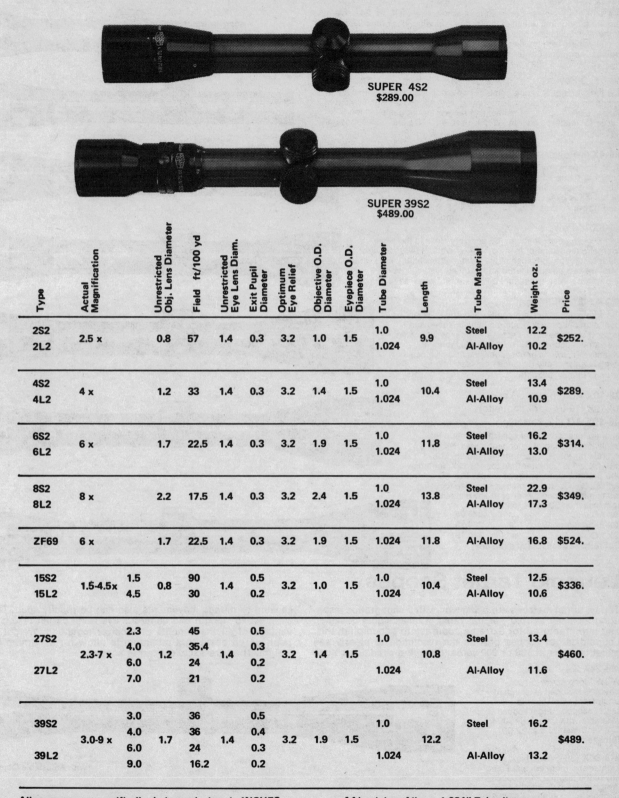

SUPER 4S2
$289.00

SUPER 39S2
$489.00

Type	Actual Magnification	Unrestricted Obj. Lens Diameter	Field ft/100 yd	Unrestricted Eye Lens Diam.	Exit Pupil Diameter	Optimum Eye Relief	Objective O.D. Diameter	Eyepiece O.D. Diameter	Tube Diameter	Length	Tube Material	Weight oz.	Price
2S2	2.5 x	0.8	57	1.4	0.3	3.2	1.0	1.5	1.0	9.9	Steel	12.2	$252.
2L2									1.024		Al-Alloy	10.2	
4S2	4 x	1.2	33	1.4	0.3	3.2	1.4	1.5	1.0	10.4	Steel	13.4	$289.
4L2									1.024		Al-Alloy	10.9	
6S2	6 x	1.7	22.5	1.4	0.3	3.2	1.9	1.5	1.0	11.8	Steel	16.2	$314.
6L2									1.024		Al-Alloy	13.0	
8S2	8 x	2.2	17.5	1.4	0.3	3.2	2.4	1.5	1.0	13.8	Steel	22.9	$349.
8L2									1.024		Al-Alloy	17.3	
ZF69	6 x	1.7	22.5	1.4	0.3	3.2	1.9	1.5	1.024	11.8	Al-Alloy	16.8	$524.
15S2	1.5-4.5x	0.8	1.5 → 90	1.4	0.5	3.2	1.0	1.5	1.0	10.4	Steel	12.5	$336.
15L2			4.5 → 30		0.2				1.024		Al-Alloy	10.6	
27S2	2.3-7 x	1.2	2.3 → 45	1.4	0.5	3.2	1.4	1.5	1.0	10.8	Steel	13.4	$460.
			4.0 → 35,4		0.3								
			6.0 → 24		0.2								
27L2			7.0 → 21		0.2				1.024		Al-Alloy	11.6	
39S2	3.0-9 x	1.7	3.0 → 36	1.4	0.5	3.2	1.9	1.5	1.0	12.2	Steel	16.2	$489.
			4.0 → 36		0.4								
			6.0 → 24		0.3								
39L2			9.0 → 16.2		0.2				1.024		Al-Alloy	13.2	

All measures not specifically designated, given in INCHES   ***Aluminium-Alloy = 1.024″ Tube diameter**

LEUPOLD RIFLE SCOPES

M8-2X (2-Power)

This scope is specially designed for a non-critical (10" to 24") eye relief, permitting mounting ahead of the receiver opening. It is primarily intended for the Winchester 94, and other rifles where a rear-mounted scope would interfere with top ejection. Also used on handguns, such as the popular Thompson Center single-shot pistol. Adjustable eyepiece.
$134.15   M8-2.5X Compact **$143.30**

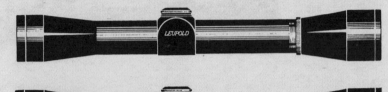

M8-3X (3-Power)

This light, compact scope combines an extra-wide field-of-view for getting on game quickly in heavy cover, with adequate magnification to make it usable up to normal hunting ranges for big game. A good choice for timbered country. Widely used on 375's and 458's for hunting dangerous African game. **$152.50**

M8-4X (4-Power)

Light, compact and modestly priced, this scope has what many big-game hunters consider to be the optimum combination of a generous field-of-view and magnification. In fact, the M8-4X is by far the most popular of all Leupold fixed-power scopes. **$163.70**   M8-4X E.E.R. **$163.70**
M8-4X Compact **$163.70**

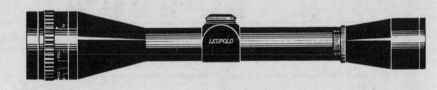

M8-6X (6-Power)

Only slightly larger than our 4X, and very close to the same external dimensions of many other 4-powers, it offers a little better resolution (because of the extra magnification) and therefore can be considered an improved long-range, big-game scope. Also excellent for light varmint rifles. **$173.90**

M8-8X AO (8-Power)

The scope has both the magnification and excellent resolution needed for hunting mountain sheep and goats. It could be excellent for antelope, as well as a fine varmint scope, too. The AO (Adjustable Objective) provides precise focusing and eliminates parallax error at any distance from less than 50 yards to infinity. **$233.05**

M8-10X AO (10-Power) and
M8-10X (10-Power Silhouette)
M8-12X AO (12-Power)

All of these scopes offer superb resolution for precision shooting at extended ranges, thus are naturals for long-range varmint hunting. The M8-10X is 1½" shorter than the M8-12X, for those who prefer a more compact scope. The AO (Adjustable Objective) provides precise focusing and eliminates parallax error at any distance from less than 50 yards to infinity.

10X AO	**$233.05**
10X Silhouette	236.15
12X AO	236.15

Dot reticles available at extra cost

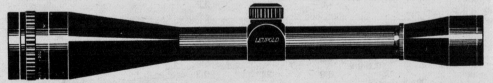

Leupold Target Scopes

Today, target matches are being won with 5-shot groups measuring as small as .100", at 100 yards. It takes sights designed and manufactured for extreme accuracy to accomplish this. Leupold target scopes provide the resolution to clearly see bullet imprints at 100 or 200 yards. Changing conditions, such as wind or mirage movements also can be readily seen. Their compact 15" length and generous eye relief permit taking advantage of all the benefits of receiver mounting. Weight has been pared down to a minimum to allow for maximum rifle weight. They are excellent target scopes.

M8-24X (24-Power)

A 2½" long screw-on sunshade is included as standard equipment with Leupold target scopes. Target scopes available with Crosshair $304.50
Conventional Dots $322.00
Sunshade $8.50

M8-36X (36-Power)

Lighter and more compact than any of the popular 24X scopes. Weight: 15.5 oz.; length: 13.9". Sunshade included.   **$328.95**

*With Adjustable Objective

LEUPOLD RIFLE SCOPES

The "GOLD-MEDALLION" Vari-X III Series

The introduction of Leupold's newest series, the Vari-X III scopes, advances the state-of-the-art of scope technology another step. In scientific terms, these scopes feature a new "Anastigmat" power-changing system that is similar to the sophisticated lens systems in today's finest cameras. Some of the improvements are subtle, such as the extremely accurate internal control system which is the result of both design and time-consuming hand matching of critical mating parts. Others —the sharp, superb-contrast sight picture and the "flatness" of field—are obvious. The total result is a series of tough, dependable scopes that are superior in optical and mechanical quality . . . particularly pleasing to the discriminating sportsman who really appreciates the true value of such quality. Reticles are same apparent size throughout power range, stay centered during elevation and windage adjustments. Fog free, of course.

VARI-X III 1.5x5 (1½ to 5- Power)

This scope's 1.5X-power setting is particularly helpful for hunting whitetail deer, since they often are taken in fairly heavy cover. Also, because a large field-of-view makes it easier to get on target fast, this magnification is often used when hunting dangerous game. **$238.15**

VARI-X III 2.5x8 (2½ to 8-Power)

This scope is excellent for all types of big game and varmint hunting. It offers a versatile range of magnifications—in a compact package (approximately the same size as a Leupold M8-6X). **$268.75**

VARI-X III 3.5x10 AO (3½ to 10-Power)

The extra power and Adjustable Objective feature makes this scope the optimum choice for the year-round shooter who enjoys every phase of shooting, from big game and varmint hunting to target shooting. **$308.55**

VARI-X III 3.5x10 (3½ to 10-Power)
Without Adjustable Objective **$281.00**
With Adjustable Objective **$308.55**

VARI-X III 6.5x20 (6½ to 20-Power)
Features every magnification necessary for varmint hunting and some forms of big game hunting and target shooting. Weight: 16 oz.; length: 14.2″. **$332.15**

The PERFORMANCE-PROVED Vari-X II Series

VARI-X II 1x4 (1 to 4-Power)

This is a good magnification range for a variety of hunting. At the low end, the larger field-of-view makes it easier to make close-in shots on fast-moving game. At the high end, many hunters feel the 4X power is the optimum magnification for big-game hunting. **$200.45**

VARI-X II 2x7 (2 to 7-Power)

A compact scope, no larger than the Leupold M8-4X offering a wide range of power. It can be set at 2X for close ranges in heavy cover, or zoomed to maximum power for shooting or identifying game at longer ranges. **$218.80**

VARI-X II 3x9 and VARI-X II 3x9 AO
(3 to 9-Power)

A wide selection of powers lets you choose the right combination of field-of-view and magnification to fit the particular conditions you are hunting at the time. Many hunters use the 3x9 at the 3X or 4X setting most of the time, cranking up to 9X for positive identification of game or for extremely long shots. The AO (Adjustable Objective) eliminates parallax and permits precise focusing on any object from less than 50 yards to infinity, for extra-sharp definition.
3x9 ... **$235.10**   3x9 AO .. **$264.70**

Dot reticles available at extra cost

LEUPOLD SCOPE SPECIFICATIONS

Scope	M8												Vari-X II						Vari-X III							
													1x4		2x7		3x9/3x9[4]		1.5x5		2.5x8		3.5x10/3.5x10[4]		6.5x20[4]	
		2X[2]	4X[2]	2.5X[3]	4X[3]	3X	4X	6X	8X[4]	10X[4]/10X[5]	12X[4]	24X[4]	36X[4]	1X	4X	2X	7X	3X	9X	1.5X	5X	2.5X	8X	3.5X	10X	6.5X	20X
Actual Magnification		1.8	3.5	2.3	3.6	2.7	4.1	5.9	7.8	10.1	12.2	23.6	36.0	1.6	4.2	2.5	6.6	3.5	9.0	1.5	4.6	2.7	7.9	3.4	9.9	6.5	19.2
Field	Feet[1]	22.0	9.5	42.0	26.5	43.0	30.0	18.0	14.5	10.3	9.0	4.5	3.2	70.5	28.5	42.0	18.0	30.5	13.0	64.0	23.0	36.0	12.7	29.5	10.5	14.8	5.7
	Meter[1]	7.3	3.2	14.0	8.83	14.3	10.0	6.0	4.8	3.3	3.0	1.5	1.1	24.3	9.5	14.0	6.0	10.2	4.3	21.3	7.7	12.0	4.2	9.8	3.5	4.9	1.9
Optimum Eye Relief	inch	12-24		4.3	4.1	3.9	3.9	3.9	3.6	3.5	3.5	3.5	3.4	4.3	3.4	4.1	3.7	4.1	3.5	4.7	3.5	4.2	3.4	3.9	3.4	4.6	3.5
	mm	254-610		109	104	99	99	99	91	89	89	89	86	109	86	104	94	104	89	119	89	107	86	99	86	117	89
Length	inch	8.1	8.4	8.5	10.3	10.3	11.9	11.7	12.9	12.9	14.3	15.2	13.9	9.5		10.9		12.6		9.7		11.6		12.8		14.2	
	mm	206	213	216	262	262	302	297	328	328	363	386	353	241		277		320		246		295		325		361	
Weight	oz.	6.8	7.6	7.4	8.5	8.7	9.3	10.4	13.5	14.0 15.0	14.4	16.0	15.5	9.5		10.9		13.6 15.0		9.8		11.5		14.9		16	
	gram	193	215	210	241	247	264	295	383	397 425	408	454	440	269		309		386 425		278		326		422		454	
Adj. Scale Div. Equal	mins. angle	1	1	1	1	1	1	1	1	½ 1[6]	½	1[7]	1[7]	1		½		½		1		1		½		½	
Max. Adj. Elev. & Wind	inch[1]	100	75	100	100	100	100	80	70	68	60	60	46	50		36		26		80		60		44		40	
	cm[1]	278	208	278	278	278	278	222	194	167	167	167	128	139		100		72		222		167		122		111	

Available with these reticles.

	2X[2]	4X[2]	2.5X[3]	4X[3]	3X	4X	6X	8X[4]	10X	12X[4]	24X[4]	36X[4]	1x4	2x7	3x9	1.5x5	2.5x8	3.5x10	6.5x20
Duplex	✔	✔	✔	✔	✔	✔	✔	✔	✔	✔	—	—	✔	✔	✔	✔	✔	✔	✔
CPC	—	—	—	—	✔	✔	✔	✔	✔	✔	—	—	✔	✔	✔	✔	✔	✔	✔
Crosshair	—	—	—	—	—	—	—	—	—	—	✔	✔	—	—	—	—	—	—	—
Dot	—	—	—	—	✔	✔	✔	✔	✔	✔[8]	✔[9]	—	—	—	—	—	—	—	—

(1) @ 100 Yards/Meters
(2) Extended-eye-relief model
(3) Compact model
(4) With adjustable objective
(5) Silhouette model, with adjustable objective
(6) Silhouette model has 1-Min. divisions, with 1/2-Min. "clicks"
(7) Target models have 1-Min. divisions, with 1/4-Min. "clicks"
(8) 1/8-Min.-0.13" (3.6mm): 1/4-Min.-0.25" (6.9mm)
(9) 0.18 Min.-0.18" (5.0mm)

NOTES: A. All Leupold Scopes have self-centered, non-magnifying reticles. B. Windage and Elevation adjustments are internal. C. Diameter of all scope tubes is 1". D. We reserve the right to make design modifications and other improvements without prior notice. E. Leupold Scopes are manufactured under one or more of the following patents: No. 3,058,391; No. 3,161,716; No. 3,286,352; No. 3,297,389; No. 3,918,791 (Foreign Patents Pending).

Leupold "STD" Standard Mount

... the perfect companion to your Leupold "Golden Ring"® Scope

The Leupold "STD" Mount is carefully machined from cold-rolled bar-stock steel to provide the ultimate in strength and rugged dependability. Featuring generous windage adjustments, precision-fitted dovetail and handsome, streamlined rings, the "STD" offer a firm, slip-free mount for any 1"-tube-diameter scope. Permits quick removal and return of scope. Available for the majority of popular rifles. *Note: "STD" Mount Bases and Rings interchange with Redfield "JR" and "SR" components.*

Leupold "STD" Mount Bases fit these popular models:

Model	Firearm Model
STD BA	Browning Automatic Rifle, all calibers
STD BLA	Browning Lever Action
STD FN	FN Mauser and other rifles using this basic long action
STD HC	Husqvarna Crown Grade, J.C. Higgins (after 1955), Smith & Wesson and HVA-Carl Gustaf
STD 336R	Marlin 36 and 336 Models and Western Field M/740
STD M	Mauser 95 and 98*
STD 700RH-LA	Remington 700, 721, 725 (long actions); Ruger M/77 (round receiver); and Weatherby Mark V
STD 700LH-LA	Remington 700 (left hand, long action)
STD 700RH-SA	Remington 700, 722, 725 and 40X (short actions)
STD 700SA-Spec	Long base for Remington Short Action 700
STD 760	Remington 740, 742, 760
STD 788	Remington 788 (long and extra long actions)
STD RBH	Ruger Black Hawk and other Ruger revolvers having adjustable rear sight*
STD R77	Ruger Model 77 (short or long action) w/Dovetail receiver*
STD RM14	Ruger Mini-14*
STD R1022	Ruger 1022 Rimfire
STD 99R	Savage 99 Lever Action
STD 110RL	Savage 110, 110C, 111 (long action)
STD S&W-K	Smith & Wesson K & N-frame Revolver*
STD S	Springfield 1903*
STD S-Spec	Springfield 1903A3*
STD T/C-C	Thompson/Center Contender
STD T/C-H	Thompson/Center Hawken Rifle
STD 70A	All Winchester Model 70s above # 66,350, not including .300 H&H and .375 H&H Magnums
STD W94	Winchester Model 94 Carbine*

*Drilling and tapping required.

Leupold Reticles

Chart above shows reticles available in each Leupold scope.

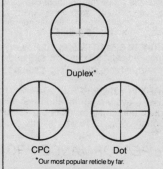

Duplex*

CPC   Dot

*Our most popular reticle by far.

Accessories

50-Ft. Focus Adapter

Allows sharp focusing for 50-foot gallery target shooting.

Sunshade

2½" long. Also acts as support for improvised "mirage tube."

Leupold Extension Ring Sets

Reversible extended front ring, regular rear ring, in 1" LOW or MEDIUM heights.

Special Colt .45 Ring Mount

Permits mounting an M8-2X or M8-4X Extended-Eye-Relief scope on a Colt .45 "Gold Cup" National Match. Cross slots must be cut by a vertical mill.

Handgun Mounts***

STD RBH—For Ruger Blackhawk and other Ruger revolvers with adjustable rear sights.

STD T/C-C — For Thompson/Center Contender.

***Single base, with two dovetail rings.

CHOICE OF 3 RING HEIGHTS — TWO SIZES: 1 in. or 26mm.**

.650"   .770"   .900"

1" LOW   1" MEDIUM 26mm MEDIUM   1" HIGH

**26mm Rings available in medium height only.

LONDON GUN SIGHTS

DOVETAIL BASE FOR EXPRESS SIGHT

Available in large and small sizes. **$20.00**

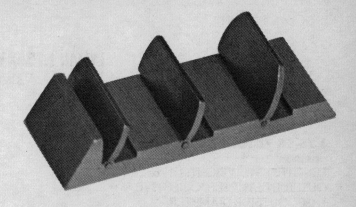

BRITISH STYLE EXPRESS SIGHT

Features one standing sight with three folding leaves. Made of steel. **$60.00**

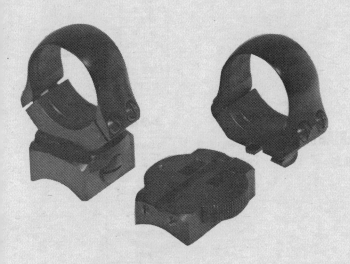

SCOPE MOUNT

Quick-detachable claw-style scope mount for Mauser 98 with 1" rings. Scope pivots to rear to detach. **$150.00**

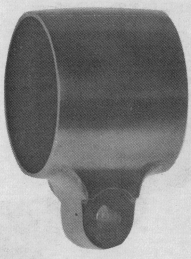

BARREL BAND FOR QUICK-DETACHABLE SWIVELS

Available in two styles: standard quick-detachable swivels (SD) & old-style Winchester quick-detachable swivels (W). Twelve sizes available from .630 through .905; all made of steel.
SD & W $16.00

LYMAN RIFLE SCOPES

LYMAN 1.75-5X VARIABLE SCOPE
$159.95

1.75-5X VARIABLE Specifications
LENGTH: 12¼", WEIGHT: 11⅓ oz.,
OUTSIDE DIAMETER, OBJECTIVE:
1.490", OUTSIDE DIAMETER,
EYEPIECE: 1.540", EYE RELIEF: 3",
FIELD OF VIEW (1.75X): 48' at 100 yds.,
FIELD OF VIEW (5X): 18' at 100 yds.,

1.75-5X

| 4 Center-range |
| Center Wire Covers |
| 2" (1.75X) at 100 yds. |
| 1" (5X) at 100 yds. |
| 4011704 |

LYMAN 2-7X VARIABLE SCOPE
$169.95

2-7X VARIABLE Specifications
LENGTH: 11⅝", WEIGHT: 10½ oz.,
OUTSIDE DIAMETER, OBJECTIVE:
1.500", OUTSIDE DIAMETER,
EYEPIECE: 1.570", EYE RELIEF: 3¼",
FIELD OF VIEW (2X): 49' at 100 yds.,
FIELD OF VIEW (7X): 19' at 100 yds.,

2-7X

| 4 Center-range |
| Center Wire Covers |
| 2" (2X) at 100 yds. |
| 1" (7X) at 100 yds. |
| 4233003 |

LYMAN 3-9X VARIABLE SCOPE
$179.95

3-9X

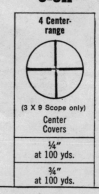

| (3 X 9 Scope only) Center Covers |
| ¼" at 100 yds. |
| ¾" at 100 yds. |

FEATURES
- Full magnification at all power settings. • Full field of view.
- Non-magnifying, constantly centered reticle • Finest quality, fully coated optical system to provide top light transmission.
- Ultra durable anodized exterior surface. • Matted interior surfaces to reduce stray light reflection. • Smooth control power ring, free of projections which could snag on clothing or straps.

3-9 VARIABLE Specifications

Length	12½"
Weight	12 oz.
Tube Dia.	1"
Click Values	½" at 100 yds.
Field of View (3x)	39' at 100 yds.
Field of View (9x)	13' at 100 yds.
Eye Relief (3x)	3½"
Eye Relief (9x)	3½"

LYMAN RIFLE SCOPES

L.W.B.R. SCOPES

20X

The L.W.B.R. series rifle scopes have been designed to fulfill the demanding needs of today's benchrest, high-power, and small-bore rifleman. They are hand-assembled for dependable performance on the range.

SPECIFICATIONS:

20x L.W.B.R.
Length: .... 17"
Weight: .... 16 oz.
Tube Diameter: ....1"
Click Values: .... ⅛" at 100 yds.
Field of View: ....5'6" at 100 yds.
Eye Relief: ....3¼"
Price with standard reticle $339.95

SPECIFICATIONS:

25x L.W.B.R.
Length: .... 17"
Weight: .... 19 oz.
Tube Diameter: ....1"
Click Value: .... ⅛" at 100 yds.
Field of View: ....4'8"
Eye Relief: ....3"
Price with standard reticle $369.95

SILHOUETTE SCOPES

These scopes are designed for metallic silhouette competition and have been carefully constructed to withstand the punishment of adverse hunting conditions, while delivering the unexcelled performance inherent in Lyman's LWBR Target Rifle Scopes. They feature Lyman's exclusive hand-fit optical/mechanical system, parallax-adjustable objective lens with positive recoil-proof locking, Lyman hand-lapped, zero-repeat, windage and elevation systems, and external adjustment controls with zero reset, a feature allowing each user to preselect the zero reference point for his guns and loads.

SPECIFICATIONS:

6X—SL
Length: ....13⅞"
Weight: ....14¼ oz.
Tube Diameter: ....1"
Click Value : .... ½" at 100 yds.

Field of View: ....20' at 100 yds.
Price with external adjustments: $229.95

8X—SL
Length: ....14⅝"
Weight: ....15¼ oz.

Tube Diameter: ....1"
Click Values: .... ⅓" at 100 yds.

Field of View: ....14' at 100 yds.
Price with external adjustments: $239.95

10X—SL
Length: ....15⅜"
Weight: ....15¼ oz.
Tube Diameter: ....1"
Click Values: .... ⅓" at 100 yds.

Field of View: ....12' at 100 yds.
Price with external adjustments: $249.95

LYMAN RECEIVER SIGHTS

LYMAN 57 RECEIVER SIGHT: An unobtrusive micrometer receiver sight for hunting or target shooting with sporter, target or military rifle.

This sight is equipped with a push-button quick-release slide that makes it ideal for alternating use on a scope-equipped rifle.

Fully adjustable with audible ¼-minute clicks for windage and elevation. Choice of coin-slotted stayset knobs for hunting or finger operated target knobs.

Slide adjustments are equipped with precision scales to aid in pre-setting sights for specific ranges or wind conditions. Slide furnished with elevation stop screw that facilitates return to "zero" if removed and re-attached.

Slide operates in dovetail channel.

No. 57 Receiver Sight, complete **$39.95**

LYMAN 66 RECEIVER SIGHT: Similar in design and construction to the No. 57 receiver sight, the model 66 was designed specifically for autoloading, pump-action and lever-action rifles. Ideally suited for use on the new Ruger .44 Carbine.

Features include ¼-minute click adjustments for windage and elevation, quick release slide, and elevation stop screw for return to "zero" if detached.

Push button release features of slide facilitates speedy removal and re-attachment.

May be had with choice of coin-slotted stayset hunting knobs or target knobs.

Like the model 48 and 57 this sight is furnished with settings scales for easy reference.

No. 66 Receiver Sight, complete **$39.95**

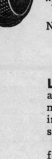

NO. 57 SIGHT

NO. 66 SIGHT

TARGET FRONT SIGHTS

SIGHT HEIGHT*

17AHB	.360″	17AMI	.445″	17AUG	.532″
17AHI	.360″	17ASF	.500″		

*From bottom of dovetail to center of aperture.

SERIES 17A TARGET FRONTS

Teamed with a Lyman receiver sight, these low silhouette front sights provide precise, X-ring accuracy on the range. Designed for use with dovetail slot mounting, they are supplied with seven interchangeable inserts (see descriptions below) that are locked into place with a threaded cap.

Price:
Series 17A Target Front Sight
Complete with Inserts....**$15.95**

INSERTS FOR USE WITH SERIES 17A SIGHTS

Set includes: two post type inserts (.100″ and .050″ wide), five aperture type inserts (1 plastic .120″ hole insert and four steel inserts with .070″, .093″, .110″, and .120″ holes).

Price: Complete Set of Inserts for Series 17A or 77 Sights............. **$5.95**

LYMAN HUNTING FRONT SIGHTS

Despite the exceptionally sharp definition provided by a fine aperture receiver sight, an equally fine front sight is necessary for consistently accurate shooting—particularly in extreme glare and overcast in the field. Lyman ivory bead front sights are the ideal field front sights. They present a flat optical surface that's equally illuminated by bright or dull light, and they keep their "color" under all light conditions. The Lyman ivory bead front sight is the perfect teammate for your favorite Lyman receiver sight, and will give you a reliable, sharply defined, glareless aiming surface, even under the worst conditions. You can fit a readily adaptable Lyman bead front sight to your rifle in minutes.

A—WIDTH   F—WIDTH

These illustrations show the size and appearance difference between the two standard base widths. In general, the outside diameter of the barrel determines the width of the base to be used. "A" width is used with most ramps.

DOVETAIL TYPE FRONT SIGHTS (first letter following number of sight gives the height, the second letter the width)

SIGHT SELECTION CHART

MODELS SUPPLIED 1/16" bead	Height Inches	Width Inches
31BA	.240	11/32
31CA	.290	11/32
3CF	.290	17/32
31FA	.330	11/32
3FF	.330	17/32
31GA	.345	11/32
3GF	.345	17/32
31HA	.360	11/32
3HF	.360	17/32
31JA	.390	11/32
3JF	.390	17/32
31KA	.410	11/32
3KF	.410	17/32
31MA	.445	11/32
3MF	.445	17/32
31SA	.500	11/32
3SF	.500	17/32
31VA	.560	11/32
3VF	.560	17/32

No. 31

O   1/16" BEAD

NO. 31 FRONT SIGHT . . . This sight is designed to be used on ramps. Standard 3/8" dovetail. Ivory bead. See Sight Selection Chart.

Price: No. 31 Front Sight **$6.95**

No. 3

O   1/16" BEAD

NO. 3 FRONT SIGHT . . . This sight is mounted directly in the barrel dovetail. 3/8" dovetail is standard. Ivory bead. See Sight Selection Chart.

Price: No. 3 Front Sight **$6.95**

RAMP FRONT SIGHTS

18E

18A   18C

NO. 18 SCREW-ON TYPE RAMP . . . The screw-on ramp is designed to be secured with a heavy 8-40 screw (it may be brazed on if desired). Screw-on ramps are ruggedly built and extremely versatile. They use A width front sights, and are available in the following heights:

18A — Low Ramp: .100" from top of barrel to bottom of dovetail.
18C — Medium Ramp: .250" from top of barrel to bottom of dovetail.
18E — High Ramp: .350" from top of barrel to bottom of dovetail.

No. 18 Screw-On Ramp Less Sight **$9.95**

LYMAN SIGHTS

LEAF SIGHTS

NO. 16 FOLDING LEAF SIGHT... Designed primarily as open rear sights with adjustable elevation, leaf sights make excellent auxiliary sights for scope-mounted rifles. They fold close to the barrel when not in use, and they can be installed and left on the rifle without interfering with scope or mount. Two lock screws hold the elevation blade adjustments firmly in place. A sight of this type could save the day if the scope becomes damaged through rough handling. Leaf sights are available in the following heights:

16A —.400″ high; elevates to .500″.
16B —.345″ high; elevates to .445″.
16C —.500″ high; elevates to .600″.

For installation on rifles without a dovetail slot, use Lyman No. 25 Base.

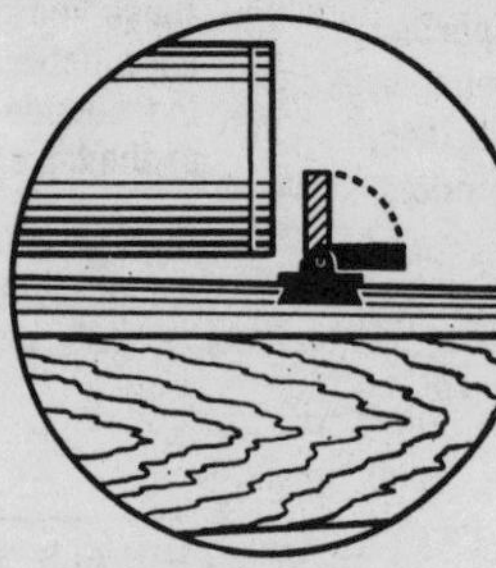

SIGHT FOLDS TO CLEAR SCOPE

GRADUATED BLADE ELEVATES BY SLIDING IN ELONGATED SCREW HOLES

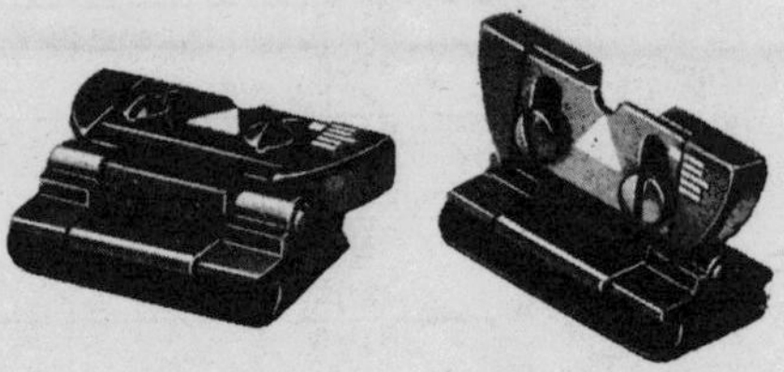

A "Patridge" type blade for the No. 16A Folding Leaf Sight is offered as an auxiliary blade.

Price:
No. 16 Folding Leaf Sight..... **$8.95**

BASES

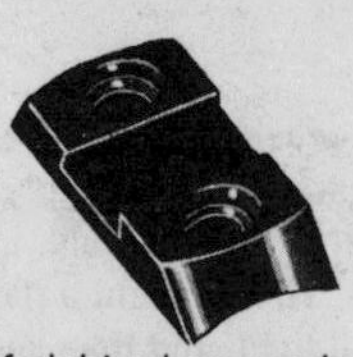

NO. 25 BASES

Permit the installation of dovetail rear sights such as Lyman 16 leaf sight on rifles that do not have dovetail cut in barrel. They also supply a higher line of sight when needed. The No. 25 Base is mounted by drilling and tapping the barrel for two 6-48 screws. Screws are supplied with base.

Price: No. 25 Base **$6.50**

STANDARD BASES	HEIGHT FROM TOP OF BARREL to BOTTOM of DOVETAIL	BARREL RADIUS
25A-Base (Low)	.025—	.875 or larger
25C-Base (High)	.125—	.875 or larger
SPECIAL BASES		
25B-Base Fits factory screw holes on Remington 740, 742, 760, 725 & replaces factory rear	.125—	.875 or larger
25D-Base For small diameter barrels, Note Radius	.025—	For Barrels under .875 dia.

NOTE: For gunsmith use — 25A, C and D bases are also available in the white (unblued), and without screw holes. Heights and radii as above. **Price: $1.25**

NO. 12 SLOT BLANKS

These Blanks fill the standard ⅜″ rear barrel dovetail when a receiver sight is installed. They are also available for front sight dovetails and ramps when a scope is being used. Three lengths are available, all fit standard ⅜″ dovetails.

No. 12S (⅜″ x ⅝″ long) for standard rear barrel slots.
No. 12SS (⅜″ x 9⁄16″ long) for standard front sight slots and some rear slots in narrow barrels.
No. 12SF (⅜″ x 11⁄32″ long) this blank has square ends and is intended for use in ramps.

Price: (all sizes) **$2.95**

SHOTGUN SIGHTS

SHOTGUN SIGHTS .... Lyman shotgun sights are available for all shotguns. Equipped with oversized ivory beads that give perfect definition on either bright, or dull days, they are easy to see under any light conditions. They quickly catch your eye on fast upland targets, and point out the lead on long passing shots. Lyman shotgun sights are available with WHITE or RED bead, and can be fitted to your gun in minutes.

NO. 10 FRONT SIGHT (Press Fit) for use on double barrel, or ribbed single barrel guns.
Sight **$2.95**

NO. 10D FRONT SIGHT (Screw Fit) for use on non-ribbed single barrel guns. These sights are supplied with a wrench. Sight & Wrench **$3.95**

NO. 11 MIDDLE SIGHT (Press Fit) This small middle sight is intended for use on double barrel and ribbed single barrel guns. Sight **$2.95**

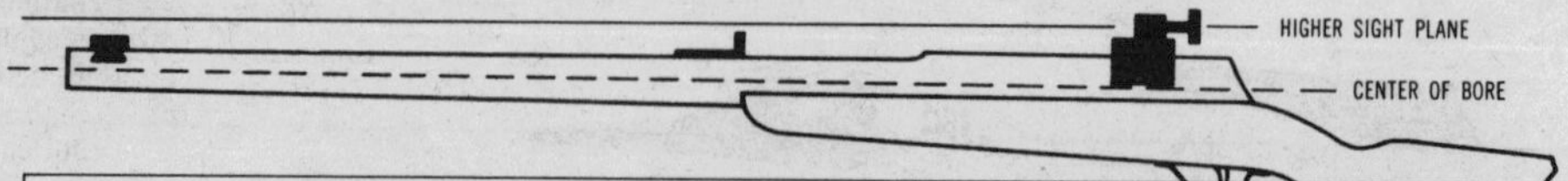

When you replace an open rear sight with a receiver sight, it is usually necessary to install a higher front sight, to compensate for the higher plane of the new receiver sight. The table below shows the increase in front sight height that's required to compensate for a given error at 100 yards.

AMOUNT OF ADJUSTMENT NECESSARY TO CORRECT FRONT SIGHT ERROR

DISTANCE BETWEEN FRONT AND. REAR SIGHTS		14″	15″	16″	17″	18″	19″	20″	21″	22″	23″	24″	25″	26″	27″	28″	29″	30″	31″	32″	33″	34″
Amount of Error at 100 Yards Given in Inches	1	.0038	.0041	.0044	.0047	.0050	.0053	.0055	.0058	.0061	.0064	.0066	.0069	.0072	.0074	.0077	.0080	.0082	.0085	.0088	.0091	.0093
	2	.0078	.0083	.0089	.0094	.0100	.0105	.0111	.0116	.0122	.0127	.0133	.0138	.0144	.0149	.0155	.0160	.0156	.0171	.0177	.0182	.0188
	3	.0117	.0125	.0133	.0142	.0150	.0159	.0167	.0175	.0184	.0192	.0201	.0209	.0217	.0226	.0234	.0243	.0251	.0259	.0268	.0276	.0285
	4	.0155	.0167	.0178	.0189	.0200	.0211	.0222	.0234	.0244	.0255	.0266	.0278	.0289	.0300	.0311	.0322	.0333	.0344	.0355	.0366	.0377
	5	.0194	.0208	.0222	.0236	.0250	.0264	.0278	.0292	.0306	.0319	.0333	.0347	.0361	.0375	.0389	.0403	.0417	.0431	.0445	.0458	.0472
	6	.0233	.0250	.0267	.0283	.0300	.0317	.0333	.0350	.0367	.0384	.0400	.0417	.0434	.0450	.0467	.0484	.0500	.0517	.0534	.0551	.0567

EXAMPLE: Suppose your rifle has a 27 inch sight radius, and shoots 4 inches high at 100 yards, with the receiver sight adjusted as low as possible. The 27 inch column shows that the correction for a 4 inch error is .0300 inch. This correction is added to the over-all height of the front sight (including dovetail). Use a micrometer or similar accurate device to measure sight height. Thus, if your original sight measured .360 inch, it should be replaced with a sight .390 inch high, such as a J height sight.

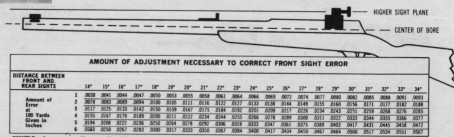

MERIT SHOOTING AIDS

MERIT IRIS SHUTTER MASTER TARGET DISC

WITH

FLEXIBLE NEOPRENE LIGHT SHIELD

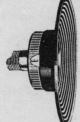

PATENT PENDING

May be cut to size

Particularly adapted for use with extension, telescope height and tang sights . . .

- The 1½" in diameter flexible neoprene light shield is permanently attached to the eye cup which is replacable by removing three screws. The shield is concentrically ribbed on its concave face for cutting to suitable size. It is more advantageous than a large metal disc since it protects the sighting equipment in case the disc is accidentally bumped.

- The Master Target Disc may be used on all sights having clearance for a disc 7/16" thick and 3/4" or larger in diameter.

Master Disc . . .	$41.25
MERIT DELUX Master Disc . . .	51.25
Replacement Shield	7.50
Delux Replacement Shield and Steel Cup	8.75

THE MERIT LENS DISC is made with any of the No. 3 Series shanks. The body of the Standard Lens Disc is 7/16" thick . . . the Master Target Lens Disc is ¾" thick . . . Outside diameters are the same as shown for No. 3 Series and Master Target Discs. The Merit Lens Disc is properly cushioned to absorb recoil shock.

MERIT DELUX No. 3 Lens Disc	$52.50
MERIT DELUX Master Lens Disc . . .	61.25

MERIT No. 4SS—Outside diameter of disc ½". Shank 5/16" long. Disc thickness ¼".   **$33.75**

MERIT No. 4LS—Outside diameter of disc ½". Shank 11/32" long. Disc thickness ¼".   **33.75**

MERIT No. 4ELS—Outside diameter of disc ½". Shank ½" long. Disc thickness ¼".   **33.75**

SIGHT CHART

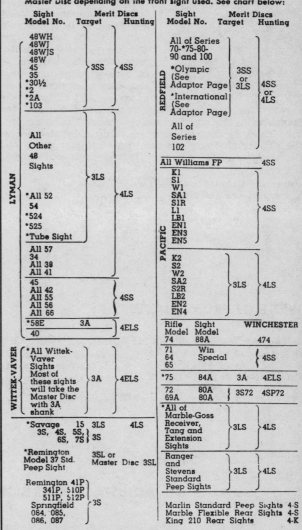

Popular Peep Sights and the proper Merit Discs to fit them. The Merit Master Target Disc may be had with any of the No. 3 series shanks. All of the sights marked ★ will take the Master Disc depending on the front sight used. See chart below:

	Sight Model No.	Target	Hunting
LYMAN	48WH, 48WJ, 48WJS, 48W, 45, 35, ★30½, ★2, ★2A, ★103	3SS	4SS
	All Other 48 Sights	3LS	
	★All 52, 54, ★524, ★525, ★Tube Sight		4LS
	All 57, 34, All 38, All 41		
	45, All 42, All 55, All 56, All 66		4SS
	★58E	3A	4ELS
	40		
WITTEK-VAVER	★All Wittek-Vaver Sights Most of these sights will take the Master Disc with 3A shank	3A	4ELS
	★Savage 3S, 4S, 5S, 6S, 7S — 15	3LS / 3S	4LS
	★Remington Model 37 Std. Peep Sight	3SL or Master Disc 3SL	
	Remington 41P, 341P, 510P, 511P, 512P Springfield 084, 085, 086, 087	3S	

	Sight Model No.	Target	Hunting
REDFIELD	All of Series 70-★75-80-90 and 100	3SS	4SS or 4LS
	★Olympic (See Adaptor Page)	3SS or 3LS	
	★International (See Adaptor Page)		
	All of Series 102		
	All Williams FP		4SS
PACIFIC	K1, S1, W1, SA1, S1R, L1, LB1, EN1, EN3, EN5		4SS
	K2, S2, W2, SA2, S2R, LB2, EN2, EN4	3LS	4LS

Rifle Model	Sight Model	WINCHESTER	
74	88A	474	
71, 64, 65	Win Special	4SS	
★75	84A	3A	4ELS
72, 69A	80A, 80A	3S72	4SP72

	Target	Hunting
★All of Marble-Goss Receiver, Tang and Extension Sights	3LS	4LS
Ranger and Stevens Standard Peep Sights	3LS	4LS

Marlin Standard Peep Sights	4-S
Marble Flexible Rear Sights	4-S
King 210 Rear Sights	4-K

THE MERIT OPTICAL ATTACHMENT WITH APERTURE IS THE ANSWER TO A SHOOTER'S PROBLEM WHEN THE EYESIGHT IS IMPAIRED.

(1) concentrates and sharpens the vision by increasing the focal depth of the eye, making pistol or rifle sights stand out sharp and clear; (2) Cuts out objectionable side lights; (3) Helps the shooter to take the same position for each shot. (This is a very vital factor in accurate shooting;) (4) Gives instant and easy choice of just the right aperture suiting your own eye and particular conditions at time of shooting.

Delux Optical Attachment Price: **$49.50**
The Delux model has swinging arm feature so that the shooter can swing the aperture from the line of vision when not shooting.
Replacement suction cup—Price **$7.00**

MICRO SIGHTS FOR HANDGUNS

The Micro Sight is small and compact. The sight is attached to models with dovetail slot for rear and removable front sights in the same manner as the factory sight. The rear sight has positive self-locking click adjustments in both windage and elevation. Each click changes point of impact ½" at twenty-five yards. Once set—the sight is constant and will not move from recoil. The sighting radius is raised, allowing for a deep notch in the rear aperture. This added depth gives the shooter sharper definition and eliminates glare. It is necessary to install a higher front sight to conform with the rear.

Front sight blades are available in : ⅛"
The styles are plain post or quick-draw.

ADJUSTABLE REAR SIGHTS with BLADE FRONT SIGHTS for the following:

1P Standard Adj. sights for Colt 45 ACP & 45 Commander; and Star Model "B" 9m/m	
2P Standard Adj. sights for Colt 38 Super, 9 MM & 38 Commander	
3P Low Mount Adj. sights for Colt 45 ACP and 45 Commander	
4P Low Mount Adj. sights for Colt 38 Super, 9 MM & 38 Commander	
5P Low Mount Adj. sights for Colt 22 Service Ace & 22/45 Conversion unit	
15P Colt M. T. Woodsman, Postwar	
16P Colt Target Woodsman, Postwar	
17P Colt M. T. Woodsman, Prewar	$28.50
19P Colt 22 Officers Model Match & Officers Model Special	
20P Colt 38 Officers Model Match & Officers Model Special	
23P Ruger 22 Standard Sport Model	
27P Browning 9MM Hi-Power LOW MT	

Adjustable Micro Rear only	$24.00
Micro Front Blade only	6.00
MICRO front ramp only—less blade	8.00
MICRO blade only for front ramp	6.00
MICRO-TITE barrel bushing for Colt 45 Govt Model	8.50
MICRO barrel bushing wrench	1.75
MICRO insert only for rear sight	1.75
MICRO white outline rear insert	6.50

WIDTH OF FRONT BLADES 1/8"

INTERCHANGEABILITY OF MICRO ADJUSTABLE REAR SIGHTS

Group #1—1P 2P QR RR 28P 3R   Group #6—BR CR DR ER FR GR
        4R 5R 7R 29P   HR IR JR KR LR MR
Group #2—3P 4P 5P 16P 17P 19P   NR OR PR ZR 8R 9R
        20P 27P 25P   Group #7—VR WR

TYPES OF MICRO FRONT BLADE SIGHTS

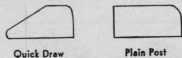

Quick Draw   Plain Post

INTERCHANGEABILITY OF MICRO FRONT SIGHTS
    Group #6—BR FR
    Group #7—ER HR

ADJUSTABLE REAR SIGHTS WITH RAMP FRONT SIGHTS
ALL $35.00

AR	Ruger Single Six	NR	Great Western 45
BR	Smith & Wesson 38 Military Police	OR	Colt New Service 38
CR	Colt 38 Official Police	PR	Colt New Service 45
DR	Colt 22 Official Police	QR	Colt Challenger 22
ER	Smith & Wesson 1917 45 Revolver	RR	Colt Sport Model Woodsman (Prewar)
FR	Smith & Wesson 38/44	VR	Supermatic Trophy & Citation
GR	Smith & Wesson 44 Special	WR	Supermatic Tournament
HR	Smith & Wesson 1950 45	ZR	Colt Scout 22
IR	Colt Single Action 22	3R	Colt Huntsman
JR	Colt Single Action 38	4R	Colt Targetsman
KR	Colt Single Action 45	5R	Colt Navy Cap & Ball
LR	Great Western 22	7R	Navy Arms 44 Rem Cap & Ball
MR	Great Western 38	8R	Hy Hunter Six Shooter 357

(Ramp style not made for 45 Govt)

PACHMAYR SCOPE MOUNTS

(FOR 1-INCH & 26 M/M SCOPES)

PACHMAYR LO-SWING® SCOPE MOUNT

Combines two important advantages in one mount. Provides instant use of open sights and a scope mounted as low as possible on your rifle. Don't let fogged lenses or a damaged scope spoil your chance for a kill. Guaranteed to maintain zero alignment no matter how many times removed or swung to the side. Side mount $30.00 top mount $35.00

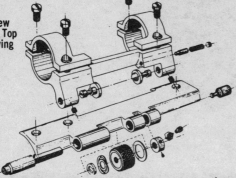

Exploded view of Lo-Swing Top Mount showing exclusive Pachmayr spherical eccentric bearing windage & elevation adjustment principle.

TOP MOUNTS   Available for: $55.00

MAKE OF GUN	GUN MODELS	MOUNT NO.
Remington	700, 721, 725 (long actions)	R700 RT
	700, 722, 725 (short actions)	R700 RT
	700 L.H. (long action)	R700 L.H.RT
	700 L.H. (short action)	R700 L.H. ST
	720, 30	R30T
	600	R600T
	(**660)	R600T
	740	
	742 Ser. 184, 499 & below	R7 40T
	742 Ser. 184, 500 & up	R742BDLT
	760 Ser. 443, 499 & below	R740T
	760 Ser. 443, 500 & up	R742 BDLT
	788 short action	R788S-T
	788 long action	R788L-T
	788 extra long action	R788X-T
	141	R141-T
Winchester	Win. 70 - 670, 770 All calibers, except .300 & .375 H&H Mag., above Serial No. 66,350	W 70T
	Win. 70 .300 / .375 H&H Mag., above Serial No. 700,000	W70MT
	Win. 70 Target	W70 TGT
	Win. 70 .300 & .375 H&H Mag., between Serial Nos. 66,350 and 700,000	W70 TGT
	Win. 70 All Cals. except .300 & .375 H&H Mag., below Serial No. 66,350	W70 T
	Win. 70 .300 & .375 H&H Mag., below Serial No. 66,350	W70 TGT
	88 & 100	W-88T
Savage	99	S-99T
	110 R.H. Long Action	S-110 RHT
	110 L.H. Long Action	S-110 LHT
	110 short action R.H	S-110 RHST
	110 short action L.H	S-110 LHST
	**24V	S-24VT
Sako	Finnbear	SK-FIT
	Forester	SK-FOT
	Vixen	SK-VT
Marlin	**336, 1895, 44	M-336T
	**1894	M-1894T
Mauser	98 (large ring long action)	MR-T
	Yugoslav 1924 (lrg. Rg. sht. act.)	YU-T
	Kar 98 (sm. ring, long action)	KA-T
	Mexican (sm. ring, short action)	Mex-T
	FN (std. FN action)	FN-T
	Santa Fe (FN action spec. hole spacing)	MSF-T
	66 (dovetail receiver)	MR66T
	2000	MR2000T
	4000	M-4000T

**Due to special stop pin lengths, these bases should be ordered only with matching loop

MAKE OF GUN	GUN MODELS	MOUNT NO.
Mossberg	800	MO-800T
	810	MO-810T
	472	MO-472T
Krico	Varmint	KRICO-T
Husqvarna	Short action (small ring)	HV-SRT
	Long action (large ring)	HV-T
Springfield	03-06	SPR-03T
	03/A3	SPR-A3T
Enfield	Eddystone	EN-T
Schultz & Larsen	Regular	SLR-T
	Magnum	SLM-T
Ruger	44	R-44T
	10/22	R-22T
	M-77 RS long (dovetail)	R77-RS-LT
	M-77 RS short (dovetail)	R77-RS-ST
	M-77 ST long (round)	R77-ST-LT
	No. 1	R. No. 1T
Browning Sako	222, 222 Magnum	B469-T
	243, 308, 22-250	B479-T
Browning	Safari	FN-T
	Short Action	BRO-S-T
	Semi-auto. rifle	BRO-SAT
	Lever action	BRO-LAT
BSA Monarch	Dovetail rec. long action	BSA-TR
	Dovetail rec. short action	BSA-TS
	Round Receiver Long Action	R 700 RT
	Round Receiver Short Action	R 700 ST
Weatherby	Mark V, left hand Vangard, LH	WLH-T
	Mark V, Vangard, RH	R700 RT
Parker Hale Harrington	1200 & P1200	FN-T
Richardson	300 & 301	FN-T
Smith & Wesson	A, B, C, D, E.	HV-SRT
Ranger Arms	Texas Maverick	RA-TMV
	Texas Magnum 458	RA-458-T
	Texas Magnum 375	RA-375-T
Interarms	Mark X	FN-T
Voere Shikar		VST

SIDE MOUNTS   Available for: $55.00

MAKE OF GUN	GUN MODELS	MOUNT NO.
Winchester	54, 70	W-70
	64, 94, Rem. 121, 241	W-94
	Model 12 shotgun	W-12
	88, 100	W-88
Remington	Enfield 30S, R720	Enf
	8, 81	R-81
	141, 14	R-14
	721, 722, 725 and 700 series	R-721
	740, 760, 742	R-740
	Shotgun 1100	R-1100
	870	R-1100
Savage	40, 45 and Ariska, Husqvarna Cr., Swedish Mauser	S-40
	20, Japanese 25	S-20
	99	S-99
	340, 342, Sako .222	S-340
	24 DL	S-24 DL
Springfield	1903, A3, 1922, Sedley-Newton	Spr.
Stevens	325C, 322 Sako L 46	S-325C
Marlin	36A, 336	M-36
	39A	M-39
Mauser	93	S-40
	98	MR
	FN 1949 Auto	FN 49A
	All FN Bolt Actions	MR
Mauser Carbine	Carbine Brno	MC
Mannlicher-Schoenauer	1950 or later	MS
Krag..		K
Garand Brng. Std.	Military auto 30/06, 308	M-1
Rem. 11	Shotguns	B-R
Military	*Carbine 30M1	M-1 Carbine
Lee Enfield	SMLE No. 1, Mk. 1, 2, 3	L-Enf A
	SMLE No. 4 Mk.1	L-Enf B
Ithaca	37	W-12
Ruger	Mini. 14	Ru-14

*Due to near vertical shell ejection, it is recommended that these bases be used with a left hand loop and a crosshair reticle scope.

PALMA METALLIC TARGET RECEIVER SIGHT

Replaces the International Match and Olympic receiver sights used by competitive shooters. Elevation staff and sighting disc block feature dovetail construction for precise, stable travel and provide a means for the shooter to correct for longtime wear. Insert in sighting disc block accepts either American or European thread. Adapter for front of sighting disc block. Optional to accept European light filters, etc. forward of the sighting disc block. Windage and elevation adjustments are ¼ MOA and can be adjusted for either a hard or soft feel by the shoulder. Repeatability error is limited to .001" per click (.012 MOA, or ⅛" @ 100 yards). Averages between .0002" to .0004".
Palma Metallic Target Receiver Sight **$173.60**

REDFIELD SURE-X DISC

SURE-X DISC

Selective aperture sizes from .028" to .042" in increments of .002". Each size is clearly stamped on the aperture wheel. Selection of the proper aperture for the prevailing light conditions provides an optimum sight picture with good contrast and crisp, round front sight aperture.
Sure-X Disc **$18.30**

REDFIELD TARGET SIGHTS

Target Sight Bases and Accessories

Redfield offers you a complete line of bases and accessories to complement the target sights shown on the previous pages. All are manufactured to the most exacting of specifications in order to provide you with the most professional and dependable sighting equipment available.

INTERNATIONAL SMALLBORE FRONT

This improved model of an old favorite allows for easy drop-in insertion of eared Skeleton (Polycarbonate) inserts, with inner sleeve which eliminates possibility of light leakage. Round, optically clear, plastic inserts accommodated with speed and ease **$46.60**

INTERNATIONAL BIG BORE FRONT

For .30 caliber shooting, same as small bore except tube shortened to approximately 2″, eyepiece same size as tube to provide greatest possible rapid fire visibility. **$46.60**
All Big Bore Fronts are within I.S.U. maximum dimension limits.

Index of Front Sight Bases

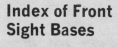

(S)

2-Step

Special base for Small Bore shooting. Height given is for the lower or 100 yard step. 50 yard step is .054″ higher. Fast, convenient, saves wear on your Receiver Sight.

S-Type $5.65-9.25
2-Step $6.95-11.70

GLOBE FRONT SIGHTS

1″ long, ½″ diam. Inserts held firmly by simple locking sleeve, which loosens but doesn't have to be removed when changing inserts.

GLOBE NO.	HEIGHT "A"	BASE	PRICE W/INSERTS
63	.483″	Uses Standard Front Base (Separate $2.95)	**$29.30**
64	.733″	Standard Front Base (separate $2.95)	**$34.50**
65	.316″	Integral male dovetail	**$23.90**
65NB	.316″	base drives into dovetail	**$22.80**
66	.595″	on barrel 66 for Spring	**$26.20**
68	.441″	field dovetail 65, 68 for	**$22.10**

Extra inserts for Globe Front Set .... **$ 6.30**

Index of Receiver Sight Bases

Receiver Sight Bases

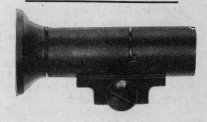

#75

Olympic and International

This base provides a series of threaded attachment holes to permit rear sight mounting locations for any shooting position. **$15.20-19.00**

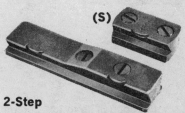

OLYMPIC DETACHABLE FRONT

Admits a greater volume of light, perfectly controlled by shading flanges. Set of 10 easy-change inserts includes five steel apertures, one post, four transparent apertures. Transparent available in clear, green or amber, with or without crosslines. Amber with crosslines will be furnished unless otherwise requested.

Olympic Front w/Inserts
(no base) **$43.60**
Extra Set Olympic Inserts ... **10.00**

REDFIELD RINGS AND BASES

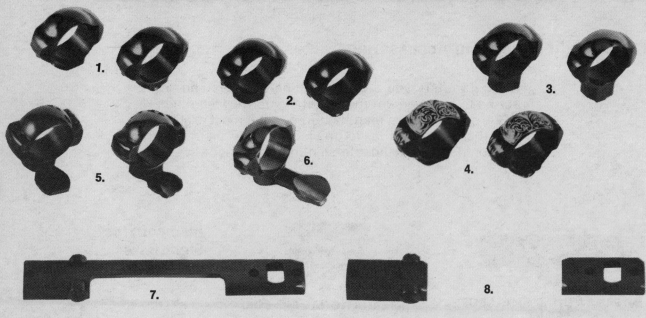

1. **Low.** For scopes up to 1.6" objective diameter. Height 0.152" **$26.50**
2. **Medium.** For scopes with 1.6" to 1.9" objective diameter. Height 0.272" **$26.50**
3. **High.** For scopes over 1.9" objective diameter. Height 0.402" **$26.50**
4. **Engraved Rings.**
   Medium, **$59.50**
5. **Standard Rear, Extension Front, Medium $36.60**
   Standard Rear, Extension Front, High **$36.60**
   Standard Rear, Long Extension Front, Medium **$38.60**
   Extension Rear, Standard Front, Medium **$38.60**
6. **Extension Rear, Extension Front, Medium $42.60**
7. **JR Bases (one piece) $17.95-21.10**
8. **SR Bases (two piece) $20.50-44.50**
9. **Colt Sauer SR Base (two piece) $44.50**
10. **Widefield See-Thru Mounts $23.30**
11. **Ring Mounts for Rimfire Rifles**
    Fit mounting grooves on most 22s. ¾" and 1" **$26.30**
12. **22 Adapter Bases**
    For 22 rifles without dovetail receiver.

Rifle	Item No.	Price
Model 39A Marlin	614002	$ 6.50
Model 57 Marlin	614003	6.50
Model 10/22 Ruger	614004	7.00
Browning Auto. 22	614009	16.50

REDFIELD SCOPES

RM 6400

The RM 6400 16x, 20x and 24x target scopes are offered with FCH reticles. These scopes combine the outstanding optical quality of the 3200 and allow the additional feature of receiver of barrel mounting.

RM target scopes weigh only 18 ounces and are only 17 inches long. The Model RM 6400 offers a 25% wider field of view than the Model 3200. For example, in 16x it's 6.5 feet at 100 yards against 5.2 feet for the Model 3200. Either ⅛ MOA or ¼ MOA click (accuracy to ± 1/32 MOA) adjustment knobs are provided. This permits immediate adjustment with pinpoint accuracy for serious target and varmint shooters. Packaged in a handsome high-impact styrene carrying case.

RETICLE		PRICE
16X FCH		**$298.70**
20X FCH		**$308.20**
24X FCH		**$317.65**

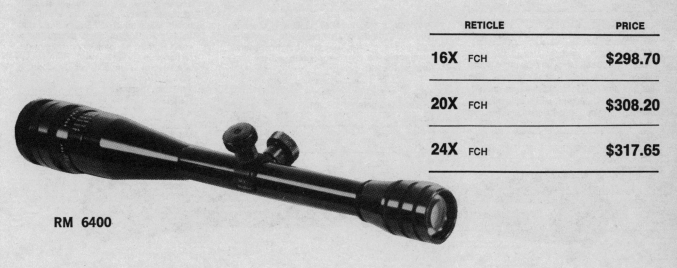

RM 6400

3200 TARGET SCOPE

The 3200 Target Scope, available in 16x, 20x, and 24x powers, was the first sealed target scope with internal adjustments. Precision machining and the use of spring-loaded, hardened steel clicker balls, give the Redfield 3200 crisp consistent ¼-minute adjustments capable of obtaining an accurate ± 1/32 MOA with every positive click.

RETICLE	PRICE
16X FCH	**$332.80**
20X FCH	**$341.75**
24X FCH	**$353.55**

⅛' and ⅜' dots are available at additional cost

REDFIELD SCOPES

Traditional
Fixed Power

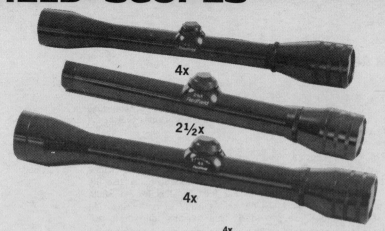

4x

2½x

4x

4x

The Traditional's ¾" tube, at 6½ ozs. and a compact 9½" long, is the perfect complement to a .22 or other small caliber rifle. This scope is hermetically sealed to prevent fogging. The Traditional features precision-ground coated glass lenses throughout for precise resolution. This tough scope is designed and tested to withstand the recoil of magnum caliber rifles.

4x
¾" Tube Diameter

Reticle	Price
4-Plex	$89.20

Lens Covers	Price
Storm Queen	$8.50

6X

This traditional 6x eyepiece gives extra magnification for longer ranges. Has all the famous Redfield features including tough aluminum alloy construction, coated lenses. Hermetically sealed, 1" tube diameter.

Reticle	Price
4-Plex	$160.65

2½x

Provides a 43' field of view for close-in type brush hunting. Complements any "slug gun package" for use on shotguns where slugs are used for deer hunting. All the features of the 4x.

2½x
1" Tube Diameter

Reticle	Price
4-Plex	$123.15
PCH	144.60

4x

Efficient performance at a moderate price for hunters who prefer a medium power scope. All the quality Redfield features: unscratchable, hard anodized finish. Magnum proof. Streamlined Redfield look. Coated glass lenses for increased light transmission. Brilliant distortion-free resolution. Hermetically sealed with O-rings to prevent fogging.

4x
1" Tube Diameter

Reticle	Price
4-Plex	$139.20

Lens Covers	Price
Storm Queen	$8.50

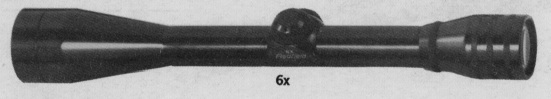

6x

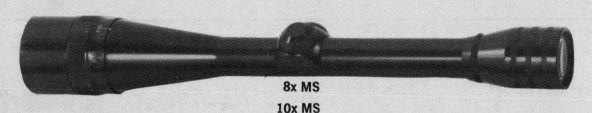

8x MS

10x MS

12x MS

Metallic Silhouette Scopes: Designed to furnish precise point of impact change at all ranges. Adjustable objective lens assembly eliminates parallax/focus error at ranges from 50 feet to infinity. Marked in yards and meters, including 385 for turkey. Also useful as a varmint scope.

8x MS
1" Tube Diameter

Reticle	Price
4-Plex	$244.60

10x MS
1" Tube Diameter

Reticle	Price
4-Plex	$255.30

12x MS
1" Tube Diameter

Reticle	Price
4-Plex	$267.80

Traditional

Variable Power

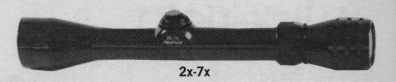

2x-7x

3x-9x

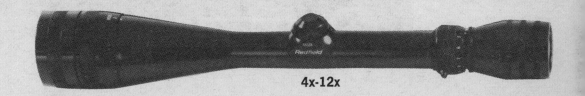

4x-12x

6x-18x

2x-7x

This model of the Traditional line gives the same advantages of the 4x Traditional, but with the added benefit of a popular variable power range.

2x-7x
1" Tube Diameter

Reticle	Price
4-Plex	$191.00
AT 4-Plex	231.20

3x-9x

Actually works like three scopes in one. At 3x, it's perfect for close-in woods and brush hunting. At 4x-6x, it handles normal open range hunting. And at 9x, it's ideal for long range spotting and shooting.

3x-9x
1" Tube Diameter

Reticle	Price
4-Plex	$210.65
3x9x Accu-Range Variable	
AT 4-Plex	$250.85

3x-9x ROYAL

A rifle scope made specially for heavy recoil magnum rifles. Offers you an extra ½" eye relief for high recoil magnum rifles. One piece tube construction. Anodized finished.

3x-9x Royal

Reticle	Price
4-Plex	$244.25

3x-9x Royal Accu-Range Variable

Reticle	Price
AT 4-Plex	$285.30

4x-12x

Power to go after everything from varmints to big game. Parallax-Focus (from 50 yards to infinity) on the objective bell is clearly marked and easy to adjust . . . an important feature for varmint and bench-rest shooters to whom the higher power range is vital. Positive stops prevent over-turning of the parallax adjusting sleeve.

4x-12x Variable
1" Tube Diameter

Reticle	Price
CH	$287.45
4-Plex	287.45
AT 4-Plex	326.75

6x-18x

A favored scope of higher power for varmint hunting and bench-rest shooting. Excellent field of view at all power settings with Parallax-Focus adjustment from 50 yards to infinity. Stops at either end prevent over-turning of this adjustment.

6x-18x Variable
1" Tube Diameter

Reticle	Price
4-Plex	$317.85
AT 4-Plex	357.10

All Lens Covers	Price
Storm Queen	$8.50

REDFIELD SCOPES

Widefield
Low Profile
Fixed Power

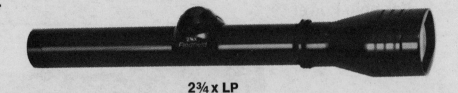

2¾ x LP

4xLP

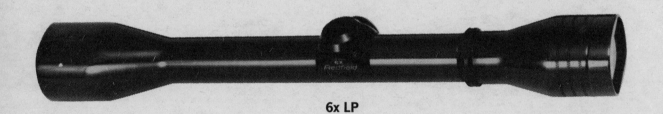

6x LP

2¾ x LP

A rugged and efficient lower magnification scope with a 55.5′ field of view at 100 yards. For comparatively short range brush and/or slug gun hunting. Even in poor light, dawn or dusk. moving targets are easy to locate.

4x LP

The most popular fixed-power member of the Widefield LP family. Outstanding field of view in an all-purpose, all-around scope with the flexibility to handle close-in shots or those at moderately long range.

6x LP

A scope for long ranges in wide open spaces or big mountain country. The combination of 6x magnification and 30% extra field of view has caused many hunters to switch from lower-powered scopes. A proven complement to all-around, flat-shooting sporting rifles for medium to long range varmint hunting.

2¾ x LP
1″ Tube Diameter

Reticle	Price
PCH	$187.45
4-Plex	166.00

Lens Covers	Price
Storm Queen	$8.50

4x LP
1″ Tube Diameter

Reticle	Price
PCH	$201.75
4-Plex	180.30

Lens Covers	Price
Storm Queen	$8.50

6x LP
1″ Tube Diameter

Reticle	Price
4-Plex	$160.65

Lens Covers	Price
Storm Queen	$8.50

REDFIELD SCOPES

widefield
Low Profile
Variable Power

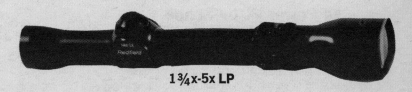

1¾x-5x LP

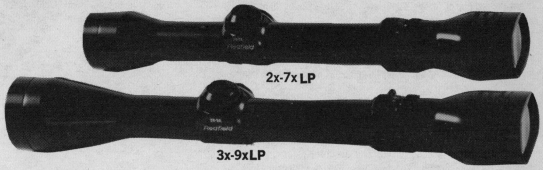

2x-7x LP

3x-9xLP

1¾x-5x LP
Ideal for fast, accurate close-in brush and slug shooting . . . the field of view at 100 yards at 1¾x is an outstanding 70 feet. Ample magnification is provided at 5x for longer ranges.

1¾x-5x Variable LP
1" Tube Diameter

Reticle	Price
PCH	$241.00
4-Plex	219.60

Lens Covers	Price
Storm Queen	$8.50

2x-7x LP
For the all-purpose hunter . . . smaller than the 3x-9x for conventional scabbards, tough enough to handle most any hunting situation or range.

2x-7x Variable LP
1" Tube Diameter

Reticle	Price
PCH	$258.90
4-Plex	237.45
2x-7x Accu-Trac Variable	
AT 4-Plex	$277.65

Lens Covers	Price
Storm Queen	$8.50

3x-9x LP
All the versatility and rugged dependability for big game and varmint hunting are built into this model. It fulfills a variety of purposes from long-range, peak-to-peak spotting and shooting to shorter ranges in wooded situations and poor light conditions.

3x-9x Variable LP
1" Tube Diameter

Reticle	Price
PCH	$285.65
4-Plex	264.25
3x-9x Accu-Trac Variable	
AT 4-Plex	$304.45

Lens Covers	Price
Storm Queen	$8.50

SPECIFICATIONS:

Power	2½x	1½x
Field @ 100 yds. (m)	9' (2.7m)	14' (4.3m)
Eye relief	14"-24"	19"-32"
	(35-60cm)	(48-81cm)
Overall length	Both 9.82" (24.9cm)	
Diameter of tube	Both 1" (2.54cm)	
Outside diameter of objective end	Both 1" (2.54cm)	
Outside diameter of eyepiece	Both 1.515" (3.8cm)	
Clear aperture of objective lens	Both .725" (1.84cm)	
Weight	Both 10.5 oz. (297g)	
Internal adjustment graduation (in @ 100 yds.) (cm @ 100m)	Both 1" (2.54cm)	
Maximum internal adjustment (in. @ 100 yds.) (m @ 100m)	Both 120" (3m)	
Reticle adjustment	Internal	Internal
Finish	Anodize H.C.	Anodize H.C.
Exit pupil	8mm	13mm
Reticles available	4-Plex	4-Plex

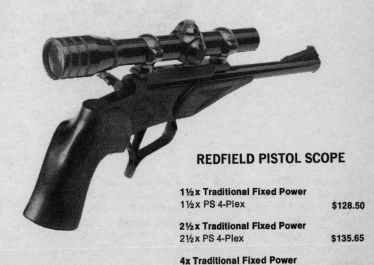

REDFIELD PISTOL SCOPE

1½x Traditional Fixed Power
1½x PS 4-Plex — $128.50

2½x Traditional Fixed Power
2½x PS 4-Plex — $135.65

4x Traditional Fixed Power
4x PS-4 Plex — $149.95

REDFIELD SCOPES

4-Power Pistol Scope
$149.95

This classic "magnum-proof" scope with its carefully designed mount system will withstand the very sharp recoil of .41 and .44 magnums without change in point of impact.

The excellent field of view (9 feet at 100 yards), the enlarged eye relief (12-22″), and the 8mm exit pupil combine to make the 4-Power Pistol Scope especially effective for both handgun hunting and target shooting.

The magnum-proof mounting system unifies the mount and pistol into virtually a one-piece system. A recoil shoulder in the scope mount base takes the recoil stress off the mounting screws and absorbs it in metal-to-metal contact with the handgun.

For positive protection against scope slippage, a double dovetail system featuring two dovetail rings is provided; for elimination of possible movement under recoil there's the Redfield ball-and-socket structural concept, which offers exceptional strength and solidity in the erector system.

The Redfield 4X scope is 9.7″ long, weighs approximately 11.1 oz. and has an outside objective diameter of 1.57″.

SAKO SCOPE MOUNTS

The scope mounting system on Sako Scopes is among the strongest in the world. Instead of using separate bases, a tapered dovetail is milled right into the reciever, to which the scope rings are mounted. A beautifully simple system that's been proven by over twenty years of use. Available in low (2½- 3-power); medium (4-power), and high (6-power). One-inch rings only.

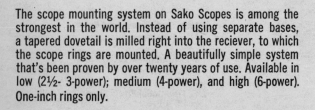

Low	$82.00
Medium	82.00
High	82.00

WEATHERBY PREMIER SCOPES

CHOICE OF RETICLES

Standard Model

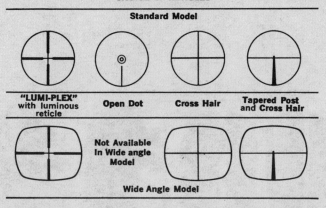

| "LUMI-PLEX" with luminous reticle | Open Dot | Cross Hair | Tapered Post and Cross Hair |

Wide Angle Model

4 POWER

This is a fixed power scope for big game and varmint hunting. Bright, clear image. "Never-wear" coated lenses for maximum luminosity under adverse conditions. 31-foot field of view at 100 yards.

WEATHERBY PREMIER SCOPES

WIDE ANGLE FIELD OF VIEW. Now, a twenty-five per cent wider field! Great for holding running game in full view.

As every hunter knows, one of his most difficult problems is keeping running game in the field of view of his scope.

Once lost, precious seconds fade away trying to find the animal in the scope again. Too much time wasted means the ultimate frustration. No second shot. Or no shot at all.

The Weatherby Wide Angle helps you surmount the problem by increasing your field of view by a full 25%!

3 TO 9 POWER

The most desirable variable for every kind of shooting from target to long range big game. Outstanding light-gathering power. Fast, convenient focusing adjustment.

2¾ POWER— AVAILABLE IN STANDARD MODEL ONLY

One of the widest fields of view on any scope . . . 45 feet at 100 yards. Ideal for big game because of its clear, bright image. Ruggedly built to withstand even the pounding of our .460 Magnum.

FEATURES

OPTICAL EXCELLENCE—NOW PROTECTED WITH NEW "NEVER-WEAR" ANTI-GLARE COATING. • FOG FREE AND WATERPROOF CONSTRUCTION. • CONSTANTLY SELF CENTERED RETICLES. • NON-MAGNIFYING RETICLE. • FINGER TIP ¼" CLICK ADJUSTMENTS. • QUICK VARIABLE POWER CHANGE. • UNIQUE LUMINOUS RETICLE. • LIFETIME NEOPRENE EYEPIECE. • EXCLUSIVE BINOCULAR TYPE SPEED FOCUSING. • RUGGED SCORE TUBE CONSTRUCTION.

SPECIFICATIONS FOR WEATHERBY PREMIER SCOPES

	STANDARD LENS			WIDE ANGLE LENS	
	2¾X40	4X40	3X - 9X40	4X40	3X - 9X40
Field of view	45' 0"	31' 0"	40' - 12'	35' 8"	43' 7" - 14' 8"
Clear aperture of objective lens	40mm	40mm	40mm	40mm	40mm
Diameter of exit pupil	14.56mm	10.0mm	13.3 - 4.4mm	10mm	13.3 - 4.4mm
Relative brightness	211.99	100.0	176.9 - 19.3	100.0	176.9 - 19.3
Eye relief	3.5"	3.5"	3.5"	3.0"	3.4" - 3.0"
Overall length	11.8"	12.7"	12.2"	11.8"	12.1"
Diameter of tube	1"	1"	1"	1"	1"
O.D. of objective end	1.85"	1.85"	1.85"	1.85"	1.85"
O.D. of ocular end	1.53"	1.53"	1.53"	1.71"	1.71"
Weight	12.3 oz.	12.3 oz.	13.7 oz.	14.1 oz.	14.8 oz.
Internal adjustment graduation	¼" clicks 1" calibration marks			¼" clicks 1" calibration marks	
Price and reticle:					
CH or TP&CH		$137.95	$142.95	$159.95	$169.95
Lumi-Plex	131.95	142.95	153.95	164.95	179.95
TRA-COM Lumi Plex					189.95

WEAVER "K" MODEL SCOPES

Model	K1.5		K2.5		K3		K4		K6		K8	
Actual Magnification	1.5	1.5	2.6	2.6	3.2	3.2	4.1	4.1	5.9	5.9	7.7	7.7
Field of View at 100 yds (ft) at 100 m (m)	55	18.3	38	12.7	34	11.3	27	9	19	6.3	15	5
Eye Distance (inches) (mm)	5¼	133.4	4½	114	4	102	4	102	3⅞	98	3½	89
Tube Diameter (inches) (mm)	1.000	25.4	1.000	25.4	1.000	25.4	1.000	25.4	1.000	25.4	1.000	25.4
Eyepiece Diameter (inches) (mm)	1.485	37.7	1.485	37.7	1.485	37.7	1.485	37.7	1.485	37.7	1.485	37.7
Front End Diameter (inches) (mm)	1.000	25.4	1.000	25.4	1.000	25.4	1.550	39.4	1.725	43.8	1.875	47.6
Length (inches) (mm)	9⅜	238	10⅜	264	10⅝	270	11¾	299	13⁷⁄₁₆	341	15	381
Weight (ounces) (grams)	9¾	276	10¼	291	10¼	291	12	340	13½	383	15½	439
Graduated Adjustments (change in inches at 100 yards, or minute of angle)	½	½	½	½	½	½	¼	¼	¼	¼	¼	¼
Reticles* Available	1,2,3,5	1,2,3,5	1,2,3,5	1,2,3,5	1,2,3,5	1,2,3,5	1,2,3,4,5	1,2,3,4,5	1,2,3,4,5	1,2,3,4,5	1,2,4,5	1,2,4,5

*RETICLES 1 Crosshair **2** Dual X
3 Post and Crosshair **4** Range-Finder
5 Dot
Reticles available as indicated: **1** and **2** at no extra cost. **3, 4,** and **5** at extra cost.
FOCUS Eyepiece of all scopes adjusts to user's vision.

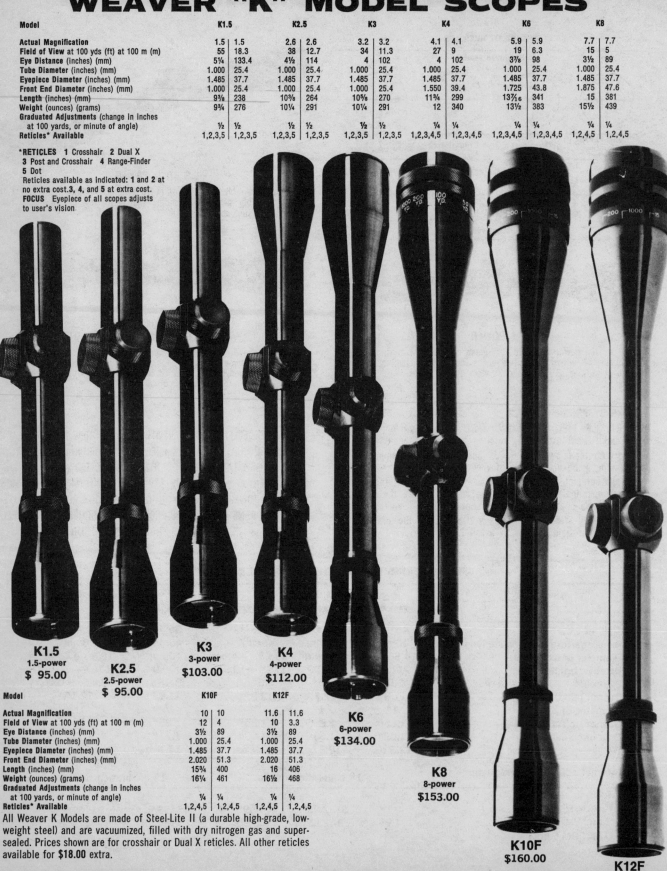

K1.5
1.5-power
$ 95.00

K2.5
2.5-power
$ 95.00

K3
3-power
$103.00

K4
4-power
$112.00

K6
6-power
$134.00

K8
8-power
$153.00

K10F
$160.00

K12F
$175.00

Model	K10F		K12F	
Actual Magnification	10	10	11.6	11.6
Field of View at 100 yds (ft) at 100 m (m)	12	4	10	3.3
Eye Distance (inches) (mm)	3½	89	3½	89
Tube Diameter (inches) (mm)	1.000	25.4	1.000	25.4
Eyepiece Diameter (inches) (mm)	1.485	37.7	1.485	37.7
Front End Diameter (inches) (mm)	2.020	51.3	2.020	51.3
Length (inches) (mm)	15¾	400	16	406
Weight (ounces) (grams)	16¼	461	16½	468
Graduated Adjustments (change in inches at 100 yards, or minute of angle)	¼	¼	¼	¼
Reticles* Available	1,2,4,5	1,2,4,5	1,2,4,5	1,2,4,5

All Weaver K Models are made of Steel-Lite II (a durable high-grade, low-weight steel) and are vacuumized, filled with dry nitrogen gas and super-sealed. Prices shown are for crosshair or Dual X reticles. All other reticles available for **$18.00** extra.

WEAVER "V" MODEL SCOPES

Model	V4.5		V7		V9		V9F		V12F	
Actual Magnification	1.6-4.3	1.6-4.3	2.5-6.7	2.5-6.7	3.3-8.8	3.3-8.8	3.3-8.8	3.3-8.8	4.4-11.8	4.4-11.8
Field of View at 100 yds (ft) at 100 m (m)	63-24	21.8	40-15	13.3-5	31-12	10.3-4	31-12	10.3-4	23-9	7.7-3
Eye Distance (inches) (mm)	4⅜-3⅞	111-98	4-3⅞	102-98	3¾-3¾	95-95	3¾-3¾	95-95	3⅞-4¼	98-108
Tube Diameter (inches) (mm)	1.000	25.4	1.000	25.4	1.000	25.4	1.000	25.4	1.000	25.4
Eyepiece Diameter (inches) (mm)	1.485	37.7	1.485	37.7	1.485	37.7	1.485	37.7	1.485	37.7
Front End Diameter (inches) (mm)	1.000	25.4	1.550	39.4	1.875	47.6	2.020	51.3	2.020	51.3
Length (inches) (mm)	10⅜	264	12⅜	314	14⅛	359	14	356	14	356
Weight (ounces) (grams)	13½	383	14½	410	17½	496	17½	496	17½	496
Graduated Adjustments (change in inches at 100 yards, or minute of angle)	½	½	¼	¼	¼	¼	¼	¼	¼	¼
Reticles* Available	1,2,3,4,5	1,2,3,4,5	1,2,3,4,5	1,2,3,4,5	1,2,3,4,5	1,2,3,4,5	1,2,3,4,5	1,2,3,4,5	1,2,3,4,5	1,2,3,4,5

*RETICLES 1 Crosshair 2 Dual X
3 Post and Crosshair 4 Range-Finder
5 Dot
Reticles available as indicated: 1 and 2 at
no extra cost. 3, 4, and 5 at extra cost.
FOCUS Eyepiece of all scopes adjusts
to user's vision.

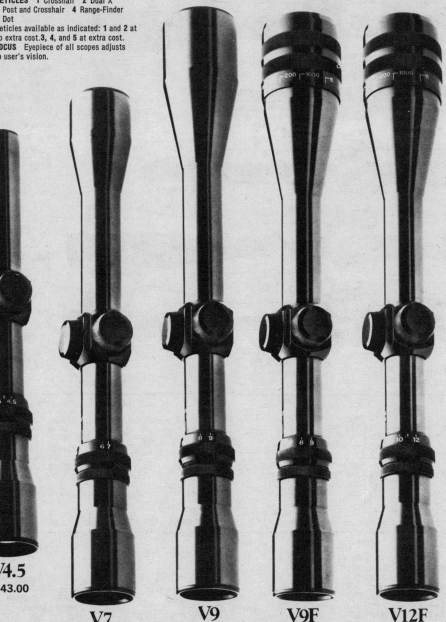

V4.5
$143.00

V7
$157.00

V9
$162.00

V9F
$176.00

V12F
$188.00

All Weaver Variable models offer a continuous and smooth power change; improved sealing and fog-proofing; the Micro-Trac Adjustment System for super-accuracy; and Steel-Lite II construction for a new dimension in lightness, toughness, and dependability.

Focus and point of impact are the same at all powers. Reticle remains constantly centered.

Precision optics are magnesium fluoride coated. Long eye relief is safe at all magnifications. Models V9F and V12F have Range-Focus. All five reticle styles are offered.

Prices shown are for crosshair or Dual X reticles. All other reticles available for **$18.00** each.

WEAVER KW & VW MODEL SCOPES

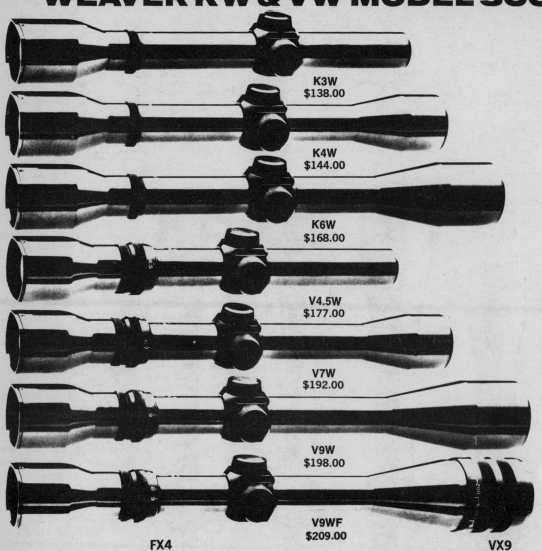

K3W
$138.00

K4W
$144.00

K6W
$168.00

V4.5W
$177.00

V7W
$192.00

V9W
$198.00

V9WF
$209.00

FX4
$149.95

VX9
$199.95

Features one-piece, machine-tooled steel tube; Micro-Trac Adjustment System. Vacuumized, nitrogen-processed and super-sealed for absolute fog-proofing. Bright, crisp, distortion-free optics. Long, safe eye relief. And Steel-Lite II finish.

Range focus now offered on the V9WF. All five reticle styles available (Range-finder not offered on the K3W).

Prices shown are for crosshair and Dual X reticles. All other reticles available for **$18.00** extra.

Model	K3W		K4W		K6W		V4.5W		V7W		V9W		V9WF	
Actual Magnification	2.9	2.9	3.7	3.7	6	6	1.6-4.2	1.6-4.2	2.6-6.9	2.6-6.9	3.3-9	3.3-9	3.3-9	3.3-9
Field of View at 100 yds (ft) at 100 m (m)	48	16	38	12.7	24	8	74-27	24-6.9	43.17	14.3-5.7	35-13	11.7-4.3	35-13	11.7-4.3
Eye Distance (in./mm)	3½	89	3⅝	92	3½	89	4¼-3¾	108-95	3⅝-3¾	92-95	3⅝-3⅝	92-92	3⅝-3⅝	92-92
Tube Dia. (in./mm)	1.000	25.4	1.000	25.4	1.000	25.4	1.000	25.4	1.000	25.4	1.000	25.4	1.000	25.4
Eyepiece Dia. (in./mm)	1.710	43.4	1.710	43.4	1.710	43.4	1.710	43.4	1.710	43.4	1.710	43.4	1.710	43.4
	x1.425	x36.2	x1.425	x36.2	x1.425	x36.2	x1.425	x36.2	x1.425	x36.2	x1.425	x36.2	x1.425	x36.2
Front End Dia. (in./mm)	1.000	25.4	1.550	39.4	1.725	43.8	1.000	25.4	1.550	39.4	1.875	47.6	2.020	51.3
Length (in./mm)	11	279	11¹³⁄₁₆	300	13¼	337	10⅜	264	12⅜	314	14⅛	359	14	356
Weight (oz./gm.)	11	312	13	368	14½	410	14¼	404	15¼	432	18¼	517	18¼	517
Graduated Adj. (change in in. at 100 yds./min. of angle)	½	½	¼	¼	¼	¼	½	½	¼	¼	¼	¼	¼	¼
Reticles* Available	1,2,3,5		1,2,3,5		1,2,3,4,5		1,2,3,4,5		1,2,3,4,5		1,2,3,4,5		1,2,3,4,5		1,2,3,4,5	

Model	FX4		VX9	
Actual Magnification	4.1	4.1	3.3-8.8	3.3-8.8
Field of View at 100 yds (ft) at 100 m (m)	27	9	31-12	10.3-4
Eye Distance (in./mm)	4	102	3.8-3.8	95-95
Tube Dia. (in./mm)	1.000	25.4	1.000	25.4
Eyepiece Dia. (in./mm)	1.485	37.7	1.485	37.7
	1.550	39.4	1.875	47.6
Front End Dia. (in./mm)	11.8	299	14.2	359
Length (in./mm)	13	368	18	510
Weight (oz./gm.)				
Graduated Adj. (change in in. at 100 yds./min. of angle)	.25	.25	.25	.25
Reticles* Available	2	2	2	2

*RETICLES 1 Crosshair 2 Dual X
3. Post and Crosshair 4 Range-Finder
5 Dot
Reticles available as indicated: **1 and 2** at no extra cost. **3, 4,** and **5** at extra cost.
FOCUS Eyepiece of all scopes adjusts to user's vision.

D4		D6		V22		Model
4.2	4.2	6.2	6.2	3-5.8	3-5.8	Actual Magnification*
29	9.7	19.75	6.6	31-16.25	10.3-5.4	Field of View* at 100 yds (ft) at 100 m (m)
2¼	57	2¼	57	1⅝-2¼	41.3-57	Eye Distance* (inches) (mm)
.875	22.2	.875	22.2	.875	22.2	Tube Diameter (inches) (mm)
1.310	33.3	1.310	33.3	1.310	33.3	Eyepiece Diameter (inches) (mm)
.875	22.2	.875	22.2	.875	22.2	Front End Diameter (inches) (mm)
11⅞	302	12⁵⁄₁₆	313	12⅜	314	Length (inches) (mm)
5.5	155.9	5.5	155.9	7	198.4	Weight (ounces) (grams)
1	1	1	1	1	1	Graduated Adjustments (change in inches at 100 yards, or minute of angle)
1 only	1 only	1 only	1 only	1,2	1,2	Reticles** Available

*Weaver-Scopes offer carefully balanced magnification, field of view, eye relief, and diaphragming to provide hunters with maximum efficiency, safety, and clarity.
**RETICLES 1 Crosshair 2 Dual X
Reticles available as indicated: 1 at no extra cost. 2 at extra cost (on V22 only).
†Weight without mount 4 ounces; with mount 5 ounces.

FOCUS Eyepiece of all scopes adjusts to user's vision.

D4
4-power

D6
6-power

V22
3- to 6-power

22 MODELS

1.
CROSSHAIR

2.
DUAL X®
(at extra cost, on V22 only)

Model D4 with Crosshair Reticle	$24.50
Model D4 with Dual X Reticle	27.00
Model D6 with Crosshair Reticle	27.00
Model D6 with Dual X Reticle	29.50
Model V22 with Crosshair Reticle	32.50
Model V22 with Dual X Reticle	35.00

Advanced D Models and V22 have outstanding features usually found only in more expensive scopes: large ⅞" tubes, matching turret of modern design, improved optics with larger eyepiece. Lighter and stronger than ever, they are made of finest materials by skilled American craftsmen.

Weaver's constantly-centered reticle permits unusual speed and ease of aim. Use is limited to light recoil rifles only because of relatively short eye relief.

Factory-equipped with Tip-Off or N Mount at no extra cost.

Crosshair reticle is standard in all three scopes; Dual X is optional in the V22 at extra cost.

K856
8-power
$210.00

Actual Mag.: 7.7
Field of View: 15 ft. at 100 yds. (5m at 100m)
Eye Distance: 3.5 in. (89mm)
Tube Diam.: 1.000 in. (25.4mm)
Eyepiece Diam.: 1.5 in. (37.7mm)
Front End Dia.: 2.5 in. (62.5mm)
Reticles: Dual X and German Post ($18.00 extra)
Length: 15 in. (381mm)
Weight: 18.7 oz. (532 grams)
Graduated Adj. (change in in. at 100 yds. or minute of angle): .25

WEAVER LENS CAPS

Transparent windows allow the scope to be used quickly with the caps in position in emergency. Durable and snug fitting, Weaver Lens Caps provide attractive, inexpensive protection for the scope's optics. Made in 13 sizes: **$5.25**

K1.5	V9F, V12F
K2.5, K3, V4.5	K3W, V4.5W
K4, V7, FX4, MI, MI-SF-TO	K4W, V7W
K6	K6W
K10F, K12F	V9W
K8, V9, VX9	V9WF
	D4, D6, V22

WEAVER SIGHTS & MOUNTS

QWIK-POINT®

QUICKEST WAY TO IMPROVE SHOTGUN AND SHORT-RANGE RIFLE SHOOTING.

S-1
for shotguns
$75.00

S-1100
for Remington 1100 and 870 shotguns
$75.00

R-1
for centerfire rifles
$75.00

R-22
for 22 rifles
$75.00

Keep your eye on the target. The blaze-orange dot is OUT THERE where your target is.

Dot is bright blaze-orange, even in dim light or heavy cover.

Weaver's amazing Qwik-Point can quickly improve natural shooting skills with shotgun, centerfire rifle, or 22.

With one or both eyes open, simply look at the target, move the blaze-orange dot to the target, and fire. The dot is focused to infinity, so it will automatically appear where eyes are focused.

Dot and target are seen simultaneously in clear, sharp focus. No changing point of focus from sight to target.

On shotguns, Qwik-Point is an effective short-cut to becoming an accomplished wingshot. Makes "swing" and "lead" easy to see, understand, and follow. Helps the expert detect where and why he missed.

Qwik-Point is shockproof, weatherproof, foolproof. Made of lightweight aluminum with durable jet-black anodizing. Easily sighted in like a scope.

Specifications:
Weight:
S-1, 7¾ ounces
S-1100, 7¾ ounces
R-1, 8¾ ounces
R-22, 7½ ounces
Length:
S-1, 6 inches
S-1100, 6 inches
R-1, 6¼ inches
R-22, 6¾ inches
Adjustments:
¼" click at 40 yards
Eye Relief: Infinite
Focus: Universal

Mounting:
Model S-1 for shotguns:
Complete with mount and base (8A) for most pumps and automatics.

Model S-1100 for Remington 1100 and 870 shotguns:
Complete with side mount and bolts; installed in minutes without special tools.

Model R-1 for center fire rifles:
Built-in mount attaches to Weaver Top Mount bases (bases extra). Special bases (77, 78) available for Model 94 Winchester.

Model R-22 for 22's: Complete with mount which fits factory-grooved receivers.

WEAVER TIP-OFF® MOUNTS

Weaver 1" Tip-Off Mount for K Models and other 1" scopes
$17.95

Weaver ⅞" Tip-Off Mount for D Models, V22, and other ⅞" scopes
$9.95

Tip-Off Mounts are made for use on 22 rifles with ⅜" dovetail receiver grooves. No bases required. They clamp into the rifle receiver grooves. No tools needed. Clamping screws tighten easily with a coin.

1" Tip-Off Mounts, a pair of split rings, are designed to mount K Models and other 1" scopes.

⅞" Tip-Off Mounts, a pair of solid rings, are designed to mount Weaver D Models, V22, and other ⅞" scopes. Also available in ¾" rings to fit ¾" scopes.

These rifles have ⅜" receiver grooves:
Anschutz Mark 10, 64MS, 141, 153, 520, 1363, 1388, 1416, 1418, 1441, 1442, 1443, 1516, 1518
Browning T-Bolt, BL-22
CIL 68, 121, 125, 167, 180, 190S, 212, 227, 300, 310, 470
Colt Colteer, Courier, Stagecoach Carbine
Cooey 64, 121, 131, 141, 250, 255, 270, 275, 290
Glenfield 10, 20, 60, 70, 75
H&R 422, 750, 751, 755, 760, 800, 865, 866
High Standard 22 Sport-King
Ithaca X5 Lightning, 72, Tikka
Kleinguenther K11, K12, K13
Kodiak 260
Lee-Enfield requires adapter TO-1 at extra cost; must be drilled, tapped
Marlin 49, 56, 57, 80, 81, 88, 89, 98, 99, 101, 122, 780, 781, 782, 783, 980, 989
Montgomery Ward 822, 832, 868, 892
Mossberg 142, 144, 146, 151, 152, 300 Series, 400, 402, 430, 432, 620, 640
Noble 235, 275, 285, 835, 875, 885
Remington 10, 11, 12, 66, 76, 77, 510, 511, 512, 513S, 521T, 540X, 541S, 550, 552, 572, 580, 581, 582, 590M, 591M, 592M
Ruger 10/22 with TO-9 base
Savage 4, 5, 6, 24, 29, 54, 60, 63, 65, 88, 90, 164, 184, 219
Stevens 34, 46, 73, 84, 85, 86, 87
Weatherby XXII
Winchester 61, 69, 72, 74, 75S, 77, 121, 131, 135, 141, 145, 150, 190, 250, 255, 270, 275, 290, 310, 320, 325, 490, 9422

WEAVER SIGHTS & MOUNTS

WEAVER-DETACHABLE MOUNTS

Detachable Top Mount made in 7/8", 1", and 1.023" (26mm) diameters; Hi-Style made in 1" diameter only **$17.95**

Extension Top Mount made in 1" diameter only **$20.95**

Detachable Side Mount made in 1" diameters **$17.95**

Detachable Long Side Mount in 1" diameter for Winchester 94 and other short-action rifles **$20.95**

Light, compact and finely finished, Weaver-Detachable Mounts can be used with complete assurance on rifles of heaviest recoil and under roughest hunting use. Installation is easy since most rifle receivers are factory drilled and tapped specifically for Weaver-Mounts.

Hi-Style Top Mounts, made in 1" diameter only, are designed to provide adequate barrel and iron sight clearance for most scopes having objective diameters greater than 1¾". Scopes of this size (1¾") can be mounted on some rifles using regular Top Mounts.

Use Hi-Style Top Mounts when installing K6, K6W, K8, K10F, K12F, V9, V9F, V9W, V9WF V12F on Remington 600, 660, 788, Marlin 336, 444, and Savage 99; K6, K6W, V9, V9F, V9W, V9WF, V12F on Remington 740, 742, 760; V9, V9F, V9W, V9WF and V12F on Remington 700, 721, 722, 725.

WEAVER-PIVOT MOUNTS

Pivot Mount open

Pivot Mount closed
$22.95

Weaver-Pivot Mounts permit choice of scope or iron sights. Top mounting gives wide spacing of mount rings, rigidity, low scope position, easy installation and removal. Replacement is accurate, alignment exact and fully dependable. Made for ¾" and 1" scopes.

Hi-Style Pivot Mounts are available in 1" diameter only. The high rings position the scope ¼" higher than the standard ring, and provide adequate barrel and iron sight clearance for scopes with objective diameters greater than 1¾". Use Hi-Style Pivot Mounts when installing K6, K6W, K8, K10F, K12F, V9, V9F, V9W, V9WF and V12F on these rifles: Remington 700, 742, 760, 600, 660; Marlin 336, 444; and Savage 99.

WEAVER N MOUNTS

Type N Mounts (side bracket design) are pressed from tough alloy steel. They are rigid, sturdy, and suitable for use on high-power rifles and 22's. Made in 7/8" diameter for D Models and V22.

The dependability of the inexpensive N Mount has been proved under all conditions and on large caliber rifles. **$9.95**

Weaver's 1100/870 Scope Mount System **$127.00**

Everything needed is conveniently pre-assembled with choice of K1.5 or K2.5 (with Dual X Reticle)

System installs quickly on Remington 1100 and 870 shotguns . . . with no drilling or tapping required

Mount a scope on Remington's 1100 or 870 shotgun with only a screwdriver. Two choices are available, pre-assembled with a Weaver K1.5 or K2.5. Just push the two existing trigger plate pins out, with the two bolts that come with the system. No drilling, no tapping of receiver.

The scope can be removed just as easily. Everything you need is conveniently pre-assembled and ready for immediate installation.

This system offers a great advantage where deer hunting with a shotgun is mandatory, or for anyone who enjoys turkey, goose, and other specialized shotgun hunting.

Make, Model of Rifle	Top Mount Rear	Top Mount Front	Side Mount	Pivot Mounts Rear	Pivot Mounts Front	N Mounts Made for ⅞" dia. Scopes
ENFIELD receiver cut down like:						
Remington 30	11	11	1			
Winchester 70†	47	46		147	146	
Remington 721†	36	35		136	135	
GARCIA 73	53			153		
74	67	66				
GOLDEN EAGLE 7000	71	71				
H&R 300, 301, 330, 370 prior to 1973	45	46	5	145	146	
300, 301 short action for 1973 and after (22-250, 243, 308)	83	84				
300, 301 long action for 1973 and after (270, 30-06, 7mm, 300 Win)	54	46		154	146	
360, 361	81					
317, 322	11	35				
317 prior to 1975 model	67	66				
Topper 30, 22 Jet, 158 prior to 1973	60					
Topper 158C for 1973 and after; 157 drilled and tapped	82					
65, 165, 150, 151 (Auto)	18	18	2			N3
264, 265, 365, 250, 251, 450, 550	18	16	2			N3
700	87		1			
HERTERS U9 BSA Action (requires drilling, tapping)	28	28				
U9 round receiver	36	35		136	135	
J9	45	46	5	145	146	
HIGH STANDARD Hi-Power	55	46	1			
INTERARMS S2 Carbine			3A			
ITHACA LSA-55, LSA-65	61	61				
JAPANESE 6.5 mm*†, 7.7mm*†	70		1	170		
KRAG (offset left for easy ejection)			2			
LEE-ENFIELD (Use TO-1 Adapter Base and Tip-Off Mount.)						
MARLIN 36, 62, 93, 336, 444, 1893, 1895, Glenfield 30, Zane Grey	63B			163A		
39A	90					
1894	63B					
455	45	46	5			
57 Magnum	58					
MAUSER FN including former Husqvarna (with receiver ring about 1.410" dia.)*; 95, 98	45	46	5	145	146	
Mark X	55	20A				
HVA Lightweight Husqvarna (with rec. ring about 1.300" dia.)*; ZB 8mm*, 7mm*, 6.5mm*, with round rec.	55	46	1	155	146	
Bauer 3000, 4000	68	46		168	146	
MOSSBERG 800	55	55		155	155	
810, RM7	25	11				
25, 26, 42, 46M, 140, 142, 146. Also late Models 45, 46 with ¾" dia. bbls.	12	13	2			N3
43, 44, 144, 46BT, 35. Also early Models 45, 46, 46A, 46B with 13/16" dia. bbls.	12	16	2			N3
40	20A	42	2			N3
400	20A	42				
472, 479, 679	80					
500AS, 600 shotguns	88					
MUSGRAVE Mark I, Mark II	54	46		154	146	
Mark III, Mark IV	45	46		145	146	
PARKER-HALE 1000, 1000C, 1100, 1200, 1700	45	46		145	146	
REMINGTON 700 Long Action in 270, 280, 25-06, 30-06, 7mm Mag., 300 Win. Mag., 264, 375, 458, 40X-L; 721; 725 in 270, 280, 30-06, 375	36	35	1	136	135	
700 Short Action in 17, 222, 222 Mag., 22-250, 243, 6mm, 308; 722, 40X-S; 725 in 222, 243, 244	36	40A	1	136	140	
740, 742, 760	62			162		
660, 600	70		1	170		
788	76	75				
30	11	11	1			
14, 141	20A	27				
12A, 121 with ¾" diameter barrels	18	13	2			
121 with 13/16" diameter barrels	18	17	2			
12C octagon barrel	18	31				N5
24, 241 (#60 1-pc. base attaches to barrel, extends back over receiver; for 1" scopes only)	60					N5
25	18	21	2			N5
10, 11, 12, 521T, 34*, 341*	43	42	2			N3
513S, 513T	43	44	2			N3
514	16	21	2			N3
541S	15	15	2			
33*	17	13	2			N3
41*	17	17	2			N3
XP-100	70					
RUGER 1	85	89				
3	85	86				
10/22	TO-9					
44 Magnum Deerstalker	47	68		147	168	
77ST round top	79	35				
SAKO Vixen (requires no drilling)	67	66				
Forester, Finnbear (requires no drilling)	67	65				
Finnwolf	53			153		
72, 75, 78	85	85				
SAVAGE 99, 1895	14	19		114	119	
110, 111, 112RH**	61	46	1	161	146	
24*	74		1			
20*, 340, 342			1			
40, 45	11	11	2			
3	16	21	2			N3
7	12	12	2			N3
19, 23	15	16	2			N3
219	12	30	2			N3
25 octagon barrel	19	31				N5
170	62			162		
2400	67	66				

Make, Model of Rifle	Top Mount Rear	Top Mount Front	Side Mount	Pivot Mounts Rear	Pivot Mounts Front	N Mounts Made for ⅞" dia. Scopes
SCHULTZ & LARSEN	54	46	1	154	146	
SEARS 50, 51	45	46	5	145	146	
51L	55	46	1	155	146	
53	47	46	1	-147	146	
54, 100			3B			
SHILEN flat top receiver	61	61				
Round receiver	35	35				
SMITH & WESSON Mauser actions with small receiver ring	55	46	1	155	146	
1500, 1600	36	35				
SPRINGFIELD 03*†	54	55	1	154	155	
03-A3*†	59	45		159	145	
STEVENS 26	22	22	2			N3
27 octagon	31	31				N5
53	16	21	2			
56, 66	12	13	2			N3
57, 76, 417½, 762	12	12	2			N3
416	18	17	2			N3
417	15	15	2			N3
418, 418½	16	16	2			N3
325, 322			1			
STEVENS-SPRINGFIELD 83	16	21	2			
872	12	12	2			N3
840			1			
THOMPSON Contender Handgun		92				
U.S. CARBINE Cal. 30 M1			M			
VOERE 2150, 2165/1, 2165/2, 2165/3, 2165/4	45	46		145	146	
2130 (must be drilled, tapped)	28	28				
WEATHERBY Mark V, Vanguard	36	35		136	135	
Mark V 22-250, 224	36	46		136	146	
Other models with FN Mauser actions	45	46	5	145	146	
WESTERNFIELD 730	25	11				
740	63B			163A		
750	67	65				
770	55	20A				
772	80					
775, 780	55	55		155	155	
WINCHESTER 70, 70A, 70 Varmint	47	46	1	147	146	
Pre-1964 70, 54*	48	46	1	148	146	
70 Target, 300 H&H, 375 H&H	49A	46	1	149	146	
70, 375 H&H after 1963	49A	46	1	139	146	
54*, early Model 70	48	46	1	148	146	
670, 770	47	46	1	147	146	
88, 100	53			153		
94			3B			
94 Big Bore 375			3C			
53, 55, 64, 65, 66, 71, 86, 92, 95			3A			
07, 05, 10	20A	17				
43	18	18				
03, 63	19	22	2			
06, 62, 62A, 90 octagon barrel	32	32				N5
61 round barrel	19	13	2			N5
61 octagon barrel	25	32				N3
60*, 67*, 68*	21	21				N3
57, 69	12	13	2			N3
69A, 72, 47	12	17	2			N3
74	12	12	2			N3
77	15	32	2			
75 Sporter	15	30	2			N3
75 Target	15	16	2			N3
52*	25	57	2			N3
52D	85	85				
9422	TO-10					
ZB 22	28	24	2			N3
Hornet, 218 Bee	39	24				
SHOTGUNS Pump shotguns except Winchester 42			8			
Winchester 42						
Auto shotguns EXCEPT Remington 11-48, 1100, Sportsman 48, 58, Winchester 50, Browning Double Auto, High Standard Auto			7			
Remington Auto 11-48, 1100, Sportsman 48, 58, Winchester 50, High Standard Auto			8			

NOTE: Top Mounts with No. 50 (long, one-piece) base can be used on double and single barrel shotguns with ribs thick enough for base screws.

New Weaver® Mount Base Systems:
No Drilling, No Tapping

Make, Model of Gun	Mount Base System
COLT Officer's Model	303
Python	304
RUGER Blackhawk, Super Blackhawk Handguns	301
Mini-14	302
Security Six	305
Mark I 22 Automatic Pistol	306
Standard 22 Automatic Pistol	306

QWIK-POINT: Installation information packed with product.

D4, D6, and V22 Scopes (like other makes designed for 22 rifles) have short eye relief, and for this reason should not be used on high-power rifles.

*Rifles so marked (and older guns in some other models) require bolt handle alteration.

**Due to wide ring spacing, V7, V7W, V9, V9F, V9W, V9WF, and V12F Models cannot be installed on Savage 110, 111, and 112 with Pivot Mount rings.

†Enfield, Japanese, and Springfield: Pivot Mount usable only on sporterized guns with suitable front and middle sights.

Dual X; Micro-Trac; Qwik-Point; Range-Finder Reticle; Tip-Off; V22; and Weaver are registered trademarks, and Marksman; SL-II; Steel-Lite II; Auto-Comp and W with design are trademarks of W. R. Weaver Company.

WARNING: Caution must be used in drilling and tapping receivers. Proper drill and tap size must be used. There must be enough metal to hold base screws. If there is a question, contact the gun manufacturer for information.

W. R. Weaver Company / El Paso, Texas 79915

WILLIAMS APERTURES & BASES

TWILIGHT APERTURE $3.15

REGULAR SERIES $2.30

SHOTGUN BIG GAME APERTURE $4.30

5D

FP

TWILIGHT APERTURES

Twilight apertures are designed for shooting under poor light conditions, early morning, late evening, and other inclement conditions. They create a sharp contrast that gives quick definition to the aperture hole, and they eliminate the "fuzz" with which many shooters have trouble.

These apertures are perhaps the greatest development in metallic sights in the last three decades—positive sighting when the light is poor but the hunting best.

Williams 'Twilight' apertures will accommodate Redfield, Lyman, etc.

TW-3/8 X .050	3/8" O.D. with .050 inner hole
TW-3/8 X .093	3/8" O.D. with .093 inner hole
TW-3/8 X .125	3/8" O.D. with .125 inner hole
TW-1/2 X .050	1/2" O.D. with .050 inner hole
TW-1/2 X .093	1/2" O.D. with .093 inner hole
TW-1/2 X .125	1/2" O.D. with .125 inner hole

SHOTGUN BIG GAME APERTURE

All Williams receiver sights can now be equipped with the new shotgun aperture. This aperture has amazing light gathering ability. Permits clear shooting even when the light is poor. Designed for aerial shooting, slug shooting and for big game rifles. PROVIDES THE FASTEST, MOST ACCURATE SIGHTING YOU CAN HAVE!

REGULAR SERIES
Buckbuster — Standard — Target

We have always felt that a disc with a small outer diameter and a large inner hole is best for hunting. For this reason, we have made the 3/8" O.D. disc with a .093 inner hole as standard equipment. Other sizes are optional.

For the shooter who wants the FASTEST sighting aperture, we can supply our BUCKBUSTER model which has a 3/8" O.D. and a large .125 inner hole. Williams discs are standard thread size and will accommodate Redfield, Lyman, etc.

R-3/8 X .050	3/8" O.D. with .050 inner hole
R-3/8 X .093	3/8" O.D. with .093 inner hole
	(STANDARD, unless otherwise specified)
R-3/8 X .125	3/8" O.D. with .125 inner hole
	(BUCKBUSTER)
R-1/2 X .050	1/2" O.D. with .050 inner hole
R-1/2 X .093	1/2" O.D. with .093 inner hole
R-1/2 X .125	1/2" O.D. with .125 inner hole
R-7/8 X .050	7/8" O.D. with .050 inner hole
	(TARGET)

NOTE: Long shank apertures for WGRS Receiver Sight are available only in the 3/8 X .093 and the 3/8 X .125 sizes.

GOLD OR SILVER METAL SHOTGUN SIGHTS
$2.00

No. 3 Front   Nos. 1 & 2 Front   No. 4 Rear

Model	Thread	Bead Dia.	Shank Length
No. 1	6-48	.175	1/8"
No. 2	3-56	.175	1/8"
No. 3	3-56	.130	1/8"
No. 4	3-56	.067	3/32"

GARAND CLIP $7.90

For hunting, most states limit the magazine capacity to five shot.

5 Shot Garand

SMLE EXTRACTOR SPRINGS
$4.15

New, and specially made from tempered spring steel. Easily fitted. Only a punch is needed.

NUMBER 1   NUMBER 4 & 5

GUNSMITH'S
DRILL AND TAP SETS

3-56 Tap ($2.75) Carbon
6-48 Tap ($2.75) Carbon
8-40 Tap ($2.75) Carbon

6-48 H.S. Tap — #31 H.S. Drill $7.50
8-40 H.S. Tap — #28 H.S. Drill   7.50
10-32 H.S. Tap — #21 H.S. Drill 7.50

SLOT BLANK
$2.40

For appearance sake—use this slot blank after removing iron sight. It will also cover up most burr marks.

Standard 3/8" (left) for Winchester, Stevens, Marlin, Remington, Savage, and other rifles.

OPEN FOLDING SIGHT BASE
$4.25

For Military and Standard Rifles. Will accommodate standard folding sights such as Marble 69, 70, 69H. 70H, Lyman 16A or 16B and Redfield 46, 47 and 48. Base furnished with 6-48 screws. Acts as a riser to give open rear sight necessary height to align properly with ramp front sights or to use with scoped rifles.

WILLIAMS TWILIGHT SCOPES

2½X	T-N-T	$ 89.50
4X	T-N-T	$ 95.90
3X-9X	T-N-T	$136.00
2X-6X	T-N-T	$129.95

The 'Twilight' series of scopes was introduced to accommodate those shooters who want a high-quality scope in the medium-priced field. The 'Twilight' scopes are the best value on the market. They are waterproof and shockproof, have coated lenses and are nitrogen filled. Resolution is sharp and clear — actually much superior to the optics of several other more expensive makes. All 'Twilight' scopes have a highly polished, rich-black, hard-anodized finish.

There are four models available — the 2½X, the 4X, the 2X-6X, and the 3X-9X. They are available in two styles of reticles — the plain crosshair and our T-N-T (which stands for thick and thin.)

TWILIGHT SPECIFICATIONS				2X - 6X		3X - 9X	
OPTICAL SPECIFICATIONS		2.5X	4X	At 2X	At 6X	At 3X	At 9X
Clear aperture of objective lens		20mm	32mm	32mm	Same	38mm	Same
Clear aperture of ocular lens		32mm	32mm	32mm	Same	32mm	Same
Exit Pupil		8mm	8mm	16mm	5.3mm	12.7mm	4.2mm
Relative Brightness		64	64	256	28	161.2	17.6
Field of view (degree of angle)		12°20'	5°30'	8°30'	3°10'	7°	2°20'
Field of view at 100 yards		32'	29'	45½'	16¾'	36½'	12¾'
Eye Relief		3.7"	3.6"	3"	3"	3.1"	2.9"
Parallax Correction (at)		50 yds.	100 yds.	100 yds.	Same	100 yds.	Same
Lens Construction		9	9	11	Same	11	Same
MECHANICAL SPECIFICATIONS							
Outside diameter of objective end		1.00"	1.525"	1.525"	Same	1.850"	1.850"
Outside diameter of ocular end		1.455"	1.455"	1.455"	Same	1.455"	Same
Outside diameter of tube		1"	1"	1"	Same	1"	Same
Internal adjustment graduation		½ min.	½ min.	½ min.	Same	½ min.	Same
Minimum internal adjustment		75 min.	75 min.	75 min.	Same	60 min.	Same
Finish		Glossy	Hard	Black	Anodized		
Length		11¼"	11¾"	11½"	11½"	12¾"	12¾"
Weight		8½ oz.	9½ oz.	11½ oz.	Same	13½ oz.	Same

WILLIAMS SIGHT-THRU MOUNTS

**MODEL 742 REM.
WITH
SIGHT-THRU MOUNT**

MODELS	Front	Rear
Winchester Models 88 and 100; Sako Finnwolf; Ithaca 3†	A	A
Remington Models 760-740-742; Savage Model 170; Remington 870† and 1100†	A	B
Winchester Models 70 Standard, 670 and 770; Browning BBR	D	C
Remington Models 700 R.H. and L.H., 721, 722, 725; Weatherby MK-V and Vanguard; BSA round top receivers; Ruger 77ST; Smith and Wesson Model 1500	D	E
Savage Models 110, 111 and 112V	D	F
Browning High Power Auto and lever action; Mossberg 800; Remington 541S†. Will also fit Ward's Western Field Model 72 and Mossberg Model 472 lever action. *See note below	G	G
Late Models Marlin 336, 1894 and 1894C	H	H
FN Mauser; Browning Bolt Action; J. C. Higgins 50-51; Interarms Mark X Mauser	D	I
Savage 99 (New Style)	J	K**
Schultz & Larsen	A	G
1917 Enfield	J	J
Ruger 10/22	L	M
Ruger 44	O	M
Ruger 77R and RS Series†	H	P

* When ordering 'G' bases for Western Field Model 72 and Mossberg Model 472, please specify that .360 screws must be furnished.
** Requires Sub Block   † Drilling and Tapping Required

The Williams Sight-Thru Mount provides instant use of scope above or iron sights below. Easily installed. Uses existing holes on top of receiver. No drilling or tapping necessary. The Sight-Thru is compact and lightweight—will not alter balance of the rifle. The high tensile strength alloy will never rust. All parts are precision machined. Completely rigid. Shockproof. The attractive streamlined appearance is further enhanced by a beautiful, hard black anodized finish.

Rings are 1″ in size

⅞″ Sleeves available at $1.00 per set.

Sight-Thru Mount complete includes front and rear mount, rings, screws **$17.75**

One Ring complete with Sight-Thru base **8.88**

** Sub Block, when required **2.00**

* Patent Pending

SIGHT-THRU MOUNT FOR 22s

These new mounts are precision made. They are designed to fasten on the dovetails of all current 22's. For those 22's not having dovetails, there are mounting plates available to attach to receiver that creates the dovetails. Base of mount can be installed in a very low position with an unobstructed, clear view right down to the top of receiver—yet scope can still be elevated approximately ¼″ additional.

These WST-D22 Sight-Thru mounts are recommended for 22's only and are available in ¾″, ⅞″ and 1″ tube diameters. Specify tube diameter when ordering—

This Remington model 552 is equipped with a WST-D22-1″ mount and a Williams 4X Twilight scope. This sighting system is much more than just a plinking piece of equipment. It is accurate and dependable for target work and excellent for shooting running game.

WST-D22 ¾″ **$7.50**
WST-D22 ⅞″ **8.15**

WILLIAMS SCOPE MOUNTS

WILLIAMS QC SIDE MOUNTS

HCO Rings place scope overbore.

Regular Rings place scope offset.

The Williams QC Side Mounts permit the shooter to have both scope and receiver sight always available for instant use. From the same base, shooter has his choice of rings that place scope directly over the bore or in the offset position.

Williams Side Mounts have positive locks. Using these locks, the mount becomes a "one piece" mount. Used optionally, the mount is quickly detached. Williams QC Mounts are provided with a limited amount of windage in the base to insure you of a good mounting job.

QC Side Mount Base	$19.25
QC Side Mount Complete, with split or extension rings	34.15
QC Side Mount Complete with HCO rings	41.60

THE QUICK CONVERTIBLE SIDE MOUNT — WITH REGULAR OR HCO RINGS

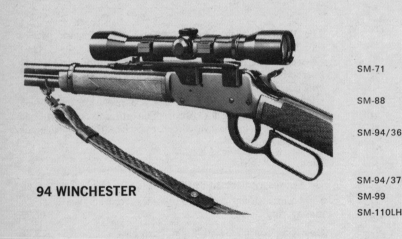

94 WINCHESTER

SM-70	Fits 70, 770, 670, 54 Winchesters; 600, 660, 700 R.H. and L.H., 721, 722 Remingtons; Mossberg 800 and 3000; Weatherby; Mauser; Enfield; Springfield; Jap; 40-45, 322-325 and 340-343 Savages; S&W and Mark X rifles; Stevens; round receivered SMLE's; Husqvarna; 7x61 S&H; Swiss 1911; 7.5; BSA; Savage 110 R.H.; and 91-93-95 small ring Mausers. (Also fits 98 Mauser large ring and 1917 Enfield large ring—request shim packs with mount.)
SM-71	Fits 36, 336, 93, 444, 44 Magnum, and 95 Marlins; 71* and 86* Winchesters; Remington 14 and 141; 7.62 Russian; and flat receivered SMLE's.
SM-88	Fits 88 and 100 Winchesters; Ruger 44 and 10/22; Winchester 150, 190, 250, 270, and 290; Weatherby 22; Browning lever action; and Sako Finnwolf.
SM-94/36	Fits 64, 65, 66, and 94 Winchesters. No drilling or tapping. On 36 and 336 Marlins drill and tap just one hole. NOTE: If mount is to be used with FP or 5D receiver sight, then use the SM-71 mount equipped with proper 94 screws.
SM-94/375	Fits Winchester 94 Big Bore .375.
SM-99	Fits 99 Savage.
SM-110LH	For the Savage 110 left-hand model (fastens on right side of receiver) and fits both short or long actions; and Weatherby Mark 5 L.H.
SM-340	Fits Savage 340 factory drilling and tapping. Also fits old 322-325 and 340-343 (drilling and tapping necessary).
SM-760/40/42	For 760-740-742 Remingtons. Regular mount base with four mounting holes. Also fits 30-M1 Garand and Carbine with mounting plate; Browning A.R.; Winchester 1200 and 1400; flat receivered shotguns such as Model 12; and flat receivered .22's such as 572 and 552.
SM-MS-52/56	For Mannlicher-Schoenauer of the modified version imported by Stoeger in 1952 and altered in 1956. Also for 1903 Greek Mannlicher modified receiver, like the 52-56. Will also fit Ithaca Model 37.
SM-Krag	For Krag* and Remington 788 right and left hand. Also, for Remington 870 and 1100.
SM-Mini-14	Fits Ruger Mini-14 .223 rifle with old or new-style receiver.
SM-Mini-14(NS)	(New Style) Fits Ruger Mini-14 .223 rifle with new style receiver.

* Will not accommodate central overbore rings.

Mounting plate for the 30-M1 carbine **$8.75**
(Attach with 8-40 fillister screws). Use the Williams SM-740 side mount base with this mounting plate. Scope can be offset or high overbore.

Mounting plate for SMLE No. 1 .... **$4.35**
(Attach with 8-40 fillister head mounting screws). This mounting plate is supplied with long 8-40 fillister head screws to replace SM-70 short screws. Use the QC SM-70 base. Mount can be installed offset or central overbore.

Mounting plate for M1 Garand rifle **$8.75**
The mounting screws for this mounting plate are 8-40 x .475 Fillister head. Use the Williams QC SM-740 (4 holes) side mount with this mounting plate.

QC SIDE MOUNT, BASES ONLY **$16.95**

QC SIDE MOUNT, COMPLETE WITH SPLIT, OR EXTENSION RINGS **$29.55**

QC SIDE MOUNT, COMPLETE WITH HCO (HIGH CENTRAL OVERBORE) RINGS **$36.00**

WILLIAMS DOVETAIL OPEN SIGHT

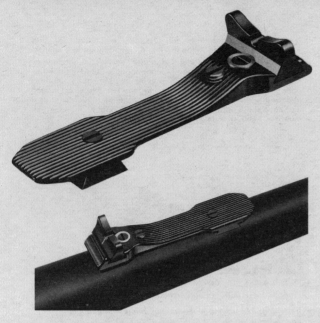

A precision sight made of lightweight high tensile strength alloy. Has steel screws and locks. Fits the standard ⅜" dovetail. Anodized black finish. Rustproof.

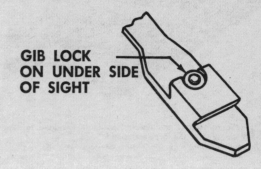

GIB LOCK ON UNDER SIDE OF SIGHT

The revolutionary design of the W.D.O.S. means **no more driving or hammering an open sight into the dovetail** of the rifle. The dovetail of the W.D.O.S. simply slides into the dovetail slot in the rifle barrel with just finger tip pressure as you tighten the locking screw it pulls the steel gib lock up snug against the dovetail on the rifle barrel and locks the sight in place.

Available in four heights with four different styles of blades — the same blades as used in the famous Williams Guide Open Sight — the U, V, SQ, and Britisher type notches.

WINDAGE ADJUSTMENT — Windage Adjustment is obtained by simply loosening the screw to unlock the steel gib lock and then the Williams Open Sight Blade can be moved either to the right or the left. In extreme cases, a double amount of windage can be obtained by getting windage in the dovetail of the barrel as well as with the blade.

ELEVATION—Elevation is obtained simply by an elevation set screw that can be turned in a full 1/16". Since the sight blades are also 1/16" from one model to another, you can get a wide range of adjustment from .281 up to .531.

The WDOS with 3/16" blade is adjustable in height from .281 to .345.

The WDOS with 1/4" blade is adjustable in height from .345 to .406.

The WDOS with 5/16" blade is adjustable in height from .406 to .468.

The WDOS with 3/8" blade is adjustable in height from .468 to .531.

MODELS: WDOS-U-281
          WDOS-U-345
          WDOS-U-406
          WDOS-U-468

The WDOS is furnished with the 'U' type blade unless otherwise ordered as the 'U' is the most popular. The 'V'—the 'SQ'—or the 'B' type may be ordered by merely substituting these letters for the 'U' in the model number.

TYPES OF BLADES

"SQ"   "U"   "V"   "B"

Sight blades are available in four styles and four heights. The "U", The "V", and "SQ" and the "B" in 3/16", ¼" 5/16" and ⅜".
EXTRA BLADES, each ------------------------------------ $3.10

BLADES

The "U" style is widely used by big game hunters and the "V" has almost as many advocates. The square notch is very popular with target shooters. However, many hunters prefer the square notch blade particularly when using a flat bladed front sight. "B" Britisher blade is exceedingly popular among African big game hunters.

Sight blades are interchangeable and may be quickly removed. Simply loosen the gib lock screw and change to any style or height of blade desired.

Extra sighting blades are just $1.95 each so that an assortment is inexpensive and will provide the shooter with a wide range of heights and styles to suit his taste or requirements.

Price with blade **$9.00**

WILLIAMS GUIDE OPEN SIGHT

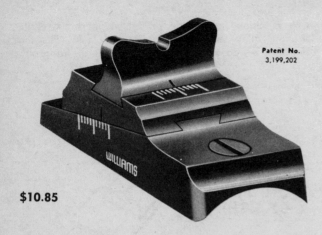

Patent No.
3,199,202

$10.85

The new Guide Open Sight was designed, engineered and field tested by the Williams. It advances a new concept in sighting.

It is compact, lightweight, and has a neat streamlined appearance. Both windage and elevation adjustments have positive locks — and various base and blade sizes permit the fitting of most any military or sporting rifle barrel in the greatest range of heights. Also used on rifles when you want iron sights high enough so that sighting plane is above a scope base on the receiver or when you want iron sights close to the height of scope sights.

Fast - the contour of the sighting blade is designed to give the shooter the greatest speed
- Made from high tensile strength metal. Will not rust.
- All parts are milled — no stampings.
- Streamlined and lightweight with tough anodized finish.
- Dovetailed windage and elevation — Adjustments quickly made by loosening one screw.
- Positive locks for windage and elevation.
- Hardened gib locks assure positive retention of zeroing.
- Fits all military and sporting rifles with ramp front sights.

- Easily installed. No dovetailing of barrel necessary. Simply fasten to barrel with two 6-48 screws.
- Interchangeable sighting blades of four different heights and four styles of notches.
- Fits the Drilling and Tapping on the 760, 740, 742, 700, 725 Remington, late 70 Win. etc. (9/16″ distance center to center on mounting screws.)

SIMPLE WAY TO DESIGNATE SIGHT DESIRED

1) SPECIFY TYPE OF SIGHT —

"WGOS" means
Williams Guide Open Sight

2) SPECIFY RADIUS OF BASE DESIRED S-M-L or FLAT
(Small - Medium - Large or Flat)

Small: for barrels .660 to .730
Medium: for barrels .730 to .830
Large: for barrels .830 to .930

SPECIAL high base is available for the model 70 Winchester with high line of sights for bbls .730 to .830.

3) SPECIFY OVERALL HEIGHT DESIRED

HEIGHT

The WGOS with 3/16″ blade is adjustable in height from .369 to .431.
The WGOS with 1/4″ blade is adjustable in height from .431 to .493.
The WGOS with 5/16″ blade is adjustable in height from .493 to .555.
The WGOS with 3/8″ blade is adjustable in height from .555 to .617.
The WGOS with flat base is .050 higher than the above standard models.
The WGOS-Special in extra large radius is .100 higher than any of the above models.
The WGOS flat base with peep sight aperture is adjustable from .481 to .543.

4) SPECIFY STYLE OF BLADE DESIRED

"SQ" - or - "U" - or - "V" or "B"

EXTRA BLADES — $2.70 each

The most popular blade is the 'U' type notch. Because of this, our WGOS are listed by models, all with the 'U' type notch blade fitted in them. You may want the other style notches as extra or as optional equipment. The following are the basic model numbers.

WGOS S 3/16″ 'U'	WGOS M 3/16″ 'U'
WGOS S 1/4″ 'U'	WGOS M 1/4″ 'U'
WGOS S 5/16″ 'U'	WGOS M 5/16″ 'U'
WGOS S 3/8″ 'U'	WGOS M 3/8″ 'U'

WGOS L 3/16″ 'U'
WGOS L 1/4″ 'U'
WGOS L 5/16″ 'U'
WGOS L 3/8″ 'U'

The WGOS can be ordered with other style blades or with the Flat bases instead of the Small (S), Medium (M) or Large (L) radii—or in the WGOS Special.

WILLIAMS SIGHTS

WILLIAMS SIGHT COMBINATION CHART

Ramp Height	Height from Base to Dovetail	Height of Williams Bead	From Top of Barrel to Top of Bead
1/8"	.035	.250	.285
1/8"	.035	.290	.325
1/8"	.035	.312	.347
3/16"	.0975	.250	.3475
1/8"	.035	.343	.378
3/16"	.0975	.290	.3875
3/16"	.0975	.312	.4095
1/8"	.035	.375	.410
3/16"	.0975	.343	.4405
1/8"	.035	.406	.441
9/32"	.191	.250	.441
9/32"	.191	.290	.481
3/16"	.0975	.375	.4725
5/16"	.2225	.250	.4725
1/8"	.035	.450	.485
9/32"	.191	.312	.503
3/16"	.0975	.406	.5035
5/16"	.2225	.290	.5125
9/32"	.191	.343	.534
5/16"	.2225	.312	.5345
3/8"	.285	.250	.535
3/16"	.0975	.450	.5475
5/16"	.2225	.343	.5655
9/32"	.191	.375	.566
3/8"	.285	.290	.575
9/32"	.191	.406	.597

Ramp Height	Height from Base to Dovetail	Height of Williams Bead	From Top of Barrel to Top of Bead
3/8"	.285	.312	.597
5/16"	.2225	.375	.5975
7/16"	.3475	.250	.5975
3/8"	.285	.343	.628
5/16"	.2225	.406	.6285
7/16"	.3475	.290	.6375
9/32"	.191	.450	.641
7/16"	.3475	.312	.6595
3/8"	.285	.375	.660
5/16"	.2225	.450	.6725
7/16"	.3475	.343	.6905
3/8"	.285	.406	.691
3/8"	.285	.450	.735
7/16"	.3475	.375	.7225
9/16"	.4725	.250	.7225
7/16"	.3475	.406	.7535
9/16"	.4725	.290	.7625
9/16"	.4725	.312	.7845
7/16"	.3475	.450	.7975
9/16"	.4725	.343	.8155
9/16"	.4725	.375	.8475
9/16"	.4725	.406	.8785
9/16"	.4725	.450	.9225

AMOUNT OF ADJUSTMENT NECESSARY TO CORRECT FRONT SIGHT ERROR

DISTANCE BETWEEN FRONT AND REAR SIGHTS		14"	15"	16"	17"	18"	19"	20"	21"	22"	23"	24"	25"	26"	27"	28"	29"	30"	31"	32"	33"	34"
Amount of	1	.0038	.0041	.0044	.0047	.0050	.0053	.0055	.0058	.0061	.0064	.0066	.0069	.0072	.0074	.0077	.0080	.0082	.0085	.0088	.0091	.0093
Error	2	.0078	.0083	.0089	.0094	.0100	.0105	.0111	.0116	.0122	.0127	.0133	.0138	.0144	.0149	.0155	.0160	.0156	.0171	.0177	.0182	.0188
at	3	.0117	.0125	.0133	.0142	.0150	.0159	.0167	.0175	.0184	.0192	.0201	.0209	.0217	.0226	.0234	.0243	.0251	.0259	.0268	.0276	.0285
100 Yards	4	.0155	.0167	.0178	.0189	.0200	.0211	.0222	.0234	.0244	.0255	.0266	.0278	.0289	.0300	.0311	.0322	.0333	.0344	.0355	.0366	.0377
Given in	5	.0194	.0208	.0222	.0236	.0250	.0264	.0278	.0292	.0306	.0319	.0333	.0347	.0361	.0375	.0389	.0403	.0417	.0431	.0445	.0458	.0472
Inches	6	.0233	.0250	.0267	.0283	.0300	.0317	.0333	.0350	.0367	.0384	.0400	.0417	.0434	.0450	.0467	.0484	.0500	.0517	.0534	.0551	.0567

When you replace an open rear sight with a receiver sight, it is usually necessary to install a higher front sight, to compensate for the higher plane of the new receiver sight. The table above shows the increase in front sight height that's required to compensate for a given error at 100 yards. Suppose your rifle has a 19 inch sight radius, and shoots 6 inches high at 100 yards, with the receiver sight adjusted as low as possible. The 19 inch column shows that the correction for a 6 inch error is .0317 inch. This correction is added to the over-all height of the front sight (including dovetail). Use a micrometer or similar accurate device to measure sight height. Thus, if your original sight measured .250 inch, it should be replaced with a sight .290 inch high.

WILLIAMS FRONT SIGHT PUSHER

$31.00

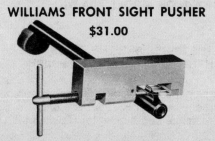

In the past there was only one accepted way to install a front sight in a ramp—pound it in with a hammer from the side. This method frequently marred a beautiful finish and loosened or damaged the ramp.

The Williams Front Sight Pusher provides the easiest and best way to install a front sight in a ramp. By equalizing the pressure on ramp and sight, it permits installation without marring or damaging, and eliminates excessive pressure on the ramp itself. Sight is smoothly and accurately moved into exact position.

The Front Sight Pusher is a precision tool for neat precision work.

WILLIAMS SIGHTS

$15.70

In most cases these sights utilize dovetail or existing screws on top of receiver for installation. They are made from an aluminum alloy that is stronger than many steels. Light. Rustproof. Williams quality throughout.

WGRS-37 — For Ithaca 37 pump shotgun.

WGRS-44 — For Ruger 44. Similar to the WGRS-RU22, but not interchangeable. Usually requires a higher front sight — .500 to .560.

WGRS-54 — For Savage-Anschutz 54, 64, 141, 141M, 153, 153S. Also Remington 541S, 552BDL, 572BDL, and Winchester 310 and 320. This is a very versatile sight in that it can be fitted on most of the dovetails on the receivers of .22 rifles. These dovetails have quite a wide tolerance and in many cases will require some hand fitting of the WGRS-54, but this can be easily accomplished by filing the bottom of the sight slightly to increase the width of the dovetail and then it is just a matter of slipping the sight on. Because most .22's do not have ramp front sights, a higher front sight is required. Use of the Williams Shorty or Streamlined ramp and a Williams beaded front sight should solve any of these problems.

WGRS-70 — For all post war Model 70 Winchesters. Will also fit the Model 670 and 770.

- Compact Low Profile
- Lightweight, Strong, Rustproof
- Positive Windage and Elevation Locks

WGRS-70 — For all post war Model 70 Winchesters. Will also fit the Model 670 and 770.

WGRS-100 — For Winchester 88 lever action and 100 automatic. (Higher front sight needed — .406 height.) Also for Sako Finnwolf.

WGRS-700 — For Remington 700, 721 and 722.

WGRS-742 — For Remington 760 and 742. Early models will require a higher front sight. For the BDL's, use the FP-740AP.

WGRS-BAR — For Browning High Power Auto rifle and lever action sporting version.

WGRS-FN — Will fit any FN type action with ½" hole spacing including the Mauser FN, S&W, Crown Grade Husqvarna (CGH), and the Browning high power bolt action, and Mark X.

WGRS-M1 CAR. — For the 30 M1 Carbine. Fits dovetail.

WGRS-M/L — For Thompson/Center Hawken and most black powder rifles with octagon barrels.

WGRS-RU-22 — Fits Ruger 10/22 without drilling or tapping. A higher front sight is normally required, usually .500 to .560.

WGRS-WR — For late Winchester and Remington slide action and autoloading shotguns. Also will fit Hopkins & Allen muzzleloaders.

OPEN SIGHT BLADES
FOR THE GUIDE OPEN SIGHT

Many shooters wish to make open sights out of receiver sights. This can be done since the blades from our Guide Open Sights are interchangeable with the apertures of the receiver sights. Any Guide Receiver Sight can be ordered special with a Guide Open Sight blade in the SQ, U, V, or B. Normally the 3/16" blade is used since it is the approximate same height as the regular peep sight aperture.

WILLIAMS STREAMLINED TOP MOUNT

SHOWN ON MODEL 70A WIN.

- AVAILABLE FOR WIDE ASSORTMENT OF FACTORY DRILLED RIFLES
- PRECISION MACHINED—LIGHTWEIGHT
- SOLID CONSTRUCTION
- ELIMINATES NEED FOR EXTENSION RINGS— ALLOWS USE OF VIRTUALLY ALL 1" SCOPES

- THE BASES ARE THE RINGS
- HARD BLACK ANODIZED FINISH

Streamline two-piece Top Mount complete **$17.75**
Streamline front or rear base only **8.88**
Streamline sub-blocks for Hawken ML (per pair) **6.45**

WILLIAMS SIGHTS & ACCESSORIES

Patent No. 2578386

THE FOOLPROOF

One of the reasons the Foolproof is so popular is that it is free from knobs and other obstructions that impair and blot-out much of the shooter's field of vision.

Internal micrometer adjustments have positive internal locks — there is nothing — no exterior knobs or posts — that could be accidentally jarred or moved to throw the sight out of adjustment.

The Foolproof is strong, rugged, dependable. The alloy used to manufacture this sight has a tensile strength of 85,000 lbs. Yet the Foolproof is light and compact, weighing only 1½ ounces.

$28.85

with Twilight Aperture—
$29.70

with Target Knobs = $34.35
with Target Knobs and Twilight
Aperture = $35.20

FOOLPROOF RECEIVER SIGHT WITH TARGET KNOBS

The FP-TK has audible micrometer click adjustments. Target knobs allow quick positive windage and elevation adjustments without the use of a screwdriver. Positive internal locks.

These Models Fit More Than 100 Guns

FP-12/37	For Winchester 12, 1200, 1400, 150, 190, 250, 255, 270 275 and 290; Ithaca 37; Remington Sportsman 48, 58, 11-48, 1100, 870* and most flat receivered pumps and autoloaders.
FP-14	For Remington 14 and 141.
FP-17	For Enfield, Remington Express and British Pattern 14.
FP-30 Car.	For Government 30 Carbine.
FP-39	For Marlin 39A lever action.
FP-52	For Win. 52 Sporter or other round receivered 52 models.
FP-70	For 70 and 54 Winchesters; 721, 722, 725 Remingtons; Mossberg 800.
FP-70AP	For new Model 70, 670 and 770 with high sight line; Remington 700; Mossberg 800 and 3000; BSA; and Smith & Wesson Model 1500.
FP-71	For Win. 95, 71, 86, 05, 07, and 10.
FP-88/100	For Win. 88 lever action; Win. 100 auto; Marlin 56, 57, 62, 99 auto-loading; and Sako Finnwolf.
FP-94/36	For Winchester Models 94, 55, 63, 64, 65, and 9422; Marlin Models 36, 336, 444, 44 Magnum, and 93; Sears and Browning centerfire lever actions.
FP-98	For military Mauser, Husqvarna, Weatherby Mark V, right and left, and BRNO without dovetailed receiver.
FP-98AP	For Browning high power bolt with high line of sights; also for Rem. 700 left hand.
FP-99	For Savage 99 lever action.
FP-99S	For late Savage 99 with top tang safety.
FP-110	For Savage 110 bolt action, right and left.
FP-121	For Remington 12 and 121.
FP-340	For 322-325-340-342 Stevens-Savage.

FP-600	For Remington 600, 660 bolt action and XP-100.
FP-740AP	For all 742 Remingtons and for the late 760-740 Remingtons with high comb (all purpose stock) and high iron sights. Also for the higher sight models of the 740 in the 30-06 and 280 calibers above serial number 207,200 and the 308 caliber above serial number 200,000. Also for Remington 572BDL and 552BDL and Savage 170.
FP-788	For Remington 788 bolt action.
FP-788LH	For Remington 788 left hand action.
FP-A3	For 03/A3 and 03 Springfields.
FP-BAR	For Browning auto-loading high power rifle.
FP-CGH	For Crown Grade Husqvarna and S&W rifle.
FP-FN	For factory drilled and tapped FN and Dumoulin, Mark X, Daisy 99 and 299.
FP-Hawken	For Thompson/Center Hawken and Renegade M/L rifles.
FP-JAP	For Jap .25 and .31 caliber rifles.
FP-Krag	For American Krag and Norwegian Krag.
FP-RU	For 44 Mag. Ruger carbine and .22 L.R. 10/22 all models.
FP-RU-77	For Ruger Model 77 bolt action.
FP-S&L	For Schultz & Larsen 54J, Model 60 and 65DL.
FP-SMLE	For British Short Magazine Lee Enfields.
FP-SSM	For square sterned auto shotguns. Also fits 8-81 Rem.
FP-SW	For 1911, Swiss 7.5.
FP-T/C	For Thompson/Center Contender Pistol.

NOTE: Add 'TK' to model number if target knobs are desired.

WILLIAMS SIGHTS & ACCESSORIES

5D-12-37

5D-22-410

5D-94-36

5D-JEMS

The Williams 5D receiver sight is made for big game rifles, shotguns, and 22 Caliber rifles. It is well made of the finest materials with positive windage and elevation adjustments. Standard thread sizes permit use of a wide range of apertures for all sighting conditions. This high-grade alloy is finished with an anodize in a deep blue-black that adds even further to the strength of the sight by creating an extra hard surface $16.40

FOR FOLLOWING MODELS

5D-12/37*   Winchester 1200, 1400, 12-25, 150, 190, 250, 255, 270, 275, and 290; Remington 1100, '58, 11-48, Spt's. 48, 870, and 31; Stevens 620; Ithaca 37; and other shotguns with flat-sided receivers.

5D-22/410   For the .22-410, 20, etc. over and under Savage or Stevens.

5D-39A   Marlin 39A lever action. No drilling or tapping necessary.

5D-49   For the Ithaca 49 Saddlegun .22 cal.

5D-56/989   For Marlin Levermatic 56, 57, 62, 99 Auto, Marlin 989 and 99's; Sako Finnwolf; Winchester 88 and 100.

5D-70   For Winchester 70, 54, 670, 770, and 74 .22 Auto; Remington 700, 721, 722, and 725; Mossberg 800 and 3000.

5D-74   For Winchester Model 74 .22 Auto.

5D-77   For Winchester 77 .22 Auto.

5D-81   For Marlin 80, 81 and A1 rifles (factory drilled and tapped).

5D-94/36   For Winchester 94, 64, 9422; Marlin 36, 336, 1894, .44 Magnum.

5D-510   For Remington 510, 511, 512, and 513 (some factory drilled and tapped), Nylon 12 tubular loading, Nylon 11 box magazine.

5D-550   For Remington 550 auto (it will also fit some of the Stevens-Savage .22's that are not drilled and tapped).

5D-572   For Remington 572, 572BDL, 552BDL .22 slide action; Kodiak 260.

5D-760N–740–742   For the Remington 760 with serial numbers above 154,965 and 740's above serial number 64,046. Also for Remington Nylon 66; Winchester new series 250, 255, 270, 275, and 290 with ramp; and Savage 170.

5D-CR-160   For Crosman air rifles model 160.

5D-JEMS   For Jap, Enfield, Mauser, and Springfield 03; Remington 700 L.H.; Daisy 99 and 299.

5D-Krag   For American Krag.

5D-03/A3   For 1903-A3 Springfield.

5D-RU   For 44 Ruger Carbine and 10/22 (all models).

5D-SH   For Sheridan Model 'C'; Benjamin 340, 342, 347. (The Benjamin needs a higher front sight).

5D-SMLE   For British Short Magazine Lee Enfield, Nos. 1, 4, & 5.

5D-SSM*   For square stern models of Remington, Browning and Savage auto shotguns. Also fits Rem. 8-81 autoloaders.

*Special shotgun aperture optional, Extra shotgun apertures $3.75
3/8'' OD Aperture with 093 inner hole furnished unless otherwise specified.

Some of the Higgins guns are made by Marlin. Usually if the model number 103 is on a Higgins gun— then it's made by Marlin. Consequently, some of the sights we have designed for Marlin will fit a few models of the Higgins.

AVAILABLE IN IVORY, RED, GOLD
Available in Ivory, Red, Gold

WILLIAMS "GUIDE BEAD" SHOTGUN SIGHTS
$3.05

Fits all shotguns. Large ⅛'' jewel finish bead has exceptional light gathering ability. Gets you on target fast. Easily installed. Screws into existing sight hole. Two thread sizes: 6-48 and 3-56, and two shank lengths, ³⁄₃₂'' and ⁵⁄₃₂''.

WILLIAMS SCOPE MOUNTS

WILLIAMS QUICK CONVERTIBLE TOP MOUNT

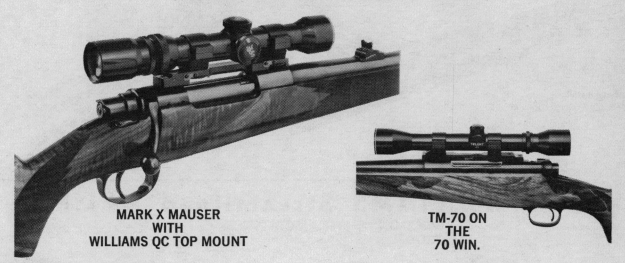

**MARK X MAUSER
WITH
WILLIAMS QC TOP MOUNT**

**TM-70 ON
THE
70 WIN.**

TM-03	For 03 Springfield.
TM-03/A3	For 03/A3 Springfield.
*****TM-7x61 (54)**	For Sharpe & Hart 7x61, 54 bolt action.
*****TM-7x61 (60)**	For Sharpe & Hart 7x61, 60 bolt action.
*****TM-14**	For Remington Model 14 slide action.
TM-17	For 1917 Enfield and 30 Express and 720 Remingtons. On the Enfield grind the receiver to the same height and radius in the rear as in the front.
TM-17 Special	For 1917 Enfield. There is enough stock left at the rear of mount base so the Model 17's not cut to standard specifications may be fitted.
TM-22 RU	For Ruger 10/22 Auto rifle.
*****TM-30**	For J. C. Higgins Model 30.
*****TM-43N**	For new Model 43 factory drilled and tapped.
*****TM-50**	For early versions of J. C. Higgins Model 50.
*****TM-52**	Fits late Winchester Model 52 Sporter and Target. (Older models are not drilled and tapped.)
*****TM-63/121**	For Win. 63 Auto and Rem. 121 slide action.
TM-70	For all factory drilled 70's and 670's, 770's except 300 H&H and 375 H&H. Rear hole spacing—center to center—.860.
*****TM-77**	For Winchester 77 .22 Auto.
TM-88	For Winchester 88 lever action, fitting factory drilling and tapping.
TM-93/95	For Mexican or Spanish Mausers (short action). It is necessary to flatten the top of receiver where the 5-shot clip enters receiver if the gun is not going to be reblued. If it is to be reblued, grind this lobe off entirely. Also for 91 Argentine Mauser, 94 Swedish Mauser.
TM-98	For 98 Mauser and standard Husqvarna. It is necessary to flatten the top of receiver where the 5-shot clip enters receiver if the gun is not going to be reblued. If it is to be reblued, grind this lobe off.
TM-99	For all 99's without tang safety.
TM-99S	For the 99 Savages 99DL and F models with tang type safety.
TM-100	For Model 100 Winchester Auto, Sako Finnwolf.
*****TM-110-L**	For Savage Model 110's, 30-06, 270, 7mm, 264, and 338 Magnum with longer action.
*****TM-110-LS**	For Savage left hand, short actions, 243 and 308.
*****TM-110-S**	For Savage Model 110, 243 and 308 short actions.

TM-336N	Fits late 336 Marlins that are factory drilled and tapped. Mounting screw holes are 8-40. Earlier models must be drilled and tapped. Includes the 444's.
TM-600	For Rem. 600, 660 bolt action, 40X and XP100 pistol.
TM-721-MK5	For factory drilled and tapped 721, 725, 700 (long action) Remingtons; Weatherby Mark 5; BSA; and Smith & Wesson Model 1500.
TM-722	Fits factory drilled and tapped 722 and 700 short action Remingtons.
TM-760	Fits 760, 740, 742 Remingtons. Most of these rifles are drilled and tapped on top for this mount. Also fits Savage 170.
*****TM-800**	For Mossberg 800.
TM-B22-241	For Browning .22 Auto and Rem. 241 with mount fastening on barrel and extending back over receiver.
TM-BAR	For Browning High Power Auto rifle and lever action.
*****TM-BRS**	For short action 243 Browning, FN Browning short action.
TM-CGH	For Crown Grade Husqvarna. Fits factory drilling and tapping. Also for Smith & Wesson rifle.
TM-FNA	For F.N. actions. Fits FN actions, Weatherby, and late J. C. Higgins Models 50 and 51, Browning High Power rifles. (Except short FN actions.)
*****TM-L-57**	For Sako medium action 243, 308, etc. Necessary to drill and tap.
TM-MK5-LH	For Weatherby Mark V L.H. and Rem. 700 L.H.
*****TM-RU**	For Ruger .44 Magnum carbine. Fits old style factory drilling and tapping with all 4 holes on receiver.
TM-SW Mauser	For Mauser Mark X.
TM-VOERE	For Voere Mauser.
TM-WBY-VM	Varmint Master, Weatherby 224 and 22/250 calibers.
TM-AR-15	For Colt AR-15 .223. (Also M-16)

QC Top Mount, Bases only $19.25

QC Top Mount, Complete 34.15

***** Discontinued — Subject To Stock On Hand.**

WILLIAMS RAMPS

Easy installation, simply insert in dovetail

The Streamlined

The Shorty

WILLIAMS Streamlined RAMPS

SWEAT-ON MODEL

STEEL MODELS

SCREW-ON MODEL

WITH HOOD **$12.20**
LESS HOOD **10.10**

The STREAMLINED

Available in heights of: 9/16", 7/16", 3/8", 5/16", 3/16".

WILLIAMS SHORTY RAMP — Steel —

MAY BE SWEATED ON

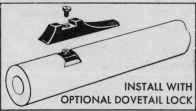

INSTALL WITH OPTIONAL DOVETAIL LOCK

SCREW ON
IN LOW ⅛" Model

ATTACH WITH ONE SCREW

A SHORTENED VERSION OF THE POPULAR STREAMLINED RAMP

The new Shorty ramp is the companion to the popular Streamlined ramp. It is much shorter, being designed especially for handguns, .22s and some of the big game rifles. The Shorty is easily installed. It can be sweated on or screwed on a Special locking device that fits the standard 3/8" dovetail cut and a 6:48 screw is also furnished. The single screw firmly locks ramp snugly to barrel for a neat perfect fit.
Four heights available: 1/8", 3/16", 9/32" and 3/8".

$7.75
HOODLESS ONLY

WILLIAMS RIFLE SIGHT ASSORTMENT KIT $147.85

Front sights available in eight heights with a 1/16" bead. Also 3/32" bead on special order. Half of the sights have a base width of .250 for the Streamlined and Shorty ramp and the other sights have a wide .340 base for the 99 Savage, 94 Winchester, 336 Marlin, etc.

Dovetail open sights available in four heights — from .281 to .468 with a "U" type notch unless otherwise **specified**.

4 Front Sights .250 high—Gold and White—Two Widths
4 Front Sights .281 high—Gold and White—Two Widths
4 Front Sights .312 high—Gold and White—Two Widths
4 Front Sights .343 high—Gold and White—Two Widths
4 Front Sights .375 high—Gold and White—Two Widths
4 Front Sights .406 high—Gold and White—Two Widths
4 Front Sights .437 high—Gold and White—Two Widths
4 Front Sights .468 high—Gold and White—Two Widths
4 Williams Dovetail Open Sights—Four Heights

Ammunition

CCI AMMUNITION

CCI 22 RIMFIRE

Part No.		Description	Retail per box	Qty. per Case	lbs. per Case
Plastic 100 PAK					
0030	P22HS	Mini-Mag Long Rifle	$4.30	5000	47
0031	P22HP	Mini-Mag Long Rifle (HP)	4.73	5000	45
0032	P22SV	Mini-Group Long Rifle	4.30	5000	47
0033	P22GT	Competition Green Tag	6.78	5000	44
0029	P22L	Mini-Mag Long	4.00	5000	39
0027	P22S	Mini-Mag Short	3.77	5000	37
0028	P22SHP	Mini-Mag Short (HP)	4.00	5000	37
0037	P22ST	Mini-Group Short Target	4.08	5000	37
0038	P22CBL	Mini-Cap Long	3.87	5000	38
0026	P22CB	Mini-Cap CB	3.87	5000	38
0039*	P22SS	Mini-Mag (Shotshell)	2.22	2000	18
Paper 50 PAK					
0034	22HS	Mini-Mag Long Rifle	2.15	5000	40
Plastic 50 PAK					
0050	STINGER	Penta-Point (LRHP)	2.85	5000	44
0023	WMR22HS	Maxi-Mag (Solid)	5.90	5000	58
0024	WMR22HP	Maxi-Mag (HP)	5.90	5000	58
0025*	WMR22SS	Maxi-Mag (Shotshell)	3.62	2000	26

CCI-SPEER LAWMAN CENTERFIRE

Plastic 50 PAK

380 AUTO					
3605	88 gr. JHP	Reserve	$14.35	1000	22
9mm LUGER					
3610	100 gr. JHP	Marshal	17.43	1000	27
3620	125 gr. JSP	M-P	17.43	1000	31
38 SPECIAL					
3710	110 gr. JHP	Special Agent	16.82	1000	30
3720	125 gr. JHP+P	Detective	16.82	1000	32
3725	125 gr. JSP+P	Patrolman	16.82	1000	32
3740	140 gr. JHP+P	Deputy	16.82	1000	34
3748	148 gr. HBWC	Match	13.80	1000	35
3750	150 gr. FMJ		16.82	1000	35
3752	158 gr. SWC L	Service	13.57	1000	37
3758	158 gr. RN L	Service	13.25	1000	37
3759	158 gr. JSP+P	Trooper	16.82	1000	37
3760	158 gr. JHP+P	S.W.A.T.	16.82	1000	37
3708	#9 SHOTSHELL		17.75	1000	31
3709**	#9 SHOTSHELL	(10-PAK)	4.34	1000	33
357 MAGNUM					
3910	110 gr. JHP	Special Agent	18.43	1000	35
3920	125 gr. JHP	Detective	18.43	1000	36
3925	125 gr. JSP	Patrolman	18.43	1000	36
3940	140 gr. JHP	Deputy	18.43	1000	38
3950	150 gr. FMJ		18.43	1000	40
3959	158 gr. JSP	Trooper	18.43	1000	39
3960	158 gr. JHP	S.W.A.T.	18.43	1000	39
Plastic 25 PAK					
44 MAGNUM					
3972	200 gr. JHP	Sheriff	12.02	500	30
3974	240 gr. JSP	Sheriff	12.02	500	30
3979**	#9 SHOTSHELL	(10-PAK)	5.79	1000	50
45 AUTO					
3965	200 gr. JHP	Inspector	9.93	500	29

*20 rounds per box
**10 rounds per box—10 boxes per carton—10 cartons per shipper

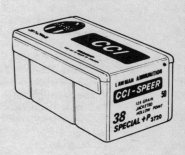

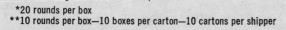

FEDERAL CENTERFIRE AMMUNITION

RIFLE CARTRIDGES

NO.	CALIBER	WT. GRS.	BULLET STYLE	FACTORY PRIMER NO.	BOX OF 20
222A	222 Remington	50	Soft Point	205	$8.50
222B	222 Remington	55	Metal Case Boat-tail	205	8.50
22250A	22-250 Remington	55	Soft Point	210	9.30
223A	223 Remington (5.56mm)	55	Soft Point	205	9.30
223B	223 Remington (5.56mm)	55	Metal Case Boat-tail	205	9.30
6A	6mm Remington	80	Soft Point	210	11.60
6B	6mm Remington	100	Hi-Shok Soft Point	210	11.60
243A	243 Winchester	80	Soft Point	210	11.60
243B	243 Winchester	100	Hi-Shok Soft Point	210	11.60
2506A	25-06 Remington	90	Hollow Point	210	12.60
2506B	25-06 Remington	117	Hi-Shok Soft Point	210	12.60
270A	270 Winchester	130	Hi-Shok Soft Point	210	12.60
270B	270 Winchester	150	Hi-Shok Soft Point	210	12.60
7A	7mm Mauser	175	Hi-Shok Soft Point	210	12.85
7RA	7mm Remington Magnum	150	Hi-Shok Soft Point	215	15.60
7RB	7mm Remington Magnum	175	Hi-Shok Soft Point	215	15.60
30CA	30 Carbine	110	Soft Point	205	8.10
30CB	30 Carbine	110	Metal Case	205	8.10
3030A	30-30 Winchester	150	Hi-Shok Soft Point	210	9.90
3030B	30-30 Winchester	170	Hi-Shok Soft Point	210	9.90
3006A	30-06 Springfield	150	Hi-Shok Soft Point	210	12.60
3006B	30-06 Springfield	180	Hi-Shok Soft Point	210	12.60
3006C	30-06 Springfield	125	Soft Point	210	12.60
3006D	30-06 Springfield	165	Soft Point Boat-tail	210	13.15
3006E	30-06 Springfield	200	Soft Point Boat-tail	210	13.15
300A	300 Savage	150	Hi-Shok Soft Point	210	12.70
300B	300 Savage	180	Hi-Shok Soft Point	210	12.70
300WB	300 Winchester Magnum	180	Hi-Shok Soft Point	215	16.45
308A	308 Winchester	150	Hi-Shok Soft Point	210	12.60
308B	308 Winchester	180	Hi-Shok Soft Point	210	12.60
8A	8mm Mauser	170	Hi-Shok Soft Point	210	13.00
32A	32 Winchester Special	170	Hi-Shok Soft Point	210	10.55
35A	35 Remington	200	Hi-Shok Soft Point	210	11.65
44A	44 Remington Magnum	240	Hollow Soft Point	150	9.60
4570A	45-70 Government	300	Hollow Soft Point	210	14.35
3030C	30-30 Winchester	125	Hollow Point	210	9.90

PISTOL CARTRIDGES

NO.	CALIBER	WT. GRS.	BULLET STYLE	PRIMER NO.	BOX OF 50
25 AP	25 Auto Pistol (6.35mm)	50	Metal Case	100	$12.25
32AP	32 Auto Pistol (7.65mm)	71	Metal Case	100	14.00
380AP	380 Auto Pistol	95	Metal Case	100	14.35
380BP	380 Auto Pistol	90	Jacketed Hollow Point	100	14.35
9AP	9mm Luger Auto Pistol	123	Metal Case	100	17.40
9BP	9mm Luger Auto Pistol	115	Jacketed Hollow Point	100	17.40
38A	38 Special (Match)	148	Lead Wadcutter	100	13.80
38B	38 Special	158	Lead Round Nose	100	13.25
38C	38 Special	158	Lead Semi-Wadcutter	100	13.55
38D	38 Special (High Vel + P)	158	Lead Round Nose	200	14.70
38E	38 Special (High Vel + P)	125	Jacketed Hollow Point	200	16.80
38F	38 Special (High Vel + P)	110	Jacketed Hollow Point	200	16.80
38G	38 Special (High Vel + P)	158	Lead Semi-Wad Cutter Hollow Point	200	14.40
38J	38 Special (High Vel + P)	125	Jacketed Soft Point	200	16.80
38H	38 Special (High Vel + P)	158	Lead Semi-Wadcutter	200	13.55
357A	357 Magnum	158	Jacketed Soft Point	200	18.40
357B	357 Magnum	125	Jacketed Hollow Point	200	18.40
357C	357 Magnum	158	Lead Semi-Wadcutter	200	15.60
357D	357 Magnum	110	Jacketed Hollow Point	200	18.40
357E	357 Magnum	158	Jacketed Hollow Point	200	18.40
44SA	S & W Special	200	Semi-Wadcutter Hollow Point	150	18.25
44B	44 Remington Magnum		Jacketed Hollow Point	150	21.80
45A	45 Automatic (Match)	230	Metal Case	150	19.20
45B	45 Automatic (Match)	185	Metal Case S.W.C.	150	19.85
45C	45 Automatic	185	Jacketed Hollow Point	150	19.85
45LCA	45 Colt	225	Lead Semi-Wad Cutter Hollow Point	150	17.75

FEDERAL RIMFIRE AMMUNITION

HI-POWER 22's with copper-plated bullets. A high velocity load for that extra-hard blow you need when hunting small game or pests. Their flat trajectory and accuracy provide an advantage at normal ranges. All have a non-corrosive, non-mercuric priming mixture that has long-term stability and will not cause barrel rust. Packed 50 per box except where noted.

NO.	CALIBER	WT. GRS.	BULLET STYLE	PER BOX
701	22 Short Hi-Power	29	Lead, Solid	$1.88
703	22 Short Hi-Power Hollow Point	29	Lead, HP	2.00
706	22 Long Hi-Power	29	Lead, Solid	2.00
710	22 Long Rifle Hi-Power	40	Lead, Solid	2.15
712	22 Long Rifle Hi-Power Hollow Point	38	Lead, HP	2.37
716	22 Long Rifle Hi-Power Shot	25	No. 12 Shot	4.36
810	22 Long Rifle Hi-Power (100 pack)	40	Lead, Solid	4.30
812	22 Long Rifle Hi-Power Hollow Point (100 pack)	38	Lead, HP	4.74

CHAMPION standard velocity 22's. A standard velocity load with a lubricated lead bullet for plinking, short range hunting, and informal target shooting where consistent accuracy is needed. All have non-corrosive, non-mercuric priming mixture which will not cause barrel rust. Packed 50 per box except where noted.

NO.	CALIBER	WT. GRS.	BULLET STYLE	PER BOX
711	22 Long Rifle	40	Lead, Solid	$1.88
811	22 Long Rifle (100 pack)	40	Lead, Solid	4.30

FEDERAL SHOTSHELLS

Gauge	Load No.	Shell Length Inches	Dram Equiv.	Shot Charge Oz.	Shot Sizes	Price Per Box
SUPER MAGNUM LOADS						
▲10	F103	3½	4¼	2	BB,2,4	$22.95
▲12	F131	3	4	1⅞	BB,2,4	15.35
▲12	F129	3	4	1⅝	2,4,6	14.20
▲12	F130	2¾	3¾	1½	BB,2,4,5,6	12.85
▲16	F165	2¾	3¼	1¼	2,4,6	12.65
▲20	F207	3	3	1¼	2,4,6,7½	11.90
▲20	F205	2¾	2¾	1⅛	4,6,7½	10.55
HI-POWER LOADS						
12	F127	2¾	3¾	1¼	BB,2,4,5,6,7½,8,9	9.90
16	F164	2¾	3¼	1⅛	4,5,6,7½	9.50
20	F203	2¾	2¾	1	4,5,6,7½,8,9	8.70
28	F283	2¾	2¼	¾	6,7½,8	8.75
.410	F413	3	Max.	11⁄16	4,5,6,7½,8	8.15
.410	F412	2½	Max.	½	6,7½	6.90
WATERFOWL STEEL SHOT LOADS						
12	W147	2¾	3¾	1⅛	1,2,4 Steel	12.40
▲12	W148	2¾	3¾	1¼	BB1,2,4 Steel	14.90
▲12	W149	3	3½	1⅜	BB1,2,4 Steel	16.60
▲10	W104	3½	4¼	1⅝	BB2 Steel	20.85
▲20	W209	3	3¼	1	4 Steel	11.90
FIELD LOADS						
12	F125	2¾	3¼	1¼	7½,8	9.30
12	F124	2¾	3¼	1¼	7½,8,9	8.75
12	F123	2¾	3¼	1⅛	4,5,6,7½,8,9	8.45
16	F162	2¾	2¾	1⅛	4,6,7½,8	8.45
20	F202	2¾	2½	1	4,5,6,7½,8,9	7.65
GAME LOADS						
12	F121	2¾	3¾	1	6,7½,8	6.85
16	F160	2¾	2½	1	6,7½,8	6.80
20	F200	2¾	2½	⅞	6,7½,8	6.25
DUCK & PHEASANT LOADS						
12	F126	2¾	3¾	1¼	4,5,6,7½	8.55
16	F163	2¾	3¼	1⅛	4,6,7½	8.40
20	F204	2¾	2¾	1	4,6,7½	7.70

Gauge	Load No.	Shell Length Inches	Dram Equiv.	Shot Charge Oz.	Shot Sizes	Price Per Box
RIFLED SLUG LOADS						
12	F127	2¾	Max.	1	Rifled Slug	$ 3.20
▲12	A127	2¾	Max.	1	Rifled Slug	16.00
16	F164	2¾	Max.	⅘	Rifled Slug	3.20
20	F203	2¾	Max.	⅝	Rifled Slug	2.95
.410	F412	2½	Max.	⅕	Rifled Slug	2.80
TARGET LOADS						
12	F115	2¾	2¾	1⅛	7½,8,9	7.55
12	F116	2¾	3	1⅛	7½,8,9	7.55
12	C117	2¾	2¾	1⅛	7½,8,8½,9	7.35
12	C118	2¾	3	1⅛	7½,8,9	7.35
12	T122	2¾	3	1⅛	9	7.55
20	F206	2¾	2½	⅞	8,9	7.05
20	S206	2¾	2½	⅞	9	7.05
28	F280	2¾	2	¾	9	8.55
.410	F412	2½	Max.	½	9	6.90
HI-POWER® BUCKSHOT LOADS						
10	G108	3½	Mag.		4 Buck—54 Pellets	4.70
12	F131	3	Mag.		000 Buck—10 Pellets	3.55
12	F131	3	Mag.		00 Buck—15 Pellets	3.55
12	F131	3	Mag.		1 Buck—24 Pellets	3.55
12	F131	3	Mag.		4 Buck—41 Pellets	3.55
▲12	A131	3	Mag.		4 Buck—41 Pellets	17.75
12	F130	2¾	Mag.		00 Buck—12 Pellets	3.10
12	F130	2¾	Mag.		1 Buck—20 Pellets	3.10
12	F130	2¾	Mag.		4 Buck—34 Pellets	3.10
▲12	A130	2¾	Mag.		4 Buck—34 Pellets	15.50
12	F127	2¾	Max.		000 Buck— 8 Pellets	2.80
12	G127	2¾	Max.		00 Buck— 9 Pellets	2.80
12	F127	2¾	Max.		00 Buck— 9 Pellets	2.80
12	F127	2¾	Max.		0 Buck—12 Pellets	2.80
12	F127	2¾	Max.		1 Buck—16 Pellets	2.80
12	F127	2¾	Max.		4 Buck—27 Pellets	2.80
▲12	A127	2¾	Max.		4 Buck—27 Pellets	14.00
16	F164	2¾	Max.		1 Buck—12 Pellets	2.80
20	F207	3	Mag.		2 Buck—18 Pellets	3.10
20	F203	2¾	Max.		3 Buck—20 Pellets	2.80

Buckshot and rifled slugs packed 5 rounds per box, except ▲ 25 rounds per box. All other shotshells packed 25 rounds per box.

FIOCCHI RIMFIRE AMMUNITION

22 Rimfire Cartridges

CALIBER	BULLET WEIGHT IN GRAINS	BULLET TYPE	CALIBER	BULLET WEIGHT IN GRAINS	BULLET TYPE	CALIBER	BULLET WEIGHT IN GRAINS	BULLET TYPE
22 SHORT TRAINING	29	Lead	22 SHORT "Z"	29	Lead	22 L.R. ULTRASONIC	40	Lead
22 SHORT NOMALE	29	Lead	22 LONG	28	Lead	22 L.R. EXPANSIVE	37	Lead
22 SHORT OLIMPIONICO	31	Lead	22 LONG "Z"	29	Lead	22 L.R. COMPETIZIONE	40	Lead
22 SHORT V 50	28	Lead	22 LONG L.R. MAXAC	40	Lead	22 L.R. PISTOLA LIBERA	40	Lead
22 SHORT EXPANSIVE	28	Lead	22 L.R. CARB. BERETTA	40	Lead	22 EXTRA LONG	40	Lead

Short

Short H.P.

Short Spatterpruf

Long Rifle

Long Rifle H.P.

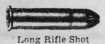
Long Rifle Shot

Long Rifle Match

W.R.F. (Rem. Spec.)

Winchester Magnum

H. P.—Hollow Point   LUB.—Lubricated   L. V.—Low Velocity

FIOCCHI CENTERFIRE AMMUNITION

Centerfire Cartridges for Pistols

CALIBER	BULLET WEIGHT IN GRAINS	BULLET TYPE
25 A.C.P. 6.35mm	50 / 50	F.M.C. / Lead
.30 MAUSER 7.63mm Mauser	88	F.M.C.
32 A.C.P. 7.65mm	73 / 75	F.M.C. / Lead
30 LUGER PARABELLUM 7.65mm	93	F.M.C.
ROTH-STEYR 8mm	113	F.M.C.
380 A.C.P. 9mm (short M34)	93	F.M.C.
9mm LUGER 9mm (long M38)	115	F.M.C.
9mm GLISENTI	123	F.M.C.
9mm LUGER PARABELLUM	123	F.M.C.
9mm STEYR	115	F.M.C.
30 MI CARBINE	111	F.M.C.
38 A.C.P. 38	129	F.M.C.
45 A.C.P. 45	230	F.M.C.

Centerfire Cartridges for Revolvers

CALIBER	BULLET WEIGHT IN GRAINS	BULLET TYPE
5.5mm VELO DOG REVOLVER 5.75 VELO DOG	43	F.M.C.
SWISS ORDNANCE 7.5mm	107	F.M.C.

CALIBER	BULLET WEIGHT IN GRAINS	BULLET TYPE
7.62 NAGANT	97	F.M.C.
8mm LEBEL	111	F.M.C.
8mm GASSER	126	F.M.C.
ITALIAN ORDNANCE 10.4mm	177	F.M.C.
32 SMITH & WESSON SHORT	85 / 85	F.M.C. / Lead
32 SMITH & WESSON LONG	98 / 98	F.M.C. / Lead
320 SHORT	82 / 82	F.M.C. / Lead
320 LONG	82 / 82	F.M.C. / Lead
38 SMITH & WESSON SHORT	145 / 145	F.M.C. / Lead
38 SPECIAL	158 / 158	F.M.C. / Lead
38 SPECIAL WAD CUTTER	148	Lead
380 SHORT	125 / 125	F.M.C. / Lead
380 LONG	125 / 125	F.M.C. / Lead
44 SMITH & WESSON RUSSIAN	247	Lead
450 SHORT	226	Lead
455 MK II	262	Lead
357 MAGNUM	158	J.S.P.

HORNADY FRONTIER CARTRIDGES

RIFLE AMMUNITION

222 REM.
- #8010   50 gr. SX .... $ 8.40
- #8015   55 gr. SX .... $ 8.40

223 REM.
- #8025   55 gr. SP .... $ 9.25
- #8027   55 gr. FMJ .... $ 9.25

22-250 REM.
- #8030   53 gr. HP .... $ 9.25
- #8035   55 gr. SP .... $ 9.25
- #8037   55 gr. FMJ .... $ 9.25

220 SWIFT
- #8120   55 gr. SP $12.95
- #8122   60 gr. HP $12.95

243 WIN.
- #8040   75 gr. HP $11.50
- #8043   80 gr. FMJ $11.50
- #8045 100 gr. SP $11.50

270 WIN.
- #8050 110 gr. HP $12.50
- #8055 130 gr. SP $12.50
- #8056 140 gr. BTSP $12.65
- #8058 150 gr. SP $12.50

7MM REM. MAG.
- #8060 154 gr. SP $15.50
- #8065 175 gr. SP $15.50

30 M1 CARBINE
- #8070 110 gr. RN $20.10
- #8077 110 gr. FMJ $20.10

30-30 WIN.
- #8080 150 gr. RN .... $ 9.80
- #8085 170 gr. FP .... $ 9.80

308 WIN.
- #8090 150 gr. SP $12.50
- #8095 165 gr. SP $12.50
- #8098 165 gr. BTSP $12.95
- #8097 168 gr. BTHP Match $14.60

30-06 SPRINGFIELD
- #8110 150 gr. SP $12.50
- #8115 165 gr. BTSP $12.95
- #8117 168 gr. BTHP Match $14.60
- #8118 180 gr. SP $12.50

300 WIN. MAG.
- #8200 180 gr. SP $16.35

PISTOL AMMUNITION

  NEW

25 AUTO
- #9000   50 gr. FMJ-RN $12.15

380 AUTO
- *#9010   90 gr. JHP $14.20
- *#9015 100 gr. FMJ $14.20

9MM LUGER
- *#9020   90 gr. JHP $17.25
- *#9023 100 gr. FMJ $17.25
- *#9025 115 gr. JHP $17.25
- *#9027 124 gr. FMJ-FP $17.25

38 SPECIAL
- *#9030 110 gr. JHP $16.35
- *#9032 125 gr. JHP $16.35
- *#9033 125 gr. JFP $16.35
- *#9043 148 gr. HBWC Match .. $14.05
- *#9036 158 gr. JHP $16.35
- *#9038 158 gr. JFP $16.35
- *#9045 158 gr. LRN $13.40
- *#9046 158 gr. SWC $13.40

357 MAG.
- *#9050 125 gr. JHP $18.25
- *#9053 125 gr. JFP $18.25
- *#9056 158 gr. JHP $18.25
- *#9058 158 gr. JFP $18.25
- *#9065 158 gr. SWC $15.45

44 REM. MAG.
- #9080 200 gr. JHP .... $ 9.50
- #9085 240 gr. JHP .... $ 9.50
- #9087 240 gr. SWC .... $ 8.05

45 ACP
- #9090 185 gr. JHP .... $ 8.05
- #9095 185 gr. SWC Target ..... $ 8.70
- #9110 200 gr. SWC .... $ 7.45
- #9097 230 gr. FMJ-RN .... $ 8.05
- #9098 230 gr. FMJ-FP .... $ 8.05

BBWC—Bevel Base Wadcutter	HP—Hollow Point
BT—Boat Tail	RN—Round Nose
DEWC—Double End Wadcutter	SJ—Short Jacket
FMJ—Full Metal Jacket	SP—Spire Point
FP—Flat Point	SWC—Semi-Wadcutter
HBWC—Hollow Base Wadcutter	SX—Super Explosive

* PACKED 50 PER BOX. ALL OTHERS PACKED 20 PER BOX

NORMA CENTERFIRE RIFLE AMMO

NO.	WT. GRAINS	BULLET STYLE	PER BOX OF 20
220 SWIFT:			
15701	50	Soft Point Semi Pointed	**$18.00**
222 REMINGTON:			
15711	50	Soft Point Semi Pointed	**9.60**
15712	**50**	**Full Jacket**	**11.70**
15714	53	Soft Point Semi Pointed Match Spitzer	**9.60**
22-250 :			
15733	53	Soft Point Semi Pointed Match Spitzer	**9.70**
22 SAVAGE HIGH POWER: (5.6x52 R):			
15604	71	Soft Point Semi Pointed	**21.70**
15605	71	Full Jacketed Semi Pointed	**21.70**
243 WINCHESTER:			
16002	100	Full Jacketed Semi Pointed	**13.00**
16003	100	Soft Point Semi Pointed	**13.00**
6.5 JAP:			
16531	139	Soft Point Semi Pointed Boat Tail	**21.00**
16532	156	Soft Point Round Nose	**21.00**
6.5 x 55:			
16550	77	Soft Point Semi Pointed	**21.00**
16557	139	Plastic Pointed "Dual-Core"	**21.00**
16552	156	Soft Point Round Nose	**21.00**
6.5 CARCANO:			
16535	156	Soft Point Round Nose	**21.00**
16536	139	Plastic Pointed "Dual-Core"	**21.95**
270 WINCHESTER:			
16902	130	Soft Point Semi Pointed Boat Tail	**14.20**
16903	150	Soft Point Semi Pointed Boat Tail	**14.20**
7 x 57 (7MM MAUSER):			
17002	150	Soft Point Semi Pointed Boat Tail	**15.00**
7 x 57 R:			
17005	150	Soft Point Semi Pointed Boat Tail	**22.50**
17006	150	Full Jacketed Pointed Boat Tail	**22.50**
7MM REM. MAGNUM:			
17021	150	Soft Point Semi Pointed Boat Tail	**18.30**
7 x 64:			
17013	150	Soft Point Semi Pointed Boat Tail	**22.50**
17015	175	Soft Point Nosler	

NO.	WT. GRAINS	BULLET STYLE	PER BOX OF 20
280 REMINGTON (7MM EXPRESS):			
17050	150	Soft Point Semi Pointed Boat Tail	**$14.75**
7.5 x 55 SWISS:			
17511	180	Soft Point Semi Pointed Boat Tail	**22.00**
30 U.S. CARBINE:			
17621	110	Soft Point Round Nose	**12.60**
7.62 x 39 SHORT RUSSIAN:			
17672	**125**	**Soft Point**	**17.00**
7.62 RUSSIAN:			
17634	180	Soft Point Semi Pointed Boat Tail	**22.35**
30-06 SPRINGFIELD:			
17640	130	Soft Point Semi Pointed Boat Tail	**14.15**
17643	150	Soft Point Semi Pointed Boat Tail	**14.15**
17648	180	Soft Point Round Nose	**14.15**
17653	180	Plastic Pointed "Dual-Core"	**14.15**
17656	**180**	**Plastic Pointed "Dual-Core"**	**7.10** (10 pack)
30-30 WINCHESTER:			
17630	150	Soft Point Flat Nose	**13.30**
17631	170	Soft Point Flat Nose	**13.30**
308 WINCHESTER:			
17623	130	Soft Point Semi Pointed Boat Tail	**14.15**
17624	150	Soft Point Semi Pointed Boat Tail	**14.70**
17628	180	Plastic Pointed "Dual-Core"	**16.35**
308 NORMA MAGNUM:			
17638	180	Plastic Pointed "Dual-Core"	**27.90**
7.65 ARGENTINE:			
17701	150	Soft Point Semi Pointed	**21.95**
303 BRITISH:			
17712	150	Soft Point Semi Pointed	**15.70**
17713	180	Soft Point Semi Pointed Boat Tail	**15.70**
7.7 JAP:			
17721	130	Soft Point Semi Pointed	**22.50**
17722	180	Soft Point Semi Pointed Boat Tail	**22.50**
8 x 57 J (.318"):			
17901	196	Plastic Pointed "Dual-Core"	**23.00**
8 x 57 JS (8 MM MAUSER):			
18003	196	Soft Point Round Nose	**15.50**
358 NORMA MAGNUM:			
19001	250	Soft Point	**27.95**
9.3 x 57:			
19302	286	Plastic Pointed "Dual-Core"	**19.75**
9.3 x 62:			
19314	286	Plastic Pointed "Dual-Core"	**19.75**

NORMA CENTERFIRE PISTOL AMMUNITION

NO.	WT. GRAINS	BULLET STYLE	PER BOX OF 50
30 LUGER:			
17612	93	Full Jacketed Round Nose	$26.70
32 ACP:			
17614	77	Full Jacketed Round Nose	18.35
9MM LUGER:			
19021	115	Hollow Point	24.90
19022	116	Full Jacketed Round Nose	24.90
19026	116	Soft Point Flat Nose	24.90
38 SPECIAL:			
19114	158	Full Jacketed Semi-Wad Cutter	23.35
19119	110	Jacketed Hollow Point Magnum	29.20
19110	148	Lead Wad Cutter	15.90
19112	158	Lead Round Nose	15.90

NO.	WT. GRAINS	BULLET STYLE	PER BOX OF 50
38 SPECIAL:			
19124	158	Soft Point Flat Nose	$20.90
19125	158	Hollow Point	20.90
357 MAGNUM:			
19101	158	Hollow Point	25.90
19106	158	Full Jacketed Semi-Wad Cutter	30.00
19107	158	Soft Point Flat Nose	25.90
44 MAGNUM:			
11103	240	Power Cavity (Box of 20)	14.35
44 AUTO MAGNUM:			
11105	240	Flat Point	45.00

REMINGTON CENTERFIRE PISTOL & REVOLVER CARTRIDGES
with "KLEANBORE" PRIMING

22 Remington "Jet" Magnum

No.	Bullet weight	Bullet style	Wt. case, lbs.	Per box
R22JET	40 gr.	Soft Point	12	$21.00

50 in a box, 500 in a case.

32 Short Colt

No.	Bullet weight	Bullet style	Wt. case, lbs.	Per box
R32SC	80 gr.	Lead	10	$11.75

50 in a box, 500 in a case.

221 Remington "Fire Ball"

No.	Bullet weight	Bullet style	Wt. case, lbs.	Per box
R221F	50 gr.	PTd. Soft Point	12	$9.70

20 in a box, 500 in a case.

32 Long Colt

No.	Bullet weight	Bullet style	Wt. case, lbs.	Per box
R32LC	82 gr.	Lead	10	$12.25

50 in a box, 500 in a case.

25 (6.35mm) Auto. Pistol

No.	Bullet weight	Bullet style	Wt. case, lbs.	Per box
R25AP	50 gr.	Metal Case	28	$12.25

50 in a box, 2,000 in a case.

32 (7.65mm) Auto. Pistol

No.	Bullet weight	Bullet style	Wt. case, lbs.	Per box
R32AP	71 gr.	Metal Case	36	$14.00

50 in a box, 2,000 in a case.

REMINGTON CENTERFIRE PISTOL AND REVOLVER CARTRIDGES

32 S & W

No.	Bullet weight	Bullet style	Wt. case, lbs.	Per box
R32SW	88 gr.	Lead	41	$11.85

50 in a box, 2,000 in a case.

32 S & W Long

No.	Bullet weight	Bullet style	Wt. case, lbs.	Per box
R32SWL	98 gr.	Lead	46	$12.25

50 in a box, 2,000 in a case.

357 Magnum

No.	Bullet weight	Bullet style	Wt. case, lbs.	Per box
R357M7	110 gr.	Semi-Jacketed Hollow Point	63	$18.40
R357M1	125 gr.	Semi-Jacketed Hollow Point	71	18.40
R357M2	158 gr.	Semi-Jacketed Hollow Point	77	18.40
R357M3	158 gr.	Soft Point	77	18.40
R357M4	158 gr.	Metal Point	77	18.15
R357M5	158 gr.	Lead	77	15.60
R357M6	158 gr.	Lead (Brass Case)	77	15.60

50 in a box, 2,000 in a case.

9mm Luger Auto. Pistol

No.	Bullet weight	Bullet style	Wt. case, lbs.	Per box
R9MM1	115 gr.	Jacketed Hollow Point	54	$17.40
R9MM2	124 gr.	Metal Case	56	17.40

50 in a box, 2,000 in a case.

38 S & W

No.	Bullet weight	Bullet style	Wt. case, lbs.	Per box
R38SW	146 gr.	Lead	63	$13.15

50 in a box, 2,000 in a case.

38 Special

No.	Bullet weight	Bullet style	Wt. case, lbs.	Per box
R38S1	95 gr.	Semi-Jacketed Hollow Point (+P)	52	$16.80
R38S10	110 gr.	Semi-Jacketed Hollow Point (+P)	56	16.80
R38S2	125 gr.	Semi-Jacketed Hollow Point (+P)	65	16.80
R38S3	148 gr.	Targetmaster Lead Wadcutter	66	13.80
R38S4	158 gr.	Targetmaster Lead Round Nose	70	13.80
R38S5	158 gr.	Lead	70	13.25
R38S6	158 gr.	Lead Semi-Wad-cutter	70	13.55
R38S7	158 gr.	Metal Point	70	16.80
R38S8	158 gr.	Lead (+P)	70	14.70
R38S12	158 gr.	Lead Hollow Point (+P)	69	14.40
R38S9	200 gr.	Lead	82	14.15

50 in a box, 2,000 in a case.

38 Short Colt

No.	Bullet weight	Bullet style	Wt. case, lbs.	Per box
R38SC	125 gr.	Lead	14	$12.90

50 in a box, 500 in a case.

38 Super Auto. Colt Pistol

Adapted only for 38 Colt Super and Colt Commander Automatic Pistols.

No.	Bullet weight	Bullet style	Wt. case, lbs.	Per box
R38SUI	115 gr.	Jacketed Hollow Point (+P)	56	$15.15
R38SUP	130 gr.	Metal Case (+P)	62	15.75

50 in a box, 2,000 in a case.

38 Auto. Colt Pistol

Adapted only for 38 Colt Sporting, Military and Pocket Model Automatic Pistols.

No.	Bullet weight	Bullet style	Wt. case, lbs.	Per box
R38ACP	130 gr.	Metal Case	62	$15.65

50 in a box, 2,000 in a case.

(+P) Ammunition with (+P) on the case headstamp is loaded to higher pressure. Use only in firearms designated for this cartridge and so recommended by the gun manufacturer.

REMINGTON CENTERFIRE CARTRIDGES PISTOL/REVOLVER

380 Auto. Pistol

No.	Bullet weight	Bullet style	Wt. case, lbs.	Per box
R380A1	88 gr.	Jacketed Hollow Point	45	$14.35
R380AP	95 gr.	Metal Case	45	14.35

50 in a box, 2,000 in a case.

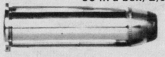

41 Magnum

No.	Bullet weight	Bullet style	Wt. case, lbs.	Per box
R41MG1	210 gr.	Soft Point	52	$24.20
R41MG2	210 gr.	Lead	49	20.70

50 in a box, 1,000 in a case.

44 S&W Special

No.	Bullet weight	Bullet style	Wt. case, lbs.	Per box
R44SW	246 gr.	Lead	25	$18.55

50 in a box, 500 in a case.

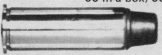

44 Remington Magnum

No.	Bullet weight	Bullet style	Wt. case, lbs.	Per box
R44MG1	240 gr.	Lead, Gas-Check	57	$23.50
R44MG4	240 gr.	Lead	57	20.05

50 in a box, 1,000 in a case.

R44MG2	240 gr.	Soft Point	29	9.60
R44MG3	240 gr.	Semi-Jacketed Hollow Point	29	9.60
R44MG5	180 gr.	Semi-Jacketed Hollow Point	29	8.75

20 in a box, 500 in a case.

45 Colt

No.	Bullet weight	Bullet style	Wt. case, lbs.	Per box
R45C	250 gr.	Lead	26	$17.80

50 in a box, 500 in a case.

45 Auto.

No.	Bullet weight	Bullet style	Wt. case, lbs.	Per box
R45AP1	185 gr.	Targetmaster Metal Case Wadcutter	43	$19.85
R45AP2	185 gr.	Jacketed Hollow Point	43	19.85
R45AP3	230 gr.	Targetmaster Metal Case	49	19.85
R45AP4	230 gr.	Metal Case	49	19.20

50 in a box, 1,000 in a case.

45 Auto. Rim

No.	Bullet weight	Bullet style	Wt. case, lbs.	Per box
R45AR	230 gr.	Lead	27	$20.50

50 in a box, 500 in a case.

REMINGTON CENTER FIRE BLANK

No.	Caliber	No. in case	Wt. case, lbs.	Per box
R32BLNK	32 S & W	5,000	37	$11.70
R38SWBL	38 S & W	2,000	25	14.15
R38BLNK	38 Special	2,000	28	14.25

50 in a box.

RIFLE

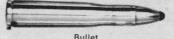

17 Remington

No.	Bullet weight	Bullet style	Wt. case, lbs.	Per box
R17REM	25 gr.	Hollow Point "Power-Lokt"	12	$10.80

20 in a box, 500 in a case.

22 Hornet

No.	Bullet weight	Bullet style	Wt. case, lbs.	Per box
R22HN1	45 gr.	Pointed Soft Point	9	$19.90
R22HN2	45 gr.	Hollow Point	9	19.90

50 in a box, 500 in a case.

222 Remington

No.	Bullet weight	Bullet style	Wt. case, lbs.	Per box
R222R1	50 gr.	Pointed Soft Point	27	$8.50
★R222R4	55 gr.	Metal Case	27	8.50
R222R3	50 gr.	Hollow Point "Power-Lokt"	27	9.25

20 in a box, 1,000 in a case.

222 Remington Magnum

No.	Bullet weight	Bullet style	Wt. case, lbs.	Per box
R222M1	55 gr.	Pointed Soft Point	15	$9.65
R222M2	55 gr.	Hollow Point "Power-Lokt"	15	10.30

20 in a box, 500 in a case.

22-250 Remington

No.	Bullet weight	Bullet style	Wt. case, lbs.	Per box
R22501	55 gr.	Pointed Soft Point	42	$9.30
R22502	55 gr.	Hollow Point "Power-Lokt"	42	10.00

20 in a box, 1,000 in a case.

(*) May be used in rifles chambered for .244 Remington.

★ **New for 1981**

REMINGTON CENTERFIRE RIFLE CARTRIDGES

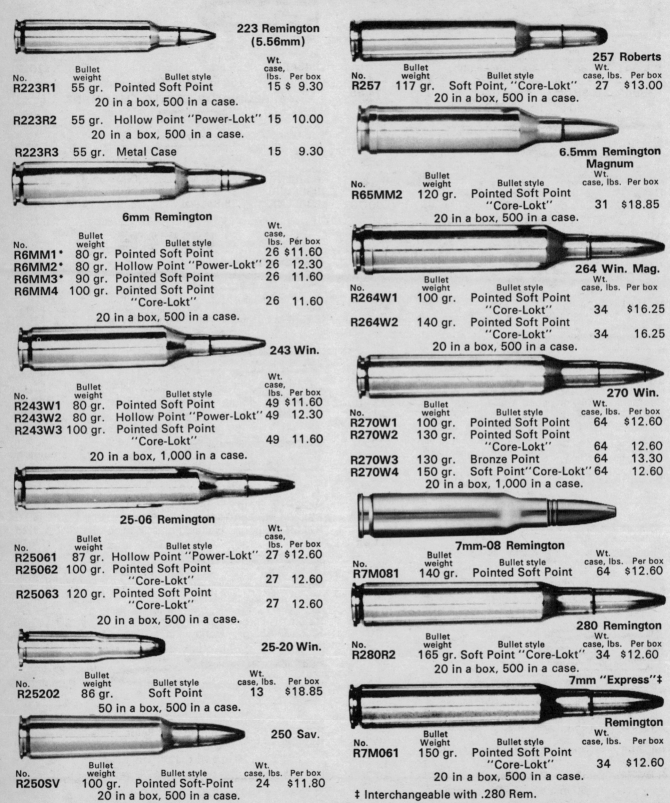

223 Remington (5.56mm)

No.	Bullet weight	Bullet style	Wt. case, lbs.	Per box
R223R1	55 gr.	Pointed Soft Point	15	$ 9.30

20 in a box, 500 in a case.

| R223R2 | 55 gr. | Hollow Point "Power-Lokt" | 15 | 10.00 |

20 in a box, 500 in a case.

| R223R3 | 55 gr. | Metal Case | 15 | 9.30 |

6mm Remington

No.	Bullet weight	Bullet style	Wt. case, lbs.	Per box
R6MM1*	80 gr.	Pointed Soft Point	26	$11.60
R6MM2*	80 gr.	Hollow Point "Power-Lokt"	26	12.30
R6MM3*	90 gr.	Pointed Soft Point	26	11.60
R6MM4	100 gr.	Pointed Soft Point "Core-Lokt"	26	11.60

20 in a box, 500 in a case.

243 Win.

No.	Bullet weight	Bullet style	Wt. case, lbs.	Per box
R243W1	80 gr.	Pointed Soft Point	49	$11.60
R243W2	80 gr.	Hollow Point "Power-Lokt"	49	12.30
R243W3	100 gr.	Pointed Soft Point "Core-Lokt"	49	11.60

20 in a box, 1,000 in a case.

25-06 Remington

No.	Bullet weight	Bullet style	Wt. case, lbs.	Per box
R25061	87 gr.	Hollow Point "Power-Lokt"	27	$12.60
R25062	100 gr.	Pointed Soft Point "Core-Lokt"	27	12.60
R25063	120 gr.	Pointed Soft Point "Core-Lokt"	27	12.60

20 in a box, 500 in a case.

25-20 Win.

No.	Bullet weight	Bullet style	Wt. case, lbs.	Per box
R25202	86 gr.	Soft Point	13	$18.85

50 in a box, 500 in a case.

250 Sav.

No.	Bullet weight	Bullet style	Wt. case, lbs.	Per box
R250SV	100 gr.	Pointed Soft-Point	24	$11.80

20 in a box, 500 in a case.

257 Roberts

No.	Bullet weight	Bullet style	Wt. case, lbs.	Per box
R257	117 gr.	Soft Point, "Core-Lokt"	27	$13.00

20 in a box, 500 in a case.

6.5mm Remington Magnum

No.	Bullet weight	Bullet style	Wt. case, lbs.	Per box
R65MM2	120 gr.	Pointed Soft Point "Core-Lokt"	31	$18.85

20 in a box, 500 in a case.

264 Win. Mag.

No.	Bullet weight	Bullet style	Wt. case, lbs.	Per box
R264W1	100 gr.	Pointed Soft Point "Core-Lokt"	34	$16.25
R264W2	140 gr.	Pointed Soft Point "Core-Lokt"	34	16.25

20 in a box, 500 in a case.

270 Win.

No.	Bullet weight	Bullet style	Wt. case, lbs.	Per box
R270W1	100 gr.	Pointed Soft Point	64	$12.60
R270W2	130 gr.	Pointed Soft Point "Core-Lokt"	64	12.60
R270W3	130 gr.	Bronze Point	64	13.30
R270W4	150 gr.	Soft Point "Core-Lokt"	64	12.60

20 in a box, 1,000 in a case.

7mm-08 Remington

No.	Bullet weight	Bullet style	Wt. case, lbs.	Per box
R7M081	140 gr.	Pointed Soft Point	64	$12.60

280 Remington

No.	Bullet weight	Bullet style	Wt. case, lbs.	Per box
R280R2	165 gr.	Soft Point "Core-Lokt"	34	$12.60

20 in a box, 500 in a case.

7mm "Express"‡ Remington

No.	Bullet Weight	Bullet style	Wt. case, lbs.	Per box
R7M061	150 gr.	Pointed Soft Point "Core-Lokt"	34	$12.60

20 in a box, 500 in a case.

‡ Interchangeable with .280 Rem.

REMINGTON CENTERFIRE RIFLE CARTRIDGES

7mm Remington Magnum

No.	Bullet weight	Bullet style	Wt. case, lbs.	Per box
R7MM2	150 gr.	Pointed Soft Point "Core-Lokt"	37	$15.60
R7MM3	175 gr.	Pointed Soft Point "Core-Lokt"	37	15.60

20 in a box, 500 in a case.

7mm Mauser

No.	Bullet weight	Bullet style	Wt. case, lbs.	Per box
R7MSR	175 gr.	Soft Point	32	$12.85

20 in a box, 500 in a case.

30 Carbine

No.	Bullet weight	Bullet style	Wt. case, lbs.	Per box
R30CAR	110 gr.	Soft Point	15	$20.25

50 in a box, 500 in a case.

30-30 Win.

No.	Bullet weight	Bullet style	Wt. case, lbs.	Per box
R30301	150 gr.	Soft Point "Core-Lokt"	53	$9.90
R30302	170 gr.	Soft Point "Core-Lokt"	53	9.90
R30303	170 gr.	Hollow Point "Core-Lokt"	53	9.90

20 in a box, 1,000 in a case.

30-30 "Accelerator"

No.	Bullet weight	Bullet style	Wt. case, lbs.	Per box
R3030A	55 gr.	Soft Point	36	$11.00

20 in a box, 1,000 in a case.

30 Remington

No.	Bullet weight	Bullet style	Wt. case, lbs.	Per box
R30REM	170 gr.	Soft Point "Core-Lokt"	26	$12.75

20 in a box, 500 in a case.

30-40 Krag

No.	Bullet weight	Bullet style	Wt. case, lbs.	Per box
R30401	180 gr.	Soft Point "Core-Lokt"	32	$13.25
R30402	180 gr.	Pointed Soft Point "Core-Lokt"	32	13.25

20 in a box, 500 in a case.

30-06 Spfd.

No.	Bullet weight	Bullet style	Wt. case, lbs.	Per box
R30061	125 gr.	Pointed Soft Point	69	$12.60
R30062	150 gr.	Pointed Soft Point "Core-Lokt"	69	12.60
R30063	150 gr.	Bronze Point	69	13.30
R30068	165 gr.	Pointed Soft Point	62	12.60
R30064	180 gr.	Soft Point "Core-Lokt"	69	12.60
R30065	180 gr.	Pointed Soft Point "Core-Lokt"	69	12.60
R30066	180 gr.	Bronze Point	69	13.30
R30067	220 gr.	Soft Point "Core-Lokt"	69	12.60

20 in a box, 1,000 in a case.

30-06 "Accelerator"

No.	Bullet weight	Bullet style	Wt. case, lbs.	Per box
R30069	55 gr.	Pointed Soft Point	52	$14.00

20 in a box, 1,000 in a case.

300 Sav.

No.	Bullet weight	Bullet style	Wt. case, lbs.	Per box
R30SV1	150 gr.	Soft Point "Core-Lokt"	58	$12.70
R30SV2	150 gr.	Pointed Soft Point "Core-Lokt"	58	12.70
R30SV3	180 gr.	Soft Point "Core-Lokt"	58	12.70
R30SV4	180 gr.	Pointed Soft Point "Core-Lokt"	58	12.70

20 in a box, 1,000 in a case.

300 H & H Mag.

No.	Bullet weight	Bullet style	Wt. case, lbs.	Per box
R300HH	180 gr.	Pointed Soft Point "Core-Lokt"	39	$16.90

20 in a box, 500 in a case.

300 Win. Mag.

No.	Bullet weight	Bullet style	Wt. case, lbs.	Per box
R300W1	150 gr.	Pointed Soft Point "Core-Lokt"	39	$16.45
R300W2	180 gr.	Pointed Soft Point "Core-Lokt"	39	16.45

20 in a box, 500 in a case.

REMINGTON CENTERFIRE RIFLE CARTRIDGES

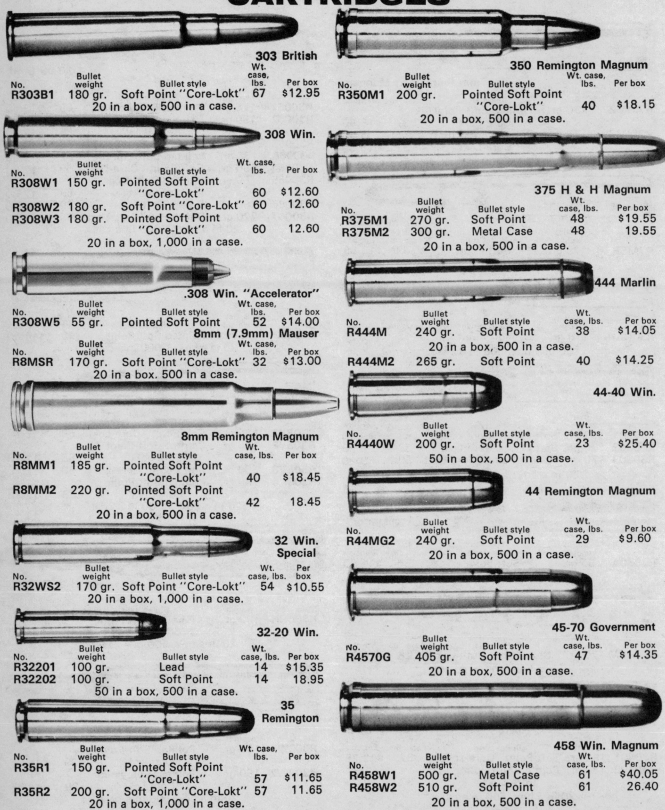

303 British

No.	Bullet weight	Bullet style	Wt. case, lbs.	Per box
R303B1	180 gr.	Soft Point "Core-Lokt"	67	$12.95

20 in a box, 500 in a case.

308 Win.

No.	Bullet weight	Bullet style	Wt. case, lbs.	Per box
R308W1	150 gr.	Pointed Soft Point "Core-Lokt"	60	$12.60
R308W2	180 gr.	Soft Point "Core-Lokt"	60	12.60
R308W3	180 gr.	Pointed Soft Point "Core-Lokt"	60	12.60

20 in a box, 1,000 in a case.

.308 Win. "Accelerator"

No.	Bullet weight	Bullet style	Wt. case, lbs.	Per box
R308W5	55 gr.	Pointed Soft Point	52	$14.00

8mm (7.9mm) Mauser

No.	Bullet weight	Bullet style	Wt. case, lbs.	Per box
R8MSR	170 gr.	Soft Point "Core-Lokt"	32	$13.00

20 in a box. 500 in a case.

8mm Remington Magnum

No.	Bullet weight	Bullet style	Wt. case, lbs.	Per box
R8MM1	185 gr.	Pointed Soft Point "Core-Lokt"	40	$18.45
R8MM2	220 gr.	Pointed Soft Point "Core-Lokt"	42	18.45

20 in a box, 500 in a case.

32 Win. Special

No.	Bullet weight	Bullet style	Wt. case, lbs.	Per box
R32WS2	170 gr.	Soft Point "Core-Lokt"	54	$10.55

20 in a box, 1,000 in a case.

32-20 Win.

No.	Bullet weight	Bullet style	Wt. case, lbs.	Per box
R32201	100 gr.	Lead	14	$15.35
R32202	100 gr.	Soft Point	14	18.95

50 in a box, 500 in a case.

35 Remington

No.	Bullet weight	Bullet style	Wt. case, lbs.	Per box
R35R1	150 gr.	Pointed Soft Point "Core-Lokt"	57	$11.65
R35R2	200 gr.	Soft Point "Core-Lokt"	57	11.65

20 in a box, 1,000 in a case.

350 Remington Magnum

No.	Bullet weight	Bullet style	Wt. case, lbs.	Per box
R350M1	200 gr.	Pointed Soft Point "Core-Lokt"	40	$18.15

20 in a box, 500 in a case.

375 H & H Magnum

No.	Bullet weight	Bullet style	Wt. case, lbs.	Per box
R375M1	270 gr.	Soft Point	48	$19.55
R375M2	300 gr.	Metal Case	48	19.55

20 in a box, 500 in a case.

444 Marlin

No.	Bullet weight	Bullet style	Wt. case, lbs.	Per box
R444M	240 gr.	Soft Point	38	$14.05

20 in a box, 500 in a case.

| R444M2 | 265 gr. | Soft Point | 40 | $14.25 |

44-40 Win.

No.	Bullet weight	Bullet style	Wt. case, lbs.	Per box
R4440W	200 gr.	Soft Point	23	$25.40

50 in a box, 500 in a case.

44 Remington Magnum

No.	Bullet weight	Bullet style	Wt. case, lbs.	Per box
R44MG2	240 gr.	Soft Point	29	$9.60

20 in a box, 500 in a case.

45-70 Government

No.	Bullet weight	Bullet style	Wt. case, lbs.	Per box
R4570G	405 gr.	Soft Point	47	$14.35

20 in a box, 500 in a case.

458 Win. Magnum

No.	Bullet weight	Bullet style	Wt. case, lbs.	Per box
R458W1	500 gr.	Metal Case	61	$40.05
R458W2	510 gr.	Soft Point	61	26.40

20 in a box, 500 in a case.

REMINGTON RIMFIRE CARTRIDGES

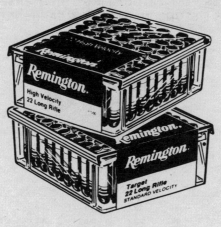

"HIGH VELOCITY" CARTRIDGES with "Golden" Bullets

22 Short

No.	Bullet weight and style	Wt. case, lbs.	Per box
1022	29 gr., Lead	29	$1.88
1122	27 gr., Lead, Hollow Point	28	2.00

50 in a box, 5,000 in a case.

22 Long

No.	Bullet weight and style	Wt. case, lbs.	Per box
1322	29 gr., Lead	31	$2.00

50 in a box, 5,000 in a case.

22 Long Rifle

No.	Bullet weight and style	Wt. case, lbs.	Per box
1522	40 gr., Lead	40	$2.15
1622	36 gr., Lead, Hollow Point	38	2.37

50 in a box, 5,000 in a case.

100 Pack

1500	40 gr., Lead	40	$4.30
1600	36 gr., Lead, Hollow Point	38	4.74

100 in a box, 5,000 in a case.

5mm Remington Magnum

No.	Bullet weight and style	Wt. case, lbs.	Per box
1050	38 gr., "Power Lokt" H.P.	21	$13.52

50 in a box, 2,000 in a case.

"TARGET" STANDARD VELOCITY CARTRIDGES

22 Short

No.	Bullet weight and style	Wt. case, lbs.	Per box
5522	29 gr., Lead	29	$1.88

50 in a box, 5,000 in a case.

22 Long Rifle

No.	Bullet weight and style	Wt. case, lbs.	Per box
6122	40 gr., Lead	40	$2.15

50 in a box, 5,000 in a case.

.22 Long Rifle, Target
100 pack.

No.	Bullet weight and style	Wt. case, lbs.	Per box
6100	40 gr., Lead	40	$4.30

100 in a box, 5,000 in a case.

"YELLOW JACKET" CARTRIDGES Hyper-Velocity

22 Long Rifle

No.	Bullet weight and style	Wt. case, lbs.	Per box
1722	33 gr. Truncated Cone, Hollow Point	36	$2.63

50 in a box, 5,000 in a case.

MATCH CARTRIDGES

Rifle Match 22 Long Rifle 100 pack.

No.	Bullet weight and style	Wt. case, lbs.	Per box
6600	40 gr., Lead	39	$7.18

100 in a box, 5,000 in a case.

Pistol Match 22 Long Rifle

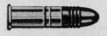

No.	Bullet weight and style	Wt. case, lbs.	Per box
6800	40 gr., Lead	39	$7.18

100 in a box, 5,000 in a case.

SHOT

22 Long Rifle Hi-Speed

No.	Wt. case, lbs.	Per box
9322	33	$4.36

50 in a box, 5,000 in a case.

BLANK

22 Short

No.	Wt. case, lbs.	Per box
9022	7	$12.38

250 in a box, 5,000 in a case.

REMINGTON PLASTIC SHOTSHELLS
SHOTGUN SHELLS
REMINGTON "EXPRESS" and "NITRO MAG" HIGH BASE PLASTIC SHELLS
with "POWER-PISTON" WADS and "KLEANBORE" PRIMING

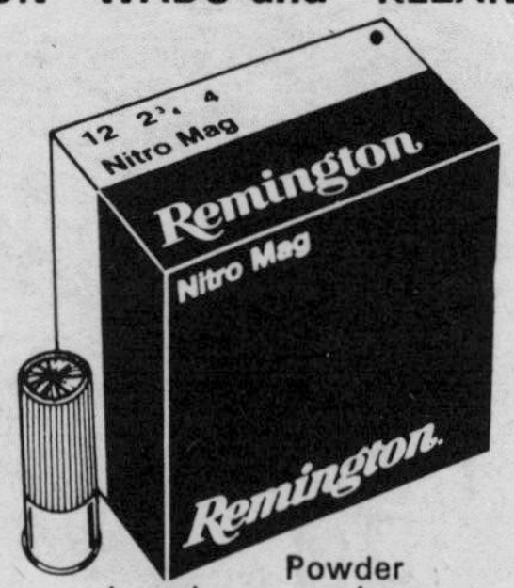

	No.	Gauge	Length shell, in.	Powder equiv. drams	Shot, oz.	Size shot	Wt. case, lbs.	Per box
"EXPRESS" LONG RANGE LOADS	SP10	10	2⅞	4¾	1⅝	4	74	$14.15
	SP12	12	2¾	3¾	1¼	BB 2 4 5 6 7½ 9	58	9.90
	SP16	16	2¾	3¼	1⅛	4 5 6 7½ 9	52	9.50
	SP20	20	2¾	2¾	1	4 5 6 7½ 9	46	8.70
	SP28	28	2¾	2¼	¾	6 7½	37	8.75
	SP410	410	2½	Max.	½	4 6 7½	22	6.90
	SP4103	410	3	Max.	¹¹⁄₁₆	4 5 6 7½ 9	31	8.15

‡ 28 ga. and 2½", 410 bore No. 9 shot marked "Skeet Load."

	No.	Gauge	Length shell, in.	Powder equiv. drams	Shot, oz.	Size shot	Wt. case, lbs.	Per box
"NITRO MAG" HIGH PERFORMANCE MAGNUM LOADS	SP12SNM	12	2¾	Max.	1½	2 4	66	$13.65
	SP12NM	12	3	4	1⅝	2 4	70	14.90

	No.	Gauge	Length shell, in.	Powder equiv. drams	Shot, oz.	Size shot	Wt. case, lbs.	Per box
"EXPRESS" MAGNUM LOADS	SP10Mag●	10	3½	Max.	2	BB 2 4 (Mag.)	45	$22.95
	SP12Mag●	12	3	4	1⅝	2 4 6 (Mag.)	37	14.20
	SP12SMag●	12	2¾	Max.	1½	2 4 5 6 (Mag.)	34	12.85
	SP12HMag●	12	3	Max.	1⅞	BB 2 4 (Mag.)	41	15.35
	SP16CMag●	16	2¾	Max.	1¼	2 4 6 (Mag.)	29	12.65
	SP20SMag●	20	2¾	Max.	1⅛	4 6 7½ (Mag.)	28	10.55
	SP20HMag●	20	3	Max.	1¼	2 4 6 7½ (Mag.)	30	11.90

	No.	Gauge	Length shell, in.	Powder equiv. drams	Shot, oz.	Size shot	Wt. case, lbs.	Per box
STEEL SHOT WATER FOWL LOADS New! Magnum	STL12	12	2¾	Max.	1⅛	1 2 4	55	$12.40
	STL12Mag	12	3	Max.	1¼	1 2 4	60	16.10

	No.	Gauge	Length shell, in.	Powder equiv. drams	Shot, oz.	Size shot	Wt. case, lbs.	Per box
RIFLED SLUG LOADS	SP12RS-5PK●	12	2¾	3¾	1	Rifled Slug "Slugger"	26	$3.20
	SP16RS-5PK●	16	2¾	3	⅘	Rifled Slug	24	3.20
	SP20RS-5PK●	20	2¾	2¾	⅝	Rifled Slug	19	2.95
	SP410RS-5PK●	410	2½	Max.	⅕	Rifled Slug	8	2.80

	No.	Gauge	Length shell, in.	Powder equiv. drams	Shot, oz.	Size shot	Wt. case, lbs.	Per box
"Power Pakt" "EXPRESS" BUCKSHOT LOADS	SP12BK-5PK●	12	2¾	3¾	...	000 Buck— 8 Pellets	31	$2.80
	SP12BK-5PK●	12	2¾	3¾	...	00 Buck— 9 Pellets	29	2.80
	SP12BK-5PK●	12	2¾	3¾	...	0 Buck—12 Pellets	32	2.80
	SP12BK-5PK●	12	2¾	3¾	...	1 Buck—16 Pellets	32	2.80
	SP12BK-5PK●	12	2¾	3¾	...	4 Buck—27 Pellets	31	2.80
	SP16BK-5PK●	16	2¾	3	...	1 Buck—12 Pellets	26	2.80
	SP20BK-5PK●	20	2¾	2¾	...	3 Buck—20 Pellets	24	2.80

	No.	Gauge	Length shell, in.	Powder equiv. drams	Shot, oz.	Size shot	Wt. case, lbs.	Per box
"Power Pakt" "EXPRESS" MAGNUM BUCKSHOT LOADS	SP12SMagBK-5PK●	12	2¾	4	...	00 Buck—12 Pellets	34	$3.10
	SP12SMagBK-5PK●	12	2¾	4	...	1 Buck—20 Pellets	34	3.10
	★SP12HMagBk-5PK●	12	3	4½	...	000 Buck—10 Pellets	40	3.55
	SP12HMagBK-5PK●	12	3	4½	...	00 Buck—15 Pellets	40	3.55
	SP12HMagBK-5PK●	12	3	Max.	...	1 Buck—24 Pellets	40	3.55
	SP12HMagBK-5PK●	12	3	4½	...	4 Buck—41 Pellets	42	3.55

★ New for 1981

● Packed 250 per case.
25 in a box, 500 in a case.

REMINGTON PLASTIC SHOTSHELLS
SHOTGUN SHELLS
**REMINGTON "SHURSHOT" LOW BASE PLASTIC SHELLS AND REMINGTON TARGET LOADS
with "POWER-PISTON" WADS and "KLEANBORE" PRIMING**

REMINGTON FIELD LOADS

	No.	Gauge	Length shell, in.	Powder equiv. drams	Payload size. oz.	Size shot	Wt. case, lbs.	Per box
"SHUR SHOT" PLASTIC FIELD LOADS With "Power Piston" Wad	R12H	12	2¾	3¼	1⅛	4 5 6 7½ 8 9	51	$8.45
	RP12H▲	12	2¾	3¼	1¼	7½ 8	58	8.75
	R16H	16	2¾	2¾	1⅛	4 5 6 7½ 8 9	51	8.45
	R20M	20	2¾	2½	1	4 5 6 7½ 8 9	45	7.65

▲ Contains Extra Hard Shot

	No.	Gauge	Length shell, in.	Powder equiv. drams	Payload size. oz.	Size shot	Wt. case, lbs.	Per box
"SHUR SHOT" PLASTIC SCATTER LOADS With Special Wad Column	RSL12	12	2¾	3	1⅛	8	51	$9.00

REMINGTON TARGET LOADS

	No.	Gauge	Length shell, in.	Power equiv. drams	Payload size, oz.	Size shot	Wt. case, lbs.	(No suggested Retail Price) Per box
12 GAUGE "BLUE MAGIC" TRAP AND SKEET	PTL12M	12	2¾	3	1⅛	7½ 8 9	54	
	PTL12L	12	2¾	2¾	1⅛	7½ 8	54	
12 GAUGE INTERNATIONAL TARGET LOADS With "Power Piston" Wad	★SP12L	12	2¾	3¼	1¼	7½ 8	58	
	SP12H	12	2¾	3¼	1⅛	7½ 8	54	
	NSP12H	12	2¾	3¼	1⅛	7½ 8 (nickel)	54	
REMINGTON	XR20	20	2¾	2½	⅞		9 41	
PLASTIC SKEET LOADS	SP28	28	2¾	2	¾		9 37	
	SP410	410	2½	Max.	½		9 22	

25 in a box, 500 in a case.

★ New for 1981   **Prices Subject to Change Without Notice**

S&W CENTERFIRE PISTOL/REVOLVER CARTRIDGES

Symbol Number	Cartridge	Bullet Weight	Bullet Style		Average Case Weight	Rounds Per Box	Price Per Box
● S357M5	357 Magnum	110	J.H.P.		33	50	
● S357M7	357 Magnum	125	J.S.P.		34	50	
● S357M6	357 Magnum	125	J.H.P.		34	50	$18.40
● S357M8	357 Magnum	158	J.H.P.		39	50	
● S357M9	357 Magnum	158	J.S.P.		39	50	15.60
● S357M3	357 Magnum	158	S.W.C.		39	50	
● S357M10	357 Magnum	158	S.W.C.H.P.		39	50	16.40
● S9MM4	9 mm	100	F.M.C.		25	50	
● S9MM5	9 mm	115	F.M.C.		27	50	
● S9MM3	9 mm	115	J.H.P.		27	50	17.40
● S9MM6	9 mm	115	M.C.S.W.C.		27	50	
● S38S2	38 Special	158	R.N.	Small Pistol	35	50	13.25
● S38S6	38 Special	148	H.B.W.C.		33	50	13.80
● S38 + P5	38 Sp. + P	110	J.H.P.		28	50	
● S38 + P6	38 Sp. + P	125	J.H.P.		32	50	
● S38 + P7	38 Sp. + P	125	J.S.P.		32	50	16.80
● S38 + P8	38 Sp. + P	158	J.H.P.		35	50	
● S38 + P9	38 Sp. + P	158	J.S.P.		35	50	
● S38 + P3	38 Sp. + P	158	S.W.C.		35	50	13.55
● S38 + P10	38 Sp. + P	158	S.W.C.H.P.		35	50	14.40
● S380AP1	380 Auto	84	J.H.P.		21	50	14.35
● S380AP2	380 Auto	95	F.M.C.		23	50	
● S44M1	44 Magnum	240	J.H.P.		29	20	9.60
● S45A1	45 Automatic	185	M.C.S.W.C.		43	50	19.85
● S45A2	45 Automatic	230	F.M.C.		49	50	19.20
NYCLAD Ammunition							
● N3573N	357 Magnum	158	S.W.C.		39	50	16.50
● N35710N	357 Magnum	158	S.W.C.H.P.		39	50	17.30
● N9MM7N	9 mm	125	S.W.C.		29	50	16.05
● N382N	38 Special	158	R.N.		35	50	14.10
● N386N	38 Special	148	H.B.W.C.		33	50	14.65
● N383N	38 Special	158	S.W.C.		35	50	14.40
● N3879	38 Special	125	S.W.C.H.P.		32	50	15.30
● N38P7N	38 Sp. + P	125	S.W.C.H.P.		32	50	15.30
● N38P3N	38 Sp. + P	158	S.W.C.		35	50	14.50
● N38P10N	38 Sp. + P	158	S.W.C.H.P.		35	50	15.30

Bullet style explanation:

J.H.P.—jacketed hollow point
J.S.P.—jacketed soft point
M.C.—metal case
M.C.S.W.C.—metal case semiwadcutter

R.N.—round nose, lead
H.B.W.C.—hollow base wadcutter, lead
S.W.C.—semiwadcutter, lead
S.W.C.H.P.—semiwadcutter, lead hollow point

WEATHERBY CENTERFIRE RIFLE CARTRIDGES

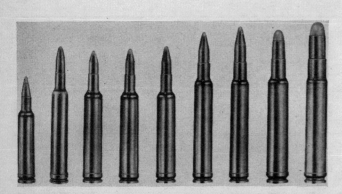

Weatherby Magnum Cartridges: Left to Right—.224 W.M., .240 W.M., .257 W.M., .270 W.M., 7mm W.M., .300 W.M., .340 W.M., .378 W.M., and .460 W.M.

Cartridge	Ammunition 20 per box	Unprimed Cases 20 per box
224—50 or 55 gr.	$21.95	$13.25
240—70, 87 or 100 gr.	21.95	13.25
—100 gr. Nosler	29.95	
257—87, 100 or 117 gr.	22.95	13.25
—100 or 117 gr. Nosler	31.95	
270—100, 130 or 150 gr.	22.95	13.25
—130 or 150 gr. Nosler	31.95	
7mm—139.154 or 175 gr.	22.95	13.25
—140 or 160 gr. Nosler	31.95	
300—110, 150, 180 or 220 gr.	22.95	13.25
—150, 180 or 200 gr. Nosler	31.95	
340—200 or 250 gr.	24.20	13.25
—210 or 250 gr. Nosler	38.95	
375—300 gr. RN or		not available
—300 gr. FMJ	30.95	
378—270, or 300 RN	39.25	22.95
—300 gr. FMJ	44.95	
460—500 RN	42.95	25.95
—500 RMJ	49.95	

WINCHESTER-WESTERN CENTERFIRE PISTOL/REVOLVER CARTRIDGES

WINCHESTER WESTERN SYMBOL	WINCHESTER AND/OR WESTERN SYMBOL	CARTRIDGE	PRIMER NUMBER	CASE CONTAINS M's	CASE WT. LBS.		SUGGESTED RETAIL PRICE PER BOX
		25 Automatic (6.35mm)					
X25AXP	—	45 gr. Expanding Point to Caliber					12.90
X25AP	—	50 gr. Full Metal Case	1½-108	2	24		12.25
		256 Winchester Magnum					
X2561P	—	60 gr. Hollow Point SUPER-X	6½-116	2	49		23.75
		30 Luger (7.65mm)					
X30LP	—	93 gr. Full Metal Case	1½-108	½	12		19.70
		32 Automatic					
X32ASHP	—	60 gr. Silvertip Hollow Point	1½-108	2	32		15.15
X32AP	—	71 gr. Full Metal Case	1½-108	2	35		14.05
		32 Smith & Wesson					
X32SWP		85 gr. Lead Bullet	1½-108	2	39		11.85
		32 Smith & Wesson Long (Colt New Police)					
X32SWLP	—	98 gr. Lead Bullet	1½-108	2	45		12.25
		32 Short Colt					
X32SCP		80 gr. Lead Bullet	1½-108	½	9		11.75
		32 Long Colt					
X32LCP		82 gr. Lead Bullet	1½-108	½	10		12.25
		32 Colt New Police	See 32 Smith & Wesson Long				
		32-20 Winchester					
X32201	32201	100 gr. Lead Bullet	6½-116	½	13		15.35
X32202		100 gr. Soft Point	6½-116	½	13		19.00
		357 Magnum					
X3573P		110 gr. Jacketed Hollow Point SUPER-X . .	1½M-108	2	62		18.45
X3576P	—	125 gr. Jacketed Hollow Point SUPER-X . .	1½M-108	2	62		18.45
X3571P	—	158 gr. Lead Bullet SUPER-X	1½M-108	2	76		15.60
X3575P	—	158 gr. Jacketed Soft Point SUPER-X	1½M-108	2	77		18.45
X3574P	—	158 gr. Jacketed Hollow Point SUPER-X . .	1½M-108	2	77		18.45
		357 Magnum Metal Piercing					
X3572P		158 gr. Met. Pierc. SUPER-X	1½M-108	2	76		18.15
		9mm Luger (Parabellum)					
X9MMJSP	—	95 gr. Jacketed Soft Point	1½-108	2	46		17.45
X9LP	—	115 gr. Full Metal Case	1½-108	2	52		17.45
X9MMSHP	—	115 gr. Silvertip Hollow Point	1½-108	2	53		18.30
		9mm Winchester Magnum Not for Arms Chambered for 9mm Luger					
X9MMWM		115 gr. Full Metal Case	1½-108	2	52		18.65
		38 Smith & Wesson					
X38SWP	—	145 gr. Lead Bullet	1½-108	2	62		13.15
		38 Special					
X38S1P	—	158 gr. Lead Bullet	1½-108	2	■48 68		13.25
X38S2P	—	158 gr. Metal Point	1½-108	2	68		16.80
X38S3P	38S3P	200 gr. Lead Bullet	1½-108	2	80		14.15
		38 Special Super-X					
X38SSHP	—	95 gr. Silvertip Hollow Point	1½-108	2	55		17.65
X38S6PH	—	110 gr. Jacketed Hollow Point SUPER-X + P	1½-108	2	59		16.80
X38S7PH	—	125 gr. Jacketed Hollow Point SUPER-X + P	1½-108	2	63		16.80
X38SPD	—	158 gr. Hollow Point SUPER-X + P	1½-108	2	■30 69		16.45
X38WCP	—	158 gr. Semi-Wad Cutter SUPER-X + P . . .	1½-108	2	69		13.55
X38S4P	—	150 gr. Lead Bullet SUPER-X + P	1½-108	2	66		14.70
X38S5P	—	150 gr. Metal Piercing SUPER-X + P	1½-108	2	66		16.80

11% Excise tax included
+ P = Ammunition with (+ P) on the case head stamp is loaded to higher pressure.
Use only in firearms designated for this cartridge and so recommended by the gun manufacturer.

Packed 50 per Box

§ Discontinued stock—offered subject to prior sale
■ Cases per pallet

WINCHESTER-WESTERN CENTERFIRE PISTOL/REVOLVER CARTRIDGES

WINCHESTER WESTERN SYMBOL	WINCHESTER AND/OR WESTERN SYMBOL	Packaged 50 per Box CARTRIDGE	PRIMER NUMBER	CASE CONTAINS M's	CASE WT. LBS.	SUGGESTED RETAIL PRICE PER BOX
		38 Special Match				
X38SMRP		148 gr. Mid-Range (Sharp Corner) Match .	1½-108	2	■50 65	13.80
X38SMP		158 gr. Lead (Optional) SUPER-MATCH . . .	1½-108	2	68	13.80
		38 Short Colt				
X38SCP	—	130 gr. Lead Bullet	1½-108	½	14	12.95
		38 Long Colt				
X38LCP		150 gr. Lead Bullet	1½-108	½	17	19.45
		38 Automatic Super-X (For use only in 38 Colt Super and Colt Commander Automatic Pistols)				
X38A3P		125 gr. Jacketed Hollow Point + P	1½-108	2	56	15.75
X38A1P		130 gr. Full Metal Case + P	1½-108	2	58	15.15
		38 Automatic (For all 38 Colt Automatic Pistols)				
X38A2P	38AZP	130 gr. Full Metal Case	1½-108	2	59	15.65
		380 Automatic				
X380ASHP	—	85 gr. Silvertip Hollow Point	1½-108	2	40	15.00
X380AP		95 gr. Full Metal Case	1½-108	2	43	14.35
		38-40 Winchester				
X3840	—	180 gr. Soft Point	7-111	½	23	24.05
		41 Remington Magnum Super-X				
X41MP	W41MP	210 gr. Lead Bullet	7M-111F	1	49	20.70
X41MJSP		210 gr. Jacketed Soft Point	7M-111F	1	50	24.25
X41MHP	—	210 gr. Jacketed Hollow Point	7M-111F	1	50	24.25
		44 Smith & Wesson Special				
X44SP	—	246 gr. Lead Bullet	7-111	½	28	18.55
		44 Remington Magnum Super-X				
X44MP		240 gr. Lead Bullet (Gas Check)	7M-111F	1	57	23.50
•X44MHSP		240 gr. Hollow Soft Point	7M-111F	1	57	9.60
		44-40 Winchester				
X4440	—	200 gr. Soft Point	7-111	½	24	25.40
		45 Colt				
X45CP		255 gr. Lead Bullet	7-111	½	28	18.85
		45 Automatic				
X45A1P	—	230 gr. Full Metal Case	7-111	1	47	19.20
•X45ASHP	—	185 gr. Silvertip Hollow Point	7-111	1	43	8.05
		45 Automatic Super-Match				
X45AWCP		185 gr. Full Metal Case (Clean Cutting) . . .	7-111	1	42	19.85
		45 Winchester Magnum Not for Arms Chambered for Standard 45 Automatic				
X45WM	W45WM	230 gr. Full Metal Case	7M-111F	1	47	20.55

11% Excise tax included   • 20 Per Box

CENTERFIRE RIFLE CARTRIDGES

WINCHESTER WESTERN SYMBOL	WINCHESTER AND/OR WESTERN SYMBOL	CARTRIDGE	PRIMER NUMBER	CASE CONTAINS M's	CASE WT. LBS.	SUGGESTED RETAIL PRICE PER BOX
		218 Bee				
•X218B	•218B	46 gr. Hollow Point SUPER-X	6½-116	½	10	29.40
		22 Hornet				
•X22H1	—	45 gr. Soft Point SUPER-X	6½-116	½	9	19.90
•X22H2	—	46 gr. Hollow Point SUPER-X	6½-116	½	9	19.90
		22-250 Remington				
X222501	—	55 gr. Pointed Soft Point SUPER-X	8½-120	1	41	9.30

11% Excise tax included   • 50 Per Box—All Others 20 Per Box   D = Disintegrating

WINCHESTER-WESTERN CENTERFIRE RIFLE CARTRIDGES

WINCHESTER WESTERN SYMBOL	WINCHESTER AND/OR WESTERN SYMBOL	CARTRIDGE	PRIMER NUMBER	CASE CONTAINS M's	CASE WT. LBS.	SUGGESTED RETAIL PRICE PER BOX
		222 Remington				
X222R	—	50 gr. Pointed Soft Point SUPER-X	6½-116	1	28	8.50
X222R1	—	55 gr. Full Metal Case SUPER-X	6½-116	1	30	8.50
		223 Remington				
X223R	—	55 gr. Pointed Soft Point SUPER-X	6½-116	½	15	9.30
X223R1	223R1	55 gr. Full Metal Case SUPER-X	6½-116	½	18	9.30
		225 Winchester				
X2251	—	55 gr. Pointed Soft Point SUPER-X	8½-120	1	38	10.15
		243 Winchester (6mm)				
X2431	—	80 gr. Pointed Soft Point SUPER-X	8½-120	1	47	11.60
X2432	—	100 gr. Power-Point (S.P.) SUPER-X	8½-120	1	50	11.60
		6mm Remington				
X6MMR1	—	80 gr. Pointed Soft Point SUPER-X	8½-120	½	24	11.60
X6MMR2	—	100 gr. Pointed Soft Point SUPER-X	8½-120	½	24	11.60
		25-06 Remington				
X25061	—	90 gr. Positive Expanding Point SUPER-X	8½-120	½	26	12.60
X25062	—	120 gr. Positive Expanding Point SUPER-X .	8½-120	½	28	12.60
		25-20 Winchester				
—	•§25201	86 gr. Lead Bullet	6½-116	½	12	17.00
•X25202	—	86 gr. Soft Point	6½-116	½	12	18.85
		25-35 Winchester				
X2535	—	117 gr. Soft Point SUPER-X	8½-120	1	45	12.90
		250 Savage				
X2501	—	87 gr. Pointed Soft Point SUPER-X	8½-120	½	22	11.80
X2503	—	100 gr. Silvertip Expanding SUPER-X	8½-120	½	23	12.45
		256 Winchester Magnum				
•X2561P	—	60 gr. Hollow Point SUPER-X	6½-116	2	49	23.75
		257 Roberts				
—	§2571	87 gr. Pointed Soft Point SUPER-X	8½-120	½	24	10.50
X2572	2572	100 gr. Silvertip Expanding SUPER-X	8½-120	½	24	13.70
X2573	—	117 gr. Power-Point (S.P.) SUPER-X	8½-120	½	25	13.00
		264 Winchester Magnum				
X2641	W2641	100 gr. Pointed Soft Point SUPER-X	8½-120	½	32	16.30
X2642	W2642	140 gr. Power-Point (S.P.) SUPER-X	8½-120	½	35	16.30
		270 Winchester				
X2701	—	100 gr. Pointed Soft Point SUPER-X	8½-120	1	55	12.60
X2705	—	130 gr. Power-Point (S.P.) SUPER-X	8½-120	1	59	12.60
X2703	—	130 gr. Silvertip Expanding SUPER-X	8½-120	1	59	13.30
X2704	—	150 gr. Power-Point (S.P.) SUPER-X	8½-120	1	62	12.60
		284 Winchester				
§X2841	—	125 gr. Power-Point (S.P.) SUPER-X . . .	8½-120	1	60	13.15
X2842	W2842	150 gr. Power-Point (S.P.) SUPER-X	8½-120	1	63	14.60
		7mm Mauser (7 x 57)				
X7MM	—	175 gr. Soft Point SUPER-X	8½-120	½	30	12.85
		7mm Remington Magnum				
X7MMR3	—	125 gr. Power-Point (S.P.) SUPER-X	8½-120	½	33	15.65
X7MMR1	—	150 gr. Power-Point (S.P.) SUPER-X	8½-120	½	35	15.65
X7MMR2	—	175 gr. Power-Point (S.P.) SUPER-X	8½-120	½	37	15.65
		30 Carbine				
•X30M1	—	110 gr. Hollow Soft Point	6½-116	1	30	20.25
•X30M2	—	110 gr. Full Metal Case	6½-116	1	30	20.25

11% Excise tax included   •50 Per Box—All Others 20 Per Box   §Discontinued stock—offered subject to prior sale   (S.P.) = Soft Point

WINCHESTER-WESTERN CENTERFIRE RIFLE CARTRIDGES

WINCHESTER WESTERN SYMBOL	WINCHESTER AND/OR WESTERN SYMBOL	CARTRIDGE	PRIMER NUMBER	CASE CON-TAINS M's	CASE WT. LBS.	SUGGESTED RETAIL PRICE PER BOX
		30-30 Winchester				
X30301	—	150 gr. Hollow Point SUPER-X	8½-120	1	51	9.90
X30306	—	150 gr. Power-Point (S.P.) SUPER-X	8½-120	1	51	9.90
X30302	—	150 gr. Silvertip Expanding SUPER-X	8½-120	1	51	10.45
X30303	—	170 gr. Power-Point (S.P.) SUPER-X	8½-120	1	54	9.90
X30304	—	170 gr. Silvertip Expanding SUPER-X	8½-120	1	54	10.45
		30-06 Springfield				
X30060	—	110 gr. Pointed Soft Point SUPER-X	8½-120	1	56	12.60
X30062	—	125 gr. Pointed Soft Point SUPER-X	8½-120	1	58	12.60
X30061	—	150 gr. Power-Point (S.P.) SUPER-X	8½-120	1	62	12.60
X30063	—	150 gr. Silvertip Expanding SUPER-X	8½-120	1	62	13.30
X30064	—	180 gr. Power-Point (S.P.) SUPER-X	8½-120	1	66	12.60
X30066	—	180 gr. Silvertip Expanding SUPER-X	8½-120	1	66	13.30
X30068	—	220 gr. Power-Point (S.P.) SUPER-X	8½-120	1	72	12.60
X30069	—	220 gr. Silvertip Expanding SUPER-X	8½-120	1	72	13.30
		30-40 Krag				
X30401	30401	180 gr. Power-Point (S.P.) SUPER-X	8½-120	½	31	13.30
X30403	30403	180 gr. Silvertip Expanding SUPER-X	8½-120	½	31	14.00
		300 Winchester Magnum				
X30WM1	—	150 gr. Power-Point (S.P.) SUPER-X	8½-120	½	36	16.50
X30WM2	—	180 gr. Power-Point (S.P.) SUPER-X	8½-120	½	38	16.50
X30WM3	—	220 gr. Silvertip Expanding SUPER-X	8½-120	½	41	17.35
		300 H. & H. Magnum				
X300H2	W300H2	180 gr. Silvertip Expanding SUPER-X . . .	8½-120	½	38	16.95
§X300H3	—	220 gr. Silvertip Expanding SUPER-X	8½-120	½	41	16.05
		300 Savage				
X3001	—	150 gr. Power-Point (S.P.) SUPER-X	8½-120	1	54	12.75
X3003	—	150 gr. Silvertip Expanding SUPER-X	8½-120	1	54	13.40
X3004	—	180 gr. Power-Point (S.P.) SUPER-X	8½-120	1	58	12.75
X3005	—	180 gr. Silvertip Expanding SUPER-X	8½-120	1	58	13.40
		303 Savage				
X3032	—	190 gr. Silvertip Expanding SUPER-X	8½-120	½	29	15.00
		303 British				
X303B1	—	180 gr. Power-Point (S.P.) SUPER-X	8½-120	1	62	12.95
		308 Winchester				
X3081	—	110 gr. Pointed Soft Point SUPER-X	8½-120	1	50	12.60
X3087	—	125 gr. Pointed Soft Point SUPER-X	8½-120	1	52	12.60
X3085	—	150 gr. Power-Point (S.P.) SUPER-X	8½-120	1	56	12.60
X3082	—	150 gr. Silvertip Expanding SUPER-X	8½-120	1	56	13.30
X3086	—	180 gr. Power-Point (S.P.) SUPER-X	8½-120	1	62	12.60
X3083	—	180 gr. Silvertip Expanding SUPER-X	8½-120	1	61	13.30
X3084	—	200 gr. Silvertip Expanding SUPER-X	8½-120	1	63	13.30
		32 Winchester Special				
X32WS2	—	170 gr. Power-Point (S.P.) SUPER-X	8½-120	1	54	10.55
X32WS3	—	170 gr. Silvertip Expanding SUPER-X	8½-120	1	54	11.15
		32-20 Winchester				
•X32201	•32201	100 gr. Lead Bullet	6½-116	½	13	15.35
•X32202	—	100 gr. Soft Point	6½-116	½	13	19.00
		8mm Mauser (8 x 57; 7.9)				
X8MM	—	170 gr. Power-Point (S.P.) SUPER-X	8½-120	1	62	13.00

11% Excise tax included   •50 Per Box—All Others 20 Per Box   §Discontinued stock—offered subject to prior sale   (S.P.) = Soft Point

WINCHESTER-WESTERN CENTERFIRE RIFLE CARTRIDGES

WINCHESTER WESTERN SYMBOL	WINCHESTER AND/OR WESTERN SYMBOL	CARTRIDGE	PRIMER NUMBER	CASE CONTAINS M's	CASE WT. LBS.	SUGGESTED RETAIL PRICE PER BOX
		338 Winchester Magnum				
X3381	—	200 gr. Power-Point (S.P.) SUPER-X	8½-120	½	39	19.80
§X3382	—	250 gr. Silvertip Expanding SUPER-X	8½-120	½	43	18.75
X3383	—	225 gr. Soft Point SUPER-X	8½-120	½	41	19.80
		348 Winchester				
X3482	W3482	200 gr. Silvertip Expanding SUPER-X	8½-120	½	37	24.00
		35 Remington				
X35R1	—	200 gr. Power-Point (S.P.) SUPER-X	8½-120	1	62	11.65
X35R3	—	200 gr. Silvertip Expanding SUPER-X	8½-120	1	62	12.30
		351 Winchester Self-Loading				
•X351SL2	—	180 gr. Soft Point	6½-116	½	22	32.25
		358 Winchester (8.8mm)				
X3581	—	200 gr. Silvertip Expanding SUPER-X	8½-120	1	64	18.40
		375 Winchester				
X375W	—	200 gr. Power-Point (S.P.) SUPER-X	8½-120	½	32	15.05
X375W1	—	250 gr. Power-Point (S.P.) SUPER-X	8½-120	½	35	15.05
		375 H. &. H. Magnum				
X375H1	—	270 gr. Power-Point (S.P.) SUPER-X	8½-120	½	45	19.60
X375H2	—	300 gr. Silvertip Expanding SUPER-X	8½-120	½	48	20.65
X375H3	—	300 gr. Full Metal Case SUPER-X	8½-120	½	48	19.60
		38-40 Winchester				
•X3840	—	180 gr. Soft Point	7-111	½	23	24.05
		38-55 Winchester				
X3855	—	255 gr. Soft Point	8½-120	½	35	14.00
		44 Remington Magnum Super-X				
•X44MP	—	240 gr. Lead Bullet (Gas Check)	7M-111F	1	57	23.50
X44MHSP	—	240 gr. Hollow Soft Point	7M-111F	1	57	9.60
		44-40 Winchester				
•X4440	—	200 gr. Soft Point	7-111	½	24	25.40
		45-70 Government				
X4570H	—	300 gr. Jacketed Hollow Point	8½-120	½	39	14.35
		458 Winchester Magnum				
X4580	W4580	500 gr. Full Metal Case SUPER-X	8½-120	½	59	40.10
X4581	W4581	510 gr. Soft Point SUPER-X	8½-120	½	61	26.45

11% Excise tax included   •50 Per Box—All Others 20 Per Box   §Discontinued stock—offered subject to prior sale   (S.P.) = Soft Point

CENTERFIRE BLANK CARTRIDGES

		32 Smith & Wesson				
32BL1P	W32BL1P	No Bullet Smokeless	1½-108	5	37	11.70
32BL2P	—	No Bullet Black Powder	1½-108	5	40	11.70
		38 Smith & Wesson				
38BLP		No Bullet Smokeless	1½-108	2	22	14.15
		38 Special				
38SBLP	—	No Bullet Smokeless	1½-108	2	24	14.25

11% Excise tax included

WINCHESTER-WESTERN RIMFIRE AMMUNITION

SUPER-X 22 RIMFIRE CARTRIDGES (HIGH VELOCITY)

Symbol No.	Cartridge	Bullet or Shot Wt. Grs.	Type of Bullet	Suggested Retail Per Box
X22S	22 Short SUPER-X	29	Lubaloy — K	1.88
X22SH	22 Short H.P. SUPER-X	27	Lubaloy — K	2.00
X22L	22 Long SUPER-X	29	Lubaloy — K	2.00
X22LR	22 L.R. SUPER-X	40	Lubaloy — K	2.15
X22LR1*	22 L.R. SUPER-X	40	Lubaloy — K	4.30
X22LRD	22 L.R. DYNAPOINT SUPER-X (Semi H.P.)	40	Lubaloy — K	2.37
X22LRH	22 L.R. H.P. SUPER-X	37	Lubaloy — K	2.37
X22LRH1*	22 L.R. H.P. SUPER-X	37	Lubaloy — K	4.74
X22LRS	22 L.R. Shot SUPER-X	25	No. 12 Shot	4.37
X22WMR	22 Win. Magnum SUPER-X	40	Jacketed H.P.	5.91
X22MR1	22 Win. Magnum SUPER-X	40	Full Metal Case	5.91

H P — Hollow Point   L.R. — Long Rifle   *Packed 100 per box — all others 50   K — Kopper Klad

T22 RIMFIRE CARTRIDGES (STANDARD VELOCITY)

XT22S	22 Short	29	Lead, Lub.	1.88
XT22LR	22 L.R.	40	Lead, Lub.	2.15

T22 Long Rifle cartridges are designed to give a high degree of accuracy and are especially recommended for all-around shooting and target practice with rifles and pistols.
L.R. — Long Rifle   Lub. — Lubricated

SUPER-MATCH RIMFIRE CARTRIDGES

SM22LR4	22 L.R. SUPER-MATCH Mark IV Pistol	39	Lead	4.68

Super-Match cartridges are especially recommended for the highest degree of accuracy in all match shooting with rifles and pistols.
L.R. — Long Rifle

OTHER RIMFIRE CARTRIDGES

22BL	22 Short Blank	—	—	2.48
WW22CBS2	22 Short C.B.	29	Lead	9.55

SHOTSHELLS

SUPER-X MARK 5 LONG RANGE LOADS

Symbol No.	Gauge	Length Shell Inches	Powder Dram Equiv.	Oz. Shot	Shot Sizes	Suggested Retail Per Box
X10	10	2⅞	Max.	1⅝	4	$14.15
X12	12	2¾	3¾	1¼	BB, 2, 4, 5, 6, 7½, 9	9.90
X16H	16	2¾	3¼	1⅛	4, 5, 6, 7½, 9	9.50
X20	20	2¾	2¾	1	4, 5, 6, 7½, 9	8.70
X28	28	2¾	2¼	¾	6, 7½	8.75
X41	410	2½	Max.	½	4, 6, 7½	6.90
X413	410	3	Max.	¹¹⁄₁₆	4, 5, 6, 7½, 9	8.15

SUPER-X MARK 5 LONG RANGE MAGNUM LOADS

X10M	10	3½ Mag.	4¼	2	2	23.00
X12H	12	2¾ Mag.	4	1½	2, 4, 5, 6,	12.85
X12M	12	3 Mag.	4	1⅝	2, 4, 6,	14.20
X123	12	3 Mag.	4	1⅞	BB, 2, 4,	15.35
X16M	16	2¾ Mag.	3¼	1¼	2, 4, 6	12.65
X20H	20	2¾ Mag.	2¾	1⅛	4, 6, 7½	10.55
X20M	20	3 Mag.	3	1¼	4, 6, 7½	11.90

SUPER DOUBLE X FIELD LOADS

X103X	10	3½ Mag.	4½	2¼	BB, 2, 4	24.65
XG12X	12	2¾	3¾	1¼	2, 4, 6	10.75
X12X	12	2¾ Mag.	Max.	1½	BB, 2, 4, 6	14.60
X123X	12	3 Mag.	4	1⅞	BB, 2, 4, 6 New	16.45
XG20X	20	2¾	2¾	1	4, 6	9.65
X203X	20	3 Mag.	3	1¼	2, 4, 6	13.05

SUPER-X STEEL SHOT

X12SSF	12	2¾	Max.	1¼	BB, 1, 2, 4	14.90
X12SSM	12	3	Max.	1½	BB, 1, 2, 4	18.25

SUPER-X MARK 5 SUPER BUCKSHOT LOADS

X12RB	12	2¾	Max.	—	00 Buck— 9 Pellets	14.00
X124B	12	2¾	Max.	—	4 Buck—27 Pellets	14.00

SUPER-X MARK 5 SUPER BUCKSHOT LOADS — 5 ROUND PACK

X12000B5	12	2¾	Max.	—	000 Buck— 8 Pellets	2.80
X12RB5	12	2¾	Max.	—	00 Buck— 9 Pellets	2.80
X120B5	12	2¾	Max.	—	0 Buck—12 Pellets	2.80
X121B5	12	2¾	Max.	—	1 Buck—16 Pellets	2.80
X124B5	12	2¾	Max.	—	4 Buck—27 Pellets	2.80
X16B5	16	2¾	Max.	—	1 Buck—12 Pellets	2.80
X20B5	20	2¾	Max.	—	3 Buck—20 Pellets	2.80

SUPER-X MAGNUM MARK 5 SUPER BUCKSHOT LOADS

X12MB	12	3 Mag.	Max.	—	4 Buck—41 Pellets	17.75

SUPER-X MAGNUM MARKS 5 SUPER BUCKSHOT LOADS — 5 ROUND PACK

X104B5	10	3½ Mag.	Max.	—	4 Buck—54 Pellets	4.70
X123000B5	12	3 Mag.	Max.	—	000 Buck—10 Pellets	3.55
X12B5	12	2¾ Mag.	Max.	—	00 Buck—12 Pellets	3.10
X123B5	12	3 Mag.	Max.	—	00 Buck—15 Pellets	3.55
X12M1B5	12	2¾ Mag.	Max.	—	1 Buck—20 Pellets	3.10
X1231B5	12	3 Mag.	Max.	—	1 Buck—24 Pellets	3.55
X12MB5	12	3 Mag.	Max.	—	4 Buck—41 Pellets	3.55

SUPER-X RIFLED SLUG LOADS — 5 ROUND PACK

X12RS15	12	2¾	Max.	1	Rifled Slug New	3.20
X16RS5	16	2¾	Max.	⅘	Rifled Slug	3.20
§X20RS5	20	2¾	Max.	⅝	Rifled Slug	2.65
X20RSM5	20	2¾	Max.	¾	Rifled Slug New	2.95
X41RS5	410	2½	Max.	⅕	Rifled Slug	2.80

UPLAND MARK 5 FIELD LOADS

Symbol No.	Gauge	Length of Shell Inches	Powder Dram Equiv.	Oz. Shot	Shot Sizes	Suggested Retail Per Box
UW10BL	10	2⅞	8	—	•Blank	$17.90
UW12H	12	2¾	3¼	1⅛	4, 5, 6, 7½, 8, 9	8.45
UW12P	12	2¾	3¼	1¼	6, 7½, 8	8.75
UW12BL	12	2¾	6	—	•Blank	14.50
‡£UW16H	16	2¾	2¾	1⅛	4, 5, 6, 7½, 8, 9	8.45
£UW20H	20	2¾	2½	1	4, 5, 6, 7½, 8, 9	7.65

WESTERN FIELD TRIAL POPPER LOAD

XP12FBL	12	2¾	—	—	Blank	6.30

AA PLUS TRAP LOADS

WW12AAP	12	2¾	2¾	1⅛	7½, 8	8.10
WW12MAAP	12	2¾	3	1⅛	7½, 8	8.10

DOUBLE A INTERNATIONAL TRAP LOADS

WWIN12AH	12	2¾	3¼	1⅛	7½, 8 (Nic. Pl. Shot)	10.35
WWIN12A	12	2¾	3¼	1⅛	7½, 8	8.80

AA PLUS SKEET LOADS

WW12AAP	12	2¾	2¾	1⅛	9	8.10
WW12MAAP	12	2¾	3	1⅛	9	8.10
WW20AAP	20	2¾	2½	⅞	9	7.05
WW28AAP	28	2¾	2	¾	9	8.55
WW41AAP	410	2½	Max.	½	9	6.95

DOUBLE A INTERNATIONAL SKEET LOAD (No shot protectors)

WWAA12IS	12	2¾	3½	1⅛	9	8.80

SUPER TARGET LOADS (Paper not plastic)

WW12	12	2¾	2¾	1⅛	7½, 8, 9	7.85
WW12M	12	2¾	3	1⅛	7½, 8, 9	7.85

SUPER PIGEON TARGET LOADS

WW12SP	12	2¾	3¼	1¼	7½, 8	9.90

‡9 Shot recommended for Skeet.
§Discontinued Stock — Offered subject to prior sale
£7½ or 8 Shot recommended for Trap Shooting.
•Black Powder
Shotshells packed 25 per box except where indicated.

Ballistics

FEDERAL BALLISTICS

25AP   32AP   380AP   9AP   9BP   38B 38D   38C 38G 38H   38E 38F 38J   357A 357B 357D 357E   44SA   45A   45B

Automatic Pistol Ballistics (Approximate)

Federal Load No.	Caliber	Bullet Style	Bullet Weight in Grains	Velocity in Feet Per Second Muzzle	50 yds.	Energy in Foot/Lbs. Muzzle	50 yds.	Mid-range Trajectory 50 yds.	Test Barrel Length
25AP	25 Auto Pistol (6.35mm)	Metal Case	50	810	775	73	63	1.8"	2"
32AP	32 Auto Pistol (7.65mm)	Metal Case	71	905	855	129	115	1.4"	4"
380AP	380 Auto Pistol	Metal Case	95	955	865	190	160	1.4"	3¾"
380BP	380 Auto Pistol	Jacketed Hollow Point	90	1000	890	200	160	1.4"	3¾"
9AP	9mm Luger Auto Pistol	Metal Case	123	1120	1030	345	290	1.0"	4"
9BP	9mm Luger Auto Pistol	Jacketed Hollow Point	115	1160	1060	345	285	0.9"	4"
45A	45 Automatic (Match)	Metal Case	230	850	810	370	335	1.6"	5"
45B	45 Automatic (Match)	Metal Case, S.W.C.	185	775	695	247	200	2.0"	5"
45C	45 Automatic	Jacketed Hollow Point	185	950	900	370	335	1.3"	5"

Revolver Ballistics—Vented Barrel* (Approximate)

Federal Load No.	Caliber	Bullet Style	Bullet Weight in Grains	Velocity in Feet Per Second Muzzle	50 yds.	Energy in ft./lbs. Muzzle	50 yds.	Mid-range Trajectory 50 yds.	Test Barrel Length
38A	38 Special (Match)	Lead Wadcutter	148	710	634	166	132	2.4"	4"
38B	38 Special	Lead Round Nose	158	755	723	200	183	2.0"	4"
38C	38 Special	Lead Semi-Wadcutter	158	755	723	200	183	2.0"	4"
▲ 38D	38 Special (High Velocity + P)	Lead Round Nose	158	915	878	294	270	1.4"	4"
38E	38 Special (High Velocity + P)	Jacketed Hollow Point	125	945	898	248	224	1.3"	4"
▲ 38F	38 Special (High Velocity + P)	Jacketed Hollow Point	110	1020	945	254	218	1.1"	4"
▲ 38G	38 Special (High Velocity + P)	Lead, Semi-Wadcutter Hollow Point	158	915	878	294	270	1.4"	4"
▲ 38H	38 Special (High Velocity + P)	Lead Semi-Wadcutter	158	915	878	294	270	1.4"	4"
▲ 38J	38 Special (High Velocity + P)	Jacketed Soft Point	125	945	898	248	224	1.3"	4"
357A	357 Magnum	Jacketed Soft Point	158	1235	1104	535	428	0.8"	4"
357B	357 Magnum	Jacketed Hollow Point	125	1450	1240	583	427	0.6"	4"
357C	357 Magnum	Lead Semi-Wadcutter	158	1235	1104	535	428	0.8"	4"
357D	357 Magnum	Jacketed Hollow Point	110	1295	1094	410	292	0.8"	4"
357E	357 Magnum	Jacketed Hollow Point	158	1235	1104	535	428	0.8"	4"
NEW 44SA	44 S&W Special	Semi-Wadcutter Hollow Point	200	900	830	360	305	1.4"	6½"
** 44A	44 Rem. Magnum	Jacketed Hollow Point	240	1180	1081	741	623	0.9"	4"
** 44B	44 Rem. Magnum	Jacketed Hollow Point	180	1610	1365	1045	750	0.5"	4"
45LCA	45 Colt	Semi-Wadcutter Hollow Point	225	900	860	405	369	1.6"	5½"

*To simulate service conditions, these figures were obtained from a 4" length vented test barrel with a .008" cylinder gap and with the powder positioned horizontally inside the cartridge case. 44SA and 45LCA data from revolvers of indicated barrel length.

▲This ammunition is loaded to a higher pressure, as indicated by the "+P" marking on the case headstamp, to achieve higher velocity. Use only in firearms especially designed for this cartridge and so recommended by the manufacturer.

**Both 44A and 44B can be used in either pistols or rifles of this caliber. However, the 44B is accurate only in pistols.

22 Caliber Rimfire Cartridges

	Federal Load Number	Cartridges Per Box	Cartridge	Bullet Type	Bullet Wt. in Grains	Velocity in Ft. Per Sec. Muzzle	100 yds	Energy in Foot/lbs. Muzzle	100 yds	Bullet Drop In Inches at 100 yds	Drift In 10 mph Cross-wind 100 yds	Height of Trajectory Inches above line of sight if sighted in at ⊕ yardage. Sight .9" above bore.					
												50 yds	100 yds	150 yds	50 yds	100 yds	150 yds
HI Power	701	50	22 Short	Solid	29	1095	905	77	53	16.8	5.3"	⊕	−8.0	−26.8	+4.0	⊕	−14.7
	703	50	22 Short	Hollow Point	29	1120	905	81	53	16.4	5.9"	⊕	−7.9	−26.4	+3.9	⊕	−14.6
	706	50	22 Long	Solid	29	1240	960	99	60	14.1	6.9"	⊕	−6.8	−23.0	+3.4	⊕	−12.8
	710	50	22 Long Rifle	Solid	40	1255	1015	140	92	13.2	5.5"	⊕	−6.2	−20.8	+3.1	⊕	−11.5
	712	50	22 Long Rifle	Hollow Point	38	1280	1020	138	88	12.9	5.9"	⊕	−6.1	−20.6	+3.1	⊕	−11.4
	716	50	22 Long Rifle	No. 12 Shot	25	—	—	—	—	—	—						
100 Pack	810	100	22 Long Rifle	Solid	40	1255	1015	140	92	13.2	5.5"	⊕	−6.2	−20.8	+3.1	⊕	−11.5
	812	100	22 Long Rifle	Hollow Point	38	1280	1020	138	88	12.9	5.9"	⊕	−6.1	−20.6	+3.1	⊕	−11.4
Champion Standard Velocity	711	50	22 Long Rifle	Solid	40	1150	975	117	85	15.0	4.4"	⊕	−7.0	−23.2	+3.5	⊕	−12.6
	811	100	22 Long Rifle	Solid	40	1150	975	117	85	15.0	4.4"	⊕	−7.0	−23.2	+3.5	⊕	−12.6

Unless otherwise noted, these ballistic specifications were derived from test barrels 24 inches in length.
All specifications are nominal; individual guns may vary from test barrel figures.

FEDERAL BALLISTICS

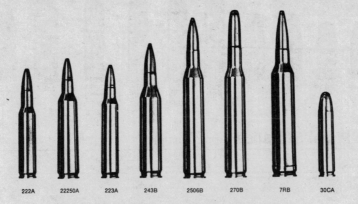

222A 22250A 223A 243B 2506B 270B 7RB 30CA

Centerfire Rifle Cartridge Ballistics

Federal Load No.	Caliber	Bullet Weight in Grains	Bullet Style	Factory Primer	Velocity In Feet Per Second						Energy In Foot Pounds					
					Muzzle	100 yds	200 yds	300 yds	400 yds	500 yds	Muzzle	100 yds	200 yds	300 yds	400 yds	500 yds
222A	222 Remington	50	Soft Point	205	3140	2600	2120	1700	1350	1110	1090	750	500	320	200	135
NEW 222B	222 Remington	55	Metal Cs. Boat-T.	205	3020	2740	2480	2230	1990	1780	1115	915	750	610	485	385
22250A	22-250 Remington	55	Soft Point	210	3730	3180	2700	2260	1860	1520	1700	1240	885	620	425	280
223A	223 Remington	55	Soft Point	205	3240	2750	2300	1910	1550	1270	1280	920	650	445	295	195
223B	223 Remington	55	Metal Cs. Boat-T.	205	3240	2880	2540	2230	1940	1680	1280	1010	790	610	460	340
6A	6mm Remington	80	Soft Point	210	3470	3060	2690	2350	2040	1750	2140	1670	1290	980	740	540
6B		100	Hi-Shok S.P.	210	3130	2860	2600	2360	2130	1910	2180	1810	1500	1230	1000	810
243A	243 Winchester	80	Soft Point	210	3350	2955	2595	2260	1950	1670	1995	1550	1195	905	675	495
243B		100	Hi-Shok S.P.	210	2960	2700	2450	2220	1990	1790	1950	1620	1330	1090	880	710
2506A	25-'06 Remington	90	Hollow Point	210	3440	3040	2680	2340	2030	1750	2360	1850	1440	1100	825	610
2506B		117	Hi-Shok S.P.	210	3060	2790	2530	2280	2050	1840	2430	2020	1660	1360	1100	875
270A	270 Winchester	130	Hi-Shok S.P.	210	3110	2850	2600	2370	2150	1940	2790	2340	1960	1620	1330	1090
270B		150	Hi-Shok S.P.	210	2900	2550	2230	1930	1650	1420	2800	2170	1650	1240	910	665
7A	7mm Mauser	175	Hi-Shok S.P.	210	2470	2170	1880	1630	1400	1220	2370	1820	1380	1030	765	575
7RA	7mm Remington Magnum	150	Hi-Shok S.P.	215	3110	2830	2570	2320	2090	1870	3220	2670	2200	1790	1450	1160
7RB		175	Hi-Shok S.P.	215	2860	2650	2440	2240	2060	1880	3180	2720	2310	1960	1640	1370
*†30CA	30 Carbine	110	Soft Point	205	1990	1570	1240	1040	920	840	965	600	375	260	210	175
*†30CB	30 Carbine	110	Metal Case	205	1990	1600	1280	1070	950	870	970	620	400	280	220	190
3030A	30-30 Winchester	150	Hi-Shok S.P.	210	2390	2020	1680	1400	1180	1040	1900	1360	945	650	460	355
3030B		170	Hi-Shok S.P.	210	2200	1900	1620	1380	1190	1060	1830	1360	990	720	535	425
3030C		125	Hollow Point	210	2570	2090	1660	1320	1080	960	1830	1210	770	480	320	260
3006A	30-'06 Springfield	150	Hi-Shok S.P.	210	2910	2620	2340	2080	1840	1620	2820	2280	1830	1450	1130	875
3006B		180	Hi-Shok S.P.	210	2700	2470	2250	2040	1850	1660	2910	2440	2020	1670	1360	1110
3006C		125	Soft Point	210	3140	2780	2450	2140	1850	1600	2740	2150	1660	1270	955	705
3006D		165	Boat Tail S.P.	210	2800	2610	2420	2240	2070	1910	2870	2490	2150	1840	1580	1340
3006E		200	Boat Tail S.P.	210	2550	2400	2260	2120	1990	1860	2890	2560	2270	2000	1760	1540
300WB	300 Winchester Magnum	180	Hi-Shok S.P.	215	2960	2745	2540	2345	2155	1980	3500		2580	2195	1860	1565
300A	300 Savage	150	Hi-Shok S.P.	210	2630	2350	2100	1850	1630	1430	2300	1850	1460	1140	885	685
300B		180	Hi-Shok S.P.	210	2350	2140	1940	1750	1570	1410	2210	1830	1500	1220	985	800
308A	308 Winchester	150	Hi-Shok S.P.	210	2820	2530	2260	2010	1770	1560	2650	2140	1710	1340	1050	810
308B		180	Hi-Shok S.P.	210	2620	2390	2180	1970	1780	1600	2740	2290	1900	1560	1270	1030
**8A	8mm Mauser	170	Hi-Shok S.P.	210	2510	2110	1740	1430	1190	1040	2380	1670	1140	770	530	400
32A	32 Winchester Special	170	Hi-Shok S.P.	210	2250	1920	1630	1370	1170	1040	1910	1390	1000	710	520	410
35A	35 Remington	200	Hi-Shok S.P.	210	2080	1700	1380	1140	1000	910	1920	1280	840	575	445	370
*†44A	44 Remington Magnum	240	Hollow S.P.	150	1760	1380	1090	950	860	790	1650	1015	640	485	395	330
*4570A	45-'70 Government	300	Hollow S.P.	210	1880	1650	1425	1235	1105	1010	2355	1815	1355	1015	810	680

Unless otherwise noted, ballistic specifications were derived from test barrels 24 inches in length.
†Test Barrel Length 20 Inches.   *Without Cartridge Carrier.
**Only for use in barrels intended for .323 inch diameter bullets. Do not use in 8mm Commission Rifles (M1888) or sporting arms of similar bore diameter.

FEDERAL BALLISTICS

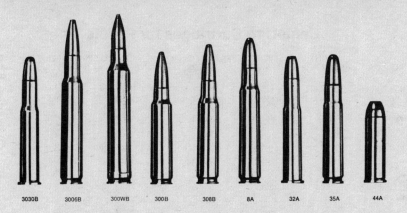

3030B 3006B 300WB 300B 308B 8A 32A 35A 44A

Centerfire Rifle Cartridge Ballistics

Bullet Drop In Inches From Bore Line					Drift In Inches In 10 mph Crosswind					Height of Trajectory — Inches above line of sight if sighted in at ⊕ yards. For sights .9″ above bore.												
100 yds	200 yds	300 yds	400 yds	500 yds	100 yds	200 yds	300 yds	400 yds	500 yds	50 yds	100 yds	150 yds	200 yds	250 yds	300 yds	100 yds	150 yds	200 yds	250 yds	300 yds	400 yds	500 yds
2.0	9.2	24.3	51.6	98.2	1.7	7.3	18.3	36.4	63.1	+0.5	+0.9	⊕	−2.5	−6.9	−13.7	+2.2	+1.9	⊕	−3.8	−10.0	−32.3	−73.8
2.0	8.6	21.0	40.8	68.2	0.9	3.4	8.5	16.8	26.3	+0.5	+0.8	⊕	−2.1	−5.4	−10.8	+1.9	+1.6	⊕	−2.8	−7.7	−22.7	−45.3
1.4	6.2	16.0	32.6	59.4	1.2	5.1	12.3	23.9	41.2	+0.2	+0.5	⊕	−1.5	−4.3	−8.4	+2.2	+2.6	+1.9	⊕	−3.3	−15.4	−37.7
1.8	8.4	21.5	44.4	81.8	1.4	6.1	15.0	29.4	50.8	+0.4	+0.8	⊕	−2.2	−6.0	−11.8	+1.9	+1.6	⊕	−3.3	−8.5	−26.7	−59.6
1.8	7.8	19.2	37.7	65.4	1.0	4.2	10.1	19.2	32.1	+0.4	+0.7	⊕	−1.9	−5.1	−9.9	+1.7	+1.4	⊕	−2.8	−7.1	−21.2	−44.6
1.6	6.9	17.0	33.4	58.3	1.0	4.1	9.9	18.8	31.6	+0.3	+0.6	⊕	−1.6	−4.5	−8.7	+2.4	+2.7	+1.9	⊕	−3.3	−14.9	−35.0
1.9	8.0	19.4	37.0	62.3	0.8	3.3	7.8	14.5	23.8	+0.4	+0.7	⊕	−1.9	−5.1	−9.7	+1.7	+1.4	⊕	−2.7	−6.8	−20.0	−40.8
1.7	7.4	18.3	36.0	63.0	1.0	4.3	10.4	19.8	33.3	+0.3	+0.7	⊕	−1.8	−4.9	−9.4	+2.6	+2.9	+2.1	⊕	−3.6	−16.2	−37.9
2.1	9.0	21.7	41.6	70.2	0.9	3.6	8.4	15.7	25.8	+0.5	+0.9	⊕	−2.2	−5.8	−11.0	+1.9	+1.6	⊕	−3.1	−7.8	−22.6	−46.3
1.6	7.0	17.2	33.8	58.9	1.0	4.1	9.8	18.8	31.3	+0.3	+0.6	⊕	−1.7	−4.5	−8.8	+2.4	+2.7	+2.0	⊕	−3.4	−15.0	−35.2
2.0	8.4	20.4	39.0	65.9	0.8	3.5	8.2	15.3	25.2	+0.5	+0.8	⊕	−2.0	−5.4	−10.3	+1.8	+1.5	⊕	−2.9	−7.3	−21.2	−43.4
1.9	8.1	19.4	37.0	62.1	0.8	3.2	7.4	13.9	22.7	+0.4	+0.7	⊕	−1.9	−5.1	−9.7	+1.7	+1.4	⊕	−2.7	−6.8	−19.9	−40.5
2.2	9.9	24.6	48.8	85.4	1.2	5.2	12.5	23.9	40.2	+0.6	+1.0	⊕	−2.5	−6.8	−13.1	+2.2	+1.9	⊕	−3.6	−9.3	−28.1	−59.7
3.1	13.7	34.1	67.8	119.3	1.5	6.2	15.0	28.7	47.8	+0.4	⊕	−2.2	−6.6	−13.4	−23.0	+1.5	⊕	−3.6	−9.7	−18.6	−46.8	−92.8
1.9	8.2	19.7	37.8	63.9	0.8	3.4	8.1	15.1	24.9	+0.4	+0.8	⊕	−1.9	−5.2	−9.9	+1.7	+1.5	⊕	−2.8	−7.0	−20.5	−42.1
2.2	9.5	22.5	42.5	70.8	0.7	3.1	7.2	13.3	21.7	+0.6	+0.9	⊕	−2.3	−6.0	−11.3	+2.0	+1.7	⊕	−3.2	−7.9	−22.7	−45.8
5.2	24.8	67.2	142.0	257.6	3.4	15.0	35.5	63.2	96.7	+0.9	⊕	−4.5	−13.5	−28.3	−49.9	⊕	−4.5	−13.5	−28.3	−49.9	−118.6	−228.1
5.1	24.1	64.5	135.1	244.1	3.1	13.7	32.6	58.7	90.3	+0.9	⊕	−4.3	−13.0	−26.9	−47.4	+2.9	⊕	−7.2	−19.7	−38.7	−100.4	−200.5
3.4	15.4	39.9	82.3	149.8	2.0	8.5	20.9	40.1	66.1	+0.5	⊕	−2.6	−7.7	−16.0	−27.9	+1.7	⊕	−4.3	−11.6	−22.7	−59.1	−120.5
4.0	17.7	44.8	90.3	160.2	1.9	8.0	19.4	36.7	59.8	+0.6	⊕	−3.0	−8.9	−18.0	−31.1	+2.0	⊕	−4.8	−13.0	−25.1	−63.6	−126.7
3.0	14.2	38.0	81.0	148.7	2.2	10.1	25.4	49.4	81.6	+0.1	⊕	−2.0	−7.3	−15.8	−28.1	+3.2	+2.4	⊕	−5.5	−15.8	−51.7	−112.3
2.2	9.5	23.2	44.9	76.9	1.0	4.2	9.9	18.7	31.2	+0.6	+0.9	⊕	−2.3	−6.3	−12.0	+2.1	+1.8	⊕	−3.3	−8.5	−25.0	−51.8
2.5	10.8	25.9	49.4	83.2	0.9	3.7	8.8	16.5	27.1	+0.2	⊕	−1.6	−4.8	−9.7	−16.5	+2.4	+2.0	⊕	−3.7	−9.3	−27.0	−54.9
1.9	8.3	20.6	40.6	70.7	1.1	4.5	10.8	20.5	34.4	+0.4	+0.8	⊕	−2.1	−5.6	−10.7	+1.8	+1.5	⊕	−3.0	−7.7	−23.0	−48.5
2.2	9.5	22.7	42.8	71.0	0.7	2.8	6.6	12.3	19.9	+0.5	⊕	−1.1	−4.2	−8.8	−14.3	+2.1	+1.8	⊕	−3.0	−8.0	−22.9	−45.9
2.6	11.2	26.6	59.7	81.6	0.6	2.6	6.0	11.0	17.7	+0.6	⊕	−2.7	−6.0	−12.4	−18.8	+2.3	+1.8	⊕	−4.1	−9.0	−25.6	−51.3
2.1	8.8	20.9	39.4	65.3	0.7	2.8	6.6	12.3	20.0	+0.5	+0.8	⊕	−2.1	−5.5	−10.4	+1.9	+1.6	⊕	−2.9	−7.3	−20.9	−41.9
2.7	11.7	28.7	55.8	96.1	1.1	4.8	11.6	21.9	36.3	+0.3	⊕	−1.8	−5.4	−11.0	−18.8	+2.7	+2.2	⊕	−4.2	−10.7	−31.5	−65.5
3.4	14.3	34.7	66.4	112.3	1.1	4.6	10.9	20.3	33.3	+0.4	⊕	−2.3	−6.7	−13.5	−22.8	+1.5	⊕	−3.6	−9.6	−18.2	−44.1	−84.2
2.3	10.1	24.8	48.0	82.4	1.0	4.4	10.4	19.7	32.7	+0.2	⊕	−1.5	−4.5	−9.3	−15.9	+2.3	+1.9	⊕	−3.6	−9.1	−26.9	−55.7
2.7	11.5	27.6	52.7	88.8	0.9	3.9	9.2	17.2	28.3	+0.2	⊕	−1.8	−5.2	−10.4	−17.7	+2.6	+2.1	⊕	−4.0	−9.9	−28.9	−58.8
3.1	14.2	36.8	76.7	141.2	1.9	8.5	21.0	40.6	67.5	+0.4	⊕	−2.3	−7.0	−14.6	−25.7	+1.6	⊕	−3.9	−10.7	−21.0	−55.4	−114.3
3.8	17.1	43.7	88.9	159.3	1.9	8.4	20.3	38.6	63.0	+0.6	⊕	−2.9	−8.6	−17.6	−30.5	+1.9	⊕	−4.7	−12.7	−24.7	−63.2	−126.9
4.6	21.5	56.9	118.9	215.6	2.7	12.0	29.0	53.3	83.3	+0.8	⊕	−3.8	−11.3	−23.5	−41.2	+2.5	⊕	−6.3	−17.1	−33.6	−87.7	−176.3
6.7	32.4	87.0	179.8	319.6	4.2	17.8	39.8	68.3	102.5	⊕	−2.7	−10.2	−23.6	−44.2	−73.3	⊕	−6.1	−18.1	−37.4	−65.1	−150.3	−282.5
4.3	21.5	57.2	112.8	NA	1.7	7.6	18.6	35.7	NA	⊕	−2.4	−8.2	−17.6	−31.4	−51.5	⊕	−4.6	−12.8	−25.4	−44.3	−95.5	NA

Trajectory figures show the height of bullet impact above or below the line of sight at the indicated yardages. Aim low indicated amount for + figures and high for − figures. Zero ranges indicated by circled crosses.

NOTE: These trajectory tables were calculated by computer and are given here unaltered. The computer used a standard modern scientific technique to predict trajectories from the best available data for each round. Each trajectory is expected to be reasonably representative of the behavior of the ammunition at sea level conditions, but the shooter is cautioned that trajectories differ because of variations in ammunition, rifles, and atmospheric conditions.

FIOCCHI BALLISTICS

Centerfire Cartridges for Pistols

CALIBER	BULLET WEIGHT IN GRAINS	VELOCITY IN FT./SEC. MV	VELOCITY IN FT./SEC. 50 YDS.	ENERGY IN FOOT LBS. MV	ENERGY IN FOOT LBS. 50 YDS.	BARREL LENGTH INCHES
25 A.C.P.	50	754.6	698.8	62.2	53.5	2⅜″
6.35mm	50	656.2	607.00	47.00	40.5	2⅜″
.30 MAUSER 7.63mm Mauser	88	1443.6	1253.3	400.00	301.6	5½″
32 A.C.P.	73	951.5	879.3	147.6	125.9	3⅜″
7.65mm	75	885.8	826.8	130.2	113.6	3⅜″
30 LUGER PARABELLUM 7.65mm	93	1181.1	1066.3	287.2	233.6	4¹⁷⁄₃₂″
ROTH-STEYR 8mm	113	1082.7	1010.5	293.7	255.3	5″
380 A.C.P. 9mm (short M34)	93	984.3	876.00	199.6	157.7	3⅜″
9mm LUGER 9mm (long M38)	115	1345.2	1158.2	462.2	342.8	7⅞″
9mm GLISENTI	123	1230.3	1072.9	415.2	315.4	7⅞″
9mm LUGER PARABELLUM	123	1312.4	1122.1	472.3	345.00	7⅞″
9mm STEYR	115	1181.1	1000.7	356.6	256.1	5″
30 MI CARBINE	111	1968.5	1804.5	956.2	803.6	20″
38 A.C.P. 38	129	1148.3	1004.00	377.6	288.6	6⅓₂
45 A.C.P. 45	230	820.2	777.6	343.6	308.9	5″

Centerfire Cartridges for Revolvers

CALIBER	BULLET WEIGHT IN GRAINS	VELOCITY IN FT./SEC. MV	VELOCITY IN FT./SEC. 50 YDS.	ENERGY IN FOOT LBS. MV	ENERGY IN FOOT LBS. 50 YDS.	BARREL LENGTH INCHES
5.5mm VELO DOG REVOLVER	43	853.00	777.6	70.2	57.9	3¾″
SWISS ORDNANCE 7.5mm	107	1115.5	997.4	296.6	237.2	5″
7.62 NAGANT	97	1049.9	987.6	238.00	210.5	6″
8mm LEBEL	111	885.8	839.9	193.8	174.3	5″
8mm GASSER	126	885.8	856.3	219.2	204.7	4¾″
ITALIAN ORDNANCE 10.4mm	177	951.5	895.7	356.6	316.1	5″
32 SMITH & WESSON SHORT	85	738.2	708.7	102.7	94.8	5″
	85	721.8	639.8	98.4	77.4	5″
32 SMITH & WESSON LONG	98	836.6	784.1	151.2	133.1	5″
	98	820.2	771.00	145.4	128.7	5″
320 SHORT	82	820.2	790.7	122.2	113.6	5″
	82	787.4	744.8	112.8	100.5	5″

FIOCCHI BALLISTICS

Centerfire Cartridges for Revolvers

CALIBER	BULLET WEIGHT IN GRAINS	VELOCITY IN FT./SEC. MV	50 YDS.	ENERGY IN FOOT LBS. MV	50 YDS.	BARREL LENGTH INCHES
320 LONG	82	853.00	803.8	132.4	117.2	3⅜″
	82	820.2	764.4	122.2	106.3	3⅜″
38 SMITH & WESSON SHORT	145	754.6	721.8	183.7	167.8	5″
	145	721.8	682.4	167.8	149.7	5″
38 SPECIAL	158	918.7	876.00	296.6	269.8	6″
	158	685.8	820.2	275.6	236.5	6″
38 SPECIAL WAD CUTTER	148	787.4	669.3	203.3	146.8	6″
380 SHORT	125	820.2	790.7	186.6	173.6	5″
	125	787.4	734.9	172.1	149.7	5″
380 LONG	125	853.00	800.5	201.8	177.9	7⅞″
	125	820.2	761.2	186.6	160.6	7⅞″
44 SMITH & WESSON RUSSIAN	247	820.2	790.7	368.9	342.8	6½″
450 SHORT	226	853.00	813.7	365.3	332.7	7½″
455 MK II	262	853.00	816.9	423.9	389.1	7½″
357 MAGNUM	158	1378.00		667.6		7⅝″

22 Rimfire Cartridges Short-Long-Long Rifle-Extra Long

CALIBER	BULLET WEIGHT IN GRAINS	VELOCITY IN FT./SEC. MV	50 YDS.	ENERGY IN FOOT LBS. MV	50 YDS.	BARREL LENGTH INCHES
22 SHORT TRAINING	29	1049.9	948.2	71.6	58.6	22″
22 SHORT NORMALE	29	951.5	849.5	59.3	47.00	22″
22 SHORT OLIMPIONICO	31	787.4	702.1	42.7	34.00	5″
22 SHORT V 50	28	1181.1	987.6	86.1	60.00	22″
22 SHORT EXPANSIVE	28	1181.1	931.8	86.1	53.5	22″
22 SHORT "Z"	29	853.00	764.4	47.7	38.8	22″
22 LONG	28	1246.7	1013.8	96.2	63.7	27¼″
22 LONG "Z"	29	820.2	748.00	44.1	36.9	27¼″
22 LONG L.R. MAXAC	40	1148.3	1063.00	117.9	100.5	27¼″
22 L.R. CARB. BERETTA	40	1099.1	1033.5	107.8	95.5	27¼″
22 L.R. ULTRASONIC	40	1328.8	1197.5	157.7	128.00	27¼″
22 L.R. EXPANSIVE	37	1345.2	1210.7	149.00	120.8	27¼″
22 L.R. COMPETIZIONE	40	1082.7	1023.6	104.2	93.3	27¼″
22 L.R. PISTOLA LIBERA	40	1049.9	1013.8	98.4	91.9	9″
22 EXTRA LONG	40	1410.8	1325.5	177.2	157.00	27¼″

All specifications are nominal. Individual guns may vary from test barrel figures.

NORMA BALLISTICS

Caliber Bullet weight Prod.no	Velocity – Feet per sec. Muzzle	100 yards	200 yards	300 yards	Energy–Foot pounds Muzzle	100 yards	200 yards	300 yards	Sight at yards	25 yards	50 yards	100 yards	150 yards	200 yards	300 yards
220 Swift 50 gr/3.2 g 15701	4110	3611	3133	2681	1877	1448	1090	799	100 180 200	−0.9 −0.8 −0.8	−0.5 −0.3 −0.2	0 +0.4 +0.6	−0.2 +0.4 +0.7	−1.2 −0.4 0	−5.9 −4.7 −4.1
222 Rem. 50 gr/3.2 g 15711	3200	2650	2170	1750	1137	780	520	340	100 180 200	−0.8 −0.5 −0.4	−0.3 +0.3 +0.5	0 +1.2 +1.6	−0.9 +0.8 +1.5	−3.2 −0.9 0	−12.9 −9.4 −8.2
222 Rem. 50 gr/3.2 g 15712	3200	2610	2080	1630	1137	756	480	295	100 180 200	−0.7 −0.4 −0.3	−0.2 +0.5 +0.7	0 +1.4 +1.9	−1.1 +1.0 +1.7	−3.7 −1.0 0	−15.7 −11.6 −10.1
222 Rem. 50 gr/3.2 g 15713	2790	2235	1755	1390	863	554	341	214	100 180 200	−0.6 −0.1 +0.1	±0.0 +1.0 +1.4	0 +2.1 +2.9	−1.7 +1.5 +2.6	−5.8 −1.5 0	−23.4 −17.1 −14.8
222 Rem. 50 gr/3.2 g 15715	3200	2610	2080	1630	1137	756	480	295	100 180 200	−0.7 −0.4 −0.3	−0.2 +0.5 +0.07	0 +1.4 +1.9	−1.1 +1.0 +1.7	−3.7 −1.0 0	−15.7 −11.6 −10.1
222 Rem. 53 gr/3.4 g 15714	3117	2670	2267	1901	1142	838	604	425	100 180 200	−0.7 −0.4 −0.3	−0.2 +0.4 +0.6	0 +1.3 +1.7	−1.0 +0.9 +1.6	−3.5 −0.9 0	−14.0 −10.1 −8.7
22–250 53 gr/3.4 g 15733	3707	3192	2741	2332	1616	1198	883	639	100 180 200	−0.9 −0.7 −0.6	−0.4 −0.1 +0.1	0 +0.7 +1.0	−0.5 +0.5 +1.0	−1.9 −0.6 0	−8.6 −6.6 −5.7
5.6x52 R 71 gr/4.6 g 15604	2790	2296	1886	1558	1226	831	561	383	100 180 200	−0.6 −0.2 0	−0.1 +0.8 +1.1	0 +1.8 +2.4	−1.5 +1.2 +2.1	−4.8 −1.2 0	−18.6 −13.2 −11.4
5.6x52 R 71 gr/4.6 g 15605	2790	2296	1886	1558	1226	831	561	383	100 180 200	−0.6 −0.2 0	−0.1 +0.8 +1.1	0 +1.8 +2.4	−1.5 +1.2 +2.1	−4.8 −1.2 0	−18.6 −13.2 −11.4
243 Win. 100 gr/6.5 g 16002	3070	2790	2540	2320	2090	1730	1430	1190	100 180 200	−0.7 −0.5 −0.4	−0.2 +0.3 +0.5	0 +1.1 +1.4	−0.9 +0.7 +1.3	−2.9 −0.7 0	−10.6 −7.4 −6.3
243 Win. 100 gr/6.5 g 16003	3070	2790	2540	2320	2090	1730	1430	1190	100 180 200	−0.7 −0.5 −0.4	−0.2 +0.3 +0.5	0 +1.1 +1.4	−0.9 +0.7 +1.3	−2.9 −0.7 0	−10.6 −7.4 −6.3
6.5 Jap. 139 gr/9.0 g 16531	2430	2280	2130	1990	1820	1605	1401	1223	100 130 200	−0.5 −0.4 +0.1	±0.0 +0.4 +1.4	0 +0.6 +2.7	−1.8 −0.8 +2.3	−5.4 −4.1 0	−18.8 −16.9 −10.8
6.5 Jap. 156 gr/10.1 g 16532	2065	1871	1692	1529	1481	1213	992	810	100 130 200	−0.3 ±0.0 +0.8	+0.4 +0.9 +2.5	0 +1.1 +4.3	−2.9 −1.2 +3.5	−8.5 −6.3 0	−29.2 −26.0 −16.4
6.5 Carcano 139 gr/9 g 16536	2576	2379	2192	2012	2046	1745	1481	1249	100 180 200	−0.6 −0.1 ±0.0	±0.0 +0.9 +1.2	0 +1.8 +2.3	−1.5 +1.1 +2.0	−4.7 −1.1 0	−16.6 −11.3 −9.6
6.5 Carcano 156 gr/10.1 g 16535	2430	2208	2000	1800	2046	1689	1386	1123	100 180 200	−0.5 ±0.0 +0.2	+0.1 +1.2 +1.5	0 +2.2 +2.9	−1.9 +1.4 +2.4	−5.7 −1.3 0	−20.2 −13.7 −11.7
6.5x55 77 gr/5.0 g 16550	2725	2362	2030	1811	1271	956	706	562	100 180 200	−0.6 −0.2 ±0.0	−0.1 +0.8 +1.1	0 +1.8 +2.4	−1.5 +1.2 +2.1	−4.8 −1.2 0	−18.1 −12.7 −10.9
6.5x55 80 gr/5.2 g 16528	3002	2398	1886	1499	1604	1023	633	400	100 180 200	−0.7 −0.3 ±0.0	−0.2 +0.7 +1.0	0 +1.7 +2.3	−1.4 +1.2 +2.1	−4.7 −1.2 0	−19.3 −14.2 −12.3
6.5x55 139 gr/9.0 g 16551	2854	2691	2533	2370	2512	2233	1978	1732	100 180 200	−0.7 −0.6 −0.2	−0.2 +0.4 +0.5	0 +1.3 +1.7	−1.0 +0.8 +1.5	−2.3 −0.8 0	−12.3 −8.6 −7.4
6.5x55 139 gr/9.0 g 16557	2790	2630	2470	2320	2402	2136	1883	1662	100 180 200	−0.7 −0.3 −0.2	−0.2 +0.5 +0.8	0 +1.4 +1.8	−1.1 +0.9 +1.6	−3.7 −0.9 0	−13.3 −9.2 −7.8
6.5x55 156 gr/10.1 g 16552	2495	2271	2062	1867	2153	1787	1473	1208	100 180 200	−0.6 ±0.0 +0.1	+0.2 +1.0 +1.3	0 +2.0 +2.6	−1.7 +1.3 +2.2	−5.3 −1.3 0	−18.8 −12.7 −10.9
270 Win. 130 gr/8.4 g 16902	3140	2884	2639	2404	2847	2401	2011	1669	100 180 200	−0.8 −0.5 −0.4	−0.3 +0.2 +0.4	0 +1.0 +1.4	−0.8 +0.7 +1.3	−4.1 −0.7 0	−10.7 −7.7 −6.6
270 Win. 150 gr/9.7 g 16903	2800	2616	2436	2262	2616	2280	1977	1705	100 180 200	−0.7 −0.3 −0.2	−0.2 +0.5 +0.7	0 +1.4 +1.8	−1.1 +0.9 +1.6	−3.6 −0.9 0	−13.1 −9.0 −7.7
7x57 150 gr/9.7 g 17002	2755	2539	2331	2133	2530	2148	1810	1516	100 180 200	−0.7 −0.3 −0.2	−0.1 +0.6 +0.9	0 +1.5 +2.0	−1.2 +1.0 +1.7	−3.9 −1.0 0	−14.3 −9.8 −8.4
7x57 R 150 gr/9.7 g 17005	2690	2476	2270	2077	2411	2042	1717	1437	100 180 200	−0.6 −0.2 −0.1	−0.1 +0.7 +1.0	0 +1.6 +2.1	−1.3 +1.1 +1.8	−4.2 −1.0 0	−15.2 −10.4 −8.9
7x57 R 150 gr/9.7 g 17006	2690	2476	2270	2077	2411	2042	1717	1437	100 180 200	−0.6 −0.2 −0.1	−0.1 +0.7 +1.0	0 +1.6 +2.1	−1.3 +1.1 +1.8	−4.2 −1.0 0	−15.2 −10.4 −8.9
7 mm Rem. M 150 gr/9.7 g 17021	3250	2960	2638	2440	3519	2919	2318	1983	100 180 200	−0.8 −0.6 −0.5	−0.3 +0.1 +0.3	0 +0.9 +1.2	−0.7 +0.6 +1.1	−2.4 +0.6 0	−9.5 −6.8 −5.8
7x64 150 gr/9.7 g 17013	2890	2598	2329	2113	2779	2449	1807	1487	100 180 200	−0.7 −0.4 −0.3	−0.2 +0.4 +0.6	0 +1.2 +1.7	−1.0 +0.9 +1.5	−3.3 −0.8 0	−12.5 −8.8 −7.5
7x64 175 gr/11.3 g 17015	2725	2516	2339	2198	2884	2460	2126	1878	100 180 200	−0.7 −0.3 −0.2	−0.1 +0.6 +0.8	0 +1.4 +1.8	−1.2 +0.9 +1.6	−3.6 −0.9 0	−12.7 −8.5 −7.2
280 Rem. 150 gr/9.7 g 17050	2900	2683	2475	2277	2802	2398	2041	1727	100 180 200	−0.7 −0.4 −0.3	−0.2 +0.4 +0.7	0 +1.2 +1.7	−1.0 +1.1 +1.5	−3.4 −0.8 0	−12.4 −8.6 −7.4
7.5x55 Swiss 180 gr/11.6 g 17511	2650	2441	2248	2056	2792	2380	2020	1690	100 180 200	−0.6 −0.2 −0.1	−0.1 +0.7 +1.0	0 +1.6 +2.1	−1.4 +1.1 +1.8	−4.3 −1.0 0	−15.3 −10.4 −8.9

	Muzzle	100 yards	200 yards	300 yards	Muzzle	100 yards	200 yards	300 yards		25 yards	50 yards	100 yards	150 yards	200 yards	300 yards
30 US Carbine 110 gr/7.1 g 17621	1970	1595	1300	1090	948	622	413	290	100	−0.1	+0.6	0	−4.1	−12.4	−45.7
									130	+0.3	+1.4	+1.5	−1.8	−9.3	−41.1
									200	+1.4	+3.7	+6.2	+5.2	0	−27.0
7.62 Russian 180 gr/11.6 g 17634	2625	2415	2222	2030	2749	2326	1970	1644	100	−0.6	−0.1	0	−1.4	−4.4	−15.7
									180	−0.2	+0.8	+1.7	+1.1	−1.1	−10.7
									200	−0.1	+1.0	+2.2	+1.9	0	−9.1
30−06 130 gr/8.4 g 17640	3205	2876	2561	2263	2966	2388	1894	1479	100	−0.8	−0.3	0	−0.8	−2.7	−10.8
									180	−0.5	+0.2	+1.0	+0.7	−0.7	−7.8
									200	−0.4	+0.4	+1.4	+1.3	0	−6.7
30−06 146 gr/9.5 g 17651	2772	2549	2336	2133	2485	2102	1765	1472	100	−0.7	−0.1	0	−1.2	−3.9	−14.3
									180	−0.3	+0.6	+1.5	+1.0	−1.0	−9.9
									200	−0.2	+0.8	+2.0	+1.7	0	−8.4
30−06 150 gr/9.7 g 17643	2970	2680	2402	2141	2943	2393	1922	1527	100	−0.7	−0.2	0	−1.0	−3.4	−12.9
									180	−0.4	+0.4	+1.3	+0.9	−0.9	−9.1
									200	−0.3	+0.6	+1.7	+1.5	0	−7.8
30−06 180 gr/11.6 g 17648	2700	2477	2261	2070	2914	2430	2025	1713	100	−0.6	−0.1	0	−1.3	−4.1	−14.9
									180	−0.3	+0.7	+1.6	+1.0	−1.7	−10.2
									200	−0.1	+0.9	+2.1	+1.8	0	−8.7
30−06 180 gr/11.6 g 17649	2700	2494	2296	2109	2914	2487	2107	1778	100	−0.6	−0.1	0	−1.3	−4.1	−14.8
									180	−0.3	+0.7	+1.5	+1.0	−1.0	−10.2
									200	−0.1	+0.9	+2.0	+1.8	0	−8.7
30−06 180 gr/11.6 g 17653	2700	2494	2296	2109	2914	2487	2107	1778	100	−0.6	−0.1	0	−1.3	−4.1	−14.8
									180	−0.3	+0.7	+1.5	+1.0	−1.0	−10.2
									200	−0.1	+0.9	+2.0	+1.8	0	−8.7
30−30 Win. 150 gr/9.7 g 17630	2410	2075	1790	1550	1934	1433	1066	799	100	−0.5	+0.1	0	−2.2	−7.0	−26.1
									130	−0.3	+0.6	+0.8	−1.0	−5.4	−23.6
									200	+0.4	+1.9	+3.5	+3.0	0	−15.6
30−30 Win. 170 gr/11.0 g 17631	2220	1890	1630	1410	1860	1350	1000	750	100	−0.4	+0.3	0	−2.7	−8.1	−29.2
									130	−0.1	+0.8	+1.0	−1.2	−6.1	−26.3
									200	+0.6	+2.3	+4.0	+3.4	0	−17.1
308 Win. 130 gr/8.4 g 17623	2900	2590	2300	2030	2428	1937	1527	1190	100	−0.7	−0.2	0	−1.1	−3.7	−14.2
									180	−0.4	+0.5	+1.4	+1.0	−0.9	−10.0
									200	−0.2	+0.8	+1.9	+1.7	0	−8.6
308 Win. 146 gr/9.5 g 17622	2812	2589	2375	2172	2558	2168	1824	1526	100	−0.7	−0.1	0	−1.3	−4.1	−15.6
									180	−0.3	+0.6	+1.5	+1.1	−1.0	−11.0
									200	−0.2	+0.9	+2.1	+1.8	0	−9.4
308 Win. 150 gr/9.7 g 17624	2860	2570	2300	2050	2725	2200	1760	1400	100	−0.7	−0.2	0	−1.2	−3.8	−14.2
									180	−0.3	+0.6	+1.4	+1.0	−1.0	−10.0
									200	−0.2	+0.8	+1.9	+1.7	0	−8.5
308 Win. 180 gr/11.6 g 17628	2610	2400	2210	2020	2725	2303	1952	1631	100	−0.6	−0.1	0	−1.4	−4.5	−16.2
									180	−0.2	+0.8	+1.7	+1.1	−1.1	−11.0
									200	±0.0	+1.1	+2.3	+1.9	0	−9.4
308 Win. 180 gr/11.6 g 17635	2610	2400	2210	2020	2725	2303	1952	1631	100	−0.6	−0.1	0	−1.4	−4.5	−16.2
									180	−0.2	+0.8	+1.7	+1.1	−1.1	−11.0
									200	±0.0	+1.1	+2.3	+1.9	0	−9.4
308 Win. 180 gr/11.6 g 17636	2610	2393	2185	1988	2724	2287	1906	1578	100	−0.6	±0.0	0	−1.5	−4.6	−16.5
									180	−0.2	+0.8	+1.7	+1.1	−1.1	−11.3
									200	±0.0	+1.1	+2.3	+2.0	0	−9.6
308 Norma M 180 gr/11.6 g 17638	3020	2798	2585	2382	3646	3130	2671	2268	100	−0.8	−0.3	0	−0.8	−2.6	−10.1
									180	−0.5	+0.2	+1.0	+0.7	−0.7	−7.1
									200	−0.4	+0.4	+1.3	+1.2	0	−6.1
7.65 Argentine 150 gr/9.7 g 17701	2920	2630	2355	2105	2841	2304	1848	1476	100	−0.7	−0.2	0	−1.0	−3.6	−12.9
									180	−0.4	+0.5	+1.3	+0.9	−0.9	−9.1
									200	−0.3	+0.7	+1.7	+1.5	0	−7.8
303 British 150 gr/9.7 g 17712	2720	2440	2170	1930	2465	1983	1569	1241	100	−0.6	−0.1	0	−1.4	−4.4	−16.3
									180	−0.2	+0.7	+1.7	+1.1	−1.1	−11.3
									200	−0.1	+1.0	+2.2	+1.9	0	−9.7
303 British 180 gr/11.6 g 17713	2540	2340	2147	1965	2579	2189	1843	1544	100	−0.6	±0.0	0	−1.6	−4.9	−17.3
									130	−0.4	+0.3	+0.6	−0.7	−3.7	−15.6
									200	±0.0	+1.2	+2.4	+2.1	0	−10.0
7.7 Jap. 130 gr/8.4 g 17721	2950	2635	2340	2065	2513	2004	1581	1231	100	−0.7	−0.2	0	−1.1	−3.5	−13.5
									180	−0.4	+0.5	+1.3	+0.9	−0.9	−9.5
									200	−0.3	+0.7	+1.8	+1.6	0	−8.2
7.7 Jap. 180 gr/11.6 g 17722	2495	2292	2101	1922	2484	2100	1765	1477	100	−0.6	±0.0	0	−1.7	−5.2	−18.1
									130	−0.4	+0.3	+0.6	−0.8	−3.9	−16.3
									200	+0.1	+1.3	+2.6	+2.2	0	−10.4
8x57 J 196 gr/12.7 g 17901	2525	2195	1894	1627	2778	2097	1562	1152	100	−0.6	±0.0	0	−1.8	−5.8	−21.4
									130	−0.4	+0.4	+0.7	−0.8	−4.4	−19.3
									200	+0.2	+1.5	+2.9	+2.5	0	−12.7
8x57 JS 108 gr/7.0 g 18009	2976	2178	1562	1129	2122	1137	585	305	100	−0.6	−0.1	0	−1.8	−6.1	−27.1
									150	−0.4	+0.5	+1.2	0	−3.8	−23.5
									200	−0.1	+1.5	+3.1	+4.0	0	−17.9
8x57 JS 196 gr/12.7 g 18003	2525	2195	1894	1627	2778	2097	1562	1152	100	−0.6	±0.0	0	−1.8	−5.8	−21.4
									130	−0.4	+0.4	+0.7	−0.8	−4.4	−19.3
									200	+0.2	+1.5	+2.9	+2.5	0	−12.7
8x57 JS 196 gr/12.7 g 18007	2525	2195	1894	1627	2778	2097	1562	1152	100	−0.6	±0.0	0	−1.8	−5.8	−21.4
									130	−0.4	+0.4	+0.7	−0.8	−4.4	−19.3
									200	+0.2	+1.5	+2.9	+2.5	0	−12.7
358 Norma M 250 gr/16.2 g 19001	2800	2493	2231	2001	4322	3451	2764	2223	100	−0.7	−0.1	0	−1.2	−4.0	−14.3
									180	−0.3	+0.6	+1.5	+1.0	−1.0	−9.8
									200	−0.2	+0.9	+2.0	+1.7	0	−8.3
9.3x57 286 gr/18.5 g 19302	2065	1818	1595	1404	2714	2099	1616	1252	100	−0.3	+0.4	0	−3.1	−9.1	−32.0
									130	±0.0	+1.0	+1.1	−1.3	−6.8	−28.5
									200	+0.9	+2.7	+4.6	+3.8	0	−18.3
9.3x57 286 gr/18.5 g 19303	2065	1818	1595	1404	2714	2099	1616	1252	100	−0.3	+0.4	0	−3.1	−9.1	−32.0
									130	±0.0	+1.0	+1.1	−1.3	−6.8	−28.5
									200	+0.9	+2.7	+4.6	+3.8	0	−18.3
9.3x62 286 gr/18.5 g 19314	2360	2088	1815	1592	3544	2769	2092	1700	100	−0.5	+0.1	0	−2.1	−6.5	−23.5
									180	+0.1	+1.4	+2.5	+1.6	−1.6	−16.0
									200	+0.3	+1.8	+3.3	+2.8	0	−13.7
9.3x62 286 gr/18.5 g 19315	2360	2088	1815	1592	3544	2769	2092	1700	100	−0.5	+0.1	0	−2.1	−6.5	−23.5
									180	+0.1	+1.4	+2.5	+1.6	−1.6	−16.0
									200	+0.3	+1.8	+3.3	+2.8	0	−13.7

REMINGTON BALLISTICS

Remington Center Fire Pistol and Revolver Cartridges

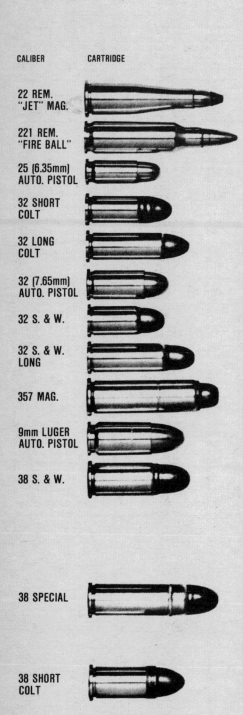

CALIBER	CARTRIDGE
22 REM. "JET" MAG.	
221 REM. "FIRE BALL"	
25 (6.35mm) AUTO. PISTOL	
32 SHORT COLT	
32 LONG COLT	
32 (7.65mm) AUTO. PISTOL	
32 S. & W.	
32 S. & W. LONG	
357 MAG.	
9mm LUGER AUTO. PISTOL	
38 S. & W.	
38 SPECIAL	
38 SHORT COLT	

REM-INGTON	BULLET Primer No.	Wt.-Grs.	Style	VELOCITY—FEET PER SECOND Muzzle	50 Yds.	100 Yds.	ENERGY—FOOT POUNDS Muzzle	50 Yds.	100 Yds.	MID-RANGE TRAJECTORY 50 Yds.	100 Yds.	BARREL
R22JET	6½	40*	Soft Point	2100	1790	1510	390	285	200	0.3"	1.4"	8⅜"
R221F	7½	50*	Pointed Soft Point	2650	2380	2130	780	630	505	0.2"	0.8"	10½"
R25AP	1½	50*	Metal Case	810	775	700	73	63	54	1.8"	7.7"	2"
R32SC	1½	80*	Lead	745	665	590	100	79	62	2.2"	9.9"	4"
R32LC	1½	82*	Lead	755	715	675	100	93	83	2.0"	8.7"	4"
R32AP	1½	71*	Metal Case	960	905	850	145	130	115	1.3"	5.4"	4"
R32SW	5½	88*	Lead	905	855	810	129	115	97	1.4"	5.8"	4"
R32SWL	1½	98*	Lead	705	670	635	115	98	88	2.3"	10.5"	4"
R357M7	5½	110	Semi-Jacketed H.P.	1295	1094	975	410	292	232	0.8"	3.5"	4"
R357M1	5½	125	Semi-Jacketed H.P.	1450	1240	1090	583	427	330	0.6"	2.8"	4"
R357M2	5½	158	Semi-Jacketed H.P.	1235	1104	1015	535	428	361	0.8"	3.5"	4"
R357M3	5½	158	Soft Point	1235	1104	1015	535	428	361	0.8"	3.5"	4"
R357M4	5½	158	Metal Point	1235	1104	1015	535	428	361	0.8"	3.5"	4"
R357M5	5½	158*	Lead	1235	1104	1015	535	428	361	0.8"	3.5"	4"
R357M6	5½	158	Lead (Brass case)	1235	1104	1015	535	428	361	0.8"	3.5"	4"
R9MM2	1½	124*	Metal Case	1115	1047	971	341	280	241	0.9"	3.9"	4"
R9MM1	1½	115	Jacketed H.P.	1110	1030	971	339	292	259	1.0"	4.1"	4"
R38SW	1½	146*	Lead	685	650	620	150	135	125	2.4"	10.0"	4"
R38S1	1½	95	Semi-Jacketed H.P. (+P)†	1175	1044	959	291	230	194	0.9"	3.9"	4"
R38S10	1½	110	Semi-Jacketed H.P. (+P)†	1020	945	887	254	218	192	1.1"	4.9"	4"
R38S2	1½	125	Semi-Jacketed H.P. (+P) +	945	898	858	248	224	204	1.3"	5.4"	4"
R38S3	1½	148	"Targetmaster" Lead W.C.	710	634	566	166	132	105	2.4"	10.8"	4"
R38S4	1½	158	"Targetmaster" Lead Round Nose	755	723	692	200	183	168	2.0"	8.3"	4"
R38S5	1½	158*	Lead	755	723	692	200	183	168	2.0"	8.3"	4"
R38S6	1½	158	Semi-Wadcutter	755	723	692	200	183	168	2.0"	8.3"	4"
R38S7	1½	158	Metal Point	755	723	692	200	183	168	2.0"	8.3"	4"
R38S8	1½	158	Lead (+P)	915	878	844	294	270	250	1.4"	5.6"	4"
R38S12	1½	158	Lead H.P. (+P)	915	878	844	294	270	250	1.4"	5.6"	4"
R38S9	1½	200	Lead	635	614	594	179	168	157	2.8"	11.5"	4"
R38SC	1½	125*	Lead	730	685	645	150	130	115	2.2"	9.4"	6"

*Illustrated

"JET", "FIRE BALL", and "Targetmaster" are trademarks registered in the United States Patent and Trademark Office by Remington Arms Company, Inc.

Note B: Ammunition with (+P) on the case headstamp is loaded to higher pressure. Use only in firearms designated for this cartridge and so recommended by the gun manufacturer.

REMINGTON BALLISTICS

Remington Center Fire Pistol and Revolver Cartridges

CALIBER	CARTRIDGE	REM-INGTON	Primer No.	Wt.-Grs.	Style	Muzzle	50 Yds.	100 Yds.	Muzzle	50 Yds.	100 Yds.	50 Yds.	100 Yds.	BARREL
					BULLET	**VELOCITY— FEET PER SECOND**			**ENERGY— FOOT POUNDS**			**MID-RANGE TRAJECTORY**		
38 SUPER AUTO. COLT PISTOL		R38SU1	1½	115*	Jacketed H.P. (+P)†	1300	1147	1041	431	336	277	0.7"	3.3"	5"
		R38SUP	1½	130	Metal Case (+P)†	1280	1140	1050	475	375	320	0.8"	3.4"	5"
38 AUTO. COLT PISTOL		R38ACP	1½	130*	Metal Case	1040	980	925	310	275	245	1.0"	4.7"	4½"
380 AUTO. PISTOL		R380AP	1½	95*	Metal Case	955	865	785	190	160	130	1.4"	5.9"	4"
		R380A1	1½	88*	Jacketed H.P.	990	920	868	191	165	146	1.2"	5.1"	4"
41 REM. MAG.		R41MG2	2½	210	Lead	965	898	842	434	376	331	1.3"	5.4"	4"
		R41MG1	2½	210*	Soft Point	1300	1162	1062	788	630	526	0.7"	3.2"	4"
44 S. & W. SPECIAL		R44SW	2½	246*	Lead	755	725	695	310	285	265	2.0"	8.3"	6½"
44 REM. MAG.		R44MG5	2½	180	Semi-Jacketed H.P.	1610	1365	1175	1036	745	551	**0.5"**	**2.3"**	6½"
		R44MG1	2½	240*	Lead Gas Check	1350	1186	1069	971	749	608	0.7"	3.1"	4"
		R44MG2	2½	240	Soft Point	1180	1081	1010	741	623	543	0.9"	3.7"	4"
		R44MG3	2½	240	Semi-Jacketed H.P.	1180	1081	1010	741	623	543	0.9"	3.7"	4"
		R44MG4	2½	240	Lead (Med. Vel.)	1000	947	902	533	477	433	1.1"	4.8"	6½"
45 COLT		R45C	2½	250*	Lead	860	820	780	410	375	340	1.6"	6.6"	5½"
45 AUTO.		R45AP4	2½	230*	Metal Case	810	776	745	335	308	284	1.7"	7.2"	5"
		R45AP1	2½	185	Metal Case Wad Cutter	770	707	650	244	205	174	2.0"	8.7"	5"
		R45AP3	2½	230	Metal Case Targetmaster	810	776	745	335	308	284	1.7"	7.2"	5"
		R45AP2	2½	185	Jacketed H.P.	940	890	846	363	325	294	1.3"	5.5"	5"
45 AUTO. RIM		R45AR	2½	230*	Lead	810	770	730	335	305	270	1.8"	7.4"	5½"

"Specifications are nominal." Ballistics figures established in handguns, individual guns may vary in cylinder gap, chamber and bore dimensions, etc.

REMINGTON CENTERFIRE RIFLE BALLISTICS

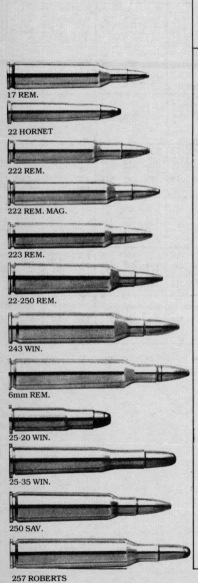

17 REM.

22 HORNET

222 REM.

222 REM. MAG.

223 REM.

22-250 REM.

243 WIN.

6mm REM.

25-20 WIN.

25-35 WIN.

250 SAV.

257 ROBERTS

Remington Ballistics

CALIBERS	REMINGTON Order No.	BULLET Wt.-Grs.	BULLET Style	Primer No.
17 REM.	R17REM	25*	Hollow Point Power-Lokt®	7½
22 HORNET	R22HN1	45*	Pointed Soft Point	6½
	R22HN2	45	Hollow Point	6½
222 REM.	R222R1	50	Pointed Soft Point	7½
	R222R3	50*	Hollow Point Power-Lokt	7½
	R222R4	**55**	**Metal Case**	7½
222 REM. MAG.	R222M1	55*	Pointed Soft Point	7½
	R222M2	55	Hollow Point Power-Lokt	7½
223 REM.	R223R1	55	Pointed Soft Point	7½
	R223R2	55*	Hollow Point Power-Lokt	7½
	R223R3	55	Metal Case	**7½**
22-250 REM.	R22501	55*	Pointed Soft Point	9½
	R22502	55	Hollow Point Power-Lokt	9½
243 WIN.	R243W1	80	Pointed Soft Point	9½
	R243W2	80*	Hollow Point Power-Lokt	9½
	R243W3	100	Pointed Soft Point Core-Lokt®	9½
6mm REM.	R6MM1	80**	Pointed Soft Point	9½
	R6MM2	80**	Hollow Point Power-Lokt	9½
	R6MM3	90**	Pointed Soft Point Core-Lokt®	9½
	R6MM4	100*	Pointed Soft Point Core-Lokt	9½
25-20 WIN.	R25202	86*	Soft Point	6½
25-35 WIN.	R2535W	117*‡	Soft Point Core-Lokt	9½
250 SAV.	R250SV	100*	Pointed Soft Point	9½
257 ROBERTS	R257	117*	Soft Point Core-Lokt	9½
25-06 REM.	R25061	87	Hollow Point Power-Lokt	9½
	R25062	100*	Pointed Soft Point Core-Lokt	9½
	R25063	120	Pointed Soft Point Core-Lokt	9½
6.5mm REM. MAG.	R65MM2	120*	Pointed Soft Point Core-Lokt	9½M
264 WIN. MAG.	R264W1	100‡	Pointed Soft Point Core-Lokt	9½M
	R264W2	140*	Pointed Soft Point Core-Lokt	9½M
270 WIN.	R270W1	100	Pointed Soft Point	9½
	R270W2	130*	Pointed Soft Point Core-Lokt	9½
	R270W3	130	Bronze Point	9½
	R270W4	150	Soft Point Core-Lokt	9½
7mm MAUSER	R7MSR	175*	Soft Point	9½
7mm-08 REM.	R7M081	140*	**Pointed Soft Point Core-Lokt**	**9½**
280 REM.††	R280R2	165*	Soft Point Core-Lokt	9½
7mm EXPRESS REM.	R7M061	150*	Pointed Soft Point Core-Lokt	9½
7mm REM. MAG.	R7MM2	150*	Pointed Soft Point Core-Lokt	9½M
	R7MM3	175	Pointed Soft Point Core-Lokt	9½M
30 CARBINE	R30CAR	110*	Soft Point	6½
30 REM.	R30REM	170*	Soft Point Core-Lokt	9½
30-30 WIN. "ACCELERATOR"	R3030A "Accelerator"	55*	Soft Point	9½
30-30 WIN.	R30301	150*	Soft Point Core-Lokt	9½
	R30302	170	Soft Point Core-Lokt	9½
	R30303	170	Hollow Point Core-Lokt	9½

Cartridge illustrations not actual size.

†† 280 Rem. and 7mm Express Rem. are interchangeable.
*Illustrated   **Interchangeable in 244 Rem.   ‡Subject to stock on hand.

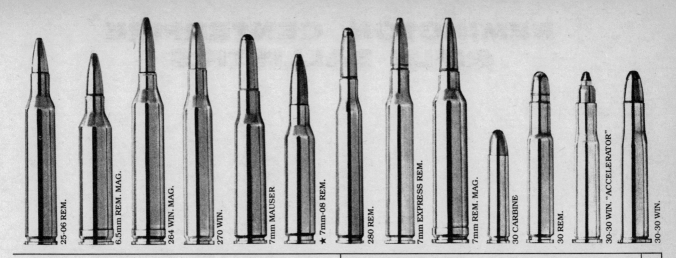

25-06 REM. · 6.5mm REM. MAG. · 264 WIN. MAG. · 270 WIN. · 7mm MAUSER · ★ 7mm-08 REM. · 280 REM. · 7mm EXPRESS REM. · 7mm REM. MAG. · 30 CARBINE · 30 REM. · 30-30 WIN. "ACCELERATOR" · 30-30 WIN.

TRAJECTORY† 0.0 Indicates yardage at which rifle was sighted in.

VELOCITY FEET PER SECOND						ENERGY FOOT-POUNDS						SHORT RANGE (Bullet does not rise more than one inch above line of sight from muzzle to sighting-in range.)						LONG RANGE (Bullet does not rise more than three inches above line of sight from muzzle to sighting-in range.)							BARREL LENGTH
Muzzle	100 Yds.	200 Yds.	300 Yds.	400 Yds.	500 Yds.	Muzzle	100 Yds.	200 Yds.	300 Yds.	400 Yds.	500 Yds.	50 Yds.	100 Yds.	150 Yds.	200 Yds.	250 Yds.	300 Yds.	100 Yds.	150 Yds.	200 Yds.	250 Yds.	300 Yds.	400 Yds.	500 Yds.	
4040	3284	2644	2086	1606	1235	906	599	388	242	143	85	0.1	0.5	0.0	-1.5	-4.2	-8.5	2.1	2.5	1.9	0.0	-3.4	-17.0	-44.3	24"
2690	2042	1502	1128	948	840	723	417	225	127	90	70	0.3	0.0	-2.4	-7.7	-16.9	-31.3	1.6	0.0	-4.5	-12.8	-26.4	-75.6	-163.4	24"
2690	2042	1502	1128	948	840	723	417	225	127	90	70	0.3	0.0	-2.4	-7.7	-16.9	-31.3	1.6	0.0	-4.5	-12.8	-26.4	-75.6	-163.4	
3140	2602	2123	1700	1350	1107	1094	752	500	321	202	136	0.5	0.9	0.0	-2.5	-6.9	-13.7	2.2	1.9	0.0	-3.8	-10.0	-32.3	-73.8	24"
3140	2635	2182	1777	1432	1172	1094	771	529	351	228	152	0.5	0.9	0.0	-2.4	-6.6	-13.1	2.1	1.8	0.0	-3.6	-9.5	-30.2	-68.1	
3000	**2544**	**2130**	**1759**	**1439**	**1192**	**1099**	**790**	**554**	**378**	**253**	**174**	**0.6**	**1.0**	**0.0**	**-2.6**	**-7.1**	**-13.9**	**2.3**	**1.9**	**0.0**	**-3.9**	**-10.0**	**-31.5**	**-69.9**	
3240	2748	2305	1906	1556	1272	1282	922	649	444	296	198	0.4	0.8	0.0	-2.2	-6.0	-11.8	1.9	1.6	0.0	-3.3	-8.5	-26.7	-59.5	24"
3240	2773	2352	1969	1627	1341	1282	939	675	473	323	220	0.4	0.8	0.0	-2.1	-5.8	-11.4	1.8	1.6	0.0	-3.2	-8.2	-25.5	-56.0	
3240	2747	2304	1905	1554	1270	1282	921	648	443	295	197	0.4	0.8	0.0	-2.2	-6.0	-11.8	1.9	1.6	0.0	-3.3	-8.5	-26.7	-59.6	24"
3240	2773	2352	1969	1627	1341	1282	939	675	473	323	220	0.4	0.8	0.0	-2.1	-5.8	-11.4	1.8	1.6	0.0	-3.2	-8.2	-25.5	-56.0	
3240	2759	2326	1933	1587	1301	1282	929	660	456	307	207	0.4	0.8	0.0	-2.1	-5.9	-11.6	1.9	1.6	0.0	-3.2	-8.4	-26.2	-57.9	
3730	3180	2695	2257	1863	1519	1699	1235	887	622	424	282	0.2	0.5	0.0	-1.5	-4.3	-8.4	2.2	2.6	1.9	0.0	-3.3	-15.4	-37.7	24"
3730	3253	2826	2436	2079	1755	1699	1292	975	725	528	376	0.2	0.5	0.0	-1.4	-4.0	-7.7	2.1	2.4	1.7	0.0	-3.0	-13.6	-32.4	
3350	2955	2593	2259	1951	1670	1993	1551	1194	906	676	495	0.3	0.7	0.0	-1.8	-4.9	-9.4	2.6	2.9	2.1	0.0	-3.6	-16.2	-37.9	24"
3350	2955	2593	2259	1951	1670	1993	1551	1194	906	676	495	0.3	0.7	0.0	-1.8	-4.9	-9.4	2.6	2.9	2.1	0.0	-3.6	-16.2	-37.9	
2960	2697	2449	2215	1993	1786	1945	1615	1332	1089	882	708	0.5	0.9	0.0	-2.2	-5.8	-11.0	1.9	1.6	0.0	-3.1	-7.8	-22.6	-46.3	
3470	3064	2694	2352	2036	1747	2139	1667	1289	982	736	542	0.3	0.6	0.0	-1.6	-4.5	-8.7	2.4	2.7	1.9	0.0	-3.3	-14.9	-35.0	24"
3470	3064	2694	2352	2036	1747	2139	1667	1289	982	736	542	0.3	0.6	0.0	-1.6	-4.5	-8.7	2.4	2.7	1.9	0.0	-3.3	-14.9	-35.0	
3190	2863	2558	2273	2007	1760	2033	1638	1307	1032	805	619	0.4	0.7	0.0	-1.9	-5.2	-9.9	1.7	1.4	0.0	-2.8	-7.0	-20.8	-43.3	
3130	2857	2600	2357	2127	1911	2175	1812	1501	1233	1004	811	0.4	0.7	0.0	-1.9	-5.1	-9.7	1.7	1.4	0.0	-2.7	-6.8	-20.0	-40.8	
1460	1194	1030	931	858	797	407	272	203	165	141	121	0.0	-4.1	-14.4	-31.8	-57.3	-92.0	0.0	-8.2	-23.5	-47.0	-79.6	-175.9	-319.4	24"
2230	1905	1613	1363	1169	1041	1249	943	676	483	355	281	0.6	0.0	-3.0	-8.8	-17.9	-31.0	2.0	0.0	-4.8	-13.0	-25.1	-64.2	-128.7	24"
2820	2504	2210	1936	1684	1461	1765	1392	1084	832	630	474	0.2	0.0	-1.6	-4.7	-9.6	-16.5	2.3	2.0	0.0	-3.7	-9.5	-28.3	-59.5	24"
2650	2291	1961	1663	1404	1199	1824	1363	999	718	512	373	0.3	0.0	-1.9	-5.8	-11.9	-20.7	2.9	2.4	0.0	-4.7	-12.0	-36.7	-79.2	24"
3440	2995	2591	2222	1884	1583	2286	1733	1297	954	686	484	0.3	0.6	0.0	-1.7	-4.8	-9.3	2.5	2.9	2.1	0.0	-3.6	-16.4	-39.1	24"
3230	2893	2580	2287	2014	1762	2316	1858	1478	1161	901	689	0.4	0.7	0.0	-1.9	-5.0	-9.7	1.6	1.4	0.0	-2.7	-6.9	-20.5	-42.7	
3010	2749	2502	2269	2048	1840	2414	2013	1668	1372	1117	902	-0.5	0.8	0.0	-2.1	-5.5	-10.5	1.9	1.6	0.0	-2.9	-7.4	-21.6	-44.2	
3210	2905	2621	2353	2102	1867	2745	2248	1830	1475	1177	929	0.4	0.7	0.0	-1.8	-4.9	-9.5	2.7	3.0	2.1	0.0	-3.5	-15.5	-35.3	24"
3320	2926	2565	2231	1923	1644	2447	1901	1461	1105	821	600	0.3	0.7	0.0	-1.8	-5.0	-9.7	2.7	3.0	2.2	0.0	-3.3	-16.6	-38.9	24"
3030	2782	2548	2326	2114	1914	2854	2406	2018	1682	1389	1139	0.5	0.9	0.0	-2.0	-5.4	-10.2	1.8	1.5	0.0	-2.9	-7.2	-20.8	-42.2	
3480	3067	2690	2343	2023	1730	2689	2088	1606	1219	909	664	0.3	0.6	0.0	-1.6	-4.5	-8.7	2.4	2.7	1.9	0.0	-3.3	-15.0	-35.2	24"
3110	2823	2554	2300	2061	1837	2791	2300	1883	1527	1226	974	0.4	0.8	0.0	-2.0	-5.3	-10.0	1.7	1.5	0.0	-2.8	-7.1	-20.8	-42.7	
3110	2849	2604	2371	2150	1941	2791	2343	1957	1622	1334	1087	0.4	0.7	0.0	-1.9	-5.1	-9.7	1.7	1.4	0.0	-2.7	-6.8	-19.9	-40.5	
2900	2550	2225	1926	1653	1415	2801	2165	1649	1235	910	667	0.6	1.0	0.0	-2.5	-6.8	-13.1	2.2	1.9	0.0	-3.6	-9.3	-28.1	-59.7	
2440	2137	1857	1603	1382	1204	2313	1774	1430	998	742	563	0.4	0.0	-2.3	-6.8	-13.8	-23.7	1.5	0.0	-3.7	-10.0	-19.1	-48.1	-95.4	24"
2860	**2625**	**2402**	**2189**	**1988**	**1798**	**2542**	**2142**	**1793**	**1490**	**1228**	**1005**	**0.6**	**0.9**	**0.0**	**-2.3**	**-6.1**	**-11.6**	**2.1**	**1.7**	**0.0**	**-3.2**	**-8.1**	**-23.5**	**-47.7**	24"
2820	2510	2220	1950	1701	1479	2913	2308	1805	1393	1060	801	0.2	0.0	-1.5	-4.6	-9.5	-16.4	2.3	1.9	0.0	-3.7	-9.4	-28.1	-58.8	24"
2970	2699	2444	2203	1975	1763	2937	2426	1989	1616	1299	1035	0.5	0.9	0.0	-2.2	-5.8	-11.0	1.9	1.6	0.0	-3.1	-7.8	-22.8	-46.7	24"
3110	2830	2568	2320	2085	1866	3221	2667	2196	1792	1448	1160	0.4	0.8	0.0	-1.9	-5.2	-9.9	1.7	1.5	0.0	-2.8	-7.0	-20.5	-42.1	24"
2860	2645	2440	2244	2057	1879	3178	2718	2313	1956	1644	1372	0.6	0.9	0.0	-2.3	-6.0	-11.3	2.0	1.7	0.0	-3.2	-7.9	-22.9	-45.8	
1990	1567	1236	1035	923	842	967	600	373	262	208	173	0.9	0.0	-4.5	-13.5	-28.3	-49.9	0.0	-4.5	-13.5	-28.3	-49.9	-118.6	-228.2	20"
2120	1822	1555	1328	1153	1036	1696	1253	913	666	502	405	0.7	0.0	-3.3	-9.7	-19.6	-33.8	2.2	0.0	-5.3	-14.1	-27.2	-69.0	-136.9	24"
3400	2693	2085	1570	1187	986	1412	886	521	301	172	119	0.4	0.8	0.0	-2.4	-6.7	-13.8	2.0	1.8	0.0	-3.8	-10.2	-35.0	-84.4	24"
2390	1973	1605	1303	1095	974	1902	1296	858	565	399	316	0.5	0.0	-2.7	-8.2	-17.0	-30.0	1.8	0.0	-4.6	-12.5	-24.6	-65.3	-134.9	24"
2200	1895	1619	1381	1191	1061	1827	1355	989	720	535	425	0.6	0.0	-3.0	-8.9	-18.0	-31.1	2.0	0.0	-4.8	-13.0	-25.1	-63.6	-126.7	
2200	1895	1619	1381	1191	1061	1827	1355	989	720	535	425	0.6	0.0	-3.0	-8.9	-18.0	-31.1	2.0	0.0	-4.8	-13.0	-25.1	-63.6	-126.7	

† Inches above or below line of sight. Hold low for positive numbers, high for negative numbers. Specifications are nominal.
Ballistics figures established in test barrels. Individual rifles may vary from test-barrel specifications.

REMINGTON CENTERFIRE RIFLE BALLISTICS

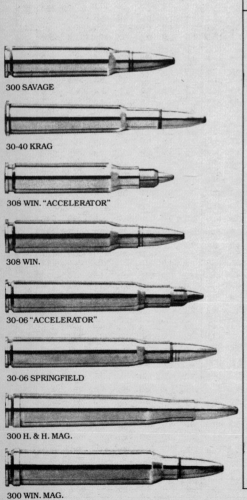

300 SAVAGE

30-40 KRAG

308 WIN. "ACCELERATOR"

308 WIN.

30-06 "ACCELERATOR"

30-06 SPRINGFIELD

300 H. & H. MAG.

300 WIN. MAG.

Remington Ballistics

CALIBERS	REMINGTON Order No.	BULLET			Primer No.
		Wt.-Grs.	Style		
300 SAVAGE	R30SV1	150	Soft Point Core-Lokt		9½
	R30SV2	150*	Pointed Soft Point Core-Lokt		9½
	R30SV3	180	Soft Point Core-Lokt		9½
	R30SV4	180	Pointed Soft Point Core-Lokt		9½
30-40 KRAG	R30401	180	Soft Point Core-Lokt		9½
	R30402	180*	Pointed Soft Point Core-Lokt		9½
308 WIN "ACCELERATOR"	R308W5 "Accelerator	55*	Pointed Soft Point		9½
308 WIN.	R308W1	150*	Pointed Soft Point Core-Lokt		9½
	R308W2	180	Soft Point Core-Lokt		9½
	R308W3	180	Pointed Soft Point Core-Lokt		9½
30-06 "ACCELERATOR"	R30069 "Accelerator"	55*	Pointed Soft Point		9½
30-06 SPRINGFIELD	R30061	125	Pointed Soft Point		9½
	R30062	150	Pointed Soft Point Core-Lokt		9½
	R30063	150	Bronze Point		9½
	R3006B	165*	Pointed Soft Point Core-Lokt		9½
	R30064	180	Soft Point Core-Lokt		9½
	R30065	180	Pointed Soft Point Core-Lokt		9½
	R30066	180	Bronze Point		9½
	R30067	220	Soft Point Core-Lokt		9½
300 H. & H. MAG.	R300HH	180*	Pointed Soft Point Core-Lokt		9½ M
300 WIN. MAG.	R300W1	150	Pointed Soft Point Core-Lokt		9½ M
	R300W2	180*	Pointed Soft Point Core-Lokt		9½ M
303 BRITISH	R303B1	180*	Soft Point Core-Lokt		9½
32-20 WIN.	R32201	100	Lead		6½
	R32202	100*	Soft Point		6½
32 WIN. SPECIAL	R32WS2	170*	Soft Point Core-Lokt		9½
8mm MAUSER	R8MSR	170*	Soft Point Core-Lokt		9½
8mm REM. MAG.	R8MM1	185*	Pointed Soft Point Core-Lokt		9½ M
	R8MM2	220	Pointed Soft Point Core-Lokt		9½ M
35 REM.	R35R1	150	Pointed Soft Point Core-Lokt		9½
	R35R2	200*	Soft Point Core-Lokt		9½
350 REM. MAG.	R350M1	200*	Pointed Soft Point Core-Lokt		9½ M
375 H. & H. MAG.	R375M1	270*	Soft Point		9½ M
	R375M2	300	Metal Case		9½ M
38-40 WIN.	R3840W	180*‡	Soft Point		2½
44-40 WIN.	R4440W	200*	Soft Point		2½
44 REM. MAG.	R44MG2	240	Soft Point		2½
	R44MG3	240	Semi-Jacketed Hollow Point		2½
444 MAR.	R444M	240*	Soft Point		9½
	R444M2	265	Soft Point		9½
45-70 GOVERNMENT	R4570G	405*	Soft Point		9½
458 WIN. MAG.	R458W1	500	Metal Case		9½ M
	R458W2	510*	Soft Point		9½ M

Cartridge illustrations not actual size.   ‡Subject to stock on hand.
                                               *Illustrated

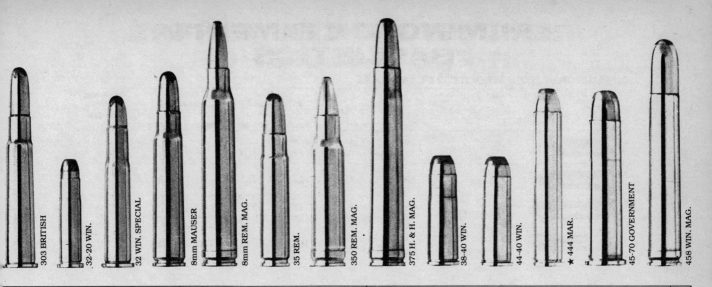

303 BRITISH · 32-20 WIN. · 32 WIN. SPECIAL · 8mm MAUSER · 8mm REM. MAG. · 35 REM. · 350 REM. MAG. · 375 H. & H. MAG. · 38-40 WIN. · 44-40 WIN. · ★ 444 MAR. · 45-70 GOVERNMENT · 458 WIN. MAG.

VELOCITY FEET PER SECOND						ENERGY FOOT-POUNDS						TRAJECTORY† SHORT RANGE						TRAJECTORY† LONG RANGE							BARREL LENGTH
Muzzle	100 Yds.	200 Yds.	300 Yds.	400 Yds.	500 Yds.	Muzzle	100 Yds.	200 Yds.	300 Yds.	400 Yds.	500 Yds.	50 Yds.	100 Yds.	150 Yds.	200 Yds.	250 Yds.	300 Yds.	100 Yds.	150 Yds.	200 Yds.	250 Yds.	300 Yds.	400 Yds.	500 Yds.	
2630	2247	1897	1585	1324	1131	2303	1681	1198	837	584	426	0.3	0.0	-2.0	-6.1	-12.5	-21.9	1.3	0.0	-3.4	-9.2	-17.9	-46.3	-94.8	24"
2630	2354	2095	1853	1631	1433	2303	1845	1462	1143	886	685	0.3	0.0	-1.8	-5.4	-11.0	-18.8	2.7	2.2	0.0	-4.2	-10.7	-31.5	-65.5	
2350	2025	1728	1467	1252	1098	2207	1639	1193	860	626	482	0.5	0.0	-2.6	-7.7	-15.6	-27.1	1.7	0.0	-4.2	-11.3	-21.9	-55.8	-112.0	
2350	2137	1935	1745	1570	1413	2207	1825	1496	1217	985	798	0.4	0.0	-2.3	-6.7	-13.5	-22.8	1.5	0.0	-3.6	-9.6	-18.2	-44.1	-84.2	
2430	2098	1795	1525	1298	1128	2360	1761	1288	929	673	508	0.4	0.0	-2.4	-7.1	-14.5	-25.0	1.6	0.0	-3.9	-10.5	-20.3	-51.7	-103.0	24"
2430	2213	2007	1813	1632	1468	2360	1957	1610	1314	1064	861	0.4	0.0	-2.1	-6.2	-12.5	-21.1	1.4	0.0	-3.4	-8.9	-16.8	-40.9	-78.1	
3770	**3215**	**2726**	**2286**	**1888**	**1541**	**1735**	**1262**	**907**	**638**	**435**	**290**	**0.2**	**0.5**	**0.0**	**-1.5**	**-4.2**	**-8.2**	**2.2**	**2.5**	**1.8**	**0.0**	**-3.2**	**-15.0**	**-36.7**	24"
2820	2533	2263	2009	1774	1560	2648	2137	1705	1344	1048	810	0.2	0.0	-1.5	-4.5	-9.3	-15.9	2.3	1.9	0.0	-3.6	-9.1	-26.9	-55.7	
2620	2274	1955	1666	1414	1212	2743	2066	1527	1109	799	587	0.3	0.0	-2.0	-5.9	-12.1	-20.9	2.9	2.4	0.0	-4.7	-12.1	-36.9	-79.1	24"
2620	2393	2178	1974	1782	1604	2743	2288	1896	1557	1269	1028	0.2	0.0	-1.8	-5.2	-10.4	-17.7	2.6	2.1	0.0	-4.0	-9.9	-28.9	-58.8	
4080	3485	2965	2502	2083	1709	2033	1483	1074	764	530	356	0.4	1.0	0.9	0.0	-1.9	-5.0	1.8	2.1	1.5	0.0	-2.7	-12.5	-30.5	24"
3140	2780	2447	2138	1853	1595	2736	2145	1662	1269	953	706	0.4	0.8	0.0	-2.1	-5.6	-10.7	1.8	1.5	0.0	-3.0	-7.7	-23.0	-48.5	
2910	2617	2342	2083	1843	1622	2820	2281	1827	1445	1131	876	0.6	0.9	0.0	-2.3	-6.3	-12.0	2.1	1.8	0.0	-3.3	-8.5	-25.0	-51.8	
2910	2656	2416	2189	1974	1773	2820	2349	1944	1596	1298	1047	0.6	0.9	0.0	-2.2	-6.0	-11.4	2.0	1.7	0.0	-3.2	-8.0	-23.3	-47.5	
2800	2534	2283	2047	1825	1621	2872	2352	1909	1534	1220	963	0.7	1.0	0.0	-2.5	-6.7	-12.7	2.3	1.9	0.0	-3.6	-9.0	-26.3	-54.1	24"
2700	2348	2023	1727	1466	1251	2913	2203	1635	1192	859	625	0.2	0.0	-1.8	-5.5	-11.2	-19.5	2.7	2.3	0.0	-4.4	-11.3	-34.4	-73.7	
2700	2469	2250	2042	1846	1663	2913	2436	2023	1666	1362	1105	0.2	0.0	-1.6	-4.8	-9.7	-16.5	2.4	2.0	0.0	-3.7	-9.3	-27.0	-54.9	
2700	2485	2280	2084	1899	1725	2913	2468	2077	1736	1441	1189	0.2	0.0	-1.6	-4.7	-9.6	-16.2	2.4	2.0	0.0	-3.6	-9.1	-26.2	-53.0	
2410	2130	1870	1632	1422	1246	2837	2216	1708	1301	988	758	0.4	0.0	-2.3	-6.8	-13.8	-23.6	1.5	0.0	-3.7	-9.9	-19.0	-47.4	-93.1	
2880	2640	2412	2196	1990	1798	3315	2785	2325	1927	1583	1292	0.6	0.9	0.0	-2.3	-6.0	-11.5	2.1	1.7	0.0	-3.2	-8.0	-23.3	-47.4	24"
3290	2951	2636	2342	2068	1813	3605	2900	2314	1827	1424	1095	0.3	0.7	0.0	-1.8	-4.8	-9.3	2.6	2.9	2.1	0.0	-3.5	-15.4	-35.5	24"
2960	2745	2540	2344	2157	1979	3501	3011	2578	2196	1859	1565	0.5	0.0		-2.1	-5.5	-10.4	1.9	1.6	0.0	-2.9	-7.3	-20.9	-41.9	
2460	2124	1817	1542	1311	1137	2418	1803	1319	950	687	517	0.4	0.0	-2.3	-6.9	-14.1	-24.4	1.5	0.0	-3.8	-10.2	-19.8	-50.5	-101.5	24"
1210	1021	913	834	769	712	325	231	185	154	131	113	0.0	-6.3	-20.9	-44.9	-79.3	-125.1	0.0	-11.5	-32.3	-63.8	-106.3	-230.3	-413.3	24"
1210	1021	913	834	769	712	325	231	185	154	131	113	0.0	-6.3	-20.9	-44.9	-79.3	-125.1	0.0	-11.5	-32.3	-63.6	-106.3	-230.3	-413.3	
2250	1921	1626	1372	1175	1044	1911	1393	998	710	521	411	0.6	0.0	-2.9	-8.6	-17.6	-30.5	1.9	0.0	-4.7	-12.7	-24.7	-63.2	-126.9	24"
2360	1969	1622	1333	1123	997	2102	1463	993	671	476	375	0.5	0.0	-2.7	-8.2	-17.0	-29.8	1.8	0.0	-4.5	-12.4	-24.3	-63.8	-130.7	24"
3080	2761	2464	2186	1927	1688	3896	3131	2494	1963	1525	1170	0.5	0.8	0.0	-2.1	-5.6	-10.7	1.8	1.6	0.0	-3.0	-7.6	-22.5	-46.8	24"
2830	2581	2346	2123	1913	1716	3912	3254	2688	2201	1787	1438	0.6	1.0	0.0	-2.4	-6.4	-12.1	2.2	1.8	0.0	-3.4	-8.5	-24.7	-50.5	
2300	1874	1506	1218	1039	434	1762	1169	755	494	359	291	0.6	0.0	-3.0	-9.2	-19.1	-33.9	2.0	0.0	-5.1	-14.1	-27.8	-74.0	-152.3	24"
2020	1646	1335	1114	985	901	1812	1203	791	551	431	360	0.9	0.0	-4.1	-12.1	-25.1	-43.9	2.7	0.0	-6.7	-18.3	-35.8	-92.8	-185.5	
2710	2410	2130	1870	1631	1421	3261	2579	2014	1553	1181	897	0.2	0.0	-1.7	-5.1	-10.4	-17.9	2.6	2.1	0.0	-4.0	-10.3	-30.5	-64.0	20"
2690	2420	2166	1928	1707	1507	4337	3510	2812	2228	1747	1361	0.2	0.0	-1.7	-5.1	-10.3	-17.6	2.5	2.1	0.0	-3.9	-10.0	-29.4	-60.7	24"
2530	2171	1843	1551	1307	1126	4263	3139	2262	1602	1138	844	0.3	0.0	-2.2	-6.5	-13.5	-23.4	1.5	0.0	-3.6	-9.8	-19.1	-49.1	-99.5	
1160	999	901	827	764	710	538	399	324	273	233	201	0.0	-6.7	-22.2	-47.3	-83.2	-130.8	0.0	-12.1	-33.9	-66.4	-110.6	-238.3	-425.6	24"
1190	1006	900	822	756	699	629	449	360	300	254	217	0.0	-6.5	-21.6	-46.3	-81.8	-129.1	0.0	-11.8	-33.3	-65.5	-109.5	-237.4	-426.2	24"
1760	1380	1114	970	878	806	1650	1015	661	501	411	346	0.0	-2.7	-10.0	-23.0	-43.0	-71.2	0.0	-5.9	-17.6	-36.3	-63.1	-145.5	-273.0	20"
1760	1380	1114	970	878	806	1650	1015	661	501	411	346	0.0	-2.7	-10.0	-23.0	-43.0	-71.2	0.0	-5.9	-17.6	-36.3	-63.1	-145.5	-273.0	
2350	1815	1377	1087	941	846	2942	1755	1010	630	472	381	0.6	0.0	-3.2	-9.9	-21.3	-38.5	2.1	0.0	-5.6	-15.9	-32.1	-87.8	-182.7	24"
2120	**1733**	**1405**	**1160**	**1012**	**920**	**2644**	**1768**	**1162**	**791**	**603**	**498**	**0.7**	**0.0**	**-3.6**	**-10.8**	**-22.5**	**-39.5**	**2.4**	**0.0**	**-6.0**	**-16.4**	**-32.2**	**-84.3**	**-170.2**	
1330	1168	1055	977	918	869	1590	1227	1001	858	758	679	0.0	-4.7	-15.8	-34.0	-60.0	-94.5	0.0	-8.7	-24.6	-48.2	-80.3	-172.4	-305.9	24"
2040	1823	1623	1442	1237	1161	4620	3689	2924	2308	1839	1469	0.7	0.0	-3.3	-9.6	-19.2	-32.5	2.2	0.0	-5.2	-13.6	-25.8	-63.2	-121.7	24"
2040	1770	1527	1319	1157	1046	4712	3547	2640	1970	1516	1239	0.8	0.0	-3.5	-10.3	-20.8	-35.6	2.4	0.0	-5.6	-14.9	-28.5	-71.5	-140.4	

TRAJECTORY† — 0.0 Indicates yardage at which rifle was sighted in.

SHORT RANGE: Bullet does not rise more than one inch above line of sight from muzzle to sighting-in range.

LONG RANGE: Bullet does not rise more than three inches above line of sight from muzzle to sighting-in range.

†Inches above or below line of sight. Hold low for positive numbers, high for negative numbers. Specifications are nominal.
Ballistics figures established in test barrels. Individual rifles may vary from test-barrel specifications.

REMINGTON RIMFIRE BALLISTICS

REMINGTON "HIGH VELOCITY" 22 CARTRIDGES

		Bullet		Velocity— Ft. Per Second		Energy— Foot-Pounds		Mid-Range Trajectory
		Wt. Grs.	Style	Muzzle	100 Yds.	Muzzle	100 Yds.	100 Yds. Inches
	22 Short	29	Lead	1095	903	77	52	4.5
		27	Hollow Point	1120	904	75	49	4.4
	22 Long	29	Lead	1240	962	99	60	3.9
	22 Long Rifle	40	Lead	1255	1017	140	92	3.6
		36	Hollow Point	1280	1010	131	82	3.5
	22 Long Rifle "Yellow Jacket"	33	Truncated Cone Hollow Point	1500	1075	165	85	2.8

"TARGET" STANDARD VELOCITY 22 CARTRIDGES

		Wt. Grs.	Style	Muzzle	100 Yds.	Muzzle	100 Yds.	100 Yds. Inches
	22 Short	29	Lead	1045	872	70	49	4.8
	22 Long Rifle	40	Lead	1150	976	117	85	4.0

MATCH LONG RIFLE AND SPECIAL CARTRIDGES

		Wt. Grs.	Style
	22 Long Rifle (Rifle Match)	40	Lead
	22 Long Rifle (Pistol Match)	40	Lead
	22 Long Rifle Shot Cartridges	—	Dust
	22 Short	—	Blank

*May be used in guns chambered for 22 rim fire magnum cartridges.
†Not for use in handguns.

	Bullet		Velocity— Ft. Per Second		
	Wt. Grs.	Style	Muzzle	100 Yds.	150 Yds.
	38	"Power-Lokt" Hollow Point	2105	1609	1401

	Energy— Foot Pounds			Trajectory (Rifle sighted in at 100 yds.)	
	Muzzle	100 Yds.	150 Yds.	100 Yds.	150 Yds.
5mm Remington Magnum	374	218	166	0	-4.2

WEATHERBY BALLISTICS

Note: Any load having an average breech pressure of over 55,000 p.s.i. should not be used, and is shown for reference only. All ballistic data were compiled using Weatherby cartridge cases, Hornady or Nosler bullets and powder and primers as indicated. Loads shown with Norma powder are factory-equivalent loads. Other powders shown are DuPont IMR 3031, 4350 and 4064, and Hodgdon 4831. Velocities from 24" barrels for all calibers are approximately 90 fps less than those listed.

.224 WEATHERBY MAGNUM VARMINTMASTER

Primer: Federal #215   Overall cartridge length: 2⁵⁄₁₆"

Charge	Powder	Bullet	Muzzle Velocity in 26" Barrel	Avg. Breech Pressure	Muzzle Energy in Foot-Pounds
29.5 grs	3031	50 gr	3500-FPS	45,700-PSI	1360
30.0 grs	3031	50 gr	3560	47,500	1410
30.5 grs	3031	50 gr	3620	50,000	1455
31.0 grs	3031	50 gr	3670	52,000	1495
31.5 grs	3031	50 gr	3695	52,600	1515
32.0 grs	3031	50 gr	3740	55,200	1550
29.0 grs	3031	55 gr	3390	46,700	1405
29.5 grs	3031	55 gr	3450	48,000	1455
30.0 grs	3031	55 gr	3470	49,100	1470
30.5 grs	3031	55 gr	3525	53,200	1520
31.0 grs	3031	55 gr	3580	56,200	1570

WEATHERBY BALLISTICS

.240 WEATHERBY MAGNUM

Primer: Federal #215   Overall cartridge length: 3¹/₁₆″

Charge	Powder	Bullet	Muzzle Velocity in 26″ Barrel	Avg. Breech Pressure	Muzzle Energy in Foot-Pounds
53 grs	4350	70 gr	3684	48,530	2110
54 grs	4350	70 gr	3732	50,440	2163
55 grs	4350	70 gr	3780	52,270	2221
56 grs	4350	70 gr	3842	54,840	2293
55 grs	4831	70 grs	3533	44,680	1937
56 grs	4831	70 gr	3598	47,630	2011
57 grs	4831	70 gr	3708	52,070	2136
58.3 grs	Norma MRP	70 gr	3850	53,790	2304
54.1 grs	Norma MRP	87 gr	3500	53,420	2366
50 grs	4350	90 gr	3356	48,970	2246
51 grs	4350	90 gr	3424	51,270	2340
52 grs	4350	90 gr	3507	54,970	2453
53 grs	4831	90 gr	3325	48,630	2205
54 grs	4831	90 gr	3395	50,860	2299
55 grs	4831	90 gr	3451	52,410	2374
54.0 grs	Norma MRP	100 gr	3395	52,900	2560
49 grs	4350	100 gr	3223	50,680	2302
50 grs	4350	100 gr	3308	53,400	2425
51 grs	4350	100 gr	3367	56,190	2512
51 grs	4831	100 gr	3157	48,850	2208
52 grs	4831	100 gr	3222	50,950	2297
53 grs	4831	100 gr	3268	51,760	2370
54 grs	4831	100 gr	3362	54,740	2502

.257 WEATHERBY MAGNUM

Primer: Federal #215   Overall cartridge length: 3¹/₄″

Charge	Powder	Bullet	Muzzle Velocity in 26″ barrel	Avg. Breech Pressure	Muzzle Energy in Foot-Pounds
68 grs	4350	87 gr	3698	51,790	2644
69 grs	4350	87 gr	3715	53,270	2666
70 grs	4350	87 gr	3831	56,120	2835
69 grs	4831	87 gr	3521	44,750	2390
71 grs	4831	87 gr	3617	48,140	2532
73 grs	4831	87 gr	3751	52,470	2717
75 grs	4831	87 gr	3876	57,910	2901
74.1 grs	Norma MRP	87 gr	3825	50,700	2825
65 grs	4350	100 gr	3450	52,860	2638
66 grs	4350	100 gr	3520	54,860	2747
67 grs	4350	100 gr	3588	57,130	2857
66 grs	4831	100 gr	3315	43,640	2435
68 grs	4831	100 gr	3418	48,190	2593
70 grs	4831	100 gr	3543	53,410	2786
71 grs	4831	100 gr	3573	55,690	2833
71.3 grs	Norma MRP	100 gr	3555	51,730	2806
62 grs	4350	117 gr	3152	50,020	2573
64 grs	4350	117 gr	3262	54,860	2755
63 grs	4831	117 gr	3152	46,650	2573
65 grs	4831	117 gr	3213	48,520	2679
67 grs	4831	117 gr	3326	53,930	2867
67.1 grs	Norma MRP	117 gr	3300	53,050	2830

WEATHERBY BALLISTICS

.270 WEATHERBY MAGNUM

Primer: Federal #215   Overall cartridge length: 3¼"

Charge	Powder	Bullet	Muzzle Velocity in 26" Barrel	Avg. Breech Pressure	Muzzle Energy in Foot-Pounds
70 grs	4350	100 gr	3636	49,550	2934
72 grs	4350	100 gr	3764	54,540	3148
74 grs	4350	100 gr	3885	58,200	3353
74 grs	4831	100 gr	3492	43,800	2700
76 grs	4831	100 gr	3594	47,790	2865
77 grs	4831	100 gr	3654	50,940	2966
78 grs	4831	100 gr	3705	52,890	3048
77.2 grs	Norma MRP	100 gr	3760	51,400	3139
65 grs	4350	130 gr	3184	46,780	2922
66 grs	4350	130 gr	3228	49,130	3006
67 grs	4350	130 gr	3286	52,120	3108
68 grs	4350	130 gr	3345	55,210	3224
68 grs	4831	130 gr	3076	43,320	2730
70 grs	4831	130 gr	3178	47,600	2913
71 grs	4831	130 gr	3242	51,150	3024
72 grs	4831	130 gr	3301	52,980	3138
73 grs	4831	130 gr	3335	54,350	3206
74 grs	4831	130 gr	3375	56,520	3283
73.3 grs	Norma MRP	130 gr	3375	50,260	3285
65 grs	4350	150 gr	3085	52,120	3167
67 grs	4350	150 gr	3150	57,560	3299
66 grs	4831	150 gr	2920	46,470	2840
67 grs	4831	150 gr	2971	48,380	2939
68 grs	4831	150 gr	3014	50,580	3027
69 grs	4831	150 gr	3069	53,720	3140
70 grs	4831	150 gr	3124	56,960	3246
68.5 grs	Norma MRP	150 gr	3245	51,800	3508

7MM WEATHERBY MAGNUM

Primer: Federal #215   Overall cartridge length: 3¼"

Charge	Powder	Bullet	Muzzle Velocity in 26" Barrel	Avg. Breech Pressure	Muzzle Energy in Foot-Pounds
68 grs	4350	139 gr	3250	51,930	3254
69 grs	4350	139 gr	3308	54,310	3375
70 grs	4350	139 gr	3373	57,960	3500
72 grs	4831	139 gr	3147	45,990	3047
73 grs	4831	139 gr	3233	49,700	3223
74 grs	4831	139 gr	3291	52,570	3335
75 grs	4831	139 gr	3328	54,520	3417
74.1 grs	Norma MRP	139 gr	3300	50,300	3360
66 grs	4350	154 gr	3055	49,960	3191
67 grs	4350	154 gr	3141	54,500	3365
68 grs	4350	154 gr	3175	55,210	3439
70 grs	4831	154 gr	3013	46,940	3109
71 grs	4831	154 gr	3066	49,160	3212
72 grs	4831	154 gr	3151	53,010	3387
73 grs	4831	154 gr	3183	53,520	3462
71.0 grs	Norma MRP	154 gr	3160	51,250	3414
71.8 grs	Norma MRP	160 gr Nosler	3150	53,700	3525
71.0 grs	Norma MRP	*175 gr	3070	53,350	3662
63 grs	4350	*175 gr	2828	46,900	3112
65 grs	4350	*175 gr	2946	53,830	3369
68 grs	4831	*175 gr	2852	49,470	3157
69 grs	4831	*175 gr	2885	49,930	3234
70 grs	4831	*175 gr	2924	52,680	3323
71 grs	4831	*175 gr	2975	55,800	3439

*The 175 grain bullet is recommended for use only in 7mm W.M. rifles having 1 in 10" twist barrels.

WEATHERBY BALLISTICS

.300 WEATHERBY MAGNUM

Primer: Federal #215   Overall cartridge length: 3-9/16"

Charge	Powder	Bullet	Muzzle Velocity in 26" Barrel	Avg. Breech Pressure	Muzzle Energy in Foot-Pounds
86 grs	4350	110 gr	3726	48,950	3390
88 grs	4350	110 gr	3798	51,180	3528
90 grs	4350	110 gr	3863	53,460	3649
81.0 grs	Norma 203	110 gr	3900	53,050	3714
82 grs	4350	130 gr	3488	49,540	3510
84 grs	4350	130 gr	3567	52,570	3663
86 grs	4350	130 gr	3627	54,730	3793
80 grs	4350	150 gr	3343	48,000	3710
82 grs	4350	150 gr	3458	52,380	3981
84 grs	4350	150 gr	3538	56,230	4167
84 grs	4831	150 gr	3305	47,620	3632
86 grs	4831	150 gr	3394	51,990	3831
88 grs	4831	150 gr	3470	54,570	4004
88.0 grs	Norma MRP	150 gr	3545	53,490	4185
77 grs	4350	180 gr	3066	50,830	3755
78 grs	4350	180 gr	3110	53,130	3857
79 grs	4350	180 gr	3145	53,610	3946
80 grs	4831	180 gr	3060	50,240	3742
82 grs	4831	180 gr	3145	54,310	3946
84 grs	4831	180 gr	3223	57,370	4147
81.8 grs	Norma MRP	180 gr	3245	51,800	4208
77.2 grs	Norma MRP	200 gr Nosler	3000	49,000	3996
76 grs	4831	200 gr Nosler	2858	46,480	3632
78 grs	4831	200 gr Nosler	2926	50,620	3800
80 grs	4831	200 gr Nosler	3029	54,690	4078
73 grs	4350	220 gr	2878	54,890	4052
75 grs	4350	220 gr	2926	56,510	4180
74 grs	4831	220 gr	2740	47,920	3667
76 grs	4831	220 gr	2800	51,060	3830
78 grs	4831	220 gr	2881	55,760	4052
77.2 grs	Norma MRP	220 gr	2905	52,850	4122

WEATHERBY BALLISTICS

.340 WEATHERBY MAGNUM

Primer: Federal #215   Overall cartridge length: 3-9/16"

Charge	Powder	Bullet	Muzzle Velocity in 26" Barrel	Avg. Breech Pressures	Muzzle Energy in Foot-Pounds
80 grs	4350	200 gr	3075	48,290	4200
82 grs	4350	200 gr	3151	53,180	4398
84 grs	4350	200 gr	3210	54,970	4566
84 grs	4831	200 gr	2933	43,240	3824
86 grs	4831	200 gr	3004	45,940	4012
88 grs	4831	200 gr	3066	48,400	4172
90 grs	4831	200 gr	3137	52,730	4356
91.0 grs	Norma MRP	200 gr	3210	50,185	4575
92.0 grs	Norma MRP	210 gr Nosler	3180	51,290	4714
84 grs	4350	210 gr Nosler	3115	51,450	4515
85 grs	4350	210 gr Nosler	3148	53,300	4618
86 grs	4350	210 gr Nosler	3172	54,960	4675
74 grs	4350	250 gr	2741	49,240	4168
76 grs	4350	250 gr	2800	51,370	4353
78 grs	4350	250 gr	2862	55,490	4540
80 grs	4831	250 gr	2686	44,970	4005
82 grs	4831	250 gr	2764	49,180	4243
84 grs	4831	250 gr	2835	53,370	4460
85 grs	4831	250 gr	2860	54,400	4540
86 grs	4831	250 gr	2879	55,500	4605
87 grs	4831	250 gr	2886	56,270	4623
84.9 grs	Norma MRP	250 gr	2850	49,600	4508

.378 WEATHERBY MAGNUM

Primer: Federal #215   Overall cartridge length: 3-11/16"

Caution: Use only the #215 primer in reloading the .378 W. M.

Charge	Powder	Bullet	Muzzle Velocity in 26" Barrel	Avg. Breech Pressure	Muzzle Energy in Foot-Pounds
106 grs	4350	270 gr	3015	44,800	5446
107 grs	4350	270 gr	3015	49,700	5713
108 grs	4350	270 gr	3112	54,620	5786
116 grs	4831	270 gr	3080	50,190	5689
117 grs	4831	270 gr	3102	50,930	5748
118 grs	4831	270 gr	3128	51,930	5862
101 grs	4350	300 gr	2831	49,500	5334
103 grs	4350	300 gr	2922	54,300	5679
110 grs	4831	300 gr	2897	51,050	5583
111 grs	4831	300 gr	2933	52,270	5736
112 grs	4831	300 gr	2958	53,410	5835

.460 WEATHERBY MAGNUM

Primer: Federal #215   Overall cartridge length: 3¾"

Caution: Use only the #215 primer in reloading the .460 W. M.

Charge	Powder	Bullet	Muzzle Velocity in 26" Barrel	Avg. Breech Pressure	Muzzle Energy in Foot-Pounds
115 grs	4350	500 gr	2513	44,400	6995
118 grs	4350	500 gr	2577	47,460	7390
120 grs	4350	500 gr	2601	48,330	7505
122 grs	4350	500 gr	2632	50,370	7680
124 grs	4350	500 gr	2678	52,980	7980
126 grs	4350	500 gr	2707	55,130	8155
102 grs	4064	500 gr	2486	49,000	6860
104 grs	4064	500 gr	2521	51,340	7050
106 grs	4064	500 gr	2552	53,280	7220
92 grs	3031	500 gr	2405	49,530	6420
94 grs	3031	500 gr	2426	50,170	6525
96 grs	3031	500 gr	2470	53,560	6775

WINCHESTER-WESTERN RIMFIRE CARTRIDGE BALLISTICS

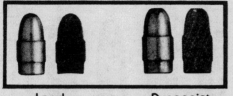

Lead   Dynapoint

Hollow Point   Jacketed Hollow Point   Full Metal Case

RIMFIRE RIFLE CARTRIDGES

Cartridge	Bullet		Velocity (ft/s)		Energy (ft. lbs.)		Nominal Mid-Range Traj. (In.)
	Wt. Grs.	Type	Muzzle	100 yds.	Muzzle	100 yds.	100 yds.
22 Short Super-X	29	L *	1095	902	77	52	4.5
22 Short H.P. Super-X	27	L *	1120	904	75	49	4.4
22 Long Super-X	29	L *	1240	961	99	59	3.9
22 Long Rifle Super-X	40	L *	1255	1016	140	92	3.6
22 Long Rifle DYNAPOINT Super-X	40	L *	1255	1016	140	92	3.6
22 Long Rifle H.P. Super-X	37	L *	1280	1013	135	84	3.5
22 Long Rifle Shot Super-X (#12 Shot)	—	—	—	—	—	—	—
22 Long Rifle Xpediter H.P.	29	L *	1680	1079	182	75	2.5
22 Winchester MAGNUM R.F. Super-X	40	JHP	1910	1326	324	156	1.7
22 Winchester MAGNUM R.F. Super-X	40	FMC	1910	1326	324	156	1.7
22 Short T22	29	Lead *	1045	872	70	49	4.8
22 Long Rifle T22	40	Lead *	1150	975	117	84	4.0
22 Short Blank	—	—	—	—	—	—	—
22 Short C.B.	29	Lead *	715	—	33	—	—

RIMFIRE PISTOL AND REVOLVER CARTRIDGES

Cartridge	Bullet		Barrel Length	Muzzle Velocity (ft/s)	Muzzle Energy (ft. lbs.)
	Wt. Grs.	Type			
22 Short Blank	—	—	—	—	—
22 Short Super-X	29	L *	6"	1010	66
22 Short T22	29	Lead *	6"	865	48
22 Long Super-X	29	L *	6"	1095	77
22 Long Rifle Super-X	40	L *	6"	1060	100
22 Long Rifle T22	40	Lead *	6"	950	80
22 Long Rifle Super-Match Mark IV	40	Lead *	6¾"	1060	100
22 Winchester MAGNUM Rimfire Super-X	40	JHP	6½"	1480	195
22 Winchester MAGNUM Rimfire Super-X	40	FMC	6½"	1480	195

FMC—Full Metal Case   *—Wax Coated   L—Lubaloy   JHP—Jacketed Hollow Point

Specifications are nominal. Test barrels are used to determine ballistics figures. Individual firearms may differ from these test barrel statistics.

WINCHESTER-WESTERN CENTERFIRE PISTOL & REVOLVER BALLISTICS

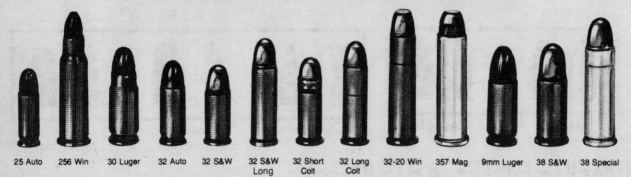

| 25 Auto | 256 Win | 30 Luger | 32 Auto | 32 S&W | 32 S&W Long | 32 Short Colt | 32 Long Colt | 32-20 Win | 357 Mag | 9mm Luger | 38 S&W | 38 Special |

CALIBER	BULLET			SYMBOL	PRIMER
	WT. GRS.	TYPE			
25 Automatic (6.35mm)	50	FMC		X25AP	1½-108
256 Winchester Magnum Super-X	60	OPE(HP)		X2561P	6½-116
30 Luger (7.65mm)	93	FMC		X30LP	1½-108
32 Automatic	71	FMC		X32AP	1½-108
32 Automatic	60	STHP		X32ASHP	1½-108
32 Smith & Wesson (inside lubricated)	85	Lead		X32SWP	1½-108
32 Smith & Wesson Long (inside lubricated)	98	Lead		X32SWLP	1½-108
32 Short Colt (greased)	80	Lead		X32SCP	1½-108
32 Long Colt (inside lubricated)	82	Lead		X32LCP	1½-108
357 Magnum Jacketed Hollow Point Super-X	110	JHP		X3573P	1½-108
357 Magnum Jacketed Hollow Point Super-X	125	JHP		X3576P	1½-108
357 Magnum Super-X (inside lubricated)	158	Lead		X3571P	1½-108
357 Magnum Jacketed Hollow Point Super-X	158	JHP		X3574P	1½-108
357 Magnum Jacketed Soft Point Super-X	158	JSP		X3575P	1½-108
357 Magnum Metal Piercing Super-X (inside lubricated, lead bearing)	158	Met. Pierc.		X3572P	1½-108
9 mm Luger (Parabellum)	95	JSP		X9MMJSP	1½-108
9 mm Luger (Parabellum)	100	JHP		X9MMJHP	1½-108
9 mm Luger (Parabellum)	115	FMC		X9LP	1½-108
9 mm Luger (Parabellum)	115	STHP		X9MMSHP	1½-108
9 mm Winchester Magnum Super-X	115	FMC		X9MMWM	1½-108
38 Smith & Wesson (inside lubricated)	145	Lead		X38SWP	1½-108
38 Special (inside lubricated)	158	Lead		X38S1P	1½-108
38 Special Metal Point (inside lubricated, lead bearing)	158	Met. Pt.		X38S2P	1½-108
38 Special Super Police (inside lubricated)	200	Lead		X38S3P	1½-108
38 Special Super-X Jacketed Hollow Point+P	110	JHP		X38S6PH	1½-108
38 Special Super-X Jacketed Hollow Point+P	125	JHP		X38S7PH	1½-108
38 Special Super-X+P	95	STHP		X38SSHP	1½-108
38 Special Super-X (inside lubricated)+P	150	Lead		X38S4P	1½-108
38 Special Metal Piercing Super-X (inside lubricated, lead bearing) +P	150	Met. Pierc.		X38S5P	1½-108
38 Special Super-X (inside lubricated)+P	158	Lead-HP		X38SPD	1½-108
38 Special Super-X Semi-Wad Cutter (inside lubricated) +P	158	Lead-SWC		X38WCP	1½-108
38 Special Super-Match and Match Mid-Range Clean Cutting (inside lubricated)	148	Lead-WC		X38SMRP	1½-108
38 Special Super Match (inside lubricated)	158	Lead		X38SMP	1½-108
38 Short Colt (greased)	130	Lead		X38SCP	1½-108
38 Long Colt (inside lubricated)	150	Lead		X38LCP	1½-108
38 Automatic Super-X (For use only in 38 Colt Super and Colt Commander Automatic Pistols)	125	JHP		X38A3P	1½-108
38 Automatic Super-X +P (For use only in 38 Colt Super and Colt Commander Automatic Pistols)	130	FMC		X38A1P	1½-108
38 Automatic (For all 38 Colt Automatic Pistols)	130	FMC		X38A2P	1½-108
380 Automatic	95	FMC		X380AP	1½-108
380 Automatic	85	STHP		X380ASHP	1½-108
41 Remington Magnum Super-X (inside lubricated)	210	Lead		X41MP	7-111F
41 Remington Magnum Super-X Jacketed Soft Point	210	JSP		X41MJSP	7-111F
44 Smith & Wesson Special (inside lubricated)	246	Lead		X44SP	7-111
44 Remington Magnum Super-X (Gas Check) (inside lubricated)	240	Lead		X44MP	7-111F
45 Colt (inside lubricated)	255	Lead		X45CP	7-111
45 Automatic	185	STHP		X45ASHP	7-111
45 Automatic	230	FMC		X45A1P	7-111
45 Automatic Super-Match Clean Cutting	185	FMC-WC		X45AWCP	7-111
45 Winchester Magnum Super-X	230	FMC		X45WM	7-111

Met. Pierc.-Metal Piercing   FMC-Full Metal Case   SP-Soft Point   JHP-Jacketed Hollow Point   JSP-Jacketed Soft Point   Met. Pt.-Metal Point
OPE-Open Point Expanding   HP-Hollow Point   PP-Power Point   WC-Wad Cutter   SWC-Semi Wad Cutter   STHP-Silvertip Hollow Point
Specifications are nominal. Test barrels are used to determine ballistics figures. Individual firearms may differ from these test barrel statistics.

WINCHESTER-WESTERN CENTERFIRE PISTOL & REVOLVER BALLISTICS

38 Special S.M. | 38 Short Colt | 38 Long Colt | 38 Auto | 380 Auto | 38-40 Win | 41 Rem Mag. | 44 S&W | 44 Rem Mag. | 44-40 Win | 45 Colt | 45 Auto | 45 Auto S.M.

VELOCITY-FPS			ENERGY FT-LBS.			MID-RANGE TRAJECTORY INCHES		BARREL LENGTH INCHES
MUZZLE	50 YDS.	100 YDS.	MUZZLE	50 YDS.	100 YDS.	50 YDS.	100 YDS.	
810	755	700	73	63	54	1.8	7.7	2
2350	2030	1760	735	550	415	0.3	1.1	8½
1220	1110	1040	305	255	225	0.9	3.5	4½
905	855	810	129	115	97	1.4	5.8	4
970	895	835	125	107	93	1.3	5.4	4
680	645	610	90	81	73	2.5	10.5	3
705	670	635	115	98	88	2.3	10.5	4
745	665	590	100	79	62	2.2	9.9	4
755	715	675	100	93	83	2.0	8.7	4
1295	1094	975	410	292	232	0.8	3.5	4 V
1450	1240	1090	583	427	330	0.6	2.8	4 V
1235	1104	1015	535	428	361	0.8	3.5	4 V
1235	1104	1015	535	428	361	0.8	3.5	4 V
1235	1104	1015	535	428	361	0.8	3.5	4 V
1235	1104	1015	535	428	361	0.8	3.5	4 V
1355	1140	1008	387	274	214	0.7	3.3	4
1320	1114	991	387	275	218	0.7	3.4	4
1155	1047	971	341	280	241	0.9	3.9	4
1225	1095	1007	383	306	259	0.8	3.6	4
1475	1264	1109	556	408	314	0.6	2.7	5
685	650	620	150	135	125	2.4	10.0	4
755	723	693	200	183	168	2.0	8.3	4 V
755	723	693	200	183	168	2.0	8.3	4 V
635	614	594	179	168	157	2.8	11.5	4 V
1020	945	887	254	218	192	1.1	4.8	4 V
945	898	858	248	224	204	1.3	5.4	4 V
1100	1002	932	255	212	183	1.0	4.3	4 V
910	870	835	276	252	232	1.4	5.7	4 V
910	870	835	276	252	232	1.4	5.7	4 V
915	878	844	294	270	250	1.4	5.6	4 V
915	878	844	294	270	250	1.4	5.6	4 V
710	634	566	166	132	105	2.4	10.8	4 V
755	723	693	200	183	168	2.0	8.3	4 V
730	685	645	150	130	115	2.2	9.4	6
730	700	670	175	165	150	2.1	8.8	6
1245	1105	1010	430	340	285	0.8	3.6	5
1280	1140	1050	475	375	320	0.8	3.4	5
1040	980	925	310	275	245	1.0	4.7	4½
955	865	785	190	160	130	1.4	5.9	3¾
1000	921	860	189	160	140	1.2	5.1	3¾
965	898	842	434	376	331	1.3	5.4	4 V
1300	1162	1062	788	630	526	0.7	3.2	4 V
755	725	695	310	285	265	2.0	8.3	6½
1350	1186	1069	971	749	608	0.7	3.1	4 V
860	820	780	420	380	345	1.5	6.1	5½
1000	938	888	411	362	324	1.2	4.9	5
810	776	745	335	308	284	1.7	7.2	5
770	707	650	244	205	174	2.0	8.7	5
1400	1232	1107	1001	775	636	0.6	2.8	5

+P Ammunition with (+P) on the case head stamp is loaded to higher pressure. Use only in firearms designated for this cartridge and so recommended by the gun manufacturer.

V-Data is based on velocity obtained from 4" vented barrels for revolver cartridges (38 Special, 357 Magnum, 41 Rem. Mag. and 44 Rem. Mag.) and unvented (solid) test barrels of the length specified for 9mm and 45 auto pistols.

WINCHESTER-WESTERN CENTERFIRE RIFLE BALLISTICS

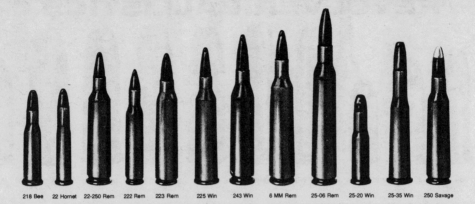

218 Bee　22 Hornet　22-250 Rem　222 Rem　223 Rem　225 Win　243 Win　6 MM Rem　25-06 Rem　25-20 Win　25-35 Win　250 Savage

WINCHESTER FIREARM SELECTOR	CARTRIDGE	GAME SELECTOR GUIDE	BULLET WT. GRS.	BULLET TYPE	SYMBOL	PRIMER	BARREL LENGTH INCHES	VELOCITY IN FEET PER SECOND MUZZLE	100	200	300 YARDS	400	500
	218 Bee Super-X	S	46	OPE(HP)	X218B	6½-116	24	2760	2102	1550	1155	961	850
	22 Hornet Super-X	S	45	SP	X22H1	6½-116	24	2690	2042	1502	1128	948	840
	22 Hornet Super-X	S	46	OPE(HP)	X22H2	6½-116	24	2690	2042	1502	1128	948	841
■ □	22-250 Remington Super-X	S	55	PSP	X222501	8½-120	24	3730	3180	2695	2257	1863	1519
■ □	222 Remington Super-X	S	50	PSP	X222R	6½-116	24	3140	2602	2123	1700	1350	1107
■ □	222 Remington Super-X	S	55	FMC	X222R1	6½-116	24	3020	2675	2355	2057	1783	1537
	223 Remington Super-X	S	55	PSP	X223R	6½-116	24	3240	2747	2304	1905	1554	1270
	223 Remington Super-X	S	55	FMC	X223R1	6½-116	24	3240	2877	2543	2232	1943	1679
	225 Winchester Super-X	S	55	PSP	X2251	8½-120	24	3570	3066	2616	2208	1838	1514
■ □	243 Winchester Super-X	S	80	PSP	X2431	8½-120	24	3350	2955	2593	2259	1951	1670
■ □	243 Winchester Super-X	D,O/P	100	PP(SP)	X2432	8½-120	24	2960	2697	2449	2215	1993	1786
	6 MM Remington Super-X	S	80	PSP	X6MMR1	8½-120	24	3470	3064	2694	2352	2036	1747
	6 MM Remington Super-X	D,O/P	100	PP(SP)	X6MMR2	8½-120	24	3130	2857	2600	2357	2127	1911
■	25-06 Remington Super-X	S	90	PEP	X25061	8½-120	24	3440	3043	2680	2344	2034	1749
■	25-06 Remington Super-X	D,O/P	120	PEP	X25062	8½-120	24	3010	2749	2502	2269	2048	1840
	25-20 Winchester	S	86	SP	X25202	6½-116	24	1460	1194	1030	931	858	798
	25-20 Winchester	S	86	Lead	X25201	6½-116	24	1460	1194	1030	931	858	798
	25-35 Winchester Super-X	D	117	SP	X2535	8½-120	24	2230	1866	1545	1282	1097	984
	250 Savage Super-X	S	87	PSP	X2501	8½-120	24	3030	2673	2342	2036	1755	1504
	250 Savage Super-X	D,O/P	100	ST	X2503	8½-120	24	2820	2467	2140	1839	1569	1339
	256 Winchester Mag. Super-X	S	60	OPE(HP)	X2561P	6½-116	24	2760	2097	1542	1149	957	846
	257 Roberts Super-X	S	87	PSP	X2571	8½-120	24	3170	2802	2462	2147	1857	1594
	257 Roberts Super-X	D,O/P	100	ST	X2572	8½-120	24	2900	2541	2210	1904	1627	1387
	257 Roberts Super-X	D,O/P	117	PP(SP)	X2573	8½-120	24	2650	2291	1961	1663	1404	1199
●	264 Winchester Mag. Super-X	S	100	PSP	X2641	8½-120	24	3320	2926	2565	2231	1923	1644
●	264 Winchester Mag. Super-X	D,O/P	140	PP(SP)	X2642	8½-120	24	3030	2782	2548	2326	2114	1914
■	270 Winchester Super-X	S	100	PSP	X2701	8½-120	24	3480	3067	2690	2343	2023	1730
■	270 Winchester Super-X	D,O/P	130	PP(SP)	X2705	8½-120	24	3110	2849	2604	2371	2150	1941
■	270 Winchester Super-X	D,O/P	130	ST	X2703	8½-120	24	3110	2823	2554	2300	2061	1837
■	270 Winchester Super-X	D,L	150	PP(SP)	X2704	8½-120	24	2900	2632	2380	2142	1918	1709
	284 Winchester Super-X	D,O/P	125	PP(SP)	X2841	8½-120	24	3140	2829	2538	2265	2010	1772
	284 Winchester Super-X	D,O/P,L	150	PP(SP)	X2842	8½-120	24	2860	2595	2344	2108	1886	1680
	7 MM Mauser (7x57) Super-X	D	175	SP	X7MM	8½-120	24	2440	2137	1857	1603	1382	1204
●	7 MM Remington Mag. Super-X	D,O/P	125	PP(SP)	X7MMR3	8½-120	24	3310	2976	2666	2376	2105	1852
●	7 MM Remington Mag. Super-X	D,O/P	150	PP(SP)	X7MMR1	8½-120	24	3110	2830	2568	2320	2085	1866
●	7 MM Remington Mag. Super-X	D,O/P,L	175	PP(SP)	X7MMR2	8½-120	24	2860	2645	2440	2244	2057	1879
	30 Carbine	S	110	HSP	X30M1	6½-116	20	1990	1567	1236	1035	923	842
	30 Carbine	S	110	FMC	X30M2	6½-116	20	1990	1596	1278	1070	952	870
★	30-30 Winchester Super-X	D	150	OPE	X30301	8½-120	24	2390	2018	1684	1398	1177	1036
★	30-30 Winchester Super-X	D	150	PP(SP)	X30306	8½-120	24	2390	2018	1684	1398	1177	1036
★	30-30 Winchester Super-X	D	150	ST	X30302	8½-120	24	2390	2018	1684	1398	1177	1036
★	30-30 Winchester Super-X	D	170	PP(SP)	X30303	8½-120	24	2200	1895	1619	1381	1191	1061
★	30-30 Winchester Super-X	D	170	ST	X30304	8½-120	24	2200	1895	1619	1381	1191	1061
	30 Remington Super-X	D	170	ST	X30R2	8½-120	24	2120	1822	1555	1328	1153	1036
■	30-06 Springfield Super-X	S	110	PSP	X30060	8½-120	24	3380	2843	2365	1936	1561	1261
■	30-06 Springfield Super-X	S	125	PSP	X30062	8½-120	24	3140	2780	2447	2138	1853	1595
■	30-06 Springfield Super-X	D,O/P	150	PP(SP)	X30061	8½-120	24	2920	2580	2265	1972	1704	1466
■	30-06 Springfield Super-X	D,O/P	150	ST	X30063	8½-120	24	2910	2617	2342	2083	1843	1622
■	30-06 Springfield Super-X	D,O/P,L	180	PP(SP)	X30064	8½-120	24	2700	2348	2023	1727	1466	1251
■	30-06 Springfield Super-X	D,O/P,L	180	ST	X30066	8½-120	24	2700	2469	2250	2042	1846	1663
■	30-06 Springfield Super-X	L	220	PP(SP)	X30068	8½-120	24	2410	2130	1870	1632	1422	1246
■	30-06 Springfield Super-X	L	220	ST	X30069	8½-120	24	2410	2192	1985	1791	1611	1448

WINCHESTER FIREARMS SELECTOR CODE

■ = Models 70 XTR & 70A XTR　● = Models 70 XTR Magnum　★ = Model 94　S = Small game
□ = Model 70 XTR Varmint　○ = Model 70A XTR Magnum　D = Deer

GAME SELECTOR CODE

O/P = Open or Plains shooting (i.e. Antelope, Deer)　XL = Extra Large game (i.e. Kodiak bear)
L = Large game (i.e. Moose, Elk)

WINCHESTER-WESTERN CENTERFIRE RIFLE BALLISTICS

256 Win   257 Roberts   264 Win   270 Win   284 Win   7 MM Mauser   7 MM Rem Mag.   30 Carbine   30-30 Win   30 Rem   30-06 Springfield

TRAJECTORY Inches above (+) or below (-) line of sight   0 = Indicates yardage at which rifle is sighted in.

| ENERGY IN FOOT POUNDS | | | | | | SHORT RANGE | | | | | | LONG RANGE | | | | | | |
MUZZLE	100	200	300 YARDS	400	500	50	100	150	200 YARDS	250	300	100	150	200	250 YARDS	300	400	500
778	451	245	136	94	74	0.3	0	-2.3	-7.2	-15.8	-29.4	1.5	0	-4.2	-12.0	-24.8	-71.4	-155.6
723	417	225	127	90	70	0.3	0	-2.4	-7.7	-16.9	-31.3	1.6	0	-4.5	-12.8	-26.4	-75.6	-163.4
739	426	230	130	92	72	0.3	0	-2.4	-7.7	-16.9	-31.3	1.6	0	-4.5	-12.8	-26.4	-75.5	-163.3
1699	1235	887	622	424	282	0.2	0.5	0	-1.5	-4.3	-8.4	2.2	2.6	1.9	0	-3.3	-15.4	-37.7
1094	752	500	321	202	136	0.5	0.9	0	-2.5	-6.9	-13.7	2.2	1.9	0	-3.8	-10.0	-32.3	-73.8
1114	874	677	517	388	288	0.5	0.9	0	-2.2	-6.1	-11.7	2.0	1.7	0	-3.3	-8.3	-24.9	-52.5
1282	921	648	443	295	197	0.4	0.8	0	-2.2	-6.0	-11.8	1.9	1.6	0	-3.3	-8.5	-26.7	-59.6
1282	1011	790	608	461	344	0.4	0.7	0	-1.9	-5.1	-9.9	1.7	1.4	0	-2.8	-7.1	-21.2	-44.6
1556	1148	836	595	412	280	0.2	0.6	0	-1.7	-4.6	-9.0	2.4	2.8	2.0	0	-3.5	-16.3	-39.5
1993	1551	1194	906	676	495	0.3	0.7	0	-1.8	-4.9	-9.4	2.6	2.9	2.1	0	-3.6	-16.2	-37.9
1945	1615	1332	1089	882	708	0.5	0.9	0	-2.2	-5.8	-11.0	1.9	1.6	0	-3.1	-7.8	-22.6	-46.3
2139	1667	1289	982	736	542	0.3	0.6	0	-1.6	-4.5	-8.7	2.4	2.7	1.9	0	-3.3	-14.9	-35.0
2175	1812	1501	1233	1004	811	0.4	0.7	0	-1.9	-5.1	-9.7	1.7	1.4	0	-2.7	-6.8	-20.0	-40.8
2364	1850	1435	1098	827	611	0.3	0.6	0	-1.7	-4.5	-8.8	2.4	2.7	2.0	0	-3.4	-15.0	-35.2
2414	2013	1668	1372	1117	902	0.5	0.8	0	-2.1	-5.5	-10.5	1.9	1.6	0	-2.9	-7.4	-21.6	-44.2
407	272	203	165	141	122	0	-4.1	-14.4	-31.8	-57.3	-92.0	0	-8.2	-23.5	-47.0	-79.6	-175.9	-319.4
407	272	203	165	141	122	0	-4.1	-14.4	-31.8	-57.3	-92.0	0	-8.2	-23.5	-47.0	-79.6	-175.9	-319.4
1292	904	620	427	313	252	0.6	0	-3.1	-9.2	-19.0	-33.1	2.1	0	-5.1	-13.8	-27.0	-70.1	-142.0
1773	1380	1059	801	595	437	0.5	0.9	0	-2.3	-6.1	-11.8	2.0	1.7	0	-3.3	-8.4	-25.2	-53.4
1765	1351	1017	751	547	398	0.2	0	-1.6	-4.9	-10.0	-17.4	2.4	2.0	0	-3.9	-10.1	-30.5	-65.2
1015	586	317	176	122	95	0.3	0	-2.3	-7.3	-15.9	-29.6	1.5	0	-4.2	-12.1	-25.0	-72.1	-157.2
1941	1516	1171	890	666	491	0.4	0.8	0	-2.0	-5.5	-10.6	1.8	1.5	0	-3.0	-7.5	-22.7	-48.0
1867	1433	1084	805	588	427	0.6	1.0	0	-2.5	-6.9	-13.2	2.3	1.9	0	-3.7	-9.4	-28.6	-60.9
1824	1363	999	718	512	373	0.3	0	-1.9	-5.8	-11.9	-20.7	2.9	2.4	0	-4.7	-12.0	-36.7	-79.2
2447	1901	1461	1105	821	600	0.3	0.7	0	-1.8	-5.0	-9.7	2.7	3.0	2.2	0	-3.7	-16.6	-38.9
2854	2406	2018	1682	1389	1139	0.5	0.8	0	-2.0	-5.4	-10.2	1.8	1.5	0	-2.9	-7.2	-20.8	-42.2
2689	2088	1606	1219	909	664	0.3	0.6	0	-1.6	-4.5	-8.7	2.4	2.7	1.9	0	-3.3	-15.0	-35.2
2791	2343	1957	1622	1334	1087	0.4	0.7	0	-1.9	-5.1	-9.7	1.7	1.4	0	-2.7	-6.8	-19.9	-40.5
2791	2300	1883	1527	1226	974	0.4	0.8	0	-2.0	-5.3	-10.0	1.7	1.5	0	-2.8	-7.1	-20.8	-42.7
2801	2307	1886	1528	1225	973	0.6	0.9	0	-2.3	-6.1	-11.7	2.1	1.7	0	-3.3	-8.2	-24.1	-49.4
2736	2221	1788	1424	1121	871	0.4	0.8	0	-2.0	-5.3	-10.1	1.7	1.5	0	-2.8	-7.2	-21.1	-43.7
2724	2243	1830	1480	1185	940	0.6	1.0	0	-2.4	-6.3	-12.1	2.1	1.8	0	-3.4	-8.5	-24.8	-51.0
2313	1774	1340	998	742	563	0.4	0	-2.3	-6.8	-13.8	-23.7	1.5	0	-3.7	-10.0	-19.1	-48.1	-95.4
3040	2458	1972	1567	1230	952	0.3	0.6	0	-1.7	-4.7	-9.1	2.5	2.8	2.0	0	-3.4	-15.0	-34.5
3221	2667	2196	1792	1448	1160	0.4	0.8	0	-1.9	-5.2	-9.9	1.7	1.5	0	-2.8	-7.0	-20.5	-42.1
3178	2718	2313	1956	1644	1372	0.6	0.9	0	-2.3	-6.0	-11.3	2.0	1.7	0	-3.2	-7.9	-22.7	-45.8
967	600	373	262	208	173	0.9	0	-4.5	-13.5	-28.3	-49.9	0	-4.5	-13.5	-28.3	-49.9	-118.6	-228.2
967	622	399	280	221	185	0.9	0	-4.3	-13.0	-26.9	-47.4	2.9	0	-7.2	-19.7	-38.7	-100.4	-200.5
1902	1356	944	651	461	357	0.5	0	-2.6	-7.7	-16.0	-27.9	1.7	0	-4.3	-11.6	-22.7	-59.1	-120.5
1902	1356	944	651	461	357	0.5	0	-2.6	-7.7	-16.0	-27.9	1.7	0	-4.3	-11.6	-22.7	-59.1	-120.5
1902	1356	944	651	461	357	0.5	0	-2.6	-7.7	-16.0	-27.9	1.7	0	-4.3	-11.6	-22.7	-59.1	-120.5
1827	1355	989	720	535	425	0.6	0	-3.0	-8.9	-18.0	-31.1	2.0	0	-4.8	-13.0	-25.1	-63.6	-126.7
1827	1355	989	720	535	425	0.6	0	-3.0	-8.9	-18.0	-31.1	2.0	0	-4.8	-13.0	-25.1	-63.6	-126.7
1696	1253	913	666	502	405	0.7	0	-3.3	-9.7	-19.6	-33.8	2.2	0	-5.3	-14.1	-27.2	-69.0	-136.7
2790	1974	1366	915	595	388	0.4	0.7	0	-2.0	-5.6	-11.1	1.7	1.5	0	-3.1	-8.0	-25.5	-57.4
2736	2145	1662	1269	953	706	0.4	0.8	0	-2.1	-5.6	-10.7	1.8	1.5	0	-3.0	-7.7	-23.0	-48.5
2839	2217	1708	1295	967	716	0.6	1.0	0	-2.4	-6.6	-12.7	2.2	1.8	0	-3.5	-9.0	-27.0	-57.1
2820	2281	1827	1445	1131	876	0.6	0.9	0	-2.3	-6.3	-12.0	2.1	1.8	0	-3.3	-8.5	-25.0	-51.8
2913	2203	1635	1192	859	625	0.2	0	-1.8	-5.5	-11.2	-19.5	2.7	2.3	0	-4.4	-11.3	-34.4	-73.7
2913	2436	2023	1666	1362	1105	0.2	0	-1.6	-4.8	-9.7	-16.5	2.4	2.0	0	-3.7	-9.3	-27.0	-54,9
2837	2216	1708	1301	988	758	0.4	0	-2.3	-6.8	-13.8	-23.6	1.5	0	-3.7	-9.9	-19.0	-47.4	-93.1
2837	2347	1924	1567	1268	1024	0.4	0	-2.2	-6.4	-12.7	-21.6	1.5	0	-3.5	-9.1	-17.2	-41.8	-79.9

HSP-Hollow Soft Point   PEP-Positive Expanding Point   PSP-Pointed Soft Point   PP(SP)-Power-Point Soft Point
FMC-Full Metal Case   SP-Soft Point   HP-Hollow Point   OPE-Open Point Expanding   ST-Silvertip

Specifications are nominal. Test barrels are used to determine ballistics figures. Individual firearms may differ from these test barrel statistics.

WINCHESTER-WESTERN CENTERFIRE RIFLE BALLISTICS

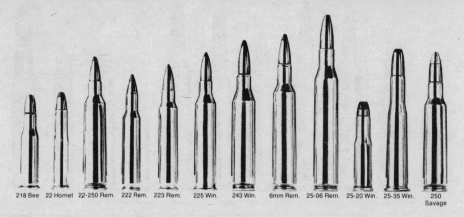

218 Bee 22 Hornet 22-250 Rem. 222 Rem. 223 Rem. 225 Win. 243 Win. 6mm Rem. 25-06 Rem. 25-20 Win. 25-35 Win. 250 Savage

WINCHESTER FIREARM SELECTOR	CARTRIDGE	GAME SELECTOR GUIDE	BULLET WT. GRS.	BULLET TYPE	SYMBOL	PRIMER	BARREL LENGTH INCHES	MUZZLE	100	200	300	400	500
											YARDS		
	30-40 Krag Super-X	D	180	PP(SP)	X30401	8½-120	24	2430	2099	1795	1525	1298	1128
	30-40 Krag Super-X	D	180	ST	X30403	8½-120	24	2430	2213	2007	1813	1632	1468
	30-40 Krag Super-X	L	220	ST	X30404	8½-120	24	2160	1956	1765	1587	1427	1287
● 0	300 Winchester Mag. Super-X	D,O/P	150	PP(SP)	X30WM1	8½-120	24	3290	2951	2636	2342	2068	1813
● 0	300 Winchester Mag. Super-X	O/P,L	180	PP(SP)	X30WM2	8½-120	24	2960	2745	2540	2344	2157	1979
● 0	300 Winchester Mag. Super-X	L,XL	220	ST	X30WM3	8½-120	24	2680	2448	2228	2020	1823	1640
	300 H.&H. Magnum Super-X	O/P	150	ST	X300H1	8½-120	24	3130	2822	2534	2264	2011	1776
	300 H.&H. Magnum Super-X	O/P,L	180	ST	X300H2	8½-120	24	2880	2640	2412	2196	1991	1798
	300 H.&H. Magnum Super-X	L,XL	220	ST	X300H3	8½-120	24	2580	2341	2114	1901	1702	1520
	300 Savage Super-X	D,O/P	150	PP(SP)	X3001	8½-120	24	2630	2311	2015	1743	1500	1295
	300 Savage Super-X	D,O/P	150	ST	X3003	8½-120	24	2630	2354	2095	1853	1631	1434
	300 Savage Super-X	D	180	PP(SP)	X3004	8½-120	24	2350	2025	1728	1467	1252	1098
	300 Savage Super-X	D	180	ST	X3005	8½-120	24	2350	2137	1935	1745	1570	1413
	303 Savage Super-X	D	190	ST	X3032	8½-120	24	1940	1657	1410	1211	1073	982
	303 British Super-X	D	180	PP(SP)	X303B1	8½-120	24	2460	2233	2018	1816	1629	1459
■	308 Winchester Super-X	S	110	PSP	X3081	8½-120	24	3180	2666	2206	1795	1444	1178
■	308 Winchester Super-X	S	125	PSP	X3087	8½-120	24	3050	2697	2370	2067	1788	1537
■	308 Winchester Super-X	D,O/P	150	PP(SP)	X3085	8½-120	24	2820	2488	2179	1893	1633	1405
■	308 Winchester Super-X	D,O/P	150	ST	X3082	8½-120	24	2820	2533	2263	2009	1774	1560
■	308 Winchester Super-X	D,O/P,L	180	PP(SP)	X3086	8½-120	24	2620	2274	1955	1666	1414	1212
■	308 Winchester Super-X	D,O/P,L	180	ST	X3083	8½-120	24	2620	2393	2178	1974	1782	1604
■	308 Winchester Super-X	L	200	ST	X3084	8½-120	24	2450	2208	1980	1767	1572	1397
	32 Win. Special Super-X	D	170	PP(SP)	X32WS2	8½-120	24	2250	1870	1537	1267	1082	971
	32 Win. Special Super-X	D	170	ST	X32WS3	8½-120	24	2250	1870	1537	1267	1082	971
	32 Remington Super-X	D	170	ST	X32R2	8½-120	24	2140	1785	1475	1228	1064	963
	32-20 Winchester	S	100	SP	X32202	6½-116	24	1210	1021	913	834	769	712
	32-20 Winchester	S	100	Lead	X32201	6½-116	24	1210	1021	913	834	769	712
	8mm Mauser (8x57) Super-X	D	170	PP(SP)	X8MM	8½-120	24	2360	1969	1622	1333	1123	997
●	338 Winchester Mag. Super-X	D,O/P	200	PP(SP)	X3381	8½-120	24	2960	2658	2375	2110	1862	1635
●	338 Winchester Mag. Super-X	L,XL	225	SP	X3383	8½-120	24	2180	2572	2374	2184	2003	1832
●	338 Winchester Mag. Super-X	L,XL	250	ST	X3382	8½-120	24	2660	2395	2145	1910	1693	1497
	348 Winchester Super-X	D,L	200	ST	X3482	8½-120	24	2520	2215	1931	1672	1443	1253
	35 Remington Super-X	D	200	PP(SP)	X35R1	8½-120	24	2020	1646	1335	1114	985	901
	35 Remington Super-X	D	200	ST	X35R3	8½-120	24	2020	1646	1335	1114	985	901
	351 Winchester S.L.	D	180	SP	X351SL2	6½-116	20	1850	1556	1310	1128	1012	933
	358 Winchester Super-X	D,L	200	ST	X3581	8½-120	24	2490	2171	1876	1610	1379	1194
	358 Winchester Super-X	L	250	ST	X3582	8½-120	24	2230	1988	1762	1557	1375	1224
★	375 Winchester	D,L	200	PP(SP)	X375W	8½-120	24	2200	1841	1526	1268	1089	980
★	375 Winchester	D,L	250	PP(SP)	X375W1	8½-120	24	1900	1647	1424	1239	1103	1011
●	375 H.&H. Magnum Super-X	L,XL	270	PP(SP)	X375H1	8½-120	24	2690	2420	2166	1928	1707	1507
●	375 H.&H. Magnum Super-X	L,XL	300	ST	X375H2	8½-120	24	2530	2268	2022	1793	1583	1397
●	375 H.&H. Magnum Super-X	L,XL	300	FMC	X375H3	8½-120	24	2530	2171	1843	1551	1307	1126
	38-40 Winchester	D	180	SP	X3840	7-111	24	1160	999	901	827	764	710
★	38-55 Winchester	D	255	SP	X3855	8½-120	24	1320	1190	1091	1018	963	917
	44 Remington Magnum Super-X	D	240	HSP	X44MHSP	7M-111F	20	1760	1362	1094	953	861	789
	44-40 Winchester	D	200	SP	X4440	7-111	24	1190	1006	900	822	756	699
	45-70 Government	D,L	405	SP	X4570	8½-120	24	1330	1168	1055	977	918	869
●	458 Winchester Mag. Super-X	XL	500	FMC	X4580	8½-120	24	2040	1823	1623	1442	1287	1161
●	458 Winchester Mag. Super-X	L,XL	510	SP	X4581	8½-120	24	2040	1770	1527	1319	1157	1046

WINCHESTER FIREARMS SELECTOR CODE

■ = Models 70 XTR   ● = Models 70 XTR Magnum   ★ = Model 94
□ = Model 70 XTR Varmint

WINCHESTER-WESTERN CENTERFIRE RIFLE BALLISTICS

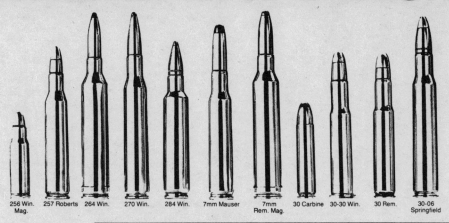

256 Win. Mag.   257 Roberts   264 Win.   270 Win.   284 Win.   7mm Mauser   7mm Rem. Mag.   30 Carbine   30-30 Win.   30 Rem.   30-06 Springfield

TRAJECTORY Inches above (+) or below (-) line of sight   0 = Indicates yardage at which rifle is sighted in.

MUZZLE	ENERGY IN FOOT POUNDS 100	200	300 YARDS	400	500	SHORT RANGE 50	100	150	200 YARDS	250	300	LONG RANGE 100	150	200	250 YARDS	300	400	500
2360	1761	1288	929	673	508	0.4	0	-2.4	-7.1	-14.5	-25.0	1.6	0	-3.9	-10.5	-20.3	-51.7	-103.9
2360	1957	1610	1314	1064	861	0.4	0	-2.1	-6.2	-12.5	-21.1	1.4	0	-3.4	-8.9	-16.8	-40.9	-78.1
2279	1869	1522	1230	995	809	0.6	0	-2.9	-8.2	-16.4	-27.6	1.9	0	-4.4	-11.6	-21.9	-53.3	-101.8
3605	2900	2314	1827	1424	1095	0.3	0.7	0	-1.8	-4.8	-9.3	2.6	2.9	2.1	0	-3.5	-15.4	-35.5
3501	3011	2578	2196	1859	1565	0.5	0.8	0	-2.2	-5.5	-10.4	1.9	1.6	0	-2.9	-7.3	-20.9	-41.9
3508	2927	2424	1993	1623	1314	0.2	0	-1.7	-4.9	-9.9	-16.9	2.5	2.0	0	-3.8	-9.5	-27.5	-56.1
3262	2652	2138	1707	1347	1050	0.4	0.8	0	-2.0	-5.3	-10.1	1.7	1.5	0	-2.8	-7.2	-21.2	-43.8
3315	2785	2325	1927	1584	1292	0.6	0.9	0	-2.3	-6.0	-11.5	2.1	1.7	0	-3.2	-8.0	-23.3	-47.4
3251	2677	2183	1765	1415	1128	0.3	0	-1.9	-5.5	-11.0	-18.7	2.7	2.2	0	-4.2	-10.5	-30.7	-63.0
2303	1779	1352	1012	749	558	0.3	0	-1.9	-5.7	-11.6	-19.9	2.8	2.3	0	-4.5	-11.5	-34.4	-73.0
2303	1845	1462	1143	886	685	0.3	0	-1.8	-5.4	-11.0	-18.8	2.7	2.2	0	-4.2	-10.7	-31.5	-65.5
2207	1639	1193	860	626	482	0.5	0	-2.6	-7.7	-15.6	-27.1	1.7	0	-4.2	-11.3	-21.9	-55.8	-112.0
2207	1825	1496	1217	985	798	0.4	0	-2.3	-6.7	-13.5	-22.8	1.5	0	-3.6	-9.6	-18.2	-44.1	-84.2
1588	1158	839	619	486	407	0.9	0	-4.1	-11.9	-24.1	-41.4	2.7	0	-6.4	-17.3	-33.2	-83.7	-164.4
2418	1993	1627	1318	1060	851	0.3	0	-2.1	-6.1	-12.2	-20.8	1.4	0	-3.3	-8.8	-16.6	-40.4	-77.4
2470	1736	1188	787	509	339	0.5	0.9	0	-2.3	-6.5	-12.8	2.0	1.8	0	-3.5	-9.3	-29.5	-66.7
2582	2019	1559	1186	887	656	0.5	0.8	0	-2.2	-6.0	-11.5	2.0	1.7	0	-3.2	-8.2	-24.6	-51.9
2648	2061	1581	1193	888	657	0.2	0	-1.6	-4.8	-9.8	-16.9	2.4	2.0	0	-3.8	-9.8	-29.3	-62.0
2648	2137	1705	1344	1048	810	0.2	0	-1.5	-4.5	-9.3	-15.9	2.3	1.9	0	-3.6	-9.1	-26.9	-55.7
2743	2066	1527	1109	799	587	0.3	0	-2.0	-5.9	-12.1	-20.9	2.9	2.4	0	-4.7	-12.1	-36.9	-79.1
2743	2288	1896	1557	1269	1028	0.2	0	-1.8	-5.2	-10.4	-17.7	2.6	2.1	0	-4.0	-9.9	-28.9	-58.8
2665	2165	1741	1386	1097	867	0.4	0	-2.1	-6.3	-12.6	-21.4	1.4	0	-3.4	-9.0	-17.2	-42.1	-81.1
1911	1320	892	606	442	356	0.6	0	-3.1	-9.2	-19.0	-33.2	2.0	0	-5.1	-13.8	-27.1	-70.9	-144.3
1911	1320	892	606	442	356	0.6	0	-3.1	-9.2	-19.0	-33.2	2.0	0	-5.1	-13.8	-27.1	-70.9	-144.3
1728	1203	821	569	427	350	0.7	0	-3.4	-10.2	-20.9	-36.5	2.3	0	-5.6	-15.2	-29.6	-76.7	-154.5
325	231	185	154	131	113	0	-6.3	-20.9	-44.9	-79.3	-125.1	0	-11.5	-32.3	-63.6	-106.3	-230.3	-413.3
325	231	185	154	131	113	0	-6.3	-20.9	-44.9	-79.3	-125.1	0	-11.5	-32.3	-63.6	-106.3	-230.3	-413.3
2102	1463	993	671	476	375	0.5	0	-2.7	-8.2	-17.1	-29.8	1.8	0	-4.5	-12.4	-24.3	-63.8	-130.7
3890	3137	2505	1977	1539	1187	0.5	0.9	0	-2.3	-6.1	-11.6	2.0	1.7	0	-3.2	-8.2	-24.3	-50.4
3862	3306	2816	2384	2005	1677	1.2	1.3	0	-2.7	-7.1	-12.9	2.7	2.1	0	-3.6	-9.4	-25.0	-49.9
3927	3184	2554	2025	1591	1244	0.2	0	-1.7	-5.2	-10.5	-18.0	2.6	2.1	0	-4.0	-10.2	-30.0	-61.9
2820	2178	1656	1241	925	697	0.3	0	-2.1	-6.2	-12.7	-21.9	1.4	0	-3.4	-9.2	-17.7	-44.4	-87.9
1812	1203	791	551	431	360	0.9	0	-4.1	-12.1	-25.1	-43.9	2.7	0	-6.7	-18.3	-35.8	-92.8	-185.5
1812	1203	791	551	431	360	0.9	0	-4.1	-12.1	-25.1	-43.9	2.7	0	-6.7	-18.3	-35.8	-92.8	-185.5
1368	968	686	508	409	348	0	-2.1	-7.8	-17.8	-32.9	-53.9	0	-4.7	-13.6	-27.6	-47.5	-108.8	-203.9
2753	2093	1563	1151	844	633	0.4	0	-2.2	-6.5	-13.3	-23.0	1.5	0	-3.6	-9.7	-18.6	-47.2	-94.1
2760	2194	1723	1346	1049	832	0.5	0	-2.7	-7.9	-16.0	-27.1	1.8	0	-4.3	-11.4	-21.7	-53.5	-103.7
2150	1506	1034	714	527	427	0.6	0	-3.2	-9.5	-19.5	-33.8	2.1	0	-5.2	-14.1	-27.4	-70.1	-138.1
2005	1506	1126	852	676	568	0.9	0	-4.1	-12.0	-24.0	-40.9	2.7	0	-6.5	-17.2	-32.7	-80.6	-154.1
4337	3510	2812	2228	1747	1361	0.2	0	-1.7	-5.1	-10.3	-17.6	2.5	2.1	0	-3.9	-10.0	-29.4	-60.7
4263	3426	2723	2141	1669	1300	0.3	0	-2.0	-5.9	-11.9	-20.3	2.9	2.4	0	-4.5	-11.5	-33.8	-70.1
4263	3139	2262	1602	1138	844	0.3	0	-2.2	-6.5	-13.5	-23.4	1.5	0	-3.6	-9.8	-19.1	-49.1	-99.5
538	399	324	273	233	201	0	-6.7	-22.2	-47.3	-83.2	-130.8	0	-12.1	-33.9	-66.4	-110.6	-238.3	-425.6
987	802	674	587	525	476	0	-4.7	-15.4	-32.7	-57.2	-89.3	0	-8.4	-23.4	-45.6	-75.2	-158.8	-277.4
1650	988	638	484	395	232	0	-2.7	-10.2	-23.6	-44.2	-73.3	0	-6.1	-18.1	-37.4	-65.1	-150.3	-282.5
629	449	360	300	254	217	0	-6.5	-21.6	-46.3	-81.8	-129.1	0	-11.8	-33.3	-65.5	-109.5	-237.4	-426.2
1590	1227	1001	858	758	679	0	-4.7	-15.8	-34.0	-60.0	-94.5	0	-8.7	-24.6	-48.2	-80.3	-172.4	-305.9
4620	3689	2924	2308	1839	1496	0.7	0	-3.3	-9.6	-19.2	-32.5	2.2	0	-5.2	-13.6	-25.8	-63.2	-121.7
4712	3547	2640	1970	1516	1239	0.8	0	-3.5	-10.3	-20.8	-35.6	2.4	0	-5.6	-14.9	-28.5	-71.5	-140.4

GAME SELECTOR CODE

S = Small game
D = Deer

O/P = Open or Plains shooting (i.e. Antelope, Deer)
L = Large game (i.e. Moose, Elk)

XL = Extra Large game (i.e. Kodiak bear)

Reloading

HORNADY RIFLE BULLETS

■ 17 CALIBER (.172)

	Price Per 100 Retail
25 gr. HP............#1710	$ 7.55

■ 22 CALIBER (.222)

40 gr. Jet............#2210	$ 6.55

■ 22 CALIBER (.223)

45 gr. Hornet........#2220	$ 6.55

■ 22 CALIBER (.224)

45 gr. Hornet........#2230	$ 6.55
50 gr. SPSX..........#2240	$ 6.65
50 gr. SP............#2245	$ 6.65

■ 22 CALIBER MATCH

52 gr. BTHP.........#2249	$ 8.00

■ 22 CALIBER MATCH

53 gr. HP............#2250	$ 8.00
55 gr. SPSX..........#2260	$ 6.80
55 gr. SP............#2265	$ 6.80
55 gr. SP w/c........#2266	$ 7.25
55 gr. FMJ-BT w/c..#2267	$ 7.25
60 gr. SP............#2270	$ 7.25
60 gr. HP............#2275	$ 8.00

■ 22 CALIBER (.227)

70 gr. SP............#2280	$ 8.90

■ 6MM CALIBER (.243)

70 gr. SP............#2410	$ 8.45
75 gr. HP............#2420	$ 8.55

6MM Caliber (.243) continued

	Price Per 100 Retail
80 gr. FMJ...........#2430	$ 9.25
87 gr. SP............#2440	$ 8.90
87 gr. BTHP..........#2442	$ 9.90
I 100 gr. SP ....#2450	$ 9.25
100 gr. BTSP ....#2453	$ 9.55
I 100 gr. RN...........#2455	$ 9.25

■ 25 CALIBER (.257)

60 gr. FP.............#2510	$ 8.45
75 gr. HP............#2520	$ 8.90
87 gr. SP............#2530	$ 9.20
I 100 gr. SP ....#2540	$ 9.45
I 117 gr. RN...........#2550	$10.10
I 120 gr. HP ....#2560	$10.25

■ 6.5MM CALIBER (.264)

100 gr. SP............#2610	$10.10
I 129 gr. SP ....#2620	$10.90
I 140 gr. SP ....#2630	$11.10
I 160 gr. RN...........#2640	$12.25

■ 270 CALIBER (.277)

100 gr. SP ....#2710	$ 9.80

270 Caliber (.277) continued

	Price Per 100 Retail
110 gr. HP ....#2720	$10.00
I 130 gr. SP ....#2730	$10.55
I 140 gr. BTSP ....#2735	$11.20
I 150 gr. SP ....#2740	$11.10
I 150 gr. RN...........#2745	$11.10

■ 7MM CALIBER (.284)

120 gr. SP ....#2810	$10.20
120 gr. HP ....#2815	$10.20
I 139 gr. SP ....#2820	$10.65
I 154 gr. SP ....#2830	$11.35
I 154 gr. RN ....#2835	$11.55

■ 7MM MATCH

162 gr. BTHP ....#2840	$13.65
162 gr. BTSP ....#2845	$12.75
I 175 gr. SP ....#2850	$12.55
I 175 gr. RN ....#2855	$12.55

■ 30 CALIBER (.308)

100 gr. SJ............#3005	$ 6.55
110 gr. SP ....#3010	$ 9.25
110 gr. RN...........#3015	$ 8.45

"I" denotes interlock bullets.

Prices effective January 15, 1981 *(All prices subject to change without notice.)*

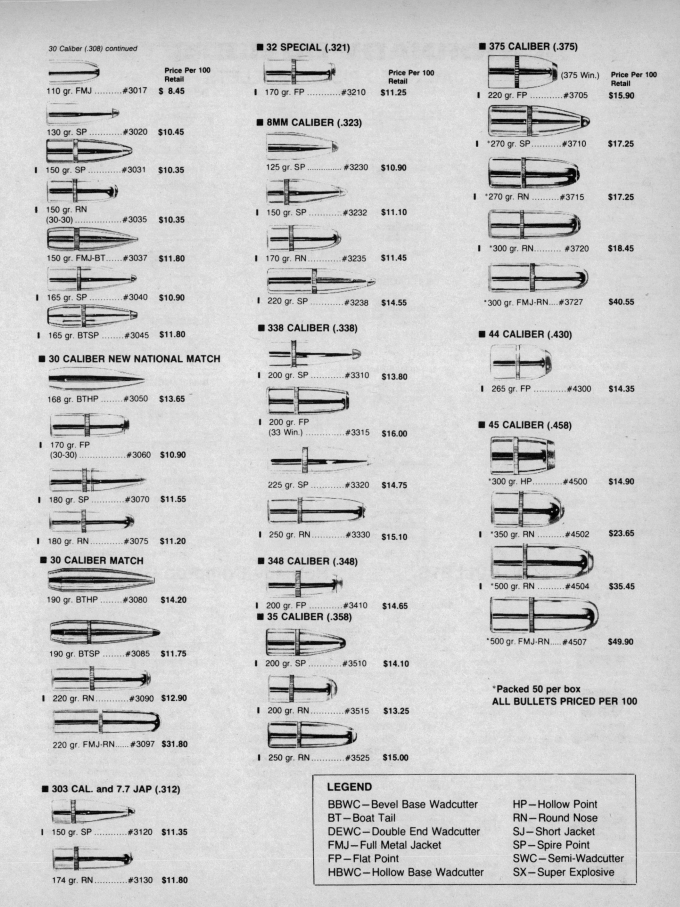

30 Caliber (.308) continued

		Price Per 100 Retail
110 gr. FMJ	#3017	$ 8.45
130 gr. SP	#3020	$10.45
150 gr. SP	#3031	$10.35
150 gr. RN (30-30)	#3035	$10.35
150 gr. FMJ-BT	#3037	$11.80
165 gr. SP	#3040	$10.90
165 gr. BTSP	#3045	$11.80

■ 30 CALIBER NEW NATIONAL MATCH

168 gr. BTHP	#3050	$13.65
170 gr. FP (30-30)	#3060	$10.90
180 gr. SP	#3070	$11.55
180 gr. RN	#3075	$11.20

■ 30 CALIBER MATCH

190 gr. BTHP	#3080	$14.20
190 gr. BTSP	#3085	$11.75
220 gr. RN	#3090	$12.90
220 gr. FMJ-RN	#3097	$31.80

■ 303 CAL. and 7.7 JAP (.312)

150 gr. SP	#3120	$11.35
174 gr. RN	#3130	$11.80

■ 32 SPECIAL (.321)

		Price Per 100 Retail
170 gr. FP	#3210	$11.25

■ 8MM CALIBER (.323)

125 gr. SP	#3230	$10.90
150 gr. SP	#3232	$11.10
170 gr. RN	#3235	$11.45
220 gr. SP	#3238	$14.55

■ 338 CALIBER (.338)

200 gr. SP	#3310	$13.80
200 gr. FP (33 Win.)	#3315	$16.00
225 gr. SP	#3320	$14.75
250 gr. RN	#3330	$15.10

■ 348 CALIBER (.348)

200 gr. FP	#3410	$14.65

■ 35 CALIBER (.358)

200 gr. SP	#3510	$14.10
200 gr. RN	#3515	$13.25
250 gr. RN	#3525	$15.00

■ 375 CALIBER (.375)

(375 Win.)

		Price Per 100 Retail
220 gr. FP	#3705	$15.90
*270 gr. SP	#3710	$17.25
*270 gr. RN	#3715	$17.25
*300 gr. RN	#3720	$18.45
*300 gr. FMJ-RN	#3727	$40.55

■ 44 CALIBER (.430)

265 gr. FP	#4300	$14.35

■ 45 CALIBER (.458)

*300 gr. HP	#4500	$14.90
*350 gr. RN	#4502	$23.65
*500 gr. RN	#4504	$35.45
*500 gr. FMJ-RN	#4507	$49.90

*Packed 50 per box
ALL BULLETS PRICED PER 100

LEGEND

BBWC—Bevel Base Wadcutter	HP—Hollow Point
BT—Boat Tail	RN—Round Nose
DEWC—Double End Wadcutter	SJ—Short Jacket
FMJ—Full Metal Jacket	SP—Spire Point
FP—Flat Point	SWC—Semi-Wadcutter
HBWC—Hollow Base Wadcutter	SX—Super Explosive

HORNADY BULLETS
JACKETED PISTOL BULLETS

■ 25 CALIBER (.251)

Price Per 100
Retail

50 gr. FMJ-RN.......#3545 $ 7.20

■ 9MM CALIBER (.355)

90 gr. HP............#3550 $ 7.45

100 gr. FMJ ....#3552 $ 7.65

115 gr. HP ....#3554 $ 7.75

124 gr. FMJ-FP......#3556 $ 8.20

■ 38 CALIBER (.357)

110 gr. HP ....#3570 $ 7.75

125 gr. HP ....#3571 $ 7.90

125 gr. FP ....#3573 $ 7.90

---

38 Caliber (.357) continued

Price Per 100
Retail

158 gr. HP............#3575 $ 8.25

158 gr. FP ....#3578 $ 8.25

160 gr. FMJ ....#3579 $ 9.55

■ 41 CALIBER (.410)

210 gr. HP ....#4100 $10.00

■ 44 CALIBER (.430)

200 gr. HP ....#4410 $10.00

240 gr. HP ....#4420 $10.90

240 gr. FMJ-FP......#4427 $11.65

■ 45 CALIBER (.451)

Price Per 100
Retail

185 gr. HP, ACP ....#4510 $10.35

185 gr. Target
SWC, ACP............#4513 $10.65

230 gr. FMJ-RN .....#4517 $10.90

NEW

230 gr. FMJ-FP......#4518 $10.90

■ 45 CALIBER (.452)

250 gr. Long
Colt HP ....#4520 $11.10

LEGEND

BBWC—Bevel Base Wadcutter   HP—Hollow Point
BT—Boat Tail   RN—Round Nose
DEWC—Double End Wadcutter   SJ—Short Jacket
FMJ—Full Metal Jacket   SP—Spire Point
FP—Flat Point   SWC—Semi-Wadcutter
HBWC—Hollow Base Wadcutter   SX—Super Explosive

Packed 50 per box. All others packed 20 per box.

LEAD PISTOL BULLETS

Boxed Price Per 100
Bulk Price Per 1000

Retail

38 cal. (.358)
148 gr. ....#3580 $ 5.35
BBWC ....*#3581   42.00

38 cal. (.358)
148 gr. ....#3582 $ 5.35
HBWC ....*#3583   42.00

NEW
38 cal. (.358)
148 gr. ....(Bulk only)
DEWC ....*#3585 $42.00

38 cal. (.358)   #3586 $ 5.55
158 gr. RN ......*#3587   45.00

38 cal. (.358)   #3588 $ 5.55
158 gr. SWC ....*#3589   45.00

44 cal. (.430)   #4430 $ 8.00
240 gr. SWC ....*#4431   66.00

45 cal. (.452)   #4526 $ 7.00
200 gr. SWC ....*#4527   60.55

500 Per Box except 44, 400 Per Box

Hornady Crimp-on Gas Checks

Designed with open edges thicker than sidewalls. Size die crimp assures tight fit to the bullet. They're permanent.

Before sizing on bullets   **After** sizing on bullets

	Price Per 1000 Retail			Price Per 1000 Retail
22 cal. ....#7010	$ 8.80		32 cal. (8mm)....#7080	$10.00
6mm cal......... #7020	8.80		338 cal.............#7090	10.00
25 cal. ....#7030	8.80		348 cal.............#7100	10.00
6.5mm cal. ......#7040	8.80		35 cal. ....#7110	8.80
270 cal. ....#7050	10.00		375 cal.............#7120	10.00
7mm cal. ....#7060	10.00		44 cal. ....#7130	12.75
30 cal. ....#7070	10.00		45 cal. ....#7140	12.75

NOSLER BULLETS

PARTITION™ BULLETS

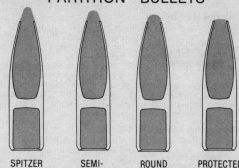

| SPITZER | SEMI-SPITZER | ROUND NOSE | PROTECTED POINT |

While Nosler bullets resemble traditional bullet styles outwardly, the cutaway drawings illustrate some basic inside design features that put these bullets in a class of their own.

The Partition bullet, easily recognized by the lead core visible in the base end, is a unique concept in hunting bullet design. This lead core, held in position by the integral partition, retains more than half the bullet weight, providing controlled expansion and deeper penetration and game-stopping power on heavy game.

The Solid Base bullet, featuring a thick copper base, is a superbly accurate bullet for all types of shooting.

Both bullet styles are manufactured by a special impact-extrusion process which allows absolute control over wall thickness, weight distribution and concentricity for better radial and axial balance.

SOLID BASE BOAT TAIL BULLETS

SPITZER BOAT TAIL   HOLLOW POINT

CAL.	DIAMETER	BULLET WEIGHT AND STYLE	100 PER BOX
22	.224	50 Gr. Spitzer	$ 7.50
	.224	50 Gr. Hollow-Point	7.55
	.224	50 Gr. Hollow-Point, Match	9.75
	.224	52 Gr. Hollow-Point	8.95
	.224	52 Gr. Hollow-Point, Match	10.50
	.224	55 Gr. Spitzer	7.95
	.224	60 Gr. Spitzer	8.25
6MM	.243	70 Gr. Hollow-Point	10.25
	.243	70 Gr. Hollow-Point, Match	13.30
	.243	85 Gr. Spitzer	10.50
	.243	100 Gr. Spitzer	11.05
25	.257	100 Gr. Spitzer	11.20
	.257	120 Gr. Spitzer	12.00
6.5 mm	.264	120 Gr. Spitzer	12.35
270	.277	100 Gr. Spitzer	11.35
	.277	130 Gr. Spitzer	12.60
	.277	150 Gr. Spitzer	13.20
7MM	.284	120 Gr. Spitzer	12.00
	.284	140 Gr. Spitzer	12.70
	.284	150 Gr. Spitzer	13.10
30	.308	150 Gr. Flat Point	12.85
	.308	150 Gr. Spitzer	12.85
	.308	150 Gr. Hollow-Point	12.85
	.308	150 Gr. Hollow-Point, Match	16.10
	.308	165 Gr. Spitzer	13.25
	.308	168 Gr. Hollow-Point	13.30
	.308	168 Gr. Hollow-Point, Match	16.80
	.308	170 Gr. Flat Point	13.25
	.308	180 Gr. Spitzer	13.60

CAL.	DIAMETER	BULLET WEIGHT AND STYLE	50 PER BOX
6MM	.243	95 Gr. Spitzer	$12.45
	.243	100 Gr. Semi-Spitzer	12.65
25	.257	100 Gr. Spitzer	12.65
	.257	115 Gr. Spitzer	13.20
	.257	117 Gr. Semi-Spitzer	13.20
6.5MM	.264	140 Gr. Spitzer	14.15
270	.277	130 Gr. Spitzer	13.70
	.277	150 Gr. Spitzer	14.35
	.277	160 Gr. Semi-Spitzer	14.60
7MM	.284	140 Gr. Spitzer	14.15
	.284	150 Gr. Spitzer	14.35
	.284	160 Gr. Spitzer	14.70
	.284	175 Gr. Semi-Spitzer	15.10
30	.308	150 Gr. Spitzer	14.30
	.308	165 Gr. Spitzer	14.70
	.308	180 Gr. Spitzer	15.35
	.308	180 Gr. Protected Point	15.35
	.308	200 Gr. Round Nose	15.65
338	.338	210 Gr. Spitzer	19.65
	.338	250 Gr. Round Nose	21.05

REMINGTON BULLETS

"Core-Lokt® Bullets"

The "Number One Mushroom"—a name given by hunters everywhere to the Remington center fire cartridges with "Core-Lokt" bullets.

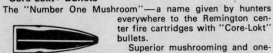

Superior mushrooming and one-shot stopping power are the results of the advanced design of "Core-Lokt" bullets: metal jacket and lead core are locked together by the jacket's heavy mid-section. "Core-Lokt" bullets are available in a wide variety of types and weights.

Bronze Point Expanding Bullet

A top performing all-around bullet of a unique design for extra long range accuracy and controlled expansion. Travels in a flat trajectory and has great wind bucking qualities.

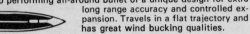

NEW ORDER NO.	OLD ORDER NO.		DESCRIPTION	WT. (LBS.) PER 100
17 cal. (.172)				
B1705	B22936		25 gr. PLHP	0.3
22 cal. (.224)				
B2210	B22704		45 gr. SP	0.7
B2220	B27710		50 gr. PSP	0.7
B2230	B22708		50 gr. MC	0.7
B2240	B22950		50 gr. PLHP	0.7
B2250	B22956		50 gr. PL Match	0.7
B2260	B22948		52 gr. HPBR	0.8
B2270	B22924		55 gr. PSP	0.8
B2280	B22952		55 gr. PLHP	0.8
B2290	B22958		55 gr. PL Match	0.8
B2265	B23558		55 gr. MC WO/C	0.8
6mm (.243)				
B2420	B22966		80 gr. PSP	1.2
B2430	B22954		80 gr. PLHP	1.2
B2440	B22960		80 gr. PL Match	1.2
B2460	B22920		100 gr .PSPCL	1.5
25 cal. (.257)				
B2510	B22752		87 gr. PLHP	1.4
B2520	B22730		100 gr. PSPCL (25-06)	1.5
B2540	B22736		120 gr. PSPCL (25-06)	1.8
6.5mm (.264)				
B2610	B22926		120 gr. PSPCL	1.8
270 cal. (.277)				
B2710	B23744		100 gr. PSP	1.5
B2720	B22746		130 gr. PSPCL	1.9
B2730	B22748		130 gr. BrPt	1.9
B2740	B22750		150 gr. SPCL	2.2
7mm (.284)				
B2830	B22756		150 gr. PSPCL	2.2
B2850	B22918		175 gr. PSPCL 7mm Rem.	2.6
30 cal. (.308)				
B3010	B22796		110 gr. SP Carbine	1.6
B3020	B22770		150 gr. BrPt (30-06)	2.2
B3025	B22774		150 gr. SPCL (30-30)	2.2
B3030	B22776		150 gr. PSPCL	2.2
B3040	B23594		165 gr. PSPCL	2.4
B3050	B22782		170 gr. SPCL	2.5
B3060	B22784		180 gr. BrPt	2.6
B3070	B22786		180 gr. SPCL	2.6

* .360 dia. for best accuracy. † Also available in bulk pack.

"Power-Lokt"® Bullets

Remington "Power-Lokt" bullets are uniquely designed with the core and jacket electrolytically bonded into a one-piece unit. This exclusive process produces a better balance and more concentric bullet of uniformly high performance, rapid expansion and amazing accuracy.

ABBREVIATIONS

BrPt—Bronze Point
CL—Core-Lokt
GC—Gas Check
HP—Hollow Point
J—Jacketed
LD—Lead
MC—Metal Case
PL—Power-Lokt
PSP—Pointed Soft Point
SJ—Semi-Jacketed
SP—Soft Point
WC—Wadcutter
SWC—Semi-Wadcutter

NEW ORDER NO.	OLD ORDER NO.		DESCRIPTION	WT. (LBS.) PER 100
30 Cal. (.308) Cont'd				
B3080	B22788		180 gr. PSPCL	2.6
B3090	B22792		220 gr. SPCL	3.2
32 cal. (.320)				
B3250	B22828		170 gr. SPCL	2.5
8mm (.323)				
B3270	B22984		185 gr. PSPCL	2.8
B3280	B22986		220 gr. PSPCL	3.3
35 cal. (.358)				
B3510	B22868		200 gr. SPCL	2.9
9mm (.354)				
B3550	B22942		115 gr. JHP	1.8
B3552	B22842		124 gr. MC	1.9
38 cal.				
B3810	B22944		95 gr. SJHP	1.4
357/38 cal. (.357)				
B3570	B23586		110 gr. SJHP	1.6
B3572	B22866		125 gr. SJHP	1.9
B3574	B22846		158 gr. SP	2.3
B3576	B22938		158 gr. SJHP	2.3
357 cal. (.358)				
B3578	B22856		158 gr. LEAD SWC†	2.3
38 cal. (.360)*				
B3830	B22850		148 gr. LD WC†	2.2
38 cal. (.358)				
B3840	B22854		158 gr. LEAD†	2.3
B3850	B23568		158 gr. LEAD HP	2.3
41 mag. (.310)				
B4110	B22888		210 gr. SP	3.1
41 mag. (.411)				
B4120	B22922		210 gr. LEAD	3.1
44 cal. (.430)				
B4405	B23588		180 gr. SJHP	2.8
B4410	B22906		240 gr. SP	3.5
B4420	B22940		240 gr. SJHP	3.5
44 cal. (.432)				
B4430	B22884		240 gr. LEAD GC	3.5
B4440	B22768		240 gr. LEAD	3.5
45 cal. (.451)				
B4530	B22892		230 gr. MC†	3.4
B4510	B22890		185 gr. MCWC†	2.7
B4520	B22586		185 gr. JHP	2.7

REMINGTON BULLETS

Remington brass cases with 5% more brass for extra strength in head section—annealed neck section for longer reloading life—primer pocket dimension controlled to .0005 inch to assure precise primer fit—heavier bridge and sidewalls—formed and machined to exacting tolerances for consistent powder capacity—choice of seventy-one center fire rifle, pistol and revolver cases—

Rifle Cases (Unprimed)

	QTY. PER BOX	"KLEANBORE" PRIMER NO.	PRICE PER BOX
17 REMINGTON • U17REM ★	20	7½	$6.11
22 HORNET • U22HRN	50	6½	8.89
222 REMINGTON • U222R	20	7½ .	4.27
222 REMINGTON MAGNUM • U222MG	20	7½	4.83
22-250 REMINGTON • U22250	20	9½	6.11
★ 223 REMINGTON • U223	20	7½	5.28
6mm REMINGTON • U6MM	20	9½	6.11
243 WINCHESTER • U243	20	9½	6.11
25-06 REMINGTON • U2506	20	9½	6.44
270 WINCHESTER • U270	20	9½	6.44
7mm-08 REMINGTON • U7MM08	20	9½	6.11
7mm EXPRESS REMINGTON • U7MM06 ‡	20	9½	6.44
7mm REMINGTON MAGNUM • U7MMAG	20	9½M	8.00
30 CARBINE • U30CAR	50	6½	9.26
30-06 SPRINGFIELD • U3006	20	9½	6.44
30-30 WINCHESTER • U3030	20	9½	5.53
300 WINCHESTER MAGNUM • U300W	20	9½M	8.00
8mm REMINGTON MAGNUM • U8MMAG	20	9½M	8.45
308 WINCHESTER • U308	20	9½	6.11
45-70 GOVERNMENT • U4570	20	9½	5.94

Pistol and Revolver Cases

	QTY. PER BOX	"KLEANBORE" PRIMER NO.	PRICE PER BOX
357 MAGNUM (BRASS) • U357B	50	5½	6.95
9mm LUGER AUTO PISTOL • U9MLUG	50	1½	8.89
38 SPECIAL (BRASS) • U38SPB	50	1½	6.30
41 REMINGTON MAGNUM • U41MAG	50	2½	9.36
44 REMINGTON MAGNUM • U44MAG	50	2½	9.44
45 COLT • U45CLT	50	2½	9.44
45 AUTO • U45AP	50	2½	8.89

* Designed for Remington No. 7½ primer only. Substitutions not recommended. U number is unprimed.

‡ Interchangeable with 280 Rem.

★ NEW for 1981.

Bench Rest Cases

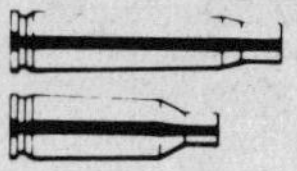

	QTY. PER BOX	"KLEANBORE" PRIMER NO.	PRICE PER BOX
	20	7½	$6.20

Order No. URBR Remington .308 BR case ready for sizing, shortened and necked down to .224, 6mm, or 7mm.

Remington "Kleanbore" CENTER FIRE PRIMERS

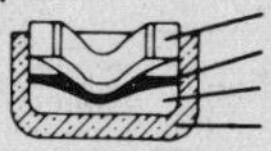

ANVIL
PAPER DISC
PRIMER MIX
PRIMER CUP

PRIMER NO.	ORDER NO.	DESCRIPTION
Small Pistol 1½	X 22600	Brass. Nickel-plated. For small revolver and pistol cartridges.
Large Pistol 2½	X 22604	Brass. Nickel-plated. For large revolver and pistol cartridges.
Small Pistol 5½	X 22626	Brass. Nickel-plated. Specially designed for 32 S & W and 357 Magnum cartridges.
Small Rifle 6½	X 22606	Brass. Nickel-plated. For small rifle cartridges other than those noted under Primer No. 7½.
Small Rifle Bench Rest 7½	X 22628	Brass. Copper-plated. Specially designed for 17 Rem., 221 Rem., "Fire Ball," 222 Rem., 222 Rem. Mag., 22 Rem. BR and 223 Rem. cartridges.
Large Rifle 9½	X 22608	Brass. For large rifle cartridges.
Magnum Rifle 9½M	X 22622	Brass. For use in belted magnum cartridges, 264 Win., 6.5mm Rem. Magnum., 7mm Rem. Magnum, 300 Win. Magnum, 300 H&H Magnum, 8mm Rem. Magnum, 350 Rem. Magnum, 375 H&H Magnum, 458 Win. Magnum cartridges.

PERCUSSION CAPS

SIZE	INSIDE DIA.	ORDER NO.	DESCRIPTION
10	.162"	X 22616	A hotter primer mix to assure more reliable ignition of both black powder and substitutes. Uniform, dependable performance. F.C. trimmed edge, foil-lined, center fire. Identical in length, priming mixture, weight of charge.
11	.167"	X 22618	
12	.172"	X 22620	

All Remington Center Fire Primers and Percussion Caps packed 100 per box (PC caps—tin), 1,000 per carton, 5,000 per case.

SIERRA BULLETS

Stock No.	Description	Price
.22 Caliber .223" Diameter Hornet		
1100	40 gr. Hornet	$7.20
1110	45gr. Hornet	7.20
.22 Caliber .224" Diameter Hornet		
1200	40 gr. Hornet	$7.20
1210	45gr. Hornet	7.20
.22 Caliber .224" Diameter High Velocity		
1300	45gr. SMP	$7.20
1310	45gr. SPT	7.20
1320	50gr. SMP	7.29
1330	50gr. SPT	7.29
1340	50gr. Blitz	7.29
1350	55gr. SMP	7.28
1355	55gr. FMJBT **NEW**	9.90
1360	55gr. SPT	7.38
1365	55gr. SBT	8.46
1370	63gr. SMP	7.65
.22 Caliber .224" Diameter MatchKing		
1400	53gr. HP	$9.72
1410	52gr. HPBT	9.90
6MM .243" Diameter		
1500	60gr. HP	$9.00
1505	70gr. HPBT MatchKing	11.07
1510	75gr. HP	9.54
1520	85gr. SPT	9.90
1530	85gr. HPBT	10.80
1540	100gr. SPT	10.08
1550	100gr. SMP	10.17
1560	100gr. SBT	11.52

Stock No.	Description	Price
.25 Caliber .257" Diameter		
1600	75gr. HP	$9.99
1610	87gr. SPT	10.08
1615	90gr. HPBT	11.07
1620	100gr. SPT	10.17
1630	117gr. SBT	12.33
1640	117gr. SPT	10.98
1650	120gr. HPBT	12.33
6.5MM .264" Diameter		
1700	85gr. HP	$10.62
1710	100gr. HP	11.16
1720	120gr. SPT	11.25
1730	140gr. SBT	13.50
1740	140gr. HPBT MatchKing	14.85
.270 Caliber .277" Diameter		
1800	90gr. HP	$10.80
1810	110gr. SPT	10.89
1820	130gr. SBT	13.23
1830	130gr. SPT	11.25
1840	150gr. SBT	14.04
1850	150gr. RN	11.88
7MM .284" Diameter		
1900	120gr. SPT	$10.89
1910	140gr. SPT	11.70
1915	150gr. HPBT MatchKing **NEW**	15.21
1920	160gr. SBT	14.04
1930	168gr. HPBT MatchKing	15.75
1940	175gr. SBT	15.12
1950	170gr. RN	12.87

SIERRA BULLETS

Stock No.	Description		Price
.375 Caliber .375" Diameter			
3000	300gr. SBT		$13.50*
.45-70 Caliber .458" Diameter			
8900	300gr. HP		$8.10*
9MM .355" Diameter			
8100	90gr. JHP		$7.74
8110	115gr. JHP		$8.01
8120	125gr. FMJ	NEW	$8.19
.38 Caliber .357" Diameter			
8300	110gr. JHC		$7.83
8310	125gr. JSP		8.01
8320	125gr. JHC		8.01
8330	150gr. JHC		8.19
8340	158gr. JSP		8.19
8350	170gr. FMJ Match		10.89
.41 Caliber .410" Diameter			
8500	170gr. JHC		$11.07
8520	210gr. JHC		11.34
8530	220gr. FMJ	NEW	11.97
.44 Magnum .429" Diameter			
8600	180gr. JHC		$11.34
8605	220gr. FMJ Match		11.97
8610	240gr. JHC		11.61
.45 Caliber .451" Diameter			
8800	185gr. JHP		$11.43
8810	185gr. FMJ Match		11.79
8815	230gr. FMJ Match		12.15
8820	240gr. JHP		11.52
.30 Caliber .307" Diameter			
2000	150gr. FN		$11.34
2010	170gr. FN		11.79
2020	125gr. HP		11.07

Stock No.	Description		Price
.30 Caliber .308" Diameter			
2100	110gr. RN		$8.64
2105	110gr. FMJ		8.64
2110	110gr. HP		10.53
2120	125gr. SPT		10.80
2125	150gr. SBT		12.78
2130	150gr. SPT		11.25
2135	150gr. RN		11.43
2140	165gr. HPBT		13.86
2145	165gr. SBT		13.86
2150	180gr. SPT		11.97
2160	180gr. SBT		14.31
2165	200gr. SBT		16.20
2170	180gr. RN		12.06
2180	220gr. RN		13.68
.30 Caliber .308" Diameter MatchKing			
2190	150gr. HPBT	NEW	$15.21
2200	168gr. HPBT		15.75
2210	190gr. HPBT		17.10
2220	180gr. HPBT		16.74
2230	200gr. HPBT		17.55
2240	220gr. HPBT		19.71
.303 Caliber .311" Diameter			
2300	150gr. SPT		$12.60
2310	180gr. SPT		13.23
8MM .323" Diameter			
2400	150gr. SPT		$12.42
2410	175gr. SPT		12.96
2420	220gr. SBT		9.90*
.338 Caliber .338" Diameter			
2600	250gr. SBT		$10.44*
.35 Caliber .358" Diameter			
2800	200gr. RN		$7.02*

SPEER BULLETS

Jacketed Pistol Bullets
(Packed 100 Per Box)

9mm CALIBER (.355)

88 grain Hollow Point, #4000 **$7.45**

100 grain Hollow Point, #3983 **7.45**

125 grain Soft Point, #4005 **8.00**

38 CALIBER (.357)

110 grain Hollow Point, #4007 **7.75**

125 grain Hollow Point, #4013 **7.90**

125 grain Soft Point, #4011 **7.90**

140 grain Hollow Point, #4203 **8.25**

146 grain Hollow Point, #4205 **8.40**

158 grain JHP, #4211 **8.25**

158 grain Soft Point, #4217 **8.25**

160 grain Soft Point, #4223 **8.30**

41 CALIBER (.410)

200 grain Hollow Point, #4405 **10.00**

220 grain Soft Point, #4417 **10.50**

44 CALIBER (.429)

200 grain Magnum HP, #4425 **10.00**

225 grain Hollow Point, #4435 **10.50**

240 grain Soft Point, #4447 **10.70**

240 grain Magnum HP, #4453 **$10.90**

240 grain Magnum SP, #4457 **10.90**

45 CALIBER (.451)

200 grain HP, #4477 **10.90**

225 grain Magnum HP, #4479 **11.15**
260 grain Hollow Point, #4481 **12.20**

Lead Pistol Bullets
(Packed 100 Per Box)

9mm CALIBER (.356)

125 grain RN, #4601 **6.25**

38 CALIBER (.358)

148 grain BBWC, #4605 **5.90**

148 grain HBWC, #4617 **5.90**

158 grain Semi-Wadcutter, #4623 **6.20**

158 grain Round Nose, #4647 **6.20**

44 CALIBER (.430)

240 grain SWC, #4660 **8.55**

45 CALIBER (.452)

200 grain SWC, #4677 **7.55**

230 grain Round Nose, #4690 **9.20**

250 grain SWC, #4683 **$9.20**

Rifle Bullets
(Packed 100 per box)

22 CALIBER (.223)

40 grain Spire Point #1005 **6.85**   45 grain Spitzer #1011 **6.55**

22 CALIBER (.224)

40 grain Spire Point #1017 **6.85**   45 grain Spitzer #1023 **6.55**

50 grain Spitzer, #1029 **6.65**

52 grain Hollow Point, #1035 **7.10**

55 grain Spitzer Soft Point #1049 **7.25**

55 grain Full Metal Jacket, #1045 **7.05**

55 grain Spitzer, #1047 **6.85**

70 grain Semi-Spitzer, #1053 **8.95**

6mm CALIBER (.243)

75 grain Hollow Point, #1205 **8.70**

80 grain Spitzer, #1211 **8.55**

85 grain Boat Tail Spitzer Soft Point, #1213 **9.95**

90 grain Full Metal Jacket, #1215 **9.30**

90 grain Spitzer, #1217 **8.90**

105 grain Round Nose, #1223 **9.45**

105 grain Spitzer, #1229 **9.3C**

25 CALIBER (.257)

87 grain Spitzer, #1241 **9.20**

100 grain Hollow Point, #1407 **10.90**

100 grain Spitzer, #1405 **$9.50**

120 grain Spitzer, #1411 **10.15**

6.5mm CALIBER (.263)

120 grain Spitzer, #1435 **10.70**

140 grain Spitzer, #1441 **11.15**

270 CALIBER (.277)

100 grain Hollow Point, #1447 **10.00**

100 grain Spitzer, #1453 **9.80**

130 grain Spitzer, #1459 **10.55**

130 grain Grand Slam, #1465 **11.50**

150 grain Spitzer, #1605 **11.10**

150 grain Grand Slam, #1608 ***12.15**

7mm CALIBER (.284)

115 grain Hollow Point, #1617 **10.20**

130 grain Spitzer, #1623 **10.45**

145 grain Spitzer, #1629 **10.70**

160 grain Spitzer, #1635 **11.35**

160 grain Grand Slam, #1638 ***12.70**

◔ HOT-COR BULLETS

* Packed 50 per box
** Packed 500 per box

SPEER BULLETS

160 grain Magnum *MAG-TIP*, #1637 — $13.60

175 grain Magnum *MAG-TIP*, #1641 — 13.10

175 grain Grand Slam, #1643 — *13.05

30 CALIBER (.308)

100 grain PLINKER,® #1805 — 6.55

110 grain HP VARMINTER, #1835 — 7.65

110 grain Round Nose, #1845 — 8.45

110 grain Spire Point, #1855 — 9.25

130 grain Hollow Point, #2005 — 10.90

130 grain Flat Soft Point, #2007 — 10.50

150 grain Flat Nose, #2011 — 10.35

150 grain Round Nose, #2017 — 10.35

150 grain Boat Tail Spitzer Soft Point, #2022 — 12.75

150 grain Spitzer, #2023 — 10.35

150 grain Magnum *MAG-TIP*, #2025 — $12.50

165 grain Round Nose, #2029 — 11.05

165 grain Boat Tail Spitzer Soft Point, #2034 — 12.00

165 grain Spitzer, #2035 — 10.90

165 grain Grand Slam, #2038 — *13.40

170 grain Flat Nose, #2041 — 10.90

180 grain Round Nose, #2047 — 11.20

180 grain Boat Tail Spitzer Soft Point, #2052 — 12.35

180 grain Spitzer, #2053 — 11.55

180 grain Magnum *MAG-TIP*, #2059 — 14.10

180 grain Grand Slam, #2063 — *13.70

200 grain Spitzer, #2211 — *6.45

303 CALIBER (.311)

150 grain Spitzer, #2217 — 11.50

180 grain Round Nose, #2223 — 12.00

32 CALIBER (.321)

170 grain Flat Nose, #2259 — $11.25

8mm CALIBER (.323)

150 grain Spitzer, #2277 — 11.10

170 grain Semi-Spitzer, #2283 — 11.45

200 grain Spitzer Soft Point, #2285 — 6.70

338 CALIBER (.338)

200 grain Spitzer, #2405 — *6.90

275 grain Semi-Spitzer, #2411 — 7.70

35 CALIBER (.358)

180 grain Flat Nose, #2435 — 13.90

250 grain Spitzer, #2453 — *7.50

375 CALIBER (.375)

235 grain Semi-Spitzer, #2471 — *8.10

45 CALIBER (.458)

400 grain Flat Nose, #2479 — *10.80

HOT-COR BULLETS

* Packed 50 per box

** Packed 500 per box

DOMESTIC PRIMERS

MAKE	PRIMER NUMBER	TYPE	DIA.	PRICE PER 1,000	DESCRIPTION	CALIBERS		
For Small Pistol Cartridges								
Remington	1½	Small Pistol	.175"	$12.70	Brass. Nickel-plated. For centerfire Pistol and Revolver cartridges.	25 Automatic 30 Luger Auto 32 Automatic 32 S&W 32 S&W Long 32 Short Colt	32 Colt New Police 9mm Luger Automatic 38 S&W 38 Special	38 Long Colt 38 Colt New Police 38 Super-Auto Colt 38 Automatic 38 Automatic Colt 380 Automatic
Remington	5½	Small Pistol	.175"	14.60				
Winchester Western	1½-108	Small Pistol	.175"	12.75				
CCI	500	Small Pistol	.175"	11.30				
CCI	550	Mag. Sm. Pistol	.175"		Brass. Nickel-plated. For centerfire revolver cartridges.	357 Magnum		
Winchester Western	1½M-108	Mag.Sm. Pistol	.175"	14.50				
For Large Pistol Cartridges								
Remington	2½	Large Pistol	.210"	12.70	Brass. Nickel-plated. For centerfire pistol and revolver cartridges, also brass shot shells except .410 gauge.	38-40 Winchester 44 S&W Special 44-40 Winchester 45 Colt	45 Auto Rim 45 Automatic	
Winchester Western	7-111	Large Pistol	.210"	12.75				
CCI	300	Large Pistol	.210"	12.75				
CCI	350	Mag. Lg. Pistol	.210"	14.60		41 Magnum		
Winchester Western	7M-111F	Mag.Lg. Pistol	.210"	14.50		44 Magnum		
For Small Rifle Cartridges								
Remington	6½-116	Small Rifle	.175"	12.70	Brass. Nickel-plated. For centerfire rifle and revolver cartridges.	218 Bee 22 Hornet 25-20 Winchester	30 Carbine 32-20 Winchester	
Winchester	6½-116	Small Rifle	.175"	12.75				
CCI	400	Small Rifle	.175"	12.75				
CCI	BR-4	Small Rifle	.175"	18.95				
Remington	7½	Small Rifle BR	.175"	14.70	Brass. Copper plated. For centerfire rifle and XP-100 pistol cartridges.	221 Remington "Fireball" 222 Remington 22 Remington "Jet" Magnum	222 Remington Mag. 223 Remington (5.56mm) 22 BR Remington 7mm BR Remington	17 Remington 256 Winchester Magnum
CCI	450	Mag. Sm. Rifle	.175"	14.60				
For Large Rifle Cartridges								
Remington	9½	Large Rifle	.210"	12.70		220 Swift 22-250 Remington 25-06 Remington 243 Winchester 6mm Remington 225 Winchester 25-35 Winchester 250 Savage 257 Roberts 270 Winchester 280 Remington 284 Winchester	7mm Express Remington 7mm-08 Remington 7mm Mauser 30-30 Winchester 30 Remington 30-06 Springfield 30-40 Krag 300 Savage 303 Savage 303 British 308 Winchester 32 Winchester Special	32 Remington 32-40 Winchester 8mm Mauser 348 Winchester 35 Remington 358 Winchester 38-55 Winchester 444 Marlin 45-70 Government
Winchester Western	8½-120	Large Rifle	.210"	12.75				
CCI	200	Large Rifle	.210"	12.75				
CCI	BR-2	Large Rifle	.210"	18.95				
Remington	9½M	Large Rifle	.210"	14.70	Brass. Nickel-plated. For centerfire belted Magnum Rifle.	264 Winchester Magnum 6.5mm Remington Magnum 7mm Remington Magnum 300 H&H Magnum 300 Winchester Magnum	338 Winchester Magnum 350 Remington Magnum 375 H&H Magnum 8mm Remington Magnum 458 Winchester Magnum	
CCI	250	Mag. Lg. Rifle	.210"	14.60				

For Shotgun Shells (Battery Cup Type)

MAKE	No.	DESCRIPTION	PRICE PER 1,000
Remington	97 (209 Size)	Battery Cup. Used in Remington 12-and 20-gauge target loads and all 28-gauge loads with plastic base wad.	$23.10
Remington	57	Battery Cup. Used in all Remington 10-, 12-, 16-, 20- and 28-gauge shells (except 12 and 20 plastic target loads and all 28-gauge shells with plastic base wad.)	24.10
Remington	97-4	Battery Cup. Used in 410 Gauge, 2½ and 3" plastic shotshells with solid plastic base wad.	24.10

MAKE	No.	DESCRIPTION	PRICE P 1,000
Winchester Western	209	Battery Cup. Used in 10, 12, 16, 20, 28 and .410 gauge.	$22.95
CCI	109	Battery Cup. (Winchester Size).	24.35
CCI	157	Battery Cup. (Remington Size).	24.35
CCI	209	Trap and Skeet	22.75

FEDERAL PRIMERS

Code Number	Type	Use	Nominal Diameter in Inches	Color Coding	Per 1000
100	Small Pistol	Standard velocity pistol and revolver loads.	.175	Green	$12.90
150	Large Pistol	Standard velocity and magnum pistol and revolver loads.	.210	Green	12.90
200	Small Rifle	Rifle; high velocity and magnum pistol and revolver loads.	.175	Red	12.90
205	Small Rifle	Thick cup design especially for 17 Rem. and 22 centerfire loads.	.175	Purple	12.90
210	Large Rifle	Standard rifle loads.	.210	Red	12.90
215	Large Magnum Rifle	Magnum rifle loads.	.210	Purple	14.85
205M	Small Rifle Match	Match version of No. 205.	.175	Purple	17.85
210M	Large Rifle Match	Match version of No. 210.	.210	Red	17.85
209	Shotshell	Standard and magnum loads in 12, 16 and 20 gauge.	.243		23.35
410	Shotshell	For .410 and 28-gauge loads.	.243		23.35

FEDERAL UNPRIMED CASES

RIFLE—Unprimed

Code Number	Caliber	No. Per Box	Recommended Federal Primer Number for Handloads	Per Box
222 UP	222 Remington	20	200 or 205	$4.10
223 UP	223 Remington	20	200 or 205	5.10
22250 UP	22-250 Remington	20	210	5.90
243 UP	243 Winchester	20	210	5.90
2506 UP	25-06 Remington	20	210	6.20
270 UP	270 Winchester	20	210	6.20
7R UP	7mm Rem. Magnum	20	215	7.70
30C UP	30 Carbine	20*	200	3.55
3030 UP	30-30 Winchester	20	210	5.35
3006 UP	30-06 Springfield	20	210	6.20
300W UP	300 Win. Magnum	20	215	7.70
308 UP	308 Winchester	20	210	5.90
8 UP	8mm Mauser	20	210	6.70
222M UP	222 Rem. Match†	20*	205M	5.05
308M UP	308 Win. Match†	20*	210M	6.80

*Packed in partitioned carton, without plastic "Cartridge Carrier pack.
†Nickel-plated case.

PISTOL—Unprimed

Code Number	Caliber	No. Per Box	Recommended Federal Primer Number for Handloads	Per Box
380 UP	380 Auto Pistol	50	100	$5.85
9 UP	9mm Luger Auto Pistol	50	200	8.60
38 UP	38 Special	50	100*	6.10
357 UP	357 Magnum	50	200	6.65
44 UP	44 Rem. Magnum	50	150	9.10
45 UP	45 Automatic	50	150	8.60
45 LCA UP	45 Colt	50	50	9.10

Packed 50 per box, 20 boxes per case of 1000.
*For standard velocity loads only. No. 200 recommended for high velocity loads.

UNPRIMED CASES

WINCHESTER CENTERFIRE RIFLE CARTRIDGE CASES
(Packed 20 per Box)

Cartridge Case Caliber & Symbol	Per 100
*218 Bee U218B Unprimed	$17.30
*22 Hornet U22H Unprimed	17.30
22-250 U22250 Unprimed	29.70
220 Swift U220S Unprimed	29.70
222 Remington U222R Unprimed	20.80
223 Remington U223R	25.65
225 Winchester U225 Unprimed	25.65
243 Winchester U243 Unprimed	29.70
6mm Remington U6MMR	29.70
*25-20 Winchester U2520 Unprimed	19.80
*256 Winchester Magnum U256P	19.80
250 Savage U250 Unprimed	31.90
25-06 Remington U2506 Unprimed	31.25
257 Roberts U257 Unprimed	31.90
264 Winchester Magnum U264 Unprimed	38.90

Cartridge Case Caliber & Symbol	Per 100
270 Winchester U270 Unprimed	$31.25
284 Winchester U284 Unprimed	33.65
7 mm Mauser U7MM Unprimed	33.65
7 mm Remington Magnum U7 Mag. Unprimed	38.90
*30 Carbine UW30M1 Unprimed	17.95
30-30 Winchester U30C Unprimed	26.90
30-06 Springfield U3006 Unprimed	31.25
30-40 Krag U3040 Unprimed	33.65
300 Winchester Magnum U30WM Unprimed	38.90
300 H & H Magnum U300H Unprimed	42.80
300 Savage U300	31.90
303 British UW303B Unprimed	33.65
308 Winchester U308 Unprimed	29.70

*Packed 50 to the box—all others 20 per box.

Cartridge Case Caliber & Symbol	Per 100
32 Winchester Special U32W Unprimed	$28.85
*32-20 Winchester U3220 Unprimed	19.80
8 mm Mauser U8MM Unprimed	33.65
338 Winchester Magnum U338 Unprimed	38.90
348 Winchester U348 Unprimed	41.25
35 Remington U35R Unprimed	31.90
358 Winchester U358 Unprimed	33.65
375 H & H Magnum U375H Unprimed	45.75
*38-40 Winchester U3840 Unprimed	19.80
38-55 Winchester	38.00
*44-40 Winchester U4440 Unprimed	18.30
* 44 Remington Magnum U44M	18.30
45-70 Government U4570 Unprimed	28.90
458 Winchester Magnum U458 Unprimed	45.75
375 Winchester U375W Unprimed	38.90

WINCHESTER PISTOL & REVOLVER CARTRIDGE CASES
(Packed 50 per Box)

Cartridge Case Caliber & Symbol	Per 100
25 Automatic U25A Unprimed	$12.15
256 Winchester Magnum U256 Unprimed	19.80
32 Automatic U32A Unprimed	11.70
32 S & W U32SW Unprimed	10.50
32 S & W Long U32SWL Unprimed (32 Colt New Police)	10.50

Cartridge Case Caliber & Symbol	Per 100
357 Magnum (nickel-plated) U357 Unprimed	$13.55
U9 mm Luger Unprimed	17.40
38 S & W (38 Colt New Police) U38SW Unprimed	11.70
38 Special U38S Unprimed	12.30

Cartridge Case Caliber & Symbol	Per 100
38 Automatic (& 38 Super) U38A Unprimed	$14.30
380 Automatic U380A Unprimed	11.70
41 Remington Magnum U41M	18.15
44 S & W UW44S Unprimed	15.35
44 Magnum U44M Unprimed	18.30
45 Colt U45C Unprimed	18.30
45 Automatic U45A Unprimed	17.40

NORMA EMPTY UNPRIMED RIFLE CASES

Caliber	Box 20
220 Swift	$9.75
222 Remington	5.95
22 SAV High Power	9.75
243 Winchester	8.60
6.5 Jap	9.75
6.5 Norma (6.5x55)	9.75
6.5 Carcano	9.75
270 Winchester	9.30
7mm Mauser	9.30
7x57 R (Rimmed)	10.35
7mm Rem. Mag.	11.00
7x64	10.35
7.5x55 (7.5 Swiss)	10.00

Caliber	Box 20
30 U.S. Carbine	$4.90
7.62 Russian	11.00
30-06 Springfield	8.60
22-250 Rem.	8.60
30-30 WIN	9.35
308 Winchester	8.60
308 Norma Magnum	12.70
7.65 Argentine Mauser	10.00
303 British	8.60
7.7mm Jap	10.00
8x57J (.318 dia.)	10.00
8mm Mauser (.323 dia.)	8.60

Caliber	Box 20
358 Norma Belted Magnum	$13.00
9.3x57 Dual Core	11.70
9.3x62 Dual Core	11.70

NORMA EMPTY UNPRIMED PISTOL CASES

	Box 50
9mm Luger	$14.20
38 Special	9.20
357 Magnum	15.00
44 Magnum	17.55
44 Auto Mag	19.20

DU PONT SMOKELESS POWDERS

SHOTSHELL POWDER

Hi-Skor 700-X Double-Base Shotshell Powder. Specifically designed for today's 12-gauge components. Developed to give optimum ballistics at minimum charge weight (means more reloads per pound of powder). 700-X is dense, easy to load, clean to handle and loads uniformly.

PB Shotshell Powder. Produces exceptional 20- and 28-gauge skeet reloads; preferred by many in 12-gauge target loads,

it gives 3-dram equivalent velocity at relatively low chamber pressures.

SR-4756 Powder. Great all-around powder for target and field loads.

SR-7625 Powder. A fast growing "favorite" for reloading target as well as light and heavy field loads in 4 gauges. Excellent velocity-chamber pressure.

IMR-4227 Powder. Can be used effectively for reloading .410-gauge shotshell ammunition.

RIFLE POWDER

IMR-3031 Rifle Powder. Specifically recommended for medium-capacity cartridges.

IMR-4064 Rifle Powder. Has exceptionally uniform burning qualities when used in medium- and large-capacity cartridges.

IMR-4198. Made the Remington 222 cartridge famous. Developed for small- and medium-capacity cartridges.

IMR-4227 Rifle Powder. Fastest burning of the IMR Series. Specifically designed for the 22 Hornet class of cartridges.

SR-4759. Brought back by shooter demand. Available for Cast bullet loads.

IMR-4320. Recommended for high-velocity cartridges.

IMR-4350 Rifle Powder. Gives unusually uniform results when loaded in magnum cartridges. Slowest burning powder of the IMR series.

IMR-4831. Produced as a canister-grade handloading powder. Packaged in 1 lb. canister, 8 lb. caddy and 20 lb. kegs.

IMR-4895 Rifle Powder. The time-tested standard for caliber 30 military ammunition is now being manufactured again. Slightly faster than IMR-4320. Loads uniformly in all powder measures. One of the country's favorite powders.

PISTOL POWDER

PB Powder. Another powder for reloading a wide variety of center-fire handgun ammunition.

IMR-4227 Powder. Can be used effectively for reloading "magnum" handgun ammunition.

"Hi-Skor" 700-X Powder. The same qualities that make it a superior shotshell powder contribute to its excellent

performance in all the popular handguns.

SR-7625 Powder. For reloading a wide variety of center-fire handgun ammunition.

SR-4756, IMR-3031 and IMR-4198. Three more powders in a good selection—all clean burning and with uniform performance.

HERCULES SMOKELESS POWDERS

Eight types of Hercules smokeless sporting powders are available to the handloader. These have been selected from the wide range of powders produced for factory loading to provide at least one type that can be used efficiently and economically for each type of ammunition. These include:

Powder	Packaging				
	1-lb Canisters	4-lb Canisters	5-lb Canisters	8-lb Keg	15-lb Keg
Bullseye	X	X		X	X
Red Dot	X	X		X	X
Green Dot	X	X		X	X
Unique	X	X		X	X
Herco	X	X		X	X
Blue Dot	X		X		
Hercules 2400	X	X		X	X
Reloder 7	X				

BULLSEYE®

A high-energy, quick-burning powder especially designed for pistol and revolver. The most popular powder for .38 special target loads. Can also be used for 12 gauge-1 oz. shotshell target loads.

RED DOT®

The preferred powder for light-to-medium shotshells; specifically designed for 12-gauge target loads. Can also be used for handgun loads.

GREEN DOT®

Designed for 12-gauge medium shotshell loads. Outstanding in 20-gauge skeet loads.

UNIQUE®

Has an unusually broad application from light to heavy shotshell loads. As a handgun powder, it is our most versatile, giving excellent performance in many light to medium-heavy loads.

HERCO®

A long-established powder for high velocity shotshell loads. Designed for heavy and magnum 10-, 12-, 16-, and 20-gauge loads. Can also be used in high-performance handgun loads.

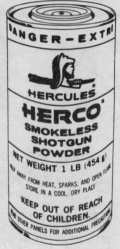

BLUE DOT®

Designed for use in magnum shotshell loads, 10-, 12-, 16-, 20- and 28-gauge. Also provides top performance with clean burning in many magnum handgun loads.

HERCULES 2400®

For use in small-capacity rifle cartridges and .410-Bore shotshell loads. Can also be used for large-caliber magnum handgun cartridges.

RELODER® 7

Designed for use in center-fire rifle cartridges. Has outstanding accuracy in small-capacity rifle cartridges used in bench rest shooting.

HODGDON SMOKELESS POWDER

RIFLE POWDER

H4227 and H4198
H4227 is the fastest burning of the IMR series. Well adapted to Hornet, light bullets in 222 and all bullets in 357 and 44 magnum pistols. Cuts leading with lead bullets. H4198 was developed especially for small and medium capacity cartridges.
1 lb. can $11.75; 8 lb. keg $88.50

H322
A new extruded bench-rest powder which has proved to be capable of producing fine accuracy in the .22 and .308 Bench-rest guns. This powder fills the gap between H4198 and BL-C(2). Performs best in small to medium capacity cases.
1 lb. can $11.75; 8 lb. keg $88.50

SPHERICAL BL-C®, Lot No. 2
A highly popular favorite of the Bench-rest shooters. Best performance is in the 222, and in other cases smaller than 30/06.
1 lb. can $10.95; 8 lb. keg $82.35

SPHERICAL H335®
Similar to BL-C(2), H335 is popular for its performance in medium capacity cases, especially in 222 and 308 Winchester.
1 lb. can $10.95; 8 lb. keg $82.35

4895®
4895 may well be considered the most versatile of all propellants. It gives desirable performance in almost all cases from 222 Rem. to 458 Win. Reduced loads, to as low as 3/5 of maximum, still give target accuracy.
1 lb. can $11.75; 8 lb. keg $88.50

SPHERICAL H380®
This number fills a gap between 4320 and 4350. It is excellent in 22/250, 220 Swift, the 6mm's, 257 and 30/06.
1 lb. can $10.95; 8 lb. keg $82.35

SPHERICAL H414®
A new development in spherical powder. In many popular medium to medium-large calibers, pressure velocity relationship is better.
1 lb. can $10.25; 8 lb. keg $75.00

SPHERICAL H870®
Very slow burning rate adaptable to overbore capacity magnum cases such as 257, 264, 270 and 300 mags with heavy bullets.
1 lb. can $5.95; 8 lb. keg $38.00

SPHERICAL H450®
A powder well adapted to maximum loads in most cartridges. Gives excellent performance in 30/06.
1 lb. can $10.25; 8 lb. keg $75.00

H4831®
Here is a new batch of the original 4831. The most popular of all powders. Use same loading data as our original surplus powder. Outstanding performance with medium and heavy bullets in the 6mm's, 25/06, 270 and magnum calibers.
1 lb. can $11.75; 8 lb. keg $88.50

SHOTGUN AND PISTOL POWDER

HP38
A fast pistol powder for most pistol loading. Especially recommended for mid-range 38 special.
12 oz. can $7.50; 8 lb. keg $67.50

TRAP 100
Trap 100 is a spherical trap and light field load powder, also excellent for target loads in centerfire pistol. Mild recoil.
8 oz. can $4.75; 8 lb. keg $64.75

HS-6 and HS-7
HS-6 and HS-7 for magnum field loads are unsurpassed since they do not pack in the measure. They deliver uniform charges and are dense so allow sufficient wad column for best patterns.
HS-6 and HS-7 1 lb. can $8.95; 8 lb. keg $64.75

H110
A spherical powder made especially for the 30 M1 carbine. H110 also does very well in 357, 44 Spec., 44 Mag. or 410 ga. Shotshell. Magnum primers are recommended for consistent ignition.
1 lb. can $8.95; 8 lb. keg $64.75

NORMA SMOKELESS POWDER

RIFLE POWDERS

NORMA 200
A fast-burning powder, for small capacity cartridge cases as the 222, but also for use with light bullets and/or light loads in larger calibers. **400 g. canister $18.30**

NORMA 201
Slower than the 200, used with lighter bullets in medium-size cases, or with big-caliber cartridges where a large bore volume is to be filled up quickly by expanding gases. case capacity. **500 g. canister $22.50**

NORMA 202
A rifle powder of medium-burning rate that makes it the right choice for cartridges in the 6. 5mm-7mm—30-06 caliber range of regular **500 g. canister $22.50**

NORMA 204
A slow-burning powder, adapted for cartridges with a large case capacity and/or using heavy bullets in relation to the caliber. **500 g. canister $22.50**

NORMA MAGNUM RIFLE POWDER
Exceptionally slow-burning, high-energy powder for highest velocity with large capacity cases. A must for Magnums. **400 g. canister $18.30**

HANDGUN POWDERS

NORMA POWDER R-1
Is a fast-burning, easily-ignited powder especially adapted for revolver cartridges with lead bullets, such as 38 Special target loads. It is clean burning, and the granules are of such size and shape that they flow easily in the powder measure and without binding the cylinder. It also handles very easily in the spoon or powder trickler for shooters who prefer weighing their loads. **275 g. canister $21.95**

NORMA POWDER R-123
Is a slow-burning handgun powder for heavier loads in cartridges such as 357 and 44 Magnum, especially when using jacketed bullets. This powder gives a lower breech pressure and the charge weight can therefore be increased for higher bullet velocities.
400 g. canister $33.35

NORMA RELOADING POWDERS

Rifle Powders/Pulver für Büchsenpatronen

Caliber	Bullet index no.	Bullet weight grains	Max Cartridge length inch	mm	Norma primer	Norma powder	Load grains	grams	Muzzle vel. Feet per sec.	Meter per sec.	Pressure[1] psi	bar
220 Swift	65701	50	2.62	66.5	LR	202	39.3	2.55	3980	1213	53700	3700
222 Rem.	65701 + 65702	50	2.11	53.5	SR	200	21.0	1.36	3200	975	46400	3200
						200	20.2	1.31	3000	914	46400	3200
						200	17.7	1.15	2790	850	46400	3200
	65704	53	2.16	55.0	SR	200	20.8	1.35	3115	950	46400	3200
22-250	65704	53	2.38	60.5	LR	202	36.6	2.37	3710	1130	53700	3700
5.6x52 R	65604	71	2.50	63.5	LR	202	27.0	1.75	2835	864	42100	2900
	65605	71	2.50	63.5	LR	202	27.0	1.75	2835	864	42100	2900
243 Win.	66002 + 66003	100	2.62	66.5	LR	204	45.1	2.92	3070	936	52200	3600
						204	43.8	2.84	2870	875	52200	3600
						204	42.0	2.72	2670	814	52200	3600
6.5 Jap.	66531	139	2.82	71.5	LR	202	30.9	2.00	2270	692	32200	2220
						201	28.2	1.83	2230	680	32200	2220
						200	24.0	1.55	2030	618	32200	2220
	66532	156	2.89	73.5	LR	202	28.2	1.83	2035	620	32200	2220
						201	24.7	1.60	1865	568	32200	2220
						200	20.5	1.33	1665	508	32200	2220
6.5x55	66551	77	2.62	66.5	LR	200	33.2	2.15	2725	830	45000	3100
						200	37.8	2.45	3115	950	45000	3100
						200	34.1	2.21	2915	889	45000	3100
	66512	139	2.99	76.0	LR	204	46.6	3.02	2790	850	45000	3100
						MRP	49.4	3.20	2815	858	45000	3100
						MRP	47.8	3.10	2740	835	45000	3100
	66532	156	3.07	78.0	LR	204	44.2	2.86	2495	760	45000	3100
						204	42.5	2.75	2295	700	45000	3100
						204	39.8	2.58	2095	639	45000	3100
6.5 Carc.	66532	156	2.97	75.5	LR	202	35.5	2.30	2340	713	37700	2600
						200	25.2	1.63	1800	549	37700	2600
270 Win.	66902	130	3.15	80.0	LR	204	57.0	3.69	3140	957	52200	3600
						204	55.0	3.56	2940	896	52200	3600
						204	52.0	3.37	2740	835	52200	3600
	66903	150	3.23	82.0	LR	204	52.4	3.39	2800	853	52200	3600
						204	50.5	3.27	2600	792	52200	3600
						204	46.7	3.02	2400	731	52200	3600
7x57	67002	150	3.05	77.5	LR	202	44.0	2.85	2690	820	49300	3400
						201	40.0	2.59	2555	779	49300	3400
						201	36.5	2.36	2355	718	49300	3400
7x57 R	67002 + 67003	150	3.02	76.7	LR	202	42.9	2.78	2620	799	43500	3000
						201	36.3	2.35	2290	698	43500	3000
Super 7x61	67002	150	3.19	81.0	LR	MRP	67.4	4.37	3165	965	55100	3800
						204	58.5	3.79	2950	899	55100	3800
						204	55.3	3.58	2750	838	55100	3800
7 mm Rem. M.	67002	150	3.25	82.5	LR	MRP	71.4	4.63	3250	990	55100	3800
						204	66.6	4.31	3060	933	55100	3800
						204	62.4	4.04	2860	872	55100	3800
7x64	67002	150	2.13	84.0	LR	204	57.1	3.70	2890	880	52200	3600
						204	52.9	3.43	2690	819	52200	3600
						204	49.5	3.21	2490	758	52200	3600
	67036	175	2.13	84.0	LR	MRP	56.6	3.67	2725	830	52200	3600
						MRP	51.7	3.35	2475	754	52200	3600
						MRP	48.3	3.13	2275	693	52200	3600
280 Rem.	67002	150	3.29	83.5	LR	MRP	59.4	3.85	2980	910	50800	3500
7.5x55 Swiss	67625	180	2.91	74.0	LR	204	52.2	3.38	2650	808	45000	3100
						204	54.0	3.50	2690	820	45000	3100
7.62 Russ.	67623	130	2.66	67.5	LR	201	51.4	3.33	3100	945	47900	3300
	67624	150	2.75	70.0	LR	201	47.8	3.10	2800	853	47900	3300
	67625	180	2.82	71.5	LR	202	47.1	3.05	2595	791	47900	3300
						201	37.2	2.41	2225	678	47900	3300

Caliber	Bullet index no.	Bullet weight grains	Max Cartridge length inch	mm	Norma primer	Norma powder	Load grains	grams	Muzzle vel. Feet per sec.	Meter per sec.	Pressure[1] psi	bar
30 US Carb.	67621	110	1.67	42.5	SR	-	-	-	1970	600	46400	3200
30-06	67621	110	2.87	73.0	LR	201	54.5	3.53	3280	1000	50800	3500
	67623	130	3.11	79.0	LR	202	56.3	3.65	3205	977	50800	3500
	67624	150	3.13	79.5	LR	202	52.5	3.40	2955	901	50800	3500
						MRP	62.4	4.04	2820	860	50800	3500
	67628	180	3.17	80.5	LR	204	56.3	3.65	2700	823	50800	3500
						202	48.5	3.14	2645	806	50800	3500
						201	41.6	2.69	2300	701	50800	3500
	67648	180	3.15	80.0	LR	204	56.3	3.65	2700	823	50800	3500
						202	48.5	3.14	2645	806	50800	3500
						201	41.6	2.69	2300	701	50800	3500
30-30 Win.	67630	150	2.50	63.5	LR	201	35.5	2.30	2410	735	43500	3000
						201	32.5	2.10	2210	674	43500	3000
						200	26.1	1.69	2010	613	43500	3000
	67631	170	2.50	63.5	LR	201	32.4	2.10	2220	677	43500	3000
						200	26.3	1.70	2020	616	43500	3000
						200	23.3	1.51	1820	555	43500	3000
308 Win.	67621	110	2.38	60.5	LR	200	40.1	2.60	2740	835	52200	3600
	67623	130	2.62	66.5	LR	200	40.6	2.63	2900	884	52200	3600
						200	38.2	2.47	2700	823	52200	3600
						200	35.1	2.27	2500	762	52200	3600
	67624	150	2.65	67.5	LR	201	45.5	2.95	2860	872	52200	3600
						201	43.3	2.80	2660	811	52200	3600
						201	40.6	2.63	2460	750	52200	3600
	67628	180	2.70	68.5	LR	202	42.1	2.73	2525	770	52200	3600
308 Norma M.	67623	130	3.17	80.5	LR	204	78.4	5.08	3545	1080	55100	3800
	67624	150	3.21	81.5	LR	204	76.7	4.97	3330	1015	55100	3800
	67628	180	3.25	82.5	LR	MRP	74.3	4.81	3020	920	55100	3800
						204	71.8	4.65	2900	884	55100	3800
						204	70.0	4.53	2700	823	55100	3800
7.65 Arg.	67701	150	2.85	72.5	LR	201	47.8	3.10	2920	890	49300	3400
						201	44.0	2.85	2720	829	49300	3400
						201	42.5	2.75	2520	768	49300	3400
303 British	67701	150	2.95	75.0	LR	201	44.6	2.89	2720	829	46400	3200
						201	41.4	2.68	2520	768	46400	3200
						200	33.9	2.19	2320	707	46400	3200
	67713	180	2.97	75.5	LR	202	43.0	2.79	2540	774	46400	3200
						202	43.5	2.82	2600	792	46400	3200
						201	36.2	2.34	2140	652	46400	3200
7.7 Jap.	67711	130	2.84	72.0	LR	202	51.7	3.35	3005	916	39200	2700
	67713	180	3.03	77.0	LR	202	46.0	2.98	2515	767	39200	2700
8x57 J	67901	196	2.97	75.5	LR	202	48.0	3.11	2485	757	48500	3300
						201	39.8	2.58	2125	648	48500	3300
8x57 JS	68003	196	2.95	75.0	LR	202	48.3	3.13	2485	757	49300	3400
						200	36.4	2.36	2125	648	49300	3400
	68007	196	2.97	75.5	LR	202	48.3	3.13	2485	757	49300	3400
						200	36.4	2.36	2125	648	49300	3400
358 Norma M.	69001	250	3.23	82.0	LR	202	66.3	4.30	2710	826	53400	3700
						201	57.0	3.69	2400	731	53400	3700
9.3x57	69303	286	3.01	76.5	LR	201	44.6	2.89	2065	630	36300	2500
						201	40.6	2.63	1865	569	36300	2500
						200	34.2	2.22	1665	508	36300	2500
9.3x62	69303	286	3.23	82.0	LR	201	54.7	3.54	2360	720	49300	3400
						201	51.2	3.32	2160	659	49300	3400
						200	44.0	2.85	1960	598	49300	3400

NORMA RELOADING POWDERS

MRP/Magnum Rifle Powder

An exceptionally slow burning, high-energy powder for highest velocity with large capacity cases. Replaces the famous Norma 205 powder. A must for magnums.

Caliber	Bullet index no.	Bullet weight grains	Max Cartridge length inch.	mm	Norma primer	Norma powder	Load grains	grams	Muzzle vel. Feet per sec.	Meter per sec.	Pressure psi	bar
243 Win.	—	80	2.54	64.5	LR	MRP	50.6	3.28	3347	1020	52200	3600
243 Win.	66003	100	2.62	66.5	LR	MRP	49.2	3.19	3199	975	52200	3600
6 mm Rem.	66003	100	2.82	71.6	LR	MRP	46.4	3.01	3117	950	54400	3750
6 mm Rem.	66003	100	2.82	71.6	LR	MRP	48.2	3.12	3248	990	54400	3750
6.5 Carc.	66551	77	2.52	64.0	LR	MRP	46.5	3.01	2965	904	37700	2600
6.5 Carc.	66522	80	2.50	63.5	LR	MRP	46.6	3.02	2950	899	37700	2600
6.5 Carc.	66512	139	2.85	72.5	LR	MRP	43.2	2.80	2570	783	37700	2600
6.5 Carc.	66510	144	2.95	75.0	LR	MRP	43.2	280	2550	777	37700	2600
6.5 Carc.	66532	156	2.95	75.0	LR	MPR	42.4	2.75	2435	744	37700	2600
6.5 Jap.	66512	139	2.81	71.5	LR	MRP	37.7	2.44	2335	712	37700	2600
6.5 Jap.	66532	156	2.89	73.3	LR	MRP	38.1	2.47	2310	704	37700	2600
6.5x55	66531	139	2.99	76.0	LR	MRP	47.8	3.10	2740	835	45000	3100
6.5x55	66512	139	2.99	76.0	LR	MRP	49.4	3.20	2815	858	49300	3400 [2]
6.5x55	66510	144	3.05	77.5	LR	MRP	48.6	3.15	2780	847	49300	3400 [2]
6.5x55	66532	156	3.07	78.0	LR	MRP	48.0	3.11	2645	806	49300	3400 [2]
270 Win.	—	110	3.15	80.0	LR	MRP	61.5	3.98	3166	965	52200	3600
270 Win.	66902	130	3.15	80.0	LR	MRP	60.9	3.95	3133	955	52200	3600
270 Win.	66903	150	3.23	82.0	LR	MRP	58.4	3.78	2969	905	52200	3600
7x57	67002	150	3.03	77.0	LR	MRP	50.9	3.30	2615	797	49300	3400
7x57 R	67002	150	3.02	76.7	LR	MRP	51.3	3.32	2690	820	43500	3000
7x57 R	—	160	3.06	77.7	LR	MRP	50.4	3.27	2608	795	43500	3000
7x61 Super	—	160	3.19	81.0	LR	MRP	66.5	4.31	3100	945	55100	3800
7x61 Super	—	175	3.19	81.0	LR	MRP	64.8	4.20	2904	885	55100	3800
7x64	67002	150	3.27	83.0	LR	MRP	59.6	3.86	2960	902	52200	3600
7 mm Rem.	—	160	3.19	81.0	LR	MRP	70.2	4.55	3166	965	55100	3800
7 mm Rem.	—	175	3.21	81.5	LR	MRP	68.0	4.41	2986	910	55100	3800
7.5x55	67621	110	2.56	65.0	LR	MRP	60.9	3.95	3085	940	45000	3100
7.5x55	67623	130	2.80	71.0	LR	MRP	60.2	3.90	3060	933	45000	3100
7.5x55	67602	146	2.81	71.5	LR	MRP	57.1	3.70	2920	890	45000	3100
7.5x55	67624	150	2.80	71.0	LR	MRP	57.1	3.70	2890	881	45000	3100
7.5x55	67625	180	2.80	71.0	LR	MRP	55.6	3.60	2730	832	45000	3100
30–06	67624	150	3.13	79.5	LR	MRP	62.4	4.04	2822	860	50800	3500
30–06	67628	180	3.17	80.5	LR	MRP	60.1	3.89	2658	810	50800	3500
30–06	—	200	3.23	82.0	LR	MRP	59.4	3.85	2608	795	50800	3500
30–06	67628	180	3.17	80.5	—	MRP	61.7	4.00	2790	850	50900	3500

Loading data for Weatherby Magnums/Ladedata für Weatherby Magnum Patronen

Caliber	Bullet index no.	Bullet weight grains	Max Cartridge length inch.	mm	Norma primer	Norma powder	Load grains	grams	Muzzle vel. Feet per sec.	Meter per sec.	Pressure psi	bar
240 WM	—	70	3.15	80.0	—	MRP	59.4	3.85	3838	1170	55100	3800
240 WM	—	85	3.15	80.0	—	MRP	54.9	3.56	3497	1066	55100	3800
240 WM	—	87	3.15	80.0	—	MRP	54.5	3.53	3497	1066	55100	3800
240 WM	—	100	3.15	80.0	—	MRP	54.0	3.50	3395	1035	55100	3800
257 WM	—	87	3.42	87.0	—	MRP	74.1	4.80	3757	1145	55100	3800
257 WM	—	100	3.42	87.0	—	MRP	71.3	4.62	3555	1084	55100	3800
257 WM	—	117	3.42	87.0	—	MRP	67.1	4.35	3300	1006	55100	3800
270 WM	—	100	3.42	87.0	—	MRP	77.2	5.00	3760	1146	55100	3800
270 WM	—	130	3.42	87.0	—	MRP	73.3	4.75	3375	1029	55100	3800
270 WM	—	150	3.42	87.0	—	MRP	71.7	4.65	3245	990	55100	3800
7 mm WM	—	139	3.42	87.0	—	MRP	74.1	4.80	3300	1006	55100	3800
7 mm WM	—	154	3.42	87.0	—	MRP	72.8	4.72	3160	963	55100	3800
7 mm WM	—	160	3.42	87.0	—	MRP	72.5	4.70	3150	960	55100	3800
7 mm WM	—	175	3.42	87.0	—	MRP	71.0	4.60	3070	935	55100	3800
300 WM	—	110	3.58	91.0	—	MRP	81.0	5.25	3900	1189	55100	3800
300 WM	—	150	3.58	91.0	—	MRP	88.0	5.70	3545	1081	55100	3800
300 WM	—	180	3.58	91.0	—	MRP	83.3	5.40	3245	990	55100	3800
300 WM	—	200	3.58	91.0	—	MRP	78.7	5.10	3000	914	55100	3800
300 WM	—	220	3.58	91.0	—	MRP	79.2	5.13	2905	885	55100	3800
340 WM	—	200	3.70	94.0	—	MRP	91.0	5.90	3210	978	55100	3800
340 WM	—	210	3.70	94.0	—	MRP	91.0	5.90	3180	969	55100	3800
340 WM	—	250	3.70	94.0	—	MRP	85.2	5.52	2850	869	55100	3800
378 WM	—	270	3.70	94.0	—	MRP	115.5	7.48	3180	969	58785	4055
378 WM	—	300	3.70	94.0	—	MRP	111.8	7.20	2925	892	58785	4055

Handgun Powders

Caliber	Bullet index no.	Bullet weight grains	Max Cartridge length inch.	mm	Norma primer	Norma powder	Load grains	grams	Muzzle velocity Feet per sec.	Meter per sec.	Pressure psi	bar
9 mm Luger	69010	116	1.16	29.5	SP	R-1	3.8	0.246	1115	340	36300	2500
38 Special	69110	148	1.16	29.5	SP	R-1	2.5	0.162	800	244	17000	1170
	69112	158	1.50	38.0	SP	R-1	3.5	0.227	870	265	20000	1380
	69107	158	1.48	37.5	SP	R-1	4.2	0.272	900	274	20000	1380
	69101	158	1.46	37.0	SP	R-1	4.2	0.272	900	274	20000	1380
357 Mag.	69101	158	1.59	40.5	SP	R-123	13.9	0.900	1450	442	40600	2800
	69107	158	1.59	40.5	SP	R-123	13.9	0.900	1450	442	40600	2800
38 S & W	—	146	1.16	29.5	SP	R-1	2.0	0.130	730	222	13800	950
44 Mag.	61103	240	1.61	41.0	LP	R-123	19.1	1.240	1675	511	40600	2800

BONANZA RELOADING TOOLS

CO-AX PRESS

Snap-in and snap-out die change, positive spent primer catcher, automatic self-acting shell holder, floating guide rods, perfect alignment of die and case is assured, good for right- or left-handed operators, uses standard ⅞ x 14 dies.

MODEL 68 PRESS

No obstructions to visibility of operator, open working space, upright mounting, equal thrust distribution, simple in construction, heavy duty, constructed of automotive-type casting, ram is machined and fitted.

BONANZA MODEL 68 PRESS . . . . $ 60.60
BONANZA CO-AX PRESS (B-1) less dies 113.15
EXTRA SET JAWS for Co-Ax . . . . set 15.40

PISTOL DIES

BONANZA PISTOL DIES are three-die sets. The 38 Spl. & 357 Mag., and the 44 Spl. & 44 Mag. are so designed that each set may be used to load the two calibers. You need not buy extra dies to load the magnums. The Bonanza Cross Bolt Lock Ring is standard on all Bonanza dies. A special taper crimp die is available for 45 ACP and 38-357 and 9mm Luger.

Bonanza Three-Die Pistol Set $25.78
Bonanza Taper Crimp Die 12.65
Bonanza Two-Die Pistol Set 24.85

CO-AX RIFLE DIES

All Bonanza Dies are made with ⅞ x 14 threads and can be used on various other makes of presses. The CO-AX SEATER can be adjusted to crimp or not to crimp. All calibers crimp. The Sizer, with elevated expander button, is the same as is supplied with the Bench Rest Dies. This "E-Z" OUT expander button is drawn through the case neck while the operator uses the full mechanical advantage of the press.

Bonanza CO-AX Die Set $24.85
Bonanza CO-AX Seating Dies only 10.98
Bonanza CO-AX Sizing Die only 17.35
Bonanza Three-Die Rifle Set 25.98

BONANZA RELOADING TOOLS

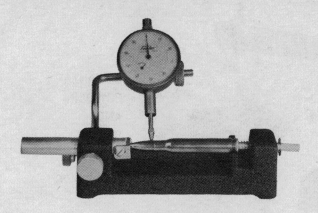

CO-AX INDICATOR

Gives a reading of how closely the axis of the bullet corresponds with the axis of the cartridge case. Spring-loaded plunger holds against cartridges **a recessed, adjustable rod** supported in a "V" block.

BONANZA CO-AX INDICATOR, less Indicator Dial $21.35

Indicator Dial only 31.35

CASE TRIMMER MODEL "66"

Neck case pilot eliminates the need for a collet and shell holder. Reversible mandrell and four-blade case-mouth trimmer. Dull cutter is exchanged for a sharpened cutter.

BONANZA CASE TRIMMER, complete with Pilot
(state caliber) $20.75
extra Pilots (state caliber) 1.40
extra Cutter 3.20
Cutter Sharpening "Exchange" 2.30

BONANZA BULLS-EYE PISTOL POWDER MEASURE

Measure has fixed-charge rotor. Supplied with a quick detachable bracket for use on a bench, or it can be held by hand.
Bonanza Pistol Powder Measure and One Rotor .. $27.45
Extra Rotor or Blank Rotor 4.60

BONANZA BENCH REST POWDER MEASURE

Powder is metered from the charge arm.
Measure will throw uniform charges from 2½-grains bulls-eye to 95-grains 4320.
Measure empties by removing charge bar from charge arm, letting contents flow through charge arm into powder container.
BBRPM Bonanza Bench Rest Powder Measure $38.70
Stand (extra) fits either Pistol or Bench Rest Measure 18.50

BONANZA RELOADING TOOLS

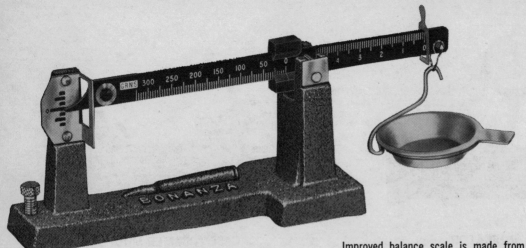

BONANZA POWDER AND BULLET SCALE

MODEL "C"

Improved balance scale is made from "Marlon-Lexon," an inert, non-magnetic material. Allows greater sensitivity, precision alignment and bearing, eliminates static electricity, accuracy guaranteed to 1/10 grain, sensitivity guaranteed to 1/20 grain.

Bonanza Powder and Bullet Scale Model "C" $28.60

BONANZA "M" MAGNETIC DAMPENED SCALE

505 grain capacity, tempered stainless steel right hand poise, diamond polished agate "V" bearings, non-glare white markings, three point suspension base, strengthened beam at pivot points, powder pan for right or left pouring, guaranteed accurate to 1/10 grain, sensitivity guaranteed to 1/20 grain.

Bonanza "M" Magnetic Dampened Scale $35.85

BONANZA CO-AX PRIMER SEATER

The Bonanza Primer Seater is designed so that primers are seated Co-Axially (primer in line with primer pocket). Mechanical leverage allows primers to be seated fully without crushing. With the addition of one extra set of Disc Shell Holders and one extra Primer Unit, all modern cases, rim or rimless, from .222 up to .458 Magnum can be primed. Shell Holders are easily adjusted to any case by rotating to contact rim or cannelure of the case.

Bonanza Primer Seater $33.45
Primer Tube 2.90

BONANZA RELOADING TOOLS

CO-AX CASE TRIMMER
Model 80000

The cutter shaft rides within a honed bearing for turning of the crank handle when trimming. Hardened and ground cutter teeth remove excess brass. Case to be trimmed is locked in a collet case holder, case is seated against the collet then locked, cases are trimmed to the same length regardless of rim thickness or head diameter. For accuracy of setting to proper trim length a collar stop is provided on the shaft. Cases may be trimmed to a tolerance of .001" or less.

Case Trimmer with one collet and one pilot	$30.60
Case Trimmer less collet and pilot	26.60
Case Trimmer Pilot 8009 (give caliber)	1.40
Case Trimmer Collet 0102-(No. 1, 2, or 3)	4.35
Case Trimmer Cutter Shaft 0107 (Standard)	8.65
Case Trimmer Cutter Shaft 0107 — .17 caliber	8.65
Case Trimmer Pilot for .17 caliber	1.40

(Above two items are accessories and not offered with a trimmer. Not interchangeable with standard shaft.)

Short Base 0104-S	6.10
Long Base 0104-L	6.10

CO-AX BENCH REST
RIFLE DIES

BONANZA BENCH REST DIES are glass hard for long wear and minimum friction. Interiors are polished mirror smooth. Special attention is given to headspace, tapers and diameters so that brass will not be overworked when resized. Our sizing die has an elevated expander button which is drawn through the neck of the case at the moment of the greatest mechanical advantage of the press. Since most of the case neck is still in the die when expanding begins, better alignment of case and neck is obtained. **Our Bench Rest Seating Die** is of the chamber type. The bullet is held in alignment in a close fitting channel. The case is held in a tight fitting chamber. Both bullet and case are held in alignment all the while the bullet is being seated. These dies represent the first improvement in design since 1924. The set costs less than some are charging for a straight line seater alone. As a bonus you get our cross bolt lock ring.

Bench Rest Die Set	$31.15
Full Length Sizer	17.35
Bench Seating Die	17.35

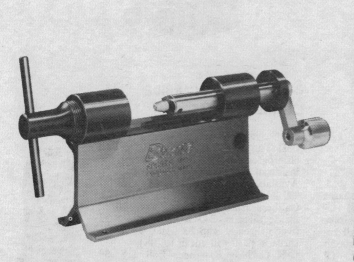

C-H RELOADING TOOLS

C-H RELOADING DIES

C-H reloading dies are available in all popular calibers. The outside has a non-glare satin finish. The outside threads are ⅞x14 and will fit all standard presses. C-H die lock rings feature a nylon ball lock inside the set screw to prevent damage to the threads and facilitate readjustment.

C-H TRIM DIES

By using these C-H Trim Dies you can shorten the neck of your cases with a file or a fine-tooth hacksaw. Dies are hardened and will not be effected by the filing. Available in the following calibers: 222 Rem., 22-250, 225 Win., 243 Win., 6mm R, 257 Robts., 25-06, 257 Wea., 6.5x55, 270 Win., 7x57 Mauser, 7mm Rem. Mag., 7mm Wea., 308 Win., 30-06, 300 Win. Mag., 300 Wea., 8x57.
File Trim Die **$10.00**

AUTO CHAMPION MARK IV

Available for 38 Special/357; 45 ACP; 44 Mag. and 9 mm Luger. Features: Reloading capability of 500 rounds per hour. Fully progressive loading. Powder measure cam allows you to "jog" the machine without dispensing powder. Simple powder measure emptying device included with each unit. Tungsten-carbide sizing die at no extra cost. Unit comes with your choice of powder bushing and seating stem (round nose, wadcutter or semi-wadcutter). Seating die cavity-tapered for automatic alignment of the bullet. One 100-capacity primer tube, two 15-capacity case tubes and tube coupling also included at no extra cost **$699.00**

STANDARD CALIBER DIE SETS

Series 'A' Full Length Sizer and Seater Die ..**$21.50**
Series 'B' Sizer, Expander-Decapper and Seater Die **21.50**
Series 'C' Sizer-Decapper, Expander and Seater Die **21.50**
Series 'D' Neck Sizer and Seater Die **21.50**
Series 'E' Full Length Sizer, Neck Sizer and Seater Die **27.00**
Series 'F' Sizer, Expander-Decapper and Speed Seater Die **23.00**
Series 'G' Carbide Sizer, Expander-Decapper and Seater Die **38.00**
Series 'H' Carbide Sizer, Expander-Decapper and Speed Seater Die **39.00**
Decapping Pin, Specify caliber (standard or heavy duty) **1.00**
pkg. of 5

C-H CHAMPION PRESS

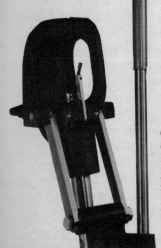

Compound leverage press for all phases of re-loading. Heavyweight (26#) C-Hampion comes complete with primer arm, ⅞x14 bushing for use with all reloading dies. Spent primers fall through back of press into waste basket. 'O' frame design will not spring under any conditions. Ideal press for swaging bullets. Top of frame bored 1¼x18 for use with special dies and shot-shell dies.

$199.50

C-H TUNGSTEN CARBIDE EXPANDER BALLS

Now available as an accessory, the C-H Tungsten Carbide Expander Ball eliminates the need for lubricating the inside of the case neck.

Available in the following calibers: 22, 243, 25, 270, 7mm, 30, 320, 322. Calibers 7mm and larger have 10-32 inside threads, 243 to 270 have 8-32 inside threads and 22 has 6-32 inside threads. (270 will not fit RCBS)
C-H Carbide Expander Ball ..**$5.50**
For the RCBS 22 expander unit we can provide a complete rod with carbide expander that will fit their die body.
C-H Carbide Expander Ball to fit....
22 cal. RCBS die **$6.50**

C-H RELOADING TOOLS

CHAMPION Jr. RELOADING PRESS

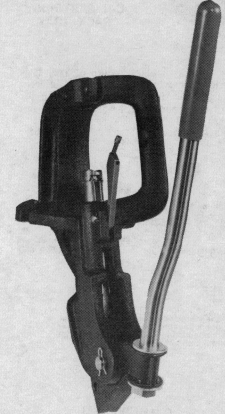

CHAMPION Jr. Heavy Duty Reloading Press—semi steel (cast iron) "O" press offset so the opening is 210 degrees for better access. Solid steel handle is offset to match opening.

Positioning of toggle pin provides maximum leverage—so powerful that a 30/06 case can be forced into a 250 full length resizing die. In addition to usual 2 bolt fastening we put a 3rd bolt so the "big" jobs using maximum power won't break off your bench.

Weight 13½ lbs.

Uses standard detachable shell holders.

Price complete w/primer arm and 1 shell holder $52.50

Price complete with 1 die set $70.50

C-H DIE BOX

Protect your dies from dust and damage with a C-H 3-compartment plastic Die Box. High-impact plastic—will not break. Easy to label and stack.
No. 700 C-H Die Box $1.25

BULLET SWAGING DIE EJECTOR

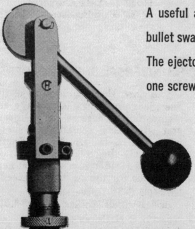

A useful accessory for use with the new C-H jacketed bullet swaging dies.

The ejector attaches easily to the swaging die body with one screw. Can be used with either the core seating die or the swage die. Ejects the seated core or finished bullet with ease. No more tapping the top of the die.

Price $18.65

FROM C-H 3/4 JACKETED PISTOL BULLET

SWAGING DIES

- Any bullet weight from 110 gr. to 250 gr. with same set of dies
- Can be used in any good 7/8 x 14 loading tool
- Absolutely no leading
- Complete — no extras to buy
- Increased velocity
- Solid Nose or hollow point (hollow point $2.50 extra)
- Available in 38/357, 41 S & W 44 Mag. and 45 colt calibers

PRICE
$38.45

FROM C-H NEW SOLID STEEL

CANNELURE TOOL

PRICE
$24.75

- Will work on all sizes of bullets, from 17 to 45
- Completely adjustable for depth and height
- One set will process thousands of bullets
- Necessary for rolling in grooves on bullets prior to crimping
- Hardened cutting wheel, precision machined throughout.

C-H RELOADING ACCESSORIES

NO. 725 POWDER and BULLET SCALE

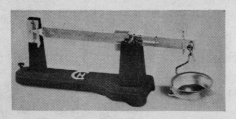

Chrome plated, brass beam. Graduated in 10 gr., 1 gr. and 1/10th gr. increments. Convenient pouring spout on pan. Leveling screw on base. All metal construction. 360 gr. capacity. **Price** **$24.95**

C-H CARTRIDGE RACK TRAY

Holds 60 cartridges. Comes in black, white or red. It is handy for the reloader who works up cases for different loads, etc. Holes are 15/16" deep which is too deep for 38 Spl. Holes are not large enough for 45/70 or 348 but hold all sizes up to 375 H&H.
No. 403 Cartridge Rack Tray **$1.65**

C-H CASE TRIMMER
No. 301
This design features a unique clamp to lock case holder in position. Ensures perfect uniformity from 22 cal. thru 45 cal. whether rifle or pistol cases. Complete including hardened case holder . . . **$21.95**
Extra case holders (hardened & hand-lapped) . . . **$3.50**

C-H POWDER MEASURE

The new steel drum is designed so the handle can be placed on either the right or left side, and the charge can be dropped on either the up or down stroke. Or reverse for use with micrometer either front or back. Base threads are ⅞ x 14. The rifle micrometer adjusts precisely and permits up to 100 grains of 4831. The Pistol micrometer permits up to 12 grains of Bullseye.
A baffle plate is supplied with the optional 10" production hopper.

No. 502 Powder Measure *Specify Rifle*
  or Pistol $34.95
No. 502-1 Stand ⅞" thread **6.95**
No. 502-2 Micrometer *Specify Rifle or*
  Pistol **9.75**
No. 592-3 10" Production Hopper
  (*with baffle*) **5.50**

C-H UNIVERSAL PRIMING ARMS

Accommodates all standard rifle and pistol primers. Made of fine metal—not a stamping, for extra strength and dimensional stability. Packaged in clear acetate tube.

No. 414 C-H Universal
  "C" Priming Arm . . **$4.25**

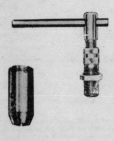

C-H BULLET PULLER
C-H Bullet Puller features positive die-locking action, removes the bullet easily without any damage to housing or bullet. The detachable handle is constructed of ⅜" stock and adjusts to any position. The hex nut for crescent wrench adjustment locks the die into firm position. Extra long internal thread for extra locking leeway.
No. 402 with Collet .**$10.50**
No. 402-1 Extra Collet **3.25**

C-H UNIVERSAL SHELL HOLDERS

Up to now, shell holders came in one piece and you had to have as many shell holders as the calibers you wished to reload. However, with the C-H Universal Shell Holder all the reloader needs is the Shell Holder ram and then get the heads for the calibers desired.
No. 408 C-H Universal "C"
  or "H" Shell Holder Head **$4.00**
No. 407 C-H Universal "H"
  Shell Holder Ram **5.25**
No. 412 C-H Universal "C"
  Shell Holder Ram **5.50**

LYMAN RELOADING TOOLS

FOR RIFLE OR PISTOL CARTRIDGES

LYMAN 310 TOOL

The 310 Tool is a compact, portable reloading kit that can be used anywhere—home, hunting camp, in the field, on the range. Using the 310 Tool, the novice can start reloading with a small investment. The 310 Tool performs all the operations required for reloading metallic cartridges for handguns and rifles. It removes the old primer, resizes the cartridge neck, it inserts a new primer, and seats the new bullet. A practiced reloader can load, fire, adjust and reload his charge right on the range, test firing until he determines his best load.

310 Tool Handles Only (large or small) **$19.95**

310 Dies (rifle or handgun)—Set consists of five pieces: Neck Resizing and Decapping Die, Priming Chamber, Neck Expanding Chamber, Bullet Seating Chamber and an Adapter Die **$27.50**

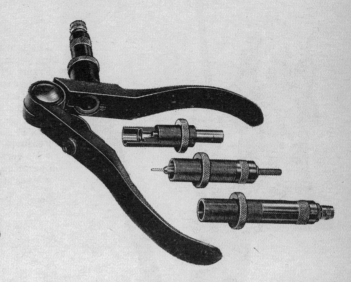

GROUP V AA BENCH REST 2-DIE SETS

Bench Rest Set includes a micrometer seating die for ultra-precise seating depth control and bullet to case alignment; a neck sizing die designed to consistently retain the cartridge's precise fire-formed dimensions and a true micrometer head. Micrometer head may be repositioned within the die body—no special shell holders are ever needed, no matter how short your cartridge. Because there's no port, the full contact alignment sleeve is precisely centered throughout the entire bullet seating operation. It cannot lose concentric alignment right at the point when alignment is critical. Sizing die only sizes the neck of the case so cartridges retain the exact fire-formed shape of the gun chamber. The die is machined to hold maximum concentricity between the neck of the shell and the body of the die.

Die Set **$49.95**
Micrometer Seating Die **39.95**
Neck Sizing Die **16.50**

LYMAN SHOTSHELL HANDBOOK

The second edition of the Lyman Shotshell Handbook features an authoritative study devoted exclusively to shotshell reloading—a reloading handbook which covers every aspect of modern shotshell reloading. Dealing with the latest components it is an indispensable reference book which belongs on every reloading bench. Complete "How To Reload" section on choosing a load, factory velocities, assembling shotshells, etc. Reference section covers up-to-date pressure information, four color case identification chapter, plus chapters on wads, patterns, powder and primers. Over 1000 tested loads covering all gauges 10, 12, 16, 20, 28 and 410. Contains suggested reloads using modern components from all of the major manufacturers **$10.95**

LYMAN RELOADING TOOLS
FOR RIFLE OR PISTOL CARTRIDGES

LYMAN SPAR-T TURRET PRESS

The Lyman Spar-T Press combines the maximum speed of turret loading with the operating ease, and strength of the ever popular C Frame Press. It's massive frame, and 6 station Turret, are ruggedly constructed of high-silicone, iron-steel castings (not aluminum alloy). It's Verti-Lock Turret is firmly secured to the frame by a heavy duty ¾" steel stud. Positive stop, audible click action insures foolproof cartridge to die alignment and rapid operation. Uses standard ⅞ x 14 dies.

Features: • Lock nut rigidly locks turret in one position for swaging. • Powerful toggle-link leverage (25 to 1) • UP or DOWN STROKE operation. • Alignment ramp positions Shell Holder at top of stroke. • Uses standard Spartan accessories.

Spar-T Press with ram and primer arm $94.95

SPAR-T SET: Consists of Spar-T Press, Spar-T Auto-Primer Feed, Spartan Primer Arm, Spartan Ram, Spartan Shell Holder Head, Complete set of All-American Dies. $114.95

SPARTAN SET: Consists of Spartan Press, Spartan Ram, Spartan Shell Holder Head, Spartan Primer Arm, Complete set of All American Dies (standard ⅞" by 14). Spartan Primer Catcher.................... $79.95

SPARTAN SPAR–T ACCESSORIES

PRIMER CATCHER: Made of heavy-duty plastic, this unit may be used on either the Spartan or Spart-T Press. Locks securely to press, yet allows for easy removal when emptying primers. $3.95

RAM: Designed for perfect alignment. Fits Lyman Spartan press. Pacific Standard, RCBS, Jr., C & H Super C. $6.00

DETACHABLE SHELL HOLDER: Precision cut and hardened to ensure perfect case fit. Used with the Spartan Ram on the Spartan Press and on many other presses. $4.50

UNIVERSAL PRIMING ARM: Seats all sizes and types of primers. Supplied with two priming sleeves (large and small) two flat priming punches (large and small), and two round priming punches (large and small). $6.95

AUTO-PRIMER FEED: Eliminates handling of primer with oily fingers, speeds loading. Supplied with two tubes (large and small) Spartan and O-Mag. Spar-t $12.95

LYMAN SPARTAN RELOADING PRESS

The Lyman Spartan Press is a massive, 11 lb. heavy-duty iron frame press which reloads all rifle and pistol cases quickly, accurately and easily. Its powerful toggle-link mechanism multiplies the force applied to the handle 25 times and takes the hard work out of full-length resizing and case forming, and is even rugged enough for bullet swaging.

• Uses Lyman All-American (standard ⅞" x 14) dies • Simple changeover to either up- or down-stroke • Alignment ramp positions shell holder at top of each stroke • Precision bored frame ensures perfect alignment • Maximum serviceability at extremely low cost.

Spartan Press With ram and priming arm. $62.95

LYMAN RELOADING TOOLS

FOR RIFLE OR PISTOL CARTRIDGES

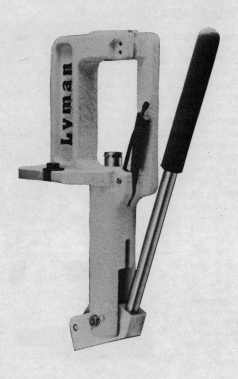

LYMAN O-MAG

Lyman has fitted its O-Mag with some unexpected extras that truly make it the magnum press for every serious reloader. These extras include a 4½-inch opening that easily accommodates even the largest cartridge, a longer, slip-free grip and a hole behind the mounting (in addition to the two conventional side holes) for an extra measure of stability and leverage. The Lyman O-Mag is also the first magnum press to introduce a flat work surface above and behind the die station for mounting racks and accessories. Set includes the O-Mag press and primer catcher, universal primer arm, ram, detachable shell holder and a complete set of standard AA dies (state caliber).

Also available as a companion to the Lyman O-Mag is the Powder Measure Stand, which features the standard ⅞" x 14" thread and raises any measure high enough to position cases beneath the powder drop tube.

O-Mag Set (18 lbs.) **$99.95**
O-Mag Press only w/ram and universal primer arm . 79.95
Powder Measure Stand 12.95

T-MAG SET

Our T-Mag Set includes the T-Mag Press, plus the tools you need to turn out top-quality reloads for your rifle or handgun:
- T-Mag Press
- O-Mag Primer Catcher
- Universal Primer Arm
- Ram
- Detachable Shell Holder
- Complete Set of standard AA Dies (state caliber)

T-Mag Set (18 lbs.) **$99.95**

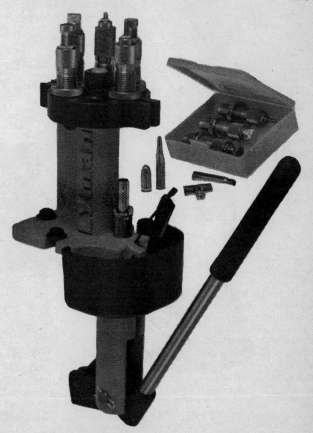

T-MAG TURRET RELOADING PRESS (shown)

With the T-Mag you can mount up to six different reloading dies on our turret. This means you can have all your dies set up, precisely mounted, locked in and ready to reload at all times. The T-Mag works with all ⅞ x 14 dies. It's built with O-Mag strength and uses standard O-Mag primer feed and O-Mag primer catcher. The T-Mag turret is held in rock-solid alignment by a ¾-inch steel stud.

T-Mag Press only with Ram and Universal Priming Arm (17 lbs.) **$79.95**

LYMAN RELOADING ACCESSORIES

PRIMER POCKET REAMER

Cleans and removes rough metal edges from a primer pocket. This tool is a must for military type primers. Available in large or small—see priming punch size in cartridge table.

Price **$6.95**

THE NO. 55 POWDER MEASURE

This Powder Measure and dispensing device charges any number of cases with black, or smokeless, powder loads that are consistent within a fraction of a grain. Its three-slide micrometer adjustable cavity adjusts the load accurately, and locks in place to provide accurate charging. The 2400 grain capacity plastic reservoir gives a clear view of the powder level. The reservoir is fabricated from blue-tinted polyvinyl-chloride plastic that resists chemical action of double base powders, and filters out light rays that would damage powders. An optional 7000 grain reservoir is available. The measure clamps securely to the loading bench, or mounts directly to any turret press by means of threaded drop tubes (supplied with measure). A knocker mounted on the side of the measure insures complete discharge of powder directly into the cartridge case. No funnel is required.

No. 55 POWDER MEASURE **$48.95**
Optional 7000 grain capacity reservoir .. **7.95**
⅞" x 14 Adapter for Turret Mounting **2.00**

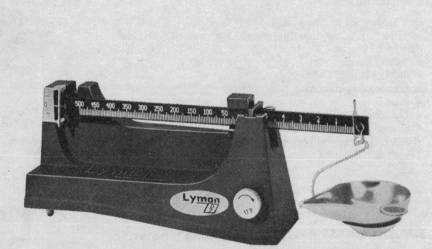

The unique three-slide micrometer adjustable cavity is the key to the unfailing accuracy of the 55 Powder Measure. Micrometer adjustments for both width and depth provide a dependable, consistent measure that minimizes cutting of coarse powder.

POWDER FUNNEL

This plastic powder funnel is designed to fill cases from 22 Hornet through 45-70 without inserts or adjustments.
Price: **$1.95**

Powder Dribbler **$7.50**

LYMAN D-7 SCALE

Dial markings are white on jet black for easy reading. The pointer, and dial, are placed on the same plane to eliminate parallax error. Its high capacity of up to 505 grains, permits the heaviest charges and even bullets to be weighed. Features magnetic damping. Genuine agate bearings guarantee one tenth of a grain of sensitivity. **Lyman D-7 Scale** **$42.95**

LYMAN RELOADING DIES

The All-American Dies shown on this page are designed for use with the Lyman Spartan, Spar-T, AA Turret, and all other reloading presses having 7/8" x 14" thread die stations. AA die sets are offered in either 2 or 3 die combinations, depending on shape of cartridge case, and type of bullet to be loaded.

Outer surfaces of all dies are chrome-plated. All bullet seating dies are adjustable to crimp or not crimp the bullet. Sizing dies for bottleneck cartridges are vented to prevent air traps.

THREE-DIE RIFLE SET

Required to load straight-taper cartridge cases, and all other cartridges when using cast bullets.

This set consists of: full-length resizing and decapping die, a 2-step neck expanding die, and a bullet seating and crimping die. The added advantage of the three-die set is in the use of the 2-step neck expanding die which allows the bullet to enter the case freely, without cutting or marring lead. This method of neck-expanding insures precise case neck tension on seated bullet.

Standard Three-die rifle set
(complete with wrench) **$25.50**

TWO-DIE RIFLE SET

These sets consist of two dies. The first die full-length resizes, decaps, and expands, while the second die seats the bullet and crimps when desired. Two die sets are specifically designed for loading bottleneck shape cartridge cases using jacketed bullets. These sets are not offered for straight-taper shape cases. They should not be used with cast bullets unless in conjunction with an "M" die (see below).

Two-die rifle set (complete with wrench) **$24.50**

THREE-DIE PISTOL SETS

Available for all pistol calibers this set can be used with either cast of jacketed bullets.

Set consists of: full-length resizing and decapping die, a 2-step neck expanding die, and a bullet seating and crimping die. Available for various bullet styles.

Standard Three-die pistol set
(complete with wrench) **$25.50**

T-C* PISTOL DIE

***Tungsten Carbide Resizing & Decapping Die for handgun cartridges.**

A lifetime of reloads, some 200,000 rounds can be pushed through this Full-Length Sizing and Decapping Die without a sign of wear. Its diamond-like sizing surface of polished tungsten carbide creates far less friction (75% less) than steel dies. With the Lyman T-C Die, cases need not be lubricated and even dirty cases come out of the die with a polished burnished appearance. T-C Dies are available for the following pistol cartridges.

38 S & W (also fits 38 ACP & 38 Super)	44 Special (also fits 44 Magnum)
38 Special (also fits 357 Magnum)	45 ACP
	45 Colt
41 Magnum	

T-C Pistol Die **$31.50**

TWO-STEP "M" NECK-EXPANDING DIE FOR CAST RIFLE BULLETS

Available for all rifle cases this die is required when loading cast bullets, and will also improve the accuracy of jacketed bullet reloads. The first step expands the neck of the cartridge to slightly under bullet diameter. The second step expands the first 1/16" of the neck to slightly over bullet diameter, allowing the bullet to enter the case freely, without cutting lead. This die insures precise case neck tension on seated bullet. **$10.95**

LYMAN RELOADING

AA Bench Rest 2-Die Sets
(for jacketed bullets)

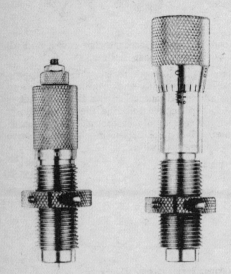

Cartridge	Die Set Number	Micrometer Seating Die	Neck Sizing Die
22-250 (22 Varminter)	7690012	7161012	7135012
220 Swift	7690013	7161013	7135013
222 Remington	7690005	7161005	7135005
223 Remington (5.56mm)	7690006	7161006	7135006
243 Winchester	7690015	7161015	7135015
6mm Remington (244 Rem.)	7690016	7161016	7135016
25-06	7690024	7161024	7135024
270 Winchester	7690033	7161033	7135033
7mm Remington Magnum	7690039	7161039	7135039
7mm Mauser (7 x 57mm)	7690035	7161035	7135035
30-06 (7.62 x 63mm)	7690049	7161049	7135049
300 Winchester Magnum	7690051	7161051	7135051
308 Winchester (7.62 x 51mm Nato)	7690047	7161047	7135047
Price:	**$49.95**	**$39.95**	**$16.50**

Match grade performance through the use of proven bench rest techniques. The set consists of a neck sizing die and our AA Micro-Seat Die. This combination enables you to get neck sizing and truly precise bullet seating from a traditional reloading press.

AA Multi-Deluxe Pistol Die Sets

Here's one innovative die set that does the reloading work of two, four or even six premium die sets. Bullet styles are changed quickly and easily because each set includes two or three seating screws that screw out of the top of the die. Multi-Deluxe Pistol Dies feature Tungsten-Carbide rings for friction-free sizing without the mess of lubrication, a two-step neck expanding die, which loads lead alloy bullets without lead shaving and distortion. A Special-Magnum advantage permits loading of the 38-Special and 357 Magnum with the same die set. Multi-Deluxe Pistol Die Set (1 lb. 10 oz.) **$46.95**

LYMAN RELOADING
DIE REFERENCE CHART

This handy chart can direct you to the correct die sets and accessories needed for reloading any of the cartridges listed.

Die Group column gives you the die set or sets that may be used for the cartridge.

Shell Holder column gives you correct number for appropriate caliber.

Primer column lets you know large or small size for choosing Primer Punches, pocket reamers and cleaners.

Trimmer Pilot column lists appropriate trimmer pilot. Lyman's Universal Trimmer requires no other collets — just the inexpensive pilot.

PISTOL CARTRIDGE	Die Group	Shell Holder Number	Primer Punch & Sleeve	Case Trimmer Pilot Number
25 ACP	NA	NA	small	25A
7mm TCU	V. VIII	26	small	28
30 Mauser	VIII	12	small	30
30 Herrett	VII	6	large	30
32 ACP	VIII	23	small	30
32 Smith & Wesson	VIII	9	small	31
38 Super Auto	VIII	12	small	9mm
38 Smith & Wesson	VIII	21	small	35
380 Auto	VIII	26	small	9mm
9mm Luger	VIII	12	small	9mm

PISTOL CARTRIDGE	Die Group	Shell Holder Number	Primer Punch & Sleeve	Case Trimmer Pilot Number
38 Special/357 Magnum	VII. IX	1	small	35
41 Magnum	VII. IX	30	small	41
44 Magnum/44 Special	VII. IX	7	large	44
44-40 Winchester	VII	14B	large	44A
45 ACP	VII. IX	2	large	45A
45 Colt	VII. IX	11	large	45A

RIFLE CARTRIDGE	Die Group	Shell Holder Number	Primer Punch & Sleeve	Case Trimmer Pilot Number
22 Hornet	II	4	small	22
22-250	I. V	2	large	22
220 Swift	II. V	5	large	22
221 Fireball	II	26	small	22
222 Remington	I. V	26	small	22
222 Remington Magnum	II	26	small	22
223 Remington (5.56mm)	I. V	26	small	22
243 Winchester	I. V	2	large	24
6mm Remington (244 Rem.)	II. V	2	large	24
25-06	I. V	2	large	25
250 Savage (250-3000 Sav.)	II	2	large	25
264 Winchester Magnum	II	13	large	26
6.5 x 55mm Swedish Mauser	II	27	large	26
270 Winchester	I. V	2	large	27
7mm Remington Magnum	I. V	13	large	28
7mm x 57 Mauser (7mm Mauser)	II. V	2	large	28
7mm Mauser (also loads 7 x 57R)	II. V	13	large	28
280 Remington (7mm Exp. Rem.)	II	2	large	28
30 M1 Carbine	III	19	small	30
30-30 Winchester (30 WCF)	I	6	large	30

RIFLE CARTRIDGE	Die Group	Shell Holder Number	Primer Punch & Sleeve	Case Trimmer Pilot Number
30-06 (7.62 x 63mm)	I. V	2	large	30
7.65 Argentine Mauser	II	2	large	31
30-40 Krag	II	7	large	30
300 H&H Magnum	II	13	large	30
300 Savage	II	2	large	30
300 Weatherby Magnum	II	13	large	30
300 Winchester Magnum	II. V	13	large	30
308 Winchester	I. V	2	large	30
303 British	II	7	large	31
32 Winchester Special	II	6	large	32
32-20 Winchester	III	10	small	32
32-40 Winchester	IV	6	large	32
8mm Mauser (8 x 57mm. 8 x 57JSmm. 7.9 x 57mm)	II	2	large	8mm
8mm Mauser (also loads 8 x 57JRSmm)	II	14B	large	8mm
8mm Remington Magnum	II	13	large	8mm
338 Winchester Magnum	II	13	large	33
35 Remington	II	8 or 2	large	35
375 Winchester	IV	6	large	37
375 H&H Magnum	II	13	large	37
444 Marlin	IV	14B	large	44
45-70 Government	IV	17	large	45
50-70 Government	IV	22	large	NA

LYMAN BULLET SIZING EQUIPMENT

450 BULLET SIZER

450 BULLET SIZER:

The 450 Bullet Sizer and Lubricator sizes the bullet to the correct diameter, forces lubricant under pressure into the bullet grooves, and will seat gas checks, if required—all in one rapid, accurate operation. Adaptable to all bullets by changing "G" and bullet sizing assembly "H & I". Use with Ideal Bullet Lubricant **$74.95**

G, H & I DIES "WITH SWAGING ACTION":

Cast bullets as much as ten thousandths oversize can be easily formed to size by the use of these dies. Lyman bullet sizing dies have been newly designed to supply a swaging rather than shearing action in reducing bullet diameters. The mouth of the "H" die contains a gentle taper which allows the gas check and bullet to start into the die easily. This tapering of the mouth combined with the exact tolerance and ultra-smoothness of the hardened inner chamber, completely eliminates shearing of lead and produces a perfectly cylindrical bullet. As this swaging action compresses and work hardens the alloy, a tougher, smoother, and more accurate bullet results.

"G" TOP PUNCH: Top Punches are designed to fit the contour of the bullet point. **$3.95**

"H & I" SIZING DIE ASSEMBLY: H & I Dies should be supplied as one unit. Their diameter should correspond to the groove diameter of your rifle, or pistol. The listing below shows the basic groove diameter for many popular calibers. A complete listing of all available sizes is also shown for the shooter who wishes to experiment with different bullet diameters or for those who have rifles with worn or non-standard bores **$10.95**

"G"

"H"

"I"

IDEAL BULLET LUBRICANT . . . Special grease developed especially for use as a cast bullet lubricant. One stick lubricates 2500 small of 500 large bullets.

Ideal Bullet
Lubricant **$2.50**
ALOX Bullet
Lubricant **2.50**

BASIC GROOVE DIAMETER FOR RIFLES

Caliber	Groove Dia.	Caliber	Groove Dia.
All 22 cal. (except 22 Hi-power)	.224	338 Win. & 33 Win.	.338
.22 Hi-Power	.226	348 Win.	.348
.243, .244, 6 M/M	.243	35 Win. S. L. & 351 S. L.	.352
.256 Win. & All 25 cals.	.257	9 x 56 M/M & 9 x 57 M/M	.354
.264 Win., 6.5 M/M	.264	35 cal.	.358
.270 Win.	.277	375 H & H Mag.	.375
7 M/M, .280 Rem., .284 Win.	.284	38/55	.379
7.35 Carcano	.299	38/40	.400
30 cals.	.308	401 S.L.	.406
7.62 Russian	.310	405 Win.	.412
32/20 Win.	.311	44/40 Win. Rifles	.428
7.65 Mauser	.311	44/40 Rem. Rifles	.425
.303 British, 7.7 M/M Jap.	.313	444 Marlin	.430
8 M/M Mauser (J.Bore)	.318	11 Mauser	.439
8 M/M Mauser (S Bore)	.323	45/70 & 458 Win.	.457
32 Win. Spec. 32 S. L. & 32 Rem.	.321		

BASIC GROOVE DIAMETER FOR PISTOLS

Caliber	Groove Dia.	Caliber	Groove Dia.
22 Jet	.222	38/40	.400
30 Mauser	.309	41 Colt	.406
30 Luger	.310	41 S & W Mag.	.410
32 Auto	.311	44/40 (revolver)	.425
32/20	.312	44 S & W Spec. & 44 Russian	.429
32 S & W & 32 Colt N.P.	.314	44 Mag. (S & W & Ruger)	.430
9 M/M Luger	.354	45 A.C.P.	.450
38 Special & 357 Mag. (Colt),		45 Auto Rim	.451
38 A.C.P. & 380 Auto	.355	45 Colt (post-war)	.451
38 Special & 357 Mag. (S & W)	.357	45 Colt (pre-war)	.454
38 S & W	.360	.455 Webley	.457

SIZING DIE DIAMETERS

.224	.225	.243	.244	.251	.257	.258
.264	.277	.278	.280	.284	.285	.301
.308	.309	.310	.311	.312	.313	.314
.321	.322	.323	.325	.338	.350	.352
.354	.355	.356	.357	.358	.359	.360
.375	.377	.378	.379	.400	.401	.410
.427	.428	.429	.430	.431	.450	.451
.452	.454	.457	.458	.459	.509	.512

LYMAN BULLET SIZING EQUIPMENT

MOULD MASTER XX

Lyman's Mould Master XX electric casting furnace features greatly increased capacity with lighter overall weight. It operates on household current. The thermostat housing has been relocated to one side allowing the caster a better view of the bottom-pour spout. Furthermore, access to the pot for ladle casting has been improved by replacing the over-arm stop with a metering thumbscrew in the lever hinge. Other features include:
- 20 lb. pot capacity.
- Calibrated thermostat permits controlled heat throughout the casting spectrum.
- Available in 115V A.C.

Furnace w/mould guide **$149.95**

MOULD MASTER BULLET CASTING FURNACE—

Heavy-duty, 11 lb. capacity furnace. Operates on standard household power—115 volts, A.C. or D.C., 1000 Watts. Calibrated dial control heats from 450° to 850° F. within 20°. Discharge spout is controlled by a lever operated valve.

Mould Master Furnace complete with Ingot
Mould and Mould Guide **$129.95**
Extra Ingot Mould **6.50**
Mould Guide **13.95**

DEBURRING TOOL—

Lyman's deburring tool can be used for chamfering or deburring of cases up to 45 caliber. For precise bullet seating, use the pointed end of the tool to bevel the inside of new or trimmed cases. To remove burrs left by trimming, place the other end of the deburring tool over the mouth of the case and twist. The tool's centering pin will keep the case aligned **$7.95**

MOULD HANDLES—

These large hardwood handles are available in three sizes—single, double and four-cavity. Single-cavity handles (for small block, black powder and specialty moulds) (9 oz.) **$10.95**
Double-cavity handles (for two-cavity and large-block single-cavity moulds) (9 oz.) **10.95**
Four-cavity handles (1 lb.) **14.95**

RIFLE MOULDS—

All Lyman rifle moulds are available in double cavity only, except those moulds where the size of the bullet necessitates a single cavity (12 oz.) **$29.50**

HOLLOW-POINT BULLETS—

Hollow-point moulds are cut in single-cavity blocks only and require single-cavity handles (9 oz.) **$34.50**

NRA-DESIGN, PAPER-PATCH BULLET MOULDS—

These mould-cast bullets of NRA design for paper-patch experimentation, in modern 30 caliber rifles **$34.50**

COMPOSITE CAST PISTOL BULLETS—

Kit includes single-cavity moulds for the nose/core and jacket, a special nose punch designed to fit the jacket's cavity during resizing, basic casting instructions and special information on preparing these new two-piece bullets. Requires single-cavity handles (1 lb. 2 oz.) **$69.50**

SHOTGUN SLUG MOULDS—

Available in 12 or 20 gauge and do not require rifling. Moulds are single cavity only cut on the larger double-cavity block and require double-cavity handles (14 oz.) **$34.50**

LEAD DIPPER—

Dipper with cast iron head. Spout is shaped for easy, accurate pouring that prevents air pockets in the finished bullet. **$6.50**

INERTA BULLET PULLER—

Quickly and easily removes bullets from cartridges **$19.95**

UNIVERSAL TRIMMER

This trimmer with patented chuck head accepts all metallic rifle or pistol cases, regardless of rim thickness. To change calibers, simply change the case head pilot. Other features include coarse and fine cutter adjustments, an oil-impregnated bronze bearing, and a rugged cast base assures precision alignment and years of service.

Trimmer less pilot **$38.95**
Extra pilot (state caliber) **1.75**
Replacement cutter head **2.25**

PILOTS AVAILABLE IN THE FOLLOWING SIZES $1.95

17	All 17 caliber rifle cases
22	All 22 caliber rifle cases
24	All 6 M M rifle cases
25A	25 ACP pistol cases
25	All 25 caliber rifle cases
26	All 6.5 M M and 264 caliber rifle cases
27	All 270 caliber rifle cases
28	All 7 M M and 284 caliber rifle cases
29	7.35 M M Italian rifle cases
30	All 30 caliber rifle plus 30 Mauser, 30 Luger and 32 Auto pistol cases
31	303 British, 7.65 M M Argentine, 7.7 M M Japanese, 32 20 rifle, plus 32 Colt and 32 S & W pistol cases
32	All 32 caliber rifle cases
8MM	8M M rifle (.323" dia.) cases
33	All 33 caliber rifle cases
9MM	9M M Luger, 38 ACP, 38 Super, 380 Auto pistol cases
34	348 Winchester rifle cases
35A	351 Winchester rifle cases
35	All 35 caliber rifle cases plus 38 Special 357, Magnum, 38 Colt and 38 S & W pistol cases
37	375 H & H, 378 Weatherby Mag., 38 55 rifle plus 41 Long Colt pistol cases
39	38 40, 301 Winchester rifle cases
41	41 S & W Magnum pistol plus 405 Winchester rifle cases
44A	44 40 rifle and pistol cases
44	44 Special, 44 Magnum pistol plus 444 Marlin and 43 Spanish rifle cases
45A	45 ACP, 45 A.R., 45 Colt, 455 Webley pistol, plus 11 M M Mauser rifle cases
45	45 70, 458 Winchester Mag., 460 Weatherby Mag. rifle cases

GAS CHECKS—

Gas checks are gilding metal caps which fit to the base of cast bullets. These caps protect the bullet base from the burning effect of hot powder gases and permit higher velocities. Easily seated during the bullet sizing operation, only Lyman gas checks should be used with Lyman cast bullets.

22 through 45 caliber (per 1000)
Note: .38 Special same as 35 caliber. **$13.50**
Also available in 45 caliber **15.50**

LEAD POT

Cast iron pot and holder for melting lead alloy using any source of heat. Pot capacity is 10 pounds of alloy. Holder keeps pot secure and level, prevents lead from splashing on stove or burner **$6.50**

MEC RELOADING

GRABBER 76

The Grabber grabs and squeezes the shell to dimensions well within commercial tolerances for new shells. Grabber resizing completely reforms the metal portion of the fired shotgun shell to factory standards in **all** respects. (Low brass 2¾" shells.) Resizing is done as an integral part of the reloading sequence and without undue agitation that might affect the uniformity of the charges. The measure assembly has been designed for strength and safety. Large capacity shot container holds 17+ pounds.

- AUTOMATIC PRIMER FEED
- GRABBER RESIZING
- EXCLUSIVE CHARGE BAR WINDOW
- FLIP TYPE MEASURE
- EXCLUSIVE PRIMER SEATING
- LARGE CAPACITY SHOT CONTAINER

12, 16, 20, 28 or 410 gauges fitted in durable chrome

price complete

$289.56

HUSTLER 76

The Grabber with its revolutionary resize chamber, combined with the MEC hydraulic system, becomes the Hustler. It gives you your own miniature reloading factory, but one that resizes to under industry standards for minimum chamber. The motor operates on regular 110 volt household current and the pump supplies instant, constant pressure. The entire downstroke and upstroke functions are utilized and synchronized to allow continuous action. Every stroke of the cylinder piston is positive and performs all operations at six reloading stations. Every downstroke of the reloader produces one finished shell.
Reloader less pump and hose...**$369.63**

- ALL THE FINE FEATURES OF THE GRABBER PLUS HYDRAULIC POWER

12, 16, 20, 28 or 410 gauges fitted in durable chrome

price complete

$778.03

600 JR.
THE PLASTIC MASTER

Any MEC reloader can be used for reloading plastic shells, but the "600 jr." positively masters the process. The PLASTIC MASTER is a single stage tool, but is designed to permit rapid, progressive operation. Every step from fired shell to the fresh-crimped product is performed with a minimum of motion. An exclusive shell holder positions and holds the shell at each station. No transfer die is required . . . resizing dies at reconditioning and crimping stations give your shell its proper form.

- CAM-ACTUATED RECONDITIONING STATION
- SPINDEX STAR CRIMP HEAD
- ADJUSTA-GUIDE WAD FEED
- CAM-LOCK CRIMP
- HARDENED CHARGING BAR
- TOGGLE LINKAGE
- FLIP-TYPE MEASURE
- ALL STEEL CONSTRUCTION
- PRIMER CATCHER

Choice of 10, 12, 16, 20, 28 or .410 gauges— fitted in beautiful lifetime chrome

price complete

$105.19

700
VERSAMEC
THE SINGLE STAGE ULTIMATE

The exclusive Platform Cam which provides the longer ejection stroke necessary to eject existing field shells at the resize station. No adjustments or part changes are required, regardless of brass length. The Pro-Check, which programs the charge bar and wad guide. This ingenious device programs the measure assembly to position the charge bar in the correct sequence. Even the hunter who reloads once or twice a year cannot err . . . the Pro-Check eliminates mistakes . . . automatically. The paper crimp starter which assembles into the Spindex Crimper. Only seconds are required to change from the 6 or 8 point plastic crimp spinner to the smooth cone for fired paper shells.

- CAM-ACTUATED RECONDITIONING STATION
- PRO-CHECK
- SPINDEX STAR CRIMP HEAD
- ADJUSTA-GUIDE WAD FEED
- CAM LOCK CRIMP
- HARDENED CHARGING BAR
- TOGGLE LINKAGE
- FLIP TYPE MEASURE
- PRIMER CATCHER
- ALL STEEL CONSTRUCTION

Choice of 12, 16, 20, 28 or .410 gauges— fitted in beautiful lifetime chrome.

price complete

$120.41

MEC RELOADING

650
THE RELOADER WITH A MEMORY

Up to 12 operations on 6 individual shells are performed simultaneously with one stroke of the press handle. Outstanding features of the 650 include a revolutionary Star Crimp Head, Automatic Primer feeding, exclusive Resize-Deprime apparatus, Toggle linkage, cam operated crimping die and Auto-Cycle charging sequence. The Auto-Cycle charging sequence automatically maintains the correct operating sequence of the charge bar. The charge bar can be actuated only when a shell is properly located to receive the powder. The MEC 650 can even handle the 3 inch shells . . . high-base, low base and light or heavy plastics. It's all steel with an extra heavy base-column. Tool comes completely assembled, tested and ready to use . . . without adjustment.

- AUTOMATIC PRIMER FEED.
- AUTOMATIC POWDER AND SHOT CHARGING
- FLIP-TYPE MEASURE
- HARDENED CHARGING BAR
- OPEN BASE
- PRIMER CATCHER
- EXCLUSIVE CAM-OPERATED CRIMP
- EXCLUSIVE RESIZE-DEPRIME APPARATUS
- 12 OPERATIONS WITH 1 STROKE
- SPINDEX STAR CRIMP HEAD
- AUTO-CYCLE

Choice of 12, 16, 20, 28 or 410 gauges — fitted in beautiful lifetime chrome

price complete

$211.32

THE MINIATURE RELOADING FACTORY

Take the 650 or the Super 600 reloader and marry it to a hydraulic system . . . the result is the hydraMEC, today's most advanced concept in high-volume reloaders. The hydraulic system is compact, lightweight and designed for long, trouble-free service. The motor operates on regular 110 volt household current and the pump supplies instant, constant pressure . . . no slowdown, no misses. The entire downstroke and upstroke functions are utilized and synchronized to allow continuous action. Every stroke of the cylinder piston is positive and performs up to 12 operations on six reloading stations. Every downstroke of the reloader produces one finished shell. The operator inserts empty shells and wads . . . the hydraMEC does the rest . . . automatically.

Tool linked for hydraulic operation to include base and cylinder.
hydraMEC 650 .... **$302.58**

HYDRAULIC UNIT ONLY—Hydraulic unit to include pump, motor, cylinder, controls, base, links and bolts required to attach to reloader with instructions. **$531.28**

650 HYDRAMEC

- AUTOMATIC PRIMER FEED
- AUTOMATIC POWDER & SHOT CHARGING
- FLIP-TYPE MEASURE
- HARDENED CHARGING BAR
- PRIMER CATCHER
- EXCLUSIVE CAM-OPERATED CRIMP
- EXCLUSIVE RESIZE-DEPRIME APPARATUS
- TOGGLE LINKAGE
- FOOL PROOF HYDRAULIC SYSTEM
- 12 OPERATIONS WITH 1 STROKE

$700.17

Choice of 12, 16, 20, 28 or .410 gauges — fitted in beautiful lifetime chrome

---

ACCESSORY EQUIPMENT

SPINDEX STAR CRIMP HEAD
The SPINDEX STAR CRIMP HEAD is a revolutionary crimp starter that prepares plastic shells for a perfect crimp . . . everytime. The SPINDEX automatically engages the original folds of each shell. No prior indexing of the shell is required . . . even on some of the earlier, unskived plastics that show no impressions of the original crimp folds. Because it employs a pressed metal part that spins into alignment with the original folds, the SPINDEX starts every crimp perfectly. And even better . . . you have a choice of an 8-segment, 6-segment, or smooth crimp starter, depending on the shells you are reloading.

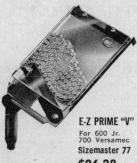

E-Z PRIME "V"
For 600 Jr.
700 Versamec
Sizemaster 77
$26.38

COMPLETELY AUTOMATIC PRIMER FEED
FROM CARTON TO SHELL WITH SECURITY, IT PROVIDES SAFE, CONVENIENT PRIMER POSITIONING AND INCREASES RATE OF PRODUCTION. REDUCES BENCH CLUTTER, ALLOWING MORE FREE AREA FOR WADS AND SHELLS.
- PRIMERS TRANSFER DIRECTLY FROM CARTON TO RELOADER — ELIMINATING TUBES AND TUBE FILLERS.
- POSITIVE MECHANICAL FEED (NOT DEPENDENT UPON AGITATION OF PRESS)
- VISIBLE SUPPLY
- AUTOMATIC — ELIMINATES HAND MOTION
- LESS SUSCEPTIBLE TO DAMAGE
- ADAPTS TO ALL DOMESTIC AND MOST FOREIGN PRIMERS WITH ADJUSTMENT OF THE COVER
- MAY BE PURCHASED SEPARATELY TO REPLACE TUBE TYPE PRIMER FEED OR TO UPDATE YOUR PRESENT RELOADER.

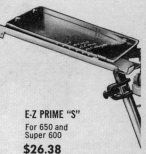

E-Z PRIME "S"
For 650 and Super 600
$26.38

SPINDEX STAR CRIMP HEAD
Dual Purpose 6 & 8 Fold (specify gauge and model of press)

434 for Model 400	$6.54
534 for all Models 600 Jr., and 700	6.54
600 Super and 650	6.54

ACCESSORIES

301L13X BH & Cap Accy.	$1.31
453P Wad Finger Ptlc.	.87
634P Crimp St. Paper	3.19
8042 Magnum Container	2.90
15CA Ez Pak Accy.	3.19

FOR THE MEC 600 JR.

741P Die Set (12, 16, 20, 28, 410) specify gauge	$36.28
741P-O Pie Set (10 gauge)	40.62
73 Kit VersaMEC 700 Modification	15.96
ProCheck	3.19
63 Kit for 3" shells (12 and 20 gauge)	3.92

FOR THE VERSAMEC 700

741V Die Set (10, 12, 16, 28, 410) specify gauge	$40.62

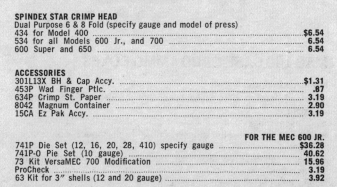

MEC E-Z PAK
Here's how to pack shot shell reloads the easy way. As each shell is reloaded, they're placed in E-Z PAK, exactly as if they were being placed in the box. After each 25 shells, original box is slipped over E-Z PAK, which is then inverted, and removed. Nothing easier — nothing neater. Available in all gauges.

$3.19

MEC SIZEMASTER 77
- SINGLE-STAGE
- PRECISION SHELL HOLDER
- EXCLUSIVE RESIZING CHAMBER
- AUTOMATIC PRIMER FEED
- POSITIVE REPRIMING
- CHARGE BAR WINDOW
- PRO-CHECK
- ADJUSTA-GUIDE WAD FEED
- WAD PRESSURE GAUGE
- WAD HEIGHT GAUGE
- EXTRA CAPACITY SHOT CONTAINER
- SPINDEX CRIMP STARTER
- CAM-ACTUATED CRIMPING STATION

Size Master 77 (includes Primer Feed)	$161.15
77 Die Set 12, 16, 20, 28 and 410	60.67
77 10-gauge Die Set	71.22

MTM

CASE-GARD 50 SERIES RIFLE AMMO CASES

Features include
- versatility - cases for every caliber from 222 to 458 Win.
- durability - material doesn't warp, crack, chip, peel, expand, or contract.
- each case rests in its own individual compartment.
- unique hinge is designed to keep the cover in the open position when reloading.
- Snap-lok latch protects contents from inadvertent spilling.
- each CASE-GARD 50 ammo box is supplied with a form for recording load and sight data.

Available in MTM Green or Light Brown

RS-50 (Small Rifle)	222 to 222 Mag	$3.19
RM-50 (Medium Rifle)	22-250 to 308 Win	3.19
RL-50 (Large Rifle)	220 Swift to 458 Win	3.19
RS-S-50	22 & 6mm PPC's, 22 & 6mm Rem. BR's	3.19
22 Horn	22 Hornet only	3.19

CASE-GARD H50 SERIES DELUXE AMMO CASE

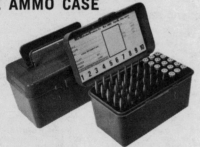

Features include:
- handle for ease of carrying.
- scuff resistant, texturized finish.
- extra space between rounds to facilitate removal when wearing gloves.
- design that allows belted magnums to be carried rim up or down.

Available in MTM Green or Light Brown

H50-RS	17 Rem. to 223 Rem.	$4.39
H50-RM	22-250 to 308 Win.	4.39
H50-RL	6mm Rem. to 30-06	4.39
H50-R MAG	264 Win. Mag to 470 KYNOCH	4.39

CASE-GARD 22 MATCH AMMO BOX

CASE-GARD® 22 Match Ammo Box— For the Small Bore Competitor. Precision molded body designed to hold 30 rounds - 3 strings - projectile-down for easy handling; plus box of ammo and loose rounds, if desired. Inside of lid equipped with supports for stop watch. The lid holds the watch at a 40° angle, for ease of reading by shooter. The Case-Gard 22 Match Ammo Box features Snap-lok latch, virtually indestructible integral hinge, and leather-like textured finish.

Available in MTM Green or Light Brown

SB-22	$5.10

CASE-GARD 9 AMMO WALLET

CASE-GARD 9 Ammo Wallet[T.M.] ammunition carrier holds 9 rounds in pocket or saddlebag. Provides absolute protection for ammunition.

Available in Dark Brown

W-9 SM	22-250 to 30-30	$3.10
W-9 LM	22-250 to 375 Mag	3.10

CASE-GARD 50 SERIES HANDGUN AMMO CASES

Features include:
- versatility - cases for every caliber from 9mm to 44 Mag.
- durability - virtually indestructible material doesn't warp, crack, chip, peel, expand or contract.
- each round rests in its own individual compartment.
- unique hinge designed to keep the cover in the open position when reloading.
- Snap-lok latch protects contents from inadvertent spilling.

Available in MTM Green or Light Brown

50-9	9mm	$1.49
PS-3	38 to 357 Mag.	1.49
PL-4	45, 41, and 44 Mag.	1.49

MAG 100 CASE-GARD AMMO BOXES

Features include:
- Snap-lok latch that protects loaded rounds from accidental spilling.
- integral hinge.
- molded of virtually indestructible high-impact polypropylene.
- pressure-sensitive label for reloading data included with each box.

Available in MTM Green or Light Brown

P-100-3	38 Special and 357 Mag.	$2.95
P-100-4	45 Auto, 41 Mag. and 44 Mag.	2.95

MTM

CASE-GARD AMMO WALLET
CASE-GARD 6, 12 AND 18

MTM offers 3 different models of varying capacity. All share common design features:
- textured finish looks like leather, and provides good gripping surface, even when wet.
- Snap-lok latch protects contents from damage, even if unit is dropped.
- integral hinge.
- contents are protected from dust and moisture.
- each round is carried securely in its own individual rattle-proof recess.

Available in Dark Brown

CALIBER→ CAPACITY↓	380 Auto & 9mm	38 & 357 Mag	41 Mag	44 Mag	45 Auto
6 Round	W6-9 $2.49	W6-38 $2.49	W6-41 $2.49	W6-44 $2.49	W6-45 $2.49
12 Round	W12-9 $2.69	W12-38 $2.69	W12-41 $2.69	W12-44 $2.69	W12-45 $2.69
18 Round	18-9 $2.99	18-38 $2.99	18-41 $2.99	18-44 $2.99	18-45 $2.99

CASE-GARD AMMO WALLET FOR 22's

Special **CASE-GARD Ammo Wallet** carrier holds 30 rounds, 22 Longs or 22 Mags . . . a convenient way to carry ammo to the range or field. Design features are:
- leather-like finish.
- Snap-lok latch protects case against inadvertent opening, even if dropped.
- each round is carried securely in its own recess.
- virtually indestructible hinge.

Available in Dark Brown
30-22M $3.10

MTM HANDLOADER'S LOG

MTM Handloader's Log. Space provided for 1,000 entries covering date, range, group size or score, components, and conditions. Book is heavy duty vinyl, reinforced 3-ring binder.
HL-74 .... $8.59
HL-50 extra pages 4.89

CASE-GARD 100 AMMO CARRIER FOR SKEET AND TRAP

THE MTM^(T.M.) CASE-GARD® 100 Round Shotshell Case carries 100 rounds in 2 trays; or 50 rounds, plus 2 boxes of factory ammo; or 50 rounds plus sandwiches and insulated liquid container; or 50 rounds, with room left for fired hulls.
- stainless steel hinge pin
- center balanced handles facilitate carrying and can be padlocked for security
- high-impact material supports 300 pounds, and will not warp, split, expand or contract
- dustproof and rainproof

Each **CASE-GARD 100** Shotshell case is supplied with 2 50-round trays.

Available in Textured Black
S100-12 .... 12 gauge $11.69
S100-16 .... 16 gauge 11.69
S100-20 .... 20 gauge 11.69

FUNNELS

MTM Benchrest Funnel Set designed specifically for the benchrest shooter. One fits 222 and 243 cases only; the other 7mm and 308 cases. Both can be used with pharmaceutical vials popular with benchrest competitors for storage of pre-weighed charges. Funnel design prevents their rolling off the bench.
BF-2 .... $2.39
MTM Universal Funnel fits all calibers from 222 to 45.
UF-1 .... $1.36
Patented MTM Adapt 5-in-1 Funnel Kit includes funnel, adapters for 17 Rem., 222 Rem. and 30 through 45. Long drop tube facilitates loading of maximum charges: 222 to 45.
AF-5 .... $2.95

PACIFIC

105 SHOTSHELL RELOADER

00-7 PRESS

MULTI-POWER 'C'

- All the features of expensive reloaders . . . without sacrificing quality.
- Crimps shells perfectly. Floating crimp starter automatically aligns with original crimp folds. Final crimp die is fully adjustable.
- Seats wads easily with built-in wad guide.
- Eliminates guesswork . . . all operations end on positive stop.

105 SHOTSHELL RELOADER Complete with charge bushings.	**$95.00**
105 DIE SET For quick-change conversion to different gauge.	**30.00**
105 MAGNUM CONVERSION SET Converts 2¾" dies to load 3" shells of same gauge, or vice versa.	**11.00**
105 CRIMP STARTER (8-point crimp starter standard equipment with loader and with Die Sets).	**2.50**
EXTRA CHARGE BUSHINGS	**2.00**

- "Power-Pac" linkage multiplies lever-to-ram power.
- Frame of press angled 30° to one side, making the "O" area of press totally accessible.
- More mounting area for rock-solid attachment to bench.
- Special strontium-alloy frame provides greater stress, resistance—won't spring under high pressures needed for full-length resizing.

00-7 PRESS (does not include dies or shell holder) **$93.95**
00-7 AUTOMATIC PRIMER FEED (complete with large and small primer tubes) **11.00**

0-7 PRESS

- Faster priming cycle. Prime during the normal stroke of the ram without hand operation of the primer arm.
- Auto primer feed permits fast and simple delivery of primers to the seating cup.
- Easier to use. The frame of the 0-7 Press is angled 30 degrees to one side to make the "O" area totally accessible.
- Delivers maximum energy with minimum effort during the critical final half-inch stroke.
- More mounting area for better attachment to bench.
- No springing or alignment problems.

0-7 PRESS (does not include dies or shellholder) **$65.95**
0-7 AUTOMATIC PRIMER FEED (complete with large and small primer tubes) **11.00**

- Pacific's patented primer system for convenient and positive primer seating.
- Pacific's patented automatic primer feed easily attached.
- "O" frame of high-density annealed cast iron insures perfect alignment of die and shell holder. Impossible for frame to spring even when swaging large caliber bullets.
- Swinging toggle multiplies leverage for easy operation when resizing and case forming.
- Steel links for maximum strength.
- All bearing surfaces hardened and precision ground.

MULTI-POWER 'C' complete press (does not include dies, primer catcher or shell holder). ....**$ 92.50**
MULTI-POWER 'C' PACKAGE (Series I & II full-length die sets only). Includes Multi-Power 'C' press, complete set of Dura-chrome dies, primer catcher, primer arm and removable head shell holder. **115.00**
MULTI-POWER 'C' PACKAGE with carbide sizing die. (Series II only). **133.50**

PACIFIC

155 SHOTSHELL RELOADER

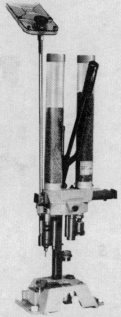

The 155 resizes entire length of the shell including head and rim. Spring-loaded finish die produces perfect tapered crimp. 113 interchangeable shot and powder bushings and handles both plastic and paper shells. Quick-change die sets let you load everything from 3-inch 12-gauge shells to 2½-inch .410 gauge shells. Dies are polished steel with deep blued finish. All operations end on a positive stop, including fully adjustable wad seating.

155 SHOTSHELL RELOADER 10 Ga. $161.00
155 SHOTSHELL RELOADER 12 & 20 Ga.
$139.95
155 SHOTSHELL RELOADER 16, 28 & .410 Ga. $144.95
Complete with standard charge bushings. (Does not include automatic primer feed.)
155 APF SHOTSHELL RELOADER 12 & 20 Ga. $161.00
155 APF SHOTSHELL RELOADER 16, 28 & .410 Ga. $166.00
Complete with standard charge bushings.

155/155 APF DIE SET 12 & 20 Ga. $45.00
155 10 Ga. DIE SET (Special Order—Loader must be returned to factory.) $60.00
155/155 APF DIE SET 16, 28 & .410 Ga. $45.00
155/155 APF MAGNUM CONVERSION SET $20.50
Converts 2¾" dies to load 3" shells of same gauge, or vice versa.
AUTOMATIC PRIMER FEED CONVERSION UNIT $28.00
EXTRA CRIMP STARTERS 2.50
EXTRA CHARGE BUSHINGS 2.00

266 SHOTSHELL RELOADER

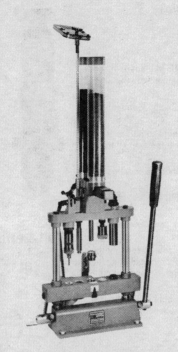

The most advanced loader in its price range. Right or left-hand operation to suit the operator. New wad guide with unbreakable spring fingers prevents wad tipping. Two-way adjustable crimper assures precise crimp depth and taper. Automatic primer feed automatically drops primer when preceding shell is powder charged.

SAFE AND CONVENIENT—Charging assembly constructed for no-spark safety. Shot and powder assembly removes completely for fast, easy load change.

266 SHOTSHELL RELOADER
Complete with charge bushings.
12 & 20 ga. $208.00; 16, 28 & .410 ga.* $214.00
266 DIE SET
For conversion to different gauge.
12, 16, 20 28 & .410 ga. $49.00

266 MAGNUM CONVERSION SET $20.50
Converts 2¾" dies to load 3" shells of same gauge, or vice versa.
EXTRA CRIMP STARTER $2.50
EXTRA CHARGE BUSHINGS 2.00

Automatic primer feed does not operate in .410.

366-AUTO SHOTSHELL RELOADER

The 366-Auto features full-length resizing with each stroke, automatic primer feed, swing-out wad guide, three stage crimping featuring Taper-Loc for factory tapered crimp, automatic advance to the next station and automatic ejection. The turntable holds 8 shells for 8 operations with each stroke. The primer tube filler is fast; automatic charge bar loads shot and powder; right or left hand operation; interchangeable charge bushings, die sets and magnum dies and crimp starters for 6 point, 8 point and paper crimps.

366-AUTO SHOTSHELL RELOADER 12, 16, 20 or 28 gauge $399.95
Complete with standard charge bushings.

366—AUTO ● ADVANCE $44.00
The Auto ● Advance automatically advances the shells to the next station. It is standard equipment on 366 loaders manufactured after November 1, 1975 and it can be added to any earlier models.
—SHELL DROP $48.00
Makes it unnecessary to manually remove loaded shells from the shell plate. Standard on 366-Auto loaders manufactured after February 1, 1976. The shell drop can be installed on earlier models; please return your 366 to Pacific postpaid for factory installation (specify gauge).
366—SWING-OUT WAD GUIDE AND SHELL DROP COMBO $110.00
Return your 366 to Pacific postpaid (specify gauge).
366—SWING-OUT WAD GUIDE $75.00
Makes insertion of the wad easier. Return 366 to Pacific postpaid for installation.
366—SHOT/POWDER SHUTOFF $27.50
Now standard on Pacific's 366 loaders, the unit fits any 366 loader and can be purchased separately.

366-AUTO DIE SET 12 & 20 Ga. $77.00
366-AUTO DIE SET 16 & 28 Ga. 82.50
366-AUTO MAGNUM CONVERSION SET $20.50
Converts 2¾" dies to load 3" shells of same gauge, or vice versa.
EXTRA CRIMP STARTERS $2.50
EXTRA CHARGE BUSHINGS 2.00

PACIFIC

DURACHROME DIES

GUARANTEED FOR LIFE
For All Popular Rifle & Pistol Calibers

- **LIFETIME DURACHROME FINISH** — satin-hard chrome protection that keeps dies looking and working like new. Guaranteed never to chip, crack or peel.
- **HEXAGON SPINDLE HEADS** — for easy removal of stuck cases and more positive adjustment.
- **PRECISION-ROLLED** ⅞ x 14 threads held to perfect size and pitch. Fits most other tools because this pioneer Pacific development has been widely copied.
- **FAST CONVENIENT ADJUSTMENT** is made possible by Pacific's all-steel lock rings.
- **BUILT IN PROVISION FOR CRIMPING** provided on all bullet seating dies.
- **ALL STEEL CONSTRUCTION** — no inexpensive substitute metals.
- **PRECISE DIMENSIONS** — minimum tolerances maintained throughout. After chambering, dies are hardened for lifetime wear, then polished to insure perfect dimensions and smooth interior surfaces.
- **HEAVY DUTY STORAGE BOX**, sample of Pacific Die Lube and spare decap pin are included with each set.

2 DIE SETS *(for bottleneck cases)*   **3 DIE SETS** *(for straight sided cases)*

Full-Length Sizing Sets
Series I **$24.50**
Series III **28.00**

Neck Sizing Set
Series I & III **$24.50**

For Series II Only
Standard	Carbide
$25.50	**$44.95**

#1 CARBIDE SIZE DIES
For 3 Die Sets
The ideal answer for large volume reloading. Diamond-hard finish won't scratch cases, no lubrication needed. Cases need not be cleaned.

METALLIC SILHOUETTE & BENCH REST DIE SETS
2 and 3 Die Sets **$28.00**

FILE TYPE TRIM DIE $11.95
Uses a fine grade file to insure precision case length. The most inexpensive and practical way to trim and form rifle cases. Made of finest steel with lifetime Durachrome finish. Available in most rifle calibers.

TAPER CRIMP DIE $11.00
The taper crimp die, used for applying proper crimp to autoloading pistols, may be added to 3-die pistol sets, for improved feeding and functioning.

REMOVABLE HEAD SHELL HOLDER $4.50
Precision machined from hardened steel then heat treated to prevent wear and give lifetime operation. Each Shell Holder is specifically designed for case to assure accurate alignment and eliminate tipping and side movement. Fits all tools using Pacific "C" design.

CUSTOM DIE SETS
Manufactured to order. See Die Reference Chart ... **$32.00**

PACIFIC DIE REFERENCE CHART

2 DIE SETS (Rifle)

CARTRIDGE	Die Group	Primer Punch Size	Shell Holder	Trimmer Pilot	Bullet Puller Collet
17 Rem. [.172]	I*	Small	16	Order Pilot & Cutter as one unit for all 17 cal.	1
17/222 [.172]	Custom*	Small	16		1
17/223 [.172]	Custom*	Small	16		1
218 Bee [.224]	III	Small	7	1	2
219 Zipper [.224]	Custom	Large	2	1	2
221 Rem. [.224]	I	Small	16	1	2
222 Rem. [.224]	I*	Small	16	1	2
222 Rem. Mag. [.224]	I*	Small	16	1	2
22 Hornet [.224]	I	Small	3	1	2
22 K-Hornet [.224]	Custom	Small	3	1	2
22 RCFM-Jet [.224]	Custom	Small	6	1	2
22 PPC [.224]	Sil & BR Dies	Small	6	1	2
5.6 x 50 Mag. [.224]	Custom	Small	16	1	2
5.6 x 52R [.227]	Custom	Large	2	1	2
5.6 x 57 [.224]	Custom	Large	1	1	2
223 Rem. [.224]	I*	Small	16	1	2
22/250 [.224]	I*	Large	1	1	2
220 Swift [.224]	I*	Large	4	1	2
22 Sav. HP [.227]	Custom	Large	2	1	2
224 Wby. [.224]	Custom*	Large	17	1	2
225 Win. [.224]	III	Large	4	1	2
240 Wby. [.243]	III	Large	1	3	3
243 Win. [.243]	I*	Large	1	3	3
244/6MM [.243]	I*	Large	1	3	3
6MM Int. [.243]	Sil & BR Dies*	Large	1	3	3
6MM/223 [.243]	Sil & BR Dies*	Small	16	3	3
6MM/PPC [.243]	Sil & BR Dies	Small	6	3	3
6MM/284 [.243]	Custom*	Large	1	3	3
6 x 47 Rem. [.243]	Sil & BR Dies*	Small	16	3	3
250 Sav. [.257]	III	Large	1	4	4
25/06 [.257]	I*	Large	1	4	4
257 Rbts. [.257]	III*	Large	1	4	4
25/20 Win. [.257]	Custom	Small	7	4	4
25/35 Win. [.257]	III	Large	2	4	4
256 Win. [.257]	Custom	Small	6	4	4
257 Wby. [.257]	III	Large	5	4	4
25 Rem. [.257]	Custom	Large	12	4	4
25/284 [.257]	Custom*	Large	1	4	4
6.5 x 55 [.264]	I*	Large	19	5	4
6.5/06 [.264]	Custom*	Large	1	5	4
6.5 Rem. Mag. [.264]	Custom*	Large	5	5	4
6.5 Mann. [.264]	Custom	Large	20	5	4
6.5 Carc. [.264]	Custom	Large	21	5	4
6.5 Jap. [.264]	Custom	Large	34	5	4
6.5 x 57 [.264]	III	Large	1	5	4
6.5 x 68 [.264]	III	Large	30	5	4
264 Win. Mag. [.264]	I	Large	5	5	4
270 Win. [.270]	I*	Large	1	6	5
270 Wby. [.270]	Custom	Large	5	6	5
7MM Mau. (7x57) [.284]	I*	Large	1	7	6
7MM/08 [.284]	Sil & BR Dies	Large	1	7	6
7MM Rem. Mag. [.284]	I*	Large	5	7	6
7MM Rem. BR [.284]	Sil & BR Dies	Large	1	7	6
7MM TCU [.284]	Sil & BR Dies*	Large	16	16	9
7MM Merrill [.284]	Sil & BR Dies	Large	4	N/A	N/A
7 x 65R [.284]	Custom	Large	13	7	6
7MM Wby. [.284]	III*	Large	5	7	6
7 x 64 [.284]	Custom	Large	1	7	6
7MM/223 Ingram [.284]	Sil & BR Dies*	Small	16	7	6
7 x 47 Helm [.284]	Sil & BR Dies*	Small	16	7	6
7 x 61 S & H [.284]	Custom*	Large	35	7	6
280 Rem. (7MM Rem. Exp.) [.284]	III*	Large	1	7	6
284 Win. [.284]	III*	Large	1	7	6
7.35 Carc. [.300]	Custom	Large	21	8	7
30/30 Win. [.308]	I*	Large	2	8	7
300 Sav. [.308]	I	Large	1	8	7
30 Luger [.308]	III	Large	8	8	7
30 Merrill [.308]	Sil & BR Dies	Large	4	N/A	N/A

*Neck size die available.

[Bullet Diameter]

2 DIE SETS (Rifle)

CARTRIDGE	Die Group	Primer Punch Size	Shell Holder	Trimmer Pilot	Bullet Puller Collet
30 Herrett [.308]	Sil & BR Dies*	Large	2	8	7
303 Sav. [.308]	Custom	Large	33	9	7
308 Win. [.308]	I*	Large	1	9	7
30/40 Krag [.308]	III	Large	11	9	7
30/06 [.308]	I*	Large	1	9	7
300 H & H [.308]	Custom	Large	5	9	7
300 Win. Mag. [.308]	I	Large	5	9	7
300 Wby. [.308]	III*	Large	5	9	7
308 Norma Mag. [.308]	Custom*	Large	5	9	7
7.62 Russ. [.308]	I	Large	23	9	7
7.5 Swiss [.308]	III	Large	30	9	7
7.7 Jap. [.312]	III	Large	1	10	7
303 Brit. [.312]	I*	Large	11	10	7
7.65 Belg. [.312]	III	Large	24	10	7
32 Win. Spl. [.321]	III	Large	2	11	8
32/20 Win. [.310]	Custom	Small	7	10	7
8MM Mau. [.323]	I*	Large	1	10	8
8MM/06 [.323]	Custom*	Large	1	10	8
8MM Rem. Mag. [.323]	III	Large	5	10	8
8 x 60S [.323]	Custom	Large	1	10	8
8 x 68S [.323]	Custom	Large	30	10	8
8.15 x 46R [.337]	Custom	Large	2	11	8
338 Win. Mag. [.338]	I	Large	5	13	8
33 Win. [.338]	I	Large	14	3	8
340 Wby. [.338]	III	Large	5	13	8
348 Win. [.348]	Custom	Large	25	14	9
35 Rem. [.358]	I*	Large	26	15	9
35 Whelen [.358]	Custom	Large	1	15	9
357 B & D [.358]	Sil & BR Dies	Large	30	15	9
350 Rem. Mag. [.358]	Custom*	Large	5	15	9
357 Herrett [.357]	Sil & BR Dies*	Large	2	15	9
358 Win. [.358]	III	Large	1	15	9
375 H & H [.375]	III*	Large	5	16	9
378 Wby. [.375]	Custom	Large	14	16	9
9.3 x 74R [.366]	Custom	Large	13	15	9
9.3 x 57 [.366]	Custom	Large	1	15	9
9.3 x 62 [.366]	Custom	Large	1	15	9
10.3 x 60 [.415]	Custom	Small	25	N/A	N/A
460 Wby. [.458]	Custom	Large	14	19	14

3 DIE SETS

CARTRIDGE	Die Group	Primer Punch Size	Shell Holder	Trimmer Pilot	Bullet Puller Collet
25 ACP [.251]	II	Small	37	4	4
30 M1 Carb. [.308]	II	Small	22	9	7
32 ACP [.312]	Custom	Small	22	10	7
32 S&W Long [.312]	II	Small	36	10	7
32 S&W Short [.312]	Custom	Small	36	10	7
9MM Luger [.355]	II	Small	8	15	9
380 Auto [.355]	II	Small	16	15	9
38 Super Auto [.357]	Custom	Small	8	15	9
38 S&W [.357]	Custom	Small	28	15	9
38 Spl. [.357]	II	Small	6	15	9
357 Mag. [.357]	II	Small	6	15	9
375 Win. [.375]	II	Large	2	16	9
38/40 Win. [.400]	Custom	Large	9	16	11
41 Mag. [.410]	II	Small	29	17	12
44 Spl. [.430]	II	Large	30	18	12
44 Mag. [.430]	II	Large	30	18	12
44 Auto Mag. [.430]	Custom	Large	1	18	12
44/40 Win. [.429]	Custom	Large	9	18	12
45 Auto Rim [.451]	Custom	Large	31	19	13
45 ACP [.451]	II	Large	1	19	13
45 Colt [.451]	II	Large	32	19	13
444 Marlin [.430]	II	Large	27	18	12
45/70 Govt. [.458]	II	Large	14	19	13
459 Win. [.458]	II	Large	5	19	13
45 Win. Mag. [.451]	Sil & BR Dies	Large	1	19	13

PACIFIC

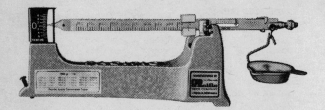

MAGNETIC PACIFIC DELUXE SCALE

Single balance beam teams with three counterpoises to give you added speed and accuracy. Graduated over/under scale lets you check powder charge or bullet weight variation without adjustments. Accepts weights up to 500 grains. Your choice of grain or gram measurements **$42.00**

MESUR-KIT™

An accurate, inexpensive portable measure at home, in the field or on the bench. Simple to use. Precise graduations make adjustable tube easy to set. Shearing action of Mesur-Kit arm gives precise charge leveling. Complete with chart for more than 1,000 load settings. Includes universal powder can. **$13.25**
Extra adjustable measure tube **11.00**

ALUMINUM POWDER FUNNEL

All-aluminum construction of Pacific's powder funnel eliminates the static electricity and powder clinging that occurs with plastic funnels. Available in 17, 22/270 and 28/45 calibers. **$2.25**

CASE CARE KIT

An invaluable aid in preparing deprimed cases for priming and loading. The kit contains a case lube pad with a reloading block in the lid, plus an assortment of popular case items including: accessory handle, three case neck brushes, large and small primer pocket cleaners, chamfering and deburring tool and bottle of case lube. **$21.95**

MULTI-DELUXE POWDER MEASURE

Fast, accurate measurement of all powder types. Standard 7/8-14 threads for mounting on reloading press or its bench stand. Includes both rifle and pistol metering assemblies, two powder-drop tubes (22-30 caliber and 30-45 caliber); large capacity hopper; blued-steel bench stand; Sure-Loc lock ring. Converts easily for left-hand operation.
Multi-Deluxe Powder Measure **$55.00**
Extra Rifle Metering Assembly **11.00**
Extra Pistol Metering Assembly **11.00**

PISTOL POWDER MEASURE

Sliding charge bar with interchangeable bushings gives a wide selection of loads. Standard 7/8-14 threads for mounting on reloading press, bench or stand. Can be also hand held above loading block.
Pistol Powder Measure complete with stand and Sure-Loc lock ring. Does not include bushing **$25.00**
Bushings **2.00**

PISTOL POWDER MEASURE BUSHING CHART

Stock No.	Bushing Size No.	Dupont 700X	Dupont 4227	Dupont SR7625	Dupont SR4756	Dupont PB	Hercules Bullseye	Hercules 2400	Hercules Red Dot	Hercules Unique	Hercules Herco	Hercules Blue Dot	Hodgdon HP38	Hodgdon Trap 100	Hodgdon HS-5	Hodgdon HS-6	Hodgdon HS-7	Hodgdon H-110	Hodgdon H-4227	Norma R1	Norma R123	Winchester 231	Winchester 296	Winchester 630	Winchester 680
290006	1	2.0	NR	NR	NR	NR	2.6	NR	NR	NR	NR	NR	3.0	2.3	4.1	3.9	4.0	4.2	3.6	1.9	NR	3.0	NR	4.0	NR
290007	2	2.1	NR	NR	NR	NR	2.8	NR	NR	NR	NR	NR	3.2	2.5	4.5	4.2	4.4	4.5	3.9	2.0	NR	3.3	NR	4.2	NR
290008	3	2.3	NR	NR	NR	NR	3.0	NR	NR	NR	NR	NR	3.6	2.8	5.0	4.6	4.8	5.0	4.3	2.3	NR	3.6	NR	4.9	NR
290009	4	2.7	NR	NR	NR	NR	3.4	NR	NR	3.4	NR	NR	4.0	3.1	5.6	5.2	5.5	5.6	4.9	2.6	NR	4.1	NR	5.6	NR
290010	5	2.9	NR	3.1	NR	2.9	3.7	NR	NR	3.6	NR	NR	4.3	3.4	6.1	5.8	6.0	6.1	5.3	2.9	NR	4.5	NR	6.1	NR
290011	6	3.0	NR	3.5	NR	3.1	3.9	NR	NR	3.9	NR	NR	4.5	3.6	6.4	6.0	6.2	6.4	5.5	3.1	NR	4.6	NR	6.3	NR
290012	7	3.2	NR	3.6	NR	3.2	4.1	NR	NR	4.3	3.6	NR	4.8	3.9	6.9	6.3	6.7	6.9	6.0	3.2	NR	4.8	NR	6.5	NR
290013	8	3.5	NR	4.1	NR	3.3	4.4	NR	NR	4.5	3.8	NR	5.0	4.0	7.4	7.0	7.3	7.4	6.5	3.7	NR	5.3	NR	7.2	NR
290014	9	3.7	NR	4.2	3.7	3.4	4.5	NR	NR	4.6	3.9	NR	5.2	4.2	7.7	7.4	7.6	7.7	6.7	3.8	NR	5.5	NR	7.5	NR
290015	10	4.0	7.3	5.0	4.6	4.0	5.1	NR	NR	5.3	4.3	NR	6.1	4.9	8.5	7.9	8.4	8.6	7.5	4.3	NR	6.3	NR	8.4	NR
290016	11	4.3	7.5	5.1	4.6	4.6	5.2	7.3	NR	5.4	4.5	NR	6.4	5.1	8.9	8.2	8.8	9.0	7.7	4.5	NR	6.4	NR	8.7	8.8
290017	12	4.6	8.0	5.5	4.8	4.8	NR	7.9	2.2	5.8	4.8	NR	6.8	5.3	9.4	9.0	9.3	9.5	8.2	4.8	NR	6.9	NR	9.2	9.5
290018	13	5.0	8.8	6.0	5.6	5.3	NR	8.7	3.3	6.5	5.3	NR	7.6	5.8	10.3	9.7	10.1	10.4	9.0	5.3	NR	7.6	10.3	10.2	10.5
290019	14	5.5	9.4	6.4	6.0	5.8	NR	9.3	3.5	6.8	5.7	NR	8.1	6.4	11.1	10.5	11.0	11.1	9.6	5.7	NR	8.1	11.0	10.8	11.2
290020	15	5.8	9.9	6.8	6.4	6.0	NR	9.8	3.7	7.2	5.9	NR	8.5	6.7	11.8	11.1	11.6	11.8	10.2	6.0	NR	8.5	11.6	11.5	11.9
290021	16	6.1	10.3	7.1	6.7	6.4	NR	10.3	4.2	7.5	6.2	8.9	8.9	7.0	12.4	11.5	12.3	12.4	10.7	NR	NR	8.9	12.2	12.2	12.6
290022	17	6.5	11.5	7.9	7.6	7.0	NR	11.4	4.8	8.4	6.8	9.7	9.8	7.7	13.7	12.8	13.5	13.7	11.8	NR	NR	9.9	13.6	13.4	13.8
290023	18	NR	12.1	8.1	7.8	7.3	NR	12.0	5.3	8.7	7.3	10.1	10.2	8.0	14.1	13.3	13.9	14.0	12.2	NR	10.1	NR	14.0	13.8	14.3
290024	19	NR	12.3	8.6	8.3	7.6	NR	12.7	6.0	9.2	7.7	10.8	10.6	8.4	15.0	13.9	14.6	14.9	12.9	NR	10.8	NR	14.7	14.6	15.1
290025	20	NR	13.4	9.1	8.8	8.0	NR	13.4	6.4	9.7	8.1	11.4	11.4	8.8	15.7	14.9	15.6	15.6	13.6	NR	11.5	NR	15.6	15.5	16.0
290026	21	NR	14.7	9.9	9.7	8.9	NR	14.7	7.2	10.6	8.7	12.5	12.6	9.7	17.6	16.2	17.1	17.5	15.1	NR	12.5	NR	17.1	16.8	17.5
290027	22	NR	15.7	10.4	10.2	9.4	NR	15.5	7.5	11.4	9.5	13.2	13.2	10.4	18.0	17.0	17.7	17.9	15.9	NR	13.2	NR	17.9	18.0	18.3

NOTE: All Powder Designated in Grains.   NR = Not Recommended.

PONSNESS-WARREN

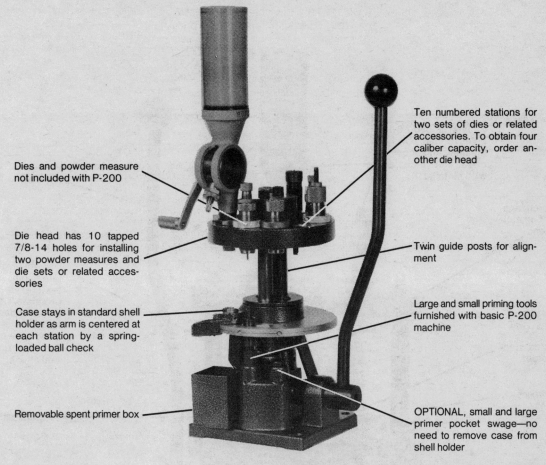

Dies and powder measure not included with P-200

Die head has 10 tapped 7/8-14 holes for installing two powder measures and die sets or related accessories

Case stays in standard shell holder as arm is centered at each station by a spring-loaded ball check

Removable spent primer box

Ten numbered stations for two sets of dies or related accessories. To obtain four caliber capacity, order another die head

Twin guide posts for alignment

Large and small priming tools furnished with basic P-200 machine

OPTIONAL, small and large primer pocket swage—no need to remove case from shell holder

METAL-MATIC P-200

Straight-wall case loader

The Metal-Matic P-200 has been designed to hold two calibers at one time. Conversion from one caliber to another is accomplished in less than five minutes. The P-200 uses standard 7/8-14 die sets and powder measure. Castings are heavy die cast aluminum coated with a silver vein black plastic applied with electrostatics and baked on for durability. Under normal conditions a person can load 200 rounds per hour, with some exceeding this average. The P-200 is designed for straight-wall cartridges.

Metal-Matic P-200 Complete (with small and large primer seating tools, less dies and powder measure). **$275.00**

Accessories:

Extra die head	**$ 34.00**
Large primer pocket swaging tool	**19.50**
Small primer pocket swaging tool	**19.50**
Case height stop assembly	**18.50**
Powder measure extension	**18.00**

METAL-MATIC P-200 PRIMER FEED

Primer feed fits standard 7/8-14 threads of the P-200 die head. Handles both large and small primers and has a shielded primer tube protector **$38.50**

PONSNESS-WARREN

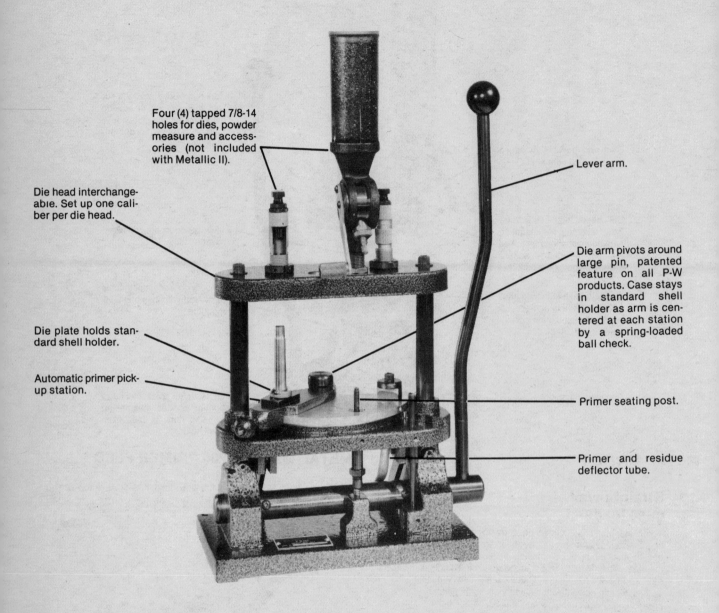

Four (4) tapped 7/8-14 holes for dies, powder measure and accessories (not included with Metallic II).

Die head interchangeable. Set up one caliber per die head.

Die plate holds standard shell holder.

Automatic primer pickup station.

Lever arm.

Die arm pivots around large pin, patented feature on all P-W products. Case stays in standard shell holder as arm is centered at each station by a spring-loaded ball check.

Primer seating post.

Primer and residue deflector tube.

Metallic M-II Rifle / pistol loader

The Metallic M-II is a totally unique and innovative loader capable of loading 150 rounds or more an hour with utmost precision. The Metallic M-II has power to spare for reforming brass, resizing cases, or loading tough calibers. The M-II uses standard dies, powder measure and shell holder. The die head has four tapped 7/8-14 holes to accept standard dies, powder measure and other accessories. Castings are heavy die case aluminum coated with a silver vein black plastic and baked on for durability.

Once the case is inserted into the shell holder, it is not removed until the case has been resized, new primer seated, powder dropped, and bullet seated and crimped. A depriming tube removes spent primer and residue, keeping the priming area clean. The Metallic M-II has an automatic primer feed. Optional features which can be purchased include additional die heads (for additional caliber capacity), and a powder measure extension to accommodate any standard powder measure.

Metallic M-II Complete (with small and large primer seating tools, automatic primer feed, large and small primer tubes, less dies, powder measure and shell holder) . . . **$440.00**

Accessories:

Extra die head . . . . **$ 34.00**
Powder measure extension **18.00**

CAL-die, bullet seating die . .**$ 33.00**
CAL-die, additional bullet retaining
    sleeves . . . . **$ 6.50**

PONSNESS-WARREN

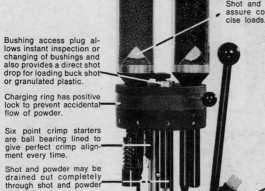

Bushing access plug allows instant inspection or changing of bushings and also provides a direct shot drop for loading buck shot or granulated plastic.

Charging ring has positive lock to prevent accidental flow of powder.

Six point crimp starters are ball bearing lined to give perfect crimp alignment every time.

Shot and powder may be drained out completely through shot and powder drop tube.

Double post construction for greater leverage and wear.

Absolute resizing, shell stays in full length sizing die through entire operation.

Handy, removable spent-primer box.

Large shot and powder reservoirs.

Shot and powder baffles assure consistently precise loads.

Trouble free tip-out wad

Sizing die is centered at each station by spring-loaded ball check.

Patented

Magn-O-Matic 10*

Special 10 gauge shotshell reloader

The Big 10 is here! Because of the growing interest in 10 gauge reloading, we have redesigned our popular Du-O-Matic into a special 10 gauge reloader, the Magn-O-Matic 10. It has all the features of its twin, the Du-O-Matic, with the exception of being convertible to other gauges. The Magn-O-Matic 10 is an exclusive 10 gauge tool for 3½ inch magnum shells. A special shot drop tube allows up to BB shot to be loaded easily, without bridging in the drop tube, while a special bushing access plug allows direct shot drop for even larger sizes. New shot and powder bushings will accommodate all 10 gauge loads up to 2¼ ounces. The Magn-O-Matic 10 possesses all of Ponsness-Warren's exclusive features. Factory-perfect reloads are made consistently by moving a shell encased in a full-length sizing die around the five station loading plate. The full length siz-

ing die and tooling are precision ground, then polished or richly blued. All castings are of the finest grade aluminum, precision machined and handsomely finished in baked-on, black wrinkle varnish. The Magn-O-Matic 10 will handle all types of 10-gauge 3½" shells at a rate of 4 to 6 boxes of shells per hour.

*No separate case resizer or conditioner needed

Pricing data

Magn-O-Matic 10 complete with
  6 point crimp starter **$305.00**

Accessories:

Magn-O-Matic crimp starter complete (6 point)	**$ 22.50**
Magn-O-Matic crimp starter head only (6 point)	**$ 12.50**
Additional shot or powder bushings	**$ 3.25**
Additional wad guide fingers . . .	**$ 1.85**

S.T.O.S. Lubricant

This special lubricant, besides being ideal for our reloading tools, for all firearms and as a case sizing lubricant, is also excellent for any bearing, gear or caming surface—wherever friction-free performance is required.

S.T.O.S.
2 oz. Jar . . . . **$ 3.25**

Shot and Powder bushings

Our bushings are manufactured with extreme care to assure absolute accuracy and consistent performance. Shot and powder bushings are of different diameters to eliminate any possibility of their being reversed. Aluminum powder bushings absolutely eliminate sparking. All bushings are clearly and permanently marked.

Shot or Powder Bushing . . . . **$ 3.25**

Crimp starters

Our six and eight point crimp starters are ball bearing lined and have sensitive automatic pick-up fingers to assure perfect crimp alignment every time. The crimp heads are interchangeable, so to broaden the loading capabilities of the tools, additional crimp heads can be attached to the original crimp starter housing.

Crimp Starter Complete (6 or 8 Point) **$19.00**
  (Specify model)
Crimp Starter Head Only (6 or 8 Point) **$10.00**

Special paper crimp assembly

This paper crimp conversion kit is intended for shooters who reload paper shells predominately. The crimp assembly which is standard on all Ponsness-Warren tools is designed primarily for plastic shells, and while paper shells can be loaded adequately, this special paper crimp assembly provides optimum appearance for paper shells. Installation can be accomplished easily in just a few minutes.

Special Paper Crimp Assembly. **$16.00**
  (Specify gauge)

Wad guide fingers

Our engineers, taking advantage of recent developments in the plastics industry, have developed a wad guide finger with longer life and greater spring action than any available before. Our wad guide fingers handle all types of wad and are adaptable to most shotshell reloading tools. They are available in 10, 12, 16, 20, 28 and 410 gauge.

Wad Guide Fingers . **$ 1.85**

PONSNESS-WARREN SHOTSHELL RELOADING TOOLS

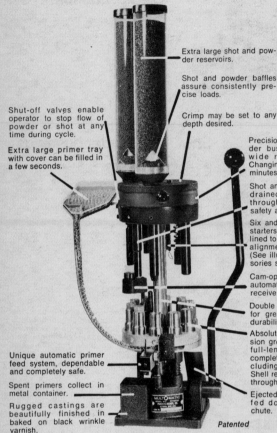

Extra large shot and powder reservoirs.

Shot and powder baffles assure consistently precise loads.

Crimp may be set to any depth desired.

Shut-off valves enable operator to stop flow of powder or shot at any time during cycle.

Extra large primer tray with cover can be filled in a few seconds.

Precision shot and powder bushings provide a wide range of loads. Changing takes but a few minutes.

Shot and powder may be drained out completely through drop tube for safety and convenience.

Six and eight point crimp starters are ball bearing lined to give perfect crimp alignment every time. (See illustration in Accessories section.)

Cam-operated wad carrier automatically tips out to receive all types of wads.

Double post construction for greater leverage and durability.

Absolute resizing — precision ground and polished full-length sizing dies completely resize case including brass and rim. Shell remains in sizing die through entire operation.

Ejected shells are gravity fed down handy shell chute.

Unique automatic primer feed system, dependable and completely safe.

Spent primers collect in metal container.

Rugged castings are beautifully finished in baked on black wrinkle varnish.

Patented

Large shot and powder reservoirs.

Shot and powder baffles assure consistently precise loads.

Bushing access plug allows instant inspection or changing of bushings and also provides a direct shot drop for loading buck shot or granulated plastic.

Charging ring has positive lock to prevent accidental flow of powder.

Tool head can hold two gauges simultaneously.

Six and eight point crimp starters are ball bearing lined to give perfect crimp alignment every time.

Shot and powder may be drained out completely through shot and powder drop tube.

Trouble-free tip-out wad guide.

Double post construction for greater leverage and wear.

Absolute resizing, shell stays in full length sizing die through entire operation.

Sizing die is centered at each station by spring-loaded ball check.

Handy, removable spent-primer box.

Photo shows Du-O-Matic with 12 and 20 gauge tooling attached.

Patented.

Mult-O-Matic*
New Model 600B

Du-O-Matic*
Model 375

Mult-O-Matic 600B Complete (with 6 or 8 point crimp starter) 12, 16, 20, 28 or 410 gauge **$525.00**

The 28 and 410 gauge 600's are designed primarily to load plastic casings using one piece plastic wads.

Accessories:

600B Additional Tooling Set Complete (with 6 or 8 point crimp starter) 12, 16, 20, 28 or 410 gauge	**$185.00**
600B 3″ Conversion Kit (12 and 20 gauge only)	**185.00**
(For 20 gauge, brand of ammunition to be loaded should be specified)	
Crimp Starter Head Only (6 or 8 point)	**10.00**
Special Paper Crimp Assembly (12 or 20 gauge only) . .	**16.00**
600B Crimp Starter Complete (6 or 8 point)	**19.00**

Du-O-Matic 375, One gauge complete; 12, 16, 20, 28 or 410 gauge, (with 6 or 8 point crimp starter) **$275.00**

NOTE: 10 gauge available as accessory tooling set only.

Du-O-Matic 375, 10 gauge complete with 6-point crimp starter **$305.00**

Accessories:

375 Additional Tooling Set 12, 16, 20, 28 or 410 gauge . .	**$105.00**
(Crimp starter or head extra)	
375 Special 10 gauge (3½″) magnum additional tooling set	**154.00**
(Includes tool head, tooling and 6 point crimp starter)	
375 Crimp Starter Complete (6 or 8 point)	**19.00**
Crimp Starter Head Only (6 or 8 point)	**10.00**
375 3″ Conversion Kit (12, 20 or 410 gauge)	**16.00**
(For 20 gauge, brand of ammunition to be loaded should be specified)	
375 2½″, 12 gauge conversion kit	**31.00**
(for international 65/67.5mm 12 gauge shells only)	
375 Tool head (No tooling included)	**33.50**
Special Paper Crimp Assembly	**16.00**

PONSNESS-WARREN SHOTSHELL RELOADING TOOLS

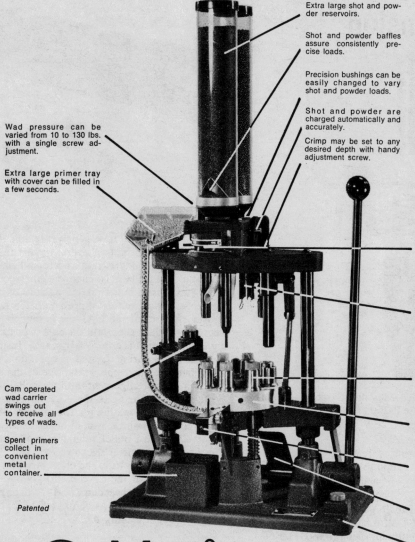

Extra large shot and powder reservoirs.

Shot and powder baffles assure consistently precise loads.

Precision bushings can be easily changed to vary shot and powder loads.

Shot and powder are charged automatically and accurately.

Crimp may be set to any desired depth with handy adjustment screw.

Wad pressure can be varied from 10 to 130 lbs. with a single screw adjustment.

Extra large primer tray with cover can be filled in a few seconds.

Shut off switches enable operator to stop flow of powder or shot at any time during cycle. Switches include a drain feature which permits complete draining of reservoirs.

Six and eight point crimp starters are ball bearing lined to assure perfect crimp alignment automatically.

Absolute resizing. Shell remains in full length, precision die through the entire operation, eliminating feeding and chambering problems and assuring increased case life.

Cylinder indexes automatically. A factory perfect shell is produced with every pull of the handle.

Cam operated wad carrier swings out to receive all types of wads.

Spent primers collect in convenient metal container.

Unique automatic primer feed system is dependable and completely safe.

Finished shell is automatically ejected by knock out rod down convenient shell chute at rear.

Rugged aluminum castings are finished in a handsome baked-on black wrinkle varnish.

Patented

Size-O-Matic

Model 800B

This is the ultimate shotshell reloader, the tool for the shooter who demands the finest in all the world—unequaled performance. It is an incredibly efficient machine. One reasonably experienced operator can load shells at a rate of 700 rounds per hour; two operators, 1200 rounds; three operators, as many as 1800 rounds per hour. Individual rates will vary slightly according to the experience and dexterity of the operator or operators. The Size-O-Matic has an ingenious automatic primer feed system with no tubes to fill and primers always in full view of the operator. A full box of 100 primers loads in just seconds. Each shell is held in a full-length sizing die through the entire loading operation, affording consistently perfect reloads, guaranteed to feed and chamber into any firearm. All tooling is ground to exacting specifications, then polished or richly blued. Nylon liners virtually eliminate wear. The Size-O-Matic will handle paper or plastic shells, either high or low base, with unmatched ease and speed.

*No separate case resizer or conditioner needed

Size-O-Matic 800B Complete (with 6 or 8 point crimp starter) 12, 20, 28 or 410 gauge **$840.00**
The 28 and 410 gauge 800B's are designed primarily to load plastic casings using one piece plastic wads.

Accessories:

800B Crimp Starter Complete (6 or 8 point)	**$ 19.00**
Crimp Starter Head only (6 or 8 point)	**10.00**
Special Paper Crimp Assembly (12 or 20 gauge only) ...	**16.00**
Additional Shot or Powder Bushings	**3.25**
Additional Wad Guide Fingers	**1.85**
Wood grip shovel handle	**25.00**

PONSNESS-WARREN

Powder Measure Extension

CAL-die

The Ponsness-Warren CAL-die bullet seating dies for rifle cases is for use on P/W's new Metallic M-II rifle/pistol loader. The CAL-die has several unique features. Only one housing or die body is required for all diameters between .224 and .358 caliber. To change calibers, only the purchase of an inexpensive bullet retaining sleeve or collet is required (see chart) and is easily slipped into the housing. Another unusual feature of the CAL-die is that the bullet retaining sleeve holds the bullet until the case is pushed into the housing and the bullet is completely seated. Instead of having to hold the bullet during the seating operation, you merely drop the bullet through a port in the side of the housing where it is held in proper alignment until the bullet is seated.

Standard packaging of the CAL-die consists of the housing, a large bullet seating pin for calibers .30 and larger (installed in the housing), a small bullet seating pin for calibers under .30, and a bullet retaining sleeve in .308 diameter. This one .308 diameter sleeve will load all .30 caliber bullets including those shown in the chart below.

The addition of the CAL-die to your Metallic M-II rifle press, or any press threaded 7/8-14, will approximately double the volume output as compared to loading with a conventional bullet seating die.

The Ponsness/Warren Powder Measure Extension is designed for both the Metal-Matic P-200 and the Metallic M-II loaders.

This extension lifts the powder measure above the dies, thus enabling the loader to change or replace dies or powder measure without having to remove adjacent tooling.

The extension consists of three main parts: a spring (B-36-2) and a powder drop insert (PW-1-2 for large size, PW-1-3 for small size) which fit into the knurled housing (PW-1-1). Both large and small powder drop inserts are supplied with the extension.

Powder Measure Extension **$18.00**

CAL-die (complete with the housing, two bullet
seating pins, and the .308 diameter bullet sleeve) . . . **$33.00**
Each additional sleeve **6.50**

Bullet Retaining Sleeve Diameter	Calibers*
.224	22
.243	243, 244, 6mm
.257	all 25
.264	6.5mm
.270	270
.284	280, 284, 7mm
.308	All 30, 30-06, 30-30

Bullet Retaining Sleeve Diameter	Calibers*
.32	32 Special, 8mm
.338	338
.358	All 35

*The list shows only the most generally used calibers and does not reflect the complete coverage of the sleeves shown.

PONSNESS-WARREN
Shot and Powder BUSHINGS

SHOT BUSHINGS

1 – 1/2 oz. 4 – 7/8 oz. 7 – 1-1/4 oz. 10 – 1-5/8 oz. 13 — 2 oz.
2 – 5/8 oz. 5 – 1 oz. 8 – 1-3/8 oz. 11 – 1-3/4 oz. 14 — 2-1/4 oz.
3 – 3/4 oz. 6 – 1-1/8 oz. 9 – 1-1/2 oz. 12 – 1-7/8 oz.

POWDER BUSHINGS
(UNITS SHOWN IN GRAINS)

THIS IS NOT A LOADING TABLE, BUT RATHER A CHART BASED ON RELATIVE HOLE SIZES, SHOWING THE APPROXIMATE NUMBER OF GRAINS DROPPED BY PONSNESS-WARREN POWDER BUSHINGS.
(All shot bushings meet N.S.S.A. and A.T.A. requirements)

	DU PONT					HERCULES							WINCHESTER					HODGDON			ALCAN		
	700-X	PB	SR 7625	SR 4756	IMR 4227	BULLSEYE	RED DOT	GREEN DOT	BLUE DOT	HERCO	UNIQUE	2400	296	452AA	473AA	540	571	HS-5	HS-6	H-110	AL-5	AL-7	AL-8
1A					12.1							12.1	13.7							13.7			
2A					12.6							12.6	14.8							14.8			
3A					14.0							13.9	15.6			15.3				15.6			
A	8.8	9.3	10.0	10.5	15.9		8.0	8.0		10.0	11.3	15.8	17.5			16.8	17.1	18.2	16.8	17.5	13.2	13.2	
B	9.5	9.7	11.0	11.0	16.8		8.5	8.5		10.6	12.1	16.7	18.8			17.6	18.2	19.5	17.7	18.8	14.1	14.1	
C	10.0	10.3	11.5	12.0	17.8		9.3	9.3		11.3	12.7	17.7	20.0			18.5	18.8	20.7	18.8	20.0	14.6	14.6	
C1	10.3	10.4	11.9	12.4	18.2		9.5	9.5		11.7	13.2	18.0				19.6	20.1	21.1	19.2	20.6	14.9	14.9	
D	10.8	11.1	12.5	13.0	19.1		9.8	9.8		12.1	13.8	19.2				20.4	21.0	22.3	20.5	21.5	16.0	16.0	
D1	11.4	12.3	13.6	13.7	19.9		10.7	10.7		13.2	14.5	20.0			15.5	21.3	22.4	23.4	21.9		16.8	16.8	
E	12.4	13.1	15.0	15.0	22.6	15.0	11.5	11.5		14.6	16.2	22.5			16.8	23.5	24.2	25.5	24.2		18.7	18.7	
E1	12.9	13.8	15.6	15.8	23.9	15.3	12.1	12.1	19.1	15.3	17.0	23.7			17.1	24.0	24.7	28.3	25.5		19.7	19.7	
E2	13.6	14.5	16.8	16.6	25.2	17.0	12.8	12.8	21.7	16.0	17.9	25.3		15.0	18.0	26.1	26.5	28.9	26.8		20.8	20.8	
F	14.5	15.3	18.0	17.5	26.5	17.5	13.5	13.5	22.0	16.7	18.8	26.3		15.6	19.6	27.5	28.5	30.4	28.0		21.9	21.9	17.8
F1	15.0	16.1	19.2	18.4	27.9	18.0	14.1	14.1	22.4	17.7	19.7	27.7		16.4	20.1	28.3	29.3	31.5	29.4		23.0	23.0	18.6
G	16.3	17.0	20.5	19.5	29.3	19.5	14.7	14.7	24.5	18.6	20.6	29.0		18.3	22.7	31.2	32.3	33.6	30.7		24.1	24.1	19.5
G1	17.0	18.4	21.7	21.1	31.5	20.2	15.9	15.9	26.2	19.9	22.6	31.4		19.0	23.0	32.7	33.4	36.4	33.1		26.1	26.1	21.4
H	17.9	18.8	22.0	21.5	32.1	21.4	16.5	16.5	27.0	20.2	23.1	32.1		19.9	24.1	34.0	34.8	37.0	33.6		26.7	26.7	21.9
I	18.5	19.2	22.5	22.0	33.0		17.0	17.0	27.8	20.7	23.5	33.0		20.3	24.7	34.4	36.5	38.3	35.0		27.3	27.3	22.4
J	19.0	19.7	23.0	22.5	34.0		17.2	17.2	28.2	21.5	24.4	34.0		21.5	25.4	35.5	37.1	39.5	36.2		28.2	28.2	23.2
J1	19.6	20.3	24.2	23.2	35.4		17.9	17.9	29.3	22.2	25.4	35.4		22.3	26.8	36.9	38.8	40.7	37.2		29.1	29.1	23.7
K	20.0	20.9	24.5	24.0	35.9		18.2	18.2	29.5	22.7	25.8	36.0		22.5	27.0	37.1	39.0	41.9	38.3		29.9	29.9	24.2
L	21.0	21.7	26.3	25.5	37.4		19.0	19.0	31.3	24.2	27.3	37.5		23.4		39.5	41.1	43.8	39.4		31.0	31.0	25.3
M	22.0	23.0	27.3	26.5	39.6		19.9	19.9	32.7	25.3	28.1	39.5		24.0		41.2	42.8	45.9	41.8		32.9	32.9	26.8
N	23.5	24.5	28.8	28.0	42.0		21.2	21.2	35.0	26.4	30.3	41.8		26.5		44.7	46.4	48.7	44.6		34.8	34.8	28.5
O	24.0	24.7	29.3	28.5	42.4		21.5	21.5	35.5	26.8	30.5	42.5				45.5	46.9	49.4	45.3		35.4	35.4	28.7
P	24.5	25.8	30.3	29.5	43.8		22.0	22.0	36.0	27.1	30.9	43.8				46.4	48.0	49.9	45.5		36.0	36.0	29.5
Q	25.0	26.2	30.8	30.0	44.8		22.8	22.8	37.5	28.1	32.2	45.0				47.7	49.3	52.4	47.6		37.4	37.4	30.3
R	25.5	26.6	31.3	30.5	45.4		23.3	23.3	38.5	29.3	32.8	45.5						53.0	49.5		38.3	38.3	31.0
S	26.5	27.7	32.8	32.0	47.2		23.8	23.8	39.2	29.9	33.8	47.2						54.7	49.9		38.9	38.9	32.2
T	28.0	29.2	33.8	33.5	49.9		25.2	25.2	42.0	31.6	36.1	49.9						57.8	52.6		41.7	41.7	33.8
U	29.5	30.9	36.3	35.5	52.8		26.7	26.7	45.1	32.7	38.1	52.8						61.4	56.9		43.8	43.8	35.8
V	30.5	31.9	36.8	36.5	54.5		27.5	27.5	46.3	33.7	38.9	54.5						63.0	57.4		45.0	45.0	37.1
W	32.5	33.7	39.3	39.0	57.5		28.9	28.9	48.1	35.9	41.8	57.5						66.8	61.2		47.8	47.8	39.3
X	33.0	34.1	39.8	39.5	58.1		29.4	29.4	48.7	36.4	42.1	58.1									48.5	48.5	39.6
Y	34.0	35.7	41.3	41.0	60.6		30.8	30.8	50.3	37.9	43.7	60.6									50.5	50.5	41.3
Z	38.0	39.3	45.8	45.5	67.2		33.9	33.9	56.3	42.8	48.2	67.2									55.5	55.5	46.1
AA	41.0	42.2	49.3	49.0	72.4		37.1	37.1	60.6	46.0	52.2	72.4									60.4	60.4	49.6

All Ponsness-Warren reloaders and additional tooling sets come with one shot bushing and one powder bushing included. If you have need to vary your loads, additional bushings are available.

Drops from powder bushings will vary slightly depending on the model of tool, the stability of the loading bench and the individual operator as well as for the reasons stated below. *We recommend that you weigh a powder charge prior to each reloading session so that you can be assured of the exact powder drop you are getting.*

The above data has been obtained by methods and from sources that are normally reliable. Since Ponsness-Warren has no control over the actual loading, choice or condition of firearms and components, no responsibility for any use of this data is assumed or implied.

RCBS RELOADING TOOLS

RCBS AUTOMATIC PRIMING TOOL

Precision-engineered to provide fast, accurate and uniform seating of primers in one simple step. Single-stage leverage system is so sensitive it enables you to actually "feel" the primer being seated to the bottom of the primer pocket. This priming tool permits you to visually check each primer pocket before seating the primer; thus eliminating wasted motion or slowing down the reloading process.

Primers are released one at a time through the RCBS automatic primer feed, eliminating contamination caused by handling primers with oily fingers.

Both primer rod assemblies furnished with this tool will handle all large and small American-made Boxer-type rifle and pistol primers.

ECONOMY FEATURES: If you already have RCBS automatic primer feed tubes, and RCBS shell holders, they will fit this RCBS Priming Tool—thus eliminating the need to buy extras.

BERDAN PRIMER ROD ASSEMBLIES

Optional Berdan Primer Rod Assemblies are available in the three sizes shown below, and are interchangeable with the American Boxer-type Primer Rod Assemblies, furnished with the Priming Tool.

PART NO.	DESCRIPTION	PRICE
09460	Priming Tool (less Shell Holder)	$39.60

RCBS AUTOMATIC PRIMER FEED

Stop misfires — greasy hands never need to touch primers. Automatically drops primers one at a time into the Primer Plug and Sleeve of the Primer Arm. Adjustable Primer Stop Pin eliminates jamming found in other Automatic Primer Feeds. Easily mounted on RCBS and most "C" type Presses. The Primer Tubes for large and small primers are completely interchangeable with the Body.

PART NO.	AUTO. PRIMER FEED	PRICE
09589	Combo for large and small primers	$12.25

RCBS PRIMER POCKET SWAGER

For fast, precision removal of primer pocket crimp from military cases. Leaves primer pocket perfectly rounded and with correct dimensions for seating of American Boxer-type primers. Will not leave oval-shaped primer pocket that reaming produces. Swager Head Assemblies furnished for large and small primer pockets — no need to buy a complete unit for each primer size. For use with all presses with standard 7/8"-14 top thread, except RCBS "A-3" Press. The RCBS "A-2" Press requires the optional Case Stripper Washer.

PART NO.	POCKET SWAGER	PRICE
09495	Combo for large and small primers	$13.25

RCBS UNIVERSAL PRIMER ARM

ONE PRIMER ARM HANDLES ALL PRIMERS

RCBS Primer Arms are designed for fast, accurate seating of primers. Interchangeable Primer Plugs and Sleeves eliminate necessity of having to buy a complete new Primer Arm for each primer size. Primer Plugs and Sleeves furnished for large and small primers. Body cast of rust-resistant zinc alloy. The Universal Primer Arm is designed for use with RCBS Rock Chucker and J.R. as well as most "C" type Presses.

PART NO.	UNIVERSAL PRIMER ARM	PRICE
09500	For large and small primers	$5.50
09502	Plug and Sleeve for large primers	1.90
09503	Plug and Sleeve for small primers	1.90

RCBS PRIMER TRAY

For fast, easy handling of primers and loading Automatic Primer Feed Tubes, place primers in this tray, shake tray horizontally, and primers will automatically position themselves anvil side up. Sturdy plastic case.

PART NO.	PRIMER TRAY	PRICE
09477	Single Tray	$1.60

RCBS PRIMER POCKET BRUSH

A slight twist of this tool thoroughly cleans residue out of primer pockets. Interchangeable stainless steel brushes, for large and small primer pockets, attaches easily to Accessory Handle.

PART NO.	PRIMER POCKET BRUSH	PRICE
09574	Complete, Combo	$7.70

RCBS RELOADING TOOLS

RCBS CASE LUBE KIT

Everything you need for proper case lubrication! Kit contains RCBS Case Lube Pad, 2 ounce tube RCBS Resizing Lubricant and RCBS Accessory Handle with .22 and .30 caliber Case Neck Brushes. See descriptions of items below.

PART NO.	DESCRIPTION	PRICE
09335	Case Lube Kit	$9.30

RCBS RESIZING LUBRICANT

A must for proper lubrication of cases before sizing or forming. Easily applied to cases with an RCBS Case Lube Pad. Packaged in convenient 2 ounce tube.

PART NO.	RESIZING LUBRICANT	PRICE
09300	Single Tube	$1.10

RCBS CASE NECK BRUSH

A handy tool for removing dirt and powder residue, and for lightly lubricating the insides of case necks to ease neck expanding operation. Accessory Handle accepts interchangeable nylon bristle Case Neck Brushes in the calibers shown below. Order Accessory Handle, and Brush in caliber of your choice.

SMALL	22- 25 caliber	$1.25
MEDIUM	270- 30 caliber	1.25
LARGE	35- 45 caliber	1.25

RCBS CASE LUBE PAD

This companion to RCBS Resizing Lubricant is ideal for lubricating cases before sizing or forming. Cases rolled lightly across Pad pick up just the right amount of lubricant. Plastic cover to protect pad.

PART NO	CASE LUBE PAD	PRICE
09307	1 Pad	$4.50

RCBS MODEL 5-10 SCALE

A major improvement in reloading scales. Gives fast, accurate weighings of powder charges and cartridge components, from 1/10th to 510 grains. **NEW Micrometer Poise** permits fast precision adjustments from 1/10th to 10 grains by merely rotating micrometer-type cylinder. **NEW Approach-to-Weight** Feature visually tells reloader when he is approaching the pre-set weight. **Easy-to-read scale beam** is graduated in 1/10th grain increments; has conventional large poise and extra-deep notches. **Magnetic Damper** eliminates beam oscillation. All-metal base and extra-large leveling foot reduce tipping. Weighted, anti-tip pan hanger, and pan platform accommodate long cartridges and components.

PART NO.	DESCRIPTION	PRICE
09070	Reloading Scale	$56.70
09072	Metric	64.90

RCBS POWDER TRICKLER

For fast, easy balancing of scales with precision powder charges. Merely twist knob and powder trickles into the scale pan a kernel at a time. Has large capacity powder reservoir. Extra large base minimizes tipping.

PART NO.	DESCRIPTION	PRICE
09094	Powder Trickler	$6.75

RCBS POWDER MEASURE STAND

Now more height — a full seven inches from the reloading bench to the bottom of the threads! The ideal accessory for raising Powder Measure to proper working height. Permits placing of Reloading Scale or cases in loading block under Powder Measure Drop Tube. Easily bolts to loading bench. For all Powder Measures with standard 7/8" - 14 thread.

PART NO.	DESCRIPTION	PRICE
09030	Powder Measure Stand	$12.95

RCBS UNIFLOW POWDER MEASURE

This tool saves the time of having to weigh every powder charge when reloading a quantity of cases. With it you will be able to throw consistently accurate and uniform powder charges directly into cases. RCBS Precisioneered Measuring Cylinder pours powder into case to eliminate clogging that occurs in powder measures that "dump" charges. Adjusts quickly and easily from one charge to another without emptying powder hopper. Powder level visible at all times. Includes stand plate for mounting on press or bench, and two drop tubes to fit from .22 to .45 caliber cases. Optional .17 caliber drop tube also available. Choice of large measuring cylinder for rifle cases, or small measuring cylinder for bench rest or pistol cases.

PART NO.	POWDER MEASURE	PRICE
09001	With Large Measuring Cylinder	$39.50
09002	With Small Measuring Cylinder	39.50
09000	Combo with Large & Small Measuring Cylinders	47.50
09003	Large Measuring Cylinder Assembly*	11.80
09004	Small Measuring Cylinder Assembly*	11.80
09028	Drop Tube .17 caliber	4.20

*Consists of Measuring Cylinder and Measuring Screw.

RCBS POWDER FUNNEL

For powder charging just a few cases at a time. Large, easy-to-use, plastic Powder Funnel in two sizes: .22 to .45 calibers, and .17 caliber. Specially designed drop tube prevents powder spills around case mouths. Antistatic treatment prevents powder from sticking. Square lip stops Funnel from rolling.

PART NO.	POWDER FUNNEL	PRICE
09087	22-45 calibers	$1.90
09086	17 caliber	1.90

RCBS RELOADING TOOLS

RELOADER SPECIAL
RCBS R.S. PRESS COMBINATION OFFER

Costs less than 9 boxes of .30-06 cartridges

This RCBS J.R. Press is the Ideal setup to get started reloading your own rifle and pistol ammo — from the largest Magnums down to .22 Hornets. This Press develops ample leverage and pressure to perform all reloading tasks including (1) resizing cases their full length, (2) forming cases from one caliber into another, (3) making bullets. Rugged Block "O" Frame, designed by RCBS, prevents Press from springing out of alignment — even under tons of pressure. Extra-long ram-bearing surface minimizes wobble and side play. Comfort grip handle. Converts to up or down stroke in minutes. Standard ⅞"-14 thread accepts all popular dies and reloading accessories. Price includes: PRIMER CATCHER, to collect ejected primers; RCBS UNIVERSAL PRIMER ARM with large and small primer plugs and sleeves; RCBS SHELL HOLDER; one set of RCBS DIES in choice of calibers shown below.

PART NO.	R.S. PRESS, LESS DIES	PRICE
09356	Less Shell Holder	$65.00

$89.50

ROCK CHUCKER "COMBO"
RCBS R.C. PRESS COMBINATION OFFER

For Heavy-Duty Reloading

U.S. Pat. No. 2,847,895

The Rock Chucker Press, with Patented RCBS Compound Leverage System, delivers up to 200% more leverage than most presses for heavy-duty reloading of even the largest rifle and pistol cases. Rugged, Block "O" Frame prevents Press from springing out of alignment — even under the most strenuous operations. It case-forms as easily as most presses full-length size; it full-length sizes and makes bullets with equal ease. Shell Holders snap into sturdy, all-purpose shell holder ram. Non-slip handle with convenient grip. Operates on down-stroke for increased leverage. Standard ⅞"-14 thread. Price includes: PRIMER CATCHER to collect spent primers; RCBS UNIVERSAL PRIMER ARM with large and small primer plugs and sleeves; one RCBS SHELL HOLDER; one set of RCBS DIES in choice of calibers shown below.

PART NO.	ROCK CHUCKER PRESS, LESS DIES	PRICE
09366	Less Shell Holder	$92.50

$115.50

PART NUMBERS FOR RELOADER SPECIAL COMBO & ROCK CHUCKER COMBO.

Reloader Special Combo	Rock Chucker Combo	Caliber	Reloader Special Combo	Rock Chucker Combo	Caliber
RIFLE CALIBERS			15371	15381	300 Winchester Magnum
10671	10681	22-250	15571	15581	308 Winchester
10971	10981	222 Remington			
11171	11181	223 Rem (5.6mm Rem.)	18278	18288	357 Magnum/38 Special (RN) (SWC) (WC)
11471	11481	243 Winchester			
13571	13581	270 Winchester			
13671	13681	7mm Rem. Magnum	18678	18688	44 Magnum/44 Special (RN) (SWC)
14671	14681	30-30 Winchester			
14871	14881	30-06 Springfield	18978	18988	45 Auto (45 ACP) (RN) (SWC)

NOTE: The following abbreviations are used to indicate bullet seater plug types: (RN) Roundnose, (SWC) Semi-Wadcutter, (WC) Wadcutter.

RCBS RELOADING TOOLS

IMPORTANT
Before checking these tables for the Die Set you require, refer to Die Reference Table. When you find the caliber you want, note the letter in Die Group column. This letter tells you which Group your caliber will be listed under in this section (Group A, B, C, etc.).

Each of these Full Length Die Sets includes a Full Length Sizer Die with Expander-Decapping Assembly and a Seater Die with built-in crimper.

GROUP A — $25.00 — Full Length Die Set 1½ lbs.

.17 Remington	17201
.218 Bee	10001
.22 Hornet	10201
.22 Remington Jet	10401
.22-250 (.22 Varminter)	10601
.220 Swift	10701
.221 Remington Fire Ball	10801
.222 Remington	10901
.222 Remington Magnum	11001
.223 Remington (5.56mm)	11101
.243 Winchester	11401
6mm Remington (.244 Remington)	11501
.25-06	12001
.25-20 Winchester	11801
.25-35 Winchester	12101
.250 Savage (.250-3000 Savage)	12201
.257 Roberts	12501
.257 Weatherby Magnum	12601
.264 Winchester Magnum	12701
6.5mmx55 Swedish Mauser	13201
.270 Weatherby Magnum	13401
.270 Winchester	13501
7mm Remington Magnum	13601
7mm Weatherby Magnum	13701
7mmx57 Mauser (7mm Mauser)	13801
.280 Remington	14001
.284 Winchester	14101
7.65mmx53 Mauser (Belgian)	14301
7.7mmx58 Japanese Arisaka	14401
.30-30 Winchester	14601
.30-40 Krag	14701
.30-06 Springfield	14801
.300 Holland & Holland Magnum	15001
300 Savage	15101
.300 Weatherby Magnum	15201
.300 Winchester Magnum	15301
.303 British	15401
.308 Winchester	15501
.308 Norma Magnum	15601
.32 Winchester Special	15701
8mmx57 Mauser (8mm Mauser)	15901
8mm Remington Magnum	16001
.338 Winchester Magnum	16301
.35 Remington	16501
.375 Holland & Holland Magnum	16901
.30 Herrett	**17401**

GROUP B — $25.00-$26.50 — 3-Die Set 1½ lbs.

.30 M1 Carbine (RN)	18005
.32-20 Winchester (RN)	18105
.357 Magnum (RN)	18205
.357 Magnum (SWC)	18206
.357 Magnum (WC)	18207
.38 Special (RN)	18305
.38 Special (SWC)	18306
.38 Special (WC)	18307
.41 Magnum (RN)	18505
.41 Magnum (SWC)	18506
.41 Magnum (WC)	18507
.44 Magnum (RN)	18605
.44 Magnum (SWC)	18606
.44 Magnum (WC)	18607
.44 Special (SWC)	18706
.44-40 Winchester (.44 Win.) (RN)	18805
.45 Automatic (.45 ACP) (RN)	18905
.45 Automatic (.45 ACP) (SWC)	18906
.45 Automatic (.45 ACP) (WC)	18907
.45 Colt (RN)	19105
.45 Colt (SWC)	19106

(RN) = Roundnose, (SWC) = Semi-Wadcutter, (WC) = Wadcutter.

GROUP D — $32.50 — Full Length Die Set 1½ lbs.

.219 Zipper	26001
.22 K-Hornet	26201
.224 Weatherby Magnum	32301
.240 Weatherby Magnum	33201
.256 Winchester Magnum	33301
.257 Improved (40°)	32201
6.5mm Remington Magnum	33401
6.5mm-06	27801
6.5mmx50 Japanese Arisaka	32401
6.5mmx52 Carcano	27601
6.5mmx54 Mannlicher-Schoenauer	27701
6.5mmx57	32801
7mmx64 Brenneke	34001
7.5mm Schmidt-Rubin	33501
7.62mm Russian	29001
7.62mmx39	32901
.30 Remington	29201
.30-338 Winchester Magnum	29401
.303 Savage	29601
.32-40 Winchester	32501
8mm-06	32601
.33 Winchester	30501
.340 Weatherby Magnum	30601
.348 Winchester	33601
.22 Savage High Power	**33801**
.225 Winchester	**33901**
.35 Whelen	30701
.350 Remington Magnum	33701
.358 Norma Magnum	31001
.358 Winchester	32701
.30 Luger (7.65mm Luger)	25001
.30 Mauser (7.63mm Mauser)	25101

These 3-Die Sets include a Sizer Die with Decapping Unit, Expander Die with Expander and Seater Die with built-in Crimper.

GROUP C — $30.00 — 3-Die Set 1½ lbs.

.444 Marlin	20704
.458 Winchester Magnum	20804
.45-70 U.S. Government	20904
.25ACP (.25 Automatic)	21004
.32 ACP (7.65mm Automatic)	20004
.32 Smith & Wesson, Long (RN)	20104
.32 Smith & Wesson, Long (WC)	20107
.38 Colt Super Automatic	20204
.38 Smith & Wesson	20304
.380 Auto Pistol	20404
9mm Luger	20504

GROUP F — $37.95 — 3-Die Set 1½ lbs.

.38-55 Winchester & Ballard	36504
.50-70 U.S. Government	38704
8mm Nambu	36404

RCBS originated 3-Die (and 4-Die) sets for straight wall rifle and pistol cases to avoid "overworking" of the brass case. Sizing is done in one Die, expanding in another, and seating in the final die.

The 3-Die Sets include a Sizer Die, Expander Die with Expander-Decapping Assembly and Seater Die with built-in crimper.

GROUP E — $32.50 — 3-Die Set 1½ lbs.

.357 Auto Magnum	35505
.38-40 Winchester (RN)*	35605
.45 Auto Rim (RN)	35705

*Jacketed bullets only — others on Special Order at extra cost.

RCBS RELOADING TOOLS

SMALL BASE DIES
GROUP A

A must for sizing small base cases to minimum dimensions, thereby ensuring smooth functioning in the actions of automatic, pump, slide and some lever action rifles. Each Small Base Die Set includes a Small Base Sizer Die with Expander-Decapping Assembly and a Seater Die with built-in crimper.

GROUP A Caliber	Small Base Die Set 1½ lbs. $25.00	Small Base Sizer Die ¾ lb. $16.50
.223 Remington (5.6mm) (SB)	11103	11131
.243 Winchester (SB)	11403	11431
6mm Remington (.244 Remington) (SB)	11503	11531
.270 Winchester (SB)	13503	13531
.280 Remington (SB)	14003	14031
.284 Winchester (SB)	14103	14131
.30-06 Springfield (SB)	14803	14831
.300 Savage (SB)	15103	15131
.308 Winchester (SB)	15503	15531
7mm Remington Magnum (SB)	13603	13631
300 Winchester Magnum (SB)	15303	15331

NECK DIES
GROUP A

These Dies size only the neck of the case, not the shoulder or body, just enough to grip the bullet. Each Neck Die Set includes a Neck Sizer Die with Expander-Decapping Assembly and a Seater Die with built-in crimper.

GROUP A Caliber	Neck Die Set 1½ lbs. $25.00	Neck Sizer Die ¾ lb. $16.50
.22-250 (.22 Varminter)	10602	10630
.222 Remington	10902	10930
.223 Remington (5.56mm)	11102	11130
.243 Winchester	11402	11430
6mm Remington (.244 Remington)	11502	11530
.25-06	12002	12030
.270 Winchester	13502	13530
7mm Remington Magnum	13602	13630
7mmx57 Mauser (7mm Mauser)	13802	13830
.30-06 Springfield	14802	14830
.300 Winchester Magnum	15302	15330
.308 Winchester	15502	15530
17 Remington	17202	17230
220 Swift	10702	10730

To store and protect dies.

RCBS TRIM DIE
TO CUT CASES DOWN TO SIZE.

A sure way of checking and adjusting case lengths. Insert a case into this Trim Die and if it sticks out above the top it's too long. So simply file case down until it is flush with Die top. Don't worry about ruining Die with file – it's been specially heat treated to withstand a file bearing against the top.

After filing, just remove the burrs from outside of case and bevel the inside with an RCBS Burring Tool.

These Dies have precision-machined Sizer Die Chambers, but with slightly larger necks, to guarantee accuracy in gauging case lengths. Headspace is kept to minimum tolerances to avoid accidentally changing the case length when it's run into the Trim Die.

Trim Die 1/2 lb.	$13.50
Caliber	Part No.
GROUP A	
.22-250 (.22 Varminter)	10665
.220 Swift	10765
.222 Remington	10965
.223 Remington (5.56mm)	11165
.243 Winchester	11465
6mm Remington (.244 Remington)	11565
.25-06	12065
.270 Winchester	13565
7mm Remington Magnum	13665
7mmx57 Mauser (7mm Mauser)	13865
.30 Herrett	17465
.30-30 Winchester	14665
.30-06 Springfield	14865
.300 Winchester Magnum	15365
.308 Winchester	15565
8mmx57 Mauser (8mm Mauser)	15965
GROUP B	
.357 Magnum (RN, SWC, WC)†	18265
.38 Special (RN, SWC, WC)†	18365
.44 Magnum (RN, SWC, WC)†	18665
.45 Automatic (45 ACP) (RN, SWC, WC)†	18965

†Extended shell holder required for trimming or forming.

NOTE: Trim dies other than those listed are available in any caliber on special order.

RCBS RELOADING TOOLS

TUNGSTEN CARBIDE DIES
GROUP B

The most extravagant Dies made, these are for the perfectionist who loads large quantities on a regular basis and wants to eliminate the need for lubing cases. Each 3-Die Carbide Set, 4-Die Carbide Set and 4-Die Carbide Set with Tamper Crimp includes a Carbide Sizer Die, Expander Die with Expander-Decapping Assembly. The 3-Die Carbide Set has Seater Die with built-in crimper, while the 4-Die Carbide Sets have a Seater Die without crimper and therefore a separate roll Crimper Die. Either roll or taper. The 4-Die Carbide Sets with Taper Crimp have a Seater Die without crimper and a Taper Crimp Die.

GROUP B Caliber	Carbide Sizer Die ½ lb.	4-Die Carbide Set 1½ lbs.	4-Die Carbide Set With Taper Crimp 1½ lbs.	Taper Crimp Die ½ lb.
30 M-1 Carbine (RN)	18037	—		—
357 Magnum (RN)	18237	18217		18264
357 Magnum (SWC)	18237	18218		18264
357 Magnum (WC)	18237	18219		18264
38 Special (RN)	18237	18317		18264
38 Special (SWC)	18237	18318		18264
38 Special (WC)	18237	18319		18264
41 Magnum (RN)	18537	18517		—
41 Magnum (SWC)	18537	18518		—
41 Magnum (WC)	18537	18519		—
44 Auto Magnum (SWC)	—	—		19264
44 Auto Magnum (WC)	—	—		19264
44 Magnum (RN)	18637	18617		—
44 Magnum (SWC)	18637	18618		—
44 Magnum (WC)	18637	18619		—
44 Special (SWC)	18637	18718		—
45 Automatic (RN)	18937	18917		18964
45 Automatic (SWC)	18937	18918		18964
45 Automatic (WC)	18937	18919		18964
45 Colt (RN)	19137	19117		—
45 Colt (SWC)	19137	19118		—
44 Auto Magnum (SWC)			*19226	
44 Auto Magnum (WC)			*19227	

*4-Die set includes regular sizer die. Tungsten Carbide sizer die not available in this caliber.

TUNGSTEN CARBIDE DIES
GROUP C

Identical to above Carbide Dies but for Group C calibers. Each 3-Die Carbide Set includes a Carbide Sizer Die with Decapping Assembly, Expander Die with Expander, and Seater Die with built-in crimper. The 3-Die Set is easily converted to a 4-Die Set by purchasing the optional Taper Crimp Die.

GROUP C Caliber	Carbide Sizer Die ½ lb.	3-Die Carbide Set 1½ lbs.	Taper Crimp Die ½ lb.
32 ACP (7.65mm Automatic)	20037	20009	—
32 Smith & Wesson Long (RN)	20137	20109	20164
32 Smith & Wesson Long (WC)	20137	20111	20164
38 Colt Super Automatic	20237	20209	—
380 Auto Pistol	20437	20409	20464
9mm Luger	20537	20509	20564

Note: Browning Automatic Rifles in .243 Winchester, .270 Winchester, .30-06 and .308 Winchester calibers require *Small Base Dies* shown above. The .338 caliber rifle requires *Standard Dies.*

(RN) — Roundnose, (SWC) — Semi-Wadcutter, (WC) — Wadcutter.

RCBS RELOADING TOOLS

MODEL 5-10

The model number has changed but this is the same scale that reloaders have been using for years. Weighs powder, bullets or complete cartridges up to 510 grains instantly and accurately thanks to a micrometer poise, an approach-to-weight indicator system, large easy-to-read graduations, magnetic dampening, agate bearings and an anti-tip pan. Guaranteed to 0.1 grain sensitivity. Also available in metric readings.

Model 5-10 Scale	09070	2 lbs.
Model 5-10 Metric Scale	09072	2 lbs.

MODEL 5-0-5

This 511 grain capacity scale has a three poise system with widely spaced, deep beam notches to keep them in place. Two smaller poises on right side adjust from 0.1 to 10 grains, larger one on left side adjusts in full 10 grain steps. The first scale to use magnetic dampening to eliminate beam oscillation, the 5-0-5 also has a sturdy die cast base with large leveling legs for stability. Self-aligning agate bearings support the hardened steel beam pivots for a guaranteed sensitivity to 0.1 grains.

Model 5-0-5 Scale	09071	1½ lbs.

MODEL 10-10

UP TO 1010 GRAIN CAPACITY.

Normal capacity is 510 grains, which can be increased, without loss in sensitivity, by attaching the included extra weight.

Features include micrometer poise for quick, precise weighing, special approach-to-weight indicator, easy-to-read graduations, magnetic dampener, agate bearings anti-tip pan, and dustproof lid snaps on to cover scale for storage. Sensitivity is guaranteed to 0.1 grains.

Model 10-10 Scale	09073	3 lbs.

A smart investment to protect the model 5-0-5 or 5-10 scale when not in use. Soft, vinyl dust cover folds easily to stow away, or has loop for hanging up.

Scale Cover	09075	1/8 lb.

Model 5-0-5	**$39.90**
Model 5-10	**56.70**
Model 5-10 Metric	**64.90**
Model 10-10	**67.20**

Du-O-Measure, 5-0-5 and 10-10 are Registered Trademarks of Ohaus Scale Corporation.

RCBS ROTARY CASE TRIMMER
PRECISIONEERED®
09369 CASE TRIMMER WITHOUT COLLET OR PILOT $29.70

CASE TRIMMER PILOT $1.65			
PART NO.	PILOT CAL.	PART NO.	PILOT CAL.
09377	.17	09387	.33
09378	.22	09388	.34
09379	.24	09390	.36
09380	.25	09391	.37
09381	.26	09392	.40
09382	.27	09393	.41
09383	.28	09394	.44
09384	.30	09395	.45
09385	.31	09396	.45-R
09386	.32		

This tool is used to (1) trim to standard length those cases which have stretched after repeated firings; (2) to trim a quantity of cases to the same length for uniform bullet seating; (3) to correct uneven case mouths.

The RCBS Rotary Case Trimmer works just like a lathe. To trim a brass case to the desired length — quickly, easily, and accurately — you lock the case into the trimmer collet. Then adjust the cutting blade to the length you wish case trimmed . . . turn the handle a few times . . . and your case is trimmed. Neatly and accurately. Bevel and deburr the trimmed case mouth with an RCBS Burring Tool and you're ready to reload it! Interchangeable quick-release collets, available for all popular calibers (.17 to .45), lock cases securely into place for trimming. Trimmer Pilots are Precisioneered to the exact dimension of the case mouth, and lock into the cutter with a setscrew. This eliminates wobbling and ensures perfect vertical and horizontal alignment of case. Pilots are inter-

CASE TRIMMER COLLET $5.00			
PART NO.	COLLET NO.	PART NO.	COLLET NO.
09371	1	09373	3
09372	2	09374	4

changeable and available in twenty sizes to fit from .17 to .45 caliber cases.

Double lock rings on the cutting assembly permit any quantity of cases to be trimmed to the same length with a single adjustment. Cutter blades are made of hardened mill-type steel for extended service life, and removable for sharpening.

The RCBS Case Trimmer is 100 percent metal — no wood or plastic. Has slots for holding extra collets and pilots. Base can be secured to bench with screws.

RCBS RELOADING TOOLS

MODEL 304 SCALE

PART NO.	DESCRIPTION	SHPG. WT.	PRICE
09074	Model 304 Scale	4¾ lbs.	$166.50

The 304 is a laboratory-quality scale offering an easy-to-set **direct reading** dial in values from 0.1 to 10 grains. Instead of the usual single beam, it has **two** tiered beams (10 to 100 grains and 100 to 1000 grains). Both beams have center-reading poises. The magnetic damper, plus agate bearings provide both speed of operation and accuracy. Guaranteed sensitivity 0.1 grain. Includes platform for holding powder trickler.

RCBS STUCK CASE REMOVER

Removes stuck cases from Sizer Dies quickly and efficiently. To use, back Die Expander-Decapping unit away from case head, drill case head and tap. Then place RCBS Stuck Case Remover on top of case head and turn hexhead screw until stuck case pulls free!

PART NO.	DESCRIPTION	PRICE
09340	STUCK CASE REMOVER	$8.00

RCBS BULLET PULLER

A valuable tool for pulling bullets from cases that have wrong powder charges, or for salvaging bullets from old ammo. Pulls bullets of any length or shape without damaging or marking them. Soft lead bullets may distort. Interchangeable Bullet Puller Collets work like a draw collet on a lathe, securely holding the bullet as the case is pulled away. Each Collet is precision-machined internally to the exact bullet diameter. Fits all reloading presses with standard ⅞"-14 thread. Order Bullet Puller plus one Collet in caliber of your choice from chart below.

PART NO.	DESCRIPTION		PRICE
09440	BULLET PULLER (less Collet)		$8.50
	BULLET PULLER COLLETS		5.00
PART NO.	**CALIBER**	**PART NO.**	**CALIBER**
09419	.17	09428	32/8mm
09420	.22	09429	348
09421	6mm	09430	35/ 38 Spec.
09422	.25	09431	375
09423	6.5mm	09432	40
09424	.270	09433	41
09425	7mm	09435	44/11mm
09426	.30/7.35 Carc	09436	45
09427	.338		

RCBS BURRING TOOL

For beveling and removing burrs from case mouths of new factory cases, newly formed and trimmed cases. To bevel, insert pointed end of tool into case mouth and twist slightly. To remove burrs, place other end of tool over case mouth and twist. Centering pin keeps case aligned during deburring. Precision-machined and hardened for years of usage. Knurled for use by hand or in lathe. For .17 to .45 calibers.

PART NO.	DESCRIPTION	PRICE
09349	Burring Tool	$7.75

RCBS SETSCREW WRENCH

Here's a handy item for every reloading bench. The convenient hexagonal plastic handle will not roll off bench. Size is stamped in large easy-to-read numbers for quick identification. Available in two sizes to fit all popular RCBS products as shown below:

3/32″ Dies/Trim Dies/Case Forming Dies/Automatic Primer Feed attaching screws, bullet molds.

5/64″ Universal Primer Arm (new)•Case Trimmer

PART NO.	SETSCREW WRENCH	PRICE
09646	Combo	$4.00

RCBS RELOADING TOOLS

LUBE-A-MATIC Lubricator

The Lube-A-Matic frame, housing, and lubricant reservoir are cast in one piece—from sturdy cast iron—for strength, rigidity, and simplicity. The ram-bearing surface, and the Die housing, are drilled and reamed straight through, in one operation. This guarantees perfect alignment of the Top Punch with the Bullet Sizer Die below. The construction, combined with the link-leverage system, permits the largest cast bullets to be swaged in one short, continuous stroke, without strain on the sizer-lubricator.

Lube-A-Matic Bullet Sizer Dies—available in many different bullet diameters—lock firmly into the Die housing with a hexagonal Locking Cap.

Intercangeable Top Punches are available to fit the nose of any bullet design, and lock rigidly into the steel ram with an Allen set-screw.

The Lube-A-Matic Bullet Sizer-Lubricator is available completely equipped as shown. Lube-A-Matic Bullet Sizer Dies and Top Punches available separately—are listed below.

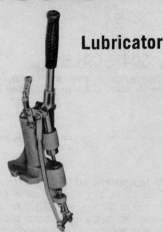

Lubricator

PART NO.	DESCRIPTION	SHPG. WT.	PRICE
80060	Lube-A-Matic—less Sizer Die and Top Punch	8 lbs.	$78.00

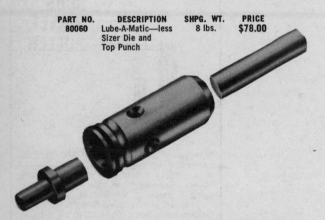

LUBE-A-MATIC BULLET SIZER DIES

Lube-A-Matic Sizer Dies are designed to swage bullets—with or without gas checks—to their correct diameters without shaving lead. This swaging action work-hardens the alloy through compression and produces a perfectly cylindrical bullet of increased strength, smoothness and accuracy.

BULLET SIZER DIE
SHPG. WT. ¼ lb. $11.00

Part No.	Sizer Die	Part No.	Sizer Die
82200	.224"	82222	.357"
82236	.228"	82223	.358"
82201	.243"	82224	.375"
82203	.257"	82225	.400"
82204	.264"	82238	.406"
82205	.277"	82226	.410"
82208	.284"	82227	.427"
82211	.308"	82228	.429"
82212	.309"	82230	.439"
82213	.310"	82239	.446"
82217	.321"	82231	.450"
82237	.323"	82232	.451"
82218	.338"	82233	.452"
82219	.354"	82234	.454"
82220	.355"	82235	.457"
82221	.356"	82240	.512"

LUBE-A-MATIC TOP PUNCHES

These Top Punches are designed for use in the RCBS Lube-A-Matic Bullet Sizer-Lubricator or with most other popular sizer-lubricators. Each Top Punch is precision machined for a perfect fit to the contour of the bullet nose. Locks into Bullet Sizer-Lubricator ram with Allen setscrew.

LUBE-A-MATIC TOP PUNCH
SHPG. WT. ⅛ lb. $3.85

Part No.	Top Punch	Part No.	Top Punch	Part No.	Top Punch	Part No.	Top Punch
82504	#115	82534	#460	85535	#535	85585	#585
82506	#190	82536	#465	85540	#540	85590	#590
82513	#311	82541	#495	85546	#546	85595	#595
82515	#344	85500	#500	85550	#550	85600	#600
82519	#374	85505	#505	85555	#555	85605	#605
82522	#402	85510	#510	85560	#560	82544	#610
82527	#421	85516	#516	85565	#565	85615	#615
82528	#424	85520	#520	85570	#570	85620	#620
82529	#429	85525	#525	85575	#575	82545	#680
82543	#445	85530	#530	85580	#580		

45 BASIC BRASS CASES

45 Basic Brass is ideal for the reloader who wants to produce unusual calibers of cartridges, or calibers that are no longer available from the factory. They can be formed into many different calibers with RCBS Case Forming Dies. With proper reloading, each case can be reloaded up to 20 times.

PART NO.	DESCRIPTION	SHPG. WT.	PRICE
79001	45 Basic Brass Cases	1 lb.	$21.00

REDDING RELOADING TOOLS

IMPROVED "C" PRESS
MODEL No. 7

New improvements include: Stronger frame (ASTM 30 alloy) for the heaviest reloading task; extremely shallow throat eliminates deflection; stronger (alloy steel) lower linkage; added rear mounting lug—prevents springing and "bench splitting;" snap-in shell holder may be rotated to any position; accepts all standard ⅞-14 threaded dies and all universal shell holders. Press includes primer arm for seating both large and small primers.

No. 7 "C" Press, complete	$64.00
No. 7K Kit includes press, shell holder, and one set of dies	86.00
No. 19 Automatic Primer Feeder	12.00
No. 20 Primer Catcher	6.00
No. 11 Shellholders (Universal Snap-in)	4.75

SUPER 32
SHOTSHELL RELOADER

Turret-type press capable of producing up to 300 reloads/hr. All operations are performed at one station without shell handling. Will handle high or low brass cases from 2½" to 3" without complicated adjustments or conversion kits. Quick change—pull pin die head allows user to change to a different gauge in about 60-90 seconds without die adjustments. Press comes complete with all necessary bushings, dies, etc. for one gauge.

CONVERSION KIT FOR SUPER 32

All the parts necessary to change from one gauge to another.
Includes complete die head assembly, dies, crimp starter, shellholder, bushings and quick release pin.

Conversion Kit Super 32, 12 or 20 ga.	$ 58.00
16, 28 or 410 ga.	66.00
Super 32, complete, 12 or 20 ga.	164.95
16, 28 or .410 ga.	172.95

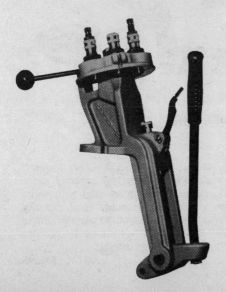

TURRET RELOADING PRESS
MODEL 25:

Extremely rugged, ideal for production reloading. Choice of four or six Station Turrets. No need to move shell, just rotate turret head to positive alignment. Ram accepts any standard snap-in shell holder. Includes primer arm for seating both small and large primers.

No. 25 Press, complete	$164.95
No. 25K Kit, includes press, shell holder, and one set of dies	186.50
No. 25T Extra Turret (6 Station)	38.00
No. 19T Automatic Primer Feeder	14.00

REDDING RELOADING TOOLS

BENCH STAND
MODEL RS-6

Convenient bench stand for Redding Master Powder Measure. Stand is not threaded. Powder measure is secured with a lock ring permitting quick dump of reservoir. Fits all powder measures with ⅞-14 thread mounting.
$13.95

MASTER POWDER MEASURE
MODEL 3

Universal- or pistol-metering chambers interchange in seconds. Measures charges from ½ to 100 grains. Unit fitted with lock ring for fast dump with large "clear" plastic reservoir. "See-thru" Drop Tube accepts all calibers from .22 to .600. Precision-fitted rotating drum, critically honed to prevent powder escape. Knife-edged powder chamber shears coarse-grained powders with ease, ensuring accurate charges.

No. 3 Master Powder Measure, (Specify Universal- or Pistol-Metering chamber) **$52.00**
No. 3K Kit Form, includes both Universal and Pistol chambers. .. **62.00**
No. 3-12 Universal or Pistol chamber. **12.00**

POWDER TRICKLER
MODEL No. 5

Brings underweight charges up to accurate reading, adding powder to scale pan a granule or two at a time by rotating knob. Speeds weighing of each charge. Solid steel, low center of gravity. "Companion" height to all reloading scales; weighs a full pound No. 5 Powder Trickler. **$9.95**

MASTER CASE TRIMMER
MODEL No. 1400

This unit features a universal collet that accepts all rifle and pistol cases. This trimmer is also unique in that it chamfers and deburrs the case neck at the same time it is trimmed to length. The frame is solid cast iron with storage holes in the base for extra pilots. Both coarse and fine adjustments are provided for case length.

The case-neck cleaning brush and primer pocket cleaners attached to the frame of this tool make it a very handy addition to the reloading bench.

Trimmer comes complete with the following:
* New speed cutter shaft
* Two pilots (.22 cal. and .30 cal.)
* Universal collet
* Two neck cleaning brushes (.22 thru .30 cal.)
* Two primer pocket cleaners (Large and Small)

No. 1400 Master Case Trimmer complete **$42.50**
No. 1500 Pilots **1.75**

STANDARD POWDER AND
BULLET SCALE
MODEL No. RS-1

For the beginner or veteran reloader. Only two counterpoises need to be moved to obtain the full capacity range of 1/10 grain to 380 grains. Clearly graduated with white numerals and lines on a black background. Total capacity of this scale is 380 grains. An over and under plate graduate in 10th grains allows checking of variations in powder charges or bullets without further adjustments.

Model No. RS-1 .... **$32.95**

REDDING RELOADING TOOLS

MASTER POWDER AND BULLET SCALE MODEL No. 2

Guaranteed accurate to less than 1/10 grain. Master model has magnetic dampening for fast readings. 1/10 grain graduated over/under plate permits checking powder charge variations without moving counterpoises. Features also include: 505-grain capacity; high-visibility graduated beam; pour-spout pan; stable cast base; large convenient leveling screw; hardened and honed, self-aligning beam bearings for lifetime accuracy.

No. 2 Scale $42.00

RELOADING DIES MODEL No. 10

Redding dies are made from alloy steels heat treated and hand polished. All Redding dies are lifetime guaranteed and use no aluminum parts or plating. Standard ⅞-14 thread to fit most presses. Available in 2 Or 3 die rifle sets, 3 die pistol sets and 4 die pistol sets with taper crimp.

Series A $24.50
Series B 29.50
Series C 34.50

All Redding dies are packaged in the combination plastic storage box/loading block.

Neck sizing dies are available in most bottleneck calibers for those who wish to resize only the necks for longer case life and better accuracy.

Custom made dies are available on special order.

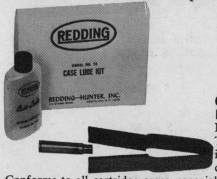

CASE LUBE KIT MODEL No. 12

New Case Lube Tongs simplify and increase speed of case lubrication. Conforms to all cartridge cases, especially useful to ensure proper case neck lubrication. Eliminates stuck cases and pulled rims. Prolongs life of dies and simplifies case reforming. Includes 2 oz. plastic bottle of Redding case lube.

No. 12 Case Lube Kit $7.50
No. 21 Case Lube only, 2 oz. Bottle 2.50

"SUPERCHARGER" POWDER MEASURE KITS MODEL No. 101 AND 102

Supercharger Kit No. 101
Contains: Model No. RS-1 Standard Powder and Bullet Scale, Model No. 3 Master Powder Measure, Model No. 5 Powder Trickler and Model No. RS-6 Bench Stand.

No. 101 .... $98.00

Supercharger Kit No. 102
Contains: Model No. 2 Master Powder and Bullet Scale, Model No. 3 Powder Measure, Model No. 5 Powder Trickler and Model No. RS-6 Bench Stand.

No. 102 .... $106.00

TITANIUM CARBIDE PISTOL Dies Model No. 10-TIC

Titanium carbide has the highest hardness of any readily available carbide yet is not as brittle. Its smooth, rounded micrograins present a slippery, nongalling surface, unattainable with other carbides. Lubrication is a thing of the past and the inserts are tapered, to prevent belts or shoulders on your cases.

No. 10-TIC Pistol Die Sets $59.00
No. 10-TIC Sizing Die Complete 45.00
No. 1021 R Decapping Rod Assembly 6.00

SELF-INDEXING STAR CRIMP STARTER MODEL 23

In reloading some plastic and new paper cases, a good folded crimp can only be obtained by use of a Star Crimp Starter. The Redding Self-indexing Star Crimp Starter attaches to the No. 32 Shotshell Reloader and is available in 6 or 8 point star. Fired cases must be recrimped with the same number of folds as in the original for best results. Available in 12, 16, 20 Ga., 6 & 8 point—28 & .410 Ga., 6 point only.

Model No. 23 Crimp Starter, 6 or 8 point. $7.50

CASE PREPARATION KIT MODEL NO. 18

All the tools you need in one package for removing dirt and powder residue from the inside of case necks and primer pockets. Kit comes complete with accessory handle, large and small primer pocket cleaners and three case neck brushes to handle all cartridges from 22 thru 45 caliber.
$7.95

TEXAN RELOADING TOOLS

MODEL RT 6-STATION

The Model RT6-Station with adjustable wad pressure has the Texan split bar arrangement, self-aligning nylon crimp starter, all steel crimper for Texan Taper Crimp, double-link leverage. It features an indexing turret, primer catcher box right in front. It is designed for high speed production of shotgun shells and is ideally suited for skeet and trap shooters' high volume requirements.

12 and 20 gauge only $239.95
Crimp Starter (specify gauge and number of points) may be used on
FW, GT, AP and DP Models 5.95

MODEL M-IV

The MIV has a smooth self-indexing action which moves cases through all stations to produce a completed shell for each pull of the handle. The automatic priming system functions only if there is a case in position to be reprimed. It features a wad guide, which prevents deformed cases, easy to adjust and read wad pressure system, shell retention system, self-aligning crimp starter. It includes 6- and 8-point* crimp starters, shell ejector, cam, shell catcher, primer catcher, automatic primer feed and shot and powder bushings for both target and field loads.

RT-6

MIV

MV	New Loader with Brass Resizing station plus all features of MIV Complete with primer feed, shell ejector and catcher and automatic index. 12, 16, 20, 28 410 gauges $579.95
MIV	Loader 12, 16, 20, 28, 410 gauges with primer feed, shell ejector, and catcher $454.95
MIV	Loader - "Basic" without primer feed, ejector or shell catcher 12, 16, 20, 28, 410 ga. $339.95
MIV-CS	Crimp Starter. (Specify gauge and number of points) ....$ 5.95

MODIFICATIONS
Modernize the Texan systems of the MV. The following systems may be installed without drilling, reaming or otherwise modifying the basic tool:

MIV-APF*	Complete Priming System .... $ 62.95 *Red Model M requires additional deprime punch for Primer Feed conversion .... $ 3.79
MIV-WG	Complete Self Lowering Wad Guide System, including Nylon Wad Guide Finger .... $ 12.59 (Specify Gauge)
MIV-WP	Complete Wad Pressure System ....$ 12.59 (Specify Gauge)
MIV-STAGE	with Plate, Springs and Ejection Cam ......$ 55.95
MII, MIIA/MIV	Change Over Package (Specify Gauge) Complete— Includes Priming, Wad Guide, Wad Pressure, and Stage $125.95
MV, MIV	New Sizer Package to fit Models MIIA and MII (Press Head, Measure Cam holder, and All sizer parts) $125.95

Factory overhaul of any Model M, MII, MIIA or MIV for parts and transportation, $25.00 flat rate labor.

TEXAN RELOADING TOOLS

MODEL 101-T-11

The 101T11 is a seven-station turret-type press that provides space for three two-die rifle sets or two three-die pistol sets plus one station for powder measure or other accessory. All stations threaded 7/8-14 to accept all popular rifle and pistol die sets. Interchangeable universal shell holder heads allow fast easy caliber changes. Rugged cast iron base and powerful leverage plus rigid two-post construction to insure ease of operation. Optional primer feed eliminates handling of primers and speeds up reloading operation.

101-T-II Press with primer feed	**$219.95**
101-T-II Press without primer feed	**191.95**
191-PF Primer feed complete	**28.95**
101-T Primer post, large or small	**3.25**
191-T Primer feed post, large or small	**3.25**

MODEL 256 DOUBLE C PRESS

The Model 256 double C press is a heavy duty press with a rugged malleable cast frame. Precise alignment of the die and ram is insured by precision broaching. Threaded 7/8-14 to accept all popular dies. Universal primer arm includes cups and punches to seat both large and small primers. Equipped with universal shell holder ram and primer arm.

Model 256 C Press **$56.95**
(with primer arm and ram)

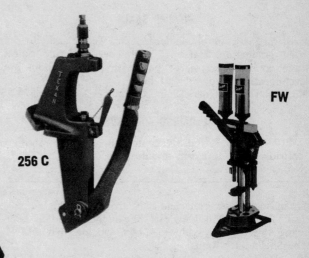

FW

256 C

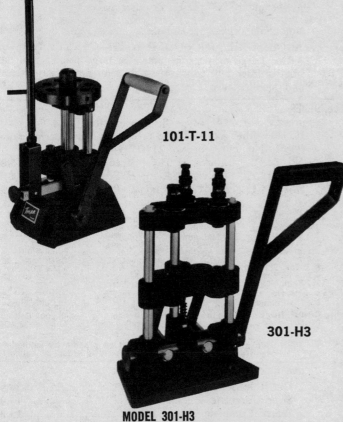

101-T-11

301-H3

MODEL 301-H3

Uses 3-die pistol or 2-die rifle sets in one press without changing dies during the reloading operation. Stations are threaded 7/8-14 to accept all standard rifle and pistol dies. Uses H-type Universal rams and Universal shellholder heads. Three-column design maintains positive alignment for exacting reloading and smooth operation. Includes both large and small primer seating posts and three Universal H-type rams. Heavy-duty cast metal brass drilled for bench mounting.

Press with handle, 3 Universal H-type Shellholder Rams, large and small primer seating posts	**$126.95**
H-3 Primer Post, large or small	**3.25**

MODEL FW

The FW features rugged aluminum castings and two column design plus double, toggle-action linkage. Cam action ejects high or low brass cases from resize die without adjustment. Repriming is positive with full base wad support to eliminate concaving case head. Shell mouth spreader opens shell mouth to aid in effortless seating of all types of wads through the self-lowering wad guide. Wad pressure is completely adjustable for all type wads. Self-aligning crimp starter seeks out original folds and final crimp die produces "Taper Crimp." Swivel top allows easy draining of powder or shot and convenient changing of powder or shot bushings. Unique base design allows operation without being bolted to bench or table. Conversion to other gauges is simple. All parts, including shot and powder bushings, are included in kit.

FW Loader, 12, 16, 20, 28, 410 gauge	**$114.95**
FW Loader, 12, 20, or 410 gauge 3"	**119.95**
FW Loader with Primer Feed Installed 12, 16, 20, 28 or 410 gauge	**126.95**
FW-CK 2¾" Conversion Kit, 12, 16, 20, 28, 410 gauge	**44.95**
FW-SPL-CK Conversion Kit, 2¾" to 3", 12, 16, 20, 28, 410 gauge	**50.95**
FW-CK 3" Conversion Kit, 12, 20 or 410 ga. 3" regular	**24.95**
FW-APF Automatic Primer Feed	**21.95**

(Specify gauge and number of points)
The FW crimp starter may be used on Texan RT and FW loaders.

TEXAN RELOADING TOOLS

MODEL R-1 SHOTSHELL RECONDITIONER

Recommended for use in conjunction with the Texan models M-IV and other automatic reloaders. Reconditions both plastic and paper cases to fit all makes of shotguns. One pull of the handle resizes, deprimes, flattens bulged or concaved case head and reseats base wad. Makes possible reloads that look and perform like new.

Model R1 12, 16, 20, 28 or 410 guage $44.95
Model R1-CK Conversion Kit 12, 16, 20, 28 or 410 gauge $12.95

POWDER SCALE

With magnetic or oil damped beam. Tenth grain to 500 grain graduation. Hardened knife-edged fulcrum points, three counterpoises, large pan with pouring spout and leveling screw. Rugged cast base.

No. 304 with magnetic damped beam $24.95

RELOADING ACCESSORIES

DEBURRING TOOL. Chamfers or deburrs mouth of cartridge cases to clean, smooth edge.

No. 259 .... $4.75

TEXAN DIE LUBE. Specially formulated lubricant. Exacting companion to Texan Micro-Bore dies.

2 oz. $1.00

BULLET PULLER. Will not mar or scratch bullet. Standard ⅞-14 thread.

No. 302 Bullet Puller without collet $7.45
No. 302 Collet of Special Caliber (specify) 3.45

CASE TRIMMER. Collets and pilots for all size cases. Accurate precision trimming.

No. 303 Case Trimmer and Pilot $31.95
No. 303 Collet 4.00
No. 303 Pilot (specify caliber) 1.25

CASE LUBE PAD. The fast, easy way to lubricate. Eliminates dents caused by excess lube.

Use with Texan die lube $2.95

"C" TYPE PRIMER ARM. For No. 256 "C" press. Fits most standard "C" presses or other makes.

No. 255 .... $4.95

ACCESSORIES INCLUDED WITH "C" TYPE PRIMER ARM. Large primer pin, concave; large primer pin, flat; small primer pin, concave; small primer pin, large sleeve and small sleeve $2.95

SHELLHOLDER

Texan Shellholder heads and rams are made of high quality steel. The No. 214 Universal Shellholder Head is interchangeable between both No. 214 C-type and No. 214 H-type Shellholder Rams.

The No. 214 C-type fits Texan Model "C" and other "C" presses. No. 214 H-type fits Texan Model 101-T-II, 301-H3 and other make H-type presses. When ordering rams, specify No. 214-C or No. 214-H type.

No. 214   Universal Head (specify number) $3.89
No. 214-H   Universal Ram, H-Type 4.95
No. 214-C   Universal Ram, C-Type 4.95

NO. 214 SHELLHOLDER HEAD GROUP NUMBERS

GROUP NO. 1	7mm - 270	GROUP NO. 2	30 Remington	8mm - 338	30 - 40 Krag	38 Super Auto	GROUP NO. 15
225 Win.	280 Remington	219 Zipper	32 Remington	338 Winchester	303 British	GROUP NO. 12	221
22/250 (22 Var.)	7.7 Jap	219 Donaldson	351 Winchester	35 Newton	35 WCF	22 Super Jet	222 Rem.
243 Winchester	30 - 06	22 Sav. Hi-Power		358 Norma Mag.	44 Special	22 Rem. Jet	222 Rem. Mag.
243 Rockchucker	300 Savage	25-35	GROUP NO. 6	375 Wea. Mag.	44 Magnum	256 Win. Mag.	223 Rem.
244 Remington	308 Winchester	30-30	257 Wea. Mag.	375 H & H Mag.	44 Russian	357 Magnum	380 Auto
6mm Remington	7.9 Mauser	32 Special	264 Winchester	11mm Mauser	.444 Marlin	38 Special	9 MM Short
228 Ack. Mag.	8mm Mann. Sch.	32 - 40	264 - 270	458 Winchester	GROUP NO. 9	38 Long Colt	GROUP NO. 16
257 Roberts	284 Winchester	38 - 55	270 Wea. Mag.	ALL Ack. Sh. Mag.	38 - 40	GROUP NO. 13	9 MM Luger
250/3000 (250 Sav.)	8mm Mauser		275 H & H Mag.	6.5 Rem. Mag.	44 - 40	6.5 x 55	GROUP NO. 17
250 Donaldson	8 x 51	GROUP NO. 3	276 Dubiel	350 Rem. Mag.	GROUP NO. 10	7.65 Belgian	41 Mag.
25/06	8 x 60	218 Bee	7 x 61 Sharpe & Hart		32 Long Colt	Mauser	GROUP NO. 18
6.5 x 57	8mm - 06	25 - 20 Repeater	7mm Wea. Mag.	GROUP NO. 7	32 S & W	GROUP NO. 14	45 Auto Rim.
6.5 x 06	333 OKH	32 - 20	7 mm Rem. Mag.	8 x 57 Rimmed	GROUP NO. 11	.35 Rem.	SPECIALS
6mm - 06	35 Whelen		300 Wea. Mag.		30 Luger	6.5 Carcano	45 Long Colt
256 Newton	358 Winchester	GROUP NO. 4	300 H & H Mag.	GROUP NO. 8	30 Mauser	7.35 Italian	30 M1 or 32 ACP
270 WCF	9mm Mauser	220 Swift	300 Winchester	25 - 303			
7mm Mauser	9mm Mann. Sch.	220 Rocket	308 Norma Mag.				
7 x 57	9.3 x 72	240 Cobra	30 - 338				
7 x 64	45 ACP	GROUP NO. 5	30 Newton				
		25 Remington					

All other shellholder heads must be ordered by caliber as they are not interchangeable with this group of calibers.

MICRO-BORE PISTOL AND RIFLE DIES

Texan two-die sets, for bottle neck cases, and three-die sets for straight wall cases are constructed from special alloy steel, micro-bored and polished to rigid specifications. Each die body is treated inside and out, for protection against wear, rust or corrosion. Precision dies that feature the hex body design and double hex lock rings for secure, mar-free wrench adjustment. Every set packaged in attractive plastic display and storage box

2 Die Rifle Set $24.95
Sizer Complete 13.00
Seater Complete 13.00
3 Die Pistol Set 24.95
Sizing Die Complete 11.00
Expander Die Complete 10.00
Plastic Die Storage Box Only 2.00

Caliber Available	No. Dies in Set	Shell Holder	Caliber Available	No. Dies in Set	Shell Holder	Caliber Available	No. Dies in Set	Shell Holder
222 Rem.	2	15	280 Rem.	2	1	350 Rem. Mag.	2	6
222 Rem. Mag.	2	15	284 Win.	2	1	38 S&W	3	SPL
223 Rem. (AR)	2	15	7MM Rem. Mag.	2	6	38 Super Auto	3	11
22-250 Rem.	2	1	30 Mi. Car.	3	SPL 30 MI	380 Auto	3	15
243 Win.	2	1	30-30	2	2	9MM Luger	3	16
244 Rem.	2	1	300 Savage	2	1	38 Special	3	12
6MM Rem.	2	1	308 Win.	2	1	357 Mag.	3	12
257 Roberts	2	1	30-06	2	1	41 Mag.	3	17
25-06 Rem.	2	1	300 Win. Mag.	2	6	44 Special	3	8
264 Win.	2	6	303 British	2	8	44 Mag.	3	8
6.5 Rem. Mag.	2	6	8MM Mauser (8 x 57)	2	1	45 Auto. Rim.	3	18
270 Win.	2	1	338 Win. Mag.	2	6	45 A.C.P.	3	1
7MM Mauser (7 x 57)	2	1	35 Rem.	2	14	45 Long Colt	3	SPL 45 LC

Directory of Manufacturers and Suppliers

Air Rifle Headquarters *(Feinwerkbau, Gamo, Weihrauch, Wischo air guns)*
247 Court Street
Grantsville, West Virginia 26147
(304) 354-6193

Anschutz
(rifles available through Savage Arms; air guns available through Beeman's)

Astra
(handguns available through Interarms; shotguns available through L. Joseph Rahn, Inc.)

BSA *(air guns)*
(available through Precision Sports)

Baikal International Trading Corp.
(shotguns)
12 Farview Terrace
Paramus, New Jersey 07652
(201) 845-8710

Bauer Firearms Corporation *(handguns)*
34750 Klein Avenue
Fraser, Michigan 48026
(313) 294-9130

Beeman's Precision Air Guns, Inc. *(also Anschutz, Feinwerkbau, Webley, Weihrauch, Wischo air guns)*
47 Paul Drive
San Rafael, California 94903
(415) 472-7121

Benjamin Air Rifle Company
Eight and Marion Streets
St. Louis, Missouri 63104
(314) 321-4469

Beretta U.S.A. Corp. *(handguns, shotguns)*
17601 Indianhead Highway
Acco Keck, Maryland 20607
(301) 283-2191

Bernardelli *(handguns)*
(available through Interarms)

Bersa *(handguns)*
(available through Interarms)

Bonanza Sports Manufacturing Co.
(reloading tools)
412 Western Avenue
Faribault, Minnesota 55021
(507) 332-8676

Browning *(handguns, rifles, shotguns, black powder guns)*
Route 1
Morgan, Utah 84050
(801) 876-2711

Maynard P. Buehler, Inc. *(mounts, screws)*
17 Orinda Highway
Orinda, California 94563
(415) 254-3201

Burris Company, Inc. *(scopes, mounts)*
331 East Eighth Street
Greeley, Colorado 80632
(303) 356-1670

Bushnell Optical Company *(scopes)*
(Div. of Bausch & Lomb)
2828 East Foothill Boulevard
Pasadena, California 91107
(213) 577-1500

CCI *(ammunition, primers)*
(see Omark Industries, Inc.)

CVA *(black powder guns)*
Connecticut Valley Arms, Inc.
Saybrook Road
Haddam, Connecticut 06438
(203) 345-8511

C-H Tool & Die Corporation
(reloading)
P.O. Box L
Owen, Wisconsin 54460
(715) 229-2146

Charter Arms Corporation *(handguns, rifles)*
430 Sniffens Lane
Stratford, Connecticut 06497
(203) 377-8080

Colt Industries, Firearms Division
(handguns, rifles, black powder guns)
150 Huyshope Avenue
Hartford, Connecticut 06102
(203) 278-8550

Crosman Air Guns
980 Turk Hill Road
Fairport, New York 14450
(716) 223-6000

Daisy *(air guns; also Power Line)*
P.O. Box 220
Rogers, Arkansas 72756
(501) 636-1200

Dakota *(handguns)*
(see E.M.F. Company, Inc.)

Dixie Gun Works, Inc. *(black powder guns)*
Gunpowder Lane
Union City, Tennessee 38261
(901) 885-0561

E. I. Du Pont de Nemours & Co., Inc.
(gunpowder)
Explosives Department
1007 Market Street
Wilmington, Delaware 19898
(302) 774-1000

Dynamit Nobel of America, Inc. *(Rottweil shotguns)*
105 Stonehurst Court
Northvale, New Jersey 07647
(201) 767-1660

E.M.F. Company, Inc. *(Dakota handguns)*
1900 East Warner Avenue, One D
Santa Ana, California 92705
(714) 966-0202

Euroarms of America *(black powder guns)*
1501 Lenoir Drive
Winchester, Virginia 22601
(703) 662-1863

Fabrique Nationale Sports *(rifles)*
(available through Steyr Daimler Puch)

Federal Cartridge Corporation
(ammunition, primers, cases)
2700 Foshay Tower
Minneapolis, Minnesota 55402
(612) 333-8255

Feinwerkbau *(air guns)*
(available through Air Rifle Headquarters, Beeman's)

FIAS *(shotguns)*
(available through Kassnar Imports)

FIE *(shotguns, black powder guns)*
P.O. Box 4866 Hialeah Lakes
Hialeah, Florida 33014
(305) 685-5966

Fiocchi Munizione S.P.A. *(ammunition)*
Via Santa Barbara, 4
22053 Lecco, Italy

Fox *(rifles and shotguns)*
(see Savage Arms)

Franchi *(shotguns)*
Luigi Franchi S.P.A.
Via del Serpente
Fornaci (Brescia), Italy

Freedom Arms *(handguns)*
One Freedom Lane
Freedom, Wyoming 83120
(307) 883-2468

J. L. Galef & Son, Inc. *(shotguns)*
85 Chambers Street
New York, New York 10007
(212) 267-6727

Renato Gamba *(handguns, rifles, shotguns)*
(available through Steyr Daimler Puch)

Gamo *(air guns)*
(available through Stoeger Industries, Air Rifle Headquarters)

Garbi *(shotguns)*
(available through L. Joseph Rahn, Inc.)

Griffin & Howe, Inc. *(sights, mounts)*
589 Broadway
New York, New York 10012
(212) 966-5323

Harrington & Richardson, Inc.
(handguns, rifles, shotguns)
Industrial Rowe
Gardner, Massachusetts 01440
(617) 632-9600

Heckler & Koch *(handguns, rifles, shotguns)*
933 North Kenmore Street, Suite 218
Arlington, Virginia 22201
(703) 243-3700

Hercules, Inc. *(gunpowder)*
910 Market Street
Wilmington, Delaware 19899
(302) 575-5000

High Standard Inc. *(handguns)*
31 Prestige Park Circle
East Hartford, Connecticut 06108
(203) 289-9531

Hodgdon Powder Co., Inc.
7710 West 63rd Street
Shawnee Mission, Kansas 66202
(913) 362-5410

Hopkins & Allen Arms *(black powder guns)*
3 Ethel Avenue
Hawthorne, New Jersey 07507
(201) 427-1165

Hornady Manufacturing Company *(reloading, ammunition, bullets)*
P.O. Box 1848
Grand Island, Nebraska 68801
(308) 382-1390

Interarms *(handguns, black powder guns; also Astra handguns, Bernardelli, Bersa, Star, Walther)*
10 Prince Street
Alexandria, Virginia 22313
(703) 548-1400

International Distributors, Inc.
(Taurus handguns)
7290 S.W. 42nd Street
Miami, Florida 33155
(305) 264-9321

Ithaca Gun Company, Inc. *(shotguns)*
123 Lake Street
Ithaca, New York 14850
(607) 273-0200

Paul Jaeger, Inc. *(mounts)*
211 Leedom Street
Jenkintown, Pennsylvania 19046
(215) 884-6920

Iver Johnson's Arms, Inc. *(handguns, rifles)*
Wilton Avenue off South Avenue
Middlesex, New Jersey 08846
(201) 752-4994

Kahles of America *(scopes)*
Main Street
Margaretsville, New York 12455
(914) 586-4103

Kassnar Imports *(rifles, black powder guns; Kassnar/Zabala, FIAS shotguns, Parker-Hale rifles)*
P.O. Box 6097
Harrisburg, Pennsylvania 17112
(717) 652-6101

Kimber *(rifles)*
9039 S.E. Jannsen Road
Clackamas, Oregon 97015
(503) 656-1704

Kleinguenther's Inc. *(rifles)*
P.O. Box 1261
Seguin, Texas 78155
(512) 379-8141

Krieghoff Gun Company *(shotguns)*
P.O. Box 52-3367
Miami, Florida 33152
(305) 871-6550
(Other Krieghoff shotguns available through Shotguns of Ulm)

Leupold & Stevens, Inc. *(scopes, mounts; Nosler bullets)*
P.O. Box 688
Beaverton, Oregon 97075
(503) 646-9171

Llama *(handguns)*
(available through Stoeger Industries)

London Guns *(sights, mounts)*
1528 20th Street
Santa Monica, California 90404
(213) 828-8486

Luger *(handguns)*
(see Stoeger Industries)

Lyman Products Corporation *(black powder guns, sights, scopes, reloading tools)*
Route 147
Middlefield, Connecticut 06455
(203) 349-3421

MEC, Inc. *(reloading tools)*
Mayville Engineering Company, Inc.
P.O. Box 267
Mayville, Wisconsin 53050
(414) 387-4500

MTM Molded Products Company *(reloading tools)*
5680 Webster Street
Dayton, Ohio 45414
(513) 890-7461

Mandall Shooting Supplies, Inc.
(Sig-Hammerli air guns)
7150 East Fourth Street
Scottsdale, Arizona 85252
(602) 945-2553

Mannlicher *(rifles)*
(see Steyr Mannlicher)

Marksman Products, Inc. *(air guns)*
2133 Dominguez Street
Torrance, California 90509
(213) 775-8847

Marlin Firearms Company *(rifles, shotguns)*
100 Kenna Drive
North Haven, Connecticut 06473
(203) 239-5621

Merit Gunsight Company *(optical aids)*
318 Sunnyside North
Sequim, Washington 98382
(206) 683-6127

The Merrill Company *(handguns)*
704 East Commonwealth
Fullerton, California 92631
(714) 870-8530

Micro Sight Company *(sights)*
242 Harbor Boulevard
Belmont, California 94002
(415) 591-0760

O. F. Mossberg & Sons, Inc. *(rifles, shotguns)*
7 Grasso Avenue
North Haven, Connecticut 06473
(203) 288-6491

Navy Arms Company *(handguns, black powder guns, replicas; Parker-Hale black powder guns)*
689 Bergen Boulevard
Ridgefield, New Jersey 07657
(201) 945-2500

Norma Precision *(ammunition, gunpowder, reloading cases)*
(see Precision Sports)

Nosler Bullets, Inc.
(available through Leupold & Stevens, Inc.)

Omark Industries, Inc. *(CCI, RCBS, Speer)*
Box 856
Lewiston, Idaho 83501
(208) 746-2351

Pachmayr Gun Works, Inc. *(scope mounts)*
1220 South Grand Avenue
Los Angeles, California 90015
(213) 748-7271

Pacific Tool Company *(reloading tools)*
(Div. of Hornady Manufacturing Company)

Parker-Hale
(black powder guns available through Navy Arms; rifles available through Kassnar Imports)

Ponsness-Warren, Inc. *(reloading tools)*
P.O. Box 8
Rathdrum, Idaho 83858
(208) 687-1331

Power Line *(air guns)*
(see Daisy)

Precise International *(air guns)*
3 Chestnut Street
Suffern, New York 10901
(914) 357-6200

Precision Sports *(BSA, Norma)*
(Div. of General Sporting Goods Corporation)
798 Cascadilla Street
Ithaca, New York 14850
(607) 273-2993

RCBS, Inc. *(reloading tools)*
(see Omark Industries, Inc.)

L. Joseph Rahn, Inc. *(Astra, Garbi
shotguns)*
201 South Main Street
First National Building, Room 502
Ann Arbor, Michigan 48104
(313) 994-5089

Redding-Hunter, Inc. *(reloading tools)*
114 Starr Road
Cortland, New York 13045
(607) 753-3331

Redfield *(sights, scopes)*
5800 East Jewell Avenue
Denver, Colorado 80224
(303) 757-6411

Remington Arms Company, Inc. *(rifles,
shotguns, ammunition, primers)*
939 Barnum Avenue
Bridgeport, Connecticut 06602
(203) 333-1112

Rossi *(handguns, rifles, shotguns)*
(available through Interarms)

Rottweil *(shotguns)*
(available through Dynamit Nobel of America,
Inc.)

Ruger *(handguns, rifles, shotguns, black
powder guns)*
(see Sturm, Ruger & Company, Inc.)

Sako *(rifles, scope mounts)*
(available through Stoeger Industries)

Savage Arms *(shotguns, rifles; also Fox,
Stevens, Savage Anschutz)*
Springdale Road
Westfield, Massachusetts 01085
(413) 562-2361

Sheridan Products, Inc. *(air guns)*
3205 Sheridan Road
Racine, Wisconsin 53403
(414) 633-5424

Shiloh Products Co., Inc. *(black powder guns)*
37 Potter Street
Farmingdale, New York 11735
(516) 249-2801

Shotguns of Ulm *(also Krieghoff)*
P.O. Box 253
Milltown, New Jersey 08850
(201) 297-0573

Sierra Bullets
10532 South Painter Avenue
Santa Fe Springs, California 90670
(213) 941-0251

Sig-Hammerli *(air guns)*
(available through Mandall Shooting Supplies,
Inc.)

Smith & Wesson Ammunition Company
2399 Forman Road
Rock Creek, Ohio 44084
(216) 563-3660

Smith & Wesson *(handguns, shotguns)*
2100 Roosevelt Avenue
Springfield, Massachusetts 01101
(413) 781-8300

Speer *(bullets)*
(see Omark Industries, Inc.)

Springfield Armory *(rifles)*
420 West Main Street
Geneseo, Illinois 61254
(309) 944-5138

Star *(handguns)*
(available through Interarms)

Sterling Arms Corporation *(handguns)*
211 Grand Street
Lockport, New York 14094
(716) 434-6631

Stevens *(rifles, shotguns)*
(see Savage Arms)

Steyr *(handguns)*
(See Steyr Daimler Puch)

Steyr Mannlicher *(rifles)*
(See Steyr Daimler Puch)

Steyr Daimler Puch of America Corporation
*(Fabrique Nationale, Renato Gamba, Steyr,
Steyr Mannlicher)*
Sporting Arms Division
85 Metro Way
Secaucus, New Jersey 07094
(201) 865-2284

Stoeger Industries *(Gamo, Llama, Luger, Sako)*
55 Ruta Court
South Hackensack, New Jersey 07606
(201) 440-2700

Sturm, Ruger & Company, Inc.
(Ruger firearms)
Lacey Place
Southport, Connecticut 06490
(203) 259-7843

Taurus *(handguns)*
(available through International Distributors, Inc.)

Texan Reloaders, Inc. *(reloading tools)*
444 Cips Street
Watseka, Illinois 60970
(815) 432-5065

Thompson/Center Arms *(black powder guns)*
Farmington Road
Rochester, New Hampshire 03867
(603) 332-2333

Tikka *(rifles)*
SF-41160
Tikkakoski, Finland

Ventura Imports *(shotguns)*
P.O. Box 2782
Seal Beach, California 90740
(213) 596-5372

Walther *(air guns, handguns)*
(available through Interarms)

Weatherby, Inc. *(rifles, shotguns, scopes,
ammunition)*
2781 Firestone Boulevard
South Gate, California 90280
(213) 569-7186

W. R. Weaver Company *(sights, scopes,
mounts)*
P.O. Box 20010
El Paso, Texas 79998
(915) 778-5281

Webley *(air guns)*
(available through Beeman's)

Weihrauch *(air guns)*
(available through Air Rifle Headquarters,
Beeman's)

Dan Wesson Arms, Inc. *(handguns)*
293 Main Street
Monson, Massachusetts 01057
(413) 267-4081

Western *(ammunition)*
(see Winchester-Western)

Williams Gun Sight Company *(sights, scopes,
mounts)*
7389 Lapeer Road
Davison, Michigan 48423
(313) 653-2131

Winchester-Western *(rifles, shotguns,
ammunition, primers, cases)*
275 Winchester Avenue
New Haven, Connecticut 06504
(203) 789-5000

Winslow Arms Company *(rifles)*
P.O. Box 783
Camden, South Carolina 29020
(803) 432-2938

Wischo *(air guns)*
(available through Air Rifle Headquarters,
Beeman's)

RIFLE/SHOTGUN COMBINATION GUNS, DOUBLE RIFLES DRILLINGS

Index